COMPENDIUM OF THE WORLD'S LANGUAGES

Review of the first edition

> 'Campbell's *Compendium* achieves the near-impossible.... It succeeds in presenting the most characteristic features of several hundred languages.'
>
> (Stephen Matthews, University of Hong Kong)

This second edition of George Campbell's astounding survey of world languages has been thoroughly updated, revised, and expanded. It presents a comprehensive cross-section of languages, ranging from the familiar and well-documented to the relatively obscure.

Twenty completely new entries on exotic languages such as Comanche, Shona, and Wotapuri have been added to the more than 300 descriptions of the many forms taken by human speech worldwide. Also included are numerous articles on non-Roman scripts, not featured in the first edition. 'Dead' languages associated with the great cultures of the past – Classical Chinese, Sanskrit, Classical Greek, and Latin – are featured, as well as intriguing isolates like Etruscan and Tangut.

Throughout, the treatment is simple and factual: technical terminology is used only where necessary. The articles are ordered alphabetically and have a standardized structure for ease of reference.

This two-volume work comprises an unsurpassed study of world languages.

George L. Campbell, formerly of the BBC World Service, is a polyglot linguist and translator.

COMPENDIUM OF THE WORLD'S LANGUAGES

SECOND EDITION

GEORGE L. CAMPBELL

VOLUME I: ABAZA TO KURDISH

London and New York

First published 1991
by Routledge
11 New Fetter Lane, London EC4P 4EE

Simultaneously published in the USA and Canada
by Routledge
29 West 35th Street, New York, NY 10001

Routledge is an imprint of the Taylor & Francis Group

Second edition published 2000

© 1991, 2000 George L. Campbell

Typeset in Times and Frutiger by Taylor & Francis Books Ltd

Printed and bound in Great Britain by Biddles Ltd,
Guildford and King's Lynn

All rights reserved. No part of this book may be reprinted or reproduced or utilised in any form or by any electronic, mechanical, or other means, now known or hereafter invented, including photocopying and recording, or in any information storage or retrieval system, without permission in writing from the publishers.

British Library Cataloguing in Publication Data
A catalogue record for this book is available from the British Library

Library of Congress Cataloging in Publication Data
Campbell, George L.
Compendium of the world's languages / George L. Campbell. – [2nd, rev., updated, and enl. ed.]
p cm.
Includes bibliographical references.
Contents: v. 1. Abaza to Kurdish (v. 1: alk. paper).
v. 2. Ladakhi to Zuni (v. 2: alk paper).
1. Language and languages. I. Title.
P371.C36 2000 99–15194
403–dc21 CIP

ISBN 0–415–20298–1 (Set)
ISBN 0–415–20296–5 (Volume I)
ISBN 0–415–20297–3 (Volume II)

CONTENTS

VOLUME I

Introduction vii
Abbreviations xv
List of languages xvii

COMPENDIUM OF THE WORLD'S LANGUAGES
Abaza to Kurdish 1

VOLUME II

COMPENDIUM OF THE WORLD'S LANGUAGES
Ladakhi to Zuni 931

Bibliography 1819

INTRODUCTION

'Les langues imparfaites,' complained Mallarmé, 'en cela que plusieurs, manque la suprême.' ('Languages [are] imperfect, in that there are many [of them], [but] the supreme [one] is lacking.) (*Variations sur un sujet: Crise de Vers.*) In some ways, this is a puzzling remark. Exactly what does *plusieurs* refer to? If it is to the multiplicity of natural languages, there need be no disagreement, on this point at least. Languages have indeed proliferated on the planet; the most recent and most comprehensive count (Merritt Ruhlen 1988) records around five thousand languages which are or have been spoken, some by millions, most by several thousands, and some by only a few hundred people. We have no way of gauging how many languages, once existent, have now vanished without trace. It seems unlikely, however, that Mallarmé had made first-hand acquaitance with all or even many of the natural languages, or had been able to assess in what degree they fell short of perfection. One might have expected him to find much to his taste in Classical Chinese or Classical Arabic poetry. Moreover, how and why could or should one language be 'supreme'.

The sentence begins perhaps to make more sense if we take *plusieurs* to refer to *levels* of language, particularly since Mallarmé goes on to deplore the *numéraire facile* – the 'easy currency' – of everyday speech, which is non-convertible into *la notion pure*. Given this non-convertibility, it is the poet's job to transcend natural language and communication by providing what Mallarmé calls *un complément supérieur* – a 'higher complement'. In Mallarmé's hands, the higher integration functions in a realm of autonomous verbal creativity, yielding a kind of cerebral algebra of images, hardly if at all anchored in the world of everyday experience and communication. It is a construct which we acclaim as arcane and beautiful poetry.

But the *numéraire facile* rejected by Mallarmé as 'imperfect' represents something even more mysterious and far more valuable: the original mapping of the shared human environment and shared human experience onto the plane of speech. This construct is initiated and sustained by an innate human competence, whose nature we can hardly even guess at. Key factors in the mapping are the remembered use of words, and their division into constants which can be transposed, and operators and operational codes which cannot.

The 'easy currency' has enabled man *qua* Robinson Crusoe to plot his position, catalogue his possessions, and tabulate his actions. Far from being divorced from natural experience, natural language might be defined as the audible inventory of that experience, and words are its bench-marks. In contrast, the conscious creation of alternative and idiosyncratic worlds has to do rather with a secondary mimetic mapping from the spoken to the written plane.

Intentional language has played a fundamental role in man's mimetic re-creation of the material universe; so, one would reasonably expect to find that we know a great deal deal about its origins and evolution. In fact, we know virtually nothing; we know far more about the origins and life-cycles of the stars than we do about the pre-history of the languages we speak. The history of language is *ipso facto* the history of its only begetter – Homo sapiens, whose remote ancestors appeared on Earth about a million years ago: that is, fourteen billion years after the original creation of space-time, energy, and matter. By 250,000 BC Homo sapiens was equipped with a brain which Professor E. Wilson in *Consilience* has described as 'the most complex object known in the universe: known, that is, to itself (1998: 97). We can assume that Homo sapiens was using intentional language by 50,000 BC to 30,000 BC, when he was already in Europe, on his way to colonizing and monopolizing the planet. The factual record does not begin until 3,000 BC when three languages – Archaic Chinese, Old Egyptian, and Sumerian – suddenly, thanks to the invention of writing, emerged fully fledged from the darkness. This suggests a lengthy period of anterior development. But, for the period 250,000 BC to 3,000 BC, we are reduced to guess-work.

Various scenarios have been put forward; these tend to fall into either of two categories: (a) dramatic intervention (The Tower of Babel is a powerfully mythopoeic example) or the great leap forward; and (b) gradual evolutionary process over thousands of years.

(a) Here, the most interesting theory is that offered by Professor T. Crow of Oxford University who postulates a chance mutation on the Y-chromosome of a male Homo sapiens (the Y-chromosome is found only in males). This could have led to a specialization in the left cerebral hemisphere, with a consequent upsurge in the creative use of intentional language. In this scenario there is a price to pay: the attendant threat of that breakdown in intentional communication which we know as schizophrenia. (And the recent global chaos in cyberspace as a result of a virus that paralysed the computer world (May 2000) is a timely reminder that man's mimetic re-creation even has room for a 'do-it-yourself' Tower of Babel.)

(b) Professor M. Nowak (Princeton), working with Dr D. Krakauer, starts from the traditional view of proto-language distilling and congealing from the 'primeval soup' of natural noises, grunts, and squeals, but goes on to underpin it with the mathematics of the theory of games (John von Neumann and Oskar Morgenstern (1944) *Theory of Games and Economic Behaviour*, New York) in order to quantify and validate the statistical chances of a language getting a 'winning hand' and so gaining evolutionary advantage. Where there is a multiplicity of players, combinations can be arrived at which minimalize losses for all participants.

These are attractive concepts for fiercely contested fields like war and big business; but languages have not normally been in competition with one another. For example, English did not 'defeat' Tasmanian: the white settlers simply eliminated the Tasmanians. In digloss situations, boundaries are usually agreed by mutual consent.

But, whatever the scenario, the central enigma persists: exactly how are impulses in the brain 'bodied forth' as selected phonemes which generate a recollected lexicon of lexemes? Is the human brain created to create language? If so, why? Perhaps an enigmatic (but not irrelevant) Arabic tradition is appropriate here:

كُنْتُ كَنْزاً مَخْفِيّاً فَأَحْبَبْتُ أَنْ أُعْرَفَ فَخَلَقْتُ الْخَلْقَ لِكَيْ أُعْرَفَ

'I was a hidden treasure, and I wished to be known, and I created mankind (or: the creation) that I might be known.'

* * *

The natural inventory is not, of course, entirely homogeneous. There are local nuances of modality and circumstance. This or that facet of a nominal or verbal event is stressed in one language, ignored in another. Thus, where Indo-European languages tend to use adjectival and adverbial modifiers, in many American Indian languages such information inheres in the verb stem itself. In verbal systems, some languages adopt the standpoint of temporal sequence – tense, that is – while others prefer to make an aspectual distinction between completed and uncompleted action. But these are surface variations. From the Egyptian, Sumerian, and Archaic Chinese of 3,000 BC to modern Russian, German, and Arabic, from Old Norse and Sanskrit to Navajo and Quechua, there is general consensus on the fundamental parameters of existence: the spatio-temporal matrix, and the kinetic operational paradigms which underlie the surface diversity. *Vis-à-vis* Mallarmé's *notion pure* and *complément supérieur*, the world's natural languages may indeed be askew; but they are orthogonalities for their users, and none is superfluous. As Sir Thomas Browne said: 'There are no Grotesques in Nature, not anything framed to fill up empty Cantons and unnecessary spaces.'

The construct yielded by the primary mapping is not immutable. Over long periods of time, phonological and morphological systems are subject to superficial erosion and replacement. Declensions are reduced, class and gender taxonomies are amended, verbal structures simplified. Essential linguistic profiles do not seem to be affected. The relative brevity of the written record, with a cut-off point at around the third millennium BC, limits our perspectives here; extrapolation is risky. But it is difficult to imagine that Chinese was, or ever could be, 'like' Sanskrit, or Hawai'ian like Ket, though the same 'generational template' underlies all four.

Innovation where it occurs is largely a surface phenomenon, involving transposition of constants and local differentiation. Like Mallarmé, the great Tang poet Tu Fu can score brilliant aesthetic effects by transposing semantic nuclei – in Chinese, a far more radical step than it is in French (see, for example, lines 5–6 of *Wàng yuè*, 'On a Prospect of T'ai-Shan', in David Hawkes (1967) *A Little Primer of Tu Fu*, Oxford University Press). Arabic, on the other hand, prefers to make novel, not to say unheard-of, utterances via a cerebral play upon words, and a kind of phonological mirror-imagery (see, for example, the *Maqāmāt*, the 'Assemblies', of the eleventh-century poet al-Ḥarīrī, especially Assembly 32). But essential linguistic profiles are not much affected by such innovations; al-Ḥarīrī could no more insert the Arabic adjective between the article and the noun than Tu Fu could mark his verbs for gender, number, and person. If the surface diversity of languages is the main subject of this book, the underlying consensus emerges, it is hoped, as a corollary.

For reasons of space, certain other properties of language receive less than the attention due to them. For example, in a sense (not that of Mallarmé), words carry their own *complément supérieur* in the form of a mythopoeic potential or charge, which seems to be latent in them from the outset, and which is activated in literary creativity, and, most particularly, in any language which is the vehicle of a religion or taboo system. Words resonate beyond themselves into more or less adjacent semantic fields. Hugo von Hofmannsthal in his wisdom put it beautifully: 'und dennoch sagt der viel, der "Abend" sagt' ('and yet he says much, who says "evening"'; *Ballade des äuszeren Lebens*).

The first eight verses of Chapter 1 of St John's Gospel, which, where available, follow each article, serve not only to exemplify the language in question, but also to show how readily co-ordinates can be tacitly transformed, so that spatio-temporal markers that are meaningful in one frame of reference appear to remain semantically invariant, that is, meaningful, in another: '*in the* beginning', '*was the* Word', '*with* God'.

The late twentieth century witnessed an increasing tendency for both primary and secondary mappings to cede status at least to a derivatory mapping – their instantaneous and infinite electronic multiplications, with or without visual display: 'I heard it on TV'. It is too early to assess the full implications of our reliance on images, but we all know what happened to the Lady of Shalott when she was suddenly deprived of them.

While it is not difficult for someone in a given language to find the relevant geographical and demographic facts concerning it, it is not always so easy to find a simple account in English of how it actually works – of its nuts and bolts. There is, of course, no shortage of books on the major languages of the West, or on the more important Oriental languages such as Chinese, Japanese, and Arabic; and today's students are fortunate in having ready to hand such invaluable exotica as Hewitt's *Abkhaz* and Aronson's *Georgian* to name only two of the best examples. But the quixotically curious – those who might turn to a single reference work in the hope of finding out at one and the same time how the Navajo verb and the Andi nominal system work, why vowel harmony has been eroded in Uzbek, and what sort of script the Cambodians use – are not so well catered for. It has been my hope and intention that this book should provide basic guidance in simple language, and point the reader, via the bibliography, towards the more competent and more detailed accounts, to which I gratefully acknowledge my indebtedness.

The first edition of the *Compendium of the World's Languages* was published by Routledge in 1991. This second edition has been considerably expanded: firstly by the inclusion of some two dozen new articles dealing with such languages as Comanche, Newārī, Shona, Sotho, the Orkhon-Yenisei inscriptions, and the Lü language of southern Yunnan; and secondly by the extensive rewriting of most of the articles taken over from the first edition. Thus Old Mon, for example, which originally occupied a few paragraphs, has grown to six pages. The revision makes far more use of illustrative examples, with particular attention being paid to syntax. The script tables have been adapted from my *Handbook of Scripts and Alphabets* (Routledge 1997) and are now integrated with the new text: thus Devanāgarī, for example, follows Sanskrit; Roman follows Latin.

In general, the articles follow the same lay-out, sub-divided as follows:

1. *Head-word*: background note on the language, its affiliation, location, and number of speakers; dialects; where relevant, some remarks on the literature of which it is the vehicle.
2. *Script*: if other than Roman, the script used by a language is described after the Introduction or appears as a separate section with accompanying tables at the end of the article.
3. *Phonology*: for the most part, the phonological inventories are set out in terms of mode of utterance; that is, consonants are sub-divided into stops, affricates, fricatives, nasals, laterals, semi-vowels; vowels into oral and nasal series. In a few special cases, for example Sanskrit, a positional grid is used, showing the phonemes of the language in terms of labial, palatal, dental, retroflex, and velar series. This positional grid is also retained in the case of certain Caucasian languages, for example, which make a phonemic distinction between uvular, pharyngeal, and glottal series. Tone, if relevant, is also described here.

   Wherever possible, phonological inventories are in IPA symbols. Exceptions to this general rule are provided by languages, long dead, whose phonological values are conjectural, and by languages such as Andamanese or Chimu for which no IPA values seem to be available. Transcription is broad.
4. *Morphology and syntax*: the main sub-headings are: article; noun;

adjective; pronoun; numerals; verb; pre/postpositions; word order. For reasons of space, only very general questions of syntax are taken up.

5. *Illustrative text*: verses 1–8 of the first chapter of St John's Gospel have been chosen as a suitable example, available in most of the languages described. Alternative biblical specimens are substituted, and identified, in cases where a translation of St John's Gospel is not available.
6. *Bibliography*: arranged alphabetically by language.

Selection and classification

My aim was to include all of the world's literary languages, along with certain other languages which, though lacking a written literature, were nevertheless felt to be of sufficient interest and importance to warrant inclusion. The list of 1,000 languages, given by David Crystal (1988) on pp. 463 – 44 of his *Encyclopaedia of Language* served as a general base, extended where necessary by specialist works such as Bernard Comrie (1981), *The Languages of the Soviet Union*. In Crystal's list, the cut-off point for number of speakers is 10,000. I have included several languages with much smaller, even minimal tallies, e.g. certain members of the Caucasian, Palaeo-Siberian, and North American Indian groupings.

Classification

Here again, I follow David Crystal's middle course between 'lumpers' – linguists who seek to identify genetic or at least typological relationships connecting ever wider and more numerous groups of languages – and 'splitters' – linguists who, on the contary, sub-divide large putative groupings into smaller, well-defined and demonstrably coherent units. Thus, the Semito-Hamitic languages are described as forming part of the Afro-Asiatic family, and Bantu as Niger-Congo; but Indo-European and Japanese are not classified as 'Euroasiatic', nor are Quechua and Cree lumped together as 'Amerind'. Nor is there, perhaps mistakenly, any mention of 'Nostratic' or 'Austric'.

Sources

The books which have been used in the preparation of this work are listed in the Bibliography. Examples in the text, mainly in the section on Morphology and Syntax, fall into two categories. In the case of languages with which I have worked over the years, examples are drawn partly from the standard works listed in the Bibliography, partly from other sources. In the case of languages with which I am not actively familiar, all examples are taken from the works listed. Thus, for example, all Ainu examples are taken from Refsing (1986); the Nama examples are from Hagman (1977); Bambara from Brauner (1974); Samaritan from Vil'sker (1974), and so on. I am especially indebted to two Russian collective works: *Jazyki Narodov SSSR* and *Jazyki Azii i Afriki*.

Permissions

In conclusion, I would like to express my gratitude to all those who have worked on this project, and have helped in various ways to turn a very daunting text into a printed book. Mary Ann Kernan, Sophie Oliver, and Jan McNellie were actively involved in the early stages, and I thank them for their help and encouragement. I am particularly grateful to Ceri Prenter (project manager) and Vicki Damen (typesetter) who were constantly in touch with me throughout the production process; also to James Folan, who solved many of the problems that arose. My thanks also to Shomit Dutta, whose deep knowledge of Classical Greek was very much appreciated, and to Techbooks, who captured the data very efficiently; to Sean Harrop and Nigel Marsh. For the New Testament examples appended to most of the articles I have to thank once again the Rev. Alan Jesson (now retired) and Rosemary Mathew, both of the Bible Society's Library in Cambridge University.

Finally, I have to thank Mr Gareth King, who read the whole text in draft, and made many valuable suggestions and corrections.

G.L.C.

ABBREVIATIONS

abl.	ablative
abs.	absolute
acc.	accusative
adess.	adessive
adit.	aditive
affirm.	affirmative
Afr.	Afrikaans
anim.	animate
Ar.	Arabic
Assyr.	Assyrian
aux.	auxilliary
Azer.	Azerbaijani
Bel.	Belorussian
BI	Bahasa Indonesian
BP	Brazillian Portuguese
Ch.	Chinese
Ch.Ap.	Chiricahua Apache
CPR	Chinese People's Republic
Chip.	Chipewyan
cl.	class
CL	Classical Latin
com.	comitative
comp.	comparative
conj.	conjunctive
D	Dutch
dat.	dative
def.	definite
dep.	dependent
EArm.	Eastern Armenian
EP	European Portuguese
erg.	ergative
ESlav.	Eastern Slavonic
excl.	exclusive
fam.	familiar
fem.	feminine
Fin.	Finnish
Fr.	French
fut.	future
gen.	genitive
Gk	Greek
Gm	German
hon.	honorific
IE	Indo-European
illat.	illative
imper.	imperative
imperf.	imperfect
impers.	impersonal
inanim.	inanimate
incl.	inclusive
Ind.	Indonesian
indef.	indefinite
iness.	inessive
instr.	instrumental
It.	Italian
Jap.	Japanese
K	Krâmâ (Javanese)
Lat.	Latin
lk	link
loc.	locative
masc.	masculine
ME	Middle English

MF	Middle French
MSC	Modern Standard Chinese
N	Ngoko (Javanese)
Nav.	Navajo
neg.	negative
neut.	neuter
nom.	nominative
O/obj.	object
obl.	oblique
obv.	obviative
OE	Old English
OF	Old French
OI	Old Irish
Old Ch. Slav.	Old Church Slavonic
opt.	optative
Osc.	Oscan
p.	person
part.	partitive
pass.	passive
perf.	perfective
pl.	plural
Pol.	Polynesian
poss.	possessive
pp.	past participle
prep.	preposition(al)
pres.	present
pret.	preterite
prog.	progressive
pron.	pronoun
prox.	proximate
refl.	reflexive
rel.	relative
Romy	Romany
Russ.	Russian
S/sbj.	subject
SC	Serbo-Croat
sing.	singular
Skt	Sanskrit
Sl.	Slovene
Slav.	Slavonic
Som.	Somali
Sp.	Spanish
SSlav.	Southern Slavonic
subj.	subjunctive
trans.	transitive
Ukr.	Ukrainian
V	verb
Viet.	Vietnamese
VN	verbal noun
voc.	vocative
WArm.	Western Armenian

LIST OF LANGUAGES

The use of bold type or small capital letters indicates that there is an article on an individual language or language family respectively. Normal type indicates that a language is covered within an article on the cross-referenced language or language family, or is an alternative name for that language.

Abaza
Abelam *see* PAPUAN LANGUAGES
Abkhaz
ABKHAZ-ADYGE LANGUAGES
Aceh *see* **Achinese**
Achinese
Adamawa Eastern *see* NIGER CONGO LANGUAGES
Adyge
Afrikaans
Agul
Ahom *see* **Assamese**
Ainu
Āka-Bēa-da *see* **Andamanese**
Akan
Ākar-Bālē *see* **Andamanese**
Akhvakh *see* ANDI LANGUAGES
Akkadian
Albanian
Aleut
ALTAIC LANGUAGES
Altay
Alyutor see **Koryak**; PALAEO-SIBERIAN LANGUAGES
Amharic
ANATOLIAN LANGUAGES
Andamanese
ANDEAN-EQUATORIAL LANGUAGES
ANDI LANGUAGES
Anglo-Saxon *see* **English**
Ao *see* NAGA LANGUAGES
Apabhraṁśa *see* **Prakit**
Apache
Arabic
Aramaic *see* SEMITIC LANGUAGES
Arapaho
Araucanian *see* **Mapudungu**
Arawakan *see* ANDEAN-EQUATORIAL LANGUAGES
Ardhamāgadhī *see* **Prakit**
Arin *see* **Ket**
Armenian, Classical
Armenian, Modern Standard
Aromanian *see* **Romanian**
Ashkenazi *see* **Yiddish**
Aṣkun *see* DARDIC LANGUAGES
Asmat *see* PAPUAN LANGUAGES
Assamese
Assan *see* **Ket**
Athabaskan
Āūkāū-Jūwōī *see* **Andamanese**
Aukštait *see* **Lithuanian**
AUSTRALIAN LANGUAGES
AUSTRO-ASIATIC LANGUAGES
AUSTRONESIAN LANGUAGES
Ava *see* PAPUAN LANGUAGES
Avar
Avestan
Aymará
Azerbaijani

Aztec *see* **Nahuatl**
AZTEC-TANOAN LANGUAGES

Bactrian *see* IRANIAN LANGUAGES
Bagval *see* ANDI LANGUAGES
BAHNARIC LANGUAGES
Balinese
BALTIC LANGUAGES
BALTO-FINNIC MINOR LANGUAGES
Baluchi
Bambara
Banning *see* PAPUAN LANGUAGES
BANTU LANGUAGES
Bao'an *see* MONGOLIAN LANGUAGES OF CHINA
Bashkir
Baśkārik *see* DARDIC LANGUAGES
Basque
Batak
Bats *see* NAKH LANGUAGES
Bella Coola *see* NORTH AMERICAN INDIAN ISOLATES
Belorussian
Beludzh see **Baluchi**
Bengali
Benue-Congo *see* NIGER CONGO LANGUAGES
Berber
Bhili *see* **Gujarati**; NEW INDO-ARYAN LANGUAGES
Bikol
Blackfoot
Bohairic *see* **Coptic**
Bolmaç *see* **Avar**
Bongu *see* PAPUAN LANGUAGES
Botlikh *see* ANDI LANGUAGES
Brahui
Brazilian *see* **Portuguese**
Breton
Bribrí
Brythonic *see* CELTIC LANGUAGES
Buginese
Bulgarian
Bulgarian, Old *see* TURKIC LANGUAGES
Burmese
Burushaski
Buryat
Bushman *see* **!Kung**
Buyi *see* TAI LANGUAGES

Cambodian
Canaanite *see* SEMITIC LANGUAGES
Čače rom *see* **Romany**
Caddoan *see* MACRO-SIOUAN LANGUAGES
Cantonese *see* **Yue**
Carib
Carib Island, *see* ANDEAN-EQUATORIAL LANGUAGES
Carrier *see* NA-DENE LANGUAGES
Catalan
Catawba *see* MACRO-SIOUAN LANGUAGES
CAUCASIAN LANGUAGES
Cayuga *see* MACRO-SIOUAN LANGUAGES
Cebuano
CELTIC LANGUAGES
Chagatay *see* TURKIC LANGUAGES
Cham
Chamalal *see* ANDI LANGUAGES
Chamorro
Chari-Nile *see* NILO-SAHARAN LANGUAGES
Chechen
Cheremis *see* **Mari**
Cherokee
Cheyenne
Chibcha
Chickasaw *see* **Choctaw**
Chimú
Chinese
Chinese, Archaic
Chinese, Classical
Chinese, Modern Standard
CHINESE, DIALECTS
Chinook *see* PENUTIAN LANGUAGES
Chipewyan
Chiricahua *see* **Apache**
Choctaw
Chrau *see* BAHNARIC LANGUAGES
Chukchi
Chulim *see* TURKIC LANGUAGES

Chuvash
Circassian *see* **Kabard-Cherkes**
Citrali *see* DARDIC LANGUAGES
Cœur d'Alene *see* NORTH AMERICAN INDIAN ISOLATES
Comanche
Coos *see* **Penutian**
Coptic
Cornish
Cornouaille *see* **Breton**
Cree
Creek *see* MACRO-ALGONQUIAN LANGUAGES
Crow
Cuang *see* **Juang**
Czech

DAGESTANIAN LANGUAGES
Dagur *see* MONGOLIAN LANGUAGES OF CHINA
Dai *see* TAI LANGUAGES
Dakota
Danish
DARDIC LANGUAGES
Dargin *see* **Dargva**
Dargva
Delaware *see* MACRO-ALGONQUIAN LANGUAGES
Demeli *see* DARDIC LANGUAGES
Digor *see* **Ossetian**
Dinka
DRAVIDIAN LANGUAGES
Drindari *see* **Romany**
Dutch
Dyirbal *see* AUSTRALIAN LANGUAGES
Dyula *see* **Bambara**

Easter Island *see* POLYNESIAN LANGUAGES; **Rapanui**
Efik
Egyptian
Elamite
Ellice Islands *see* POLYNESIAN LANGUAGES
English
Epigraphic South Arabian
Erlides *see* **Romany**
Erzyan *see* **Mordva**
Eskimo *see* **Inuit**; ESKIMO-ALEUT LANGUAGES
ESKIMO-ALEUT LANGUAGES
Estonian
Ethiopic
Euskara *see* **Basque**
Etruscan
Even
Evenki
Ewe

Faeroese
Fijian
Finnish
Fintike roma *see* **Romany**
Flemish *see* **Dutch**
Fore *see* PAPUAN LANGUAGES
Frafra *see* **Gurenne**
French
Fulani
Fulbe *see* **Fulani**
Fulfulde *see* **Fulani**
Futunan *see* POLYNESIAN LANGUAGES

Gadsup *see* PAPUAN LANGUAGES
Gaelic *see* **Scottish Gaelic**
Gagauz
Galatian *see* CELTIC LANGUAGES
Galla *see* **Oromo**
Gan *see* CHINESE, DIALECTS
Garo
Garwi *see* DARDIC LANGUAGES
Gawar(bati) *see* DARDIC LANGUAGES
Ge'ez *see* **Ethiopic**
Georgian
German
GERMANIC LANGUAGES
Gheg *see* **Albanian**
Gilyak *see* **Nivkh**
Goajiro *see* ANDEAN-EQUATORIAL LANGUAGES
Godaba *see* DRAVIDIAN LANGUAGES
Godoberi *see* ANDI LANGUAGES
Goideḷic *see* CELTIC LANGUAGES
Gold *see* **Nanay**

Golden Horde *see* TURKIC LANGUAGES
Goṇḍi
Gondwana *see* DRAVIDIAN LANGUAGES
Gorontalo
Gothic
Greek, Classical
Greek, Modern Standard
Guaraní
Gujarati
Gur, *see* NIGER-CONGO LANGUAGES
Gurbeti *see* **Romany**
Gurenne

Haida *see* NORTH AMERICAN INDIAN ISOLATES
Haitian Creole *see* PIDGINS AND CREOLES
Hakka *see* CHINESE, DIALECTS
Hattic *see* ANATOLIAN LANGUAGES
Hausa
Hawai'ian
Hebrew
Hidatsa *see* MACRO-SIOUAN LANGUAGES
Hiligaynon *see* **Cebuano**
Hindi
Hittite
Hokan *see* MACRO-SIOUAN LANGUAGES
Hopi
Hsi-Hsia *see* **Tangut**
Hungarian
Hunnic *see* TURKIC LANGUAGES
Hupa *see* NA-DENE LANGUAGES
Hurrian

Icelandic
Igbo
Ilokano
INDO-ARYAN LANGUAGES (NEW) *see* NEW INDO-ARYAN LANGUAGES
INDO-EUROPEAN LANGUAGES
Indonesian
Ingrian *see* BALTO-FINNIC MINOR LANGUAGES
Ingush *see* **Chechen**
Inuit
IRANIAN LANGUAGES
Irish
Irish, Old
Iron *see* **Ossete**
Iroquois *see* MACRO-SIOUAN LANGUAGES
Ishkashim *see* PAMIR LANGUAGES
Italian
Itelmen
Ivrit

Jain-Mahārāṣṭrī *see* **Prakit**
Jain-Śaureseni *see* **Prakit**
Japanese, Literary
Japanese, Modern Standard
Javanese
Javanese, Old
Jicarilla *see* **Apache**
Juang

Kabard-Cherkes
Kabyle *see* **Berber**
Kachin
Kalāṣa *see* DARDIC LANGUAGES
Kalispel *see* NORTH AMERICAN INDIAN ISOLATES
Kalmyk
Kam *see* TAI LANGUAGES
Kamoro *see* PAPUAN LANGUAGES
Kannada
Karachay-Balkar
Karakalpak
Karata *see* ANDI LANGUAGES
Karelian
Karen
Karluk *see* TURKIC LANGUAGES
Kartvelian *see* **Georgian**
Kashmiri
Kashubian
Katī *see* DARDIC LANGUAGES
Kawi *see* **Old Javanese**
Kazakh
Kekavyari *see* **Romany**
Kelderari *see* **Romany**
Kerek *see* PALAEO-SIBERIAN LANGUAGES

Keres *see* MACRO-SIOUAN LANGUAGES
Keresan *see* AZTEC-TANOAN LANGUAGES
Ket
Keva *see* PAPUAN LANGUAGES
Khakas
Khalkha *see* **Mongolian, Modern**
Khandeśi *see* NEW INDO-ARYAN LANGUAGES
Khanty
Khari-Bholi *see* **Hindi**
Khasi
Khazar *see* TURKIC LANGUAGES
Kherwari *see* **Muṇḍāri**
Khmer *see* **Cambodian**
Khotanese *see* IRANIAN LANGUAGES
Khowar *see* DARDIC LANGUAGES
Khwarezmian *see* IRANIAN LANGUAGES
Kiowa *see* NA-DENE LANGUAGES
Kipchak *see* TURKIC LANGUAGES
Kirgiz
Klamath-Modoc *see* PENUTIAN LANGUAGES
Kodagu *see* DRAVIDIAN LANGUAGES
Kol *see* AUSTRO-ASIATIC LANGUAGES
Kolami *see* DRAVIDIAN LANGUAGES
Komi
Konkani *see* **Marathi**
Korean
Koryak
Kota *see* DRAVIDIAN LANGUAGES
Kott *see* **Ket**; PALAEO-SIBERIAN LANGUAGES
Kpelle
Kui *see* DRAVIDIAN LANGUAGES
Kumyk
!Kung
Kurdish
Kurmandji *see* **Kurdish**
Kurukh *see* DRAVIDIAN LANGUAGES
Kuvi *see* DRAVIDIAN LANGUAGES
Kwa *see* NIGER-CONGO LANGUAGES
Kwakiutl *see* NORTH AMERICAN INDIAN ISOLATES
Ladakhi
Lahndā
Lak
Lakota *see* **Dakota**
Lamut *see* **Even**
Langue d'Oc *see* **Occitan**
Lao
Lappish
Latin
Latvian
Laz
Leon *see* **Breton**
Lezgi
Lhota *see* NAGA LANGUAGES
Li *see* TAI LANGUAGES
Lingurari *see* **Romany**
Lingala
Lithuanian
Liv *see* BALTO-FINNIC MINOR LANGUAGES
Lotfika roma *see* **Romany**
Lovari *see* **Romany**
Lü
Luganda
Lusatian
Luvian *see* ANATOLIAN LANGUAGES
Lycian *see* ANATOLIAN LANGUAGES
Lydian *see* ANATOLIAN LANGUAGES

Maasai
Macassarese
Macedonian
MACRO-ALGONQUIAN LANGUAGES
MACRO-SIOUAN LANGUAGES
Madurese
Māgadhī *see* **Prakit**
Mahārāṣṭri *see* **Prakit**
Mahl *see* **Sinhalese**
Maiduan *see* PENUTIAN LANGUAGES
Maiyā̃ *see* DARDIC LANGUAGES
Malagasy
Malayalam
Malinke *see* **Bambara**
Maltese
Malto *see* DRAVIDIAN LANGUAGES
Mam
Manchu

Mandaean *see* SEMITIC LANGUAGES
Mandan *see* MACRO-SIOUAN LANGUAGES
Mandingo *see* **Bambara**
Mangarevan *see* POLYNESIAN LANGUAGES
Mansi
Manx
Maonan *see* Tai languages
Maori
Mapudungu
Marathi
Margi
Mari
Marind *see* PAPUAN LANGUAGES
Marquesan *see* POLYNESIAN LANGUAGES
Maya
Median *see* IRANIAN LANGUAGES
Melanesian *see* AUSTRONESIAN LANGUAGES
Mende
Menomini
Meroitic
Mescalero *see* **Apache**; NA-DENE LANGUAGES
MIAO-YAO LANGUAGES
Micmac *see* MACRO-ALGONQUIAN LANGUAGES
Micronesian *see* AUSTRONESIAN LANGUAGES
Middle English *see* **English**
Middle Persian *see* **Pehlevi**
Min *see* CHINESE, DIALECTS
Minangkabau
Mingrelian
Miskito
Miwok-Costanoan *see* PENUTIAN LANGUAGES
Mixtec
Mobilian *see* **Choctaw**
Mohawk *see* MACRO-SIOUAN LANGUAGES
Mohican *see* MACRO-ALGONQUIAN LANGUAGES
Mokshan *see* **Mordva**
Mon, Old
Mongolian, Classical
MONGOLIAN LANGUAGES OF CHINA
Mongolian, Modern
Monguor *see* MONGOLIAN LANGUAGES OF CHINA
Mon-Khmer *see* AUSTRO-ASIATIC LANGUAGES
Mordva
Mordvinian *see* **Mordva**
Mortlokese *see* **Trukese**
Motu *see* PAPUAN LANGUAGES
Mulam *see* TAI LANGUAGES
Multani *see* **Lahndā**
Muṇḍārī
Mundži *see* PAMIR LANGUAGES
Muskogean *see* MACRO-ALGONQUIAN LANGUAGES
Muysca *see* **Chibcha**
Mycenaean *see* **Greek, Classical**

NA-DENÉ LANGUAGES
NAGA LANGUAGES
Nahuatl
Naiki *see* DRAVIDIAN LANGUAGES
NAKH LANGUAGES
Nakota *see* **Dakota**
Nama
Nanay
Nasioi *see* PAPUAN LANGUAGES
Natchez *see* MACRO-ALGONQUIAN LANGUAGES
Navajo
Naxi
Negidal
Nenets
Nepali
Newārī
NEW INDO-ARYAN LANGUAGES
Nez Perce *see* PENUTIAN LANGUAGES
Nicobarese
NIGER-CONGO LANGUAGES
NILO-SAHARAN LANGUAGES
Niue *see* POLYNESIAN LANGUAGES
Nivkh
Nogay *see* TURKIC LANGUAGES
Norse, Old
NORTH AMERICAN INDIAN ISOLATES

NORTH AMERICAN INDIAN LANGUAGES
Norwegian
Nubian

Occitan
Oguz *see* TURKIC LANGUAGES
Oirat
Oirot *see* **Altay**
Ojibwa *see* MACRO-ALGONQUIAN LANGUAGES
Old Church Slavonic
Old English *see* **English**
Oneida *see* MACRO-SIOUAN LANGUAGES
Ono *see* PAPUAN LANGUAGES
Onondaga *see* MACRO-SIOUAN LANGUAGES
Oriya
Orkhon-Yeṇisei
Oroch *see* **Udege**
Orok *see* **Nanay**
Oromo
Osage *see* MACRO-SIOUAN LANGUAGES
Ossete
Ostyak *see* **Khanty**
OTOMANGUEAN LANGUAGES
Otomi *see* OTOMANGUEAN LANGUAGES

Pahari *see* NEW INDO-ARYAN LANGUAGES
Paiśācī *see* **Prakit**
Paiute *see* AZTEC-TANOAN LANGUAGES
PALAEO-SIBERIAN LANGUAGES
Palaic *see* ANATOLIAN LANGUAGES
Palaung
Pali
PAMIR LANGUAGES
Panjabi
Papago *see* AZTEC-TANOAN LANGUAGES
PAPUAN LANGUAGES
Parji *see* DRAVIDIAN LANGUAGES
Parthian *see* IRANIAN LANGUAGES
Paṣai *see* DARDIC LANGUAGES
Pashto
Pawnee *see* MACRO-SIOUAN LANGUAGES
Pecheneg *see* TURKIC LANGUAGES
Peguan *see* **Mon, Old**
Pehlevi
Pelasgian *see* **Greek**, **Classical**
PENUTIAN LANGUAGES
Permic, Old *see* **Komi**
Permyak *see* **Komi**
Persian
Perv̌ika roma *see* **Romany**
Phalūṛa *see* DARDIC LANGUAGES
Phoenician
PIDGINS AND CREOLES
Piman *see* AZTEC-TANOAN LANGUAGES
Plaščunuya *see* **Romany**
Polish
Polovets *see* TURKIC LANGUAGES
POLYNESIAN LANGUAGES
Portuguese
Potawatomi *see* MACRO-ALGONQUIAN LANGUAGES
Prakrit
Prasun *see* DARDIC LANGUAGES
Provençal *see* **Occitan**
Puchikwar *see* **Andamanese**
Puluwatese *see* **Trukese**
Punic *see* **Phoenician**; SEMITIC LANGUAGES

Quechua
Quiché

Rajasthani *see* NEW INDO-ARYAN LANGUAGES
Rapanui
Raratonga *see* POLYNESIAN LANGUAGES
Riff *see* **Berber**
ROMANCE LANGUAGES
Romanian
Romany
Runa Simi *see* **Quechua**
Ruska roma *see* **Romany**
Russian

Ryu-Kyu *see* **Japanese, Modern Standard**

Saami *see* **Lappish**
Sabaean-Himyaritic *see* SEMITIC LANGUAGES
Sahaptian *see* PENUTIAN LANGUAGES
Sahidic *see* **Coptic**
Saka *see* IRANIAN LANGUAGES
Salishan *see* NORTH AMERICAN INDIAN ISOLATES
Samaritan
Samoan
Sango *see* NIGER-CONGO LANGUAGES
Sanskrit
Sanskrit, Buddhist Hybrid *see* **Prakit**
Santa *see* MONGOLIAN LANGUAGES OF CHINA
Santali
Sarcee *see* NA-DENE LANGUAGES
Sarikoli *see* PAMIR LANGUAGES
Śauraseni *see* **Prakit**
Scottish Gaelic
Scythian *see* IRANIAN LANGUAGES
Seljuk *see* TURKIC LANGUAGES
Seminole *see* MACRO-ALGONQUIAN LANGUAGES
SEMITIC LANGUAGES
Seneca
Sephardic *see* **Ivrit**; **Yiddish**
Serbo-Croat
Servi *see* **Romany**
Servika roma *see* **Romany**
Sgaw *see* **Karen**
Shawia *see* **Berber**
Shawnee *see* MACRO-ALGONQUIAN LANGUAGES
Shilluk
Shluh *see* **Berber**
Shoshonean languages *see* AZTEC-TANOAN LANGUAGES
Shona
Shughn-Roshan
Siamese *see* **Thai**
Ṣiṇā *see* DARDIC LANGUAGES
Sindhi
Sinhala *see* **Sinhalese**
Sinhalese
SINO-TIBETAN LANGUAGES
Sinti *see* **Romany**
Siraiki *see* **Lahndā**; **Sindhi**
SLAVONIC LANGUAGES
Slavonic, Old Church *see* **Old Church Slavonic**
Slovak
Slovene
Sogdian *see* IRANIAN LANGUAGES
Somali
Sonoran *see* AZTEC-TANOAN LANGUAGES
Sora *see* **Khasi**
Sorani *see* **Kurdish**
Sorbian *see* **Lusatian**
Sotho
Spanish
Squamish *see* NORTH AMERICAN INDIAN ISOLATES
Stieng *see* BAHNARIC LANGUAGES
Sui *see* TAI LANGUAGES
Sumasti *see* DARDIC LANGUAGES
Sumerian
Sundanese
Svan
Swahili
Swedish
Syriac

Tabasaran
Tagalog
Tahitian
TAI LANGUAGES
Tairora *see* PAPUAN LANGUAGES
Takelma *see* PENUTIAN LANGUAGES
Tajik
Talaing *see* **Mon, Old**
Talysh
Tamahaq *see* **Berber**
Tamazight *see* **Berber**
Tamil
Tangut

Tanoan-Kiowa *see* AZTEC-TANOAN LANGUAGES
Tapanta *see* **Abaza**
Tarahumar *see* AZTEC-TANOAN LANGUAGES
Tasmanian
Tat
Tatar
Telefol *see* PAPUAN LANGUAGES
Telugu
Thai
Tibetan
Tigre
Tigrinya
Tindi *see* ANDI LANGUAGES
Tiraki *see* DARDIC LANGUAGES
Tlingit
Toba *see* **Batak**
Tocharian
Toba *see* DRAVIDIAN LANGUAGES
Tokelau *see* POLYNESIAN LANGUAGES
Tongan
Tonkawa *see* MACRO-ALGONQUIAN LANGUAGES
Tōrwālī *see* DARDIC LANGUAGES
Tosk *see* **Albanian**
Treguier *see* **Breton**
Trukese
Trukhmen *see* TURKIC LANGUAGES
Tshimshian *see* PENUTIAN LANGUAGES
Tuamotuan *see* POLYNESIAN LANGUAGES
Tuareg *see* **Berber**
Tulu *see* DRAVIDIAN LANGUAGES
Tunica *see* MACRO-ALGONQUIAN LANGUAGES; MACRO-SIOUAN LANGUAGES
Tupí
TURKIC LANGUAGES
Turkish
Turkmen
Tuva *see* **Tuvinian**
Tuvinian
Twi *see* **Akan**
Tzotzil *see* **Maya**

Ubykh
Udege
Udmurt
Ugaritic
Ukrainian
Ulcha *see* Nanay
Ungrika roma *see* **Romany**
URALIC LANGUAGES
Urartian
Urdu
Ursari *see* **Romany**
Uto-Aztecan *see* AZTEC-TANOAN LANGUAGES
Uvean, East *see* POLYNESIAN LANGUAGES
Uygur
Uygur, Old
Uzbek

Vaigalī *see* DARDIC LANGUAGES
Vakh *see* PAMIR LANGUAGES; **Khanty**
Vannes *see* **Breton**
Vedic *see* **Sanskrit**
Veps *see* BALTO-FINNIC MINOR LANGUAGES
Veri *see* PAPUAN LANGUAGES
Vietnamese
Visayan *see* **Cebuano**
Vogul *see* **Mansi**
Volokhuya *see* **Romany**
Volšenenge kale *see* **Romany**
Voltaic *see* NIGER-CONGO LANGUAGES
Vot *see* BALTO-FINNIC MINOR LANGUAGES
Votapuri *see* DARDIC LANGUAGES
Votyak *see* **Udmurt**

Wakashan *see* NORTH AMERICAN INDIAN ISOLATES
Walmatjari *see* AUSTRALIAN LANGUAGES
Warrgamay *see* AUSTRALIAN LANGUAGES
Welsh
Wendish *see* **Lusatian**
Wenli *see* **Chinese, Classical**
Weršikwar *see* **Burushaski**

West Atlantic *see* NIGER-CONGO LANGUAGES
Western Desert Language *see* AUSTRALIAN LANGUAGES
Wichita *see* MACRO-SIOUAN LANGUAGES
Winnebago *see* MACRO-SIOUAN LANGUAGES
Wintun *see* PENUTIAN LANGUAGES
Wolof
Wu *see* CHINESE, DIALECTS

Xiang *see* CHINESE, DIALECTS
Xibo *see* **Manchu**
!Xũ *see* **!Kung**

Yagnob
Yakut
Yazgulyam *see* PAMIR LANGUAGES
Yi
Yiddish
Yidiny *see* AUSTRALIAN LANGUAGES
Yokutstan *see* PENUTIAN LANGUAGES
Yoruba
Yuchi *see* MACRO-SIOUAN LANGUAGES
Yue
Yukagir
Yuki *see* MACRO-SIOUAN LANGUAGES
Yupik *see* **Inuit**; ESKIMO-ALEUT LANGUAGES
Yurok *see* MACRO-ALGONQUIAN LANGUAGES

Zapotec
Žemait *see* **Lithuanian**
Zend/Zand *see* IRANIAN LANGUAGES
Zletari *see* **Romany**
Zulu
Zuni
Zyryan *see* **Komi**

ABAZA

INTRODUCTION

Abaza belongs to the Abkhaz-Adyge sub-group of North-West Caucasian. There are about 25,000 speakers in the Karachaevo-Cherkessia Republic Region, and many in Turkey who migrated there after the Shamil uprising in the mid-eighteenth century. The Tapanta dialect affords the basis for the literary standard.

SCRIPT

Since 1938 a Cyrillic-based script has been used for Abaza. Since Abaza is so close, both phonologically and morphologically, to Abkhaz that some authorities consider it to be an Abkhaz dialect, a common script for the two languages might have seemed a sensible proposition. The two notations differ, however, in a very confusing way. Thus the non-Cyrillic sign *I*, widely used in Caucasian languages, appears in Abaza as the ejective marker, but is absent in Abkhaz, where the unmarked consonant graph is used to notate the ejective. For example, the labial ejective stop is notated as п in Abkhaz, as п*I* in Abaza; п in Abaza is the unvoiced stop, represented as ҧ in Abkhaz. Similarly, the labialized pharyngeal ejective is ҟь in Abkhaz, къь in Abaza.

Altogether, the Abaza script has over 70 graphs, including 28 digraphs and 12 trigraphs.

PHONOLOGY

The phonology of Abaza is close to that of Abkhaz, with some divergencies in the spirant and affricate alveolar series. The vocalic system reduces to a basic contrast between *a* and *ι*. Some authorities (e.g. Allen 1956) give Abaza only one vowel – /ə/. Lomtatidze (1967) gives /a/ and /ı/ as basic, with positional allophones /e, o, u/.

MORPHOLOGY AND SYNTAX

Largely as in Abkhaz. Hewitt (1981) points to Circassian influence on Abaza verb structure *vis-à-vis* Abkhaz.

ABKHAZ

INTRODUCTION

Abkhaz belongs to the North-West Caucasian or Abkhaz-Adyge sub-group of Caucasian languages. Abkhaz is very closely connected to Abaza; indeed the Abkhaz-Abaza complex can be described in terms of four dialects: Southern – Bzyb and Abžui, the latter providing the basis for the Abkhaz literary language; and Northern – Aškhar and Tapanta, on which the Abaza literary language is based.

In 1979 there were some 90,000 speakers of Abkhaz, of whom about 95 per cent claimed Abkhaz as their mother tongue. Most Abkhazians live in the Abkhaz Autonomous Region (capital Sukhumi), with a residue in Mingrelia and in Turkey.

Abkhaz oral literary tradition possesses a version of the *Narts* saga, which is regarded as more archaic than the parallel Ossetian version. The saga combines mythological accounts of the origins of Iranian society and its culture with records, which may be historical, of migration and warfare. The fact that the Greeks seem to have borrowed some of the material (e.g. the Prometheus motif) goes to suggest that the *Narts* saga may date from at least 1000 BC.

The first Abkhaz newspaper, *Apsne*, was launched in 1917 by Drmit Gulia (1874–1960), who is generally recognized as the father of literature in Abkhaz. He translated widely from Russian and Georgian, and wrote a novel on social themes, *Kamačič*.

SCRIPT

In 1862 a Cyrillic-based script was devised by Uslar. Between 1928 and 1954 various experiments were made with Romanization and with Georgian script. The present Cyrillic-based script, in use since 1954, has the following extra characters: џ, ҧ, ө.

PHONOLOGY

Consonants

stops: /p, b, p'; t, d, t'; k, g, k'; q'/. The ejectives p', t', k' are notated as *ṗ*, *ṭ*, etc. The dental and velar series and /q'/ occur labialized: /t°, d°, t'°; k°; g°, k'°, q'°/. The velar series and /q'/ occur palatalized: /k′, g′, k''; q''/.

affricates: /ts, dz, ts'; tʃ, dʒ, dʒ'/; labialized: /ts°, dz°, ts'°/; retroflex: /tʂ, dʐ, tʂ'/ (notated as *ḍẓ*, *c.*, *ç.*)
fricatives: /f, v, s, z, ʃ, ʒ, x, ɣ, x°, ɣ°, x′, ɣ′/; labialized: /ʃ°, ʒ°/; retroflex: /ʂ, ʐ/; pharyngeals: /ħ, ħ°, ʕ°/y°/: Hewitt (1979) describes this latter sound as a 'radico-pharyngeal voiced pulmonic fricative labialized'.
nasals: /m, n/
lateral and roll: /l, r/
semi-vowels: /j, w/

Vowels

The Abkhaz vowel system is based on a simple distinction between an open vowel /a/ and a closed vowel /ı, ə/. /a/ is the prevalent vowel in Abkhaz. Depending on phonetic environment, both /a/ and /ı, ə/ may be realized as [e, i, o, u], e.g. the present-tense marker *-wa-* becomes [o] when followed by /j/.

MORPHOLOGY AND SYNTAX

Gender in Abkhaz, though marked in the pronoun, which distinguishes masculine/feminine in the 2nd and 3rd singular, is not marked in the noun. The pronominal gender distinction is, of course, carried via the pronominal markers to the verbal complex. Further, the class of human referents is distinguished from the non-human. *See* **Pronoun**, below.

Noun

Nouns are definite or indefinite. In citation form, with an *a-* prefix they are definite: e.g. *a.çla* 'the tree'; *a.xaça* 'the man'. The indefinite marker is suffixed *-ḳ*: e.g. *çla.ḳ* 'a tree'; *xaça.ḳ* 'some man or other'; *la.ḳ* 'a dog'.

PLURAL MARKERS

Suffixed *-c°a* for human referents, *-k°a* for non-human: e.g. *apsa.c°a* 'Abkhazians'; *ač̣ḳun.c°a.ḳ* 'some children'; *a.çla.k°a* 'the trees'; *çla.k°a.ḳ* 'some trees'.

-aa is a collective plural marker: e.g. *aps.w.aa* 'the Abkhaz people'.

A numeral may be prefixed to a nominal with or without a plural marker: e.g. with *pš-* 4; *pš.la.(k°a).(ḳ)* 'the four dogs/four dogs'.

In the absence of any sort of case inflection, syntactic relationships are expressed by affixes, supported where necessary by adverbial postpositions.

POSSESSION

Possessor precedes possessed: X's Y is expressed as X *lk* Y, where *lk* is the possessive linking particle, agreeing in number and, partially, in gender with X. *See* **Pronoun**, below.

DIRECT AND INDIRECT OBJECT

While nominals are not themselves marked, their status as subject or object is signalled by the presence of pronominal markers in the verbal complex. These markers are set out in the section on the **Pronoun**, below. Here, the system may be illustrated by an example from Hewitt 1979:

(sara) a.x°ə č̣.k°a a.š°q°.k°a Ø.rə.s.to.yṭ
'I give the books to the children'

where *sara* denotes the independent 1st p. pronoun 'I'; *a.x°ə č̣.k°a* denotes 'children'; *a.š°q°.k°a* denotes 'books'; *to* is the root 'to give'; *yṭ* is the characteristic of the finite verb, used to express the present tense; ***rə*** is the 3rd p. pl. indirect object marker: 'to them'; ***s*** is the 1st p. pronominal copy of *sara* 'I', subject of the transitive verb; and Ø indicates the position where a 3rd p. non-human pronominal marker would be inserted if necessary, referring to 'books'; here it is not necessary.

Adjective

The adjective in Abkhaz does not differ formally from the noun. Predicate adjectives are stative verbs. The attributive adjective usually follows its noun, whose indefinite marker, if any, is transferred to the adjective, which may also take the plural marker: e.g. *la bzəya.**ḳ*** 'a good dog', *a.la.(k°a) bzəya.k°a* 'the good dogs', *pš.la bzəya.ḳ* or *a.la bzəya.k°a.pš.ba* 'four good dogs', *a.bzəya.k°a* 'the good ones'.

A comparative is made with the formants *-aasta*, *-eyħa*, or *-aç̣ḳ'əs*: e.g. *a.ph°əs a.xaça y.aasta də.ħaraḳ.ə.w.p̣* 'the woman is taller than the man', where *a.ph°əs* is 'woman', *y-* a pronominal marker for 3rd p. sing. masc., *də.ħaraḳ* 'tall', and *-əwp̣* is the copula. Cf. *yara zeg' **r**.eyħa də.harak.ə.w.p̣* 'he is taller than all (*zeg'*) of them (*r-*)'.

Pronoun

Abkhaz has independent personal pronouns, possessive pronominal prefixes, and bound personal pronominal markers.

The independent series is:

		Singular	Plural			
1		sa(ra)	ħa(ra)	*incl.*		
			ħart	*excl.*		
2	human masc.	wa(ra)	š°a(ra)	*incl.*	š°art	*excl.*
	human fem.	ba(ra)				
3	human masc.	ya(ra)	da(ra)			
	human fem.	la(ra)				

-xata may be added to a reduplicated pronominal deixis for emphasis: e.g. ***sa(ra)**s.xata* 'I myself'.

The reflexive pronoun is *a.xə* 'head'.

POSSESSIVE PREFIXES

These are provided by the short forms of the independent series: *sa*, *wa*, etc. in certain cases with vocalic reduction: e.g. *sə.ç̣la* 'my tree', *ħa.ç̣la* 'their tree'.

BOUND PRONOMINAL MARKERS

These can be grouped in three series, each with specific functions:

Series 1

	Singular	*Plural*	
1	s(ə)	ħ(a)	Markers in this series occupy first slot in the pre-radical verbal complex. Note that 2nd sing. distinguishes masc. (*w*) from fem. (*b*) while 3rd sing. has generic distinction between human (*d*) and non-human (*y*). These markers provide the subject pronouns of intrans. verbs, and the direct objects of trans. verbs.
2	w(ə)	š°(ə)	
	b(ə)		
3	d(ə)	y(ə)	
non-human	y(ə)		

Series 2

1	s(ə)	ħ(a)/aħ	Series 2 provides indirect-object markers, following directly on Series 1. Note that 3rd sing. makes both gender and class distinction.
2	w(ə)	š°(ə)	
	b(ə)		
3	y(ə)	r/d(ə)	
	l(ə)		
non-human	a(ə)		

Series 3

1	s/z(ə)	Plural forms as in Series 2	Series 3, occupying third place in the pre-radical complex, provides the pronominal subject markers of transitive verbs. Again, 3rd sing. makes both gender and class distinction.
2	w(ə)		
	b(ə)		
3	y(ə)		
	lə)		
non-human	(n)a		

E.g. ***də.r.*** *beyṭ* 'they (***r.***) saw him (***də***)'; ***y.bə.r.****toyṭ* 'they (***r.***) give that (***y***) to you (fem.) (***bə***)'.

DEMONSTRATIVE PRONOUN

There are three degrees of distancing: the proximate form, suggesting nearness to 1st person, is sing. *a(b)rəy*, pl. *(ab)art*; distal but within purview of 1st and 2nd p. is sing. *a(b)nəy*, pl. *(ab)ant*; the second distal set, sing. *wəy/wəbrəy*, pl. *wərt/wəbart*, is used for referents beyond the purview of either 1st or 2nd person.

INTERROGATIVE PRONOUN

d.*arban* 'who?', where ***d-*** can be replaced by other 1st slot pronominal markers; *zaḳ°əy* 'what?'; *yanba* 'when?'; *yaba* 'where?'

There is no relative pronoun in Abkhaz. A slot 1 marker + *-an(ə)* can be used for a temporal relative clause; a slot 1 marker + *-ax (ə)* for a locative. An example of the latter from Hewitt (1979: 166):

> sara **yə.z.**boyṭ Merab **d.**ax'ə.n.xo a.y°nə
> 'I see the house where Merab lives'

where *sara* denotes 'I'; ***yə*** 'it'; ***z.*** is the pronominal subject marker 'I'; *bo.yṭ* 'see' (finite); ***d.*** is the pronominal subject marker 'he'; *axə* 'where'; *n* is the preverb; *xo* 'to live'; and *a.y°nə* 'the house'.

Numerals

The system is vigesimal, and reflects the human/non-human dichotomy. Here, the cardinals 1–10 are set out as they appear with non-human referents. For human referents, these numbers from 3 inclusive onwards take *w* instead of *pa/ba*: *a.ḳə, y°.ba, x.pa, pš.ba, x°.ba, f.ba, bež.ba, aa.ba, ž°.ba, ž°a.ba*; 11 is *ž°e.y.za*; 12–18: *ž°a/z°ə* + unit root form, in some cases abbreviated; thus 15, for example, is *ž°ə.x°*; 17 is *ž°ə.bž*; 19 is *ze.y.ž°*; 20 is '2.10' *y°a.ž°a*, to which the units are then added; 30 *y°a.ž°əy. z°a.ba*; 40 *y°ən y°a.ž°a*; 60 *xən y°a.ž°a*; 80 *pšən y°a.ž°a*; 100 *š°.ḳə*; 200 *y°ə.š°*; 1,000 *zḳə*. For example, *a.la.k°a pš.ba* = *pš.la.ḳ* '(the) four dogs'.

Both article and plural marker are discarded if the numeral lacks the generic marker *ba/pa*: e.g. *wasa y°ə°s°* '200 sheep'. Ordinals are formed by affixation of *-ṭ°əy* to the cardinal.

Verb

Abkhaz verbs are stative (resultative) or dynamic, transitive or intransitive, mono- or polypersonal. Monopersonal verbs are intransitive: e.g. ***d.****ceyṭ* 'he went', ***s.****ceyṭ* 'I went'. Polypersonal verbs may be either transitive or intransitive, depending on the sense of the root and the valencies assigned to it in Abkhaz. There is no passive voice in Abkhaz. A dynamic base can, however, be converted to a stative by means of the stative marker *-wp̣* and concomitant realignment involving the use of postpositional forms denoting agency.

A causative is made by inserting pre-radical *-r-*: e.g. *yə.b.sə.r.qa.çeyṭ* 'I made you do it'; where *yə* denotes 'it', *b* 'you' (fem.), *sə* 'I', *r* causative formant, *qa* is a preverb, and *çeyṭ* 'make/do' the finite form.

INDICATIVE MOOD (PRESENT AND PAST)

Choice of marker here depends on (a) whether the verb is stative or dynamic, and on (b) whether a finite or a non-finite form is required:

Stative finite present:	*s.ṭ°o.**wp̣***	'I stand', 'am standing'
Stative finite past:	*s.ṭ°a.**n***	'I was standing'
Dynamic finite present:	*yə.z.bo.**yṭ***	'I see it'
	*s.co.**yṭ***	'I go'
Dynamic finite past:	*yə.z.be.**yṭ***	'I saw it'
	*s.ce.**yṭ***	'I went'

Dynamic future (two forms are made):	*s.ca.**p***	'I'll go' (inaugurative)
	s.ca.ṣṭ	'I'll probably go'
A stative future is made with the characteristic *zaa*:	*də.ṭ°a.zaa.weyṭ*	'He will be sitting'
The characteristic of the dynamic perfective finite is *x'a/x'e*:	*s.ca.x'e.yṭ*	'I've gone' (my going is over and done with)

Five dynamic imperfective forms (three past, two conditional) have an *-n* suffix in place of the perfective *p/ṭ*: e.g. *s.co.**n*** 'I was going'; *s.ca.rə.**n*** 'I would go', where *rə* is the conditional characteristic; cf. *wəy də.z.ba.**r*** 'that one, if I see her'.

The non-finite correlatives of these ten finite forms take the format: pronominal marker + root (+ characteristic or aspect marker); cf. *yə.co* 'he who goes', *yə.ca* 'he who went', *yə.ca.ra* 'he who will go', *yə.co.z* 'he who was going'.

IMPERATIVE

The stem is used with the 2nd p., sing. or pl., subject marker if the verb is intransitive; 2nd p. pl. only if it is transitive, i.e. the marker for singular transitive imperative is zero.

The negating format *-m-/-m* is added to the complex to provide a prohibitive, and *-n* (associated with the imperfective aspect) is added: e.g. *š°ə.**m**.ṭ°a.**n*** 'don't you (pl.) sit'. For the negative marker, cf. *s.co.**m*** 'I'm not going', *s.co.**mə**.z.ṭ* 'I was not going'.

SUBJUNCTIVE MOOD

A subjunctive mood is made with the formant *-aa.yṭ*: e.g. *yə.l.g.aa.yṭ* 'let her (*l*) take it', and an inferential with *-zaa.p*: e.g. *də.šta.zaa.p* 'it seems he's lying down'.

POTENTIAL

The verb *a.l.ṣa.ra* 'to be able' is used: e.g. *a.ca.ra Ø.sə.l.ṣo.yṭ* 'I can go', where *a.ca.ra* is a verbal noun 'the going', Ø marks the position of the unexpressed 3rd p. subject ('it'), *sə* is 'to me', and *l* is a preverb; *ṣa.wa.yṭ* > *ṣo.yṭ* 'is possible'.

DIRECTIONAL PRE-VERBS

For example, *-aa-* 'hither', *-na-* 'thither', *-y°a-* 'upwards', *-la-* 'downwards'. These are inserted in the verbal complex: e.g. *yə.b.z.**aa**.z.ge.yṭ* 'I bring it for you (fem.)', where *yə* denotes 'it', *b* 'you' (fem.), *z(ə)* 'for' (postposition), *z.* 'I', *ge* 'bring', and *yṭ* the finite marker.

Postpositions

There is a wide inventory of spatio-temporal postpositions, which are often combined with directional preverbs in the verbal complex. Where required, pronominal markers belonging to the second series are prefixed to postpositions: e.g. ***s.**qənṭ°* 'from me', ***yə.**qənṭ°* 'from him'.

Some examples:

at: ***a**.ṭṣ̦;ə* 'at it (***a***)'; *a.voḳzal* ***a**.ṭṣ̦ə* 'at the station' (Russian loanword)
inside: ***a**.y°nə c̣q̣a*; ***a.**y°nə a.y°n c̣q̣a* 'inside the house'
behind: ***a**.šta.x′*; *a.y°nə* ***a**.šta.x′ də.q̣o.wp̣* 'he is behind the house'
above: ***a**.xəx′*; *a.y°nə* ***a.**xəx′* 'above the house'
on: ***a**.k°c°a*; *a.c̣la* ***a**.k°c°a* 'on top of the tree'
among: ***rə**.y°nə c̣q̣a*; *a.c̣la.k°a* ***rə**.y°nə c̣q̣a* 'among the trees'

Adverbs

Several affixes produce adverbs from nouns or adjectives, e.g. *-nə*, which requires the root to be marked either by the neutral (non-human) pronominal prefix *yə-*, or by the Series 1. pronominal marker in concord with the verbal subject. Hewitt gives the following example:

sara **yə.**las.**nə** **s.**nəq̣°o.yṭ 'I walk quickly'
s .las.**nə** **s.**nəq̣°o.yṭ

Word order

SOV is normal. For pronominal subject/indirect and direct object order in the verbal complex, *see* **Pronoun** and **Verb**, above.

1. Аханàт̆ дѷqан Àзка, у̀і Àзка Анц̡à іĕѷ дѷqан; у̀і Àзка дѵ'-Нц̡àн.

2. У̀і Àзка Анц̡à іĕѷ аханàт̆ дѷqан.

3. Зеќѷ У̀і ìла іqалѵèіт, У̀і ìда акќѷ азѷqамлѵеіт ìqалаз.

4. У̀і абзàзара ìлан, У̀і ібзàзара ауаà рзѵ лашàран.

5. Àлашара àлаӥцара аĕѷ ілашѵуòіт,— àлаӥцара Іарà ізѵіхàмђеіт.

6. Дѷqан Анц̡à іqнѷт̆ іаàӥђѵз аʃѷ; у̀і Іоàнн ìх̇ʒѵн.

7. У̀і даàіт шаhàђѵс Àлашàра дѵізѷшаhађразѵ,— іарà ìла зеќѷ дхàртц̡аразѵ.

8. Іарà длашàрамѵзт, ахà (дааӥђѷн) àлашара зхѷлтц̡ѵуа дѵìђушаhађхаразѵ.

ABKHAZ-ADYGE LANGUAGES

INTRODUCTION

These languages fall into three groups: (a) Abkhaz and Abaza; (b) Adyge and Kabard-Cherkes; (c) Ubykh. Genetically, these languages are closely related, but the three groups are not mutually intelligible. As an isolated outlier, Ubykh (now extinct) diverges considerably from (a) and (b). The Ubykh people moved *en bloc* to Turkey in the middle of the nineteenth century. The other languages are spoken by about half a million people in the Abkhaz Autonomous Region, in Georgia, the Karachaevo-Cherkessia Republic, the Adygeia Republic, and the Kabardino-Balkaria Republic.

SCRIPT

Ubykh was unwritten; the other four are in use as literary languages. The Cyrillic script is used, but in highly inconsistent fashion; the same Cyrillic letters being used in different languages to represent different sounds. In Abkhaz, the script is extended by three non-Cyrillic graphs.

PHONOLOGY

All of these languages are characterized by a possibly unique proliferation of consonants, on the one hand, and by a very simple, rudimentary vowel system, on the other. Thus, Ubykh had a basic vocalic opposition in /ə/ – /a/ plus an inventory of some 80 consonantal phonemes. Similarly, Abaza has two vowels and 66 consonants; Abhaz has 58. Clearly, such inventories can be achieved only by means of secondary articulation – glottalization, palatalization, labialization, aspiration – and each of the languages has specific refinements on these lines. For example, two dialects of Adyge extend the normal three-term series: voiced stop – unvoiced aspirate – ejective, with a semi-ejective, unaspirated member: e.g. /b – p – p' – p̄/.

For detailed inventories, *see* **Abkhaz** and **Kabard-Cherkes**.

MORPHOLOGY AND SYNTAX

Noun

The human/non-human dichotomy underlies the nominal system. Nouns are also marked for definiteness/indefiniteness, number, and the genitive relationship. Adyge, Kabard-Cherkes, and Ubykh have nominative/ergative opposition; Abkhaz and Abaza have virtually no case system. Gender is marked in second and third person forms in Abkhaz/Abaza.

Verb

Abkhaz-Adyge verbs are dynamic or stative; transitive or intransitive; monopersonal or polypersonal; and are marked for person, number, tense, mood. The verbal complex contains, if required, interrogative and negative markers. Causativity, reciprocity, potentiality, and involuntary action are also indicated by markers in verbal complex.

In a tripersonal verbal complex the sequence of personal pronominal markers is: direct object (nominative) – oblique object (ergative) – subject (ergative). The combination of polysynthetic structure on this scale and polypersonalism leads, as might be expected, to the formation of long and complex verbal forms, in which root and markers alike often consist of a single consonant.

Kumakhov (1979: 144) gives the following, admittedly somewhat extreme, example from Kabard-Cherkes:

w-a-qə-də-d-ej-z-ɣe-šə-žə-f-a-te-qəm-əj

analysed as follows:

w-	2nd p. sing. direct obj. prefix
a-	3rd p. pl. indirect obj. prefix
qə	directional marker: 'hither'
də-	comitative marker
d-	locative marker
ej-	3rd p. sing. obj. prefix
z-	1st p. sing. sbj. prefix
ɣe-	causative prefix
šə-	root of verb *še-n* 'to bring'
-žə	reflexive suffix
-f	suffix of potentiality
-a	past-tense suffix
-te	temporal suffix: 'then'
-qəm	suffix of negation
-əj	modal suffix

That is, root + 8 prefixes + 6 suffixes. The whole complex means: 'So then I was not able to get him to bring you back from there along with them.' Further simpler examples showing the arrangement of subject and object markers will be found in the articles on Abkhaz and Kabard-Cherkes.

Two basic syntactic constructions are found: the nominative sentence (subject in nominative; intransitive verb) and the ergative sentence (subject in ergative; direct object in nominative; transitive verb).

ACHINESE

INTRODUCTION

Achinese belongs to the Malayo-Polynesian branch of Austronesian, and is spoken by over 2 million people in northern Sumatra. The Indonesian spelling is *Aceh*. The language may be related to the Cham languages in Vietnam and Cambodia (*see* **Cham**). The Achinese have been Muslims since the thirteenth/fourteenth centuries.

SCRIPT

Traditionally Arabic, now replaced by romanization with diacritics denoting vowel quality. Transcription here is broad.

PHONOLOGY

Consonants

Achinese has labial, dental, palatal, and velar series of the type: unvoiced stop – voiced stop – nasal, e.g. /p, b, m; k, g, ŋ/. Other sounds: /s/ > [θ]; /l, r, h/, glottal stop or hamza; /w, j/. /p, b, t, c, k, s, h, r/, and hamza have nasalized counterparts. Stop + /r/l/ is fairly frequent: /dr-, pl-, bl-/, etc. Cf. *bloe* 'buy', *ple* 'pour', *klo* 'deaf', *grah* 'thirst', *jroh* 'beautiful', *croh* 'fried' (Indonesian *goreng*).

Vowels

/i, ɪ, ɛ, a, ə, ɔ, o, u/. /ə/ has two values: /ə/ notated as *eu*, /ə̆/ = /ʌ/ notated as *ë*. [ɪ] and [ə̆] prolong vocalic finals in colourless off-glide. All diphthongs have [ə/ə̆] as second element. /i, ɛ, a, o/ are nasalized in contact with nasal vowels, but not necessarily nasalized in contact with the nasalized counterparts of the stops (see above). Diphthongized vowels: cf. *ujeuen* (Ind. *hujan*) 'rain', *ureueng* (Ind. *orang*) 'person, man'. Cf. diphthongization of vowels in Cambodian.

MORPHOLOGY AND SYNTAX

Noun

No grammatical gender, no marking for case or number. Reduplication may be used to suggest vague quantities: *macam-macam* 'all sorts of…'.

POSSESSION

Possessor follows: *pinto rumoh* 'the door of the house'; *alat rumoh* 'household goods'.

Adjective

As attribute, the adjective follows the noun: *ureueng tuha* 'old man', *nanggroë Aceh* 'the Achinese country'.

Pronoun

The independent personal forms are:

	Singular	*Plural*
1	keë, ulon	*incl.* geutanyoë, *excl.* kamoë
2	kah, gata	droeneuh
3	jih, gobnyan	droeneu

Related (truncated) forms act as verbal prefixes recapitulating the overtly expressed independent form, and there is a related series of possessive enclitics: e.g. for 1st p. sing. *lampoh.lon* 'my garden'; *rumoh.ku* 'your house'; *blang.meuh* 'our (excl.) paddy field'; *sikula.teuh* 'our (incl.) school'; *meuneukat.neuh* 'your (pl.) goods'.

VERBAL PREFIXES

Si N. **ji**jak u peukan ngon ma**jih**
'N. goes to market with her mother'

Gobnyan **geu**.teuka di Jawa
'He is returning from Java'

Gobnyan **geu**.beuet basa Aceh
'He is learning Achinese'

Droeneuh bandum **neu**.teuka singoh bak teumpat nyoe
'You are all to come here (to this place) tomorrow'

Cf. forms without independent pronoun: *ku.duek* 'I sit'; *meu.duek* 'we (excl.) sit', *geu.duek* 'he/they sit'. Cf.

lon lon.woe ngon gobnyan
'I'm coming back with him'

gigoe.jih meuh = meuh gigoe.jih
'his teeth are (of) gold'

geutanyoe ta.deungö ngon punyueng, ta.ngieng ngon mata
'we hear with our ears, and see with our eyes'

peue geutanyoe ta.mudek atawa ta.ek u laot singoh?
'Shall we go to the mountain(s) (*mudek*) or shall we go sailing tomorrow?'

DEMONSTRATIVE PRONOUN/ADJECTIVE

nyan, *nyoe*: *rumoh nyan* 'this house'

INTERROGATIVE PRONOUN

soë 'who?': *Bak soë* ***ta****.kheun* 'To whom did you say that?; *Rumoh soë nyan* 'Whose house is that?'

RELATIVE PRONOUN

Nyang

Ureueng nyang le ji.troh meuih pirak
'People who have lots (*le*) of gold (*meuih*) and silver (*troh* = BI *taruh* 'have in one's possession')

Ureung nyang jak baroë ka **ji**.woë
'The man who went away yesterday has come back'

leumo.geuh nyang ji.pök le moto
'his cow which was hit by a car . . .'

limong droe ureueng nyang ba beude sajan ka ji.droh le pulisi
'five men who were carrying weapons were arrested by the police'

nyang rayeuk
'what is big'

nyang trok baroe
'he who arrived yesterday'

abu geu.bloe eungkot mi nyang ta.guen
'father buys fish, ma is the one who cooks it'

Verb

Since Achinese has no verbal inflection, and since there is no overt or formal difference between transitive and intransitive verbs, the sense of a statement depends on (a) the ordered syntax of pronominal components, (b) the use of adverbials, and (c) the use of prefixes, infixes, and suffixes.

There is a broad division into verbs expressing intentional action, and verbs expressing chance or unintentional action.

As noted above, the verbal personal prefix recapitulates the personal pronoun.

TENSE MARKERS

Present unmarked, past has *ka*. The present progressive may be marked by *teungoh*: *teungoh geu.jak* 'he is now going'; *gobnyan teungoh geu.beuet basa Aceh* 'he is now learning the Achinese language'.

gohlom (= Ind. *belum*) signifies 'not yet': *gohlom teungeut* 'not yet asleep'; *tapike dilee si.gohlom ta.pubuet* 'think before you act'.

Specimen past tense: *jak* 'to go' (pronounced /ja'/):

lon ka lonjak	'I went'
kah ka kajak	'you went'
jih ka jijak	
gobnyan ka geujak	'he/she went'
geutanyoë ka tajak	'we (incl.) went', etc.

PREFIXES

For example, *meu-/mu-* 'having', 'provided with': *peng* 'money', *mupeng* 'moneyed'; *lampoh* 'garden', *meulampoh* 'having a garden'. *Meu-/mu-* is also a formant for denominative verbs: *madat* 'opium', *mumadat* 'to smoke opium'; and also for reciprocals: *rab* 'close', *meurab* 'to approach one another'.

Peu-/pu-:

(a) causative: *beuët* 'to recite/learn', *pubeuët* 'to instruct';
(b) forms denominative verbs: *teumon* 'sleep', *peuteumon* 'put to sleep'; *pungoh* 'crazy', *pupungoh* 'drive crazy'; *lampoh nyan geu.peu, timang le gobnyan* 'this garden was laid out by him'.

Teu-/tu- makes passives: *pula* 'to sow', *teupula* 'to be sown'; *bloe* 'to buy', *teubloe* 'to be bought'.

INFIXES

-eun-: forms nouns from verb stems: e.g. *bloe* 'to buy', ***beun**aloe* 'a purchase'; *bantu* 'to help', ***beun**antu* 'a helper'; *surat* 'to write', ***seun**urat* 'a writing'; *puga* 'to sow', *p.eun.uga* 'crops';

-eum-/-um-: forms verbs: *pateh* 'to obey', ***pum**ateh* 'to be docile'; *gobnyan geu.jak s.**eum**.uga u blang* 'he goes to sow seed in the paddy field'; *koh* 'piece', *k.**eum**.eu.koh* 'cut to pieces'.

NEGATIVE

Han(a) is a general negating particle: *lon hana peng* 'I have no money'; *aneuk lon hana dalam rumoh nyan* 'my child is not in the house'.

The prohibitive particle is *bek*: *bek meunan ta.kheun* 'don't speak so!'

pi 'also': *lon lon.woe jih.pi ji.woe* 'I go back, so does he'; *haba pi habeh, malam pi jula* 'story-so-finish, evening-so-late', i.e. 'by the time the story was finished, it was late in the evening'.

Parallel sentences linked by *di*: *di lon lon.bloe bakang, di gata ta.bloe ranub keu nek* 'I buy tobacco, you buy betel for grannie'. Cf. *meunyo gata han ta.tem.jak, di lon.pi han sit* 'if you don't go, then neither do I'.

Prepositions

Examples:

bak 'to', 'in', 'on', etc.: *ta.jak bak teungku* 'go to the tungku'; *jih han jeuet ji.jak bak sikula* 'he can't/couldn't go to school';

keu 'at', 'towards,' etc.: *jih na gaseh keu lon* 'he likes me' (has sympathy (*gaseh* = BI *kasih*) towards me);

oe 'to', etc.: *lon.jak oe peukan* 'I go to market';

di 'from': *srot di.bubong* 'fall(en) from the roof';

ngon 'with', 'than': *ngon lon rayeuk gata* 'you are bigger than I am'; *lon lonwoe ngon gobnyan* 'I come back with him'; *kamoe meu.jak ngon moto* 'we (excl.) go by car'; *kayee geu.koh ngon parang* 'the wood was cut with a knife'.

For 'because' Aceh uses either *sabab* (Arabic) or *kareuna* (< Sanskrit).

Word order

SVO

1 Bak saboh watèë Jesus teungoh geumeudo'a disaboh teumpat.
Watèë Gobnjan geupijôh nibak meudo'a, sidroë nibak murid^{2}geuh
djikheuën ubak Gobnjan: „Gurèë, neupeurunoëkeuh kamoë meudo'a,
lagèë njang geupeurunoë lé Jahja keu murid^{2}geuh." 2 Djaweuëb
Jesus keu awak njan: „Meunjoë gata tameudo'a, takheuën lagèë njoë:
Ja Bapa, beuneupeusutjikeuh Nan Droëneuh; beuteukakeuh Keuradjeuën
Droëneuh. 3 Neubrikeuh keu kamoë tiëp^2 uroë makanan kamoë njang
tjukôb, 4 dan Neupeuampônkeuh dèsja kamoë, sabab kamoë pih peuampôn
tiëp^2 ureuëng njang meusalah keu kamoë; dan bèkkeuh Neuba kamoë u
dalam peutjuba'an."

(Luke 11.1–14)

ADYGE

INTRODUCTION

Adyge belongs to the Abkhaz-Adyge sub-group of North-West Caucasian. There are about 100,000 speakers in the Adyge region, plus communities in Turkey, Syria, and Jordan. The literary language is based on the Temirgoi dialect, and dates from 1918. Until 1927 an adaptation of the Arabic script was used, then replaced by Latin. Since 1938 Cyrillic + *I* which here marks the ejective series.

PHONOLOGY

See **Abkhaz-Adyge Languages**.

Consonants

Peculiar to the Shapsug and Bžedug dialects of Adyge is the 'semi-ejective' (unaspirated plosive) stop which extends the normal three-way opposition – e.g. /b, p, p'/ – to a four-way opposition: /b, p, p', p̄/. This phoneme is not found elsewhere in Caucasian.

Labialization is a marked feature of Adyge, extending even to the glottal stop: '°.

Vowels

Long /a/, short /ə/, and /ɪ/.

MORPHOLOGY AND SYNTAX

See **Kabard-Cherkes, Abkhaz-Adyge Languages.**

AFRIKAANS

INTRODUCTION

Afrikaans belongs to the West Germanic branch of Indo-European, and is derived from the same sixteenth-century Dutch dialect, Frankish in origin, which underlies modern Dutch. It took shape first in the Cape Colony, where Jan van Riebeeck had arrived in 1652, and spread to the rest of South Africa, from the seventeenth century onwards. It has been a literary language for a little over a century. On both counts, it is the youngest of the Germanic languages. At present, it is spoken by about 6 million people.

The language was originally known as Kaaps-Hollands or Plat-Hollands. The designation 'Afrikaans' was adopted towards the end of the nineteenth century. From 1910 till 1925, Dutch and English were the joint official languages of the Union of South Africa; in 1925 Afrikaans replaced Dutch. The use of Afrikaans is mainly characteristic of the Cape Province, the Orange Free State, and the Transvaal.

SCRIPT

Roman, 26 letters as in English; *c*, *q*, *x*, *z* are rarely used. The circumflex is used to mark the long open *ê*, *ô*: *lê* = /lɛː/.

PHONOLOGY

Consonants

stops: p, b, t, d, k, g, ʔ; palatalized k′
affricates: ts, tʃ
fricatives: f, v, s, ʃ, j, x, ɦ
nasals: m, n, ɲ, ŋ
lateral and flap: l, r
/z/ occurs in a few loanwords

[g] and [x] are allophones: cf. *berg* 'mountain', /bɛr**x**/, pl. *berge*, /bɛrgə/. /p, t, k/ are non-aspirate, /b, d/ in final position are unvoiced → [p, t]. Dutch /sx-/ = Afrikaans /sk-/, and Dutch final *-t* drops: e.g. *nacht* > *nag* /nax/, 'night'; *nest* > *nes* 'nest'.

Vowels

front: i, iː, e, ɛ, ɛː, y, yː

middle: ə, əː, a, ɵ, ɪ, ɪː
back: ɑ, ɔ, ɔː, oː, u, uː, ʊ

/eː/ is realized as [e(ː)ə] or [ɪə]; /oː/ as [o(ː)ə] or [ʊə]. /a, ɛ, ɔ/ are nasalized when followed by *n* + fricative: e.g. *mense* [mɛ̃ːsə] 'people'; *aangesig* [ãːxəsɪx] 'face'.

DIPHTHONGS

Simple (short) or lengthened; all are falling.

short: əy, oʊ, œy (= Dutch /ʌy/), ɑi ɔi, ui
long: ɑːi, oːi/ɔːi, eːu

Stress

Stress is free, associated with pitch. The main stress is normally on the root. In separable verbs, however, the stress is transferred to the prefix.

MORPHOLOGY AND SYNTAX

Noun

The division into common and neuter nouns, retained in Dutch, has been lost in Afrikaans. A single definite article – *die* – applies to all nouns, singular and plural: e.g. *die vader* 'the father' – *die moeder* 'the mother' – *die kinders* 'the children'. '*n* = [ə] is used as singular indefinite article: e.g. '*n vliegtuig* 'a plane'.

NUMBER

-e is a frequent plural marker, with phonetic adjustment, where necessary, at juncture; *-s* and *-ers* are also used: e.g. *wolf* 'wolf' – *wolwe*; *skip* 'ship' – *skepe*; *dag* 'day' – *dae*; *oom* 'uncle' – *ooms*; *kind* 'child' – *kinders.*

CASE

There is no inflection for case in Afrikaans; the genitive relationship is expressed periphrastically with the particle *se*: e.g. *sy vader se huis* 'his father's house'; *Pretoria se koerante* 'Pretoria's newspapers, the Pretoria newspapers'.

The indirect objective case of a personal noun is marked by the preposition *vir* 'for, to': *gee... vir die arme kind* 'give the poor child...'; *Sê vir oom, hy moet tuis kom* 'Tell uncle to come home.' The use of *vir* with a direct personal object seems to be possible. Mironov (1969) gives the example: *Jan slaan vir Piet* 'Jan strikes Piet.'

COMPOUNDING

Compounding, along the familiar German/Dutch lines, is a prolific source of new words in Afrikaans: e.g. *tand.arts* 'dentist'; *speel.goed.afdeling* 'toy department'; *woord.verwerking* 'word processing'; *snel.heids.grens* 'speed limit'; *derde.party.versekering* 'third-party insurance'; *skoon.maak* 'to (make) clean'.

DIMINUTIVES

Diminutives are very widely used in Afrikaans. The ending is *(C)ie*, where C is *(t)j*, *k*, or *p*. Cf.

boek + ie: boekie 'small book'
tand + jie: tandjie 'small tooth'
boom + pie: boompie 'small tree'

Adjective

As attribute, adjective precedes noun. After either article, *-e* is normally added to all polysyllabic and some monosyllabic adjectives: e.g. *die Nederlandse taal* 'the Dutch language'. The addition of *-e* may induce change in stem final: e.g. *Die kind is **goed***; but, *Dit is 'n **goeie** kind* 'This/he/she is a good child.' Many adjectives remain uninflected: e.g. *Dit is 'n donker nag* 'It's a dark night.'

COMPARATIVE

Made with *-er*: phonetic change at junctures: e.g. *donker* 'dark' – *donkerder*; *doof* 'deaf' – *dower.*

Pronoun

Some vestiges of common Germanic inflection survive in the singular forms: the third person singular forms are marked for gender:

		Singular			*Plural*	
		Subject	*Object*	*Possessive adjective*	*Subject/ object*	*Possessive adjective*
1		ek	my	my	ons	onse
2		jy	jou	jou	julle	julle se
		U	U	U	U	U
3	masc.	hy	hom	sy		
	fem.	sy	haar	haar	hulle	hulle se
	nt.	dit	dit	—		

The predicative possessive forms are *myne, joune, U sy'n/s'n, syne, haar se*; pl. *ons sy'n, julle sy'n, hulle sy'n*: e.g. *my boek – die boek is myne – die boek is julle s'n. U* is the polite address form.

REFLEXIVE PRONOUN

The forms are:

	Singular	*Plural*
1	(my)self	onsself
2	jou/u.self	julle/u.self
	hom/haar.self	hulle.self

DEMONSTRATIVE PRONOUN/ADJECTIVE

E.g. *hierdie* 'this', *daardie* 'that'.

INTERROGATIVE PRONOUN

wie 'who?'; *wat* 'what?: e.g. *In wie se naam?* 'In whose name?'

RELATIVE PRONOUN

wat is used for all referents: e.g. *die boek wat daar lê* 'the book that is lying there'; *die man/die vrou wat daar woon* 'the man/woman who lives there'. 'Whose' is rendered as *wie se*: *die man wie se huis verkoop sal word* 'the man whose house is to be sold'.

Numerals

As in Dutch with some changes in spelling: e.g. D. *vijf* 'five' = Afr. *vyf.*

Verb

Apart from the *ge-* prefix on most past participles, all verbal inflection has been lost. The verbal base is identical with the present tense of the indicative mood: e.g. *val* 'to fall', *ek/hulle val* 'I/they fall'. Auxiliaries such as *het, is, sal, word* are used to make composite tenses. The typical Germanic past-tense forms, whether strong or weak (*see* **German**), have disappeared, leaving the composite form with *het* as the sole past tense in Afrikaans (apart from *was*, the past tense of *is*) (cf. **Yiddish**): e.g. *ek het geval* 'I fell/have fallen'. If the verb begins with an inseparable prefix, e.g. *be-*, *er-*, *her-*, *ver-*, etc., the *ge-* of the past participle is dropped; i.e. here, the past participle coincides with the stem and the present tense.

SEPARABLE VERBS

The order of components in the tense structure of verbs with separable prefixes may be illustrated as follows, for *saambring* 'to bring along with one':

present: *ek bring my broeder saam* 'I'm bringing my brother along with me'
past: *ek het my broeder saam.ge. bring* 'I brought/I've brought . . . '
future: *ek sal my broeder saam.bring* 'I shall bring . . . '
split infinitive: *om saam te bring* '(so as) to bring along with one'

PASSIVE

The modal auxiliary *word* is used:

present: *die huis word gebou* 'the house is being built'
past: *die huis gebou word* 'the house was built'
past anterior: *die huis had gebou word* 'the house had been built'
future: *die huis sal gebou word* 'the house will be built'

IMPERATIVE MOOD

A simple imperative form is once again identical with stem and present tense; and, as in the present tense, a separable prefix follows: e.g. *oppas* 'to take care', *Pas op*! 'Take care!' A polite hortative form can be made with the auxiliary *moet*: e.g. *jy moet weggaan* 'you should/must go'. *Moet* + *nie* → *moenie* provides a negative imperative: e.g. *Moenie hier staan nie!* 'Don't stand here!'

Various auxiliaries, single or conjoint, are used to express possibility (realized or unrealized), obligation, desirability, etc.:

ek sou skryf as ek kan 'I'd write if I could'
ek moes dit gedoen het 'I should have done this'
hy hoef dit nie te doen nie 'he need not do it'
hy wou hulle help 'he wanted to help them'
dit sou kon gebeur het 'that could have happened'

NEGATIVE

The negating particle is *nie*: *ek praat nie* 'I don't speak', 'I'm not speaking'. In composite verbal forms, where an object is explicitly mentioned, *nie* is recapitulated as final component of the sentence:

hy het nie gekom nie 'he didn't come'
hy het niks gedoen nie 'he didn't do anything'
ek ken nie die man nie 'I don't know the man'

Similarly in stative verbs with adjectives:

die gebou is nie klein nie 'the building is not small'

NON-FINITE FORMS

The infinitive form is heavily eroded: e.g. *hê* (< *heb* < *hebben*) 'to have'; *sê* (< *seg* < *seggen*) 'to say'.

The present participle retains its original Germanic form: e.g. *lesende* 'reading'; *vallende* 'falling'; *Al pratende het hulle uit die kamer gestap* 'Talking, they left the room.'

Past participle: *ge*-prefix, except in verbs with an inseparable prefix; cf.

Hy het die boek gelees 'He read/has read the book.'
Hy het die boek vertaal 'He translated/has translated the book.'

Strong past participles inherited from Dutch function in general as attributive adjectives. Cf.

deur.dink 'to think through', 'consider': *'n deur.**dagte** plan* 'a carefully considered plan' (cf. German *denken – dachte – gedacht*);
sluit 'to close': *agter **geslote** deure* 'behind closed doors'.

Prepositions

Prepositions require the objective form of personal pronoun: e.g. *met haar* 'with her'; *Ek hou nie van hom nie* 'I don't like him' (lit. 'hold not with him'); *Ek wil môre graag by jou kom kuier* 'I'd like to come and visit you tomorrow' (*graag* = Gm. *gerne*).

As in German and Dutch, prepositions fuse with demonstrative and interrogative pronouns, in reverse order and with certain modifications:

*met wat > waarmee 'with what?'
*van dit > daarvan 'from this'
*op wat > waarop 'on what'

e.g. ek hou van rolprente 'I like films'
ek hou daarvan 'I like this'

Word order

SVO in principal clause; in subordinate clause SOV; if the subordinate clause precedes the principal clause, the word order in the latter is VSO.

Subordinate clause, past tense: OSV aux.: e.g. *die motorkar wat ek gister gekoop het* 'the car I bought yesterday'.

Subordinate clause, future tense: OS aux. V: e.g. *die brief wat ek môre sal ontvang* 'the letter which I'll get tomorrow'.

If a modal auxiliary is present, the order is SO aux. modal aux. V: e.g. (*Hy het gesê dat*) *hy ons môre sou kan help* '(He said that) he would be able to help us tomorrow.'

1 [a]**IN die begin was** [b]**die Woord, en die**
Woord was [d]**by God, en die Woord**
[e]**was God.**
2 Hy was in die begin by God.
3 [g]**Alle dinge het deur Hom ontstaan,**
en sonder Hom het nie een ding ontstaan
wat ontstaan het nie.
4 [i]**In Hom was lewe, en die lewe was**
die lig van die mense.
5 En [j]**die lig skyn in die duisternis, en**
die duisternis het dit nie oorweldig nie.
6 Daar was 'n man [l]**van God gestuur,**
wie se naam [m]**Johannes was.**
7 Hy het tot 'n getuienis gekom om van
die lig te getuig, sodat almal deur hom
sou glo.
8 Hy was nie die lig nie, maar hy moes
van die lig getuig.

(Genesis 1.1–18)

AGUL

INTRODUCTION

Agul belongs to the Eastern Lezgi group of Dagestanian languages. Agul is spoken by about 14,000 people, whose villages are located in ravines high in the mountains. Communications are difficult, and the language varies, often quite considerably, from one village to another. The Aguls use Lezgi in communication with their neighbours, and Lezgi is, along with Russian, the language of education. The administrative centre of the Agul region of the Dagestan Republic is Tpig.

SCRIPT

Agul is unwritten. For pedagogic purposes, the language has been notated in Georgian script, in romanization, and in Cyrillic + *I* as ejective marker. In his 1970 grammar of the language, Magometov uses romanization; his article on Agul (in *Jazyki Narodov USSR* (1966–8)) uses Cyrillic.

PHONOLOGY

Consonants

The labial, dental, and velar stops appear in four-term series: voiced plosive – voiceless unaspirated geminate – voiceless aspirate – ejective: e.g. /b – pp – p – p'/. The pharyngeal series lacks the voiced plosive: /Ø – qq – q – q'/. The affricate series are /Ø – tts – ts – tș/, /dʒ – ttʃ – tʃ – tʃ'/.

Fricative series: /w/v, ff, f; ʒ, ʃʃ, ʃ; z, ss, s; j, x'x', x'; γ, xx, x/. There are two pharyngeals: /ʕ, ħ/; and two glottals: /h, ʔ/. The /dʒ/ and /ʒ/ series have labialized values [dz°], etc. (not in all dialects). Ejectives are notated here as *p̣*, etc.

Vowels

i, e, a, u, y

/o/ is absent, and there is no nasalization.

MORPHOLOGY AND SYNTAX

Noun

In Agul, the division of nouns into grammatical classes by class marker (*see*, for example, **Avar**) is atrophied, though petrified class markers signalling four grammatical classes can be identified in nouns, pronouns, adjectives, and numerals.

NUMBER

The plural marker of consonantal endings is *-ar*; for vocalic endings, *-bur/wur/yar*: e.g. *is* 'year', pl. *isar*; *gada* 'son', pl. *gadawur.*

DECLENSION

There are 28 cases: four basic (nominative, ergative, genitive, dative) + 24 locative–directional cases arranged in eight series of three terms each, specifying (a) rest in given locus; (b) motion towards speaker; (c) motion away from speaker. The nominative provides the base for the ergative, which is, in turn, the base for all the other cases. For example, the basic cases of *gaga* 'father':

nominative	gaga
ergative	gagadi
genitive	gagadin
dative	gagadis

-di is only one of many endings marking the ergative; others are *-i*, *-u*, *-a*, *-ni*, etc. The logical subject of a transitive verb is in the ergative, the direct object in the nominative. The subject of a verb of perception is in the dative: *zus wun agwaja* 'I see you'.

The locative–directional series: the eight locus markers are: (1) 'behind': *q*; (2) 'under': *kk*; (3) 'on': *k*; (4) 'in front of': *h*; (5) 'on': *l*; (6) 'at': *w/f*; (7) 'in':'; (8) 'between/among': γ. For example: *usttuli**l** aldi'a kitab* 'on the table (*stul*) lies a book (*kitab*)'. These markers can be affixed to personal pronouns, and recapitulated in the verb:

za**h**kitab **h**aja	'in front of me there is a book'
za**f**kitab **f**aja	'at me there is a book' (i.e. 'I am holding a book')
za**kk** kursi **kk**eja	'below me there is a stool'

Adjective

Independent and predicative adjectives take number marker and class marker; also case if used as nominal. As attribute, they are invariable. Thus *idž**ed*** 'good', ergative, *idže**di***, etc. *-n*, *-s*; pl. *idže**dar***; but *Idže∅ insan**di** hhuč ḳini* 'The good man killed the wolf' (subject in ergative).

Pronoun

PERSONAL PRONOUN

	Singular		*Plural*
1	zun	*incl.*	x'in
		excl.	čin
2	wun		kun

These are declined in the four basic cases. Most dialects make no distinction between nominative and ergative, e.g. *zun* and *wun* being used for both. Forms for 3rd p. are supplied from the demonstrative series *me*, *te,* etc.

The genitive form provides the possessive pronoun: *ze čuj* 'my brother'.

DEMONSTRATIVE PRONOUN

me 'this', *te* 'that'; *ge* 'that (down there)'; *le* 'that (up there)', marked for case and number.

INTERROGATIVE PRONOUN

fiš/fuš 'who'; declined with oblique base in *hin-*; *fi* 'what?'. E.g. *hina ķine hhuč* 'who killed the wolf?', where *hina* is the ergative case of *fiš* 'who'; *hhuč* 'wolf' is in the nominative case.

RELATIVE PRONOUN

None; a participial construction is used:

kitab xuraje geda	'the boy who is reading the book'
kitabar zaš ruxuttare	'the books which I read'
xurunaje kitab	'the book which was read'
mi kitab.ar, waš ruxuban.ttare	'these (are) the books which you must read', where *waš* is the ergative case of *wun*

Note metathesis of consonants: *rux-/xur-*; both forms of the root occur in spoken Agul.

Numerals

1–10: *sad, qüd, x'ibud, jaqud, jüfud, jegx'id, jerid, mujid, jerķüd, jiçud*; 11–19 are made by prefixing *çi-* to units. 20 *qqad*; 30 *x'imçur*; 40 *jaγçur*; 100 *werš*.

Verb

Like Lezgi, Agul has lost the grammatical class system which is typical of Dagestanian languages, and has not replaced it with inflection by personal endings. Conjugation is, therefore, analytic, on the model: personal pronoun – sense-verb in non-finite form – auxiliary (marked for present/past, affirmative/negative).

The non-finite forms used in the formation of tenses are:

(a) The infinitive in *-s*, linked to stem by *-a-* or *-e-* depending on stem vowel: *ruxas* 'to read'; *liķes* 'to write'. This is the base form for future and subjunctive.
(b) Present gerund in *-di, d'*: the base for imperfective forms.
(c) Past gerund in *-na*: base for perfective forms.

AUXILIARY VERB

'To be' is defective: the present is *i/e*; negative, *dawai*, past *idi*/variants; negative, *dawadi*. For example *wun idemi e* 'you are a man'; *wun idemi dawa* 'you are not a man'; *zakas idemi x'ase* 'I shall be a man' (lit. 'from-me a man will become').

Example of tense formation:

zun/zas kitab xuruna.i → xuruni	'I read (past) the book'
wun/was kar aq̣una.i → aq̣uni	'you did the work'
zun/zas kitab xuras.e	'I shall read the book'

NEGATIVE FORMS

The infinitive is negated by prefixing *d*(V)-; *aq̣as* 'to do': *daq̣as* 'not to do'. If a preverb is present, the negative marker follows it: *qi. ḳas* 'to open': *qi.di.ḳas* 'not to open'. The *-tt-* infix in a verb changes that verb to its antonym: *qacas* 'to put on (clothes)': *qattacas* 'to take (clothes) off'.

VOICE

Active and passive are not formally distinguished. The participial form *xuruf*, for example (with petrified class marker *-f*), can mean, with reference to *kitab* 'book', '(he) who reads... ' or 'which was read'.

PARTICIPLE

-a- is present marker; *-u-* past. The participle takes the plural (class) marker: *aquf*, pl. *aquttar* 'doing (in past)', where *-f* and *-tt-* are class markers.

The participle of the auxiliary verb *de/re*, plus the petrified class marker *-f*, is used to form subordinate clauses: *i.de.f* 'being', pl. *i.de.ttar*, neg. *da.wa.f* 'not being', pl. *da.wa.ttar*; e.g. *zas 'ax' x'eri, wun idʒe insan iref* 'I know you being a good man', i.e. 'I know that you are a good man'.

MODAL AFFIXES

E.g. *gana/hana* 'when... ': *wun adi.gana* 'when you came... '; *zun xura.gana* 'when I was reading... '.

In addition to the indicative mood there are subjunctive, conditional, imperative, and necessitative moods, the latter formed by attaching participial endings to the genitive form of the verbal noun: *aqub.**an.f*** 'what has to be done (sing.)'; pl. *aqub.**an.tt.ar**.*

LOCATIVE–DIRECTIONAL MARKERS

(*See* **noun**, above.) These markers are prefixed to verbs as preverbs.

Postpositions

The case system is, in general, sufficiently rich; where necessary, adverbs of place/time can be used as postpositions.

Word order

SOV is usual; SVO occurs.

AINU

INTRODUCTION

The Ainu survive, in small and decreasing numbers, in Hokkaidō, and, at least until recently, in Sakhalin and the Kurile Islands. It is difficult to assess how many of them retain any knowledge of the Ainu language; but certainly none of them are monoglot, and the language appears to be on the verge of extinction. There has never been a written Ainu language. A considerable body of traditional or folk literature in both prose and verse exists, however, and Shibatani (1990) calls the language of these texts Classical Ainu. Prominent among the Classical Ainu texts are the heroic tales known as *yukar*, or *kamuy yukar* 'god-story'.

Ainu has no known congeners. Similarities between it and Korean have been detected, and it has been compared with several other language families: with Polynesian (Gjerdman 1926), with Hebrew (Batchelor), and with Indo-European (Naert 1958).

In no case, however, has any consistent and convincing relationship been established. R.A. Miller (1967) identifies the Ainu with the non-Yamato Aboriginals, who were driven northwards by the Yamato people (*see* **Japanese, Literary**).

By the twentieth century, two main dialect divisions had crystallized: Sakhalin and Hokkaidō. These appear to be highly divergent, almost to the point of mutual unintelligibility. The forms set out here are mainly those of the Shizunai dialect of Hokkaidō, as described by Refsing (1986). Additional examples are from Shibatani (1990).

PHONOLOGY

Consonants

labial: p (→ [b]), m
dental: t (→ [d]), n (→ [ŋ]), s (→ tʃ), r (→ [ɖ])
velar: k (→ [g])
glottal: h (→ [ɦ])

The semi-vowels /j, w/ occur as glide sounds between vowels: /io/ = [ijo]/, /ue/ = [uwe]. /ɖ/ is notated as *ḍ*.

Vowel harmony

Vowel harmony in Ainu is postulated by Chiri Mashio (1952) in terms of three vocalic groups: a, u / o / i, e, where i, e are compatible with a, u, and with o, while a, u are not compatible with o. Shibatani (1990) rejects the Chiri case for vowel harmony on grounds of its inconsistency.

MORPHOLOGY AND SYNTAX

Noun

There is no grammatical gender. Nouns are mainly mono- or disyllabic: *pet* 'river', *cise* 'house', *upas* 'snow', *ni* 'tree'. A plural marker *utar* exists: *aynu.utar* 'men'; but nominals are usually unmarked for number (cf. Japanese). On the other hand, plurality is marked in the verb.

CASE SYSTEM

This is marked by affix. The ending -(*h*)V, where V is a harmonic echo of the last stem vowel (i.e. a kind of vowel harmony), is used for a genitive or construct relationship, especially where inalienable ownership is concerned: cf. *apa* 'relative(s)', *apaha* '. . . 's relative(s)'; *caro* 'mouth', *caro.ho* '. . . 's mouth'; *nea aynu maci.hi* 'that man's wife'. This third example is from Shibatani (1990), who denies the existence of a genitive case in Ainu.

The vowel *i* is neutral (cf. Altaic languages): *imak* 'tooth', *imaki* '. . . 's tooth; *hon* 'stomach', *honi* '. . . 's stomach'; this relational form is also used in a partitive sense: *cep* 'fish', *cep rurihi* 'fish (its) broth'.

The postposition *un* acts as a link between two nouns, the first of which is the locus or origin of the second: *kim un kamuy* 'god of the mountain', i.e. 'bear' (*kamuy* appears to be a Japanese loanword: *kami*).

A noun may modify another noun without marker: *kamuy cep* 'god fish', i.e. 'salmon'; *kas kamuy* 'protector god'.

The verb *kor* 'to have' functions as an alienable possession marker: *ku kor menoko* 'my woman/wife'.

Other cases are constructed with postpositions as follows:

locative: *ta*: *sine to ta* 'in one day'; Batchelor has *atpaketa* for 'in the beginning' (St John's Gospel 1.1); *poro cise ta* 'in the big house'
allative: *un*: *toon nay or.un* (directional prefix *e-/o-* + *-un* > *erun/orun*) 'into that swamp'; *e.kim.un* 'into the mountains'; *Tookyoo un arpa* 'went to T'
ablative: *orwa*: *Kusur un kotan orwa* 'from the village of Kusur'
comitative: *tura*: *ponnispa tura* 'along with the young gentleman'
instrumental: *ari*: *tek ari kar.pe* 'something made by hand'
topicalizing affix: *anak* (corresponding to Japanese *wa*): *toon poro nupur anak* 'that big mountain' (cf. Jap. *ano ookii yama wa*)

Adjective

The Ainu adjective is best treated as a stative verb. When used attributively, as in the above example, it precedes the noun.

Pronoun

The personal independent first- and second-person forms, with their subject and object copies, as given by Refsing, are:

		Independent	*Subject affix*	*Object affix*
singular	1	kuani	ku-	en-
	2	eani	e-	e-
plural	1	cioka	ci-/-as	un-
	2	ecioka	eci-	eci-

E.g. *e.un.nukar.a* 'you (sing.) are looking (*nukar*; *.a* is a durative modal affix) at us'; *eci.un.kore* 'you (pl.) gave (*kore*) to us'.

Third-person forms are supplied from the demonstrative series, plus nominalizers: *toon kur* 'that person', *toon pe* 'that thing'; *pe* is a nominalizing particle.

DEMONSTRATIVE PRONOUN/ADJECTIVE

The base forms are *ta* (proximate), *to* (distal).

INTERROGATIVE PRONOUN

The base form is *ne*: *nen* 'who?', *nep* 'what?', *neyta* 'where?', *nepkusta* 'why?'

RELATIVE PRONOUN

None: Ainu treats the relative adjunct as qualifying material in the adjectival position preceding the nominal. Shibatani's example is: *tumpa.oran oka menoko* 'the/a woman (*menoko*) who stayed (*oka*) in (*oran*) the room (*tumpa*)'. Cf. *ekimne kusu soyene nispa* 'the man (*nispa*) who had gone out (*soyene*) to hunt (*ekimne kusu*)'.

NOMINALIZERS

E.g. *-p*(*e*): *pirka* 'good', *pirka.p* 'something good'; *ray* 'to die', *ray.pe* 'the dead'; *a.yanene.p* 'what I dislike'. *-ike* forms abstract nouns: *pirka.ike* 'goodness'.

Numerals

1–10: *sine*, *tu*, *re*, *ine*, *asikne*, *iwan*, *arwan*, *tupesan*, *sinepesan*, *wan*. If things are being counted, *-p*(*e*) is added: *sinep*, *tup*, *rep*, etc. For enumerating persons, *-n*/*-iw* is added: *sinen*, *tun*, *ren*, etc., e.g. *waniw* 'ten people'; 11–19: construction with *ikasma* 'more than', e.g. 12 *tu ikasma wan*; 20 *hotnen*; 30 *wan e tu hotne*; 40 *tu hotne*; 50 *wan e re hotne*, etc.; 100 *asikne hotne* (5×20).

Verb

Ainu verbs are transitive or intransitive. In the language of the classical epics, specific subject and object markers are used as follows:

1st p. sing. and pl. subject: trans. *a*-; intrans. *-an*;
2nd p. sing. and pl. subject: trans. and intrans. sing. *e*-; pl. *eci*-;

1st p. sing. and pl. object: trans. and intrans. *i-*;
2nd p. sing. object: *e-*; pl. *eci-*;
In all cases, the 3rd p. marker is Ø.

A generalized object is represented by prefixed *i-*, with accompanying switch from transitive to intransitive status. Shibatani gives the example:

ya a.ske 'I knit a net (*ya*)' (*a-* is the transitive subject marker)
i.ske.an 'I do it-a-knitting' (*-an* is the intransitive subject marker)

The same transition takes place when the reflexive pronoun *yay* is used with a transitive verb: *yay.rayke.an* 'I do a self-killing', i.e. 'I kill myself'. Similarly, a direct object may be incorporated in a verbal complex, which is then treated as an intransitive, e.g. (again from Shibatani):

transitive: *inaw a.ke* 'I make an *inaw* (cult object made of wood)'
intransitive: *inaw.ke.an* 'I am-a-maker-of-*inaw*'

Adjectives and adverbs may also be thus incorporated.

COPULA AND EXISTENTIAL VERB

The copula *ne* is used in an equative sense: *taan pe seta ne* 'this is a dog'. The existential verb is marked for number: sing. *an*; pl. *oka*: *aynu he an? kamuy he an?* 'Was he a human being (*aynu*)? Was he a god?'

Refsing (1986) classifies the Ainu verb as follows:

(a) non-affixing verbs denoting natural phenomena: *aptoas* 'it's raining';
(b) intransitive verbs, incompatible with the object affix: *ahun* (pl. *ahup*) 'to enter';
(c) adjectives: *cep pirka* 'the fish is good', *pirka cep* 'a good fish';
(d) transitive verbs, taking subject and object pronominal prefixes.

Verbs take prefixes (intensifying, moderating, etc.) and suffixes (e.g. of causality). There are no tenses: aspect (perfective, imperfective, terminative, and concomitant) is distinguished, as is modality (durative, iterative, hortative, imperative, desiderative, etc.). The verb is not conjugated for person.

The perfective aspect is marked by *isam*, linked to the verb by *wa*: *cep ku.Ø.e.wa.isam* 'I (*ku-*) ate (*e*) the fish (*cep*) and finished (*isam*) it Ø'. The existential sing./pl. markers, *an*, *oka*, reappear as characteristics of the imperfective aspect.

MOODS

Both durative and iterative moods are expressed by reduplication of stem. For the imperative, the bare stem is used, without pronominal affix. For other moods various markers are in use (ibid.: 201): e.g.

necessitative: *nankor na*: *e nu.nankor.na* 'you must listen' (*nu* 'to listen')
desiderative: *rusuy*: *e e.rusuy.cik* 'if you want to eat it' (*e* 'to eat', *cik* 'if')
intentional: *kusu ki*: *e oman.kusu.ki* 'you intend to go' (*oman* 'to go')

potential: *askay* (affirmative) and *aykap* (negative) preceded by summarizing particle *e*: *ku apkas.e.aykap* 'I can't walk' (*apkas* 'to walk')
reciprocal: *u-*: *nukar* 'to see': *u-nukar* 'to confer'
causative: *-re/te*, *-ke*, *-yar*: e.g. *e* 'to eat': *e.re* 'cause to eat', 'serve'; *hopuni* 'to rise': *hopuni.re* 'cause to rise, awaken'; *hure* 'to be red': *hure.ka* 'to dye red'

-(*y*)*ar* is used for a plural referent: e.g. *nukar* 'to see': *nukar.ar* 'to show sth. to people'.

Several verbs have distinct singular and plural stems: e.g. *arpa* (sing.), *paye* (pl.) 'to go'; *ek* (sing.), *arki* (pl.) 'to come'. See Shibatani (1990: 50–4) for a detailed discussion of plural verb forms.

The verb *kor* 'to have' may be added to the root to denote possession of the quality expressed in the root: e.g. *tum* 'strength': *tum.kor* 'to be strong'.

Interrogative sentences are marked by final *ya* (cf. Japanese *ka*, Korean *kka*).

THE APPLICATIVE CONSTRUCTION

This is Shibatani's name for what Refsing calls the 'adjunct-increasing prefixes'. Briefly, application of one of the prefixes, *o-*, *e-*, *ko-*, to a verb with an indirect object renders the normal construction with a postposition superfluous; that is, the noun + postposition construction is replaced by applicative prefix + verb, where the prefix carries the semantic deixis of the postposition. Cf.

(a) poro cise.ta horari 'he lives in a big house'
(b) poro cise e-horari 'he inhabits a big house'

(b) is construed as transitive, (a) as intransitive.

The general negating particle is *somo*, which in the following two examples precedes the pronominal subject marker:

somo ku.ku 'I don't smoke' (*ku* 'to smoke')
somo e.ye yakka 'even though (*yakka*) you (*e-*) don't say (*ye*) (it)'

In prohibitions *iteke* is used. Some verbs have negative versions: e.g. *amkir* 'know', *eramiskari* 'not know'; *easkay* 'be able', *eapkay* 'be unable'.

PASSIVE VOICE

Since verbal roots never change their form, use of the term 'passive voice' in Ainu depends on the assumption that the root is neutral as to voice. The question then arises: By what grammatical means is it identifiable as 'passive'? Kindaichi and Chiri (quoted by Shibatani) give very interesting examples, as does Refsing. Cf.

Kindaichi: X Y *ray.ke* 'X killed Y'
Y X.*orwa a.ray.ke* 'Y was killed by X'
Shibatani: Y X.*orwa an.omap* 'Y was loved by X'
Refsing: Y X.*orwa a.koyki wa a.ronnu* 'Y was attacked by X and killed by X'

Refsing glosses *a-* as 'indefinite person marking the passive', and this is one of the meanings given to *a-* by Kindaichi. Basically, *a-* is, of course, the *transitive* subject marker, and thus it appears that the logical patient is 'not really an object, but a subject' (Shibatani). Strong support for this interpretation comes from the fact that, in the language of the Yukar, honorary plural verbs are used with reference to what Indo-European regards as the logical patient; but honorary verbs can only be used of *subject* forms in Ainu (see Shibatani 1990: 55–60 on this point).

Postpositions

See **Noun**, above.

Word order

SOV is normal; under certain conditions OSV is found.

1 Atpaketa anak ne Itak an, Itak anak Kamui tura
2 an, Itak anak ne Kamui ne ruwe ne. Nei Itak anak
3 ne atpaketa Kamui tura no an nisa ruwe ne. Obitta
no an okaibe anak ne nei Itak orowa no akara,
orowa, akarape shinep ne yakka Shinuma isama no
4 akara shomoki nisa ruwe ne Shinuma otta inotu
5 an, inotu anak ne utara pekere ne ruwe ne. Nei
pekere kunne-i ta at, kunne-i anak ne nei ambe
6 eramushkare nisa ruwe ne. Kamui orowa no
ateshkara ainu an, reihei anak Yoannes ne ruwe ne.
7 Nei guru paweteshu-i gusu ek, utara obitta shinuma
gusu aeishokore kuni ne nei pekere gusu paweteshu
8 ki nisa ruwe ne na. Shinuma anak ne nei a pekere
shomo ne, nei pekere gusu paweteshu ki kuni gusu
9 an gun'ne.

AKAN or TWI

INTRODUCTION

This language is spoken in two major dialects, Ashanti and Fante, by up to 8 million people in Ghana. Akan belongs to the Kwa group of the Niger-Congo family. The form described here is Ashanti, the dialect spoken by the great majority of the Akan-speaking population.

The Basler Evangelische Missionsgesellschaft undertook the task of creating a Twi literary language in the 1840s, and the next 40 years saw the appearance of a Twi Bible, a definitive grammar, and a dictionary, mostly the work of J.G. Christaller. This early literary activity was based on the minor but politically and geographically accessible Akuapem dialect. Through the first half of the twentieth century, however, Ashanti began to be recognized as the proper base for a national literary language. Though certain scholars (e.g. Danquah) continued to write in Akuapem, others like Nketia and Tabi switched to Ashanti. In 1968 A.C. Denteh launched the important literary periodical *Odawuru* (*ɔ.dáwúru*, defined by Christaller as 'a kind of drum struck by the town crier').

SCRIPT

Roman plus ɛ, ɔ. In 1961 the Bureau of Ghana Languages devised a common standardized script for all forms of Akan. Tone is not normally marked, nor is nasalization. The correspondence between the script and the actual sounds of Akan is rather weak.

PHONOLOGY

Consonants

stops: p, b, t, d, k, g, ɖ
affricates: tʃ, dʒ
fricatives: f, ɸ, s, ʃ (ç), h
nasals: m, n, ɲ, ŋ
trill: r

Note: all consonants tend to be palatalized before front vowels, and stops tend to affricates.

There is a labialized series: /k°, g°, h°, n°, ŋ°/; /v/ and /l/ occur in foreign words. /ɖ/ is notated as *ḍ*; /ɸ/ as *w*.

Vowels

i, ɪ, e, ɛ, æ, å, ɔ, o, ŭ, u, y

/e/ and /å/ have no nasalized counterparts; all other vowels take nasalization.

VOWEL HARMONY

lax series: ɪ, ɛ, ɑ, o, ʊ̂
tense series: i, e, a, o, u

This division is important for vowel harmony: briefly, a *lax* vowel followed by /i/, /a/, or /ʊ/ is promoted to the next-highest vowel in the *tense* series, e.g. the sequence /ɪ . . . ʊ/ → /i . . . u/.

Vowel harmony determines the vocalic structure of the possessive and subject pronouns.

Tone

Three tones, which are phonemic: high, middle, and low. The tones in Akan are characteristically 'terraced', i.e. successive highs begin on a slightly lower level. This in turn affects successive middle tones, but low pitch is not affected.

MORPHOLOGY AND SYNTAX

Noun

Most Akan nominals consist of a stem with a prefix. The stem is neutral in the sense that it is not coded for function. Noun-forming prefixes may be oral: *a, ɛ, e, ɔ, o*; or nasal: *(a)m/n/ŋ*.

ɔ and *o* are used to form nouns denoting animates: *o.nípa* 'man', *ɔ.sebɔ́* 'leopard', and exceptionally for some inanimates: *ɔ.bó* 'stone', *o.sú* 'rain'; also, certain abstract nouns: *ɔ.kɔ́m* 'hunger'.

a- forms animates: *a.gyá* 'father'; inanimates: *a.kyené* 'drum'; abstracts: *à.bóro* 'injury'. The homorganic nasal, sometimes preceded by *a-*, forms nouns denoting collectives and substances: *n.sú* 'water', *ŋ.ŋó* 'oil', *m.fɔ́té* 'termites', *nna* < *n.da* 'sleep'.

Suffixes may be added: *didi* 'to eat', *a.didi.i* 'eating place'. *-ni* following the stem X indicates 'one who does/suffers X': *ohĩá* 'poverty', *ohĩá.ní* 'poor man'.

COMPOUNDS

Noun + adjective/noun: e.g. *ade.bòné* 'bad (*bòné*) thing (*a.dé*)' = 'evil', which can also be expressed by *ɛ.bòné* (note change in tonal pattern); *sika.guá* 'gold(en) stool' (enshrining and symbolizing the soul of the Ashanti people).

Compounds containing three components plus prefix are frequent: *o.fie.asétrǎ.sɛm* literally 'home – life – matters' = 'the affairs of this life'.

Example of word-building: base *yaré* 'to be sick':

ɔ.yàré 'sickness'
ɔ.yaré.dɔ́m 'epidemic'
ɔ.yaré.fó 'sick person'
ɔ.yare.súsow 'to be an invalid'
a.yare.sá 'the act, art of healing'
a.yare.sá.bèa 'hospital' (*bèa* is a locative marker)
a.yare.sá.de 'fee for curing a disease'
ɔ.yare.sá.fò 'doctor'

Nouns may also be expressed as construct forms, i.e. noun + annexed noun; e.g. from *ɔ.héne* 'king' and *o.fi* 'house' Akuapem makes *ahem.fi* 'king's house' = 'palace'. Here, Akan has (*Asante*).*héne.fié* 'the king of Ashanti's palace'. In a compound AB, A may retain its isolate tone, while B takes the annexed nominal tone(s).

The normal possessive order in Akan is possessor–possessed: *Ghánà mãn* 'the country of Ghana'. A pronominal link marked for person may be inserted: *abofára nó nhómã* 'the child (his) book'.

This word order – noun plus annexed noun – is reversed in compounds involving the word *kwa* < *akoá* 'slave': *kwà.safo* 'belonging to the community'. In boys' names the *kwa* component is followed by a truncated version of the name of the jinn presiding over the relevant day of the week: Ayísi over the first day, Adwó over the second. Thus a boy born on the first day of the week is called Kwàsí, on the second day Kwàdwó, and so on. Corresponding female names are Akosuwa, Adwowa. See Christaller 1933: 599 for a full list. As Christaller points out, the departure from normal Akan (Kwa) construct order, and the presence of feminine inflection, suggest that these forms originate in a non-Kwa sociolinguistic milieu.

CASE

Case is reflected in the prevailing SVO order: *ɔ.frɛ́.nò* 'he (*ɔ*) calls him (*nò*)'. Indirect object precedes direct object:

ɔ.mã́à me akutù 'he gave (*ɔ.mã́à*) to-me (*me*) an orange (*akutù*)'
ɔ.mã́ no biribí 'he gave him something'

Action which many languages express by means of an instrumental case is expressed in Akan as the product of two verbs, e.g.

ɔ.de pomá bɔɔ̀ no 'he took stick struck him', i.e. 'he struck him with a stick' (*de* 'take', *pomá* 'stick', bɔ 'strike')
ɔ.de siká yɛɛ̀ kaá 'he took gold made ring', i.e. 'he made a ring from gold' (*siká* 'gold', *kaá* 'ring')

There are several ways of making a singular noun plural. *-nṍm* is a pluralizing suffix: *ɔyére* 'wife', pl. *ɔyérenṍm*.

Pluralizing prefixes:

m-: *ɔba* 'child', pl. *mma*;
a-: *ɔkérãmãñ* 'dog', pl. *akérãmãñ*;
n-: *ɛdá* 'day', pl. *nná*.

Some plurals are suppletive: *osáni* 'warrior', pl. *asáfoɔ*.

Adjective

As attribute, adjective follows noun, and is often reduplicated: *mmára fófòro pii* 'many new laws' (*mmára* 'law', *fófòro* 'new'); *búùku kétewaa tuntum̀* 'a small black book' (*tuntum̀* 'dark in colour').

Exceptionally, some adjectives make a plural form.

Comparative is made with *sẽñ*: *eyé duru* 'it is heavy', *eyé duru sẽñ búùku nɔ̃́* 'It is heavier than the book.'

Pronoun

Emphatic personal independent + subject markers (here + copula):

	Singular		*Plural*	
	Independent	*Subject marker*	*Independent*	*Subject marker*
1	mẽ	mẽyɛ	yɛ́ŋ	yɛyɛ
2	wó	wóyɛ̀	mɔ̃́	mɔ̃yɛ̀
3	ɔnɔ̃́	ɔyɛ	wɔ́ŋ	wɔyɛ
impersonal	ɛnɔ̃́	ɛyɛ	ɛnɔ̃́	ɛyɛ

The objective forms: *mẽ, wo, nɔ̃* are reduced as verbal suffixes to *-m̀*, *-ẁ*, *-ǹ*.

DEMONSTRATIVE PRONOUN

(ɛ)há 'this/here'; *(ɛ)hó* 'that/there'. *Eyí* is a demonstrative adjective: *nhɔ̃́mã yí* 'this book'.

INTERROGATIVE PRONOUN

ɛhẽna 'who?'

RELATIVE PRONOUN

nea, áà; *ɔyaresáfóɔ áà ɔ́ɔkɔ* 'the doctor who is going'

Numerals

1–10: *baakɔ̃́*, *mmienṹ*, *mmiensã́*, *ɛnnã́n*, *enṹm*, *ensĩá*, *ɛnsɔ̃́n*, *ɛŋwɔtwé*, *ɛŋkorɔ̃́ŋ*, *edú*; 11 *dúbàakɔ̃́*; 12 *dúmìenṹ* ... 20 *aduonũ*; 21 *aduonṹbàakɔ̃́* ... 30 *aduasã́*; 40 *aduanã́ñ*; 100 *ɔhá*; 101 *ɔhá né baakɔ̃́* ....

The item enumerated precedes the cardinal, and the nominal prefix is retained: *nnuá dú* 'ten trees'; *ɔ.bó biakɔ̃* 'one stone'.

Verb

The stem is formally immutable, but may be reduplicated. Also, Akan euphony requires initial *b-* to mutate to *m-* when in contact with the negating element *-m-*: e.g. *bisa* 'to ask', *mmisá* 'do not ask'. Similarly in the perfect tense: *wammisá* 'he has not asked'.

Subject markers prefixed to stem: *hu*(*nu*) 'to see', present tense:

	Singular	*Plural*
1	mĩhu	yehũ
2	wúhũ	mű̃hũ
3	ohũ	wohũ

Negated by a low-tone nasal prefixed to stem: *mẽte Twíì* 'I speak Twi'; *mẽnté Twíì* 'I don't speak Twi'.

Prefixed pronominal object: *mẽte aséɛ* 'I understand' (*aséɛ* 'meaning'), e.g.:

mẽte	**w**ásè	I understand	you	ɔte	**m**ase	he understands	me
	nasè		him		**w**ase		you
	másè		you (pl.)		**wɔn** ase		them

TENSE AND MOOD MARKERS

Progressive tense: the pronominal vowel is lengthened: *mẽkấ* 'I speak': */mẽekã/* 'I'm speaking' (lengthening not notated in script).
Future positive: prefix *bɛ́*: *wóbɛko* 'you will go' (+ tonal changes).
Immediate future: with *kɔ* 'to go': (+ lengthening of vowel as in progressive): *mẽekɔtɔ́ nsuomnám* 'I'm going to buy fish' (*tɔ* 'to buy').
Past tense: lengthening or gemination of final vowel: *-y* is added for intransitives: *mẽbaay* 'I came'.
Perfect: *a-* prefix + specific tonal pattern + contractions. For example, *kɔ* 'to go':

	Singular	*Plural*
1	makɔ	yɛakɔ
2	woakɔ	moakɔ
3	wakɔ	wɔakɔ

The *past* negative is the *perfect* affirmative + low-tone nasal before stem; the *perfect* negative is the *past* affirmative + low-tone nasal before stem: e.g. *mẽŋkɔɔ* 'I haven't gone'; *mẽŋkóhũù* 'I haven't gone to see it'; *mi**n**nii* 'I haven't eaten'; *o**n**nii* 'he hasn't eaten'; *wo**n**nii* 'they haven't eaten'.

CAUSATIVE

ma + low-tone nasal prefix on verb: *mã nõ ŋkò* 'have him go!'

SUBJUNCTIVE

Low-tone nasal prefix + high tone on verb.

IMPERATIVE

Stem + low tones; the plural prefix is *mɔ̃́n-* + high tones: *mɔ̃́nkasa* 'would you please talk'.

CONSECUTIVE FORM

a- prefix: e.g. with *tumí* 'to be able', *mĩtumí àkɔ̀* 'I can go'.

THE VERB IN THE AKUAPEM LITERARY LANGUAGE (SUMMARY OF TENSE FORMS)

Present: bare stem with prefixed personal marker: *ɔ́.fà* 'he takes', negated by nasal infix plus tonal change: *ɔ.m.fà* 'he doesn't take'.

Stative: stem changes tone; *-e* or *-i* may be suffixed: *sɔ̃̀* 'large': *ɔ̀.sɔ̃* 'he is large', negated by nasal infix: *ɔ.n.sɔ̃́* 'he is not large'.

Preterite: stem has high tone; *-e*/*-i* suffix or gemination of final: *ɔ.fá.è* 'he took it', negative: *ɔ.m.fá.è.*

Perfect: *a-* is prefixed: *ɔ.a.fa* > *wá.fà* 'he has taken', negative: *wa.m.fá.*

Progressive: *re-* prefix: *ɔ.ré.fà* 'he is taking', negative: *ɔ́.re.m̀.fá.*

Future I (unspecified): *bɛ-* prefix: *ɔ̀.bɛ́.fa* 'he will take', negative: *ɔ̀.mm̀.fá*, where *-mm-* represents coalescence of stem initial with nasal infix.

Future II (immediate): *re-* + *bɛ-* prefixes: *ɔ.re.bɛ.fa* 'he will take right now', negative: *ɔ.re.m̀m ɛ.fá.*

Resultative: (Christaller calls this tense 'consecutive') *a-* prefix as in perfect, but tone changes: (*na*) *wafá* 'that he may/should/might take' (cf. perfect *wáfà*), negative: *wa.m.fá.*

Imperative I bare stem: *fá* 'take', negative: *m.fá* (2nd person only)

Imperative II: *ɔ̀mfa* 'he is to take' (the *-m-* here is not the negative marker).

Postpositions

Nouns are used to define spatial relationships: e.g. *ɛso* 'upper part (of sth.)', *ɔpɔ̃́ŋ nɔ̃́ só* 'on the table('s top)'; *ase* 'lower part', *ɔ.póŋ* (*no*) *ase* 'under a/the table'; *emu* 'interior', *a.dáká no mù* 'in the box'; *akyi* 'back', *ɔ.dáŋ akyì* 'behind the house'.

Word order

Any part of speech can be stressed by being promoted to initial position, and additionally stressed, if a noun, by the topicalizer *déɛ*. SVO is normal.

1. Mfiase no na Ase̱m no wo̱ ho̱, na
Ase̱m no nė Nyaṅkōpo̱ṅ na e̱wo̱ ho̱, na
Ase̱m no ye̱ Onyame.
2 O̱noara na mfiase no o̱-nė Nyaṅkō-
po̱ṅ wo̱ ho̱.
3 E̱nam no so na wo̱ye̱e̱ ade nnyinā,
na wo̱aṅkwati no anye̱ biribiara a wo̱ye̱e.
4 No mu na ṅkwā wo̱, na ṅkwā no
ne nnipa hāṅṅ;
5 na haṅṅ no hyere̱ṅ wo̱ sūm mu, na
esūm no annye no.
6 ¶ Onipa bi wo̱ ho̱ a Onyaṅkōpo̱ṅ so-
maa no a ne diṅ de Yohane;
7 o̱no na o̱baa adansedi se̱ orebedi
haṅṅ no hō adanse, se̱ nnipa nnyinā mfa
no so nnye nni.
8 E̱nye̱ o̱no ne haṅṅ no, na se̱ orebedi haṅṅ no hō adanse.

AKKADIAN

INTRODUCTION

This north-eastern outlier of the Semito-Hamitic family is the oldest known Semitic language. For more than 2,000 years, from the middle of the third millennium BC onwards, it was in use in southern Mesopotamia, whence it spread as the language of international communication and diplomacy to most of the Near East and to Egypt. The language as we know it is not pure Semitic, being, even in its earliest stages, much influenced by Sumerian, which continued, indeed, to act as joint liturgical language of the Assyro-Babylonian Empire. About 2000 BC the language – known up to this point as Old Akkadian – split up into Babylonian (southern Mesopotamia) and Assyrian (northern Mesopotamia).

The most important example of Akkadian literature, the Assyrian version of the Sumerian epic of Gilgamesh, was found in Assurbanipal's library at Nineveh. Other works found here and at other sites such as Uruk, Nippur, and Kültepe, include the Etana myth, the *Enuma Elish*, and *Ludlul bel Nemeqi*, a specimen of Akkadian wisdom literature.

Of particular interest in Old Babylonian literature are the so-called 'omen-texts', haruspicatory documents which are couched in a standardized two-part formula. First comes a protasis, in which some unusual (and therefore ominous) feature of a still-born or sacrificial animal is described. Lungs, entrails, and, especially, the liver and gall-bladder were closely scrutinized for abnormalities. In this way an esoteric vocabulary of technical terms was built up, not all of which has been successfully correlated with parts or characteristics of the relevant organs. Thus, while *bāb ekallim*, 'the palace gate' (see below), certainly refers to the space between the two lobes of the liver, in which the gall-bladder is sited, it is not clear exactly what is meant by *ṣibtum* 'excrescence'.

On the basis of his findings, the officiating priest proceeded to forecast (in the apodosis) the likely implications of the omen(s) for the ruler in particular, and for society in general. A parallel with divination practice in ancient China suggests itself (*see* **Chinese, Archaic**).

The protasis generally begins with the word *šumma* 'if', 'when': e.g.

šumma martum ṣalmat
'if/when the gall-bladder (*martum*) is dark (*ṣalmat*)'

šumma martum pānū.ša ana šumēlim šaknū

‘if the front (*pānū*) (*ša* ‘its’) of the gall-bladder lies/tends (*šaknū*) towards (*ana*) the left’

šumma bāb ekallim kajjānum šakin.ma šanum u.šappil.ma warkat amūtim šakin
‘when the “palace gate” is normal, and a second palace gate lies-below (*šappil*) and behind (*warkat*) the liver (*amūtum*, gen. *amūtim*)’

Typical forecasts in the apodosis are:

ajjābū.ka ana abullī.ka irrubūnim
‘thy (*-ka*) enemies (*ajjābū*) will-come-in (*irrubūnim*: *irrub* is the present stem of *erēbum* ‘to come in’) at/by (*ana*) thy (*-ka*) door (*abullī*: genitive case of *abullu*(*m*) ‘door’)’

ūmum irrup.ma šamūm ul izannum
‘the day (*ūmum*) will become overcast (*irrup*) but rain (*šamūm*) not (*ul*) will-fall (*izannu*)’

ebūr mātim ul iššēr
‘the harvest (*ebūr*) of the land (*mātim*, gen. of *mātum* ‘land’) not (*ul*) will-thrive (*iššēr*)’

(Based on Riemschneider 1969, where many more examples will be found.)

SCRIPT

Akkadian adopted the wholly unsuitable Sumerian cuneiform script (*see* **Sumerian**): not only the syllabic system but also the logographic elements, the ideograms to which Akkadian values were given. For example, when the Sumerian ideogram LUGAL ‘king’ occurred in an Akkadian text, it could be read as *šarrum* ‘king’ (Akkadian). Conversely, the Akkadian scribe wishing to write the word *šarrum* could chose either the Sumerian ideogram LUGAL or the phonetic/syllabic writing *ša-ar-ru-um*. The Sumerian use of determinatives, or generic markers, was also adopted. In transcription, determinatives are written in index position to the nominal. For example ^{d} (shorthand for *dingir* – ‘god’ in Sumerian) precedes Akkadian names of gods: ^{d}*Marduk*. Similarly, ^{ki} (‘place’, in Sumerian) follows placenames: *Bābili*^{ki} ‘Babylon’ (in Akkadian).

A minority of signs are phonetically single-valued, but most have many possible readings: e.g. the simple sign ▷– has at least 15 readings, ranging from V*s*/*š*/*z* to *rum*, *šup*, *dal*. Conversely, the sound /a/ has several different graphs in cuneiform.

Where more than one Akkadian reading of a Sumerian ideogram was possible, the final syllable of the required reading was added in phonetic script; and these phonetic complements were used to distinguish cases in Akkadian. Thus:

LUGAL-ru-um read as šarrum = nominative case, ‘the king’
LUGAL-**ra-am** read as šarr**am** = accusative case, ‘the king’

PHONOLOGY

Consonants

labial: p, b, m, w
dental: t, d, n, s, z, l, r; emphatic dentals: ŧ, ꞩ /[ts]
palatal: ç, ʃ, j
velar: k, g, ḫ
uvular: q, ', ʿ

Note: ' is basically hamza, but also does duty for /h, ɦ/, *gh* (/ɣ/); ʿ = Arabic ʿain.

Vowels

Four vowels are notated in the script: common Semitic /a, i, u/ + /e/ as secondary vowel. Traces of vowel harmony may be due to Sumerian influence.

Sandhi: the language is characterized by an extensive system of environmentally induced consonant and vowel change, regressive assimilation, consonant and vowel loss, epenthetic vocalization.

MORPHOLOGY AND SYNTAX

Noun

The triliteral root is basic in the language (*see* **Semitic Languages**). Nouns are masculine or feminine. The masculine marker is Ø, feminine is *-t*: *mār-u*(*m*) 'son'; *mar****t****-u*(*m*) 'daughter'; *bēl-u*(*m*) 'lord'; *bē****lt****-u*(*m*) 'mistress'.

Mimation was regular in the Old Akkadian period, but lost in the later Assyrian–Babylonian period.

Many very old Akkadian feminine nouns have no *-t* marker: *ummu*(*m*) 'mother'; *īnu* 'eye'; *lišānu*(*m*) 'tongue'; *mātu*(*m*) 'land'; *nāru*(*m*) 'river'.

STATE

Absolute or construct. In the construct, the two items are treated as a unit, with the stress on the second: *bīt ábi*(*m*) 'the father's house'; or with pronoun enclitic: *harrān-ša* 'her way'. The construct case unit remains invariable for all cases: *šar mātim* 'the king of the land (nom., acc., gen., dat.)'.

Cf. *ubānu šarrim ša qāti.šu* 'a finger of the king's hand', where *ubānu* is 'finger'; *šarru*(*m*) 'king', genitive case *šarri*(*m*); *qātu* 'hand', genitive *qāti*; *ša* relativizing determinative (*see* **Relative clause**, below); *šu* 3rd p. masc. possessive enclitic 'his': 'finger of-king it/that one of-his-hand'.

NUMBER

Singular, dual, and plural. In the oldest period use of the dual was generalized, i.e. it could be used of any two referents. From Old Babylonian on, use of the dual was restricted to paired parts of the body: *īnān* 'the eyes'; *šēpān* 'the feet'.

The masculine plural is formed (a) by lengthening the final vowel; (b) by changing *-ānu* to *-āni*. Some nouns may have both forms.

Most feminine nouns take *-ātu*: *ummu* 'mother' – *ummātu*; *šarra* 'empress' – *šarrātu*.

In the later period, the oblique forms (see below) *-āni/-āti* seem to have ousted the direct forms *-ānu/-ātu*.

CASE

The characteristic pattern (especially in Babylonian texts) is nom. *-u*, gen. *-i*, acc. *-a* in the singular, i.e. triptote, with diptote in dual and plural: *-a/-i, e*; *-u/-i, e*: e.g.

masc.	sing.	nom.	šarru(m),	gen.	šarri(m), *acc.* šarram
	dual		šarrān	gen.–acc.	šarrīn
	pl.		šarrū		šarrī *or* šarrānū – šarrānī
fem.	sing.		bēltum	bēltim	bēltam;
	pl.		bēlētum	bēlētim	

Adjective

As attribute, the adjective follows noun and agrees with it in gender, number, and case: e.g. *nakrum* 'hostile':

masc. sing.	nakrum – nakrim – nakram	pl.	nakrūtum – nakrutīm
fem.	nak**art**um – nakrim – nakram	pl.	nak**rāt**um – nak**rāt**im

Pronoun

The independent personal pronouns are:

					Enclitic forms	
	Singular			*Plural*	*Singular*	*Plural*
1		anāku		nīnu	-i, -ja	-ni
2	masc.	attā	masc.	attunu	-ka	-kunu
	fem.	attī	fem.	attina	-ki	-kina
3	masc.	šū	masc.	šunu	-šu	-šunu
	fem.	šī	fem.	šina	-ša	-šina

These are declined for gen.–acc. and dative: e.g. for *anāku*: gen.–acc. *jāti*, dative (*ana*) *jāšim*.

The enclitic forms are added to nouns to act as possessive pronominal endings: *bēli* 'my lord', *bēl**ka*** – *bēl**ki***, etc. These are nominative–accusative forms, and are declined for genitive: *bēlī**ja***, *bēlī**ka***, etc.

Cf. *ilū mātam izzibū.šī* 'the gods leave the land' (*ilu* 'god', pl. *il(ān)ū*); *ezēbum 'to leave'*: 3rd p. pl. base stem present *i.zzibū*; *šī* 3rd p. fem. pronominal enclitic, i.e. the direct object *mātam* (fem.) is copied (*šī*) in the verb).

DEMONSTRATIVE PRONOUN

šu, fem. *ši*; pl. *šunu – šina; annu*(*m*), fem. *annītu*(*m*). The oblique forms vary very considerably; the dual is very rare.

INTERROGATIVE PRONOUN

mannu(*m*) 'who?'; *mīnu*(*m*) 'what?' These are not marked for person, number, or gender, but take three-fold case pattern, *-u*, *-i*, *-a*.

RELATIVE PRONOUN

šu, fem. *šat*; pl. *šūt*, *šāt*. These have genitive forms. For relative-clause formation, see below.

Numerals

1–10: *ištēn, šena, šalaš, erbe, ḫamiš, šiššu* (?), *sebe, samāne, tiše, ešer*; these are masculine forms. The feminine forms are: *ištiat*, *šitta*, *šalāšat*, *erbet*, etc. From 3 to 10 a masculine noun takes a feminine numeral, and vice versa (cf. **Arabic**); 20 to 50: decades are the dual forms of the corresponding units, e.g. 40 *erbā*, etc.; 100 *me'at*.

Verb

The root is typically CCVC: **mḫur* 'to receive'. Verbs are active or stative; formally they are grouped as: (a) strong verbs (triliterals, including strengthened biliterals); (b) weak verbs; (c) verbs doubly or triply weak; (d) quadriliterals. There are finite and non-finite forms. Finite forms show gender, person, and number. The non-finite forms are treated as nouns; the infinitive has case, but is not marked for person or number. The following moods are distinguished: indicative, imperative, optative, allative, subjunctive.

Instead of the typical Semitic division into perfective and imperfective aspects, Akkadian has an idiosyncratic quadruple segmentation which corresponds broadly to a present/preterite/perfect system, with the fourth member acting as a kind of stative. This stative includes adjectival verbs: e.g. *damiq* 'he is good'.

A ventive form is made by adding *-am* to the verbal stem: cf.

illik	'he went'	} note *i/a* ablaut, rare in Akkadian
illak	'he goes'	
illak.**am**	'he comes'	

Cf. *mīlum gapšum illakam* 'the great flood will come' (*mīlu*(*m*) 'flood', *gapšu*(*m*) 'great'). Cf. *i.qrib.am* 'he approached'.

The forms here set out are for Version I (*see* **Versions**, below):

Indicative

Present: the formants are prefix + gemination of second radical + suffix: ***imaḫḫaṣa*** 'he strikes'; ***tamaḫḫaṣa*** 'you (pl.) strike'.

Preterite: prefix + root: *imḫaṣ* 'he struck'.

Perfect: prefix + root with *-ta-* infix: *im**ta**ḫaṣ* 'he has struck'. This form is peculiar to Akkadian.

Stative: root + personal suffixes: *bēl* 'he is lord'; *bēlēta* 'you (masc.) are lord'.

Imperative: second person only. Formally, the second person prefix *ta-* of the preterite is dropped, and an epenthetic vowel inserted: (***ta**prus*, *Øprus*) ***pu**rus* 'cut!'

Optative particle *lū/lu* + preterite: ***lu**špur* 'I want to write' (*ašpur* 'I wrote'); *lū salim* 'may he prosper!'

Allative present, preterite, and stative take *-am* (consonantal final) or *-nim* (vocalic final); the form expresses benefactive mode, or motion towards speaker: *išpu**ram*** '(from there) he wrote (to me)'. The form is often used with the indirect object: *irrubū.nim.kum* → *irrubūnikkum* 'they come in to you'; *ašpurakkuššu* 'I sent him to you' (← *ašpur.am.kum.šu*).

Subjunctive: used in subordinate clauses only; the marker is *-u*: *sa . . . iksud**u*** '(that) he conquer . . . ' (*iksud* 'he conquered').

CONJUGATION

Three specimen paradigms follow:

(a) present tense of base stem *maqātu*(*m*) 'to fall';
(b) preterite tense of base stem *maḫāṣu*(*m*) 'to strike';
(c) denominative stative verb: *bēl* 'he is lord, master'.

			a	*b*		*c*
singular	3	masc.	imaqqut	imḫaṣ		bēl
		fem.	imaqqut*	imḫaṣ		bēlet
	2	masc.	tamaqqut	tamḫaṣ		bēlēta
		fem.	tamaqqutī	tamḫaṣī		bēlēti
	1	com.	amaqqut	amḫaṣ		bēlēku
dual	3	com.	imaqqutā	imḫaṣā		bēlā
plural	3	masc.	imaqqutū	imḫaṣū		bēlū
		fem.	imaqqutā	imḫaṣā		bēlā
	2	com.	tamaqqutā	tamḫaṣā	masc.	bēlētunu
	1	com.	nimaqqut	nimḫaṣ	fem.	bēlētina
					1	bēlēnu

* A form with the general Semitic fem. prefix *ta-* might be expected here, and is, in fact, found in Old Akkadian: *tamaqqut*. The form is retained in Old Babylonian verse.

VERSIONS

(Cf. *binyanim* in **Hebrew**; derived stems in **Arabic**):

1. Base stem.
2. Second radical geminated: intensifies and forms active verbs from passive stems. Thus, from *ḫalāqu*(*m*) 'to be destroyed':

naker.ka māt.ka u.ḫā**ll**aq 'thy enemy will-destroy thy country' (*nakru*(*m*) 'enemy', construct form *nakir*/*naker*)

3. The so-called *š*-stem, which is made by prefixing *š*(*a*)-: causative in meaning, e.g. *naqāru*(*m*) 'to be destroyed': *š*-stem **u.šanqar* > *ušaqqar* 'causes to be destroyed'.
4. The *n*-stem: made by prefixing *n*(*a*)-: passive. The *n*- is assimilated to the first consonant of the root. Thus, **i.**n**.šakkan* > *i.ššakkan* 'will be/is put, placed'. In the perfect: **i.**n**.ta.škan* > *i.ttaškan* 'has been made'; *alum ana šena illete* (< *i.**n**.lete*) 'the town (*alum*) will-be-split into two parts'.
5. -*ta*- infix following the first radical in stems 1, 2, or 3; reciprocals. Cf. *iṭṭul* 'he looked towards', *it.ta.ṭlu* 'they looked at each other'.
6. -*tan*(*a*) infix following the first radical in stems 1 or 2, or following the first pre-radical formant in stems 3 and 4; iterative.

NEGATION

ul(*a*) negates the predicate in the principal clause; *lā* is used in subordinate clauses, and as the particle of prohibition.

RELATIVE CLAUSE

Relative clauses are genitival complements introduced by *ša*; the verb is in the subjunctive:

ḫammurabi ša Šamaš kīnātim išruku-šum
Hammurabi, on whom Šamaš conferred the truth...

Cf. *šarram **ša** ittī.ka nakru ina kakki ta.dakma* 'thou-shalt-kill (*tadakma*) a king (*šarram*) who (*ša*) (is) with-thee (*ittī.ka*) an enemy (*nakru*) with (*ina*) a weapon (*kakku*(*m*), gen. *kakki*)'.

Ša may be omitted: *bīt ipušu* 'the house he built'.

Prepositions

Preposition and noun are in construct relationship, i.e. the noun takes the genitive ending: *ina bīti*(*m*) 'in the house'; *ana jāšim* 'to me'; *ana nāri*(*m*) 'to the river'; *eli šarrāni* 'against the emperors'; *adi ḫamšim warḫim* 'till the fifth month'. Thus with *išti*/*itti*: *išti.šu* 'with him'; *itti.ja* 'with me'; *itti.ka* 'with thee'; *ina gegunnim* 'in the high temple'.

Word order

SOV is normal, OSV is possible; relegation of the verb to final position is untypical of Semitic, and may be due to Sumerian influence.

Example of an Old Akkadian royal inscription

šarrukin šar mātim ^{d}Enlil māḫira la iddinu.śum
tiāmtam 'alitam u śapiltam ^{d}Enlil iddinu.śum

TRANSLATION

'Šarru.kin, King of the land, to-him the divine Enlil gave no rival of equal birth, to-him Enlil gave the upper and the lower sea.'

šar(ru)(m): 'king'
mātim: genitive case of *mātu(m)* 'land'
^{d}Enlil: the index ^{d} is the short-hand exponent for the Sumerian word *DINGIR* 'god'.
māḫira: oblique case of *māḫiru(m)* 'contestant/rival of equal birth', *la*: negating particle.
iddinu.śum: the root is *nadānu(m)* 'to give'; Old Akk. *pret. iddin*; *śum* is the Old Akk. 3rd p. indirect pronoun enclitic 'to him'. This /ś/ is found only in Old Akk.; by the Old Babylonian period it had coalesced with /š/.
tiamtam/ti'āmtam: acc. of *tiāmtu(m)* 'sea'; the diphthongs /ia/, /iu/ are stable in Old Akk.
'alitam: adjective in acc. agreeing with *tiamtam* 'upper'
śapiltam: 'lower'

The language of Old Babylonian verse differs in certain respects from that of the omen-texts and of royal correspondence. Archaic forms present include: (a) a locative/adverbial case in *-u*(*m*): e.g. *rēš.um.ša* > *rešušša* 'on his head', and (b) a terminative in *-iš*: ištin.iš 'together'.

There follows a short extract from an Old Babylonian version of the Sumerian epic *Gilgameš* (the main Semitic version of this epic is in Assyrian).

Enkidug ša arāmmu.ma danniš
itti.ja ittallaku kalu marṣātim
illik.ma ana šimatu awīlūtim
urri u muši eli.šu abki
ul addiššu ana qebērīm

'Enkidu, whom I greatly love, who ever went with me through all difficulties, has gone to the fate of all mankind; day and night have I wept for him, I have not given him to burial.'

arāmmu: *rāmu* 'to love': *a.rāmmu* is 1st p. sing. present tense of base form
danniš 'very much'
itti.ja: 'with me'
ittallaku: the root is *alāku(m)* 'to go', i.e. 'he went'
kalu: 'all'
marṣātim: oblique case of *marṣātum* 'difficulties'
illik: root *alāku(m)* 'to go'
ana: 'to'
šimatu/šimtu(m): 'fate'; *ana šimti alākum* 'to go to fate', i.e. 'to die'
awīlūtim: gen. of *awīlūtu(m)* 'humanity'
urri u muši: 'day and night'

eli.šu: 'for him'
abki: the root is *baku(m)* 'to weep', 'I wept'
ul: 'not'
addiš.šu: the root is *nadānu(m)* 'to give': *addin.šu* > *addiš.šu* 'I gave him'
ana qebērīm: 'to burial'; *qebēru(m)* 'burial'

ALBANIAN

INTRODUCTION

Generally regarded as the sole survivor of the Illyrian branch of Indo-European languages, Albanian (*gjuha shqipe*) is spoken today in two main dialects: Tosk (southern) and Gheg (northern). The boundary between the two forms is roughly marked by the river Shkumbini. The total number of speakers of both dialects within Albania is about 3 million. In addition, there are some 2 million Gheg speakers in Kosovo, and a few thousand speakers of a third dialect, Arbëresh, in southern Italy and Greece. Albanian literature, mainly in Gheg, dates from the sixteenth century (1555, Buzuku's *Meshari*). Tentative steps towards the creation of a unified national language culminated first in the adoption of the Roman alphabet (1908, Congress of Manastir) and secondly in the selection of the Elbasan (central) dialect (a form of Gheg) as the most suitable base for such a language. From 1920 to the 1950s both dialects were used for literary purposes. In 1952, however, Tosk was officially declared as the base for the new standardized literary language. In Kosovo, Gheg continues to prosper as both spoken and literary language. Tosk and Gheg are mutually intelligible, and differ indeed only in certain points – most importantly in the rhotacism of Tosk: Gheg -V*n*V- = Tosk -V*r*V-; e.g. Gheg *zani* 'voice', Tosk *zëri*; and in the formation of the future tense (*see* **Verb**, below).

SCRIPT

As noted above, the Congress of Manastir (1908) provided Albanian with a standardized script based on the Roman alphabet plus *ç* and *ë; w* is not used. The following digraphs are used: *th* = /θ/, *dh* = /ð/, *sh* = /ʃ/, *zh* = /ʒ/, *xh* = /dʒ/, *gj* = /g′/, *nj* = /ɲ/, *ll* = /ł/, *rr* = /rr/.

PHONOLOGY

Consonants

stops: p, b, t, d, k, g; k′, g′
affricates, ts, dz, tʃ, dʒ
fricatives: f, v, θ, ð, s, z, ʃ, ʒ, j, h
nasals: m, n, ɲ, ŋ
laterals: l, ł, r, rr

Vowels

Tosk has seven vowel phonemes; Gheg has twelve, including five nasal vowels. The Tosk series:

i, e, a, ə, o, u, y

/ə/ is notated as *ë*.

Stress

Stress is frequently on the penultimate syllable.

MORPHOLOGY AND SYNTAX

Noun

Albanian has two genders, masculine and feminine, with traces of an old neuter, limited now to very few words.

There are two articles, definite and indefinite. The latter is sing. *një*, pl. *ca* or *disa*; thus, *një shok* 'a comrade', *disa shokë* 'comrades'.

The definite article is affixed to the noun and is coded for gender (cf. **Bulgarian** and **Romanian**):

Masculine affixes: *-i*, *-u*, *-ri/-ni*, *-a*: *mal* 'mountain', *mal**i*** 'the mountain'; *zog* 'bird', *zog**u*** 'the bird'.
Feminine affix: *-a*: *shtëpi* 'house', *shtëpi**a*** 'the house'; *motër* 'sister', *motr**a*** 'the sister'.

PLURAL

Typical masculine plural endings are *-a*, *-e*, *-nj*, *-q(e)*, *-gj(e)*, *-ë*: e.g. *mësim* 'lesson' – *mësime*; *mal* 'mountain' – *male*; *ari* 'bear' – *arinj*; *mik* 'friend' – *miq*; *pyll* 'forest' – *pyje*; *punëtor* 'worker' – *punëtorë*.

Feminine plural: *-a*, *-e*; often no change: e.g. *lule* 'flower' – *lule*; *dhomë* 'room' – *dhoma*.

Umlaut occurs in some masculine nouns: *breg* 'coast' – *brigje*; *plak* 'old man' – *pleq*. The plural nominative definite form ends in *-t(ë)*.

CASE

The following two paradigms show a masculine and a feminine noun declined with and without definite article, in four cases and two numbers.

Masculine: *mal* 'mountain'

	Singular		*Plural*	
	Indefinite	*Definite*	*Indefinite*	*Definite*
nom.	mal	mali	male	malet
gen.	mali	malit	maleve	malevet
dat.	mali	malit	maleve	malet
acc.	mal	malin	male	malevet

	Feminine: *shtëpi* 'house'			
	Singular		*Plural*	
	Indefinite	*Definite*	*Indefinite*	*Definite*
nom.	shtëpi	shtëpia	shtëpi	shtëpitë
gen.	shtëpie	shtëpisë	shtëpive	shtëpivet
dat.	shtëpie	shtëpisë	shtëpive	shtëpivet
acc.	shtëpi	shtëpinë	shtëpi	shtëpitë

Adjective

The attributive adjective follows the noun to which it is connected by the inflected article, e.g. masc.:

	Indefinite 'a good friend'		*Definite 'the good friend'*	
	Singular	*Plural*	*Singular*	*Plural*
nom.	mik i mirë	miq të mirë	miku i mirë	miqt e mirë
gen.–dat.	miku të mirë	miqve të mirë	mikut të mirë	miqvet të mirë
acc.	mik të mirë	miq të mirë	mikun e mirë	miqt e mirë

Following a feminine definite noun the gen.–dat. link is *-së-*, which becomes *-të-* if it is preceded in the syntagma by other qualifying material: e.g. *Partisë **së** Punës **të** Shqipërisë*, literally 'the Party of Work of Albania', i.e. the Albanian Workers' Party.

Certain adjectives, e.g. those derived from nouns or verbs, do not take the connecting article: *një shkollë fillore* 'an elementary school' (*fillore* ← *filloj* 'to begin').

A few adjectives have four specific forms for gender/number: e.g. *ri* 'new': masc. sing. *i ri*, pl. *të rinj*; fem. sing. *e re*, pl. *të reja*.

An adjective which takes the article in attributive position keeps it in predicative position: *vendi është i bukur* 'the place is beautiful', *vendet janë të bukura* (pl.).

It is interesting that in the plural many masculine nouns are given feminine concord: cf. *qyteti është i madh* (masc.) 'the town is big' and *qytetet janë **të mëdha*** 'the towns are big'.

Pronoun

The base forms are:

	Singular		*Plural*	
	Subject	*Oblique*	*Subject*	*Oblique*
1	unë	më	na/ne	na
2	ti	të	ju	ju

Third-person forms are supplied by the demonstrative series (see below).

DEMONSTRATIVE PRONOUN/ADJECTIVE

The proximate series is based on *ky*, fem. *kjo*; the distal series is *ai*, fem. *ajo*.

The series *ai*, *ata*; *ajo*, *ato* is used for the third-person pronoun, with oblique forms *e* 'him, her', and *i* 'to him, to her'.

These forms fuse with other oblique pronouns: e.g. *më* + *e* → *ma*: *ma dha librin* 'he gave me the book'.

A noun as complement is anticipated by a pronominal copy:

Do t'**i** them edhe Abazit '**I**'ll tell A. as well'
E njihte mirë Dini**n** 'He knew D. well'
Unë **i** fola asaj vajz**e** 'I spoke to this girl'

Cf. in the relative clause: *njeriu që **e** kam parë* 'the man whom I saw him', i.e. 'the man I saw'.

POSSESSIVE PRONOUN

These follow the noun possessed; here, the singular and plural nominative forms are given for each person:

libri im	'my book'	librat e mi	'my books'	libri ynë	'our book'
				librat tanë	'our books'
libri yt	'your book'	librat e tu	'your books'	libri juaj	'your (pl.) book'
				librat tuaj	'your (pl.) books'
libri i tij	'his book'	librat e tij	'his books'	libri i tyre	'their book'
				librat e tyre	'their books'

INTERROGATIVE PRONOUN

kush 'who?', inflected for case only; *çka* 'what?'; *cili* 'which?' is inflected for gender, number, and case: *cili djal dhe cila vajzë* 'which boy and which girl?'

RELATIVE PRONOUN

që is not inflected; *i cili*, etc. is inflected; e.g.

nje ndërtesë e vogël, e cila ndryshonte fare pak nga shtëpitë e tjera
'a small building which differed little from the other houses'
(*ndërtesë* (fem.) 'building'; *ndryshoj* 'to differ'; *tjeter*, (pl.) *tjerë* 'other')

Numerals

1–10: *një*, *dy*, *tre/tri* (the only numeral marked for gender), *katër*, *pesë*, *gjashtë*, *shtatë*, *tetë*, *nëndë*, *dhjetë*; 11 *njëmbëdhjetë*; 12 *dymbëdhjetë*... 20 *njëzet*; 30 *tridhjetë*; 40 *dyzet*, i.e. *dyzet* is a vigesimal form; 60 and 80, however, revert to decimal form: *gjashtëdhjetë*, *tetëdhjetë*; 100 (*një*)*qind*.

Verb

The Albanian verb has two voices, active (unmarked), and medio-passive, the latter having a specific set of endings. There are six moods and eight tenses; only the indicative mood has all of these tenses, the other moods – subjunctive, conditional, optative, admirative – have present and perfect tenses, to which the subjunctive and the admirative add an imperfect and a pluperfect. The imperative mood has a present form only.

In the absence of an infinitive, Albanian verbs are generally classified in terms of the 1st person singular present, varying endings of which yield the following conjugational types: (a) vowel + *-j*: *punoj* 'I work'; (b) vowel: *pi* 'I drink'; (c) consonant: *flas* 'I speak'. The 1st person singular of the present active is one of the three basic forms from which, in theory, all other forms of the Albanian verb can be derived, the other two being the 1st person singular aorist, and the past participle: thus, *dal – dola – dalë* 'give'; *flas – fola – folur* 'speak'. The 1st person singular present, for example, is the base for the imperative, the imperfect, the subjunctive, the future, and the conditional. The two examples given are, however, enough to show that the information provided by the three bases does not extend to internal flection and/or suppletive forms. There are several ablaut series in the Albanian verbal system: two examples have already been given. Cf. *hedh – hodha – hedhur* 'throw'; *ndjek – ndoqa – ndjekur* 'follow'. Ablaut also affects the present tense of many verbs: e.g. for *flas*:

	Singular	*Plural*
1	flas	flasim
2	flet	flisni
3	flet	flasin

Suppletive forms: e.g. *shoh – pashë – parë* 'see'; *bie – prura – prurë* 'bring'; *jap – dhashë – dhënë* 'give'.

Tenses may be further sub-divided by aspect into perfective and imperfective categories. Finite forms are marked throughout for person and number.

Tenses are primary or analytical; the latter are formed by means of the auxiliaries: *jam* 'I am', and *kam* 'I have'.

THE AUXILIARIES

The basic forms of *jam* and *kam* are:

present:	*jam, je, është*; pl. *jemi, jeni, janë*
imperfect:	*isha, ishe*
aorist:	*qeshë, qe*...
subjunctive:	*të jem, të jesh*...
past participle:	*qenë*

present:	*kam, ke, ka*; pl. *kemi, keni, kanë*
imperfect:	*kisha, kishe*
aorist:	*pata, pate*...

subjunctive:	*të kem, të kesh . . .*
past participle:	*pasur*

MODAL VERBS

Two important modals are: *dua* 'I want' and *mund* 'I can'.

SPECIMEN CONJUGATION

Vocal stem, *kërkoj* 'I ask for, seek'.

Indicative	
present:	*kërko**j**, **-n**, **-n***, pl. *kërko**jmë**, **-ni**, **-jnë***
imperfect:	*kërko**ja**, **-je**, **-nte***; pl. *kërko**nim**, **-nit**, **-nin***
aorist:	*kërko**va**, **-ve**, **-i***; pl. *kërk**uam**, **-uat**, **-uan***
perfect:	*kam, ke*, etc. *kërkuar*
future:	*do të kërko**j**, do të kërko**sh**. . .* (subjunctive endings, see below).

This is the Tosk form of the future tense; the Gheg model is *kam me* + infinitive.

Subjunctive	
present:	*të kërkoj, **-sh**, **-jë***; pl. as indicative present
imperfect:	*të* + indicative imperfect forms
Admirative	
present:	*kërkua**kam**, kërkua**ke***, etc. (i.e. *kërkua* + present tense of *kam*)
Optative	
present:	*kërko**fsha**, **-fsh**, **-ftë***; pl. *kërko**fshim**, **-fshi**, **-fshin***
Imperative:	sing. *kërko*; pl. *kërko**ni***
Past participle:	*kërkuar*

Medio-passive voice: vocalic stems have the augment *-h-* in the present:

present:	*kërko**hem**, **-hesh**, **-et***; pl. *kërko**hemi**, **-heni**, **-hen***
imperfect:	*kërko**hesha**, **-heshe**. . .*
aorist:	*u-kërko**va**, u-kërko**ve**, u-kërk**ua***; pl. *u-kërk**uam**, **-uat**, **-uan***
perfect:	*jam kërkuar . . .*, etc.

The subjunctive is much used in Albanian. The form is preceded by *të* which fuses with a pronominal precursor: *të* + *e* > *ta*: *ai fillon të punojë* 'he begins to work'; *dua **ta** vizitoj* 'I want to visit him/it'. Preceded by *të*, the past participle with the affix *-it* yields a verbal noun: *të punuarit* 'working'; *të qeshurit* 'laughing'.

The particle *duke* is used with the past participle to express an adverbial participial construction: *duke punuar* 'while working'.

NEGATIVE

nuk and *s'* are general negating particles; *kemi* 'we have'; *s'kemi* 'we don't have'; *Goni nuk flet anglisht* 'Goni doesn't speak English.' *Mos* is used with the imperative: *mos pini duhan* 'don't smoke'.

Prepositions

(a) With nominative (usually in definite form): e.g. *nga* 'from', *tek* 'at', *gjer* 'until', etc.
(b) With accusative: e.g. *mbi* 'on', *me* 'with', *në* 'in', *pa* 'without', etc.
(c) With dative (ablative): e.g. *pranë* 'near', *kundër* 'against', *mbrapa* 'after', etc.

Word formation

(a) Compounding: e.g. noun + noun: *hekur* 'iron + *udhë* 'way': *hekurudhë* 'railway'.
(b) By suffix: e.g. *-im* forming abstract nouns: *kujtimi* 'memory' (cf. *kujtoj* 'remember'); -(*t*)*ore* denoting locus of activity: *grunore* 'wheatfield' (cf. *grunë* 'wheat').
(c) By prefixing preposition or adverb: *në*(*n*) 'below' + *punës* 'working': *nëpunësi* 'employee';
adverb + adjective: *jashtzakonshëm* (*jasht* 'outside' + *zakon* (Slav.) 'law, custom') 'unusual, extraordinary';
privative prefix *pa-*: *pakuptueshëm* 'incomprehensible' (cf. *kuptoj*, 'I understand; *kuptueshëm* 'comprehensible').

Prefixes frequently used to form derived verbs are: (*sh*)*për-*, *mb-*, *sh-*, *c-*: e.g. from

shkruaj 'to write', përshkruaj 'to describe'
jashtë 'outside', përjashtoj 'to exclude'
lidh 'tie', mbledh 'to collect'

The ablative case in *-ësh* may be used attributively to form a compound: (*një*) *kopsht-femijësh* 'a kindergarten'.

Word order

SVO is normal.

1 Që përpara herësë ishte Fjala, edhe Fjala
ishte me Perëndinë, edhe Fjala ishte Perëndi,
2 Këjo ishte që përpara herësë me Perëndinë.
3 Të-gjitha u bënë me anë t' asaj; edhe pa
atë nuk' ubë as ndonjë *gjë* që është bërë.
4 Nd' atë ishte jetë, edhe jeta ishte drita e
5 njerësvet. Edhe drita ndrit nd' errësirët, edhe
errësira nuk' e kupëtoj.
6 Qe *një* njeri dërguarë nga Perëndia, i-
7 cili *e kishte* emërinë Joan. Ky erdhi për dëshmim, që të apë dëshmim. Dritënë, që të be-
8 sonjënë të-gjithë me anë t' ati. Ay nuk' ishte
Drita, po *qe dërguarë* që të apë dëshmim
për Dritënë.

(Tosk dialect)

ALEUT

INTRODUCTION

Aleut is distantly related to the Eskimo (Inuit) languages; a proto-Aleut/ Eskimo language seems to have been spoken in prehistoric times in the western seaboard (Bering) area of Alaska. Today, Aleut is spoken by small numbers in the Aleutian Islands and the Alaskan Peninsula. Krauss (1979) estimated that out of 2,000 Aleuts on US territory, about 700 spoke at least some Aleut. Pedagogic efforts to revive the language are being made at the Alaska Native Language Centre in Fairbanks. There are two main dialects: Western (Attuan) and Eastern (Unalaskan). Early in the nineteenth century, the Commander Islands, lying to the east of Kamchatka, were colonized by Aleutians representing both dialects. When Menovshchikov described the Unalaskan form (in *JaNSSSR*, Vol. V, 1968) only about fifty elderly people spoke the language, which may now be presumed to be extinct. The Aleutians in the Commander Islands called themselves /anʁaʁinas/ 'inhabitants'. A note on this form of Aleutian is included in this article. /ʁ/ is notated here as *ṛ*, /ŋ/ as *ṅ*.

SCRIPT

In the 1830s the Russian scholar I.E. Veniaminov used an adaptation of Cyrillic to notate Aleut, and laid a substantial foundation for the study of the language. Cyrillic continued to be used for religious texts and instruction even after the Alaska Purchase (1867). In the twentieth century the Roman script was adopted.

PHONOLOGY

Consonants

The consonantal inventory is notable for the absence of the labial series, apart from /w/ and /m/. The dental series includes /t/ → [θ] and /d/ → [ð]: lateral /ɬ/. There are parallel velar and uvular series: /k/q, x/χ, g/γ./ Here, *ṅ* = /ŋ/.

Vowels

The basic vowel pattern is /a, i, u/; /i/ blends into [ɛ], /u/ into [ɔ]. Veniaminov distinguished four values of *a*: over-short, short, long, and over-long.

MORPHOLOGY AND SYNTAX

Noun

All stems are potentially nominal and verbal. Most nouns are disyllables: e.g. *táṅakh* 'water'; *kannogh* 'heart'. The final *-kh*/*-gh* is discarded before the case endings are added: e.g. *ádakh* 'father': *áda.n* 'the fathers', *áda.m* 'of the father'.

A stem treated as nominal has three numbers: e.g. *agitudakh* 'the brother', *agituda.kek* 'the two brothers', *agituda.n* 'the brothers'.

Veniaminov's paradigms show, in addition to nominative, accusative (= nom.), and genitive (*-m*), a dative (*-man*), and a relative genitive in *-gan*, apparently used obviatively (cf. Algonquian 4th person). Cf. *-p*/*-ata* in **Inuit**. Example: *agôghum aṅále.gan tunó* 'the word of the kingdom of God'.

Other case relationships are supplied by postpositions: e.g. *ésik* 'with', *khulèn* 'for', *ko'an* 'on' take the genitive: *áda.m ésik* 'with the father'; *alèghu.m ko'an* 'on the sea'. Note that the number marker moves to the end of the postpositional phrase if the noun is in the relative genitive: e.g. *tána.gan il.kek* 'in the two lands' (*il.in* 'in', *kek* = dual marker).

Pronoun

PERSONAL PRONOUN

Subject and object forms with possessive enclitics:

	Singular	*Possessive*	*Dual*	*Plural*
1	thiṅ	-ṅ	toman	toman
2	txen	-n	txidhek	txiče
3	iṅan	-n	iṅakux	iṅakun

There are also dative forms, e.g. for first person *noṅ – tumanan – tumanen*.

DEMONSTRATIVE PRONOUN/ADJECTIVE

Three grades of distancing with many sub-divisions specifying locus, modality, etc.

POSSESSIVE MARKERS

For example, *áda.ṅ* 'my father'; *áda.n.ṅ* → *áda.neṅ* 'my father's'. The third person is distinguished from the second by stress shift (vowel lengthening): e.g. *áda.n* 'thy father', *adá.n* 'his father'. The possessive-marker grid is, thus, 9×3, the middle term being a double dual: e.g. *tána.keṅen* 'the two lands of us two'. All possessive forms can be declined.

INTERROGATIVE PRONOUN

kin 'who?'; *alhkhotakh* 'what?'

Numerals

1–5: *attákan, 'álak, khánkun, síčen, čáṅ*; 6–10: *attóṅ, ullyóṅ, khamčiṅ, sečiṅ, 'átkekh. Khankódhem 'áthekh* 30, where *-dhem* = 'times'. *Sísikh* 100.

Verb

The verb shows class, mood, tense, person, number, voice, and version (affirmative or negative). Examples of tense formation, indicative mood:

present: *-ku-*, e.g. *táňa.ku.kh* 'he drinks'
past indef.: *-na-*, e.g. *táňa.na.kh* 'he was drinking'
perfective: *-kha-*, e.g. *táňa.kha* 'he drank'
future: *-doka.(ku)-*, e.g. *táňadóka.ku.kh* 'he will drink'
semelfactive: *-kha.gan-*, e.g. *táňa.kha.gan* 'he will drink once'
conditional: *-gu-*, e.g. *táňa.gu.n* 'if he drinks'
imperative: markers are *-da*, *-dhek*, e.g. *táňa.da/dhek!* 'drink!'

The above forms apply to the great majority of Aleut verbs; a few vary.

Negative version: three particles are used: *óluk*, affixed to conjugational endings, and *laka/laga* added to stem, preceding modal and tense markers: e.g. *táňa.laka.kh* 'he doesn't drink', *táňa.nagh.óluØ.theň* 'I haven't drunk'.

Prohibitive: *táňa.laga.da/dhek!* 'don't drink!'

PERSONAL ENDINGS

There are several sets, each with specific usages: e.g.

	Singular	*Dual*	*Plural*
1	kheň/theň	1, 3 kek	neň
2	xtxen	xtxidhek	xtiče
3	kh		ňen

These are used for affirmative version in present, past indefinite, and future, and for the negative version in *oluk*, etc.: e.g. *táňa.ko.kheň* 'I drink', *táňa.laka.kheň* 'I don't drink', *táňa.ko.xtxen* 'you drink'.

PASSIVE

-lga-/-ghe- infixed immediately after stem: e.g. *táňa.lga.kukh* 'it is drunk/one drinks it'; *táňa.lga.da* (passive imperative).

FINITE VERB WITH PRONOMINAL OBJECT

The verb agrees in person with the subject, in number with the object: e.g. *thiň imdhek exxta.ko.kek* 'I speak to you two', where *-kek* is first person dual. Participles marked for tense are available in both versions and all three voices, including reflexive: e.g. *táňa.na.kh* 'who drank'; *táňa.dóka.kh* 'having to drink, about to drink'; *táňa.dóka.na.ghóluk* 'not having to drink'.

AUXILIARY CONJUGATION WITH *Á-*

ákukh 'is/are'; *axta.kukh* (durative); *axkhakukh* 'becomes'; *aghekukh* 'has/have': e.g.

táňa.**ňan**.aghe.kó.kheň 'I'm drinking right now'
(*ňan* is first person infinitive marker)

táṅa.**men**.aghe.kó.**xtxen** 'you are drinking right now'
(*men* is second person infinitive marker)

The periphrastic conjugation with *á-* can be used with all moods, versions, tenses. Note that the *-ghe-* infix in *aghekukh* 'he has' is the passive marker. Cf.

ádakh axtakukh → ádaxtakukh 'he is a father' ⎰ both forms can then
ádakh aghekukh → ádaghekukh 'he has a father' ⎱ be conjugated in full

That is, 'he has a father' is treated as the passive of 'he is a father'.

There is in addition a wide inventory of verbal infixes expressing many nuances: causative *-čxhi-*; terminative *-kada-*; inchoative *-kali-*; desiderative *-tu-*; potential *-masyo-*: collective *-gya-*, etc. Example: *táṅa.kali.gó.men* 'if you start to drink'.

Word formation

For example, agentive, *-takh*/*-nakh*: e.g. *tayá* 'sell', *tayánakh* 'seller'. Possessive, *-ghekh*: 'endowed with': e.g. *makha* 'riches', *makhághekh* 'wealthy'. Instrumental, *-sekh*: e.g. *mayaghá* 'to fish', *mayaghásekh* 'harpoon'. *-lukh* indicates locus: e.g. *tayá* 'sell', *tayálukh* 'market'.

Compounding occurs, but is not prolific.

THE DIALECT OF THE COMMANDER ISLANDS

The nominal markers are: sing. *-χ*; dual *-x*; pl. *-s*, e.g. *ayχasiχ*, *ayχasix*, *ayχasis* 'boat, two boats, boats'.

These number markers are discarded before the possessive enclitics are added:

ayχasi.**ṅ** 'my boat'
ayχ asi.**ki.ṅ** 'my two boats' (*-ki-* is the dual object marker, with sing. sbj.)
ayχasi.**ni.ṅ** 'my boats' (*-ni-* is the plural object marker, with sing. sbj.)
ayχasi.**n** 'thy boat'
ayχasi.**mas** 'our boat'
ayχasi.**čix** 'your (pl.) boat'
ayχasī 'his boat' (note vowel lengthening for 3rd p. possessive)

The relative case marker *-m* is found only in the singular: cf.

ayχasi.**m** uxasiṅis 'the oars of the boat'

In the dual and the plural, the absolute case with *-x*/*-s* markers is found:

ayχasi.**x** uxasiṅis 'the oars of the two boats'
ayχasi.**s** uxasiṅis 'the oars of the boats'

Possessive enclitics with noun in genitive: cf.

ayχasi.**ṅ** uxasiṅis 'the oars of my boat'

ayχasi.**ki.ṅ** uxasiṅis 'the oars of my two boats'
ayχasi.**ni.ṅ** uxasiṅis 'the oars of my boats'
ayχasi.**gan** uxasiṅis 'the oars of his boat'

Menovshchikov gives an example of the double izafet form with *-gan-*:

ada.**ṅ** kamṛi.**gan** hig.**ī** čilgalana
'of my father – of his head – its headdress – got torn', i.e. 'my father's headdress got torn'

Commander Island independent personal pronouns:

	Singular	*Dual*	*Plural*
1	tiṅ	–	timas
2	tin	tidix	tičix

Dative/benefactive forms are also found: *ṅus* 'to/for me'; *amas/imas* 'to/for us'; *amdix* 'to/for you two'; *imčix* 'to/for you (pl.)'.

DEMONSTRATIVE PRONOUNS

The base forms underlying about twenty paradigms are:

proximate: *wan – wakux – wakus*
distal: *iṅan – iṅakux – iṅakus*
remote: *akan – akakux – akkakus*

Verb

TENSE

The present-tense marker *-ku-* and the past marker *-na-* are shared with Alaskan Aleutian. In addition, CI can combine *-ku-* or *-na-* with *maya* to form a recent past. The future characteristic is *(qali).aa.qali.**gan** aṛiku* 'he will sleep'.

The interrogative mood is marked by *-ī*: e.g. *qaχ suχ.ī* 'did he catch fish?', the imperative by *-da*: e.g. *awa.da* 'work!'

MODAL/ASPECTUAL MARKERS

-li- for continuing action:

saṛa.**li**.ku.χ 'he just goes on sleeping'

-dada-: repetitive/frequentative:

aygagi.**dada**.ku.χ 'he often goes…'

-yukati-: prolongation of action:

awa.**yukati**.ku.χ 'he goes on and on working for ages'

-qali-: inceptive (cf. future-tense marker, above):

awa.**qali**.ku.χ 'he starts work'

NEGATION

-ṛula- and *-laka-* negate verbals: e.g. *aygagi.**ṛula**.χ* 'he doesn't go'.

INTRANSITIVE AND TRANSITIVE

Example of intransitive present tense: root *haka-* 'go':

	Singular	*Dual*	*Plural*
1	haka.ku.q	alagal haka.ku.s	haka.ku.s
2	haka.ku.χt	haka.ku.χt.xidix	haka.ku.χt.xičix
3	haka.ku.χ	haka.ku.x	haka.ku.s

Transitive present: SOV

tiṅ uxasiχ haka.**sa**.qa.**ṅ** 'I carry an oar'
tiṅ uxasix haka.**sa**.qa.ki.ṅ 'I carry two oars'
tiṅ uxasis haka.**sa**.qa.ni.ṅ 'I carry oars'
timas uxasiχ haka.**sa.**qa.mas 'we carry an oar'
timas usaxix haka.**sa**.qa.mas 'we carry two oars'
timas uxasis haka.**sa**.qa.mas 'we carry oars'

Word order

Increasingly, according to Menovshchikov, the idiomatic ergative construction in an SOV sentence, where S and O are nominals, fell into disuse, and both S and O began to appear in the absolute form. Menovshchikov gives the example:

Laχ uxasis haka.sa.ku.χ 'the boy carries oars'

where *laχ* is in the absolute case, and contrasts it with the idiomatic rendering:

la**m** uxasiχ haka.sa.**qa** 'the boy carries an oar'

where *lam* is in the ergative (relative) case, while the verb is marked for person and number of O. Cf.

la**m** uxasis haka.sa.**qaṅ.is** 'the boy carries oars'

д҃. Умата́ликъ [1] камга-
да́чи: туманинъ А́дакъ [2],
А́манъ акухтхинъ ининъ ку-
нинъ! Асанъ амчугасҗдагта [3];
і҃. Аҥалинъ акагта; Ану-
хтанатхинъ малгагтанъ и-
нимъ куганъ каюхъ танамъ
куганъ;
аі҃. Калгадамъ анухтана
нинъ акача [+] уажмъ;
ві҃. Каюхъ туманинъ а-
дунъ нинъ игнида, амакунъ
туманъ каюхъ малгалигинъ
нинъ адугинанъ игнидакунъ;
гі҃. Каюхъ туманъ сугла-
тачхиганахтхинъ; тага ада-
лудамъ илжнъ туманъ аггича.
Аҥалинъ, Каюнъ каюхъ Алгу-
насҗдаусинъ ауанъ усюганъ
акунинъ маликъ. Аминь.

(Mark 6.9–15)

ALTAIC LANGUAGES

Three contiguous groups of languages – Turkic, Mongolian, and Tungusic – occupy a broad swathe of territory in Inner Asia, extending from the borders of China in the east and north to the Urals and the Mediterranean in the west. While they are mutually unintelligible, these three groups share so many common features that genetic relationship seems probable. They are accordingly united under a collective title as the 'Altaic' languages, after the mountain range which cuts diagonally through their territory, dividing Mongolian and Tungusic in the north and east from Turkic in the west. Internally, all three groups are remarkably homogeneous.

The salient common features may be listed as follows:

1. A rather simple consonantal inventory based on the series /b, p, m; d, t, n; g, k, ŋ/; + /r, l/, one or two sibilants, some palatalized consonants and velar fricatives like /x/ and /γ/. The vowel systems are well developed, usually containing rounded vowels: /œ, y/.
2. Vowel harmony is observed throughout the family, except where alien influence has been strong (e.g. in the case of Uzbek, a Turkic language affected by long contact with the Iranian language Tajik). In general, back vowels are followed by back, front by front, with /i/ neutral.
3. All Altaic languages are basically agglutinative; suffixation is used to the virtual exclusion of prefixation.
4. There is no grammatical gender; no articles.
5. In the 1st person plural a distinction is often made between inclusive and exclusive forms.
6. All member languages have case endings showing a basic parallelism. The number of cases in individual languages varies from about a dozen in the Tungusic languages to five or six in Turkic.
7. There is a recurrent parallelism between the personal possessive markers and the verbal personal endings.
8. Absence of verb meaning 'to have'; possession indicated by dative or postpositional constructions.
9. Absence of relative pronoun; relative clauses are turned into participial constructions.
10. Modifier precedes modified; attributive adjective precedes noun without concord (exceptions in Tungusic).
11. The singular is used with numerals.
12. No prepositions; postpositions are used throughout the family.
13. Lexicon: evidence here for a Proto-Altaic parent language rests mainly on establishing sets of regular phonological correspondences between

the three families, yielding referents at least belonging to related semantic fields. In several cases it has proved possible to extend these equations to Korean and Old Japanese, and the Altaic family has been correspondingly expanded. By means of glottochronological techniques, a separation date for Korean and the Tungusic languages has been put at 3500 BC.

The thesis of a common 'Altaic' origin is not universally accepted. It has been pointed out that the common features listed above, along with others, may be due to sociolinguistic contact and mutual interaction over the millennia. Contemporary evidence of such contact in action can be seen, for example, in the mutual interaction of the Turkic language Yakut with Evenki, which is Tungusic.

The undoubted similarities between the three groups would then be typological rather than genetic, and they can be shown to be shared with other languages which are in no way connected with the Altaic question.

At present, some 40 Altaic languages are spoken by about 100 million people, more than half of this total being made up by one language – Turkish. Proof that Korean and Japanese are Altaic languages would, of course, increase the number of speakers by about 200 million.

See **Turkic Languages**, **Altay**, **Azerbaijani**, **Bashkir**, **Chuvash**, **Gagauz**, **Karachay-Balkar**, **Karakalpak**, **Kazakh**, **Khakas**, **Kirgiz**, **Kumyk**, **Tatar**, **Turkish**, **Turkmen**, **Tuvinian**, **Uzbek**; **Buryat**, **Kalmyk**, **Mongolian (Classical** and **Modern)**, **Mongolian Languages of China**, **Oirat**; **Even**, **Evenki**, **Manchu**, **Nanay**, **Negidal**, **Nenets**, **Udege**; **Korean**; **Japanese (Literary** and **Modern Standard)**.

ALTAY

INTRODUCTION

Altay belongs to the Kirgiz-Kipchak group of Eastern Turkic, with about 50 to 60 thousand speakers in the Gornoy-Altay Republic of the Altay Kray. Prior to Russian colonization in the eighteenth century, the Altay region, inhabited by several Turkic tribes, formed part of the Dzhungaria Khanate. In the early years of Soviet rule, the Altay peoples were collectively known as 'Oirots'. They are now officially designated as 'Altay'. Northern and southern dialects of the language differ markedly, the former tending towards the Uigur-Oguz group (in Baskakov's 1966 classification). The modern literary language is based on southern usage. Literature in Altay is almost exclusively post-1920. At least one newspaper and some periodicals appear in the language.

At least two forms of taboo language are found in Altay. The primary words for certain objects in the environment are also used as male proper names: e.g. *malta* 'axe' (Turkish, *balta*). Accordingly, if her husband's name is Malta, a woman is required to use the acceptable substitute word *keziner* for 'axe', instead of the taboo word *malta*.

Similarly, there is a specific hunter's lexicon of taboo words denoting animals: e.g. the wolf must be called *bööstoy* instead of *börÿ*.

SCRIPT

As far back as 1845, a Cyrillic script was provided by missionaries. As usual in the case of minority languages of the Soviet Union, the 1930s saw a period of experimental romanization. The Cyrillic script now in use has the following additional letters: *j*, *ö*, *ÿ*. *j* = /dʒ/ → [d'], *ÿ* = /y/.

PHONOLOGY

Consonants

stops: p, b, t, d, k, g
affricates: tʃ/ts, dʒ/d′
fricatives: (f, v) s, z, ʃ, ʒ, x, ɣ
lateral and trill: l/l′, r
nasals: m, n, ŋ

[x] and [γ] are allophones of /k/, /g/; *l* in the script represents both /l/ and /l′/.

Vowels

a, ɛ, o, œ, ı, i, y, u

All occur short or long; when long, they are written doubled: *aa*, etc. Here *ö* = /œ/, *ü* = /y/.

VOWEL HARMONY

Front (/ɛ, i, œ, y/) followed by front; back (/a, ı, o, u/) by back; rounded followed by rounded, unrounded by unrounded.

Stress

Stress is on the final syllable, with secondary stresses within the word. Exceptionally for a Turkic language, the negative infix is stressed: e.g. *barbázım* 'I shan't go'. Stress is phonemic in homonymous forms: e.g. *algánım* 'I took'; *alganím* 'taken by me'.

MORPHOLOGY AND SYNTAX

(*See also* **Turkic Languages**.)

Noun

The noun has two numbers and five cases. The plural marker is *-lar*^{12}. The index $+^{12}$ indicates that the combination of three possible initials with four vowels (a, e, o, œ) gives the following twelve forms: *l*-series: *-lar, -ler, -lor, -lör*; similarly for *d*-series and *t*-series: *dar/tar*, etc.

CASE

Basic forms, all with six to twelve variants:

genitive: -*n*V*ŋ*: *balanıŋ* 'of the boy'
dative: -*g*V: *balaga* 'to the boy'
accusative: -*dı*: *koldı* 'the hand (acc.)'
locative: -*d*V/*t*V: *atta* 'on the horse'
ablative: -*d*V*ŋ* *baladaŋ* 'from the boy'

The possessive suffixes are added to the noun, preceding case endings: sing. 1 -V*m*; 2 -V*ŋ*; 3 -(*z*)V; pl. 1 -(*ı*)*bıs*/(*i*)*bis*; 2 (*ı*)*gar*/(*i*)*ger*; 3 = sing.: e.g. *ada.m.naŋ* 'from my father'; *ada.bıs.taŋ* 'from our father'.

Adjective

As attribute, adjective precedes noun, and is invariable.

Pronoun

Sing. 1 *men*, 2 *sen*, 3 *ol*; pl. 1 *bis*(*ter*), 2 *sler*(*ler*), 3 *olor*. These are declined in all cases; the oblique base of *ol* is *on-*.

DEMONSTRATIVE PRONOUN/ADJECTIVE

bu 'this', *ol* 'that'. The oblique base of *bu* is *mın-*, e.g. *mınıŋ* (genitive).

INTERROGATIVE PRONOUN

kem 'who?'; *ne* 'what?'

RELATIVE PRONOUN

None; as in Turkic languages generally, participial forms are used in relative constructions. *See* **Verb**, below.

Numerals

1–10: *bir, eki, üč, tört, beš, altı, jeti, segis, togus, on*; 11 *on bir*; 12 *on eki*; 20 *jirme*; 30 *odus*; 40 *tört on* or *kırık*; 100 *jüs.*

Verb

The Altay verb has voice, mood, tense, marked for number and person; the non-finite forms – participles, gerunds – play a crucial role in the syntax, as in other Turkic languages. All forms have from two to six or more allophones.

VOICE

The passive voice marker is -V*l*, with assimilation of stem final: e.g. *tök-* 'to pour': *tögül* 'to be poured':

reflexive: -(V)*n*: e.g. *al-* 'to take', *alın-* 'to take for oneself'
reciprocal: -(V)*š*: e.g. *ber-* 'to give', *beriš-* 'to give each other'
causative: *-d/t*V*r*: e.g. *bil-* 'to know', *bildir-* 'to inform'

MOODS

Indicative, imperative, conditional, optative, subjunctive. The imperative has a specific set of endings: sing. 1 *-ayın*, 2 *-gın*, 3 *-zın*; pl. 1 *-alık*, 2 *-ıgar*, 3 *-zın*.

The participial markers may be listed here, as they reappear in the tense system:

(a) of definite past time: *dı*
(b) of indefinite past time: *gan*
(c) imperfective aspect: *galak*
(d) present/future time: *atan*
(e) future indefinite: V*r*
(f) conditional: *sa*
(g) optative: *gay*

The most important gerund is in *-ıp* marking concomitant or immediately preceding action; used in compound-tense formation.

TENSE FORMATION

The personal endings (*see* **Turkic Languages**) have been truncated: e.g. *mın* > *m*, *zıŋ* > *ŋ*, and scarcely differ from the possessive enclitics.

The main tenses in the indicative mood are, for root *bar-* 'to go':

past definite: *bar.dı.m* 'I went'; *bar.dı.ŋ* 'you went', etc.
past indefinite: *bar.gan.ım* 'I went' (at some unspecified time)
future indefinite: *bar.ar.ım* 'I shall go'
conditional mood: *bar.za.m* 'if I go'
optative mood: *bar.gay.ım* 'that I may go'

Compound tenses are made with various auxiliaries; the sense verb is typically in the *-ıp* gerundial form: e.g. *bar.ıp jadım* 'I'm going now'; *bar.ıp turum* '(it appears that) I went'.

RELATIVE CLAUSE

Participial constructions: e.g. *bargan* 'he/she came'; 'he/she who came'; *barar* 'he/she will come'; 'he/she who will come'; *ayıl.ga kirgen* 'he/she who had gone into the village'.

Postpositions

Primary or derived:

primary: e.g. *učun* 'for: *meniŋ učun* 'for me'; *le* 'with': *sen le* 'with you'.
derived: e.g. *ara* 'interval': *arazında* 'among, between'; *agaštıŋ arazında* 'among the trees'.

Word order

SOV

1. Баш-башкыда Сӧс болгон, Сӧс Кудайда болгон, ол Сӧс Кудай болгон.

2. Ол башкыда Кудайда болгон.

3. Ончо ончозы Анан̄ пўткен; неле пўткен Анан̄ пўтпей пўткен эмес.

4. Аныn̄ Бои тўрў болгон, Аныn̄ тўрўў кижилерге јарык полгон.

5. Јарык карачкыда јарып, карачкаа пўркетпеди.

6. Кудайдан̄ іилген кижи болгон, аныn̄ ады Іоанн.

7. Ол, јарыкты керелеирге, керее келген, ончолор анан̄ ары пўтсин, деп.

8. Ол бои јарык полгон эмес, јарыкты керелеирге іилгенболгон.

AMHARIC

INTRODUCTION

This Afro-Asiatic (Semito-Hamitic) language is South Semitic in origin (*see* **Ethiopic**) but has acquired a very considerable non-Semitic element, presumably through contact with neighbouring Cushitic languages such as Oromo. The word *Amhara* is the ethnonym of the 14 million people in central and north-western Ethiopia (an area which includes the capital, Addis Abbeba) who speak *amarəñña*. As the official language of Ethiopia, Amharic is also used as a second language by about a third of the total population of Ethiopia. The main dialects are those of Gondar, Gojjam, and Shoa.

Before the late nineteenth century little was written in Amharic. Missionary activity involving the use of written Amharic was encouraged for political reasons by the Emperors Menelik II and Haile Selassie I. The first printing press for Amharic books was established in the 1880s. Through the twentieth century there has been a gradual drift from the total religious commitment of previous Ethiopian writing, towards cautious experimentation in such Western genres as the novel and the stage play, which allow social and economic issues to be raised.

SCRIPT

The Ethiopic syllabary of 26 characters (*see* **Ethiopic**), written from left to right, has been extended by seven letters denoting specifically Amharic sounds. Phonological reduction from Ethiopic to Amharic has resulted in some redundancy; thus, there are, for example, four graphs for /h/. A major omission in the script is the absence of a sign denoting gemination, which is very important, usually phonemic, in Amharic. Signs for the numerals up to 20 are derived from Greek. Words are sometimes separated from each other by the marker ':'.

PHONOLOGY

Consonants

stops: p, b, p', t, d, t', k, g, k' ʔ
affricates: tʃ, dʒ, tʃ'
fricatives: f, v, s, z, s', ʃ, ʒ, h
semi-vowels: j, w
nasals: m, n, ɲ, (ŋ)
lateral and flap: l, r;

The emphatics, i.e. glottalized consonants, are notated here as *p̣, ṭ, ḳ, ṣ*; /k'/ is often notated as *q*. Most consonants occur labialized. In the case of the velar series and /h/, this labialization is notated for all vowels by a specific series of graphs; in realization, however, /k°/, /g°/, /k'°/, and /h°/ precede /a/; before other vowels, the labialization tends to be lost.

Vowels

i, e, ɛ, a, ə, u, o

/ɛ/ is notated here as *ä*.

Stress

Very weak.

MORPHOLOGY AND SYNTAX

Noun

In contrast to Tigrinya and Tigre, gender is not formally marked. Nouns are treated as masculine or feminine for reasons of natural gender or by convention; thus, *färäs* 'horse' is masculine, but *baqlo* 'mule' is feminine. Inanimate objects are usually treated as masculine, but there are exceptions. Words like *ləj* 'child', can be made more specific by the addition of *wənd* 'male', or *set* 'female': *wənd ləj* 'boy'. Gender is specifically marked in the affixed definite article, the demonstratives and the second and third persons of the verb. The Semitic feminine ending *-t* reappears in certain words, e.g. *mušərri**t*** 'bride' (*mušərra* 'bridegroom').

The concept of gender merges in Amharic with that of dimension, giving rise to an opposition between normal size/masculine and diminutive/feminine. Thus, concord fluctuates: a noun which takes 'masculine' concord when the referent is of normal dimensions may take 'feminine' concord when departure from the norm is to be stressed; cf. *yih bet tələq* ***nəw*** 'this house is big', but *yih bet bäṭam tənnəš* ***nəč*** 'this house is very small'.

Conversely, nouns like *ṣähay* 'sun', *çäräqa* 'moon', *kokäb* 'star', which normally take feminine/diminutive concord, acquire masculine status when unusual size is stressed; cf. *kokäb wəṭ**ṭač*** 'a star came out', but *talaq kokäb kä.sämay* ***wädäqä*** 'a great star fell from heaven' (Revelation 8.10).

DEFINITE ARTICLE

-u/*-w* identifies a singular noun as masculine; the feminine affix is *-wa*/*-itu*: e.g. *bet* 'house', *bet**u*** 'the house'; *lam* 'cow', *lam**wa*** 'the cow'.

NUMBER

The plural affix is *-očč*, which takes the definite article: e.g. *bet.očč.u* 'the houses'. There are some traces of a broken plural. The numeral *and* 'one' can be used as an indefinite article. The accusative is marked by *-n*: e.g. *innatwa.**n*** *ayyəč* 'she saw her mother'.

Genitive: the particle *yä* precedes the noun: e.g. ***yä.*** *Yohannəs innat* 'John's mother'; ***yä**.Ityopya häzb* 'the people of Ethiopia'. Further examples: *yä.däbub Afrika yä.tor awroplan* 'a South African warplane'; *yä.wədajən-nät.na yä.təbəbbər səməmmənnät* 'a treaty (*səməmmənnät*) of friendship and cooperation' (*-na* is the connective 'and').

yä is not used after prepositions: *b.abbat.e bet wəsṭ* 'in my father's house' instead of **bä yä* . . . .

Other case relationships are expressed with the help of prefixes, circumfixes, and affixes: *see* **Postpositions**, etc., below.

Adjective

The attributive adjective precedes the noun and is formally unmarked: e.g. *təlləq bet* 'big house'. If the noun is definite, the article is affixed to the adjective: e.g. *təllə**qu** bet* 'the big house'; and similarly for the case ending in *-n*. The adjective may take the plural marker: e.g. *addis.očč bet.očč* 'new houses'.

The possessive marker *yä* precedes the attributive adjective: *yä ḳonjo set* 'of the beautiful woman'.

COMPARATIVE

kä or *tä* precedes the word compared: e.g. ***kä**.Gondar Addis Ababa təlləq näw* 'Addis Abbeba is bigger than Gondar.'

Pronoun

The independent personal pronouns with copula and enclitic markers:

		Singular		*Plural*	
1		əne näññ	-ññ	əñña nän	-n
2	masc.	antä näh	-h	ənnantä naččəhu	-ččəhu
	fem.	anči näš	-š		
3	masc.	əssu näw	-w/-t	ənnässu naččäw	-ččäw
	fem.	əsswa näčč	-t		

The enclitic markers are shown in characteristic form without the linking vowels that usually precede them. They are used as the object pronouns of transitive verbs: e.g. *Bä.gäbäya ayyu.**t*** 'They saw him/her at market'; and may be anticipated by a noun or the relevant pronoun in the accusative case: e.g. *əssu.**n** ayyu.*(***t***) 'they saw him'. Some additional examples: *ayyä.hu.t* 'I saw him/it'; *ayyä.hu.w.at* 'I saw her'; *ayyä.hu.w.aččə hu* 'I saw you (pl.)'; *ayyä.ññ* 'he saw me'; *ayyä.ččə hu* 'he saw you (pl.)'.

There are respectful forms for independent second and third persons: second *ərswo*; third *əssaččäw*.

POSSESSION

This may be expressed by the affixed personal markers: sing. 1 *-e*, 2 *-əh/š*, 3 *-u/wa*i; pl. 1 *-aččən*, 2 *-aččəh*, 3 *-aččäw*: e.g. *bet**e*** 'my house'; *bet**aččən*** 'our house'.

'To have' is expressed in Amharic by means of the verb *allä* 'there is'; the past tense is *näbbärä*. In this construction *allä* is conjugated in concord with the possessed object, and to these inflections the pronominal enclitic identifying the possessor by person, gender, and number is added. Thus, the form *all.ä.ññ* indicates that a masc. sing. object (*-ä-*) is (*all-*) to-me (*ññ*), i.e. 'I have a (masculine singular object)'. The form *all.äččə.ññ* identifies the possessed object as feminine. Similarly, *all.u.ññ*: 'I have (plural object)'. Cf. *all.ä.w* 'he has' (masculine singular object), *all.äččə.w* 'he has' (feminine singular object), *all.u.t* (for plural object). *allä* is negated by *yälläm*: *yäll.ä.ññ.əm* 'I do not have' (masculine singular object). Past tense (affirmative): *näbbär.ä.ññ* 'I had' (masc. sing. obj.).

DEMONSTRATIVE PRONOUN/ADJECTIVE

'This': masc. *yəh*, fem. *yəčč*, pl. *ənnäzzih*; 'that': masc. *ya*, fem. *yačč*, pl. *ənnäzziya*.

INTERROGATIVE PRONOUN

man 'who?'; *mən*(*dən*) 'what?'

RELATIVE PRONOUN

See relative clause in **Verb**, below.

Numerals

1–10: *and*, *hulätt*, *sost*, *aratt*, *amməst*, *səddəst*, *säbatt*, *səmmənt*, *zäṭäññ*, *assər*; 11 *asra and*; 12 *asra hulätt*; 20 *haya*; 30 *sälasa*; 40 *arba*; 100 *mäto*.

Verb

Roots are mainly two-, three-, or four-radical, the majority being triliterals. A few verbs have five radicals, and there is one monoradical – *ša* 'to want'. The citation form is, as customary in Semitic languages, the third person masculine past tense (more accurately, perfective): e.g. *mätta* 'he came', *fällägä* 'he wanted'. A typical triliteral perfective is conjugated as follows:

singular 3 masc. *fällägä*, fem. *fällägä**čč***; 2 masc. *fällägh*, fem. *fällägš*; 1 *fällägh**hu***;
plural 3 common, *fälläg**u***; 2 common, *fälläg**aččəhu***; 1 common, *fälläg**ən***.

IMPERFECTIVE, OR PRESENT-FUTURE FORM

The stem is modulated by prefix and affix to provide this form, which is not predictable from the perfective form. There are two patterns, which hinge on differing treatment of the geminated second radical: that is to say, if **1**, **2**, **3** are the radicals, **1***ä***22***ä***3** may yield *yə***1***ä***23***al* or *yə***1***ä***22***ə***3***al* as present-future form: thus, *fällägä* yields *yə***F***ä***LL***ə***G***al*; but *säbbärä* yields *yə***S***ä***BR***al*.

This is, in fact, a composite form. The *-al* component is a shortened form of the existential verb *allä*, and the pronominal object is therefore infixed between the stem and the *-al* component: cf. some examples with **F***ä***LL***ä***G***ä*:

əFäLLəGä.w.allähu 'I want him/it': ***-w-*** is the third person masculine pronominal object, and ***ə*** . . . ***hu*** is the present-future circumfix for first-person singular.

təFäLLəGə.ññ.alläh 'you (masc. sing.) want me': *-ññ-* is the first person pronominal object, ***tə...h*** is the second person singular masculine circumfix.

The prefixes in this verbal form are the familiar Semitic series: sing. 3 *yə-/tə-*, 2 *tə-*, 1 *ə-*; pl. 3 *yə-*, 2 *tə-*, 1 *ənnə-*; and the affixes are forms of the existential verb + personal markers.

Biliterals are conjugated essentially as triliterals: e.g. *qomä* 'he stood'; *qom**ku*** 'I stood'; ***yə**qom**al*** 'he stands'; ***ə**qom**allähu*** 'I stand'.

Amharic has an imperative mood used only in the second person singular, and a jussive, used in the first and third person singular and plural and in second plural. The verbal noun takes the prefix *mä-*: e.g. *mäfalläg* 'wanting'; *mähed* 'going'. These forms can take the personal affixes: e.g. *kä.mähede bäfit* 'before I went' (for the form *kä... bäfit*, *see* **Postpositions**, etc., below).

GERUND

The base patterns are: **1***ä***23**, or **1***ä***22ə3**: the gerund takes personal affixes similar to the possessive series: *fälləg**o*** 'wanting...he ...'; *fälləg**än*** 'wanting...we...', e.g. *Betun šəṭo yət agər məhed yəfälləgal?* 'Having sold his house, to which country does he want to go?' *fälləgä.š.aččäw* 'you (fem.) having wanted them...'.

DERIVED STEMS

(a) *-a* prefixed to base stem changes intransitive to transitive: e.g. *moqä* 'he was warm'; ***a**moqä* 'he warmed sth. up';
(b) *-tä-* passive of transitive, e.g. *anäbbäbä* 'he read': ***tä**nabbäbä* 'it was read';
(c) *as-*: causative, e.g. *wässädä* 'he took'; ***as**wässädä* 'he had sth. taken'.

THE SHORT IMPERFECTIVE FORM

This is the present-future form minus the *-allä* component. It is used, e.g. in subordinate temporal and causal clauses introduced by such pre-posited relational conjunctions as *sə-*, *lə-*, *bə-*, *əndə-*, etc. (with juncture sandhi). That is to say, the short imperfective stem cannot be used by itself; it must be preceded by one of the relational affixes. Examples: *Almaz **si**mäṭṭa wädä bet əhedallähu* 'When A. comes, I'll go home'; *Yohannəs mäṣhafun **si**fälläg* 'when John was looking for the book'. And in negative: *baburu **sa.y.**mättä* 'the train not coming' = 'before the train comes'.

A conditional form is made by prefixing the relational particle *b(ə/i)* to the short imperfective: *bi.mäṭa, ə.hed.allähu* 'if he comes, I'll go'; *gize bi.nor.ä.ññ* 'if I had time'. The corresponding negative form is *b.ay.nor.ä.ññ.*

Volition/intention is expressed by the relational affix *l(ə/i)* + short imperfective: e.g. *mäṣhaf li.yanäb yəfälləgal* 'he wants to read a book'.

NEGATION

For the perfective, the circumfix *al...m* is used: e.g. ***al**fällägä**m*** 'he didn't want'; ***al**fälläghu**m*** 'I didn't want'. The circumfix for the imperfective negative is: *a*C*...m*, where C varies: cf. ***ay**fälləgə**m*** 'he doesn't want';

anfälləgəm 'we don't want'. With infixed pronoun object: *alfälləgä**w**əm* 'I don't want it'; *ayfälləgaččəhum* 'he doesn't want you (pl.)'.

RELATIVE CLAUSES

These are treated as qualifiers preceding the headword: *yä-* introduces a relative clause in the perfective; *yämmə-* in the imperfective. Cf. ***yämäṭṭaw*** *säw* 'the man (*säw*) who came'; ***yämäṭṭut*** *säwočč* 'the men who came'; *gänzäb* ***yäṭ****äffabbat säw* 'the man who lost his money'; ***yämmə****norəbbat bet yəhäw* 'This is the house in which I live.'

In a negative relative clause the *-əm* component of the negating circumfix is dropped: *yämm.al.fäll ə ggäw mäṣhaf* 'the book I don't want'.

Prepositions and postpositions

Circumfix: e.g.

bä 'in': *bä.kätäma* 'in the city';
kä 'from': *Kä.yät mäṭṭa* 'From where has he come?';
wädä 'towards, to': *kä.gära wädä ḳäññ* 'from left to right';
kä... bəhwala 'after': *Kä.hullu bəhwala mäṭṭa* 'He came after all the others';
bä... mäkakäl 'among, between': *bä.säwočč mäkakäl* 'among people';
lä... silə 'for, on behalf of': *lä.ageru silə motä* 'to die for one's country'.

Also *bä... lay* 'on', *bä... wəsṭ* 'inside'; *kä... bäfit* 'before', etc.

Word order

SOV; OSV is permissible.

በመጀመሪያው ቃል ነበረ ፥ ቃልም በእግዚአብሔር ፩ ፤
ዘንድ ነበረ ፤ ቃልም እግዚአብሔር ነበረ ። ይህ በመጀመ ፪ ፤
ሪያው በእግዚአብሔር ዘንድ ነበረ ። ሁሉ በእርሱ ሆነ ፥ ፫ ፤
ከሆነውም አንዳች ስንኳ ያለ እርሱ አልሆነም ። በእርሱ ፬ ፤
ሕይወት ነበረች ፥ ሕይወትም የሰው ብርሃን ነበረች ። ብር ፭ ፤
ሃንም በጨለማ ይበራል ፥ ጨለማም አላሸነፈውም ።
ከእግዚአብሔር የተላከ ስሙ ዮሐንስ የሚባል አንድ ፮ ፤
ሰው ነበረ ፤ ሁሉ በእርሱ በኩል እንዲያምኑ ይህ ስለ ብር ፯ ፤
ሃን ይመሰክር ዘንድ ለምስክር መጣ ። ስለ ብርሃን ሊመ ፰ ፤
ስክር መጣ እንጂ ፥ እርሱ ብርሃን አልነበረም ።

ANATOLIAN LANGUAGES

From the mid-nineteenth century onwards, archaeological excavation has been instrumental in bringing to light the existence of several languages which were used in Anatolia during the three millennia preceding the Christian era. These languages were all virtually extinct by the turn of the millennia, though it is possible that isolated pockets of spoken Hetto-Luwian may have survived into the early years of our era.

The languages can be classified in two ways:

1. Genetically: Hittite, Luwian, Palaic, Carian, Lycian, and Lydian are Indo-European languages. This group can be further subdivided into:

(a) Hetto-Lydian (including Carian)
(b) Luwian-Lycian (including Palaic)

Three languages – Hattic, Hurrian, and Urartian – are non-Indo-European.

2. Epigraphically:

(a) The oldest stratum, 1700–1200 BC, is represented by languages written in Sumero-Akkadian cuneiform: these are Hittite, Luwian, Palaic, Hattic, Hurrian, Urartian.
(b) Languages written in hieroglyphic script in south-eastern Anatolia between 1400 and 800 BC: these are Hieroglyphic Hittite and Hieroglyphic Luwian.
(c) Languages written in alphabetic script of Greek type between 700 and 300 BC: these are Lycian, Lydian, Carian.

So far, only one of these languages – Hittite – is attested in sufficient quantity, and is, because of its Indo-European structure, sufficiently accessible to us to permit in-depth study. *See* **Hittite**, **Hattic**, **Hurrian**, **Urartian**. Here follow brief descriptions of Hieroglyphic Luwian, Lycian, and Lydian.

HIEROGLYPHIC LUWIAN

Luwian dialects were spoken in the south coastal regions of Anatolia, and in northern Syria, from the middle of the second millennium BC to about the close of the pre-Christian era. Here we consider the Eastern Luwian of the neo-Hittite states (late second to early first millennium BC), written in hieroglyphic script. For parallel forms of the older Luwian dialect found in the Bogaz-köy archives (cuneiform script), *see* **Hittite**.

SCRIPT

Lists of all the Hetto-Luwian hieroglyphic characters known up to 1960 are given in E. Laroche (1960) and in I.M. Dunayevskaya (1969). In the texts, much use is made of the so-called 'phonetic complement': roots are denoted by hieroglyphs, while phonetic signs are added to denote base auslaut and nominal/verbal inflection (cf. Japanese, where Chinese roots are followed by inflectional sequences in *kana*). About 500 characters are known, including from 50 to 100 phonetic signs.

Ideograms may combine; cf.  'temple', read as *hajani*. This compound ideogram consists of  'god' plus 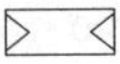 'house' (read in isolation as *parna*). The script is boustrophedon.

PHONOLOGY

The inventory given by Korolev (1976) in *JaAA*, Vol. 1, shows /p, t, k, k°; m, n, w, l, r; s, h, ts/. The hieroglyphic script does not distinguish between voiced and unvoiced consonants, so that /b, d, g/ are possible values of the /p, t, k/ series.

Vowels

i, e, a, u

The absence of *o* is typical of Anatolian languages in general.

MORPHOLOGY

Noun

Common and neuter genders are distinguished, with two numbers, singular and plural. In the singular, the case markers are: nominative *-s*, accusative *-n* (common; the neuter marker is *-i*), dative *-a*, ablative *-ti*, genitive *-s*. These are preceded by the stem vowel *i* or *a*: thus *-is*/*-as*, *-in*/*-an*, etc., though the ablative shows *-ati* for both stems. Plural nominative/accusative forms are: *-ii*, *-ai*; there is no genitive in the plural. In addition to a singular genitive case, Hieroglyphic Luwian possessed a declinable adjectival possessive in *-asi-*. The adjective is declined as a nominal.

Pronoun

The first person nominative singular form is *amu*, which has an enclitic *-mu*; *amu* serves also as accusative and dative case. A second person singular enclitic is known: *-ti*. The third person is also known from its enclitic form: *-as*, *-an*, *-tu*. These are common gender forms. The nominative/accusative neuter singular form is *-ata*, which comes to function as the plural nom./acc.

DEMONSTRATIVE PRONOUN/ADJECTIVE

The proximate form is *is*, distal *apas*. Both are fully attested, with *-n* accusative and *-s* genitive in the singular. The interrogative/relative pronoun is *k°as* (?) (cf. Cuneiform Luwian and Hittite *kwis*, Lydian *qis*).

Numerals

Two is attested in the plural accusative form *tuwai*.

Verb

The Hieroglyphic Luwian verbal system, in so far as it is attested, seems to be largely analogous to the Hittite *mi*-paradigm (*see* **Hittite**); *ḫi*-forms have been tentatively identified. A medio-passive voice is theoretically postulated, but hardly attested. The active voice has an indicative mood with two tenses – present and past – and an imperative. Thus for the stem *as*- 'to be' the following forms are attested:

present: singular 1 *ami*, 3 *asti*; plural 3 *asanti*
preterite: singular 1 *asha*, 3 *asta*; plural 3 *asanta*
imperative: singular 2 *astu*; plural *asantu*

As in Cuneiform Luwian, the infinitive ends in *-un*(*a*). An active participle in *-nt* is attested.

Postpositions

These function also as preverbs: e.g. *anta* 'in', *arha* 'out of', *katta* 'under', *paran* 'before', *inan* 'among'.

Some Hieroglyphic Luwian bases:

hali-	'day'	nanaśra-	'sister'	arha-	'border, frontier'
ziti-	'man'	nawani-	'son'	pia-	'give'
pati-	'foot'	ta-	'brother'	aśu-	'horse'

LYCIAN

One of the first Anatolian languages to be deciphered, Lycian is known to us from a corpus of inscriptions, about 150 in all, dating from the period 500–200 BC. The Lycians, a sea-faring and trading people, were settled along the south-western coast of Anatolia throughout the latter half of the first millennium BC, and their language appears to be connected with a Luwian dialect, which was spoken in the same area a thousand years earlier. Lycian is written in an alphabetic script, which is, at least in part, based on Greek characters.

Lycian shares certain features with Hittite, but is in general closer to Luwian. Cf.

	Lycian	*Hieroglyphic Luwian*	*Hittite and Cun. Luwian*	
'man'	ziti	ziti		
'to do'	a(i)-	aja-	ija-	
'moon-god'	ermm̃e-		arma-	
'horse'	esbe-	aśu(wa)-		
'give'	pije-	pia-	pija-	
'foot'	pede-	pata-	pati-	pata-
'year'	uha-			ussa-

PHONOLOGY

Consonants

The consonantal inventory shows: *p, b, t, d, k, g, k°*; *ts, dz*; *β, ð, s, x, h*; *m, m̃, n, ñ; l, r, w.*

Vowels

The oral series is *i, e, a, u*; as in Luwian, *o* is absent. The vowel system is notable for the presence of at least two nasalized vowels: *ã, ẽ.* It seems likely that *i* and *u* also had nasalized values.

MORPHOLOGY

Noun

Typically for Late Anatolian languages, Lycian has an accusative singular marked by a nasal (*n, Ṽ*); there is a dative/locative in *-i(j)a*, and an ablative/instrumental in *-di* (cf. Luwian *-ti*). The adjectival possessive marker in -(V)*h*(V) (Luwian *-assi-*) tends to replace the old genitive case.

Pronoun

As in Hieroglyphic Luwian and in Lydian, the first person singular nominative – *emu* – (cf. Hieroglyphic Luwian and Lydian *amu*) functions also as accusative and dative/locative. The possessive form *emi* 'my', 'our' is also found in Lydian. The third person singular pronominal base represented in Hetto-Luwian as *apa-* appears in Lycian as *ebe-*.

Verb

First and third person endings are known for present and past tenses of the indicative mood; first, second, and third person endings for the imperative mood.

present: 1 -wi (archaic), -m
3 -di/ti

A second person ending in *-si* is postulated.

past: 1 velar + a
3 dental + e/a

Imperative mood: 1 *-lu*, 2 Ø, 3 -dental + *u*

LYDIAN

INTRODUCTION

This apparently Indo-European language is attested in sixty-four inscriptions, including a few bilinguals, mostly of a funerary and votive nature, dating from the seventh to the fourth centuries BC. The most ancient was found in Egypt. The Lydian capital was Sardis in western Anatolia.

SCRIPT

The Lydian script was probably borrowed from the Anatolian Greeks early in the seventh century BC, though an indigenous origin is possible. It runs generally from right to left with additional characters for sounds alien to Greek, e.g. the nasalized vowel /e/ notated as Ỿ. Eight vowels are notated.

PHONOLOGY

Consonants

The following consonants figure in the script:

stops: b, t, d, k, q
fricatives: f, v, s, ś
nasals: m, n
lateral and flap: l, r

/t, d, l, n/ seem to have palatalized counterparts, notated by researchers as τ, ↑, λ, ν.

r, l, m, n function both as consonants and as vowels: *m/m̥, n/n̥, l/l̥, r/r̥*.

Vowels

a, ã, e, ẽ, i, o, u

Also a vowel transliterated as *y*, which may indicate closed /ẹ/.

MORPHOLOGY AND SYNTAX

Noun

Lydian had two genders, common and neuter, with two numbers, singular and plural. Common nouns have a nominative ending in *-s/ś*, which also appears in Hittite, Palaic, and Luwian. Similarly, the common accusative in *-n/v* is shared with these three languages. There is a dative/locative in -λ; cf. *vãnaś* 'tomb': acc. *vãnav*, loc. *vãnaλ*.

Plural: nominative and accusative in *-(a)ś;* dative/locative in *-av*.

Pronoun

The following forms are known: sing. 1 *amu* 'I', *ẽmi* 'mine'; sing. 3 *bi* 'he', *bili* 'his'. The possessive pronoun form *ẽmi* has nom. *ẽmis*, acc. *ẽmv*, dat./loc. *ẽmλ*.

DEMONSTRATIVE PRONOUN

es 'this'; *eś.ś – es.v – es.λ.* Neuter accusative in *es.t.*

RELATIVE PRONOUN

qi, which takes the *-s*, *-v*, *-λ* endings, with a neuter nominative and accusative in *-d*: *qid*.

Verb

Certain present-future and past-tense forms have been identified: e.g. present-future: sing. 1 *-u/-v*, 2 *-s*, 3 *-d/-t* (the plural forms seem to be identical); past: sing. 1 *-v*, sing./pl. 3 *-l*.

Some Lydian bases:

bi-	'to give'	da-	'to give'
bira-	'house'	e-	'to be'
borli-	'year'	ēna-	'mother'
brafr-	'brother'	istamin-	'family'
kofu-	'water'	laλe-	'speak'

Bira- 'house' may be compared with Hittite *pir.*

Examples of inscriptions

Here follow five lines from one of the two known Lydian–Aramaic bilingual inscriptions, as interpreted by Ševoroškin (1967):

ak.it n[āqi.s]
es.λ mru.λ buk es.λ vāna.λ buk esva.v
laqirisa.v buk.it kud ist es.λ vāna.λ bλtarvo.[d]
ak.t.in nāqi.s qel.λ.k fēnsλifi.d fak.m.λ artimu.ś
ibśimsi.s artimu.k kulumsi.s aara.λ bira.λ.k
kλida.λ kofu.λ.k qira.λ qel.λ.k bil.λ v↑baqēn.t

ŠEVOROŠKIN TRANSLATES

If anyone does harm to this stele or to this tomb or to these walls, or to anything else appertaining to this tomb, verily to him Artemis of Ephesus and Artimis of Cholcis (?) will destroy his belongings in house and yard, on land and water.

ak.it	*ak-* inceptive particle, intensified by *-it*; 'now lo . . . '
nāqi.s	whosoever (*qis* 'who')
es.λ	*es-* proximate demonstrative pronoun + -λ dat./loc. marker
mru.λ	dat./loc. case in -λ of *mru.d* 'stele'
buk	conjunction 'or'
vāna.	dat./loc. case of *vāna.ś* 'tomb'
esνaν	plural (?) dat./loc. case of *es-*: 'to these'
laqirisa.ν	dat./loc. case; meaning doubtful; Ševoroškin translates 'to these walls', i.e. of the tomb
kud	'where'
ist	preposition 'in'
bλtarvo.[d]	'property'
qel.λ.k	dat./loc. case of *qesi* 'anything'; *-k* is a conjunction 'and'
fēnsλifi.d	3rd p. sing. of pres./fut. tense; *fēn-* is a preverb; the Aramaic version suggests 'do harm to'
fak.m.λ	-λ here is the dat./loc. case of the 3rd p. enclitic *-i*; *-m-* is an intensifier: 'now verily to him'
artimu.ś	Artemis; *-ś* is the nom. sing. marker, common gender
ibsimsi.s	adjective in concord with *artimu.ś*: 'Ephesian'
artimu.k	'and Artemis' with elision of nom. sing. case ending
kulumsi.s	adjective 'of Cholo-'
aara.λ	'in the courtyard'
bira.λ.k	'and in the house'
kλida.	'to/on earth'
kofu.λ.k	'and to/on water'
qira.λ	dat./loc. case of *qirad* 'belongings'
qel.λ.k	'and (*-k*) to whatever . . . '
bil.λ	dat./loc. case of *bili-* 'his'
$v_{\uparrow}$ba.qēn.t	the root is *qēn*, Hetto-Luwian *kuen* 'slay'; the verb form is 3rd p. pl. of pres./fut. tense: '(may) they destroy'; $v_{\uparrow}$ and *ba-* are both verbal prefixes

ANDAMANESE

INTRODUCTION

Andamanese may be an isolate like Basque or Burushaski. Recently, it has been tentatively linked with the Indo-Pacific group, which includes the Papuan languages. In 1898, M.V. Portman's *Notes on the Languages of the South Andamanese Group of Tribes* – a work forming a part of his *Record of the Andamanese*, 'undertaken for the British Museum and the Government of India' – was published in Calcutta. In his Preface, Portman, who was 'Officer in Charge of the Andamanese', describes the Andamanese race as 'almost extinct'.

The work is a very valuable and detailed study of five South Andamanese languages: Āka-Bēa-da, Ākar-Bālē, Pūchikwār, Āūkāū-Jūwōī, and Kol, with a comparative vocabulary of 2,286 words, specimens of Andamanese songs, and much anthropological information of great interest.

PHONOLOGY

Consonants

Portman gives the following inventory of consonants:

stops: p, b, t, d, k, g
affricates: ts, dʒ, tʃ
fricatives: s, h
semi-vowels: j, w
nasals: m, n, ɲ, ŋ
lateral and flap: l, r

/dʒ/ is notated here as *ǰ*.

Vowels

iː, ɪ, eː, ɛ, ə, ʌ, a, aː, ɔ, o, oː, œ, u, uː

Diphthongs: ai, aw, ow, oi. Long vowels are notated here as *ī*, *ē*, etc.

MORPHOLOGY AND SYNTAX

Roots are modulated by prefixes, which indicate physical properties of the referent – roundness, softness, length, flexibility, etc. – and by suffixes which are functional, i.e. they mark syntactical relationships in nominals, temporal/aspectual distinctions in verbs.

Portman classifies Andamanese roots into the following:

(a) parts of the human body; roots relating to mankind in general;
(b) natural objects, animate or inanimate;
(c) functional roots;
(d) pronouns;
(e) postpositions, adverbs, conjunctions, exclamations, proper names.

Nouns

Examples of class (a) roots in Pūchikwār:

ōte-tā-da 'head': *ōte* is the prefix marking roundness, *-da* /də/ is the nominal marker;
ōng-tā-da 'foot': *ōng-* is the prefix used to denote hands or feet.

Similarly, *ēr-kawdak-da* 'eye', *īr-bo-da* 'ear'. The prefixes function, that is to say, like class markers in Bantu languages, though the motivation for the Andamanese taxonomy is often no longer clear. For example, with root *yōp.(da)* 'soft':

with prefix *ōt-* (round things): *ōt-yōp-da* 'a sponge';
with prefix *auto-* (long, thin things): *auto-yōp-da* 'a cane';
with prefix *āka-* (pointed things): *āka-yōp-da* 'a pencil'.

In association with class (a) nouns (parts of the body), the prefixes are construed as third person possessive pronouns, and take plural forms. Thus, number, normally ignored in Andamanese, may be shown by the third person pronominal prefixes: cf. *ōt-chēta-da* 'his/her/its head'; *ong-kaura-tek* 'by his hand(s)'; *ōtōt-chēta-da* 'their heads'.

Adverbial roots expressing the notion of plurality = more than one may also be used: thus, in Āka-Bēa-da, *rōko-da* 'canoe': *rōko l'ar-dūru-da* 'lots of canoes'.

Relational affixes in Āka-Bēa-da: root *chāng-da* 'hut': *chāng-lia* 'of a/belonging to a hut', *chāng-len* 'in a hut', *chāng-lat* 'to a hut', *chāng-tek* 'by a hut'; *X-liaērem-len* 'in the land of X'.

Modifiers follow modified root: e.g. *ōgar-da* 'the moon'; *ōgar-dērēka-da* '"baby" moon' (i.e. 'new moon'); *ōgar-chao-da* '"big" moon' (i.e. 'full moon'). Cf. *jūrū chao* 'big sea' (i.e. 'the open sea').

Pronouns

The Pūchikwār forms are:

	Singular	*Plural*
1	tū-le	mū-le
2	ngū-le	ngū-wel
3	ū-le	nū-le

POSSESSIVE PRONOUN

Have full and shortened forms:

	Singular		*Plural*	
	Full	*Short*	*Full*	*Short*
1	tiye-da	d’	mīye-da	m’
2	ngīye-da	ng’	ngīyil-da	ng’. . . *l*
3	īye-da	∅	nīye-da	n’

A specific series of pronominal subject forms is used with verbs. The Āka-Bēa-da set is:

	Singular	*Plural*
1	dō	moicho
2	ngō-	ngoicho
3	dā-	ēda

For example, *dō māmi-kē* ‘I sleep, shall sleep’; *dō wōlij̆-kē* ‘I shall drink’; *tuk mōli-kē* ‘I sleep, shall sleep’ in Pūchikwār.

Numerals

The Āka-Bēa-da set 1–5 is: *ūbatūl*, *ik-paur*, *ēd-ār-ūbāī*, *ē-īj̆i-pagi*, *ār-dūru*.

Verb

Functional suffixes attached to verbals:

-kē	for	present-future tense
-kā		imperfect
-rē		perfect
-ba		negative
-nga		present participle

E.g. *māmi-nga* ‘sleeping’; *Lūratūt-la chāpa tāp-nga ōmō-rē* ‘Luratut (proper name) came stealing fire’ (Āka-Bēa-da language; *-la* is an honorific affix; *chāpa* ‘fire’; *tāp-nga* = present participle; *-rē* = perfect marker).

The personal pronouns appear to change their form in association with certain tenses; e.g. *dō-māmi-kē* ‘I (shall) sleep’, but ***dā*** *māmi-ka* ‘I was sleeping’; ***dā*** *māmi-rē* ‘I slept’; ***dōna*** *ī-dai-nga yāba-da* ‘I do not understand’ (*yāba-da* ‘not’).

Word order

SOV is usual.

ANDEAN-EQUATORIAL LANGUAGES

This very extensive grouping of South American Indian languages stretches the full length of the continent, from Central America to Tierra del Fuego. Its four most important branches are:

1. Quechuamaran: demographically, the largest unit of American Indian languages, with about 10 million speakers in Ecuador, Peru, Bolivia, Colombia, and Argentina. Quechua itself is spoken by about 6 million in Peru, Bolivia, and Ecuador. Aymará, in Peru and Bolivia, has over 1 million speakers.
2. Tupí: Guaraní, the principal Tupian language, has semi-official status alongside Spanish in Paraguay, where it is spoken by some 3 million people. Many Tupian languages of Brazil are moribund or already extinct.
3. Arawakan: a very extensive, but deeply fragmented, branch, found in enclaves in Brazil, Venezuela, and Central America. Goajiro, spoken by about 40,000 in Colombia and Venezuela, is the main Arawakan language.
4. Island Carib is spoken by about 30,000 in Honduras, Guatemala, and some parts of the West Indies.

Some authorities regard Mapudungu as an Andean-Equatorial language (but *see* **Penutian Languges**).

The 250 Andean-Equatorial languages are spoken by around 15 million people.

See **Aymará**, **Quechua**, **Guaraní**, **Tupí**.

ANDI LANGUAGES

INTRODUCTION

Genetically a sub-division of North-East Ibero-Caucasian, the Andi languages are spoken by about 50,000 people in the south-west corner of Dagestan. Andi itself accounts for about a quarter of the total number of speakers. The other members of the sub-group are: Botlikh, Godoberi, Karata, Akhvakh, Bagval, Tindi, and Chamalal. None are written languages. Avar (*see* **Avar**) is used as a lingua franca and as a literary language throughout the Andi-speaking area.

PHONOLOGY

The velar stops, and the dental and alveolar affricates appear in the four-term series: simple stop/affricate – geminate – ejective – ejective geminate: e.g. /k – kk – ḳk – ḳḳ/. Andi has six laterals, including *ɬ*, *kɬ*, *ḳɬ*, *l*, ɬ̵. The vocalic system is simple /i, e, a, o, u/; nasalization of vowels occurs throughout the group. Stress is weak and movable.

MORPHOLOGY AND SYNTAX

Noun

As in Avar, nouns in the Andi languages are arranged in grammatical classes. Broadly speaking, male and female human classes are distinguished from those comprising animals, inanimate objects, and natural phenomena. Most Andi languages have three classes in the singular, two in the plural. Andi itself has five classes in both singular and plural; Chamalal has five in the singular, two in the plural.

The taxonomy in Andi is as follows:

Class		*Singular marker*	*Plural*
1	human male	w-	w
2	human female	y-	y
3	all other animates	b-	y
4, 5	inanimate objects	b-	r

Taxonomies vary: e.g. classes 4 and 5 in Chamalal contain certain animals, reptiles, birds.

In contrast with Avar, where verbal and adjectival recapitulation of a given nominal class is grammatically automatic, the Andi languages have developed a degree of option in the selection of classifiers. In Chamalal, for example, there may be a semantic element in the selection (Bokarev 1949). Position of classifier: usually prefix or suffix, sometimes both; rarely infix. Cf. in Chamalal:

Class 1	***w**eçaṭu heḳwa*	'black man'
Class 2	***y**eçaṭw**i** yah*	'black woman'
Class 3	***b**eçaṭu**b** çcatw*	'black horse'
Class 4	***y**eçaṭu**l** tay*	'black foal'
Class 5	***y**eçaṭw**i** yeła*	'black night'

Evidence for a noun's class has to be sought in material in concord with that noun. Nouns themselves do not carry class markers, though petrified class markers occur: e.g. in Chamalal, ***w**ac* 'brother', ***y**ac* 'sister'; here, the initials do not change in the plural form, as they would if the *w-/y-* were still construed as class markers.

As explained above, the plural form first of all requires replacement of the singular class prefix by the corresponding plural prefix: e.g. *b-* → *r-/y-*. In addition, however, pluralizing suffixes are attached. These are based on permutations of the group -/(V)b/d V 1/: e.g. *-(o)bil*, *-(o)dul*, *-dobil*, *-ibdul*. Thus, *yocci* 'sister', pl. *yocci.**bol***.

DECLENSION

As in Avar, the division into basic cases (absolute, ergative, genitive, dative) + several series of locative cases, is usual. The absolute form does not always provide the base for the oblique cases.

A typical Andi declension pattern is:

absolute case: Ø
ergative case: *-di*
genitive case: -class marker of object possessed
dative case: *-y*
affective case: -class marker of referent + *-o*

This basic paradigm is expanded by certain elements: e.g. *-ṣu-* (Cyrillic *щ*) or *-łł-* (Cyrillic ЛЪЛЪ) following the stem. E.g. Andi *heḳa* 'man':

ergative: *heḳa.ṣu.di*
genitive: *heḳa.ṣu.* + class marker
dative: *heḳa.ṣu.y*
affective: *heḳa.ṣu.* (class marker)*.o*

The genitive case: cf. base *ima* 'father':

(a) *imu.**w** **w**occi* 'father's brother'
(b) *imu.**y** **y**occi* 'father's sister'
(c) *imu.**b** ḳotu* 'father's horse'
(d) *imu.**w.ul** wocc.**ul*** 'father's brothers'
(e) *imu.**y.il** yocci.**bol*** 'father's sisters'

The ***w**-*, ***y**-* initials of *wocci* and *yocci* are petrified class markers, which do not invalidate the general principle that nouns in Andi are not marked for class (cf. Chamalal example above): *ḳotu* 'horse', in (c) above, is formally identified as belonging to Class 3 only by the ***-b*** in the genitive ending.

Note the pluralizing suffixes in (d) and (e).

LOCATIVE CASES

Relative location ('on', 'at', 'under', etc.) and motion relative thereto ('towards', 'from') are elaborately defined in the Andi languages by a series of seven categories, each of which has two or three cases. In Andi itself, Category I defines contiguity: 'at'; III also defines contiguity, with an emphasis on proximity: 'near'; II defines superimposition: 'on'; IV, VI, and VII define locus: 'in' something (IV for plural, VII for singular referent); the locus of referents in V is 'under' something. Each category in Andi has three cases:

(a) locative, i.e. rest in a place;
(b) allative, motion towards referent;
(c) ablative/elative: 'from, out of'.

In addition to its purely locative function, the locative case of IV is used to mark the indirect object of *verba dicendi*:

bosan imu.ʿi 'told (to) father'

and also serves as an instrumental case:

besuno.ʿi 'with a knife'.

In Akhwakh the superimposition series has a *-g-* characteristic, the contiguity series has *-xar-*, while the *-ḷʿi-* characteristic marks location within something.

Some examples (Magomedbekova 1967):

beča.**g**.e 'on the mountain'
beča.**g**.a 'onto the mountain'
beča.**g**.u 'from the mountain'
wacc.o.**xar**.i 'near the brother'
wacc.o.**xar**.u 'from close to the brother'
ixwa.ḷʿ.a 'into the butter/oil'

Adjective

The attributive adjective precedes the noun, and may take class markers:

	w.očuxa ima	'big daddy', i.e. grandfather
	y.ečuxa ila	'big mama', i.e. grandmother
but	**Ø**čonči **w**ošo	'good son'
	Øčonči **y**oši	'good daughter'
	Øčonči ḳotu	'good horse'

Pronoun

The singular first and second persons are true pronouns with suppletive plurals. In Andi:

	Singular		*Plural*
1	din/den	*excl.*	iṣṣil
		incl.	iḷ'il
2	min/men		bissil

The *min/din* forms are used by men, *den/men* by women.

The third person forms are supplied from the demonstrative series, and take classifiers:

singular: *how*, *hoy*, *ho**b***, *hor*
plural: *how.ul*, *hoy.il*, *ho**b**.ul*, *hor.ul*

This is the proximate series. There are several distal series, some of which distinguish relative location in the vertical plane ('up', 'down').

Verb

Verbs are transitive or intransitive. In all members of the group, the verb is marked for number, tense, and mood. One member, Akhvakh, also distinguishes person. Not all verbs are marked for grammatical class: the classifier, where it occurs, copies the subject of an intransitive verb, the direct object of a transitive verb.

Number is, as a rule, identifiable from the vowel following the class marker (if any). In very general terms, the closed vowel of the singular is replaced by a more open vowel for the plural: cf. (examples from Tsertsvadze 1967):

Intransitive:

wocci **w.u.**lon 'the brother went away'
wocc.ul **w.o.**lon 'the brothers went away'
yocci **y.i.**qo 'the sister came'
yocci.bol **y.o.**qo 'the sisters came'

Transitive:

imu.di çul **r.u.**qqi 'father was cutting a stick'
imu.di çuli.bol **r.a.**qqi 'father was cutting sticks'
ilu.di ḳorḳon **r.i.**ɬon 'mother was boiling an egg'
ilu.di ḳorḳo.mil **r.o.**ɬon 'mother was boiling eggs'

It will be seen from these examples that the logical subject of a transitive verb is in the ergative case in *-di*, while the logical object is in the absolutive.

TENSE

In general, the Andi languages are equipped to express present, future, and past in verbal form. Indicative, imperative, optative, and two conditional (real and unreal) moods are usually present.

There are two conjugations:

1. with the characteristic formant *-i/ud-* + tense/mood marker;
2. with the characteristic formant *-i/un-* + tense/mood marker.

Principal forms:

Conjugation 1:	stem *bek* 'to till'	Conjugation 2:	stem *bax* 'to sew'
infinitive:	*bekɨ.**id**.u*		*bax.**inn**.u*
present:	*bekɨ.id.o*		*bax.inn.o*
future:	*bekɨ.id.iya*		*bax.inn.iya*
participle:	*bekɨ.id.iya*		*bax.inn.iya*
aorist:	*bekɨ.i*		*bax.on*
imperative:	*bekɨ.o*		*bax.on*
conditional:	*bekɨ.i.bor*		*bax.om.or*
optative:	*bekɨ.i.do*		*bax.on.do*
past participle:	*bekɨ.i.b*		*bax.on.b* > *om*
present participle:	*bekɨ.i.rado.ssi*		*bax.o.mado.ssi*
verbal noun:	*bekɨ.ir*		*bax.on*

Several composite tenses are formed by means of auxiliary verbs.

As mentioned above, the Akhvakh verb exhibits both the class system (Akhvakh has three classes: I male humans; II female humans; III everything else) and a system of personal endings, in which first person is opposed to second/third person, and singular is opposed to plural. Thus, for an intransitive verb with subject markers:

wu.ḳɨ.ari 'I (male) died'
yi.ḳɨ.ade 'I (female) died'
ba.ḳɨ.widi 'we (humans) died'
yi.ḳɨ.ari 'you (female)/she died'
ri.ḳɨ.wari 'they (non-human) died'

Transitive verb:

1 kɨ.waredo 'I killed him (human)'
2 kɨ.wareri 'you/he killed him (human)'
1 kɨ.warede 'I killed her'
1 kɨ.waridi 'I killed them (humans)'
1 kɨ.warede 'I killed them (non-human)'

In Andi a frequentative aspect is made by reduplication of the stem: a causative by addition of such formants as *-ol/on* with allophones: *bekɨ.id.u* 'to till': *bekɨ.oll.u* 'to cause to till'.

In *verba sentiendi* the logical subject is in the affective case, the class marker copying the direct object:

imu.**w**.o haḳɬ.id.o wocci 'father sees the brother'
imu.**y**.o haḳɬ.id.o yocci 'father sees the sister'

NEGATION

The negating suffix is -*ss*(*u*): *din heva wuq.id.o.ss.iya* 'I shall not come here'.

In Botlikh, the negative affix is differentiated for grammatical class: *ɬiç̣i* for animates, *xuç̣i* for inanimates; *guç̣i* is neutral, although in practice all three are normally reduced to -*ç̣*V: e.g. *qwarde.u.ç̣i* 'does not write'.

Postpositions

This category is weakly represented in the Andi languages; the highly developed case system covers most requirements. Some postpositions are found in Botlikh, Bagval, and Chamalal: e.g. Botlikh *γalu* 'for', *dera* 'up to', *xxindu* 'to'.

Word order

SOV and SVO are possible.

APACHE

INTRODUCTION

Along with Navajo, the Apachean languages form the southernmost branch of the Athabaskan family (*see* **Athabaskan**). The Western Apache languages – Chiricahua, Mescalero, Jicarilla – are very closely interrelated and have much in common with Navajo; the eastern form – Kiowa – is completely or very nearly extinct. The total number of Apache speakers is estimated at about 15,000. The form described here is Chiricahua, after Hoijer (1946). At present, the Chiricahua – in the mid-nineteenth century the most warlike of the Apache tribes – live with the Mescalero in the Mescalero Reservation in New Mexico.

PHONOLOGY

Standard Athabaskan, and very close to the Navajo system (*see* **Navajo**).

MORPHOLOGY AND SYNTAX

As in other Athabaskan languages the main division of words is into particles, nouns, and verbs. Particles are never inflected.

Noun

Nouns may be basic monosyllables, e.g. *ḳàa* ‘arrow’, bound stems, e.g. *bì.kèe* ‘his foot’, thematic nouns (i.e. stem + affix), e.g. *kòo.γą̀* ‘camp’, compounds, e.g. *ḳàa.béeš* ‘arrow-head’, nominalized verbal, e.g. *dìγì* ‘it is holy’→ ‘ceremony’, or verbal + relative marker, e.g. *ńłčì’diłxìł.í* ‘that wind which is black’ = ‘tornado’ (*-í’* relative marker, *ńłči* ‘wind’, *díłxíł* ‘it is black’).

The possessive markers: first person, *ši-*; second person, *ni-*; third person, *bi-*; obviative, *go-*; indefinite, *’i*; + dual and plural forms. The objective pronominal forms, infixed in verbal complex, are very similar. Affixing the possessive marker may induce phonetic change in the stem, and a vowel may be added: e.g. *béeš* ‘knife’; *nì.béež.è* ‘your knife’.

Verb

(For general structure, *see* **Athabaskan**.)

Hoijer analyses the preverbal stem complex as follows:

Position	*Theme*	*Adverbial prefixes*	*Paradigmatic prefixes*
1			indirect object
2		postposition	
3		adverbial prefix	
4	theme prefix		
5			iterative mode
6			number prefix
7			direct object
8			deictic prefix
9		adverbial prefix	
10			tense prefix
11			modal prefix
12			subject prefix
13			classifier
14	stem		

Some points with reference to the above model:

1. Stems modulate for mode/aspect/tense. In Chiricahua, three stems are usual, though five or six may occur.
2. Adverbial prefixes, here exemplified with the theme *'àa* 'to handle a round object':

   \+ prefix *dàh.yí* 'upon, on top': *dàh.yí . . . 'àa* 'to put a round object on top of something';
   \+ prefix *céh* 'into a fire': *céh . . . 'ą́* 'to have put a round object into the fire' (*'ą́* is perfective stem).

3. Certain components are in complementary distribution; e.g. if position 5 is occupied, 10 and 11 must be vacant.
4. Choice of subject markers: deictic prefix position (8) or pronominal position (12). The former is used for the fourth person (obviative), the indefinite subject, or a subject marking time or locus. The twelfth slot contains any pronominal marker except for third person. Where both positions 8 and 12 are empty, third person subject is understood. That is, the third person subject marker in Apachean is Ø.
5. Apart from third person, the choice of subject pronoun depends on which classifier is used in position 13: Ø, *d*, *l*, or *ł* (*see* **Athabaskan**), and on which mode of the stem is being conjugated. There are two sets of subject pronoun, virtually identical except for the first person singular, which is *š-* in set (a) and *í-* in set (b). In Chiricahua, the latter set is used with the perfective stem of **Ø**- and *ł*-class verbs. Extensive assimilation takes place here. Thus, for the *si*-perfective of **Ø**- and *ł*-class verbs the first three singular personal markers are: *sí-*, *síǹ-*, *sì-*; for *d-* and *l*-class verbs, the equivalent forms are: *sìš-*, *síǹ-*, *sì-*.

6. Markers for other modal/temporal paradigms: progressive, *ho-*; future, *do-*; iterative, *ná-*; optative, *ho-*.

1 Dantsé godeyaadá’ Yati’ golį́į́ lę́k’e, Yati’ Bik’ehgo’ihi’n̲ań yił nlįį, Yati’íí Bik’ehgo’ihi’n̲ań nlįį.

2 Yati’íí dantsé godeyaadá’ Bik’ehgo’ihi’n̲ań yił nlįį.

3 Áń dawahá áyíílaa; áń doo hak’i dayúgo dawahá álzaahíí doo álzaa le’at’éé da.

4 Ihi’n̲aahíí biyi’ golį́į́; áí ihi’n̲aahíí nn̲ee yee daago’įį.

5 Got’iiníí godiłhiłyú idindláád; godiłhiłíí got’iiníí doo yitis nlįį da.

¶6 Bik’ehgo’ihi’n̲ań nn̲ee John holzéhi yides’a’.

7 Áń Begot’ínihíí nn̲ee yił nagoln̲i’go nyáá, bíí bee nn̲ee dawa da’odląą doleełgo.

8 John doo Begot’iiníí nlįį da, áídá’ Begot’iiníí yaa nagoln̲i’go nyáá.

(Western Apache)

ARABIC

INTRODUCTION

Arabic belongs to the South Central Semitic branch of the Semito-Hamitic family. Modern standard literary Arabic (*al-fuṣḥa*) is the official language of some 20 countries, ranging from Morocco on the Atlantic seaboard of Africa to the Persian Gulf states. As such, it is used in the press and other media, and is the language of diplomacy and official communication between Arab states. Basically, this literary standard is the language of the Qur'ān and the Hadith, lexically enriched, of course, largely from Arabic's own generative resources. Modernisms abound, but they are additions to a core structure which has hardly changed in a thousand years. Colloquial Arabic is spoken as mother tongue, in various dialect forms, by an estimated 165 million people. And again, as the canonical language of Islam, Arabic is understood up to a point by many millions of people, wherever the Qur'ān is taught – in Iran, Pakistan, Indonesia, East and West Africa, etc. Finally, one should mention the thousands of Arabic words that have been borrowed by Iranian, Turkic, Indian, and African languages, with little or no reciprocal borrowing by Arabic.

Arabic literature, one of the world's richest, dates from the sixth century AD, i.e. from the period immediately preceding the composition of the Qur'ān and the birth of Islam. The following periods may be broadly distinguished:

1. Pre-Islamic paganism (*al-jāhiliyya*, 'the period of ignorance').
2. The Qur'ān and the Hadith (to mid-seventh century).
3. The Umayyad period (to mid-eighth century).
4. The 'Abbāsid' period, the 'golden age' of Arabic literature (to mid-thirteenth century).
5. The age of decadence (thirteenth to nineteenth centuries).
6. The nineteenth-century revival (*al-nahḍa*).
7. The twentieth century. Confrontation with European modes of thought and expression, and vast proliferation of literature in all genres.

SCRIPT

See **Script** at end of article.

PHONOLOGY

Consonants

labial: b, f, m, w
dental: t, d, n, θ, ð, s, ʃ, z, l, r
velarized emphatic: ŧ, đ, ꞩ, ž̃
palatal: dʒ, j
velar: k, χ, ɣ
uvular: q
pharyngeal: ħ, ʕ(')
glottal: h, ʔ(')

Emphatic /ŧ/, etc. are notated here as *ṭ*, etc.

ASSIMILATION

The so-called 'sun letters': the *-l* of the article is assimilated to a following initial dental or an emphatic, e.g., *al-šamsu* → [eʃ-ʃamsu] 'the sun'; *al-nāru* → [ɛn-nɛːru] 'the fire'; *al-tājiru* → [ɛt-tɛːjiru] 'the merchant'; *al-ṭabīb* → [uŧ-ŧɔbiːb] 'the doctor'.

Vowels

long and short: i, a, u

Long vowels are notated as *ā*, etc. Initial /i, a, u/ are supported by alif in the script, and pronounced with glottal onset (hamza). /a, aː/ tend towards [ɛ, ɛː]; after the emphatic consonants, *a* → [ɔ]: e.g. *ḍaraba* → [đɔraba], 'he struck'. In proximity to *l*, /a/ → [ɛ]: *malik* → [mɛlik], *kalb* → [kɛlb].

Stress

Primary stress tends to fall on the penultimate if this is long. If the last two syllables are short, stress moves to the antepenultimate: e.g. *fallā́hun* 'a peasant'; *šáriba* 'he drank'.

MORPHOLOGY AND SYNTAX

Noun

The form of an Arabic word (*wazn*, pl. *awzān*) is related to its function. Thus, if we use C_1, C_2, and C_3 to denote the components of a triliteral root:

C_1*a*C_2C_2*ā*C_3 denotes the practitioner of the verbal action: e.g. *NaJJār*(*un*) 'carpenter'; *XuBBāZ*(*un*) 'baker'.
maC_1C_2*a*C_3 is a noun of place: e.g. *MaDRaS*(*un*) 'school'; *ma*ṬBaX(*un*) 'kitchen'.
C_1*a*C_2*ī*C_3(*un*) is often an adjective; may also be infinitive or broken plural (see below): e.g. *KaRīM* 'noble'; *JaMīL* 'beautiful'.

For a general note on the triliteral root, *see* **Semitic Languages**.

There are two genders, masculine and feminine, and three numbers.

ARTICLE

Indefinite status is indicated by nunation: e.g. *malik**un*** 'a king'. The definite article for all genders and numbers is prefixed *al-*: e.g. *al-maliku* 'the king'. As pointed out above, the *-l* of the article assimilates with the 'sun letters'.

GENDER

A common feminine marker is *-at*, written with tā' marbūṭa, i.e. *-h* with two dots, in the singular, but reverting to ordinary *t* in the plural: e.g. *xādimun* 'a servant': *xādim*__at__*un* 'a female servant'. Several common nouns are feminine, though not so marked: e.g. *al-'arḍu* 'the earth', *al-nāru* 'the fire', *al-šamsu* 'the sun'.

NUMBER

Singular, dual, and plural. The plural form may be sound or broken. The sound plural is in *-ūna*, oblique *-īna*; feminine, *-ātun*, oblique *-ātin*. Broken plural: the form of a broken plural is unpredictable, though there are certain recurrent patterns. Thus, with radicals $C_1C_2C_3$:

'*a*C_1C_2*i*C_3ā'*u* is a plural of C_1*a*C_2*ī*C_3*un*: e.g. *ṢaDīQun* 'friend', pl. *'aṢDiQā'u*;
maC_1*ā*C_2*i*C_3*u* is a plural of *ma*C_1C_2*a*C_3 *un*: e.g. *maKTaBun* 'school', pl. *maKāTiBu*.

Common broken plural forms are (omitting nunation):

C_1*u*C_2*ū*C_3: e.g. *QaLB*, pl. *QuLūB* 'heart';
C_1*i*C_2*ā*C_3: e.g. *KaLB*, pl. *KiLāB* 'dog';
C_1*u*C_2*u*C_3: e.g. *KiTāB*, pl. *KuTuB* 'book'.

Dual: masc. *-āni*, obl. *-aini*. In the feminine *-t-* is inserted: *-tani*, obl. *-taini*. Nunation drops in construct: e.g. *bābāni* 'two doors': *bābā***Ø***.l-bait* 'the two doors of the house'. Formally, a broken plural is a feminine singular collective noun, and therefore takes a feminine singular adjective.

CASE

Most nouns are triptotes with three cases, nominative, genitive, accusative, with characteristic vowels *-u* (nom.), *-i* (gen.), *-a* (acc.). Diptotes have nominative in *-u* and general oblique in *-a*: e.g. triptote *al-bait**u*** 'the house'; *daxala baita.ka* 'he went into your (*-ka*) house'; *fi.**l**-bait**i*** 'in the house'. In the colloquial, the endings *-u*, *-a*, *-i* tend towards Ø.

THE CONSTRUCT

(Ar. *'iḍāfa*) Noun defined by noun. In Arabic, the two nouns are put in the construct relationship, whereby the first, the defining member, necessarily loses its article: thus, with *al-baitu* 'the house'; *al-rajul* 'the man': ***Ø****baitu.l-rajuli* [baitu.**r**-rajul], 'the man's house'. Similarly, *al-šubbāku* 'the window': ***Ø****šubbaku.l-baiti* 'the window of the house'. (Cf. **Hebrew** and, interestingly, Celtic. In Arabic, there is no obligatory stretto of first component.)

Plural and dual in construct: *kutubu.l-mu'allimīna* 'the teachers' books';

kitābā.r-rajuli 'the man's two books'; *waladai.l-wazīri* 'the wazir's two sons' (acc.).

Adjective

Certain awzān (*see* **Noun**, above) are adjectives, e.g. $C_1\bar{a}C_2iC_3$, $C_1aC_2\bar{\imath}C_3$, $C_1aC_2\bar{u}C_3$: e.g. *ṣādiq* 'just, upright'; *kabīr* 'big'; *jahūl* 'very ignorant'. The attributive adjective follows the noun and takes the article, if definite: e.g. *al-baitu.l-kabiru* 'the big house'; *al-bintu.l-ḥasanatu* 'the beautiful girl'. As pointed out above, broken plural forms are construed as feminine singular for purposes of concord: e.g. *durūsun sa'**ba**tun* 'difficult lessons'. But broken plural adjectives may be used to qualify broken plural nouns denoting male humans: e.g. *rijālun ṭiwālun* 'tall men' (*ṭawīl* 'tall').

Adjectives denoting colours or bodily defects have the following pattern: masc. sing. $'aC_1C_2aC_3u$ (i.e. no nunation), fem. $C_1aC_2C_3\bar{a}u$, pl. $C_1uC_2C_3un$: e.g. *'aḥmaru* 'red', fem. *ḥamrā'u*, pl. *ḥumrun*; *'aṭrašu* 'deaf', fem. *ṭaršā'u*, pl. *ṭuršun*. The masculine form of this pattern is used for the elative (comparative); thus from *kabir* 'big', *'akbar* 'bigger'; from *jahil* 'ignorant', *'ajhal* 'more ignorant'.

Pronoun

Independent and enclitic:

	Singular		*Dual*		*Plural*	
	Independent	*Enclitic*	*Independent*	*Enclitic*	*Independent*	*Enclitic*
1	'anā	-ya, -(n)ī			naḥnu	-nā
2 masc.	'anta	-ka	'antumā	-kumā	'antum	-kum
fem.	'anti	-ki			'antunna	-kunna
3 masc.	huwa	-hu/hi	humā	-humā	hum	-hum
fem.	hiya	-hā			hunna	-hunna

The enclitics are bound forms attached to verbs as object pronouns, and to nouns as possessive markers. They also follow prepositions: e.g. *walad**uhu*** 'his son'; *ḍarabtu**hu*** 'I struck him'; *'alai**kum*** 'on you (pl.)'. The following sentence ilustrates all three usages:

Ba'aθat**ni** 'umm**i** 'ilai**ka**
'My mother sent me to you' (*ba'aθa* 'he sent'; *'umm* 'mother'; *'ila* 'to')

DEMONSTRATIVE PRONOUN/ADJECTIVE

Masc. *hāðā*, dual, *haðāni*, pl. *hā'ulā'i*; fem. *hāðihi*, dual, *hatāni*, pl. *hā'ulā'i* 'this, these'. Masc. *ðālika*, fem. *tilka* (no plural) 'that'. The demonstrative adjective precedes the noun, which is definite: e.g. *hāðā.l-kitāb* 'this book'; *tilka.l-jibāl* 'those mountains'.

INTERROGATIVE PRONOUN

man 'who?'; *mā* 'what?' (or, *māðā*). The introductory interrogative particle is *hal* or *'a*: e.g.

wa hal b'imkāni.l-bašari 'an ya'rifū.l-ḥaqīqata?
'and is it in the power of men to know the truth?' (Gibran Khalil Gibran)

RELATIVE CLAUSES

Where the antecedent is indefinite, no link is required: e.g.

baṭalun wahaba ḥayātahu li.bilādihi
'a hero who laid down his life for his country'

bayānun ṣadara fī London
'a communiqué which appeared in London'

Where the antecedent is definite, the linking pronoun *allaði*, fem. *allati*, is used. This has dual, plural, and oblique forms: *al-šaix . . .*, *allaði zāra London 'axīran* 'Sheikh . . ., who visited London recently'.

Numerals

Professor Tritton's definition of the Arabic numerals as 'the nightmare of a bankrupt financier' is celebrated.

1: This is a pronoun agreeing in gender with its referent: masc. *'aḥadun*, fem. *'iḥdā*. The form *wāḥidun*, fem. *wāḥidatun*, is an adjective.

2: *'iθnāni*, fem. *'iθnatāni* (with oblique and construct forms), is a noun in concord with referent. The dual form of the noun may also be used to indicate duality: *'usbū'aini* 'two weeks'.

3–10: The Arabic equivalents for these numerals are fully declined nouns which obey the law of inverse polarity, i.e. feminine form for masculine referent, and vice versa: e.g. *θalāθ**atu** rijālin* 'three men' (lit. 'a threesome of men'); *θalāθu marratin* 'three times'. The base forms of the numbers 3–10 are: *θalāθ-*, *'arbaʿ-*, *xams-*, *sitt-*, *sabʿa-*, *θamān-*, *tisʿa-*, *ʿašar-*.

11, 12: Here, both components agree in gender with the referent: *'aḥada ʿašara* (masc.) 13–19: partial polarity. The ten is in concord with referent, the unit is not: e.g. *xamsa ʿašrata sanatan* '15 years'. 20–99: the tens are diptotes, the units triptotes; 100 *mi'atun*; 200 *mi'atāni*; 300 *θalāθu mi'atin*.

Verb

The dictionary form is the third person masculine singular perfective: e.g. *KaTaBa* 'he wrote'. The strong verb has three radical letters; hamza, *yā*, and *wāw* are excluded. Weak verbs have hamza, *yā*, or *wāw* in initial, medial, or final position; doubly weak verbs have initial, medial, or final hamza + *yā* or *wāw*; thus, *ra'ā* 'he saw' is medial hamza + final *yā*.

Roots may have four radicals, or may be doubled verbs, i.e. geminated second radical: e.g. *ZaXRaFa* 'to adorn'; *MaRRa* 'to pass'.

Aspect rather than tense is denoted by the finite forms: perfective and imperfective. The vowel following the second radical may be *a*, *i*, or *u*, and is known as the characteristic: e.g. *KaTaBa* 'he wrote'; *ŠaRiBa* 'he drank'; *KaRuMa* 'he was noble'. The perfective is marked by suffix for person, number, and, in part, gender; the imperfective is marked by prefix and suffix for person, number, and gender (except for 1st person singular and plural): e.g.

perfective, *kataba* 'he wrote' (Arabic order of person is maintained):

		Singular	*Dual*	*Plural*
3	masc.	kataba	katab**ā**	katab**ū**
	fem.	kataba**t**	katab**tā**	katab**nā**
2	masc.	katab**ta**	katab**tumā**	katab**tum**
	fem.	katab**ti**	katab**tumā**	katab**tunna**
1		katab**tu**		katab**nā**

imperfective indicative:

3	masc.	**ya**ktub**u**	**ya**ktub**āni**	**ya**ktub**ūna**
	fem.	**ta**ktub**u**	**ta**ktub**āni**	**ya**ktub**na**
2	masc.	**ta**ktub**u**	**ta**ktub**āni**	**ta**ktub**ūna**
	fem.	**ta**ktub**īna**		**ta**ktub**na**
1	common	**'a**ktub**u**		**na**ktub**u**

From the imperfective indicative are formed, with slight changes in final vowel, the subjunctive, and the jussive.

IMPERATIVE

E.g. from *KaTaBa*: *'uKTub*, pl. *'uKTubū*, fem. *'uktubī*, *'uktubna*. The negative imperative: here the jussive is used: *lā taKTuB* 'do not write!'

THE DERIVED STEMS

These correspond to the *binyanim* in Hebrew (*see* **Hebrew**). Servile letters are added to and/or inserted in the base form to generate extensions and modifications of the base meaning. (I is the base form; R = radical.)

Form		*Meaning*	*Example*
II:	geminate of R_2	intensive	*KaSaRa* 'he broke': *KaSSaRa* 'he smashed'
III:	vowel following R_1 lengthened	extension of meaning to involve addressee of action	*KaTaBa* 'he wrote' *KāTaBa* 'he wrote to, corresponded with'
IV:	*'a* prefix	causative trans. ← intrans.	*JaLaSa* 'he sat': *'aJLaSa* 'he seated'

V:	*ta*-prefixed to II	reflexive of II	*FaRRaQa* 'to separate': *taFaRRaQa* 'to be scattered'
VI:	*ta*-prefixed to III	reciprocal	*ḤaRiBa* 'to be furious': *taḤāRaBa* 'to fight each other'
VII:	*n*-prefix with liaison	reflexive passive	*KaSaRa* 'he broke': *'inKaSaRa* 'it got broken'
VIII:	*-t-* inserted after R_1 + liaison	heterogeneous	*NaðaRa* 'he saw, expected': *'iNtaðaRa* 'he expected, awaited'
IX:	alif-prefix with liaison; V_1 dropped, R_3 geminated	used for colours and bodily defects	*'iḤMaRRa* 'to turn red' (cf. *ḤaMMaRa* 'to make red'; *'aHMaR* 'red': *see* **Adjective**)
X:	*sta-* prefixed with liaison	to seek, pursue, require action denoted by root	*XaLaFa* 'he remained behind': *istaXLaFa* 'he appointed a successor' (*XaLiFa* 'caliph') *akbar* 'great': *istaK BaRa* 'he regarded... as great' *ḤaSuNa* 'to be handsome': *istaḤSaNa* 'he thought well of...'

PASSIVE

The Arabic passive is made by internal flection – *-u* after first radical – e.g. from *KaTaBa*: ***KuTiBa*** 'it was written'; ***yuKTabu*** 'it is being written'. Similarly for the derived stems, e.g. in VIII: *'iNtaðaRa* 'he expected': ***'uNtuðiRa*** 'it was expected'. If a passive verb is used, the agent cannot be overtly specified, i.e. *ḍuriba X* 'X was struck'; but if Y, the striker, is mentioned, the sentence must be rephrased in the active voice: *ḍaraba Y X*.

NEGATIVE

Arabic has several negating particles:

lā is a general negating particle followed by a noun in the accusative or by a verb in the imperfective: e.g. *lā mahalla li.l-'ajab* 'there is no need to be surprised'; *lā yaktubu* 'he doesn't/didn't write'.

mā denies verbal sentences in either aspect: e.g. *mā kataba* 'he didn't write'; *mā yaktubu* 'he doesn't write'.

lam with the jussive = *mā* with perfective: *lam yaktub* = *mā kataba* 'he didn't write'.

lan + subjunctive denies the future: e.g. *lan yaktub**a*** 'he will not write'.

laisa 'is not/are not': *laisa lī 'a'dā'u* 'I have no enemies'.

PARTICIPLES

E.g. from *kataba* 'he wrote':

active: *kātib*(*un*) 'writing' → 'writer';
passive: *maktūb*(*un*) 'written' (with a plural form *makātību*).

Prepositions

The noun following a preposition is in the genitive case: e.g. *fī.l-bait**i*** 'in the house'. The enclitic forms of the pronouns follow prepositions: e.g. *min.hum* 'of them, from them'; *fī.hā* 'in her'.

Word formation

Originally and essentially, word-building in a 'God-given' language is reduced to the regular process of expansion of the triliteral root in accordance with the established moulds or patterns (*awzān*). A root capable of natural semantic expansion may have as many as 44 verbal nouns; and any root not hitherto so exploited could be used to generate new, but orthodox and therefore intelligible forms by analogy (*al-qiyās*). Permutation of the 28 consonants of Arabic yields over 3,000 potential bases 'theoretically existent with all their regular derivatives' (Massignon, quoted in Monteil 1960: 107). (But note phonotactic constraints on formation of roots, e.g. in neighbourhood of emphatics.) *Al-qiyās* was a fertile source of lexical enrichment in the Umayyad-'Abbāsid period.

Since the Indo-European predilection and aptitude for the formation of compound words is alien to Arabic, the problem of how best to provide the language with equivalents for modern scientific, technical, and political terms has proved a difficult one. Monteil (1960) gives an interesting account of tentative steps in this field. Many of the proposed equivalents are paraphrases rather than compounds, along the lines of, for example, *mā fawqa.l-banafsajī* 'ultraviolet' (lit. 'what-is-beyond-violet-ness'). However, the truncated root *kahra-* (← *kahraba* 'to electrify') has been successfully used in many compound forms: e.g. *kahra-jābī* 'electro-positive'; *kahra-rākid* 'electrostatics'. Scientific and political terms with the privative prefixes *a-*, *an-*, *non-* go readily into Arabic by means of *lā-*, *γayr*, or *'adam*: e.g. *lā-iš'ā'ī* 'non-radioactive'; *γayr mustaqīm* 'non-linear'; *'adam al-i'tida'* 'non-aggression'.

Word order

VSO is normal in verbal sentences, though inversions are found. SV in nominal sentences.

١ فِي ٱلْبَدْءِ كَانَ ٱلْكَلِمَةُ وَٱلْكَلِمَةُ كَانَ عِنْدَ ٱللهِ وَكَانَ
٢ ٱلْكَلِمَةُ ٱللهَ * ٢ هٰذَا كَانَ فِي ٱلْبَدْءِ عِنْدَ ٱللهِ * ٣ كُلُّ شَيْءٍ بِهِ
٤ كَانَ وَبِغَيْرِهِ لَمْ يَكُنْ شَيْءٌ مِمَّا كَانَ * ٤ فِيهِ كَانَتِ ٱلْحَيٰوةُ وَٱلْحَيٰوةُ
٥ كَانَتْ نُورَ ٱلنَّاسِ * ٥ وَٱلنُّورُ يُضِيءُ فِي ٱلظُّلْمَةِ وَٱلظُّلْمَةُ لَمْ
تُدْرِكْهُ
٦ كَانَ ٦ إِنْسَانٌ مُرْسَلٌ مِنَ ٱللهِ ٱسْمُهُ يُوحَنَّا * ٧ هٰذَا جَاءَ
٨ لِلشَّهَادَةِ لِيَشْهَدَ لِلنُّورِ لِكَيْ يُؤْمِنَ ٱلْكُلُّ بِوَاسِطَتِهِ * ٨ لَمْ يَكُنْ هُوَ
ٱلنُّورَ بَلْ لِيَشْهَدَ لِلنُّورِ * ٩

SCRIPT

Arabic is written from right to left in an alphabet of 28 letters, all of which are consonants. The language has six vowels, three short and three long. The three short vowels are fatḥa (*a*), kasra (*i*), and ḍamma (*u*). Fatḥa and ḍamma are written above, and kasra below the line. Thus, with the consonant *b*:

بُ bu بِ bi بَ ba

The short vowels are not normally written except in pedagogical texts, and, of course, in the Qur'ān, texts of which are always fully vocalized. Long vowels *ā*, *ī*, and *ū* are represented systematically in the script by the consonants ', *y*, and *w* respectively.

The three consonants alif, wāw, and yā' are used in the notation of the three long vowels, *ā*, *ī*, *ū*, with their short counterparts, fatḥa, kasra, and ḍamma, on the preceding consonant: thus, again with *b*:

بُو bū بِي bī بَا bā

Twenty-two of the letters are connected in writing both to the preceding and to the following letter; the relevant initial, medial, and final forms are set out in the accompanying table. It will be seen, however, that six letters have no medial form: that is, they cannot be joined to a following letter.

Additional signs used in Arabic script:

(a) *Nunation*. An Arabic noun is either definite or indefinite. For most nouns, indefiniteness is expressed by nunation, i.e. the addition of the ending *-un*, marked as ـٌ superscript (in the nominative; the marker changes to ـً /-an/ and ـٍ /-in/ in the oblique cases). For example:

مَدِينَةٌ *madinatun* مَدِينَةً *medinatan* مَدِينَةٍ *madinatin* ('town')

(b) *Sukūn*. The superscript marker ° over a consonant indicates that that consonant is vowelless: e.g. شَرْق 'East', where rā' is marked by sukūn.
(c) *Hamza*. The marker ء indicates the glottal stop. The bearer for initial hamza is always alif, with fatḥa, kasra, or ḍamma as required. Medially, hamza may be carried by alif, wāw, or yā'; finally, it is placed on the line of script.
(d) *Shadda*. A doubled consonant (geminate) is written as a single consonant with the sign ـّ over it. This is called shadda or tashdid. Cf.

كَسَرَ 'he broke'

كَسَّرَ 'he smashed to pieces'

(e) *Madda*. If long alif follows the glottal stop, the hamza sign is dropped, and one alif is written as superscript over a second: آ = /'aː/. Madda may occur medially, notably in the word قُرْآن *qur'ānun* 'Qur'ān', 'Koran'. Arabic has no capital letters.

The Arabic script is a derivative of the Nabataean consonantal script, which was used for inscriptions in Petra from the second century BC to the second century AD. The earliest manuscripts of the Qur'ān (eighth to tenth century) are written in a style known as Kufic, i.e. associated with the city of Kūfah in Mesopotamia, though this provenance has been questioned. It is the source of the *maghribī* style, which developed in Spain and which is still used in the Arab states of North Africa.

From the eleventh century onwards, the beautiful flowing cursive style known as *naskhī* was developed and perfected to become the Arabic script *par excellence*. This is the form which underlies most contemporary typefonts. A somewhat simplified form, known as *ruq'a*, has been used for ordinary purposes of handwriting (as distinct from calligraphy) since the Ottoman period. This utilitarian form does not, however, depart from *naskhī* in the way that 'grass script' (*cǎo shū*), for example, distorts Chinese standard characters.

There are several offshoots of *naskhī*, such as the ornate and exquisite *ta'līq* (or *nasta'liq*), much used for poetry in Persian and Urdu, and *dīvānī*, the script of the Ottoman Turkish imperial chancellery. The supreme *tour de force* of the *dīvānī* style is the *tuğra* – the monogram or cipher specifically designed for each Sultan. Nowhere is the curious alchemy of the Arabic script made more manifest than in the *tuğra*: the jinn of pure formal beauty emerges from the bottle of the script. **Figure 1** shows the wondrous emblem created for Suleyman the Magnificent.

The Arabic script is, or has been, used to notate many other languages.

Among those which have abandoned Arabic script for Roman are Indonesian (Malay), Hausa, Somali, Sundanese, Swahili, and Turkish. Several Caucasian languages, e.g. Chechen, Kabardian, Lak, Avar, and Lezgi, used the Arabic script until, after a short period of experimental romanization, Cyrillic was imposed on them. At present, Arabic is retained for a number of important languages, including Persian, Urdu, Pashto, Baluchi, Kurdish, Lahndā, Kashmiri, Sindhi, and Uighur. Since the phonological inventories of these languages differ, in some cases markedly, from that of Arabic, the script has had to be augmented and adapted to meet the new demands made upon it. An extreme case is provided by Sindhi, in which certain Arabic letters have been adapted to denote the six retroflex sounds, six aspirates, four implosives, and two nasals found in Sindhi. In both Persian and Sindhi certain Arabic letters are redundant, in that two or more Arabic phonemes are reduced to one sound. Thus in Persian the four letters ذ (Ar. /ð/), ز (Ar. /z/), ض (Ar. ḍ) ظ (Ar. /ẓ/) are all realized as /z/. Similarly, the three Arabic phonemes /θ/, /s/, and /ṣ/ fuse to give /s/.

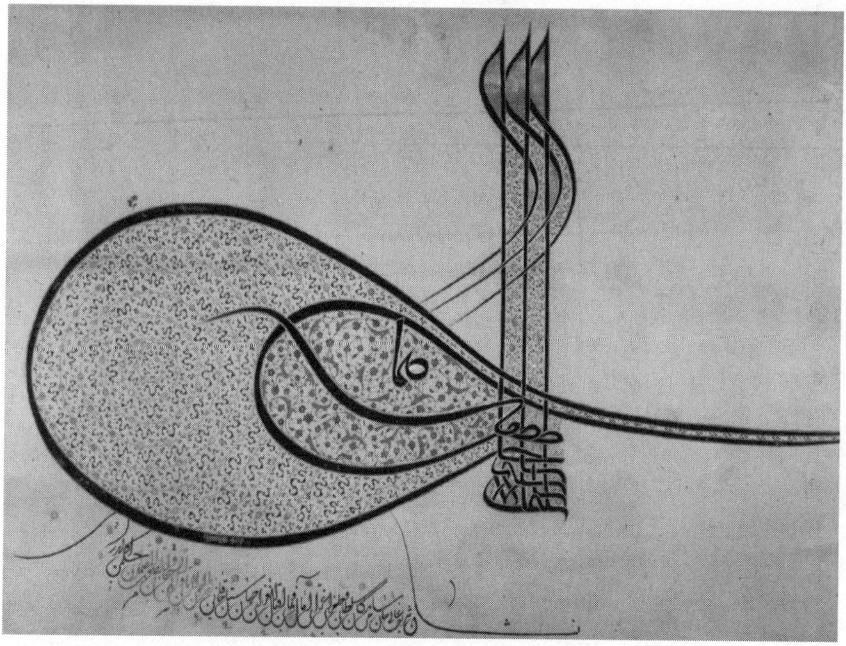

Figure 1

THE ARABIC SCRIPT

THE ALPHABET

Transliteration	*Final*	*Medial*	*Initial*	*Alone*	*Name*
ā	ـا			ا	ʔalif
b	ـب	ـبـ	بـ	ب	bāʔ
t	ـت	ـتـ	تـ	ت	tāʔ
θ	ـث	ـثـ	ثـ	ث	θaʔ
ǰ	ـج	ـجـ	جـ	ج	ǰīm
ħ	ـح	ـحـ	حـ	ح	ħāʔ
x	ـخ	ـخـ	خـ	خ	xāʔ
d	ـد			د	dāl
ð	ـذ			ذ	ðāl
r	ـر			ر	rāʔ
z	ـز			ز	zāy
s	ـس	ـسـ	سـ	س	sīn
š	ـش	ـشـ	شـ	ش	šīn
ṣ	ـص	ـصـ	صـ	ص	ṣād
ḍ	ـض	ـضـ	ضـ	ض	ḍād
ṭ	ـط	ـطـ	طـ	ط	tāʔ
ð	ـظ	ـظـ	ظـ	ظ	ðaʔ
ʕ	ـع	ـعـ	عـ	ع	ʕayn
ɣ	ـغ	ـغـ	غـ	غ	ɣayn
f	ـف	ـفـ	فـ	ف	fāʔ
q	ـق	ـقـ	قـ	ق	qāf
k	ـك	ـكـ	كـ	ك	kāf
l	ـل	ـلـ	لـ	ل	lām

Transliteration	*Final*	*Medial*	*Initial*	*Alone*	*Name*
m	ـم	ـمـ	مـ	م	mīm
n	ـن	ـنـ	نـ	ن	nūn
h	ـه	ـهـ	هـ	ه	hāʔ
w	ـو			و	wāw
y	ـى	ـيـ	يـ	ى	yāʔ

Source: Kaye, A.S. (1987) 'Arabic', in B. Comrie (ed.) *The World's Major Languages*, London: Routledge.

NUMERALS

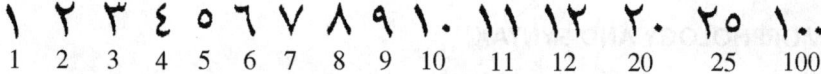

١	٢	٣	٤	٥	٦	٧	٨	٩	١٠	١١	١٢	٢٠	٢٥	١٠٠
1	2	3	4	5	6	7	8	9	10	11	12	20	25	100

ARAPAHO

INTRODUCTION

This member of the Algonquian family is spoken by about 1,000 people in the borderlands of Oklahoma and Wyoming.

PHONOLOGY

The sparse consonantal inventory includes /b, w, t, θ, s, n, tʃ, j, k, x, h, ʔ/ + allophones. The vowels are /i, e, o, u/. High and low tones.

MORPHOLOGY AND SYNTAX

Noun

The noun may be simple or compound, dependent or independent; the latter are absolute or possessed. Examples: *néč* 'water'; *hinén* 'man'; *heebeθiinen* 'big man'. Some Arapaho stems are ambivalent, i.e. can be treated as nouns or verbs. The basic dichotomy between animate and inanimate (on non-Indo-European lines) affects concord: e.g. *hinén nonoohówoot X* 'a/the man sees X-animate'; *hinén nonoohóóto' X* 'a/the man sees X-inanimate'.

Plural: animate plurals are, for example, *-o'*, -V*n*, *-uu/ii*; inanimate *-o*, -V*n*, -V. The stem itself may be altered before the plural affixes: e.g. *henééčee* 'buffalo', pl. *henééčeen*; *wóx* 'bear', pl. *wóxuu*; *nééčee* 'chief', pl. *nééčeen*; *wóxhoox* 'horse', pl. *wóxhooxebii*; *bééte'* 'bow', pl. *béétéíí*.

Dependent nouns occur only in possessed form; the indefinite possessive marker is *b-/w-*: ***b**étee* '(one's) heart'; ***b**éíčiθ* '(one's) tooth'. The first person singular personal possessive marker is *n-*: ***n**étee* 'my heart'; second person *h-*: ***h**éíčiθ* 'your tooth'; plural of object possessed: e.g. ***n**éíčito* 'my teeth'; plural of possessor, suffix -**V́***noo* is added: *heteθebiib**ínoo*** 'your (pl.) dogs' (*he*θ 'dog').

The first person plural distinguishes inclusive and exclusive forms.

Verb

An Arapaho verb consists of a stem plus prefixes and suffixes. Transitive verbs are inflected for agent and for object/target; intransitive verbs are inflected for agent only. In each version, the distinction between animate and inanimate categories is observed.

There are four tenses – present, future, preterite, and narrative (aorist).

The main verbal prefixes are:

interrogative marker: *koo/kuu*
narrative tense: *hee'ih*
first person pronoun singular: *ne/né*
second person pronoun singular: *he/hé*
obviative: *h*V/Ø
preterite: *nih*
future: *hoot*
negative: *-ihoowu-*; *-cii-*

Transitive verbs have suffixed inflections specifying the subject/object pronominal relationship. Thus, for a first person singular acting upon a second person singular the ending is *-eθen* (if the object is animate). Similarly, *-ún* indicates action by second person singular on first person singular animate; *-ót* specifies action by second person singular on obviative animate (the so-called fourth person), etc. Examples:

nihnoohob**éθen** 'I saw you' (where *nih-* is the preterite-tense prefix)
nonoohob**éθen** 'I see you'
héíhoowunoohob**eθébe** 'I don't see you (pl.)' (*-ihoowu-* is the negative prefix)
heetnéíhoowunoohob**eθébe** 'I shan't see you (pl.)' (*heet* = *hoot*, future marker)
koohonoohob**eθ**? 'do I see you (sing.)?'
nonóóhow**ún** 'you (sing.) see me'
níhnóóhow**ót** 'you (sing.) saw him (obv.)'

Word order

The verb tends to be final.

1 Nau hethauwuu, henee, daunausuvevethahede haedaunanenee, hāejenedaude, hanesāhenith hethauguhādaune hathāhuk, Vahadāhene, jeechauhauthehāa hadnesevevethahee, waude Jaun jea neesechauhauthehaude hethauguhādaunau.
2 Nau hanaāāedauwunaude, hāene nananena vanevethahenā jeenanesenehena, Hāsaunaunene Nananede hanedaude hejavaa, Vadanauha Nananene haneseede. Nananene hanajanede hanājaunauau. Nananene hathanavāane hadnaasedaunee hasauau hejavaa, nau jee nuu vedauauwuu.
3 Hejevenāa hadauchusenee hayauwusenee vethewau.
4 Nau jejaegudanauwunāa hewauchudaudenedaunau hanau nechau nejaegudanauwunade haunauude hanesāde nethāesayānedanauwunāade. Nau jevaechauhāa nedauvasehadee; hau haugaunayauhāa hehethee hadau wausauau.

(Luke 11.1–14)

ARAUCANIAN

See **Mapudungu.**

ARMENIAN, CLASSICAL

INTRODUCTION

A branch of Indo-European, Armenian seems to have reached its present location, to the south of the main range of the Caucasus, during the second millennium BC, when Indo-European-speaking invaders from the Balkans or the Pontic area (*see* **Indo-European Languages**) overthrew the Urartian kingdom (*see* **Urartian**).

Though traces of some kinship with Hellenic are discernible, Armenian is in two senses something of an isolate within the Indo-European family: in contrast to such groupings as Indo-Iranian, Italo-Celtic, Balto-Slavonic, it has no correlative; and, secondly, its Indo-European phonological identity has been crucially modified by long sojourn in a non-Indo-European phonological environment. The close analogy between the Armenian and Georgian sound systems has been emphasized by authorities on the two languages, e.g. A. Meillet.

Specifically, the term 'Classical Armenian' denotes the language as fixed early in the fifth century AD, by Mesrop Mashtots, who provided it with an alphabet, and who initiated the translation into it of the Bible and the writings of the Church Fathers. Mesrop himself seems to have translated the New Testament into Armenian.

Thus codified, the classical language, known as *grabar* or 'book language' continued to be used as the written language of Armenia up to the nineteenth century, a literary norm from which the spoken forms had by then long diverged. (Compare the Katharevousa–Demotike situation in Greek.) *Grabar* is still in use as the liturgical language of the Armenian Church.

SCRIPT

See **Script** at end of article.

PHONOLOGY

Consonants

stops: b, p, p'; d, t, t'; g, k, k'
affricates: dʒ, tʃ, tʃ' dz, ts, ts'
fricatives: v, s, ʃ, ʒ, x, h
nasals: m, n
liquids: r, rr, l, ł

semi-vowels: j

Central to Armenian phonology is the distinction between a voiced consonant, its unvoiced aspirate, and glottalized counterpart, for labial, dental, palatal, and velar series. Glottalized sounds are notated here with subscript dots. *ç* = /ts/.

Vowels

i, e, ə, a o, u
diphthongs: ui, ai

/ə/ occurs in consonantal clusters as an epenthetic vowel which is not notated; e.g. ***marṭnčel*** 'to fight' is pronounced [marṭ'ənčɛl]. /e/ is realized as [e] and [ɛ]. The digraph **ու** may be read as /u/ or /vo/: **տուն** = /ṭ'un/; **զինուոր** = /zinvor/. When Classical Armenian is being read aloud, either modern standard Oriental or Occidental pronunciation may be used.

Stress

Stress is fixed on final full syllable.

MORPHOLOGY AND SYNTAX

As an Indo-European language, Armenian presumably had gender originally, but there is no trace of it in the historical record.

Article

DEFINITE

There are three forms of the definite article: *-s*, *-d*, *-n*. These are suffixed to the noun, and are associated with the three persons of the pronominal system. They are found also in the demonstrative series: cf.

ṭun**s** ay**s** 'this house (near me)'
ṭun**t** ay**d** 'that house (near you)'
ṭun**n** ay**n** 'that house (yonder, near third person)' (*ṭun* 'house')

This postfixed article may also be added to a noun in apposition to a subject pronoun: e.g. *yes ṭers yev vardapeṭs* 'I, lord and master . . . '.

The numeral *mi* 'one' may be used as an indefinite article following the noun: e.g. *er ayr mi* 'there was a man . . . ' (John 3.1). The plural marker is *-k* with various link vowels; often the stem is subject to elision and umlaut, and there are many irregularities: e.g. *ṭun* 'house', pl. *ṭun**k***; *kałak* 'town', pl. *kałak**ək***; *hayr* 'father', pl. *har**k***; *gin* 'woman', pl. *gan**ayk***. The definite article is added to the plural marker: *geṭ**k.n*** /get'əkn/ 'the rivers'.

Noun

DECLENSION

There are seven regular declensions depending on the vowel used to form the genitive singular. This vowel may be added to the nominative singular or inserted before the final consonant if this is *-n*, *-ł*, or *-r*.

Example of declension: *geṭ* 'river' (external flection):

	Singular		*Plural*
nom., acc.	geṭ	nom.	geṭ**k**
		acc.	geṭs
gen., dat.	geṭ**uy**		geṭ**oc**
abl.	**i** geṭ**uy**		**i** geṭ**oc**
instr.	geṭ**ov**		geṭ**ovk**

A definite object is marked by *z-* prefixed to the accusative: e.g.

Hanel č.garen **z**.dev.n
'They cannot expel the demon'
(*hanel* 'to expel', *garel* 'to be able', *č.* 'not', *dev* 'demon')

Accusative plural in *-s*: examples:

Indefinite: *ḳov.k eš.***s** *voč çnanin* 'cows do not give birth to asses'.

Definite: *ḳoče arr inkn z.yerḳoṭasan.***s.n**. 'he called the twelve to him' (*ḳočel* 'to call', *arr* 'to(wards)'); *ziard voč pašṭes z.di.***s** *mer* 'why do you not worship our gods?'.

Genitive: possessor may precede or follow possessed: e.g. *Voč sa e hivsann vordi?* 'Is this not the carpenter's son?' (Matthew 13.55); *luys mardḳan* 'the light of men' (John 1.4).

Adjective

As attribute, adjective may precede or follow noun, and may or may not be in concord. The non-attributive adjective is declined as a noun, with plural in *-k*. There are a few irregular formations, e.g. *pokr* 'small', pl. *pokunk*.

Irk havasṭi**k** paṭmin 'They relate things that are certain' (concord marked, adjective follows noun)

yev tnán noca arḳaneli**s** spiṭaḳ**s** 'and they were given white robes' (Revelation 6.11) (concord in acc. pl.)

Snoṭi∅ ban**k** en 'These are vain words' (no concord, adjective precedes noun)

Comparative: there are three ways of making a comparative:

(a) positive + *kan* + acc.: e.g. *čar kan zṭer* 'more evil than the master'
(b) adverb + positive: *aveli čar*...
(c) *-aguyn* added to positive: *čaraguyn*...

Pronoun

PERSONAL PRONOUN

The basic independent forms are:

sing. 1 *yes*, 2 *du*, 3 *na*; pl. 1 *mek*, 2 *duk*, 3 *noka*

These are declined in all cases; e.g. for first person singular:

acc. *zis*, gen. *im*, dat. *inj*, abl. *yinen*, loc. *is*, instr. *inev*

Examples:

yev yecuyc **inj** makur geṭ 'and he shewed me a pure river' (Revelation 22.1)
porjea **z**is, Ṭer 'examine me, Lord' (Armenian Liturgy)

The possessive forms are:

	Singular	*Plural*
1	im	mer
2	ko	jer
3	sora, **d**ora, **n**ora	soca, **d**oca, **n**oca

The genitive forms have acquired nominative status, and act as bases for a secondary series of four cases (nominative, accusative, genitive, dative). For example, *im*, which is itself the genitive of *yes* 'I', has a genitive form *imo*, dative *imum*. Cf. Matthew 15.10: *ṭesamen z.yeṛes.s Hor imo* 'they behold the face of my Father'.

DEMONSTRATIVE PRONOUN/ADJECTIVE

Three-degree series (*see* **Article**, above): sing. *ays*, *ayd*, *ayn*; pl. *aysk*, *aydk*, *aynk*. These are fully declined in all cases.

The demonstrative pronouns/adjectives *sa*, *da*, *na* (with three-person deixis) make a plural with infixed *-k-* marker: *so**k**a*, *do**k**a*, *no**k**a*.

The *-s*, *-d*, *-n* markers reappear in the directional accusative articles *ay**s**r*, *ay**d**r*, *a**n**dr*, which follow the accusative case. Cf. *arḳanen z. Yovnani i çov* ***andr*** 'they threw Jonas into the sea', where the neutral article *-n* is replaced by the accusative directional article *andr*.

INTERROGATIVE PRONOUN

zi 'who? what?'; *vov* 'who?'; *inč* 'what?'

The sign ՞ is placed over the focused word in an interrogative sentence: e.g.

Zînč čar arar
'What evil hath he done?' (Matthew 27.23)

Aržân e mez Ḳayser harḳs ṭal te voč
'Is it lawful for us to give tribute to Caesar, or no?' (Luke 20.22)

RELATIVE PRONOUN

Sing. *vor*, pl. *vork*. Use of plural form with singular antecedent is optional. e.g.

Zînč en ban.k.n, **zor** duk.d asek 'What words are these that you say?'

Čarik.n, **vor** gorçin ķamaçink en yev voč bnaķank 'The evils which are committed are intentional, not natural.'

Numerals

1–10: *mi*, *yerķu*, *yerek*, *čork*, *hing*, *vec*, *yutn*, *ut*, *inn*, *ţasn*; 11–19: unit + link + *ţasan*, e.g. 18 *ut.ev.ţasn*; 20 *ksan*; 30 *yeresun*; 40 *karrasun*; 100 *haryur*.

Mi, *yerķu*, *yerek*, and *čork* are declined and may precede or follow a noun. The other numbers up to 9 may be declined.

Verb

The infinitive ending is *-al/-el/-ul*. *-el* verbs are further sub-divided into those which retain the *-e* as characteristic vowel, and those that change it to *-i*. There are thus four basic conjugations.

The modal and tense structure is built on two aspectual bases:

the imperfective (present) = the infinitive minus *-l*;
the perfective (aorist) = the root, often extended by -V*c*.

From the imperfective base are formed the present, the imperfect, the first future tense, and the prohibitive mood. The imperfect is often used as a subjunctive (there is no optative in Classical Armenian). The perfective aspect provides the aorist, the second future, the imperative, and the hortative. (The original distinction between 'first' and 'second' future seems to have been aspectual: 'first' is based on the present root, hence imperfective; 'second' on the aorist root, hence perfective.)

PRESENT TENSE

The endings for all verbs are *-m*, *-s*, *-y*; pl. *-mk*, *-yk*, *-n*: e.g. *lavana***m**, *lavanas*, *lavanay* 'I wash, you wash, he washes'.

Passive forms are made from active present-tense verbs by change of characteristic vowel to *-i*: e.g. *sirem ayl voč sirim* 'I love but am not loved'.

FIRST FUTURE

The endings are *-ycem*, *-yces*, *-yce*, etc. The first future form conveys a future, subjunctive, or conditional sense:

tołucuys z.gorç.s ko?
'will you leave your affairs?'

çrag luys ţa amenacun vor i ţan.nisen
'the lamp gives light to all those who are (*qui soient*) in the house'

Voč ķare kałak takčel, vor i veray lerin ķa**yce**
'A city that (of such a kind) is set on a hill cannot be hid' (Matthew 5.14)

PROHIBITIVE

Negative particle *mi* + singular form in *-r*, pl. in *-ayk*. This form is used in place of the missing negative imperative: e.g.

> Ṭer, **mi** hamari**r** toca z.ays meł.s
> 'Lord, lay not this sin to their charge' (Acts 7.59)

AORIST

Two sets of endings: active and passive. The two forms are not available for all verbs. For example, in the *-el* series, while all verbs have the active forms, only four verbs have the passive. 'Passive' here includes middle voice: e.g. *zarmac**ay*** 'I was surprised'.

The active endings are: sing. *-i, -er, -Ø*; pl. *-ak, -ek, -in*. Passive endings: sing. *-ay, ->ar, -av*; pl. *-ak, -ayk, -an*. Example: *Vor inč grec**i**, grec**i*** 'what I have written, I have written' (John 19.22).

Short aorist passive forms may take an augment *ye-*: e.g. *ṭes* = *yeṭes* 'he saw'; *giṭ* = *yegiṭ* 'he found'.

SECOND FUTURE

This has both future and subjunctive sense. The endings are: *-ic, -ces, -ce*; pl. *-cuk, jik, -cen*. *-e* → *-i* for passive. Example: *Mi xrroves**cin** sirṭk jer* 'Let not your hearts be troubled' (John 14.1).

PARTICIPLES

The participle in *-eal* may be used as a noun, and is then declined as, for example, *gorçk arrakeloc* 'the Acts of the Apostles' (*arrakeal* 'the one who is sent'). A perfect tense is made with this participle and the auxiliary *yem* 'I am'. The forms of *yem* are: sing. *yem, yes, e*; pl. *yemk, yik, yin*: e.g. *ṭeseal yem* 'I have seen'; *ṭeseal ei* 'I had seen'. Here, the logical subject can be in the genitive case with the auxiliary in third person singular: e.g. *i bazum paṭerazmuns mṭeal e **im*** 'and of me there has been a going into many wars' = 'I have been in many wars'.

Future participle: *-oc* is added to the infinitive: e.g. *Krisṭos yayṭneloc e* 'Christ will reveal himself.'

IMPERATIVE

Made from aorist root, is found in second person only, and is always positive: e.g. from *havaṭal* 'to believe': *havaṭ**a***!, pl. *havaṭa**cek***!

HORTATIVE

Aorist root + *-jir* (sing.), *-jik* (pl.).

NEGATION

The general verbal negator is *voč* (→ *č-* preceding verb): e.g. *voč yertayḳ* = *čertayk* 'you do not go'. The prohibitive takes the negating particle *mi*.

CAUSATIVE

Aorist root + *-ucanel* (restricted use): e.g. from *ç̣anačel* 'to know', *ç̣anucanel* 'to cause to know'.

Prepositions

There are six basic prepositions: *arr*, *z-*, *ənd*, *i*(*y*), *əsṭ*, *c-*. Each of these can be used with more than one case, and each varies accordingly in meaning. Thus, *arr* with the accusative means 'at, towards'; with the dative/ablative, 'because of'; with the instrumental 'beside, at the time of'. Examples:

Mi yerḳnčir arrnul **arr kez** z.Mariam gin ko
'Fear not to take unto thee Mary thy wife' (Matthew 1.20)

ənd with dative:
yes **ənd jez** em . . . minčev i ḳaṭaraç ašxarhi
'and I am with you even unto the end of the world' (Matthew 28.20)

arr, *ənd*, *əsṭ*, *i* are written separately; *z-* and *c-* are prefixed to the noun, as is *y-*, the form taken by *i* before an initial vowel: cf. *ase **i** hogi iur* 'he says in his soul' (*iur* is the genitive of *inkn* 'he himself': *suus*); but ***y***. (*y*)*eresun avr* 'in 30 days'.

As noted above, *z-* also marks the accusative case: *ḳoče z.kez arr inkn* 'he calls you to him(self)'.

Word formation

Armenian is rich in compound and derived words. A very frequent model is X-*a*-Y, where X is usually a noun or adjective, and Y is a noun, adjective, or verb: e.g. *arçat.a.ser* 'silver-loving' = 'miser'; *meç.a.ṭun* '(having) a big house' = 'rich'. The link element may be assimilated after *-i* stem-final: e.g. *gin.**e**.ber* 'wine producing' (from *gin**i*** 'wine').

Derivation is by prefix: e.g. the privative prefixes *an-*, *ap̣-*, *ṭž-*, etc.: *ṭžgoh* 'dissatisfied'; *anmardi* 'inhuman'; *apyeraxṭ* 'ungrateful'; and by suffix, of which there are many: e.g.

-anoc, *-aran*: making nouns of place, e.g. *çalḳanoc* 'flower garden';
-ak, *-iḳ*: diminutives, e.g. *navaḳ* 'small boat';
-avor: bearer of . . . , e.g. *daṭavor* 'judge';
ič, *-ord*: agent, e.g. *orsord* 'hunter';
pes: formant for adverbs;
-utyun: makes abstract nouns, e.g. *canḳutyun* 'desire'.

Word order

Very free.

1 ԲԿ. Ի ՍԿԶԲԱՆԷ էր Բանն, եւ
Բանն էր առ Աստուած, եւ Աստուած
2 էր Բանն։ Նա էր ի սկզբանէ առ Աս-
3 տուած։ Ամենայն ինչ նովաւ եղեւ,
եւ առանց նորա եղեւ եւ ոչ ինչ որ
4 ինչ եղեւն։ Նովաւ կեանք էր, եւ
5 կեանքն էր լոյս մարդկան. Եւ լոյսն ի
խաւարի անդ լուսաւորէ, եւ խաւար
նմա ոչ եղեւ հասու։
6 Եղեւ այր մի առաքեալ յԱստուծոյ,
7 անուն նմա Յովհաննէս։ Սա եկն ի
վկայութիւն զի վկայեսցէ վասն Լուսոյն, զի ամենեքին հաւատասցեն նո-
8 վաւ։ Ոչ էր նա Լոյսն, այլ զի վկայեսցէ վասն Լուսոյն։

THE ARMENIAN SCRIPT

THE ALPHABET

Capitals	*Lower case*	*Transliteration*	*Cursive*	
Ա	ա	*a*	Ա	ա
Բ	բ	*b*	Բ	բ
Գ	գ	*g*	Գ	գ
Դ	դ	*d*	Դ	դ
Ե	ե	*e*	Ե	ե
Զ	զ	*z*	Զ	զ
Է	է	*ē*	Է	է
Ը	ը	*ə*	Ը	ը
Թ	թ	*t'*	Թ	թ
Ժ	ժ	*ž*	Ժ	ժ
Ի	ի	*i*	Ի	ի
Լ	լ	*l*	Լ	լ
Խ	խ	*x*	Խ	խ
Ծ	ծ	*c*	Ծ	ծ
Կ	կ	*k*	Կ	կ
Հ	հ	*h*	Հ	հ
Ձ	ձ	*j*	Ձ	ձ
Ղ	ղ	*ł*	Ղ	ղ
Ճ	ճ	*č*	Ճ	ճ
Մ	մ	*m*	Մ	մ
Յ	յ	*y*	Յ	յ
Ն	ն	*n*	Ն	ն
Շ	շ	*š*	Շ	շ
Ո	ո	*o*	Ո	ո
Չ	չ	*č'*	Չ	չ
Պ	պ	*p*	Պ	պ
Ջ	ջ	*ǰ*	Ջ	ջ

Capitals	*Lower case*	*Transliteration*	*Cursive*	
Ռ	ռ	*ṙ*	Ռ	ռ
Ս	ս	*s*	Ս	ս
Վ	վ	*v*	Վ	վ
Տ	տ	*t*	Տ	տ
Ր	ր	*r*	Ր	ր
Ց	ց	*c'*	Ց	ց
Ւ	ւ	*w*	Ւ	ւ
Փ	փ	*p'*	Փ	փ
Ք	ք	*k'*	Ք	ք

Source: Adapted from Minassian, M. (1976) *Manuel pratique d' Arménien ancien*, Paris Librairie Klincksieck.

ARMENIAN, MODERN STANDARD

INTRODUCTION

This Indo-European language is spoken by about 5 million people in Armenia, in Georgia and elsewhere in the former Soviet Union; and, in a slightly different form, by about a million people in several Middle Eastern countries (Turkey, Lebanon) and by émigré colonies throughout the world. This second form is known as Western Armenian; Eastern Armenian is the written and spoken language used in the former Soviet Union. The two forms are mutually intelligible, indeed very close to each other. Within Eastern Armenian the sub-dialectal system is very complex: Garibian distinguishes over 50 dialects, sub-divided into seven groups, according to the method used to form the present tense.

For Old Armenian language and literature, *see* **Armenian, Classical**.

Classical Armenian continued to be used as a written language until the nineteenth century and was the medium for the notable and very important renaissance of Armenian culture initiated by the Mekhitarist Order in Venice from the early eighteenth century onwards. In Armenia itself, the first steps towards the creation and development of a new literary language, closer to the spoken norm, were taken in the early nineteenth century by Khachatur Abovian and Ghevond Alishan. The late nineteenth century produced many outstanding writers, notably the novelists Raffi and Shirvanzade, the poets Tumanian and Isahakian, and the playwright Sundukian.

SCRIPT

See **Armenian, Classical**.

PHONOLOGY

Consonants

stops: b, p, p’, d, t, t’, g, k, k’
affricates: dz, ts, ts’, dʒ, tʃ, tʃ’
fricatives: f, v, s, z, ʃ, ʒ, x, h
nasals: m, n
lateral and flap: r, rr, l, ł (→[γ])
semi-vowel: j

The ejectives are notated here as dotted letters; like Ossete, Armenian seems to have taken these phonemes from the Caucasian languages which surround this small Indo-European enclave. There are thus five series (three of stops, two of affricates) consisting of voiced member – aspirate surd – voiceless ejective: e.g. /b – p – p'/. The contrast between the aspirate and the ejective is often phonemic: cf. *yerek* 'three'; *yereḳ* 'yesterday'. Final voiced consonants are unvoiced: e.g. *yerb* 'when' → [yer**p**]. In this article *c* = /ts/.

Vowels

front: i, e ([e] and [ɛ])
mid: a, ə
back: o, u

The vowel /ə/, represented in the script by the letter Ը, occurs unnotated in many consonant clusters: thus **գրել** 'to write', is pronounced [gərel]. It is more convenient, however, to transliterate such words without the epenthetic vowel, which is in any case fleeting and often close to a shwa: *grel.*

Stress

Stress is virtually always on the final syllable.

MORPHOLOGY AND SYNTAX

Noun

There is no grammatical gender. Armenian has two numbers. The definite article is affixed to the noun: *-ə*/*-n*: e.g. *ṭun* 'house', *ṭunə* 'the house'; *gini* 'wine'; *gini**n*** 'the wine'. In Eastern Armenian, the indefinite article is *mi* preceding the noun; in Western it follows in the form *mə*: thus, EArm. *mi mard* = WArm. *mard mə* 'a man'. The plural marker is *-er* for monosyllables, *-ner* for polysyllables: e.g. *ṭun.er* 'houses'; *ṭun.er.ə* 'the houses'; *kaɣak.ner* 'towns', *kaɣak.ner.ə* 'the towns'.

DECLENSION

There are seven cases. Various types of declension are distinguished in the singular, differing mainly in the formation of the genitive and dative cases. There are no irregularities in the plural, as all nouns take -(*n*)*er*. Specimen declensions: *banvor* 'worker'; *gari* 'barley'; *or* 'day'.

	Singular	*Singular*	*Singular*
nom.	banvor	gari	or
gen.	banvor**i**	gar**u**	or**va**
dat.	banvor**i**	gar**u**	or**va**
acc.	banvor	gari	or
abl.	banvor**ic**	gar**uc**	orvan**ic**
instr.	banvor**ov**	gar**ov**	or**ov**
loc.	—	gar**um**	or**um**

Examples of anomalous genitive formation: *hayr* 'father' – *hor*; *kuyr* 'sister'

– *kroč*. All nouns in -*tyun* have a genitive in -*tyan*. Very many Armenian nouns are formed from two root words linked by -*a*-: e.g. *mayr* 'mother' + *kaɣak* 'town': *mayr**a**kaɣak* 'capital city'; *hay* 'Armenian' + -*sṭan* 'place': *Hay**a**sṭan* 'Armenia'.

Adjective

As attribute, adjective precedes noun and is invariable: e.g. *lav bareḳam* 'good friend'; *lav bareḳam.ner.i* 'of good friends'.

COMPARATIVE

With *aveli* 'more than': e.g. *spiṭaḳ* 'white': *aveli spiṭaḳ* 'whiter'. The compared nominal is in the ablative: e.g. *Yerevan.**ic*** (*aveli*) *meç* 'bigger than Yerevan'.

Pronoun

PERSONAL

The independent forms of the personal pronouns, with accusative case:

	Singular		*Plural*	
	Nom.	*Acc.*	*Nom.*	*Acc.*
1	yes	inj	menk	mez
2	du	kez	duk	jez
3	na	nran	nrank	nranc
	ink	iren	irenk	irenc

The full declension of *yes* 'I', for example, is: *yes – im – inj – inj – injnic – injnov – injnum*: *asek inj* 'tell me'; *inj asacin, vor…* 'they told me that…'.

POSSESSIVE ADJECTIVES

These are provided by the genitive forms of the above listed personal pronouns (*im – ko – ir*, etc.) and are paralleled by a series of personal possessive affixed markers for first, second, and third person: -*s*, -*d*, -*n*. Thus, ***im*** *anunə* = *anunəs* 'my name' (in both cases, with the definite article).

DEMONSTRATIVE PRONOUN/ADJECTIVE

Three forms closely connected with the personal endings: *ays/sa* 'this' (Lat. *apud me*), *ayd/da* (Lat. *apud te*), *ayn/na* (Lat. *apud eum*). These have plural forms: *srank*, *drank*, *nrank*; as adjectives they are invariable: e.g. *ayd ç̣ašaran.ner.um* 'in these restaurants'.

INTERROGATIVE PRONOUN

vov 'who?'; *inč* 'what?'

RELATIVE PRONOUN

Sing. *vor*, pl. *vronk*: e.g. *duk, vor uzum ek sovorel hayeren* 'you who wish to learn Armenian'. Relative clauses may also be made with participles (see below): e.g. *ayn gnac**oɣ*** *usanoɣ* 'the student who is walking over there' (*gnal* 'to go, walk').

Numerals

1–10: *meḳ, yerḳu, yerek, čors, hing, vec, yot, ut, inn, ṭas*; 11 *ṭas.n.meḳ*; 12 *ṭas.n.yerḳu*; 20 *ksan*; 30 *yeresun*; 40 *kar̆asun*; 100 *haryur.*

Verb

The Armenian verb has active and passive voices and four moods: indicative, optative, conditional–subjunctive, and imperative. Only the indicative mood has a full set of tenses.

The infinitive ends in *-el/al*; as in Old Armenian, two bases are formed from the infinitive:

(a) The present base, formed by dropping the *-el/al*: e.g. *grel* 'to write': present base *gr-*; *ḳardal* 'to read': present base *ḳard-*; *mṭnel* 'to go': *mṭn-*.
(b) The aorist base: *-l→aç* or *-acaç*: *grel*: aorist base *graç*; *ḳardal*: *ḳardacaç*.

From the present base are formed the optative, the subjunctive, the conditional, the imperfective participle in *-um*, and the future participle in *-u*. From the aorist base are formed the simple past tense and the participle in *-o*. The past participle is identical with the second base: *graç*, *ḳardacaç*.

The main auxiliary used in conjugation is *yem* = I am:

present sing.: 1 *em*, 2 *es*, 3 *ē*; pl. 1 *enk*, 2 *ek*, 3 *en*; *y-* anlaut if necessary
past sing.: 1 *ēi*, 2 *ēir*, 3 *ēr*; pl. 1 *ēink*, 2 *ēik*, 3 *ēin*

Specimen conjugation: *grel* 'to write'; indicative mood (main forms):

present: *grum em, es*, etc.
past imperfect: *grum ēi, ēir*, etc.
future: *grelu yem, yes*, etc., or with particle *ḳə*: *ḳə grem* (optative)
preterite: *grel em*, etc.
pluperfect: *grel ēi*, etc.
perfect: *graç em*, etc.
simple aorist: sing. *greci, grecir, grec*; pl. *grecink, grecik, grecin*
optative: sing. *grem, gres, gri*; pl. *grenk, grek, gren*

GERUNDS

The present gerund ends in *-um* (the form used in the present and imperfect tenses above) or in *-elis/alis*; the latter form is used to denote action upon which a second action is contingent: e.g. *Senyaḳ mṭ**nelis** girkəs hanum em* 'Upon entering the room, I take my book.' The future gerund is seen as a tense formant in the future: *grelu yem*, etc. It can also be used as an infinitive of purpose: e.g. *Gnaci gradaran girk ḳarda**lu*** 'I went to the library to read a book'; and attributively: e.g. *ḳardalu girk* 'a book to be read'.

IMPERATIVE

Sing. *grir!* 'write!', pl. *grecek!*

HORTATIVE

Optative form preceded by *ḅiṭi*: e.g. *ḅiṭi grem* 'I am to/have to write'.

PASSIVE
The marker is *-v-*: e.g. *sirel* 'to love'; passive, *sirvel* 'to be loved'; *Vočnčacvec meķ řmbaķoçič* 'One bomber was destroyed.'

CAUSATIVE
-V*cn-*: e.g. *nsțel* 'to sit', ***nsțecnel*** 'to ask someone to be seated'.

NEGATIVE
The negative particle *čə* is prefixed to the auxiliary if there is one; the auxiliary then precedes the sense verb: e.g. *grum ēi* 'I was writing', ***čei*** *grum* 'I wasn't writing'; *grelu e* 'he will write': ***či****grelu* 'he will not write'. The negative particle for the imperative mood is *mi*.

Prepositions and postpositions

Armenian uses both.

PREPOSITIONS
With genitive case: *ařanc* 'without': e.g. *ařanc ķasķaçi* 'doubtless'; and with accusative case: *depi* 'towards': e.g. *gnum em depi hyusis* 'I am going northwards'.

POSTPOSITIONS
Usually follow the genitive case: e.g.

hamar 'for': e.g. *hayreniki hamar* 'for the motherland';
masin 'about': e.g. *Xosum enk girki masin* 'We're talking about the book';
heț 'with': e.g. *nra heț gnaci* 'I went with him';
vra 'on': e.g. *seγani vra* 'on the table'.

Word order

SVO is basic; can be altered for emphasis.

1 Սկզբումն էր Բանը. և Բանն Աստուծոյ մօտ էր. և Աստուած էր
2 Բանը։ Նա սկզբումն Աստուծոյ
3 մօտ էր։ Ամէն ինչ նորանով ե-
ղաւ, և առանց նորան ոչինչ չե-
4 ղաւ, ինչ որ եղաւ։ Նորանով էր
կեանք, և կեանքը մարդկանց լոյսն
5 էր։ Եւ լոյսը խաւարումը լոյս է տա-
լիս, և խաւարը չիմացաւ նորան։
6 Մի մարդ եղաւ Աստուածանից
ուղարկուած, անունը Յովհաննէս։
7 Սա վկայութեան համար եկաւ,
որ այն Լուսոյ համար վկայ է.
որ ամէնքը նորանով հաւատան։
8 Նա չէր Լոյսն, այլ որ Լուսոյն
համար վկայէ։

ASSAMESE

INTRODUCTION

This Eastern New Indo-Aryan language derives, like Bengali and Oriya, from the Māgadhī Prakrit. It is spoken by around 12 million people in the state of Assam, which forms linguistically an enclave between Tibeto-Burman and Mon-Khmer territories. There are two dialects, Eastern (Sibsagar) and Western (Kamarupa). The literary standard is based on the former. The dialectal split dates from the fifteenth/sixteenth century. Assamese is one of the fourteen official languages recognized in the Indian constitution.

From the thirteenth to the nineteenth century the Tai invaders, known as the Ahom, ruled the country, their power culminating in the early eighteenth century. The Ahom, who seem to have been relatively few in number, lost their own Tai language, and adopted the IE prakrit which was spoken by the inhabitants of the conquered territory (cf. the adoption of a Slavonic language by the Old Bulgars). 'Ahom' is the normal Assamese pronunciation of the word *asam* (IE sibilants are reduced to /h, x/ in Assamese: *see* **Phonology**, below).

In the early nineteenth century the British administration introduced Bengali as the official language of Assam. Popular opposition to this move was widespread and effective, and in 1882 Bengali was finally replaced by Assamese, though the Bengali script was retained.

Literature in Assamese is recorded from the fourteenth century onwards. The father of Assamese literature is Śaṅkaradeva, who was born in 1449 and seems to have died, aged 119, in 1568. To his valuable reworking of Sanskrit epic and religious material, Śaṅkaradeva added a large output of original Kṛṣṇaite and *bhakti* poems and plays. His effect on the development of Assamese as a literary language was profound. A distinctive and specifically Assamese genre is the historical chronicle, many of which were produced during the last two centuries of Ahom rule: they are known by their Ahom name, *Buronji*, and nearly all are prudently anonymous. The first Assamese novel – Ranjanikānt Bardaloi's *Mirijiyari* – was published in 1895. The short story was introduced by Lakṣmīnāth Bezbaṛuā, the founder, in 1889, of the important literary periodical *Jonaki*. A key work for the study of Assamese literature is the *Asamiya Sahityar Chaneki* (*Typical Selections from Assamese Literature*) of Hemchandra Gosvāmī (1923–9).

The Assamese lexicon comprises:

(a) A main core of *tadbhava* words (pronounced /tɔdbhɔb/ in Assamese) (*see* **New Indo-Aryan Languages**).
(b) *Tatsama* words (Assamese /tɔtsɔm/), providing a repertory of scholarly terminology for literature, politics, economics, and the sciences.
(c) Loanwords from several sources, including *deśi* words, shared with Bengali and Oriya.

SCRIPT

The Bengali script, introduced in the nineteenth century, is used for writing Assamese. There is an extra letter for /w/, which has no counterpart in Bengali. Also, Assamese *r* differs from Bengali *r*.

There is an extremely poor correspondence between script and sound in this language, in that 49 graphs are available for 33 phonemes.

PHONOLOGY

Consonants

stops: p, b, t, d, k, g; with aspirates ph, bh, th, dh, kh, gh
fricatives: s, z, x, h
nasals: m, n, ŋ
laterals and flap: l, r, rh
semi-vowels: j, w

It will be noticed that, in comparison with the standard New Indo-Aryan inventory, the palatal series, *c, ch, j, jh,* and the retroflex, *ṭ, ṭh, ḍ, ḍh,* are missing from the above table. In Assamese the palatals have turned into /s/, /z/, while the IA cerebrals have merged with the dental series, and the IA sibilants are represented by /x/ and /h/.

Sandhi rules reflect both Classical Sanskrit practice (*see* **Sanskrit**) and a later series of accommodations at junctures.

Vowels

a = [ɐ], i, e, æ, a = [ɔ], o, u

These occur nasalized, and the following palatalized variants are found: [œ,y]. Diphthongs: /oi, ou/. Nasalization is marked by candrabindu ँ.

VOWEL HARMONY

/ɔ/, /o/ followed by /i/ → [u]: e.g. *khora* 'lame man' – fem. *khuri*; /æ/ followed by /i/, /u/ → [e]: e.g. *bæta* 'son' – *beti* 'daughter'.

Stress

In Eastern dialect stress is on the penultimate syllable.

MORPHOLOGY AND SYNTAX

Noun

The basic dichotomy is between humans (masculine and feminine) and non-human (neuter). The distinction between masculine and feminine may be reflected morphologically: thus, -(*n*)*i* is a feminine marker: e.g. *burha* 'old man', *burhi* 'old woman'; *asamiyani* /ɔhɔmiyani/ 'Assamese woman'.

NUMBER

The plural is formed with the help of various agglutinative suffixes: thus, *-bilak* for humans, *-bor* for animals: *manuh.bilak* 'people', *ghora.bor* 'horses'. *-sakal* /xɔkɔl/ is an honorific suffix: *dewta.sakal* 'gods'.

SPECIMEN DECLENSION

manuh 'man, human being':

	Singular
nom./agentive	manuh**e**
acc.	manuh**ak**
gen.	manuh**ar**
instr.	manuh**ere**, manuh**ar ddara**
	(*ddara* is a postposition)
dat.	manuh**ak**, manuh**lai**
abl.	manuh**ar para**
loc.	manuh**at**

The same endings are added to the plural markers: e.g. *manuhbilake*, *manuhbilak**ak***. There is no article as such in Assamese, but a singular animate noun may acquire some degree of definiteness by the insertion of *-to-* between base and case ending: e.g. *manuh**tok*** 'to that man (already mentioned)'. This enclitic seems to be an importation from contiguous non-Indo-European linguistic stock. Non-Indo-European influence is also seen in the Assamese practice of adding personal markers to kinship terms in the singular: e.g. with *bopa* 'father': *bopai* 'my father', *baper* 'thy father', *bapera* 'your father' *bapek*, 'his/her father'.

Adjective

The adjective is not sharply distinguished from the noun, and can be declined as such. As attribute it is invariable for case, but takes fem. *-i* where necessary: *kala balad* 'black bull', *kali gai* 'black cow'.

COMPARISON

A comparative form is made by means of *koi/kari* following the locative case: e.g. *Xei ghar**at** **koi** ei ghar daŋar* 'This house is bigger than that house.' The *tatsama* comparative in *-tar* /tɔr/ is also used.

Pronoun

The independent personal forms are:

	Singular	*Plural*
1	mai/mɔi/	ami
2	tai/tɔi/	tahãt
hon. 2	apuni	aponasakal

In the third person the demonstratives, *i* (masc.), *ei* (fem.); *xi/xei* (masc.), *tai* (fem.), are used, with honorary forms *eõ̃* and *tēõ̃*.

The base forms are declined, e.g. for *mai*: acc. *mok*, instr. *more/mor ddara*, abl. *mor para*, gen. *mor*, loc. *mot*: e.g. *mor bandhu* 'my friend'.

DEMONSTRATIVE PRONOUN

Not declined when used attributively: e.g. *ei manuhak* 'of this man'. The plural marker may be added to either the noun or the demonstrative, not both: e.g. *ei manuhbilake* = *eibilak manuhe* 'these people'.

INTERROGATIVE PRONOUN

kih 'who?'; *kon* 'what, which?': e.g. *kon manuh/kitap* 'which man/book?'

RELATIVE PRONOUN

yi /zi/, pl. *yibilake*. These have oblique bases: *yā-* /zaː/ for humans, *yiha-* for non-human.

Verbal participle + the particle *thaka* is also used for relative constructions: e.g. *kitap parhi thaka manuh* 'the man who is reading the book'.

Numerals

1–10: *æk*, *dui*, *tini*, *sāri*, *pãs*, *say*, *xāt*, *āth*, *na*, *dah*; 11–19 have synthetic forms; 20 *bis*; 30 *tris*; 40 *sallis*; 100 *xa*. Formation of numerals up to 100 is not predictable.

Verb

Has active and passive voices, and the following moods: indicative, imperative, subjunctive, conditional, presumptive.

Personal endings (see table) are the same for both numbers; where necessary *-hãk* may be added to mark plural. Gender is nowhere specified.

Personal endings:

		Present	*Past*	*Future*
1		-isõ,	-(i)lõ	-(i)m
2	familiar	-a, -isa	-(i)li	-(i)bi
	neutral	-ā, -isā	-(i)lā	-(i)bā
2 and 3	hon.	-e, -ise	-(i)lē	-(i)ba

The past forms are composed of the past passive participle + personal markers. The auxiliary *ach* /as/ is used with the present participle to make an analytical present tense: e.g. *mai kitap parhi achõ* /asõ/ 'I am reading a/the book'. Similarly with past indefinite: *mai kitap parhi achõilõ* /asõilõ/ 'I was reading a/the book'.

Invariable particles enter into the composition of the subjunctive, the presumptive, and the conditional. The three moods are also specifically associated with tense – the subjunctive with the past tense + *hẽten*, the presumptive with the present tense + *habalā*, the conditional with the non-finite form in *-ā* + *hẽten*: e.g. *mai gəlo hẽten* 'I'd have gone'; *xi ahise habalā* 'he must have come'.

NON-FINITE FORMS

Infinitive in *-(i)ba*: e.g. *buliba* 'to speak'. Present participle in *-i*; past participle in *-a*. Perfective conjunctive in *-i*. Negative: *na* /nɔ/ is prefixed to verb: e.g. *mai **na**karõ* 'I don't do'.

PASSIVE VOICE

The auxiliaries *ya* /za/ and *ha* /hɔ/ are used + transitive past participle. Where *ya* is used, the logical subject is in the instrumental, the logical object in the nominative: e.g. *mor ddara ei kamto kara zay* 'by me this work is done' = 'I do this work'.

Ha construction: the logical object is in the accusative, subject is in the instrumental + third person of *ha*: e.g. *Tar ddara tomak mara nahaba* 'You will not be beaten by him' (examples from Babakaev 1961).

CAUSATIVES

As in Hindi, first and second causative endings are added to the base stem, forming a triad: e.g. *dekh-* 'to look', *dekhā* 'to show', *dekhowā* 'to cause someone to show'. The first causative ending is *-ā*, *-uwā*, etc., with euphonic adjustment at junctures, and, possibly, change of root vowel: *rākh* 'to protect': *rakha* /rɔkha/ 'to cause to protect'; *gā* 'to sing': *gowā* 'to cause to sing'. Formally, the second causative often coincides with the first; it emphasizes the role of an intermediary.

Postpositions

Assamese has about three dozen New Indo-Aryan postpositions: e.g. *āge* 'before', *upare* /upɔre/, 'on', *ddara* 'through/by means of', *loi* 'for', and a few drawn from Arabo-Persian: e.g. *bade* 'after'.

Word order

Normally SOV.

১ আদিতে[১] বাক্য[২] আছিল, আরু বাক্য ঈশ্বরে সৈতে আছিল,
২ আরু বাক্যেই আপুনি ঈশ্বর। তেওঁ আদিতে ঈশ্বরে সৈতে আছিল।
৩ তেওঁর দ্বারায় সকলোৰেই হল ;[৩] আরু যি যি হল, সেইবোরর
৪ এটাও, তেওঁর বিনে নহল। জীৱন তেওঁতেহে ;[৪] সেই জীৱনেই
৫ মানুহর পোহর।[৫] পোহর আন্ধারত প্রকাশিত হৈ আছে ;
৬ কিন্তু আন্ধারে তাক গ্রহণ* নকরিলে। ঈশ্বরর পরা পঠোৱা যোহন[৬]
৭ নামেরে এজন মানুহ আছিল ; তেওঁর দ্বারায় সকলোৰে যেন
বিশ্বাস করে, এই নিমিত্তে, সেই পোহরর সাক্ষ্য দিবলৈ[৭] তেওঁ
৮ সাক্ষ্যর অর্থে আহিছিল। তেওঁ আপুনি সেই পোহর নাছিল,
৯ কিন্তু পোহরর সাক্ষ্য দিবলৈহে আহিছিল।

ATHABASKAN

INTRODUCTION

In his 1929 classification of the North American Indian languages Edward Sapir placed Athabaskan as the major branch of the Na-Dene phylum, to which he also allocated Tlingit and Haida. This grouping is retained in the Voegelin classification of 1966.

Athabaskan itself falls into three major divisions:

1. Northern: about a dozen languages including Chipewyan, Dogrib, Sarsi, Carrier; a total of perhaps 10,000 speakers.
2. Californian: included Hupa and half a dozen other languages. All extinct.
3. Apachean: an internally closely related sub-group including Navajo, Western Apache, Chiricahua and Mescalero Apache, Jicarilla Apache, Kiowa (extinct). Estimated total of *c.* 135,000 speakers, of whom *c.* 120,000 are Navajo.

PHONOLOGY

In general, Athabaskan languages are marked by nasalization, glottalization, and the presence of tones. There is often extensive differentiation of the lateral and velar–uvular series: e.g. Chiricahua Apache has five laterals, Navajo has nine affricates in the dental–alveolar series. /p/ and /r/ are often absent. For inventories of Athabaskan consonants, *see* **Apache**, **Chipewyan**, **Navajo**.

Vowels

Typically, /i, e, a, o, (u)/, extended by length distinction and by nasalization.

MORPHOLOGY AND SYNTAX

Some main features:

Nominals

There is a basic common stock of monosyllabic nouns: e.g. Nav. *béésh*, Ch. Ap. *béésh*, Chip. *bes* 'knife'.

Many nouns have a dual base – absolute form and possessed form: e.g. Nav. *béésh* 'knife', ***-béézh*** '. . . 's knife'. Inalienable possession (bodily parts, kinship terms) is denoted by bound forms: e.g. Nav. *'ajaad* 'one's leg' → 'leg'.

Verbals may be nominalized: e.g. Nav. *ólta'* 'reading is done' = 'school'; Chip. *nátsər* 'he is strong' = 'strength'.

Personal pronominal possessive markers are prefixed to nouns: e.g. Nav. *shí-*, Ch. Ap. *shì-*, Chip. *sɛ-* for first person singular: Ch. Ap. *shì.dìbéhé* = Nav. *shi.dibé* 'my sheep'.

Typical pronominal markers are:

				Example
sing.	1	sh/s	Ch. Ap.	shí
	2	n		ní
3rd sing. pl.		b		bi
	4	h	Nav.	ha/ho
pl.	1/2	nVh		nihi

Personal pronominal markers can be prefixed to postpositions: e.g. Nav. *shi.ḳi* 'on me', *ni.ḳi* 'on you'.

There is extensive use of directional and relational postpositive enclitics, plus non-affixed postpositions.

VERBALS

The typical Athabaskan verbal paradigm comprises a verbal stem preceded by a strictly ordered sequence of prefixes. If these are numbered 1 to 10, the stem is in tenth position; the pronominal subject prefix occupies position 8, the pronominal object, if any, is in 4 (in other words, slot 4 is empty for intransitive verbs). Some positions are in complementary distribution: for example, if the iterative marker is present in slot 2, slot 7 – the position for non-iterative moods and aspects – must be vacant.

Position 9 is obligatorily occupied by the verbal classifier. The division by classifier – Ø, /d, l, ł/ – into transitive, intransitive, and passive verbal paradigms runs right through Athabaskan. In some of the languages the classifiers have merged, and may be represented by their phonetic reflexes. Together with aspect, the class of verb determines the form of the subject pronominal series in position 8. For example, in Apachean the first person singular marker is *-sh-* or *-éli*, depending on class and aspect.

The stem itself is monoform if the verb is stative. Active verbs, however, modulate into several stems to denote different aspects and modes. A Navajo active verb, for example, modulates into progressive, imperfective, perfective, iterative, and optative modes, which will be listed in a Navajo dictionary. For example the stem meaning 'to handle a round, bulky object' has the following five stems:

'ááł, 'aah, 'ą̨, 'ááh, 'ááł

The stems are unpredictable, as is their functional relationship to each other. Often the progressive and iterative stems are identical. In the Chiricahua Apache verb 'to copulate' four stems are identical and only the perfective varies by a change of tone from high to falling, and *ł* → *l*: *’į́įł*, *’į́įł*, *’į̀įł*, *’į́įł*, *’į́įł*.

TENSE

Future, past, present. The future tense is expressed by the progressive mode, the present by the imperfective or progressive, the past by the perfective. The objective pronoun is incorporated in the verb complex (position 4). Formal means exist for expressing passive, reciprocal, reflexive, inchoative, and other nuances, assisted by a great many sense-modulating verbal prefixes.

For detailed description of the Athabaskan verb system, *see* **Navajo**, **Apache**, **Chipewyan**.

AUSTRALIAN LANGUAGES

INTRODUCTION

In the late eighteenth century, when Europeans first reached Australia, some 200 native languages were spoken on the continent. Even in the earliest days of the convict settlement near present-day Sydney, a few exceptional individuals paid some attention to local Aboriginal speech. Dixon (1980) cites the case of Lieutenant Dawes, who actually set about compiling a grammar of the now-extinct Sydney language. By and large, however, neither convicts and jailers nor the settlers who followed them took any interest in their new-found Caliban or in the 'grunts and groans' which seemed to them to constitute his speech. What else were they to expect from the bearers of a culture which was described by one nineteenth-century zoologist – Carl Lumholtz – as 'the lowest to be found among the whole genus homo sapiens' (Dixon 1980: 14).

This was the generally accepted view of Aboriginal culture and language, which persisted virtually unchanged into the twentieth century. A few honourable exceptions deserve to be mentioned: L.E. Threlkeld, Captain George Grey, and E.M. Curr. But it was not until the middle of the twentieth century that native Australian languages began to receive the serious scientific attention that was their due. By then, the cultural damage had been done: of the original 200 languages, 50 were now extinct, and about a hundred were in various stages of obsolescence, many of these close to extinction. Only about 50 are officially rated as 'stable', with numbers of speakers ranging from 6,000 – the Western Desert language – to a few hundreds. There is an obvious parallel with the plight of native languages in the USA and Canada.

In 1974 a School of Australian Languages was opened at Darwin, and professional linguists are now busily engaged in recording, analysing, and comparing Aboriginal languages. These are fairly evenly distributed across the continent, with somewhat denser incidence in Arnhem Land, northern Queensland, Victoria, and New South Wales. All but a handful can be shown to belong to one 'Australian' family. In accordance with these data, it seems plausible to postulate a proto-Australian language, though here the time-scale is doubtful.

The human imprint in Australia dates from around 80,000 to 50,000 BC. These early inhabitants may have spoken the proto-language. However, a second wave of immigrants, who may just as well have been its bearers, seems to have made an Australian landfall much more recently, possibly as late as

4,000 years ago, bringing the dingo with them. At all events, there is no evidence of any connection with any other family of languages.

As it now stands, the Australian family can be further sub-divided into genetically compatible groups, each such group having up to ten members. A genetic relationship is often difficult to distinguish from areal typological features.

Various classifications have been put forward. Schmidt (1919) drew a dividing line between northern and southern Australian languages. In 1956 Capell proposed a formal classification between languages which use both prefixes and suffixes, and languages which use suffixes only. Then in the 1960s Kenneth Hale made a typological distinction between the Pama-Nyungan languages, covering 90 per cent of the continent, and the non-Pama-Nyungan languages of Arnhem Land and north-west Western Australia, which are endowed with, or have developed, complex verbal systems of the polysynthetic type.

With an upsurge of interest in the native languages of Australia has come a degree of understanding of the powerful mythopoeic insights which inform the Aboriginal culture. The Australian people conceived of the creation as a 'dreamtime' in which the elaborate totemic system by which they lived was initiated and mapped on to their language. This confers an oneiric dimension upon its sequences and structures, wherein the life of the individual is integrated with the social unit, the tribe, with its totemic origins and specific identity, with the natural environment and the ley lines that thread it, oneiric, topographical, melodic, and linguistic. For an authoritative account of these matters, see Dixon (1980), especially pp. 23–68. See also B. Chatwin (1987) *The Song Lines.*

SCRIPT

No Australian language was written. Adaptations of the English alphabet are in use for a few of the major languages: e.g. the retroflex series in Yolŋu is marked by underlining: ḏ, ṯ, ṉ, ḻ, and ' denotes the glottal stop.

PHONOLOGY

Sound systems, both consonantal and vocalic, show a surprising degree of homogeneity over the whole continent. A standard and typical inventory comprises:

Consonants

stops and fricatives: b, d, ɖ, ð, ʒ, g
associated nasals: m, n, n′, ɳ, ŋ
laterals: l, ʎ, ɭ
rhotics: r
semi-vowels: w, y
vowels: a, i, u

Fricatives and sibilants are almost unknown in Australian languages. Where they occur, they are due to phonological change leading to enhancement of, or subtraction from, the typical inventory. Thus, a few languages have developed greatly augmented vowel systems, up to 12 phonemes in some cases. The six standard stops have voiceless allophones; the contrast between [b] and [p], for example, is, however, not phonemic.

Areal typological factors have to be taken into account; thus, the dental/retroflex contrast is missing in most eastern languages, but is typically found throughout the central and western areas.

Typical of the whole field is the word pattern CVC(C)V(C).

MORPHOLOGY AND SYNTAX

Dixon (1980) lists these word classes: nominals (including adjectives), pronouns, verbs, adverbs, locative and temporal qualifiers, particles, interjections.

Nominals

Three numbers are usually found: singular, dual, plural. Plural number is optionally marked, often by reduplication. The numeral 'two' may accompany the dual affix.

Some northern languages, e.g. in Arnhem Land, have class systems on Bantu lines (*see* **Bantu Languages**). The noun class prefix is recapitulated in the adjective and echoed in the verb. A different kind of class system is found in Dyirbal, where gender-marked determinatives act as articles: masc. *bayi*, fem. *balan*, neuter *bala*. A fourth form, *balam*, indicates edible, but non-flesh, foodstuffs.

Widespread use is made of genetic markers, to which specific terms are added: e.g. in Dyirbal the feminine class marker will precede a nominal denoting a bird (since the Dyirbal believe that women turn into birds when they die).

CASE

In most languages five or six cases are found; coverage varies. The absolute case, usually with Ø inflection, provides the subject of an intransitive verb and the object of a transitive. The ergative case affix marks the subject of a transitive verb. The genitive affix is used for alienable possession; inalienable possession is expressed by simple apposition (cf. **Chinese**). Other cases are: dative, allative and ablative locatives, purposive, instrumental. Australian languages may be unique in having an 'aversive' case, used in such contexts as 'for fear of the dog'.

A typical set of endings may be taken from Yidiny:

absolute	-Ø
ergative	-ŋgu/du
genitive	-ni
locative and instr.	-da/la/ŋga
ablative	-mu/m

dative	-nda
purposive	-gu
aversive	jida/yida

All show sandhi at junctures. Analogous endings are found in many languages, though, as noted above, the semantic boundaries of the cases are fluid.

Adjective

As attribute, the adjective follows the noun and takes its case: Dixon gives an example from Warrgamay: *ŋulmburu.**ŋgu** wurrbi.bajun.**du*** '(by) the very big woman (ergative)'.

Pronoun

There are singular, dual, and plural forms; trial and paucal also occur. The first person dual/plural is marked for inclusive/exclusive possession. This is average practice. More complicated systems take kinship degree into account. Only the forms for first and second persons are true personal pronouns; the third person forms are supplied from the demonstrative pronominal series, on a scale of relative proximity: e.g. in Western Desert Language:

ngaa- 'this'	he, she... (close at hand)
pala- 'that'	he, she... (further away)
nyarra- 'that'	he, she... (remote)
palunya 'that'	he, she... (not visible)

In some languages the personal pronouns have absolute, ergative, object, genitive forms.

Bound pronominal clitics appear in many languages. Where these are available, use of free pronouns is optional: e.g. in Western Desert, singular:

	Subject	*Object*
1	-rna	-rni
2	-n	-nta
3	-Ø	-lu

There are corresponding series for dual and plural. Dixon gives the following example from the Western Desert language: *pu.ngku.rna.nta* 'I will hit you' (*pu-* = stem; *-ngku* = future marker; *-rna-* = 1st p. sbj. marker; *-nta-* = 2nd p. obj. marker).

DEMONSTRATIVE PRONOUN

See **Pronoun**, above.

INTERROGATIVE PRONOUN

A widespread pattern is: *w/n – a – n'a*: e.g. Dyirbal, *wanya*, Western Desert, *ngana* 'who?'; Dyirbal, *minya*, Western Desert, *nyaa* 'what?'

Numerals

The concepts unity, duality, triality are covered by singular, dual, and plural inflection. There are no numbers in Aboriginal languages higher than three. For everyday purposes, the English numerals are used.

Verb

Roots do not occur without inflection. Most languages have anything up to half-a-dozen different conjugations, distinguished by phonetic criteria, not semantic. A comparison of five languages in Dixon (1980) shows that transitivity is in general associated with the *-l-* conjugation; intransitive verbs are generally in the *y/Ø* conjugation. Typical markers are: *Ø*, *ŋ*, *n*, *l*, *rr* (these taken from Walmatjari).

Derivational/modal affixes may appear. If present, they are sited between the stem and the inflection. They give reflexive, causative, inceptive, habitual, semelfactive connotation to the stem. Transitive verbs are made from intransitives by the addition of a suffix: e.g. *bala.n* 'to be open', in Yidiny: *bala.**ŋa**.l* 'to open' (transitive). Similarly, intransitives can be formed from transitives: *wawa.l* 'to look at something': *wawa.**aji.n*** 'to look' (intransitive) (Dixon 1980: 278).

Almost all Australian languages have an imperative mood; the negative imperative may be a distinct form.

TENSE

Many languages have past, present, and future inflections. The precise frame of reference varies from one language to another: in some, the future is contrasted with the non-future, i.e. past and present are lumped together; in others, past is contrasted with non-past.

In typical inflection patterns the conjugation marker is followed by the tense marker; in Walmatjari the tense endings for an *-l-* conjugation verb are:

imperative: *-nyja*
future: *-lku*
past: *-rni*
customary: *-lany*
subordinate: *-rnu*

As will be seen from the last entry in this list, there is a specific marker for the verb in a subordinate clause in Walmatjari, as there is for switch reference.

It should be pointed out that in many cases a conjugation has very few members: e.g. the *-n-* conjugation in Walmatjari has only three members: *ya.n* 'to go', *ma.n* 'to do', and *la.n* 'to pierce'.

In sentences with a nominal subject, transitive verb, and direct object an ergative construction is general throughout the entire field: noun + ergative marker (usually *-ŋu/du*) with object in absolutive (nominative) case: the nominative marker is usually zero. A corollary of this model is a rather free word order. However, if the subject is a personal pronoun (1st or 2nd person), a nominative–accusative model is used.

Negation is by particle.

EWANGELIA JOHANNAKA

KAP. I.

1 **TJONTINJALA** ankatja nitjama, ankatja Altjiragata
nitjama, Altjira ankatja nitjama tuta.
2 Nanatoa tjontinjala Altjiragata nitjama.
3 Inkarakima nanalela mbaramala, nanaraba itja mbaramala, nanatoa mbaramalanga.
4 Ekurala etata nitjita, nana etata nitjita bartja rellirbe
raka.
5 Bartja bartjima tabatabala, tabatabala nana erkutji-
makana.
6 Atua ninta tnaka, erina Altjirala jainamala, retna ekura
Johannes.
7 Lenatoa pitjika tjartjatunjaka, era tjartjatutjika bartjibera, nakaguia inkarakala ekuralela tnakitjika.
8 Era bartja nitjimakana, era bula tjartjatutjika bartjibera.

(Aranda)

AUSTRO-ASIATIC LANGUAGES

This is the designation adopted for a collocation of three typologically comparable but not necessarily genetically related groups of languages. They are:

1. Mon-Khmer languages: spoken in Vietnam, Laos, and Cambodia, with extensions into Burma and Malaysia. One member – Khasi – is in India. Estimates of the total numbers of Mon-Khmer speakers depend on whether Vietnamese is or is not regarded as a member of the family (*see* **Vietnamese**). With Vietnamese, the total comes to around 70 million; without it, to about 10 million.
2. Munda languages: also known as Kol. These languages are spoken in the Indian states of Bihar, Orissa, and Madhya Pradesh. Their original distribution must have been far wider, and their presence in the subcontinent antedates the coming of the Aryans in the third/second millennium BC. About 6 million people speak a dozen Munda languages, of which the most important by far are Santali and Muṇḍārī.
3. Nicobarese: spoken by around 18,000 in the Nicobar Islands.

See **Khmer**, **Vietnamese**, **Mon**, **Khasi**, **Palaung**, **Bahnaric Languages**, **Santali**, **Muṇḍārī**, **Nicobarese**.

AUSTRONESIAN LANGUAGES

This very extensive family of some 700 languages, spoken by about 270 million people, falls naturally into two divisions, which intersect close to the island in which the whole Austronesian family is believed to have originated – New Guinea.

The Western division centres on Indonesia and the Philippines, with outliers in Taiwan, Madagascar, and Micronesia. Ninety-eight per cent of the total number of speakers of Austronesian languages are to be found in this division.

The Eastern division has not more than 2 million speakers, who inhabit thousands of islands scattered over a vast area of the Pacific Ocean. Three main sub-divisions are distinguished: Polynesian, Melanesian, and Micronesian languages.

While the Polynesian languages form a remarkably homogeneous group, the genetic affiliation between them and the Melanesian and Micronesian groups is not obvious, and was only finally demonstrated by Otto Dempwolf in the middle of the twentieth century. Since then, progress has been made on the reconstruction, by comparative methods, of the parent language, or Proto-Austronesian.

Recent research goes to show that Proto-Austronesian split, about 4,000 years ago, into two branches which are, today, highly divergent: Formosan (small and dwindling; about 100,000 speakers in the mountains of Taiwan) and Malayo-Polynesian.

See **Polynesian Languages**, **Achinese**, **Balinese**, **Batak**, **Minangkabau**, **Indonesian**, **Javanese**, **Sundanese**, **Madurese**, **Gorontalo**, **Buginese**, **Macassarese**, **Hawaiian**, **Samoan**, **Tongan**, **Maori**, **Tagalog**, **Cebuano**, **Ilokano**, **Bikol**, **Trukese**, **Chamorro**, **Cham**, **Malagasy**, **Fijian**, **Tahitian**, **Rapanui**.

AVAR

INTRODUCTION

Avar belongs to the Avaro-Andi-Dido group of the Dagestani branch of the Ibero-Caucasian family. There is a basic split into northern and southern dialectal forms. The literary standard is based on *bolmaç*, a kind of lingua franca developed on a northern variety of Avar for trade and communication purposes. The Avars form by far the largest ethnic group in the Dagestan Republic, with an estimated number of speakers now approaching the half-million mark. The earliest record of Avar is found in bilingual inscriptions (with Georgian) dating from the tenth century AD. The Avar Khanate, which arose from the ruins of Mongol dominion in the Caucasus, reached its zenith in the seventeenth to eighteenth centuries, and the Avar literary tradition is of equivalent age. Until relatively recently, however, Arabic was the main, not to say sole, literary language. The late nineteenth century saw the emergence of creative writing in Avar (Mahmud of Kahabroso, Hamzat Tsadasa, and, in the mid-twentieth century, Rasul Hamzatov). The Avar press dates from the early Soviet period; newspapers, journals, and some books are published in the language.

SCRIPT

Arabic until 1928, followed by ten years of experimental romanization. Since 1939 Cyrillic + *I*, which is here in general the marker for ejective consonants, but note ʅ and x*I*, both of which are pharyngeal fricatives.

PHONOLOGY

Consonants

There are 44 consonants, including a rich inventory of fricatives, affricates, and sibilants. A typical series is affricate – geminate – ejective affricate – geminated ejective: e.g. /tʃ, ttʃ, tʃ', ttʃ'/. In this article, gemination is marked by the macron, and the subscript dot indicates an ejective consonant.

There are at least four laterals, here transcribed as *ḳƚ̣*, *ƚ̣*, *ƚ̄*, *l*. The velar series – /g, k, kk, k', k'k'/ – is extended deeper into the throat by consonantal phonemes described as uvular (five values based on /q/), pharyngeals (/ʕ/ and /ħ/), and laryngeals (/ʔ/ and /h/).

Vowels

front: i, ɛ

central: a
back: o, u

Stress

Weak, free, usually on first or second syllable.

MORPHOLOGY

Noun

Nouns are marked for number and case, and are divided into three classes: male persons, female persons, animals, and objects. Specific markers for these classes are affixed as prefixes to verbs, and as suffixes to adjectives. Pronouns and adverbs also reflect class. Thus the class markers articulate the sentence as syntactic relay points (cf. **Bantu Languages**). For class 1, male persons, the marker is *v-/-v*; for class 2, *y-/-y*, and for class 3, *b-/-b*. The plural marker for all three classes is *r-/-l* (*r-* for verbs, *-l* for adjectives). Examples:

emen **v**aç̌ana 'the father came'
ç̌užu **y**aç̌ana 'the woman came'
ču **b**aç̌ana 'the horse came'
vasal **r**aç̌ana 'the boys came'

Nominal class distinction extends even to cetain adverbs: cf. from *ruq̄* 'house', *ruq̄ob* (adverb) 'at home', where the final *-b* is a class 3 marker: hence, *emen ruq̄o***v** ***v****ugo* 'father is at home'; *ebel ruq̄o***y** ***y****ugo* 'mother is at home'; *łimal ruq̄o***r** ***r****ugo* 'the children are at home'.

NUMBER

Plural markers, e.g. *-zabi*, *-zal*, *-bi*, *-al*, are suffixed to noun stems: e.g. *khur* 'field', pl. *khurzal*; *ber* 'eye', pl. *beral*; *halmaγ* 'comrade'; *halmaγzabi* 'comrades'.

CASE SYSTEM

The basic cases are: nominative, ergative, genitive, dative. In addition, Avar has three series of locative cases specifying (a) rest in a place; (b) motion towards a focus; and (c) motion out of, away from a focus. Each of these series is further sub-divided into five referential frames, depending on whether the rest or motion is related to the surface of something, contiguity with something, inclusion in something, being underneath something, or, lastly, being inside something. Thus, *šaharalda* 'in the town'; this is a class (a) locative (rest in a place) with reference to a surface: *Dos hudulasde kaγat qvana* 'He wrote a letter to a friend'; here, *hudulasde* is a class-(b) locative (motion towards something → indirect object) with reference to contiguity.

Using the ergative singular ending as criterion, we get three declensions: (1) ergative in *-s*; (2) ergative in *-ł*; (3) ergative in *-ca*.

Specimen declension: first declension, *vas* 'son'; *ç̌užu* 'woman':

	Singular	*Plural*	*Singular*	*Plural* (suppletive)
nominative	vas	vasal	ç̌užu	ručabi
ergative	vasas	vasaz	ç̌užuyał	ručabaca
genitive	vasasul	vasazul	ç̌užuyałul	ručabazul
dative	vasase	vasaze	ç̌užuyałe	ručabaze

To each paradigm 30 locative cases must be added.

Adjective

Attributively, the adjective precedes the noun and is in class concord with it, by suffixed marker in the singular only; for a plural referent, the adjective is marked for number, not for class: e.g. *tiriya**v** vas* 'lively boy'; *tiriya**l** vasal* 'lively boys'; *tiriya**y** yas* 'lively girl'. Only when used substantively is the adjective marked for case.

Pronoun

PERSONAL PRONOUN

The basic personal forms are: sing. 1 *dun*; 2 *mun*; plural: 1 incl. *nił*; excl. *niž*; 2 *nuž*. Demonstrative pronouns are used for the third person forms. The personal pronouns are declined in the basic cases + two locatives: e.g. for first person singular: *dun, dica, dir, die*; *dida, diq*. They do not take class markers. Possessive forms precede noun: e.g. *dir halmaγ* 'my comrade'.

DEMONSTRATIVE PRONOUN

A three-degree series of relative proximity is further complicated by a distinction in relative altitude, above or below speaker. Thus, *he**v*** suggests a class 1 (male) person in distal relationship with speaker; *ho**v*** further identifies him as being situated lower down than the speaker. That is, the demonstratives take the class markers.

INTERROGATIVE PRONOUN

Also takes class marker: *ši**v*** 'who?' (class 1), *šib* 'what?' The plural is *šal.*

RELATIVE PRONOUN

None.

Numerals

The root forms for 1–10 are: *co, ḳi, łab, unq, šu, anł, anḳł, miḳł, iç̌, anç. -go* is added to form the cardinals. Formation of the decades may be decimal or vigesimal: 20 *qogo*; 30 *łebergo*; 40 *ḳiqogo* = 2×20; 100 *nusgo.*

Verb

Transitive and intransitive; syntactically, verbs of perception and affective verbs form specific sub-divisions.

TRANSITIVE VERBS

Logical subject in ergative case, verb in class concord with logical object in nominative (absolute) case: e.g. *Ebelaɬ vas vačana* 'The mother brought her son'; *Ebelaɬ yas yačana* 'The mother brought her daughter.' With certain verbs, the pronominal class marker is an infix: e.g.

Muslimatica vas ha**v**una 'Muslimat bore a son'
Muslimatica yas ha**y**una 'Muslimat bore a daughter'
Muslimatica ɬumal ha**r**una 'Muslimat bore children'

INTRANSITIVE VERBS

Subject in nominative (absolute) case: e.g. *cŭ bač̣ana* 'the horse came'.

Affective verbs: subject in dative: verb in class concord with logical object: e.g. *Muradie yas yoḳɬ̣ula* 'Murad loves (his) daughter.'
Verbs of perception: subject in class (a) locative, verb in class concord with logical object: e.g. *Ebelalda vas vixana* 'The mother saw the son'; *Insuda yas yiẋana* 'The father saw the daughter.'

'To have' is expressed by the relevant tense of *vuḳine* 'to be' plus the genitive case of the logical subject: *dos.ul* ***v****as* ***v****ugo* 'he has a son'; *mašhur.***ab** *ču* ***b****ugo doz.ul* 'they have a famous horse' (*mašhur* 'famous' is an Arabic loanword).

MOODS

There are four moods – indicative, imperative, conditional (subjunctive), and interrogative. The indicative mood has three tenses: a general/aorist tense, a past, and a future. These may be illustrated with the stem *c̣ali(ze)* 'to read': general, *c̣alula*; past, *c̣alana*; future, *c̣alila* (this root is marked with initial geminate in Saidov's dictionary). The general tense and the future are negated by affixing *-ro*; *c̣alularo*. The past is negated by adding *-č̣o*.

The conditional/subjunctive marker is *-ni*, negated by *č̣oni*: *c̣ala.ni* 'if he read(s)'; negative *c̣alič̣oni*. The participial forms are negated by infix: e.g. future, *c̣alileb*, neg. *c̣alilareb*. Similarly, negative past participial form, *č̣alič̣eb*. The existential verb is negated by *guro*: *hab ču guro*, *'orc̣en* ***b****ugo* 'this is not a horse, it is a mule'.

Postpositions

Several of these, e.g. *žanib* 'inside', *ṭad* 'on', do little more than resume the meaning of the spatial case series. Others, like *horɬ* 'between, among', *naqa* 'behind', *dande* 'against', serve to extend or amplify the spatial series:

Poyezdalda ṭad reḳana dov
'He boarded (onto) the train'

Stolalda ṭad ɬe dir sa'at
'Lay my watch on the table'
(*poyezd*, *stol* are Russian loanwords, 'train', 'table'; *sa'at* 'watch' is an Arabic loanword)

Word formation

By affixation or by compounding. Thus, *-či* and *-qan* form nouns denoting agent from verbal stems: e.g. *ħalṭuqan* 'worker' (*ħalṭize* 'to work'). Compounding: e.g. *kver* 'hand' + *bač̣*, root of the verb *bač̣ize* 'to clean'; *kverbač̣* 'handkerchief'.

Word order

SOV is normal in ergative construction, but note intransitive and imperative constructions in examples of postpositions above.

1. АВАЛАЛДА вукIана Калам. Гьев вукIана Аллагьгун, ва Гьев вукIана Аллагъ.

2. Авалалдасаго Гьев Аллагъгун вукIана.

3. Гьесдасахун тIолабгояб бижизабуна; Гьев гъечIого щибниги лъугьинчIо.

4. Гьесулъ букIана гIумру, ва чагIазе гъеб гIумру букIана нур.

5. Гьеб нур кенчIола бецIлъуда, ва бецIлъиялда кIвечIо гьеб свинабизе.

6. Аллагьас витIана, жинда ЯхIя-ян абулев цо чи.

7. Гьес гIадамазда нур бихьизабизе кколаан, гьелдалъун цинги киналго гьелда божизе гIоло.

8. Гьев живго гьеб нурлъун вукIинчIо; гьесул тIадкъай букIана гIицIго, гьес гьеб нур бихьизаби.

AVESTAN

INTRODUCTION

Avestan belongs to the Iranian branch of Indo-European, and is one of the oldest attested Indo-European languages. Textual material in Avestan may be divided by content into (a) the religious texts of Zoroastrianism, in part dating from the middle of the first millennium BC; and (b) a poetic corpus embodying the mythology and the heroic traditions of ancient Iran; some of this material is pre-Zoroastrian. Neither sector was recorded in writing until long after Avestan had ceased to be a spoken language. Both were handed down by word of mouth until the first known codification, which took place between the fourth and sixth centuries AD, during the Sasanid period. For this purpose the Pehlevi script was available (*see* **Pehlevi**), and it was forthwith adapted and amplified so as to accommodate the richer phonological inventory of the ancient language. To this codification the name *avesta* was given, while the accompanying translation and commentary in Pehlevi were known as *zand*. It is probable that the material thus codified was far more extensive than that extant today, the losses being due in part at least to the Muslim invasions. The content as now known comprises:

(a) The Zoroastrian canon: the *Yasna*, including the *Gāthās* and the *Homyašt*: in part very old, in part rewritten.
(b) The 'little Avesta', a collection of Zoroastrian hymns, including some of the most ancient.
(c) The *Yašts*: an ancient heroic and mythological stratum reworked in the spirit of Zoroastrian homiletics by the priesthood.

SCRIPT

The 16-letter Pehlevi script was expanded to 48; some of the graphs are positional variants. There are 14 vowel signs; the rest denote consonants. Some Pehlevi ligatures were adopted.

PHONOLOGY

No one phonological inventory can be given for the different strata in the Avestan corpus; what is valid for one stratum is invalid for another. The authorities in this field – Emile Benveniste, G. Morgenstierne – have reconstructed an 'idealized' inventory, in the light of Sanskrit/Vedic congeners and the general principles of Indo-European philology. The proposed 'idealized' system comprises:

Consonants

labials: /p, b, f, v, m/
dentals: /t, θ, d, n, s, z, r/
alveolar–palatals: /tʃ, dʒ, j, ʃ, ʒ/
velars: /k, g, x/
glottal: /h/; + allophones

The absence of /l/ is striking.

Vowels

long and short: i, a, u

There are also signs for the allophones [e, ə, əː, a, oː] (long vowels are here indicated by a macron). The basic diphthongs are: /ai, aːi, au, aːu/. Vocalic /r̥/ seems to be present, though not notated.

VOWEL GRADATION

(*See* **Sanskrit**.) Gradation is present, but not always strictly observed: /Ø – a – aː; r̥ – ar – aːr/, etc.

CONSONANT GRADATION

E.g. alternation of /k/tʃ/: e.g. root *vak* 'to speak', perfect *vavača*.

Tone and stress

Internal evidence in the *Gāthās*, along with parallel evidence in the congener languages, points to the existence in the oldest Avestan period of a tonal system similar to that in Vedic (*see* **Vedic**). In later stages, tone was replaced by a stress accent on the penultimate if this was long, otherwise on the ante-penultimate.

MORPHOLOGY AND SYNTAX

Noun

The structure of Avestan is synthetic and flectional. Nominals, including nouns and adjectives, are marked for gender (masculine, feminine, neuter), number (singular, dual, plural), and case (eight cases).

Examples of Avestan stems (in idealized notation) with Sanskrit equivalents:

Avestan	*Sanskrit*	*Translation*
māh	mās	'month'
xšap	kṣap	'night'
zr̥d	hr̥d	'heart'
pada	pada	'step'
sata	śata	'hundred'
gari	giri	'mountain'
tanū	tanu	'body'

Examples of formative suffixes shared by Avestan and Sanskrit:

	Avestan	*Sanskrit*	*Translation*
-tṛ/ -tar/ -tār	dā.tar	dhātṛ/dhātar	'creator'
-ra	sux.ra	śukra	'red'
-at/-ant	bṛzant	bṛhat/bṛhant-	'tall, big'

DECLENSION

A broad division into (a) thematic and (b) athematic stems may be made. Examples of thematic stems with their Modern Persian reflexes: *aspa-* 'horse', Persian *asp*; *zasta-* 'hand', Persian *hast*; *martya-* 'man', Persian *mard*; and athematic: *pād-* 'foot', Persian *pāy*; *āp* 'water', Persian *āb.*

Bases in -(v)*at*/-(v)*ant*: *mazat*/*mazant* 'big'; *dvišyat*/*dvišyant* 'enemy'.
Bases in *-r*/*-ar*/*-ār*: *dātar* 'creator'; *pitar* 'father'; *mātar* 'mother'; *vadar* 'weapon'.
Bases in *-n*/*-an*/*-ān* (these are masculine, feminine, or neuter): *xšafn*/*xšapan* 'night'; *čašman* 'eye', Persian *čašm*; *asman* 'sky', Persian *āsmān*.
Bases in *-u*/*ū*, *-i*/*ī*: *ahu* 'world'; *manyu* 'spirit'; *pasu* 'cattle'; *vahu* 'good'.

Vahu, fem. *vahvī*, is a typical example of the idealized spelling. Some of the forms actually attested in the Gāthās are:

nominative singular: masc. *vaŋhuš*, fem. *vaŋuhi*, neuter *vahū*
accusative singular: masc. *vohūm*, fem. *vaŋuhīm*, neuter *vohū*
genitive singular: masc. *vaŋhə̄uš*, fem. *vaŋhuyā*
ablative singular: masc. *vaŋhaoθ*
nominative plural: masc. *vaŋhavō*, fem. *vaŋuhīš*
genitive plural: masc. *vohunãm*
locative plural: masc. *vaŋhušu*

The case endings are analogous to those in Sanskrit. As a specimen, here is the full set of endings for a masculine *-a* stem:

	Singular	*Dual*	*Plural*
nom.	-as → ō	-ā	-ā, -a
acc.	-m	-ā	-əŋg
gen.	-ahe	-ayā	-ānam
abl.	-āt → -āθ	-aēibya	-aē^{i}byō
dat.	-ai		-aē^{i}byō
instr.	-ā		-āiš
loc.	-ōi, -e, -aya	-ayō	-aēšu
voc.	-a, -ā		

There are analogous paradigms for stems in *-ā*, *-i*/*-ī*, *u*/*ū*, *-āu*, and consonantal stems. Not all possible forms are actually attested, though the record is very much fuller than it is for Old Persian: e.g. the *-ant*/*-at* paradigm is fully attested in Avestan, whereas for Old Persian only the nominative, accusative, and genitive singular are known.

Some examples of case formation:

-*a* stems:

aspa 'horse', *aspahe* (gen.) 'of a horse'
ahura 'lord', *ahurā* (voc.) 'Oh Lord!'
spāda 'army', *spādā* (dual nom.) 'two armies'
zast- 'hand', *zastōibya* (dual instr.) 'with both hands'

-*ā* stems:

daēnā 'religion' *daēnayā* 'of religion'
gaēθā 'being', *gaēθanām* 'of the beings'

-*ī* stem:

xšaθrī 'woman', *xšaθrišu* 'in the women'

-*u* stem:

pasu 'cattle', *pasvō* (acc. pl.)
vaŋhu- 'good', *vaŋhubyō* 'to the good (ones)' (dat. pl.)

Consonant stems:

sna^{i}θiš 'weapon', *snaiθīžbya* 'to/with/from the two weapons'

-*n*:

urvān- 'soul', *urvānəm* (acc. sing.)
čašman- 'eye', *čašmanat* [-aθ] 'from the eye'

Adjective

Nouns and adjectives are similarly declined. Adjectives form a comparative grade in -*yaṣ* > -*yah*: *vahu* 'good', *vah.yah* 'better'; or in -*tara*: *aka-* 'bad', *aka.tara* 'worse'.

Adjectives are marked for gender. Masc./neuter nominative: -*a*/-*ant*; feminine -*ā*, -*ī*, -*yā*. If the stem is changeable, the feminine endings are added to the weak grade: *bṛzant* 'high', feminine *bṛzatī*.

Pronoun

PERSONAL PRONOUN

The following 1st and 2nd personal forms are attested:

Singular: 1 *azəm*; 2 *tvəm*
Plural: 1 *vaēm*; 2 *yūžəm* (cf. Lithuanian, Latvian, Albanian)

Oblique forms attested include:

Singular: genitive 1 *mana*, 2 *tava*; accusative 1 *mām*, 2 *θuam* (*t* > *θ*); instrumental 2 *θuā*

Plural: dative 1 *ahmaibyā*, 2 *yūšmaibyā*; instrumental 2 *xšmā*

Only two dual forms are known – the first person accusative, *əəāva*, and the second person genitive, *yavākəm*.

The third person forms are drawn from the demonstrative series, and are therefore marked for gender.

DEMONSTRATIVE PRONOUN

In the idealized spelling the proximate demonstrative pronouns are presented as *ayam*, *hvaṣ*, *aišaṣ*, attested in the Avestan text as *aēm*, *hō*, *aēšō*. These are masculine nominative forms. The oblique base of *ayam* is *ta-*; of *hvaṣ*, *ima-/ana-*. The feminine of *ayam* is attested as *īm* (*iyam* in the idealized notation); of *hvaṣ*, *hā/hī*; of *aēšō*, *aēša*.

Distal: masculine singular nominative: *hāu*, *avam* (both in idealized notation), feminine *hāu*. The oblique forms for both genders, as attested (the neuter forms are hardly attested), are made from *avam*; *hāu* appears to be used in the nominative only; cf. *hāu maza mərəγō* 'that big bird' (cf. Persian *morγ*). The masc. sing. accusative: *īm*, fem. *hīm*, neuter *īt*.

RELATIVE PRONOUN

This is attested as *yō*. Apart from dual forms, the relative pronoun is widely attested in the Avestan text. Sokolov (1961) points out that this is partly because of its use in a kind of izafet construction, e.g. *mərəγō yō parō.darš nāma* 'a bird of Parō.darš' name', i.e. 'a bird by the name of Parō.darš'. The relative pronoun also functions as a pre-nominal (compared by Sokolov to the definite article): *azəm yō ahurō mazdā* 'I (who am) Ahura Mazda'.

INTERROGATIVE PRONOUN

This is attested as *ka-/kā-*, e.g. *kō mām stavāθ kō yazāite* 'Who extols me, who does sacrifice to me?' The base *-či/-čai* is added (cf. Sanskrit *kaś.čit*, *kā.čit*, *kiṃ.čit*): *kas.čit martyanām* 'someone of the people'.

Numerals

1–10: the idealized notation is here followed by an attested form. Where idealized and attested forms coincide, only one form is given: 1 *aiva-*, *aēvō*, 2 *dva*, 3 *ṭri-* (fem. *tiṣr-*), *θrāyō* (fem. *tišrō*), 4 *čatur*, *caθwārō*, 5 *panča*, 6 *xšvaš*, 7 *hapta*, 8 *aštā*, 9 *nava*, 10 *dasa*. 20, *vīsaiti*; 300, 400, 500 are attested as *θrisatəm*, *čaθwarəsatəm*, *pančasatəm*; (formally these are accusatives); 100 *satam*, *satəm*; 1,000 *hazahram*, *hazaŋrəm*.

Verb

Avestan has active and middle voices. Middle-voice forms are mainly characteristic of the older stratum in the language; there are four moods – indicative, imperative, subjunctive, and optative. Tense distinction is found only in the indicative mood. Tenses are marked for number and person.

There are three bases – present, aorist, perfect – each generating relevant tense forms. Personal inflections vary according to tense.

TENSE FORMS

From present base: present, imperfect. The imperative mood is also formed from this base. From aorist base: aorist. From perfect base: perfect, pluperfect. The subjunctive and optative moods are made from any base. The subjunctive marker is *-a/-ā*, the optative marker is *-i*: e.g. *kərᵊnavāne* 'that I may do' (middle voice, subj. of *kərᵊnav.* 'to do').

Example of present tense: *bara-* 'to carry, bear'. Active voice:

			cf. *Sanskrit*
singular	1	barāmi	bharāmi
	2	barahi	bharasi
	3	baraⁱti	bharati
plural	1	barāmahi	bharāmaḥ
	2	(barayaθā)	bharatha
	3	barənti	bharanti

In both the imperfect and the aorist the *a-* augment is optional. As in Sanskrit, there is a sigmatic aorist (IE *-s* > Av. *š/h*) and an asigmatic: e.g. (*aivi-*) *visəm* 'I saw'.

The perfect tense is formed from the perfect base by reduplication: e.g. *susruye* 'I have heard'; *yayata* 'he has moved'; *dadāθa* 'thou hast created'.

NEGATION

The general negating particle (prepositive) for the indicative tense system is *nōit* → *nōiθ*. The imperative is negated by *mā*. Use of either negating particle is optional in the subjunctive and the optative.

PREVERBS

These are mainly directional and very widely used: e.g.

fra-: indicating motion forwards;
niš-/niž-: motion towards something;
para-: motion away from something;
aⁱti-: motion through something;
ava-: motion downwards.

NON-FINITE FORMS

Each of the three bases has an active and a middle-voice participle. The present active participle, for example, is in *-nt*, fem. *-ntī*, and is declined like a noun in *-nt*. There is also a passive past participle made from the Ø grade stem + *-ta*: e.g. *gatō* (masc. nom.) from root *gam-*.

Prepositions and postpositions

Attested forms include *antar* 'in', *pasča* 'after', *upairi* 'on', *anu* 'according to', *avi/aivi* 'towards'.

It is sometimes not clear whether a particular form is a preverb or a postposition. Sokolov gives the example: *asmanam avi frašusāni zām avi ni.urvisyāni*, where *avi* can be construed either as a postposition meaning 'towards', or as a directional preverb: *avi.fra.šusa* 'to go to(wards)'. With either reading, the sentence means 'Am I to go to heaven, or am I to turn back to earth?' It may be noted that the accusative case (here, *asmanam*, *zā̃m*) in itself carries a directional sense: cf. *kam zā̃m āyenī* 'to which land am I to go?'

Word order

Free.

The first stanza of *Yasna* 29 follows, as an example of Avestan scriptural verse.

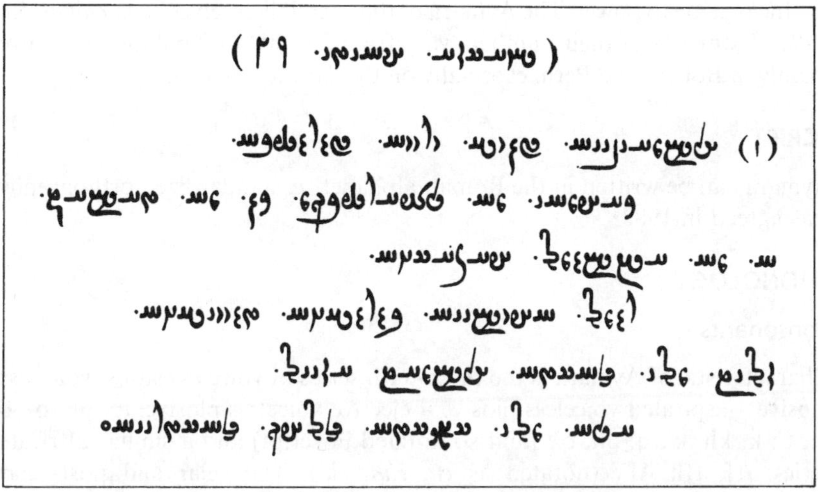

xšmaibyā gə̄uš urvā gərəždā
kahmāi mā θwarōždūm? kə̄ mā tasaθ?
ā.mā aēšəmō hazas.čā; āhišāyā dərəščā təviščā
nōiθ mōi vāstā xšmaθ anyō aθ mōi sastā vohu vāstryā
To you, the spirit of the Bull complained: to what purpose did you make me? Who created me? Passion and tyranny, ruthlessness and brutality threaten me: other than you there is for me no Herdsman. Grant me, therefore, (the bounty of) your good herding.
(For vāstryā, see last paragraph of Indo-European Languages. Compare Svetāśvataropaniṣad I).

AYMARÁ

INTRODUCTION

This language belongs to the Quechumaran group of the Andean-Equatorial family. 'Aymará' is an umbrella term for about a dozen ethnic groups, some of which, e.g. the Colla and the Lupaka, had formed independent states before the Incas came to power. The Aymará of today call themselves '*la nacionalidad qulla*'. Estimates of their numbers vary from 500,000 to 2 million. They live mainly in Bolivia and Peru, especially on the Titicaca plateau.

SCRIPT

Aymará can be written in the Roman alphabet. A standardized orthography was agreed in 1983.

PHONOLOGY

Consonants

Characteristic of Aymará is the three-term series of voiceless stops: voiceless plosive – aspirated voiceless plosive – ejective voiceless plosive: /p, ph, p'; t, th, t'; k, kh, k'; q, qh, q'/ (and so notated in script) and a similar affricate series: /tʃ, tʃh, tʃ'/ (notated as *ch*, *chh*, *ch'*). The velar and post-velar fricatives /x/γ/ and /χ/ʁ/ are present, along with alveolar /s/. There are three nasals: /m, n, ɲ/; two laterals: /l, ɬ/; one trill: /r/; two semi-vowels: /j, w/. The voiced plosives are missing. The velar and post-velar fricatives are denoted by *j* and *x*.

Vowels

short and long: i, u, a

Final short vowels are regularly elided unless they are sentence-final.

Stress

Stress seems to be mainly on the penultimate, as in Quechua, but may move to final, e.g. postposition *-takí*.

MORPHOLOGY AND SYNTAX

Noun

There is no grammatical gender. There are two numbers, singular and plural;

the plural marker is *-naka*. Native Aymará usage requires only one member of a plural complex to be so marked (numerals, for example, take the singular) but Spanish influence is leading to reduplication. Thus *aka**naka**x qala**naka**wa* 'these are stones' might now be heard instead of the more idiomatic *aka**naka**x qala**Ø**wa*. (In this phrase, *-x* is a subject marker, *-wa* is a confirming particle.)

CASE

Cases are formed by the addition of suffixes; in the plural, these follow the plural marker.

The genitive marker is *-n*(*a*); the noun denoting the object possessed takes the appropriate possessive marker (as in Turkic): e.g. *awki.xa.**n** uta.**pa**.x* 'my father's house' (*-xa-* is 1st p. poss. marker; *-pa-* is 3rd p. poss. marker); *jila.ma.**n** yapu.**pa**.x* 'your brother's chacra' (*-ma-* is 2nd p. poss. marker).

Other case endings:

ablative, *-ta*: *marka**t**(**a**)*... *alta* 'I bought... from the market';
comitative, *-mpi*: *awki.xa.**mpi*** 'with my father';
inessive, *-n*: *uta**n*** 'in the house';
benefactive, *-taki* 'for': *wawa.ma.**taki*** 'for your son';
terminative, *-kama*: *Marka.**kama**.w* 'It's as far as the market', *Qharur-**ukama*** 'Until tomorrow!'

A personal indirect object can be marked by *-r*(*u*).

The interrogative affix is *-ti*; a negative of the copula is *-kiti* preceded by *jan*(*iw*): e.g. *Uka.x anu.wa* 'That (*uka*) is a dog (*anu*)'; *Anu**ti**?* 'Is it a dog?'; ***Jan**(**iw**)* *anu**kiti*** 'It isn't a dog.'

Adjective

As attribute, adjective precedes the noun and is invariable: e.g. *Machaq*(*a*) *marka.ti?* 'Is it a new market/village?'; *Mirq'i marka.wa* 'It is an old village.'

COMPARISON

A comparative can be made with *juk'ampi* + *-ta* case: e.g. *misk'**ita** juk'ampi muxsa* 'sweeter than honey'.

Pronoun

Personal independent + enclitic possessive:

	Singular	*Enclitic*	*Plural*	*Enclitic*
1	naya	-xa	jiwasa (*incl.*)	-sa
			nanaka (*excl.*)	
2	juma	-ma	jumanaka	
3	jupa	-pa	jupanaka	

Examples: *uta**xa**x* 'my house'; *uta.naka.**pa**.x* 'his houses'; *qawra.naka.**sa**.x* 'our llamas'.

DEMONSTRATIVE PRONOUN

Three degrees of relative distance: *aka – uka – khaya*.

INTERROGATIVE PRONOUN

khiti 'who?'; *kuna* 'what?' supported by -*s*(*a*), the interrogative marker: e.g. *Khiti**sa**jupa.xa?* 'Who is he?'

RELATIVE PRONOUN

The interrogative *khiti* may be used with -*ti* added to the subject, and -*k*- inserted in the verb: e.g. *khiti warmi.mpi.**ti** jupa.x sarnaḳ**ke***...'the woman with whom he went...'; or the relative clause may be rephrased as two principal clauses: e.g. *Jaqi.x jut.**k**.i uka.x jach'awa* 'The man who has come is big' (*jutaña* 'to come').

Numerals

1–10: *maya, paya, kimsa, pusi, phisqa, suxta, paqallqu, kimsaqallqu, llātunka, tunka*; 11 *tunkamayani*; 12 *tunkapayani*; 20 *pātunka*; 30 *kimsatunka*; 100 *pataka*.

Verb

All infinitives end in -*ña*: e.g. *saraña* 'to go', *munaña* 'to want'. Moods: indicative, imperative, subjunctive, optative, dubitative. Tenses: present, progressive, future, preterite, pluperfect, conditional. Verbs are conjugated for number and person; there are inclusive and exclusive forms of first person plural.

TENSES

Present tense of *saraña* 'to go':

	Singular		*Plural*
1	sarta	*incl.*	sarapxta
		excl.	sarapxtan
2	sarta		sarapxta
3	sari		sarapxi

Note: -*px*- is the plural infix for all tenses.

Progressive: the infix is -*sk*- in present tense: e.g. *Markar sara**sk**iwa* 'He's going to the village.'

Future: *sarā, sarāta, sarani*; pl. *sarapxā*, etc.

Preterite: infix is -*yā*-: e.g. *sara**yāt**(w)a* 'I went', *sara.pxa.**yā**.ta(n)* 'we went'

Pluperfect: infix is -*tā*-: e.g. *sara.pxa.**tā**.ta* 'we had gone'.

Conditional: -*tixa* (sbj. marker) + -*xa* (verbal marker): e.g. *Juma**tix**(**a**) munta**xa**, naya.x jutā**wa*** 'If you like, I'll come.'

NEGATION

The negative circumfix is *janiw/jan ... ti*. In the verb, this is supported by the negative infix -*k*-. Thus, in the present: *jan sarkti* 'I don't go', in the plural -

px- → **pk**: *jan(iw) sarapkti* 'we don't go'. Future: *jan sarkāti* 'I shan't go'; l. *janiw sarapkāti.*

IMPERATIVE

Abrupt in *-m*: *saram!* 'go!'; pl. *sarapxam*. Negative: *jan saramti!* 'don't go!'

SUBJUNCTIVE

Infinitive + personal marker + *-taki* for terminative, *-layku* for causative: e.g. *manq'aña.**xa.taki*** 'so that I may eat'; *manq'a.**pxa**.ña.**sa.taki*** 'so that we may eat' (note pl. *-px-* infix in inifinitive).

PRONOMINAL FORMS

Specific conjugations provide forms coded for subject, indirect object, and tense. Thus, for *churaña* 'to give':

present tense:	*chursma*	'I give to you' → 'I have given to you'
	churista	'you give to me'
	churitu	'he gives to me'
future tense:	*churāma*	'I shall give to you'
	churitāta	'you will give to me'
	churitani	'he will give to me'

Similarly for other tenses. The plural forms are ambiguous; thus, *churapxāma* may mean 'I shall give... to you (pl.)' or 'we shall give... to you (sing.)'.

Examples:

naya**x** qullq chur**sma** 'I have given you money'
naya**x** qullq chur**āma** 'I shall give you money'
naya**x** qulq chur**ayāsma** 'I gave you money'

PARTICIPLES

The past participle in *-ta* can be used adjectivally: e.g. from *usuña* 'to be/fall ill': ***usuta** warmi.pa.taki* 'for his sick wife'. This form may also be used as a verbal noun: e.g. *juta**ta**.pa.kama* 'until his arrival' ('until he is having-come').

Present participle: *-sa-* is the marker if both principal and subordinate clauses have the same subject, *-ipan(a)-* otherwise: *Mark sarasaw jupar uñjta* 'I saw him (when I was) going to the market'; *Pīrun mark sar**ipan**xa sarayātanwa* 'When Pedro went to the market, we went away'; *Naya mark sar**ipan**xa jumax parlta* 'While I was going to market, you were speaking.'

Where the action in the subordinate clause is the object of the principal verb, *-iri-* is used: e.g. *Pirur mark sar**ir**/sar**kir**t uñjtan* 'We saw Pedro going to the market' (i.e. 'Pedro was going...').

Examples of other affixes:

benefactive, *-rapi-*: Yapuxa irnaqa**rapi**ta 'He works my farm for me';
causative, *-ya-*: Chachaxar manq'a**ya**twa 'I feed (make to eat) my husband' (*-r(u)* marks indirect object).

The order in which affixes are attached to stems is fixed. The main inflectional items occur in the following order: possessive marker – case endings – locative markers – *r*(*u*) of direction – interrogative marker.

Word order

SOV

1 KALLTANJJA Arünwa, Arusti Diosampïnwa, Arusti Diosänwa.
2 Kalltanjja ucajj Diosampïnwa.
3 Take cunanacawa jupan lurata; jan jupampisti janiu cuna luratasa luratäquiti.
4 Jacañajj jupancänwa, jacañasti jakenacan khanapänwa.
5 Khanasti ch'amacanac taypinjja khaniwa; ch'amacanacasti janiu ucjja catokapquiti.

Juanan Khanañchäwipa

6 Diosan qhitanita mä jakewa utjäna, ucasti Juan sutinïnwa.
7 Ucawa khanañchañataqui juti, khanata khanañchañataqui, takeni jupa toke iyausapjjañapataqui.
8 Janiu jupajj khanäcänti, ucatsipana khanata khanañchiriu juti.

AZERBAIJANI

INTRODUCTION

Generally treated as a member of the Oguz-Seljuk group of Turkic, a group which also includes Osmanli Turkish and Turkmen. It is spoken by about 4 million in Azerbaijan, where it is joint official language (with Russian). In addition, Azerbaijani is spoken by at least 3½ million people in north-western Iran, and by smaller communities in Georgia, Armenia, and Dagestan. There are four main dialect divisions.

The earliest writer in Azerbaijani Turkish is also its greatest master – Füzuli (fl. early sixteenth century), the author of the mystical epic *Leylâ ve Mecnûn* and the *Šikâyetnâme.* Modern Azerbaijani literature is probably, in terms of quality and quantity, second only to Uzbek among the smaller Turkic languages. Newspapers and periodicals have been appearing since the mid-nineteenth century.

SCRIPT

Initially Arabic. As far back as in the middle of the nineteenth century Akhundzadä proposed the introduction of the Roman alphabet, but this reform had to wait until the general period of experimental romanization in the 1920s–30s. The Cyrillic script was introduced in 1939 and variously amended over the following 20 years: e.g. я and ю were discarded in 1958 and replaced by *ja*, *jy.* The alphabet includes the following non-Cyrillic letters: ә, θ, ү, ҝ, ҹ, һ.

PHONOLOGY

Consonants

stops: p, b, t, d, k, g; palatalized: g′
affricates: tʃ, dʒ
fricatives: f, v, s, z, ʃ, ʒ, j, x, γ, h
nasals: m, n
lateral and flap: l, r

Vowels

There are nine vowels:

high: i, ı
mid: e/ɛ, œ, y, u, o

low: ə = [ɛ], a

/œ/ is notated as *ö*; /ɛ/ is notated as *ä*.

VOWEL HARMONY

See **Turkic Languages**. The assimilation processes are normal in Azerbaijani, but note that /e, œ, o/ cannot appear in certain, indeed most, affixes: that is, rounding (labial harmony) is progressively cancelled. Certain very important affixes have only a two-way choice between *-a-* and *-ä-*: e.g. ***bilmäk*** 'to know'; ***görmäk*** 'to see'; ***bašlamak*** 'to start'.

MORPHOLOGY AND SYNTAX

(For a general conspectus of Turkic morphology, *see* **Turkic Languages**.)

Noun

In Azerbaijani the case endings are:

genitive: *-ın*^{4}, *-nın*^{4} (i.e. four allomorphs: *ın*, *in*, *un*, *ün*)
dative: *-(j)a*^{2}
accusative: *-(n)ı*^{4} (contrast with Bashkir: *-nı*^{16})
locative: *-da*^{2}
ablative: *-dan*^{2}

The plural marker is *lar*/*lär*, the latter used with high and mid vowel-stems: e.g. *ev* 'house', pl. *evlär*.

The predicative and possessive suffixes:

	Predicative		*Possessive*	
	Singular	*Plural*	*Singular*	*Plural*
1	-(j)am^2	-(j)ıg^4	-m, -ım^4	-(ı)mız^4
2	-san^2	-sınız^4	-n, -ın^4	-(ı)nız^4
3	-dır^4	-(dır)lar^2	-ı, -sı^4	-ı, -sı^4

Adjective

Follows general Turkic model.

Pronoun

PERSONAL INDEPENDENT

Sing. 1 *män*, 2 *sän*, 3 *o*; pl. 1 *biz*, 2 *siz*, 3 *onlar*. These are declined in all cases: e.g. for *män*: *mänim*, *mänä*, *mäni*, *mändä*, *mändän*.

DEMONSTRATIVE PRONOUN

bu 'this'; *o* 'that'

INTERROGATIVE PRONOUN

kim 'who?'; *nä* 'what?'

Numerals

1–10: *bir, iki, üč, dörd, beš, altı, yeddi, säkkiz, dogguz, on*; 20 *iyirmi*; 30 *otuz*; 40 *gırx*; 100 *yüz*.

Verb

The verb in Azerbaijani has voice, mood, tense, and non-finite forms. Voice and mood markers are standard: passive *-ıl*^{4}, reciprocal *-š*, reflexive *-n/l*, conditional: *sa*^{2}, etc.

TENSE SYSTEM

The indicative mood has simple and composite tense forms: these latter for past tense only.

present: *-ır*^{4}: ***alıram*** 'I take'; 2 *alırsan*, 3 *alır*; pl. *alırız*, *-sınız*, *-lar*
definite future: *-adžag*^{2}: e.g. *aladžaγam* 'I shall take'
definite past: *-dı*^{4}: e.g *aldım* 'I took'
perfect: two forms:

(a) *-mıš*^{4}: e.g. *almıšam* 'I've taken';
(b) *-(dž)ıb*^{4}+predicative affix: e.g. *o alıb.dır* 'he has taken'. No first person.

Composite tenses are formed with the auxiliary *i-* (defective): e.g. *alır idim* → *alırdım* 'I took'.

A continuous tense is made with the formant *-magda*^{2}*-* + predicative affix: e.g. *almagdayam* 'I am taking'; composite past continuous: *almagda idim* → *almagdajdım* 'I was taking'.

NEGATION

The standard Turkic negating infix *-m*(V)- follows the stem: e.g. *aldım* 'I took', *al**ma**dım*; *aladžaγam* 'I shall take', *al**ma**jadžaγam*.

PARTICIPLES

Present in *-an*^{2}, -(*j*)ır^{12}; past in *-mıš*^{4}.

Verbal nouns: there are two: *-dıg*^{4}, relating to present and past, and *-adžag*^{2}, future. They are neutral as to voice, expressing both active and passive: e.g.

mänim (i.e. gen. case) oxuduγu**m** kitab
'the book which I am/was reading'

atamın yazdıγı mäktub
'the letter which my father is writing/wrote'

onun yazadžaγı mäktub
'the letter which he is going to write'

The gerund in *-(j)ıb*^{4} is used where two finite verbs denote concomitant or consecutive actions: e.g. *g'äl**ib** söjlädi* 'he came and said' (lit. 'coming, he said'). There are several more gerundial endings denoting specific relationships between actions: e.g. *-arag*², *-anda*².

RELATIVE CLAUSES

The examples given above in illustration of the *-dıg* form also show the normal transfer of an Indo-European right-branching clause to participial form preceding the headword. Exposure to Iranian influence, however, has led to the use in Azerbaijani of a relative construction with *ki* + right-hand branching: e.g. *Adam var ki, hejvan ondan jaxšıdır*, lit. 'There are people who – animals are better than they.'

Postpositions

Follow several cases: e.g.

following dative: *g′örä* 'according to', e.g. *onun dedijine g′örä* 'according to what he said';
following ablative: *sonra* 'after', e.g. *därsdän sonra* 'after the lesson';
following nominative/genitive: *kimi* 'like, as', e.g. *guš kimi učur* 'flies like a bird'.

Word order

As in Turkic generally.

١ ٢ ابتداده کلمه وار ایدی وکلمه اللّهن یاننده ایدی وکلمه الله ایدی ☆ بو ابتداده اللّهن
٣ یاننده ایدی☆ هر زاد اونن واسطه‌لغی اینن موجود اولدی و هیچ بر موجود اولمش
٤ زاد اونسز وجوده کلمدی☆ اونده حیات وار ایدی و او حیات آدملرن نوری ایدی☆
٥ ٦ و نور ظلمتده اشیغ ویرر ایدی امّا ظلمت اونی درك ایلمر ایدی☆ اللّه طرفندن کوندرلمش
٧ بر آدم وار ایدی آدی یحیی☆ بو شهادت ایچون کلدیکه نورن خصوصنده شهادت
٨ ویرسون تا که هامی اونن واسطه‌لغی اینن ایمان کتورسونلر☆ اوزی او نور دکل ایدی
٩ آنجق کلدی که او نورن خصوصنده شهادت ویرسون☆

AZTEC-TANOAN LANGUAGES

This grouping formed one of Edward Sapir's (1929) six superstocks of North American Indian Languages. It included Zuni. The Aztec-Tanoan phylum, included in the 1965 classification of Voegelin and Voegelin, is very much the same as Sapir's, with the exclusion, however, of Zuni. The grouping falls into two parts: Uto-Aztecan, including Nahuatl, Hopi, Piman (Sonoran), and Shoshonean (with Comanche and Paiute); and Tanoan-Kiowa. It is possible that Keresan is also an Uto-Aztecan language; in the 1965 classification it is treated as an isolate.

The most important Aztec-Tanoan language in terms of numbers is Nahuatl with about a million speakers in Mexico. Classical Nahuatl was the language of the Aztec Empire, overthrown by Cortés. Two other member languages in Mexico, Tarahumar and Papago (Pima) have, respectively, 50,000 and 20,000 speakers.

The Shoshonean languages are spoken in the southern United States. *See* **Nahuatl**, **Hopi**, **Zuni**.

BAHNARIC LANGUAGES

INTRODUCTION

The Bahnaric languages form a branch of Mon-Khmer, spoken by about 750,000 people in Southern Vietnam. There are three main divisions: northern, including Bahnar itself; western, about half-a-dozen small languages; southern, including Stieng and Chrau. In all, about 20 or 22 languages.

All are unwritten, apart from translations of some parts of the Bible.

This article ends with a short description of Chrau, based on Thomas (1971).

PHONOLOGY

Consonants

A typical Bahnaric consonantal inventory includes:

p, ɓ, b/v, m, w
t, ɗ, d, n, l, r, s
ts, dz, ɲ, j
k, g, ŋ
ʔ, h

/ɓ/ and /ɗ/ are implosive, e.g. in Chrau, and may show Vietnamese influence. Bahnar has aspirated consonants: /ph, th, kh/ and such initial clusters as /ml, mr, hn, br/: e.g. Bahnar *bri* 'forest', *kram* 'bamboo', *klik* 'deaf', *klan* 'python'.

Vowels

The vowel system is relatively simple in comparison with certain other branches of Mon-Khmer. The short vowels in Bahnar are /i, e, ɛ, a, œ, ə, o, ɔ, u/. In Chrau, long vowels tend towards diphthongization.

Some northern Bahnaric languages have a rudimentary tone system.

MORPHOLOGY AND SYNTAX

The typical Bahnar root is CVC, often with a prefix: $C_1VC_2VC_3$ where C_2 may be a cluster, and C_1V- is usually a reduced syllable (Cə): e.g. *klik* 'deaf': *pəklik* 'to deafen'.

Noun

As there is no inflection of any kind, word order is crucial, and certain markers are used, e.g. in Bahnar *kœ* for dative: e.g. *an kœ iɲ* 'give (to) me'.

POSSESSION

X's Y is YX: e.g. *hnam bahnar* 'the Bahnar's house'.

NUMBER

Singularity and plurality inhere in the word; number can be made more precise by the use of numerical classifiers, e.g. *nu* for human beings: Bahnar *kədrang bar nu* 'two men' (lit. 'man – two – classifier'). Similarly, *to* is used for animals and objects in the plural, *pōm* for an animal or object in the singular: e.g. *min pōm hnam* 'one house'; *peng to hnam* 'three houses'.

Order fluctuates in both Chrau and Bahnar: numeral – classifier – noun *or* noun – numeral – classifier.

Adjective

Follows noun attributively: Chrau *ca măq* 'big fish', Bahnar *ka tih*.

Pronoun

Chrau has a gender distinction in the second person singular: masc. *mai*, fem. *ay*. Both Bahnar and Chrau have inclusive and exclusive forms in first person plural. Bahnar has a dual series: *ba* 'we two'; *bre* for animals: *bre rœmo* 'the two bullocks'.

Numerals

The Chrau series 1–10 is: *muôi, var, pe, puôn, prăm, prau, pŏh, pham, su'n, mât*; 20 *var jât*; 100 *rayeng*.

Verb

The stem is invariable. Markers are used for tense/mood distinctions; in Bahnar:

present: Ø
imperfect: *kəmlung* (cf. Thai *gamlang*)
past: *ji, klaih*, etc.; these precede the stem
future: *gô*, e.g. *iɲ gô an kœ e* 'I shall give it to you' (*iɲ* = Chrau *ănh* /aɲ/ 'I'; *an* 'to give'; *e* 'you')

Bahnar has a participial form with the preposition *pang* 'with, by': e.g. *pang bœ ma dap hoan* 'by working with all one's strength' (*dap* 'all'; *bœ* 'to work manually').

NEGATIVE MARKER

uh (*kœ*)

Word formation

In Bahnar, roots with simple initial consonant make a derived form by infixing *-œ-*; usually noun from verb, but other forms of derivative occur: e.g. *dol* 'to support': ***dœ**nol* 'pillar'; *kœl* 'head': *k**œn**œl* 'pillow'. Roots with initial cluster have *-œd-* infix: e.g. *krol* 'to roll down': *k**œd**rol* 'cascade'.

Prefixes: *pœ-* (← *pœm* 'to do, make') forms causatives: e.g. *et* 'to drink': ***pœ**et* 'to give to drink'; *dek* 'quick': ***pœ**dek* 'to hasten'. *Tœ-* forms reciprocals: e.g. *go* 'to wait': ***tœ**go* 'to await each other'; *kœ-* is a passive formant: e.g. *dap* 'to cover': ***kœ**dap* 'to be covered'.

Word order

SVO

CHRAU

Intonation

Thomas (1971) describes the basic Chrau intonation pattern as a 'level mid-tone over the sentence, with a rise or rise-fall on the last syllable'. Pitch is largely associated with grammatical class; interrogatives like *lŭh* 'why?', *ví* 'where?', *camvú* 'who?' having the highest pitch. Negatives and intensifiers also have high pitch. Final particles have low pitch.

PHONOLOGY

Vowels

Chrau has ten long vowels (counting *ia/u'a* as one vowel) and six short (again counting *i/u'* as one). Thomas makes the important point that the long vowels are not simply protracted versions of their short correlatives: they are phonetically different (cf. Vietnamese).

MORPHOLOGY AND SYNTAX

Noun

Root monosyllables, e.g. *chho'* 'tree', *ca* 'fish', or composite: generic + specific: *chho' rapaq* 'guava'; Chinese-type compounds $\int_{B}^{A} \geqq C$, AB = C are also found: *trôq ntěh* 'sky-earth', i.e. 'the world, universe'.

CLASSIFIERS

Three or four dozen classifiers are available, most of them used with small, closed classes of object; almost all can be replaced by the all-purpose *lâm* (cf. Chinese *ge*). The order is: numeral – classifier – noun: *var lâm khananh* 'two item person' > 'us'.

In enumeration involving classifiers, *du* is used for 1 (otherwise *muôi*): *du vum alăc* 'a mouthful of wine'.

Pronoun

PERSONAL PRONOUN

	Singular	*Plural*
1	ănh	vo′n (*incl.*), kha.nanh (*excl.*)
2	mai (*masc.*), ay (*fem.*)	
3	něh	

Kinship terms are used as pronouns in address: *co* 'grandfather' is a term of respect to older males; *pi* 'in-law' is an informal address among men.

DEMONSTRATIVE PRONOUN/ADJECTIVES

heq 'this', *nŏq* 'that', *to′q* 'that' (distal): *iĕr ănh* 'my chicken', *iĕr ănh heq* 'this chicken of mine'.

INTERROGATIVE PRONOUN

camvú 'who?', *păch n′hya* 'what?': *păch n′hya mai ôp?* 'what are you (masc.) doing?'

Numerals

The cardinal numbers are: 1–10: *muôi, var, pe, puôn, prăm, prau, pŏh, pham, su′n, mât*; 11 *mât muôi*; 20 *var jât*; 100 *rayĕng*.

Verb

Thomas (1971) distinguishes preverbal particles, auxiliary verbs, and intentional verbs as components, in that order, of the maximum verbal phrase.

Preverbal particles include several negatives: *có, êq, sáy*, etc., *phai* 'must', *lĕq* 'completely', *co′nh* 'almost': *ănh êq sây nĕh* 'I didn't see him'.

The auxiliary verbs include *saq*, which marks inceptive or progressive action, and *gŭq*, marking inaction, absence of change:

ănh saq păh chho′ 'I set about chopping trees'
ănh gŭq lĩnh 'I'm stuck in the army'
nĕh gŭq nhai 'he just went on talking'

Intentional verbs: *co′nh* 'want to' and *lĕq* 'complete action' reappear here (see preverbal particles above). In their role as verbs of intent, however, these lexemes can be negated: *ănh êq gĕh co′nh saq* 'I really don't want to go'.

Main verbs comprise transitives, intransitives, and verbs of state, colour, condition: *sa* 'eat', *saq* 'go', *măq* '(be) big'.

Composite verbs on the Chinese model (Chinese *huílái* 'return', *líkāi* 'leave', *wàngjì* 'forget') are common.

A causative is made with prefix *ta-*: *chu′t* 'die', *ta.chu′t* 'kill'. Reduplication is often used for onomatopoetic effect. The second member may be modified to give a partial echo: *chwŏc rawŏc* 'smashed to bits'.

A remarkable feature of Chrau syntax is a fondness for starting a new sentence with a partial resumption of the preceding sentence. (See Thomas 1971: 169).

Word order

The basic word order is SVO.

BƠR PÔH TRONG. **1 - Dơng tơm, tơnŏk dei I. Kon, mă I. Kon duh oei atŭm păng B.I.. mă I. Kon duh adoi B.I.. 2 - Kơna dơng tơm xơ̆ Di xang oei atŭm lơm B.I.. 3 - Tôm tơdrong ling dơng Di xang pơjing; uh dei kikiơ xang dei, mă bĭ dơng Di pơjing. 4 - Lơm Di dei tơdrong erih, tơdrong erih ji Ang chră kơ kon bơngai. 5 - Ang pơrang lơm măng-mu, chŏng bơngai lơm măng-mu uh gơnăl kơ ang. 6 - Dei minh nu mă B.I. xang phai, măt di ji Joang. 7 - Di truh oă pơtil, ji pơtil gah ang, oă kơ tôm bôl gơh lui, gơnơm kơ di bơtho. 8 - Kơxĭ kơ di ji ang. chŏng ji oă pơtil kơ de gah ang mơnoh dik.**

(Bahnar)

BALINESE

INTRODUCTION

A member of the Malayo-Polynesian branch of Austronesian, Balinese is spoken by 3 to 4 million people in the island of Bali and some smaller adjacent islands. It has three sociolinguistic registers:

1. Basa *ketah* (K): everyday Balinese for family and friendly use.
2. Basa *madia* (M): basically *ketah* with an injection of more formal words for use in situations where low *ketah* would be unacceptable.
3. Basa *singgih* (S): corresponds to Javanese *kråmå*; a somewhat artificial construct containing many Sanskrit and Javanese words.

Many *ketah* words have no *singgih* equivalents, and have to be promoted to *singgih* status when the latter is being used. For many key concepts, however, each register has its own word: cf.

	Ketah	*Madia*	*Singgih*
'eat'	naar	neda	ngadjengang
'dead'	mati	padem	séda
'live'	idup	urip	njeneng

According to Kersten (1948), stricter attention is paid to correct social register in the Balinese spoken on Lombok.

SCRIPT

Originally Javanese. A standard romanization, based on Dutch spelling, was provided by H.J. Schwartz in Batavia in the early twentieth century.

PHONOLOGY

In the main, as in Malay. Final /k/ is not entirely glottalized. The vowel *a* in such prefixes as *pa-*, *ka-*, *ma-* is /ə/; final *a* tends to /œ/. Final *h* tends to /ç/ or /x/.

Stress

Tends to be on the penultimate syllable.

MORPHOLOGY AND SYNTAX

The definite article is affixed -(*n*)*é*: e.g. *batuné* 'the stone'; *guruné* 'the teacher'. Before proper nouns the article *i* is used.

The great majority of Balinese stems are disyllabic. Nasalization of a monosyllabic base requires an initial bearer syllable: cf. *djoh* 'far' whose transitive derivative verb is *nge.djoh.ang* (not **njohang*).

NOMINAL FORMS

Simple and derived; the latter are made with such prefixes as the following:

(a) *pa-*: forms verbal nouns, e.g. *rérén* 'to stop': *pa.rérén* 'the stopping'; *pa-* + ... *-an*: *pa.réré.an* 'the stopping place'; denotes agent or instrument: *peseng* 'to press, squeeze': *pa.peseng.an* 'press'; or locus: *saré* 'to lie': *pa.saré.an* 'bed'; often as modifier preceded by negator *tan*: *tan pa.tulung.an* 'helpless'.
(b) *para-/pra-*: forms collectives, e.g. *parawanita* 'women'.
(c) *ka ... an*: forms abstract concepts, e.g. *ka.djegég.an* 'beauty'.

Adjective

Invariable; as attribute, adjective follows noun: e.g. *anaké odah ento* 'the old man' (*odah* 'old'). A comparative/superlative form is made by means of *-an*: *kelih.an* 'older'; *gedé.n.an* 'bigger'; *wénten.an* 'is better'.

Pronoun

Number is not distinguished.

First person (excl.): S form is *titiang*; M form, *tiang*; K form, *itjang*.

Second person: K forms are *tjai* (masc.) and *njai* (fem.). For polite address, e.g. to strangers, *djero* can be used, at least until the caste situation has been clarified. The Malay form *tuan* is replacing the old Balinese forms. In very elevated S speech, *tjokor i ratu*/*tjokor i déwa* may be used, the latter to a prince.

Third person: the caste forms were *dané* for a vaiśya, *ida* for a satria or brahman, and these forms are still in use where such distinctions are called for. Omnibus forms are S *ipun* and K *ia*.

There is a general tendency to use the polite third person form when speaking of first or second person.

anak is widely used as a general personal pronoun.

POSSESSION

Possessed – possessor: in first and second person the personal pronoun is used: e.g. *umah tiang(é)* 'my house'. Third person: the K form is *né*, e.g. *limanné* 'his hand', *abian iané* 'his field' (the gemination in the first example is necessary to distinguish the form from noun + definite article, *limané* 'the hand'). S and M form: *-ipun*, e.g. *somahipun* = *rabinida* 'his wife' (*ida* is S 3rd p. pron.)

DEMONSTRATIVE PRONOUN

S *puniki* = K *ené* 'this'; S *punika* = K *ento* 'that'.

INTERROGATIVE PRONOUN

S *sira* = K *njén* 'who?'; S *punapi* = K *apa* 'what?'

RELATIVE PRONOUN

S *sané* = K *ané*; or *sang*/*kang*: e.g.

anaké ané **n**ulungin tjai 'the man who helped you'
anaké ané **t**ulungin tjai 'the man who was helped by you'
mémé bapa sang sampun nguripin titiang 'my parents who gave me life'
(*nguripin* 'life')

Numerals

1–10: *sa*, *dua*/*kalih*, *telu*/*tiga*, *empat*, *lima*, *enem*, *pitu*, *akutus*, *asia*, *adasa*. These have positional variants: (a) reduplicated; (b) with *-ng*: e.g. *dua* – *dadua* – *duang*. The reduplicated form is used where the numeral is treated as a nominal; the *-ng* form where the numeral immediately precedes a noun.

Verb

Stems are neutral, and become transitive or intransitive by morphophonemic change. Nearly all intransitive verbs in Balinese have a non-nasal initial: e.g. *lunga* 'to go', *urip* 'to live'. Transitive verbs may focus either on subject or on object: if on subject, the initial is a nasal: e.g. *batuné ané mara gebeg* 'the stone was polished'; *tiang né* ***ng****ebeg batuné* 'I polished the stone'.

Stems may be made transitive by affixation of *-ang*: e.g. *takén* 'to ask', *takén****ang*** 'to ask someone for something'. Also, transitive verbs can be intensified by addition of *-ang*: e.g. *mireng* 'to hear', *mireng****ang*** 'to pay attention to'; *ngelah* 'to own', *ngelah****ang*** 'to exercise rights of ownership'; or made causative: e.g. *uning* 'to know', *uning****ang*** 'to bring something to someone's knowledge'. Note nominal particularization of root: *adjeng* 'eat': *adjeng.an* 'eatables' → 'rice'; *djukut* 'greens': *djukut.an* 'weeds'.

-ang also makes verbs from adjectives and nouns: *utama* 'excellent', *utama****ang*** 'to regard something as excellent'; *soré* 'afternoon', ***njoréang*** 'to do something in the afternoon'; *sugih* 'rich', ***njugihang*** 'to get richer'.

The Balinese verb appears in four forms (plus or minus affixation): (1) the simple (weak) form; (2) the strong (nasalized) form; (3) the *ka-* form; (4) the *ma-* form.

1. The simple form: the agent follows the verb: e.g.

   Buku punika tumbas tiang di pidan adji limang rupiah
   'I bought the book formerly for 5 guilders.'

2. Some examples of the nasalized form have been given above.
3. The *ka-* form focuses on verbal action; normally + *-ang*/*-in* affix, though this is not used for first or second person: e.g. ***ka****tulung****in*** *baan bapanné* 'helped by his father'; ***Ø****tulung****in*** *itjang*/*tjai* 'helped by me/you'.
4. The *ma-* form: if the base is intransitive, so is the *ma-* form; if the base is

transitive, the *ma-* form is usually intransitive → passive, e.g. *padiné jén suba **ma**tebuk*... 'once the rice has been pounded...'; *padi ané **ma**tebuk* 'the pounded rice'.

The verbal modifiers *adjak*, *selag*, *anggon*, meaning 'with the help of', 'using', 'accompanied by', are used in their base form when the referent is definite; when the referent is a collective or an indefinite number they are nasalized: cf.

lantas ia luas maboros adjak.a tjitjingné ané selem ento
'so he went hunting with his black dog'; but:

lantas ia luas maboros ngadjak tjitjing
'so he went hunting with dogs'

nunun kamben nganggon mesin
'when weaving one uses the machine'

dugas njait kambené ento anggon tiang mesin pisagané kali.kangina
'when sewing the garment, I used a machine belonging to my neighbours on the east'

petengé ia mabalih njamanné selaga
'in the evening he sat watching among his little brothers'

petengé ia mabalih njelag anak tua
'... among older people'

The adverb *lantas* 'so', 'consequently' introduces a principal clause Y following a subordinate clause X: X *lantas* Y. It is interesting that *lantas* is often nasalized in this position, which gives it a verbal character: *mapamité uli di.Gagelang ngalantas Ida ka Singasari*: 'Taking leave of Gagelang, he thereupon-went to Singasari.'

NEGATION

K. *tusing*, *tura*, *tera*; M. *nenten*, *ten*; S. *tan* (*wénten*)

tiang tusing kema, kerana tusing ka.undang
'I didn't go because I didn't have to'

titiang tan wénten purun nakénang penjungkanidané
'I did not ask what his illness was'

In K. *tidong* = Malay *bukan*, S. form *boja*: *boja.dja ipun sané*... 'it was not he, who...'.

Word order

Depends on verbal construction: SVO, VSO, OVS are possible.

1 Sadurung jagate puniki kaadakang antuk Ida Sang Hyang Widi Wasa, Sang Sabda sampun wenten. Sang Sabda punika sinarengan ring Ida Sang Hyang Widi Wasa, tur Sang Sabda punika taler maraga Widi. 2 Saking pangawit Sang Sabda punika sinarengan ring Ida Sang Hyang Widi Wasa. 3 Malantaran Sang Sabda punika Ida Sang Hyang Widi Wasa ngadakang saluiring sane wenten. Tur tan wenten sane kaadakang sane tan malantaran Sang Sabda. 4 Sang Sabda punika maraga wit urip, tur uripe punika dados galang manusane. 5 Galange punika macahya ring tengah petenge, tur petenge punika tan mrasidayang ngaonang galange punika.

6 Ida Sang Hyang Widi Wasa sampun ngutus utusan Idane, sane mapesengan Yohanes. 7 Dane rauh jaga midartayang pariindik galange punika ring i manusa, mangda manusane sami miragiang tur percaya. 8 Boya ja dane Yohanes ngaraga galange punika, nanging rauh danene buat midartayang indik galange punika.

BALTIC LANGUAGES

This branch of Indo-European is of special interest in comparative linguistics because of its retention of certain very archaic features, both phonological and morphological. Baltic is genetically close to, and seems to have been always geographically contiguous with, Slavonic and Germanic. East and West forms of Baltic are distinguished. Of several East Baltic languages known to have existed, only two survive – Lithuanian and Latvian. Evidence for the extinct congeners is entirely toponymic; thus the name of the Curonians survives in Courland (Latvian: *kurzeme*). The sole attested West Baltic language – Old Prussian – survived into the seventeenth century.

The toponymic evidence shows that Baltic was formerly spoken over an area considerably exceeding its present limitations: south-eastwards across White Russia towards the Dniepr, and southwards into what is now Poland. This original habitat shrank as Baltic stock gave ground to Slavonic and Germanic. To a lesser extent, local Finno-Ugric languages have been absorbed or ousted by Baltic (*see* **Liv**, under **Balto-Finnic Minor Languages**).

The oldest written records in Baltic are Old Prussian texts of the fourteenth century. Records in Lithuanian and Latvian date from the sixteenth century.

Both Lithuanian and Lativan are tonal, exhibit archaic Indo-European features, and share an extensive common vocabulary. In spite of this homogeneity, however, they are usually treated as belonging to different areal groupings. Thus, on areal criteria, Gyula Décsy classifies Lithuanian along with Polish, Ukrainian, Belorussian, and Kashubian; Latvian with Estonian, Vot, and Liv.

The total number of people speaking Baltic languages is probably about 5 million (including émigré populations).

See **Lithuanian, Latvian, Balto-Finnic Minor Languages**.

BALTO-FINNIC MINOR LANGUAGES (Ingrian, Liv, Veps, Vot)

INGRIAN

Ingrian, also known as Izhor, is spoken by fewer than a thousand people, all of whom are bilingual (with Russian), in the Kingisepp and Lomonosov areas, immediately to the west of Leningrad. Genetically, Ingrian is close to Karelian, and has been influenced by Vot, Estonian, Finnish, and Russian. Some attempt to write Ingrian in the Roman alphabet was made in the 1930s. The language is now unwritten.

The vowel system is practically identical to the Karelian one. All vowels occur long or short; the difference is phonemic. Long *ō*, *ē*, *ȫ* in initial syllables are raised in speech above the register of short *o*, *e*, *ö*, and tend towards /ū, ī, ǖ/.

The consonant inventory is notable for the presence of half-voiced labial, dental, and velar stops, notated in pedagogical literature as *B*, *D*, *G*, *Z*. Both consonant gradation and vowel harmony are present: cf. *otta* 'to take', *oDan* 'I take'; *iskiä* 'to strike', *iZen* 'I strike', *jalGa* 'foot', *jalaD* 'feet'.

Nouns have the usual Balto-Finnic cases, with a nominative plural in -D: e.g. *katto* 'roof', gen. *kaDon*, part. *kattoa*, pl. nom. *kaDoD*. *Katto* is a single-base noun; an example of a two-base noun is the Germanic loanword *lammaz* 'sheep', gen. *lampähan*, pl. *lampāhaD*. Exceptionally for Finno-Ugric, the plural marker may be added to the possessive affix: e.g. *veneh.emme.D* 'our boats'.

The adjectival system has a comparative marker in *-mB*: *sūr* 'big', *sūremB*.

Compound tenses are made with *olla*, as in Finnish, etc., and the past participle is marked for number: e.g. *olen ommelD* 'I have sewn', *olemma ommellēD* 'we have sewn'.

Negation: sing. 1 *en*, 2 *eD*, 3 *ei*; pl. 1 *emmä*, 2 *että*, 3 *eväD*: *en kuo* 'I do not weave', past: *en kuttōnD*, where *kuttōnD* is the past participle.

Examples of Ingrian sentences (*JaNSSSR*, Vol. III):

mēheD pütäD kallā
'the men catch fish'

hä tekkö tōDä hüvast
'he docs-work well'

kolt kertä näin sūrD nälkä
'three times I saw great hunger'

meijen kolhoZi oli hüvä ribaz kolhoZi
'our kolkhoz was a good, rich kol'

mō̃ tahoimma sinne Lavvassārē pässä no mō̃ kuingkā sinne emmä pässēD
'we wanted to go there, to Lavvassaari, but however (we tried) we couldn't get there'

LIV

From a former position of dominance in Courland and Livonia (Livland), where they had been settled for about 2,000 years, the Livs are now reduced to a remnant of some 300 persons who live in fishing villages at the tip of the Courland peninsula. It is estimated that most of these people, who call themselves 'fisher folk' – *kalamiez* – still use the language in their homes; but Latvian is otherwise in general use.

Some portions of the New Testament were translated into Liv in the 1860s, and some revival of Liv writing and culture took place under the auspices of the Latvian Republic (up to 1939). Today, Liv is unwritten.

The half-voiced stops *B*, *D*, *G* are present, and palatalization is a major feature of Liv phonology. Consonant gradation has been lost, as have the vowels /œ, y/. The historical presence of *h*, now lost, is marked by a broken intonation or glottal stop: e.g. *rā'* 'money' (cf. Finnish *raha*); *lē'D* 'leaf, page' (cf. Finnish *lehti*). Consonantal clustering, unusual in Finno-Ugric languages, is tolerated in medial position.

The nominal declension includes a dative (in *-n*), unique in Balto-Finnic. The plural marker, nominative, is *-D*.

In the verbal system, the first and third person singular endings have coalesced: *ma luguB* 'I read', *ta luguB* 'he/she reads'; past: *ma lugiz* 'I read', *ta lugiz* 'he, she read'; *ma vol' lu'ggən* 'I had read', *ta vol' lu'ggən* 'he/she had read'. Similarly, *ma volks lu'ggən* 'I would have read'; *mi'nnən vol' lu'ggəməst* 'I had to read'; *ma lu'ggiji* '(it seems) I am reading'.

The negative conjugation is remarkable in that some forms are doubly marked.

Negative present:

	Singular	*Plural*
1	ma äb lu'G 'I don't read'	mēg ä**b** lu'gg**əm**
2	sa äd lu'G	tēg ä**d** lu'gg**ət**
3	ta äb lu'G	ne ä**b** lu'gg**ət**

Negative past:

	Singular	*Plural*
1	ma iz lu'G	mēg iz lu'gg**əm**
2	sa ist lu'G	tēg ist lu'gg**ət**
3	ta iz lu'G	ne iz lu'gg**ət**

(*Contrast* **Finnish** and **Estonian**.)

Certain verbs continue to take oblique cases, e.g. *ied* 'to become' with the translative: *iel kezizəks* 'he's getting angry'; *ulzə tūlda* 'to come forth from' with the elative: *suiš' tul metsast ulzə* 'the wolf came out of the forest'.

Also interesting is the presence of Liv roots with Latvian prefixes: e.g. Latv. *aiz-* + Liv *lä'də* 'to go': *aiz.lä'də* 'to go away' (= Latv. *aiziet*).

Example of a Liv sentence: *rāndališt jelabət säl, kus um vālda jeuG* 'the shore-dwellers (i.e. the Livs) live there, where is white sand'.

VEPS

Veps is spoken in the area to the south of the Karelian Republic, bounded by Lakes Ladoga and Onega and the Bjeloje Ozero. Estimates of numbers vary greatly. Crystal (1988) gives 6,000–7,000, Comrie (1981) 3,000. Décsy (1973) gives a figure of 15,000 from contemporary Soviet sources, of whom about 6,000 spoke Veps as mother tongue. It is only the Southern Veps who call themselves *beps(a)/veps(a)*. Elsewhere in Veps territory the term *t'ähin'e/ t'ägälain'e* 'I/we here' is used. The term *l'üd'in'ik/l'üd'il'ain'e* (from Russian *l'ud'i* 'people') is also used.

Veps is unwritten. There was an attempt to create a literary language in the 1930s.

As in Liv, palatalization is a major feature of the phonology: all consonants, except the semi-vowel /j/, have soft, i.e. palatalized, counterparts. Consonant gradation has been lost; and vowel harmony is observed only in the first two or three syllables of a word.

Eleven cases are distinguished in two numbers: cf. *k'irvez* 'axe', pl. *k'irvehed*; gen. sing. *k'irvhen*, gen. pl. *k'irvh'id'e(n)*. The case system can be extended by agglutinative affixes; e.g. *-nou*, indicating proximity, can be added to the genitive case ending; *laps'id'en.**nou*** 'along with the children (where they are)', *minunnou* 'near me'. Similarly *-pai* is added to the allative case: *jarvele.**pai*** 'in the direction of the lake' (cf. *-nost*: *jarven. nost* 'to the lake'.

As in Finnish, the negative marker is conjugated preceding the sense-verb in stem form marked for number: e.g. *joksen* 'I run', *en jokse* 'I don't run'; *joksemai* 'we run', *emai joks**koi*** 'we don't run'.

Veps has an inceptive mood, with the marker *-škand/ška-*:

k'ir'juta**škand**en 'I'll begin to write'
k'ir'juta**škanz'**in' 'I began to write'
en k'ir'juta**škande** 'I shan't begin to write'
en k'ir'juta**škannuiz** 'I would not have started to write'

The direct object following a transitive verb in Veps may be in the partitive or the accusative, with no difference in meaning. Cf. the following example from *JaNSSSR*, Vol. III:

m′in′ä kaikutcou p′äiv′än s′ön s′ent′, bolad, l′iib′äd, void′ (partitive)
m′in′ä kaikutcou p′äiv′än s′ön s′en′en, bolan, l′iib′än, voin′ (accusative)
'Every day I eat mushrooms, whortleberries, bread, butter.'

VOT

The ethnonym is *vad′d′alain*. Décsy (1973) describes the Vots as the original inhabitants of Ingermanland, historically the province between present-day Leningrad and the river Narva. Today, the language is virtually extinct, spoken by a few dozen people in the Kingisepp area. Vot has never been a written language.

As described by Adler in *JaNSSSR* (1966), Vot has standard vowel harmony and a very elaborate system of consonant gradation: according to Adler the most elaborate of any Finno-Ugric language. Such oppositions as /ttʃ–d′d′/ are found: e.g. *väittšiä* 'to call' – *väd′d′i!* 'call!' Consonant gradation extends even to the affix system.

The noun is declined in 14 cases. Plural marker is *-D* (nominative), i.e. the half-voiced plosive, as in Ingrian and Liv.

Present indicative of *tehä* 'to do':

singular: *tēn, tēD, tēB*; pl. *tēmmä, tēttä, tetševäD*
negative: *en, ed, ep tē*; *emmä, että, eivät tē*

Perfect: *elen tehnü*; negative: *en ele tehnü*.

Word order

SVO is frequent; if adverbial material introduces sentence, VSO is used.

1. Ȳrgandõksõs voļ Sõna ja Sõna voļ Jumal jūs ja Jumal voļ Sõna.

2. Ȳrgandõksõs ta voļ Jumal jūs.

3. Amad ažad āt leb täm tiedõt ja ilm tǟnda äb ūo mittõ midagist tiedõt, mis um tiedõt.

4. Täms voļ jelami ja jelami voļ rovz sieldõm.

5. Ja sieldõm pāistiz pimdõms ja pimdõm iz võta tǟnda rastõ.

6. Ykš rišting, nimtõt Jāņ, sai Jumalst kaimdõt.

7. Ta tuļ tapartõks pierast, ūndam tapartõkst yļ sieldõm, laz amad uskõgõd leb täm.

8. Ta iz ūo sieldõm, aga tämmõn voļ yļ sieldõm tapartõmõst.

(Liv)

BALUCHI (Beludzh)

INTRODUCTION

Baluchi belongs to the North-West Iranian group of languages. The ethnonym is *balūč* or *balūdž*. The original habitat of the Baluchi people seems to have been near the southern shores of the Caspian Sea, whence they migrated during the first millennium AD to their present habitat in south-east Iran and south-west Pakistan. East and west Baluchi are divided from each other by the Brahui enclave (*see* **Brahui**).

Between 2 and 4 million people speak Baluchi, of whom 1 million are in Pakistan, and well over half a million in Iran. There are about 200,000 speakers in Afghanistan, and smaller communities in India, the Arabian Peninsula, and the former Soviet Union.

The Baluchi people have a rich oral tradition in folk literature, the main feature being the *daptar* – heroic ballads in stereotyped format, recounting the origins of the Baluchi, their wars, and wanderings. The twentieth century has produced several notable writers in Baluchi; newspapers and periodicals in the language appear in Quetta and Karachi. The Baluchi in the former Soviet Union use Turkmen as their literary language.

SCRIPT

Arabo-Persian. Attempts made in the 1930s to provide a Roman script for the Baluchi in the USSR were abandoned.

PHONOLOGY

Consonants

stops: p, b, t, d, ʈ, ɖ, k, g
affricates: tʃ, dʒ
fricatives: s, z, ʃ, ʒ, x, γ, h
nasals: m, n, ŋ
lateral and flap: l, r
semi-vowels: j, w

The eastern dialects have additional series of labial, dental, retroflex, and velar aspirates, plus the fricatives /θ, ð, f/. Stops in western dialects are often represented by fricatives in eastern; thus western *dāta* 'given' = eastern *dāθa*; *lōg* 'house' = *lōγ*; *āp* 'water' = *āf*.

The outline given here refers essentially to western Baluchi.

Vowels

long: aː, iː, eː, uː, oː
short: a, i, u

Baluchi preserves the Middle Persian series; and this quantitative opposition between long and short vowels links Baluchi to Middle Persian in contradistinction to other present-day Iranian languages, whose vocalic structure turns on a qualitative difference between vowels. Long vowels in Baluchi tend to be articulated clearly with a certain amount of tension; short vowels are slacker and reduced.

Stress

Stress is usually on the final syllable, excluding affixes and indefinite marker.

MORPHOLOGY AND SYNTAX

Noun

Parts of speech fall under two headings: nominals and verbals. There is no grammatical gender. A plural marker in *-ān* is, in general, optional in nominative.

CASE SYSTEM

Typical endings are:

	Singular	*Plural*
nominative	Ø	(-ān)
genitive	-a	-ani
accusative	-ā, -ārā	-ān(r)ā
prepositional	-ā	-ān

The accusative case may also denote the indirect object: e.g. *mardumār* '(to) the man'. An enclitic *-ē*, which can take case endings, is used as an indefinite article: e.g. *mard* 'man'; *mardē* = *yak mard* 'a man'; genitive: *mardēa.*

Adjective

Adjectives do not change for number or case when used attributively but take the affix *-ēn*: e.g. *šarr**ēn** mard* 'good man'. Used predicatively, they take the ending -V*nt*[2]: e.g. *Ān mard šarr**ant*** 'These people are good.' When used as an independent nominal, the adjective is declined for number and case, and takes the indefinite marker.

COMPARISON

A comparative is made with *-tir* + *či*: e.g. X *či* Y *šarr**tir**.in* 'X is better than Y.'

Pronoun

PERSONAL INDEPENDENT

Sing. 1 *man*, 2 *ta*(*u*), 3 *ē*, *ēš*, *ā*; pl. 1 (*a*)*mā*, 2 *š*(*u*)*mā*, 3 *ē*, *ēšān*; *ā*, *āyān*. The declension of the personal pronouns is subject to much dialectal variation.

ENCLITIC FORMS

These are (sing. and pl.) 1 *-un*, 2 *-it*, 3 sing. *-ī/ē*, pl. *-iš*. These are used both as possessive markers and as direct-object markers. According to Frolova (1960), they also figure in the so-called ergative construction as subject markers.

DEMONSTRATIVE PRONOUN

ē 'this', *ā*(*n*) 'that'; pl. *ēšān*, *āyān*. Not declined when used attributively.

INTERROGATIVE PRONOUN

kai 'who?'; *či* 'what?'

Numerals

1–10: *yak*, *dō*, *say*, *čār*, *panč*, *šaš*, (*h*)*apt*, (*h*)*ašt*, *nō*, *dah*; 11 *yāzdah*; 12 *dwāzdah*; 20 *gīst*; 30 *sī*; 100 *sad/saθ*.

Verb

As in other Iranian languages, the Baluchi verbal system is constructed on two bases, the present and the past, each of which is used to generate a series of appropriate tenses. The past base is normally the present base plus -(*i*)*t*. There are several irregular formations, some suppletive:

regular: *guš* – *gušt* 'say';
irregular: *nind* – *ništ*;
suppletive: *gind* – *dīst* 'see'.

There are two voices, active and passive; and three moods: indicative, subjunctive, imperative. The passive is rare. The auxiliary verb *bayag* 'to be' is used. Imperative: second person only. The prefix is *b*(*i*)-. Subjunctive: this is represented by the aorist tense (prefix *b*(*i*)-) and the form expressing unreal conditions. *See* **Tense system**, below.

TENSE SYSTEM

Two prefixes are used, *ak/a*, with phonetic variants, and *b*(*i*)-: *ak-* is used in the present/future tense and the past continuous; *b*(*i*)- in aorist, imperative, and unreal conditional tense.

The personal endings:

	Singular	*Plural*
1	-ān, -ūn, etc.	-an, -in, -ēn
2	-ē, -ay	-it
3	-it, -t, -i	-ant, -en

The copula is (*h*)*ast-* + above endings for both present and past tense.

TENSES ON PRESENT BASE

Present/future: prefix *ak-* (or variant) + stem + ending. In certain phonetic conditions the *a* and *k* of the prefix are treated as separable, the *a* being attached to the preceding word, the *k* prefixed to the verb: e.g. *Laškar.**a*** ***k**.āyt* 'the army is coming'.

Aorist: the *b*(*i*)- prefix is attached to the present-future form; sandhi at juncture: b + surd → p, b + n → m, b + b → Ø: e.g. ***m**nīndit* 'so that you should sit down'; ***p**kanit* 'so that you should do'.

TENSES ON PAST BASE

The distinction formerly made here between transitive verbs with ergative construction and intransitive verbs with nominative construction appears to be unstable. Frolova (1960) gives the following examples: *bādšāh**ā*** (i.e. oblique case in *-ā*) *ā mard* (direct case) *kuštag* 'the emperor killed that man'; *bādšāh**ā** man**ārā*** (accusative) *kuštag* 'the emperor killed me'.

A peculiarity of Baluchi is the use of the 'ergative' construction with certain verbs which are semantically intransitive: e.g. *bādšāh**ā** kandıta* 'the emperor began to laugh'.

SPECIMEN TENSES

present-future: e.g. *guš**un**, guš**ay***, 'I/you (will) say'
simple past: e.g. *gušt.**un**, gušt.**ay***
perfect: past participle in *-a*(*g*) + shortened copula: e.g. *guštagun, guštagay, guštagØ*
aorist: e.g. ***b**gušun*, ***b**gušay*

UNREAL CONDITIONS

The suffix *-en-* is added to the past base followed by personal endings: e.g. (***b***)*gušt**ēnan***, (***b***)*gušt**ēne***, (***b***)*gušt**ēnØ*** 'I, you, he/she would have spoken'.

INFINITIVE

Is in *-ag*: e.g. *guštag* 'to speak'.

PARTICIPLES

A present-future participle in *-ī* suggests intention: e.g. *šutinī* 'intending/ having to go'.

NEGATION

The negating prefix is *na-* in the indicative mood, *ma-* in the subjunctive and the imperative. It is interesting that where *-a* and *k-* are separated as present-future tense markers, *-na-* is inserted between them. Frolova gives the example: *tayatt.**a.na.k**.ārit* '. . . can't stand it'.

RELATIVE CLAUSE

Relative clauses are made with connecting particle *ki*: e.g.

Ō manī pit, či mālā har bahar **ki** manīg bīt, manārā bidai
'Father, give me each (= that) part of the property which is to be mine.' (Grierson 1921)

Prepositions

For example, *pa*(*r*) 'on', 'for' *aš/šalač* 'about', 'from', etc.; *gō*(*n*) 'with'.

There are a few postpositions: e.g. *sarā* 'on'; *lāpā* 'in'; *padā* 'after', 'behind'. These are used along with prepositions: e.g. ***ša*** *mašmay* ***padā kāyt*** 'he comes behind us' (*mašmay* is an inclusive 1st p. pl. pron. characteristic of the former Soviet Union Baluchi).

Word order

SOV

1 Pesha awula nyama hawe KALAM ath, o hawe KALAM go HUḌHA
2 de gon ath, wa HUḌHA hawe KALA'M de astath. Hawesh awwula
nyáma go HUḌHA gon ath. Durust chie
eshi márifata bithaghant, wa azh eshiya siwa hech na bitha, an chie ki
4 bitha. Eshi nyama ZINDAGHI ath, wa an ZINDAGHI an NUR in-
5 sanegh ath. Wa an NUR maṉ thahára chimkaghe, wa thahárá anhi
6 sama na girt. Marde bitha Hudhá shashthatha eshi nám Yuhanna.
7 Hawan pha sháhidi aḳhtá ki NU'R phara shahidi khat, ki darnst mardán 'sh
8 eshiya iman khanant. Hamesh an NUR niyath, bale ki an NURA phara
shahidi khat.

BAMBARA

INTRODUCTION

This member of the Mande group of the Niger-Congo family is the main language of the Republic of Mali, where it is spoken by about 2 million people. The similarity between Bambara and its sister languages Malinke and Dyula is such that the three were grouped by Delafosse (1901, 1929–55) as one language which he called Mandingo.

SCRIPT

In the 1960s a standardized script was adopted; this uses the Roman alphabet plus *è* = /ɛ/ and *ò* = /ɔ/.

PHONOLOGY

Consonants

stops: p, b, t, d, k, g
affricates: tʃ, dʒ
nasals: m, n, ɲ, ŋ
fricatives: f, s, z, ʃ, h
lateral and flap: l, r
semi-vowels: j, w

Vowels

i, e, ɛ, a, ɔ, o, u

The contrast between /e/ and /ɛ/ is phonemic: cf. /kelel/ 'one'; /kɛlɛl/ 'war'. Nasalization is notated by vowel + nasal consonant: *dan* /dã/. The apostrophe is used to mark vowel elision.

TONE

High and low; the contrast is phonemic: cf. *sá* 'snake'; *sa* 'die, death'.

MORPHOLOGY AND SYNTAX

Noun

Natural gender can be indicated by affix: *kè* (male), *muso* (female): e.g. *den**kè*** 'son'; *den**muso*** 'daughter'. There is no inflection. A plural marker is *-u*/*-Cu*, where C is, for example, *r*: e.g. *mogo* 'man', *mogo**u*** 'men'; *den* 'child', *denu* = /dẽu/, 'children'; *bááràkèlá* 'worker', *bááràkèláu* 'workers'.

POSSESSION

X of Y = YX: e.g. *nègè sira* 'way of iron' = 'railway'; *Mali bááràkèláu* 'the workers of Mali'.

Adjective

As attribute, adjective follows noun, and appears in doublets: XØ and X*man*: e.g. *kòrò* = *kòròman* 'old'; *misira ba* 'the big mosque'; *tasuma ble* 'the red light'.

COMPARATIVE

X *ka...ni* Y *ye* 'X is...er than Y'.

Pronoun

	Singular	*Plural*
1	ne	an
2	i, e	au
3	a	u

When using these as possessives, a distinction is made between material and non-material possession (often inalienable): for the former *ka* is added: e.g. *n'teri* 'my friend'; *n'fa* 'my father'; *n'**ka** fali* 'my donkey'; *n'**ka** faliu* 'my donkeys'. But see also postpositions *fè*, *la*, *na*.

DEMONSTRATIVE PRONOUN/ADJECTIVE

nin 'this'; *o* 'that'. These may precede or follow the noun; if following, they take the plural marker: e.g. *nin watiri kurau* = *watiri kurau nin**u*** 'these new cars'.

RELATIVE PRONOUN

min, pl. *minu*: e.g. *dunan* ***min*** *na.na* 'the foreigner who came'.

Numerals

1–10: *kele(n)*, *fila*, *saba*, *naani*, *duuru*, *wòoro*, *wolonfla*, *segi*, *kònòntò*, *tan*; 20 *mugan*; 30 *bi saba*; 40 *bi naani*; 100 *kèmè*.

Verb

Brauner (1974) distinguishes four predicating particles: *do* and *ye* identify; *ka* is descriptive; *bè* localizes. The infinitive marker is *ka*: e.g. *ka cike* 'to plough'.

TENSE MARKERS

Present: *bè*, negative *tè*: e.g. *m'be taga* 'I go' (/n'/ → /m'/ before /b/); *n'tè taga* 'I don't go'.

Perfect: *-ra*, *-la*, *na* depending on stem final: e.g. *ne taga.ra* 'I went'; *a yele.la* 'he laughed'.

These are negated by *ma*: *m'ma taga* 'I didn't go'. The future marker is *di/be na*: negated by *te na*.

There are forms for imperfect, immediate present, and pluperfect.

IMPERATIVE

Singular expressed by bare stem; plural marked by *a ye*: e.g. *a ye ta(g)a*! 'go!'

CONDITIONAL

tunna: e.g. *n' tunna a fò* 'I'd say it'.

SUBJUNCTIVE

Affirmative *ka*; negative *kana*: e.g. *n'ka a fò* 'that I should say'; neg. *n'kana a fò*.

VERBAL NOUN

E.g. from *mi* 'to drink': *mini* 'drinking'.

PARTICIPLES

Present -*tò*; past -*le*/-*ne* (with passive sense): e.g. *Mali tla**le** do yòrò saba* 'Mali was (= is) divided into three regions'; *Liwru kalan**na** an fè* 'The book was read by us' (*kalan* 'to read').

Postpositions

Examples:

- *bè* 'with', 'at': used to express possession: e.g. *so bèn'fè* 'I have a house (*so*)';
- *fè* 'by': e.g. *an fè* 'by us';
- *la*, *kònò* 'in', 'within': e.g. *so kònò* 'inside the house';
- *cè*, *cè la* 'among'.

Word formation

Mainly by suffixation, though prefixes and compounding are also found. Examples:

- -*ni*: forms diminutives, e.g. *den* 'child', *den**ni*** 'small child';
- -*ya*: forms abstracts, e.g. *muso* 'woman', *muso**ya*** 'femininity';
- -*la*/-*na*: indicates agent, e.g. *sènè* 'agriculture', *sènè**la*** 'peasant';
- -*bali* is privative, e.g. *balo* 'life', *balo**bali*** 'lifeless'; *balobaliya* 'lifelessness';
- -*tò* makes qualitative adjectives, e.g. *kongo* 'hunger', *kongotò* 'hungry';
- -*ta* gives potential sense, e.g. *ye* 'see', *ye**ta*** 'visible';
- -*lan* indicates instrument or means, e.g. *gosi* 'strike', *gosi**lan*** 'hammer'.

Word order

SOV

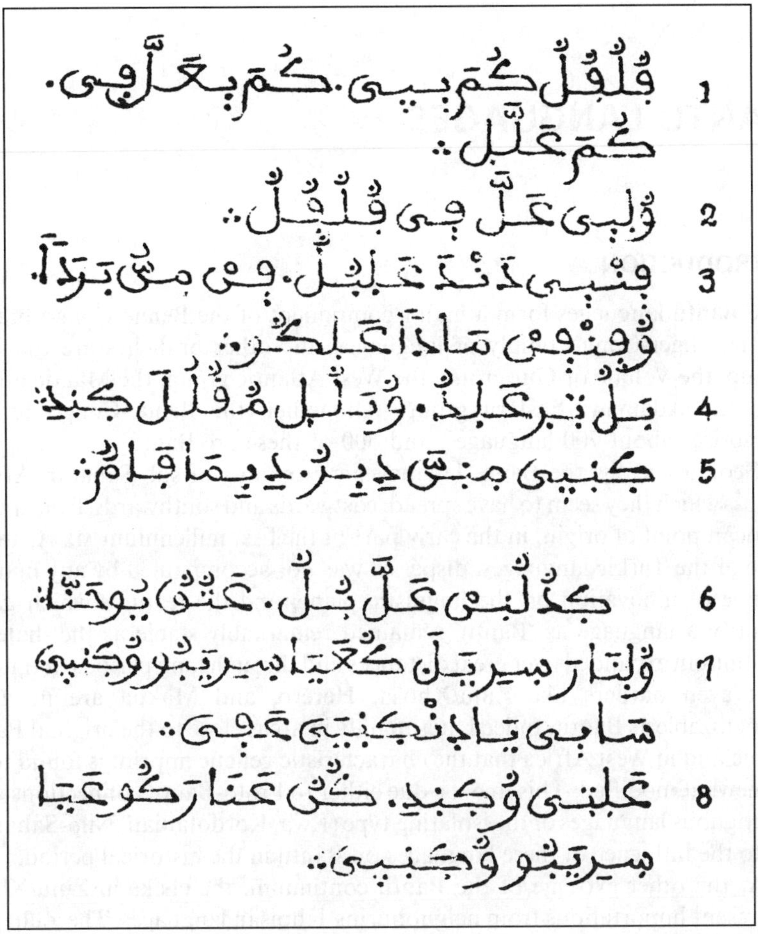

BANTU LANGUAGES

INTRODUCTION

The Bantu languages form a major component of the Benue-Congo branch of the Niger-Congo family of languages; the other branches are the Kwa group, the Voltaic or Gur group, the West Atlantic group, the Mande group, and the Adamawa-Eastern group. Altogether, the Benue-Congo branch comprises about 700 languages, and 500 of these are Bantu.

Geographically, the Bantu languages cover most of sub-Saharan Africa, across which they seem to have spread, eastwards and southwards, from a West African point of origin, in the early part of the first millennium AD. As in the case of the Turkic languages, dispersal was not accompanied by any marked degree of innovation on the linguistic plane; and the features which go to identify a language as 'Bantu' remained remarkably stable as the dialectal continuum expanded over great distances and through long periods of time, so that even outliers like Zulu/Xhosa, Herero, and Makua are instantly recognizable as Bantu. Indeed, it is mainly in areas close to the original Bantu homeland in West Africa that the characteristic genetic imprint is found to be somewhat modified. This may be due either to Proto-Bantu connections with contiguous languages of the isolating type (Kwa, Kordofanian, Nilo-Saharan) or to the influence of these languages on Bantu in the historical period.

At the other extreme of the Bantu continuum, the clicks in Zulu/Xhosa represent importations from neighbouring Khoisan languages. The Zulu grid of click sounds, for example, shows a labio-velar, a dental–velar, and a lateral–velar series, each containing four phonemes – a surd, its aspirate, its voiced allophone, and its nasal, e.g. in the dental–velar series /q, qh, gq, nq/.

The earliest descriptions of Bantu languages date from the mid-seventeenth century – e.g. Giacinto Brusciotto's Latin grammar of Kongo, published in 1659. The task of providing an internal classification of the Bantu languages based on scientific criteria, was first undertaken by W.H.J. Bleek (1862–9), who coined the name *Bantu* to designate the people and their languages. The word is a plural form meaning 'people', and functions as such in many Bantu languages: cf.

	Singular	*Plural*
Rwanda	umu.ntu 'man'	aba.ntu
Kongo	mu.ntu	ba.ntu
Zulu	umu.ntu	aba.ntu
Herero	omu.ndu	ova.ndu

Swahili	m.tu	wa.tu
Lingala	mo.to	ba.to
Sotho	mō.thō	bā.thō
Shona	mu.nhu	va.nhu
Luganda	omu.ntu	aba.ntu

The Common Bantu prototype, of which these are reflexes, has been reconstructed as sing. **mo.to*; pl. **ba.nto.*

Bleek was followed by Carl Meinhof (1901) and Sir Harry Johnston (1919). In 1948, Professor M. Guthrie published the first part of his definitive *Classification of the Bantu languages* (complete edition, 4 vols, 1967–70). This classification lists about 700 languages (including those which Guthrie calls 'semi-Bantu') divided into 16 areal groupings, each grouping having specific phonological and morphological features.

The Bantu languages are spoken by a total of about 160 million people. Numbers for individual languages vary very considerably; between 50,000 and 100,000 is about average. Rwanda tops the list as the mother tongue of at least 10 million, followed by Swahili, Zulu/Xhosa, and Makua (in Mozambique) with 5–6 million each. The picture changes if second-language status is taken into account: Swahili, with some 50 million, then easily outstrips all its congeners.

A broad areal division, based on Guthrie's 16 zones, with the names of some of the most important representative members, is given:

1. North-West Central Africa: Duala, Fang, Buja, Lingala/Losengo.
2. West and South-West Central Africa: Kongo, Songe, Herero, Ciokwe.
3. East Central: Swahili, Sango, Bemba, Tonga, Nyanja.
4. North-East Central: Luganda, Gikuyu, Nyankole, Soga, Rundi, Rwanda, Nyamwesi.
5. South-East: Shona, Tsonga, Ronga, Makua, Yao.
6. South: Sotho, Swazi, Tswana, Zulu/Xhosa.

PHONOLOGY

Consonants

The parent Proto-Bantu language had a relatively simple inventory of stops /p,t,k/, plus /tʃ/ with their voiced, nasal, and pre-nasalized (both voiced and unvoiced) allophones: e.g.

p, b, m, ^{m}p, ^{m}b; t, d, n, ^{n}t, ^{n}d

The plural forms in the *umuntu*/*abantu* chart illustrate reflexes in modern Bantu languages of the unvoiced pre-nasalized series. In Swahili, for example, the nasal has been lost, *wa.tu*; in Herero, the unvoiced has merged with the voiced series, *ova.**ndu*** (cf. a.***ndu*** in Thagicu); while in Shona the stop has been lost, *va.nhu* (cf. *wa.nu* in the Luguru language of Tanzania).

Common Bantu seems to have had no sibilants, while /s/ and several other fricatives – /ʃ, z, h, f, v/ – are widespread in the successor languages. In many of these, the fricatives and some sonants are reflexes of the parent voiced series.

Vowels

Proto-Bantu had seven vowels, /i, e, ɛ, a, ɔ, o, u/, an inventory which is characteristic today of two of Guthrie's areal groupings (North-East and North-West Central), and is also found (along with the five-vowel system) in seven others. The five-vowel system, /i, ɛ, a, ɔ, u/, is found in about 60 per cent of Bantu languages.

Tone

Proto-Bantu was probably a tone language, and tone is a general characteristic of present-day Bantu languages, where it is often phonemic. The curious phenomenon of tone reversal has been noted in Western Congo languages (high tone for Common Bantu low, and vice versa). Tone has been lost in Swahili.

Stress

Stress normally tends to the penultimate syllable.

MORPHOLOGY AND SYNTAX

Noun

It seems clear that Proto-Bantu was already in possession of the class prefix system which is now the most general and the most typical feature of Bantu morphology. Proto-Bantu had 19 classes, an inventory which has been retained in many of the daughter languages, and much reduced (usually by syncretic processes) in others; Sotho, for example, has only seven classes. Class 1, the class of human beings, is largely homogeneous over the whole field; the other classes are heterogeneous, though some of them are associated, at least in part, with certain semantic fields: e.g. trees are often in class 3, animals in class 9. In origin, the classes may well have been associated with an elaborate system of classifiers such as are found in South-East Asia. The class system has nothing to do with gender; nor is it, at least in origin, connected with an animate/inanimate dichotomy. The animate concord which is now a feature of Swahili and some other East Central languages is a recent development.

Class is marked in nouns by prefix which is then echoed by concordial coefficients in all associated parts of speech, thus producing a kind of semantic alliteration: e.g. Swahili:

wageni **wa**zungu **w**engi **wa**lifika Kenya (ili) **wa**pande mlima wa Kilimanjaro; nime**wa**ona.

'Many European visitors came to Kenya to climb Mount Kilimanjaro; I have seen them.'

(*-fika* 'to arrive, come'; *-geni* 'strange'; *Mzungu* 'European'; *-ingi* 'many';

-pande 'to climb'; *mlima* 'mountain'; *-li* = past-tense marker; *-me-* = perfect-tense marker; *-ona* 'to see')

Classes are normally paired: a class containing singular nouns is followed by the class containing the respective plurals. Classes 1 and 2, containing singular and plural nouns denoting human beings, have been illustrated above: *umu.ntu*/*aba.ntu*, etc. Similarly, class 3 comprises singular nouns with a *m-*/*mw-*/*mu-* prefix; class 4, the relevant plurals with a *mi-* prefix. The semantic field in classes 3/4 is heterogeneous, basically animate, e.g.

	Class 3	*Class 4 plurals*
Swahili	m.ti. 'tree'	mi.ti
Kongo	n.ti	mi.ti
Zulu	umu.thi	imi.ti
Shona	mu.ti	mi.ti
Lingala	mw.ete	mi.ete
Luganda	omu.ti	emi.ti
Gikuyu	mu.ti	mi.ti

It will be noticed that certain prefixes – e.g. *m-* in classes 1 and 3 – are duplicated. This can only give rise to confusion in citation form; in connected utterance, oral or written, specific concordial sequence ensures semantic discrimination.

Some classes are at least partially correlated with specific semantic fields, the obvious example being class 1/2. This is on the whole atypical, however, and not consistent. *See* **Swahili** for a specific set of classes. For comparative purposes, here is the Luganda system, which is notable for the retention of classes which have been lost in other North-East Central Bantu languages:

Class	*Prefix*	*Class features and examples*
1	omu-	class of human beings: ***omu**ntu* 'man'
2	aba-	plurals of nouns in cl. 1: ***aba**ntu* 'men, people'
3	omu-	plants, trees, etc.: ***omu**ti* 'tree'
4	emi-	plurals of nouns in cl. 3: ***emi**ti* 'trees'
5	li-/eri-	with sandhi at junctures; heterogeneous field: ***ejj**inja* 'stone' (*li* + *j-* > (*e*)*jj*)
6	ama-	plurals of nouns in cl. 5: ***ama**yinja* 'stones'
7	eki-	human artefacts: ***eki**zimbe* 'building'; may have disparaging nuance: ***eki**renzi* 'overgrown youth'
8	ebi-	plurals of cl. 7 nouns: ***ebi**zimbe* 'buildings'
9	en-	heterogeneous; includes some animals: ***en**jovu* 'elephant'
10	zi-	provides plural forms for nouns belonging to various classes
11	olu-/olw-	class of long and/or thin objects: ***olu**tindo* 'bridge'
12	otu-	nouns denoting small quantities of something: ***otu**zzi* 'drops of water'

13	aka-	heterogeneous field: ***aka**mwa* 'mouth'; ***aka**ntu* 'something small'; ***aka**wungeezi* 'evening'
14	obu-/obw-	plurals of nouns in cl. 13: ***obu**mwa* 'mouths'
15	oku-	actions: ***oku**genda* 'going' (< *-genda* 'to go')
20	ogu-	augmentatives based on nouns in other classes: ***ogu**ntu* 'giant' (cf. *omuntu* 'man')
22	aga-	plurals of nouns in cl. 20: ***aga**ntu* 'giants'

It is worth pointing out here that Luganda has, in addition, a series of prefixes denoting high rank, which draw on class 1 for their concordial agreement, e.g. *sse-*, *nna-*, with plural forms *basse-*, *banna-*: e.g. *ssabasajja Kabaka* 'His Highness the Kabaka'.

Classes 16, 17, and 18, left blank in the above table, are the locational classes with prefixes *pa-*, *ku-*, *mu-* indicating, respectively, definite locus, indefinite locus, and locus within something: cf. Swahili *nyumba.ni* ***mw**a mwalimu* 'in the house of the teacher' (*-ni* is a locative suffix; *nyumba* 'house'; *mwalimu* 'teacher').

Adjective

There are very few root adjectives in Bantu. Examples are:

	'Large'		*'Bad'*
Zulu	-kulu	Zulu	-bi
Swahili	-kuu	Herero	-i
Nyanja	-kulu	Luganda	-bi
Tswana	-xolo	Kongo	-bi
		Swahili	-baya

Attributively, root adjectives follow the noun qualified, taking the proper class prefix: e.g. with root *-ema* 'good', in Swahili: *mtu mw.ema* 'a good person'; *watu wema* 'good people'; *-dogo* 'small': *wa.toto wa.dogo wa.wili* 'two small children' (*-wili* 'two') (cl. 2). Often, a relative construction is preferred, e.g. in Zulu: *umu.ntu o.na.amandhla* 'a strong man' (lit. 'a man who is strong'; relative $-a + u \rightarrow o$).

Pronoun

The conjunctive pronouns, subjective and objective, are remarkably homogeneous over most of the Bantu area. Meinhof (1906) gives the Common Bantu forms for the subject verbal prefixes as:

	Singular	*Plural*
1	ni	ti/tî
2	γu	mî/mu
3	γa, γyu	βa

Reflexes of first person singular: e.g. Swahili *ni*; Zulu *ngi*; Luganda *n* (with variants); Kongo *n* (with variants); Duala *na*; Rundi *n/ndi*; Yao *ni*.

In Meinhof's table of 38 languages (1906: 88), only two – Makua and Sotho – are non-conformist, each with a *ke/ki* form for the first person singular.

DEMONSTRATIVE PRONOUNS

Three degrees of relative distance are normally distinguished; *see* **Swahili**.

RELATIVE PRONOUN

Many Bantu languages have no relative construction. Where such a construction exists it may take various forms:

(a) with demonstrative in the *(hu) yo* → *ye*, *(ha)o* form; with tense marker: e.g. *a.li.**ye**.soma* 'he who read'; pl. *wa.li.**o**.soma* (*-li-* is the past-tense marker);
(b) subject prefix + stem + relative particle: e.g. *(mtu) a.soma.ye* '(the man) who reads';
(c) relative pronoun: e.g. in Sotho, *mōthō ea rutang* 'a person who teaches'; *bathō ba rutang* 'persons who teach';
(d) analytical construction with *amba-* (in Swahili) + relative particle: e.g. *mtu amba**ye** a.na.kuja* 'the man who is coming' (*-na-* is the present-tense marker).

Indirect relative: the concordial object pronoun precedes the verb + suffixed relative form agreeing with object: e.g. *(kitu) ni.**ki**.taka.**cho*** 'the thing I want', where *kitu* is a class 7 noun, *-ki-* is the class 7 subject/object prefix, and *-cho-* is the class 7 relative pronominal form.

Verb

Most primary roots are disyllables. Derived stems are formed by suffixation, e.g. the reciprocal in *-ana*. This marker is found in many Bantu languages:

Swahili:	pendana 'to love each other'
Lingala:	lingana 'to love each other'
Zulu:	bonana 'to see each other'
Rwanda:	ku.bonana 'to see each other'
Sotho:	ho.bonana 'to see each other'
Shona:	onana 'to see each other'
Luganda:	yombagana 'to quarrel with each other'

Similarly, with the causative ending in -V*sha* in Swahili (e.g. *weza* 'be able to', *weze**sha*** 'to enable'); this ending appears as *-ithia* in Gikuyu, as *-isa* in Zulu, as -V*sa*-V*dza*/-V*tsa* in Shona, as -V*sa* in Sotho, as *-a/-e* in Luganda, as *-isa* in Lingala, and as *-itha* in Herero.

Other derived stems: passive, in -(*i*)*wa*, with variants: cf.

Zulu:	bon.wa 'to be seen'
Gikuyu:	igu.(w)o 'be heard'

Luganda: lab.wa 'be seen'
Sotho: ho rōngŏa 'be sent' (← *rōma* 'to send': /m/ → [ŋg] before /w/)
Swahili: ku.on.wa 'be seen'

The Lingala passive is in *-ema*/*ama*: e.g. *ekosalema* 'to be done'.

Some Bantu languages have a neutral passive of state in -V*ka*(*la*), e.g. in Zulu *inkanyezi ya.bona.ka.la* 'the star was visible'; cf. *thandwa* 'to be loved', *thand.eka* 'be loving, affectionate'.

Prepositional or benefactive: e.g. -V*la*/*ra* in Zulu, *-ri*/*-er* in Shona, depending on vowel harmony; Zulu *hlala* 'to wait', *hlal.ela* 'to wait for someone'; *hamba* 'to travel'; *hambela* 'to go to visit someone'.

Antonymous: typically -V*l*/*ra*: e.g. Gikuyu, *hinga* 'to shut'; *hingura* 'to open'.

MOODS

Moods are generally marked by suffix. Most Bantu languages have seven moods: infinitive, indicative, imperative, subjunctive, perfect, continuative, relative.

The infinitive is a noun (Swahili *ku-* class, corresponding to *uku-* in Zulu, *hō-* in Sotho). The infinitive (or gerund), the indicative, and the direct imperative usually have *-a* final; the subjunctive has *-e*, the negative *-i*. Cf. Swahili.

ku.soma 'reading, to read'
ni.ta.soma 'I shall read'
soma! 'read'
ni.som**e** (*nini*)? 'What shall I read?', 'What am I to read?'
si.som**i** 'I do not read'

Negative tense formation provides one of the criteria by which Bantu languages may be internally classified. Negation by tone pattern occurs in some, e.g. in Fang, but the use of a negative infix is much more usual and typical. For a characteristic set of negative tenses, *see* **Swahili**. Cf. Zulu:

past affirm.	*nga hamba* 'I travelled'
neg.	*a.ngi.hamba.nga* 'I didn't travel'
pres. affirm.	*ngi hamba* 'I travel'
neg.	*a.ngi.hambi* 'I don't travel'
proximate future affirm.	*ngi.za.uku.hamba* 'I shall travel shortly'
neg.	*a.ngi.zi.uku.hamba* 'I shall not travel shortly'

In Gikuyu the negative particle *-ti-* is used to negate plural verbs in principal clauses, e.g. with stem *gwāta* 'to get, take hold of'; present habitual negative plural: first person *tuti.gwat.aga*; second person *muti.gwat.aga*; third person *mati.gwat.aga*, where *-aga* is the habitual present-tense marker.

The singular forms are negated by modification of the pronominal prefix:

1	affirm.	ni.ngwat.aga
	neg.	**ndi**.gwat.aga
2	affirm.	u.gwat.aga
	neg.	**ndu**.gwat.aga

The *-ti-* negative forms of certain tenses are used in an *interrogative* sense only: e.g. immediate past perfect, positive *(ni)nd.a.gwat.a* 'I did not get'; *-ti-* neg. *ndi.a.gwat.a?* 'Did I not get?' To negate such a tense, the negative of another past tense (the *-īte* perfect) must be used.

The negative particle may be reduplicated, e.g. Kongo *ke be.tonda ko* 'they do not love'; and may precede or follow the personal prefix, e.g. Nyanja *si.ndi.dziwa(i)*, Shona *ha.ndi.ziwe* 'I do not know', but Duala *na.si.loma* 'I don't read'.

In general, the negative particle tends to follow the subject pronoun in the subjunctive mood, the relative version, and the participial forms: e.g. Zulu, indicative *a.ngi.hambi* 'I do not go'; subjunctive *ngi.nga.hambi* 'I may not go'. Some negative tenses in Bantu have no affirmative correlatives.

The typical Bantu verbal complex consists of prefix (subject concord marker) – tense marker – object marker – stem – modal/voice marker (with negative particle variously sited): e.g., in affirmative version, Swahili *ni.li.ki.soma* Ø 'I read (past) it' (where *ni-* is the personal subject marker for first person singular; *-li-* is the past-tense marker; *-ki-* is a class 5 object marker, referring presumably to *kitabu* 'book'; *soma* 'to read'; Ø is the null marker for the indicative mood). Similarly, *ni.ta.ku.ele.za* 'I shall explain (it) to you' (*-ta-* is the future marker; *-ku-* is the second person singular object marker; *ele.za* is the causative of *elea* 'to be clear'). Cf. Gikuyu *Ni.ma.a.tu.ona?* 'Did they see us?' (*ni-* is the interrogative marker; *ma* = third person plural subject; *-a-* is the immediate past marker; *-tu-* is first person plural object marker; *ona* 'to see'). Examples from other Bantu languages:

Zulu	*u.ya.yi.thanda*	'he loves it'
	ngi.ya.ba.thanda	'I love them'
Shona	*ndi.cha.mu.ona*	'I shall see him/her' (*cha* is future marker)
Sotho	*kēa mō ruta*	'I teach him'
	oa n.thata	'she loves me' (the root is ***r****ata* 'to love'; *rata* → ***th****ata* following /n/)
	ba m.pona	'they see me' (**n.bona* > ***m.p****ona*)
Lingala	*ako.li.mona*	'he sees it' (*-li-* is cl. 5 marker)
	bako.lo.yoka	'they hear us'

TENSE MARKERS

Considerable variation; the Swahili set is: present *-na-*; past *-li-*; future *-ta-*; perfect *-me-*; conditional *-ki-*; present indefinite *-a-*; habitual *-hu-*; narrative: *-ka-*.

Numerals

The numerals 1 to 5 inclusive are Common Bantu stock; so is the word for 10. 6, 7, 8, 9 vary very condsiderably from language to language; often they are missing and have to be expressed by compounds: 5 + 2, etc.

Word order

SVO is basic.

1 Yoi linaliyaaki ena limatsako, ko Yoi linaliki la
Yakomba, ko Yoi linaliki Yakomba. 2 Ende ayaaki la
Yakomba ena limatsako; 3 toma tohatotu tonunola-
maki l'ende, efan'iyema imoko iniciki inik'ende ata-
nunola. 4 Liiko li-yaaki eneyal'ende, ko liiko lo-yaaki
fololo en'ato: 5 koko fololo eololoma ena liucu, ko
liucu lit'umbak'eho. 6 Bot'omonyi am'enya, onoki
Yakomba otomaka, lina linande liyaaki Yoane. 7 E-
nde ayaki oyalama bosumoli, lacina asumola bosimo
bona fololo, lacina bato bahatu bimedya l'ende. 8 Ende
atayalaki fololo eho, ende ayaki lacina asumola bosimo
bona fololo.

(Lingala)

1 1 Pakutanga Shoko raivako, Shoko raiva kuna Mwari,
iro Shoko raiva Mwari. 2 Irori pakutanga raiva kuna
Mwari. 3 Zvinhu zvose zvakaitwa naye; kunze kwake
hakuna kuitwa kunyange chinhu chimwe chete chakaitwa.
4 Maari ndimo maiva noupenyu; ihwo upenyu hwaiva chiedza
chavanhu. 5 Zvino chiedza ichi chinovenekera murima, asi
rima harina kuchikunda. 6 Kwakanga kuno munhu wakanga
atumwa naMwari; zita rake wainzi Johane. 7 Iyeyu wakauya
kuzopupura, kuti apupure zvechiedza ichi kuti vose vatende
naye. 8 Iyeyu wakanga asati ari icho chiedza kwete, asi
wakauya kuti azopupura zvechiedza.

(Shona)

1 Tshimolohong Lentswe le ne le le teng, mme Lentswe
le ne le le ho Modimo, mme Lentswe e ne e le Modimo.
2 Le ne le le ho Modimo tshimolohong. **3** Dintho tsohle
di bile teng ka lona, mme ha ho letho le bileng teng ha
e se ka lona. **4** Bophelo bo ne bo le ka ho lona, mme bophelo e ne e le lesedi la batho; **5** lesedi le kganya lefifing,
mme lefifi ha le a ka la le hlola.

(Sotho)

1 Ekuqaleni libeliko I-
lizwi, Ilizwi libelikwano-
Tixo, ne-Lizwi lalingu-Ti-
xo.
2 Elo libeliko ekuqale-
ni kwano-Tixo.
3 Zonke izinto zadalwa
lilo ; akudalwanganto eya-
dalwa lingeko lona.
4 Kulo bekuko Ubomi;
nobomi bebulukanyiso lwa-
bantu.
5 Ukanyiso luyakanyi-
sa ebumyameni; koko ubu-
mnyama abuluqondanga.
6 Kwabekuko indoda
eyatunywa ivela ku-Tixo,
egama libelin-gu-Yohan-
nes.
7 Yona yeza ukuze i-
belinqina galo Ukanyiso,
ukuba bonke abantu ba-
kolwe lulo.
8 Yona ibingelulo olo-
kanyiso ; koko yatunywa
ukuze inqine golokanyiso.

(Xhosa)

EKUQALENI wa be e ko-
na uLizwi, uLizwi wa
be e noTixo, uLizwi wa be
e nguTixo.
2 Yena lowo wa be e no-
Tixo ekuqaleni.
3 Konke kwenziwa uye;
ngapandhle kwake a kwe-
nziwanga uto olwenziwayo.
4 Kwa be ku kona ukupi-
la kuye; ukupila kwa ku
ukukanya kwabantu.
5 Ukukanya kwa kanya
ebumnyameni; kepa ubu-
mnyama a bu kwamkela-
nga.
6 Kwa ku kona umuntu e
tunyiwe uTixo, igama lake
la li nguJohane.
7 Yena weza ukuqinisa,
ukuba a qinise ngokuka-
nya, ukuba bonke ba ko-
lwe ngaye.
8 Yena wa be e nge siko lo-
kukukanya, kodwa wa tu-
nyelwa ukuqinisa ngoku-
kanya.

(Zulu)

BASHKIR

INTRODUCTION

Bashkir belongs to the Kipchak group of Western Turkic (Baskakov's 1966 classification) and is at present spoken by about 900,000 people in the Bashkortostan Republic. It is close to Tatar (*see* **Tatar**), towards which Bashkir gravitated till the 1930s, when a new literary norm was introduced on the basis of the eastern (mountain) dialect. In the past, Tatar had been used as a literary langauge by the Bashkirs, much as Avar is used by the Andi-speaking people in Dagestan. Newspapers, journals, and some books are now published in Bashkir.

SCRIPT

Until 1929 Arabic. Following the typical period of experimental romanization in the 1930s, a Cyrillic script was introduced, with additional letters for specifically Bashkir sounds, e.g. the dental fricatives.

PHONOLOGY

Consonants

stops: p, b, t, d, k, g, q, ʔ; palatalized: t′
affricates: tʃ
fricatives: f, s, z, θ, ð, ʃ, ʒ, x/χ, γ, h
nasals: m, n, ŋ
lateral and flap: l, ł, r
semi-vowels: j, w

The alveolar /ts/ occurs only in loanwords.

Vowels

front: i, y, ə, œ, ɛ, e
back: u, ı, o, a

Note that front vowel /i/ has no back correlate. /œ/ is notated as *ö*, /ɛ/ as *ä*, /y/ as *ü*.

VOWEL HARMONY

Both palatal and labial (*see* **Turkic Languages**).

Stress

Vowels in unstressed syllables tend to be reduced: e.g. *keše*, → [k'šə], 'person'. Stress is on the final syllable in Turkic words (with certain constraints, e.g. never on negative or interrogative marker).

MORPHOLOGY AND SYNTAX

Noun

All case-forming affixes are affected by juncture sandhi and by the laws of vowel harmony. Thus the accusative ending has 16 allomorphs: 4 initials (*n*, *d*, *t*, *ð*) × 4 vowels (*ı*, *e* = [ə], *o*, *ö*).

Specimen declension: *bala* 'child', pl. *balalar*:

	Singular	*Plural*
genitive	bala**nıŋ**	bala.lar**ðıŋ**
dative	bala**γa**	bala.lar.**γa**
accusative	bala**nı**	bala.lar.**ðı**
locative	bala**la**	bala.lar**ða**
ablative	bala**nan**	bala.lar.**ðan**

Plural affix: *lar*[8] (i.e. 4 initials × 2 vowels: *l*, *t*, *d*, *ð*, *a*/*ä*): e.g. *kül* 'lake', pl. *kül**där***; *taw* 'mountain', pl. *taw**ðar***.

THE POSSESSIVE AFFIXES

Specimen paradigm as attached to *bala* 'boy':

	Singular possessor	*Plural possessor*
1	bala**m**	bala**bıð**
2	bala**ŋ**	bala**γıð**
3	bala**hı**	bala**ları**

Example: *bašqort tele(**neŋ**) grammatika**hı*** 'a grammar of the Bashkir language' (*tele* = Turkish *dil* 'language').

Adjective

As attribute, adjective precedes noun and is invariable. When independent, it behaves as nominal, taking all case affixes, the plural marker, and the possessive markers. Also used adverbially: e.g. *yaqšı bala* 'good boy'; *yaqšı uqıy* 'he reads well'.

Pronoun

PERSONAL INDEPENDENT

Sing. 1 *min*, 2 *hin*, 3 *ul*; pl. 1 *bəð*, 2 *həð*, 3 *ular*. These are declined in all cases: e.g. for *min*: *mineŋ*, *miŋə*, *mine*, *minən*, *mində*.

DEMONSTRATIVE PRONOUN

bıl 'this'; *šul* 'that'

INTERROGATIVE PRONOUN

kəm 'who?'; *ni* /nəy/, 'what?'

Numerals

1–10: *ber, ike, ös, dürt, biš, altı, ete, higeð, tuγıð, un. e* here is /ə/. Thus, *ete* is /yətə/. 20 *egerme* /yəgərmə/; 30 *utıð*; 40 *qırq*; 100 *yöð*. Numerals are followed by the singular of the noun enumerated.

Verb

JaNSSSR, Vol. II, lists five voices and six moods, with standard markers (*see* **Turkish Languages**) in their Bashkir format. Thus, for example, the conditional marker – in Turkish *-sa-* – appears here as *-ha-*: *bar.**ha**.m* 'if I go'.

MOODS

Moods may be sub-divided into (a) those that take the predicative suffixes, and (b) those that take the possessive suffixes with certain changes: e.g. the ending of the first person plural is *-q* instead of *-bıð*; of third person sing. Ø.

(a) The predicative suffixes are:

	Singular	*Plural*
1	-mVn	-bVð
2	-hVn	-hVgVð
3	-Ø	-Ø + 1Vr (*or* -1VrðV$_2$r)

where V = *ə, ı, ö, o*, and V$_2$ = *a*/*ä*.

Only the intentional mood takes the predicative affixes; the marker is *-maqsı-*: *bar.maqsı.min* 'I intend to go'.

(b) Moods taking possessive affixes:

conditional: *bar.ha.**m*** 'if I go'
necessitative: *bar.ahım.bar* 'I have to go'
subjunctive: *barır ine**m*** 'that I should go'

The imperative mood has Ø in second person singular; *-gı* in second person plural.

The tenses of the indicative mood are similarly sub-divided by predicative or possessive ending:

(a) Predicative ending:

present: *bar.a.mın* 'I go'
future: *bar.a.saq.mın* 'I shall go'
reported past: *bar.γan.mın* '(it seems that) I went'

(b) Possessive suffixes:

past definite: *bar.dı.m* 'I went'
past habitual: *bar.a.torγanı.m* 'I was in the habit of going'
relative past: *bar.a.inem* 'when I went . . .'

PASSIVE VOICE

The marker is *-l/n-*.

NEGATION

The general negative marker is *-ma/mä-*, unstressed, following the stem: e.g. *yaha* 'to make', *yaháma* 'not to make'; *kit-* 'to go', *kitmä* 'not to go'. To negate certain verbal forms, e.g. those with *-asaq-*, *-bar-*, the negating particles *yoq* and *tügel* are used: e.g. *barγanım yoq* 'I didn't go (in general)'.

PARTICIPIAL FORMS

-γan, *-ır*, *-γas* are used in the formation of compound tenses and of relative clauses: e.g.

barır keše/barasaq keše 'the man who is coming/will come'
kilgänende belmänem 'I didn't know you had come'
uqıy torγan kitap 'the book that is being read'

Postpositions

Examples:

following nominative: *menən* 'with'; *ösön* 'for', e.g. *xalıq ösön* 'for the people';
following genitive of pronoun: *menən* 'with', e.g. *hineŋ menən* 'with you';
following dative: *saqlı* 'until', e.g. *bıyılγa saqlı* 'until this year';
following ablative: *birle* 'since, from', e.g. *köððən birle* 'from autumn onwards'.

Such postpositions as /aθ/ 'down', /œθ/ 'up', *art* 'behind' follow dative, locative, or ablative as required for sense (rest in a place or motion towards/from a place).

Loanwords in Bashkir

Russian and Arabic loans are illustrated in the following sentence:

Sovyet vlase yıldarında bašqort xalqının əðəbiəte həm iskusstvohı ısınısından səskə atıuγa ölgəšte.
'In the years of Soviet rule the literature and art of the Bashkir people really came to bloom.'

Vlase < *vlast′* 'power, rule' (Russian); *iskusstvo* 'art' (Russian); *sovyet* 'Soviet' (Russian); *xalq* 'people' (Arabic); *əðəbiət* 'literature', 'culture' (Arabic).

Word order

As normal in Turkic.

> Тäўлä Г̇ÿз̆ булган. Г̇ÿз̆ Хоз̆айз̆а булган. Г̇ÿз̆ Хоз̆ай булган. Ул тäўлä Хоз̆айз̆а булган. Бар нäрс̆ä лä Ул (Г̇ÿз̆) аркыры була баштаган; нейгенä була башта̇ға ла, Анг̇ыз̆ була баштамаган. Анд̄а теректек булган, теректек кешелäрз̆ен йактыг̇ы булган. Йакты карангылыкта йактырыб тора, карањгылык аны йенг̆ä-алмай. Хоз̆айз̆ан йебäрелгäи бер кеше булган; анын исеме Іоаниъ (булган). Ул таныктык итäргä килгäи, ул аркыры бары̄г̇ыла эшäнг̇ендäр тиб, йактыны таныктарга (килгäн). Ул йактылык булмаган, ул йактылыкты таныктар ӧсӧн йебäрелгäн.

BASQUE

INTRODUCTION

Euskara, as the Basques call their language, is an isolate, with no known congeners. Structural analogies with Caucasian languages have been pointed out, and from time to time attempts are made to connect Basque with various other languages and language families. No conclusive evidence has been adduced, however, and it seems safer to regard Basque as a relic of the prehistoric language or languages spoken in the Iberian peninsula before the arrival of Indo-European.

Basque is spoken today by over half a million people in *Euskal Herria*, the Basque country in North-Western Spain (Guipuzcoa, Vizcaya, Navarra), and by about 100,000 in the Pyrénées-Atlantiques region of France.

The language is attested in fragmentary form from *c.* AD 1000 onwards. The first Basque printed book appeared in 1545. Writing in Basque is now recovering from the period of proscription following the Spanish Civil War.

SCRIPT

Roman alphabet; the orthography, which is not yet stable, has been influenced by Spanish.

PHONOLOGY

Consonants

stops: /p, b, t, k, g/; Saltarelli (1988) includes two palatal plosives /tj, dj/, which are notated in Basque orthography as *tt*, *dd*.
affricates: /ts, ʦ/, tʃ/: notated in the orthography as *tz*, *ts*, *tx*; /ts/ is lamino-alveolar; /ʦ/ is apico-alveolar. The difference is phonemic: cf. *atzo* 'yesterday', *atso* 'old'.
fricatives: /f, z̠, s̠, ʃ/; the lamino-alveolar /z/ is notated as *z*, the apico-alveolar /s̠/ as *s*; /ʃ/ is notated as *x*. /z̠/ and /s̠/ have voiceless allophones before voiceless consonants or vowels.
nasals: /m, n, ɲ/.
laterals and flaps: /l, ʎ, r, rr/.

Vowels

i, e, a, o, u

Diphthongs: au, ai, ei, oi, ui.

MORPHOLOGY AND SYNTAX

Basque has no grammatical gender, though a gender distinction is made in the second person singular of the synthetic conjugation: cf. *hik daukak* 'you (fam. masc.) have', *hik dauka**n*** 'you (fam. fem.) have'.

ARTICLES

The definite article is affixed: *-a* (sing.), *-ak* (pl.): e.g. *mendi* 'mountain', *mendia* 'the mountain', *mendi**ak*** 'the mountains'. As indefinite article, the numeral *bat* 'one' may be used: e.g. *gizon bat* 'a man'. *Bat* may take the case endings: e.g. *mendi bat.**en** igaera* 'the ascent of a mountain'.

Noun

DECLENSION

Nine cases may be distinguished, but several additional endings occur. Basic cases of *gizon* 'man':

nominative	gizon	comitative	gizon**arekin**
ergative	gizon**ak**	inessive	gizon**an**
dative	gizon**ari**	aditive	gizon**ara**
genitive	gizon**ako** (of origin)	ablative	gizon**atik**
	gizon**aren** (of possession)		

The plural endings may be illustrated with *etxe* /etʃe/, 'house':

nominative	etxe**ak**	comitative	etxe**ekin**
ergative	etxe**ek**	inessive	etxe**etan**
dative	etxe**ei**	aditive	etxe**etara**
genitive	etxe**en**/etxe**etako**	ablative	etxe**etatik**

The distinction between the two genitive forms is seen in a phrase such as *Bilbo**ko** arte eder**ren** museoa* 'the museum of (poss.) fine art of (origin) Bilbao' (*eder* 'beautiful, fine'; -(*r*)*en* = gen. ending) Cf. *Manuren semea* 'Manu's son'; *nere aitarekin* 'with my father'; *etxean* 'in the house'; *menditik* 'from the mountain'.

Adjective

As attribute, adjective follows noun, e.g. *asto txuri bat* 'a white donkey', and takes the definite article: e.g. *etxe**Ø** eder**ra*** 'the beautiful house'; *gure ahuntz polit**ak*** 'our pretty goats' (*polit* 'pretty'). Case endings are also transferred to the adjective: e.g. *ardo berria za*(*ha*)*gi berri**etan*** 'new wine in(to) old bottles' (*ardo* 'wine'; *berri* 'new'; *za*(*ha*)*gi* 'bottle').

Pronoun

The personal forms with the present tense of *izan* 'to be' are:

	Singular	*Plural*
1	ni naiz	gu gara
2	hi haiz	zu zara; zuek zarete
3	hura da	haiek dira

The resumed characteristic (*n-* in first person singular, *g-* in first person plural, *z-* in second person plural) is found throughout the verbal system (*d-* is characteristic of third person).

The ergative forms are: *nik*, *hik*, *hark*; *guk*, *zuk/zuek, haiek*.

The personal pronouns may take other cases: cf. *zuek Nigan, eta Ni zuengan* 'ye in me, I in you' (St John's Gospel 14.20), but see note on verbal system, below.

The possessive forms are: *nire*, *zure*, *bere*; *gure*, *zuen*, *beren*.

DEMONSTRATIVE PRONOUN

Three degrees of relative distance: *hau* 'this' – *hori* 'that' – *hura* 'that (yonder)'; these are postpositional: *gizon hori* /ɔri/ 'that man'.

INTERROGATIVE PRONOUN

nor 'who?' – with ergative, *nork*; *zer* 'what?'

RELATIVE PRONOUN

See **Verb**, below.

Numerals

1–10: *bat*, *bi*, *hiru*, *lau*, *bost*, *sei*, *zazpi*, *zortzi*, *bederatzi*, *hamar*; 11 *hamaika*; 12 *hamabi*; 13 *hamahiru*; 20 *hogei*; 30 *hogei eta hamar*; 40 *berrogei*; 60 *hirurogei*; 70 *hururogei eta hamar*; 80 *laurogei*; 100 *ahun*. That is, a vigesimal system. Apart from *bat*, which follows its noun, the numerals precede the noun, which is in the singular: e.g. *bost seme* 'five sons'.

Verb

As in Georgian, a relatively simple nominal system is accompanied by a very complicated verbal system. But, whereas in Georgian the complication lies in the proliferation of permutations and combinations to which the sense-verb is subjected, in Basque the sense-verb itself usually appears in simple stem or participial form, accompanied by an enormously rich network of auxiliary forms which are deictically coded for person and regimen, and which are quasi-bound in the sense that they only acquire full meaning when associated with a sense-verb stem. For example, by itself *diot* indicates action by first person singular directed in some way at third person singular, i.e. it specifies a deictic relationship. Following the stem *eman* 'to give', plus a noun, e.g. *liburu* 'book', *liburu eman* **diot**, *diot* generates the meaning 'I give

him a book'. If the deixis code is changed by substituting *dizut* for *diot*, the meaning becomes 'I give **you** a book'. A quantitative change can also be introduced by changing *dizut* to *dizkizut*: this indicates that '**I** gave **you** more than one object – books'.

With this sort of deictic relational network at its disposal, Basque makes very sparing use of personal pronouns. Nouns continue to be marked: e.g. *Gizon**ari** liburua eman diot* 'I give the book **to the** man.'

All Basque verbs can be conjugated thus, analytically or periphrastically, but half a dozen crucially important auxiliaries and a few other verbs – e.g. *joan* 'to go', *etorri* 'to come', *eduki* 'to have', *jakin* 'to know', *esan* 'to say', *ikusi* 'to see' – retain a synthetic form of conjugation, which seems to have been formerly more widespread. As an example of a synthetic conjugation, here are the present and past tenses of *etorri* 'to come':

	Present		*Past*	
	Singular	*Plural*	*Singular*	*Plural*
1	ni nator	gu gatoz	ni nentorren	gu gentozen
2	hi hator	zu zatoz	hi hentorren	zu zentozen
3	hura dator	haiek datoz	hura zetorren	haiek zetozen

THE ANALYTICAL CONJUGATION

The most important auxiliaries are (present and past forms):

da – zen: used to conjugate intransitive verbs;
du – zuen: used to conjugate transitive verbs;
zaio – zitzaion: with indirect object; subject in possessive case;
dio – zion: polypersonal (direct and indirect objects).

Altogether, these four auxiliaries produce about a thousand forms, which are:

1. Coded for person and deixis: e.g. *diot – dizut*, as shown above.
2. Coded for number:
   (a) of subject: *du – dizut*, as shown above;
   (b) of object: *diot* indicates singular object; *dizkiot* indicates plural object.
3. Tense: from *du*, *nauzu* indicates second person/first person singular in present; *ninduzun* in past.
4. Mood: e.g. *niezaioke* indicates potential action of first person singular on third person singular, involving singular object; *niezazkioke* indicates the same deixis but involving plurality of object; *zeniezazkigukeen* indicates potential action in past by second person plural on first person plural involving a plurality of objects.

SOME NOTES ON THE MAIN AUXILIARIES

Izan 'to be'; the present tense is given above (*see* **Pronoun**); the past tense is *ni nintzen, hi hintzen, hura zen; gu ginen, zu zinen/zuek zineten, haiek ziren.*

The general negating particle is *ez*: e.g. *ni euskalduna naiz* 'I am a Basque'; *ni euskalduna ez naiz* 'I am not . . . '. In the negative, *ez* plus auxiliary precede the sense-verb: e.g. *ni etorri naiz* 'I have come', *ni ez naiz etorri* 'I haven't . . . '. Future: participle in *-ko* + auxiliary: e.g. *ni etorri.ko naiz* 'I'll come'.

Du – zuen: this auxiliary is used in the conjugation of transitive verbs; the nominal/pronominal subject is in the ergative with *-k*: e.g. with *ikusi* 'see': (*zu**k***) *ikusi nauzu* 'you have seen me'; (*gu**k***) *ikusi zaitugu* 'we have seen you', where *nauzu* encodes second person action on first person and *zaitugu* encodes first person plural action on second person. In *ekarri**ko** zituen* 'he was going to bring them', *zituen* encodes third person singular action on third person plural. A further example: *Maite* ***zintudan***, *baina zuk ez* ***ninduzun*** *maite* 'I loved you, but you did not love me'.

Zaio – zitzaion: this auxiliary is used with stative verbs, intransitive verbs with ethic dative, and verbs whose subject is in possessive case, and is usually translated in English as transitive verb + direct object: e.g. (*niri*) *jausi zait* 'to-me it has fallen' = 'I've dropped it'; (*niri*) *jausi zaizkit* 'to-me they have fallen' = 'I've dropped them'; *gozo zaio* 'pleasant to him' = 'he likes it'; *haurrak joan zaizkio* 'the children have gone off on-him' = 'his children have left him' (where *zaizkio* indicates indirect action on third person singular by third person plural); *liburua galdu zait* 'the book has gone lost on me' = 'I've lost my book'.

Altogether, the *zaio – zitzaion* paradigm, including present, past, conditional, resultative, potential, subjunctive, and imperative forms for all persons and both numbers, has a total of about 280 forms, not all of them in everyday use.

Dio – zion: this auxiliary is used in polypersonal verbs with direct and indirect objects, of the type 'I gave it to him', *eman* ***nion***: cf. *eman dizkiot* 'I give him things'; *eman nizkion* 'I gave him things'; *gutun bat idatzi zion* 'he wrote him a letter'.

The *dio – zion* paradigm has a total of about 700 forms.

RELATIVE FORMS

-(*e*)*n* is added to the relevant auxiliary form: *da* → *den*; *gizon**ari** eman dio**ten*** *ogia* 'the man to whom I gave the bread' (*ogi*); *ogi**a** eman dit**en** gizon**a*** 'the man who gave me the bread'.

As mentioned above, in connection with *zaio – zitzaion*, the deictic grid has full conditional, subjunctive, potential, resultative, and imperative versions. Cf. *ekar* ***ziezagun*** 'so that he might bring us (a singular object)'; *ekar* ***ziezazkigun*** 'so that he might bring us (a plurality)'.

Ba- is a characteristic prefix for auxiliaries in the conditional mood: e.g. *erosi nai* ***ba.dituzu*** 'if you want (*nai*) to buy (*erosi*) . . . '.

Postpositions

These may follow plain stem or case ending: e.g. *bostak aldean* 'about 5 o'clock'; *bihar arte* 'until tomorrow'. Following genitive: *euskaldun**en** artean* 'among the Basques'; *gerla zibil**aren** ondo.**tik*** 'since the (time of) the Civil War'; *mahai(a.**ren**) azpian* 'on the table'.

Word order

Free.

Asieran Itza ba-zan,
ta Itza Yainkoagan zan,
ta Itza Yainko zan.
2 Asieran Bera Yainkoagan zan.
3 Dana Berak egiña da,
ta Bera gabe ez da egin
egindako ezer ere.
4 Beragan bizitza zan,
ta bizitza gizargia zan;
5 ta argia iluntan ageri da,
ta ilunak ez zun aŕtu.
6 Gizon bat azaldu zan
Yainkoak bidalia;
aren izena Yon.
7 Aitoŕtzat au etoŕi zan,
argiaren aitoŕtzat,
aren bidez guziek siñesteko.
8 Ez zan ori argia,
argiaz aitoŕ egitekoa baño.

BATAK (Toba)

INTRODUCTION

Batak belongs to the Malayo-Polynesian branch of Austronesian, and is spoken by about 2½ to 3½ million people in Northern Sumatra. The Batak have a rather rich traditional literature, consisting mainly of folk-tales in prose, orations, panegyrics, and ritual texts for use in divination and invocation. Van der Tuuk in his grammar (1864–7) describes special forms of Batak, e.g. the language of keening, the esoteric language of the 'muttered invocation', and the private language of the camphor-gatherers. There are several widely differing dialects.

SCRIPT

See **Script** at end of article.

PHONOLOGY

Consonants

stops: p, b, t, d, k, g; palatalized: t′, d′/d
nasals: m, n, ŋ
fricatives: s, h
lateral and flap: l, r
semi-vowels: w, j

There is extensive juncture sandhi, especially of nasals with homorganic stops: e.g *t′an.pasaribu* → [t′a**p**pasaribu].

Vowels

i, e, ε, a (→ [ɔ]), ɔ, o, u

Stress

Stress is a function of word class and of morphophonology.

MORPHOLOGY AND SYNTAX

Noun

Natural gender is marked by lexical means: e.g. *hoda* 'horse', *hoda tunggal* 'stallion'. Nominals are primary (e.g. *biyang* 'dog', *gadja* 'elephant') or derived. The latter form an open class, drawn regularly from transitive/

intransitive verbal stems. This process is two-way, in that verbal valencies may be applied to nominal stems. Van der Tuuk relates the derived nominal to the passive form of the verb:

the passive imperative form of a transitive verb = stem = nominal form;
the passive imperative form of an intransitive verb = stem = nominal form with stress shift.

If the verb has a *pa-* or *mar-* prefix, the nominal form = active verbal substantive: e.g. *mar.mahan*: *par.mahan* 'a herdsman'.

NUMBER

Not normally marked. Plurality is inherent in certain verb forms, e.g. *mar.habang.an* 'to fly' (where a flock of birds is concerned).

POSSESSION

Positional, or with linker *di*: e.g. *isi ni huta* 'the contents/inhabitants of the village' (ni < di).

Adjectives

The adjectival verbs have the *ma-* prefix; the prefix is discarded to give an attributive form: e.g. *ma.rára bunga on* 'this flower is red' (verb *ma.rára* 'to be red'); *rará bunga on* 'red – this flower'. Cf. *balgá biyang on* 'this dog is large/this large dog'; *biyang na balga* 'a dog that is large' (*na* is a relative pronoun).

Pronoun

Personal independent with enclitic forms:

	Singular		*Plural*	
	Independent	*Enclitic*	*Independent*	*Enclitic*
1	au	-hu	*incl.* hta, *excl.* hami	-ta, -nami
2	ho	-mu	hamu	-muna
3	ibana	-na	nasida	-nasida

DEMONSTRATIVE PRONOUN

on 'this'; *an* 'that'; *aduwi* 'that yonder'

INTERROGATIVE PRONOUN

ise 'who?'; *aha* 'what?'

RELATIVE PRONOUN

na

Numerals

1–10: *sada*, *duwa*, *tolu*, *opat*, *lima*, *onom*, *pitu*, *uwalu*, *siga*, *sappulu*; 11 *sappulu.sada*; 12 *sappulu.duwa*; 20 *duwa pulu*; 30 *tolu pulu*; 100 *sa.ratus*.

Verb

A few simple stems are in use, e.g. *lao* 'to go', *hundul* 'to sit', *tindang* 'to stand', but the great majority of Batak verbs are derivatory. Derivation takes place by means of (a) simple prefix, often plus suffix, e.g. *mang-* – *mang-*… *-hon*; or (b) composite prefix, again often with associated suffix, e.g. *ma.si-* stem (*-hon*). With these affixes a very extensive and subtly differentiated lexicon of verbal forms is generated, not only from primary verbal stems but also from numerals, nominals, adjectival stems, etc. The underlying stem itself may not always be attested. The forms express many shades of modality and relationship to locus and nature of action, the involvement of other persons as direct or indirect objects, beneficiaries (coded for number); nuances which cut across the simple active/passive, transitive/intransitive oppositions. The class is open.

Van der Tuuk (1864 (1971)) classifies verbs in terms of formation, version (broadly, transitive/intransitive), and meaning. The most important prefixes are:

(a) Simple: *ma-*, *mang-*, *mar-*, *pa-*, *ha-*; used with zero suffix or with *-i*, *-hon*, *-an*. The infixes *-um-*, *-ur-/-al-/-ar-* are also found.
(b) Composite: *ma.hi-*, *ma.si-*, *ma(ng).hu-*, *mang.si-*, *pa.tu-*; again, + suffixes. There is extensive use of sandhi at junctures.

Some representative examples:

ma-: qualitative and stative verbs, e.g. *ma.rára* 'to be red'; *ma.timbo* 'to be high'; *ma.bugang* 'to be wounded'.
mang-: intransitive, e.g. *mambuwat boru* 'to get married' (of male) (/ŋ/ > /m/ before labial).

involuntary action, e.g. *mang.embang* 'to unfold' (as a flower); involuntary action on something, e.g. *maninggang* 'to fall accidentally on sth.'.

mang-… *-i*: transitive, e.g. *mang.a.napuran.i* 'give betel to someone' (*napuran* 'betel').
mang-… *-hon*: with reference to a desired or intended result, e.g. *man.angi.hon* 'to listen for something'; *mang.adop.pon* 'to turn to face someone; make use of something', e.g. *mang.ultop.pon* 'to blow (arrow) from blowpipe'.
mar-: to own object denoted by nominal, e.g. *mar.hoda* 'to own a horse'.
mar-… *-hon*: causal, e.g. *mar.bada.hon* 'to have a quarrel over something'.
mar-… *-an*: indicates plurality in action, e.g. *mar.songgop.an* 'to roost, perch' (many birds).
-um-: involuntary action, e.g. *s.um.urut* 'to recoil involuntarily'.
pa-: reciprocity, e.g. *pa.djuppa* 'to meet each other'; plus reduplication, e.g. *pa. djuppa-djuppa* 'to meet each other often'.
pa-… *-hon*: cause someone to enter a certain state or condition, e.g.

pa.pande.hon 'to make someone a labourer'; *pa.pahat.ton* 'to make an animal eat'; to express ordinal, e.g. *pa.duwa.hon* 'to be second'.

ma.si-: to acquire the object denoted by stem, e.g. *ma.si.hotang* 'to get cane'.

ma.si-...-an: plural reciprocity, e.g. *ma.si.pangan.an napuran* 'to eat each other's betel'.

mar.si...: onset of action leading to intended or desired result, e.g. *mar.si.gorgor* 'to flame up' (of funeral pyre).

TENSE

Expressed by adverbs of time (of which there are several, expressing in addition aspect) or it is deduced from context. Demonstrative adverbs of place or time are made by prefixing prepositions: e.g. *i-* is a demonstrative pronoun of past time, e.g. *pidong i* 'the bird referred to' (i.e. not visible); *di s.i* 'at that time'; this can be used as a past-tense marker.

NEGATIVE

The particle is *inda(d)ong*, abbreviated to *indang*: e.g. *indang/indaong hu.boto* 'I don't know'; *indang adong* 'is not there'.

Sowada 'neither': e.g. *Sowada hu.ida sowada hu.boto* 'I haven't seen it and I don't know about it.'

PASSIVE FORMS

In place of a simple passive form available for all verbs in mechanical fashion, Batak has several passives, whose usage depends on the circumstances attending the action, and on such factors as agency, intention, accident, completion/non-completion, etc. The relationship between the passive form and the derived nominal has already been mentioned.

1. Pronominal marking for agent may be suppressed, especially in third person where *di-* is prefixed to the nominal form: e.g. *di.buwat* 'is taken by him/her'; *di.timbung ma tu aek* 'the river was jumped into by him' (*aek* 'river'; *tu* 'towards, into'; *ma* is particle of continuing action).
2. Practicability of action is expressed by the prefixes *tar-*, *ha-*: e.g. *tar.tuhor hita* 'it can be bought by us'. Chance occurrence: e.g. *tar.podom ibana* 'falling-asleep by him' = 'he has fallen asleep'. With qualitative verbs: e.g. *tar.gorsing* 'be yellowish'.
3. Nominal form + preposition *ni*: e.g. *ni.ultopmi* 'the thing shot at by you with your blowpipe'; *pidong na ni.ultopmi* 'the bird (which is) the thing shot at...'. Hence, many substantives are formally passives of this type: e.g. (*na*)*pinahan* 'the things that have been fed' = 'the cattle'.

Prepositions

Examples: *di* 'in', 'at', 'because of', etc.: *di au* 'because of me'; *dibana* 'at his place, with him'; *tu* 'towards': *tu tonga ni uma* 'to (the place of) the field'. The preposition may not require a verb of motion: e.g. *tu aek ibana* 'he goes/has gone/will go to the river' (*aek*).

Compound words

a.b. where b qualifies a: e.g.

ari.logo 'dry weather', *ari.udan* 'wet weather' (*ari* 'day');
anak.tubu 'newly born child' (*anak* 'male child'); separable for pronominal enclitic, e.g. *anak**ku**.tubu i* 'my newly born child';
pande 'skilled at . . .', e.g. *pande.bodil* 'gunsmith' (*mamodil* 'to shoot at something with a gun');
gondang.dalan 'path-music' = 'music for the journey'.

Word order

Basically SVO.

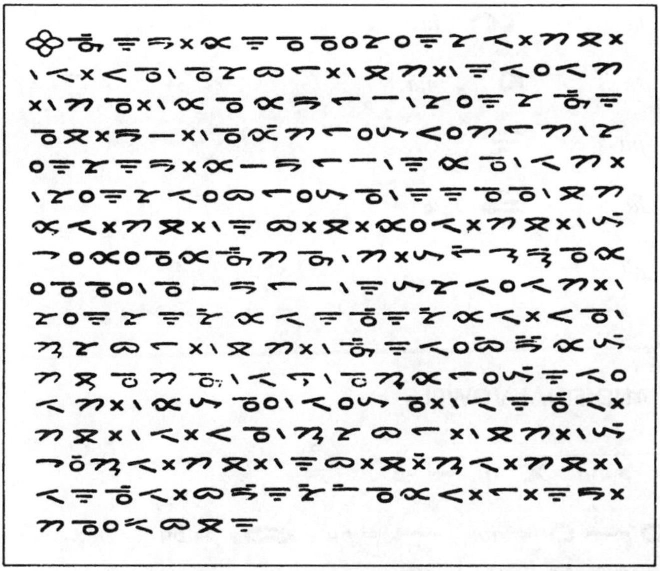

(Mark 3.31–5)

SCRIPT

Much of the literature of the Batak people has been recorded in a script based ultimately on an Indic model. Originally used on bark and bamboo, the script is now losing ground to Roman.

THE BATAK SCRIPT

THE ALPHABET

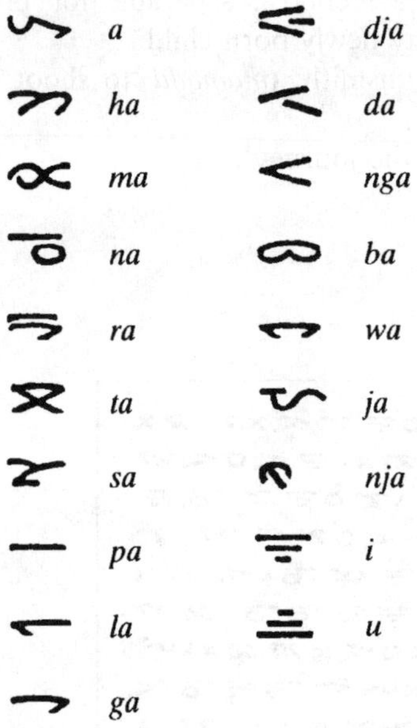
a
dja
ha
da
ma
nga
na
ba
ra
wa
ta
ja
sa
nja
pa
i
la
u
ga

MEDIAL AND FINAL VOWELS

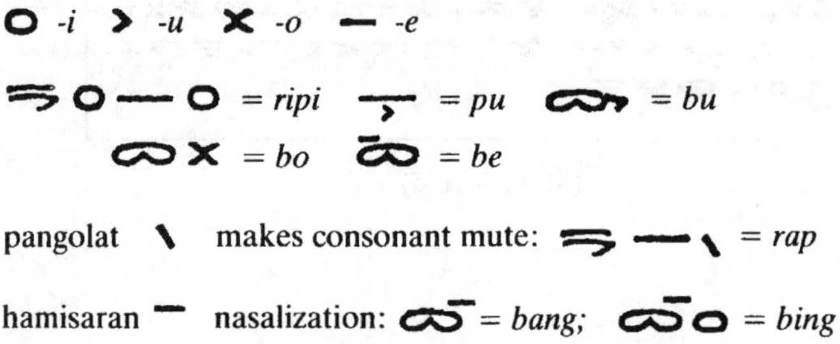
-i
-u
-o
-e
= ripi
= pu
= bu
= bo
= be
pangolat
makes consonant mute:
= rap
hamisaran
nasalization:
= bang;
= bing

BELORUSSIAN

INTRODUCTION

Belorussian is a member of the East Slavonic group of the Slavonic branch of Indo-European. Often regarded in the past as a dialect of Russian, it has now achieved official status as the language of Belarus (capital Minsk). It derives from a complex of West Russian dialects which were spoken in the large area between the Pripet and the western Dvina, and which, from the thirteenth century onwards, coalesced towards a common norm. This process was hastened by the fact that an ecclesiastical form of West Russian was the official language of the Grand Duchy of Lithuania (thirteenth to sixteenth centuries). By the same token, Polish influence on Belorussian is due to Polish ascendancy within the Grand Duchy (Lithuanian itself was not used as a written language till the sixteenth/seventeenth centuries). Under the Russian tsars, Belorussian was proscribed. Since 1917, the language has been codified and standardized, and is now the vehicle for a considerable literature.

Belorussian means 'White Russian'. Exactly what 'white' means here is not clear. The authors (Birillo, Bulaxov, Sudnik) of the article on Belorussian in *JaNSSSR*, Vol. I, 1966, interpret 'white' as meaning 'free' in contrast to the 'black' territories which were the first to succumb to the Grand Duchy in the thirteenth century.

Today, Belorussian is spoken in Belarus and in the adjoining republics by about 7½ million people. All are bilingual in Belorussian with Russian or Ukrainian.

SCRIPT

Cyrillic (*see* **Russian**). The alphabet, fixed in 1933, is identical to the Russian alphabet, minus и, and plus the letter I /i/ and ў /w/. The digraphs *dž* and *dz* occur.

PHONOLOGY

Consonants

stops: p, b, t, d, k, (g)
affricates: ts, dz, tʃ, dʒ
fricatives: f, v, s, z, ʃ, ʒ, x, γ, h
nasals: m, n
lateral and flap: ł, r
Semi-vowels: j, w

Followed by soft vowels, the following consonants are soft, i.e. palatalized: /p, b, f, v, m, s, z, n, l, k, g (= [h]), x, γ/. /t/ and /d/ are hard only: their soft correlatives are the affricates /ts′/, /dz′/. These two phonemes are specifically notated in the script as ц and дз. See *ciekańnie* and *dziekańnie*, below. Note, however, that the same two letters are used to notate etymologically original /ts/, /dz/, which are hard consonants, as in *tsaná* 'price'. As regards the other thirteen consonants listed above, one and the same letter serves to notate both hard and soft values.

Vowels

hard: ı, e, a, o, u
soft: i, ye, ya, yo, yu

/ı/ is notated as ы; /i/ as *i*; the remaining four soft vowels are notated as in Russian. Where Russian uses the soft sign ь to mark palatalization before a soft vowel, Belorussian uses the apostrophe ': cf. Russian пью 'I drink', Belorussian п'ю; Russian семья 'family', Belorussian сям'я. The apostrophe is also used to divide a consonantal prefix, or one ending in a consonant, from a soft initial, i.e. where Russian uses the hard sign ъ. Cf. Russian съезд, Belorussian з'езд 'congress'. The Cyrillic soft sign ь is used to mark /l, n, z, s, ts, dz/ as soft, e.g. in word-final position: e.g. *pisac′* 'to write' (*-i-*, here, being invariably soft, does not require marking). In this entry, ı = hard, /ı/; i = soft, /i/.

Some characteristics of the Belorussian phonological system:

1. *ciekańnie*: Russ. *t′* = Bel. *c′*: e.g. *t′en′* 'shadow' = *c′en′*.
2. *dziekańnie*: Russ. *d′* = Bel. *dz′*: e.g. *d′en* 'day' *dz′en′*.
3. Initial *o* = /vo/, initial *u* = /vu/: e.g. *voka* 'eye', *vuxa* 'ear'.
4. Presence of voiced velar fricative: *gorad* 'town', /γorat/.
5. The shift of unstressed /o, ɛ/ to /a/ is regular in Russian, where, however, it is not notated in the orthography; in Belorussian it is notated, which complicates the inflectional system. Thus, *zólata* 'gold' – *z**a**latí* 'golden'.
6. As in Russian and Ukrainian, an unvoiced consonant preceding a voiced consonant is itself voiced, and vice versa; in Belorussian this assimilation takes place even if palatalization is present: cf. /pros′ba/ > /proz′ba/ 'request'. /d/, /z/ + /ts, tʃ, ʃ, ʒ / > gemination of second component: e.g. *d.ts* > /tsts/.

Stress

On any syllable and movable.

MORPHOLOGY AND SYNTAX

Noun

Three genders: masculine, feminine, and neuter. Three declensions are distinguished:

1. *a*-stems: mostly feminine, e.g. *rabóta* 'work', pl. *rabótı*;
2. *o*-stems: masculine and neuter, e.g. *stól* 'table', pl. *st**a**lí*;
3. *i*-stems: feminine, *mıš* 'mouse', pl. *míšı*.

A few neuter nouns can be declined either in a specific form or as (2) above: e.g. *imya* 'name' may have plural *imyonı* or *imi*.

Specimen declension of first declension feminine noun: *galava* 'head':

	Singular	*Plural*
nom.	galavá	galóvı
acc.	galavú	galóvı
gen.	galaví	galów
dat.	galavyé	galóvam
instr.	galavóy	galóvami
prep.	galavyé	galóvax

The nominal paradigms have a great many variants depending on phonetic environment: e.g. consonantal alternation in the prepositional case: *ruka* 'hand' – prep. *ruce*; *narod* 'people' – *naro**dz**e*; *malako* 'milk' – *malace*. Note also the alternation between stressed *o* /vo/ and *a* /a/: *aknó* 'window', pl. *vóknı*; *vóz′era* 'lake', pl. *azyórı*.

As in Russian, an animate/inanimate distinction is observed in the formation of the second declension masculine singular and the plural of all nouns: e.g. *brat* 'brother' – *brat**a*** – *brat**ow*** (gen. sing./pl.). For all nouns denoting inanimates, the accusative = the nominative.

Adjective

In general, as in Russian.

Pronoun

The first and second person series behave much as in Russian, with spelling differences: e.g. from *tı*, acc./gen. *cjabje*, but dative: *tabje*. The third person series is unique in Slavonic in that the palatalized onset of the oblique cases is also present in the nominative: *jon* – fem. *jana* – nt. *jano*, plural for all three genders: *janı*.

DEMONSTRATIVE PRONOUN/ADJECTIVE

getı 'this'; *toj* 'that'

INTERROGATIVE PRONOUN

xto 'who?'; *što* 'what?'

In the oblique cases of the interrogative pronoun *xto*, *x* > *k*: acc./gen. *kago*, dat. *kamu*, instr./prep. *kim*. Similarly, /ʃ/ > /tʃ/ in the oblique cases of *što*: gen. *čago*, dat. *čamu*, instr./prep. *čim*.

RELATIVE PRONOUN

As interrogative.

Numerals

Formally as in Russian, apart from spelling differences. As in Ukrainian, however, and in opposition to Russian, 2, 3, 4 are followed by nominative/accusative plural: e.g. *dva stalı* 'two tables'; *čatırı bratı* 'four brothers'.

Verb

The aspect/mood/tense system of Russian and Ukrainian is shared by Belorussian. Most Belorussian verbs are paired for aspect. The infinitive is in *-c′*, *-c* (*-čı* after velar).

ASPECT

Many perfective forms are made from imperfective by prefixation.

Imperfective	*Perfective*
isci 'to go'	pa.isci
pisac′ 'to write'	na.pisac′
magčı 'to be able'	z.magčı

The reverse process, imperfective form from perfective, may use, e.g. *-va-*: *vıpisac′* 'to write out'; imperfective: *vıpisvac′* 'to be writing out'.

VERBS OF MOTION

As in Russian and Ukrainian, the imperfective aspect is equipped to distinguish between a generalized concept and a particular application thereof: the latter can then be made perfective: e.g. *jezdzic′* 'to travel' (in general) – *jexac′* 'to make a specific journey': perf. *pa.jexac′*.

TENSES

There are two conjugations:

(a) verbs in *-(v)ac′*, *-jec′*, *-nuc′*, etc.
(b) verbs in *-ic′*, *-ıc′*, *-jec′*, etc.

Specimen present tense: conjugation (a), consonant stem: *nasıc′* 'to carry' (stress on final syllable throughout):

Singular	*Plural*
njasu	njasjom
njasješ	njesja**cjé**
njasje	njasuc′

It is noteworthy that the *-e-* of the second person singular ending does not change to *-o-* under stress.

Past tense: as in Russian and Ukrainian; in masculine form, *-l* → *-w*: e.g. *čıtaw* 'I (masc.) read'.
Future:

(a) Perfective: formally, the present endings of the imperfective: e.g. *skažu* 'I shall say'.
(b) Imperfective: future tense of *bıt'* + imperfective infinitive: e.g. *ja budu čıtac'* 'I shall read/be reading'.

SUBJUNCTIVE MOOD
Past tense + invariable particle *bı*.

IMPERATIVE
There are forms for second person singular and first and second person plural: e.g. from *kupic'* 'to buy': *kupi*; *kupjem*, *kupicje*.

PARTICIPLES
Only the past passive participle is regularly used in spoken Belorussian: e.g. *napisanı-* 'written'; *kupljenı* 'bought'; *uzjatı* 'taken'.

Prepositions

Prepositions govern the oblique cases. Many prepositions can take more than one case, with corresponding changes in meaning. Usually, however, there is a preferred case, e.g. *dlya* 'for' with the genitive, *k/ka* 'to' with the dative, *ab* 'concerning' with the prepositional.

Word order

As in Russian.

В начале было Слово, и Слово было у Бога, и Слово было Бог.
2. Оно было в начале у Бога.
3. Все чрез Него на̀чало быть, и без Него ничто не на̀чало быть, что̀ на̀чало быть.
4. В Нем была жизнь, и жизнь была свет человеков;
5. И свет во тьме светит, и тьма не объяла его.
6. Был человек, посланный от Бога; имя ему Иоанн.
7. Он пришел для свидетельства, чтобы свидетельствовать о Свете, дабы все уверовали чрез него.
8. Он не был свет, но *был послан*, чтобы свидетельствовать о Свете.

BELUDZH

See **Baluchi**.

BENGALI

INTRODUCTION

This Eastern New Indo-Aryan language is the official language of Bangladesh, where it is spoken by about 110 million people, and the official regional language for another 55 million people in the Indian state of West Bengal. There are also sizable Bengali-speaking communities in Orissa, Assam, Bihar, Tripura, and Meghalaya. Along with its close congeners, Oriya and Assamese, Bengali crystallized from the Magadhi Apabhraṁśa, roughly between AD 1000 and 1200. Texts dating from this period (e.g. the esoteric Buddhist–Tantric hymns known as *Caryāpada*) show general Magadhan areal features, but are usually described as being in Old Bengali. Middle Bengali was the vehicle for a very rich literature on traditional Indian themes, which is remarkable in view of the fact that by then Bengal was Muslim; indeed, Bengal remained part of the Mughal Empire until the eighteenth century. The British take-over in the nineteenth century added a third strand to an already composite cultural scene. Bengal now became the focal point of European cultural influence in India, and literary genres, alien to the sub-continent, began to appear: e.g. the novel, first in imitation of Scott, but soon developing to culminate in the socio-political realist novel of criticism and protest. The list of outstanding names includes Sáratcandra Caṭṭopādhyāy and one figure of world stature – Rabindranāth Ṭhākur. A key role in the formation and education of a secularized and anti-traditionalist reading public was played by critical, often pro-Marxist periodicals such as *Kallol* (1923 onwards). Mention should also be made of the rich Bengali folk-literature, the songs of the *Bāuls*, or wandering minstrels, and the *yātrās*, nocturnal celebrations of Hindu gods and goddesses.

The numerous dialects are classified by most authorities on a broad east/west basis. Some are highly divergent, e.g. the Chittagong dialect. Until the twentieth century, Bengali was written in a somewhat artificial, heavily Sanskritized book-language known as *sādhu-bhāṣā*. Modern writing is almost entirely in *calit-bhāṣā*, a demotic based on the Calcutta colloquial. Even here, however, the distinction between book-language and spoken language persists; that is, even modern *calit-bhāṣā* is, in a sense, an artificial medium. Wherever philosophical or scientific terminology is required, of course, the limitless Sanskrit reservoir is always available. In addition, it should not be forgotten that most Bengalis are Muslim; and the language now contains several thousand Arabo-Persian words.

SCRIPT

See **Script** at end of article.

PHONOLOGY

Consonants

stops: p, b, t, d, ṭ, ḍ, k, g
aspirated: ph, (bh > β), th, dh, ṭh, ḍh, kh, gh
affricate: unaspirated: tʃ, dʒ
aspirated: tʃh, dʒh
fricatives: ʃ, s, h
nasals: m, n, ŋ
laterals and flaps: l, r, ṛ, ṛh

In Bengali, as typically in the Magadhan daughter languages, the three sibilants of Sanskrit (dental, retroflex, and palatal) have coalesced to give /ʃ/, with a tendency towards /s/, especially in Bangladesh.

Conjunct consonants are formed, as in Devanāgarī, by means of juxtaposition and superimposition. Consonant clusters are simplified in pronunciation: e.g. *laksya* is realized as /lɔkk^{h}o/, *anekkṣan* as /ɔnekk^{h}on/, *pakši* as /pokkhi/.

Vowels

i, e, æ, a, ɔ, o, u

All occur nasalized. Difference in length is not phonemic. The inherent vowel in the base consonantal form is /ɔ/, corresponding to Sanskrit/Hindi /a/. In the section on **Morphology and Syntax** below, *a* = /aː/, *ă* = /ɔ/.

'Vowel raising', a form of vocalic assimilation, is a characteristic feature of Bengali phonology. It can be broadly summarized as follows:

/ɔ, e, o/ →	[o, i, u] if the following syllable contains /i/ or /u/
/i, u, e/ →	[e, o, æ] if the following syllable contains /ɔ, a, e/ or /o/
/a/ →	[e] if the preceding syllable contains /i/
/a/ →	[o] if the preceding syllable contains /u/

For example, *cali* 'I go' is pronounced [coli]: /ɔ/ raised to [o] before /i/; from *šona* 'to hear': *šuni* 'I hear': /o/ → [u] before /i/; *iccha* 'wish' → *icche*: /a/ → [e], as preceding syllable countains /i/. The /ɔ/ → [o] and /e/ → [æ] shifts affect pronunciation only; the others are notated in the script. Both short and long *i* and *u* still figure in the Bengali vocalic inventory, but the distinction in length is no longer phonologically significant.

Stress

On first syllable in citation form, on headword of phrase in speech.

MORPHOLOGY AND SYNTAX

Noun

Bengali has lost the grammatical gender system of Indo-Aryan, and has replaced it with a natural taxonomy of animate versus non-animate categories. Animates make a plural form in -(*e*)*ra*. For non-animates, there is a variety of affixes, e.g. *-guli/-al-o*, *-šăkăl*, *-šăb*, *-šămăšto*, etc. Some vestiges remain of the typical Indo-Aryan association of certain endings with gender, e.g. the *-a/-i* opposition: *buṛa* 'old man', *buṛi* 'old woman'.

CASE

Only the genitive marker -(*e*)*r* is obligatory. There follow specimen declensions of animate *manuṣ* 'man', and non-animate *nădi* 'river':

	Singular	*Plural*	*Singular*	*Plural*
nom.	manuṣ /maːnus/	manuṣera	nădi	nădiguli
gen.	manuṣer	manuṣder (ke)	nădir	nădigulir
dat.	manuṣke	manuṣder	nădike	nădigu-like
acc.	manuṣke	manuṣder	nădi	nădiguli
loc.	manuṣe	—	nădite	—

These endings are typical; for all cases except the genitive, however, there is a choice of ending. There is a tendency for the agglutinative plural suffixes *-šăb*, *-šăkăl*, etc. to be used with animates as well.

The enclitics *-ṭa/ṭi* may act as defining articles: e.g. *Năgărṭa khub băṛo* 'The town is very big.'

Adjective

As attribute the adjective is indeclinable and precedes the noun. A periphrastic comparative is made by means of *ceye* (the perfective participle of *caoya /tʃawa/* 'to look at') + genitive case: e.g. *Še amar ceye băṛo* 'He is older than I am.'

Pronoun

PERSONAL INDEPENDENT

In contrast to the dual base pattern found in the pronominal system of Western New Indo-Aryan, Bengali uses single bases to which endings are added agglutinatively: sing. 1 *ami*; 2 *tumi* (familiar), *apni* (polite); 3 *še* (familiar), *tini* (polite). The plural forms are: *amra*, *tomra*, *apnara*, *tãhara/tara*. These are declined as nouns: *ami*, *amar*, *amake*, etc.: e.g. *Tini amader kache prătidin ašten* 'He came to us every day' (the postposition *kache* 'to', 'at' takes genitive case).

DEMONSTRATIVE PRONOUN

Three degrees of removal are recognized: *e*, *iha*, *ini* 'this' (proximate); *o*, *uha*, *uni*, 'that' (distal); *še*, *taha*, *ta* 'that' (not visible but known).

INTERROGATIVE PRONOUN

ke 'who?'; *ki* 'what?'

RELATIVE PRONOUN

ǰe/*ǰini*/*ǰa* + correlative: e.g. *ǰe* . . . *še*; *ǰini* . . . *tini*

> **ǰe** lokṭa kal ekhane chilo, **še** abar eseche
> 'the man who was here yesterday has come again'
>
> Tumi **ǰ**ekhane thakbe, ami.o **š**ekhane thakba
> 'Where you will be, there shall I be also.'

Numerals

1–10: *œk*, *dui*, *tin*, *car*, *pãc*, *chɔĕ*, *šat*, *aṭ*, *nɔĕ*, *dɔš*. 11–19: the forms are based on the units, ending in *-o*: e.g. *œgaro*, *baro*, *tœro*, *coddo*, *pɔnero*. 20 *biš*; 30 *triš*; 40 *colliš*; from 20 to 99 the forms are unpredictable, though decade + 9 is always related to the following decade: e.g. 30 *triš*, 39 *unɔcolliš*; 40 *colliš*; 49 *unɔpɔ̃caš*; 50 *pɔ̃ncaš*. 100 /šɔto/ (the word is written as *šɔtɔ*: the second *ɔ* is raised to /o/).

Verb

Roots are mono- or disyllabic. Many derived bases are made from nouns by adding *-a*: e.g. *ghum* 'sleep': *ghum**a**na* 'to sleep'. The rules for vowel harmony (see above) apply throughout the verbal system: e.g.

> root *căla* 'to go': /tʃɔlo/ 'you go', /tʃ**o**li/ 'I go';
> root *dekha* 'to see': /d**æ**kho/ 'you see', /d**e**khi/ 'I see';
> root *lekha* 'to write': /l**e**kho/ 'you write', /l**i**khi/ 'I write'.

On the basis of such alternations, Chatterji (cited in Zograph 1982) has divided Bengali verbs into seven classes.

Aspect/tense markers are added to the stem before the personal inflections: e.g. *-ch-* for imperfective/continuative, *-b-* for future, *-l-* for past.

TENSE SYSTEM

Number is not marked. The first person has one form for both singular and plural: e.g. *jani* 'I know/we know'. The second person has three forms depending on status of addressee: familiar, everyday polite, and respectful; typical endings are *-i*, *-e*, *-en*/*-iš*, *-o*, *-en*. The third person has an ordinary form in *-e*/*-o* and a respectful one in *en*. Thus, the form *janen*, for example, may mean 'you know' (sing./pl.), 'he/she knows', or 'they know'. The correct meaning can be fixed by the personal pronoun.

As an example of tense formation, here are the third person ordinary forms of the indicative mood of the root *kɔra* 'to do' (*calit-bhaṣa* forms as pronounced):

simple present	kɔre 'does'
imperfective present	korche 'is doing'
perfective present	koreche 'has done'
simple past	korlo 'did'
imperfective past	korchilo 'was doing'
perfective past	korechilo 'had done'
habitual past	korto 'would do'
future	korbe 'will do'
imperative mood	koruk 'let him/her (etc.) do'

NON-FINITE FORMS

There are two verbal nouns: present *-a/-wa/-na*, etc., and future in *-(i)ba*. Participles: imperfective in *-(i)te*, perfective in *-iya/-e* and conditional in *-(i)le*: e.g. *Ami kichu kărte pari na* 'I can't do anything'; *Še kătha šune apni ki bălechilen?* 'What did you say when you heard that?'

CAUSATIVE

The marker is *-a-* between stem and ending: e.g.

jana 'to know': *janana* 'to inform' (/janano/)
dekha 'to see': *dekhana* 'to show' (/dekhano/)

PASSIVE

An impersonal construction involving nominalization is preferred: e.g. the use of the verbal noun in *-a*, etc. plus an auxiliary, /jawa/ 'to go', or /hɔwa/ 'to be'. The auxiliary does not agree with the logical subject: e.g. *amake pawa gœlo* 'to-me finding it-went' = 'I was found'; *E rasta diya jawa jay na* 'this street going-along goes not' = 'One cannot go along this street.'

NEGATIVE

The particle is *na*, with allophones [ne, ni]. It is never stressed. Example: *Tar sambandhe kichui jani ne* 'I know nothing about it.'

Postpositions

Postpositions follow either the nominative or the genitive: e.g. *ṭebiler upăr* 'on the table'; *ghărer bhităre* 'inside the house'.

The perfective participles of certain verbs, e.g. /dewa/ 'to give', /newa/ 'to take', act as postpositions: e.g. from /tʃawa/ 'to look at', /tʃeye/ has come to mean 'than' (*see* **Adjective**, above). Similarly, /theke/ from /thaka/ 'to stay', means 'from'; /diye/ from /dewa/ means 'through': *Janala diye dekhi* 'I look through the window.'

Word order

SOV is normal.

১ আদিতে বাক্য ছিলেন, এবং বাক্য ঈশ্বরের
কাছে ছিলেন, এবং বাক্য ঈশ্বর ছিলেন।
২,৩ তিনি আদিতে ঈশ্বরের কাছে ছিলেন। সকলই
তাঁহার দ্বারা হইয়াছিল, যাহা হইয়াছে, তাহার কিছুই
৪ তাঁহা ব্যতিরেকে হয় নাই। তাঁহার মধ্যে জীবন ছিল,
৫ এবং সেই জীবন মনুষ্যগণের জ্যোতি ছিল। আর সেই
জ্যোতি অন্ধকার মধ্যে দীপ্তি দিতেছে, আর অন্ধকার
তাহা গ্রহণ * করিল না।
৬ এক জন মনুষ্য উপস্থিত হইলেন, তিনি ঈশ্বর হইতে
৭ প্রেরিত হইয়াছিলেন, তাঁহার নাম যোহন। তিনি
সাক্ষ্যের জন্য আসিয়াছিলেন, যেন সেই জ্যোতির
বিষয়ে সাক্ষ্য দেন, যেন সকলে তাঁহার দ্বারা বিশ্বাস
৮ করে। তিনি সেই জ্যোতি ছিলেন না, কিন্তু আসিলেন,
৯ যেন সেই জ্যোতির বিষয়ে সাক্ষ্য দেন

SCRIPT

The derivative of Brāhmī in which Bengali (Bāṅlā) is written is also used for Assamese, Khasi, and a few other local languages.

Signs used in Bengali script:

Sanskrit *anusvāra*, Bengali *ɔnušar*: in Sanskrit, the sign ̇ , superscript above the letter which it follows, marks the unmodified nasal. In Bengali it is notated as ং and may be replaced in some words by the velar nasal ঙ. As in Devanāgarī, vowels may also be nasalized by the sign ঁ.

ঃ Sanskrit *visarga*, Bengali *bišɔrgo*. In some Bengali words the sign indicates strong aspiration; in others it marks a lengthening of the preceding consonant. For rules of sandhi affecting *visarga*, *see* **Devanāgarī**.

্ *hasanta*. This corresponds to Devanāgarī *virāma*. It cancels the vowel sound inherent in a consonant:

Bengali ক্ = Devanāgarī क् /k/.

The accompanying table shows the consonantal inventory of Bengali, the independent vowels, and the secondary vowel signs in combination with /k/.

THE BENGALI SCRIPT

CONSONANTS

ক *k*	খ *k*	গ *g*	ঘ *gh*	ঙ *ṅ*		
চ *c*	ছ *ch*	জ *j*	ঝ *jh*	ঞ *ñ*		
ট *ṭ*	ঠ *ṭh*	ড *ḍ*	ঢ *ḍh*	ণ *ṇ*		
ত *t*	থ *th*	দ *d*	ধ *dh*	ন *n*		
প *p*	ফ *ph*	ব *b*	ভ *bh*	ম *m*		
য় *y*	র *r*	ল *l*	ব *v*			
শ *ś*	ষ *ṣ*	স *s*	হ *h*	য *z*	ড় *ṛ*	ঢ় *ṛh*

VOWELS

(a) Independent:

অ *a*	আ *ā*	ই *i*	ঈ *ī*	উ *u*	ঊ *ū*	ঋ *ri*
এ *ē*	ঐ *ai*	ও *ō*	ঔ *au*	অং *aṅ*	অঃ *a'*	

(b) In combination with /k/:

কা *kā*	কি *ki*	কী *kī*	কু *ku*	কূ *kū*
কৃ *kri*	কে *kē*	কৈ *kai*	কো *kō*	কৌ *kau*

NUMERALS

১	২	৩	৪	৫	৬	৭	৮	৯	০
1	2	3	4	5	6	7	8	9	0

BERBER

INTRODUCTION

Berber is a member of the Afro-Asiatic (Semito-Hamitic) family. For the Greeks and Romans who colonized North Africa, the local inhabitants were βάϱβαϱοι, *barbari*, who spoke a 'barbarous' tongue. The designation found its way into Arabic, and into English as Berber. An ethnonym for the mainstream of Berber tribes is *amažiγen*; the language is *tamažiγt*.

Berber seems to have been originally spoken in a strip of North African territory stretching from the Atlantic coast to the borders of Egypt. Over the last thousand years, Berber-speaking populations have spread beyond this original habitat, and today two or three hundred Berber dialects are spoken in about a dozen North African countries: Egypt, Libya, Tunisia, Algeria, Morocco, Mauretania, Mali, Burkina Faso, Niger, Chad. The total number of Berber speakers is put at *c*. 12 million. The principal dialects are: Shluh, Tamazight, and Riff in Morocco; Kabyle and Shawia in Algeria; Tamahaq (Tamashek) or Tuareg in several Saharan countries. Shluh is also known as *tašelḥait*, Shawia as *tašawit*, and Kabyle as *taqbaylit*. All of these dialects are essentially spoken colloquials, with no written literature. Nevertheless, a script for the notation of Berber consonants had been devised more than 2,000 years ago, as is shown by two bilingual (Punic-Berber) inscriptions found in the Roman city of Dugga in Tunisia. Many hundreds of Berber inscriptions have also been discovered in Libya. These are in Roman script, but are of great value as they are vowelled.

SCRIPT

See **Script** at end of article.

PHONOLOGY

A basic inventory includes the following phonemes:

Consonants

stops: b, d, ɖ, t, k, g
affricates (in Kabyle and elsewhere): ts, dz, tʃ, dʒ
fricatives: f, s, z, ʐ, ʃ, ʒ, γ,
nasals: m, n
lateral and flap: l, r
semi-vowels: j, w

/ŧ, đ/ emphatics appear in Kabyle and other northern dialects. Several Arabic sounds – /ȿ, q, ʕ (= 'ain), ħ, ḫ/ – have been widely borrowed.

Consonants are long or short; long consonants are tense and held: C̄, not C.C. The contrast between C and C̄ is fundamental in Berber phonology.

Vowels

The basic contrast is between full grade /i, a, u/ and reduced or null grade /ə/ or Ø. Central Atlas Tamazight has the following inventory:

front: i, ɪ, e
central: ɛ, a, ə
back: o, ʊ, u

All with allophones.

MORPHOLOGY AND SYNTAX

Most roots have two or three radicals; mono- and quadriliterals also occur. Common Afro-Asiatic features in Berber are: *t* as feminine marker, *k* as second person marker; the prefix/suffix conjugational paradigm; broken plural.

Noun

There are two genders in Berber, masculine and feminine. All feminine nouns have *t-* initial, and feminine nouns with a final root consonant also take *-t* following this consonant: e.g. *agmar* 'horse', ***t**agmar**t*** 'mare'; *afunas* 'bull', ***t**afunas**t*** 'cow'; in Tamahaq *əkahi* 'cock', ***t**əkahi**t*** 'hen'. The feminine *t . . . t* circumfix is also used for certain natural phenomena: e.g. ***t**afuk**t*** 'sun'; ***t**aka**t*** 'fire' (both of these are also feminine in Arabic).

The formal structure of the Tamahaq noun can be summarized as follows:

masc. sing. has *a, e, i,* or *u* initial; plural, *i* initial;
fem. sing. and pl., *t-* initial.

There are exceptions: for example, some masculine nouns have a consonantal initial, including even the normal feminine characteristic: *ti* 'father'; *midden* 'men'. On the other hand, some feminine nouns do not have *t-*, e.g. *(am)ma* 'mother'; and some do not take the normal final *-t*: *timsi* 'fire', *tes* 'cow'.

NUMBER

(a) By broken plural; (b) sound plural by affix.

(a) For example, *(a)drar* 'mountain', pl. *durar* or *(i)drarən*. In the broken plural, *-a-* is typical vocalization between R_2 and R_3 (R = radical): cf. *tamazirt* 'garden', pl. *timaz**a**r*. In Tamahaq *atri* 'star', pl. *itr**a**n*; *amagur* 'old camel', pl. *imug**a**r*.

(b) Suffixation: the characteristic ending is *-wən* (masc.), *(w)in* (fem.): e.g. *amɣar* 'man', pl. *imɣar**ən***; *tamɣart* 'women', pl. *timɣar**in***.

DECLENSION

Nouns are free or annexed; free nouns have vocalic initial (masc.), or *t-* + vowel (fem.). In the annexed state, expressing the genitival/relational link, masculine nouns take *w-*; feminine nouns do not change (i.e. = free state).

The genitival/relational construct is also expressed by the *-n-/-l-* link realized as /ən/ /nə/ /əl/ /lə/: e.g. Tamahaq *amγar **n** aγerem* 'the sheikh of the town'; *aiis wareγ **n** abba* 'this horse of my father'; Central Atlas Tamazight *tamazirt **l** lmγrib* 'the country of Morocco'; *ssuq **l** l.ḥdd* 'Sunday market'; Kabyle *ab̲rid̲ **n** ssuq* 'the road to market'.

Accusative:

As nominative:

inγa abeggi 'he killed a jackal'

Dative (marked in Tamahaq by *i*):

ikfa i ales 'he gave to the man'

Ablative (marked in Tamahaq by *s*):

igmedh s aγerəm 'he came forth from the town'.

Adjective

No specific form; a participial construction is used: e.g. Tamahaq *yulaγən* 'being good' (masc.); *tulaγət* (fem.); *illa γur.i aiis yulaγən* 'I have a good horse' (*illa* 'there is'; *γur.i* 'to me'). Tamazight: *lāil amẓẓian* 'small boy', pl. *luašum imẓẓian*; *tarbat tamẓẓiant* 'small girl', pl. *tirbatin timẓẓiamin*.

A comparative form is made with the preposition *fəll* (Tamahaq *full*) 'on': *kəmmu təhusid full ult.ma.m* 'you are prettier than your sister' (*ult.ma* is 'mother's daughter'; *-m* is the second person singular feminine marker).

Pronoun

Free and affixed forms. The free forms are used only for emphasis; the set is remarkable for having feminine forms for all persons and both numbers, with the sole exception of the first person singular (in Kabyle).

The Kabyle forms for emphatic free and post-prepositional affix are:

		Singular		*Plural*	
		Free	*Affix*	*Free*	*Affix*
1	masc.	nəkk	-i	nukni	-nəγ
	fem.	–	–	nukə nti	-ntəγ
2	masc.	kəčč	-k	kunwi	-wən
	fem.	kəm	-m	kunə mti	-nkwətt
3	masc.	nətta	-s	nut̲ni	-nsən
	fem.	nəttat̲	-s	nut̲ə nti	-nsətt

For example, in Tamahaq: *akal n.nəγ* 'our country'; *akal n awən* 'your (masc. pl.) country'.

There are also pronominal affix series for kinship terms and for direct and indirect object; these sets do not differ greatly from the one tabulated above. Cf. in Tamahaq:

əkfiγ **ak** 'I gave you (masc.)'
ikfa has**en** 'he gave them (masc.)'

ənniγ **am** 'I told you (fem.)'
inna has 'he said to him/her'

With prepositions: Tamahaq *γur.**i*** 'at my home'; *dat **əm*** 'before you (fem.)'; *gar aw**ən*** 'among/between you (masc. pl.)'.

DEMONSTRATIVE PRONOUN

In Tamahaq and Kabyle: *wa* (masc.), pl. *wi*; *ta* (fem.), pl. *ti*. Cf. Tamahaq:

wa hin 'mine' (the referent is masc. sing.)
ta nnək 'thine' (the referent is fem. sing.)
wi nnit 'his' (the referent is pl.)

warəγ/wadəγ 'this' follows a noun: *ales wadəγ yulaγən* 'this man is good'; cf. *warəγ ales yulaγən* 'this is a good man'.

INTERROGATIVE PRONOUN

ma 'who?', 'what?', e.g. *ma issanən* 'who knows?'; *ma tərhid* 'what do you want?'. The dative of *ma* is *mis* (Tamahaq): *mis təkfid tirawt* 'to whom did you give the letter?'

RELATIVE PRONOUN

The *wa* series can be used + resumptive pronoun, e.g. in Tamahaq: *ales **wa as** əkfiγ triawt* 'the man who to-him I gave the letter', (i.e. . . . to whom . . .); *arabən **wi asən** əkfiγ əhari'n azrəf* 'the Arabs to whom I gave money'.

Numerals

The older (indigenous) numerical system is best preserved in Tamahaq and in the Tašelhayt of the High Atlas. Masculine and feminine forms are distinguished. The masculine forms, 1–10: *ya*(*n*), *sin*, *kṛaḍ*, *ḳḳuẓ*, *səmmus*, *sḍis*, *sa*, *tam*, *tẓa*, *mra*; the feminine forms add *-t* to these (with some variants, e.g. the feminine of *sin* is *snat*).

This indigenous series has been largely replaced by the Arabic numerals from 3 onwards.

After the numerals 2 to 10, the noun is in the plural: *səmmus iisan* 'five horses'. From 11 onwards, the formula is: base decade + noun in plural + unit: Tamahaq: *məraw iisan d.iien* 'ten horses and one', i.e. 'eleven horses'; *məraw iisan d.kəṛadh* 'thirteen horses'.

Verb

Three bases are distinguishable: (1) C_1C_2; (2) $C_1C_2C_2 + a$; (3) $C_1C_2 + i/a$; i.e. base 1 is unmarked for vocalization, bases 2 and 3 are marked. It is customary to designate these bases (1) aroist–imperative, (2) strengthened aorist, (3) preterite.

Exactly how these bases are related to tense and mood – if, indeed, the categories of tense and mood can be usefully applied to the Berber verb – is a controversial question. Different researchers have distinguished an aorist and a preterite, a past tense from a present/future, a present/past from a future; some make an aspectual distinction between perfective and imperfective. Hanoteau in his grammar of Tamahaq (1896) uses the term 'aorist' for his '*mode unique*', which can refer equally to present, past, or future: this 'aorist' can be modulated by vocalization, e.g. by *-a-* between the second and third radicals: cf. *əlkemeγ* 'I follow, have followed', *əlkem**a**γ* 'I am now following'.

The general paradigm of personal markers, prefixal and suffixal, is:

	Singular	*Plural*
1	ø R -əγ	nə- R ø
2	tə- R -t/-d	tə- R -əm
		tə- R -əmt
3 masc.	y/i- R ø	ø R -ən
fem.	tə- R ø	ø R -ən(t)

DERIVED FORMS

s- causative; *t-* passive; *n-* reflexive/passive: e.g. Tamahaq forms of *əγbər* 'to kick':

səγbər 'to cause to beat', 'kick'
təγbər 'to be beaten', 'kicked'
nəγ**b**ə**r** 'to beat', 'kick each other'

Further examples of the derived forms in Tamahaq:

Causative *s-*:

ərhin 'to be ill': sərhin 'to make someone ill'
əlməd 'to learn': səlməd 'to teach', e.g. əlmədəγ tamaheq; ma ha.k tet isəlmədən 'I have learned Tamahaq; who taught you?' (*ha.k* 'to you'; *tet* 'it' fem. sing. referent).

Passive (the Tamahaq characteristics are *tu-* or *m-*):

ənγ 'to kill': i.**tu**.nəγ 'he has been killed'
əkš 'to eat': i.**tu**.əkš 'it has been eaten'
əsu 'to drink': i.**m**.su.a 'it has been drunk'

Reciprocal (*nim-*):

ilal 'to help': ə.**nim**.alal.ən 'they helped each other'

Habitual action (this is expressed by a *t*- characteristic, or by gemination of the second radical):

as 'to go': **t**.as 'to go habitually'; əlməd 'to learn': lammədəγ 'I learn habitually'

Subjunctive (this is expressed in Tamahaq by the *mode unique*, or by the future):

ərhiγ addias 'I want – he will come', i.e. 'I want him to come'

PARTICIPLES

y/i...n is a frequent formula: e.g. in Tamahaq *ilkəm* 'follow', participle *ilkəmən*; in Kabyle, *əkšəm* 'go in', participle *ikəšmən.*

NEGATION

In Tamahaq, *ur* is a general negator: e.g. *ur essineγ* 'I don't know'. Similarly in Tamazight, *ur d.idzi* 'he didn't come'. In Kabyle and some other dialects, /j/ acts as a negator in the past tense: e.g. *unfəγ* 'I left', *un**i**fəγ* 'I didn't leave'.

Prefixed particles may be tense formants, e.g. *kelad* (imperfect), *ad* (future), in Tamahaq: *kəlad irəgeh dat.i* 'he was walking in front of me'. -*d* and -*n* are directional markers: e.g. *awi* 'to take', *awi**d*** 'to bring', *awi**n*** 'to take away'.

In Tamahaq, *ad* is prefixed to singular 1 and 3 (masc.) and to plural 3 (masc. and fem.); *att* to singular 2 (fem.) and to plural 2 (both genders); *ann* to plural 1. E.g. ***ad**.əlkəm.əγ* 'I shall follow', ***att**.əlkəm.əmt* 'you (fem. sing.) will follow'.

The verb 'to be': in Tamahaq, *ili* is used: *əlliγ*, *təllid*, *illa*, etc. Coupled with the preposition *γur* (marked for person) this expresses possession: *illa γur.**i*** *aiis* 'I have a horse'; *kəlad illa γur.**i** aiis* 'I had a horse'. Similarly, ***t**əlla γur.**i*** ***t**ibəgaw**t** tulaγə**t*** 'I have a good mare'; *əllanət γur.**sən** tibəgawin yulaγənin* 'they have good mares'.

Prepositions

Examples: *dat* 'before', *dəγ* 'in', *s* 'from', *γur* 'at the home of': e.g. Tamahaq *dəγ aγerem* 'in town'; *s akal ənnit* 'from his country'.

Word order

VSO

G'LIḂD́Ā illa Aoual; Aoual illa ƒor Rebbi, Aoual 1
illa d́'Rebbi. Ouagi illa ġ'lib̆d́ā ƒor Rebbi. Irkoul 2 3
elh̆aouaïdj tsououqement yīs; oulach ain our-netsouou-
qem ara yīs, d́eg irkoul ain itsououqemen. D'eg-s ai 4
thella thoud́erth, thoud́erth thella tsafath g-ergazen.
Thafath thechâcha ġe-ṭlam, ṭlam our ts-ifh̆im ara. 5
Illa íoun ourgaz, ism-is Yah̆yā, itsouchegâ-d s'ƒor 6
Rebbi. Yousa-d ad́-yili d́' inígi, íouakken ad́-ichehed́ ƒef 7
thafath, íouakken ad́-amnen irkoul fedéma en-*chehād́a*-s.
Our ill'ara entsa s'iman-is tsafath, lamâna *itsouchegâ-d* 8
íouakken ad́-ichehed́ ƒef thafath.

(Kabyle dialect)

SCRIPT

The two inscriptions found at Dugga are in a script identical, or at least very close, to the *tifinagh* script, which is still in use among the Tuareg people. The word *tifinagh* is the Tamahaq plural form of *tafineq*, which means 'letter', and is a Berberization of the Latin word *punica*.

Tifinagh is a purely consonantal script, written from right to left. It has no way of indicating initial or medial short vowels, though the point called *tagherit* (see the accompanying table) may be used to indicate final /a, i/ or /uː/ or /uː/. Further, the letters : and ⵣ can be used as the counterparts of the Arabic /uː/ and /iː/. There is no way of indicating gemination, which is of phonemic importance in Berber.

THE BERBER SCRIPT

THE ALPHABET

Tar′erit	·	*a, i, u*	Iel	ǁ	*l*
Ieb	◫ ⴲ	*b*	Iem	⊐	*m*
Iet	+	*t*	Ien	I	*n*
Ied	⊓ ∧ ⊔	*d*	Iek	·:	*k*
Iej	ⵊ	*j*	Iak′	···	*q*
Iez	#	*z*	Ier′	⋮	*ɣ*
Iez′	ⵥ ⵥ	*z′*	Iech	ʚ	*ʃ*
Ier	□ ○	*r*	Iah	⁞	*h*
Ies	⊡ ⊙	*s*	Iadh	Ǝ	*ḍ, ṭ*
Ieg	.!. ï	*g*	Iakh	∷	*χ*
Ieg′	⋈	*g′*	Iaou	:	*ū*
Ief	ⵂ ⵊ	*f*	Iéy	≤	*ī*

COMBINED LETTERS

Iebt	+◫	*bt*	Ielt	ǁ+	*lt*
Iezt	#+	*zt*	Iemt	+⊐	*mt*
Iert	⊞	*rt*	Ient	†	*nt*
Iest	+⊡	*st*	Iecht	+ʚ	*ʃt*
Iegt	‡	*gt*	Ienk	·†·	*nk*
Ieg′t	+⋈	*g′t*			

Source: Hanoteau, A. (1980) *La Langue Tamachek*, Algiers.

BIKOL

INTRODUCTION

This language belongs to the Philippine group of Malayo-Polynesian languages. It forms a dialect complex sited between the Tagalog and Visayan speech areas in Southern Luzon and in the offshore islands. The standard dialect is that of Naga city. The standard language is used in local broadcasting and journalism. There are many Spanish loanwords.

SCRIPT

Romanization. Spanish loanwords are reproduced in Bikol spelling.

PHONOLOGY

As in Tagalog, with addition of palatalized series: /t′, d′, s′, n′, l′/.

Stress

Stress is mobile: e.g. in the verb it shifts as tense, aspect, and modal markers are added.

MORPHOLOGY AND SYNTAX

Noun

Nouns are introduced by specific markers: *si*/*an* for focused items, *ki*/*ni*/*nin*/*kan* for non-focused items. These have plural forms, and there is a locative series in *ki*/*sa*: e.g. *nagpuli' si Carlos* 'Carlos went home'; *inapod ako nin maestro* 'a teacher called (*inapod*) me'; *nagbakal ako nin tinapay* 'I bought bread'; *nagbakal ako nin tinapay sa sa' od* 'I bought bread in the market.'

POSSESSION

The linker is *-ng*/*na*: e.g. *an mga linguahe.**ng** Pilipino* 'the languages of the Philippines'; or by simple apposition, e.g. *an lapis kan maestro* 'the teacher's pencil'. The word *mga* in the example above is pronounced /maŋa/ and is a plural marker: cf. *lalaki* 'boy', *mga lalaki* 'boys'.

Adjective

As attribute, adjective precedes noun, to which it is linked by *-ng*/*na*: e.g. *dakula* 'big', *an dakula**ng** lapis* 'the big pencil'; *magayon* 'beautiful', *magayon **na** babayi* 'beautiful woman'. Adjectives are divided into *ma-* stems, *ha-*

stems, and Ø- stems. The plural of *ma-* adjectives is made by reduplicating the first syllable after *ma-*: e.g. *magayon*, pl. *ma**ga**gayon*. *ha-* stems insert *-r* with echo vowel: e.g. *halangkaw* 'tall', pl. *ha**ra**langkaw*.

COMPARATIVE

The Spanish *más* is generally used.

Pronoun

There are four sets corresponding to the marker series: in the *si* class the singular forms are: *ako*, *(i)ka*, *siya*; pl. *kami/kita*, *kamo*, *sinda*. The *ni* class has singular *ko*, *mo*, *niya*; pl. *mi/ta*, *nindo*, *ninda*. The forms for the *ki* and locative classes are identical: sing. *sakuya*, *saimo*, *saiya*: pl. *samuya'/satuya'*, *saindo*, *sainda*. The second form in the paired forms for first person plural is the inclusive form. For example, *Ika an nagapod* 'Was it you that called?'; *Inapod ka niya* 'He called you.'

Locative class: *Nagiba siya saindo* 'Did he go with you?'; *Nagiba siya sakuya'* 'He went with me'; *Binakal ko an libro saimo* 'I bought the book from you (sing.)'; *Binakal ko an libro sainda* 'I bought a book from them.'

DEMONSTRATIVE PRONOUN

Like the personal pronouns, these are correlated with the *si/ni/ki* locative classes: three degrees of relative distance + linker: e.g. *ini*, *iyan*, *ito*; *an libro.ng ini* = *ini.ng libro* 'this book'; *sa lalaki.ng iyan* 'that boy'.

INTERROGATIVE PRONOUN

Appears as *si'isay*, *ni'isay*, *ki'isay*: i.e. correlated with the pronominal and marker series.

RELATIVE PRONOUN

an can often be used: e.g. *Ano an itina'o saimo* 'What was (that which was) given you?'

Numerals

The Bikol numbers 1–10 are: *saro'*, *duwa*, *tulo*, *apat*, *lima*, *anom*, *pito*, *walo*, *siyam*, *sampulo'*. The Spanish numerals may be used for these, and are the sole forms for numbers beyond 10. They are spelled according to Bikol orthography: e.g. *katorse* 14.

Verb

INTRANSITIVE

The prefix is *mag-*, with a past-tense form in *nag-* or *pig-*. The agent is focused; if pronominal, from the *si* class: e.g. *mag.balik* 'to return', *Nag.balik ako alas kuatro* 'I came back at 4 o'clock.'

TRANSITIVE

Here, by definition, either agent or patient can be focused. If the agent is focused, the primary prefixes are *mag-/nag-* as in intransitive verbs; if patient is stressed, the prefix *i-* or the suffixes *-an/-on* are used. Subject and object pronouns cannot be from the same class. Example: *inapod ko siya* 'I called him' (*ko* – subject – is *ni* class; *siya* – object – is *si* class).

TENSE STRUCTURE

Past, progressive, and future tenses are formally distinguished.

Past: *nag-* and *pig-* are past-tense markers. The infix *-in-* can also be used following a consonant initial: e.g. *kakan* 'to eat', past ***kinakan*** (or *pig.kakan/nag.kakan*: *Pig.kakan mo an ice cream na ini?* 'Have you eaten the ice-cream?').

Future: usually by reduplication of first base syllable: e.g. *gibohon* 'to do', future *gigibohon*; *tabangan* 'to help', future *tatabangan*.

Progressive: the future form + infix *-in-*: the final *-on* of *-on* verbs drops: *gibohon* – future *gigibohon* – prog. *ginigibo*: e.g. *Ano an ginigibo mo?* 'Where (is it that you) are (you) going?' *mag-* verbs add the prefix *nag-* to the progressive: *mag.hugas* 'to wash', progressive *nag.hu.hugas.*

POTENTIAL VERBS

Verbs denoting change or accidental happening. Three basic prefixes are used: *ma-* with focus on object; *maka-*, focus on subject; *ika-*, focus on recipient, beneficiary, etc. Examples: from verb *tumba* 'to fall': *matumba* 'to trip over something and fall'; *makatumba* 'to knock something over by accident' (onus on agent). These have tense forms: e.g. *matungtungan* 'get stepped on'; past *natungtungan*; future *matutungtungan*; progressive = past.

CAUSATIVE

The characteristic marker is *pa-*: e.g. for *mag-* verbs, *magpa-* with focus on agent, and *pa-...-on* with focus on patient. Cf. stem *basa* 'read': *pa.basa. hon* 'to have X read something'; *ipa.basa* 'to have something read by X'. These have tense forms, e.g. from *pa.basa.hon*: past *pinabasa/nagpa-/ pigpa.basa*; future *papabasahon*; from *ipabasa*: past *ipinabasa*, future *ipapabasa*, prog. *ipinapabasa*.

The above is a simplifed outline of basic formulae. Additional prefixes and variant forms proliferate: e.g. the *maki-/paki-* series used in making requests, the *para-* series for reiteratives, and *magka-* series giving a terminative or perfective sense to the verb.

Pag- is a formant applied to both transitive and intransitive stems to generate nominals or adverbial turns of phrase: e.g. *an pagbalik mo* 'your return'; *pagbalik mo* 'when you came back . . . '. The general negating particle is *da'i*: e.g. *da'iko aram* 'I don't know'.

Prepositions

The basic formula is *sa* + noun + article: e.g. *sa likod sa'od* 'at the back of the market' = 'behind the market'; *sa tahaw kan laguerta* 'in the (middle of) the orchard'.

Word order

SVO/VSO, depending on construction.

1 Sa caenotenote sia iyo an Verbo, asin an Verbo nasa caibahan nin Dios, asin an Verbo iyo an Dios.
2 Sia sa caenotenote nasa Dios.
3 An gabos na magña bagay guinibo nia, asin cun day sia day nin anoman na naguibo sa naguinibo.
4 Sa saiya duduman an buhay; asin an buhay iyo an ilao nin magña tauo.
5 Asin an ilao minaliuanag sa magña cadiclomán, alagad an magña cadicloman day namansayan an ilao.
6 Iguá nin saróng tauo, na sinogô nin Dios, na gñinagña-ranan si Juan.
7 Ini napadigdi sa pagsacsi, ta gñaning mapatotoohan an dapit sa ilao, ta gñaning an gabos magturubod huli sa saiya.
8 Bacô sia an ilao, condi napadigdi sa pag-patotoo dapit can ilao;

BLACKFOOT

INTRODUCTION

This Algonquian language is spoken today by about 6,000 Indians, divided into two groups, one in Montana, the other in Alberta.

PHONOLOGY

Consonants

Blackfoot has no voiced stops or fricatives. The consonantal inventory is /p, t, k; c, ç, χ; s; m, n; h, ʔ/. /ç/ is notated as *x*; a notable feature of the phonology is the presence of clusters based on *k* and *x*: *xk* = /çk/, *xts* = /çc/, *ksts* = /ksc/, *xp* = /çp/, etc.

Vowels

aː, ă, ɔ, ɔː, ʌ, eː, ɛ, iː, oː, u

This is Uhlenbeck's list (1938). Uhlenbeck makes the point that [e, i] and [u,o] are likely to be variants of two phonemes.

There is a strong tonic accent; it is free and may be accompanied by prolongation of stressed vowel.

MORPHOLOGY

Noun

For a more detailed description of an Algonquian congener, *see* **Cree**. Blackfoot is also characterized by a fundamental dichotomy between animate and inanimate categories, a dichotomy which, from the Indo-European point of view, is not logically followed through. Thus, some trees are animate, others are not. Parts of the body are inanimate. Uhlenbeck quotes the interesting case of *motokis* 'skin, hide', which is animate but becomes inanimate after processing. Nouns denoting geographical terms are inanimate.

NUMBER

Animate nouns make a plural in *-iks*(*i*): e.g. *imita* 'dog', pl. *imitaiks*; *ponoka* 'elk', pl. *ponokaiks*. An inanimate plural form is in *-ists*(*i*): e.g. *nitummo* 'hill', pl. *nitummoists*. There are many variant forms: e.g. *ake* 'woman', pl. *akeks*.

CASE

There is no declension, in an Indo-European sense. Congruence in the verb determines syntactical relations.

Genitive: possessor precedes possessed: e.g. *ninna otănni* 'my father's daughter'.

Obviative: (*see* **Cree**): obviative forms are used in Blackfoot for third person singular forms topically subordinate to focused (third) person. The focused third person may be implicit, e.g. *unni* 'his father': the form *unni* is obviative because the third person form actually though covertly focused is 'son'.

Most animate nouns have a primary form in *-ua*, *-a* /wa/, with obviative in *-ai*/*-i*: e.g. for root *-nn-* 'father': *ninna* 'my father'; obv. *ninni*; *kinna* 'your father'; obv. *kinni*. The third person form *unni* (obv.) has no primary form.

Many kinship terms and designations for parts of the body are always accompanied by the indefinite personal possessive prefix *mo-*.

Adjective

A small number of independent adjectives precede or follow the noun as attributives: e.g. *ponokāmitaiks aχsiks* 'the good horses' (*aχsi* 'good'). Qualifying material is usually prefixed to the noun; there is a large number of such adjectival prefixes: e.g.

inak- 'small', e.g. *aatsista* 'rabbit', ***inak**aatsista* 'small rabbit';
ino- 'long', e.g. ***ino**kinistsiu* 'he has long arms';
man- 'new', e.g. ***man**okimiu* 'he has a new lodge' (*oki* 'lodge');
matsiu 'good-looking', e.g. *matsoake* 'good-looking woman';
sik- 'black', e.g. ***sik**sika* 'Blackfoot tribe'.

Pronoun

Emphatic (independent) and possessive/verbal subject or object (prefixed):

	Singular			*Plural*	
	Emphatic	*Prefix*		*Emphatic*	*Prefix/Suffix*
1	nistoa	ni(t)-, ho-	*excl.*	nistunan	ni(t)-. . . (i)nan
			incl.	ksistunan	ki(t)-. . . (i)nun
2	ksistoa	ki(t)-, ko-		ksistoau	ki(t)-. . . oau
3	ostoi	o-, ot-		ostoauai	o-. . . oauai

Example of possessive declension, stem *-kos* 'child': ***nokos*** 'my child':

	Singular		*Plural*
1	nokos	*excl.*	nokosinan
		incl.	kokosinun
2	kokos		kokosoau

3 okos	okosoauai

DEMONSTRATIVE PRONOUN

amo 'this' ('here-being'); *oma* 'that' ('there-being'). These are declined for singular and plural, animate and inanimate, and the forms can be verbalized.

INTERROGATIVE PRONOUN

taka 'who?'; *tsala*χ*sa* 'what?'. Often combined with relative pronoun (see below): e.g. *Taka anna*χ*k ninauaxk?* 'Who is (it that is) the chief?' (*ninau* 'chief').

RELATIVE PRONOUN

anna/anni+ χ*ka* (singular); many variants. The form is marked for number and category, animate/inanimate: e.g. *Anni*χ*k nit.axpummai***χk** *napioyisk ikomaxko* 'The house which I bought is very large.'

Numerals

Three sets, simple or neutral, animate, and inanimate. The neutral series 1–10: *nitokska*, *natoka*, *niuokska*, *nisoo*, *nisito*, *nau*, *ixkitsika*, *naniso*, *pixkso*, *kepo*. 11–19: primary + *koputo*. 20 *natsippo*; 30 *nippo*; 40 *nisippo*; 100 *kekippo*.

Animate/inanimate series: coded endings are added to the neutral series: e.g. the rows for 7, 8, are:

ixkitsikami	inanimate:	ixkitsikaii
	nanisoyimi	nanisoyi

Numerical correlatives can also be prefixed to nouns: e.g. *Niuokskaitapiau* 'There are three people.'

Verb

The basic division is into transitive and intransitive verbs, with each of which classes a specific set of endings is associated. Whereas there is only one paradigm for most intransitive verbs, the transitive verb has two paradigms, depending on whether the object is animate or inanimate. Thus, *nit.siksipau* 'I bite him (anim.)'; *nit.sikstsixp* 'I bite it (inanim.)'. Structurally, passive forms underlie the transitive paradigms: cf. *siksipau*, which is an indefinite passive animate form 'he is bitten by somebody'. The same form *siksipau* also means 'we (incl.) bite him (indic. trans. anim.)'. To this form the personal prefixes are added: *nit.siksipau* 'I bite him' (lit. 'he is bitten by me').

The verbal paradigm is marked for two numbers, three persons, and obviative.

MOODS

The indicative is not specifically marked. There are three versions: affirmative, negative, and interrogative.

As a specimen of Blackfoot conjugation: here are the singular forms of the

-siksi- stem 'to bite', in three persons plus obviative; intransitive and transitive affirmative.

	Intransitive	*Transitive animate*	*Transitive inanimate*
1	nit.ai.sikstaki	nit.(ai).siksipau	nit.(ai).sikstsixp
2	kit.ai.sikstaki	kit.(ai).siksipau	kit.(ai).sikstsixp
3	Ø ai.sikstakiu	Ø siksipiu	Ø sikstsim
4	Ø ai.sikstakinai	Ø siksipinai	Ø sikstsiminai

The paradigm continues with forms for plural 1, 2, 3, plus forms for plural object, animate, and inanimate.

There are several other moods: e.g. the causative, formed from the intransitive stem + *-ats-* + transitive animate ending: e.g. *nit.ai.simi* 'I drink' (intrans); *nit.ai.simi.**ats**.au* 'I cause/give him to drink'. (NB *-ai-* in the above example and in the paradigm is the durative marker). Similarly, the imperative, benefactive, translative, conditional, subjunctive, and optional moods have specific markers. The negative marker is *-mat-*.

The many hundreds of forms thus generated in the basic conjugation of the Blackfoot verb are infinitely extended by means of composition with nominal stems, and by modal prefixes of manner, locus, time, degree, etc. For example, almost any noun denoting a part of the body can be compounded with any relevant verb in any form, and with any relevant affix of manner. This leads naturally to rather long words. One example from Uhlenbeck (1938):

osotămomaχkakaiitapisaksitokaie
'Then he was suddenly shot by him (obv.) in the thigh, so that there was a gap in it'

The nominal component here is *mo.apisk* 'thigh'. Uhlenbeck lists about 150 modal prefixes.

1 Oki. Isskoohtsika itsaoma'paistotoahpi ksaahkomma
iikayissitsstsiiwa annaahkayii iihto'tsstsiiwa aamo
iihkana'paisiiyi. Annahkao'ka annaahka Jesus Christ.
Itohpoka'paitapiimiwa anniska A'pistotookiiyiska. Ki
noohkattamiwa A'pistotooki. 2 Awaanio'pa
iikayissitsstsiiwa itsaoma'paistotoahpi ksaahkomma.
Iitohpoka'paitapiimiwa anniska A'pistotookiiyiska.
3 Kana'paisi iihtsistapitsstsiiwa ostoyi.
Matoohkitsstsiihpa aahksaohtsistapitsstsii ostoyi,
imaki'tokska. 4 Iihtsistapitsstsiiwa aissksipaitapi'ssini
ostoyi. Ki amiiksiska iihkotaiksi amohka
niipaitapi'ssinihka akohkottohtsistapohta'pawaawahkaayaawa
ksistsikoinattsii. 5 Ki amohka ksistsikoinattsiiyihka
itapsstsiiwa amiiksiska ita'pawaawahkaaiksi
isskii'nattsi. Ki amohka isskii'nattsiyihka
mataonoao'tsitsksskonata'pssatoomaatsi ksistsikoinattsi.
Ki annihkayii matakonoawaahtsaaka'siwa amiia
ksistsikoinattsiiyi.

6 Oki. Aamayii matapiiwa, A'pistotookiwa
otssksksimo'taani aanistawa John Awaatoa'pistotakiwa.
7 Ostoyi ota'po'takssinayi maahkitaokakianistahsi
matapiiyi. Iihtokamo'tsi'poyiwa anniska iihkokkiiyiska
aahkita'pawaawahkaao'si ksiistsikoinattsi. Ki annihkayii
otapi'ssina ayaakomai'takiiksi maahkitomai'takssi. 8 John
matamiiwaatsi anniska iihkokkiiyiska
aahkita'pawaawahkaao'si ksistsikoinattsi.

BRAHUI

INTRODUCTION

Brahui is a Dravidian outlier. The language seems to have been separated from the mainstream of Dravidian, about three or four thousand years BC, before the latter embarked on the southward migration to India. At present, Brahui is spoken in an enclave between Eastern and Western Baluchi, in Western Pakistan, by about 360,000 people, many of whom are bilingual in Brahui and Baluchi. There are also sizable Brahui communities in Hyderabad and Karachi; and nomad Brahui groups are found in Afghanistan and Iran. The language shows Iranian, specifically Baluchi, influence.

According to Andronov (1971), the *-hui* part of the ethnonym is identical with the *Kui*, *Kuvi*, which appears in the ethnonyms of other Dravidian peoples, and means 'mountain' (cf. Tamil *kō̄*). Andronov analyses the name as *vaṛa-kō̄-ī* > *brā'ūī* 'northern mountain people'.

SCRIPT

Brahui is unwritten, but the Arabic script has been used to notate its folk literature.

PHONOLOGY

Consonants

stops: p, b, t, d, ʈ, ɖ, k, g, ʔ
affricates; tʃ, dʒ
fricatives: f, v, s, z, s′, z′, x, γ
nasals: m, n, ɲ, ŋ
laterals and flaps: l, ɬ, r, ɽ

Retroflex consonants are notated with a dot in the following text.

Vowels

i, iː, e, eː, a, aː, oː, u, uː

Stress

Stress is weak, tending towards the beginning of a word.

MORPHOLOGY AND SYNTAX

Noun

The noun has two numbers; the plural marker is -(*ā*)*k* for the nominative; -(*ā*)*t* is the base for plural oblique cases. /γ/ may figure as a link element: e.g. *urā* 'house', pl. *urāk*; *xal* 'stone', pl. *xalk*; *īṛ* 'sister', pl. *īṛk*; *bāva* 'father', pl. *bāvaγāk*; *lumma* 'mother', pl. *lummaγāk*. The oblique base in -(*ā*)*t* is specific to Brahui, and is not found in other Dravidian languages. In the light of the Caldwell thesis (*see* **Dravidian Languages**) this -*t* has been compared with the -*t* plural formant in Uralic.

CASE SYSTEM

Ten case endings are added to the singular stem, to plural oblique base:

genitive: sing. -*nā*, pl. -*ā*; e.g. *kaŋ**nā** īlum**nā** 'ullī* 'my brother's horse'
dative: -*ki* (with link vowel); e.g. *mār* 'son', *māra**ki*** 'to the son'
accusative: -*e*; e.g. *mār**e*** 'the son'
instrumental: -*aṭ*, pl. -*eaṭ*; e.g. *mār**aṭ*** 'by the son'; *māt**eaṭ*** 'by the sons'
comitative: -*tō* (with link vowel); e.g. *māra**tō*** 'with the son'
ablative: -*ān* (with link vowel); e.g. *māte**ān*** 'from the sons'
locative: -*ṭī* (with link vowel); e.g. *urā**ṭī*** 'in the house'; *o kanā s′ a' ra**ṭī** tūlik* 'he lives in our village'
aditive: -*āy*; e.g. *urā**āy*** 'into the house'
adessive: -*isk*; e.g. *dūn**isk*** 'at the well'
terminative: (*is*)*kā*; e.g. *draxt* 'tree' (Iranian loanword), *draxt**iskā*** 'as far as the tree'

Adjective

Qualitative adjectives have short, indefinite, and definite forms: e.g. short *djān* 'good'; indefinite *juānō*; definite *juan**āl**-aŋgal-**īkō***. The short form is used predicatively, the other two as prepositive attributes: e.g. *marγun**ā** kasar* 'the long road'; *rāst**īkō** dū* 'the right hand'.

COMPARISON

A comparative is made with -*tir* (= Iranian -*tar*): e.g.

Dā 'ullī juān aff, asi juān.**tir.ō**' ullī-as 'ata
'This horse is no good, bring me a better one.'

Pronoun

PERSONAL INDEPENDENT

	Singular	*Base*	*Plural*	*Base*	
1	ī	kan-	nan	nan-	
2	nī	ne-	num	num-	
3	dād	dād/dāṛ	dāfk	daft-	proximate
	ōd	ōd/ōṛ	ōfk	ōft-	intermediate

ēd	ēd/ēṛ	ēfk	ēft-	remote

These are declined in all cases: e.g. for first-person singular: *ī*, *kanā*, *kanḳi*, *kane*, *kaneaṭ*, *kantō*, etc.

DEMONSTRATIVE PRONOUN

Three degrees of proximity: *dā* – *ō* – *ē*. These are invariable.

INTERROGATIVE PRONOUN

dē(*r*) 'who?; *ant* 'what?' Declined in most cases.

RELATIVE PRONOUN

The Iranian loanword *ki* is used.

Numerals

Only the words for 1, 2, and 3 are Dravidian: *asi*(*ṭ*), *iraṭ*/*irā*, *musi*(*ṭ*). All other numerals are borrowed from Iranian.

Verb

For almost all positive forms there is a parallel set of negative forms (*see* **Dravidian Languages**; **Finnish**).

Finite forms are marked for mood, tense, number, and person; non-finite forms are participles, gerunds, and verbal nouns (infinitive).

In the great majority of cases, personal and non-personal forms are made from a single base form, which is the verbal noun minus the ending -(*i*)*ŋg*: e.g. *biniŋg* 'to hear', base *bin*-; *salīng* 'to stand', base *salī*-. Some verbs have three or more bases, which may be suppletive: e.g. '*iniŋg* 'to go' has two bases, '*in* and *kā*.

INDICATIVE MOOD

The present/future tense has the endings *-iva*, *isa*-, *-ik*; *-ina*, *-ire*, *-ira*, added directly to the base, optionally preceded by *a*: e.g. (*a*)*tix**iva*** '***I*** put', (*a*)*tix**ik*** 'he puts'. Simple past: tense markers are added to the base; *-ā-* is the most common. The personal endings for the past are: *-ṭ*, *-s,* *-Ø*; *-n*, *-re,* *-r*: e.g. *maxiŋg* 'to laugh', *max**āṭ*** 'I laughed'. There are similar sets of endings for past continuous, past perfective, past anterior.

NEGATIVE CONJUGATION

The markers are *-p*(*a*)(*r*)-/-*f*(*a*)(*r*)-/-*t*(*a*)-, to which specific sets of personal endings are added for the various tenses. For example, the endings for the present/future tense are:

	Singular	*Plural*
1	-ra	-na
2	-ēsa	-ēre
3	-k	-sa

Examples: *xam-pa-ra* 'I do not see'; (*a*)*tix.p.ēre* 'you do/will not put'.

In the past tense the tense marker *-v-* follows the negative marker *-ta*, and a specific set of personal endings is added: e.g. *ī urāṭī pē'i.ta.v.aṭ* 'I didn't go into the house'; *tix.ta.v.as* 'they did not put'.

POTENTIAL MOOD

No specific marker; specific set of endings: e.g. *tix**e*** 'he may put'.

IMPERATIVE MOOD

Singular markers are *-a(k)*, -Ø, pl. *-bō*: e.g. *tix**Ø*** 'put!', pl. *tix**bō***. Negative: *-pa/-fa*: e.g. *tix**pa*** 'don't put!'; *ba**fa*** 'don't come!' (*banniŋg* 'to come').

CONDITIONAL MOOD

The marker is *-ōs-*: e.g. *bin**ō**suṭ* 'if I should hear'.

AUXILIARY VERB

anniŋg 'to be'. The present tense is: *uṭ, us, e; un, ure, ō*. This verb is used with the genitive case in the sense of 'to have': e.g. *kanā irā mār ō* 'I have two sons'. The negative is *affaṭ* 'I am not'; *allavaṭ* 'I wasn't': e.g. *ī brā'ūī-as affaṭ* 'I am not a Brahui'.

NON-FINITE FORMS

There are two participles, in *-ōk* and in *-ōī*. The former is invariable and is not related to any specific tense. The form in *-ōī*, also invariable, is linked with the future: e.g. *Ī dā kārēme karōī uṭ* 'I am the one who has to do this work.'

Preposition

Some prepositions have been borrowed from Baluchi, and there are a few postpositions, e.g. *bā(r)* 'like', which follows the ablative case: e.g. *'ullīām bā* 'like a horse'.

Word order

SOV

مُستَمِبکو باب

١ موھنااوّ لِیکو تیٹِي ھندا کلام اس اوھندا کلام خدا توا س
۲ و خُدا ھمو کلام اس ۲ ھمو موھنا اوّ لیکو تا خدا تو اس ۳ کل
اونا معرِفتت مسوبنو و بغیر ھموران ھیچِرہ متوَ ھندا اِگراس
۴ کہِ مسولي ۴ دالِیٹ زندِگي اس وھمي زنِدگي ھے اِنصان نا
۵ نور اس ۵ وَھمي نور تھارمِٹي نوري روشنَیا کیک و
تھار ما لودي تِیتوَ کہ
۷ نزِینس بسَ خدا اَنان موت تِروک اس دانا پن یوحنّا ۷ لوشاھدي کے
۸ بس لہ نور نا بابتت شاھدِي ایقي کہِ کُل بندغاک ھندران ایمان ھتر ۸
ھموا نور اَلّو یلے اے خاطران کہِ نور نا شاھدِي ایقي

BRETON

INTRODUCTION

Breton belongs to the Brythonic branch of Celtic (i.e. P-Celtic; *see* **Celtic Languages**). In 1930 75 per cent of the Breton population in North-Western France, totalling about 1½ million, spoke the language; fifty years on, the percentage had dropped to just over 40 per cent. With an estimated half a million speakers, however, Breton is still outstripped only by Irish among Celtic languages. Middle Breton was used as a literary language up to the nineteenth century. The modern language is spoken in four main dialects: Léon (*leoneg*), Cornouaille (*kerneveg*), Tréguier (*tregerieg*), and the divergent dialect of Vannes (*gwenedeg*).

The Bretons – *ar Vretoned* – call their language *Brezhoneg* /brɛzɔ̃:nəg/; in *gwenedeg*, /brɛhɔ̃:nəg/.

SCRIPT

The Roman alphabet minus q and x. The 1941 orthography known as *zedacheg* is in general use. The tilde marks nasalization. ch=/s, z/, c′h = /x, γ/, zh = /z/ (or /h/ in *gwenedeg*).

PHONOLOGY

Consonants

stops: p, b, t, d, k, g; labalized k°, g°
fricatives: f, v, s, z, ʃ, ʒ, x, γ, h
nasals: m, n, ɲ, ŋ
laterals: l, λ
rolled: r
semi-vowels: w, j

The only consonants which can be geminated are *l*, *m*, *n*, *r*. Such gemination identifies the preceding vowel as short: cf. *krenan* /kre:nã/ 'tremble', *krennan* /krɛnã/ 'shorten'. *ñ* is not pronounced and simply represents nasalization of the preceding vowel.

Vowels

i, e, ɛ, a, ɔ, o, œ, ø, u, y

All vowels can be long or short, and all can be nasalized, with marked variation in degree of closure. /ø/ is notated as *ö*, /y/ as *ü* in the following text.

There are several diphthongs, e.g. /εa, ao, εi, ε̃ɔ̃/.

Stress is movable.

Mutation

(*See also* **Celtic Languages**). In Breton, mutation takes four main forms:

(a) Lenition: /p, t, k/ → /b, d, g/; /b, d, g/ → /v, z, x/γ/; /m/ → /v/. This mutation occurs regularly after articles (with constraints on gender, see below), certain possessive adjectives, prepositions, verbal particles, etc.: e.g. *tad* 'father': *e* ***dad*** 'his father'; *mamm* 'mother': *ar* ***vamm*** 'the mother'; *Bretoned* 'Bretons': *ar* ***Vretoned*** 'the Bretons'. Following the definite article, lenition occurs in feminine singular and masculine plural nouns only; thus, *ar* ***vamm***; but *mor* 'sea', being masculine, does not mutate: *ar* ***mor*** 'the sea'. Example of mutation in attributive adjective: *merc'h* 'girl'; *brav* 'pretty': *ar* ***verc'h vrav*** 'the pretty girl'.

(b) Spirantization: /p, t, k/ → /f, z, x/. This mutation occurs after certain possessive adjectives, e.g. *ma* 'my', *he* 'her', *o* 'their': *ki* 'dog': *ma* ***c'hi*** 'my dog'; *penn* 'head': *ma* ***fenn*** 'my head'; *tad* 'father': *he* ***zad*** 'her father'.
  Since *e* 'his' and *he* 'her' are homophones, the presence or absence of mutation in the following initial is phonemic: *e* ***vreur*** 'his brother'; *he* ***breur*** 'her brother' (*breur* 'brother').

(c) Hardening: /b, d, g/ → /p, t, k/. This mutation occurs after *ho*(*c'h*) 'your (pl.)', *az*/*ez* 'your (sing.)': e.g. *dent* 'teeth': *ho* ***tent*** 'your teeth'; *daouarn* 'hands': *ho* ***taouarn*** 'your hands'.

(d) Mixed: /b, d, g/ → /v, t, x/; /g°/ → /w/; /m/ → /v/. This occurs after the verbal particles *e* and *o*: e.g. *gwelout* 'to see': *o* ***welout*** 'seeing'.

MORPHOLOGY AND SYNTAX

Noun

The presence of an indefinite article, *un*/*ur*/*ul*, is unique in Celtic. Similarly, the definite article has three forms, *an*/*ar*/*al*, depending on following initial.

GENDER

Masculine and feminine. Gender and mutation are co-related.

NUMBER

There is a wide inventory of plural terminations, some of which induce vowel change in stem. Some common endings are:

-*ed*: e.g. *loen* 'animal', pl. *loened*;
-*ez*: *ti* 'house', pl. *tiez*;
-(*i*)*ou*: pl. form for many inanimates: e.g. *tra* 'thing', pl. *traou* (but note exceptions such as *tadou* 'fathers', *mammou* 'mothers');

-*i* + umlaut: e.g. *bag* 'boat', pl. *bigi*; Ø ending + umlaut: *maen* 'stone', pl. *mein*.

Stress may shift in the plural: e.g. *michérour*, pl. *micheróurien*: 'workers'.

Traces of a former dual appear in the prefix *daou-/div-*: e.g. *an daoulagad* 'the eyes'; *an div.skouarn* 'the (two) ears'.

The ending *-enn* is added to collective plurals to make the singular: e.g. *ar gwez* '(the) *trees*': *gwezenn* 'a tree'; *askol* 'thistles': *askolenn* 'a thistle'.

Plural nouns take a singular verb.

POSSESSION

Possessor follows possessed object: e.g. *breur Yann* 'John's brother'. As in the Semitic construct, the noun denoting the possessed object loses the article: e.g. *gouleier an ti* 'the lights of the house'. However, other words can be interposed between N_1 and N_2, which is impossible in Semitic: e.g. *Økador vras ar bugel bihan* 'the small child's big chair' (*bras* 'big').

Adjective

As attribute, adjective follows noun, and is invariable apart from initial mutation: e.g. *an ti kozh* 'the old house'; *un den pinwidig* 'a rich man'; *ur skol vihan* 'a small school' (*bihan* 'small').

Following a masculine dual the adjective mutates: *daou.laged c'**h**las* 'blue eyes', but *div.skouarn **b**ihan* 'small ears'.

COMPARISON

The comparative is made with the ending *-oc'h* + *eget* 'than': e.g. *koant* 'pretty': *koantoc'h* 'prettier'.

Suppletive forms: *mat* 'good': *gwelloc'h* 'better'; *drouk* 'bad': *gwashoc'h* 'worse'.

Pronoun

PERSONAL PRONOUN

Gender is distinguished in third singular only.

	Singular		*Plural*	
	Base form	*Possessive*	*Base form*	*Posessive*
1	me	ma	ni	hon
2	te	da	c'hwi	ho
3 masc.	eñ	e	int	o
fem.	hi	he	int	o

Used as subject or direct object, these base forms always precede the verb, which is itself preceded by the particle *a*: e.g. *me a welit* 'you see me' (*gwelout* 'to see').

The possessive pronouns can also be used as direct object pronouns: e.g. *Da kwelout a raimp* (*warc'hoazh*) 'We'll see you (tomorrow).'

By adding personal pronominal affixes to prepositions, the ubiquitous 'conjugated prepositional' form is obtained: e.g. with *gant* /gã/ 'by', 'with', 'for', etc.

		Singular	Plural
1		ganin 'by (etc.) me'	ganeomp
2		ganit 'by you'	ganeoc'h
3	masc./fem.	gantan/ganti	ganto

Similarly with *da* 'to': *din, dit, dezhan/dezhi; dimp, deoc'h, dezho.*

The prepositions *a* 'to' and *eus* 'from' share the extended bases *ac'han-* for first and second person, *anezh-* for third, and provide direct and indirect object forms: e.g. *C'hwi a gavo ac'hanon war ar blassenn* 'You'll find me in the square.'

DEMONSTRATIVE PRONOUN

Three degrees of relative distance are marked by masc. *hemañ – hennezh – henhont*; fem. *houmañ – hounnezh – hounhont*. The plural for both genders is: *ar re-mañ – ar re-se – ar re-hont.*

Enclitic forms: *an ti-mañ* 'this house'; *an ti-se – an ti-hont.*

INTERROGATIVE PRONOUN

piv 'who?'; *petra* 'what?' Interrogative sentences are introduced by (*daoust*) *ha*(*g*): e.g. *Daoust ha brav eo am amzer?* 'Is the weather fine?' (*amzer* 'weather').

RELATIVE PRONOUN

Lacking in Breton. The verbal particle *a* is used: e.g. *ar paotr a welit* 'the boy whom you see'; *Setu ar paotr a zo klanv e dad* 'This is the boy whose father is ill.' *an dud a oa ganin dec'h* 'the people who were with me (*gan.in*) yesterday'.

Numerals

1–10: *unan, daou, tri, pevar, pemp, c'hwec'h, seizh, eizh, nav, dek*; 11 *unnek*; 12 *daouzek*; 20 *ugent*; 21 *unan warn-ugent*; 30 *tregont*; 40 *daou-ugent*; 50 *hanter-kant*; 60 *tri-ugent*; 100 *kant.*

Following a numeral, the noun is in the singular: *deg vloaz* 'ten years' (*bloaz* 'year').

In expressions involving composite numbers and a nominal, there is a fixed order of sequence: unit – nominal – conjunction – decade/hundred: e.g. *tri den ha tri-ugent* 'three man and sixty', i.e. 'sixty-three men'; *eizh vloaz ha daou-ugent eo* 'eight year and twenty he-is', i.e. he is twenty-eight.

Verb

Breton has active and passive voices. The active voice has three moods – indicative, imperative, conditional. The indicative has past, non-past, and future tenses, and distinguishes perfective, habitual, punctual, and continuous aspects. There are three persons, singular and plural, plus an impersonal form. Tense forms may be (a) synthetic: here the verb is marked for person and number; (b) analytic: the verb is unmarked, and the personal pronoun must be present; (c) mixed, with auxiliary *bezañ* 'to be', or *ober* 'to do, make'; if *bezañ* is used, the verb is marked for person and number. For example, the present tense of *labourat* 'to work', in three versions:

(a) Synthetic:

	Singular	*Plural*
1	bremañ e labouran 'I work now'	bremañ e labouromp
2	bremañ e labourez	bremañ e labourit
3	bremañ e labour	bremañ e labouront

Impersonal: e labourer 'one is working'

(b) Analytic, e.g.:

1 me a labour bremañ 'I am working now'
2 te a labour bremañ

(c) Mixed, e.g.: with *bezañ* → *bez*':

1 bez' e labouran
2 bez' e labourez
3 bez' e labour

with *ober*: base of *ober* is *gra-*, e.g:

1 labourat a ran bremañ 'I'm working now'
2 labourat a rez bremañ
3 labourat a ra bremañ

The three versions differ slightly in stress/focus.

Past:

(a) marked: e.g. *dec'h e labouren*, *e laboures*, *e laboure* (*-e-* is past discriminator);
(b) unmarked: e.g. *me a laboure*, *te a laboure*, etc.

Future:

(a) marked: sing. *e labourin, e labouri, e labouro*: pl. *e labourimp*, *e labouroc'h*, *e labourint* (*-i-/-o-* discriminators).

The (c) forms for past and future, with *ober* 'to do', are:

past, e.g.: sing. *labourat a raen*, *a raes*, *a rae*; pl. *a raemp*. . . ;
future, e.g.: sing. *labourat a rin*, *a ri*, *a raio*; pl. *a raimp*. . . .

where *gra-* > *ra-* after the verbal particle *a*.

The markers *a* and *e* precede the finite verb form; *a* induces lenition, *e* the mixed mutation.

a is the syntactic linker between the subject and the verb, or between the fronted object and verb. It appears in the (b) conjugation above: *Me a labour bremañ* 'I'm working now'; *Bara a zebran bremañ* 'Bread it is I'm eating now.'

e links attributive or adverbial material, or indirect object to verb: e.g. *Er gegin e tebran* 'It's in the kitchen I'm eating now' (*kegin* 'kitchen').

Alone among Breton verbs, *kaout*/*kaoud* 'to have' is always in concord with its subject in person, number, and (in 3rd p. sing.) gender. The present, past, and future tenses of *kaout* have two components:

(a) Marked as follows:

	Singular	*Plural*
1	am	hon/hor
2	az	ho
3	en/he	o

where *en*/*he* indicates a choice of gender; *hon*/*hor* is a matter of euphony.

(b) A tense marker whose three forms do duty for both singular and plural; its initial mutates.

Singular/*Plural*	*Present*	*Past*	*Future*
1	eus	boa	bo
2	peus	boa	po
3	deus	doa	do

Thus *en deus* 'he has', *he deus* 'she has'. Either S or O must precede this verb: *O en deus* S = S *en deus* O, 'S has O'.

The auxiliary *bezañ* has three sets of forms, expressing (a) state, (b) habitual action, and (c) spatio-temporal localization. *Bezañ* is used to make composite tenses from intransitive stems, with the past participle in *-et* (invariable). *Kaout* is used in the same way with transitive verbs. Cf.

am eus dastumet an avalou 'I have gathered the apples'
am boa dastumet an avalou 'I had gathered the apples'
am bo dastumetan avalou 'I shall gather the apples'

As an example of the passive construction we may take: *ar voger.mañ zo bet savet gant ma zad* 'this wall (***moger***) has been built by my father'; *an ti.mañ zo bet savet gantañ* 'this house has been built by him'.

The passive may also be expressed by the impersonal form in *-r*: *al levr a lenner* 'the book is being read'.

The conditional is marked by *-f-* inserted between base and past endings: e.g. *bremañ de labourfen* = *bez'e labourfen* = *labourat a rafen bremañ* 'if I worked/were working now'.

IMPERATIVE

The 2nd sing. is identical with the base; the 1st pl. ends in *-omp*, the 2nd pl. in *-it*: *komz – komzomp – komzit brezhoneg* 'speak – let us speak – speak (pl.) Breton'.

NEGATIVE

The negative is expressed by a circumfix: *ne... ket*. Only the marked conjugation can be negated; both *a* and *e* are then discarded: e.g. *ne labouran ket, ne labourez ket, ne labour ket*, etc.

Prepositions

Most are compatible with the personal endings (*see* **Pronoun**, above). Examples of prepositions without personal endings: *eus ar mor* 'from the sea'; *edan an douar* 'under the earth'; *goude ar bresel* 'after the war'; *e-kichen an ti-post* 'next to the post-office'. Some prepositions take an infixed personal marker: e.g. *war.lerc'h* 'after': *war-ma-lerc'h, war-da-lerc'h, war-e-lerc'h*, etc.

Word formation

By prefix, suffix, or compounding:

(a) Prefixation: e.g. *di-/dis-/diz-* is privative: e.g. *dizaon* 'fearless'; *dizampart* 'awkward'. *Peur-* gives a perfective sense: e.g. *peurskrivañ* 'to finish writing'; *enep-* 'contrary to': e.g. *enepreizh* 'injustice'; *hanter-* 'half-': e.g. *hanterzigor* 'half-open'.
(b) Suffixation: e.g. *-ded/-der* (masc./fem., no plural forms) make abstract nouns: e.g. *uhelded* 'nobility' (*uhel* 'high'). *-our* forms noun denoting agent, subject of action, or state: e.g. *klañvdiour* 'nurse'. *-erezh* forms abstract nouns: e.g. *bruderezh* 'publicity'.
(c) Compounding: various combinations, e.g. *bag-pesketa* 'fishing-boat'; *mont-dont* 'coming and going'; *pinwidig-mor* 'very rich'.

Word order

A basic formula is: focused topic (S, O, or adverbial modifier) followed by V. V(S)O is frequent, where V is, for example, past participle + auxiliary: *gwerzhet en deus ar... din.me* 'he sold me the...'.

1 Er gommansamant e oa ar Ger, hag ar Ger a oa gand Doue, hag ar Ger a oa Doue.

2 He-ma a oa er gommansamant gand Doue.

3 An holl draou a zo bet grëd drezan, hag hepzan n'eo bet grët netra hag a zo bet grët.

4 Ennan e oa ar vuez, hag ar vuez a oa goulou an dud.

5 Hag ar goulou a sclera en devalien, hag an devalien n'e deus ked e resevet.

6 Bez' e oe un den caset gand Doue, hanvet Ian.

7 He-ma a zeuaz da desteni, evit rei testeni diwarben ar goulou, evit ma credche an holl drezan.

8 Ne ket hen a oa ar goulou, mes *cased e oa* evit rei testeni diwarben ar goulou.

(Léon dialect)

BRIBRÍ

INTRODUCTION

Bribrí and Cabécar, spoken by a joint total of 2 or 3 thousand in Costa Rica, are very closely related members of the Talamanca group of Chibchan languages. William Gabb, writing at the end of the nineteenth century, described Bribrí as having a very deficient vocabulary of between 15 hundred and 2 thousand words (Gabb 1891–6). Gabb found that while all Cabécars spoke Bribrí, the language of the dominant tribe in the region, very few Bribrís spoke Cabécar.

PHONOLOGY

Consonants

According to Arroyo (1972), Bribrí has most of the Spanish consonantal inventory, apart from /θ/, /f/, and /ʎ/. /ʃ/ and /ts/ are present. /ʃ/ is notated by Arroyo, and here, as *x*.

Vowels

i, e, a, o, u

Both oral and nasal series. Arroyo describes /o/ as tending to be raised to [ø] and /e/ to [i].

MORPHOLOGY AND SYNTAX

Noun

There is no gender; where necessary, lexical items are used, e.g. for persons *wib* 'man' and *arákr* 'woman': e.g. *yará wib* 'son', *yará arákr* 'daughter'. A plural can be made with *-pa*, e.g. *wibpa* 'men'; or *tsotséi* 'many', can be used: *kar tsotséi* 'lots of trees'. Possessive relationship by apposition: e.g. *arákr urá* 'the woman's hand'; *kar máma* 'the tree's blossom'.

Adjective

The attributive adjective follows the noun, and is often reduplicated: e.g. *wib deríri* 'strong man'; *baba* 'hot'; *sese* 'cold'.

Pronoun

PERSONAL PRONOUN

	Singular	*Plural*
1	yé	sá
2	bé	já
3	yié	yiépa

These are both subject and object forms, and have many variants.

POSSESSION

Marked by *-cha*: e.g. *yécha* 'my, mine'; *beicha* 'your'.

DEMONSTRATIVE PRONOUN

Three degrees by relative distance: *jí* 'this' – *basé* 'that' – *jerkí auir* 'that (yonder)'. These have plural forms.

Verb

The infinitive is in -V*k*, -*k*V, *-wa*, *-ta*, etc. Tense formation is highly unpredictable and irregular. As specimen, the main parts of two verbs are given:

tsuk 'to sing'

present	tsuke	passive participle	tsé
preterite	tsí	active participle	tsúmbra
future	mike tsuk	gerund	itsúkedak
perfect	tsírure		

xege 'to eat'

present	xegegé	passive participle	xagajká
preterite	xagajká	gerund	xegegé
future	ma xege		

Word order

SOV

1. Kéue eror Sibu ufto, ufto e tso Sibu ta̰ eta ufto eror Sibu.
2. Ih ror kéue Sibu ta.
3. Iyir ulítane yoh ie-ror; eta ie ke kupa ema iẏir tso yor-ule ke ku̱n.
4. Ieh ta sauac tso, eta sauac eror koñina uepa urítane e-ia.
5. Eta ko tsetse-a̰ ko̰uoñin; ére ko tsetse ke en-a ia̰na.
6. Ieh̰ ror uéb apatke Sibu to, uak kie Juan.
7. Ih débite eh biyo-ie, ko̰ñin ufte amuk se-ia, o̰s se urítane to ieh bikeitso.
8. K̃e ieh ror koñin; irir koñin ufte amuk se-ia̰.

BUGINESE

INTRODUCTION

A member of the Malayo-Polynesian branch of Austronesian, Buginese is spoken by about 4 million people in Southern Sulawesi (Celebes). Originally Buddhist, the Buginese were converted to Islam, along with the Macassarese, in the seventeenth century. The ethnonym is *(w)ugi'* or *to.ugi'* (*to* < *tau* 'man'); the language is *basa (w)ugi'*.

Buginese has a very rich traditional literature, still largely in manuscript form. The enormous cycle of anonymous mythological poems, in five-syllable lines, known as *surə' Galigoe* or *Lagaligo*, dates from the sixteenth century. These poems portray in considerable detail an ethnic Sulawesi culture, which is neither Hindu nor Islamic. Central to the cycle are the doings, over several generations, of a highly aristocratic race claiming divine origins, thanks to which its members are *ma'dara-takku* 'having blood white as milk'. An archaic society of seafarers, built on feudal lines, is portrayed. A keyword, extracted by Sirk (1975) from Matthes (1874) is *kassuiaŋ*, denoting the 'honourable homage' rendered by a free man (not a slave) to his leader.

Lyric poetry: Buginese is rich in the genre known as *eloŋ* or *elompugi'*, which are short haiku-like poems preserved in oral tradition, which seem to have been stylistically refurbished in the nineteenth century. They make considerable use of *kenning*-type metaphors (*see* **Norse, Old**) and phonetic puns. Sirk gives the following excellent example: instead of the word *kəssiŋ* 'beauty', the phrase *lomip.walənnae* 'bottom of the river' may be used. The point here is that the bottom of the river is covered by sand – *kəssi'* in Buginese, which suggests, by phonetic association, *kəssiŋ*.

The *senusenurəŋ* is a kind of lyrical epic, concerned mainly with erotic motifs.

Prose: historiography is represented by the *attoriolоŋ*, *itihāsa*-type accounts of the doings of gods and men, including genealogies; the *surə'.bilaŋ* offer brief accounts in diary style of important events.

SCRIPT

See **Script** at end of article.

PHONOLOGY

Consonants

stops: p, b, t, d, k, g, ʔ

affricatives: tʃ, dʒ
fricatives: ɸ, s
nasals: m, n, ɲ, ŋ
lateral and trill: l, r
semi-vowels: j, w

Vowels

i, e, a ə, o, u

/e/ and /o/ have positional variants.

Stress

Tends to penultimate syllable, but may be on ante-penultimate or on final, depending on the structure and composition of a word or complex. Enclitics may take the stress.

MORPHOLOGY AND SYNTAX

Article

An enclitic article is *-e* (with allomorphs), which can be added to the complex: e.g. *bola.e* 'the/a house'; *bola aruŋŋ.e* 'princely house, the chief's house'; *utti u.tanəŋŋ.e* 'the bananas which I planted'. The article also serves to substantivize such units as extended verbs: e.g. *mallopi* 'to go by ship', *mallopi.e* 'a voyage'. The personal articles *i-la* (masc.) and *i-we* (fem.) are applied to Buginese proper nouns, names of boats, weapons, etc.

Noun

Buginese nouns are primary or derivatory; the latter mainly by prefixation: *pa*C-, for example, forms nouns of agency. The suffix *-aŋ* suggests something connected with or the result of the activity denoted by the base: e.g. *daŋkaŋ* 'trade', *daŋkaŋəŋ* 'goods'. Circumfix is also used: cf. from *musu'* 'war', *am.musu.r. əŋ* 'warlike actions'. This word illustrates the Buginese phonetic rule that before the suffix *-aŋ* or *-i*, the glottal stop changes to /k, r, s/. Cf. *-gau'* 'to do': *gaurən* 'to do for someone'.

A possessive–relational nexus is expressed by the izafet-type construction with the particle *na*: *pammulan.**na**.ro surə'.e* 'the beginning of that letter' (*pammulan* 'beginning', cf. Bahasa Indonesia *permulaan*; notice that the distal demonstrative *ro* follows the relational marker *na*). Cf. (Sirk: 81):

ambo'.na səllao.na 'the father of his friend'
səllao.na ambo'.na 'the friend of his father'

where the relational marker *na* must be distinguished from the third person possessive suffix *-na*.

As there is no case system of any kind in Buginese, word order is of crucial importance. Sirk gives the following example:

paŋŋulu.joa'.e mmita.i. bali.e 'the commander sees the enemy'
bali.e mmita.i paŋŋulu.joa'.e 'the enemy sees the commander'

For an explanation of *mmita.i* in this sentence, *see* **Verb**, below.

Adjective

Most adjectives have the form *ma* + stem: e.g. *ma.lampe* 'long'; *ma.loppo* 'big'. As attribute, adjective follows noun. As predicate, the adjective forms, along with transitive and intransitive verbs, the third class of verb.

agaga.e masempo **Ø** 'the things are-cheap' (*masempo* 'to be cheap')

Such a sentence is negated by *de'* or *aja'* plus the correlative personal pronominal affix from the *u-* series (*see* **Pronoun**, below): *de'.**na** masempo agaga.e* 'the things are not cheap' (where *na* is 3rd p. affix). Comparative degree: the suffix *-aŋ/əŋ* may be used, e.g. *kasirəŋ* 'poorer'.

Pronoun

There are free and bound series; three persons; a plural distinction is made only with regard to first person.

	Free series	*u- series*	*-ku series*
1	ia'	u-, ku-	-(k)ku
2	idi', iko, io	ik-, ta-, mu-	-(t)ta, -(m)mu
3	ia	na-	-(n)na

An exclusive plural first person is provided by *idikkəŋ*, *ikəŋ* in the free series. The *u-* series has exclusive first person plural *ki-*, inclusive *ta-*, and the distinction appears also in the *-ku* series, but the opposition is not strictly observed.

The *u-* series forms provide the subject pronouns for transitive verbs, e.g. *u.tarima* 'I receive'; *na.tarima* 'he receives'; and the logical object in passive constructions, e.g. *u.ri.tarima* 'and they receive me' = 'I am received' (*ri* is passive marker).

The *-ku* series forms may follow nouns or verbs. Following nouns, they denote the possessive relationship: e.g. *amak.ku* 'my father'; *lopin.na* 'his boat'. Following a verb they set up a temporal or causal relationship: e.g. *ma.bela.n.na* 'when he is far away/because he is far away'; *u.tarima.mu* 'when I received you'.

A third series of bound pronouns, the *a'* series, provides object forms for transitive verbs: e.g. *ri.tarima.i.* 'he undergoes reception' = 'they receive him'. *See* **Verb**, below.

DEMONSTRATIVE PRONOUN

Three-degree series: *-e/-we* 'this', *-tu* 'that', *-ro* 'that (far away)': e.g., combined with interrogative *aga* 'what?': *aga.e.tu* 'What is that?' (where *-e-* is the article). Cf. *Maloppo.i.tu bola.e.* 'That house is big.'

INTERROGATIVE PRONOUN

niga 'who?; *aga* 'what?'

RELATIVE PRONOUN

None. Relative constructions are formed with the help of bound pronouns.

Numerals

1–10: *seua/se'di, dua, təllu, əppa, lima, ənnəŋ, pitu, arua, asera, -pulo. Səppulo* is the base for 11–19: e.g. *səppulo lima* 15. 20 *dua.pulo*; *-ratu* is the base for hundreds.

Numerals can combine with nouns, e.g. *patattauŋ* 'four years', where *pata* is an alternative root for *əppa* 'four'.

Verb

Transitive and intransitive. Transitive verbs can take a passive construction, and are always correlated with an object (simple or composite). This object is copied or anticipated in the verbal form by a bound pronoun or deictic marker. Sirk (1975) gives the example: *ttiwirəŋŋ.i inanre ana'na* 'to bring food to her children'. Here, the root is *tiwi* 'to bring': the stem is made transitive–benefactive by addition of *-aŋŋ/-əŋŋ*, and then means 'to bring something to or for someone'. The object of the benefactive action, *ana'na* 'her children', is anticipated in the verbal form by the pronominal affix *-i*. The gemination of the stem initial: *tt-* is an allomorph of the active voice marker, which is *mm-* before a vowel initial.

As an example of transitive structure, Sirk (1975) gives the stem *lliaŋ* 'to sell':

base form: *əlliaŋ* 'sell'
active: *mməlliaŋ* 'to (proceed to) sell'
passive: *riəlliaŋ* 'to be sold'
personalized forms: ***u**əlliaŋ* 'to be sold by me' = 'I sell'; ***mu**əlliaŋ* 'to be sold by you' = 'you sell'; ***ta**əlliaŋ* 'to be sold by us/you' = 'we/you sell'

Intransitive verbs are heterogeneous in structure. Many are formed from substantives by means of prefix *(m)a'*, and then mean 'to have to do with' (object denoted by stem): e.g. *galuŋ* 'rice-field', *ma'galuŋ* 'to work (in) the rice-field, cultivate. . . '.

CAUSATIVES

The prefix is *pa*C- with allomorphs: e.g. *ita* 'to see', *p(a)ita* 'to show something to someone'.

PASSIVE

The general marker is *ri-*, which precedes a transitive stem: e.g.

u.ləlluŋŋ.**i** joŋa.e 'I hunt(ed) the deer'
ri.ləlluŋ(ŋ.**i**) joŋa.e. 'the deer is/was hunted'

A general negating particle is *təŋ*.

Both the construction of active/passive sentences, and the formation of relative clauses are illustrated in the following three sentences from Sirk:

tomacca **mm**uki'.əŋŋ.**i** surə'.**e** 'the scholar who writes the letter'
surə' **ri**uki'.**e** **ri**.tommaca.**e** 'the letter written by the scholar'
surə' **na**uki'.**e** 'the letter which he writes'

As Sirk remarks (1975: 27), it was the Dutch scholar J. Noorduyn who first drew attention (in his 1955 edition of an *attoriioloŋ*) to a kind of genitive absolute in Buginese. This involves a non-finite verbal form plus a suffixed *ku*- series pronominal marker: e.g. *pole.**ku*** 'on my arrival, when/because I arrived'; *lləttu'.**na*** *ri.bola.na.llesso'.n.**i*** *ri.aññara.n.na* 'on his drawing up close (lit. 'his-draw-up') to his house, he jumped from his horse'.

Preposition

ri- is an all-purpose preposition applying to spatio-temporal frames without differentiation: this is supplied by the verb, e.g. *lləttu' ri.dusuŋŋe* 'to enter the village'; *pole ri.dusuŋŋe* 'to come out of the village'.

Word order

SVO appears to be normal in active constructions, VSO with intransitive verbs and in the passive voice: SVO: *maelo'ka' mmanre.i. bale.we* 'I want to eat this fish'; VSO: *nrewə'.n.i suro.e* 'returned the envoy', i.e. 'the envoy returned'.

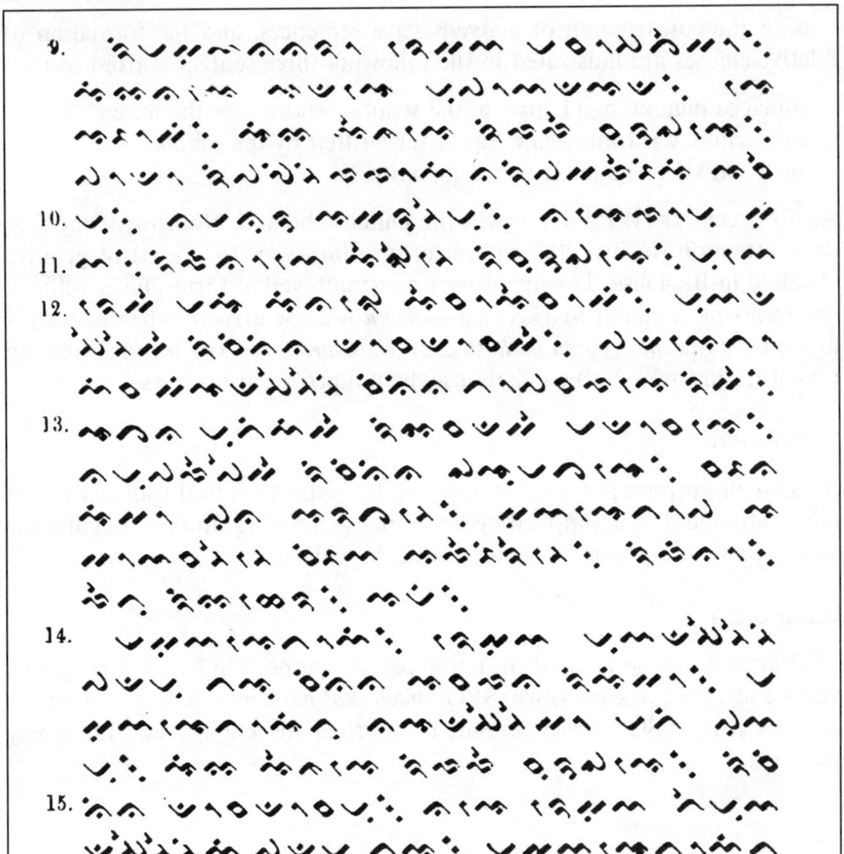

(Matthew 6.9–15)

SCRIPT

The Buginese-Macasarese syllabary known in Buginese as *hurupu' sulapa' əppa'* 'four-corner letters' (where *hurupu'* is the broken plural of Arabic *ḥarf* 'letter') is based on an Indian model, runs from left to right, and retains the typically Indian system of marking non-independent vowels as super-, subscript or collinear adjuncts to consonants. From the accompanying chart it will be seen that the Devanāgarī velar, labial, dental, and palatal series are each represented by three consonants (the aspirates are missing); and each row ends with a homorganic conjunct: *ngka*, *mpa*, *nra*, *ɲca*. The inventory is completed by the four semi-vowels *y*, *r*, *l*, *w*, the sibilant *s*, and the spirant *h*. The letter ᨕ serves (a) to notate initial *'a/a*, and (b) to act as a carrier for other vowel sounds in initial position. The vocalic diacritics are here shown in combination with the consonant *la*:

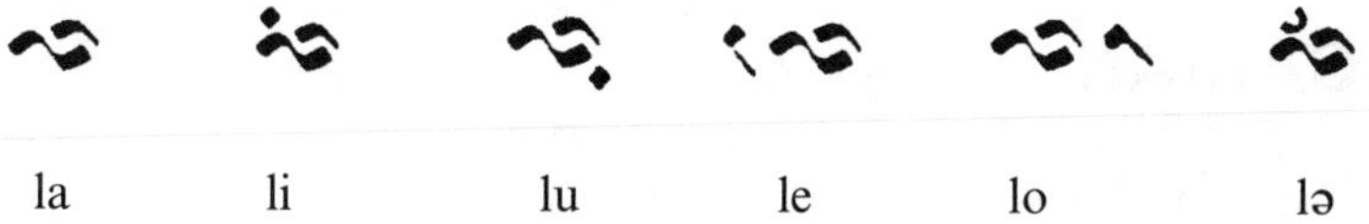
la
li
lu
le
lo
lə

Major defects in the script are its inability to notate independent vowels, and the absence of markers denoting gemination, nasalization, and glottalization. Thus ᨔᨑ can be read as *sara* 'sorrow', *sara'* 'rule', and *sarang* 'nest'. According to Sirk (1975) the conjunct graphs are not systematically used.

In Macasarese, which does not have the vowel /ə/, the diacritic ᨛ is used to indicate that the syllable so marked is followed by a nasal consonant.

THE BUGINESE SCRIPT

THE SYLLABARY

ka
pa
ta
ca
ya
sa
ga
ba
da
ja
ra
qa
nga
ma
na
ña
la
ha
ngka
mpa
nra
ñca
wa

BULGARIAN

INTRODUCTION

The ancient Bulgars were a Turkic people speaking a language classified by Baskakov as Western Hunnic; its congener, still spoken today, is Chuvash (*see* **Chuvash; Turkic Languages**). The Bulgars enter history in the seventh century AD, when they moved westwards from the Crimea area, and settled to the south of the Danube, in the Balkan peninsula. Here, they gradually merged with the Slav population already established along the Black Sea coast, and even adopted the local Slavonic language. Of the original Bulgar(ian) language, only the name remains. The language now known as Bulgarian forms, together with Macedonian, the eastern branch of South Slavonic. It is the official language of the Republic of Bulgaria where it is spoken by over 8 million people. (For the 'Old Bulgarian' literary language, *see* **Old Church Slavonic**.) Through the Middle Bulgarian period (twelfth to fifteenth centuries) and again under Turkish suzerainty from the fifteenth century onwards, Bulgarian was a spoken language only, a kind of demotic accompanying the Church Slavonic literary language. By the eighteenth century it had deviated more than any other Slavonic tongue from the common Slavonic norm. The declension of the noun had disappeared, an affixed definite article had been introduced, and the infinitive had been replaced by a construction with the particle *da* plus a finite form of the verb (these are areal features, cf. Tosk Albanian, Romanian, Serbian, and, in part, Greek). In addition, Bulgarian has developed the *preizkazano naklonenie*, a set of inferential tenses which has no parallel in other European languages (but cf. **Turkic Languages**).

The first Bulgarian writer of distinction is Khristo Botev (1848–76). Two years after Botev's death, Bulgaria gained its independence, and from then until the outbreak of the Second World War, a sustained and innovative output of verse and prose appeared in Bulgarian from such writers as Ivan Vazov, Pencho Slaveykov, Peyo Yavorov, Dimcho Debelyanov, Elin Pelin, Elisaveta Bagryana, and Nikolai Vaptsarov.

There is an east/west dialect division; literary Bulgarian is based on the western dialect.

SCRIPT

Cyrillic (*see* **Russian**) minus *ë*, *ы*, *э*. The hard sign *ъ* is used to notate the typically Bulgarian sound /ʌ/ > /ɪ/. Here, for typographical reasons, the sound will be notated as *ă*. The Cyrillic letter *щ* is /ʃt/ in Bulgarian, not /ʃtʃ/

> /ʃʃ/ as in Russian. The soft sign ь denotes palatalization of the preceding consonant: *синьо* = /sin'ɔ/.

PHONOLOGY

Consonants

stops: p, b, t, d, k, g
affricates: ts, tʃ
fricatives: f, v, s, z, ʃ, ʒ, j, x
nasals: m, n, ɲ
lateral and trill: l, r

ASSIMILATION

Voiced to unvoiced and vice versa: e.g. *gradski* = /gra**t**ski/; *velikden* = /veli**g**den/. Final voiced is unvoiced: *grad* → [gra**t**]; *vrag* → [vra**k**].

Vowels

i, ɛ, a, ə, ɔ, u, ʌ

The script distinguishes the palatalized vowels *yu*, *ya*. Diphthongs: /ai, oi/.

Vowel reduction is typical of Bulgarian pronunciation of unstressed syllables: e.g. /a/ → [ə]: *kníga* → [knigə]; /ɛ/ → [ɪ]: *zeléno* → /zɪlenɔ/; /o/ → [u]: *polé* → [pule].

Stress

Stress is free and can fall on any syllable. Bulgarian stress often agrees with Russian, but there are many exceptions.

MORPHOLOGY AND SYNTAX

Noun

There are three genders: masculine, feminine, and neuter. The case system has disappeared. The sole remaining inflectional disntinction is that between nominative and non-nominative masculine singular, where the nominative form takes the definite article (affix): e.g. *gradăt* 'the town (nom.)'; *grada* 'the town (obl.)': *v centăra na grada* 'in the middle of the town'.
Compare:

časă**t** e devet i polovina 'the time is half past nine' (nom.)
V kolko čas**a** zaminavaš 'At what time are you going?' (obl.)

DEFINITE ARTICLE

Masc. hard: *-ăt*, soft: *-yat*; fem. *-ta*: neuter: *-to*; plural, all genders: *-te*/*-ta*: e.g. *gradăt* 'the town'; *borbata* 'the struggle'; *cveteto* 'the flower'; *rabotnicite* the workers'.

PLURAL ENDINGS

Most polysyllabic masculines take *-i* with 2nd palatalization of final consonant (*see* **Slavonic Languages**) where necessary: e.g. *rabotnik* 'workers': pl. *rabotnici*; *pedagog* 'teacher': *pedagozi*; *kožux* 'fur coat': *kožusi*.

Masculine monosyllables often take *-ove*: e.g. *plod* 'fruit', pl. *plodové*, *xlyab* 'loaf', pl. *xlyábove*, *nož* 'knife', pl. *nožóve*. Note that stress may be on stem, penultimate, or final.

The feminine plural is in *-i*; neuter: final *o → a*, *e → ya/eta*, *ne → niya*: e.g. *pero* 'pen': *perá*; *cvéte* 'flower': *cvetyá*; *momče* 'boy': *momčéta*.

The particle *na* is used to indicate both genitive and dative: e.g. *knigata na deteto* 'the child's book'; *davam knigata na deteto* 'I give the book to the child'.

Adjective

Adjectives are marked for gender and number. The attributive adjective precedes the noun, and the definite article, if present, is transferred to it, the distinction between masculine nominative and oblique being maintained: e.g.

golem**iyat** grad**Ø** 'the big town (*golem* 'big', *grad* 'town')
vidždam golem**iya** grad**Ø** 'I see the big town'

Cf. *visok**ata** kăšta* 'the tall house'; *nov**oto** pero* 'the new pen'; *golem**ite** prozorci* 'the big windows'.

PREDICATIVE

knigata e červena 'the book is red'; *molivăt e červen* 'the pencil is red'.

COMPARATIVE

Comparative is made by prefixing *po-*: e.g. *dobăr* 'good', *pó-dobăr/-dobra/-dobro* 'better': e.g. *Našeto žilište e pó-xubavo ot tova* 'Our apartment is nicer than that one.'

Pronoun

The personal independent forms are:

sing. 1 *az*, 2 *ti*, 3 *toi*, *tya*, *to*; pl. 1 *nie*, 2 *vie*, 3 *te*

That is, the third person singular forms are marked for gender.

The pronouns have full and short oblique forms; thus, for first person, direct object full form: *mene*; short: *me*; indirect object full: *na mene*, short, *mi*. Example of full form used for emphasis:

Na tebe, ne na nego davam knigata
'I'm giving the book to you, not to him.'

Short forms: *viždam go* 'I see him'; *ne te viždam* 'I don't see you.' Both long and short forms may be used together: e.g. *na mene mi xaresva* 'I *do* like it.'

POSSESSIVE FORMS

Full forms:

		Singular				*Plural*	
1		moy	moya	moe	naš	naša	naše
2		tvoy	tvoya	tvoe	vaš	vaša	vaše
3	masc.	negov	negova	negovo	texen	tyaxna	tyaxno
	fem.	nein	neina	neino			

The short indirect object forms may also be used: e.g. *moyata kniga* = *knigata mi* 'my book'.

DEMONSTRATIVE PRONOUN

tozi 'this', *onya* 'that'. Both declined for gender and number.

INTERROGATIVE PRONOUN

koy 'who?'; *kakvó* 'what?' Interrogative enclitic: *li.*

RELATIVE PRONOUN

koyto/koyato/koeto; pl. *koito.* If *koyto* referes to a male person, the oblique case is *kogoto*; otherwise, *koyto*: cf.

čovekăt, **kogoto** viždam 'the man whom I see'
vlakăt, **koyto** viždam 'the train which I see'

Numerals

1 *edin/edna/edno*; 2 *dva/dve*; 3–10 *tri, četiri, pet, šest, sedem, osem, devet, deset.* 11 *edinayset*; 12 *dvanayset*; 20 *dvayset*; 30 *triyset*; 100 *sto.*

Verb

Bulgarian verbs have perfective and imperfective aspects. The present perfective form (usually with a prefix, e.g. *uča* 'I learn', perfective ***na**uča*) cannot be used independently but only in a relative capacity: cf. *trăgvam* 'I leave, start off' (imperfective); *iskam da tră**gna*** 'I want to leave'.

The citation form is the first person present imperfective.

There are active and passive voices; indicative, imperative/hortative, and conditional moods. In addition, Bulgarian has the unique inferential version of all eight indicative tenses (see below). Three types of conjugation are distinguished: *-e* stems, *-i* stems, and *-a/-ya* stems. Negative particle is *ne.*

THE COPULA

present: *săm, si, e*; pl. *sme, ste, sa*
past: *byax, be(še), be(še)*; pl. *byaxme, byaxte, byaxa*
past participle: *bil, bili*

Specimen conjugation: *četá* 'I read': indicative:

present: *četá, četeš, čete*; pl. *četem, četete, četat*
future: present forms preceded by particle *šte*: e.g. *šte četá*
past imperfective: *četyáx, četeše, četeše*; pl. *četyaxme, četyaxte, četyaxa*

past perfective: *čétox, čete, čete*; pl. *četoxme, četoxte, četoxa*
conditional mood: with auxiliary: *bix, bi, bi čel*; pl. *bixme, bixte, bixa čeli*
imperative: the endings are *-i/-ete*: *piši, pišete* 'write!'

THE INFERENTIAL VERSION

All indicative tenses have parallel forms in the indirect tense or reported-speech system. The indirect tense forms may be preceded by some such phrase as 'It is reported that . . . ' (cf. Lat. *allatum est . . .*) but the verb form in itself is enough to stamp the utterance as reported speech. The copula is used in all inferential tenses, except in the third person, where the participial form by itself (singular or plural) is used. Thus the inferential parallel for the present tense of *četa*, given above, is:

sing. *četyal săm, četyal si, četyal Ø*; pl. *četeli sme, četeli ste, četeli Ø*

E.g.

Tuk živee i semeystvoto na Ivan
'John's family too lives here'

(Čuse, če) tuk živee**lo** i semeystvoto na Ivan
'(It is said that) John's family also . . . '

Stopanstvoto ima kăm 1,000 ovce
'The farm has up to 1,000 sheep' (indicative statement)

Stopanstvoto ima**lo** kăm 1,000 ovce
'(I'm told) the farm has . . . '

As a further example, a passage from the novelist Elin Pelin in both versions:

Indicative	*Inferential*
Pisatelyat vse sedeše i vse pišeše.	Pisetelyat vse sedyal i vse pišel.
Toi ne znaeše počivka. Beše mnogo trudolyubiv.	Toi ne znael počivka. Bil mnogo trudolyubiv.

'The teacher was always sitting and writing. He never thought of taking a break. He was very much devoted to his work.'

PARTICIPLES

Use of the active past participle in *-l* has been illustrated above. The present active participle ends in *-eyki/ayki*: e.g. *pristigayki v grada . . .* 'arriving in the town . . . '. The past passive participle is in *-n* or *-t*: e.g. *pisan* 'written'; *vzet* 'taken'. This participle can be used to make passive sentences: e.g. *Vestnikăt e četen ot všicki* 'The newspaper is read by all', which can also be expressed as a reflexive verb: *vestnikăt se čete ot všicki.*

Prepositions

For example, *v* 'in'; *sled* 'after'; *kăm* 'towards'; *izvăn* 'beyond': e.g. *Tazi rabota e izvăn silite mi* 'This job is beyond my powers.'

Word formation

Derivatives mainly by sufixation: e.g.

-ar: *stol* 'chair': *stolar* 'carpenter'
-nik: *rabota* 'work': *rabotnik* 'worker'
-stvo: *bogat* 'rich': *bogatstvo* 'wealth'
-ota: *čist* 'pure': *čistota* 'purity'
-ište: *igraya* 'I play': *igrište* 'playground'

Compounding is prolific: e.g. *zelenčukproizvoditel* 'market gardener' (*zelen* 'green', *-čuk*: *zelenčuk* 'vegetable'; *-tel* suffix denoting agent; *vodya* 'I lead'; *pro-*, *iz-* are prefixes denoting 'out of', 'from').

Word order

SVO is basic.

1 Въ начало бѣ Словото; и Словото
бѣше у Бога; и Словото **бѣ Богъ.**
2 То въ начало бѣше у Бога.
3 Всичко това чрезъ Него ста-
на; и безъ Него не е станало нищо
отъ това, което е станало.
4 Въ Него бѣ животътъ и животътъ бѣ свѣтлина на човѣцитѣ.
5 И свѣтлината свѣти въ тъмнината; а тъмнината я не схвана.
6 Яви се човѣкъ изпратенъ отъ
Бога, на име Иоанъ.
7 Той дойде за свидетелство, да
свидетелствува за свѣтлината, за да
повѣрватъ всички чрезъ него.
8 Не бѣше той свѣтлината, но
дойде да свидетелствува за свѣтлината.

BURMESE

INTRODUCTION

This language belongs to the Burmic branch of the Tibeto-Burmese family. From South-West China, where its close congener, Yi, is still spoken, Burmese was carried southwards to reach its present habitat by the ninth century AD. Here it came into contact with the Mon language (*see* **Mon, Old**) and the Pali scriptures of Buddhism. The result was an amalgam: Tibeto-Burman stock with a Mon-Khmer substratum and writing system, plus a Pali–Buddhist ideological superstructure. The earliest written records in Burmese date from the eleventh century. By the twelfth century Burmese had replaced Mon as the literary language of court.

For the study of the Pali texts, a specific genre known as *nissaya* Burmese was introduced, in which Pali words are accompanied by Burmese calques (cf. **Tibetan**). An interesting feature in Burmese classical verse is the so-called 'climbing rhyme', with rhymes regressing through successive four-syllable lines:

1, 2, 3, *4*, 1, 2, *3*, 4, 1, *2*, 3, *4*, 1, 2, *3*, 4 . . . etc.

Burmese is the official language of the Republic of Burma, and is now spoken by about 21 million people. There are three main dialects: Central (the basis of the literary language), Arakanese, and Tavoi (Tenasserim). Over and above the dialectal division is a fundamental distinction between written and colloquial Burmese, with the latter exerting constant upward pressure on the former, as shown, for example, in the erosion of the old literary particles.

SCRIPT

See **Script** at end of article.

PHONOLOGY

Consonants

stops: p, ph, b, t, th, d, k, kh, g, ʔ
affricatives: ʃ, tʃh, dʒ
fricatives: θ, ð, s, sh, ʃ, z, h
nasals: m, mh, n, nh, ɲ, ŋ, ŋh
lateral and flap: l, r
semi-vowels: j, w

Sixteen of the consonants can be set out in five-term series (including aspirate sonant): surd – aspirate surd – voiced stop – sonant – aspirate sonant, e.g. for labial series: /p – ph – b – m – mh/. (There is no specific graph for the aspirate sonant, which is written with the secondary form of *h*: e.g. မ = *ma*, မှ = *hma*.) Aspiration and consonant are pronounced simultaneously, and may be conventionally notated either as C*h*, or as *h*C, where C = consonant.

Most consonants can be labialized: /p°, t°, k°/, etc.; /p, b, m/ can be palatalized.

CONSONANT GRADATION

Unvoiced stop → voiced stop in intervocalic position or following a nasal: e.g. *kauŋ* + *kauŋ* → [kauŋgauŋ]; *θwa* + *tɔ* → [θwàdɔ́].

Vowels

i, e, ɛ, a, ɔ, o, u, ə

DIPHTHONGS

ei, ou, au, ai

Diphthongs are always followed by /ŋ/ or by /ˀ/, e.g. /eiŋ/ 'house'; /kauŋ/ '(to be) good'.

Syllables are *full*, i.e. with all components receiving their full phonetic value, or *reduced*, with vowels tending to /ə/. This characteristic is not typical of Tibeto-Burman, and may indicate Mon-Khmer influence.

The Burmese syllable must contain a vowel or diphthong, which may be preceded and/or followed by a consonant: $(C_1)V(C_2)$ where V = vowel or diphthong. There is a wide choice for C_1, but C_2 can only be /ŋ/ or /k, t, p/, realized as [ˀ]. C_1 may be followed by the semi-vowel /j/ or /w/ (i.e. palatalized or labialized).

Tone

There are three tones. The level tone is unmarked; the heavy falling tone is marked in the script by visarga and in transcription by grave accent; the 'creaky' tone is marked in the script by subscript dot, and in notation by acute accent. In addition, an abrupt (implosive or choked-off) tone occurs before the glottal stop final: this is unmarked in script. Tone marking is not consistent.

MORPHOLOGY AND SYNTAX

Noun

No grammatical gender. Where natural gender has to be specified, lexical means are employed, e.g. *má* for human females: *yá.hàŋ* 'monk' – *yá.hàŋ.má* 'nun'. *Dó* is a general plural marker: *lu* 'man', *ludó* 'people'. *Myà* is a restricted plural marker: *lumyà* 'a certain (given) number of people'. Syntactic relationships are expressed by particles following the noun. Thus, *ká* is a subject marker (literary *ði*). *Ko* is an object or directional marker, *hma* is a locative, *nɛ́* an instrumental marker: e.g. *eiŋ.hma* 'in the house'; *dou'.nɛ́* 'with a stick' (literary *hníŋ*).

POSSESSION

Literary *í* = colloquial *yɛ́*; Y of X is expressed as X *í*/*yɛ́* Y. This particle can be omitted; if it is, X changes tone: e.g. *θu.yɛ́ eiŋ* = *θú.eiŋ* 'his house'. If omitted, the objective marker *ko* induces similar tonal change.

There are several numerical coefficients, e.g. *yau'*, *ù* for people; *kauŋ* for animals; *lòuŋ*, *chàuŋ* for objects according to shape, size, and so on. *Khú* is an all-purpose classifier which can replace any other (cf. Chinese 个 /ge/).

Pronoun

The independent personal pronouns are:

Singular

1 cuŋ.dɔ (masc.), cuŋ.má (fem.)

2 khìŋ.bya (formal), mìŋ (general)

3 θu

Plural markers are added to make the plural series. Possessives are made by adding *í*/*yɛ́*. Again, if this is omitted, the tone of the pronoun changes: *cuŋ.dɔ.yɛ́* = *cuŋ.dɔ́* 'mine'.

DEMONSTRATIVE PRONOUN

di 'this'; *ho* 'that'

INTERROGATIVE PRONOUN

These are based on the particle *bɛ* + modulators: *bɛ.ðu* 'who?'; *ba.go* 'what?'.

Numerals

1–10: *ti'*, *hni'*, *θòuŋ*, *lè*, *ŋà*, *chau'*, *khú.ni'*, *ši'*, *kò*, *təs*^{h}*ə*/*təse*; 20 *hni'shɛ*; 100 *təya*.

Verb

Verbs in Burmese may be simple, e.g. *θwà* 'to go', *sà* 'to eat'; or compound, i.e. root + root, e.g. *twé.myiŋ* 'to meet' ('meet' + 'see'). There is no inflection for person. The general predicative marker is *ði* (coll.)/*i* (lit.). This marker is further amplified by several specific markers for tense and mood: e.g. *mɛ* (future), *gɛ* (perfective), *ne* (progressive), *pyi* (inceptive). E.g.

tәne.θә.hnai mauŋ.lu.e youŋ.hma sɔ.zɔ shiŋ.la.**gɛ.i**
'One day, Maung Lu E came home from work early'
(*təne.θə.hnai* 'one day', 'once'; *youŋ* 'place of work'; *hma* 'from' (postposition); *sɔ.zɔ* 'early'; *shiŋ.la* 'to return'; *gɛ* perfective particle; *i* predicative marker)

kɛ́/kouŋ/pi: these are used to express perfective aspect.

NEGATION

The negative marker is *mə… phù*: e.g. *mə humaŋ phù* 'not true'.

IMPERATIVE

Command is made more polite by addition of *pa*: e.g. *θwà.**ba*** 'please go'. An interrogative marker is *la*.

MODAL VERBS

Desiderative *chiŋ*; potential *ta'/hnain*; necessitative *yá*; conditional *yiŋ*: e.g. *twé.yiŋ* 'if… meet(s)'; *θwa.yá.mɛ* '… must go'. A verbal noun is made with the ə-prefix (written အ = *a*, reduced to /ə/): e.g. *lou'* 'to work' – *ə.lou'* 'work' (noun); *hlá* 'to be pretty' – *ə.hlá* 'beauty'.

Many verbs occur in functive–stative pairs (active–passive in Indo-European terms); the functive member has an aspirate initial which is dropped in the stative:

Functive	*Stative*
hcìŋ 'to make narrow'	ciŋ 'to be narrow'
hcwá 'to raise'	cwá 'to be lifted'
hnòu 'to waken'	nòu 'to be awake'
hlu' 'to set free'	lu' 'to be free'

As in Chinese, there are many four-syllable set phrases, which may be extended to six members. These often consist of formant + rhyming word, reduplicated: e.g. *kə.pya.kə.ya* 'hurriedly'.

RELATIVE CLAUSES

May be made with the particle *tɔ*:

θwà.**dɔ̀**.lu 'the man who is going'
θwà.**gɛ́**.dɔ̀.lu 'the man who went' (with perfective marker *kɛ* → *gɛ*)
θwa.mɛ.**dɔ̀**.lu 'the man who will go' (with future marker *mɛ*)

Subjectless sentences proliferate, as in Chinese: e.g. *Pyɔ.pyɔ.ne ðe.gɛ̀.ði* 'Live well, die miserably.'

Compounding

Burmese has a very large stock of polysyllables built up by compounding from various parts of speech. An example shows two nouns and a verb forming a third polysyllabic noun: *nyá* 'night' + *ne* 'sun' + *sàuŋ* 'to lean' → *nyá.ne.zàuŋ* 'afternoon'.

Word order

SOV is normal.

၁ [၁]အစအဦး၌ [၂]နှုတ်ကပတ်တော် ရှိ၏။ နှုတ်ကပတ်
တော်သည် ဘုရားသခင်နှင့် အတူ[၃]ရှိ၏။ နှုတ်ကပတ်
၂ တော်သည်လည်းဘုရားသခင်[၄]ဖြစ်တော်မူ၏။-ထိုနှုတ်
ကပတ်တော်သည်အစအဦး၌ ဘုရားသခင်နှင့်အတူရှိ
၃ ၏။- ကိုယ်တော်သည် [၅]ခပ်သိမ်းသော အရာတို့ကိုဖန်
ဆင်းတော်မူ၏။ ကိုယ်တော်နှင့် ကင်းလွတ်လျက်၊ ဖန်
၄ ဆင်းသောအရာ တစုံတခုမျှ မရှိ။- ကိုယ်တော်၌ [၆]အ
သက်ရှိ၏။ထိုအသက်သည်လည်း[၇]လူတို့၏အလင်းဖြစ်
၅ ၏။-[၈]ထိုအလင်းသည်မှောင်မိုက်၌ထွန်းလင်း၍၊ မှောင်
၆ မိုက်သည် မသတ်မငြိမ်း စေနိုင်။-[၉]ယောဟန်အမည်ရှိ
သောသူတယောက်ကို ဘုရားသခင် စေလွှတ်တော်မူ
၇ ၏။-ထိုသူကိုလူအပေါင်းတို့သည်အမှီပြု၍၊ [၁၀]ယုံကြည်
ခြင်းသို့ရောက်မည်အကြောင်း၊ထိုသူသည် [၁၁]သက်သေ
ခံဖြစ်၍၊အလင်းတော်၏အကြောင်းကိုသက်သေခံခြင်း
၈ ငှါလာ၏။-ထိုသူသည်[၁၂]အလင်းတော်မဟုတ်၊အလင်း
တော်၏အကြောင်းကိုသက်သေခံခြင်းငှါသာလာ၏။-
၉ ဟုတ်မှန်[၁၃]သောအလင်းမူကား၊ဤလောကသို့ကြွလာ
လျက်၊ ခပ်သိမ်းသောလူအပေါင်းတို့အား အလင်းကို

SCRIPT

The Burmese script is derived from the Mon version of Brāhmī. As in all Indic scripts, each base consonant has an inherent short vowel /a/. In addition to their primary forms, all vowels and certain consonants have secondary forms. The table shows the consonantal inventory of Burmese, and the initial vowel signs and the secondary vowel signs as applied to a consonant, denoted by C.

Eleven vowels are coded for tone, i.e. they require no tone marker. Seven of these are second tone, three are first tone, and one is third. Using /k/ as bearer consonant, we then have:

Second tone

ကာ ***kā***, ကီ ***kī***, ကူ ***kū***, ကေ ***kē***, ကယ် ***kɛ̄***, ကော် ***kɔ̄***, ကို ***kō***

First tone

က ***ka***, ကိ ***ki***, ကု ***ku***

Third tone

ကဲ ***kɛ̄***

First-tone vowels other than the three specified above are marked with subscript dot, e.g.

ကေ့ ***ke,*** ကဲ့ ***kɛ,*** ကော့ ***kɔ,*** ကို့ ***ko***

Third-tone vowels are marked with ꞉ (< Sanskrit visarga): e.g.

ကား ***kā,*** ကီး ***kī,*** ကူး ***kū,*** ကေး ***kē***

THE BURMESE SCRIPT

CONSONANTS

က	ခ	ဂ	ဃ	င	စ	ဆ	ဇ	ဈ	ည	ဋ
ka	*kha*	*ga*	*ga*	*nga*	*sa*	*sa*	*za*	*za*	*nya*	*ta*
ဌ	ဍ	ဎ	ဏ	တ	ထ	ဒ	ဓ	န	ပ	
tha	*da*	*da*	*na*	*ta*	*tha*	*da*	*da*	*na*	*pa*	
ဖ	ဗ	ဘ	မ	ယ	ရ	လ	ဝ	သ	ဟ	ဠ
pha	*ba*	*ba*	*ma*	*ya*	*ya(ra)*	*la*	*wa*	*sa*	*ha*	*la*

VOWELS

(a) Independent

အ	အာ	အား	ဣ	ဤ	ဥ	ဦ
a	*ā*	*ā*	*i*	*ī*	*u*	*ū*
အေ့	ဧ	အဲ	ဪ	ဩ	အို	အံ
e	*ē*	*ɛ*	*ō*	*ō*	*ō*	*an*

(b) as used with bearer consonant, represented by C:

C *-a*   Cာ *-ā*   Cား *-ā*   Cိ *-i*   Cီ *-ī*   Cု (C|) *-u*   Cူ (C| *-ū*

ေC *-e*   ေC *-ē*   Cဲ *-ɛ*   ေCာ် *-ō*   ေCာ *-ō*   Cို *-ō*

CONJUNCT CONSONANTS

As a general rule, conjunct consonants retain their primary form and are written as subscripts, but four – ya, ra, wa, ha – have specific forms, shown here as applied to *ma*:

မ *ma*, မျ *mya*, မြ *mya*, မွ *mwa*, မှ *hma*, မျွ *mywa*, မျှ *hmya*, မြှ *hmya*, မွှ *hmwa*, မြို *myo*.

NUMERALS

၁	၂	၃	၄	၅	၆	၇	၈	၉	၀
1	2	3	4	5	6	7	8	9	0

BURUSHASKI

INTRODUCTION

Related, so far as is known, to no other language, Burushaski is spoken by about 40,000 people in isolated and inaccessible mountain valleys in the part-Indian, part-Pakistani state of Jammu and Kashmir. The Burushaski (ethnonym *burušo*) appear to be the sole residue of a pre-Indo-European population inhabiting Northern India, classified by anthropologists as 'Europeanoid'. Burushaski is unwritten. Claims that a literary Burushaski may have been in use in the very early Middle Ages rest on a reference in a Tibetan source to translation from *bruža'*. Many attempts have been made to connect Burushaski with other language families – Caucasian, Dravidian, Munda, Basque, etc. – but none are convincing, and Burushaski must, for the present, rate as a language with no known congeners.

Burushaski was formerly spoken in much of what is now Dardic territory (*see* **Dardic Languages**), and shares with the Dardic group (along with certain Tibeto-Burman languages, the Pamir languages, some North-West Indian languages, and one Dravidian) the areal features of the grouping known as 'Himalayan'. H. Berger (1959) has identified Burushaski words in Romany.

There are two main dialects, *burušaski* and *weršikwar*, which are mutually intelligible. The purest Burushaski is that of Hunza.

PHONOLOGY

Consonants

The series, surd stop – aspirated surd – voiced stop, is typical: e.g. /p, ph, b; t, th, d; ṭ, ṭh, ḍ; tʃ, ṭʃh, dʒ; k, kh, g/, etc. The dental stops and fricatives have retroflex counterparts (notated here with dots), apart from dental /n/, which has no parallel in the retroflex series. In this article /tʃ/ is notated as *č*, /ts/ as *c*.

Vowels

Long and short: i, e, a, o, u

Allophones are [ɪ, ɛ, ʌ, ə, ɔ]. Length is phonemic: cf.: *γēniṣ* 'empress', *γeniṣ* 'gold'. The presence of overlong vowels has been noted by some authorities.

Tones are present in Burushaski, but so far scarcely investigated. According to Siddheshwar Varma (1931) they are comparable to the tonal system in Panjabi.

Stress

On long vowel, if present, in disyllables, but stress is weak and seems to be largely 'irrelevant' (Morgenstierne 1945, Lorimer 1935).

MORPHOLOGY AND SYNTAX

Noun

There are four classes of noun: (1) male beings; (2) female beings; (3) other animates (animals, etc.) and some objects; (4) everything not included in (1–3).e.g.

Class 1: *hīr* 'man', *hiles* 'boy', *phūt* 'demon'
Class 2: *gus* 'woman', *dasin* 'daughter'
Class 3: *huk* 'dog', *haγur* 'horse'
Class 4: *cil* 'water', *mamu* 'milk', *γeniṣ̌* 'gold'

There are no typical class endings, though *-ṣ̌*, *-č*, and *-ŋ* are often found in class 4 nouns.

The indefinite marker *-an* is suffixed to nouns, usually in combination with the prepositive marker *hin* for classes 1 and 2, *han* for classes 3 and 4: e.g. (***hin***) *gus**an*** 'a woman, some woman'. The indefinite marker takes case endings (see below): e.g. *hin džat gusan.mo ha* 'an old woman's house'. *-ik* is a plural indefinite marker: e.g. *hir**ik*** 'some men'.

NUMBER

There are two numbers. Plural markers are extremely heterogeneous – several dozen suffixes, with assimilation at junctures. Two common suffixes are *-o* and *-anc*: e.g. *balas* 'bird', pl. *bala**šo***; *huyēlterc* 'shepherd', pl. *huyēlter**čo***; *baš* 'bridge', pl. *baš**anc***; *haγur* 'horse', pl. *haγur**išo***.

CASE SYSTEM

Simple opposition between nominative and oblique/ergative, e.g. for *hiles* 'boy': sing. nom. *hiles*, erg./obl. *hiles**e***. pl. nom. *hile**šo***, erg./obl. *hile**šue***. In class 2 nouns, a distinction is made between ergative and general oblique case; e.g. for *gus* 'woman': erg. *guse*; general obl. *gus**mo***.

Most syntactic relationships are expressed with the help of postpositions: e.g. *gus.mu.cum* 'from the woman'; *den.iŋ.ulo* 'in the years'.

POSSESSION

The proclitic personal markers are mainly used where inalienable or organic possession is concerned. They are:

	1st person	*2nd person*	*3rd person*			
			Class 1	*2*	*3*	*4*
Singular	a-	gu-	i-	mu-	i-	i-
Plural	mi-	ma-		u-		i

Examples: ***ari**ŋ* 'my hand', ***guri**ŋ* 'your hand'; ***muri**ŋ* 'her hand'.

Adjective

Hardly distinguished from noun. As attribute, adjective usually precedes noun. Plural affixes attached to adjectives may be marked for class. Thus, *cūmi**šo*** 'heavy (pl.)' with reference to classes 1–3; *cūmi**ŋ*** 'heavy (pl.)' to class 4.

COMPARISON

A comparative is made with the postposition *cum* 'from' + positive degree: e.g. *J̌a haγur īne haγur**cum** šua bi* 'My horse is better than his horse.'

Pronoun

The independent personal forms are:

	Singular	*Oblique/ergative*	*Plural*	*Oblique/ergative*
1	ǰe	ǰa	mi	mi(m)
2	ūn/ūŋ	ūŋ(e)	ma	ma(m)

The third person forms are supplied from the demonstrative series, which vary for class of referent. There are two series, proximate and distal:

	Class 1, 2	*Class 3*	*Class 4*
Proximate	kīne	guse	gute
Distal	īne	īse	īte

All with plural forms. A specific series is used only for classes 3 and 4: proximate *kōs/kōt*; distal: *ēs/ēt*.

The possessive proclitic series (see above) is used to denote direct/indirect object of verb; also, + postposition *ər*, to express a benefactive sense: e.g. ***ar*** 'to, for me'; ***gor*** 'to, for you'.

The pronominal series based on *men-*, *bes-*, etc., provide interrogative, negative, and relative forms, depending on context: e.g. *Ūŋ menan ba?* 'Who are you?'; *Besan ečam?* 'What shall I do?'

Numerals

The first three units vary for class:

	Classes 1 and 2	*Class 3*	*Class 4*
1	hin	han	han
2	āltan	ālta	ālto
3	īsken	usko	usko

4–10, all classes; *wālto, cundo, mišindo, talo, āltambo, hunčo, tōrumo*. 11–13: *turma* + class-related forms of 1, 2, 3; thereafter, *turma* + 4–9, as above. 20 *āltəran*; 30 *āltərtōrumo*; 40 *āltuwāltər*; 50 *āltuwāltər tōrumo*; 100 *tha*.

Verb

Finite forms are (a) primary (future, past tenses, imperative mood), or (b) secondary (all other tenses and moods): these secondary forms were originally compound – verb stem + *b-* auxiliary.

As in Iranian, all verbs, except the *b-* auxiliary, have two bases: past and present. The present base is made from the past by the addition of –(V)*č*/*ǰ*/*š*, depending on past base final: e.g. *sūyas* 'to bring', past base *su-*; present base *suč-*. The personal and class markers are prefixed or suffixed to, or infixed in, the verbal base. The verbal complex is negated by a negating prefix *a-* (with variants).

Prefixed markers are essentially the possessive markers (see above). They are in concord with the object of transitive verbs (the ergative construction), and with the subject of intransitive verbs (where they are, in fact, redundant).

Suffixed markers show person, number, and, in the third person, class of subject. They are vocalic in the singular, V + *n* in plural: e.g. the first person singular marker is *-a*, the plural *-an*; class 2 third person singular *-u*/*o*, plural *-an*: ***gu****yecam* 'I saw you' (*-m* is past-tense marker); ***mu****yecum.an* 'they saw her'.

TENSE

The indicative mood has six tenses, three formed from each of the two bases. For example, from *ni(y)as* 'to go': present root *nič-*; past root *ni.*

		Singular		*Plural*
1		niča ba	1	niča bān
2		niča	2	ničān
3	Class 1:	ničaii	3	ničān
	Class 2:	niču bo		ničān
	Class 3:	niči bi	3	–
	Class 4:	niči bīla		–

The future tense of the same verb is: 1st p. sing. *ničam*, 2nd *ničuma*; the class-marked forms for the 3rd p. are *ničim.**i**/**o**/**i***.

The past tense: *niam*, *nīma*; *nīmi*, *nīmo, nīmi*. The perfect has *ni*(*a*) + *b-* auxiliary: e.g.

present: *ǰe čamine ēirča ba* 'I'm dying of hunger'
future: *γenišan gučičam* 'I shall give you gold'
past: *badša haγurcum sōkimi* 'the emperor dismounted from the horse'

IMPERATIVE

The endings are sing. *-ni*, pl. *nīn*(*a*).

Certain verbs have class infixes, i.e. specific vocalic patterns.

NEGATION

Prefix *a-* (rarely *o-*, *ō-*): e.g. *dīca ba* 'I brought him'; ***a****tīca ba* 'I didn't bring him'.

NON-FINITE FORMS

infinitive: past base + *-as/ās*
first gerund: past base + -V*m*
second gerund: past base + -Vṣ̌

Example: *Ṣ̌apik* ***dicum*** *gŭsiŋanc osalǰaii* 'He sees women bringing bread' (*ṣ̌apik* 'bread').

Word order

Normally SOV.

BURYAT

INTRODUCTION

This Mongolian language, closely related to Khalkha Mongolian, is spoken by about 300,000 people in the Buryatia Republic, and by, possibly, 100,000 in the People's Republic of China. It is difficult to estimate how many people speak Buryat in China, as they are not listed separately from the Khalkha and Oirat Mongolians (total for all three *c.* 3½ million).

In addition to a long and rich oral tradition, the Buryats now have a considerable output in several literary fields. Four main dialects are distinguished. The literary norm is based on the eastern Khori dialect.

SCRIPT

Originally the Buryats had an amended version of the vertical Mongolian character. Initial experiments with Cyrillic were made in the nineteenth century. A period of romanization in the 1930s was followed by the present Cyrillic alphabet, which contains the additional letters θ, γ, h. The Cyrillic letter н does duty for both the dental and the velar sound: /n/ and /ŋ/.

PHONOLOGY

Consonants

stops: b (→ [w]), d, t, g (→ [γ])
fricatives: s, z, ʃ, ʒ, x, h
nasals: m, n, ŋ
lateral and flap: l, r
semi-vowel: j

/p, f, k, ts, tʃ/ occur in loanwords.

Vowels

front: ɪ, iː
central: y, yː, œː, e, eː, ε, εː
back: u, uː, o, oː, a, aː

Vocalic reduction takes place in all non-initial syllables. /œ/ is notated here as *ö*.

VOWEL HARMONY

The basic opposition is between central and back vowels; the high vowels /ɪ, iː/ are neutral: cf. *doloon* 'seven'; *negen* 'one'; *xorin* 'twenty'; *ygi* 'not'. Some erosion of this system is due in part to the monophthongization of old diphthongs. Thus, /aj, oj, uj/ have all become /ɛː/: cf. *axa* 'elder brother' + *tai* 'with' → *axataj* = /axatɛː/.

MORPHOLOGY AND SYNTAX

Noun

No gender, no articles. Nouns and adjectives are not formally differentiated; a noun in base form may serve as a qualifier: e.g. *modon ger* 'wood(en) house'; *aman zoxjol* 'oral literature' (lit. 'mouth creation').

PLURAL MARKERS

(C)*uud*^{2}: the index indicates that two allomorphs are possible, depending on vowel harmony: e.g. *seseg* 'flower', pl. *sesegyyd* (front vowel in stem); *gazar* 'place,' pl. *gazarnuud* (back vowel in stem). Similarly, *-nar*^{3} indicates three possible allomorphs; this marker is used as a collective affix for humans: e.g. *dyyner* 'young people'; *axanar* 'elder brothers'.

-d is used as a plural marker after unstable *-n*, and in certain words: e.g. *mori*(*n*) 'horse', pl. *morid*; *nöxör* 'friend', pl. *nöxöd*.

CASE SYSTEM

Specimen paradigms of singular forms for *gal* 'fire', *dalai* 'sea':

nominative	gal	dalai
genitive	galai	dalain
dative/locative	galda	dalaida
accusative	galiije	dalaije
instrumental	galaar	dalaigaar
comitative	galtai	dalaitai
ablative	galhaa	dalaihaa

The same endings are added to plural forms. Affixes are subject to assimilation at junctures, and, of course, to vowel harmony.

The case marker precedes the possessive affix: e.g. *axa.da.m* 'to my elder brother'.

Cases may be compounded: e.g. *temeen.tei.hee* 'from the one who has the camel'; *terge.tei.tei* 'with the one who has a cart'.

Adjective

As attribute, adjective precedes noun and may take plural marker instead of noun: e.g. *jexe* **Ø** ***gernyyd*** = *jexe**nyyd** ger* 'big houses'. Personal markers may be added to adjectives: e.g. *ulaanš* 'you (who are) red'.

Pronoun

PERSONAL INDEPENDENT

Sing. 1 *bi*, *ši*, 3 *tere* pl. 1 *bide(ner)*, 2 *ta(anar)*, 3 *tede(ner)*. These are declined in all cases. As in Khalkha, the oblique cases of *bi* 'I' are formed from a suppletive base, *nam-*, with a genitive in *minii*.

Possessive enclitic markers: these are truncated versions of the personal pronominal genitive cases: e.g. sing. 1 *minii* > *-mni/-m*; 2 *-š(ni)*; 3 *-(ii)n*. The plural forms are: *-(m)nai*, *-(t)nai*, *-(ii)n*. Thus, *šinii noxoi* 'your dog' can also be expressed as *noxoi.****šni****/noxoi.š*.

DEMONSTRATIVE PRONOUN

ene 'this', pl. *ede*; *tere* 'that', pl. *tede.*

INTERROGATIVE PRONOUN

xen 'who?', pl. *xed*; *juu(n)*; 'what?', pl. *juud.*

Numerals

1–10: *negen*, *xojor*, *gurban*, *dyrben*, *taban*, *zurgaan*, *doloon*, *naiman*, *jyhen*, *arban*. 11–19: *arban* + *negen*, etc.; 20 *xorin*; 30 *gušan*; 40 *dyšen*; 100 *zuun.*

Verb

The Buryat verb has finite and non-finite forms. Finite forms take personal endings and function only as predicates. Non-finite forms are (a) verbal nouns which function mainly as attributives, but can take case endings and function as nouns, and (b) gerunds or converbs which are always in accessory relationship with a main verb.

There are five voices and four moods, each with specific marker (Ø in active voice and indicative and imperative moods).

VOICE

passive: *-gda*^{2}*-*, e.g. *neexe* 'to open': *ne****gd****exe* 'to be opened'
causative: *-uul*^{2}*-*, e.g. *jabaxa* 'to go': *jab****uul****axa* 'to cause to go'
reciprocal: *-lda*^{3}*-/-lša*^{3}*-*, e.g. *zolgoxo* 'to meet': *zogo****ldo****xo* 'to meet each other'

MOODS

The indicative mood has three main tenses – present, past, future. The tense markers are: present *-na*^{3}*-*; past *-ba*^{3}*-/-(g)aa*^{4}; future *-xa*^{3}*-*. The personal markers are: sing. 1 *-b/m*, 2 *-š*, 3 *-Ø*; pl. 1 *-bdi*, 2 *-t*, 3 *-d/-Ø*. Examples from *jabaxa* 'to go':

present: *jaba.na.b/m* 'I go', *jaba.na.š* 'you go', *jaba-na* 'he goes'
past: *jab.aa.b/m* 'I went'
future: *jaba.xa.b/m* 'I shall go'

IMPERATIVE

Second sing. = bare stem: + *-iit* for plural, with polite form in *-gtii*: *jabagtii* 'Please go.'

OPTATIVE

The marker is *-hai*^{3}-: *jab.a.hai.bdi?* 'How about (us) going?'

DUBITATIVE

-(*g*)*uuža*^{2}-: *unuuža.b?* 'What if I were to fall?'

GERUNDIVE AFFIXES

(Converbs): examples:

- *-ža*^{3}- for concomitant action: e.g. *Gazaaguur gara**ža** laptaa naadana* 'Going out, they play a ball-game.'
- -(*g*)*aad*^{3}- marks action preceding that of the main verb: e.g. *Ger xar**aad** jabaa* 'Having seen the house, he went.'
- *-bal*^{3}- conditional: e.g. *xara**bal*** 'if... see(s)'.
- *-tar*^{3}- terminative: e.g. *zun bolo**tor*** 'until (it becomes) summer'.
- *-xalaar*^{4}- marks action immediately preceding that of main verb – 'as soon as': e.g. *Ger xara**xalaar** jabaabdi* 'As soon as we had seen the house we went.'

NEGATION

Of indicative predicative form: *ygii* + personal marker. Cf. *jabanab* 'I go'; negative *jabana ygei**b***. Other moods are negated by the particle *by*.

RELATIVE CLAUSES

Usually constructed via participial use of verbal noun forms to the left of the head-word: e.g. with *-han*^{3}; *untaxa* 'to fall asleep, be asleep', *jerexe* 'to come'. *unta**han** xyn* 'someone who has fallen asleep'; *jere**hen** xyn* 'the person who came'. With *-xa*^{3}: *jaba**xa** xargii* 'the road which... is/are to take'. *-dag*^{3} denotes constant or reiterated action: e.g. *jaba**dag** xargii* 'a road which one habitually takes'.

There are four auxiliaries, the main ones being *bol-* and *bain-*, which are fully conjugated.

Postpositions

Govern the nominative, genitive, dative, or ablative cases: e.g. *gerei xažuuda* 'near the house' (with genitive); *manai gerei urda* 'in front of our house' (with genitive).

Word order

SOV is normal, but inversions are frequent.

CAMBODIAN (Khmer)

INTRODUCTION

Cambodian belongs to the Mon-Khmer sub-division of the Austro-Asiatic family. There are about 8 million speakers in Cambodia and Vietnam. The oldest inscriptions in Khmer date from the seventh century AD. From the end of the Angkor period (twelfth century) onwards, three main divisions of Cambodian literature may be distinguished:

1. Hindu influence is exemplified in the *Ream Ker*, the Cambodian version of the *Rāmāyaṇa*; in part, this is very old.
2. Buddhist influence (Cambodia became converted to Buddhism in the twelfth century). The translation of the *Tripitaka* has proved enormously influential, as, in addition to providing much of the Buddhist canon, it gave Cambodian literature a rich supply of motifs for the specifically Cambodian genre of the verse-novel.
3. The verse-novel: Cambodians seem to be particularly addicted to romantic stories of a sentimental type in which, latterly, French influence may be discerned.

SCRIPT

See **Script** at end of article.

PHONOLOGY

Consonants

stops: p, ph, b, t, th, d, k, kh, ʔ
affricates: ts, tʃ
fricatives: s, h
nasals: m, n, ɲ, ŋ
lateral and flap: r, l
semi-vowels: j, w

Any of these may function as word/syllable initial, but the following: tʃ, s, r, ph, th, kh, b, d are excluded from the inventory of possible finals.

In Pnom Penh speech, initial and medial clusters containing /r/ tend to be reduced: cf. *craen* ('much') > *cəən*; *cumriep* ('to greet', 'salute') > *cmiep*; *bɔŋriən* ('to teach') > *b/pniən*.

Aspiration is phonemic: cf. *thaa* 'to say'; *taa* 'old man'.

Vowels

The vocalic system is of great complexity, requiring over thirty phonemic contrasts to be notated in close transcription. There are ten basic short vowels:

front: i, e, ɛ
central: ɪ, ə, a
back: u, o, ɔ, ɑ

Ten long vowels: the above vowels doubled: /ii, ee/, etc. Ten long diphthongs:

iə, ɪə, uə, ei, əɪ, ou, ae, aə, ao, ɔə

and three short:

uə, eə, oe

Cambodian is non-tonal. Stress tends to fall on the final syllable.

MORPHOLOGY AND SYNTAX

Noun

Cambodian words have no inflection of any kind, and are not readily classifiable in terms of 'parts of speech'. There are no articles: e.g. *pteəh* means 'house', 'a house', 'the house'. Number may be inferred from the context, or expressed by such modifiers as *klah* 'some', *teəng* 'all'. For example, *pii* 'two' may be added to *teəng*: *salaa.riən teəng.pii nuh* 'those two schools' (*salaa.riən* 'house of learning').

Nouns are formed from verbs by (a) prefixed formants, e.g. *b* + homorganic nasal with link vowel: *tuk* 'to put, place': *bɔntuk* 'load'; (b) by infixed nasal: *l'ɔɔ* 'be pretty': *lum'ɔɔ* 'beauty'; *som* 'to ask': *smom* 'beggar'; *klaac* 'to be afraid of': *komlaac* 'timid person'.

Compound nouns of various types are frequent in Cambodian. Some examples: *tok.tuu.kaw'ɛy* ('table-chest-chair') 'furniture'; *bɔntup.keeŋ* 'bedroom' (*bɔntup* > *ptup* 'room', *keeŋ* 'sleep'); *thŋay.bon* 'holiday' (*thŋay* 'day', *bon* 'festival'); *moha.sə mot* 'ocean' (*moha-* < Sanskrit *maha-* 'great' is a bound component). Bound components may be word-final: e.g. *-cɔɔ* 'to travel': *tehsə.cɔɔ* 'tourist' (*tehsə* 'place'); *-niyum* '-ism': *sɔŋkum.niyum* 'socialism' (*sɔŋkum* 'society').

GENDER

If necessary, gender can be expressed by such lexical additions as *proh* 'male (human)', *srəy* 'female': e.g. *koun.proh* 'son'; *koun.srəy* 'daughter'.

CASE RELATIONS

Expressed syntactically with the help of various particles, or by apposition as in the genitive: e.g. *laan əwpuk* 'father's car' (*laan* 'car'; *əwpuk* 'father'), *əwpuk neək* 'your father'; or in compound form: e.g. *tuənlee.meekong* 'the river (of the) Mekong'.

Adjective

As attribute, adjective follows noun: e.g. *salaa.riən touc* 'a small school'; *koun.srəy l'ɔɔ* 'a pretty girl'. The attribute may be another noun: *phləw laan* 'motor-way' (*phləw* 'road', *laan* 'car').

A comparative is made with *ciaŋ* 'more': *sruol* 'easy', *sruol ciaŋ* 'easier'; *pibaa'* 'difficult', *pibaa' ciaŋ*, 'more difficult'.

Pronoun

Cambodian had, and up to a point still has, a very large inventory of status-graded personal pronouns, each with correlative particles of address and response. As in the case of Lao, social change fosters the emergence of certain pronouns as neutral/polite forms of address or reference, suitable for use in most situations: e.g. for first person *khɲom*; for second person *look* (to a man), *look.srəy* (to a woman); third person *koət*. A neutral first person plural form is *yəəŋ* (*khɲom*). Plural forms may be made for these by adding *teəng.'ah*.

In the case of the second person, use of a title or a kinship term is preferred wherever possible. A full list of all status-graded forms is given in Jacob (1968: 158–63).

In their role as possessives, the personal pronouns follow the noun possessed: *mdaay khɲom* 'my mother', *pteəh look* 'your house'.

Direct and indirect object: cf. *khɲom 'aoy luy kot* (*koət*) 'I give money to-him (*kot*)'; *khɲom caŋ ñcəəñ look mɔɔk* 'I'd like (*caŋ*) to invite (*ñcəəñ*) you (*look*) to come (*mɔɔk*)'; *'aoy səphɯw khɲom bəy moh* 'give me three books'. (The word order in this last example is interesting: literally 'give book to-me three hither', i.e. the pronominal indirect object is interpolated between noun and numeral.)

DEMONSTRATIVE PRONOUN/ADJECTIVE

nih 'this/these'; *nuh* 'that/those': e.g. *laan nih* 'this car'; *siəwphɯw tlay pram nih* 'these five (*pram*) expensive (*tlay*) books'.

INTERROGATIVE PRONOUN

neə'-naa 'who?'; *'wəy* 'what?': e.g. *Neə'naa cang tɯw məəl kon?* 'Who wants to go to the cinema?' (*məəl* 'to see, watch').

Interrogative particles: *rɯ*, *tee*: *look sok.səpbaay cia tee?* 'Are you well?'; *look mɔɔk riən nɯw srok.kmae rɯ?* 'Have you come to study in Cambodia (*srok.kmae*)?'

RELATIVE PRONOUN

dael, following head-word: e.g. *Khɲom miən koun.proh məneə' dael nɯw riən nɯw laəy* 'I have a son who is still (*nɯw laəy*) at school' (*məneə'* is the classifier for person).

Numerals

1–10: *muəy, pii, bəy, buən, pram, prammuəy, prampii, prambəy, prambuən, dɔp*; 11 *dɔp.muəy*, 12 *dɔp.pii*; 20 *məphıy*; 30 *saamsəp*; 40 *saesəp*; 100 *rɔɔy*.

CLASSIFIERS

Cambodian has some two dozen numerical classifiers, representing a marked reduction from the much more extensive repertory of the older language.

The consistent use of classifiers is characteristic of the written language, e.g. *knɔɔŋ* 'buildings', *dom* 'pieces', *ne'* 'people', *kbaal* 'books', 'livestock'. Cf. *koun.səh bey ne'* 'three students' (literally 'student three person'); *kmaw.day pii daəm* 'two pencils'.

Verb

There is no inflection of any kind. Aspect, modal categories, and tense are expressed by means of auxiliary particles which may be pre- or post-verbal. Thus, *haəy* is a post-verbal particle indicating the perfective aspect; *cɔng* is a modal auxiliary expressing wish or design.

Cambodian has no genuine passive voice; many verbals can be both active and passive, the exact meaning depending on the syntactic context.

Both prefixation and infixation are used as formative processes in Cambodian. The prefix *p-/ph-*, for example, produces causatives: e.g. *dəng* 'to know' – ***p.****dəng* 'to let know, inform'; *deik* 'to sleep' – ***ph.****deik* 'to put to sleep'. Similarly, with prefix *b*V*n-*: *riən* 'to learn' – *bɔngriən* 'to teach'.

The infix -V*m-* makes transitives: e.g. *slap* 'die' – *s****ɔml****ap* 'to kill'; *krup* 'all' – ***kum****rup* 'to complete'; *s'aat* 'clean' – ***sam'****aat* 'to clean'.

The prefix *prɔ-* suggests reciprocity: e.g. *cam* 'to wait' – ***prɔ****cam* 'to wait for each other'.

Partial reduplication is used to express intensification or reiteration of action: e.g. *kaay* 'to dig' – ***kɔ****kaay* 'to dig away at'.

TENSE

Action is broadly classified as perfective, imperfective, or pending:

Perfective: expressed by *baan* or *haəy*, e.g. *Maong prambuən* ***haɔy*** 'It's gone 9 o'clock'; *khɲom sdap* **baan** 'I understood'. This form is negated by *mın ... tee*: e.g. *khɲom sdap* **min** *ban* **tee** 'I didn't understand'.

Imperfective: e.g. with *kɔmpung.tae*, corresponding to Lao *kamlang*: *Khɲom kɔmpung.tae riən phiəsaa.kmae* 'I am now learning Cambodian' (*phiəsaa* 'language', < Skt *bhāṣā*).

Pending action: e.g. with *nıng: khɲom* ***nıng*** *tıw pteəh* 'I shall go home'.

MODAL AUXILIARIES

E.g. *trəw* 'must'; *cɔng* 'want to': *khɲom trəw tıw twəə.kaa* 'I have to go to work'. *craən-tae* denotes habitual action: e.g. *khɲom craən-tae tıw psaa tŋay-can* 'I always go to market on Mondays': *dam yɔɔk krɔəp* 'to plant (*dam*) for grain'.

NEGATION

Verbals may be negated by the circumfix *mın ... tee*:

khɲom mɯn tɯw pteəh tee 'I'm not going home'
khɲom sdap mɯn baan tee 'I didn't understand'

(Note that the first component of the negation comes between sense-verb and modal; cf. *riən coul* 'be able to learn': *riən mɯn coul* (*tee*) 'was unable to learn'.)

miən 'to have' has a negative counterpart *kmiən* + *tee*: *Khɲom kmiən X tee* 'I haven't got X'.

The copula *cia* 'is/are' is negated by *mɯn mɛɛn: nih mɯn mɛɛn cia X*' 'this (*nih*) is not X'.

In rapid speech *mɯn* > *m*.

Prepositions

(a) Simple: e.g. *nɯng* 'with', *pii* 'from', *ləə* 'on'.
(b) Verbs as prepositions: e.g. *tɯw* 'to go' = 'to(wards)'; *yɔɔk* 'to take' = 'by means of, with (in instrumental sense)'.

Word order

SVO

១ ៙ ១កាលដើមដំបូងនោះមានព្រះបន្ទូល ហើយព្រះបន្ទូលគង់ជាមួយនិងព្រះដ៏
ជាអំម្ចាស់សួរគ៌ ហើយព្រះបន្ទូលជាព្រះដ៏ជាអំម្ចាស់សួរគ៌ ២កាលដើមដំបូង
ទ្រង់គង់ជាមួយនិងព្រះដ៏ជាអំម្ចាស់សួរគ៌ ។ ៣របស់ទាំងអស់បានបង្កើតមកដោយពីទ្រង់
ហើយគ្មានរបស់អ្វីសោះកើតមកដែលជាមិនបានបង្កើតមកដោយពីទ្រង់នោះគ្មាន ។
៤ក្នុងព្រះបន្ទូលនោះមានជីវិត្រ ហើយជីវិត្រជាពន្លឺរបស់មនុស្សលោក្យ ៥ពន្លឺ
បំភ្លឺក្នុងសេចក្ដីងងឹត តែសេចក្ដីងងឹតមិនបានទទួលពន្លឺទេ ។
៦មានមនុស្សម្នាក់ឈ្មោះ យ៉ូន ដែលព្រះដ៏ជាអំម្ចាស់សួរគ៌ចាត់ឲ្យមក ៧គាត់
បានមកសំរាប់ធ្វើជាទីបន្ទាល់ និងធ្វើជាបន្ទាល់ពីពន្លឺ ដើម្បីនឹងឲ្យមនុស្សទាំងអស់
ជឿដោយពីគាត់ ៨គាត់មិនមែនជាពន្លឺ តែគាត់លេចមកនិងធ្វើជាទីបន្ទាល់ពី
ពន្លឺទេ

SCRIPT

The Khmer script derives from a South Indian variant of Devanāgarī. The original Devanāgarī order is preserved (the retroflex and dental series have coalesced) as is the siting of the vowels; and, as in Devanāgarī, the consonants in their base state have a syllabic value, i.e. a back vowel inheres in each. Khmer use of this Indian material, however, introduces an essential innovation: the consonants are divided into two series or registers: the first series with base inherent vowel *-aa*; the second with base inherent vowel *-ɔɔ*. One and the same vowel sign is then realized differently depending on the series of the consonant which it vocalizes. Thus, the system doubles the vocalic inventory (Cambodian is very rich in vowels) by giving one specific value to a vowel sign following a series 1 consonant, and quite another value to the *same* vowel sign following a series 2 consonant. Formally, series 1 consonants correspond to the original Devanāgarī voiceless stops with their aspirates (including the affricate series); series 2 consonants correspond to the Devanāgarī voiced stops with their aspirates. For example, *kh* in series 1 represents Devanāgarī *kh*; *kh* in series 2 represents Devanāgarī *gh*. As illustration: *kh* in series 1 is ខ; *kh* in series 2 is ឃ; both can be followed by the vowel sign for long *ā*: ា: but ខាត់ is pronounced [khat] ('to polish'); ឃាត់ is pronounced [khoət] ('to prevent').

The consonantal phonemes of Cambodian are shown in the table. The phonemic values given are those of consonants preceding vowels. As first components in clusters, and as finals, the aspirated consonants are reduced to their non-aspirate values: /kh/ > /k/, etc.

The vowel symbols with their first and second series values are also set out in the table.

Some examples from the velar, palatal, and dental series:

Series 1			*Series 2*		
ក	ក	/kaa/ neck	គ	គ	/kɔɔ/ mute
ខ	ខាត់	/khat/ to polish	ឃ	ឃាត់	/khoə̆t/ to prevent
ច	ចា	/caa/ to inscribe	ជ	ជា	/ciə/ be
ឆ	ឆោង	chaoŋ/ interval	ឈ	ឈោង	/chooŋ/ to reach out
ញ៉	ញ៉ាំ	/ñam/ to eat	ញ	ញាំ	/ñoə̆m/ meat salad
ដ	ដុន	/don/ elephant command	ឌ	ឌុន	/dun/alike
ត	តា	/taa/ old man	ទ	ទា	/tiə/ duck

Source: Huffman, F.E. (1970) *The Cambodian System of Writing, and Beginning Reader*. Yale University Press.

As can be seen from the consonant chart, certain Cambodian phonemes are not paired, e.g. series 2 *mɔɔ* has no series 1 correlative **maa*. Where it is necessary to produce such a correlative, a consonant can be 'converted' by diacritic: ″ converts a series 2 into a series 1 consonant, e.g.:

ម៉ = *maa*

Similarly, ៊ converts a series 1 into a series 2 consonant.

Conjunct consonants are frequent in Cambodian. The second component is written as a subscript, which is usually a reduced version of the base form. There are, however, several irregularities.

The value – i.e. whether it is to be read as series 1 or 2 – of a vowel following an initial or a medial cluster depends on the nature of the components forming the cluster. Very briefly, all stops and spirants take precedence over continuants, and therefore determine vocalic sequence. Thus, in /trəy/ 'fish' the series 1 stop /t/(taa) takes precedence over the continuant /r/ and requires the vowel /əy/.

Where two stops belonging to different series form a cluster, the subscript takes precedence. For instance, in /pteəh/ 'house' the series 2 subscript /t/ (tɔɔ) prescribes the vowel; /ph/ > /p/ is a series 1 consonant.

THE CAMBODIAN SCRIPT

CONSONANTS

ក	kaa	*k*	ដ	daa	*d*	ប	baa	*b*
ខ	khaa	*kh*	ឋ (ឋ)	thaa	*th*	ផ	phaa	*ph*
គ	kɔɔ	*k*	ឌ	dɔɔ	*d*	ព	pɔɔ	*p*
ឃ	khɔɔ	*kh*	ឍ	thɔɔ	*th*	ភ	phɔɔ	*ph*
ង	ŋɔɔ	*ŋ*	ណ	naa	*n*	ម	mɔɔ	*m*

ច	caa	*c*	ត	taa	*t*	យ	yɔɔ	*y*
ឆ	chaa	*ch*	ថ	thaa	*th*	រ	rɔɔ	*r*
ជ	cɔɔ	*c*	ទ	tɔɔ	*t*	ល	lɔɔ	*l*
ឈ	chɔɔ	*ch*	ធ	thɔɔ	*th*	វ	wɔɔ	*w*
ញ	ñɔɔ	*ñ*	ន	nɔɔ	*n*	ស	saa	*s*
						ហ	haa	*h*
						ឡ	laa	*l*
						អ	qaa	*q*

Source: Huffman, F.E. (1970) *The Cambodian System of Writing, and Beginning Reader*, Yale University Press.

VOWELS

Symbol	Name	Values 1st Series	Values 2nd Series	Symbol	Name	Values 1st Series	Values 2nd Series
–	sraq qɑɑ	*aa*	*ɔɔ*	េ–	sraq qei	*ei*	*ee*
–ា	sraq qaa	*aa*	*iə*	ែ–	sraq qae	*ae*	*ɛɛ*
–ិ	sraq qeq	*e*	*i*	ៃ–	sraq qay	*ay*	*ɨy*
–ី	sraq qəy	*əy*	*ii*	េ–ា	sraq qao	*ao*	*oo*
–ឹ	sraq qəq	*ə*	*ɨ*	េ–ៅ	sraq qaw	*aw*	*ɨw*
–ឺ	sraq qəɨ	*əɨ*	*ɨɨ*	–ុំ	sraq qom	*om*	*um*
–ុ	sraq qoq	*o*	*u*	–ំ	sraq qɑm	*am*	*um*
–ូ	sraq qou	*ou*	*uu*	–ាំ	sraq qam	*am*	*oə̆m*
–ួ	sraq quə	*uə*	*uə*	–ះ	sraq qah	*ah*	*eə̆h*
េ–ី	sraq qaə	*aə*	*əə*				
េ–ឿ	sraq qɨə	*ɨə*	*ɨə*				
េ–ៀ	sraq qiə	*iə*	*iə*				

Source: Huffman, F.E. (1970) *The Cambodian System of Writing, and Beginning Reader*, Yale University Press.

CARIB

INTRODUCTION

In terms of geographical extent, the Ge-Pano-Carib group of languages is one of the largest in South America. In some classifications it is split into two groups, Cariban and Macro-Ge: the former, with nearly 100 languages, being centred on the Guianas and Northern Brazil, the latter stretching across Brazil into Paraguay and Patagonia. Cariban languages are spoken by about 40,000 people. The form of Cariban described here (after B.J. Hoff 1968) is spoken by 'several thousands' in Surinam. The language must be distinguished from Island Carib which belongs to the Arawakan family. Carib is unwritten.

PHONOLOGY

Consonants

The voiced and unvoiced pairs /b, p; d, t; g, k/ are present with associated nasals m, n; /ɲ/ does not seem to be present, but the palatal nasal /ŋ/ is. Also included in the inventory are the glottals /ʔ/ and /h/; /r, s, w/ and a sound which Hoff transcribes as *β̄* All can be palatalized except the glottals. Initial clusters consisting of nasal + stop are found, e.g. /mbo/.

Vowels

short and long: i, ɪ, e, a, o, u

Long vowels are indicated by :. There are six diphthongs, all glides to /i/, except /au/.

MORPHOLOGY AND SYNTAX

Both nouns and verbs are related to person by a series of five personal prefixes: first person Ø, second *a-*, third *i-*; third person reflexive *tɪ-*; first person pl. incl. *kɪ-*. Examples: ***Ø****tunda* 'my arriving'; ***a****tunda* 'your arriving'.

Noun

Nouns occur in isolate or in *-rɪ/-ru* form, which is used, for example, when one noun is defined in terms of another: e.g. *kuri:yara* 'boat', *kasi:ri* 'cassava': *kasi:ri ku:riya:**ran*** 'cassava boat' (with redistribution of syllabic structure).

Affixes added to nouns include:

- *-xpa* and variants: 'un-/non-'; often with *i-* prefix on noun, e.g. *ka:rai* 'blackness'; ***i****.ka:rai.****pa*** 'not black'.
- *-koβ̄/-goβ̄* is a plural marker, e.g. *wo:to* 'fish'; *wo.to****koβ̄*** (pl.).
- *-mbo* as a noun affix suggests a falling short of norm.

Nouns are turned into verbs by affixes with *-a* for intransitives, *-o* for transitives: e.g. *ɪxko:nɪ* 'dirt': *ɪxkon****da*** 'to get dirty'; *ɪxkon****do*** 'to make dirty'.

Adjective

Can be formed from nouns by circumfix *tɪ*...*Ce*: e.g. *me:nu* 'blood' – ***tɪ****me:nu.****re*** 'bloody'.

Pronoun

PERSONAL PRONOUN

Free forms seem to be lacking. *See* **Verb**, below, for coded personal prefixes; also above for possessive markers.

DEMONSTRATIVE PRONOUN

Here there is a basic two-way opposition between definite/indefinite and animate/inanimate. In addition, Carib has an intricate system of subdivisions: e.g. an indefinite inanimate demonstrative pronoun can be further modulated to express relation to place (*o:we*), to direction (*o:ya*), or to neither (*o:tɪ*). In the definite series all forms are either high-vowel-initial for proximity, or low-vowel-initial for relative distance: *i:ya* 'this (def.)', with reference to direction; *mo:e* 'that (def.) yonder', with reference to place.

INTERROGATIVE PRONOUN

no:kɪ 'who?'

Numerals

1–10: *o:wiβ̄, o:ko, o:ruwa, o:kopaime, aiyato:ne, o:winduwo:pɪima, o:kotuwo:-pɪima, o:ruwatuwo:pɪima, o:winapo:sikɪ:rɪ, aiyapato:ro.*

Verb

Stems are modulated by prefix or suffix for aspectual/modal senses, and can be extended by *-se/-ye* or *rɪ/-ru* where syntax requires. For example, the prefix *wos-* introduces the notion of reciprocal action: *e:ne* 'to see' – ***wos****.e:ne* 'to see each other'. *We-* and variants suggest that action expressed by stem does not involve second or third persons: e.g. *exke:i* 'to bake (specifically for others)'; *woxke:i* 'to be baking (for oneself?)'. The suffix *-potɪ* expresses iterative action: e.g. *e:nepotɪ* 'to go on seeing'. *-kepɪ* signals the cessation of the action expressed in the verb: e.g. *ene:kepɪ* 'to see no longer'.

A typical transitive verbal complex comprises a subject personal pronominal prefix coded for pronominal object, a stem, and a temporal or modal affix. Neither the prefix nor the affix can be used without the other.

CODED PERSONAL PREFIXES

1 acting on 3:	*s*(*i*)-
2 acting on 3:	*m*(*i*)-
1 + 2 acting on 3:	*kıs*(*i*):-
3 acting on 1:	∅ or *y*-
3 acting on 2:	*a*, *o*, or *y*
3 acting on 3:	*kıni:*/*ni*

TEMPORAL/MODAL AFFIXES

-ya, *-sa*, *-e* are used with first and second person subjects acting on first, second, or third persons; *-yaß*, *-saß*, *-:no* are used where third person acts on first, second, or third persons.

TEMPORAL MARKERS

-take for future; *-yakoß̄* for past; *-yaine* for iterative action; *-se* for purpose.

Examples:

with root *e:ne* 'to see':

*sene:**ya*** 'I see him'; *sene:ya:toß̄* 'I see them'
*sene:**yakoß̄*** 'I saw him'
*sene:**yaine*** 'I see him repeatedly'
*sene:**se*** 'so that I may see it'
kıne**:ne**yaß̄ 'he sees him'

with root *a:ro* 'to take':

*saro:**ya*** 'I take him'
maro:ya 'you take him'
kısa:roya 'we two take him'
*ya:ro**yaß̄*** 'he takes me'

A non-personal form is made with prefix *tı*/*tu*-/*t*-, depending on initial: e.g. *a:ro* 'to take' – ***ta**:ro* 'taken'.

Copula:

		Singular	*Plural*
present:	1	wa	–
	2	ma:na	mandoß̄
	1 + 2		kıta:toß̄
	3	maß̄	mandoß̄
preterite:	1	wa:koß̄	
	2	ma:koß̄	ma:tokoß̄
	1 + 2		kıta:tokoß̄
	3	kına:koß̄	kına:tokoß̄

Postpositions

Examples: *pa:to* 'on the side of'; *ta* 'in'; *uwa:po* 'before', e.g. *yu:wa:po* 'before me', ***au**:wa:po* 'before you'; *wa:ra* 'like', e.g. ***awa:raine*** 'like you (pl.)', where *-ne* is the plural marker.

1. Lidan lagumeserun Lelerun, Lelerun lumaguiñe Bondiu, Lelerun Bondiu.
2. Ligiyameme lidan lagumeserun luma Bondiu.
3. Laduga sun katey; uati adugati luï le aduguwali.
4. Lidanguiñe ibagari; ibagari igemeri woguriña.
5. Ladurulike igemeri lidan luburiga; ibidiati lun luburiga.
6. Ñeñen aban woguri hounahowti lumaguiñe Bondiu, John liña liri.
7. Ligiya liyabui lun ladimurehan, luagu larugougan lun hafiñerun sun woguriña.
8. Mama ligiya larugougan, lounahouña lun ladimurehan luagu larugougan.

CATALAN

INTRODUCTION

Catalan belongs to the Italic family of Indo-European. As the southern member of the rich and vigorous Ibero-Gallic culture which included Provençal, Catalan shares both French and Spanish traits. At present, it is spoken by *c.* 6½ million people (mostly bilingual) in the north-eastern coastal strip of Spain, stretching from Roussillon and Andorra (where it has official status, along with French) through Catalonia to Valencia and the Balearics. The standard literary language is based on the Barcelona dialect. In terms of literary output, Catalan is the most important minority language in Western Europe.

Writing in Catalan dates from the twelfth century. From the troubadour period – shared with Provençal – to the fifteenth century, Catalan literature held a leading place in Europe, and two writers of genius emerged: Ramón Llull, Neoplatonic visionary and philosopher, linguist, and apostle, whose *Ars Magna* offers a kind of universal conceptive calculus, in which Christian, Islamic, and Greek paradigms are convertible and expressible in terms of each other, and whose Catalan novel *Blanquerna* (*c.* 1284) contains the celebrated *Llibre d'amic e amat*; and Ausias March (1397–1459), the greatest poet in the Europe of his day.

From the sixteenth to the nineteenth centuries writing in Catalan virtually ceased to exist. The Catalan *renaixença* may be dated from the re-establishment of the Barcelona *Jocs Florals* in 1859, and the romantic poetry of Verdageur. A steady output of verse and prose continued until the outbreak of the Civil War, when Catalan culture was proscribed. Since the 1970s, recovery has been sustained with the help of the rich legacy of Catalan culture in exile.

The lexicon is remarkable for the large number of monosyllables of VC, CV, CVC type: e.g. *vi* 'wine', *ma* 'hand', *be* 'sheep', *ull* 'eye', *dit* 'finger', *blat* 'wheat'.

SCRIPT

The Roman alphabet, plus certain diacritics: grave, acute, cedilla.

PHONOLOGY

Consonants

stops: p, b, t, d, k, g
affricates: tʃ, dʒ

fricatives: f, v, s, z
nasals: m, n, ɲ, ŋ
laterals and flap: l, ʎ, r
semi-vowels: w, j

[ß] is a positional variant of both /b/ and /v/. *c* has three values: /s/ before *e, i*; /k/ before *a, o, u*; /ɣ/ before a voiced consonant.

/tʃ/ is represented in the script by *tx* or *ig*: e.g. *puig* /putʃ/; *cotxe* /kɔtʃə/. Doubled l is notated as *l·l* to avoid confusion with the digraph *ll* = /λ/; cf. *la pel·licula* 'the film', *la fulla* 'the leaf'.

Vowels

i, e, ɛ, a, ə, ɔ, o, u

Reductionism is an important feature of the vowel system: unstressed /e, a/ → [ə], unstressed /o/ → [u]: e.g. *patata* [pətatə], 'potato'; *forçar* [fursa], 'force' (final *-r* drops). The acute accent is used to mark the closed /e, o/; the open values /ɛ, ɔ/ are marked by the grave. The diaeresis marks a labialized vowel after /k/ or /ɣ/: *qüestio* /k°əstio/; it also marks syllabic /i/ or /u/.

Diphthongs whose second component is /i/ or /u/ are treated as monosyllables: i.e. first component + semi-vowel /w/ or /j/.

Stress

Stress is normally on penultimate of vocalic final, or on final diphthong.

MORPHOLOGY AND SYNTAX

Noun

Nouns in Catalan are masculine or feminine. The associated articles are:

	Definite		*Indefinite*	
	Singular	*Plural*	*Singular*	*Plural*
masc.	el/l'	els	un	uns
fem.	la/l'	les	una	unes

Certain prepositions fuse with the masculine definite forms: e.g. *per* + *els* → *pels.*

The plural marker is *-s*: e.g. *un gat*, pl. *uns gats* 'cats'; *el dia*, pl. *els dies* 'days'. *-os* is used for words ending in a sibilant: e.g. *el peix* 'fish', pl. *els peixos.* Addition of the plural marker may involve some change in spelling: e.g. *taronja* 'orange', pl. *taronges*; *boca* 'mouth', pl. *boques.*

Adjective

As attribute, adjective follows noun as a rule, though many of the commonest adjectives precede, e.g. *bo*/*bona* 'good', *gran* 'big', and agrees with it in gender and number. A typical row is: *blanc* – *blanca* – *blancs* – *blanques* 'white'. A few adjectives vary in meaning according to whether they precede or follow the noun.

COMPARATIVE

The comparative is made with *més* preceding adjective followed by *que* 'than'.

Pronoun

PERSONAL PRONOUN

The independent personal forms are: sing. *jo*, *tu*, *el/ella*; pl. *nosaltres*, *vosaltres*, *els/elles*. A polite form of address, corresponding to the Spanish *Usted/-es*, is *Vostè/-s*.

The forms given above are also the strong object forms, with one exception: in the first person singular *mi* replaces *jo*. The strong object forms are always governed by prepositions.

The weak object forms for direct and indirect object can precede or follow the verb; e.g. in the first person singular *em* → *m'* precedes the verb; *-me* → *'m* follows, if the verb form is an infinitive, an imperative, or a gerund: e.g. *li va parlar* 'he spoke to him'; *li'l donarem* 'we shall give it (masc.) to him/her/you'; *quan em va dir* 'when he told me'; *ajuda'm* 'help me'.

Frequently, a strong form (or a noun) is copied by a weak form attached to the verb: e.g. *a vostè no l'havia vist* 'I hadn't seen you'.

Combined weak forms: the grid for all persons and numbers yields over 200 combinations, with complex rules governing the use of full and reduced forms. The indirect precedes the direct object form: e.g. *me'l dona* 'he gives it to me'; *ha de portar-nos-els* 'he has to bring them to us'; *porta-li'ls* 'take them to him'.

POSSESSIVE ADJECTIVES

E.g., in first person, *el meu* – *la meva* – *els meus* – *les meves*, with weak forms: *mon* – *ma* – *mos* – *mes*.

DEMONSTRATIVE PRONOUN/ADJECTIVE

aquest/-a/-s/-es 'this', 'these'; *aquell/-a/-s/-es* 'that', 'those'.

INTERROGATIVE PRONOUN

qui 'who?'; *què* 'what?'; *quin/-a/-s/-es* 'what', 'which?'

RELATIVE PRONOUN

que (invariable) is used for both subject and object; in prepositional phrases *qui* refers to persons, *què* to things. The compound forms: *el/la qual*, pl. *els/les quals* can also be used: *sobre qui* = *sobre el/la qual* 'about whom'; *els nois, que*... 'the boys who'.

Numerals

1–10: *un/una*, *dos/dues*, *tres*, *quatre*, *cinc*, *sis*, *set*, *vuit*, *nou*, *deu*; 11 *onze*; 12 *dotze*; 13 *tretze*; 20 *vint*; 30 *trenta*; 100 *cent*.

Verb

As in Spanish, three conjugations are distinguished: *-ar*, *-re*, *-ir*.

(a) *-ar*: this, the largest class of verbs, is fairly regular. As in Spanish, some adjustment in spelling has to be made where consonants with hard and soft values are concerned: e.g. *-c-* alternates with *-qu-*: *tanco* 'I close', *tan**ques***.
(b) *-re*: sub-divided into classes: -(C)C*re*, *-aure*, *-eure*, *-iure*, *-oure*; e.g. *prendre* 'take', *caure* 'fall', *creure* 'believe', *escriure* 'write', *moure* 'move'.
(c) *-ir*: certain verbs in this group add the increment *-eix-* between the stem and the endings: e.g. *llegir* 'read': *llege**ix**o*.

Catalan has indicative, imperative, and subjunctive moods. The indicative mood has present, imperfect, preterite, and conditional simple tenses, plus compound tenses – perfect, pluperfect, etc. – and periphrastic tenses made with the verb *anar* 'to go'. The subjunctive mood has present, imperfect, preterite, perfect, and pluperfect forms, used, as in French and Spanish, wherever doubt, negation, possibility, apprehension, or emotion colour the utterance.

PERSONAL ENDINGS

E.g. regular verb in *-ar*, *parlar* 'to speak'.

present: sing.: *parl-o/-es/-a*; pl. *parl-em/-eu/-en*;
imperfect: sing.: *parl-ava/-aves/-ava*; pl. *parl-àvem/-àveu/-aven*;
preterite: sing.: *parl-í/-ares/-à*; pl. *parl-àrem/-àreu/-aren*;
present subjunctive sing.: *parl-i/-is/-i*; pl. *parl-em/-eu/-in*.

The periphrastic tenses: the present tense of the verb *anar* 'to go': *vaig, vas, va*; *anem, aneu, van*. *Vaig*, etc. + infinitive expresses a preterite sense: e.g. *Vaig arribar la setmana passada* 'I arrived last week.' *Vaig*, etc. + *a* + infinitive, forms the future: e.g. *Vaig a buscar les maletes* 'I'm going to look for the cases.'

The verbs *ésser* and *estar* (corresponding in sense and usage to Spanish *ser* and *estar*) share the same past participle – *estat*. *Ésser* is used with the past participle of a sense verb to make a passive: e.g. *ha estat trobat* 'has been found'; pl. *han estat trobats.*

In compound tenses, the past participle (conjugated with *haver* 'to have') is invariable, unless a third person direct pronominal object is present. Yates gives the example:

Son boníssimes aquestes prunes; jo n'he menjad**a** una i aquest se n'ha menjad**es** dues o tres
'These plums are very good; I have eaten one, and he has eaten two or three.'

Prepositions

Several are composed of locative adverb + *de*: e.g. *dins/dintre de* 'in(side)'; *damunt de* 'above'; *sota de* 'below'.

Word order

SVO is normal.

1 En lo principi era lo Verb, y lo Verb era ab Deu, y lo Verb era Deu.
2 Ell era en lo principi ab Deu.
3 Per ell foren fetas totas las cosas, y sens ell ninguna cosa fou feta de lo que ha estat fet.
4 En ell era la vida, y la vida era la llum dels homes.
5 Y la llum resplandeix en las tenebras, y las tenebras no la comprengueren.
6 Hi hagué un home enviat de Deu ques anomenava Joan.
7 Est vingué *á servir* de testimoni pera testificar de la llum, á fi de que tots creguessen per medi d'ell.
8 No era ell la llum, sinó *enviat* pera donar testimoni de la llum.

CAUCASIAN LANGUAGES

The great majority of the languages spoken in the area between the Black Sea and the Caspian, especially in the Caucasus Mountains, appear to be indigenous to the region. The only Indo-European intruders are Ossetian and Armenian, and three Turkic languages are also present – Karachay-Balkar, Kumyk, and in the extreme south-east, Azerbaijani.

There are about three dozen indigenous languages, which are classified as follows:

1. Kartvelian (e.g. Georgian, Mingrelian, Svan);
2. North-West Caucasian (the Abkhaz-Adyge languages);
3. North Central Caucasian (Chechen-Ingush – the Nakh languages);
4. Dagestanian, sub-divided as:
   (a) Avar – Andi – Dido;
   (b) Lak-Dargva;
   (c) Lezgian.

One Kartvelian language – Laz – is spoken in the Trabzon area of Turkey; apart from this one outlier, all the indigenous languages of the Caucasus are spoken in the former Soviet Union. Exile, whether voluntary (e.g. of the now extinct Ubykh people to Turkey in the 1860s, or of many Kabard-Cherkes to the Near East at about the same time) or enforced (e.g. the temporary removal of the Chechen-Ingush people to Central Asia at the end of the Second World War), has done little to alter the generally static geo-linguistic picture.

See **Georgian**, **Laz**, **Mingrelian**, **Svan**, **Abaza**, **Abkhaz**, **Abkhaz-Adyge Languages**, **Adyge**, **Agul**, **Andi Languages**, **Avar**, **Chechen**, **Dagestanian Languages**, **Dargva**, **Kabard-Cherkes**, **Lak**, **Lezgi**, **Nakh Languages**, **Tabasaran**, **Ubykh**.

CEBUANO

INTRODUCTION

In terms of numbers of native speakers, Cebuano, with around 12 million, rivals Tagalog as the major language of the Philippines, though it cannot compete with the 20 or 30 million who learn the latter as a second language. Cebuano and its two close congeners, Hiligaynon and Samaran, are often linked under the term 'Visayan'. The language is used to some extent in periodical literature, and in film and radio. Cebuano has a considerable number of Spanish loanwords.

SCRIPT

Roman.

PHONOLOGY

Identical to that of Tagalog. The stops /p, t, k/ are non-aspirated. The glottal stop is written as *q*. There are three basic vowels, /i, a, u/, with five diphthongs, /ɪ, a, u + w, y/. Short i → /ɪ/, short u → /ɔ/.

MORPHOLOGY AND SYNTAX

Noun

Nouns are root words – e.g. *balay* 'house', *tatay* 'father', *putot* 'bird', *ngipon* 'tooth' – or composite, formed by various prefixes, suffixes, and circumfixes, for example:

mag- denoting kinship, with plural *manag-*: *mag.asawa* 'husband-and-wife', 'couple', pl. *manag.asawa*;
taga- 'place of origin': *taga.Cebu* 'from Cebu';
ting- 'time of… period': *ting.init* 'hot season';
infixed *-in-*, used in names of languages: *C.in.ibuhano* 'Cebuano';
circumfix, e.g. *ka-…-an* forms collectives: *ka.balay.an* 'village', from *balay* 'house';
suffix *-an*(*an*) 'place where …': *kan.anan* 'eating-place'.

Topic, agent, oblique: in the Cebuano context, 'topic' covers not only what is the 'subject' in Indo-European languages, but also the object, target, agent, beneficiary, location of an action, or the means by which it is accomplished; any one of these can be 'focused' to make it the 'topic'. Similarly, 'agent' is used not only in the ergative sense, but also to denote source, including possession. 'Oblique' denotes the beneficiary of an action, and is also used in an ergative sense.

Common nouns, when topic-focused, are marked by *ang/-y*, and by *sa* for agentive and oblique; plural common nouns add *mga* = /manga/ to the same markers. Proper nouns have topic-focus markers: sing. *si*, plural *sila si*, with agentive forms *ni*, *nila ni*, and oblique forms *kang*, *kanila ni*. Some examples of usage:

topic-focus: *mu.adto ang babaye sa Manila* 'the woman will go to Manila';
location-focus: *gi.butang.an niya ang lamisa ug bugas* 'will-be-put by-him on the table some rice', i.e. 'he will put . . . ';
agentive-focus: *gi.tawag sa nanay ang bata* 'the mother called the child';
possession (subsumed under agentive): *sa babaye ang libro* 'the book is the woman's';
target-focus: *sa klase siya mag.tuon sa leksyon* 'he will study the lesson in class';
beneficiary-focus: *i.hatag mo ang libro sa estudyante/kang Pedro* 'give (you) the book to the student/to Pedro'.

Indefiniteness of topic/object/agent is indicated by *ug*, definiteness by *sa*. Thus, *ug saging* 'bananas', *sa saging* 'the banana'; *ang saging* 'the banana' can be eaten by *ug bata* 'a child' or by *sa bata* 'the child'.

Adjective

An adjective ending in a vowel is linked to its noun by the *-ng* ligature, otherwise by *nga*: *gwapa.ng babaye* 'pretty (Span. *guapa*) woman'; *aslum nga mangga* 'sour mango/s'; *ang libro.ng dako* 'the big book'.

Pronoun

Cebuano has four sets of personal pronouns; each set has its specific function.

Set 1 has the following subject/object forms:

	Singular	*Plural*
1	akó	kani (*excl.*) kita (*incl.*)
2	ikaw/ka	kamo
3	siya	sila

This set is correlated with:

(a) an agent marked by *ang/si*: *mu.harag siya ng kwarta* 'he/she will give money';
(b) a beneficiary: *ba.sahan siya ni Ana ug istorya* 'Ana will read (to) him/her a story'.

Set 2: *áko*, *imo*, *iya*; *amo/ato*, *inyo*, *ila*. These are used to denote possession or the source of an object: *iya ang balay* 'the house is his'; *mu.adto ako sa iya.ng balay* 'I'll go to his house'; *iya.ng kaon.on ang mansanas* 'he'll eat the apple'.

Set 3 is provided by *n-* forms: *nako*. . . , and covers much of the same ground as set 2. Correlated with non-agent(s), i.e. with *ni/sa* objects:

nag.tanum si X ng kamatis sa gardin nila 'X planted tomatoes in their garden'

nag.sugo ako niya sa pag.palit sa sinina 'I sent her/him to buy a dress'

Set 4: *k-* forms: *kanako, kanimo*. . . ; this set is correlated with objective noun/phrase, beneficiary: *i.hatag ko ang libro kaniya* 'I'll give him/her the book'; *tag.buon ko sila uban kaniya* 'I'll meet them with (*uban*) him/her'.

DEMONSTRATIVE PRONOUN

There are six classes, divided into two groups: *anhi*, *dinhi*, *nia*, *nganhi* are locational; *kini* and *niinhi* function as particularizing components in substantive phrases. Relative proximity to the speaker and hearer is made explicit. Thus in the *anhi* series: *ari* 'here' (near the speaker), *anha* 'there' (near the hearer), *anhi* 'here' (near both the speaker and the hearer). Similarly throughout the six classes.

Example of *kini* set: *ki.palit kini.ng babaye ug libro* 'this woman bought a book'; *ki.palit kini ug libro* 'this one bought a book'.

Numerals

The Spanish numerals are used.

Verb

As in Tagalog, the Cebuano verbal system is equipped to focus on any component in a sentence – agent, object, target, recipient, beneficiary, secondary agent(s), location, means (instrument) – which then becomes the 'topic', which is marked by *ang* or *si*, or by an appropriate pronoun.

Mood and aspect are also distinguished. In terms of mood in Cebuano, an action may be classified as (a) in progress or completed, (b) impending, and (c) either requested or ordered.

It will be seen that tense-based languages will construe (a) as past/present progressive, (b) as future, and (c) as optative/imperative; (c) includes the Cebuano negative system.

ASPECT

Aspect in Cebuano is broadly divided into causative and non-causative. In terms of aspect, action is sub-classified as punctual/semelfactive, durative, voluntary/involuntary, distributive/non-distributive (presence or absence of plurality of agent and/or object). Reciprocity between two agents can also be notated, and is durative or semelfactive. Thus, for example, the neutral aspect of agent-focus is marked nominally by *ang* or *si*, and verbally by the prefix *mu-*: *mu.sulat ang bata* 'the child writes'. The verbal marker for completed action is *ni-*: *ni.sulat ang bata* 'the child wrote'. Using the shorthand: (a) = factual, perfective, (b) = future/habitual progressive, the markers in the non-durative aspect with agent-focus can be listed as (a) *ni-*, (b) *mu-*, (c) Ø; in the progressive aspect with agent-focus: (a) *nag-*, (b) *mag-*, (c) *pag-*, and in the distributive aspect with agent-focus: (a) *nanga-*, (b) *manga-*, (c) *panga-*.

Some representative examples:

Non-durative aspect with target-focus: (a) *gi-*, (b) *-on*/*-hon*, (c) -(*h*)*a*/*i*: *gi.palit ni Ana ang libro* 'Ana bought the book'.

Non-durative aspect with beneficiary-focus: (a) *gi-* . . . -(*h*)*an*, (b) -(*h*)*an*, (c) -(*h*)*i*: *gi.butang.an niya ang lamisa ug bugas* 'he put some rice on the table'; *gi.telepono.han sa asawa ang iya.ng bana sa opisina* 'the wife (*asawa*) called her husband (*bana*) in the office'.

Causative-durative aspect with agent-focus: (a) *nagpa-*, (b) *magpa*, (c) *pagpa-: nagpa.lihog sila ni Pedro sa pagpa.tahi sa pantalon* 'they requested Pedro to have the trousers sewn'; *magpa.hulog kamo kanamo ug sulat* 'you (*kamo*) will have us (*kanamo*) mail a letter'.

NEGATION

The equational negator *dili* precedes the negated component: *dili ako ang lapis* 'the pencil is not mine'; *dili pobre ang tawo* 'the man isn't poor'.

wala is a locational negator: *wala sila dinhi* 'they aren't here'. *wala* also negates perfective and progressive verbal forms:

wala ma.kuha ang retrato 'the picture wasn't taken'

and the associated demonstrative pronouns:

wala sila mu.anhi 'they didn't come'

Word order

The predicate precedes the subject if neither is a pronoun. In positive sentences, the agent may precede or follow the patient.

1 Sa sinugdan mao na ang Pulong, ug ang Pulong uban sa Dios, ug Dios ang Pulong. 2 Kini siya sa sinugdan uban sa Dios. 3 Ang tanang mga butang nangahimo pinaagi kaniya; ug niadtong mga nangahimo na, walay bisan usa nga nahimo nga dili pinaagi kaniya. 4 Diha kaniya ang kinabuhi, ug ang maong kinabuhi mao ang kahayag alang sa mga tawo. 5 Ug ang kahayag nagadan-ag sa taliwala sa kangitngitan, ug ang kangitngitan wala makabuntog kaniya.

6 Dihay usa ka tawo nga ginganlan si Juan,[a] nga pinadala gikan sa Dios. 7 Siya mianhi sa pagsaksi, sa pagpang-himatuod mahitungod sa kahayag, aron ang tanan motoo pinaagi kaniya. 8 Kini siya dili mao ang kahayag, hinonoa siya mianhi aron sa pagpanghimatuod mahitungod sa kahayag.

CELTIC LANGUAGES

INTRODUCTION

If not perhaps an Urheimat, the earliest identified point of origin for Celtic expansion seems to be the area now occupied by Austria and Bohemia, where the Celts were the bearers of the La Tène (late Iron Age) culture, richly documented with artefacts of many kinds. From this base, the Celts spread out during the first millennium BC, westwards to Gaul, Britain, and Spain, eastwards to the Carpathians and Romania, southwards to Italy, Greece, and Anatolia. In the fourth century BC they could be justifiably described by a Greek writer as one of 'the four great barbarian peoples'. Nevertheless, they lead a somewhat shadowy existence until their enforced historical debut – their defeat and subjugation at the hands of the Romans, first in cisalpine Gaul, and secondly in Gaul proper, in the first century BC.

Their somewhat unruly presence in Anatolia, where they were known as 'Galatai', is documented in the third century BC. Seven hundred years later, in the fifth century AD, the Galatians were still using their Celtic language (though St Paul had written to them in Greek). Evidence for this comes from St Jerome, the translator of the Vulgate, who recognized 'Galatian' as similar to the Gaulish language he had heard spoken in Trier in his student days.

A Celtic presence in the Iberian Peninsula is recorded by Herodotus, and attested in a corpus of inscriptions written partly in Latin character and partly in an imperfectly understood Iberian script. Two Celtic words for 'hill-fort', *briga* and *dūnum*, occur in many Iberian place-names. The distribution of these words bears witness to two strata of Celtic invaders: *briga* seems to be associated with an early wave of settlers who penetrated deep into the country, *dūnum* with a later and more restricted influx into Catalonia.

At the apogee of their expansion, about 100 BC, the Celts were in control of territory stretching from the Adriatic and the Danube to Scotland, and from the Rhine to south-western Spain. A couple of hundred years later they were everywhere on the retreat, largely subjugated, and undergoing a rapid process of assimilation. By AD 400 the erstwhile presence of continental Celtic was discernible in place names only. It was in Britain alone that the Celts retained something of their national and ethnic identity.

Today, three of the four living Celtic languages – Irish, Welsh, and Breton – enjoy either some degree of political status, or, at least, overt support in the political arena. Irish, for example, has had joint official-language status (with English) since the foundation of the Free State in 1921 (the Irish name

Eire was taken in 1937), though the language is used essentially on an internal, rather than on the international, plane.

Both Welsh and Breton have been espoused by political parties or organizations, whose programmes envisage an administrative role for these languages in the future. Only recently has political support been forthcoming for Scottish Gaelic. All four languages are widely taught both at school and university level (Irish is an obligatory subject of the school curriculum in Eire, as is Welsh now in Wales), and their use as media for instruction in language and other subjects is apparently on the increase. All four, again, have locally run press, radio, and TV services.

Cornish and Manx are extinct: Cornish since the late eighteenth century, Manx since 1974, when the last native speaker died. The study of both languages is being actively promoted, however, and each can claim some hundreds of speakers.

The last hundred years have seen a steep decline in the numbers of speakers of Celtic languages. The statistics one finds in this connection are sometimes misleading. The number of people who 'know' Irish, for example, is usually given as about half a million. On closer examination, this figure is found to reflect those bilinguals who can *read* Irish, and who speak it as an acquired tongue. Only some 50,000 in western coastal areas actually speak the language as mother tongue, and virtually all of these are bilingual. In any case, the figures represent a substantial drop from the 1½ million who spoke Irish in the middle of the nineteenth century, of whom 320,000 were monoglot.

At the beginning of the twentieth century there was a total Gaelic-speaking population of about 230,000 in Scotland, mostly in Ross-shire and Inverness-shire, with 28,000 monoglot. Today's figure is *c.* 80,000, including a very small number of monoglots. There are about 3,000 Gaelic speakers in Nova Scotia. Welsh and Breton each claim about ½ million speakers; possibly none except very young children are monoglot. A few thousand people, all bilingual, speak Welsh in Patagonia.

The figures for proportional decline in the use of the Celtic languages reflect not so much a drop in populations (though emigration to North and South America has played a small part) as erosion of minority and economically weak linguistic territory by the contiguous world languages, English and French, acquisition of which is seen to be far more profitable and advantageous.

THE LANGUAGES

It was long held that Celtic stood in a special relationship with Italic, much as Baltic does with Slavonic. This thesis found some support in such linguistic phenomena as the presence of a *p*/*q* opposition in both Celtic and Italic (cf. Osc. *petora* for Lat. *quattuor*) and the parallel superlative formants: Lat. *-issimus* (IE **-isŭmo*), Proto-Celtic **-(i)samos*, OI *-(i)ssam*. For the *p*/*q* opposition, *see* **Proto-Celtic**, 5, below.

Proto-Celtic

In general, much of the Indo-European common fund is retained. Some points:

1. IE /*eː/ = Proto-Celtic /iː/: e.g. IE **rēgs*, Lat. *rēx/rēgis*: Goidelic, *rīks*, Old Irish, *rí* 'king'.
2. IE /*oː/ = Proto-Celtic (aː): e.g. IE **mōros* = Goidelic *māros*, Old Irish *már* 'big'.
3. IE aspirated and unaspirated voiced stops are collapsed; thus OI /d/ represents both IE /*d/ and /*dh/.
4. Loss of IE /*p/, a high-frequency consonant in IE: e.g.

IE	*Goidelic*	*Old Irish*	
***p**ətēr	***Ø**aþēr	ath(a)ir	'father'
***p**ro-stom		**Ø** ross	'foothill'
*ka**p**ta		ca**ch**t	'female slave'

In initial position, /*p/ seems to have gone through an intermediate fricative stage before disappearing. This stage – /h/ – is preserved in the name of the German forest **H**ercynia, from **perkus* 'oak' (Lat. *quercus*).

5. The loss of IE /*p/ was offset by the development of a secondary /p/ from IE /*k^w/ in P-Celtic, where Q-Celtic retains /k^w/. Cf. the equivalents for the numeral 'four': IE **k^wetvor.es*, Lat. *quattuor*:

	Q-Celtic		*P-Celtic*
Old Irish	ceth(a)ir	/keː.ir/	Welsh pedwar < Old Welsh petguar
Gaelic	ceithir	/kezir/	Cornish peswar/peder
Manx	kiare		Breton pevar

Insular Celtic

Insular Celtic is divided into Brythonic (Welsh, Cornish, and Breton) and Goidelic (Irish, Scottish Gaelic, and Manx).

The first Celtic colonizers of Britain, who arrived in the second half of the first millennium BC, were speakers of P-Celtic or Brythonic; and this remained the language of Britain up to and including the Roman period. From the seventh century onwards, Brythonic was squeezed more and more into western coastal areas by Anglo-Saxon pressure, while, at the same time, it came under attack from invaders belonging to Q-Celtic or Goidelic stock. It is not known when the Goidelic Celts reached Ireland, but it was from their base in Ireland that they attacked and successfully occupied western Scotland, north-western England, and the Isle of Man. The Celtic linguistic pattern thus established has remained virtually unchanged into modern times. Breton is a Brythonic enclave launched from Cornwall in the fifth to seventh centuries.

MUTATION

This is at once the most characteristic and the most striking feature of Insular Celtic. Phonological accommodation at syllable or word juncture is found in many languages, e.g. in the phenomenon of sandhi in Sanskrit, in Dravidian, in the juncture of article plus sun-letter in Arabic, in French, and in Portuguese. Typically, in these cases, accommodation at the juncture of two words A and B affects the final phoneme of A. For example, in French, *les femmes* /leːfam/ but *les enfants* /leːzāfā/. In Sanskrit, both final and initial may be affected.

The origin of mutation in the Celtic languages is precisely such accommodation at word juncture, but here it is specifically the initial of B that is affected. Under certain conditions, this initial shows a shift from voiceless to voiced stop, from stop to homorganic fricative or nasal, or to zero grade. These shifts were originally induced by such conditions as vocalic final of A. As the languages developed, the conditions inducing the shift were eroded and finally lost, but the mutation remained. And, since the mutations affected many of the most frequently occurring junctures, the whole system became grammaticalized, and, by analogy, extended.

Examples of the mutation system in practice will be found in the articles on the individual languages.

See **Breton**, **Cornish**, **Irish** (old and modern), **Manx**, **Scottish Gaelic**, **Welsh**.

CHAM

INTRODUCTION

Cham – spoken today by around 150,000 people in Vietnam and Cambodia – is the most important of the Chamic languages, which form part of the Western Austronesian family. The Indo-Chinese kingdom of Champa was established in the second century AD and lasted for some 1,500 years, reaching its political and cultural apogee from the sixth century onwards. Retaliation for Khmer invasions in the twelfth century resulted in the destruction of Angkor. Though of Austronesian stock, the Cham were completely dominated by Indian culture, an influence visible in their Gupta art forms and in the Cham script, which is based on Devanāgarī.

SCRIPT

The Devanāgarī-based script is mainly characteristic of Cambodian Cham.

PHONOLOGY

Consonants

The retroflex series is missing apart from signs for /ḍa, ḅa, ṣa/. In addition to the velar, palatal, dental, and labial series, the script has /ya, ra, la, va/, two sibilants, /sa/ and /ṣa/, and /ha/.

In Vietnamese Cham the Devanāgarī order has been lost, and the spelling is very defective: Aymonier gives the example of *sang* 'house', which is written as *pang* and pronounced as /t^{h}ang/.

Vowels

short and long: i, a, u

/eː/, /ai/, /œ/, and /o/ also occur. The vowel system has been infected by Vietnamese, and there are several diphthongs.

MORPHOLOGY

Cham marks neither gender nor number. Natural gender is indicated either by lexical item, e.g. *amoeu* 'father', *inoeû* 'mother', or by addition of classifier, *dam* (masc.), *daras* (fem.) for persons, *tanov* (masc.), *binai* (fem.) for animals.

There is no form of declension. Syntactic relationships are either positional, e.g. in genitive, *dii noethak tikuh* 'in the year of the rat' (*noethak* 'year'), or marked by particle, e.g. *kaa* for indirect object: *pvâch jhak kaa nhu* 'speak ill to him' (*pvâch* 'speak'; *nhu* 'he'). *Pak* indicates location: *pak thang* 'at home'; *pak nii* 'here'. *Dii* is an all-purpose marker for locative, ablative, instrumental cases: e.g. *dok dii thang* 'to stay at home'; *klah dii laan* 'to avoid the cold'.

NOUN FORMATION

From verbs by *-n-* infix, as in Mon-Khmer:

pvâch 'speak' – pa**n**vâch 'word'
dok 'stay' – da**n**ok 'dwelling'
jiœng 'be born' – ja**ni**œng ''

pa- is causative: e.g. *mœtai* 'to die' – *pa.mœtai* 'to kill'. The prefix *mœ-* is heterogeneous but often indicates possession or application of something: e.g. *jruu* 'poison': *mœjruu* 'to administer poison'.

NOMINAL CLASSIFIERS

E.g. *boh* for fruits, *blah* for leaves, *ôrang* for people: *pateh sa blah* 'a piece of silk'; *drēi*, the classifier for bodies is also used as a general pronoun: *arau drei* 'wash oneself'.

Adjective

The attributive adjective follows the noun.

Pronoun

PERSONAL PRONOUN

	Singular	*Plural*
1	kau	gita
2	hēû	hēû
3	nhu	nhu

These function also as possessive pronouns.

DEMONSTRATIVE PRONOUN

ni(*i*) 'this'; *nan* 'that': e.g. *ôrang ni* 'this man', *thang nan* 'that house'. Cf. Thai.

INTERROGATIVE PRONOUN

thēi 'who?'

RELATIVE PRONOUN

k(*r*)*ung* or *ya*(*a*): *ôrang ya*(*a*) *chakong* 'people who carry...'.

Verb

Tense is indicated by particle accompanying the stem, e.g. *shi*/*thi* for future, *jœû* for past (Viet. *rôi*, Khmer *hœy*). The imperative marker is *bêk*.

MODAL VERBS

E.g. *truh* 'to be able', *kiœng* 'to want to'; *kau kiœng nau* 'I want to go'.

NEGATION

ôh/*ô* precedes or follows verb, or is reduplicated: *ôh huu* = *huu ôh* = *ôh huu ô* 'there isn't'.

Word order

SVO

Specimen passage

From the *Royal Annals of Champa*, reproduced in Aymonier op. cit.:

> bloh pô Shrii Aagarang dii noegar cham tagôk rai dii noethak kubav jioeng putau dreng rai pak pluh klau thun bloh putau Shrii Aagarang lvich rai dii noethak pubêy dii bal Hingav nan joeû.

TRANSLATION

bloh 'then'; *pô* 'Lord'; *dii* 'in', 'of', 'from', etc.; *noegar* 'country', 'kingdom' (Sanskrit *nagara* 'city'); *tagôk rai* 'mount the throne'; *noethak* 'year'; *kubav* 'buffalo'; *jioeng* 'to be'; *putau* 'king'; *dreng rai* 'to rule'; *pak* 'four'; *pluh* 'ten'; *klau* 'three'; *thun* 'year'; *lvich* 'relinquish'; *pubêy* 'goat'; *bal* 'capital city'; *nan* demonstrative pronoun; *joeû* past-tense marker.

1 [1, 2]**Dahlau di bih, Anưk Pô Lingik, nặn**
Pô Êtha, hu dok thŏng Pô pajơ. Brŭk
Anưk Pô ngăk, panôch Anưk Pô sanưng jang
yau Pô Lingik, kayua Anưk Pô drơh yau Pô
Lingik. [3]**Pô Lingik bray ka Anưk Pô pajưng**
abih pakar ngŏk lingik thŏng păk la tanưh-
riya. Yau năn, biăk Anưk Pô pajưng abih.
[4, 5]**Anưk Pô dok hadiup miêt miêt jang yau**
Pô Amư dok miêt miêt. Brŭk Anưk Pô trun
lôc ni pagăp yau tanrak-hadah mưng ngŏk
lingik pasang trun tamư dalăm libĭk sup, ngăk
ka libĭk năn hadah-dai wơ̆k. Yau năn, Anưk
Pô pahadah hatai tian anưk dun-ya piơh bray
ka khol nhu thau djaup ka Pô Lingik.

CHAMORRO

INTRODUCTION

This Austronesian (Malay-Polynesian) language is related to the languages of the Philippines, and is spoken by about 60,000 in Guam and in some islands of the Marianas. There is a large stock of Spanish loanwords.

PHONOLOGY

Consonants

The labial, dental, and velar series are represented by non-aspirate voiceless + voiced stop + associated nasal: e.g. /p, b, m/. The palatal nasal /ɲ/, written *ñ*, is present, also /tʃ/, written as *ch*, and /s, l, r, h, f/ and the glottal stop. The voiced stops cannot be syllable-final, nor can /ch, l, r/; thus Spanish *verde* > *ve**t**de*, *barco* > *ba**t**co*.

Vowels

i, e, æ, a, o, u; ao, ai

Stress

Stress on penultimate, with some exceptions.

MORPHOLOGY AND SYNTAX

The definite articles are *i* for common nouns, *si* for proper. The pronominal–verbal plural marker *man-* is transferred in stative sentences to the noun component if any: e.g. *man.mediku siha* 'they are doctors' (*siha* 'they') (*see also* **Adjective**). Juncture sandhi takes place when *man-* precedes /tʃ, s, t, k, f/.

Adjective

An adjectival attribute is linked to its noun by the ligature *na* → *n*, e.g. *i betde na kareta* 'the green car'; a modifying noun follows, e.g. *batko**n** aire* 'aeroplane'.

Dual and plural markers in stative sentences are transferred to the adjective, if any. The pronominal form is the same for both dual and plural; they are distinguished by the presence of *man-* in the plural form: e.g. *dankolo ham* 'we two are big'; ***man**dankolo ham* 'we (plural) are big'.

Pronoun

PERSONAL PRONOUN

Chamorro has two sets of personal pronouns:

(a) the *yo'* pronouns:

	Singular	*Plural*
1	yo'	*excl.* ham, *incl.* hit
2	hao	hamyo
3	gue'	siha

These are used as subject forms for intransitive/stative verbs, and as objective forms after transitive verbs.

(b) the *hu* pronouns:

	Singular	*Plural*
1	hu	*excl.* in, *incl.* ta
2	un	en
3	ha	ma

These are used as subject forms with transitive verbs + definite verbs + definite object: if the latter is pronominal, a *yo'* form is used: e.g. *hu li'e'* ***gue'*** 'I saw him'; *ha li'e'* ***yo'*** 'he saw me'. The *hu* pronoun is recapitulated with a nominal subject: e.g. *i famalao'an* ***ma*** *li'e i patgon* or ***ma*** *li'e' i famalao'an i patgon* 'the women saw the child'.

THE POSSESSIVE MARKERS

Sing. 1, *-hu*/*-ku* 2, *-mu* 3, *-ña*; pl. 1 excl. *-mami*, incl. *-ta*, 2 *-miyu*, 3 *-niha*. These are used, for example, with the existential verb *guaha* to express 'to have': e.g. *guaha lepblomami* 'we have a book', *guahu salape'.hu* 'I have money'.

A further set of personal pronouns – the *guaha*, or emphatic pronouns – may be used with agent-focused verbal construction (*see* **Verb**).

DEMONSTRATIVE PRONOUN/ADJECTIVE

Three degrees of distancing: *este* – *enao* – *ayu*.

INTERROGATIVE PRONOUN

hayi 'who?'; *hafa* 'what?'

RELATIVE PRONOUN

ni is an article which functions as a relative pronoun: *i kareta ni poddong* ... 'the car which fell ... '; *Si Pedro ni hu li'e'* 'Pedro, whom I saw ... '; *l.in.i'e i palao'an ni lahi* 'what the man saw was the woman'.

Another way of making relative clauses is with the infix *-um-*. Thus, from the verb *pacha* 'to touch': *i* ***pu**m**acha*** *i lepblo* 'this one who touched the book'.

Numerals

The Spanish numerals are used as pronounced in Guam; e.g. for 12, 13, 14 – *dosse, tresse, katotse.*

Verb

As in the Philippine languages, verbal constructions in Chamorro vary according to the component – agent, target, means, etc. – emphasized or focused. Thus, *-um-* is an agent-focusing marker, *-in-* is a goal-focusing marker; cf. *guahu **lumi**'e' i lahi* 'I (not someone else) saw the man'; ***lini**'e' i lahi **nu** guahu* 'I saw the man' (*nu* is a sbj. noun marker in this construction). Similarly, *na*' focuses the causative aspect of the action: e.g. *hu **na**'li'e' i patgon ni ga'lagu* 'I let the child see the dog'. *-in-* in a similar capacity confers nominal status on verbal root: cf.

hasso 'to think' – i h.in.asso '(content of) thought'
konne' 'to catch' – i k.in.enne' 'thing caught'

DEFINITE AND INDEFINITE OBJECT

This is a crucially important distinction in Chamorro. A sentence with a definite object takes a *hu* pronoun as subject; a sentence with an indefinite object takes a *yo*' pronoun as subject + *man-* prefix on verb: e.g. ***hu** li'e' i patgon* 'I see the child'; ***manli**'e' **yo**' patgon* 'I see a child'.

TENSE

Generally, a reduplicated form indicates imperfective action: e.g. *faisen* 'to ask' – *ma **fa**faisen* 'they are asking'. A non-reduplicated form is used for the perfective aspect, i.e. usually the past tense.

Future: the general marker is *para* (Sp.); in addition, 1st person singular and 1st person plural exclusive take *bai*. A *hu* pronoun is used. Example: *para bai hu li'e' i palao'an* 'I shall see the woman'. Example of passive marker *-ma-* between plural marker *man-* and reduplicated stem: *man**ma**-lalalatde i famagu'on* 'the children are being scolded' (*lalatde* 'to scold').

NEGATION

The marker is *ti*: e.g. *Ti chumocho i patgon nigap* 'The child didn't eat yesterday' (*nigap*); *ti dankolo i tronko* 'the tree is not big'; *ti siña hit man.hanao pa'go* 'we can't go now' (*siña* is the modal verb 'can', *man-* is the pluralizing prefix, *pa'go* 'now').

Word order

VSO is normal; SVO and OSV are possible, depending on focus selected.

1 Y TUTUJONÑA gaegue y Finijo, ya y Finijo güiya yan si Yuus; ya y Finijo güiya si Yuus.

2 Güiya gaegue gui tutujonña yan si Yuus.

3 Todo y güinaja sija manmafatinas pot güiya; yaguin ti pot güiya, taya ni esta mafatinas, nu y gaegue gui finatinas sija.

4 Y linâlâ gaegue guiya güiya, ya y linâlâ, güiya y candet y toatao sija.

5 Ya y candet gui jalom jomjom maniina, ya y jemjom ti matungo.

6 Y un taotao ni manafato guine as Yuus, y naanña si Juan.

7 Güiya mamaela para testimonio, para ufannae testimonio nu y candet, para ufanmanjonggue todo y taotao pot güiya.

8 Güiya ti y candet, lao mamaela para ufannae testimonio nu y candet.

CHECHEN

INTRODUCTION

Chechen is a member of the Nakh group of North-East Caucasian (the group includes Ingush and Bats). Chechen and Ingush are very closely related; until the 1930s the same literary standard was used for both. Charged with collaboration with the Nazi invaders in the Second World War, the Chechen and the Ingush were deported to Central Asia, where they remained till 1957 when the Chechen-Ingush Autonomous Socialist Republic was reinstated. At present, Chechen is spoken by about 700,000 people, Ingush by *c.* 190,000. Both languages are written, with periodical press and occasional books.

SCRIPT

Originally Arabic; thereafter a period of romanization, since 1938 Cyrillic + *I* as glottalization marker with consonants; by itself, it is like Arabic 'ain. The Cyrillic hard sign ъ is used to indicate hamza.

Refreshing evidence that Chechen can be rationally notated in a somewhat modified Roman script is provided by N. Awde and M. Galaev (1997) *Chechen–English and English–Chechen Dictionary and Phrasebook*, which appeared in connection with West European interest in Chechnya, following the Russian invasion of the autonomous republic.

In their simplified and very practical script, Awde and Galaev notate the glottalized consonants as C', with ' representing the glottal stop: thus, *k'ant* 'boy', 'son', *k'al* 'white', *ch'ug* 'ring', *ts'ii* 'blood', *q'am* 'people', 'nation' (*Nokhchi Q'am* 'the Chechen people'). The glottal fricative (Arabic ع) is notated as ‘: *ch‘ara* 'fish', *‘azh* 'apple'. *ö* and *ü* are used for the rounded vowels, *ä* for /ɛ/. Long vowels are doubled in the script: so *ts'a vööd* 'I go home', *‘üiran* 'in the morning'.

In the Awde/Galaev transcription the personal base forms are as follows:

	Singular		Plural
1	so	*excl.*	tkho
		incl.	vai
2	h'o		shu
3	i/iza		üsh/üzash

Cf.

stag aara veelira 'the man went out'
beer aara deelira 'the child went out'

PHONOLOGY

Consonants

In general, simpler than that of the neighbouring Caucasian languages. There is only one lateral; and the ejectives are reduced to six. There are four uvulars and two pharyngeals. Altogether 34 consonants are notated in Chechen, some of these representing positional allophones, and some sounds found only in loanwords. Intensive consonants are held (geminates). The geminate/non-geminate opposition is phonemic.

Vowels

i, e, a, o, u

This basic series is greatly extended by palatalization, labialization, nasalization, and rounding. Desheriev (1967) lists 15 vowel signs, each representing two or more values. Magometov, quoted in Hewitt and Comrie (1981), lists 36 vowel sounds for Lowland Chechen. Typical rows are:

a, aː, ɛ, ɛː, ã, ãː
je, jeː, jẽ, jẽː

Stress

Normally on the first root syllable.

MORPHOLOGY AND SYNTAX

Noun

There is no gender. Nouns have class, number, and case. There are six grammatical classes of noun: the noun itself is not marked for class, which is, however, reflected in verbal concord and in certain modifiers, such as adjectives and numerals.

CLASS

Markers are:

Class	*Singular*	*Plural*	*Class members*
1	vu	du	masculine humans
2	yu	du	feminine humans
3	du	du	
4	yu	yu	heterogeneous
5	bu	bu	
6	bu	du	

PLURAL

Markers are *-š* and *-y*: e.g. *kor* 'window', pl. *kor.**a.š***; *belxalo* 'worker', pl. *belxaloy*; *nana* 'mother', pl. *nanoy*. The base may be extended, often with umlaut: e.g. *ča* 'bear', pl. *čerčiy*; *lam* 'mountain', pl. *lämnaš*.

CASE SYSTEM

Four declensions are distinguished, one criterion being the ending of the instrumental case. Specimen declension for *bedar* 'clothes', pl. *bedarš*:

	Singular	*Plural*
genitive	bedaran	bedariyn
ergative	bedaro	bedarša
dative	bedarna	bedaršna
instrumental	bedarca	bedaršca
inessive	bedarax	bedaršex
contrastive	bedaral	bedarel
locative	bedare	bedarška

Internal flection also occurs: e.g. *ça* 'house', gen. *çiynan*, pl. *çenoš*. There are several derivative locative cases, plus postpositional complexes in which the postpositions take specific case endings.

Adjective

As attribute, adjective precedes noun: e.g. *dika stag* 'good man' (*stag* 'man'). A few primary adjectives are marked for class. In attributive function, adjectives have two forms: nominative and a general form in *-č* + V, which covers all other cases: e.g. *ḳayn bepig* 'white bread'; *ḳay**ču** bäp**kan*** 'from white bread'.

COMPARISON

A comparative is made in *-x*: e.g. *dika* 'good', *dika**x*** 'better'.

Pronoun

INDEPENDENT PERSONAL PRONOUN

	Singular		*Plural*
1	so	*incl.*	way
		excl.	txo
2	ḥo		šu
3	i/iza, hara (demonstrative forms)		üš/üzaš

These are declined in all cases; specimen row, first person singular: *so*, *san*, *as*, *suna*, *söca*, *sox*, *sol*, *söga*.

DEMONSTRATIVE PRONOUN
As third person singular pronoun above.

INTERROGATIVE PRONOUN
mila, pl. *müls̆* 'who?'; *hun* 'what?' These are declined in all cases on suppletive bases.

Numerals

1–10: *cḥa'*, *ši'*, *qo'*, *di'*, *pxi'*, *yalx*, *worh*, *barh*, *iss*, *itt*; 11–19: units combined with *itt*: e.g. 11 *cħaytta*; 12 *šiytta*; 20 *tq̣a*; 30 *tq̣eitt*; 40 *šöztq̣a*; 100 *ḅ'e*.

Numeral + noun: noun is in the singular: e.g. *pxi stag* 'five men' (hamza drops). Certain numerals are marked for two cases preceding declined noun, e.g. *ši'* – *šina*, *šina govran* 'of two horses'; *di'* – *dea*, *dea berana* 'to four boys'.

Verb

The Chechen verb is marked for grammatical class, aspect, mood, tense, number (encoded in the class markers).

ASPECT
Chechen verbs are aspectually neutral, punctual, or frequentative. The distinction between the latter two aspects often reduces to the simple opposition between perfective and imperfective action, notated in Chechen by internal flection: cf. stem *qoss-* 'throw' punctual/perfective; *qiys-* 'throw' frequentative/imperfective. As in this example, perfective verbs usually have a middle-register stem vowel, which is regarded as a high-register diphthong in the imperfective: cf. perfective stem *ḥaz-* 'look', imperfective stem *ḥiez-*; perfective stem *tatt-* 'shove, push', imperfective stem *tiett-*.

MOOD
The indicative mood is not specifically marked. A polite imperative makes a distinction in number between 2nd p. sing. in *-ḥ* and 2nd p. pl. in *-š*: cf. *ala.ḥ/aliy.š* 'please say'. The optative affix is *-1*, the subjunctive *-ḥara*: *ala.ḥar.a* 'should he say...', 'that he may say'.

Specimen tenses of verb *ala* 'to say':

present: *olu*;
future: *olur*(*du*);
past: *eli* (with reference to recent past); *älla* (perfective); *olura* imperfective); *elira* (inferential).

TENSE
Tense distinction is found only in the indicative mood, which has a present characterized by a vocalic final, e.g. *ol.u* 'says', a future tense, formed by adding *-r* to the present base: *olu.r* 'will say', and several past tenses, definite and inferential: e.g. an immediate past in *-i*: *del.i* 'gave'; a recent past perfective in *-na* (with assimilation): *vaxa.na* 'went'; past imperfective definite formed by adding *-ra* to thc present base: *olu.ra* 'was saying'.

CONJUGATION

There are five models, depending on the vocalic pattern of the stem. Thus, stems with a short or long *a* form the first conjugation; stems with a diphthong the second, and so on.

Intransitive verbs show concord with subject; transitive verbs show concord with object. The class markers are prefixed to primary, i.e. non-derivatory, verbal forms; infixed in composite forms. Examples:

Intransitive:

Class	*Singular*	*Plural*
1	**v**axana 'he went'	**b**axana 'they (masc.) went'
2	**y**axana 'she went'	**b**axana 'they (fem.) went'
1	**v**ux**v**irzina 'he returned'	**b**ux**b**irzina 'they (masc.) returned'
2	**y**ux**y**irzina 'she returned'	**b**ux**b**irzina 'they (fem.) returned'

so ***v****.ux.****v****eata.* 'I (male) returned from there'

Transitive:

3	co govr yügu 'he leads the horse'	
	co govraš yügu 'he leads the horses'	
4	co ṭulg baḥa 'he brings/carries the stone'	
	co ṭulgaš **d**aḥa 'he brings/carries the stones'	

In these examples (from *JaNSSR*, Vol. IV: 200) *co* is the ergative case of the third person singular *i/iza* 'he'.

The negating particle is *ca*: e.g. *ca vaxana* 'he didn't go'.

The other moods are: imperative, hortative, optative, and subjunctive.

PARTICIPIAL FORMS

Present in *-n*, e.g. *vogu****n*** 'going'; past: recent past form minus final vowel, e.g. *vaxan* 'having gone'; future: present participle + *dolu*(*n*). These forms are used in relative clauses: e.g. *vaxan stag* 'the man who went'; *latt äxan stag* 'the man who ploughed the soil'.

Like the attributive adjective, the attributive participle is marked for only two cases: the nominative and a general oblique case in *-ču*. A negative participial form is made by adding *-za* to the imperative base: *ala* 'say!', *ala.za* 'not saying', 'not having said'.

Postpositions

E.g. *ču* 'inside', *ara* 'outside', *ṭe* 'on', *ḳel* 'under', *ṭäx'a* 'after'.

Word order

Rather free; in general, S initiates sentence, V is final.

1. **ДУЬХХЬАР** хилла Дош, и Дош Делехь хилла, Дела Дош хилла.
2. Иза хилла дуьххьара Делехь.
3. Дерриг Цуьнгахула схьадоладелла, Цуьнан лаам боцуш долчу хIуманийх хIумма хилла дац.
4. Цуьнгахь хилла дахар, дахар адамийн серло хилла;
5. Серло боданехь а къега, бодано иза дIацахьулйо.
6. Цхьа стаг хилла Дала ваийтана, цуьнан цIе хилла Яхья.

CHEREMIS

See **Mari**.

CHEROKEE

INTRODUCTION

Cherokee is a member of the Iroquoian group of the Macro-Siouan family. The language is spoken today – entirely as a second language – by about 10,000 Cherokees in Oklahoma, with a residue in North Carolina. Ousted in tribal warfare from their original habitat in the Great Lakes area, the Cherokee moved south to Georgia and the Carolinas, where they proceeded to model their way of life and institutions on those of the European settlers. By the early 1800s they had achieved a remarkable degree of administrative, economic, and cultural stability. In 1828 a Cherokee weekly newspaper, the *Cherokee Phoenix*, was launched, a unique event in the annals of the American Indian. For this publication, Sequoyah's script was used. In the circumstances, however, it was a political and economic experiment which could not last, and the wars and rigged treaties which followed led in 1838–9 to the forcible removal of the Cherokee people to Oklahoma. Descendants of the few who escaped the 'Trail of Tears' still live in North Carolina.

SCRIPT

See **Script** at end of article.

PHONOLOGY

Consonants

stops: t, d, k, g, ʔ
affricates: ts, dz/dʒ
nasals: m, n
fricatives: s, h
laterals: l, ɬ, tl/dl
semi-vowels: j, w

The velars /k/ and /g/ occur labalized: /k°, g°/; otherwise the labial series is absent, as are /z/ and /r/. In addition to the fricative /h/, there is an intrusive, pre-consonantal nasal /h̃/.

Vowels

short: ɪ, ɛ, a, u, ʌ̃
long: i, e, a, ɔ, u, ʌ̃ː

The long vowels are notated here as *i:*, *a:*, etc. Following Holmes and Smith, the nasal vowel /ʌ̃/ is notated as *v*. All final vowels are nasalized.

Stress

Long vowels may show a crescendo.

Tone

Opposition between even tone and rising/falling; tone may be phonemic.

MORPHOLOGY AND SYNTAX

Noun

Nouns are divided into two classes: animate and inanimate. The distinction becomes overt only in the plural, marked for animates by *ani-/dini-*: e.g. *a.tsu.tsa* 'boy', pl. *a.ni.tsu.tsa*, where *a.* by itself is a singular prefix.

A typical inanimate plural is made by dropping the *a-* prefix, and substituting *di/te*: e.g. *a.ye.l'.s.di* 'knife', pl. *di.ye.l'.s.di.*

Many nouns are verbal in form: e.g. *a.tsi.lv.s.gi* 'it opens out' = 'flower', pl. *a.ni.tsi.lv.s.gi.* An interesting point is that an adjective qualifying an inanimate noun may take the animate marker in the plural, even if the noun itself has the inanimate marker *di/te*; e.g.

u.ta.na tlu.kv 'a big tree'
tsu.**n'**.ta.na **te**.tlu.kv 'big trees'

where ***n'*** < *ni* is the animate marker.

Note that *di-* + *e-lu-* > *ts.*

POSSESSION

Alienable ownership and inalienable relatedness are distinguished. Movable goods and chattels are alienable; kinship terms and names for parts of the body are marked for inalienable relatedness. Clothing is optionally in either camp.

Alienable ownership is notated by a single set of markers, e.g. *-tse.li-* following pronominal bound forms of set 2 (*see* **Pronoun**, below): *a.qua.tse.li gi:tli* 'my dog'; *u.tse.li ga.lo.ge:sv* 'his farm'.

Relationship, being heterogeneous, has several sets, distinguishing, for example, kinship from possession of body parts: ***a.gi****.do.da* 'my father', ***u****.do.da* 'his father'; ***tsi****.ye.sa.dv* 'my finger', ***o.gi.na*** *li.i* 'my friend'.

Pronoun

Only two free forms exist: *a.hyv* 'I' and *ni.hi* 'you'. Their use is optional. Bound forms: there are two sets, each with ten forms (three sing., three dual, three pl., plus one collective which may include the first person).

Set 1 is as follows:

	Singular	*Dual*	*Plural*
1	ts-, g-	in-	ots-
2	h-	sd-	its-
3	ga-	osd-	a.ni-

For example, as used with the stem *wo:ni* 'speak':

tsi.wo:ni.a 'I speak'
hi.wo:ni.a 'thou speakest'
ga.wo:ni.a 'he/she speaks'

The collective form is *i.di*:

i.di.wo:ni.a 'you/others (and I) speak'

Set 2 is used by many verbs to form a present tense (marked here by *.a*).

Set 2 has the following singular forms:

1	a'.w(a) with several allophones
2	ts-
3	u-

For example:

a'.wa du.li.a 'I want'
tsa.du.li.a 'thou wantest'
u.du.li.a 'he/she wants'

Bound subject–object forms: these are coded for subject–object deixis, and infixed in the prefix position in the verbal complex. Thus, *-gv-* encodes lst p. sing. subject and 2nd p. sing. object:

gv.ge.yu.(i) 'I-thee love'
i.tsv.ge.yu 'I-you (pl.) love'
tsi.ge.yu 'I-him/her love'

There is a wide range of such forms, complicated by phonetic fusion. Not all theoretically possible forms are actually in use.

DEMONSTRATIVE PRONOUN/ADJECTIVE

hi'.a 'this' (object); *go.hi* 'this', with reference to time: e.g. *go.hi i:ga* 'this day(light)' = 'today'. *Nalna.s.gi* 'that'; *na'.ni* 'those'.

INTERROGATIVE PRONOUN

ka:ga 'who?'; *ga.do* 'what?' Certain interrogative particles may be added to a focused word: e.g. *-ke, -tsu, -tsv*: *Ga.yo:tli.ke hi.wo:ni.a tsa.la.gi?* 'Do you speak some Cherokee?' (*ga.yo:tli* 'a little'; *tsa.la.gi* 'Cherokee').

Numerals

Sequoyah experimented with a decimal system. The numerals in use today are: 1–10: *sa.wu*, *ta'.li*, *tso:(i)*, *nv:g(i)*, *hi:s.g(ii)*, *su.da.l(i)*, *ga.l(i).quo:g(i)*, *tsu.ne:l(a)*, *so.ne:l(a)*, *s.go(hi)*; 11–19: *analogous forms* + *du.(i)*; 20 *ta.l.s.go.(hi)*; 100 *s.go.hi'.s.qua*.

Verb

Cherokee verbs may be divided into those which do not require classifiers and those which do. The latter form a small minority (a couple of dozen) and are all concerned with handling objects – picking things up, putting them down, pushing, pulling, and so on. The classifiers relate to the physical properties of objects. The basic categories are: (a) flexible objects, (b) long objects, (c) nondescript objects, (d) liquids, (e) animate objects.

Thus, the English verb 'to hand something to someone' will be rendered in several different ways in Cherokee, depending on the nature of the object being handled. Cf.

gv.ne'.a 'I hand you something nondescript (probably solid)'
gv.de'.a 'I hand you something long and inflexible'
gv.nv.ne'.a 'I hand you something floppy, flexible (e.g. a cloth)'
gv.ne'.v'.si(se) 'I hand you something liquid'

The complete grid for the verb *de.s.kv.si* 'to pass something classified (in five categories) to other(s)', involving singular, dual, and plural agent(s) and recipient(s), as set out in Holmes and Smith (1976: 294–6), has 175 forms.

The classifiers surface, of course, in the Cherokee verb 'to have'. Cf.

a.gi.ha 'I have it (indefinite)'
a.gi.**ka**.ha 'I have it (animate)'
a.gi.**na**.a 'I have it (flexible)'
a.gi.**ne**.a 'I have it (liquid)'

STRUCTURE OF THE VERB COMPLEX

Prefixes – verb stem – suffixes. The main components of the prefix slot, in order, are: negative – directionals – direct object – subject, subject/object pronoun – classifiers (with certain verbs) – stem. The suffix slot includes: tense/aspect markers for durative, potential, reiterative, inferential nuances; particle indicating addressee or beneficiary of action.

First position in the prefix slot is reserved for the negative marker *tla*, which can be resumed after the stem by *yi.gi*: ***tla***.*ga.ne.li.* ***yi.gi*** 'he/she is not married' (verb base *a.ne.l* 'live with/in'; *ga* – 3rd p. sing; *-i* – recent-past marker).

Subsequent positions in the prefix slot are occupied by (a) the plural marker *d-*; (b) directional markers: *da.* for approach, *wi.* for withdrawal; (c) the *ni* marker, which generates a kind of present perfect. An example from Holmes and Smith (1976: 191) is *hni.ne.l.o*, where *hni.ne.l.* is a contraction of *ni.hi.a.ne.l*: *a.ne.l.* is the base 'live', 'dwell'; *hi* is the 2nd p. sing. from set 2; *ni* 'already + still'; *o* is the habitual-action marker: 'you have been and still are living here/there'. The last prefix position before the stem is occupied by a direct object, if any.

SUFFIXES IN THE VERB COMPLEX

Holmes and Smith list 18 suffix positions. The most important items, in slot order, are:

(a) *-'il-gi* which reverses the meaning of the verbal base: e.g. *s.du'.di* 'close', *s.du'.**i.di*** 'open'.
(b) *-doh/toh*, with allophones. This modifier has a wide range of meanings. One important function is the formation of nouns from infinitives in *-di*:

 a.tsv.s.**doh**.di 'what lights up (for him/her)', i.e. 'a light-bulb'
 a.di.**toh**.di 'what can be sipped with', i.e. 'a spoon'

(c) The indirect object marker *-(n/y)e: gv.to.lv'.**e*** 'I borrow from thee'.
(d) *s.gi*: this suffix indicates calling or profession: *a.ni.yo:**s.gi*** 'soldiers' (*ni* is the animate-plural marker).

Towards the end of the suffix sequence come the markers for habitual (*-o*), future (*-i*) action, and for the perfective aspect (*-na*).

The present-tense marker is *-a*, with several variants. The future is often indicated by the circumfix *da . . . (s)i/tsi*. There are several past-tense markers, e.g. *-(s)v*, *-ga/la*, *-na* (perfective). E.g.

ga.dv.ne'.**a** 'I am doing it'
da.ga.wo:ni.**si** 'he will speak'
u.wo.ni:**sv.i** 'he spoke'

Note the switch of 3rd p. bound pronoun: set 1 in future, set 2 in past.

INFINITIVE

The suffix is usually *s.di*, and the form necessarily includes a bound pronoun from set 2, e.g. *a.ki.wa.hi.s.di* 'to buy', where *a.ki* is the 1st p. sing. bound pronoun from set 2. The infinitive seems to have a debitive nuance: 'ought to buy'.

NEGATIVE

One marker is *tla*, which can be resumed after the verb stem by *yi.gi*: e.g. *tla ga.ne.li yi.gi* 'he/she is not married' (*g-* is 3rd p. sing.; *a.ne.l-* is the stem 'to live with'; *-i* is marker for recent past tense).

Word order

SOV, SVO.

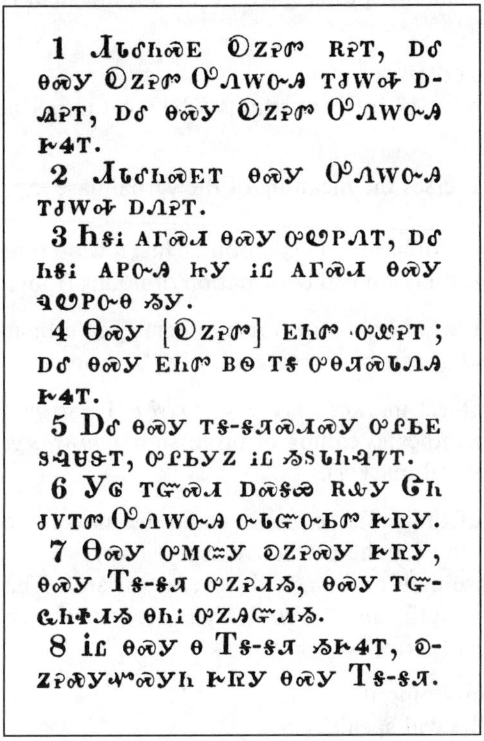

1 ᏗᏓᎴᏂᏍᎬ ᎧᏃᎮᏛ ᎡᎮᎢ, ᎠᎴ ᎾᏍᎩ ᎧᏃᎮᏛ ᎤᏁᎳᏅᎯ ᎢᏧᎳᎭ ᎠᏁᎮᎢ, ᎠᎴ ᎾᏍᎩ ᎧᏃᎮᏛ ᎤᏁᎳᏅᎯ ᎨᏎᎢ.

2 ᏗᏓᎴᏂᏍᎬᎢ ᎾᏍᎩ ᎤᏁᎳᏅᎯ ᎢᏧᎳᎭ ᎠᏁᎮᎢ.

3 ᏂᎦᎥ ᎪᎱᏍᏗ ᎾᏍᎩ ᎤᏬᏢᏁᎢ, ᎠᎴ ᏂᎦᎥ ᎪᏢᏅᎯ ᎨᎩ ᎥᏝ ᎪᎱᏍᏗ ᎾᏍᎩ ᏄᏬᏢᏅᎾ ᏱᎩ.

4 ᎾᏍᎩ [ᎧᏃᎮᏛ] ᎬᏂᏛ ᎤᏪᎮᎢ; ᎠᎴ ᎾᏍᎩ ᎬᏂᏛ ᏴᏫ ᎢᎦ ᎤᎾᏘᏍᏓᏁᎯ ᎨᏎᎢ.

5 ᎠᎴ ᎾᏍᎩ ᎢᎦ-ᎦᏘᏍᏗᏍᎩ ᎤᎵᏏᎬ ᏚᎸᏌᏕᎢ, ᎤᎵᏏᎬᏃ ᎥᏝ ᏱᏚᏓᏂᎸᏤᎢ.

6 ᎩᎶ ᎢᏳᏍᏗ ᎠᏍᎦᏯ ᎡᎲᎩ ᏣᏂ ᏧᏙᎢᏛ ᎤᏁᎳᏅᎯ ᏅᏓᏳᏅᏏᏛ ᎨᏒᎩ.

7 ᎾᏍᎩ ᎤᎷᏨᎩ ᎧᏃᎮᏍᎩ ᎨᏒᎩ, ᎾᏍᎩ ᎢᎦ-ᎦᏘ ᎤᏃᎮᏗᏱ, ᎾᏍᎩ ᎢᏳᏩᏂᏐᏗᏱ ᎾᏂᎥ ᎤᏃᎯᏳᏗᏱ.

8 ᎥᏝ ᎾᏍᎩ Ꮎ ᎢᎦ-ᎦᏘ ᏱᎨᏎᎢ, ᎧᏃᎮᏍᎩᏉᏍᎩᏂ ᎨᏒᎩ ᎾᏍᎩ ᎢᎦ-ᎦᏘ.

SCRIPT

In 1819–20, Sequoyah, a Cherokee half-breed, invented a syllabary of 86 characters, some of which are borrowed from the Roman alphabet, though with different phonetic values. The spread of literacy in this script among the Cherokees was rapid, and in 1828 a Cherokee weekly newspaper, the *Cherokee Phoenix*, was launched, a unique event in the annals of the American Indian. Parts of the Bible, tracts, and hymn-books soon appeared in the new script.

The script notates the vowels /a, e, i, o, u/ and /v/ = /ʌ̃/, and 79 combinations of consonant plus vowel. It does not notate vowel length, the intrusive /h/, or the glottal stop. It is partially inconsistent: e.g. in the velar series /ka/ and /ga/ are distinguished, the other five values are not.

THE CHEROKEE SCRIPT

THE SYLLABARY

Ꭰ *a*	Ꭱ *e*	Ꭲ *i*	Ꭳ *o*	Ꭴ *u*	Ꭵ *v*
Ꭶ *ga* Ꭷ *ka*	Ꭸ *ge*	Ꭹ *gi*	Ꭺ *go*	Ꭻ *gu*	Ꭼ *gv*
Ꭽ *ha*	Ꭾ *he*	Ꭿ *hi*	Ꮀ *ho*	Ꮁ *hu*	Ꮂ *hv*
Ꮃ *la*	Ꮄ *le*	Ꮅ *li*	Ꮆ *lo*	Ꮇ *lu*	Ꮈ *lv*
Ꮉ *ma*	Ꮊ *me*	Ꮋ *mi*	Ꮌ *mo*	Ꮍ *mu*	
Ꮎ *na* Ꮏ *hna* Ꮐ *nah*	Ꮑ *ne*	Ꮒ *ni*	Ꮓ *no*	Ꮔ *nu*	Ꮕ *nv*
Ꮖ *qua*	Ꮗ *que*	Ꮘ *qui*	Ꮙ *quo*	Ꮚ *quu*	Ꮛ *quv*
Ꮜ *sa* Ꮝ *s*	Ꮞ *se*	Ꮟ *si*	Ꮠ *so*	Ꮡ *su*	Ꮢ *sv*
Ꮣ *da* Ꮤ *ta*	Ꮥ *de* Ꮦ *te*	Ꮧ *di* Ꮨ *ti*	Ꮩ *do*	Ꮪ *du*	Ꮫ *dv*
Ꮬ *dla* Ꮭ *tla*	Ꮮ *tle*	Ꮯ *tli*	Ꮰ *tlo*	Ꮱ *tlu*	Ꮲ *tlv*
Ꮳ *tsa*	Ꮴ *tse*	Ꮵ *tsi*	Ꮶ *tso*	Ꮷ *tsu*	Ꮸ *tsv*
Ꮹ *wa*	Ꮺ *we*	Ꮻ *wi*	Ꮼ *wo*	Ꮽ *wu*	Ꮾ *wv*
Ꮿ *ya*	Ᏸ *ye*	Ᏹ *yi*	Ᏺ *yo*	Ᏻ *yu*	Ᏼ *yv*

Source: Holmes, R.B. and Smith, B.S. (1976) *Beginning Cherokee*, Norman, OK.

CHEYENNE

INTRODUCTION

This Macro-Algonquian language is spoken by 2,000 people in Montana and Oklahoma. The language was described by R. Petter (1952).

PHONOLOGY

Consonants

Petter gives the following inventory:

stops: b/p, d/t, g/k
affricates: ts/tʃ
fricatives: v/w, ç/x, h, s, ʃ, j
nasals: m, n

/q/ alternates with labialized [k°]; palatalized /t′/ alternates with the affricate [tʃ].

Vowels

ī, i, ā, ə, ō, ɔ, ɔ̄, ʌ, ε

/oː/ = [u], /a/ = [ou], /o/ = [oi], /ε/ = [ai]

Petter uses an acute accent to mark hiatus or glottalization, and a grave accent to denote closure on a soft /ç/: *nà* = /naç/. There are also whispered vowels which Petter denotes as °.

i is the dominant vowel sound in Cheyenne.

MORPHOLOGY AND SYNTAX

Noun

The sense of an indefinite article is provided by the *ma-* prefix: e.g. *ma.ex* ‘an eye, the eye (in general)’.

GENDER

The Cheyenne distinction between animate and inanimate categories surfaces in the plural marker *-eo*, specific for animates: e.g. *hetan* ‘man’, *hetaneo* ‘men’; *veces* /wεt’ɪs/ ‘bird’, pl. *vecseo*. Natural gender can be marked by lexical items: e.g. *hetan* ‘male’, *hee* ‘female’: *hetan.eham* ‘bull buffalo’; *hee.ham* ‘cow buffalo’.

There are no cases.

POSSESSION

Alienable or inalienable. The alienable inanimate paradigm is:

	Singular	Plural
1	na . . . am	na/ni . . . aman
2	ni . . . am	ni . . . amevo
3	he . . . am	he . . . amevo

Examples: *na.māme.n.am* 'my corn', pl. *na.māme.n.amoz* 'my grains'.

Inalienable possession; cf. *na.mocan* 'my shoe'; *ni.mocan* 'thy shoe'; *na.mocan.an* 'our shoe'; *na.mocan.an.oz* 'our shoes'.

KINSHIP

Many of these forms are very irregular: *nihoe* 'my father', *eijô* 'thy father', *hèhjo* 'one's father'; *nàkohe* 'my mother', *nišq* 'thy mother'; *nanis* 'my child', *ninis* 'thy child', *naniseneo* 'my children'; *nistxeo* 'my warriors (who are with me)', *estxeo* 'thy warriors'.

Pronoun

	Singular		Plural
1	na.nēhov 'I myself'	*excl.*	na.nēhov.hemê
		incl.	ni.nēhov.hemå
2	ni.nēhov		ni.nēhov.hemā
3	e.nēhov		e.nēhov.eo

DEMONSTRATIVE PRONOUN

(a) Animate:

	Singular	Plural
1	ze.nēhov.etto 'I, who . . . '	ze.nēhov.ez
2	ze.nēhov.étto	ze.nēhov.ess
3	ze.nēhov.sz	ze.nēhov.evoss

(b) Inanimate: *heto* 'this one'; *hato* 'that one'.

INTERROGATIVE PRONOUN

Animate: *nivā* 'who?', pl. *nivāseo*; inanimate: *henova* 'what?'

Verb

Petter emphasizes the great complexity of the Cheyenne verbal system, with its limitless capacity for producing *ad hoc* forms. Some basic structures are outlined here:

TENSE

Present:

	Singular		Plural
1	na.vōsan 'I see'	*excl.*	na.vōsan.hemḙ
		incl.	ni.vōsan.hemå
2	nī.vōsan		ni.vōsan.hemḙ
3	e.vōsan		e.vōsan.eo

Petter lists 35 temporal infixes: e.g. preterite: *-eše-*, e.g. *na.eše.vōsan*, *ni.eše.vōsan*; future: *-ze-*, e.g. *na.ze.vōsan*, *ni.ze.vōsan*. A simple past tense is made by modulation of the personal prefix: e.g. *nà.vōsan*, *nì.vōsan*, *è.vōsan*.

INTRANSITIVE VERBS

Four categories: (a) *-san* (with variants): these are duratives; (b) *-a*; (c) *-o*; (d) *-e*; these three categories differ from one another ontologically. To these forms are added several dozen endings denoting natural phenomena and human affection; e.g. *-éna* 'snow', *-tovao* 'smoke', *-oss* 'cold', *-eoxta* 'legged', *-ésta* 'eared', *-moxta* 'of feeling': *na.pev.o.moxta* 'I'm feeling good.'

Several endings such as *-etto*, *-tove*, *-nove*, form impersonal verbs; e.g. *-tove* converts nouns ending in *-toz* into verbs: *mesestoz* 'food' – *e.meses.tove* 'it is food'; *meàtoz* 'gift' – *e.meàtove.nsz* 'these are gifts'.

TRANSITIVE VERBS

Personal pronominal deixis expressed by personal prefix plus coded ending:

ni.vōm.az 'I see thee'
ni.vōm.e 'thou seest me'
ni.vōm.azemenȯ 'we see thee'
ni.vōm.eme 'you (pl.) see me'
na.vōm.o 'I see one'
na.vōm.on 'we (excl.) see one'
ni.vōm.on 'we (incl.) see one'

Action by third person on first or second person involves inversion of model:

na.vōm.a 'I am seen by one' = 'one sees me'
ni.vōm.ā 'thou art seen by them' = 'they see thee'
na.vōm.aen 'we are seen by one'
e.vōm.a 'he is seen by one'

Final-stem consonants are subject to sandhi.

PASSIVE PARADIGM

	Singular	Plural
1	na.vōm.an 'I am seen'	na.vōm.an.heme
2	ni.vōm.an	ni.vōm.an.heme
3	e.vōm.an	e.vōm.eo

INSTRUMENTAL INFIXES

Indicating medium (weapon, instrument, etc.) used to perform an action, e.g. *-òno* 'with a weapon'; *-éso* 'by amputation'; *-âno* 'by fire'. Examples:

na.von.âno 'I burn him'; *na.vov.èno* 'I wound him in the face'. These can be passive: e.g. *na.onexâhen* 'I am burned'; *na.vovehen* 'I am wounded in the face'.

MODAL FORMS OF VERB

Petter lists 35:

1. Indicative: simple assertion, e.g. *na.vōs.an* 'I see'; *na.vōm.o* 'I see one'; *na.vōm.az* 'I see myself'; *na.vōm.an* 'I am seen'.
2. Imperative: the personal prefix is dropped, e.g. *vehōmsz!* 'see me!'; *vehōmemeno!* 'see thou us!'
3. Hortative: also drops personal prefix. The suffixes are similar to those of the imperative, e.g. *vōsanehå* 'let him see'.
4. Negative: *-saa* is the characteristic, plus *-elhe* affix, e.g. *na.saa.vōsan.e* 'I do not see'; *na.saa.vōm.ohe* 'I do not see one'; *ni.saa.vōm.az.e* 'I do not see thee'.
5. Hypothetical: *-mo* + *-élhe*, e.g. *mo.na.vōs.an.é* 'it's likely I'll see'; *mo.na.vōm.an.é* 'it's likely I'm being seen'.
6. Interrogative: expressed by the negative or the hypothetical minus particles, e.g. *na.vōs.ané?* 'do I see?'

Among the remaining moods are an estimative, *na.pevatamo* 'I deem someone good'; a comitative, *na.veoxzemo* 'I go with someone'; a desiderative, *na.vōmatanotovu* 'I desire to see someone': further, a persuasive, a mediative, an affective, a causative, and over a dozen denoting various qualities, modes of behaviour, and appearance.

1 Hako vonoomē vovoe-ase-amexoveva ēševistävhŏ Maheone-omotom,na Maheone-omotom èvistaoxzevemhŏn Maheonȯ, na èmaheonevstavhŏ Maheone-omotom. 2 Na zenehāsz èvistaoxzevemhŏn Maheonȯ hako vonoomĕ vovoe-aseamexoveva. 3 Tāma hevetov èveše-manheneó zetohetāehovaeve,na saave-nĕhovehehŏ hovae manstŏ emsaa-eše-manehanehez'.4 Tāma hevetov envešhesse-ametanenistoveneó: na ametanenistoz ehevónamenov vostaneo. 5 Na zevónitto eoxtoxce-vóneomohetto zeáenonittoz', hotaz zeáenonitto esaanòtovaztohe zevónittoz'. 6 Nasz hetan zènmeatŏs Maheonȯ exhoènehŏ, John exheševehehŏ. 7 Zenehāsz exhoe-pânoxtahaneonevhŏ, zistose-pânoxtahaneto zevó-nittoz'. nonoxpa hevetov ememä-onisyomàtàtovó. 8 Tāma es'aameha-tó-nēhovehŏ Vónevhan óha exhoè-nehō emeheše-pânòtahanetovoss Vónevhäneheva.

CHIBCHA

INTRODUCTION

The Chibcha described here (after Middendorf, 1890–2) has been extinct since the eighteenth century. Up to the time of the Spanish Conquest, Chibcha (or Muysca as it was also called) was the language of a centralized and organized Indian civilization in what is now Colombia, and may have been spoken by as many as 500,000 people. Some Chibchan languages are still spoken. Middendorf's description is based on grammars of the language by Lugo and Uricochea.

PHONOLOGY

Consonants

/d/ and /l/ are absent, /r/ is rare, /ts/ is present.

Vowels

The vowels are as in Spanish. /y/ is described as being between /e/ and /i/.

MORPHOLOGY AND SYNTAX

Noun

Nearly all nouns end in a vowel, usually *-a*. The following typical declension is based on Lugo:

nom.	muysca 'man'
gen.	muyscaepcua/ipcua
dat.	muyscaguaca
acc.	muyscaca
ill.	muyscan/s
abl.	muyscanynši
loc.	muyscana
instr./com.	muyscabotsa

There is no special plural ending; *mabie* 'many', may be used: e.g. *gue mabie* 'many houses'; *gue mabie ipcua* 'of many houses'.

Adjective

When independent, the adjective is declined as nominal; when attributive, invariable. Normally follows noun, but may precede. Middendorf makes the point that adjectives are usually longer than the nouns they qualify: e.g. *ie afihistatsa* 'narrow way'; *fagua chinanuca* 'shining star'.

COMPARISON

Made with *ingy* 'more': e.g. *cho* 'good', *ingy cho* 'better'.

Pronoun

PERSONAL

	Singular		*Plural*	
	Independent	*Enclitic*	*Independent*	*Enclitic*
1	hycha	tsy, tse, i	chie	chi
2	mue	um	mie	mi
3	–	a, as	–	a

These are declined, e.g. for *hycha*:

nom.	hycha
gen.	hycha **tse** ipcua
dat.	hycha **tse** guaca
instr.	hycha **tse** botsa
acc.	**cha**

The enclitic forms are used as possessives: e.g. *tse gue* 'my house'.

DEMONSTRATIVE PRONOUN

as – šis – ys by relative distance: 'this' – 'that' – 'that (yonder)'. These have plural forms: *anabitsa – šinabitsa – ynabitsa*.

Numerals

1–10: *ata, botsa, mica, muyca, hycsca, ta, cuhubcua, sutsa, aca, hubchihica*; 11–19: e.g. *quicha ata, quicha botsa*; 20 *quicha hubchihica*. From 21 on, *gueta* is used for 20: 21 *gueta.s asaquy.ata*; 40 *gue botsa*; 100 *gue hysca*.

The numeral follows the noun enumerated: e.g. *muysca mica* 'three men'.

Verb

Agglutinative forms with prepositive personal pronominal enclitics. There are two voices and four moods.

INDICATIVE MOOD

Present: enclitic pronoun + stem + present marker, e.g. *tse + bquy + scua* 'I do, make'; *um.bquy.scua* 'you make'.

Past: enclitic pronoun + stem + Ø, e.g. *tse.bquyØ* 'I made/did'.

Future: enclitic pronoun + stem + future marker, e.g. *tse.bquy.nga* 'I shall do, make'.

SUBJUNCTIVE

Present form + subjunctive marker, e.g. *tse.bquy.scua.nan* 'that I may do'.

IMPERATIVE

Stem only, modified, e.g. *quyu!* 'do, make!'; pl. *quyiuva!*

PARTICIPIAL FORMS

quysca 'making/doing', e.g. '(he…) who makes/does'; past form, *quyia*; future form, *quinga*. These are used, for example in relative senses, with copula, *gue*: e.g. *hycha gue cha quysca* 'I am he who makes'; *mue gue ma quyia* 'you are the one who made'.

NEGATIVE

tsa/ts is affixed or infixed: e.g. *tse bquyscua.**tsa*** 'I do not do/make'; *tse bquy.**ts**.inga* 'I shall not do, make'; *cha quysca.**tsa*** 'I who do not …'.

PASSIVE

To form the passive of, for example *tse.bquy.scua* 'I do/make', the pronominal enclitic is put in the accusative, and the verb form is slightly changed: ***chan***, *quysca* 'he does something to me'; similarly, ***man**.quysca* 'he does something to you'.

The accusative forms of the enclitics can only be used if the agent is third person. If the agent is first or second person, the full form is used: e.g. ***a**.quity.**cha*** 'he struck me'; *mi.quity.**hycha*** 'you struck me'; *tse.quity.suca.**mue*** 'I strike you' (*-suca-* is an alternant of *-scua-*).

Chibcha used postpositions: e.g.

taca/chien 'under': e.g. *guica chien* 'under the sky', *sié taca* 'under water';
uca/uco/uquy 'under': e.g. *ts.uca* 'under me';
ubac/ubana 'before': e.g. *ts.ubana* 'before me';
suca/gahan 'behind': e.g. *ts.e.gahan* 'behind me', *i.suca* 'behind me' (*i* may replace *tse* as 1st person marker before *ch*, *n*, *s*, *š*, *t*, *ts*);
šicas 'away from': e.g. *i./tse.šicas* '(away) from me'.

Word order

SVO is usual: cf. *to a.bca cha* 'the dog bit me'.

CHIMÚ

INTRODUCTION

Chimú, the language of the ruling stratum in Peru until the coming to power of the Incas in the fifteenth century, is of doubtful genetic affiliation, and may be an isolate. It survived into the nineteenth century, and was described by Ernst Middendorf in his great work, *Die Einheimischen Sprachen Perus* (1890). The language was unwritten, and is now extinct.

PHONOLOGY

Middendorf (1890) gives the following inventory:

Consonants

Stops: p, t, d, k; the sound marked by Middendorf as ‘*t* may be a glottalized /t’/ as in Aymara.

Three velar fricatives are distinguished: *j* = Spanish /j/; *j* = hard Aymara /ʝ/; *j̇* = /ç/; the affricates *ch* = /ts/, ’*ch* = /tʝ/, *ts* = /ts/.

Also present are: f, w; m, n, ɲ; l, ʎ, r, rr; s, ss (‘sharp s’), ʃ; h

Vowels

long and short: i, e, a, o, u
diphthongs: ai, ei, ui, oi

In the diphthongs, each component vowel is given its full value. Two specifically Chimú sounds are notated by Middendorf as *ä* and *ů*: both are realized as /ɛ.u/, with /ɛ/ emphasized in the former, /u/ in the latter.

MORPHOLOGY AND SYNTAX

Noun

There is no grammatical gender; natural gender is distinguished by adjunct nouns: e.g. *chisi* ‘child’: *ñofąn chisi* ‘boy child’; *mecherräk chisi* ‘girl child’; *mecherräk rak* ‘female jaguar’. A genitive ending is made with *-är.ō/ei.ō/ngō*, depending on noun final.

The plural marker is *-än*, which precedes the genitive marker, except when this is *ngō*; *-än* is then inserted between *ng*- and *-ō*: cf. *chonkik* ‘star’, gen. *chonkik.är.ō*; pl. *chonkik.än*; gen. pl. *chonkik.än.är.ō*; *chelu* ‘falcon’, gen. *chelu.ngō*; pl. *chelu.än*; gen. pl. *chelu.ng.än.ō*. The *ō* of the genitive ending is always strongly stressed, with a hiatus between it and the preceding *-än/-är*, as though it were a postposition.

The genitive *ō* is dropped in the following circumstances:

(a) In a construct: e.g. *choj* 'boy', gen. *choj.ei.ō*; but *choj.**e** fanuss* 'the boy's dog', where *-ss* is the marker for a dependent nominal.
(b) Where a postposition governing the genitive is used: e.g. *uij* 'the earth', gen. *uij.är.ō*, *uij.är kapäk* 'on the earth'; *ōj* 'fire', *ōj.är nik* 'in the fire'.
(c) If the verb is passive, the agent is in the genitive case minus *-ō*: e.g. *c̓huvet* 'snake', *c̓huvet.är.**Ø** rranädo* 'bitten by the snake'; *ssonte* 'vulture', *ssonte.ng lletnädo* 'swallowed by the vulture'. Cf. *Mo an ang aio ñofär ef.ei.ō* 'This house is of-the-father of that man' (*mo* 'this'; *an* 'house'; *ang* 'is'; *ñofär* = *ñofän.är* 'of the man'; *ef* 'father'; *ei.ō*, genitive of dependent nominal).

THE DEPENDENT NOMINAL

The marker is always *-ss,* except for nouns ending in *-k*, which changes to *-r*: e.g. *manik* 'drinking vessel', dep. nom. *manir.* The dependent form is not used if the possessed object is separated from the possessor: cf. *mäiñ fanuss ang mo* 'my dog is this' = 'this is my dog'; but *mo fanu ang mäiñ* 'this dog is mine'. All dependent nominals have a genitive in *-ai.ō/ei.ō*.

Adjective

Not formally distinguished from the noun. Root adjectives are often monosyllabic, and precede the noun: e.g. *ñāss* 'beautiful', *ñāss tot.är.ō* 'of the beautiful face'; *ūts* 'big', *ūts nepät.är.ō* 'of the big tree'. The plural marker is added to the adjective: e.g. *ñāss.än tot* 'beautiful faces'; *ūts.än nepät* 'big trees'. But in the plural genitive the plural marker reverts to the noun: e.g. *ūts nepät.än.är.ō* 'of the big trees', realized as /uc.**o**.nepät.än.är.ō/, where *-o-* is a euphonic infix: cf. *peñ.**o**.mecharräk* 'a good woman'.

COMPARATIVE

jechna 'more' + genitive case + *lekich* (postposition): e.g. *Jechna ñāss.o fe ñing ja nech.är ja.ng lekich* 'The sea's water is better than the river's water' (*fe* = *ang* 'is'; *ñi* 'sea'; *ja* 'water'; *nech* 'river').

Pronoun

PERSONAL PRONOUN

	Singular	*Plural*
1	moiñ, gen. mäiñ.o	mäich
2	tsang	tsäich

The third person forms are supplied from the demonstrative series. These are *mo/ssio* 'this', pl. *mo.ngän/ssiong.än* 'this, these'; *aio* 'that', pl. *aiungän*.

INTERROGATIVE PRONOUN

eiñ 'who?'; *ech* 'what?'

RELATIVE PRONOUN
kan

Numerals

1–10: *onäk*, *aput*, *sopät*, *nopät*, *ejmäts*, *tsaitsa*, *ñite*, *langäss*, *tap*, *na-pong*; 11 *na-pong allo onäk*; 20 *pak pong*; 30 *sok pong*; 40 *nok pong*; 100 *na paläk*; 200 *pak paläk*.

The numeral precedes the noun, which is in the singular: e.g. *ñite.io chonkik* 'seven stars'.

Verb

THE COPULA

	Singular	Plural
1	moiñ eiñ	mäich eiš
2	tsang as	tsäich as.chi
3	aio ang	aiongän ang

There are many variant forms. *Ang/fe* can replace any of the above. In composite tenses, preferred forms are: 1 *e*, 2 *as*, 3 *fe*.

Past: the above forms plus *piñ*: e.g. *moiñ e piñ*, *tsang as piñ*. Future: the above forms plus *ka*: e.g. *moiñ e ka*.

A second substantive verb or copula is *chi*: e.g. *chi.eiñ* → *chiñ*, *chi.as* → *chis*.

CONJUGATION
Two models are possible:

(a) root + endings, coded for person and number;
(b) personal pronoun + personal marker + root.

For example, with root *tem-* 'to love, examine', present tense:

(a) *tem.eiñ*, *tem.as*, *tem.ang*; *tem.eiš*, *tem.aschi*, *tem.änang*;
(b) *moiñ e tem*, *tsang as tem*, *aiof ang tem*; *mäich eiš tem*, *tsäich aschi tem*, *aiongän ang tem*.

There is only one form for the perfect: *tem.eda.iñ*, *tem.eda.s*, *tem.eda.ng*, *tem.eda.iš*, *tem.eda.schi*, *tem.edän.ang*.

Future: *tiñ tem*, *täs tem*, *täng tem*, *tiš tem*, *täschi tem*, *täng tem än*.

Subjunctive: e.g. *tem.ema.iñ*, *tem.ema.s*, *tem.ema.ng*, or: *moiñ mang tem*, etc.

NON-FINITE FORMS
tem.äd 'to love', *tem.näm* 'in order to love', *tem.e.skäf* 'to have loved', *tem.e.läk/ssäk* 'loving'.

PASSIVE

är is added to the verbal stem: present tense, *tem.är.eiñ* = *moiñ eiñ tem.är* 'I am loved'; passive participle, *temedo* = *tem.är.edo* 'loved'.

DERIVED VERBS

Causative: the infixed marker is *-ko-*: *jep* 'burn' (intrans.) – *jep.ko.iñ* 'I ignite'; *funo* 'eat' – *funo.ko.iñ* 'I feed'; *chi* 'to be' – *chi.ko.iñ* 'I create'.

Durative: the active participle is taken as verbal theme and conjugated, e.g. *eng* 'say' – *eng.a.päk.o.iñ* 'I always say'; *kall* 'laugh' – *kallapäkoiñ* 'I laugh all the time'.

Benefactive: the infix is *-äk/ek-*, e.g. *met* 'bring' – *met.äk.eiñ* 'I bring for/to someone'.

Privative: *-un.o/unta*, *met.uno* 'without bringing'.

Postpositions

Postpositions in Chimú govern either the base form or the genitive case. With genitive:

kapäk 'on': *llemki.ng.kapäk* 'on the mountain';
-nik/nek 'in(to)': *ñi.ng.e.nik* 'in(to) the sea' (← *ni.ng.o.nik*);
tutäk 'before': *moiñ tutäk* 'before me'; *an.e tutäk* 'in front of the house';
turkich 'behind': *llemki.ng turkich* 'behind the mountain';
pän 'for': *ssiung fan.ngo pän* 'for his dog'.

With base form:

len 'with': *tsang.len* 'with you';
na 'through': *pampa.na* 'through the plains'.

NEGATION

As in Quechua, by means of circumfix, *änta . . . (e)sta*: e.g. *änta fe esta* 'it is not'; *Änta ang Dios esta mo jang mo ši* 'God is not the sun, the moon.'

Word order

Free. Verb + object: e.g. *moiñ e tem.edo tsang* 'I have loved you'; *tsang e tem.edo mäiñ* 'you were loved by me'.

CHINESE

By far the largest and most important member of the Sino-Tibetan family, Chinese is spoken today by about 1,125 million people in the Republic of China, in Taiwan, in Malaysia and other parts of South-East Asia, and in numerous Chinese communities all over the world. The umbrella term 'Chinese' covers several dialect groups which are broadly divided into (a) northern dialect (Mandarin), which accounts for about two-thirds of all Chinese speakers, and (b) the southern dialects including Wu, Gan, Xiang, Hakka, Yue, and Min. It is somewhat misleading to talk of 'dialects', as Chinese dialects are not mutually intelligible and should really be classified as languages.

Chinese has been a written language for about 3,500 years. Over this long time-span, pronunciation has changed very considerably, script and morphology comparatively little. Diachronically, the language may conveniently be considered under three main headings:

1. Archaic Chinese: fourteenth to eleventh centuries BC; the language of the Anyang inscriptions on animal bones and tortoise shells.
2. Classical Chinese (Wenli): broadly, the language and its literature – one of the world's most interesting and important – between the eleventh century BC and the eighth century AD, with an increasingly artificial prolongation well into modern times.
3. Modern Standard Chinese: *guóyŭ* ('national language') or *pŭtōnghuà* ('common language'); essentially, the vocabulary and morphology of late Classical Chinese, pruned, enlarged, and adapted for use in a modern society. Many of the Classical characters in use have been abbreviated. An official romanization is known as *pīnyīn.*

These headings are treated in the following three articles. Pīnyīn romanization is used.

CHINESE, ARCHAIC

INTRODUCTION

The earliest fragmentary examples of the Chinese writing system date from about 2000 BC. The first sizeable corpus of connected texts, however, is provided by the oracle inscriptions on animal bones and tortoise shells, which were used in divination rituals by the rulers of the Shang dynasty (*c.* 1400–1100 BC). From 1899 onwards, great numbers of these inscriptions have been excavated at the site of the ancient capital, Anyang, and elsewhere. Their content is largely stereotyped along the lines that one would expect to find in an economy based on agriculture: Is it going to rain? Will the harvest be plentiful? The question was apparently incised on one half of a shell, for example, which was then heated; the cracks which appeared in the other half were interpreted as the answer, and written in.

A typical oracle inscription falls into four sections: first, the day and place of the ritual are specified, the day being given in terms of the sixty-day cycle generated by the Ten (Heavenly Stems) and the Twelve (Earthly Branches); the name of the oracle may be added – this section always ends with the word *zhēn* 'asks'. The next section gives the text of the question, and the third section contains the answer, which is usually introduced by the stock phrase *wáng zhān yūe* 'the ruler read the answer'. Finally, the concluding section indicates the outcome of the prediction. While large numbers of inscriptions are identical as regards both content and form, small variations do occur: character sequence may change, certain words may be left out or replaced by others. Krjukov (1973) emphasizes the importance of this factor for close analysis of the Shang language. An example of a Shang oracle text is given at the end of the article, just before 'Script'.

SCRIPT

See **Script** at end of article.

PHONOLOGY

It is not possible to say with any degree of certainty how Shang Chinese was pronounced. In this entry, characters are given their modern Chinese values.

MORPHOLOGY AND SYNTAX

The Shang characters are described as semantically multivalued nuclei, with the pronouns forming an exception. Up to a point, Shang adverbs, prepositions, conjunctions, and particles are also monosemantic.

Noun and verb

In the absence of inflection of any kind, meaning depends, as far as multi-valued items are concerned, on position and function. A character may function as a noun in one context, as an active verb with a direct object in an-other, and as a passive or stative verb in a third. For example, with *huò*: 'dis-aster', 'cause/suffer disaster':

As noun: *dì fú qí jiàng huò* 'Heaven (*dì*) will not (*fú*) send down (*jiàng*) disaster' (the meaning of the adverbial *qí* is not clear).
As active verb: *cī yŭ bù wéi wŏ huò* 'this rain will not turn out to be harmful to us' (notice inversion of normal order: indirect object -(*wéi*)*wŏ*- 'for us' precedes verb *huò*; see further example below).
As stative verb: *wáng zhēn: yú huò?* 'the Wang put the question: 'shall) I (*yú*) (be) unfortunate?'

One and the same character may denote the base verb and its causative; cf. *lái* 'to come' or 'to cause to come', i.e. 'to send':

xī lái băi mă 'Xi will send a white (*băi*) horse'

Similarly, in the Shang language, *shòu* 'to receive' and *shou* 'to cause to receive', i.e. 'to give', are written with the same character 受. In the early Classical language, the latter has acquired the radical 扌 which is present in Modern Standard Chinese.

dì shòu wŏ nián 'Heaven will send us harvest'
wŏ bù qí shòu nián 'we shall get no harvest'

A general rule is that a 'verb' can take an objective complement; noun, adjective, and pronoun cannot. The adjective seems to be incompatible with the negating adverbs.

An interesting inversion of the standard SVO order occurs in negative sentences, using *bu*, with a pronominal object. Thus the negation of ***dì hàn wŏ*** 'Heaven will afflict us with drought' is *dì bú* ***wŏ hàn*** 'Heaven will not . . . '.

The verb *yŏu* 'to have', negated specifically by *mei* in MSC, has a negative counterpart in the archaic language: *wáng* 'not to have'.

Three markers are used to indicate present (*jīn*), past (*xí*), and future (*lái*) time. These also occur in an attributive capacity:

jīn lái suì wŏ shòu nián 'this year (*suì*) and next, we shall have harvest'

Pronoun

The following are attested:

1st p.	我	*wǒ* (sing. and pl.)
	余	*yú* (sing.; used only by the Shang ruler)
	朕	*zhèn*
2nd p.	汝	*rǔ*
	乃	*nǎi*

All function as subject or object; in addition, *wǒ*, *zhèn*, and *nǎi* function as attributes (e.g. possessives). There are no 3rd p. pronouns.

Numerals

The word order with numerical classifiers may be illustrated: *mǎ ěr shí bing* 'horse – two – ten – team', i.e. 'twenty teams of horses'; *niú sǎn bǎi wǔ shí wǔ niú* 'cow – three – hundred – five – ten – five – cow', i.e. '355 head of cattle'.

Prepositions

于 *yú* is an all-purpose preposition, used *inter alia* to mark the recipient or addressee of an action: *gào yú wáng* 'to inform the ruler'. It also indicates motion to a place: *bù yú shāng* 'to proceed to Shang'. In this sense, its antonym is *zì*: *bú zì shāng* 'to proceed from Shang'.

Word order

SVO is basic, but note inversion described above.

SPECIMEN ORACLE INSCRIPTION

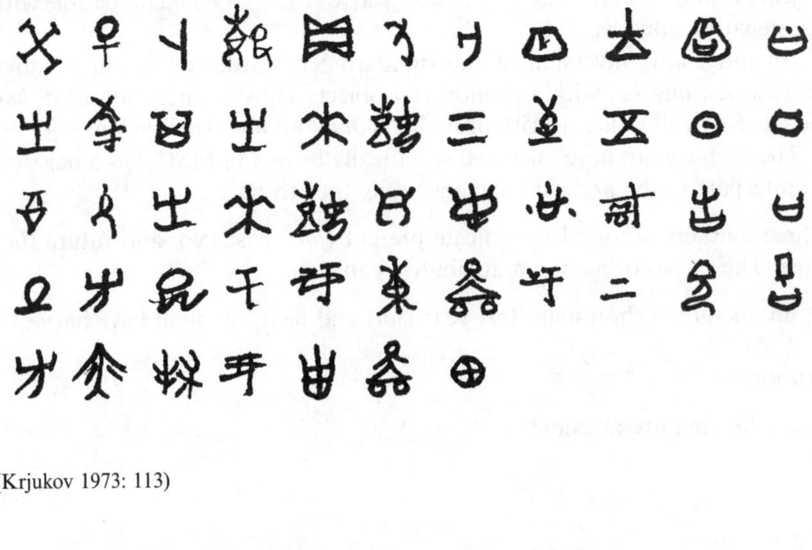

(Krjukov 1973: 113)

Transliteration into MSC (Pinyin)

gŭi-sì bŭ Que zhēn xún wáng huò wáng zhān yūe: yŏu suì qí yŏu lái jiān; qi zhì wŭ rì dĭng-yŭ yŭn lái jiān zì xī; Xĭ Zhèn gào yūe: tù fāng zhēng yú wŏ dōng bĭ cái ĕr yì; gong fāng yì qīn wŏ xī bĭ tián.

TRANSLATION

(On) the day *gui-si*, divination (took place); Que put the question: in the next ten (days) will there be no misfortune? The ruler read the answer: there will be evil, there will be danger. On the fifth day *dĭng-yŭ* indeed danger came from the west. Xi Zhen added: the Tu tribe fell upon our eastern marches and destroyed two towns; the Gong tribe also intruded on the territory of our western marches.

SCRIPT

The three basic elements – pictographs, ideographs, and phonograms – of Chinese script are all present in the Shang script, which points to a lengthy period of anterior development.

Example of Shang oracle inscription (from Krjukov 1973):

du shou wo yu du bu wo ci shou yu

Glossary: *du* 'heaven'; *shou* 'give'; *wo* 'us'; *yu* 'help'; *bu* 'not'; *ci*: an adverbial whose meaning is uncertain.

Translation: Will Heaven give us help? Heaven will not give us help.

Examples of pictographs are:

 (= modern 馬 *mă*) 'horse'

 (= modern 雨 *yŭ*) 'rain'

Examples of ideographs are:

 (= 下 *xià*) 'under', 'below'

 (=  *shàng*) 'above', 'up'

Phonograms: a phonogram is in origin a pictograph, chosen, for reasons which are not as yet clear, to notate a homophonic word. For example, the pictograph 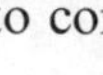 depicting the ear of wheat, came to be used to denote the word *lai* 'to come' (modern Chinese 來).

About 2,000 characters have been identified, a figure which represents a much larger corpus of 'words'. This is because the Shang characters (apart from the pronouns) might be described as semantically multivalued nuclei whose valencies depend on locus and function in the utterance as a whole. Thus,  (= modern 子) can mean any of the following: 'son', 'filial', 'to be filial', 'to regard oneself as filial', 'befitting a son', etc. Up to a point, the modern Chinese graph shares the polyvalence characteristic of both Shang and Classical Chinese.

There is, however, an essential difference between the Shang character and its Classical/Modern Standard Chinese derivative. The Shang character for 'horse', for example (see above), is like a child's drawing of the animal: it is impressionistic, and the component strokes cannot be used to make other characters. In contrast, the character 馬 – standardized since the Shuo Wen dictionary of 100 AD (*see* **Chinese, Classical**) – is a conventional diagram: it is constructed according to a prescribed order of stroke, from a prescribed number of standardized elements – in this particular case, from three horizontal strokes 三, two vertical | |, one dextro-rotary angle ㇆, and four dots 、、、、. The graph 馬 is reducible to these elements, all of which are used consistently as components in thousands of other Chinese characters. The Shang graph is not so reducible. There was no consistency in character delineation, and variants abound.

In Modern Standard Chinese, again, the great majority of 'words' combine a semantic determinant – the radical – with a phonetic element. In Shang Chinese this combination is rare; according to Krjukov (1973), only about a dozen are to be found in the Anyang corpus. In these inscriptions we see the beginnings of the diachronic process which was to yield the typical Modern Standard Chinese 'word'.

Shang characters which share a phonetic element can, on that basis, be grouped as sharing some common feature of pronunciation. But exactly what that pronunciation was remains, at best, conjectural. *See also* **Chinese, Classical**.

CHINESE, CLASSICAL (Wenli)

INTRODUCTION

In a narrow sense, the term 'Classical Chinese' refers to the Chinese language and its literature from the sixth century BC to the third century AD; a period which includes the lives and works of Confucius, Mencius, Lao Tzu, Han Fei, Mo Tzu, and Chuang Tzu, to mention only the six philosopher–sages who were to have such a far-reaching effect on subsequent Chinese thought. In a broader sense, Classical Chinese begins with the *Shih Ching* ('Book of Odes'), which was compiled between the eleventh and sixth centuries BC, and which was in fact co-opted, during the central period, to form one of the 'Five Classics' (*wu jing*). The other four are:

I Jing ('Book of Changes');
Shu Jing ('Book of History');
Li Ji ('Book of Propriety');
Chun-Chiu ('Spring and Autumn Annals').

After the Burning of the Books by the Qin Emperor Shi Huang Di (213 BC), when most of this material was destroyed, the text of the Classics had to be arduously reconstructed. This took place in the early years of the Han Dynasty, whose espousal of Confucianism determined the lineaments of Chinese literature for many centuries to come. In the Confucian hegemony three factors were crucial: (1) the sacrosanctity of the classical texts; (2) the examination system based on these texts and their commentaries; (3) the supremacy of the literati who expounded the classics and set the examinations.

Outside the examination halls, a succession of poets – especially in the Tang and Sung Dynasties – some of them disreputable by Confucian standards, went on producing a lot of the world's most attractive poetry.

SCRIPT

See **Script** at end of article.

PHONOLOGY

Reconstruction is, of course, hypothetical. The first guide to the actual pronunciation of Classical Chinese, the *Qieyun* Rhyming Dictionary, was not published until AD 601.

Consonants

Yaxontov (1965) gives the following inventory of permissible initials:

stops: p, ph, bh, t, d, th, dh, k, g, kh, gh, ʔ
affricates: ts, tʃ, dʒ
fricatives: s, ʃ, h, x
nasals: m, n, ŋ
lateral: l

The following initials were labialized: /k°, kh°, g°, gh°, n°, x°, ʔ°/. An initial consonant could be followed by *-l* and preceded by *s-* (sonants only): e.g. *bhlak* 'white' (Mod. Ch. *bai*); *smək* 'black'; *slän* 'mountain' (Mod. Ch. *shan*).

FINALS

The nasals: /p, t, k; r/.

Vowels

front: e, ɛ (+ a doubtful sound, represented here by /ɪ/)
back: ə, a, o, u

Tone

An even and a rising tone; words with /p, t, k/ ending had a specific tone, the nature of which is not clear.

MORPHOLOGY AND SYNTAX

A basic distinction is between 'full' words and 'empty' words. Pronouns count as empty words, as their exact meaning can be established only by context. The empty words – particles and pronouns – account for 25–30 per cent of all the words in a text of the central Classical period.

Given the total absence of any kind of inflection, and the polyvalent nature of Chinese words (a 'word' can be almost any part of speech in a proposition), word order is clearly of paramount importance: cf. *niǎo fēi* 'the bird flies'; *fēi niǎo* 'the flying bird': *míng kě míng* ('name' – 'can' – 'name': i.e. noun – modal verb – verb) in the first paragraph of the *Dao De Jing*, can be glossed as: *kě míng zhī míng* (modal verb – verb – relational particle – noun): 'the name that can be named'.

Pronoun

1st person: *yu* and *zhen* are inclusive; *wu* and *wo* are exclusive;
2nd person: *ru*, *ro*, *er*, *nai*;
3rd person: *qi*, *zhi*, *yan*; absence of a personal pronoun indicates 3rd person.

Choice of one or another pronoun seems to have depended on criteria which are no longer always clear. *Yu* and *zhen* are typically early Classical; *wu* and *wo* are associated with the later and post-Classical period.

Verb

The presence of paired verbs has been pointed out (e.g. Yaxontov 1965:36) which are homonyms in Modern Chinese but which varied in pronunciation in the early Classical language due to the presence, in one member of the pair, of a causative or resultative formant. For example:

{ 視 reconstructed as *dhiər* 'to see, look at'; modern reading *shì*;
示 reconstructed as *dhiəs* 'to show, exhibit'; modern reading *shì*;

{ 田 reconstructed as *dhen* 'field'; modern reading *tián*;
佃 reconstructed as *dhens* 'to till the land'; modern reading *tián*.

This phenomenon has been taken as evidence for an early Chinese inflectional system which was in desuetude by the Han period.

TENSE MARKERS

Past, past anterior, future. For example, imminent future action or state may be signalled by *jiāng*: *niǎo zhī jiāng sǐ*, *qí míng yě āi* 'when a bird is about to die, its song is sad' (*niǎo* 'bird', *sǐ* 'die', *qí* 'it(s)', *míng* 'song', *āi* 'mournful'). There is also a perfective marker.

PASSIVE VOICE

May be marked by *jiàn* (modern meaning: 'to see'): e.g. *Pen-Cheng-Guo jiàn shá* 'Pen-Cheng-Guo being slain'; *Sùi sì shí ér jiàn è yān qi zhōng yě yǐ* 'If a man of forty is disliked, that is how he is going to end' (literally: 'year – four – ten – and – suffer – dislike – then – he – end – indeed – complete').

The passive may be marked by the modal auxiliary *yú*: e.g. *shā rén* 'killed men/a man'; *shā **yú** rén* 'was killed by men/a man'.

Other modal auxiliaries are: *neng* 'to be able', *gǎn* 'to dare': e.g. *Wú shuí gǎn yuàn*? 'Against whom dare I grumble?'

PARTICLES

These form the major sector of the

虛 詞 *xū.ci*,

the 'empty words', and they are of crucial importance in the Classical style. On an average, about a third of the characters in a Wenli text are particles. They are sited throughout the discourse like signposts invested with three main functions.

1. Formally, they mark the onset, the suspension, and the conclusion of a proposition. In this role, they are not normally translatable.
2. They mark the proposition as negative, interrogative, or exclamatory; they intensify or limit its sense.
3. They have a large number of modal and prepositional (spatial and temporal) uses: concessive, causal, resultative, conditional, intentional, etc.

Some examples:

1. *fù* as initial particle:

   fù rén **zhě** jǐ yù lì **ér** lì rén
   'The man of virtue (*rén zhě*) wishing (*yù*) himself to be established (*lì*), establishes others (*rén* 'other people')'

2. *ér* as limiting agent + *yǐ fū* as final exclamatory particle:

   zǐ yūe; jūn zǐ **ěr** bù rén **zhě** you **yī fū**
   'The Master said: superior men (*jūn.zǐ*) who were not (*bù*) virtuous (*rén zhě*) there have been – and how!'

3. *ér* as concessive marker:

   zǐ yūe: pín **ér wú** yuàn nán
   'The Master said: to be poor (*pín*) and yet not (*wú*) grumble (*yuàn*) is hard (*nán*)'

Example of *zhī* as objective marker for referent known to audience:

zhī **zhī** zhě bù rú haò **zhī** zhě
'Those who know (*zhī*) it (= the Path) are not equal (*bù rú*) to those who love it'

Cf.

hǔ qiú bái shòu ér shí zhī
'a tiger caught many animals and ate them' (*hǔ* 'tiger', *qiú* 'look for and catch', *bái* 'hundred', *shòu* 'wild animal(s)', *shí* 'eat')

The very important particle *yǐ* has several meanings: e.g.

(a) By dint of, making use of: *yǐ mù zuò gōng* 'to use wood to make a bow' (*mù* 'tree, wood(en)', *zuò* 'make', *gōng* 'bow').
(b) To consider as: *yǐ guó shì wéi zhòng* 'to consider state affairs as being important' (*guó* 'country, state', *shì* 'affair(s)', *zhōng* 'important').
(c) In order to: *bǔ yǐ jué yí* 'divination (is used) in order to dispel doubt(s)' (*bǔ* 'to tell the future', 'soothsayer', *jué* 'to dispel', *yí* 'doubt(s)'.

SCRIPT

The main source for the character inventory used in the central Classical period is the *Shuo Wen* ('explain character') dictionary of the Later Han Dynasty (published *c.* AD 100). Here, the characters are arranged under 540 radicals (reduced to 214 in the late Ming Dynasty). The main categories of the *Shuo Wen* classification are:

1. Simple characters, a few hundred in number, sub-divided into:

(a) pictographs: e.g.

木 *mù* 'tree';

山 *shān* 'mountain';
門 *mén* 'gateway', 'door'.

(b) demonstratives: e.g.

二 *èr* 'two';
上 *shàng* 'above';
下 *xià* 'below'.

2. Compound characters, sub-divided into (a) ideograms, (b) phonograms:

(a) ideograms are made from two or more simple characters; e.g.

坐 *zuò* 'to sit' is formed from
人 *rén* 'man', reduplicated, placed over
土 *tǔ* 'earth'.
男 *nán* 'man' is made from
田 *tián* 'field' + 力 *lì* 'power'.

(b) phonograms – the most numerous class – are made from two elements: the radical fixing the character as belonging to this or that semantic group, and the phonetic which suggests the pronunciation. Example:

聞 *wén* 'to hear':

composed of radical

耳 *ěr* 'ear' + 門 *mén*.

That is, the following information is given: the word has to do with hearing, and should rhyme with /mén/.

The nature of the script, and one standard method of looking up characters in a Chinese dictionary, are now illustrated by means of (a) eight full-form characters in bold printed form; (b) the same eight characters in standard written form (not in the so-called 'grass script' *cǎozi*, which is a highly personalized cursive); (c) stroke order and number; (d) the radical system; (e) search procedure in a Chinese dictionary.

(a) Eight full-form printed characters:

中	海	茶	飯
zhōng	*hǎi*	*chá*	*fàn*
middle	sea	tea	food
錢	龍	聞	識
qián	*lóng*	*wén*	*shí*
money	dragon	hear	know

(b) The same characters in standard written form:

中	海	茶	飯
zhōng	*hăi*	*chá*	*fàn*
錢	龍	聞	識
qián	*lóng*	*wén*	*shí*

(c) Stroke order is illustrated here by means of four of the above characters:

chá

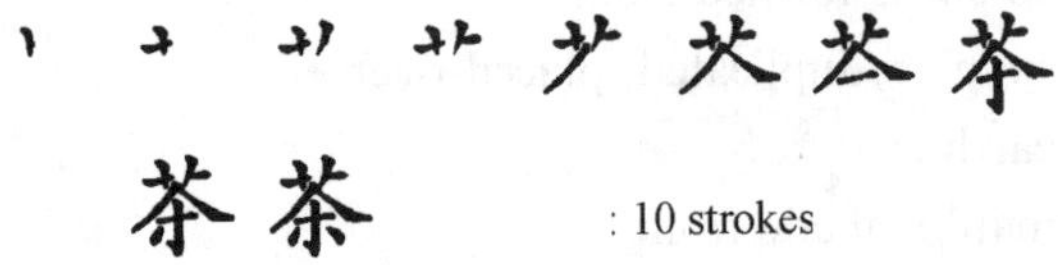

: 10 strokes

fán

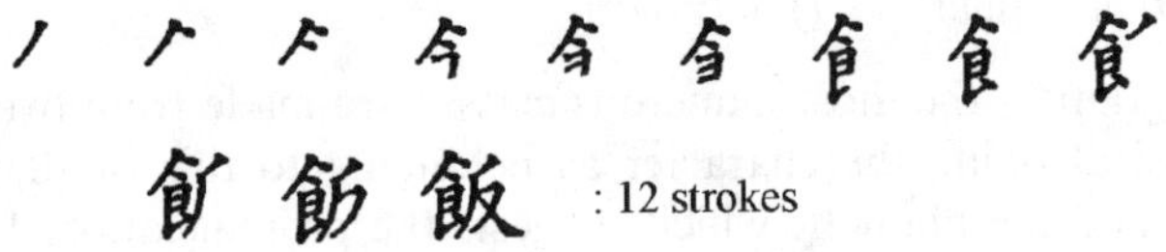

: 12 strokes

wén

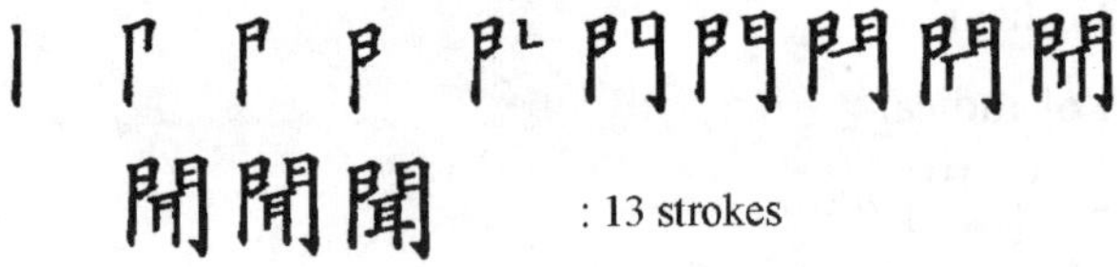

: 13 strokes

shi

: 18 strokes

It will be seen that by writing a Chinese character in the correct *order*, we arrive at the correct *number* of component strokes. The number of components underlies both the radical system and the indexing of characters in a Chinese dictionary.

(d) The radical system is set out in traditional form, as a table of 214 radicals, beginning with one stroke and rising to 17. This is reproduced from Matthews' *Chinese–English Dictionary*. The radical table is followed by a specific example – the list of all characters having the seven-stroke radical 言.

(e) To sum up: looking up characters in a Chinese dictionary involves the following steps.

1. Identify the radical; with experience this becomes automatic. The correct radical is usually obvious, but there are many cases where the radical is obscure, or where there is a choice.
2. Count the strokes remaining in the character after the radical has been subtracted.
3. Find the radical in the index of characters. All characters having this radical are listed in order of number of strokes; inspection in the correct section yields the desired character.

As example, we take the character 識 having the seven-stroke radical 言. After subtraction of radical 149, the character has twelve strokes. By inspection in the twelve-stroke section of radical 149 we find 識 numbered 5,825. Turning to 5,825 in the body of the dictionary, we find the character with translation and many examples of usage.

THE CHINESE SCRIPT

THE 214 RADICALS

1 stroke

1 一
2 丨
3 丶
4 丿
5 乙
6 亅

2 strokes

7 二
8 亠
9 人, 亻
10 儿
11 入
12 八
13 冂
14 冖
15 冫
16 几
17 凵

36 夕
37 大
38 女
39 子
40 宀
41 寸
42 小
43 尢, 兀, 尣
44 尸
45 屮
46 山
47 巛, 川, 巜
48 工
49 己
50 巾
51 干
52 幺
53 广
54 廴
55 廾
56 弋

74 月
75 木
76 欠
77 止
78 歹, 歺
79 殳
80 毋
81 比
82 毛
83 氏
84 气
85 水, 氵
86 火, 灬
87 爪, 爫
88 父
89 爻
90 爿
91 片
92 牙

110 矛
111 矢
112 石
113 示, 礻
114 禸
115 禾
116 穴
117 立

6 strokes

118 竹, ⺮
119 米
120 糸, 糹
121 缶
122 网, 罒, 罓
123 羊
124 羽
125 老
126 而

7 strokes

147 見
148 角
149 言
150 谷
151 豆
152 豕
153 豸
154 貝
155 赤
156 走
157 足
158 身
159 車
160 辛
161 辰
162 辵, 辶
163 邑, 阝
164 酉
165 釆

181 頁
182 風
183 飛
184 食
185 首
186 香

10 strokes

187 馬
188 骨
189 高
190 髟
191 門
192 鬯
193 鬲
194 鬼

11 strokes

195 魚

14 strokes

209 鼻
210 齊

15 strokes

211 齒

16 strokes

212 龍
213 龜

17 strokes

214 龠

18 刀,刂
19 力
20 勹
21 匕
22 匚
23 匸
24 十
25 卜
26 卩,㔾
27 厂
28 厶
29 又

3 strokes

30 口
31 囗
32 土
33 士
34 夂
35 夊

57 弓
58 彐,彑
59 彡
60 彳

4 strokes

61 心,忄,⺗
62 戈
63 戶
64 手,扌
65 支
66 攴,攵
67 文
68 斗
69 斤
70 方
71 无,旡
72 日
73 曰

93 牛,牜
94 犬,犭

5 strokes

95 玄
96 玉,王,王
97 瓜
98 瓦
99 甘
100 生
101 用
102 田
103 疋
104 疒
105 癶
106 白
107 皮
108 皿
109 目,罒

127 耒
128 耳
129 聿
130 肉,⺼
131 臣
132 自
133 至
134 臼
135 舌
136 舛
137 舟
138 艮
139 色
140 艸,艹
141 虍
142 虫
143 血
144 行
145 衣,衤
146 西

166 里

8 strokes

167 金
168 長,镸
169 門
170 阜,阝
171 隶
172 隹
173 雨,⻗
174 青
175 非

9 strokes

176 面
177 革
178 韋
179 韭
180 音

196 鳥
197 鹵
198 鹿
199 麥
200 麻

12 strokes

201 黃
202 黍
203 黑
204 黹

13 strokes

205 黽
206 鼎
207 鼓
208 鼠

RADICAL INDEX NOS. 147–150

148 角
149 言
150 谷

6
觥 3587
解 觧 626

7-18
觫 5504
觭 423
觷 5136
觳 2204
觴 5668
觶 970
觵 3587
觸 1416
觿 2445
〰

討 6157
訕 5634
訓 2914
訌 2385
記 431
訐 786

4
訛 4789
訥 4609
訟 5558
訦 5726
訩 2813
許 2825
訣 1700
訬 257

詢 3423
訶 2112
詒 2966
詁 3461
詞 6971
詀 131
詎 1552
評 5306
訴 5494
訹 2864
証 357
訾 6956
詆 6196
詠 7591
詖 5147
詈 3891

試 5798
詣 3011
誅 1352
詠 2308
詧 111
詳 2579
詡 2827
誄 4242
話 2215
詪 3329

7
說 5939
諙 2215
語 7651
誤 7204
誥 3288

諒 3947
諄 1490
論 4253
諊 1591
誶 5529
諏 6804
調 6298
諉 7101
誼 2994
誹 2108
誕 6051
諗 5733
課 3394
談 6078
諍 370
諂 174

諟 5795
諣 7324
諫 847
諜 6322
謀 4578
諼 2875
諶 5726
諧 2546
諡 5802
諝 7538
諸 1362
諞 2839
謂 7079
諛 7613
諻 2329
諾 4747

謐 4468
謚 5802
謠 7290
謄 6185
謅 1308
謊 2273
謔 4736
謎 4451

11
謳 4823
謫 279
謪 5674
謷 62
謾 4338
[illegible] 6734

譎 1702
䜌 4211
譁 2218
譚 6066

13
譟 5443
警 1139
譖 5386
譭 2329
譯 3064
議 3006
譫 152
譬 5167

14
譽 7617

17
讖 181
讒 161
讓 3085
讕 3797

18-22
讙 2268
讚 6681
讞 7370
讜 6096
讀 6522

150
谷 3483
谺 2513

CHINESE, MODERN STANDARD

INTRODUCTION

Essentially, Modern Standard Chinese is the Northern (Beijing) form of Chinese, written in the Classical Chinese script with certain modifications (*see* **Script**, below).

During the Sung–Yuan Dynasties (twelfth to fourteenth centuries AD) *báihuà*, 'plain speech', a form of Chinese much closer to the spoken language than the Wenli literary style, began to be used for literary purposes, e.g. in the prose passages in the Yuan drama (see, for example, the well-known *Dou E Yuan* by Guan Han-Ching). *Báihuà* was also the vehicle for the prose narrative in the great Ming novels, e.g. Hong Lou Meng, the 'Dream of the Red Chamber', and Shui-hu Chuan, the 'Water Margin'.

After the fall of the Manchu Dynasty and the establishment of the Republic (1911), the movement for a national standardized language gathered momentum, accompanied by a parallel drive for the replacement of the Chinese script by some sort of phonetic alphabet. Both of these requirements were seen as indispensable first steps if universal education was ever to become a reality in China. A key part was played by the cultural revolution known as the 4 May Movement of 1919 and the implementation of the proposals for a national language first formulated by Hu Shih in the pages of the periodical *Xin Chingnian* ('New Youth'). Finally, in 1949, *báihuà*, now known as *pŭtōnghuà*, 'common language', was officially adopted as the national language of the People's Republic of China.

SCRIPT

For notes on the origins and nature of the Chinese written character *see* **Chinese, Classical**. Modern Standard Chinese uses the same character with the following modifications:

1. Many of the ten to twelve thousand characters in use have been 'abbreviated'; i.e. the number of strokes has been reduced, often considerably, e.g. from 16 to 5, from 19 to 9: e.g.

   爲 > 为 = (co-verb): wèi 'on behalf of'

   難 > 难 = nán 'difficult';

   禮 > 礼 = lĭ 'propriety, ceremony'

2. The number of radicals has been reduced from 214 to 186. Many characters used in Classical Chinese have been discarded.

The officially adopted system of romanization is known as *pīnyīn*. The tones are indicated by diacritics: macron for high level, acute for abrupt rising, rounded breve for low rising, grave for falling.

PHONOLOGY

Consonants

INITIALS

stops: p, b, t, d, k, g
affricates: tç, ts, tʂ
fricatives: f, ç, s, ʂ, ʐ, χ
nasals: m, n, ŋ
lateral: l
semi-vowels: j, w

Phonetically /b, d, g/ are *unvoiced* and non-aspirate; /p, t, k/ are strongly aspirated. All stops occur with labialization.

/tç, ts, tʂ/ are notated as *j*, *z*, *zh*, with aspirated correlatives notated as *q*, *c*, *ch*. /ç/ is notated as *x*, /ʂ/ as *sh*, /ʐ/ as *r*, and /χ/ as *h*.

FINALS

The vowels (see below), the nasals /n, ŋ/ following various combinations of vowels, and -/r/.

Vowels

i, ɪ, ɛ, ə, a, o, u, y; *pīnyīn* /i/ is [ɪ] after the retroflex sounds. /ə/ is notated as *e* or *u*: e.g. *men* /mən/, *dun* /d°ən/.

Tone

There are four tones in Modern Standard Chinese: (1) high even; (2) rising, crescendo; (3) low dipping then rising; (4) falling from high level, diminuendo.

TONAL SANDHI

A tone 3 before another tone 3 changes to 2: e.g. *suó.yĭ* 'therefore', in citation form, both *suŏ* and *yĭ* are tone 3. Second components in disyllabic words are neutralized: e.g. *xièxiẻ* 'thank you'; *wǎnshảng* 'evening'.

MORPHOLOGY AND SYNTAX

There is no inflection of any kind. Formally, there is nothing to distinguish any one part of speech from another. Meaning in a Chinese sentence depends on due logical order assisted by certain syntactic markers such as *ba* (indicating object), *de* (many functions; see below), *le* (past marker). Grammars of modern Chinese distinguish the following parts of speech:

nouns, pronouns, numerals and measure words, transitive verbs, intransitive verbs, stative verbs, resultative verbs, auxiliary verbs and co-verbs, localizers, particles.

Noun

May be monosyllabic: these include the oldest strata of the language: e.g. *mā* 'mother'; *mǎ* 'horse'; *chá* 'tea'; *rén* 'person'; *rì* 'sun'; *mù* 'tree'. Disyllabic: *xiān.shěng* 'first-born' = 'you' (in polite address); *dì.fǎng* 'place'; *Zhong.wen* 'Chinese language'; *péng.yǒu* 'friend'. Trisyllabic: *jiě.fàng.jūn* 'Army of Liberation'; *bàn.gōng.shì* 'office'. Polysyllabic: *bǎi.huò.shāng.diàn.* 'department store' ('hundred-goods-business-place').

A pluralizing suffix *men* is available, but it is used only for pronouns and for groups; e.g. a speech may begin with the words *Tóng.zhì.**men** péng.you.**-men*** 'Comrades and friends!' The suffix is not attached to singular nouns: i.e. *shū* 'book' or 'books'.

There are a couple of dozen classifiers for specific use with objects of various types and dimensions; they are bound forms, e.g. *běn*, *kuài*, *bēi*, etc.: *nèi liǎng běn shū* 'these two books'; *zhèi zhāng zhuōzǐ* 'this table'; *yí.kuài táng* 'a piece of candy'. *Ge* is an all-purpose classifier which can replace most of the others, unless the classifier is being used specifically without a referent: cf. *sì běn* 'four books' (the classifier identifies the referent as books).

Adjective

Adjectives in Chinese are stative verbs. If used attributively they precede the noun, often followed by *de*: e.g. *lì.shǐ duǎn* ***de*** *guó.jiā* 'a country with a ṣhort (*duǎn*) history (*lìshǐ*)'. The marker *de* is a ubiquitous and very important element in Modern Standard Chinese which has the following main functions:

1. Marking attributive material, as in the above example: cf. *jīn. tián dě bào* 'today's paper'.
2. To mark alienable possession: e.g. *wǒ.de shū* 'my book' (but *wǒ.**Ø** fù* 'my father').
3. Hence, to form relative clauses preceding head-word: e.g. *wǒ.měn yǐ.jīng xué.guo.**de** cái.liǎo* 'the material we have already studied' (*xué* 'to study'; *guo* = perfective marker; *cái.liǎo* 'material').
4. After a stative verb if this is itself modified, e.g. by *hěn* 'very': cf. *shì hǎo péng.yǒu* 'is a good friend', but *hěn dà.**de** zhuōzǐ* 'a very big table'; *hěn hǎo.**de** jià.qiǎn* 'a very good price'.
5. As loose referent: e.g. *wǒ mǎi.**de*** 'the things that I bought'.
6. Categorizing particle in final position: e.g. *wǒ shi zuò fēi.jī lái.**de*** 'it was by plane that I came' = 'I came by plane'.

Pronoun

PERSONAL PRONOUN

Sing. 1 *wǒ*, 2 *nǐ*/*nín*, 3 *tā*; plural: add *men* to sing.: *wǒ.měn*, etc. These forms function both as subject and as object: e.g. *tā gěi wǒ yi.běn shū* 'he gives me a book'.

DEMONSTRATIVE PRONOUN/ADJECTIVE, OR 'SPECIFIER'

zhèi 'this', *nà/nèi* 'that'. When these are used with nouns, classifiers are inserted between the specifier and the noun: e.g. *zhèi ge rén* 'this person'; *nèi wǔ běn shū* 'those five books'.

INTERROGATIVE PRONOUN

shúi 'who?'; *shen.me* /shəmmə/, 'what?'

Numerals

1–10: *yi* (with movable tone), *èr, sān, sì, wǔ, liù, qī, bā, jiǔ, shí*; 12–19: *shí* + unit; 20 *èr.shí*; 100 *bǎi*; 1,000 *qiān*; 10,000 *wàn*.

Verb

Formally invariable; there are no tenses. Continuing or progressive action can be marked by *zhě*: e.g. *wǒ yuàn.yi̊ zhàn.zhe̊* 'I prefer to remain standing'. Impending action may be indicated by *jiù* (*yào*); the past by *gůo*: e.g. *Ní qǔ.**guo** Zhōng.guo.ma?* 'Have you ever been in China?' (*Zhong.guo* 'China'); *Wǒ méi qǔ.**guo*** 'I have never been there.'

PERFECTIVE ASPECT

le marks a change in a situation: e.g.

Dōng.xo̊ guì.**le** 'Things (lit. 'east–west') have become expensive'
Wǒ.men huì shuō Zhong.guo.huà **le** 'We can speak Chinese now' (*scil.* until now, we couldn't)
Tā hē.**le** sān píng jiǔ 'He drank up three bottles of wine'
Qì.chē pèng.zåi shù.shång **le** 'The car (*qì.chē*) ran into a tree (*shù*).'

CO-VERBS

E.g. *zài* (locational), *yòng* (instrumental), *gěi* (dative), *bǎ* ('to handle something, hold in the hands'), etc. These often have to be translated by prepositions in English: e.g. *zài fàn.guǎn.r chī.fàn* 'to eat in a restaurant'; *yòng kùai.zi̊ chī.fàn* 'to eat with chopsticks'; *wǒ gěi tā dǎ diàn.huà* 'I rang him'.

VERB + BOUND (LATENT) OBJECT

E.g. *kàn.shū* 'look at – book' → 'read'; *shuō.huà* 'say – word' → 'speak'; *chī.fàn* 'eat – rice' → 'eat'. These are separable: e.g. *tā kàn wan shū le* 'after he had finished reading . . . '.

STATIVE VERBS

E.g. *dà* 'to be big', *lěng* 'to be cold': *Jīn.tiān zhēn lěng* 'It's really cold today.'

COPULA

shì. often optional in positive, obligatory in negative: e.g. *wǒ* (*shì*) *Běijīng.rén* 'I am from Beijing'; neg. *wǒ**búshì** Běijīng.rén*.

DIRECTIONAL COMPLEMENTARY VERBS

lái 'to come', *qǔ* 'to go': e.g. *Tā yǐ.jīng dǎ.diàn.huà.**lai**.le* 'He has already rung up (incoming call)'; *nèi.běn.shū ràng.tā mǎi.**qu**.le* lit. 'that-book – by-him – bought-went' = 'he bought the book and went off'.

POTENTIAL INFIX

de/bu: e.g. *kàn.**de**.jiàn* 'able to see'; *gǎn.**bu**.shàng* 'unable to overtake'.

NEGATION

The general marker is *bu*; the verb *yǒu* 'to have' is always negated by *méi*, never by *bu*: e.g. *Gào.sů tā méi.yǒu yòng.chů* 'It's no use telling him.'

PASSIVE

There are various markers, *bèi*, *ràng*, *jiào*, *gěi*: e.g. *tā bèi chéng.fá.le yǐ.hòu* 'after he had been punished' (*chéng.fá* 'punish'; *yǐ.hòu* 'after').

MODAL VERBS

E.g. *yīng.gāi* = *bì.děi* 'have to', *huì* 'can', *xiǎng* 'want to', etc.: e.g. *wǒ.men yīng.gāi/bì.děi yóng.yǔan jì.dẻ*... 'we must always remember...'.

Four-character expressions

The Chinese have always been very fond of using set phrases consisting of four characters. These lapidary sayings were, and are, particularly popular as birthday and festive greetings, congratulations, etc.: e.g.

蟠桃集慶

pán.táo jí.qìng, which may be translated as 'long life and happiness galore'; *pán.táo* is a reference to the peach tree which grew by the *yáo.chí*, the Lake of Gems, in the Kunlun palace of the Queen Mother of the West. The fruit of the tree conferred immortality.

The sociolinguistic domain of a later and more mundane age is also punctuated by this persistent rhythm. Thus, in the 1960s, the vigilant proletarian had to eschew *sān xiáng yī miè* 'three capitulations and one cut off', observe *sì hǎo lián.duì* the 'four goods', and the *sān.bā tzuò.fēng* the 'three-eight working style', and keep his eye open for *yāo.mó gǔi.guài* 'monsters and freaks' and *niú.gǔi shé.chén* 'ox-demons and supernatural snakes', i.e. people of anti-Mao persuasion.

Word order

ba: although Chinese is essentially a SVO language, SOV is not at all uncommon. The co-verb *bǎ* provides a way of marking the object in inverted order: e.g. *wǒ **bǎ** qì.chē mǎi.**le*** 'I bought the car'.

約翰福音傳

第一章 一 元始有道、道與上帝共在、道卽上帝、二 是道元始與上帝共在也、三 萬物以道而造、凡受造者、無不以之而造、四 生在道中、生也者、人之光、五 光照於暗、暗者弗識之〇六 有上帝所遣者、名約翰、七 其至爲光作證、使衆以之而信、八 約翰非光、特爲光證耳、九 眞光者臨世、照萬人者也、十 其在世、世以之而創、世不識

Wenli

生命之道

1 宇宙被造以前，道已經存在；道與上帝同在，與上帝相同。2 在太初，道就與上帝同在。3 上帝藉着他創造萬有；在整個創造中，沒有一樣不是藉着他造的。4 道就是生命的根源，這生命把光賜給人類。5 光照射黑暗，黑暗從來沒有勝過光。

6 有一個人，名叫約翰，是上帝所差遣的使者。7 他來告訴人關於那光的事，目的要使大家聽見他的信息而相信。8 他本身不是那光，而是要爲光作證。

Guóyǔ

CHINESE, DIALECTS

Thanks to the large number of people who speak it – 1,125 million at present – and by virtue of its supreme cultural status, the language which has been described in the previous four articles has come to be known, and rightly so, as 'the Chinese language'. Organically, however, it is one member of a very extensive complex or continuum of dialects, all of which differ in varying degrees from 'Chinese', in some cases to the point of mutual unintelligibility. It is doubtful indeed whether it is appropriate to call the Amoy Min dialect, for example, 'a dialect of Chinese'. At this level of mutual unintelligibility, one is really dealing with two languages; French and Portuguese might be regarded as comparable. It should also be remembered that these minor Sinitic languages are spoken by very large populations – 80 million Wu, 55 million Yue, with comparable figures for the others.

There follow here brief profiles, mainly phonological, of the following members of the Sinitic group of Sino-Tibetan: Xiang, Hakka, Wu, Min, Gan. For Yue (Cantonese) which is by far the most important form of non-Mandarin Chinese, *see* **Yue** (Cantonese).

XIANG

The Xiang speech area centres on Hunan, and falls into two broad dialectal divisions. In one of these – urban or 'new' Xiang – the diachronic processes of consonantal mutation and lexical replacement have been accelerated by close contact with Modern Standard Chinese; so much so that, as Ramsey points out (1987: 97), between urban Xiang and Modern Standard Chinese there is a considerable degree of mutual intelligibility.

On the phonological plane, urban Xiang has replaced the voiced stops /b, d, g/, with the homorganic unvoiced, non-aspirated /p, t, k/. The voiced stops are retained in 'old' Xiang, the dialect form associated with the more backward rural communities. Thus, while the mountain peasant will talk about his ***din*** 'field', the Xiang trader and his Mandarin counterpart both call it *tián*.

About 50 million people speak the two forms of the Xiang language.

Changsha speech may be taken as typical of urban Xiang, which has six tones.

HAKKA

The Hakka are the descendants of northern Han stock who migrated during the twelfth century to southern China, where they are now very widely distributed in Guangdong, Fujian, and Jiangxi. They have long since abandoned their own form of Northern Chinese for the speech forms of their southern neighbours. The total number of Hakka speakers is estimated at something under 40 million.

Hakka has no voiced stops. The surd–aspirate series is represented by /p, p', t, t', k, k'/, with the affricates /ts, ts'/. There is no /r/. /k/-final is frequent. The Hakka reflex of the old semi-voiced stop is an aspirated surd: thus Middle Chinese *bak*, MS *bái*, Hakka *p'ak* 'white'; Middle Chinese *di*, MS *dì*, Hakka *t'i* 'younger brother'.

Final /y/ in MS is represented by Hakka /i/: MS *qū* 'to run', Hakka *ts'i*. MS /f-/ is retained in literary Hakka, but becomes /p-/ in the colloquial: MS *fēi* 'to fly', literary Hakka *fī*, colloquial *pī*.

Hakka has six vowels and six tones. The tonal system is *sui generis*, in that syllables with initial nasal or /l/ are frequently first (level) tone, a sequence normally eschewed in Sinitic languages.

WU

Wu is the form of Chinese that is spoken by about 80 million people in Shanghai and its surroundings, and in the Yangzi delta.

The distinguishing characteristic of the Wu dialects lies in the extension of the labial, dental, and velar initial stop series to include a voiced aspirate member. Thus, where Mandarin Chinese has /p, ph; t, th; k, kh/ notated in *pīnyīn* as *b, p, t, d, k, g*, Wu has /p, ph, bh; t, th, dh; k, kh gh/.

The palatal affricate series is also extended by the addition of /ẓh/ to /tṣ/, tṣh/.

Aspiration of the voiced member is carried through the syllable thus initiated, whose tone and vocal pitch are always low.

Wu has two varieties of glottal fricative /h/ and /ɦ/. Possible finals are the vowels, the glottal stop, and velar /ŋ/.

Vowels: thirteen, including a buzzing alveolar fricative, notated in transcription as *z*, which occurs in association with the dental affricates and fricatives.

Seven or eight tones are general in Wu, except in Shanghai, where only five are used. Citation tones are subject to a very elaborate system of tonal sandhi in connected speech.

As in the Yue dialects, the direct object precedes the indirect.

MIN

Min languages are spoken by around 40–50 million people in Fujian, along the south China seaboard, and in Taiwan. The Amoy dialect is perhaps the best known of the mainland forms.

The Amoy consonantal inventory shows the surd – aspirate surd – voiced stop sequence for the labial, dental, and velar series, as in Wu, but /d/ is missing, and /dz/ is present. Apart from /j/, the entire palatal series, present in Wu, is also lacking in Min, which is one of the most archaic forms of Sinitic.

There are substantial differences between literary and colloquial pronunciation in southern Min. The literary reading of standard Chinese characters retains (a) the nasals, and (b) /p, t, k/ in final position; in the colloquial language these are reduced to (a) nasalized vowels, and (b) to the glottal stop. Thus, 白 MS *bái* 'white' is read as *pik* in literary, as *pe'* in colloquial southern Min. Similarly, 門 *men* 'gate', 'door' is *bun* in literary, *bɔ̃* in colloquial.

/f/ is absent, replaced in literary Min by /h/ or /x/, in colloquial by /p/ or /p'/: e.g. MS *fēi* 'fly', literary Min *hui/xi*, colloquial *pe/puei*. MS *fu* 'rich', literary Min *hu/xu*, colloquial *pu/p'ou*.

The south Min reflex of an original nasal sonant in initial position is a voiced stop: cf. *mǎ* 'horse', Min *be*; MS *niú* 'cow', Min *gu*.

There are six vowels (/o/ and /ɔ/ are distinguished), which can be nasalized.

The Amoy dialect has seven tones, which undergo extensive sandhi in connected speech.

GAN

The Gan complex of dialects lies in Jiangxi, with some spread into adjacent regions of Hunan. In southern Jiangxi, Gan merges into Hakka; in the west of the province, into Xiang. About 25 million people speak one or another form of the Gan language.

There are six/seven tones. Each of the level, falling, and 'entering' tones has two registers, high and low; there is a single-register rising tone.

The group lacks the voiced stops /b, d, g/, which are characteristic of the neighbouring Wu dialects (*see* **Wu**, above). Treatment of final /p, t, k/ varies from one dialect to another, with complete retention found only in the extreme south. Cf. Middle Chinese *bak*, MS *bai* 'white'; Southern Gan *p'ak*; Middle Chinese *tap*, MS *dá* 'answer': Southern Gan *tap/tat*, both of which have the high entering tone. Final *p* and *k* tend towards *t*.

Phonological reductionism is more advanced in some Gan dialects than in others. Thus *fot* (MS *hŭo* 'life') in Central Gan becomes *uot* in Nan-chang on the Fujian border.

CHIPEWYAN

INTRODUCTION

Chipewyan belongs to the Northern branch of the Athabaskan family (*see* **Athabaskan**). It is the main Athabaskan language in Canada, but is now spoken by fewer than 5,500. The following sketch is based on the study of the language by Li Fang-Kuei in Hojier (1946).

PHONOLOGY

Consonants

Central to the Chipewyan inventory of sounds is the series voiced stop – unvoiced stop – ejective unvoiced stop + associated affricates: e.g.

d	t	t'
dδ	tθ	t'θ'
dz	ts	t's'

There are five laterals, /dl, tł, t'ł, ł, l/, and five velars + labialized counterparts, /g, k, k', x, γ; g°, k°, k'°, x°, γ°/. Syllabic finals are /n/ and the fricative series; /r/ cannot be initial.

Vowels

short: a, ε, e, ı, o, u
long: aː, εː, iː, uː

All, except /e/, can be nasalized (shown by cedilla).

There are two tones: high, marked by acute, and low (unmarked).

MORPHOLOGY AND SYNTAX

For a general note on Athabaskan structure, *see* **Athabaskan**. Nouns in Chipewyan can be simple: e.g. *bes* 'knife', *tθε* 'stone', 'pipe'; + suffix: *bą́n.ε* 'war party'; or marked for inalienable possession: *sε.γú* 'my tooth'.

Verbal forms may be nominalized by the relative particle *-i*: e.g. *ya.ł.tei* 'he speaks': *ya.ł.tei.**i*** 'he who speaks' = 'preacher'.

Pronoun

	Singular	*Possessive*	*Plural*	*Possessive*
1	si	sε-	nuhni	nuhε

2	nen	nɛ-	nuhni	nuhɛ
3	–	bɛ-	–	hubɛ
obviative	–	yɛ-	–	–
indefinite	–	’ɛ	–	–

The possessive suffix *ɛ́* may be added: e.g. *sɛ.ṭθ̣en.ɛ́* ‘my bone’; *dɛne.bą́n.ɛ́* ‘Indian war party’.

Various locative and directional relationships are expressed by means of postpositions: e.g. *-a* ‘for’, *-ɛ́ł* ‘with’, *ṭsén* ‘towards’. Examples: *sɛ.ṭsén* ‘towards me’; *sas.ṭsén* ‘towards the bear’; *xíł.ṭsén* ‘towards darkness’ = ‘evening’.

DEMONSTRATIVE PRONOUN

diri ‘this’, ‘these’; *’ɛyi* ‘that’, ‘those’.

INTERROGATIVE PRONOUN

The stem is *-dla-*, *-dláγ-*, *-dlį́-* + indefinite pronoun ’: e.g. *’ɛdláγį* ‘who?’; *’ɛdláγe* ‘what?’

RELATIVE PRONOUN

ṭahi ‘that which’; *ṭąhį* ‘the one who . . . ’.

Numerals

There are two sets of numerals, the first for counting things, the second for persons. Thus, *’į́łáγɛ* ‘one thing’, *’į́łą́γį* ‘one person’. Velar/nasal alternation is present: *taγɛ* ‘three things’, *tane* ‘three people’; *sasųláγɛ* ‘four things’, *sasųláne* ‘four people’.

Verb

For a general survey of Athabaskan verbal structure, *see* **Athabaskan**; *compare* **Apache** and **Navajo**.

In Chipewyan there are three aspects – imperfective, perfective, future – and five modes – neutral, punctual/transitional (Li calls this mode ‘momentaneous’), durative, habitual, progressive. Not all stems have these five modes; some have as few as two. Conversely, not all modes appear in three aspects. A rather full system may be illustrated by setting out the modal/aspectual forms of the verb meaning ‘to handle a long object such as a stick’:

neutral mode: imperfective *tą*, perfective *tą́*, future *tą́*;
punctual/transitional: imperfective *tį́*, perfective, *tą*, future *tą́*;
durative: imperfective *ten*, perfective *tą*, future *tą́*;
customary: two forms only: *tį́* – *ti*;

progressive: two forms only: *tį́ł – tįł*.

Aspectual variation may be purely tonal, as in the neutral mode set out above, or tonal plus vocalic alternation, with or without nasalization. Cf. the punctual/transitional forms of the verb meaning 'to handle a round, solid object':

'áih – 'ą – 'ał

This stem also illustrates a fairly regular feature – nasalization in the perfective aspect. Cf. the Chipewyan copula: *lɛ́ – lį – lɛ́*. The perfective often drops a final *θ*, *r*, *n*: e.g. 'to think' has *δen*, perfective *δį́*. Final *ł* is often found in the progressive mode (cf. *tį́ł*, above). In general, however, stem modulation is unpredictable; see Li op. cit.: 408.

THE VERB COMPLEX

(*Compare* **Apache**, **Navajo**.) In the case of Chipewyan, ten components precede the stem. Working backwards from the stem, these are: slot 10: occupied by the classifiers -Ø-, *-d-*, *-ł-*, *-l-*. Sandhi with stem initial is frequent, e.g. *-d-* + ' > *-ṭ-*. As in Navajo, *-ł-* is the transitive/causative classifier, *-l-* is medio-passive. Cf.

kún θɛ.**ł**.tsį 'he has made the fire' (*kún* 'fire', cf. Navajo *ko*')
hi.**1**.záih 'it is being hooked' (cf. *hį.ł.sáih* 'hook it!')

Slot 9 contains the pronominal subject forms, of which there are two sets: one for verbs using Ø and *ł* classifiers, a second set for the *d* and *l* classes. The two sets share *-s-* as 1st p. sing. imperfective and future, and *-n*(ɛ)-as 2nd p. sing. In the perfective aspect, the Ø/*ł* set has *-i-*/*-i*(*ł*)- as 1st sing., the *d*/*l* set has *-s-*. The 2nd person dual/plural *-uh-* is also common to both sets in all three aspects. As in Apache, the 3rd singular/dual/plural marker is always Ø. For example, here are the first, second, and third singular persons of the theme *cɛ́... tį* 'to eat':

	Imperfective	*Perfect*	*Future*
1	cɛ.s.tį	cɛ.γɛ.s.tį	cɛ.γwa.s.tį
2	cɛ.nɛ.tį	cɛ.γį.tį	cɛ.γwu.tį
3	cɛ.Ø.tį	cɛ.γɛ.Ø.tį	cɛ.γwa.Ø.tį

where the second person forms show assimilation of aspect and pronominal markers. *γɛ* in this example is a perfective aspectual prefix occupying slot 8 in the verbal complex. Other aspectual prefixes are: *θɛ-* (perfective), *nɛ-* (punctual/transitional), *γwa-* (future). E.g. from *tsi* 'to make it (a single object)' the future 1st person singular is *γwa.s.tsi* 'I shall make (it)'.

Slot 7 contains the modal prefixes: e.g. *tɛ-*/(*h*)*í-*/*hɛ-*, which are inceptive: cf. *d.í.gai* 'it is turning white'; *dɛ.í.γ.wa.gai* > *dúgai* 'it will turn white'. *nɛ-*/*lɛ-*/*dɛ-* is adjectival: *dɛ.l.ba* 'it is grey'; *łɛ.kan* 'it is sweet'; *nɛ.zų* 'it is good'.

(*h*)*u*- indicates target or objective: *hu.Ø.s.tas* 'I am shooting at him' where *s* is the first person subject marker, Ø marks the third person object.

Slots 5 and 6 contain third person pronominal subjects, and pronominal objects, which are formally identical with the possessive prefixes used with nominals. The third person object form *yɛ* is used only when the subject is itself third person: *yɛ.łtsi* 'he makes it'. Cf. *ṭsɛ.sɛ́.nį.ł.θer* 'he wakened me', where *ṭsɛ... θer* is the theme, and *nį*- is the *ł* class perfective reflex of the punctual/transitional marker *nɛ*-).

If noun stems are incorporated in the verbal complex, they are put into slot 4: e.g. *tθí* 'head', *na* 'eye', *sa* 'sun', *bá* 'war party', *xu* 'tooth'. Cf. *ná**bą́**hu.dɛ́ł* 'we shall go on the war-path' (*hu.dɛ́ł* 'we shall go'). The verbal complex is introduced, where relevant, by indirect/locative/adverbial material: indirect object plus governing postposition in slot 1, prefixes in slot 2. Li (1946) gives several excellent examples; e.g.

bɛ.γá.yɛ́.nił.tį 'I have given her to him'

Here, *bɛ* is the third person pronominal object governed by the postposition *γa* 'to'; *yɛ* is the third person object marker; *ni* is a fusion of *nɛ*, the punctual/transitional marker, plus *i*, the first person singular subject marker; *ł* is the transitive classifier; the stem *tį* denotes 'to handle something animate'.

A general negating adverb is *hile*: *nɛ.zų* 'it is good', *nɛ.zų hile* 'it is not good'.

Postposed particles: these include -*i*, a relative formant, which usually copies *ṭąhį* 'that which', 'he who', 'the one'. Li gives the example:

ṭąhį sas.xɛ́ł θɛtį.**i** 'the one who was sleeping with the bear'
(*sas* 'bear', Navajo *shash*, *xɛ́ł* postposition 'with', *θɛtį* 'he is sleeping')

dɛ́ 'if', *dɛ́.kúlú* 'even if':

nɛtcá.híle.dɛ́.kúlú 'even if it is not big'
(*nɛtcá* 'it is big')

Word order

Word order in Chipewyan is best treated in terms of the verbal complex (see above).

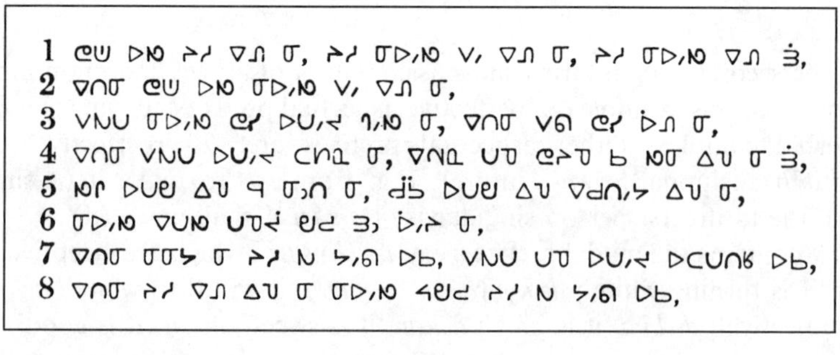

CHOCTAW

INTRODUCTION

Choctaw is a member of the Muskogean branch of the Macro-Algonquian family. Originally, the Choctaw lands were in south-eastern Mississippi and Louisiana. Here they were in contact with the French, with whom they sided in the sixteenth- to seventeenth-century wars against the British and against other Indian tribes. In the period of white expansion westwards, the Choctaw were evicted from their homelands and exiled to Oklahoma, along with the Cherokee, the Seminole, and some other tribes. Today they number about 10,000. Choctaw is very close to Chickasaw; a trade language known as *mobilian*, based on Chickasaw/Choctaw, was in use in Mississippi and Louisiana in the nineteenth century.

Translation of the Bible into Choctaw began in the early nineteenth century. A major role was played by Cyrus Byington, whose *Choctaw Grammar* – completed in 1865, after 30 years' work – was published in Philadelphia in 1870.

SCRIPT

Roman.

PHONOLOGY

Consonants

stops: p, b, t, k
affricate: tʃ
fricatives: f, s, ʃ, h
nasals: m, n
laterals: l, ł
semi-vowels: w, j

Byington (1870) distinguishes /k'/ and /x/ as allophones of /k/.

Vowels

Byington's series:

long and short: aː, ă (= [ʌ]), eː, ɛː, iː, ɪ, oː, uː, ŭ
nasalized: ã, ĩ, õ, ũ
diphthongs: ai, au

The main function of nasalization seems to be to emphasize or define more closely.

Stress

Stress in polysyllables tends to penultimate.

MORPHOLOGY AND SYNTAX

Article

Suffixed *-a*/*o*- combine with a variety of particles to express different degrees and shades of specificity, distinction, sequence, and mood (optative, presumptive, etc.). Basically, *-a* seems to define, *-o* to distinguish: e.g. *wak.a* 'the cow'; *wak.o* 'a/the cow' (e.g. not a horse). *-a* + *t* forms a frequent postpositive article: *at*, *ăt*, *et*, often following *-o* + *-k*, which is a limiting and precisioning particle: e.g. *hatak okăt* 'the man/men'; *hatak okăto* 'as for the man/men'.

The articles are applied to a vocalic stem, e.g. *peni* 'boat': *peni.ăt* 'the/a boat'; *peni.o* 'a boat' (not something else); *peni.măt* 'the boat also'; *peni.oš* 'the boat already referred to'.

Noun

The noun does not change for plural; numeral can be supplied or *lawa* 'many': e.g. *wak* 'a cow'; *wak tuklo* 'two cows'; *wak lawa* '(some) cows'.

POSSESSION

Appositional, e.g. *hatak kăllo* 'a man's strength'; *iti hishi* 'leaf of a tree'; *Chahta okla* 'the Choctaw nation'. The possessive marker may be inserted for alienable possession: e.g. *Chan in čuka* 'John his house'.

Adjective

As attribute, adjective follows noun, and is marked for number. The article is then transferred from noun to adjective: e.g. *hatak ăt mintih* 'a man is coming'; *hatak ačukma yăt mintih* 'a good man is coming'. Plural forms, e.g. of *čito* 'large': *hočito*; *yuštololi* 'short': *yuštolušli*; *falaia* 'long': *hofaloha*.

The negating particle *-ik-* may be prefixed to adjectives: e.g. *hatak kăllo* 'a strong man': *hatak **ikh**ăllo* 'a weak man'.

COMPARISON

Choctaw has an elaborate series of gradations, specifying by how much and in what way something exceeds something else.

Pronoun

EMPHATIC PERSONAL PRONOUNS

	Singular	*Plural*
1	ăno	*excl.* pišno, *incl.* hăppišno
2	čišno	hăčišno

The third person forms are supplied from the demonstrative series: *ilăppa*, *yămma*.

POSSESSIVE AFFIXES

Series 1: for inalienable possession; for alienable, add *-m*:

	Singular	*Plural*
1	sa- (si/a/o)	*excl.* pi-, *incl.* hăpi-
2	či-	hăči-
3	i-	i-

Examples: *sa(h) foni* 'my bone'; *a.ski* 'my grandmother'; *im issuba* 'his horse'.

The series 1 forms also provide the objective pronominal forms used with transitive verbs. Note, however, that for this purpose, the 3rd person sing./pl. marker is Ø, not *i-*. Examples of their use are given below, following series 2.

Series 1 forms are negated by the particle *ik*: *ik.**s*** – *ik.**či*** – *ik.**pi*** – *ik.**hači***.

Series 2: provides the bound forms which act as the subjects of active verbs: with variants

	Singular	*Plural*
1	-li (suffix)	*excl.* i(l)-, *incl.* iloh-
2	iš-	haiš-
3	Ø	Ø

These have negative forms as follows: singular 1 *ak*, 2 *čik*; plural 1 *heloh*, 2 *hačik*. Cf.

Ø.pisa.**li**.h 'I see him/them'; negative: **ak**.**Ø**.pisa.h
hači.pisa.**li**.h 'I see you (pl.)'; negative: **ak**.hači.pisa.h
iš.**sa**.pisa.h 'thou seest me'; negative: **čik**.sa.pisa.h
iš.**pi**.pisa.h 'thou seest us'; negative: **čik**.pi.pisa.h

DEMONSTRATIVE PRONOUN

ilăppa 'this'; *yămma* 'that'. Adjective: *pa* 'this'; *ma* 'that'.

RELATIVE PRONOUN

The article–pronoun is used: nominative *ăt*, *ak.oš*: oblique *ã*, *akõ*: e.g. *či pisa lik ăt* 'I who see thee' ('thee-see-I-who . . . '). Cf. *peni.at.uk* 'the boat which was . . . '; *peni.a.či* 'the boat which will be . . . '; *peni.a.hinla* 'the boat which can be . . . '.

Numerals

1–10: *ačăfa, tuklo, tukčina, ušta, tahlapi, hannali, untuklo, untučina, čakali, pokoli.* 11–19: *auah* + unit; 20 *pokoli tuklo*; 100 *tahlepa ačăfa.*

Verb

The stem is marked for person (subject and object) and tense, and is modulated by infix to express intensive, reiterative, semelfactive, diminutive aspects and moods. For example, with stem *takči* 'tie': *tãkči* 'to be busy tying'; *taiyakči* 'to tie firmly'; *tahãkči* 'to keep on tying'; *tahkči* 'to tie quickly'.

STATIVE VERBS

(a) Adjectival, with possessive pronominal-series subject: e.g. *ačukma* 'good': *im.ačukma* 'he has (= is) good'; *sa.kăllo.h* 'I am strong'.
(b) Affective, with possessive pronoun subject: *sa.lakša.h* 'I perspire'.

ACTIVE VERBS

Take series 2 pronominal subject (*see* **Pronoun**, above) and have the following moods: indicative, imperative, subjunctive, optative, potential.

TENSE MARKERS

-*tuk*, recent past; -*ttok*, remote past; -(*a*)*či*(*n*), future; -*ahinla*, potential. Examples of tense forms + pronominal subject and object:

takči.h 'he/she/it ties'; 'they tie him/her/it'
takči.li.h 'I tie'
či.takči.li.h 'I tie thee'
či.pisa.Ø.h 'he sees thee'
či.takči.li.tuk 'I have just tied thee'
či.takči.Ø.čĩ 'he will tie thee'

-*h* is used as substantive verb or copula, affixed to any part of speech, e.g. *ŭlla* 'child': *ŭlla**h*** 'it is a child'; *ăno* 'I': *ăno**h*** 'it is I'. Since -*h* cannot be added to a consonantal ending, its function is taken over by a shift in stress: *hátak* 'man': *haták* 'it is a man'.

SUBJUNCTIVE

-(*o*)*km*- infix + -*a*(*t*): e.g. *takči**km**ăt* 'if he were to tie...'.

OPTATIVE

-(*o*)*kb*- infix + *a*(*t*): e.g. *takči**kb**ăt* 'oh, that he would tie...'.

PASSIVE

Can be formed in several ways from active, e.g. *hukmi* 'to burn': *holukmi* 'to be burned'; *bohli* 'to beat': *boa* 'to be beaten'.

Prepositions

Choctaw uses directional markers in the verbal complex: e.g. *et-* 'hither', *pit-* 'thither'. A comitative marker is *iba-* 'with'.

Word order

S precedes V (but note that 1st person singular subject pronominal marker is a suffix).

1. UMMONA ka Anumpa hvt ahanta mvt, Anumpa hvt Chihowa ya̱ ai iba chvfa tok: mihmvt Anumpa hash ot Chihowa ya tok.

2. Yvmmak inli hosh vmmona ka Chihowa ya̱ ai iba chvfa tok.

3. Yvmmak atuk mak o̱ nan oklu̱ha kvt toba tok; yohmi ka nana kvt toba tok vt yvmmak o̱ keyu hokvno ik tobo ki tok.

4. Yvmmak oka isht ai okcha̱ya yvt a̱sha tok: yohmi ka isht ai okcha̱ya yvmmak ash ot hatak puta ka in tohwikeli ya tok.

5. Mihmvt tohwikeli hash ot ai okhlilika ya̱ a toho̱mmi; yohmi ka okhlilika yvt yvmmak ash o̱ ik akostinincho ki tok.

6. Hatak Chan hohchifo hosh, Chihowa nana aiahni ho̱ a̱ya tok.

7. Yvmma pulla tuk mak o̱ hatak vt momvt yimma hi o̱, yvmmak ash osh nan atokoli osh Nan-tohwikeli ash atokowa anola chi̱ hosh a̱ya tok.

CHUKCHI

INTRODUCTION

Chukchi belongs, with Koryak and Itelmen, to the Chukotko-Kamchatka group of Palaeo-Siberian languages. It is spoken in the Chukchi National Region and elsewhere over a vast area, extending from the Bering Strait to the Yakut Autonomous Region, by about 11,000 people, who fall into two groups: the Tundra Chukchi and the Maritime Chukchi. The language is in everyday use for education, administration, and journalism. Both the Chukchi and the Koryak called themselves *luoravetlat* (/ləɣˀorawətlˀat/) which means 'proper people', but the term seems to have fallen from use, as has the former specific 'women's pronunciation' of Chukchi.

SCRIPT

Cyrillic + ӈ and ӄ.

PHONOLOGY

Consonants

stops: p, t, k, q, ˀ
affricate: tʃ
fricatives: v/β, j, γ
nasals: m, n, ŋ
lateral: l
roll: r

The lateral *l* is voiceless.

Vowels

weak: i, e, u
strong: e, a, o
+ ə

That is /e/ = [ɛ] is ambivalent; /ə/ is neutral. This division underlies the Chukchi system of vowel harmony: the vowels in a word are drawn either from the weak or from the strong series, not from both. What is particularly interesting about Chukchi vowel harmony is that root vowels in a weak-series word are regraded to strong series when a strong-series affix is added to the word. This is in striking contrast with Altaic, for example, where it is the affix that takes its vocalic cue from the stem. This also happens in Chukchi: *see* **Verb** below.

Examples of regrading of weak vowels before a strong-series affix are given by Skorik in *JaNSSR*, Vol V (1968): *keŋikupren* 'sweep-net', *γa.kaŋekopra.ma* 'with the sweep-net', where weak-series *e*, *i*, *u* have been regraded as *a*, *e*, *o*, in concord with comitative case-marker *γa*... *ma*. The reverse case – the regrading of strong vowels as weak – is not found.

MORPHOLOGY AND SYNTAX

Noun

Chukchi has no grammatical gender and no articles. The basic dichotomy is between human and non-human. Skorik (1968) distinguishes three declensions: (a) non-human, (b) and (c) covering human field. All distinguish number in the nominative case, but differ in their treatment of the oblique cases, of which there are eight. In the non-human declension, there is one oblique form for both singular and plural: e.g. *milger* 'gun': nom. pl. *milger.ti*; ergative (sing./pl.): *milger.e*. The comitative form *γa.melgar.ma* shows the regrading of weak-series vowels referred to above.

In the human categories, the oblique cases have distinct singular and plural forms.

Declension of *ate* 'daddy':

	Singular	*Plural*
Nominative	ate	ate.nte
Ergative	ate.na	ate.rək
Locative	ate.na	ate.rək
Ablative	ate.ypə	ate.rəpə
Dative	ate.na	ate.rəkə
Directional	ate.γ'et	ate.rəγ'et
Designatory (Essive)	ate.no	

Nominals can be conjugated with personal endings to denote socio-economic identity and status as regards possessions:

mik.iγəm 'who am I'
ən.pənačγ.eγət 'you are an old man'
γe.ŋinqej.iγəm 'I have son(s)'
γe.ŋinqej.iγət 'you (sing.) have son(s)'
γe.req.əturi 'what do you (pl.) own?'
γe.kupre.muri 'we own a net'

Agglutinative affixation yields further declensions expressing privative, delimiting, selective, evaluative, and other nuances. E.g. privative: (V)*ke/a* suffix: *a.qora.ka* 'without a reindeer'; *e.ŋulγ.əke* 'without a belt'. Delimiting: *e/am* prefix: *em.tumγət* 'only comrades' (e.g. 'are here'); *am.walγat* 'only knives', 'knives alone'.

The evaluative forms notate admiration of, or distaste at exceptional size, large or small: the suffix is (ə)*iŋ.ən*/(ə)*čγ.ən*: thus, *a'aček* 'lad': *a'aček.əiŋ.ən* 'young giant'; *ŋewəsqet* 'woman': *nawəsqat.čəŋ.ən* 'big cow' (where *e* is regraded to *a*, though ə is neutral).

Adjective

As predicate, adjective is treated as a stative verb: e.g. *n.itč.iγəm* 'I am heavy'; *n.itč.iγət* 'you (sing.) are heavy', etc. The attributive adjective is incorporated in nominal stems. It may also take the evaluative forms (*see* **Noun**, above).

Pronoun

PERSONAL

	Singular	*Plural*
1	γəm	muri
2	γət	turi
3	ətl'on	ətri

These are declined in nine cases, and show vocalic regrading: e.g. the ergative case of *muri* 'we' is *mor.γənan*.

The possessive forms are *γəm.nin* 'my', *γən.in* 'your', *ən.in* 'his/her'. The pronouns can be marked to notate a relationship to other persons – e.g. *tur.əkekine.jγəm* expresses a relationship of first person singular to second person plural, and they can even be marked for sequence or periodicity: e.g. *γəm.r'am* 'now I . . . '; *γən.r'am* 'now you . . . '.

DEMONSTRATIVE PRONOUN

ŋotqen 'this'; *ənqen* 'that'. These are treated as nominals and declined according to whether they have human or non-human referents.

INTERROGATIVE PRONOUN

r'enut 'what?'; *meŋin* 'who?'

Numerals

Numerals have base forms uncoded for person, but usually take personal affixes. The base forms for 1–5 are: *ənnen*, *ŋireq*, *ŋəroq*, *ŋəraq*, *mətləŋen*. 6–9 are compounds: e.g. 6 *ənnenmətləŋen*. 10 *mənγətken*; 20 *qlikkin*; 40 *ŋireq qlikkin*.

Verb

Transitive (ergative construction) and intransitive (nominative construction). Verbs are marked for aspect, voice, mood, tense, person, and number. Intransitive verbs show concord with subject; transitive verbs are marked for concord with both subject and object.

Two conjugational models are applied aspectually to present, past, and future tense forms:

(a) Delimited/perfective: the model is personal prefix – root – suffix (in part marked for person): e.g.

tə.čejv.ərkən 'I go' (now, single occasion)
Ø.čejv.ərkət 'they go' (now, single occasion)
tre.čejv.rkən 'I shall go'
mətre.čejv.rkən 'we shall go'
mət.čejv.mək 'we went'

(b) Imperfective: the model is invariable prefix – root – suffix inflected for person: e.g.

nə.čejv.iγəm 'I go' (generally, habitually)
nə.čejv.iγət 'you go' (generally, habitually)
γə.čejv.iγəm 'I was going' (generally, habitually)
γə.čejv.iγət 'you were going' (generally, habitually)

Transitive/polypersonal verb: here, the prefix is subject-related, the suffix is object-related. The complete grid for any one tense gives 28 forms: e.g. from stem *l'uk* 'to see', present-tense:

tə.l'u. rkəniγət 'I see you (sing.)'
tə.l'u. rkənitək 'I see you (pl.)'
ine.l'u. rkən 'you (sing.) see me'
ne.l'u. rkəniγəm 'they see me'
ne.l'u. rkəniγət 'they see you (sing.)'

The verbal prefixes in conjugation (a) are subject to regrading in harmony with following stem vowel: e.g. *tre* → *tra*: *tra.jalγət.γ'a* 'I shall go off as nomad'.

NEGATIVE

The circumfix: (*e*)...*ke*/*kalk* negates the root meaning of the verb. Tense and personal deixis are expressed in a following composite pronominal form: e.g. *e.piri.ke mətre.ntə.ŋənet* 'we shan't take them' (*piri* 'to take'; *e*...*ke* = negative circumfix; *mətre*- 1st p. pl. future prefix; *ŋənet* = 3rd p. pl. obj. suffix).

ERGATIVE

An ergative construction is used with all transitive verbs. The logical subject is in the ergative/locative/instrumental case; the logical object in the nominative. Skorik (1968: 267) gives the following example: *tumγ.e na.ntəvat.ən kupre.**n*** 'the comrades put the net', literally: 'by the comrades – they-put-it – the net', where ***-e*** is the ergative/instrumental marker, ***-n*** is the nominative ending.

Like some American Indian languages, Chukchi can detransitivize a transitive verb by means of the prefix *ine* (→ *ena* in the following example, because of vowel regrading): *Tumγ.ət kupre.**te** **ena**.ntəvat.γ'at* 'The comrades put the net', where *tumγ.ət* is the nominative plural, and *-γ'at* is an intransitive ending.

The rich agglutinative structure of Chukchi permits the formation of composite words comprising a series of roots; equipped with the requisite formants, a whole phrase or sentence can be nominalized.

Postpostions

These normally follow nouns in locative case. Skorik (1968: 267) gives the following examples: *ətləɣ re.en.ək* 'with father'; *ɣəty.ək rəmaɣtə* 'on the other side of the lake' (where *-ək* is the locative marker).

Word order

SOV, SVO.

CHUVASH

INTRODUCTION

This, the most divergent of the Turkic languages, is spoken by a total of 1½ million people, almost equally divided between those who live in the Chuvashia Republic and those who live in the Tatarstan Republic and the Bashkortostan Republic. Baskakov's (1966) classification assigns Chuvash to the Bulgar group of West Turkic, both of whose other constituent members – Volga Bulgar and Khazar – have been long extinct. It is interesting to note that in certain common Altaic roots where Turkic in general has /z/, Chuvash joins the Mongolian branch of Altaic in having an /r/ sound. Uralic influence can be seen in the vocabulary of Chuvash and in some aspects of the morphology (see, for example, the formation of the negative imperative).

Chuvash has been a written language since the eighteenth century. It is now used in the republic for education, local media, and literature.

SCRIPT

Several versions of the Cyrillic script have been tried over the last 200 years. The present one uses the additional letters *ă*, *ĕ*, *ÿ*, *ç*.

PHONOLOGY

Consonants

stops: p, t, k (palatalized /t′/ occurs)
affricate: tʃ
fricatives: f, v, s, ʃ, ʒ′, x
nasals: m, n, ɲ
laterals and flap: l, l′, r
semi-vowel: j

/ʒ′/, notated as *ç*, is described as a palatalized fricative deriving from an original affricate /dʒ/.

Chuvash has no voiced/unvoiced opposition in the stop series; /b, d, g/ are found only in loanwords.

Vowels

front: i, ε, e, y
back: ɪ, a, u, o

Short /ă/ → short /ĕ/.

VOWEL HARMONY

The general rule, front with front, back with back, obtains in Chuvash but is not consistently applied: e.g. *yultaš.amar* 'our comrade'; *xẹr.ẹmẹr* 'our daughter'. Reduced vowels (/ă, ĕ/) are unstable. In this article, reduced vowels are dotted.

Stress

On final, unless this is a reduced vowel, when stress moves to penultimate. On initial if all vowels in a word are reduced.

MORPHOLOGY AND SYNTAX

Noun

The plural marker is *-sem/-sen*: e.g. *xula* 'town', *xulasem* (no vowel harmony).

DECLENSION

Nominative = base form + eight cases; dative and accusative have fused.

genitive: -Ṿ*n*
dative/accusative: -(*n*)*a*/-(*n*)*e*
locative: *-ra/-re, ta/te*
ablative: *-ran/-ren, tan/ten*
instrumental: *-pa/-pe, pala/pele*
privative: *-sạr/-sẹr*
benefactive: *-šạn/-šen*

Examples: *pürte* 'in the house'; *xulana kaj-* 'to go to town'; *šančạksar* 'hopeless'; *Ạval traktor.pa ẹžleme pultarat'* 'He can work with the tractor.'

POSSESSIVE AFFIXES

	Singular	*Plural*
1	-ạm/-ẹm/-m	-ạmạr/-ẹmẹr
2	-u/-ü	-ạr/-ẹr
3	-ẹ/-i	-ẹ/-i

Examples: *tusa.m* 'my friend'; *tusa.m.sem* 'my friends'; *tusẹ* 'his, her, their friend'. Possession can also be indicated by use of genitive case of personal pronoun (see below) either with or without possessive affix: e.g. *pirẹn yal* Ø = *pirẹn yal.**ạmạr*** = *yal.amạr* 'our village'.

Adjective

As attribute, adjective precedes noun and is invariable. A comparative is made with -(*ta*)*rax*/-(*te*)*rex*: e.g. *ilemlẹ.rex* 'more beautiful'; *pısạk.rax* 'bigger'.

Pronoun

Personal base forms with oblique bases:

	Singular	*Oblique base*	*Plural*	*Oblique base*
1.	epẹr	man-	epir/epẹr	pir-
2.	esẹ	san-	esir/esẹr	sir
3.	vạl	un-	vẹsem	vẹs-

These are fully declined: e.g. *manran* 'from me'; *manšạn* 'for me'; *sirẹnpe* 'by you (pl.)' *manạn vạxạt ž'uk* 'I have no time'.

DEMONSTRATIVE PRONOUN

ku 'this'; *ž'ak* 'that'; fully declined, with plural forms.

INTERROGATIVE PRONOUN

kam 'who?'; *mẹn* 'what?'

Numerals

1–10: these have full and shortened forms; the latter are used to enumerate objects: they are *pẹr, ik(ẹ), viž'ẹ, tạvat, pilẹk, ult, ž'ič, sakạr, tạxạr, vun*; 20 *ž'irẹm*. 30 *vạtạr*; 40 *xẹrẹx*; 100 *ž'ẹr*.

Verb

The Chuvash verb has four voices: active, reflexive–passive, causative, and reciprocal. There are five moods: indicative, imperative, optative, subjunctive, and concessive. The tense structure distinguishes present/future, future, and past. Aspect is not a feature of the Chuvash verb.

VOICE

Here, standard Turkic markers appear: refl./pass. in -V*l*/-V*n*, causative in *-tar*/*-ter*, reciprocal in -V*s*/-V*š*.

INDICATIVE MOOD

The present/future tense endings are: sing. 1 *-t.ạp*, 2 *-t.ạn*, 3 *-t'*; pl. 1 *-t.p.ạr*, 2 *-t.ạr*, 3 *-ž'*/*ž'e*. This tense is negated by *-mas* /*-mes*: thus *tavrạna.t.ạp* 'I (shall) return'; *tavrạn.mas.t.ạp* 'I do/shall not return'.

The past tense has the marker *-t*/*r* plus a slightly different set of endings: e.g. *tavrạn.t.ạm* 'I returned'; *tavrạn.ma.t.ạm* 'I did not return'.

IMPERATIVE

Here there are forms for all three persons and numbers, with the verbal stem providing the second person singular form: *ẹž'le!* 'work!'; *ẹž'le.tẹr* (3rd p.). The first person negative form has the particle *mar*: e.g. *ẹž'le.m mar* 'let me not work'. The second person uses the particle *an*: e.g. *an ẹž'le* 'don't work'.

The use of a prohibitive particle is alien to Turkic, though it is found in both Mongolian and Uralic.

PARTICIPIAL FORMS

Broadly divided into those with temporal significance and those with modal significance. Examples of the former are: *ẹž'le.ken* '(who is) working'; *ẹž'le.nẹ* '(who) having worked'; *ẹž''le.s* 'who will work'.

MODAL FORMS

E.g. with *malla*, giving necessitative sense; negated by *mar*: e.g. *kay.malla ž'ın* 'the man who must go'; *kay.malla mar ž'ın* 'the man who must not go'.

AUXILIARY VERBS

Used to express such modalities of action as suddenness, motion towards or away from speaker, upwards or downwards, etc.

Postpositions

Postpositions and auxiliary nouns are used, the latter declined.

Word order

SOV

I. **1.** Сăмах ţăн малтанах пур, Вăл Сăмах Турăра, Çав
2, 3 Сăмах Хăй Турă. Турăра Вăл ţăн малтанах пур. Мĕн
пулни пур те Ун урлă пулнă. Унсăр пуçне нимĕн те
4 пулман. Унăн ăшĕнţе ţĕрĕлĕх пулнă, çав ţĕрĕлĕх çын-
5 сем валли çутă пулнă. Вăл çутă тĕттĕмре çутатаť; тĕт
тĕм ăна хупласа илеймен.
6, 7 Турă йанă Іоанн йатлă çын пулнă. Хăй урлă Çут-
та пур те ĕненţţĕр тесе, вăл Çутă çинţен каласа
8 пĕлтерме килнĕ. Вăл Хăй Çутă пулман, Çутă çинţен каласа пĕлтерме йанă çын анţах пулнă.

CIRCASSIAN

See **Kabard-Cherkes.**

COMANCHE

This Uto-Aztecan language is spoken today by between two and three thousand Comanches in western Oklahoma. The original habitat of the Comanche people seems to have extended from the north-west of what is now the United States, down the Pacific coast and adjacent interior as far as a line joining Oklahoma to Mexico. Together with its closest congener, Shoshone, Comanche forms a group, whose other members include Hopi, Northern and Southern Paiute, Papago, Tarahumara, Huichol, and Tubatulabal. This article is based on Robinson and Armagost (1990).

PHONOLOGY

Consonants

bilabial: p, b > β, m, w
dental: t, ṭ, c, n, s
palatal: j, dʒ
velar: k > g, k°
glottal: ʔ, H, h

/ṭ/ is notated as *r*; /t/ > /ṭ/ following a non-front vowel; e.g. *toya* 'mountain' but *Naboo.h.roya*' /naβo:toja'/ 'Navaho Mountain'; *nʉ roya*(*bi*) 'my mountain'. Note that the *t* > *ṭ* shift is not affected by intervening /h/.
Similarly, /H/ + stop becomes /h/ + stop; Robinson and Armagost give the example of the instrumental prefix *wʉH*- which becomes *wʉh*- in *wʉh.pitʉ* 'to overtake'.

Vowels

a, e, i, o, u, ʉ with long values a:, e:, etc.

A characteristic feature of Comanche phonology is provided by the whispered vowels marked by subscript: *taabe̱* 'sun' /ta:βᵊ/. All initial vowels have glottal onset, i.e. initial *V* = /'V/.

Stress

On the first syllable of two-syllable or three-syllable words. In general, the main stress is on the first syllable of a word, with secondary stress on the final. In polysyllables, secondary stress shifts back to penultimate or antepenultimate.

MORPHOLOGY

Noun

There is no category of gender in Comanche.

In citation form, Comanche nouns appear with the absolutive suffix *-bi*: *toya.bi* 'mountain'. This suffix is discarded when the noun is inflected in any way. There are primary and compound nouns: e.g. *kuhtsu'* 'cow'; *nʉmʉ.kuhtsu'* 'buffalo', i.e. 'Comanche-people (*nʉmʉ*) cow'. Many compounds are formed with suffixes, e.g. the diminutive/endearment suffix *-htsi'*: *tuibi.htsi'* 'brave', 'young man'.

The prefix *na* marks an intrinsic relationship between components in a compound:

na'buku.waa' 'automobile'
(*puku* 'horse', *waa* 'horn sound') *p* > *b* after *V* or *V'*

Nouns formed from the imperfective verbal participle in *-tʉ* express a durative or permanent quality of the referent: RA give the following examples:

oha'ahnaka.tʉ 'one with yellow (*oha'*) underarms (*ahna-*)', i.e. coyote, *-ka-* 'having'
oha.h.poko.pi 'yellow berries (*poko*)' + generic marker, i.e. 'carrot'.

The perfective participial marker is *-Hpʉh* > *pʉ*. Nouns formed with this suffix express a completed state of affairs, the completed result of action:

tekwa.pʉ 'that which has been spoken' (*tekwa.rʉ* 'to speak'), i.e. 'word'
na.boo.pʉ 'that which has been drawn' (stem *-poo-* 'to write'), i.e. 'picture'

NOMINAL INFLECTION

The citation marker *-bi* was mentioned above. It may also take the form *-pi*, e.g. after nouns of colour: *oha.pi* 'yellow'.

NUMBER

Comanche nouns may be singular, dual, or plural. However, for non-human referents, number is normally unmarked.

kahni 'house' – dual *kahni nʉhʉ* – pl. *kahni nʉʉ*

These endings are not invariable. Thus, the *-nʉʉ* ending is reduced to *ʉ* in (polysyllabic) compounds and derivatory nouns:

oha'ahnakatʉ.ʉ̱ 'coyotes'

DECLENSION

Three cases – accusative, genitive, vocative – are marked. Formation of the vocative is unpredictable.

Accusative: the accusative marker is *-i* or *-a*. *-a* appears, for example, after finals in glottal stop: *kwasinaboo'* 'snake', acc. *kwasinaboo'**a***. Elsewhere, a low final vowel coalesces with *-i* to give *-e*: *puku* ' horse', acc. *puke*. Nouns in

-ʉ change this vowel to *-i* in the accusative: *oha'ahnakatʉ* 'coyote', acc. *oha'ahnakati*.

Nouns ending in labial + *i* make an accusative in *-hta*: *puhi**hwi*** 'money', acc. *puhihwi**hta***. Dual and plural accusative is in *-i* + anticipatory vowel harmony: *nʉhʉ* > *nihi* (dual): *nʉmʉnʉʉ* 'Comanches', acc. *nʉmʉnii*.

Genitive: possessor precedes possessed, and, if singular, may be marked by *-a* or *-Ø*: *oha'ahnakatatʉ.**n.a*** *kwasi* 'coyote's tail', where the *-n-* is historically present, though dropped in the modern language. The dual genitive marker is *-ʉ*, the plural *-Ø*.

COMPOUNDING

There are many examples of simple juxtaposition: AB = C.

tʉboo.kahni 'schoolhouse' ('writing house')
tʉboo.tahni 'postman' ('writing deliver')
puhihwi.kahni 'bank' ('money house')
puhihwi.paraiboo' 'banker' ('money boss')

Adjective

Adjectives in Comanche are simple or derived; the latter frequently occur with the aspectual markers *-tʉ/rʉ*, *-pʉ*. Cf. *tʉe'tʉ* 'small', *pʉ htʉ* 'heavy', *nasaapʉ* 'boiled' ('having reached the state of boiling'). The adjective precedes the noun, and is reduplicated for plural: *pia* 'big': *pi**bia*** *niwʉnʉ'nʉʉ* 'those (pl. marker *nʉʉ*) who talk (stem *niwʉnʉ*) big', i.e. 'a Comanche band'.

The numeral *sʉmʉ'* 'one' has a reduplicated form meaning 'some': the plural *nʉʉ* is added: *sʉsʉmʉ'nʉʉ nʉmʉnʉʉ* 'some Comanches'.

DEMONSTRATIVE ADJECTIVE

These precede the noun. Two relative degrees are distinguished for each of the three categories: proximate, distal, and dispersed. Thus, the proximate series has two sub-divisions, *i-* for close at hand, *ma-* for somewhat farther away. Similarly, the distal category has *o-* and *u-*. The common marker for the category of dispersed objects is *e-*. The *i-*, *ma-*, *o-*, and *u-* markers also function as 3rd p. pronominal stems. The imperfective participial *-tʉ/rʉ* may follow the demonstrative stems: *i.tʉ.ʉ* 'these' (relatively close to hand proximate plural).

The demonstrative adjectives take accusative and genitive inflections. An *s-* prefix (not possible in the *ma-* series) indicates that the topic now marked by the demonstrative has already been introduced, and is known to the listener.

Some examples:

s.i.t.ʉʉ 'of these': the proximate plural referent is known to the listener;
ma.hka 'this/that', acc. (*-hka* is an acc. form which occurs only in the demonstrative series);
s.u.h.rʉ 'of those two': dual, non-immediate, distal referent known to the listener.

Pronouns

PERSONAL PRONOUN

The 1st p. stem is *nʉ'*; dual and plural forms distinguish inclusive/exclusive: e.g. *nʉkwʉ*, 1st p. dual exclusive; *nʉnʉ*, 1st p. plural exclusive. The 2nd p. singular base is *ʉnʉ*; with dual and plural forms. 3rd p.: the demonstrative stems (see above) + glottal stop: *i'*, *ma'*, etc. Cf. Mark 1.11: *nʉ Rua' ʉnʉ, nʉ kamakʉna̱* 'thou (*ʉnʉ*) art my (*nʉ*) my son (*tua'* > *rua'*) my beloved (*kamakʉna̱*)'.

The personal pronouns have accusative and genitive forms. A specimen row follows: 1st p. (base *nʉ'*) genitive forms:

sing.: *nʉ* dual exclusive: *nʉhʉ*; plural exclusive: *nʉmʉ*.

The first person exclusive plural genitive is the name used by the Comanches for themselves: 'of us/ours . . . '. The word has already been given above in the Comanche term for buffalo: 'our cow'. Similar usages are: *nʉmʉ rʉborapʉ̱* 'our born-ones', i.e. the present generation of Comanches; *nʉmʉ napʉ̱* 'our shoe' = moccasin; *nʉmʉnaitʉ* 'to live as a Comanche'.

The postposition *matu* 'up to, onto' follows genitive forms to express a dative: cf.

Mark	2.18	me u.matu niwʉnʉ	(quot. *me*)	'they say to him'
	1.17	me uhrʉ.matu yʉhkwi̱	(quot. *me*)	'he said to the two' (dual)
	2.19	me urʉʉ.matu yʉhkwi̱	(quot. *me*)	'he said to them' (pl.)
	9.13	me mʉmʉ.matu yʉkwitʉ	(quot. *me*)	'I say to you'

The postposition *matu* coalesces with the proximate demonstrative *ma* to form *maatu*: an example from Robinson and Armagost: *sitʉʉ kwasinaboo' maatu tunehtsʉnʉ̱*, 'this snake ran up to him'.

INTERROGATIVE PRONOUNS AND MARKERS

Who? is expressed by *hakarʉ*: Mark 3.33:

hakarʉ.se' nʉ via' tʉasʉ nʉ rami'nʉʉ
'who is my mother, or my brethren?'
(*se'* is a contrast or concessive? marker; pia 'mother' > *via*, after vowel; *tʉasʉ* conjunction 'and'; *tami'* 'younger brother' > *rami* after vowel)

hina/hini 'what?'; *hakaniiku* 'how?'

The usual interrogative marker for a yes/no situation is *-ha* (example from Robinson and Armagost):

nʉ kahni.ha tsaa.yʉ 'is my house good?'
(*kahni* 'house'; *tsaa* 'good'; *yʉ* is a verbalizing formant)

Numerals

The following stems are known: 1 *sʉmʉ-*, 2 *waha-*, 3 *pahih-*, 4 *hayarokwe-*, 5 *mo'obe'*- (cf. *mo'o* 'hand'), 6 *naabai-*, 7 *taatsʉkwitʉ* (appears in Mark 8.5), 10 *sʉʉmarʉ*-.

Verb

The Comanche verb has a citation form (normally in *-rʉ* for low-vowel stems, in *-tʉ* for high: cf. *tekwarʉ* 'to speak'; *miarʉ* 'to go'; *wekwiitʉ* 'to enter') and a valency form, which does not occur in isolation, but always with affixes or other valencies, e.g. in compounds. Stems may vary for number, with reference to the *subject* of an intransitive, to the *object* of a transitive verb.

tʉyaaitʉ 'to die' (singular sbj.)
kooitʉ 'to die' (dual/plural sbj.)

Robinson and Armagost give the following good example from Canonge's *Comanche Texts*:

soobe'sʉ nʉnʉ su.nih.ku puhitoo'a rʉkʉ.**wasʉ**.'e.tʉ.ʉ
'long ago, we killed turkeys for food in that way'

where puhitoo' 'turkey' is not marked for plurality (*-a* is the accusative inflection); that 'turkeys' are meant, however, emerges from the verb stem, which would have been *tʉkʉ.hpehka* had only one turkey been killed (*tʉkʉ* > *rʉkʉ*, following vowel).

Like many other languages of America (cf. Haida and Kwakiutl) Comanche uses affixes to specify the means by which, and the manner in which, an action is carried out. Thus, the prefix *ku-* indicates action with the head, *kʉ(h)-* with the teeth, *sʉʉ(h)-* with the feet: *sitʉ.kʉ.se' u* ***sʉʉh****.po'tse.nu* 'he/she kicked it' (Robinson and Armagost). Direction of motion is indicated by suffixes: *-ki* for motion towards, *-kwa* for motion away from something or someone.

The Comanche verb is marked for aspect, not for tense. The following aspects are distinguished: inceptive, stative, perfective, durative, progressive, repetitive. Certain aspect markers are themselves verbs; e.g. the inceptive marker *-pitʉ* is, or at least recapitulates, the verb *pi(i)tʉ* 'to arrive'. Cf. Mark 4.37:

sʉrʉkʉ'se' kʉhtaa nʉe.hu.piitʉ
'and then it began to blow hard'
(*kʉhtaanʉetʉ* 'to blow hard, be stormy')

It will be seen that *pitʉ* is affixed to the citation form of the verb; the perfective markers *-ma* and *'i* are also added to the citation form, though a second inceptive marker, *tʉki*, takes the valency form. Cf. *urii puni'i* (perfective) he saw them (*punitʉ* 'to see'). The repetitive marker is *'e* added to the citation form.

The reflexive/passive marker is *na-*; e.g. *puni.tʉ* 'to look': ***na.b****uni* 'to look at oneself'.

The affix *-nu* functions as a narrative past marker. Cf. Mark 3.19:

wihnʉse' surʉʉ kahnikʉ̱ wekwinʉ̱ 'and they went into a house'
(*wihnʉ̱* + *se'* 'then, however…', *surʉʉ* 'they' (distal), *kahni* 'house', *-kʉ̱* postposition 'into', *wekwiitʉ* 'to go')

NEGATION

The marker is *kee* or *ke*. Negated sentences tend to be imperfective as regards aspect. There is a prohibitive marker: *keta'*: *keta' tʉrʉhkaarʉ̱* 'do not steal' (Mark 10.19).

k̠e is prefixed to stems in a privative capacity: *ke.tokwe* 'not right' *ke.bayʉmʉkitʉ* 'not moving'.

Adverb

Certain locational and directional adverbs are formed by adding the formants *k*V, *b*V, *h*V to a demonstrative stem, proximate or distal, where V harmonizes with the root vowel of the demonstrative.

Postpositions

Comanche has a plentiful supply of these, e.g. *-hi/ti* 'in, at', *-kaba* 'among', *-kuhpa* 'inside', *-kahtu* 'into', *-miihtsi'* 'near', *-tʉ̱* 'from, out of': e.g. *narʉmʉ.kahtu* 'into (the) town'; *paa.h.ku.tʉ̱* 'from out of the water' (Mark 1.10). In concatenations of postpositions, the simple forms, such as those given above, take precedence over others, with intensifiers like *-taka* or *-tuku* in final position.

Word order and syntax

Robinson and Armagost give SV for principal intransitive, SOV for principal transitive clauses, where S is in the nominative. E.g. Mark 9.13:

me nʉ' mʉmʉmatu yʉkwitʉ 'I (thus) say to you'

but note such sentences in the Robinson and Armagost dictionary as:

sarii.a (O) hipʉkatʉ (V) nʉ (S in genitive) 'I own the dog'
ʉ (O acc.) nimai(h)katʉ (V) u' (S nom.) 'he is calling you' (Mark 10.49)

SUBORDINATE CLAUSES

(a) Relative: both S and O (if present) are in the genitive. Here, Robinson and Armagost give the following excellent example:

nʉ buhiwi.hta nʉ'/narohtʉma.kʉ nʉ rʉki.'i̱h.a/**watsi.kʉ**'
'I lost my money/that I had put in a can'
(*nʉ buhiwi.hta* 'my money', acc. in *-hta*; *nʉ'* 1st p. nom.; *narohtʉma.kʉ* 'into' (*-kʉ*) 'the/a can'; *nʉ* 1st p. sing. in genitive as S of relative clause; *rʉki* < *tʉkarʉ* (sing. stem) 'to put'; *'i̱h* marks accomplished action; *watsitʉ* 'to lose'; *kʉ* causative marker; *'i̱* marks accomplished action)

(b) Complementary (adverbial): here, both S and O (if present) are in the accusative.

In both (a) and (b) duplication of pronominal forms may result. Again, Robinson and Armagost provide a good example:

urii urii maka.hka.kʉ.se' 'when they (S) had fed them (O)'

with both S and O in the accusative. The meaning is clear, however, as the infixed *-hta-* is a marker denoting subject switch.

The declarative particle *tsa'* follows the subject:

tenahpʉ tsa' aruka'a naayarʉ
'the man (*tenahpʉ*) is trailing the deer (acc.)'

1 Haya'ükünaahrü ma' tsaatü narümu'ipü̲ Jesus Christ-
kahtü God-ha Tua'.
[2] Sinihku tsa' surü Isaiah God-ha türü'a̲wewapi̲ ma voo'i̲,
me yükwiku: Kavúuni̲. Ümunakwü̲hu nü' nü nütühyoi-
wapi̲ha tühyoiitü, [ümunakwü̲hi] pühtu ü miaru'i̲ha ü
maka'mukikütu'i̲ha. [3] U tü'apeto'i̲kana tsa' pianümü-
wahtütu piarekwahkitü̲, me yükwitü: Taa Narümi'aka
pu'e maka'muuki̲. U pu'eniika tunaa müü. [4] John-se'
siku̲ pianümüwahtükü̲ nüpawühtianu̲. Surüse' John püü
suana atahpu wümüühtsi, navawühtiahtsi, ai'ku
nahanipü̲nüükü̲hu urüü ta tüsu'naaru'i̲kahti puhárekwanu̲.

COPTIC

INTRODUCTION

Coptic – the latest form of Egyptian, which belongs to the Semito-Hamitic family – was widely spoken in Egypt from the third to the sixth centuries AD. It was never the language of administration, a role which the Greek introduced by the Ptolemies continued to discharge, even under the Roman Empire. From about 100 BC onwards the old demotic script was discarded in favour of the Greek alphabetic script, and, with the spread of Christianity, Coptic began to acquire literary status. The translation of the Bible into Sahidic Coptic (mid-third century) was of enormous importance in this respect. The large number of Greek words in Coptic is part of the legacy of the Ptolemies. By the fifth century, Coptic was the literary language of Upper Egypt; one of the best-known works in Coptic literature – the biography of Shenute, the austere abbot of the White Monastery of Atrib – which appeared about 450, is in Bohairic, the dialect of Lower Egypt.

To the Arabs who conquered Egypt in the seventh century, the terms 'Egyptian' and 'Christian' were synonymous, and the name 'Copt' derives from قبطى (*qubṭi*), the Arabic version of ἀιγύπτιος. When Arabic replaced spoken Eygptian (from the twelfth century onwards), Coptic was retained as the liturgical language of the Coptic Monophysite Church (which had finally broken with the Byzantine Church in the fifth century). Today, there are about 5–6 million Copts. The liturgical language is not generally understood, and its replacement by Arabic has been urged. On the other hand, attempts have been made to revive Coptic as both a written and a spoken language.

There are six dialects, the most important being Sahidic and Bohairic, associated respectively with Upper and Lower Egypt. The present-day liturgical language is based on Bohairic. Here, in general, Sahidic forms are described.

SCRIPT

See **Script** at end of article.

PHONOLOGY

Consonants

stops: p, ḇ, t, ḏ, k, g

affricates: the pre-dental palatals: voiced ϫ = d̲′ and surd ϭ = t̲ʰ are cited as affricates; the latter in Bohairic
fricatives: β, s, ʃ, h, χ
nasals: m, n
semi-vowels: j, w
lateral and flap: l, r

/p, t, k/ are aspirates; /b̥, d̥, g̊/ are half-voiced.

Vowels

long: eː, oː, uː
short: i, e, a, o, u, ə
(long vowels are indicated here by macrons)

Stress is on the penultimate or the final syllable, long or short.

MORPHOLOGY AND SYNTAX

Coptic represents the extreme analytical stage of Egyptian. Flectional change has virtually vanished, and syntactic relationships depend on a highly developed system of articles, prefixes, prepositions, and particles.

Noun

There are two genders, masculine and feminine. In general, the old Egyptian genders are retained. The old feminine ending *-t* has disappeared in the absolute state, but reappears in the pronominal state found in certain nouns (mainly denoting parts of the body), e.g. *ro* 'mouth', pronominal state *rō*: *rō.k* 'thy mouth'; *rō.f* 'his mouth'; *hē* 'body', pronominal state *hēt*.

In theory, all nouns have two states – absolute and construct (where two nouns are directly connected, with a single stress on the second member of the collocation: *see* **Article**, below).

ARTICLE

Definite, weak form: masc. *p-*, fem. *t-*, pl. *n-*; strong: masc. *pi/pe*, fem. *ti/te*, pl. *ni/ne*. Examples: *p.rōme* 'the man', *n.rōme* 'the men'; *p.saǰe* 'the word'; *ti.polis* 'the town'; *n.halate* 'the birds'; *te.physis* 'nature'.

The indefinite article for both genders is *ou* = /w/; the plural is *hen/hən*: e.g. *w.ei* 'a house'; *hen.ei* 'houses'.

In the genitive construct, the article is attached to both components: e.g. *p.ei əm.p.ajōt* 'the house of the father'; *p.ran əm.p.ǰojs* 'the name of the Lord'; *p.kah ən.kēme* 'the land of Egypt'. In these sentences, *ən* is the genitive marker; it is *əm* before labials.

PLURAL

Marked almost exclusively by inflection in the article (see above), i.e. one and the same form of the noun serves as both singular and plural, though a few vestiges of plural inflection remain: e.g. *hōb* 'thing', pl. *hbēje*; *son* 'brother', pl. *snēj*; *ǰoj* 'ship', pl. *eǰēj*.

The category of nouns includes infinitives. Two- and three-radical nouns are most common: e.g. *sim* 'grass'; *klom* 'crown'. Four- and five-radical nouns are often reduplications of two-/three-radicals.

New formations are made by prefixation or suffixation, in the latter case showing gender: *-f* (masc.), *-s* (fem.), e.g. *sormes* 'error, delusion' (*sōrəm* 'to be mistaken').

Prefixation: e.g. *šw-* 'worthy of' – *šwmw* 'he who is worthy of death'; *šer-* 'son of' – *šerenwot* 'only son'; *bō-* 'tree of' – *bōənǰojt* 'olive tree'.

Adjective

As a separate category, the adjective does not exist in Coptic. Various verbal and nominal constructions are used: e.g. *nesōs* 'she is pretty' (< *nese-*, *nesō* 'to be pretty'). The construct formula with *ən* is frequent: e.g. *u.rōme ən.sabe* 'a man of wisdom' = 'a wise man'; *pe.f.šēre ən.wot* 'his only son'.

Pronoun

Three series: independent, suffixed, and proclitic; gender is marked in the second and third person singular:

		Singular			*Plural*		
		Independent	*Suffixed*	*Proclitic*	*Independent*	*Suffixed*	*Proclitic*
1		anok	-i/-t	ti	anon	-n	tən
2	masc.	əntok	-k/-t	k	–	–	–
	fem.	ənto	Ø/-e/-te	te	əntotən -tēutən	-tən	tetən
3	masc.	əntof	-f	f	əntow		
	fem.	əntos	-s	s			

The suffixed pronouns are used with certain nouns, usually denoting parts of the human body (*see* **Noun**, above): e.g. *rat* 'foot, leg', *toot* 'hand', *hra* 'face': *hrak* 'your face'; *hrē**tən*** 'your (pl.) face'.

The proclitic forms figure as the subject of adverbial clauses: e.g. *ti.həm pajōt* 'I am in my father' (John 14.11); *nai de* ***se****.həm p.kosmos* 'but these are in the world' (John 17.11).

DEMONSTRATIVE PRONOUN

There are three series of demonstrative pronouns, and four series of demonstrative articles. Typical of the former is the series masc. *pai*; fem. *tai*; pl. common *nai*: e.g. *Pai hən te.hweite nefšoop* 'This was in the beginning.'

The possessive prefix: masc. *pa*; fem. *ta*; pl. *na*. These precede the noun, and may be used without overt referent, as in Greek; cf. ***na*** *perro* = *ta tou pharaō* 'the things that are the Pharaoh's'.

POSSESSIVE ARTICLES

Basically, the *p-*, *t-*, *n-* series plus personal markers; thus, *tes-* is the possessive article for a feminine object possessed by a feminine third person; *netən* for a plural object possessed by second person plural: e.g. ***pe.k.***_ēi_ 'your (sing.) house'; ***netən***_.hbēje_ 'you (pl.) affairs'.

INTERROGATIVE PRONOUN

nim 'who?'; *ou* 'what?' *Nim* may be connected to a noun by *n̄* /ən/: e.g. *Nim ən.rōme?* 'What man?'; *əntək nim?* 'Who art thou?' (John 1.19); *Ou te tme?* 'What is truth?' (John 18.38). *Aš* 'who, what?': e.g. *Aš pe.***k***.ran* 'What is your name?'

RELATIVE PRONOUN

et/(e)nt < Egyptian *ntj*: e.g. *p.rōme* ***et***_.həm p.ēi_ 'the man who is in the house'; *p.rōme* ***ete*** *pa.jōt pe* 'the man who is my father'.

Numerals

The cardinals 1 to 10 and the lower teens have masculine and feminine forms: 1 *wa/wi*; 2 *snaw/sənte*; 3 *šomənt/šomte*; 4 *ftow/ftoe*; 5 *tiw/ti(e)*; 6 *sow/so(e)*; 7 *sašef/ sašfe*; 8 *šmoun/šmoune*; 9 *psis/psit*; 10 *mēt/mēte*; 20 *ǰuōt/ǰuōte*; 30 *maab/maabe*; 100 *še.*

The numerals have enclitic forms used with nouns, and specific truncated forms for use after decades: e.g. *tē* 'five' following *ǰuōt*, *maab*, etc.

Verb

The great majority of Coptic verbs are two-, three-, or four-radical. The infinitive is neutral as to voice, the transitive/intransitive opposition being alien to Egyptian. It is always masculine in gender, irrespective of whether it derives from a masculine or feminine infinitive in older Egyptian. Certain vocalic finals (*e/i*) appear where the original feminine *-t* ending has been lost.

Like the noun, the infinitive has three states: absolute, construct, and pronominal: e.g. absolute *jō* 'speak', construct *je-*, pronominal *joo.* The construct form is used with a nominal direct object, the pronominal with a pronoun.

CONJUGATION

Prefixal or suffixal. The small class of suffixal conjugations derives from the Egyptian *śǰm.f* model (*see* **Egyptian**). Examples from *peǰe* 'say': *afei ebol peǰa****f*** *naw* 'he went forth and said unto them' (John 18.4); *peǰa****w*** *naf* 'they said unto him' (John 9.12).

PREFIXAL CONJUGATION

This is the usual conjugation pattern; the model is tense marker – personal marker – stem, e.g. *a-f-sōtəm* 'he has heard'. The inventory of tenses includes three present and three future tenses, two imperfects, a future imperfect, two perfects, and a preterite, plus a series of secondary forms. Each tense has specific affirmation and negative prefixed markers, showing gender in second and third person singular: e.g. first present:

	Singular	*Plural*
1	ti	tən
2	k/te	tetən
3	f/s	se

Each tense has, in addition, a neutral marker prefixed to a nominal subject. In the 1st present, this marker is Ø. The 1st present is negated by the circumfix *ən... an*: e.g. *ti.sōtəm* 'I hear', *ən.ti.sōtəm an* 'I do not hear'; *k.eire* 'thou doest'; *əf.bōk* 'he goes'; *təm.bōk* 'we go'.

PERFECT

The prefixed personal markers are:

affirmative: sing. *ai*, *ak/are*, *af/as*; pl. *an*, *atetən*, *aw*;
negative: sing. *əmpi*, *əmpek/əmpe*, *əmpef/əmpes*; pl. *əmpen*, *əmpetən*, *əmpow*.

The tense characteristic is *a*-; the neutral marker is affirm. *a*-, neg. *mpe*-: e.g. *a.tetən shime sōtəm* 'your wife has heard'; *mpe.p.noute sōtəm erof* 'God has not heard him'.

PRESENT HABITUAL

Prefixed personal markers:

affirmative: sing: *šai*, *šak/šare*, *šaf/šas*; pl. *šan*, *šatetən*, *šaw*;
negative: sing. *mei*, *mek/mere*, *mef/mes*; pl. *men*, *metetən*, *mew*.

The tense characteristic is affirm. *šare*-, neg. *mere*: e.g. *Mere.p.noute sōtəm erok* 'God is not given to hearing you.' Similarly for other primary and secondary tenses: e.g. the conditional, with affirmative markers:

sing. *ei.šan*, *ek.šan/er.šan*, *ef.šan/es.šan*; pl. *en.šan*, *etetən.šan.ej.šan*.

The neutral marker is *eršan*: e.g. *Eršan.p.rōme šlēl p.noute na.sōtəm erof* 'If man prays, God will hear him', where *na*- is a future marker.

Conjunctive (dependent) forms have an *e*- prefix: e.g. *ef.sōtəm* 'while/as he hears'; *ef.na.sōtəm* 'while he will hear'; *ene.af.sōtəm* 'while he had heard'; *e.šaf.sōtəm* 'while he habitually hears'; *əmpat.ef.sōtəm* 'while he has not yet heard'.

COMPOUND VERBS

Infinitive in construct form + noun: e.g. *eire* 'to make, construct' *ər*-: *ər.wojn* 'to illuminate' (*wojn* 'light'). Cf. John 1.5

auō p.wojn efərwojn həm p.kake
'and the light is making-to-illuminate in the darkness'

Prepositions

Prepositions have construct and pronominal forms only, no absolute. They are simple or compound: e.g. *e-*, *ero* 'to', 'towards', 'into': *e.p.kosmos* 'into the world'; *eroi* 'to me'; *erof* 'to him'.

ən/əm marks direct object and acts as a genitive, locative, or instrumental link: e.g. *əm pei ma* 'in this place'; *p.ei əm.pa.son* 'the house of my brother'; *hən/ənhēt* 'in', 'at': *həm pei wojš* 'at this time'.

COMPOUND PREPOSITIONS

These are mostly nouns denoting parts of the body, plus simple prepositions: e.g. *ro-/ro* 'mouth' + *e-/a-*; *rat/ret* 'foot' + *e*; e.g. *Afei eratəf əmpərro* 'He came to (the feet of) the emperor.'

Word order

SVO; more precisely, in a verbal sentence, temporal prefix or neutral prenominal marker + nominal subject – infinitive – direct object – indirect object.

Ϧⲉⲛ ⲧⲁⲣⲭⲏ ⲛⲉ ⲡⲓⲥⲁϫⲓ ⲡⲉ. ⲟⲩⲟϩ ⲡⲓⲥⲁϫⲓ
ⲛⲁϥϫⲏ ϧⲁⲧⲉⲛ ⲫϯ. ⲟⲩⲟϩ ⲛⲉ ⲟⲩⲛⲟⲩϯ ⲡⲉ
ⲡⲓⲥⲁϫⲓ. [2] ⲫⲁⲓ ⲉⲛⲁϥϫⲏ ⲓⲥϫⲉⲛϩⲏ ϧⲁⲧⲉⲛ ⲫϯ.
[3] ϩⲱⲃ ⲛⲓⲃⲉⲛ ⲁⲩ|ϣⲱⲡⲓ ⲉⲃⲟⲗ ϩⲓⲧⲟⲧϥ. ⲟⲩⲟϩ
ⲁⲧϭⲛⲟⲩϥ ⲙ̅ⲡⲉ ϩⲗⲓ ϣⲱⲡⲓ ϧⲉⲛ ⲫⲏ ⲉⲧⲁϥ-
ϣⲱⲡⲓ. [4] ⲛⲉ ⲡⲱⲛϧ ⲡⲉⲧⲉⲛϧⲏⲧϥ.
Ⲟⲩⲟϩ ⲡⲱⲛϧ ⲛⲉ ⲫⲟⲩⲱⲓⲛⲓ ⲛ̅ⲛⲓⲣⲱⲙⲓ ⲡⲉ. [5] ⲟⲩⲟϩ
ⲡⲓⲟⲩⲱⲓⲛⲓ ⲁϥⲉⲣⲟⲩⲱⲓⲛⲓ ϧⲉⲛ ⲡⲓⲭⲁⲕⲓ. ⲟⲩⲟϩ
ⲙ̅ⲡⲉ ⲡⲓⲭⲁⲕⲓ ⲧⲁϩⲟϥ.
[6] Ⲁϥϣⲱⲡⲓ ⲛ̅ϫⲉⲟⲩⲣⲱⲙⲓ ⲉⲁⲩⲟⲩⲟⲣⲡϥ ⲉⲃⲟⲗ ϩⲓⲧⲉⲛ
ⲫϯ Ⲉⲡⲉϥⲣⲁⲛ ⲡⲉ ⲓⲱⲁⲛⲛⲏⲥ. [7] ⲫⲁⲓ ⲁϥⲓ ⲉⲩⲙⲉⲧ-
ⲙⲉⲑⲣⲉ ϩⲓⲛⲁ ⲛ̅ⲧⲉϥⲉⲣⲙⲉⲑⲣⲉ ϧⲁ ⲡⲓⲟⲩⲱⲓⲛⲓ.
ϩⲓⲛⲁ ⲛ̅ⲧⲉ ⲟⲩⲟⲛ ⲛⲓⲃⲉⲛ ⲛⲁϩϯ ⲉⲃⲟⲗ ϩⲓⲧⲟⲧϥ.
[8] Ⲛⲉ ⲛ̅ⲑⲟϥ ⲁⲛ ⲡⲉ ⲡⲓⲟⲩⲱⲓⲛⲓ. ⲁⲗⲗⲁ ϩⲓⲛⲁ ⲛ̅ⲧⲉϥⲉⲣ-
ⲙⲉⲑⲣⲉ ϧⲁ ⲡⲓⲟⲩⲱⲓⲛⲓ.

SCRIPT

Thanks to the use of the Greek phonetic script, Coptic is the only form of Egyptian whose pronunciation is actually attested; hence the great importance of the language for Egyptian philology.

Seven additional letters were borrowed from Demotic (*see* **Egyptian**) to denote sounds alien to Greek: ϣ / Ϣ = /ʃ/, ϥ = /f/, ϧ = /ḫ/, ϩ = ḥ, ϫ = /dʒ/ǰ/ d′/, ϭ = /k′/, ϯ = /ti/.

z was probably pronounced as /z/, not /zd/ as in classical Greek, ϩ = /ḥ/ is used for Greek ‘ (rough aspirate). The vowel marker ¯ indicates the reduced front vowel /ə/ pronounced before the bearer consonant: thus M̄ = /əm/. Abbreviations are frequent, especially in the case of *nomina sacra*: e.g. IHⲗ = ICPⲁHⲗ ‘Israel’; cⲱp = CⲰTHP ‘saviour’.

Doubled vowels are read as vowel + hamza: BⲰⲰN = /boːʔon/ ‘bad’, ‘evil’.

THE COPTIC SCRIPT

THE ALPHABET

Letter	*Transcription*
Ⲁ ⲁ	*a*
Ⲃ ⲃ	*b [b, v]*
Ⲅ ⲅ	*g*
Ⲇ ⲇ	*d*
Ⲉ ⲉ	*e [ĕ]*
Ⲍ ⲍ	*z*
Ⲏ ⲏ	*ē*
Ⲑ ⲑ	*th [t + h]*
Ⲓ ⲓ	*i [i, j]*
Ⲕ ⲕ	*k*
Ⲗ ⲗ	*l*
Ⲙ ⲙ	*m*
Ⲛ ⲛ	*n*
Ⲝ ⲝ	*x [ks]*
Ⲟ ⲟ	*o [ŏ]*
Ⲡ ⲡ	*p*

Letter	*Transcription*
Ⲣ ⲣ	*r*
Ⲥ ⲥ	*s*
Ⲧ ⲧ	*t*
Ⲩ ⲩ	*y [i, y]*
Ⲫ ⲫ	*ph [p + h]*
Ⲭ ⲭ	*kh [k + h]*
Ⲯ ⲯ	*ps*
Ⲱ ⲱ	*ō*
Ϣ ϣ	*š*
Ϥ ϥ	*f*
Ϧ ϧ	*ḫ [ch]*
Ϩ ϩ	*h*
Ϫ ϫ	*dž*
Ϭ ϭ	*č*
Ϯ ϯ	*ti*

CORNISH

INTRODUCTION

Cornish belongs to the British (Brythonic) division of the Celtic branch of Indo-European. Old Cornish is attested in various tenth-century glosses, found in Latin MSS. Middle Cornish (fourteenth to sixteenth centuries) is well known from some 20,000 lines of source material – religious drama, ecclesiastical history, etc. The last native speaker of Cornish is traditionally held to have died in 1777. In the nineteenth century, when the first serious attempts were made to revive the written and spoken language, the model chosen was not late Cornish, heavily infected as it was with English, but the comparatively pure Middle Cornish of earlier centuries. This recrudescent language, known as Unified Modern Cornish, is the product initially of the work of Henry Jenner (1848–1934) and subsequently of R. Morton Nance. The lexical repertory provided by the Middle Cornish texts has been amplified and extended by analogy with other Celtic languages. The pronunciation adopted represents a reasoned treatment of the Middle Cornish phonological material in the light of general Celtic philology. Twentieth-century and sixteenth-century Cornish are therefore in a sense synchronic.

SCRIPT

Latin alphabet minus *i*; *x* appears in borrowings from English. The following digraphs are used: *ch* = /tʃ/, *dh* = /ð/, *th* = /θ/, *gh* = /γ/, *sh* = /ʃ/.

PHONOLOGY

Consonants

stops: p, b, t, d, k, g
affricates: tʃ, dʒ
fricatives: f, v, ð, θ, s, z, ʃ, ʒ, χ, γ, h
nasals: m, n
lateral and flap: l, r
semi-vowels: j, w

Labialized /k/ and /g/ occur: [k°, g°]; also a hamza-like interruption where elision of a velar fricative has taken place: *mo'a* ('very').

For mutations see below.

Vowels

i, e, a, o, u
/i/ and /ɪ/ are represented by *y*.

The letter *e* covers /eː, ɛ, ə/; *o* covers /oː, ɔ, ɔː/; *u* covers /uː, y, ʌ/.
There are several diphthongs.

Mutation

There are four types of juncture mutation in Cornish, with traces of a fifth:

(a) Soft mutation (lenition): /b/ → /v/, /d/ → /ð/, /m/ → /v/, /k/ → /g/, /gV/ → /V/, etc. As in other Celtic languages, this mutation takes place after the definite article *an* in feminine singular nouns, in masculine plural nouns denoting persons, and elsewhere: e.g.

mam 'mother': an vam 'the mother'; dha vam 'thy mother'
dyw 'two', bre 'hill': an **dh**yw vre 'the two hills'
bugeleth 'shepherds': an vugeleth 'the shepherds'

(b) Aspiration: /k/ → /h/, /p/ → /f/, /t/ → /θ/, etc.: e.g. *pen* 'head': *ow fen* 'my head'; *tyr* 'country': *ow thyr* 'my country'.
(c) Nasalization: e.g. /d/ → /n/: *dor* 'earth': *an* ***n****or* 'the earth'.

A hard mutation: /b/ → /p/, /d/ → /t/, /g/ → /k/ (i.e. the converse of lenition) also occurs, and certain particles and adverbs generate a mixed mutation, e.g. /b/ →/f/, /d/ → /t/. This mutation is known as provection.

MORPHOLOGY AND SYNTAX

Noun

There are two genders: masculine and feminine. Certain endings are associated with gender: thus, abstracts in *-yeth*, nouns of place in *-va*/*-ek*, and nouns formed by adding *-en* to a collective plural, are feminine; abstract nouns in *-ans*, *-der*/*-ter*, nouns of place in *-jy*/*ty*, and all verbal nouns are masculine.
The definite article is *an*/*'n*. As indefinite article, *un*, a form of the numeral *onen* 'one', is used.

NUMBER

There are about a dozen plural markers: e.g. *lu* 'army': *luyow*; *bron* 'hill': *bronyon*; *pren* 'tree': *prenyer*. Some plurals are made by internal flection: *dans* 'tooth': *dyns*.
Singular nouns can be made from collectives by addition of *-en*: e.g. *derow* 'oak-trees': *derow****en*** 'an oak-tree'.
There is no inflectional system. Syntactic relationships are expressed by prepositions and by apposition. The genitive is in the construct formula or appositional: e.g. *to an chy* 'the roof of the house', with elision of the definite article belonging to the possessed component.

Adjective

Not marked for gender. As attribute, adjective may precede or follow the noun; postposition is preferred, with soft mutation in concord: e.g. after feminine singular: *an vugh vorm* 'the dun cow'. Some common adjectives always precede the noun, e.g. *keth* 'same', *ken* 'other'.

COMPARISON

es or *ages* precedes the noun compared: e.g. *whecca es mel* 'sweeter than honey'.

Pronoun

The personal pronouns have independent, infixed, and suffixed forms; the latter may be reduplicated or extended.

			Independent	*Infixed*	*Suffixed*	*Possessive*
sing.	1		my	′m	-vy, -ma, -a	ow, am
	2		ty	′th	-sy, -jy, -ta	dha, ′th
	3	masc.	ef	′n	-ef, -e, -va	y
		fem.	hy	′s	-hy	hy
pl.	1		ny	′gan, ′n	-ny	agan, an
	2		why	′gas, ′s	-why	agas, as
	3		y	′s	-y	aga

Example of infixed pronoun: *my a′**n** gwel* 'I see him/it'. The infixed pronoun often recapitulates a direct object already mentioned: e.g. *an vlejen pan y′**s** torras-**hy*** 'the flower (*an vlejen*) when she (*-hy*) picked it (*′s*)'.

DEMONSTRATIVE PRONOUN

Sing. *hemma/homma* 'this'; pl. *an rema*; sing. *henna/honna* 'that'; pl. *an rena*.

INTERROGATIVE PRONOUN

pyu 'who?'; 'what?' is expressed by various forms of the base *py*: e.g. *py lever* 'what book?'; *py* + *tra* ('thing') → *pandra* 'what?'

RELATIVE CLAUSE

See **Verb**, below.

Numerals

1–10: *onen/un, deu, try, peswar, pymp, whegh, seyth, eth, naw, dek*; 11 *unnek*; 12 *deudhek*; 20 *ugans*; 30 *dek warn ugans*; 40 *deugans*; 60 *try ugans*; 100 *cans.*

The numerals *due, try, peswar* have feminine forms *dyw, tyr, peder′*.

Verb

There are three moods: indicative, imperative, and subjunctive. The indicative mood has present/future, preterite, imperfect, and pluperfect tenses; the subjunctive has present/future and imperfect. The indicative and subjunctive have 3 + 3 personal forms, plus an impersonal.

Specimen conjugation of *prena* 'to buy': indicative mood:

	Singular	*Plural*					*Impersonal*
pres./future	pren**af**	preny**th**	pren**Ø**	preny**n**	pren**ough**	pren**ons**	preny**r**
preterite	preny**s**	pren**sys**	pren**as**	pren**en**	pren**sough**	pren**sons**	pren**as**
imperfect	pren**en**	pren**es**	pren**a**	pren**en**	pren**eugh**	pren**ens**	preny**s**

The pluperfect has the same endings as the imperfect, preceded by *-s-*: e.g. *pren**sen***. A perfect tense is made by adding the particle *re* before the preterite: e.g. ***re** prenys* 'I have bought'. The subjunctive has a specific set of endings.

THE SUBSTANTIVE VERB

bos/bones 'to be' has suppletive forms and a specific future:

Present: sing. *of*, *os*, *yu*; pl. *on*, *ough*, *yns*; the impersonal form is *or*.
Preterite: sing. *buf*, *bus*, *bu*; pl. *ben*, *beugh*, *bons*; impersonal, *bes.*
Future: sing. *bydhaf*, *bydhyth*, *byth*; pl. *bydhyn*, *bydhough*, *bydhons*; impersonal, *bydher.*
Imperfect: *en/esen*, *es/eses*, *o/esa*. . . .
Subjunctive: present/future: *byf*, *by*, *bo*. . . . Imperfect: *ben*, *bes*, *be* . . . .

IRREGULAR VERBS

There are several highly irregular verbs, exemplified here by the principal parts of:

(a) *mos/mones* 'to go':

Present/future: sing. *af*, *eth*, *a*; pl. *en*, *eugh*, *ons*; impersonal: *er.*
Preterite: *yth*, *ythys*, *eth*; *ethen*, *etheugh*, *ethons*; *es.*
Perfect: *galsof*, *galsos*, *gallas*; *galson*, *galsough*, *galsons*; no impersonal form.
Subjunctive present/future: *yllyf*, *ylly*, *ello*; *yllyn*, *yllough*, *ellons*; *eller.*

(b) *dos/dones* 'to come':

Present/future: sing. *dof*, *duth*, *de/du*; pl. *dun*, *deugh*, *dons*; impersonal: *deer.*
Preterite: *duth*, *duthys*, *deth*; *duthen*, *dutheugh*, *duthons*; *des.*
Perfect: *devef*, *deves*, *deva*; *devon*, *deveugh*, *devons*; *deves.*
Subjunctive present/future: *dyffyf*, *dyffy*, *deffo*; *dyffyn*, *dyffough*, *dyffons*; *deffoer.*

(c) *gul/gwruthyl* 'to do, make': also used as auxiliary verb 'shall, did'.

Present/future: 1st sing. *gwraf.*
Preterite: 1st sing. *gwruk.*
Subjunctive present/future: 1st sing. *gwryllyf.*

(d) *ry* 'to give':

Present/future: 1st sing. *rof.*
Preterite: 1st sing. *res.*
Subjunctive present/future: *ryllyf.*

PARTICIPLES

Present: *orth/ow* + verbal noun: e.g. *ow leverel* 'saying'.
Past: stem + *-ys*: e.g. *kemerys* 'taken'; *gwres*, *gwrys* 'done'.

NEGATIVE

Ny + soft mutation. The prohibitory negative is *na.*

Relative particles

A + soft mutation provides subject or object in relative sentence: e.g. *My a re dhys an lyver* ***a*** *dhewysyth* 'I will give you the book which you choose'; *an vugh a welys.vy* 'the cow I saw'.

Impersonal form

The characteristic is *-r*; the agent can be denoted by the particle *gans*: e.g. *redyer an lyver* 'there is a reading of the book'; *y redyer ganso* 'there is a reading by him'.

Prepositions

Simple and compound: e.g. *a* 'of', 'from', *rak* 'for'; *arak* 'before'; *aberveth yn* 'inside of'. Pronouns can be infixed between the components of a compound preposition. Some prepositions are followed by soft mutation; they take personal endings: e.g.

a: ahanaf 'of me'
a govys: a'**m** govys 'for my sake'; a'**y** wovys 'for his sake'
a ugh: a ugh**on** 'above us'
dhe: dh**ym** 'to me'
dres: dres**ough** 'over you'
war: war**nough** 'on you'

Word order

SVO in nominal clauses; VSO in verbal clauses, and obligatory in subordinate clauses; OSV is possible for reasons of emphasis.

1 Y'n dallethvos yth esa an Ger, ha'n Ger esa gans Dew, ha'n Ger o Dew.
2 An keth esa y'n dallethvos gans Dew.
3 Puptra-oll a vu gwres ganso: ha hebtho ny vu gwres travyth a vu gwres.
4 Ynno-ef yth esa bewnans; ha'n bewnans o Golow tus.
5 Ha'n golow a splan y'n tewlder, ha'n tewldre ny ylly y dhyfudha.
6 Yth esa den danvenys dyworth Dew, Jowan y hanow.
7 An keth a dheth yn tyyas rag dustunya a'n Golow may crysso pup mabden-oll dredho.
8 Nyns ova an Golow-na, mes danvenys vu rag dustunya a'n Golow.

CREE

INTRODUCTION

This is the major language of the Algonquian family in North America. It is spoken by about 70,000 Indians over a vast territory extending from Hudson's Bay in the East, across Ontario and Manitoba to Saskatchewan and Alberta, and from the grain belt northwards to Mackenzie and Kewatin. The ethnonym is *nahiyawāwak* 'the Cree people'. There are four main dialects: Plains Cree (L-dialect), Swampy Cree (N-dialect), Wood Cree in the Churchill River area, and Moose Cree, an L-dialect spoken in the Hudson's Bay country. The dialects are very largely mutually intelligible. Pre-aspiration becomes more noticeable in the western forms.

SCRIPT

See **Script** at end of article.

PHONOLOGY

Consonants

initial stops: p, t, k → medial b, d, g
affricates: tʃ after short vowels, dʒ after long
fricatives: s, ʃ, h
nasals: m, n
lateral: l
semi-vowels: j, w

Pre-aspiration of /p, t, k, tʃ/ is phonemic; it is here notated as *ḥ* (' in Hives (1948)). Initial nasal syllables, e.g. *ni-*, tend to /m̃/. The lateral /l/ is characteristic of the Plains dialect.

Vowels

The letters *a, e, i, o, u* are used to cover the following scale of values:

a = /ʌ/; *ā* = /aː ... o/; *e* (always long) = /ɛ ... e/; *i* = /ɪ ... ɛ/; ī = /iː/; *o* = /ɔ ... u/; ō = /oː ... uː/.

/ew/ and /aw/ occur very frequently in inflection; the /w/ is unstable.

MORPHOLOGY AND SYNTAX

Noun

Two key features in Cree are: (1) the all-pervasive dichotomy between animate and inanimate categories, which determines the morphological treatment of nouns, verbs, pronouns, numerals; (2) the use of the so-called 'fourth person' or obviative: once a third person noun or pronoun has been established as the subject or chief protagonist of a proposition, any other third person, subsequently introduced, is 'obviated' from true third person status, and is treated as a fourth person with its own complete set of verbal and nominal inflections. Thus, the ambiguity inherent in such English sentences as 'He saw him going down the street' is impossible in Cree, as the verbal inflections will establish which of the two third persons was going down the street. In the Hives grammar, a story is quoted which was told to Leonard Bloomsfield by Chief Coming Day: this concerns Cree Indians who were suddenly accosted by a Blackfoot raiding party. In the English translation, the frequent references to 'they' have to be glossed: does 'they' refer to the Crees or to the Blackfoot? In Cree there is no problem: the Crees being first on the scene (and the home side) are always in the true third person; the Blackfoot are in the fourth.

ANIMATES

The category of animate nouns includes several objects which would figure rather as inanimates in many other cultural taxonomies, e.g. *apwe* 'paddle', *asam* 'snowshoe', *askiḥk* 'kettle'. The plural marker for animates is -(*w*)*ak*: e.g. *aḥkik* 'seal', pl. *aḥkikwak*; *names* 'fish', pl. *namesak*; *maskwa* 'bear', pl. *maskwak*. The affix *-skaw* is used as an indicator for large numbers of something: e.g. *sakimeskaw* 'there are large numbers of mosquitoes', a nominal form which can be treated as a verb.

INANIMATES

The plural marker is *-a*: e.g. *čiman* 'canoe', pl. *čimana*. The Indo-European accusative of a specific third person referent is given an obviative ending in Cree: e.g. *Sakihew awasis***a** 'He loves-him the child' (*awasis* 'child').

LOCATIVE

In *-iḥk*/*oḥk*: e.g. *činamiḥk* 'in the canoe'; *mistikoḥk* 'in the tree'. The locative marker may be recapitulated in the verb by *-iši-*: e.g. *Čiman.***iḥk***.na kit.***iši***.apatasin?* 'Is it in the canoe that he is working?' (*-na* is an interrogative particle).

POSSESSION

The circumfix used with animate nouns:

	Singular	*Plural*
1	ni(t) . . . m/im/om	ni(t) . . . (im)inan/inaw
2	ki(t) . . . m/im/om	ki(t) . . . (im)iwaw
3	o(t) . . . a/im	o(t) . . . (im)iwaw

The inanimate markers are largely similar. The *-m/-im/-om* ending replaces *-w/-y* in citation form: e.g. *okimaw* 'boss' – ***nitokimam*** 'my boss'; *sipiy* 'river' – ***nisipim*** 'my river'; ***ničimaninan*** 'our canoe'. The locative marker follows the possessive: e.g. *nicimaninanihk* 'in our canoe'.

Bound forms: some nouns in Cree, denoting inalienable relationship, are never used without the possessive marker: e.g. ***mi**skisik* 'the eye' (i.e. someone's eye); ***ni**skisik* 'my eye'; ***mi**tanis* 'daughter'.

Double possessive: e.g. *nitanis okosisa o.čikahikan.**iyiw*** 'my daughter's son's axe', where *okosisa* is in the third person; *čikahikan* 'axe' is in the fourth person marked by the ending *-iyiw.*

Adjective

There are a few root adjectives, e.g. *kiḥči-* 'great', 'big', *mači* 'bad', *miywe-* 'good, fine', *oški-* 'new', but these are used mainly as prefixes in nominal compounds and as preverbs: e.g. *kiḥčimaneto* 'great spirit'; *kiḥči.okimaw* 'great chief'; *kiḥči.kami* 'sea'; *mači.kišikaw* 'it is a bad day'; *mači.piḥkiskwew* 'he speaks evil'.

Most adjectival meanings are conveyed by verbal roots, e.g. *kisinaw* 'it is cold'; *čiposiw* 'it is pointed'; *napakisiw* 'it is flat'.

Pronoun

PERSONAL PRONOUN

The Plains Cree forms are:

	Singular	*Plural*
1	niya	*excl.* niyanan, *incl.* kiyanaw
2	kiya	kiyayaw
3	wiya	wiyayaw

The Plains Cree forms originally had *-l-* (*nila*, *kila*, etc.), which is preserved in Moose Cree; the Swampy Cree forms have *-n-*: *nina*, *kina*, etc.

DEMONSTRATIVE PRONOUN

awa 'this' (animate), *oma* (inanimate) with obviative forms; *ana* 'that' (animate), *anima* (inanimate) with obviative forms. These have direct and obviative plural forms.

INTERROGATIVE PRONOUN

awena 'who?'; *kekwan* 'what?'

Numerals

1–10: *peyak*, *nišo*, *nisto*, *newaw*, *niyalan*, *nikotwas*, *niswas*, *niyananew*, *šank*, *mita*. 11–19 are formed with the linker *-asap*: e.g. 11 *mitataḥt peyakasap*. 20 *nisitonaw*; 30 *nistomitanaw*; 100 *mitaḥtomitanaw.*

Verb

Underlying the multitude of Cree verbal forms (Horden (1881) gives about 150 pages of paradigms, setting out some 2,000 forms) are certain basic oppositions:

transitive	intransitive
animate	inanimate
independent or proximate assertion	dependent (conjunct) assertion
direct personal deixis	inverse personal deixis

In general, Cree tends to use semantically densely ordered verbal units or complexes to express concepts which in languages of a different type require analytical strings of nouns, articles, verbs, adjectives, adverbs, etc. For example, the Watkins–Faries dictionary (1938) abounds in such entries as *puskwaskichāsin* 'It is a small open patch of burnt woods'; *tipiskiskum* 'Night overtakes him before he reaches his destination'; *nupokuskitititimunawao* 'He breaks both its shoulder blades' (these three examples are in the older spelling used in the Watkins–Faries dictionary).

INTRANSITIVE VERBS

(a) Impersonal: there are a great many of these, e.g. *taḥkwakin* 'it is autumn'; *mispon* 'it is snowing'; *kisiwayaw* 'it's warm weather'; *kimiwan* 'it's raining'.
(b) Animate intransitive verbs are sub-divided by stem vowel into several classes. A specimen paradigm follows: indicative present of *apiw* 'he is/sits at home':

		Singular	*Plural*
1		**nitapin**	*excl.* **nitapinan**, *incl.* **kitapinanaw**
2		**kitapin**	**kitapinawaw**
3	animate	**øapiw**	**øapiwak**
	inanimate	**øapimakan**	**øapimakanwa**
4	animate	**øapiyiwa**	**øapiyiwa**
	inanimate	**øapimakaniyiw**	**øapimakaniyiwa**

The conjunct (subjunctive) form drops the personal markers, which are replaced by the invariable particle *e*, and adds a new set of endings: e.g. in the singular: 1 ***e apiyān***; 2 ***e apiyan***; 3 anim. ***e apit***, *inanim.* ***e apimakak***; 4 anim. ***e apiyit***, inanim. ***e api makaniyik***.

NEGATION

mola precedes the negated word(s).

TENSE MARKERS

Future: *kitalk(a)*: e.g. *itoḥtew* 'he goes there'; *mola ni.***k***.itoḥtan* 'I'm not going there'.

Perfective: *-ki-* (positive), *-oḥči-* (negative): e.g. *Øoḥčitoḥtew* 'He didn't go there.'
Potential: *-ki-* following tense marker: e.g. *ni.ki.ki.peči.toḥtan* 'I'll be able to come' (*peči-* is a directional prefix).

INTERROGATIVE MARKER

-na is added to focused word: e.g. *Kekwan weyapaḥtaman? Čiman.na?* 'What do you see? A canoe?'

INCEPTIVE PREFIX

ati-: e.g. *Ati.kimiwan* 'It is beginning to rain.'

DESIDERATIVE PREFIX

wi-: e.g. *Winipaw* 'He wants to sleep.'

DIRECT AND INVERSE VERSIONS

First and second person pronouns take precedence over third person. Thus, for example 'you see him' can be stated directly, *ki wapamaw*; but 'he sees you' is an inverse form in Cree, ***ki*** *wapam****ik***; an English approximation is 'you are seen by him', but the passive voice is misleading. To put it another way: first and second person are covered by the direct transitive conjugation *vis-à-vis* third person: e.g. *ki.wāpam.ānawak* 'we (incl.) see them'; but the inverse conjugation has to be used when a third person is subject *vis-à-vis* first or second: e.g. *ki.wāpam.ikonawak* 'we (incl.) are seen by them' = 'they see us'.

TRANSITIVE VERB

The transitive verbal form encodes subject and target, even when a noun object is overtly expressed; i.e. in Cree, a sentence of the type 'I see X', where X is a noun, appears as 'I see-it X'. The Indo-European distinction between subject and object is not relevant in Cree, which interprets the indirect object of Indo-European languages as the *direct* object, and the direct object, if expressed, as a noun in the obviative.

CONJUNCT FORM

This is the form used in dependent clauses to express state or action concomitant with, antecedent to, or following the state or action expressed in the principal clauses; i.e. a conjunct form can only be used with reference to a direct (proximate) assertion. The form has inflected endings but no personal prefixes (see paradigm, above): e.g. *pipon* 'it is winter': ***e*** *pipo****ḥk*** 'it being winter', 'when it was winter', etc.; ***Kit****.apiñ****ānaw*** ***e*** *kimiwa****ḥk*** 'As it is raining, we are (staying) at home.'

RELATIVE

ka: cf. *ililiw ka kiḥtoḥtet* 'the person who is going away'; *ililiw ka kikiḥtoḥtet* 'the person who went away'.

Roots are modulated by prefix to express motion to or away from focus, various nuances in mode of action, inception, cessation, ingress, exit, etc. For example, from root *-asiw-* 'to sail' (*pimasiw* 'he sails'), *sipweyasiw* 'he sails off', where *sipwe-* is an inceptive prefix. Cf. *sipwečaḥkwew* 'he starts the spirit on its way' = 'he dies'.

Prepositions

Cree prepositions precede nouns in the locative case. Hives (1948) gives such examples as: *peḥce* 'in'; *peḥce waskahikaniḥk* 'in the house'.

There are also a few postpositions, e.g. *isse* 'to, towards', again with locative: *waskahikaniḥk isse* 'towards the house'.

Word order

SVO is possible in nominal sentences. A verb form, incorporating all three elements, may itself be a sentence.

MAWUTCHE nistum kẻ ẻtaw Ayumewin, mena Ayumewin kẻ wechāwāo Munetoowa, mena Ayumewin kẻ Munetoowew.

2 Āwuko owa mawutche nistum kẻ wechāwāo Munetoowa.

3 Kåkeyow kākwi weya kẻ osẻtaw; mena āka weya ỏche numoweya kākwi kitta kẻ osẻchekatāpun ka kẻ osẻtåk.

4 Weya kẻ kekeskum pimatissewin; mena pimatissewin kẻ wastānumakwuk eyinewuk.

5 Mena wastāo wasetāo wunetipiskåk; mena wunetipiskaw numoweya kẻ nissetowāyẻtumomukun.

6 ¶ Kẻ ẻtaw napāo ā issitissåwat Muneto, John ā issenỉkasoot.

7 Āwuko owa kẻ pā wẻtum, kitta wẻtumakāt oma Wastāo, kåkeyow eyinewa kitta tapwẳtumeyit weya ỏche.

8 Numoweya weya kẳchewak āwuko Wastāo, maka kẻ issitissåwaw kitta wẻtumakāt āwuko Wastāo.

SCRIPT

The Cree syllabary was developed by the Rev. James Evans in the 1830s, and by 1840 it was being used to print religious texts in Cree. As further modified and improved by the Rev. John Horden (author of *A Cree Grammar*), the syllabary has been subsequently used for the considerable body of Biblical translation and original devotional literature published in Cree from the late nineteenth century onwards.

THE CREE SCRIPT

THE SYLLABARY

	e'	i	o	a	*Finals*	
					Moose (M)	*Western (W)*
Independent Vowel	ᐁ	ᐃ	ᐅ	ᐊ		
p	ᐯ	ᐱ	ᐳ	ᐸ	ᑉ	ᑊ
t	ᑌ	ᑎ	ᑐ	ᑕ	ᑦ	ᐟ
c	ᒉ	ᒋ	ᒍ	ᒐ	ᒡ	ᐨ
k	ᑫ	ᑭ	ᑯ	ᑲ	ᒃ	ᐠ
m	ᒣ	ᒥ	ᒧ	ᒪ	ᒻ	c
n	ᓀ	ᓂ	ᓄ	ᓇ	ᓐ	ɔ.
l	ᓓ	ᓕ	ᓗ	ᓚ	ᓪ	{
s	ᓭ	ᓯ	ᓱ	ᓴ	ᔅ	ᐢ
š	ᔐ	ᔑ	ᔓ	ᔕ	ᔥ	
y	ᔦ	ᔨ	ᔪ	ᔭ	o	•
r	ᕂ	ᕆ	ᕈ	ᕋ	ᕐ	}

CROW

INTRODUCTION

Crow and Hidatsa form a sub-division of the Macro-Siouan family of North American Indian languages. At present, about 5,000 speakers live in the Crow Reservation in south-eastern Montana.

PHONOLOGY

Consonants

Basic inventory with positionally determined allophones:

stops: p/b, t/d, k/g/k′/g′
affricates: tʃ/dʒ
fricatives: β, s/ʃ, z/ʒ, x, h
liquid: r/l/n

The nasals [m] and [n] are thus construed as allophones of /w/b/ and /r/l/d/. Bilabial /β/ is realized as [w, m, b].

In general, the lenis sounds are intervocalic: cf. *wiša* 'buffalo' /biža/, transcribed as *bice* by Lowie (1941): i.e. the sound notated as *c* by Lowie is /ʃ/; his *ts* is /tʃ/; in this article, these are notated as *š* and *č*.

Kaschube (1967) describes /l/ as in free variation with /r/, and probably associated with female speakers.

Vowels

Allophones are indicated:

i/ɪ, e, a/ɛ/æ/ə, o/ɔ, u

Long values are marked here, following Kaschube (1967), with : (Lowie (1941) uses ·).

Tones

Kaschube recognizes three: falling (grave accent), high (acute), low (unmarked). Syllables with high or falling tone may be stressed.

MORPHOLOGY AND SYNTAX

There is a basic division into stems and affixes. Crow stems are not marked for morphological function; that is, there is no formal difference between nouns, verbs, adjectives, particles. Stems can, however, be classified in terms of their valencies. For example, stems which are compatible with (a) personal pronominal prefixes, and (b) the imperative modal suffixes, are classified as verbs; stems which can accept (a) but not (b) are nouns.

Verbal stems are further sub-divided, by specific restraints on choice of personal pronominal prefix, into three main classes: stative, active, mixed (the mixed class combining stative and active features). Constraints of a similar nature determine nouns as denoting alienable or inalienable possession. A concatenation of stems is classed as nominal or verbal, depending on the class of the initial component.

Some examples of Crow stems: *wára* 'tree'; *-wará:* 'money'; *-warú:* 'to fight'; *wà:ra* 'winter'; *wá:ro* 'beads'; *wirá* 'water'. Stems have allomorphs (e.g. *-wará:-/-waré:-*) which are functionally distributed.

Typically, a Crow word is composed of a succession of coded slots in three main sections: prefixes – stems – suffixes.

1. Prefixes include personal pronominal markers (see below), the past-tense marker *kara-*, reciprocal and demonstrative markers, and the spatio-temporal localizer *ar-*.

The personal pronominal markers, subjective and objective, are 1 *wih-*, 2 *rih-*, 3 *ih-*; all with series of functionally distributed allomorphs. The spelling is that of Kaschube (1967); Lowie (1941) uses initial allophones: 1 *bi·*, 2 *di·*, 3 *i·*. A 1st p. pl. form is *bare*; its exclusive correlative is *bi:ru*. The following examples are from Kaschube:

wí-hà:rik 'I finish' (*wi-* is first person marker; *-hà:ri* 'to finish'; *-k* is predicative terminator)
wí:a.ra.ká.k 'you see me' (*wí* is first person object; *a...ka* 'to see' (discontinuous stem); *ra* is medial allomorph of second person pronoun)
wá:w.wá:ríči.k 'I hit something' (*wá:w* indicates indefiniteness; *-ríči* 'to hit')
kawwá:wá:ríšši.ss.u.k 'we didn't dance' (*kar* → *kaw* = past-tense marker; *wá:* indefinite marker; *wá:* 1st person pronoun; *ríšši* 'to dance'; *-ss-* = negative marker; *-u-* plural marker; *-k* predicative terminator)
wa.sà:škia 'my horse' (*-sà:* is the alienable possession marker; *-škia* 'horse, dog')
ar.a.xap.a 'his bed' (*ar-* = spatio-temporal localizer; *a-* = third person pronoun marker; *xap* = 'to lie down'; *-a* = singular nominalizer)

The class of inalienable nouns includes those denoting parts of the body and degrees of kinship. The inalienable property markers are the personal pronominal prefixes, often with crasis: *batse*, *ditse*, *itse* 'my, your, his/her foot': *da.asuə* > *da:sua* 'your home'; *bare.asua* 'our home'. *Øra:sa* 'his (null marker) heart'.

bas-, *dis-*, *is-* mark alienable property: *is.kukuwe* 'her squashes'; *is.aračiə* > *iš.tačia* 'her garden'.

Possessive relationship with nominals: possessor precedes possessed: *isa:kšem isa:šgye* 'young-man his-horse'.

2. Suffixes: these include tense and modal markers, e.g. *-h*, *wáči* future markers; *-če* causative; *-i* durative; *-ku* benefactive; *-a/-à:ra* imperative markers. Negation markers: *-ssa-*, *ré:tá*; nominalizers: *-a* (singular), *-úa* (plural); terminators: *-k* (finalizing), *-w/-š* (holding); agentive markers: *št* (of habitual action). The suffixed definite article is *-š(e)*: *a:suə.š* 'the camp' (*a:su*(ə) is plural of *aše* 'tipi'); *axa.še* 'the Sun'; *xare.š* 'the rain'.

Plurality: by reduplication, or, by adding *-u*(ə)/-o: *wiša* 'buffalo', pl. *wiša.o*; *bače* 'man', pl. *bače.o*; *xawi* 'bad', pl. *xawa:u*; *isa.te* 'big', pl. *isa.tu*.

wá:wá:warú:w.o.h.wáči.k 'we shall fight' (*wá:* = indefinite marker; *wá:* = first person pronoun marker; *warú* = 'to fight'; *w* + *o* = first person plural marker; *-h* + *wáč* = future markers; *-k* = predicative terminator);
wú:šišt 'I'm in the habit of eating' (*w* = first person marker; *ú:ši* = 'to eat'; *-št* = habitual action).

Lowie (1941) gives the following paradigm of an aorist present tense (spelling adapted):

	Singular	*Plural*
1	ba-ka:k 'I laugh'	ba-**ku**:k
2	da-ka:k	da-**ku**:k
3	Ø-ka:k	Ø-**ku**:k

And of a discontinuous stem: *a . . . o:ri* 'to wait':

	Singular	*Plural*
1	a.wo:ri.k	a.wo:ru.k
2	a.ro:ri.k	a.ro:ru.k
3	o:ri.k	o:ruk

Some examples of Crow verb forms: *kara.xta.čeruk* 'he had forgotten' (where *čeruk* is the quotative marker: 'so it is said'); *iri.sa.čeruk* 'he spoke not' (*sa* is a negating infix); *dara:wək de.čeruk* 'flying-away (participle) it-went (predicative)'; *hine b/wiričgye.š i.kya.čeruk* 'this (*hine*) lake (*-š* definite article) he saw'; *ba:warax.dək di.əxaxua disa.ara* 'when-I-sing (*ba:warax.dək*) you-all (*di.əxaxua*) dance!' (*disa* imperative of *diši* 'to dance', *-ra* imperative plural marker): *wiša.rək dap.i.o.čeruk* 'they killed a buffalo'.

All Crow verbs have a future conjugation; active verbs have in addition an aorist present (illustrated above).

Future: the singular endings are *-bi*, *-di*, *-i/e*; the 1st plural marker is *bi:ru/wi:ru*; *di.a.wa.wiru.k* 'we'll do it'; *di.a.wa.warak. bi:ru:k* 'we'll make it for you' (*warak* expresses 1st p. deixis to 2nd).

The attributive adjective follows its noun: *šič.kya:te* 'small hill'.

Numerals

Kaschube gives the following forms for 1–5 inclusive: *hawát*, *ruhp-*, *-rà:wí-*, *šó:pá*, *čaxxo*: *i.se šo:pka:še* 'his four arrows', *hine wase.š hawate* 'one of these men'. 10 is *-piraká*.

Postpositions

Crow uses postpositions: an example is: *e:ky šiče aričia biričgyem ko:rəm* 'behind (*aričia*) that hill is a lake'.

Word order

SOV in transitive sentences, SV in intransitive.

TROOTSHID Kinjih kwịlịh, akọ Kinjih Vittukoochanchyo ha tịnchyo, akọ Kinjih Vittukoochanchyo ịlịh. 2 Ei trootshid Vittukoochanchyo ha tịnchyo. 3 Ekoochichyo kwuttutthug attun kirre zyunkwulttsuị; akọ vettun elyet ekoochichyo kwattsyah ei yoo kwulttseị. 4 Vih zit kwundui kwịlịh: akọ ei kwundui tinjih ittri ịlịh. 5 Akọ attri tseggah kwi zit ạnttri, akọ tseggah elyet kwikyittuttziitthui.
6 Tinjih kwịlịh John vazi, Vittukoochanchyo yih chile. 7 Ei yoo ket kwanduk keh njit ninịzye. Attri tsut kut kwutanduk (tinjih) tutthug kih kirre kwikyinjitetah. 8 Ei yoo elyet Attri iilyah, kọ ei Attri kut kwutanduk keh njit kwuh tsuh chile.

CUANG (Cuəŋ)

See **Juang**.

CZECH

INTRODUCTION

This Western Slavonic language is the official language of the Czech Republic, spoken by around 12 million people. Czech and Slovak are mutually intelligible. Writing in Czech dates from the thirteenth to fourteenth centuries. Historically, Czech culture and literature are orientated towards Western Europe, rather than towards Moscow and the Orthodox Church. The first flowering of Czech literature was in the reign of Charles IV (fourteenth century), with Jan Hus playing a notable role in the formation of a standardized literary language. The suppression of Czech culture, associated with the Counter-Reformation, lasted until the late eighteenth century, when contact with Western sources was re-established, and a romantic renaissance ensued. This period culminated in the abortive revolution of 1848. From the late nineteenth century to the outbreak of the Second World War, Czech was the vehicle for a very rich and extensive literature in all genres, especially poetry (e.g. Vrchlický, Bezruč, Březina) and the novel (Holeček, Hašek, Čapek).

SCRIPT

Romanization plus diacritics. The orthography was rationalized, first by Jan Hus in the fourteenth century, subsequently by the Czech Brethren in their sixteenth-century translation of the Bible.

The palatalized consonants /t', d'/ are marked by apostrophe: e.g. *ted'* 'now', *zed'* 'wall'. /t/ and /d/ are palatalized before /i/ and /je/; the latter is then written as ě. The palatal n/ɲ/ is notated as *ň*.

PHONOLOGY

Consonants

stops: p, b, t, d, k, g + palatalized t', d'
affricates: ts, tʃ
fricatives: f, v, s, z, ʃ, ʒ, j, h, x
nasals: m, n, ɲ
lateral: l
trill: r, ɼ (notated as *ř*)

/g/ occurs in foreign words only, or by assimilation; in native words, Slavonic /g/ is represented by /h/: e.g. Russian *golub*(*ka*) = Czech *holub*. The liquids /r, l/ can be syllabic: e.g. *prst* 'finger', *vlk* 'wolf'. A softened glottal stop or hamza separates vowels in final–initial contact, and in words like *naučit* 'to teach', where *-au-* is not a diphthong: *na.učit*.

Voiced consonants in final position are unvoiced: e.g. *chleb* 'bread' [xlɛ̄p]. Assimilation of unvoiced to voiced: e.g. *kdo* 'who?' [gdɔ]; *svatba* 'wedding' [sva**d**ba]. *Mě* is pronounced /mɲɛ/: e.g. *město* 'city' [mɲɛstɔ].

Vowels

short: a, ɛ, ɪ, ɔ, u
long: aː, ɛː, iː, uː

Long /oː/ occurs in foreign words only. /uː/ is notated as *ů*. /y/=/ɪ, i/ long or short. Diphthongs: /ou/ is native, e.g. *klobouk* 'hat'; /au, eu/ occur in loanwords.

In the thirteenth/fourteenth centuries vowel mutation after soft consonants (broadly, back/low vowels were raised to front/high) gave Czech its characteristic and very distinctive sound. Thus, *žena* 'woman', *duše* 'soul', with instrumental singular *ženou*, *duší*. Similarly, *nesu* 'I carry', but *píši* 'I write' (literary form).

Stress

Stress is invariably on the first syllable.

MORPHOLOGY AND SYNTAX

Noun

Three genders, two numbers. The original six declensions (*see* **Slavonic Languages**) are preserved in Czech:

-i/*-ja* feminine stems: e.g. *kost* 'bone';
-a/*-ja* stems: e.g. *žena* 'woman', *duše* 'soul';
-o/*-jo* masculine stems: e.g. *muž* 'man';
-o/*-jo* neuter stems: e.g. *místo* 'place', *moře* 'sea';
-ū stems: e.g. *církev* 'church' (feminine);
consonantal stems (masculine and neuter): e.g. *kámen* 'stone'.

There are seven cases including a vocative. Differentiation due to phonetic constraints is very considerable; some grammars give over 250 paradigms. There follow specimen declensions of a masculine noun – *muž* 'man' – and a feminine – *žena* 'woman':

	Singular	*Plural*	*Singular*	*Plural*
nom.	muž	muži	žena	ženy
gen.	muže	mužů	ženy	žen
dat.	muži/ovi	mužům	ženě	ženám
acc.	muže	muže	ženu	ženy
instr.	mužem	muži	ženou	ženami

loc.	muži	mužích	ženě	ženách
voc.	muži	–	ženo	–

Nominative, accusative forms for animate masculine nouns differ in singular and plural from those for inanimates.

POSSESSION

Possessor follows possessed: e.g. *mapa Československa* 'a map of the Czech Republic'. There are no articles.

Adjective

As attribute, adjective precedes noun, and is in full concord with it for all cases, preserving animate/inanimate distinction. Hard adjectives show gender in the nominative ending: *-ý*, *-á*, *-é*. Soft adjectives have *-í* in all three. Examples: *nový dům* (masc.) 'new house'; *stará žena* (fem.) 'old woman'; *nové divadlo* (nt.) 'new theatre'; *moderní hotel, divadlo, budova* 'modern hotel, theatre, building'.

As predicate, adjective shows concord: cf. *nový dům – dům je nový*; *nové divadlo – divadlo je nové.*

POSSESSIVE ADJECTIVES

Those based on nouns denoting males and male names: *-ův*, *-ova*, *-ovo*; females: *-in*, *-ina*, *-ino*: e.g. from *bratr: bratrův pokoj* 'the brother's room'; from *sestra*: *sestřin pokoj* 'the sister's room'. Compare *Karlův most* 'the Charles Bridge'; *Karlova Universita* 'the Charles University'.

COMPARATIVE

In *-(ej)ší*: e.g. *bohatý* 'rich' – *bohat*ší; *důležitý* e.g. 'important' – *důležitější.* There are the usual suppletives: e.g. *dobrý* 'good' – *lepší*; *špatný* 'bad' – *horší.*

Pronoun

The nominative (= subject) forms are:

sing. 1 *ja*, 2 *ty*, 3 *on/ona/ono*; pl. 1 *my*, 2 *vy*, 3 *oni*.

These forms are used for emphasis and contrast only. They are declined in all cases, and have weak and strong forms; e.g. for first person singular, acc./gen. *mě*, dat. *mi/mně*, instr. *mnou.*

The possessive adjectives are marked for gender in the singular, partially in plural:

sing. 1 *můj/má/mé*, 2 *tvůj/tvá/tvé*, 3 *jeho/její*; pl. 1 *náš/naše*, 2 *váš/vaše*.

The third person plural form *jejich* is not marked for gender.

DEMONSTRATIVE PRONOUN/ADJECTIVE

ten – ta – to 'this'; pl. *ti*; *tamten – tamta – tamto* 'that'. *-hle* may be added: e.g. *Líbí se mi tenhle klobouk* 'I like this hat.'

INTERROGATIVE PRONOUN
kdo 'who?'; *co* 'what?' These are declined.

RELATIVE PRONOUN
který/která/které 'which, that': e.g. *kniha, která leží na stole* 'the book which is lying on the table'. Replaced in colloquial by *co*. The literary form is *jenž* (masc.), *jež* (fem. and nt.): e.g. *cíl, jenž stojí před námi* 'the aim which lies before us'.

Numerals

1 *jeden/jedna/jedno*; 2 *dva/dvě*; 3 *tři*; 4 *čtyři*. These are declined in all cases. From 5 onwards, all oblique cases are in *-i*: 5–10 *pět, šest, sedm, osm, devět, deset*. 11 *jedenáct*; 12 *dvanáct*; 13 *třináct*; 20 *dvacet*; 30 *třicet*; 40 *čtyřicet*; 100 *sto*.

Verb

Taking the third person singular as criterion, we may classify Czech verbs into three groups:

(a) *-e*: e.g. *píše* 'he writes' (infinitive: *psát*);
(b) *-á*: e.g. *dělá* 'he does' (infinitive: *dělat*);
(c) *-í:* e.g. *mluví* 'he speaks' (infinitive: *mluvit*).

The *-e* groups can be further sub-divided to include-*n*- and *-uj-* stems: e.g. *tiskne* 'he presses' (infinitive: *tisknout*); *kupuje* 'he buys' (infinitive: *kupovat*). The past or *-l* form:

-e verbs take *-l*, *-nul*, or *-oval*;
-á verbs take *-al*;
-í verbs take *-il* or *-el*.

ASPECT
As in other Slavonic languages, paired verbs. Perfective formed:

(a) by prefix: e.g. *platit* 'to pay': perf. ***za**platit*; *prosit* 'to ask': perf. ***po**prosit*; *končit* 'to finish': perf. ***s**končit*; *ptát se* 'to ask' perf. ***ze**ptat se*.
(b) prefix + stem change: *odnášet* 'take away', perf. *odnést*; *přinášet* 'bring', perf. *přinést*.
(c) suppletive: *brát* 'to take': *vzít*.

Imperfectives may be formed from verbs which are inherently perfective: e.g. *padat* 'to fall': *pad**nout***; *dát* 'to give': *dá**va**t*.

Example of tense/aspect structure: *psát* 'to write':

	Past	*Present*	*Future*
imperfective:	psal jsem	píši (*coll.* píšu)	budu psát
perfective:	**na**psal jsem	**ø**	**na**píši/u

TENSE

Specimen present tense of a *-a* verb: *dělat* 'to do': imperfective:

	Singular	Plural
1	dělám	děláme
2	děláš	děláte
3	dělá	dělají

Past tense or *-l* form: the auxiliary verb is not used in the third person. The *-l* form is marked for gender and number:

	Singular	Plural
1	čekal/-a jsem 'I waited'	čekali/-y jsme
2	čekal/-a jsi	čekali/-y jste
3	čekal/-a Ø	čekali/-y Ø

FUTURE

Future tense of auxiliary *být* = *budu* + infinitive: e.g. *budu psát* 'I shall write'. This is always imperfective. The present *form* of the perfective aspect has a future meaning: e.g. ***na**píšu* 'I shall write' (= have written).

IMPERATIVE

Both aspects have imperative mood: e.g. *Čtěte!* 'Read!' (imperfective); ***Pře**čtěte cely text!* 'Read the whole text!' (perfective).

PASSIVE

(a) With *se*; this is associated with the change of transitive to intransitive: *Lidská práce mění krajinu* 'Human labour changes the countryside'; *Celá krajina **se** mění* 'The whole countryside is changing.'
(b) With auxiliary *být* + truncated verbal adjective: e.g. *byl jsem vyšetřován lékařem* 'I was examined by the doctor'.

CONDITIONAL

Provided by aux. sing. *bych*, *bys*, *by*: pl. *bychom*, *byste*, *by* + *-l* form: e.g. with *rád* 'gladly': *rád bych věděl* 'I should like to know'; *rádi bychom věděli* 'we should like to know'.

PARTICIPLES

(a) Present in *-cí* added to third person plural of imperfective present: e.g. *dělají*: *dělající*. The form is declined as an adjective.
(b) Past active participle: *-(v)ší* replaces *-l* of perfective past; declined as adjective: e.g. *udělavší* 'having done, who has done'.
(c) Past passive participle = verbal noun: *-ní/tí*: e.g. *dělání* 'doing'; *bytí* 'being'.

NEGATION

The general negating particle is *ne*, prefixed to verb: e.g. *nic neslyším* 'I hear nothing' (i.e. double negative).

Prepositions

Prepositions govern nouns in the accusative, genitive, dative, locative or instrumental cases. Some, e.g. *na* 'on/in/at', *pod* 'under', *před* 'in front of', take locative or instrumental for rest in a place and the accusative for motion towards, along, etc. e.g. *jsem na poště* 'I am in the post-office'; but *jdu na poštu* 'I go to the post-office'.

Word order

SVO is basic. Subject usually omitted if pronoun. Almost all permutations of word order are possible.

Na počàtku bylo Slovo, a to Slovo bylo u Boha, a to Slovo byl Bůh.
2 To bylo na počàktu u Boha.
3 Všecky věci skrze ně učiněny jsou, a bez něho nic není učiněno což u činěno jest.
4 V něm život byl, a život byl světlo lidí.
5 A to světlo v temnostech svítí, ale temnosti ho neobśahly.
6 Byl člověk poslaný od Boha, jemuž jméno *bylo* Jan.
7 Ten přišel na svědectvi, aby svědčil o tom světle, aby všickni uvěřili skrze něho.
8 Nebyl on to světlo, ale *přišel*, aby svědčil o tom světle.

DAGESTANIAN LANGUAGES

INTRODUCTION

These languages of the North-East and North-Central Caucasus are spoken mainly in the Dagestan Republic, with some spread into Azerbaijan, Georgia, the Chechnya Republic, and Ingushetia Republic. They can be divided on genetic grounds into the following three large groups:

1. Avar-Andi-Dido, comprising the following languages: Avar (*see* **Avar**); the Andi sub-group, consisting of Andi, Botlikh, Godoberi, Karata, Akhvakh, Bagval, Tindi, and Chamalal; total number of speakers is around 552,000, of which Avar accounts for over 500,000; the Dido or Tsez languages: Dido, Khvarsh, Ginukh, Bezhti, Gunzib. About 14,000 speakers (Dido 10,000).
2. Lezgian: comprising Lezgi, Archi, Tabasaran, Agul, Rutul, Tsakhur, Budukh, Udi, Khinalugh, Kryz. These are located in the south-eastern zone of Dagestan. The total number of speakers is *c*. 445,000, Lezgi itself having 400,000 of this total.
3. Lak (120,000 speakers) and Dargva (300,000 speakers) are spoken in the central region of Dagestan.

SCRIPT

The Dagestanian languages are unwritten apart from Avar, Lak, Dargva, Lezgi, and Tabasaran, which have been used as literary languages since the 1920s, though one or two of them have literary traditions going much further back. These five languages started their post-1917 literary activity in scripts based on Arabic, switched to a Roman-based script in the 1930s, and have, since 1938/9 been using Cyrillic + the letter *I*. This letter is generally used to mark the ejective consonants characteristic of Caucasian languages. Both the Andi and the Dido sub-groups use Avar as a literary language and as a lingua franca.

PHONOLOGY

Consonants

All the Dagestanian languages are characterized by extensive consonantal inventories allied to relatively simply vocalic systems. Many of them are particularly rich in dental, alveolar, velar, and lateral fricatives and affricatives, which usually occur in four- or five-term series of the type voiced member – simple aspirate surd – geminated aspirate surd – ejective simple surd – geminated ejective surd: e.g. /ʒ – tʃ – tʃtʃ – t'ʃ – t'ʃt'ʃ/. The geminated sounds are said to be 'tense' *vis-à-vis* their 'non-intensive' simple forms.

Vowels

The basic series, /a, e, i, o, u/, is extended by lengthening, nasalization, labialization, pharyngealization (in association with pharyngeal consonants). /ɛ/, /œ/, and /y/ also occur, e.g. in Bezhti.

MORPHOLOGY AND SYNTAX

The main common features of the Dagestanian languages are:

1. *Noun classes*: there are usually four of these. Class I normally comprises male human beings, class II female human beings; in certain languages this class also includes some inanimate objects. In the Andi sub-group, noun classes vary in number from five for both singular and plural in Andi and Chamalal to three in the others. Class III in Andi comprises animals. It is noteworthy that parity, as between singular and plural classes, is not conserved: thus four singular classes are usually reduced to two plural classes based on the simple opposition human/non-human. Otherwise, the taxonomies underlying the division into classes are not always clear. Dido is logical, from an Indo-European point of view:

Class	
I	male human beings
II	female human beings
III	animals, birds, plants
IV	inanimate objects

Tabasaran has only two classes: human/non-human. Gunzib, on the other hand, has six: I males, II females, III mixed bag, IV animals, V another mixed bag, VI contains only one word: *kəra* 'child'.

The class markers may appear as fossilized markers in nouns, but are regularly confined to marking concord in predicates, adjectives, etc. The class markers themselves are very regular: cf.

	Class	*Avar*	*Andi*	*Dido*	
singular {	I	v	v	–	} plural: r/l
	II	y	y	y	
	III	b	b	b	

2. *Very elaborate case systems*: about 40 'cases' can be distinguished in Tabasaran, for example. Most of these 'cases' are spatial, defining locus and relative motion in great detail. Thus, in Gunzib, for example, the locatives are ordered in seven series, each with two terms specifying (a) locus and (b) motion:

1. on the surface of something;
2. under something;
3. in something;
4. vertically with relation to something else;
5, 6, 7. in varying degrees of modalities of contiguity.

3. Except in Lezgi, Agul, and Udi, verbs in Dagestanian languages are conjugated by class without inflection for person. The three exceptions ignore class. Additional differentiation by person appears in Lak, Dargva, and Tabasaran. The verbal base may also contain locative and directional markers.

For more detailed descriptions of features of Dagestanian languages, *see* **Agul**, **Andi Languages**, **Avar**, **Lak**, **Lezgi**, **Tabasaran**.

DAKOTA

INTRODUCTION

Dakota is one of the major languages of the Siouan family. The word 'Dakota' is a Sioux ethnonym meaning 'friends/allies' and applies particularly to the Santee group, one of three groups known collectively as 'Dakota'; the other two are Nakota (Yankton) and Lakota (Teton).

Missionaries were active among the Dakota from 1819 onwards. A script for the language was worked out, and by the late 1880s the complete Bible and *The Pilgrim's Progress* had been translated into Dakota, and several school primers and readers had been provided.

Today the Dakota live in North and South Dakota, Montana, and Nebraska. There are 10,000–20,000 speakers.

This article comprises (a) a simplified description of Dakota, based on Riggs (1893) (reissued 1976), and (b) a more detailed account of Lakota, based on Buechel (1939).

SCRIPT

As used by Riggs (1893), the script has *ć*, *ź*, and *ś* for /tʃ, ʒ, ʃ/, ġ =/γ/, *ḣ*= /χ/, and ' = hamza. The ejective consonants are marked by subscript dot.

PHONOLOGY

Consonants

In broad transcription:

stops: p, b, p', t, d, t', k, g, k', ʔ
affricates: tʃ, t'ʃ
fricatives: s, ʃ, z, ʒ, x, γ, χ
nasals: m, n, ŋ
semi-vowels: j, w

Vowels

Riggs (1893) gives five vowels: /i, e, a, o, u/. Contraction and assimilation are frequent.

Stress

Stress is phonemic, usually on the second syllable; in many words on first: cf. *máġa* 'field', *maġá* 'goose'.

As prefixes are added, stress gravitates towards the second syllable; Riggs gives the example: *kaśká* 'to bind', *wa.káśka* 'I bind', *wićá.wa.kaśka* 'I bind them' (*wića* is the 3rd person plural objective pronoun).

MORPHOLOGY AND SYNTAX

Noun

Dakota has primary and derived nouns: examples of primary nouns are *maka* 'earth', *peta* 'fire', *ate* 'father', *ina* 'mother'. For examples of derived nouns *see* below. Natural gender is marked lexically, e.g. for humans: *wića* (male), *wiŋyaŋ* (female); for animals: *mdoka* (male), *wiye* (female).

For the plural, a distinction is made between animate and inanimate nouns. The former take *-pi*: e.g. *śuŋka* 'dog', *śuŋkapi* 'dogs'. Inanimates do not change: e.g. *ćaŋ* 'tree(s)'. The word *tipi* 'house' is a plural form used as a singular.

In Dakota, the word *śuŋka* seems to denote both 'dog' (the primary meaning) and 'horse'. The explanation given in Riggs is that the Dakota, when they first saw horses, gave them the name *śuŋka.wakaŋ* 'mysterious dog'. In Dakota, the horse is usually called *śuk.taŋka* 'great dog'; the *u* in *śuk* may be nasalized: *śũk*.

An instrumental formant is *i-*: *yumdu* 'to plough': *i.yumdu* 'a plough'. *wa-* marks the agent of an action: *i.haŋgya* 'to destroy': *wa.ihaŋgya* 'destroyer'. *wo-/wićo* form abstracta: *waśte* 'good', *wo./wićo.waśte* 'goodness'.

The diminutive marker is suffixed *-daŋ*: *mde.daŋ* 'small lake'; *hokśi.daŋ* 'boy', plural *hokś.pi.daŋ*.

The article *kiŋ* rounds off a definite phrase: e.g. *wićaśta waśte kiŋ* 'the good man'; *timdo.* ***ku*** *kiŋ* 'her brothers'. The plural marker, *-pi*, tends towards the end of the sentence, i.e. to the verb:

Dakota Beśdeke wića.kte.pi
'the Dakota – the Fox Indians – them-they-killed'

POSSESSION

Possessor precedes possessed, which may have possessive affix: e.g. *tataŋka* ***ta****wote* 'buffalo his-food'. A kinship possessive is made with the suffix *-(t)ku/-ću*, e.g. *wićaśta ćiŋkśi****tku*** 'man his-daughter'.

Adjective

As attribute, adjectives follow nouns. The adjective has a dual in *-uŋ-* as well as a plural in *-pi*: e.g. *waoŋśida* 'merciful': *waoŋśiuŋda* 'we two merciful ones'. The plural form may also be made by partial reduplication:

reduplication of first syllable: *taŋktaŋka* 'great' (plural); reduplication of final syllable: *waśteśte* 'good' (plural).

There is no formal comparative. The adverb *saŋpa* 'more' is used: *saŋpa waśte* 'better'.

Pronoun

The independent personal pronouns are:

	Singular	*Plural*	
1	miye	uŋkiye	+ *-pi*
2	niye	niye	
3	iye	iye	

There is a dual 1st person: *uŋkiye* 'I and thou'.

The possessive forms: *mitawa*, *nitawa*, *tawa*; pl. *uŋkitawapi*, *nitawapi*, *tawapi*. The dual possessive pronoun (always 1st person subject 'our') with 3rd person object is the same as the plural 1st person form, minus *-pi*.

VERBAL SUBJECT MARKERS

Sing. 1 *wa-*, 2 *ya-*; pl. 1 *un . . .* ; *pi*, 2 *ya . . .* ;*pi*: e.g. ***wa***_kaġa_ 'I make', ***ya***_kaġa_ 'you make', ***uŋ***_kaġapi_ 'we make'. These subject markers are also used with adjectives: e.g. ***ya***_ksapa_ 'you are wise'.

Assimilation occurs with verbs in *yu-*: e.g. *yuwaśte* 'to make good'; ***md***_uwaśte_ 'I make good'.

VERBAL OBJECT MARKERS

Sing. 1 *ma*, 2 *ni*; pl. 1 *uŋ . . .* ; *pi*, 2 *ni . . .* ;*pi*: e.g. ***ma***_kaga_ 'he made me'. Conjunction of 1st and 2nd person gives *-ći-*: *waśte.ći.daka* 'I love thee'. A reciprocal sense is marked by *kići* plus plural ending: *waśte.kići.da.pi* 'they love each other'. This set is used with certain verbs of state, feeling: e.g. *yazaŋ* 'to be sick', ***ma***_yazaŋ_ 'I am sick'. Also as markers for inalienable possession: e.g. ***ma***_we_ 'my blood'; ***uŋ***_taŋćaŋ_**pi** 'our bodies'.

ALIENABLE POSSESSION

Marked by *-ta-* following the *ma/mi*, *ni*, etc. markers: e.g. ***mita***_koda_ 'my friend'; *nita oŋspe* 'thy axe'.

DEMONSTRATIVE PRONOUN/ADJECTIVE

de 'this', pl. *dena*; *he* 'that', pl. *hena*.

INTERROGATIVE PRONOUN

tuwe 'who?', pl. *tuwepi*; *taku* 'what?'

Numerals

1–10: *waŋźi* (*dan*), *noŋpa*, *yamni*, *topa*, *zaptaŋ*, *śakpe*, *śakowiŋ*, *śahdoġaŋ*, *napćiŋwaŋka*, *wikćemna*. 11 *wikćemna ake waŋźidaŋ*; 20 *wikćemna noŋpa*; 30 *wikćemna yamni*; 100 *opawiŋġe*.

Verb

Roots are modulated by prefixes to become transitive verbs denoting specific modes of handling, manipulating, and using things: thus

ba- suggests cutting with a knife;
bo- denotes a directed impact from a shot, a stick, etc.;
na- signals action performed with the foot;
pa- signals action with the hand;
ya- signals action with the mouth.

Examples from root *-ksa-* 'to break off': ***ba**ksa* 'to cut with a knife'; ***ya**ksa* 'to bite off'.

Frequentative stem: *baksaksa* 'to slash with a knife'; i.e. reduplication.

Possessive, reflexive, dative, and benefactive stems are made by means of affixes/infixes: e.g. dative *-ki-*: *wowapi* ***ki**ćaġa* 'writing to-him-he-made' = 'he wrote to him'.

TENSE

Exemplified here by transitive verb with third person singular object. First and second person subjects are marked by infix (*-wa-*, *-ya-*) or by prefix (*md-*, *d-*). The third person subject marker is Ø.

There are only two tenses: an indefinite tense, not specifically marked, and a future made with the particle *kta*: *he waśte kta* 'that will be good'; *wowapi kiŋ he ma.ya, ku kta* 'thou wilt give me that book'. Context fixes the indefinite as referring to present or past. Other tenses and moods are generated with the help of adverbs.

Examples of singular and plural of root *-ksa* 'to break off' + *ba-* prefix:

singular: 1 *ba**wa**ksa* 'I cut him with a knife', 2 *ba**yaksa***, 3 *baksa*;
plural: 1 *ba**uŋ**ksa**pi***, 2 *ba**ya**ksa**pi***, 3 *baksa**pi***.

Examples with other pronominal infixes: *ba**ma**ksa* 'he cuts me with a knife'; *ba**wićuŋ**ksa* 'we cut them . . . '; *ba**uŋya**ksa**pi*** 'thou cuttest us . . . '; *ba**wićuŋ**k-sa**pi*** 'we two cut them . . . '.

IMPERATIVE

The singular suffixes are *-wo*, *-ye*; plural *-po*, *-pe*; *ćeya.wo* 'cry!', pl. *ćeya po!*' The *-o* forms seem to be more peremptory and are therefore used by males only.

PARTICIPLE

Restricted use is made of the 3rd person singular form plus *-haŋ*: thus, from *ia* 'to speak', *ia.haŋ* 'speaking'.

Riggs gives examples of a passive form in *-(wa)haŋ*: *ksa.haŋ* 'broken in two'.

Position of objective pronoun: *ma.ya.kaśka.pi* 'you (pl.) bind me (*ma*); *wića.wa.kaśka* 'I bind them'; *Ø.kaśka.pi* 'they bind him'. The last example can be construed as a passive: 'he is bound'. Similarly, *ma.kaśka.pi* 'they bind me' > 'I am bound'.

CONDITIONAL

A conditional mood is made by combining the indicative mood with either of two conjunctive particles -*kiŋhaŋ* for the present and future, *uŋkaŋś* for the past: *ya.hi kiŋhaŋ mde kta* 'if thou comest I shall go'; *ćeya uŋkaŋś* 'if he had cried'.

POTENTIAL

okihi means 'to be able', which can be negated by *śni*; there is also the verb *okitpani* 'to be unable'.

Example of *md*- conjugation:

mduśtaŋ 'I finish(ed)'
duśtaŋ 'thou finishest'
yuśtaŋ 'he/she finishes/finished'

Example of suffixed pronominal marker: *iŋ* 'to wear':

sing. 1 *hiŋ.mi*, 2 *hiŋ.ni*, 3 *iŋ*.

Example of infixed pronominal marker: *asni* 'to be/get well':

sing. 1 *a.ma.sni*, 2 *a.ni.sni*, 3 *a.Ø.sni*.

NEGATION

The adverb *śni* is placed after verb, noun, pronoun, adjective: e.g. *waćiŋ śni* 'I don't want'; *He ćaŋ śni* 'That is not wood.'

Postpositions

Many of these are separate lexemes, following nouns, or taking pronominal markers: cf.

tiŋta.ta 'on the prairie'
tipi ićahda 'by the house'
m.ikiyedaŋ 'near to me'; n.ikiyedaŋ 'near to thee'

Word order

SOV

1 Otakahe ekta Wicoie kin
hee; Wicoie kin he Wakan-
tanka kici un, qa Wicoie kin
he Wakantanka kin ee.
2 He okokahe ekta Wakan-
tanka kici un.
3 Iye eciyatanhan taku
owasin kagapi; qa taku kin
tokan tanhan takudan kagapi
śni.
4 Iye kin en wiconi; qa wiconi
kin he wicaśta iyoyamwicaye
cin hee.
5 Iyoyanpa kin hee otpaze cin
en omdesya un, tuka otpaze
cin he iyowinkiye śni.
6 Wicaśta wan Wakan-
tanka eciyantanhan u śipi,
he Johannes eciyapi.
7 He wayaotanin hi, Iyoyanpa
kin oyake kta: hecen iye
eciyatanhan owasin wica-
dapi kta.
8 Iyoyanpa kin he iye śni,
tuka iyoyanpa kin he
yaotanin kta e u śipi.

LAKOTA (Teton Sioux)

PHONOLOGY

Consonants

Each of the velar, palatal, dental, and labial rows has the three-term series: voiced stop – unvoiced aspirate – unvoiced ejective aspirate:

dʒ	ts̯’	ṭs̯’
g	k’	ḳ’
b	p’	p̯’
d	t’	ṭ’

In addition, Lakota has the following inventory of phonemes:

velar fricative: χ (g preceding /a/ > /χ/)
palatal fricative: ʒ, notated as j
dental fricatives: s, z, ṣ, s̯, ṣ (ʃ or s̯?, s̯ notated as s̍, s̯ notated as ṣ̍)
nasals: m, n

liquid: l
semi-vowels: j, w
glottal: h, ħ, ḥ, ʔ

Vowels

a, ɑ, ɛ, e, ɪ, i, o, ɔ, ʊ, u, ə; all have nasal values: ã, ã, ĩ, etc. except /e/.
Buechel uses ŋ to denote nasalization; here ~.

Buechel describes the vowels as being medium short/long in quantity. Stressed final vowels show variations in length: e.g. final *a*, *e*, *i* remain medium short, while *o*, *u*, and nasalized vowels are lengthened:

c'aŋ 'tree' /dʒã̃/i
wak'aŋ 'holy' /waʀã̃/; *cf.* wak'aŋ.t'aŋka /wak'ã.t'ã ka/ 'God'
mni 'water' /mᵊni/

Complications arise where a vowel is followed by one or more consonants. Buechel gives several pages of rules, assigning length in association with stress in such circumstances. For present purposes it is sufficient to say that both length and stress depend on phonetic environment, and that the rules are consistent.

The phoneme /ə/ is heard between the component consonants in such digraphs as *gl*, *bl*, *gw*, when initial: *ble* = /bᵊle/, *gl* = /gᵊl/, *gw* = /k°ᵊ/.

A syllabic final is normally vocalic, with or without nasalization; but emphatic ş may be added to this final vowel.

Final vowels, e.g. of suffixes, may be elided, with attendant mutation of new final consonant: e.g.

nũpa 'two' → *nũp > nũm
kaga 'to make' → *kag /kax/ > kaħ-

MORPHOLOGY

Noun

Lakota has no grammatical gender. Natural gender is reflected in the lexicon. *-wĩ* is a feminine formant, a shortened form of *wĩyã* 'female': *hok'é.wĩ* 'the woman in the moon'.

In the case of kinship nouns, one and the same referent often has two appellations, depending on the gender of the speaker. Thus 'my brother-in-law' is *ţã.hã kĩ* if a male person is speaking, *siçe kĩ* if a woman is speaking. Some examples of common nouns: *t'ípi* 'house, teepee', *mat'ó* 'bear', *p'éta* 'fire', *t'at'ã́ka* 'bull buffalo', *t'apté* 'buffalo cow', *hokśíla* 'boy'.

Animal gender may also be differentiated by use of the words *bloká* 'male', *wĩ́yela* 'female': *k'ági bloká* /kãχi.bᵊloga/ 'male crow'; *k'ági wĩ́yela* 'female crow'.

NUMBER

Formally, three numbers are distinguished: singular, dual, and plural. There is no dual marker for nominals; duality is expressed in the pronominal/verbal system. The plural marker for animate nouns is *-pi*, which can be transferred to an attributive adjective following the noun. Inanimate nouns are never marked for plurality.

hokśila 'boy' – hokśila.pi 'boys'
ptegleśka na pte.bloka c'epa.pi kĩ 'the fat cows and steers' (*c'epa* 'fat', *kĩ* is the definite article, see below)

There is no case system. Since the word order SOV is normal, it can be said that the direct object is positionally marked. An indirect object (dative) is copied in the verb complex by embedded *-ki-/-kici-*: for examples, see below.

POSSESSION

Choice of construction here depends on whether possession is felt to be real or not. To express real possession, Lakota uses either the independent possessive adjective based on *t'awa*, or the prefixed pronominal possessive markers. The possessive adjectives are: sing. 1 *mit'awa*, 2 *nit'awa*, 3 *Øt'awa*; dual: *ũkit'awa*, pl. 1 *ũkit'awa.pi*, 2 *nit'awa.pi*, 3 *t'awa.pi*. The pronominal markers are variants of these forms. Cf.

t'ipi mi.t'awa kĩ 'my house'
mak'oce mi.t'awa kĩ 'my land'

mit'a.mak'oce kĩ 'my land' ũkit'a.mak'oce.pi kĩ 'our land'

For parts of the body, *-t'a-* is dropped: *ma.ceji kĩ* 'my tongue' and a variant set of markers is employed for abstract possession: *mi.nagi kĩ* 'my soul'.

The formula X's Y is expressed as *Y X t'awa*: *śũka.wak'a X t'awa kĩ* 'X's horse'. Simple juxtaposition serves to express loose, non-possessive relationships: e.g. *mah̄piya zitkala.pi kĩ* 'the birds of the air' (*mah̄piya* 'air, cloud', *zitkala* 'bird').

The article

The definite article is *kĩ* (variant *cĩ*) following the noun:

wowapi kĩ 'the book'
wowapi waśte kĩ 'the good book'

The indefinite article is a shortened form of the numeral l: *wãji* > *wã c'ã wã* 'a tree'.

If the topic or referent has already been mentioned, or is already known to the audience, the definite article changes from *kĩ* to *ḳũ*.

Note the use of the definite article in the possessive formula: *mit'a.mak'oce* ***kĩ*** 'the my-land' = 'my land'.

Adjective

The adjective normally follows the noun, and is unmarked, though *-pi* may be used to mark plurality, if the adjective refers to an animate being. Plurality may also be expressed through reduplication:

waśte 'good' – pl. *waśteśte*
t'ãkĩyã 'great' – pl. *t'ãkĩkĩyã*

COMPARATIVE

Periphrastic, by means of adverb *sãp'a* > *sã*(*b*). Where the contrasted referent is expressed, the relational marker *i-* is prefixed to *sã*/*sam*:

hokśila kĩ atkuku kĩ **i**.sam hãska 'the boy is taller than (his) father'

The referent may be expressed by pronominal marker:

hokśila kĩ **m.i**.sam hãska 'the boy is taller than I': **n.i**.sam 'than thou'

SUPERLATIVE

The superlative is made with the adverb *iyotã* 'most'. The augmentative suffix *-ħca* may also be used: *t'ãka.ħca* 'very big', 'biggest'.

Pronoun

The independent pronouns play only a small role in Sioux, being used mainly for emphasis. For the very rich system of pronominal markers on verbs, *see* **Verb**, below. The independent forms (i.e. non-bound) are:

	Singular	*Dual*	*Plural*
1	miye	ũkiye	ũkiye.pi
2	niye		niye.pi
3	iye		iye.pi

These may be combined with a second set of emphatic independent pronouns: *miś* – *niś* – *iś*, etc. *miś.miye* 'I myself'.

DEMONSTRATIVE PRONOUN

There is a three-term series: *le* (proximate), *he* (distal), *ka* (remote) with plurals in *-na*: *léna*, *héna*, *kaná*:

he miye eca.m.õ 'it was *I* who did that, I myself did that' (which could also be expressed more idiomatically an one word: he.ca.m.õ)
lena mi.c'ĩca.pi 'these are my children'

INTERROGATIVE PRONOUN

tuwa 'who?'; *taku* 'what?'; *tukte* 'which?' (an./inan.).

RELATIVE PRONOUN

See **Verb**, **Relative clauses**, below.

NUMERALS

Cardinals 1–10: 1 *wãji*, 2 *nũpa*, 3 *yamni*, 4 *topa*, 5 *zaptã*, 6 *śakpe*, 7 *śakowĩ*, 8 *śaglogã*, 9 *napciyúka*, 10 *wikcemna*. 11–19: (*wikcemna*) *ake* + unit: e.g. 15 (*wikcemna*) *ake zaptã*. 20–90: *wikcemna* + unit: e.g. 50 *wikcemna zaptã*. 100 *opawĩge*, 200 *opawĩge nũpa*, etc. 1000 *k'oktopawĩge*.

The numerals are adjectives and follow the noun. The plural marker *-pi* is not necessary, unless plurality is being strongly emphasized.

Verb

In general, Lakota verbs are either transitive, intransitive, or reflexive. As in English, however, some roots are ambivalent. Certain prefixed markers confer absolutive status on a transitive root, and obviate the need for an object: e.g. *wa-*: cf. *wowapi wã yawa* 'he is reading a book (*wowapi*)': ***wa**.yawa* 'he is reading'. Conversely, an intransitive root becomes transitive/absolutive by addition of preverb: cf. *lowã* 'to sing' (intransitive): ***a**.lowã* 'to laud, sing the praises of someone'.

The Lakota root is not inflected and is neutral as to tense: *bla* 'I go/I went'. A future tense is made with the particle *kte*, before which root final *-a* becomes *-ĩ*: *wotĩ na iyũkĩ kte* 'he will eat and go to bed'. Some irregular verbs have more than one root: e.g. *bla* 'I go/I went'; ***mni** kte* 'I shall go'.

There is no passive voice. Buechel gives as example the sentence 'the boy was killed by the wolf', which must be expressed in Lakota as 'a wolf (*śũkmanitu wã*) killed (*kṭe*) the boy (*hokśila kĩ*): e.g. *śũkmanitu wa hokśila kĩ kṭe.*

MOODS

A subjunctive mood is marked by such particles as *ni*, *ḳeś*, *yũś*, etc. Imperative forms vary depending on the sex of the speaker. Thus, men use the particles *yo*, *wo*, *po* (in accord with phonetic environment) plus 3rd p. sing. or 3rd p. plural (with negating particle *śni*). Cf.: *hecõ po* 'do that': *hecõ śni yo* 'do not do that' (addressing one person); *hecó po* 'do that': *hecó.**pi** śni po* 'don't do that' (addressing more than one person).

That is, where several people are being addressed, the singular form of the verb is used for a positive command, the plural, marked with *-pi*, for a negative.

Women use the particles *ye*, *we*, *pi*, with similar constraints on number. Formally, verbs are classified as (a) simple base: personal pronominal markers are prefixed; (b) composite base: the pronominal markers are prefixed or infixed; (c) compound with binary base: the pronominal markers may be reduplicated.

CONJUGATION

In the absence of verbal or nominal inflection, Lakota relies on an extensive inventory of personal pronominal markers to express subject/direct-object/indirect-object deixis. The bound subject pronominal marker series for a simple transitive verb V is:

	Singular	*Dual*	*Plural*
1	wa.V	ũ.V	ũ.V.pi
2	ya.V		ya.V.pi
3	ØV		Ø.V.pi

e.g. with stem *kaśtaka*:

'to strike one': ũ.kaśtaka.pi 'we strike someone'
wa.kaśtakĩ.kte 'I shall strike someone'

Even the simple Lakota root is not an indivisible nucleus, however, as the pronominal marker(s) can be inserted into it. Cf. from *icu* 'to receive something': sing. 1 *i.**wa**.cu*, 2 *i.**ya**.cu*, 3 *icu*.

The bound-object pronominal markers' set has sing. 1 *ma*, 2 *ni*, 3 Ø; dual *ũ*(*k*); pl. 1 *ũ*(*k*), 2 *ni*, 3 *wica*. When both subject and object pronominal markers come together preceding a verbal stem, object precedes subject except in the case of 1st p. sing sbj. and 2nd p. obj./pl.: *wa.ni* 'I . . . you', *ũ.ni* 'we . . . you', but, *wica.wa* 'I . . . them', *ma.ya* 'you . . . me'. The collocation *wa.ni* 'I . . . you' is reduced to *ci*. For example, with root *kaȟniga* 'to choose someone, something':

wa.ni.kaȟniga > ci.kaȟniga > ci.caȟniga 'I choose thee' (*k* > *c* after /i/)
ũ.ya.kaȟniga.pi 'thou choosest us'
wic.ũ.kaȟniga.pi 'we choose them'

or, with infixed markers: root *naḥõ* 'to hear something':

na.ma.ya.ḥõ 'thou hearest me'
na.ũ.ni.ḥõ.pi 'we hear you'

Indirect-object markers, with prepositions *ki*/*ci* 'to', *kici*/*cici* 'for': the formula is: sbj./obj. deictic marker *-ki*/*kici* – V – (*pi*). E.g. with augmented root *ki.pazo* 'to show something to someone':

ma.ya.ki.pazo.pi 'you show it to me'
wica.ya.ki.pazo 'thou showest it to them'
ũ.ni.ci.pazo 'we show it to you' (*k* > *c* after /i/)

Infixed forms appear in, for example, *okicile* 'to seek something for someone else':

o.cici.le.pi 'I seek it for you (pl.)'
o.wic.ũ.kici.le.pi 'we seek it for them'

ki and *kici* may figure together in a verbal complex: e.g with *wace.ki.cici.ya* (absolutive) 'to pray for someone':

wace.ci.cici.ya 'I pray for thee' (*ci* 'I . . . to thee'; *cici* 'I . . . for thee')
wace.wica.ki.cici.ya.pi 'they pray for them'
wace.wic.ũ.ki.cici.ya.pi 'we pray for them'

Verbs with initial *ya-*/*yu-* have a specific set of subject markers: sing. 1 *bl*, 2 *e*, 3 Ø; dual: *ũ*(*k*); pl. 1 *ũ*(*k*), 2 *l*, 3 *y*. E.g. from *yatã* 'to praise', *blatã* 'I praise(d)', *ũ.yatã.pi* 'we praise(d)'. The object markers for this set are identical to those appearing in the verbs discussed above: *ma.yu.gica* 'he wakes me up'; with infixed subject marker: e.g. from *a.yuśtã* 'to leave someone alone', *a.bl.uśtã*

'I leave him alone'; from *o.ki.ya.ka* 'to tell someone something', *o.cici.ya.ka* 'I tell it to thee'.

REFLEXIVE PRONOUN

	Singular	*Dual*	*Plural*
1	miçi	ũkiçi	ũkiçi . . . pi
2	niçi		niçi . . . pi
3	içi		içi . . . pi

E.g.:

miçi.gnaya 'I deceive myself'
he.miçi.ye 'I say/said that to myself'

As an example of a Lakota irregular verb, we may cite *ya* 'to go', whose neutral tense is:

	Singular	*Dual*	*Plural*
1	bla	ũya	ũyãpi
2	la		lapi
3	ya		yapi

and whose future is:

	Singular	*Dual*	*Plural*
1	mni kte	ũyĩ kte	ũyã.pi kte
2	ni kte		lapi kte
3	yi kte		ya.pi kte

COMPOUND VERBS

E.g. noun + adjective/adverb > verb: *t'ipi* 'house' + (*-pi* is the plural marker) *osni* 'cold' = *t'iosni* 'to be cold in the house'; or, noun + V_1V_2: *ãpa* 'day, morning' + *icamna* 'to be stormy' = *ãpicamna* 'it's a stormy day', *cãte* 'heart' + *o.gnaka* 'to place' = *cãt.ó.wa.gnaka* 'I love someone'.

PREVERBS

These are vocalic prefixes which suggest the locus or manner of the verbal action: *a-* locus on something, *o-* in something, *e-* at something, *i-* manner of action, e.g.:

ĩyã wã **a**.hĩȟpaye 'to fall on a rock'
o.k'ata 'to be hot in something' (e.g. in *t'ipi*)
i.yuȟlata 'to scratch with something'

COPULA

The copula *e*, *e.pi* is used to identify a definite referent: (this) X is the Y:

wic'aśa kĩ le Y kĩ he.**e** 'this (*kĩ le*) man is (*e*) the Y'
he e 'that is he'
hena e.pi 'those are they'

It is not used with descriptive adjectives:

wic'aśa kĩ le waśte 'this man is good'
wa kĩ ska '(the) snow is white'

nor with personal pronouns. If an independent pronoun is used, the relevant bound form must be present in the referent:

miye **ma**.Lak'ota na niye wa.**ni**.śicũ
'I am a Lakota and you are a white man'

ho.ũ.kśila.pi 'we (*ũ*) are boys' (*hokśila* 'boy')

RELATIVE CLAUSES

A singular nominal antecedent is followed by the *indefinite* article *wã*; a plural by (*k*)*eya* 'some'; the relative clause is then nominalized and defined by the *definite* article *kĩ*. Buechel's first example is:

'the man whom you wish to see went home'

which becomes in Lakota

'a man the-you-want-you see-him went-home'
wic'aśa wã **w̃alaka yacĩ kĩ he** k'igle (*wãlaka* 'you see him', *yacĩ* 'you want')

Cf:

wic'aśa wa w̃alaka kĩ he Lak'ota kĩ heca
'a man the-you-see-him is a Lakota'

ecõ ciśi kĩ he ecõ wo
'do the-I-told-you-to-do', i.e. 'do what I told you to do'

Again, where English and many other languages use a gerundial construction, Lakota prefers nominalization with the definite article. Cf.:

mit'á.śũke kĩ num kaṭíyewicayapi kĩ íyohakab wic'áśa kĩ iyáyapi
'after (*íyohakab*) the-'they-shot' two (*num*) horses-of-mine (*mit'a.śũke*) the men went away, i.e. after shooting two of my horses, the men went away

Postpositions

Teton Sioux has a rich inventory of postpositions. Some examples follow:

akã(*l*) 'on': *mak'a akãl* 'on earth';
ekta 'in', 'at': *mah̄piya ekta* 'in heaven';
el 'in', 'at': *t'ipi kĩ le el* 'in this house';
kici 'with': *atkuku kici ũ* 'he is with his father';
ohã: 'through' *wa ohã iyaye* 'he went through the snow';
oh̄lateya 'under': *cã wã oh̄lateya* 'under a tree'.

Word order

SOV is basic:

wak'ã.t'ãka mak'a kĩ kage
'God made the earth' (*mak'a kĩ* 'the earth')

DANISH

INTRODUCTION

Danish belongs to the Scandinavian branch of the Germanic family. It is the official language of the Kingdom of Denmark, where it is spoken by over 5 million people, and joint official language of the Faeroe Islands and of Greenland. For Dano-Norwegian *see* **Norwegian**.

Writing in Danish dates from about the thirteenth century. The medieval literature is notable for its rich stock of ballads. The Bible was translated into Danish in the Reformation period. An outstanding figure of the Enlightenment was Holberg, whose influence on subsequent Danish writing was fundamental. The early nineteenth century produced one writer of world stature – Søren Kierkegaard. The modern period was inaugurated by the celebrated lectures given by Georg Brandes in the period 1870–90, the impact of which was as much socio-political as cultural (*det moderne Gennembrud* – 'the modern Renaissance'). Outstanding twentieth-century writers include Kjeld Abell, Kaj Munk, and Martin Nexø.

SCRIPT

Roman alphabet, 26 letters as in English, + *æ*, *å*, *ø*.

PHONOLOGY

Consonants

stops: p, b, t, d, k, g, ˀ
fricatives: f, v, s, ʃ, h, ð, γ, j
nasals: m, n, ŋ
lateral: l
uvular trill: ʀ

All consonants are short.

The correspondence between sound and symbol in Danish is weak. *p*, *t*, *k* are aspirate /p, t, k/ only as initials. Elsewhere, *p*, *t*, *k* and *b*, *d*, *g* tend to fuse as unaspirated /b, d, g/. Thus *lække* 'leak' and *lægge* 'lay' are both pronounced as /lɛgə/; cf. in the dental series, *sist* 'last', /sisd/. /g/ is regularly elided in certain environments: cf. *nogen* 'some', /nɔ̄n/, *spørge* 'ask', /sbœrə/, *spøg* 'joke', /sbɔiˀ/, *meget* 'much', /maiəð/.

Vowels

front: i, e, ɛ, y, ø, œ
central: a
back: ɔ, o, u
neutral: ə

DIPHTHONGS

Eight glides to /u/, two to /i/.

Stress

Normally on first syllable of root word.

Tone

The *stød* (glottal stop) corresponds in Danish to the acute tone in Swedish and Norwegian. The *stød* has phonemic force, as minimal pairs are thus distinguished: cf. *hund* 'dog', /hunˀ/ and *hun* 'she', /hun/.

MORPHOLOGY AND SYNTAX

Noun

GENDER

Danish has two genders: common and neuter. The definite article is *-en* for common nouns, *-et* for neuter; *-ene* forms the plural of both genders. If, however, an attributive adjective is present, the suffixed article is dropped, and the demonstratives *den*, *det*, *de* are used instead: e.g. *hus* 'house'; *huset* 'the house'; *det store hus* 'the big house'.

NUMBER

Three possible endings: *-e*, *-(e)r*, Ø. These may be accompanied by umlaut and gemination of the final consonant: e.g. *broder* 'brother' – *brødre*; *tand* 'tooth' – *tænder*; *fod* 'foot' – *fødder*.

CASE

Only the genitive has a specific marker: *-s*. Other cases are made as in English with the help of prepositions.

Adjective

Adjective precedes noun as attribute, and takes *-t* before a neuter singular: e.g. *et godt hus* 'a good house'. For adjective with definite noun, see above.

COMPARATIVE

In *-(e)re*, with suppletive formations as in other Germanic languages: e.g. *gammal* 'old' – *ældre; ond* 'bad' – *værre*, etc.

Pronoun

PERSONAL PRONOUN

The first and second nominative forms are: *jeg*, *du*; pl. *vi*, *I*. These have objective forms: *mig*, *dig*, *os*, *der*. The third person distinguishes gender in the singular: *han*, *hun*, *den* 'he, she, it', with corresponding objective forms *ham*, *hende*, *den*. The plural is *De*, *Dem*. *De/Dem* is also the polite second person form, singular and plural.

POSSESSIVE PRONOUN

First person *min*, *mit*, *mine*, second person *din*, *dit*, *dine*, and first person plural *vor*, *vort*, *vore*; these show concord with the object possessed. The third person forms: *hans*, *hendes*, *dens/dets* are invariable (concord, that is, with subject, not object). Similarly, the second and third person plural forms, *jeres*, *deres*, are invariable. On the analogy of *deres*, the form *vores* is replacing *vor*, *vort*, *vore*.

INTERROGATIVE PRONOUN

hvem 'who?', *hvad* 'what?'

RELATIVE PRONOUN

The interrogatives *hvem*, *hvad*, and related forms, e.g. *hvis* 'whose', are used in literary Danish, and partly in colloquial, e.g. for genitive: *Hr. Hansen, hvis broder rejser omkring i Danmark* 'Mr Hansen whose brother is travelling in Denmark'. *Som* and *der* are much used in the spoken language: *mennesker, der kan tale dansk* 'people who can speak Danish'.

Numerals

1–10: *en*, *to*, *tre*, *fire*, *fem*, *seks*, *syv*, *otte* (/-d-/), *ni*, *ti*; 11 *elleve*; 12 *tolv*; 13 *tretten*; 20 *tyve*; 30 *tredive*; 40 *fyrre*; 50 *halvtreds*; 60 *tres*; 70 *halvfjerds*; 80 *firs*; 90 *halvfems*; 100 *hundrede*.

Verb

Transitive/intransitive, weak and strong. There are active and passive voices, indicative and imperative moods, with some vestiges of a subjunctive.

NON-FINITE FORMS

Infinitive, present, and past participles. The present tense for all verbs is made by adding *-r* to the infinitive in *-e*: e.g. *jeg kommer* 'I come'. There is no inflection for person or number.

The weak/strong dichotomy affects the preterite: the weak ending is *-te/-ede*, and there may be accompanying umlaut in the root: e.g. *følge* 'to follow': pres., *jeg følger*, pret. *jeg fulgte*, /fuld/.

Strong verbs have 2- or 3-stage ablaut (including past participle): e.g. *jeg drikker* 'I drink', *jeg drak* 'I drank', *jeg har drukket* 'I have drunk'; *jeg giver* 'I give'; *jeg gav* 'I gave', *jeg har givet* 'I have given'. The ablaut sequence is often close to that in English.

Correspondence between orthography and pronunciation in the strong verb ablaut series is weak. Some examples:

drikker – drak – drukket /dregər – drag – drogəð/, 'drink'
bliver – blev – blevet /bli'r – ble' – ble:əð/, 'become'
hjælper – hjalp – hjulpet /jɛl'bər – jal'b – jolbəð/, 'help'
skriger – skreg – skreget /sgri'ər – sgrai' – sgraiəð/, 'scream'
står – stod – stået /sdɔ:'r – sdo'ð – sdɔ:əð/, 'stand'

PASSIVE

Two forms: *at blive* 'to become' + past participle, or *-s* added to infinitive: e.g. *han blev født 1805* 'he was born in 1805'; *huset ejes af Hr. H.* 'the house is owned by Mr H'.

IMPERATIVE

= stem; polite forms can be made by means of auxiliaries.

PARTICIPLES

Present in *-ende* /ənə/; past in -(*e*)*t*. The past participle can take *-en* to agree with a common gender correlative, but the modern tendency is to avoid inflection here, and to use the -(*e*)*t* form for both genders and numbers.

MODAL AUXILIARIES

E.g. *få*, *ville*, *måtte*, *gøre*, *skal*, etc. are used in many ways, including formation of a periphrastic future: e.g. *jeg skal komme i morgen* 'I shall come tomorrow'.

NEGATION

The general negating adverb is *ikke*.

Prepositions

As in English, these may be detached from the object, and take final position in the sentence: e.g. *hvad ser du på* 'what are you looking at?'

Word formation

As in German, by prefixation, suffixation, and compounding.

Word order

SVO is normal; OVS is possible, e.g. for emphasis.

I Begyndelsen var Ordet, og Ordet var
hos Gud, og Ordet var Gud.
2 Dette var i Begyndelsen hos Gud.
3 Alt er blevet til ved det, og uden det
blev intet til af det, som er.
4 I det var Liv, og Livet var Menne-
skenes Lys.
5 Og Lyset skinner i Mørket, og Mørket
fik ikke Bugt med det[1].
6 Der fremstod et Menneske, udsendt
fra Gud; hans Navn var Johannes.
7 Han kom til et Vidnesbyrd for at vidne
om Lyset, for at alle skulde komme til
Tro ved ham.
8 Selv var han ikke Lyset, men han
skulde vidne om Lyset.

DARDIC LANGUAGES

INTRODUCTION

The Dardic languages form an Indo-European language/dialect complex located in north-eastern Afghanistan (Kafiristan/Nuristan), northern Pakistan, and the extreme north-western corner of India. The exact genetic status of Dardic has been the subject of some controversy. The question is whether these languages are to be seen as a sub-division of New Indo-Aryan (henceforth NIA) (as the Pamir languages are of Iranian) or as a transitional stage between NIA and Iranian, belonging to neither but partaking of both. Sir George Grierson inclined to the latter view; Sten Konow took Dardic to be basically Iranian; while Morgenstierne regarded all Dardic languages as NIA except the Kafiristan group, which he treated as transitional. The route by which these languages reached their present site, and the dating of this migration, are equally uncertain. Grierson posited a passage via the Hindukush long after the main NIA–Iranian split; Morgenstierne argued for NIA immigration from the south. In general it can be said that New Indo-Aryan traits clearly outweigh Iranian features in most Dardic languages; and by far the most important member of the group – Kashmiri – shows several points of resemblance with Pahari and Lahnda, though here the influence of Urdu must be taken into account.

The three basic divisions with their components are:

West Dardic (Kafir): Katī, Vaigalī, Aṣkun, Prasun, Dameli;
Central Dardic: Khōwār, Kalāṣa, Paṣai, Votapuri, Sumaṣti, Gawar(bati), Tirakhi, Citrali;
East Dardic: Kāśmīrī, Baśkārik, Garwi, Tōrwālī, Maiyã, Ṣiṇā, Phalūṛa.

The total number of Dardic speakers is probably in the region of 3½ million, with Kashmiri accounting for about 3 million of this total. After Kashmiri come Khowar (*c.* 100, 000), Pashai (*c.* 100,000), and Sina (*c.* 70,000).

SCRIPT

Dardic languages are unwritten, apart from Kashmiri, which is written by the Muslim population in an expanded Arabic script, and by Hindus in either Devanāgarī or Šarada; this latter is a derivative of Brahmi. The Kaśṭawāṛī dialect of Kashmiri is written in the Kaśṭawāṛī script.

PHONOLOGY

Main points:

(a) Presence of nasalized vowels; nasalization may be phonemic (e.g. in Baśkārik).
(b) Stops and affricates generally present in three-degree series: voiced – unvoiced – unvoiced aspirate, e.g. /b, p, p'/. This is an Indo-Aryan feature, the aspirate/non-aspirate opposition being very rare in Iranian.
(c) The presence of a retroflex series again links Dardic to Indo-Aryan; but Dardic has retroflex affricates, which are not an Indo-Aryan feature.

MORPHOLOGY AND SYNTAX

Main features:

1. Gender: the feminine *-i* marker appears generally in nominal and adjectival system.
2. Number: associated with case, i.e. unmarked in base form, marked in oblique. Presence of pluralizing suffixes in some languages.
3. Case: via postpositions, which tend to become fossilized as case endings.
4. A definite/indefinite opposition is found in nearly all Dardic languages. This is more characteristic of Iranian than of New Indo-Aryan.
5. Adjectival system: wide variation, from three markers for gender, number, and case in Kashmiri to null marker in some Central Dardic languages.
6. Pronoun: forms for first and second person are everywhere present. Third person forms are supplied by the demonstrative series which usually distinguishes three degrees of relative distance from speaker or referent. There is also a pronominal enclitic series, again an Iranian trait in the main (but cf. **Vedic**, **Sindhi**, **Lahndā**).
7. Numerals: vigesimal system is widespread (not in Kashmiri).
8. Verb: varies from flectional system in West and Central Dardic to an analytic system, based on the use of participles plus auxiliaries, in Eastern Dardic. An anomaly here is provided by the Eastern Dardic language Sina, which has a future form marked by personal endings.

   An ergative construction is in general use for transitive verbs which make past tenses from old participial forms. Some languages have a specific ergative case in their declension system, and this marks the subject in the ergative construction. Where there is no specific ergative case, an oblique case is used. Normally, in such constructions, the verb agrees with the object; in some, however, with the subject, e.g. in Sina.
9. Both prepositions and postpositions are found, the latter being more usual.
10. Word order: SOV is normal.

For a description of an Eastern Dardic language, *see* **Kashmiri**. A brief description of a Central Dardic language – Wotapuri – follows here, based on Edel'man (1965).

WOTAPURI

PHONOLOGY

stops: p, ph, b, t, th, d, ṭ, ṭh, ḍ, k, kh, g
affricates: ts, ts^h, dz, tʃ, $tʃ^h$, dʒ, ṭṣ, $ṭṣ^h$
fricatives: s, z, ʃ, ṣ, x, h
nasals: m, n, ṇ
liquids: r, ṛ (ḷ), l, ƛ
semi-vowels: j, w

Vowels

i, e, a, o, u; long and short; ə

Length is phonemic; all vowels are subject to nasalization.

MORPHOLOGY

Noun

The noun in Wotapuri is marked for number and case. A gender opposition between masculine and feminine occurs in nouns referring to certain animates, which share a common consonantal base with specific vocalization: cf. *gōṛ* 'horse', *gēṛ* 'mare'; *kucur* 'dog', *kicir* 'bitch'; *kukuṛ* 'cock', *kikiṛ* 'hen'; *uštur* 'camel', *uštir* 'female camel'.

CASE AND NUMBER

Nouns are unmarked in the nominative singular, and take *-e*[3] (long, nasalized, long and nasalized) in the plural. There are two oblique cases, the first unmarked in the singular, taking *-a*/*-an*/*-ã* in the plural; the second is marked by varying values of /i(n)/ in the singular, of /ũ/ in the plural.

The nominative case functions as the subject of intransitive verbs, and of transitive verbs in non-past tenses: e.g. *maniš gā* 'the man went'.

A genitive case is formed by adding -(V)*n* to the nominative: e.g. *zūye.n puṛ* 'the woman's son'. An allative/illative sense is expressed by nominative plus -*Vŋge*: e.g. *gōṭēŋgē āū* 'he went into the house'.

The first oblique case is used to express the direct object of transitive verbs: e.g. *ta maniša au ni pīranan* 'I (*au*) don't know (*ni pīranan*) these people'.

The second oblique case functions as the subject of a transitive verb in the past tense (cf. Hindi and other Indian languages): e.g. *ṛa.ī kam kir* 'the brother worked'.

It also expresses various instrumental, locative, and adverbial senses: e.g. *au čakū.i sinan* 'I cut with a knife'; *matī̃* 'on the head'; *tēr kāli* 'last year'.

Adjective

As in certain animate nouns, the adjective in Wotapuri is marked for gender by internal vocalic flection: e.g. *gan* 'big', fem. *gen*; dūāg 'old', fem. *ḍyēg*.

Comparative: cf. *sē gām mũ gām.gesa gan thũ* 'that village (*gām* – Urdu *gaoŋ*) is bigger than our (*mũ*) village', where the postposition *-gesa* expresses 'than'.

Pronoun

The base forms are: sing. 1 *au*, 2 *tu*; pl. 1 *mũ*, 2 *thũ*. These have enclitic forms. In addition to two oblique cases, shared with the nominals, the pronouns have a genitive case: sing. 1 *men*, 2 *then*; pl. 1 *mũ*, 2 *thum*. The complete row for first person singular is then: *au, men, ma, maĩ*. The *ma* form plus *ke* provides a dative case: e.g. *te ma.ke isū* 'he said to me'; *pyānī ma.ke dē* 'give me water'. In relation to transitive/intransitive verbs, the pronominal oblique cases are used as described above for nouns: cf. ***au*** *kir karan* 'I am working'; ***maĩ*** *kam kir* 'I did work'.

The third person forms are supplied by the demonstrative series: proximate: *ai*; distal *sē*; both with two oblique cases. Cf. *ai nyāṛ ma zūye.n dū thī* 'this girl is the daughter of that woman'.

INTERROGATIVE PRONOUNS

kā 'who?' *ku* 'what?'. Both are declined.

Numerals

1–10: *yek, dū, ṭā, cawur, pandz, šō, sat, aṭ, nau, daš*; 11 *yārō̃*; 12 *bārō̃*; 13 *sidārō̃*; 20 *bīš*; 30 *bīš-o-daš*; 40 *dū-bīš*; 60 *ṭā-bīš*. 100 *pandz-bīš*.

Verb

Wotapuri economizes on accidence by using one and the same verbal form in both a finite and a non-finite capacity, i.e. the present, past, and future participles also function as the corresponding tense forms. Both as participle and as tense, the form is marked for gender and number.

Present: sing. masc. *karan* 'doing', fem. *karen*; pl. masc. *karanē*, fem. *karenē*. Thus, *karan* 'I do', 'you (masc.) do', 'he does'; *karen* 'she does'.

Past: sing. masc. *muṛ* 'having died', fem. *miṛ*; pl. masc. *muṛē*, fem. *miṛē*: e.g. *maniše gaē* 'the men went'.

Future: sing. masc. *pašun* 'about to see', fem. *pašin*; pl. masc. *pašunē*, fem. *pašinē*. Certain verbs (those with bases in *-ē-*/*-ō-*) make a future participle in -*man*, with vocalic change in root: e.g. *dē-* 'give', future participle *di.man*.

The copula is added to the past form to give a perfect tense. In addition, Wotapuri has a subjunctive, and a choice of forms expressing uncertainty and/or unreal conditions. The base is used as an imperative: e.g. *dē* 'give!'

Postpositions

Used with specific cases. Thus, *sari* 'on' follows the nominative case, *mani* 'with' the first oblique, and *yaxi* 'under' the second oblique. Allocation is not fixed, however *-sari* 'on' is also found following the second oblique case.

Word order

SOV appears to be usual. OSV occurs.

DARGVA

INTRODUCTION

Dargva belongs to the Lak-Dargva sub-group of Dagestanian languages. It is also known as Dargin; the ethnonym is *dargan*. There are about 300,000 speakers in the central part of the Republic of Dagestan, bordering the Caspian Sea.

Dargva is officially classified as one of the literary languages of Dagestan.

SCRIPT

1917–28 adaptation of Arabic; thereafter experimental period of romanization till 1938, when Cyrillic + *I* and ř was adopted.

PHONOLOGY

Consonants

stops: b, p, p', d, t, t', g, k, k', ɢ, q, q', ʔ
affricates: dz, ts, t's, dʒ, tʃ, t'ʃ
fricatives: f, v, s, z, ʃ, ʒ, j, x, γ, ʕ, h, w
nasals: m, n
lateral and flap: l, r

In this article, the ejective consonants are marked with subscript dots.

Vowels

i, e(ɛ), ə, a, u

/ə/ is notated as *a* or я.

MORPHOLOGY AND SYNTAX

Noun

Nouns are divided into three classes:

Class 1: male human beings; the concord marker is *v*-, *y*-, or Ø- in the singular; *b*- in the plural.
Class 2: female human beings; the concord marker is *r*- (sing.), *b*- (pl.).
Class 3: everything else; concord marker is *b*- (sing.), *d*- (pl.), or -*r*-infix (pl.).

Plural markers are *-bi*, *-ti*, *-ni*, etc.: e.g. *adam* 'man', pl. *adam**ti***; *dabri* 'shoe', pl. *dabr**umi***. Examples of concord: *dudeš vaḳib* 'father came'; *neš **r**aḳib* 'mother came'; *unc **b**aḳib* 'the bull came'.

DECLENSION

The cases in Dargva can be divided into two groups. Group 1 comprises nominative, ergative, dative, genitive, associative or comitative, instrumental, and a prepositional case used with verbs of discourse. Group 2 consists of 20 spatial frames, sub-divided into four series each with five cases:

Series 1	has five aditive cases: the endings are *-či*, *-zi*, *-hi*, etc.
Series 2	has five cases denoting locus without motion: the endings are those of series 1 + class markers.
Series 3	has five ablative cases: series 2 endings + *-ad*.
Series 4	has five elative cases: series 1 endings + class markers + *-əʕ*.

In the group 1 cases, the nominative has Ø ending, the ergative adds *-li*, *-ni*, *-y*; cf. *džuz* 'book', ***nuni*** *džuz* ***b**uçulra* 'I read (present tense) the book', where *nuni* is ergative of *nu* 'I', and ***b***- is the class 3 marker for *džuz*.

Either an aditive case or the ergative provides the base for the other oblique cases.

Adjective

The attributive adjective precedes the noun qualified, and may appear in base form, especially in verse: *aq dubura* 'high mountain'; *çub dəhi* 'white snow'. Certain adjectival formants may be added to the base: *aq*, for example, then appears as *aq.si* or *aq.il*. An adjective thus modulated may take the class marker of a logical referent, but does not take case endings.

Pronoun

PERSONAL PRONOUN

	Singular	*Plural*
1	nu	nuša
2	ʕu	ʕuša

These are declined as nominals, but with specific endings, sometimes suppletive. Thus *nu*: erg. ***nuni***, gen. ***dila***, dat. ***nab***, com. ***nabčil***, prep. ***nabčila***, instr. ***nabčibli***.

The third person forms are supplied by the demonstrative series, which has three degrees:

	Singular	*Plural*
neutral	iš	išdi
proximate	il	ildi
remote	it	itdi

INTERROGATIVE PRONOUN

či 'who?'; *se* 'what?'

RELATIVE PRONOUN

See **Verb**, below.

Numerals

The numerical system is decimal.

Numerals: 2–10: *ḳel, ʕəbal, aval, šel, uregal, verʕal, geʕal, urč̣emal, veçal.* 20 *γal*; 30 *ʕəbçali*; 40 *avçali*; 100 *daršal.*

The numerals can be declined as nouns.

Verb

Aspect, mood, tense, number, class, person are all expressed in a multitude of forms, all of which are based on the optative form; this has no suffixes and can be declined as a nominal, e.g. *belḳ* 'that he may/might write'.

IMPERATIVE

A vocalic marker is added to the optative base. Selection of marker vowel is correlated with the third person inflections in the past tense; e.g. when this ends in *-ib*/*-ub*, the marker is *-a* or *-i*: *kasib* 'he took' – *kas**a**!* 'take!'

There are many ways of forming the imperfective aspect from the perfective, most of them involving vocalic and consonantal change: e.g. *arses* 'to fly off' – ***u**rses* 'to be flying'. The combination of two bases (perfective and imperfective) with past, present, and future time frames generates a very wide range of verbal forms: e.g. for the past frame, a simple past, a past perfective, a past imperfective, and a past suppositive.

Examples from *vaḳes* 'to come':

simple past: *vaḳibra* 'I came' (conjugated by person: 1. *vaḳibra*, 2. *vaḳiri*, 3. *vaḳib*);
past perfective: *vaḳil(i)ri* 'I had come (before. . .)';
past imperfective: *ləvqul(i)ri* 'I was coming';
past suppositive: *vaḳiši* 'I came (it is said)'.

The latter three forms are invariable.

Specimen forms for other tenses:

present: has both aspects: perfective *vaḳil(i)ra*, *-ri*, *-say*; imperfective *ləvqul(i)ra*, *-ri*, *-say* 'I etc. am/are/is coming';
future: *ləvqəs*, *-d*, *-n*: e.g. *ləvqən* 'he will come';

future suppositive: *vaķiša*, *-ši*, *-s*.

PARTICIPLES

The formant is *-si*, *-n*, *-ri* for the singular, *-ti* for the plural. Thus a perfective present participle is *vaķib**si**-*, which is conjugated for person: *-ra*, *-ri*, *-say*. Similarly, *vaķes**si*** '(he) who will come'.

There are many gerundial forms: e.g. *vaķibla* 'since (he) came'; *vaķibʕella* 'when (he) came'; *vaķiblarhi* 'after (he) came'.

The formant *-n* makes participial forms denoting occupation, etc.: e.g. *luķan* 'he who is writing' → 'writer'.

Particles are added to these participial/gerundial forms to express a large variety of nuances: e.g. *vaķiliɢi* 'even though coming/having come'.

Postpositions

Postpositions in Dargava are petrified nouns; they follow various cases, including the nominative.

Word order

Basic SOV.

DINKA

INTRODUCTION

Dinka belongs to the Western Nilotic branch of Nilo-Saharan (Chari-Nile group) and is spoken by an estimated 1,350,000 in southern Sudan and south-western Ethiopia. The language is unwritten.

PHONOLOGY

Consonants

/p, b; t, d; tʃ, dʒ; k, g/ are present, plus associated nasals, /m, n, ɲ, ŋ/; /f, v, w, ɣ, j, r, l/ are also present. Final voiced stops tend towards voiceless /b/ → [p]. Final /tʃ/ approaches [ɟ]. In the combination /wt, wd, wn/, the /w/ is silent, but affects the pronunciation of /t, d, n/.

CONSONANT MUTATION

Final stops mutate as follows: /b, p/ → /m/, /tʃ/ → /ɲ/, /d, t/ → /n/. This takes place (a) when definite marker is added; (b) when genitive marker is added; (c) before pronominal affix; (d) before following adjective: e.g. *lyeb* 'tongue' – *lye**me*** 'the tongue'; *dit* 'bird' – *di**ne*** 'the bird' – *di**n**dia* 'my bird' – *di**n** did* 'a big bird'.

Vowels

iː, ɪ, eː, ɛ, ə, a, aː, ɔ, o, ou, u, uː

Tone

High, low, with rising and falling glide tones. Marked here where necessary by acute, grave, circumflex.

MORPHOLOGY AND SYNTAX

Noun

No grammatical gender. Natural gender in humans is distinguished lexically: e.g. *ran* 'man', *tik* 'wife'. *Tik* (*tek*) may also be used to denote the female of animals: e.g. *džonkor* 'horse', *ti**n** e džonkor* 'mare'.

DEFINITE ARTICLE

-e, pl. *-ke*.

PLURAL

Most nouns do not distinguish between singular and plural: e.g. *abuok* 'gazelle(s)'. The plural form of the definite article identifies a noun as plural: e.g. *džonkor**ke*** 'horses'. Plural may also be indicated by vowel lengthening: e.g. *tim* 'tree', pl. *tīm*; or by umlaut: e.g. *nom* 'hand', pl. *nim*; or suppletively: e.g. *tik* 'woman', pl. *dyar*.

CASE RELATIONS

Indicated by particle: e.g. *ran* 'man' (nom., acc.), *elke ran* 'of the man', *etong ran* 'to the man', *tede ran* 'from the man'.

Genitive: possessor precedes possessed: *mán nya* 'mother of the girl' (*mâ* → *mán* 'mother'). Genitive particle *elkelde* may be interpolated: e.g. *tin elde beyn.did* 'the wife of the chief' (*beŋ-did* 'chief').

Dative: e.g. *an ači kan yek ran* 'I have given that to the man' (*yek* 'to give; *kan* 'that').

Adjective

As attribute, adjective follows noun: *ran did* 'big man'; *tin puat* 'good woman'. The predicative adjective is introduced by *a*/*e*: e.g. *bâr* 'long', *Ryen **a**bâr* 'The ship is long.'

Pronoun

PERSONAL PRONOUN

Has full and abbreviated forms:

	Singular			*Plural*		
	Full	*Abbreviated*	*Possessive*	*Full*	*Abbreviated*	*Possessive*
1	ghên/an	gha/a	-dia	ghôg	gho/o/a	-da
2	yin	yi/ī	-du	uêk	ue	-dûn
3	yen	ye/e	-de	kêk	ke	-den

For plural possessed objects the possessive affixes are sing. *čia*, *ku*, *ke*; pl. *kua*, *kûn*, *ken*.

A noun may be marked for possession either by the suffixed possessive enclitic or by the prefixed abbreviated form: e.g. *lyem**dia*** = ***gha**.lyeb* 'my tongue'.

The full forms set out above act both as pronominal subject and as pronominal object.

DEMONSTRATIVE PRONOUN

kan, pl. *kak* 'this', 'these'; *ken*, pl. *kak*(*a*) 'that', 'those'.

INTERROGATIVE PRONOUN

(*ye*)*nga* 'who?'; (*ye*)*ngu* 'what?'

RELATIVE PRONOUN

e/ye/ke: e.g. *ran e yèk ghut* 'a man who built a house' (*yèk* 'build', *ghut* 'house').

Numerals

1–10: *tok*, *róu*, *dyak*, *'nguan*, *wdyeč*, *wdetem*, *wderóu*, *bêt*, *wde-nguan*, *wtyer*; 11 *wtyer ko tok*; 20 *wtyer-rou*; 30 *wtyer-dyak*; 100 *buôt*.

Verb

Most verbs are consonant-final: e.g. *tem* 'cut', *gal* 'begin', *gam* 'believe'. Root = infinitive = imperative.

TENSE

There are three basic tenses:

present: the formant is *a*, e.g. *ghên a gam* 'I believe';
perfect: *ači* → *či* + stem, e.g. *ghên/an ači nin* 'I have slept';
future: *abi* → *bi* + stem, e.g. *an abi nin* 'I shall sleep'.

PASSIVE VOICE

The stem is unchanged, the formants lengthen final vowel: e.g. *abi* → *ab*ī; *a*či → *ačī.* The combination of pronoun + formant is subject to metathesis and contraction, e.g. *ghên ači* → *ačigha* → *ača*. The resultant series is *ača*, *ači*, *ačé*; pl. *ačûg*, *ačak*, *ačik*. Similarly with *ghên*, etc. + *abi*: *aba*, *abi*, *abe*, *abû*, *abak*, *abik*.

NEGATION

The marker is *ačí* (distinguished by tone/stress from *ači*, the tense marker): e.g. *an ačí bi lo* 'I shall not go'; *kan ačí bî loy* 'that won't be done'.

The prohibitive particle is *dû*(*n*)(*e*), pl. *dunke*: e.g. *dunke lo!* 'don't go! (pl.).

PARTICIPLES

Present: *a* + stem, e.g. *a čam* 'eating'; *a nin* 'sleeping'. Perfect: *či* + stem, e.g. *Či lek* '(he) who has spoken?'

The participle can be used as a progressive tense: *ghên a čam* 'I am eating'.

Word order

SOV, SVO.

1 NE goi goc e kaŋ ke W*e*t eto, ku W*e*t eto
ke Nhialic, ku W*e*t eye Nhialic. 2 Yeneka to kene Nhialic ne goi goc e kaŋ.
3 Yeneke cak kaŋ kedhia; ku te cene yen
kacin ke ci ca ne ka ci ke ca. 4 Pir eto ne
eyic; ku pir yeneka ye ɣer de ran. 5 Ku
ɣer cya ruer tecol, ku kaci cuol ye piŋ.
6 Ran e tuoc ne Nhialic, ran col Jon.
7 Yenake dule, bi koc ya le ɣer, bi koc
kedhia biya gam ne yen. 8 Ku kacie yen
eye ɣere, e buo bi koc biya le ɣere.

DRAVIDIAN LANGUAGES

INTRODUCTION

The Dravidian stock seems to have arrived in north-west India in the fifth or fourth millennium BC. Its exact provenance is not clear. A hither/central Asian origin for the language type, if not for its present bearers, finds some support in the thesis, first advanced by Caldwell in the middle of the nineteenth century, of a lexical and morphological relationship between the Dravidian and the Uralic language families. Comparison (e.g. by Burrow 1944) of certain semantic fields seems to place a lexical relationship of some kind beyond reasonable doubt; and there are structural parallels in the tense markers, the formation of the plural, the pronominal system, and the negative conjugation. Material so far deciphered at the Mohenjo-Daro and Harappa sites also suggests a connection with Dravidian.

As regards contact between Dravidian and Indo-Aryan, it seems clear that the present polarization, with Indo-Aryan in the north and Dravidian in the south of India, is of comparatively recent date. Throughout the third and second millennia BC the two families probably coexisted in the north of India, with Dravidian gradually losing ground to Indo-Aryan. There are Dravidian words in the *Rig-Veda*, and Dravidian influence is seen in such Indo-Aryan features as the development of the retroflex series, and, later, the gradual replacement of prepositions in New Indo-Aryan by postpositions.

The process was not all one-way; the major Dravidian languages are full of Sanskrit words, and, on another front, certain features of the Dravidian outlier Brahui have been attributed to contact with its Indo-Aryan neighbour Baluchi. Andronov and Emeneau have treated parallel typological features of New Indo-Aryan and Dravidian, and their mutual interaction, as evidence of the emergence of an areal 'Indian' language type, covering New Indo-Aryan, Dravidian, and Munda.

Andronov (1965) groups the Dravidian languages as follows:

	Group	*Number of speakers* (est.)	*Location*
I	Southern		
	Tamil	52 million	Tamilnad, Sri Lanka, E and S Africa, SE Asia
	Kannada	27 million	Karnataka
	Malayalam	22 million	Kerala

	Kota	a few hundred	Kotagiri Mountains
	Toda	a few hundred	Nilgiri area
	Kodagu	90,000	Mercara area
II	South-eastern		
	Telugu	60 million	Andhra Pradesh, Tamilnad
III	South-western		
	Tulu	1 million	Mangalore
IV	Central		
	Kolami, Naiki, Parji, Godaba	200,000 (Parji, 90,000)	border regions of Andhra Pradesh, Madhya Pradesh, and Maharastra
V	Gondwana group		
	Gondi	1½ million	border regions of Andhra Pradesh, Madhya Pradesh, and Maharastra
	Kui, Kuvi	800,000	Orissa
VI	North-eastern		
	Kurukh	1,200,000	Chhota Nagpur
	Malto	50,000	Rajmahal Hills
VII	North-western		
	Brahui	1,500,000	Baluchistan

Andronov (1965) gives the following time-scale for separation stages:

4000 BC: separation of Proto-Brahui;
3500 BC: separation of Kurukh, Malto;
2500 BC: formation of Gondwana group;
1500–1100 BC: separation of Central group;
1100–900 BC: separation of Telugu;
mid-first millenniun: separation of Tulu;
turn of millennium: separation of Kannada from Tamil;
AD 1000–1300: separation of Malayalam from Tamil.

PHONOLOGY

In initial and medial position, Dravidian phonemes are remarkably stable over the entire domain, both diachronically and synchronically. Thus, Proto-Dravidian /t-/ is everywhere reflected as /t-/, and /p-/ very largely as /p-/. The same goes for alveolar /l̲/ and /r̲/: these are characteristically Dravidian phonemes.

Typologically, the Dravidian languages are agglutinative; there is a basic dichotomy into (a) human/rational and (b) non-human/non-rational. Gender distinction appears in the southern and south-eastern languages.

Typically, there are two basic cases, direct and oblique. Further case affixes are attached to the oblique form. The first person plural distinguishes inclusive and exclusive forms. A particularly interesting feature is the Uralic type of negative conjugation.

See **Tamil**, **Telugu**, **Kannada**, **Malayalam**, **Gondi**, **Brahui**.

DUTCH

INTRODUCTION

The official name of this West Germanic language is *Nederlands.* It is the official language of the Kingdom of the Netherlands, and joint official language (with French) of Belgium. There are over 14 million speakers in the Netherlands, and about 5 million in Belgium. Dutch is also the language of administration in Surinam and in the Dutch Antilles.

In the period of Germanic tribal expansion (third century AD onwards) the southern regions of what is now the Netherlands were colonized by Frankish tribes, and it was here that Old Dutch first crystallized. The transition from Middle Dutch to Modern Dutch coincided with the transfer of economic and political power to northern Holland, and the accompanying cultural polarization. It is northern (Amsterdam) usage that underlies the modern literary standard, though Brabant influence is not absent. There is a marked difference between the literary standard and the colloquials.

Writing in Old Dutch begins in the tenth century. In the subsequent history of Dutch literature three main periods may be distiguished: (a) the radiant and lyrical mysticism of fourteenth-century visionaries like Heinric van Ruysbroeck; (b) the seventeenth-century 'Golden Age'; and (c) the modern period from the mid-nineteenth century onwards: particularly rich in the social novel and in experimental verse. The novelists Multatuli, Couperus, and Schendel are outstanding. The literary monthly *De nieuwe gids* (1885 onwards) should be mentioned, as it played a seminal role in the development of Dutch culture.

SCRIPT

Roman alphabet. The standardized orthography of 1863 was revised and simplified in 1947.

PHONOLOGY

Consonants

stops: p, b, t, d, k
fricatives: f, v, s, z, x, y, j, h
nasals: m, n, ŋ
lateral: l
uvular flap: ʀ
semi-vowel: ʋ

/tj/ tends towards retroflex [ʈ].

Vowels

front: i, e, ɛ, ɪ, œ, y
middle: ɵ, a, ə
back: ɑ, ɔ, o, u

There are eight diphthongs, which are glides to /i/ or /u/.

There is assimilation, both regressive and progressive, at junctures: e.g. *afbellen* [a**v**bɛllə(n)] 'ring off'; *opvouwen* [op**f**ɔ•ʋə(n)] 'fold up'.

Voiced finals are unvoiced: (*ik*) *heb* → [hɛ**p**]; *hond* → [hənt].

/f, s/ → /v, z/ in formation of plural, and so written: *brief* 'letter' – *brieven*; *huis* 'house' – *huizen*.

Final *-n* tends to be elided: *ziekenhuis* 'hospital' → [zikəhəys].

Intrusive /ə/: e.g. *arm* /arəm/.

Stress

Normally on first syllable, disregarding weak prefixes. In compounds, stress is not always predictable.

MORPHOLOGY AND SYNTAX

Noun

Nouns are divided into those of common gender, with singular definite article in *de*, and neuters with singular definite article *het*. For both genders the plural definite article is *de*, the singular indefinite article is *een*: e.g. *de kamer* 'the room'; *het paard* 'the horse'.

The plural marker is *-en* or *-s*: e.g. *de vrouw* 'the woman', pl. *de vrouwen*; *de prijs* 'the price', pl. *de prijzen*; *de zoon* 'the son', pl. *de zoons*.

Since final *-n* is not pronounced, the opposition between singular and plural in the case of the *-en* ending is Ø/ə.

Adjective

The attributive adjective precedes the noun and takes *-e* for common-gender nouns: e.g. *een goede man* 'a good man'; but, *een goed bock*. The predicative adjective is not inflected.

COMPARATIVE

In *-er*, superlative in *-st*. Suppletive sets parallel to those in German and English occur: e.g. *goed – beter – best*; *veel – meer – meest*.

Pronoun

PERSONAL PRONOUN

For each of the six personal rows (3 singular, 3 plural) there are full and reduced subject forms, full and reduced object forms. Thus:

1st sing.	ik	'k	mij	me
3rd sing.	hij	-ie	hem	'm
	zij	ze	haar	'r

In the second person there is a choice between familiar forms: *jij*, pl. *jullie* and more formal address: *u*.

POSSESSIVE

The possessive forms are:

	Singular	*Plural*
1	mijn	ons/onze
2	jouw, je	van jullie (dat van jullie)
	uw	
3	zijn	hun
	haar	

Note: colloquial usage: *mijn broer z'n auto* = *de auto van mijn broer* 'My brother's car' = 'the car of my brother'.

DEMONSTRATIVE PRONOUN

deze, *dit* 'this', pl. *deze*; *die*, *dat* 'that', pl. *die*.

INTERROGATIVE PRONOUN

wie 'who?', *wat* 'what?'

RELATIVE PRONOUN

die with reference to common gender; *dat* with reference to neuter: e.g.

...in het decadente Haagse milieu **dat** deze schrijver kende als geen ander
'...in the decadent Hague milieu which this writer knew as no other did'

...van een levendigheid, **die** voor zijn tijd volstrekt uniek was
'...a liveliness that was quite unique for his period'

After prepositions the form is *wie* for persons, *waar* + prep. for things:

de mensen **bij wie** hij wont
'the people he lives with'

de technologische prestaties **waarop** Amerika altijd trots is geweest
'the technological achievements of which A. has always been proud'

Further to relative clauses (see above): in literary Dutch, embedding of attributive (phrase) to left of head-word is permissible: e.g. *de op de agenda staande interpellaties* 'the questions on the agenda'.

Numerals

1–10: *een, twee, drie, vier, vijf, zes, zeven, acht, negen, tien*; 20 *twintig*; 21 *een en twintig*; 30 *dertig*; 40 *veertig*; 100 *honderd.*

Verb

The citation form = infinitive, ending in -(*e*)*n*; the stem is the infinitive form minus -(*e*)*n*. A long vowel in the infinitive is written doubled in the stem: e.g. *leven* – ***leef***; *geloven* – *gel**oo**f*.

Dutch has active and passive voices, indicative and imperative moods. There are two simple tenses in the indicative: present and past.

Simple present: first person singular = stem; first plural and third plural = infinitive; second person singular and plural and third singular add -*t*: e.g. *ik kom* – *wij komen* – *hij komt*.

Formation of the simple past depends on whether the verb is weak or strong. Weak verbs add -*te*/-*ten*, -*de*/-*den* to the stem: e.g. *ik kookte* – *wij kookten*. Strong verbs make their past tense and past participle by means of single or two-stage ablaut: e.g.

bidden 'pray' – bad – gebeden
slapen 'sleep' – sl**ie**p – gesl**a**pen
liggen 'lie' – l**a**g – gel**e**gen

Past participle: *ge*- + stem + -*t*/*d* for weak; specific form for strong has to be learnt with the verb. If the verb has a stressed prefix, -*ge*- is inserted between this prefix and the stem: e.g. *aannemen* 'accept' – *aan**ge**nomen*. Unlike German, foreign verbs in -*eren* (German -*ieren*) *do* take the *ge*- in past participle.

COMPOUND TENSES

These are made with specific auxiliaries: the future with *zullen*; the perfect with *zijn* or *hebben*. *Hebben* is used with transitives; intransitives involving a change of state use *zijn* (cf. *sein* with verbs of motion in German). E.g. *hij is opgestaan* 'he (has) got up'; *wij zijn naar de stad gereden* 'we drove to town'. *Zullen* and other modal auxiliaries – e.g. *laten*, *kunnen*, *moeten* – precede the infinitive they govern: e.g.

hij is niet **kunnen** komen 'he was not able to come'
hij heeft . . . **laten** vallen 'he let . . . drop'

en ze hebben me allemaal beloofd te **zullen** komen
'and they all promised me they would come' (Couperus)

The modal auxiliary may even be inserted between an infinitive and its separable prefix. There are then three possibilities:

omdat ik in Amsterdam moet overstappen	'because I have to change in A.'
over moet stappen	
overstappen moet	

PASSIVE

Both *worden* and *zijn* are used as auxiliaries in the formation of the passive voice, the latter in the perfect tense only: e.g.

. . . zal donderdag **worden** begraven '. . . will be buried on Thursday'

het raam is gebroken 'the window is broken' (= 'the window has been broken')
uit de mededeling van thans kan **worden** afgeleid, dat...
'from the present announcement it can be inferred that...'

As dummy subject, *er* may introduce a passive sentence: e.g. *er werd veel gepraat* 'a lot of talking went on' (cf. German *es wurde viel geplaudert*).

Er also = German *da* in such constructions as: *een stuk* ***er****van = ein Stück davon*, but, contrary to German usage, *er* can be separated from the preposition: *ik heb* ***er*** *een stuk* ***van***.

NEGATION

Niet follows verb negated or its object: *ik schrijf (de brief) niet* 'I don't write the letter'; but precedes modal + infinitive groupings at end of clause: *dat boek heb ik niet kunnen kopen* 'I wasn't able to buy that book'.

Prepositions

Note that the pronoun *het* cannot be used after a preposition. Instead, *er* + prep. is used (cf. *er*, above); thus, **tegen het – ertegen*; **in het – erin*.

Word derivation

Compounds are frequent, usually two or more nouns, but other parts of speech may enter into them. Example of word-building:

antwoord 'answer'
verantwoord**elijk** 'responsible'
verantwoordelikj**heid** 'responsibility'

Stress may shift in compound: *tóeval* 'chance', *toevállig* 'by chance'.

Word order

SVO is normal; SOV in subordinate clauses; VSO in interrogation.

1 In den beginne was het Woord en het Woord was bij God en het Woord was God. 2 Dit was in den beginne bij God. 3 Alle dingen zijn door het Woord geworden en zonder dit is geen ding geworden, dat geworden is. 4 In het Woord was leven en het leven was het licht der mensen; 5 en het licht schijnt in de duisternis en de duisternis heeft het niet gegrepen.
6 Er trad een mens op, van God gezonden, wiens naam was Johannes;
7 deze kwam als getuige om van het licht te getuigen, opdat allen door hem geloven zouden. 8 Hij was het licht niet, maar was om te getuigen van het licht.

EASTER ISLAND

See **Rapanui**.

EFIK

INTRODUCTION

This language belongs to the Benue-Congo family. Efik and its close congener Ibibio are spoken by about 2,750,000 people in the Calabar area of south-east Nigeria, where the language has served as a common medium of communication between various ethnic/linguistic groups. Writing in Efik dates from 1846, when the Scottish Presbyterian Church commenced its missionary work in Calabar, and promptly set about translating parts of the Bible. A translation of *The Pilgrim's Progress* appeared in 1868. Creative writing in Efik commenced in the 1930s, and there have been several writers of note (E.N. Amuku, E.E. Okon, E.A. Edyan, and the poet Elisabeth Asibong). Efik is used for local radio services.

SCRIPT

Apart from the Roman-based alphabet provided by the missionary press, several indigenous scripts have appeared, e.g. the Nsibidhi script.

PHONOLOGY

Consonants

The labio-velar /kp/ is the syllable-initial allophone of /p/; /b/ cannot be final; /t, d, k, g, h/ are present, with /f, r, s/, and the nasals /m, n, ɲ, ŋ/. /m, n, ŋ/ appear as syllabic initials; the continuants /w/ and /j/ occur as nasal resonants.

Vowels

i/ɪ, e, ɛ, a, ɔ, o, u

There are four/five diphthongs with /i/ as second member.

VOWEL HARMONY

In prefix + stem complex, the vowel of the prefix is front or back depending on the stem vowel: e.g. *ŋ́.ke.dèp* 'I bought'; *ŋ́.kó.kùt* 'I saw'; *ŋ́.**ka**.nàm* 'I did', where *k*V is past marker, *ŋ́* is 1st person singular subject prefix.

Tone

Tone in Efik is 'terraced'; i.e. successive high tones decrease progressively in height. The relative pitch of low tones is not thereby affected.

There are two main tones, high and low, plus a rising and a falling tone. Tone plays a cardinal role in Efik grammar and syntax. For example, the 2nd and 3rd person subject prefixes are distinguished only by tone (*see* **Pronoun**, below). All Efik stems have inherent (isolate, or dictionary) tone, which is subject to specific alteration in specific grammatical constructions: e.g. *nám* 'do', but *ŋ́.ka.nàm* 'I did'.

MORPHOLOGY AND SYNTAX

There is no grammatical gender and no class system for nominals; nominals include pronouns. The noun in itself subsumes both singularity and plurality. Certain adjectives can be pluralized by prefixing a syllabic nasal: e.g. *ébot* 'goat': *èkpírì èbot* 'small goat'; *ŋ̀kpírì èbot* 'small goats' (note change of tone in noun). A few suppletive plurals are found: *éyen* 'child', pl. *ǹditɔ*; *àkámba* 'big', pl. *ìkpɔ́*.

Pronoun

The independent (long) forms are used as focused pronouns, both subject and object. The short forms are prefixed to verbs as subject:

	Singular		*Plural*	
	Focused form	*Verbal prefix*	*Focused form*	*Verbal prefix*
1	àmi	ŋ, ń, ḿ	ǹȳɪn	i
2	àfo	à (or harmonic allophone)	m̀bufo	è
3	ɛ̀ȳé	á (or harmonic allophone)	ḿmɔ̀	é

That is, tone alone distinguishes second person prefix from third: *à.nam útom* 'you are working'; *á.nàm útom* 'he is working'.

POSSESSION

A variant of the focused form follows the noun, for singular possessor: e.g. *úfɔ̀k mì* 'my house'; *úfɔ̀k fò* 'your (sing.) house'.

In case of plural possessor, full focused form follows: *úfɔ̀k m̀bufo* 'your (pl.) house'. Nominal possessor also follows: e.g. *úfɔ̀k ɔ́bɔŋ* 'chief's house'.

DEMONSTRATIVE PRONOUN/ADJECTIVE

ɛ́mì 'this', *órò* 'that', *ókò* 'that yonder': e.g. *úfɔ̀k ɛ́mì ɛ́dì ókìm* 'this house is mine'; *ɛ́mì ɛ́dì ùbóm* 'this is a canoe' where *ɛ́dì* is the identifying copula *dí*, with prefixed 3rd person verbal prefix.

INTERROGATIVE PRONOUN

ànye 'who?'; *ǹso* 'what?'

RELATIVE PRONOUN

None; relative-clause construction depends on whether the proposition is affirmative or negative. The affirmative relative clause is marked by *-dé*: e.g.

*ḿfiri ɛ́mì ì.ké.dép.**dé*** 'the fruit which we bought'; the negative suffix is *-ké*: e.g. *ŋ́kpɔ̀ ɛ́mì m̀mé.ŋ́.ko.fyɔ̀k.**ké*** 'things I didn't know' (*ŋ́kpò* 'thing', *fyɔ̀k* 'know', *ŋ́.ko*: 1st person singular verbal prefix plus contrastive construction marker *ko*).

The negative relative involves the reduction of the pronominal subject prefixes to three idiosyncratic forms: one for first person singular, one for second person singular, and one for all other personal forms: *m̀mé – m̀mú – m̀mí*.

The *de-* form is also used after *ke* 'when', *edieke* 'if', *koro* 'because', *adaŋa nte* 'as long as', etc.: e.g. (Ward 1933: 100)

Ke ndaba**de** ntre, ŋkut owo emi esine**de**... 'As I dreamt thus, I saw a man who was wearing...'

Nte nsaŋa**de** ke ikɔt ererimbot... 'As I was walking in the wilderness of the world...'

Numerals

1–10: *kyèt, ìba, ìtá, ìnaŋ, ìtyôn, ìtyôkyet, ìtyâba, ìtyâitá, ùsúk-kyèt, dwòp.* 11 *dwòp-e-kyet*; 12 *dwòp-e-ba*; 20 *édip*; 100 *ìkye.*

Numerals follow noun: e.g. *ébwa ìnaŋ* 'four dogs'.

Verb

The great majority of Efik roots are mono- or disyllabic. The root = imperative = stem for finite *prefix + stem* forms.

Perfective/imperfective action, with reference to present, past, or future, is expressed in verbal forms which combine personal prefixes, specific markers, tones, and, exceptionally, suffixes, in specific patterns. For example, for ongoing action in the present the pattern is subject prefix + stem with *low* tone: e.g. *ń.**nàm** útom* 'I am working' (*nám* – *high* tone – 'to do'); *án.**nàm** útom* 'he is working'.

PAST

Subject prefix + *ma* + subject prefix + stem: in this pattern the first subject prefix and the *ma* marker have the same tone; the second subject is high tone, and the stem has isolate = dictionary tone: e.g. *ḿmá ń.nám útom* 'I worked'; *èmà. é.nám útom* 'you (pl.) worked'.

FUTURE

Subject prefix + *yé* + stem (isolate tone): e.g. *ń.yé.bɔ́p úfɔ̀k* 'I'm going to build a house'; or, subject prefix + *dî* + stem (falling tone in monosyllable, high–low in disyllable): e.g. *Édî.kâ úfɔ̀k íbɔ̀k?* 'Is he going to go to the hospital?'

The *-di-* future is an example of what Welmers (1968) calls the 'contrastive' construction. This is found in sentences introduced by an interrogative pronoun, and also in sentences where one or another component may be optionally focused. With reference to present and past, two such constructions are possible with or without *ké* = 'is it/it is, that...'. For example, with reference to the past:

È.ké.dép ńsò	
sò **ké** ὲ.ké.dép	'What did you buy?'
ŋ́ ke.dèp ḿfiri	
ḿfiri **ke** ŋ́.ké.dép	'I bought fruit'

With reference to the present:

Ànám ńsò = ǹso **ké** ànám? 'What are you doing?'
ńnàm útom = útom **ké** ńnam 'I'm working'

NEGATIVE

The marker is a suffix: *k*V → /χ, γ/V (in Efik orthography h̲). The basic formula is given by the negative present: subject prefix + stem + negative marker with harmonic vowel: e.g. *Ń.dí.**ge** mí* 'I'm not coming here'. Similarly for past and future, with relevant tense markers preceding stem: e.g. past, *ŋ́.ke.dí.**ge** mí* 'I didn't come here'; future, *ń.dî.dî.**ge** mi* 'I shan't come here' (note change of stem tone).

Efik has, further, specific marker/tonal patterns for sequential, hortative, conditional, hypothetical, and customary forms.

Prepositions

Ké is an all-purpose location marker. Where closer definition is required, various nominals are used, e.g. *ésìt* 'in(side)'; *íso* 'face' → 'in front of': *k'íso*.

Word order

The constrastive pattern allows for SVO or OcSV, where c stands for the connective *ké*.

1 1 IKↃ okodu ke eritɔŋɔ IKↃ okonyuŋ odu ye Abasi,
2 IKↃ onyuŋ edi Abasi. Kpa Enye okodu ye Abasi ke
3 eritɔŋɔ. Edi Enye akanam kpukpru ŋkpɔ ewɔŋɔ edi;
ndien ke esiode Enye efep, ŋkpɔ baba kiet, eke ama
4 ɔwɔrɔ iwɔrɔke idi. Uwem odu Enye ke idem; uwem oro
5 onyuŋ edi uŋwana owo. Ndien uŋwana oro ayama ke
ekim; ekim inyruŋ ikanke enye.
6 Owo kiet okoto edi; Abasi osio enye ɔdeŋ; enyiŋ esie
7 ekere John. Enye ekedi nte ntiense, ete idi ntiense inɔ
uŋwana oro, kpaŋ kpukpru owo enim ke akapanikɔ
oto ke enye.
8 Enye ikedige uŋwana oro, edi ekedi man edi ntiense
9 ɔnɔ uŋwana oro.

EGYPTIAN

INTRODUCTION

One of the oldest attested languages in the world, Egyptian belonged to the Afro-Asiatic family, and showed several features shared in common with Semitic. The following stages in the development of Egyptian are distinguished:

1. Old Egyptian of the third millennium BC. Known from the Pyramid Texts, the most archaic form of Egyptian, and from funerary inscriptions of the fifth and sixth Dynasties.
2. Classical or Middle Egyptian, covering the period 2240–1780 BC (Dynasties 9 to 12).
3. Late Classical: 1780–1350 BC (Dynasties 13 to 18). The *Book of the Dead* was compiled in this period.
4. Late Egyptian: fourteenth to eighth centuries BC (Dynasties 18 to 24).
5. Demotic: eighth century BC to fifth century AD.
6. Coptic.

SCRIPT

See **Script** at end of article.

PHONOLOGY

Consonants

The consonantal inventory seems to have been as follows:

stops: p, b, t, d, k, g, q; + glottal stop ˀ (or Arabic ʾain)
affricates: tʃ, dʒ
fricatives: s/z, ʃ, h, ħ, x
nasals: m, n
lateral and flap: l, r
semi-vowels: j, w

Hamza is usually notated in transcription as ꜣ, here as ʾ. The semi-vowel /j/ in initial position is notated as *i* (also as medial). Here, /ħ/ = Ar. ح, /h/ = ه, /x/ = خ, notated as ẖ or ḫ. /tʃ/ is notated as ṯ and /dʒ/ as ḏ.

MORPHOLOGY AND SYNTAX

Noun

There are two genders, masculine and feminine. Many feminine nouns end in *-t*: e.g. *sn* 'brother', ***snt*** 'sister'. Typical Egyptian nouns are: *pr* 'house'; *pt* 'sky'; *nỉwt* 'city'; *nṯr* /nečer/ 'god'. For pronounciation, *see* **Script**, Phonograms (b).

SINGULAR, DUAL, AND PLURAL NUMBERS

The dual and plural endings are marked for gender: dual masc. *-wy*, fem. *-ty*; pl. masc. *-w*, fem. *-wt*: e.g. 'arm', '*wy* 'two arms'; *ỉrty* 'two eyes'; *nbty* 'two goddesses', with special reference to the *nebty* Name, one of the Five Great Names in the Royal Titulary. The *nebty* Name encodes the special relationship between the Pharaoh and the two queen-goddesses of pre-Dynastic Egypt: the vulture-goddess Nekhbet of Upper Egypt, and the cobra-goddess W'ḏt of Lower Egypt (both names carry the feminine marker *-t*). For the other names in the Royal Titulary, see Gardiner, Lesson VII, Excursus A.

Originally, plurality was indicated in the script by triplication, duality by duplication. This practice came to be abbreviated to three strokes for plural, two strokes for dual. Finally, the dual marker // or \\ came to be regarded as an alphabetic sign for *-y*. The three strokes reappear in many nouns denoting non-countable substances – provisions, tribute, salt, wine, etc.

CASE RELATIONS

Annexation: there is a direct construct case in which the qualifier immediately precedes the qualified, and an indirect construct using the inflected connective *n*(*y*), *n*(*t*), *n*(*y*)*w*, *n*(*yw*)*t*.

In the direct construct the first member is definite, as in Semitic; the indirect construct permits indefinite status of either component: e.g.

(a) Direct construct: *nb t'w* 'the Lord of the Lands'; *nbt pt* 'the Lady of Heaven'; *nbt sb'w* 'the Lady of the Stars'.
(b) Indirect construct: *pr **n** ỉnr* 'an administrator's house'; *'**n** nṯr* 'a god's hand'; *sḥ **n** srw* 'council of the nobles'.

Honorific transposition in direct construct: in the script, where gods and kings are concerned, the normal order is reversed: thus, for 'the son of the king' (normal order: *s' nsw*) *nsw s'* was written, but read as *s'nsw*.

Adjective

As attribute, adjective usually follows the noun, and shows concord for gender and number: e.g. *sn nfr* 'good brother'; *snt nfrt* 'good sister'. If it precedes the noun, it is invariable. When the adjective is used independently, the referent can be identified by the determinative: thus *nfr.t* may mean 'beautiful woman' (Nefertiti) or 'fine-looking cow', depending on the determinative used: or .

The plural marker -*w* tends to be dropped. Dual: cf. *rwty wrty* 'the two great doors' (*rwt* 'gate', *wrr* 'great') (Bullock 1979: 4).

Nisba adjectives are formed from nouns and prepositions by adding -*y*: e.g. *nỉwt* 'town', *nỉwty* 'urban'; *ḥr* 'on'; *ḥry* 'superior'; *m* 'in', *ỉmy* 'interior'.

COMPARISON

A comparative is made with positive + *r*: e.g. *nfr r nbw* 'finer than gold'.

Pronoun

First, the independent forms with the pronominal affixes:

		Singular		Plural	
		Independent	*Affix*	*Independent*	*Affix*
1		ỉnk	ỉ	ỉnn	n
2	masc.	ntk	k		
				nttn	
	fem.	ntṯ	ṯ		ṯn
3	masc.	ntf	f		
				ntsn	sn
	fem.	nts	s	ntsn	

There are three dual forms: 1 *ny*, 2 *ṯny*, 3 *sny*, used as suffixes. The suffixes provide the subject in conjugation: e.g. *dd.ỉ* 'I say'; *sḏm.f* 'he hears'. Following nouns they are possessive suffixes: *pr.f* 'his house'; *sn.s* 'her brother'. Affixed to prepositions they provide oblique cases: e.g. *n.f* 'for him'; *n.n* 'for us'; *ỉrmỉ,st r.f* 'I did it (= *st*, *see* **Dependent pronoun**) to him' (Bullock 1979: 60).

In sentences like 'thou art a scribe', Egyptian uses what Gardiner calls 'the m̱ of predication': *ỉw.**k** m sš* 'thou art (*ỉw.k*) by-way-of-being a scribe (*sš*)'. Cf. *ḥm.k **m** ḥr iṯt* 'Your Majesty (*ḥm.k*) is-by-way-of-being Horus (ḥr), he who conquers' (Sinuhe, B.216) (cf. use of the instrumental case in Slavonic: e.g. Polish: ***kim** on jest? On jest Polak**iem***).

DEPENDENT PRONOUN

singular: *wỉ*, 2 masc. *ṯw*, fem. *tn*, 3 masc. *sw*, fem. *st*
dual: *ny*, *ṯny*, *sny*
plural: *n*, *ṯn*, *sn*

These pronouns are used *inter alia* to provide direct objects after transitive finite forms: e.g. *dd.**tw** h'st n h'st* 'land gave you to land' (Bullock 1979: 73); *rdỉ.n.f **wỉ**...*;'he placed me...' (for the *.n.* in this sentence, *see* **verb**, below).

DEMONSTRATIVE PRONOUN

Marked for gender and number: *pw*/*tw* 'this' (masc./fem.); common pl. *nw* 'this, these'; similar form with *pf*/*tf* 'that'; *pn*/*tn*, pl. *nn*.

The demonstrative pronoun *pw* functions as a generalized pronoun with singular or plural, masculine or feminine antecedent: cf. *R*ᶜ *pw* 'it/he is Reᶜ'; *ḥmt w*ᶜ*b pw n R*ᶜ 'she is the wife (*ḥmt*) of a priest (*w*ᶜ*b*) of Reᶜ'.

INTERROGATIVE PRONOUN

m 'who?'; *ptr* 'what?'

RELATIVE PRONOUN

Masc. *nty*, fem. *ntt*, pl. *ntyw*: these can be used only if the antecedent is definite: e.g.... ***nty*** *rdi.n.i n.tn sw* 'the... which I gave (*sw* 'it' recapitulates the relative pronoun) to you (*n.tn*)'. Where the antecedent is indefinite, no link is required: the resumptive pronoun appears in the relative clause (cf. **Arabic**).

A negative relative adjective is marked for gender: *iwty*/*iwtt*: cf. *mḏ't iwtt sš.s* 'a book (*mḏ't*) which-not-is its writing', i.e. 'a book which has no writing'.

Numerals

Numerals are treated as nominals and usually follow nouns. Theoretically, both noun and numeral are masculine singular: 1–10: *w*' (with feminine form *w't*), *snw*, *ḫmt*, *fdw*, *diw*, *sisw*, *sfḫ*, *ḫmn*, *psd*, *mḏ*; 20 *ḏwty*; 30 *m'b'*; 40 *ḥm*; 100 *štt*.

Verb

Formally, an Egyptian verb consists of two, three, four, or five root consonants: e.g. *ḏd* 'speak', *mri* 'love', *sḏm* 'hear', *wstn* 'step'. Roots are classified as weak (ending in *i*, *j*, *w*), geminate, or strong. It follows that all biliterals are strong.

The citation form is the root + the enclitic masculine pronominal marker *f*: e.g. *sḏm.f* 'he hears, heard, will hear'; pronounced /sedžemef/. Essentially, this form is a verbal noun, annexed by the third person pronominal marker. It is sense-bearing, but neutral as to voice, mood, or tense. In practice, it usually serves as the active indicative present form, and is then conjugated by enclitic marker for all persons and two numbers (the dual is absorbed by the plural). The personal markers have been set out under **Pronoun** above.

The *sḏm.f* form is by far the commonest verbal form in Egyptian. The notion of tense is alien to the language, and *sḏm.f* is best regarded as an imperfective aspect indicating uncompleted or pending action. It is negated by *n* or *nn*: *nn* negates the whole proposition, *n* negates a verbal item therein. Negation of a positive verbal formula does not necessarily imply negation of the aspect/tense meaning normally associated with that formula. For example, when negated by *nn*, the *sḏm.f form* seems to refer to the future: *nn wṯs.f dšrt* 'he shall-not-wear the Red Crown (*dšrt* 'the Red Land, the desert: locus of, and by extension, the Red Crown of Lower Egypt).

When negated by *n*, the *sḏm.n.f.* form seems to generalize the temporal dimension: *n mdw.n.f* 'he does not/did not speak'.

The *sḏm.**n**.f* form is perfective, and usually refers to an action completed in the past. The *sḏm.f* and *sḏm.n.f* forms are illustrated in this sentence from the *Story of Sinuhe*: *ḏd.n.f ʿḥʾ.f ḥnʿ.i* 'He said that he would fight with me' (Bullock 1979: 48), where *ḏd.n.f* denotes completed action, *ʿḥʾ.f* imperfective/pending action. Similarly: *ḥmt.**n**.i ḫpr ḥʾ ʿyt* 'I expected that strife would arise.'

The *sḏm.n.f* form is negated by *n*, and then acquires an imperfective meaning. Among other forms taken by the Egyptian verb are the narrative form *sḏm.**in**.f*, and the sequential (with future reference) form *sḏm.**hrf***.

As was said above, the base form *sḏm* is neutral as to voice. It may have been specifically vocalized to express active or passive, but the script affords no clue here (cf. **Arabic**). A specifically passive form could be made in Egyptian, e.g. by the addition of the *-tw/-t* marker: e.g. *sḏm.**tw**.f* 'he was listened to'; *sḏm.**tw** m pr.nsw* 'it was heard in the palace'.

THE OLD PERFECTIVE

Gardiner (1969: 234) calls this the 'sole surviving relic in Egyptian of the Semitic finite verb'. Professor Bakir's (1978: 97) term 'circumstantial form' (*al-ḥāl*) is apt, as the form is neutral as to tense, used nearly always in auxiliary clauses, and, hence, essentially contingent in sense. The endings are sing. 1 *-kwi*, 2 *-ti*, 3 masc. *-w*, fem. *-ti*; pl. 1 *-wyn*, 2 *-tiwny*, 3 masc. *-w*, fem. *-ti* . Korostovtsev (1961: 60) gives the example: *gm.n.i sw rḫ.w st* 'I found him knowing this' = '. . . ;that he knew this'.

INFINITIVE

Can be masculine or feminine (then in *-t*), and is often used with *r* to denote purpose: e.g. *r sḏm* 'in order to hear'.

PARTICIPLE

Four are distinguished, denoting active/passive single or repeated action. These are marked for gender (though the masculine ending *-w* is usually omitted) and the iterative form may show gemination. Otherwise, the participles are indistinguishable from the stem; thus *sḏm*, apart from its meaning in finite forms, can signify 'hearing' (once or often), '(being) heard' (once or often), 'he who hears/is heard', etc. A common formula is: *in* + subject (noun or independent pronoun) + participle + complement, e.g. *in ḥm.f rdi ir.t(w).f* 'verily (*in*) 'His Majesty (*ḥm.f*) who caused/causes (*rdi*) its (*f*) making (root *iri* 'to make')' (*in*: cf. *inna* preceding nominal clause in Arabic).

Prepositions

Examples of these, e.g. *m*, *ḥnʿ*, *ḥr*, have appeared in sentences given above; *n* denotes the dative case: e.g. *n sn* 'to/for the brother', *n.nb.k* 'to thy lord'. *n* is also used to express the notion of having, possessing: *iw **n.k** ʿnḫ* 'life (*ʿnḫ*) is (*iw*) to-thee (n.k)', i.e. 'thou hast/shalt have life'. Another meaning of *n* is 'by reason of': *wbn.i **n** mr(w)t.**k*** 'I shine-forth (*wbn.i*) through love (*mr*(*w*)) *t* of thee (*.k*)'.

ḥr 'in, from': *ḥr Kmt* 'in Egypt'; *nbw ḥr ḫʾst* 'gold (*nbw*) from the wasteland (*ḫʾst*)'.

Word order

In verbal construction, VSO where S is a noun and O is direct (+ indirect) object; VOS where S is pronominalized: the formula here is V – indirect object – direct object – S pronominalized – (adverbial extension). Nominal construction: SV is normal, but may be inverted: e.g. *nfr ḥrrt* 'beautiful (is) this flower'.

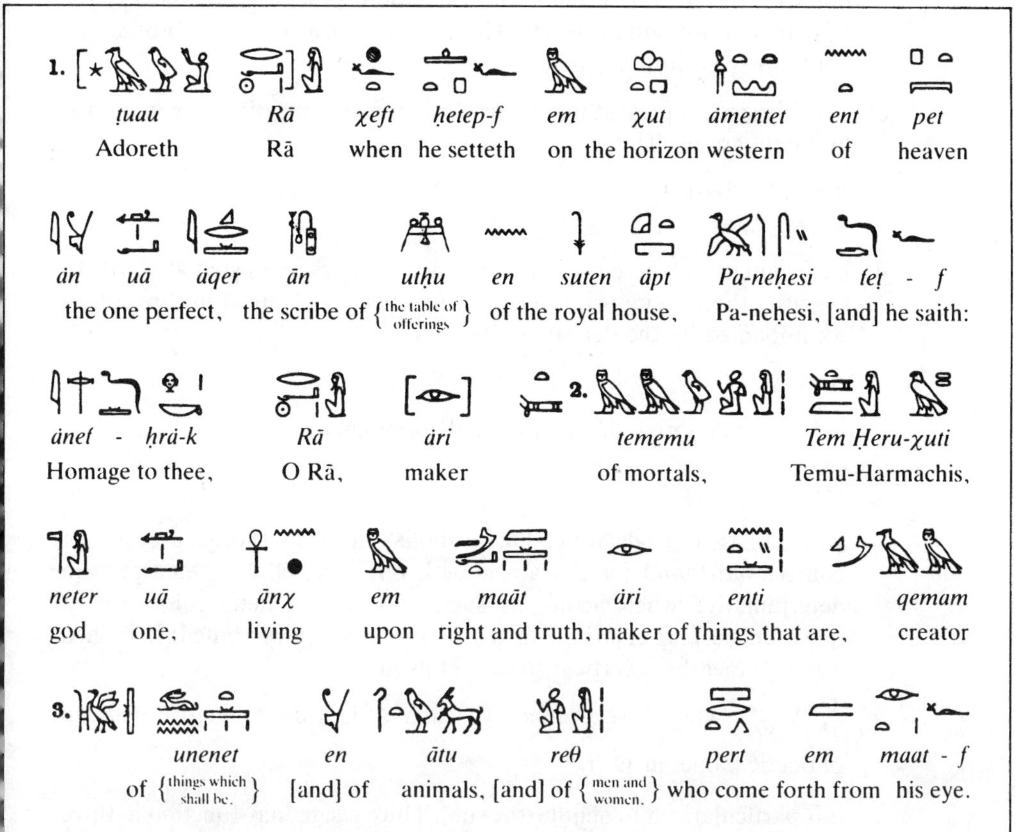

SCRIPT

The 'sacred writing' deciphered by Champollion in the 1820s is known as hieroglyphic. Several thousand hieroglyphs are known, many of them being very rare or *hapax legomena*. The hieroglyphic script is sub-divided into:

(a) Ideograms: these represent objects in purely graphic fashion with no phonetic element: e.g.

⊙ /r'/, 'day, sun';
⊓ /pr/, 'house'.

(b) Phonograms: these are particularized signs indicating pronunciation: e.g.

𓂋 /r/, 'mouth'

comes to function in the course of the centuries as the conventional sign for /r/, and a series of such single-valued signs ultimately produces an alphabet (see below). At no stage of Egyptian before Coptic are vowels notated. To facilitate pronunciation, modern practice is to vocalize the Egyptian consonants with /e/. Thus, *pr* is read as /per/; *sn* 'brother' as /sen/, *nfr* 'beautiful' as /nefer/.

(c) Syllabic signs representing two or three consonants, often accompanied by phonograms: Thus:

𓎟 /nb/, 'basket'
★ /sb'/, 'star'

(d) Determinatives: these are class or function markers posted at words to suggest their semantic field. Thus, verbs of motion are often accompanied by the determinative

𓂻

and words denoting liquids by the determinative

𓈗

(Cf. Chinese radicals, which have a similar function, though they are, of course, shorthand for characters with phonetic values). An Egyptian determinative when acting as such, has no phonetic role; it may, however, be particularized to define the object represented: it is then accompanied by a vertical stroke. Thus in

𓅱𓃀𓈖𓇳 /wbn/, 'rise', 'shine', the sign 𓇳 is a determinative with no phonetic value; in 𓇳𓏤 /r'/

it is particularized to denote 'the sun'. Thus, a sign may function in three different ways – as ideogram, as phonogram, and as determinative.

The Egyptian script is read either vertically downwards, or horizontally left to right or right to left. Ideograms representing gods, humans, or animals act as pointers to the direction in which the script is to be read: if they face to the right of the viewer, the script is read from right to left, and vice versa. Symmetry of a purely formal nature plays an important part in the arrangement of signs. There is no punctuation. The script swarms with abbreviations, formal transpositions, anomalous spellings.

A cursive form of hieroglyphic, known as hieratic, is attested from about 3000 BC. An abbreviated cursive, known as demotic, appears from about 800 BC onwards. While there is a one-to-one correspondence between a hieroglyph and its hieratic version, there is no such correspondence in demotic script, which is full of ligatures.

THE EGYPTIAN SCRIPT

THE ALPHABET

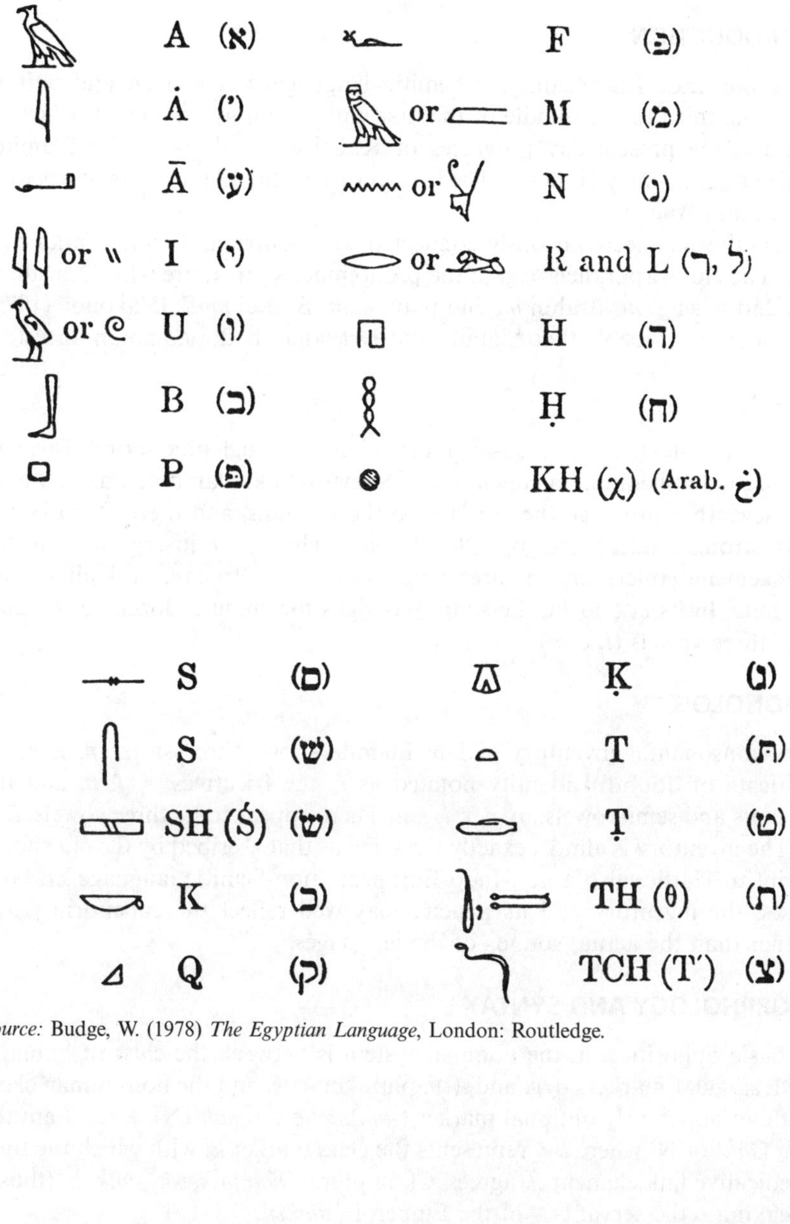

Source: Budge, W. (1978) *The Egyptian Language*, London: Routledge.

ELAMITE

INTRODUCTION

This non-Indo-European, non-Semitic language was spoken and written from the third to the middle of the first millennium BC, in a territory which covered the present-day provinces of Khuzistan and Fars. The Elamites called their country Hatamti. The best-known of the Elamite city-states were Šušen and Ančan.

Elamite has been variously connected with Hurrian, Turkic, Caucasian, etc. The closest parallels, e.g. in the pronominal system, are with Dravidian. Cf. 2nd p. sing. *ni*, Brahui *ni*; 2nd p. pl. *num*, Brahui *num*. D′akonov (1979) considers it probable that Elamite and Dravidian had a common ancestor.

SCRIPT

The earliest texts are in a so-far undeciphered hieroglyphic script. Through the second millennium a cuneiform of Sumero-Akkadian type was in use. In the seventh century BC the area fell to the Iranians, and thereafter Elamite was strongly influenced by Old Persian. The royal inscriptions of the Achaemenid rulers are in three languages – Old Persian, Akkadian, and Elamite. In its late form, the script has signs for about a dozen consonants and three vowels (*i*, *a*, *u*).

PHONOLOGY

The consonantal inventory of late Elamite shows three stops: *p*, *t*, *k*, an affricate of doubtful identity notated as *c*, the fricatives: *s*, *ʃ*, *h*, and the sonants and semi-vowels: *m*, *n*, *r*, *l*, *j*, *w*. There appear to be three vowels: *i*, *a*, *u*. The inventory is almost exactly the same as that ascribed by the cuneiform script to Hattic, also a non-Indo-European, non-Semitic language. In both cases, the inventory and its paucity may well reflect the cuneiform script rather than the actual sounds of the languages.

MORPHOLOGY AND SYNTAX

A basic opposition in the nominal system is between the class of humans, with singular markers -(*i*)*k* and -(*i*)*r*, plural in -(*i*)*p*, and the non-human class, with an apparently optional marker (*-um*)*me*: e.g. *u šak* (N). *k.i.k* 'I am the son (*šak*) of N' where *k.i.* represents the class marker *k*, with which the final predicative link element *.k* agrees. Cf. in plural: *nan.ip ker.ip sunki.p* '(those) speaking – the servants – of the Emperor (*sunki*)'.

E. Reiner suggests (*Handbuch der Orientalistik*, 1 Abt., Bd. 2) that *-k* is linked to a first person referent, *-r* to a third (cf. Armenian). *temti napp.**ip.ir*** 'ruler of the gods'; *takki.me* 'life'.

Both qualifier and qualified may take the class marker; e.g. *ruhu.**r** riša.**rra*** 'big man', or *ruhu.**Ø**.riša.rra*.

Pronoun

The base forms are:

	Singular	*Plural*
1	hu/u	*incl.* ela/elu; *excl.* niku/nika
2	nu/ni	num
3	he/e, i	ap(i)

Possessive forms: *petir.uri* 'my enemy', *rutu.uri* 'my wife', *att.uri* 'my father'.

Verb

A typical form is an agglutinative complex comprising the following slots: (1) base; (2) direct object; (3) aspectual, directional marker; (4) participial marker; (5) subject marker; (6) modal marker. Certain slots are mutually exclusive; e.g. slot 2 is occupied only if *-ma-* appears in 3: e.g. *pepši. (i)r.ma.h* 'I founded it' (*ma* is the imperfective aspect marker). The subject marker in slot 5 may be *-k*, *-t*, *-r*, etc.

Verbal nouns take class markers: *hani.**ki**.k* 'I beloved . . . ;am'; *kuši.**r*** 'built', with reference to third person sing.; *hani.**p*** 'beloved', with reference to third person pl. D′akonov gives forms for a verbal noun of action: e.g. *kuši.kk.a* 'having built, who has built'; and a gerundive form: e.g. *kuši.n* 'requiring to be, able to be built'.

INDICATIVE MOOD

The personal endings that have been identified are:

	Singular	*Plural*
1	-hu	-h.h(u)
2	-(a)t(i)	-h.t(ə)
3	-ši	-h.š(i)

The negative marker was *-in*. In late Elamite, personal class markers are found affixed to the negating element *-in-*: *in.k* 'not I/I . . . not . . . '.

Postpositions

For example, *-ma* 'on, in'; *-(i)kku* 'at, on, towards'; *-(i)mar* 'from, after'.

SPECIMEN ELAMITE SENTENCE (FROM D′AKONOV 1979)

tiri.mite.š. taššu.p. appa.pet.ip. u.me.na. inni. tiri.ma.n.pi. hupi.pi. halpi.š. man.ka 'thus I say: smite the warriors who are hostile, as they do not call themselves mine, slay them' (*tiri*... *man.ka* 'thus I say'; *mite.š* 'smite'; *taššu.p* 'warriors'; *app* 'who'; *pet.ip* 'hostile'; *u.me.na* 'mine'; *in.me* > *inni* 'they... not'; *tiri.ma.n.pi* 'as they call themselves'; *hupi.pi* 'these'; *halpi.š* 'slay!')

ENGLISH

INTRODUCTION

The West Germanic branch of Indo-European, to which English belongs, also includes Low German, Dutch, and Frisian. English itself derives from three Low German dialects spoken by the Angles, Saxons, and Jutes, who came from Denmark and North Germany to settle in England from the middle of the fifth century onwards. These dialects are marked by retention of the unvoiced stops /p, t, k/, which were mutated to the corresponding fricatives /f, θ, x/, in High German, and of the voiced stops /b, d, g/, which were likewise mutated to /p, t, k/. *See* **German**: Second Sound Shift. These mutations may be illustrated by such equations as:

Low German	*English*	*High German*
dör	**d**oor	**T**ür
pad	**p**ath	**Pf**ad
ski**p**	shi**p**	Schi**ff**
hei**t**	ho**t**	hei**ss**

Four main dialects took shape in *Englaland*, the 'land of the Angles':

1. West Saxon: spoken in the kingdom of Wessex and other parts of the south;
2. Kentish: the language of the Jutes in what is now Kent;
3. Mercian: spoken by the Angles in East Anglia and Humberside;
4. Northumbrian: the dialects of the Angles in north-east England and south-east Scotland.

Of these, West Saxon – King Alfred's *Englisc* – is by far the most important as the language in which most of Old English literature is written. (*See* **Periodization of English Literature**, below). In the eighth and ninth centuries a fresh Germanic influx came in the shape of Scandinavian settlers, whose Norse language provided English with many genetically homogeneous loanwords. From 1016 to 1042, England was, in fact, a Danish kingdom. On the linguistic plane, however, West Saxon preserved its ascendancy until the Norman invasion in 1066. The polarization of society which followed this upheaval was reflected in an equivalent polarization of language: as the language of the conquerors, Norman French assumed the dominant role, while West Saxon lost its privileged status, and joined other forms of Old English as a dialect of the English peasantry. Through the twelfth century there was little or no writing in Old English. The specific nature of Middle

English, as it emerged and was consolidated between 1100 and 1500, is largely due to three factors:

1. The widely disparate rates at which the Old English inflectional system was lost in the various dialects. This dialectal divergence reached a point at which mutual intelligibility was severely impaired or even lost. The need for an accepted common norm became more and more urgent.
2. It has been calculated that about 10,000 French words were imported in the Middle English period, 75 per cent of which are still in use today. On the one hand, this represented a considerable enhancement of a language which found itself in a new political situation; on the other hand, it implied a corresponding loss of those Old English lexical resources which were no longer immediately useful.
3. The morphological core of the emergent language remained, however, that inherited from Old English.

By the late thirteenth century, the term 'English' refers to that compromise between the East Midland (< Mercian) and South-Eastern (< Kentish) dialects, which came to be known as the London dialect. In 1258, the accession of Henry III was proclaimed in 'English'. By the middle of the fourteenth century, English had replaced French as the language of the law (Statute of Pleading, 1362) and of education; and by the end of the century, Chaucer was using the London dialect to write one of the greatest poems in English. A hundred years later, the lineaments of Early Modern English are clearly discernible.

Periodization of Modern English is meaningful mainly on the phonological plane, and, within this field, primarily with regard to change affecting the vocalic system. The consonantal inventory remained largely the same from the early Middle English period onwards, and the principal morphological reductionist processes were virtually complete by the close of that period. Thus, Old English is marked by the possession of a rich and extensive system of Germanic inflection and a purely Germanic vocabulary; Middle English by extensive erosion of the morphological apparatus, and the intake of a large number of French words; Modern English by the near-total disappearance of inflection. Four periods in the development of Modern English are distinguished: (a) 1500–1620s; (b) to 1700; (c) to the end of the nineteenth century; (d) the twentieth century. In (c) and (d), due to political and economic factors, Anglophone territory expands to global proportions, accompanied by a vast increase in the numbers of people using English as a second language. The extreme reductionism of Modern English accidence may be a contributory factor here.

Today, as the mother tongue of some 350 million people. English is demographically surpassed only by Modern Standard Chinese, which cannot, however, claim anything approaching the international status of English. The main components in this total are: USA 232 million speakers; United Kingdom 56 million; Canada 24 million; Australia and New Zealand 17 million.

In addition, English is the official language of several countries in Africa –

Zimbabwe, Nigeria, Ghana, Uganda, Liberia – and the West Indies; and it has joint official status in India (with Hindi), South Africa (with Afrikaans), and Singapore (with Chinese, Malay, and Tamil). It is the accepted global medium in the travel industry and in international communications. Increasingly, a press conference of any importance, given anywhere in the world, will be in English, or accompanied by an immediate translation into English.

One and a half thousand years after Hengist and Horsa, the local dialect they brought with them from Denmark to Kent, shows every sign of becoming the planetary lingua franca in the twenty-first century.

Periodization of English literature

1. Old English: four manuscripts, dating from *c.* 1000, contain Anglo-Saxon poetry of the eighth and ninth centuries, including the heroic poem *Beowulf* and some lyrics. In prose, the outstanding items are the works of King Alfred and the Anglo-Saxon Chronicle, which covers (with gaps) the period from Alfred's reign to the middle of the twelfth century.
2. Middle English: in the early period, the main body of work is in Anglo-Latin: e.g. Geoffrey of Monmouth's *Historia.* The transitional period includes the medieval romance *Sir Gawayne and the Grene Knight* and John Langland's *Piers Plowman*. The period ends with Chaucer.
3. Renaissance: Shakespeare and the other dramatists (Marlowe, Webster); Spenser; lyric poetry.
4. The seventeenth century: Milton; Donne and the Metaphysical poets; Dryden; Bunyan.
5. The eighteenth century: Pope; Swift; the novelists, Richardson, Smollet, Sterne; Dr Johnson; *The Tatler* and *The Spectator*: Addison and Steele; William Blake; in Scotland, Robert Burns.
6. The nineteenth century: Byron and the Romantic movement; Wordsworth, Coleridge; Keats and Shelley; Tennyson, Browning, Matthew Arnold; the novelists, the Brontë Sisters, Jane Austen, George Eliot, Dickens, Hardy.
7. The twentieth century.

OLD ENGLISH

INTRODUCTION

Script

The earliest inscriptions are runic. Old English literature is written in an Irish version of the Latin alphabet, with specific forms for *f*, *g*, *r*, *s*. Later, two runic letters, *þ* = /θ/ and *ƿ* = /w/, were added. Initially *þ* was used to indicate both /θ/ and the voiced counterpart /ð/, for which *ð* was then introduced. Used with a diphthong, the macron covers *both* letters; thus, *cēol* 'ship'.

PHONOLOGY

Consonants

stops: p, b, t, d, k, g
affricates: tʃ, dʒ (notated as *cg*)
fricatives: f, v, θ, ð, s, z, ʃ, x, γ, ç, h
nasal: m, n, ŋ
lateral and flap: l, r
semi-vowels: j, w

Vowels

short: ɑ, æ, ɛ, ə, œ, ɪ, ɔ, u, y
long: ɑː, æː, eː, œː, iː, oː, uː, yː
diphthongs: short: ea, eo; long: ēa, ēo

The long vowels never appear in the inflectional endings. They are indicated in the following text by macrons.

MORPHOLOGY AND SYNTAX

Noun

Old English had three grammatical genders: masculine, feminine, and neuter. A few nominal endings are coded for gender: e.g. *-a*, *-oþ*, *-dōm*, *-els*, *-scipe* are masculine; *-nes*, *-estre*, *-þu*, *-ung* are feminine.

DEFINITE ARTICLE

se 'the, that'; *þes* 'this'. *Se* has fem. form *sēo*, neuter *þæt*. All three are declined in five cases on a *þ*- initial base: e.g. masculine nom. *se*; acc. *þone*; gen. *þæs*; dat. *þǣ*; instr. *þȳ*. The common plural is: nom./acc. *þā*; gen. *þāra*; dat./instr. *þæm*.

Þes has fem. *þēos*, neuter *þis*. The masculine declension is: nom. *þes*; acc. *þisne*; gen. *þisses*; dat. *þissum*, *inst*. *þȳs*. The common plural is: *þās*, *þissa*, *þissum*.

DECLENSION

Five cases, the instrumental sharing a form with the dative. There are three declensions: a strong declension, the weak or *-n* declension, and a group of minor and irregular declension.

For example, masculine *a*-stem: *ceōl* 'ship':

Singular		*Plural*	
nom.	se ceōl	nom./acc.	þā ceōlas
acc.	þone ceōl		
gen.	þæs ceōles	gen.	þāra ceōla
dat./instr.	þǣm/þȳ ceōle	dat./instr.	þǣm ceōlum

Feminine *o*-stem: *rōd* 'cross':

Singular		*Plural*	
nom.	sēo rōd	nom./acc.	þā rōda
acc.	þā rōde		
gen.	þǣre rōde	gen.	þāra rōda
dat./instr.	þǣre rōde	dat./instr.	þǣm rōdum

-*n* declension: e.g. *guma* 'man': this declension has -(*a*)*n* in all four singular oblique cases, and in plural nom. and acc. The plural genitive is *gumena*, the dat./instr. *gumum*: e.g. *þǣm guman* 'to the man'; *þāra gumena* 'of the men'.

Minor declensions: e.g. *fōt* 'foot', pl. *fēt*; the mutated vowel appears in the sing. dat./instr. as well: *þæm*/*þȳ fēt* 'to/by the foot'. Cf. *bōc* 'book', pl. *bēc*; *tōþ* 'tooth', pl. *tēþ*; *mūs* 'mouse', pl. *mȳs*.

Adjective

All adjectives have a strong (indefinite) and a weak (definite) declension. The instrumental is formally distinguished from the dative in the indefinite singular: e.g. *cwic* 'living'; fem. *cwicu*, nt. *cwic*. The masculine oblique cases are: acc. *cwicne*, gen. *cwices*, dat. *cwicum*, instr. *cwice*. The neuter is identical, apart from the accusative, which remains *cwic*. For all three genders, the plural gen. is *cwicra*, the dat. *cwicum* (no instrumental).

The weak declension is used after the definite article, the demonstratives, and the possessive pronouns: e.g. *se gōda guma* 'the good man', acc. *þone gōdan guman*, dat. *þæm gōdan guman*; pl. gen. *þāra gōdra gumena*.

Cf. Luke 15.22:

bringað raðe þone sēlestan gegierelan
'bring forth the best robe' (*raðe* 'quickly'; *sēlest* suppletive superlative of *wel* 'well (good)'; *gegierele* 'robe')

Cf. John 10.11:

Ic eom gōd hierde
'I am the good shepherd'
gōd hierde selþ his līf for his scēapum
'the good shepherd giveth his life for his sheep'

COMPARATIVE

-*ra*: *earm* 'poor' – *earmra*; *bliðe* 'glad' – *bliðra*.

SUPPLETIVE FORMS

gōd 'good' – *betra*/*sēlra*; *micel* 'large' – *māra*; *yfel* 'bad' – *wiersa*; *lȳtel* 'small' – *lǣssa*.

Pronoun

The first and second persons have dual forms; the third person is marked for gender in the singular, with a common plural. Cases: nom., acc., gen., dat./instr.

	Singular	*Dual*	*Plural*
1	ic – mē – mīn – mē	wit – unc – uncer – unc	wē – ūs – ūre – ūs
2	þu – þē – þīn – þē	git – inc – incer – inc	gē – ēow – ēower – ēow
3	masc. hē – hine – his – him		
	fem. hēo – hī – hire – hire		hī – hī – hira – him
	nt. hit – hit – his – him		

Cf.

sōþ ic secge ēow 'verily I say to you'
bringað mē hider þā 'bring them hither to me' (Matthew 14.18).
and hira gōdna dæl ofslōgon 'and slew a good number of them' (*hira*)

DEMONSTRATIVE PRONOUN

See **Definite article**: *se – sēo – þœt*; *þes – þēos – þis.*

INTERROGATIVE PRONOUN

Masc. *hwā*, nt. *hwæt*; declined in five cases in the singular: *hwæðer* 'what? (which of two)'; *hwelc* 'which? (of many)'.

RELATIVE PRONOUN

þe (invariable) usually preceded by appropriate form of definite article/demonstrative *sē* (used pronominally, *se* → *sē*-).

þæt folc, þe þær binnan wæs 'the people who were inside'
se hȳra, sē þe nis hierde and sē þe nāg þā scēap
'the hireling, that is not the shepherd, and who does not own the sheep' (*nis* 'is not'; *nag* 'does not own'; *see* **Verb**, below) (John 15.12)

Numerals

1–10: *ān, twēgen, þrȳ, fēower, fīf, syx, seofon, eahta, nigon, tȳn*; 11 *endleofan*; 12 *twelf*; 13 *þrēotȳne*; 20 *twentig*; 21 *ān and twentig*, etc. 30 *þrītig*; 70 *hundseofontig*; 80 *hundeahtatig*; 90 *hundnigontig*; 100 *hundtēontig*.

Verb

As in other Germanic languages. Old English verbs are either strong (vocalic, i.e. displaying stem ablaut) or weak (consonantal). Most Old English verbs belong to the weak conjugation. There are three moods – indicative, imperative, subjunctive – and two basic tenses, present and past. The auxiliary verbs *wesan*, *bēon*, and *habban* are used to form a perfect, a pluperfect, and a future tense. The general negating particle *ne* precedes the verbal form and may fuse with it: *ne habban* → *nabban* 'not to have'. A passive can be formed periphrastically.

STRONG VERBS

The strong verbs, which form a closed set, are divided by ablaut pattern into seven classes; examples of these: infinitive – past, third singular and plural – past participle are:

1. rīsan – rās, rison – -risen 'rise'
2. bēodan – bēad, budon – -boden 'offer'
3. drincan – dranc, druncon – -druncen 'drink'
4. beran – bær, bǣron – -boren 'bear'
5. sprecan – spræc, sprǣcon – -sprecen 'speak'
6. faran – fōr, fōron – -faren 'go'
7. wēpan – wēop, wēopon – -wōpen 'weep'
   hātan – hēt, hēton – -hāten 'call'

All seven classes have various irregularities and sub-classes; classes 3 and 7 are particularly heterogeneous. Formation of second and third person singular present indicative from the stem often involves *i-* mutation: e.g.

cuman 'to come': cymst – cymþ
helpan 'to help': hilpst – hilpþ
grōwan 'to grow': grēwst – grēwþ

Specimen strong verb paradigm: *bīdan* 'to wait', class 1.

Indicative

present:	sing.	1 bīde, 2 bīdest, 3 bītt (< bīdþ)
	pl.	1–3: bīdaþ
past:	sing.	1 bād, 2 bide, 3 bād
	pl.	1–3: bidon

Subjunctive

present:	sing.	1–3: bīde; pl. 1–3: bīden
past:	sing.	1–3: bide; pl. biden

Imperative sing. *bīd*; pl. *bīdaþ*.
Participles: present: *bīdende*; past *(ge)biden*

WEAK VERBS

These were often formed from nouns and other parts of speech by means of the affix **-ja*, which induced *i-* mutation in the stem vowel of the resultant verb. According to the presence or absence of this mutation, Old English weak verbs are divided into two classes. Here, a specimen paradigm: *fremman* 'to perform' where the stem vowel represents a mutation from *-a-*:

Indicative

present:	sing.	1 fremme, 2 fremest, 3 fremeþ
	pl.	1–3: fremmaþ
past:	sing.	1 fremede, 2 fremedest, 3 fremede
	pl.	1–3: fremedon

Subjunctive

present:	sing.	1–3: fremme; pl. 1–3: fremmen
past:	sing.	1–3: fremede; pl. 1–3: fremeden

Imperative: sing. *freme*; pl. *fremmaþ*
Participles: present *fremmende*; past *gefremed*

MIDDLE ENGLISH

INTRODUCTION

The twelfth century was the century of transition between late Old English and early Middle English. Almost nothing was written in English, and very little was borrowed from French. The English dialects ceased to reflect the original tribal divisions, and tended to polarize on an areal or typological basis into two groups: Northern (including Northumbrian and Mercian, from which latter the important Midland dialect was to emerge) and Southern (comprising West Saxon and Kentish). Each of these several components developed internally in terms of its own material, and at its own specific rate.

PHONOLOGY

The process of phonological change, by which Old English became Middle English, may, however, be broadly generalized. Some salient features are:

1. Weak vowels, especially in final position, were levelled to *e*; towards the end of the Middle English period, strong diphthongs were also levelled:

Old English	*Middle English*	*Modern English*
nam**a**	nam**e**	name /nejm**Ø**/
ber**an**	ber**en**	bear
sun**u**	sun**e**	son /sʌn/
st**eo**rra	st**e**rre	star

2. /ea/ > /æ/ > /a/: e.g. ***hea**rd* > *h**æ**rd* > *h**a**rd*: Mod. Eng. *hard.*
3. Old English long vowels were largely maintained in Middle English. /yː/ became /iː/ in Northern dialects, and subsequently standard: e.g. Old English *fȳr* > Middle English *fīr* (Mod. Eng. *fire* /faiə/).
   Long vowels tended to be shortened before consonantal cluster: e.g. Old English *wīdōm* > Middle English *wisdōm*.

4. The consonantal inventory remained stable, with some changes in quantity.
5. Consonantal finals of Old English nominals were replaced by vowel finals in Middle English, originating in the oblique case: e.g. Old English *cwēn*: acc. *cwēne* > Middle English *quēne* (Mod. Eng. *queen*).

MORPHOLOGY AND SYNTAX

1. Definite article gradually reduced from the Old English inflected paradigm to the single form *þe* /θe/ > /ðə/.
2. Erosion of the article is a factor in the general loss of grammatical gender.
3. Extensive erosion of the case system; by the end of the period, only the genitive *-s* remains. Even where, for a time, a modicum of inflection persisted – e.g. in the declension of Old English feminine nouns with a plural marker in *-en* – this too was finally levelled by analogy; and a generalized plural in *-(e)s* emerges. Mutating plurals are retained: *gōs* – *gēs* 'goose, geese'; *mūs* – *mȳs* 'mouse, mice', etc., though old mutating forms in the singular are levelled.
4. The adjective becomes indeclinable.
5. Pronoun: the standard Middle English system is as follows:

		Singular		*Plural*	
			Oblique		*Oblique*
1	nom.	ī, ich	mē	wē	us
2		þow	þē	yē	yow
3	masc.	hē	him	þei	þeim
	fem.	shē	hir(e)		
	nt.	(h)it	(h)it		hem

POSSESSIVE PRONOUN

Sing.: mīn/mī – þīn, þī – his, hir(e).
Pl.: our(e) – your(e) – þeir(e), her(e).

DEMONSTRATIVE PRONOUN

Early Middle English had a full declension for all three genders, with four cases in the singular, three in the plural. This was reduced in standard Middle English to a simple opposition between 'this', 'these'/'that', 'those'.

RELATIVE PRONOUN

The relative pronoun was standardized as *that*.

Verb

The standard Middle English strong-verb paradigm shows little change from that of Old English, apart from the levelling of *-a-* and *-o-* in inflections to *-e-*, the loss of *-þ* in the present indicative plural, and the shift from *-d-* to *-g-* in the present participle. Thus, the present tense of Middle English *bīnde*(*n*) 'to bind' is: sing. *bīnde*, *bīndest*, *bīnde*; pl. common, *bīnde*(*n*). The past tense is: sing. *bǫnd*, *bounde*, *bǫnd*; pl. *bounde*(*n*). Imperative: *bīnd*, *bīnd*(*e*); subjunctive: pres. sing. *bīnde*; pl. *bīnde*(*n*); past, sing. *bounde*; pl. bounde(*n*); present participle: *bīndinge*; past participle: (*i*)*bounde*(*n*).

This represents a reduction of discriminant forms, from the twelve present in the Old English conjugation of *bindan*, to seven; Modern English reduces this to four.

A considerable number of Old English strong-verb stems were reassessed as weak in Middle English and conjugated accordingly.

MODERN ENGLISH

INTRODUCTION

The transition from Middle to Modern English:

SCRIPT

The very weak correspondence between sound and symbol, characteristic of Modern English, is due primarily to the conservation from the late Middle English period onwards of a gallicized orthography reflecting Middle English pronunciation. The orthography was consolidated by the introduction of printing (1476), and retained through a succession of phonological changes. Variant spellings were permissible into the nineteenth century.

PHONOLOGY

Vowels

The key feature in the phonological transition from late Middle to Modern English is the so-called Great Vowel Shift, which took place in the fifteenth/sixteenth centuries. Briefly, five of the long vowels were raised by one degree; the remaining two were diphthongized:

aː > æː; ɛː > eː; eː > iː; ɔː > oː; oː > uː; iː > əi > ay; uː > aw

The new long values were subsequently (through the eighteenth and nineteenth centuries) diphthongized by the introduction of a glide to reach their present values: cf.

Middle English	*Early Modern English*	*Seventeenth Century*	*Present-day*
nāme /naːmə/	/næm/	/neːm/	/neːjm/ *name*
/stɔːn/	/stoːn/	/stoːn/	/stʌun/ *stone*
/ɔpən/	/oːpən/	/oːpən/	/ʌupn̥/ *open*
/wiːn/	/wəin/	/wəin/	/wājn/ *wine*
/greːn/	/griːn/	/griːn/	/grījn/ *green*

Short vowels:

a > æ; ɪ, ɛ, u, ɔ unchanged through the sixteenth century
> ɪ, ɛ, ʌ, ɔ in the seventeenth century
> ɪ, ɛ, ɐ, ɔ in Modern English

e.g. [sune] > [sʌn] > [sɐn].

Consonants

The consonantal inventory of Modern English is:

stops, p, b, t, d, k, g
affricates: tʃ, dʒ
fricatives: f, v, θ, ð, s, z, ʃ, ʒ, h
nasals: m, n, ŋ, ɲ
lateral and flap: l, r
semi-vowels: j, w

All the stops have a measure of aspiration; /t/ and /d/ are retroflex rather than dental. All can be initial except /ŋ/; all can be medial; /h/ cannot be final. Initial /ʒ/ occurs only in loanwords: genre /ʒãːr/.

Consonantal changes in transition from late Middle English/Early Modern English to present-day Standard:

1. /θ, s, f/ are voiced in weak syllables in the modern language: e.g. in gen. case: *mannes* /manəs/ > *man's* /mænz/; *with* /wɪθ/ > /wɪð/.
2. /c/ voiced to /dʒ/: cf. Middle English *knǭwlę̄che* > /nɔlidʒ/.
3. /s/ > /z/ between weak and strong vowel: *disease* /dɪzi:z/.
4. Middle English /h/ represented /ç/ or /x^w/; both lost in Modern English:

   Middle English /nɪçt/ > /nɪht/ > /nɪːt/ > /nəit/ > /najt/ *night*
   /θɔux^{w}t/ > /θɔːt/ *thought*.

5. In Modern English /r/ tends to Ø except before a vowel; this proviso includes the so-called 'intrusive r': 'law and order' pronounced as /lɔ:r/ ənd.ɔːdə/ Cf. here = /hiə/; her = /həː/; star = /staː/.
6. /l/ was elided, from the sixteenth century onwards, between a labial vowel and a consonant: e.g. *half* > /haːf/. Cf. elision of /w/ in *towards* → /tɔːdz/.
7. /k/ dropped before /n/: *know* (sixteenth-century /knou/) > /nʌu/.

Stress

In Old and Middle English, the main stress was on the root syllable of inflected words. In Modern English, stress may be on almost any syllable of a word in citation form; often, variants are permissible, e.g. *cóntroversy/ contróversy*. In ordinary speech, stress tends to be evenly distributed over the phrasal contour, with particles, prepositions, articles in the dips. Stress is phonemic in doublets: cf. *éxtract* (noun) – *extráct* (verb); *ábsent* (adjective) – *absént* (verb).

MORPHOLOGY AND SYNTAX

The definite article is realized as /ðə/ before consonants, as /ði/ before vowels. The now prevalent use of *a/an* as an indefinite article became generalized in the Middle English period.

Noun

Only two inflections survive – the genitive *-s* = /z/ or /s/ and the plural marker *-s*, /z/ or /s/. The apostrophe is used to separate the genitive *-s* from the singular or noun; the genitive of a noun with *-s* plural is marked by ': thus, singular: *boy's*, pl.: boys'; *men's*. A few mutated plurals survive: e.g. *mouse – mice*, *goose – geese*, etc.

Adjective

All adjectives are indeclinable.

Pronoun

Up to a point, the Middle English system survives. In the first person, both singular and plural have direct and oblique forms: *I – me*; *we – us*.

In the singular, the second person is obsolete, and the plural has been levelled to a single form: *you*.

Third person: here, the gender distinction has been preserved plus oblique forms: masc. *he – him*; fem. *she – her*; nt: *it – it*. The plural is levelled to the common form: *they – them*.

Verb

Overall, there is a general reduction from the Middle English inventory to four forms: e.g. for the verb OE *bindan*, ME *bīnde(n)*, Modern English *bind*: *bind*, *binds* (3rd person present indicative), *bound* (past tense), *binding* (present participle). Archaic forms may appear in set phrases, e.g. *his bounden duty*, where *bounden* is the old past participle *(i)bounden*.

Extreme reductionism has led to confusion between certain verbs, e.g. between the intransitive *lie*, whose past tense is *lay*, and the transitive verb *lay*, the former being levelled to the latter: Standard *he lay there* being accompanied in sub-standard usage by **he laid there/he was laying there*. Such a confusion is unlikely in German, for example, where the verbs *liegen* and *legen* have remained distinct.

Prepositions

In Old English, prepositions governed the dative, the accusative, or the genitive. The static (dative case) versus dynamic (accusative case) opposition was found, as in Modern German.

In Modern English it is natural to close a sentence with a preposition, or even two (*the man I spoke to*; *what I have to put up with*) depending on the specific requirements of the sense-verb. The practice, which is also to be found in the Scandinavian languages, has been questioned on purist and stylistic grounds. Extreme simpicity of accidence, however, merits an equivalent degree of syntactical flexibility. Together, they help to make English, with its internationally enriched vocabulary of half a million words, readily accessible to, and usable by, its global community.

1. On frymðe wæs Word, and þæt Word wæs mid Gode, and God wæs þæt Word.
2. Þæt wæs on fruman mid Gode.
3. Ealle þing wǣron geworhte ðurh hyne; and nān þing næs geworht būtan him.
4. Þæt wæs līf þe on him geworht wæs; and þæt līf wæs manna lēoht.
5. And þæt lēoht lȳht on ðȳstrum; and þȳstro þæt ne genāmon.
6. Mann wæs fram Gode āsend, þæs nama wæs Iohannes.
7. Ðēs cōm tō gewitnesse, þæt hē gewitnesse cȳðde be ðām lēohte, þæt ealle menn þurh hyne gelȳfdon.
8. Næs hē lēoht, ac þæt hē gewitnesse forð bǣre be þām lēohte.

Old English (West Saxon)

1 In the bigynnynge was the word, *that*
is, Goddis sone, and the word was at
2 God, and God was the word. This was
3 in the bigynnynge at God. Alle thingis
ben maad by hym, and with outen him
is maad noȝt, that thing that is maad.
4 Was lyf in him, and the lyf was the liȝt
5 of men ; and the liȝt schyneth in derk-
6 nessis, and derknessis tooken not it. A
man was sent fro God, to whom the name
7 was Joon. This man cam in to witnessinge, that he schulde bere witnessinge of
the liȝt, that alle men schulden bileue bi
8 him. He was not the liȝt, but that he
9 schulde bere witnessing of the liȝt.

Middle English (Wyclif's translation)

IN the beginning was
that Word, and that word
was with God, and that
Word was God.
2 This ſame was in the
beginning with God.
3 All things were made by it, and
without it was made nothing that was made.
4 In it was life, and that life was the
light of men.
5 And that light ſhineth in the darkneſſe
and the darkneſſe comprehended it not.
6 ¶ There was a man ſent from God,
whoſe name *was* Iohn.
7 *This* ſame came for a witneſſe, to beare
witneſſe of that light, that all men through
him might beleeue.
8 Hee was not that light, but *was ſent* to
beare witneſſe of that light.

Early Modern English (The King James Version)

1 In the beginning the Word already was.
The Word was in God's presence, and
what God was, the Word was. 2 He was
with God at the beginning, 3and through
him all things came to be; without him
no created thing came into being. 4In
him was life, and that life was the light
of mankind. 5The light shines in the
darkness, and the darkness has never
mastered it.

6There appeared a man named John.
He was sent from God, 7and came as a
witness to testify to the light, so that
through him all might become believers.
8He was not himself the light; he came
to bear witness to the light.

Contemporary English

EPIGRAPHIC SOUTH ARABIAN

From the middle of the second millennium BC onwards, a group of highly civilized city-states developed in the south-west corner of the Arabian peninsula (corresponding roughly to modern Yemen), the most notable being Saba', Ma'īn, Qatabān, and Ḥaḍramawt. The inhabitants of these states spoke Sabaean, Minaean, Qatabanian, and Ḥaḍrami, all four being dialects of the language known as Epigraphic South Arabian. The economic success and stability of these states was based on intensive irrigation, agriculture, and an extensive network of trade-routes. The acount given in I Kings, chapter 10, of the visit of the Queen of Sheba (Saba') to King Solomon provides a fascinating glimpse of life at the top in tenth-century Arabia. Gradually through the first millennium BC the city-states declined in power and prestige, to be replaced (second century BC) by the Ḥimyaritic state, which preserved, along with a Sabaean-type dialect, much of Sabaean culture. In addition to the four dialects listed above, the group includes the nucleus of what was to become Ge'ez, the classical language of Ethiopia. The epigraphic record points to the colonization of Ethiopia from south-west Arabia early in the first millennium BC.

The dialects listed above are divided into two groups by such criteria as the formation of the demonstrative pronouns, the pronominal suffixes, and the causative marker. Sabaean, with a causative marker in *h-*, constitutes Group 1; the other three dialects, with a causative prefix in *s-*, form Group 2.

The short description which follows is mainly of Sabaean.

SCRIPT

See **Script** at end of article.

PHONOLOGY

stops; k, g, q, t, d, ṭ, ḍ, b, h, ḥ, '
fricatives: ḫ, ṯ, ḏ, s, ś, ʃ, z, ṣ, ẓ, f, ', ġ
lateral and flap: l, r
nasals: m, n
semi-vowels: w, y

MORPHOLOGY

The typical root is the triliteral: three consonants (a convenient shorthand notation is 123): e.g. *mlk* 'king', *sġr* 'small'. Weak initial (*w* or *y*) tends to be dropped in the script: *Øqh* for *wqh*; *t* may be added: *qht*. Weak 2 is usually retained in writing: *ywm* (not *ym*) 'day'; *byt* 'house' (not *bt*).

Biliteral and quadriliteral roots are found (the latter very rare). As in Arabic, irregular biliterals with hamza occur: *'b* 'father', *'h* 'brother'.

Derived nouns are made with such formants as: prefixed *'-*, *m-*, *n-*, *t-*; suffixed: *-n*, *-t*, *-y*.

The *m-* forms are mainly participial, but may also designate means or instrument: *m.'ḫd* 'lock mechanism on river'; also locus: *m.s'l* 'site of oracle'. *t-* forms abstracta and collectives: *t.šqr* 'completion'; *t.'nṯ* 'female branch of family'.

Gender: the feminine gender is marked by *-t*: *bn* 'son', *bn.t* 'daughter'; *'ḫ* 'brother', *'ḫt* 'sister'.

Number: singular, dual, and plural number is distinguished. The dual ending in Sabaean is -(*ā*)*n* or *-ain*: *wrḫyn* 'two months'; *m't.yn* 200. Plural: by prefix, suffix, or both; the broken plural also occurs.

Typical plural formations are:

'123 (probably vocalized as /'a12ā3/: *'hgr* 'towns' /*'hgār*/ (cf. *awlād* form in Arabic);
123t: e.g. *grb.t* 'people';
12y3: *ḫryf* 'years';
m123t: *m.ḍrf.t* 'canals', sing. *m.ḍrf*;
12w3 appears in Qatabani: *gzwm* 'decisions';
biliterals: e.g. *'l* 'god' makes plural *'l'l.t* 'gods'.

State

The Sabaean noun is (a) absolute, (b) definite, or (c) in construct.

(a) Absolute: in the early period of the language, mimation seems to have functioned as a postposited definite marker: *-m*; a function which was eroded by the growth of the definite postposited article *-n*. *-m*, however, continued to be used in Sabaean with place names, and with nouns denoting weights and measures (of time and space). Cf.

b.' rb'.m 'on the 4th (day)'
w.ḏn 'byt w.'rḍt.m 'and lo, houses and lands' (*-m* suffixed to final item in sequence)
w.'ln nḫl.m 'sy b.ysrn 'and these – the palm grove which he acquired in Ysrn'

Mimation is not used with nouns in the dual number.

(b) Definite: the definite state of the noun is marked by nunation: -(*a*)*n*, derived probably from the old demonstrative pronoun **hān*: *ḥrt.n* 'the canal'; *ḏt ḥrt.n* 'this canal'; *wṯn.n* 'the boundary marker'.

wṯn.n ḏ.byn... 'the boundary marker which (is placed) between...;'
š.'b.n qtbn 'the tribe of Qataban'
mlk.n ŠHR 'the Emperor ŠHR'

(c) The construct: the written form is that of the absolute minus *-m*. E.g *mlk sb'* 'the king of Sabaea'; *'dm mlk sb'* 'the slaves of the king of Sabaea'. The dual has *-y* /ai/: *'bdy bny M*. 'two slaves of the tribe of M'.

Adjective

The attributive adjective follows the noun qualified, and agrees with it in gender, number, and state: cf. *w.kl sṭr.m kbr.m f'w sġr.m* 'and all inscriptions, great or small'.

Pronoun

PERSONAL PRONOUN

Only 3rd person forms are attested in Sabaean; there are traces of a 2nd person form in Qatabani: sing. in *-k*, plural *-km*. The Sabaean forms are:

sing.	masc.	*-h(w)*		pl. masc.	*- hmw*
			dual *-hmy*		
	fem.	*-h(w)*		fem.	*-hn*

It is surprising to find a common form for singular masc./fem: e.g.

yd.hw w.lsn.hw 'his hand and his tongue'
byt.m l.hw 'his house'
w.hmw f.hmd.w 'and as regards them, they thank . . .;'
nḫl.m ḏ.b.h (y)s'l 'the palm plantation which-into-it he lays claim' (i.e. 'to which he. . . ')

DEMONSTRATIVE PRONOUN

The Sabaean forms are:

sing.	masc	*h', hw', hwt*		pl. masc.	*-hmw, hm(y)t*
			dual *-hwyt*		
fem.		*h', hy', hyt*		fem.	*hn, hnt*

In Qatabani, *s-* replaces Sabaean *h-*: *swt*, *syt*, etc.

A second demonstrative series has a *ḏ* base in the singular, with *'l* in the plural. The Sabaean forms are:

sing.	masc.	*ḏn*		pl. masc.	*'ln*
			dual *'ln/ḏyn*		
	fem.	*ḏt*		fem.	*'lt*

E.g.:

'In nḫl.n.hn 'these/those (the) palm plantations'
'lt 'hgr.m w.'bḍ'.m 'lo, these towns and regions'

RELATIVE PRONOUN

Sabaean *ḏ-/ḏt*, dual *ḏy*, pl. *'lw*, *'ly*, *'lht*: e.g.:

'wṯn.n 'ly byn nḫl.n.hn 'the boundary markers which are between the palm plantations'

w.kl hnt 'nṯn . . . ;'ly 'and of all these women who . . . ;'

Numerals

1 *'ḥd* (masc.), *'ḥt* (fem.), or *ṭd* (masc.) *ṭt*; (fem), 2 *ṯny*, 3 *šlṯ* (masc.), *šlṯt* (fem.), 4 *'rb'*(*t*), 5 *ḫms*(*t*), 6 *sdṯ*(*t*), 7 *sb'*(*t*), 8 *ṯmn*(*t*), 9 *ts'*(*t*), 10 *'šr*(*t*).

The feminine forms in *-t* are used in the enumeration of masculine nouns; conversely, the forms without *-t* are used for feminine nouns. Cf. *ḫmst hrf.n* 'the five years'; *ḫms 'mm* 'five elbows' (sing. *'mt*). 11 – 19: unit plus *'šr* (unit marked for gender), e.g.: 12 *ṯny 'šr*. 20 *'šry* (i.e. dual of *'šr* 10). 30–90 unit plus masculine dual ending: 50 *ḫmsy*, 60 *sdṯy*. 100 *m't*; 1000 *'lfm*; 2000 *ṯny 'lfm*.

w.ṯlṯ m'tm ''bl.m 'and 300 camels' (*ṯlṯ* is a late Sabaean form of *šlṯ*)

Verb

Within the limitations of the consonantal script, the verb is marked for aspect/tense, voice, mood, gender, person, and number. Verbal roots are strong or weak triliteral or biliteral; quadriliteral roots are very rare.

PERFECTIVE/PAST

The vocalization is normally reconstructed as la2a/i/u3. 3rd person forms alone are attested in the corpus of inscriptions: 123 masculine, 123t feminine, with dual in -(*t*)*y* and plural in *-w*, which is taken to reflect /u:/: *rṯd* 'he placed under his protection/patronage'; *bny.w* 'they built'.

The perfective form also functions as a positive or negative optative, e.g. following the negative particle *'l* (cf. Arabic, e.g *la raḥimahum Allah* 'may God not have mercy on them').

IMPERFECTIVE

The Sabaean forms are:

(a) without nunation:

sing. masc. y.123			pl. masc. y.123w
	dual masc. y.123y		
sing. fem. t.123			

(b) with nunation:

sing. masc. y.123.n			pl. masc.y.123.n(n)
	dual masc. y.123.yn		
sing. fem. t.123.n			pl. fem. t.123.n

The forms with nunation may derive from an emphatic form with -(*a*)*n*; cf. Arabic emphatic *-anna*.

Due to the limitations of the consonantal script, the intensive and the conative versions of the base form (Arabic II and III) cannot be distinguished from the base. Gemination, e.g. of the second radical in doubled verbs, cannot be notated, a phonemic defect to be later inherited in Ethiopic and Amharic.

The consonants *w* and *y* function both as components in diphthongs such as *u̯a, i̯a, au̯, ai̯*, and as *matres lectionis* for the long vowels /u:/, /i:/. The non-finite parts of the verb are neutral with regard to aspect, mood, and person (though it must be remembered that only the 3rd person is attested in Sabaean), in addition, the infinitive does not distinguish voice, gender, or number. Indeed, the infinitive is indistinguishable from the 3rd singular masculine perfective, except in the case of the intensive version, the infinitive of which takes prefixed *t-* (cf. Arabic).

The active participle is 123 marked for gender: *š'm.n* 'buying' (of masculine), *š 'm.t* (of feminine). The passive has an *m-* prefix: *m.qny* 'legally acquired' (of land, etc.). *m-* precedes the causative marker *h-* in *m.h.š'm.n* 'causing to buy', i.e. 'selling' (of masculine).

Prepositions

b-	'in', 'at' (time, space) *b.hgr.n mryb* 'in the town of M.'; *b.ḍr smhwtr w.qtbn* 'at (the time of) the war of Smhwtr with Qataban' *b.mqm mr'.hmw* 'by the power of their master' *b.'ṯtr* 'in (the name of) Astar'
byn	'between' *wṯn.n ḏ.byn Brd w.ḏ. tḥtn* 'the marker which (is) between Brd and Tḥt.
bn	'from, out of' *bn'ns.m* '(someone) from the people'
b'd	'after'
qdm	'before'
l-	'(up)to, for' *l.nḫl, y.hw* 'for his two palm-tree plantations'

COMPOSITE PREPOSITIONS

E.g. *b.wsṭ* 'inside', *b.'ly* 'on', 'upon', *b.'br* 'on (that/other) side'; *b./bn.tḥt*(*y*) 'under', *bn.tḥt ḏn wṯn.n* 'under this image'.

The negating particle is ', which may be followed by the verb:

'l s'l.w sb'... 'the Sabaeans cannot lay claim to...'

by the subject:

w.'l 's s'l.hmy 'and no one can lay claim to (these) two'

or by an impersonal construction with the passive of the causative:

w.'l h'ly ḏn 'tb.n 'and let not this boundary marker be transgressed' *r'* and *l-* are affirmative particles: *r′ hgb. 'y. . . ;hwt 'rḍn* 'and lo (indeed) both returned this winter'.

SCRIPT

The consonantal alphabet, which was used to write inscriptions in the South Arabian languages, is set out in the accompanying chart. This shows the monumental character typical of the older inscriptions (eighth century BC onwards), with some examples, in parentheses, of forms assumed in the later cursive. The reconstruction of South Arabian phonology and morphology is hampered by the absence of signs for the short vowels and for gemination. The exact function of the consonants *w* and *y* is not clear. In forms like *-hw* (3rd person singular masculine suffix) and *ywm* (singular noun 'day'), *w* appears to denote long /u/.

Basically the script runs from right to left. Boustrophedon texts are also found, especially in the older period. In these, non-symmetric characters such as  (*m*) and 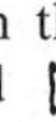 (*d*) are reversed: ,  so as to face right on the return line (cf. the similar practice as regards anthropomorphic characters, gods and men, in Egyptian hieroglyphic).

Several thousand South Arabian inscriptions of varying length (some very long) are known. They comprise oracular and votive texts, spells, incantations, military records, administrative edicts, legal documents, graffiti, burial inscriptions, etc. Two definitive collections are:

1. *Corpus inscriptionum semiticarum ad academia inscriptionum et literarum conduit atque digestum, Parisiis. Pars quarta inscriptiones himyariticas et sabaeas continens,* vols I–III. Paris, 1889–1932.
2. *'Répértoire d'épigraphie semitique' publié par la Commission du Corpus Inscriptionum Semiticarum*, vols V–VII, ed. G. Ryckmans (Inscriptions sud-arabes, Nos 2624–5106). Paris, 1929–50.

The first has photographs giving the epigraphic text plus transliteration; the second has transliteration only. See also Conti Rossini (1931), Beeston (1937).

THE EPIGRAPHIC SOUTH ARABIAN SCRIPT

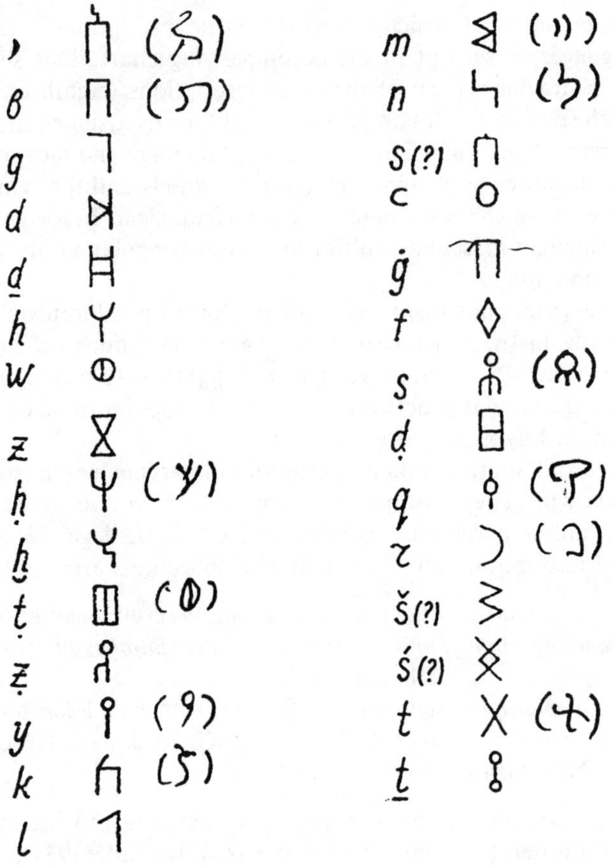

Source: Bauer, G.M. (1966) *Jazyk južnoaravijskoj pis 'mennosti,* Moscow.

ESKIMO-ALEUT LANGUAGES

Eskimo is spoken, in several dialect forms, over a vast area stretching from Greenland through the Arctic regions of Canada into Alaska and Siberia. Two main dialects are distinguished: Inuit in Greenland, northern Canada, and part of Alaska; Yupik in Alaska and Siberia. The total number of Eskimo speakers is estimated at *c*. 83,000, the overwhelming majority of whom speak Inuit. Aleut, genetically related to Eskimo, is still spoken by a few hundred people in the Aleutian Islands.

In the most recent classification of the world's languages (Greenberg 1985) Eskimo-Aleut is treated as part of a Euro-Asiatic phylum, which also includes the Indo-European family and the Altaic languages (in the wider sense, i.e. including Japanese and Korean).

See **Aleut**, **Inuit**.

ESTONIAN

INTRODUCTION

A member of the Balto-Finnic group of Finno-Ugric, Estonian is the official language of Estonia, where it is spoken by about 1 million people. There are several thousand speakers in parts of the former Soviet Union and some large *emigré* groups – for example around 70,000 in North America. The language is divided into two markedly divergent dialect groups: Northern (Tallinna keel) and Southern (Tartu keel). In their extreme forms these come close to being mutually unintelligible. The modern literary standard is based on the Northern (Tallinn) form. Centuries of German influence are reflected in the vocabulary of Estonian.

Writing in Estonian dates from the sixteenth century when religious tracts were produced in both dialects. Translation of the New Testament soon followed, and a complete Bible in 1739. A hundred years later, the appearance of Lönnroth's *Kalevala* in Finland (*see* **Finnish**) was quickly followed by the publication of a similar collection in Estonia – the *Kalevipoeg* (1857–61) edited by F.R. Kreutzwald, and by a similar upsurge of interest in the national folklore. The next important event in the history of Estonian literature was the emergence of the *Noor Eesti* group in the early twentieth century – 'Young Estonia', whose members were mainly interested in experimental verse. The period of independence in the 1920s and 1930s is the richest in Estonian literature; the main figures are the poetess Marie Under, and the novelist Anton Tammsaare, whose great novel *Tõde ja Õigus* (1926–36) offers a panoramic and detailed study of a crucial period in Estonian life, the transition from the nineteenth to the twentieth century.

SCRIPT

Roman alphabet + *ä*, *ö*, *ü*, *õ*; *c*, *f*, *q*, *w*, *x*, *y*, *z* occur only in recent loanwords. *õ* is a central vowel close to /ə/ but unrounded.

PHONOLOGY

Consonants

stops: p, t, k
fricatives: v, s, h
nasals: m, n
lateral and flap: l, r
semi-vowels: j

/p, t, k/ are unaspirated and voiceless, represented in the script by *b, d, g*; they are always short. When written as *p, t, k* they are long; when written with gemination: *pp, tt, kk* they are overlong.

PALATALIZATION

The palatalized consonants are /t′, n′, s′, l′/, not notated in script. The gradation from short to long and overlong, which affects other consonants as well as the stops, is accompanied by an increase in tenseness and a forward shift in articulation.

CONSONANT GRADATION

(*See* **Finnish**.) Exists in Estonian, although the phonological conditions which generate the phenomenon are no longer always present. For example, the typical Balto-Finnic genitive ending *-n* has been lost in Estonian; but *jalg* 'foot', still makes a genitive *jala*, representing former **jalan*. In the following table, setting out the main patterns of Estonian consonant gradation, the forms given are: strong grade – weak grade – noun in nominative – noun in genitive:

b – v: *lei**b*** 'bread'– *lei**v**a*
d – j: *sõ**d**a* 'war'– *sõ**j**a*
g – j: *sel**g*** 'back'– *sel**j**a*
mb – mm: *ku**mb*** 'which'– *ku**mm**a*
ld – ll: *ku**ld*** 'gold'– *ku**ll**a*
nd – nn: *ve**nd*** 'brother'– *ve**nn**a*
b – Ø: *tu**b**a* 'room'– *toa*
d – Ø: *ri**d**a* 'row'– *rea*
g – Ø: *vi**g**a*: 'mistake'– *vea*

Similarly, *k* is reduced to *g*, *p* to *b*, and *t* to *d*.

Vowels

front: i, e, ɛ, œ, y
middle: ə (unrounded)
back: a, o, u

Like the consonants, the vowels, too, have three degrees of phonemic length; cf. *sada* /sada/, 'hundred'; *saada* /saːda/, 'they came'; *saada* /saːːda/, 'to receive'.

VOWEL HARMONY

Has been lost in Estonian, though there are residual traces in some southern dialects.

Stress

Stress is always on the first syllable. Any vowel of any length may appear in the first syllable; in subsequent syllables, only *a, e, i, u* appear.

MORPHOLOGY AND SYNTAX

Noun

No gender; no articles. There are two numbers and 14 cases. The plural nominative marker is always *-d*. The key case endings are:

singular: nom. Ø; gen. a vowel; part. Ø, *-d/t*, or a vowel;
plural: nom. *-d*; gen. *-de/te/e*; part. *-d*.

The other cases are all constructed on the genitive base: e.g. inessive *-s*, elative *-st*, adessive *-l*, translative *-ks*.

There are seven declensions; the discriminating factors are (a) presence/absence of consonant gradation, and (b) number of syllables. Thus, declension 1 contains nouns like *puu* 'tree' with genitive *puu*, partitive *puud*: nominative plural *puud*, genitive *puude*, partitive *puid*. An example of a sixth declension noun: *jalg* 'foot' – *jala* – *jalga*; plural *jalad* – *jalgade* – *jalgu*.

Some examples of case usage:

genitive: *Eesti keele õpetaja* 'A teacher of the Estonian language';
partitive: *Leib**a** on laual* 'There is some bread on the table';
inessive: *Mina elan linnas* 'I live in the town';
elative: *Mina tulen linna**st*** 'I come out of the town';
essive: *Ta töötab arsti**na*** 'He works as a doctor';
translative: *Sõja ajal sai ta ohvitseri**ks*** 'During the war he became an officer';
adessive: *venna**l** on kirja* 'the brother has a letter';
ablative: *sain venna**lt** kirja* 'I received a letter from (my) brother';
allative: *venna**le** on see töö raske* 'this work is hard for (my) brother';
terminative: *Tallinnast Tartu**ni** on 200 kilomeetrit* 'from Tallinn to Tartu is 200 km';
abessive: *uus maja on veel katuse**ta*** 'the new house is still roofless';
comitative: *mina kirjutan sule**ga*** 'I write with a pen'.

Adjective

As attribute, adjective precedes the noun and is declined in concord with it, in most, but not all, cases: e.g. *punane raamat* 'a red book'; ***punased raamatud*** 'red books'; ***punases** raamatus* 'in a red book'; ***punastes raamatutes*** 'in red books'.

COMPARATIVE

-m is added to the genitive: e.g. *Tema on minust tugeva**m*** 'He is stronger than I am.'

Pronoun

Personal independent forms: long and short:

singular: 1 *mina/ma*, 2 *sina/sa*, 3 *tema/ta*;
plural: 1 *meie/me*, *teie/te*, 3 *nemad/nad*.

These are fully declined in 14 cases.

DEMONSTRATIVE PRONOUN

See 'this', pl. *need*; *too* 'that', pl. *tood*.

INTERROGATIVE PRONOUN

kes 'who?'; *mis* 'what?'

RELATIVE PRONOUN

As interrogative: e.g. *raamat, mis lamab laual* 'the book which is lying on the table'.

Numerals

1–10: *üks, kaks, kolm, neli, viis, kuus, seitse, kaheksa, üheksa, kümme*; 11 *üksteist*; 12 *kaksteist*; 20 *kakskümmend*; 30 *kolmkümmend*; 100 *sada*. The numerals 2–10 are fully declined in all cases; from 11 onwards, the decade component in the oblique forms is invariable in genitive form; the unit component is declined: e.g. 20 *kakskümmend*; inessive ***kahe**kümnes*; illative ***kahe**kümnesse*.

Verb

Conjugational models depend on whether the stem is mutating or not. All forms of the Estonian verb can be constructed from four basic forms:

1. 1st infinitive in *-ma*;
2. 2nd infinitive in *-da/-ta/-a*;
3. 1st person present indicative;
4. passive past participle in *-tud/-dud*.

The indicative mood has four tenses: two simple and two compound. There is no future tense. As in Finnish, the auxiliary for the compound tenses is *olema* = Fin. *olla*, with present and past forms close to those in Finnish. Again as in Finnish, all positive verb forms have parallel negative forms; but whereas the negative particle is conjugated in Finnish (*en*, *et*, *ei*, etc.), Estonian has only the single form *ei*, used with all persons and both numbers. This means that the personal pronoun must be used:

SPECIMEN CONJUGATION

kirjutama 'to write':

indicative present: sing. *kirjutan, kirjutad, kirjuta**b***; pl. *kirjutame, kirjutate, kirjutavad*;
indicative present negative version: *ei kirjuta* (preceded by personal pronoun);
indicative past: *kirjutasin, kirjutasid*, etc.;
negative: *ei kirjutanud*;
compound past tense: *mina olen kirjutanud, sina oled . . . , mina oleme . . .* ;
negative: e.g. *mina ei ole kirjutanud*.

Note reduction in Estonian to an omnibus form of the past participle, where Finnish marks number: *olen sanonut, olemme sanoneet.*

MOODS

Conditional: the marker is *-ksi-* + usual endings: e.g. *mina kirjutaksin.*

Imperative: 2nd p. sing. *kirjuta*, 2nd p. pl. *kirjutage*; negative: *ära kirjuta*, pl. *ärge kirjutage.*

Inferential: present, *-vat*; past, *olevat* + past participle: e.g. (*Ma kuulsin, et*) *tema õppi**vat** ülikoolis arstiteadust* '(I hear that) he's studying medicine at the university'; *Ta sõit**vat** homme Moskvasse* 'So he's going to Moscow tomorrow.'

IMPERSONAL FORMS

Present in *-takse/-dakse/-akse*; past in *-ti/-di*: e.g. *linnas ehi**takse** maja* 'a house is being built/they're building a house in the town' (*maja* is in nominative case); *pargis jaluta**takse*** lit. 'it-is-gone-walking' = 'one goes walking in the park'; *räägi**takse**, et* ... 'it is said that ... '.

PARTICIPLES

Present in *-v* (active and passive): e.g. *luge**v*** 'reading'; *loeta**v*** 'being read'; *luge**vad** inimesed* 'people who are reading'; *loeta**vad** raamatud* 'books that are being read'. Past in *-nud*: e.g. *Kirjuta**nud** kirja, läks ta jalutama* 'After writing the letter he went for a walk.'

The last example also illustrates the use of the infinitive in *-ma* after verbs of motion. The infinitive in *-da* is used with such modal verbs as *oskama* 'to be able to', *tahtma* 'to want to': e.g. *Tema oskab hästi laul**da*** 'He can sing well.'

It is interesting to note that the partitive/accusative opposition may be used to express tense: cf.

ostan raamatu***t*** 'I'm buying a/the book' (partitive case – present tense);
ostan raamatu**Ø** 'I shall buy the book' (accusative case – present tense with future sense).

VERBAL PARTICLES

Estonian has a rich inventory of verbal particles, whose function is (a) modification of root sense, (b) aspectual, (c) directional. They are separable: e.g. *valmis tegema* 'to complete': *ta **tegi** selle töö kiiresti **valmis*** 'he did that work quickly (and finished it)'.

Some further examples:

alla 'down': *alla tulistama* 'to shoot down';
edasi 'onwards': *edasi töötama* 'to go on working';
järele 'after': *järele jääma* 'to be left over';
kinni 'shut': *kinni võtma* 'to lay hold on'.

Cf. with *välja minema* 'to leave': *rong läheb välja* 'the train leaves'; with *pärale jõudma* 'to arrive': *rong jõnab pärale* 'the train arrives'.

Postpositions

Most take the genitive case. Some occur in more than one form, inflected in line with case endings. For example, from *äär* 'margin':

äärde 'towards': *Läheme mere äärde* 'We go towards the sea';
ääres 'at': *Istume mere ääres* 'We sit by the sea';
äärest 'from': *Tuleme mere äärest* 'We come from the sea.'

While the locative (adessive, ablative, allative) cases of the noun are usually self-sufficient, certain postpositions, which take the endings of these three cases may also be used, and then follow the genitive case. Thus, an example given above: *leiba* (partitive) *on laual* 'there is bread on the table', may also be expressed as *leiba on laua* (genitive) ***peal.***

Similarly, *pani raamatu* (partitive) *laua* ***peale*** 'he laid a book on the table'; *laua* ***pealt*** *võeti raamat* 'he took the book from the table'.

Word order

SVO is normal.

1 Alguses oli Sõna, ja Sõna oli Jumala juures, ja Sõna oli Jumal.
2 Seesama oli alguses Jumala juures.
3 Kõik on tekkinud tema läbi, ja ilma temata ei ole tekkinud midagi, mis on tekkinud.
4 Temas oli elu, ja elu oli inimeste valgus,
5 ja valgus paistab pimeduses, ja pimedus ei ole seda võtnud omaks.
6 Oli mees, Jumala läkitatud; selle nimi oli Johannes.
7 See tuli tunnistuseks, tunnistama valgusest, et kõik usuksid tema kaudu.
8 Tema ei olnud mitte valgus, vaid ta tuli tunnistama valgusest.

(Tallinn keel)

ETHIOPIC

INTRODUCTION

Ethiopic (or *Ge'z*; *lesana ge'z* 'the Ge'ez language') is in origin a South Arabian dialect carried to Ethiopia by the Semitic settlers who laid the foundations of the Aksumite Kingdom late in the last millennium BC. By the fourth/fifth century AD, Aksum had grown to be the most powerful economic and political centre in north-east Africa. It was converted to Christianity in the fourth century, and Ethiopic literature is entirely and exclusively associated with the Christian Church. In these centuries, the language lost some of its South Arabian features, and gradually split into two branches – a Northern, from which Tigrinya and Tigre were to develop, and a Southern, which is the ancestor of Amharic and of several minor Ethiopian languages (Argobba, Gafat, Sidamo, etc.).

The history of Ethiopic literature falls into three clearly defined periods:

1. The Aksum period: many pillar inscriptions of considerable historical interest, and the first Bible translation (from Greek sources). This period covers the fourth to the seventh centuries, during which Ethiopic was a living language.
2. Seventh to thirteenth centuries. After the Islamic invasions in the seventh century nothing at all seems to have been written in Ethiopic; at all events nothing remains.
3. Thirteenth to twentieth centuries. In this period a literary revival took place in Ethiopic which was no longer a living language. Bible translation recommenced, but now from Arabic sources. Original writing includes the outstanding *Kebra Nagast*, the 'Glory of the Kings', which contains *inter alia* the story of the Queen of Sheba's visit to King Solomon. There is an extensive hagiography and miracle literature, e.g. the sixteenth-century *Ta'āmra Māryām*, the 'Miracles of Mary'.

SCRIPT

See **Script** at end of article.

PHONOLOGY

Consonants

stops: p, p', b, t, t', d, d', k, q, g, ʔ; labialized q°, k°, g°
fricatives: f, s, s', ʃ, h, ħ, ḫ, ʕ; h°
nasals: m, n

lateral and flap: l, r
semi-vowels: j, w

The emphatics /t', p', s', d'/ are notated here as dotted letters: ṭ, p̣, ṣ, ḍ.

Vowels

ɛ, u, i, aː, eː, e, o

MORPHOLOGY AND SYNTAX

Noun

Nouns are masculine or feminine, the latter being usually marked by -*(a)t*. Masculine nouns are not overtly marked. The gender of a nominal is often clear from verbal and/or pronominal concord. Some nouns, e.g. *ayn* 'eye', *sayf* 'sword', *arwē* 'wild animal', are unstable in gender.

NUMBER

Singular and plural. Certain triradical patterns are used almost exclusively as plural forms: e.g. *a*.12.*ā*.3, *a*.12.*e*.3.*t*; where 1, 2, 3 are radicals; *sayf* 'sword', pl. ***asyāf***; *lebs* 'clothes', pl. ***albās;*** *bet* 'house', pl. ***abyāt***. There are, of course, many other broken plural patterns. The sound or unbroken plural is in *-ān*, *-āt*.

CASE

Ethiopic has retained an oblique (objective) case marked by -*a*/-*e*, but has lost both the nominative -*u* (retained in Classical Arabic) and, surprisingly, the genitive marker in -*i*.

The nominative -*u* reappears in some examples of pronominal affixation: e.g. *abu.hu* 'his father'.

Construct formula: X-*a* Y: e.g. *bet.**a** negus* 'the king's house'; *mangest.**a** samāyāt* 'the kingdom of heaven'. The genitive relationship may also be expressed by means of the relative pronoun *za*, or the preposition *la*: e.g. *gabr **za**.negus* 'the king's servant'; *ba.mawāʿ eli.hom.u la nagast **za**.'aksum* 'in the days of the kings of Aksum'.

Adjective

There are very few primary adjectives. Some derived adjectives are formed on such nominal formulae as 1.*a*/*e*.2.*ā*.3.*i*, e.g. *bezāwi* 'redeeming', *nabābi* 'eloquent'; or with the suffix -*awi*, e.g. *nafusāwi* 'windy', *'amānāwi* 'truthful'.

Pronoun

The independent forms with their bound objective enclitics are:

		Singular		*Plural*	
1		ana	-ya, -ni	neḥna	-na
2	masc.	anta	-ka	antemu	-kemu

	fem.	anti	-ki	anten	-ken
3	masc.	we'etu	-hu, -u, -o	emuntu/we'etomu	-homu, -omu
	fem.	ye'eti	-hā, -ā	emantu/we'eton	-hon, -on

The bound forms are used (a) as possessive markers, e.g. *faras.ka* 'your horse', *neshāhomu* 'their penitence'; (b) as objective marker, e.g. *qatal.o* 'he killed him', *qatal.ā* 'he killed her', *qatal.omu* 'he killed them'.

DEMONSTRATIVE PRONOUN/ADJECTIVE

Masc. *we'etu*, fem. *ye'eti*, pl. *we'etomu* 'this/these'; masc. *zentu*, fem. *zāti*, pl. *ellontu*, *ellāntu* 'that, those'.

INTERROGATIVE PRONOUN

mannu 'who?'; *ment* 'what?'

RELATIVE PRONOUN

The interrogatives can be used, or the relative pronoun *za* (masc.) with feminine form *enta*, and common plural *ella/ellā*;: e.g. *be'esi* ***za****.mase'a* 'the man who came'; *be'esit enta mase'at* 'the woman who came'.

Numerals

1–10: *aḥadu*, *kele'ētu*, *šalastu*, etc.: i.e. standard South Semitic forms, with feminine counterparts. As in Arabic, the law of inverse polarity holds (*see* **Arabic**). In Ethiopic, the pronominal suffix may be added to the numeral, when the referent is known to the speakers: e.g. *šalasti.****homu*** *'eḍ(aw)* = *šalasti.****hu*** *'eḍ(aw)* 'three trees'.

Verb

The Ethiopic verbal system has perfective and imperfective aspects; indicative, subjunctive, and imperative moods; and non-finite forms, e.g. gerund, present participle active, past participle passive, and infinitive. Gender is marked in the second and third persons singular and plural.

CONJUGATION

The perfective aspect and the gerund are suffixal; the imperfective and the subjunctive are circumfixal.

The perfective endings are largely standard South Semitic: e.g. *qatala* 'he killed': sing. 1 *qatal.ku*, 2 *-ka/-ki*, 3 *-a/-at*; pl. 1 *-na*, 2 *-kemu/-ken*, 3 *-u/-ā*. Examples with bound pronominal object suffix: *nagar.ku.ka* 'I said to you'; *kalā'.ku.ki* 'I forbade you (fem.)'; *qatalu.w.omu* 'they killed them'.

IMPERFECTIVE

Marked by circumfixed personal affixes; stress on 1st root syllable.

		Singular	*Plural*
1		**'e.**qatel	**ne.**qatel
2	masc.	**te.**qatel	**te.**qatl.**u**

	fem.	**te**.qatel.**i**	**te**.qatl.**ā**
3	masc.	**ye.**qatel	**ye.**qatl.**u**
	fem.	**te.**qatel	**ye**.qatl.**ā**

The subjunctive shows accent shift and crasis; stress on prefixed marker: sing. 1 *e.qtel*, 2 ***te.**qtel/**te.**qtel.**i***, 3 ***ye.**qtel*.

Imperative: masc. *qetel*; fem. *qetel.i*; pl. masc. *qetel.u*, fem. *qetel.ā*.

GERUND

E.g. from *nagara* 'to speak, say': *nagi**r**.eya* 'when I said', *nagir.akal-ki* 'when you said', *nagir.ol-a*.

DERIVED FORMS

In Ethiopic these are represented by

(a) a causative with *a-* prefix: e.g. ***a**.qtala* 'to cause to kill';
(b) reflexive–passive in *ta-*: ***ta**.qatla* 'to kill oneself';
(c) causative–reflexive in *asta-*: e.g. from *gabra* 'to do', ***asta**.gbara* 'to set to work'.

Intensive and durative aspects are formed, the first by gemination of the second radical, the second by lengthening the first vowel. As in Arabic, weak and hollow verbs, and verbs with a laryngeal radical have specific paradigms.

NEGATIVE

The marker is *'i*: e.g. *'i.qatala* 'did not kill'; *'i.yeqatel* 'does not kill'.

Prepositions

Three are written prefixed to the noun: *la*, *ba*, and *'em*: e.g. *labet* 'to the house'; *la'ālama 'ālam* 'for all eternity'; *babet* 'in the house'; *bakenefa nafus* 'on the wing of the wind'; *'embeḥēr sābā* 'from the land of Saba'.

The remaining prepositions are written separately: e.g. *'enta* 'in, towards', *'eska* 'as far as, up to', *diba* 'upon', *dehar* 'after'.

Word order

VSO is normal.

ምዕራፍ ፡ ፩ ፡

፩ ፡ ቀዳሚሁ ፡ ቃል ፡ ውእቱ ፡ ወውእቱ ፡ ቃል ፡ ኀበ ፡ እግዚአብሔር ፡
፪ ፡ ውእቱ ፡ ወእግዚአብሔር ፡ ውእቱ ፡ ቃል ። ወዝንቱ ፡ እምቀዲሙ ፡ ኀበ ፡
፫ ፡ እግዚአብሔር ፡ ውእቱ ። ኵሉ ፡ በቱ ፡ ኮነ ፡ ወዘእንበሌሁሰ ፡ አልቦ ፡ ዘኮ
፬ ፡ ነ ፡ ወኢምንትኒ ፡ እምዘኮነ ። በቱ ፡ ሕይወት ፡ ውእቱ ፡ ወሕይወትሰ ፡ ብር
፭ ፡ ሃኑ ፡ ለእጓለ ፡ እመሕያው ፡ ውእቱ ። ወብርሃንሰ ፡ ዘውስተ ፡ ጽልመት ፡ ያ
፮ ፡ በርሀ ፡ ወያርኢ ፡ ወጽልመትኒ ፡ ኢይረክቦ ። ወሀሎ ፡ አሐዱ ፡ ብእሲ ፡ ዘ
፯ ፡ ተፈነወ ፡ እምኀበ ፡ እግዚአብሔር ፡ ዘስሙ ፡ ዮሐንስ ። ወውእቱ ፡ መጽአ ፡
ለስምዕ ፡ ሰማዕተ ፡ ይኩን ፡ በእንተ ፡ ብርሃን ፡ ከመ ፡ ኵሉ ፡ ይእመን ፡ በ
፰ ፡ ቱ ። ወለሊሁሰ ፡ ኢኮነ ፡ ብርሃነ ፡ ዳእሙ ፡ ሰማዕተ ፡ ይኩን ፡ በእንተ ፡ ብር
፱ ፡ ሃን ። ዘውእቱ ፡ ብርሃን ፡ ጽድቅ ፡ ዘያበርሀ ፡ ለኵሉ ፡ ሰብእ ፡ ዘይመጽእ ፡ ው
፲ ፡ ስተ ፡ ዓለም ። ወውስተ ፡ ዓለም ፡ ሀሎ ፡ ወዓለምኒ ፡ በቱ ፡ ኮነ ፡ ወዓለምሰ ፡
ኢያእመሮ ።

SCRIPT

The Ethiopic syllabary is derived from the South Arabian consonantal script, which was used in south-west Arabia from about 1500 BC to the second century BC (cf. **Epigraphic South Arabian**). Through the first millennium BC, Ethiopia was gradually colonized by Sabaean merchants and settlers, who brought with them the nucleus of what was to become Ge'ez, the classical language of Ethiopia.

By the fourth century AD, the South Arabian script, as used in the Aksumite state in Ethiopia (by then Christianized), had undergone two modifications of fundamental importance: the direction of writing was reversed, possibly under the influence of Greek, to run from left to right, in place of the typically Semitic right to left; second, the consonantal graphs were individually modulated, so as to notate their vocalization. Thus arose the Ethiopic syllabary of seven vocalic orders, which is set out in the accompanying table. The first of the seven orders consists of the base form of the consonant with the inherent vowel /a/.

Five Sabaean letters were discarded as superfluous in Ethiopic, while six new letters were introduced: four of these denote the labialized velar phonemes q°, h°, k°, g°. As will be seen from the table, these do not have forms for the second and seventh orders, as labialization *per se* involves the rounded vowels /u/ and /o/.

Serious shortcomings in the Ethiopic script are: (1) the absence of some means of denoting the gemination which is so important, usually phonemic, both in Ethiopic itself and in the daughter languages. In the seventeenth century an attempt was made to remedy this defect by introducing the Arabic *tashdid* but this did not catch on. (2) Similarly, Ethiopic has nothing corresponding to the Arabic *sukun*, used to indicate that the bearer consonant is vowelless. Where conjunct non-vocalized consonants occur, e.g. in words like *medr* 'earth', *sayf* 'sword', the convention is to write them in the sixth order, i.e. with short *e*: thus, *medr* is written as *medere*, and correct reading as *medr* depends on the reader's awareness that the only possible pattern (Arabic *wazn*, *awzān*) here is $C_1eC_2C_3$ *medr*.

The Ethiopic syllabary is used to write the daughter languages Amharic, Tigrinya, and Tigre, and has been used for other languages such as Somali and Oromo (Galla). In the case of Amharic, the syllabary was, early in the seventeenth century, extended by seven letters denoting specifically Amharic phonemes.

Words are divided from each other by the punctuation mark :.

THE ETHIOPIC SCRIPT

THE SYLLABARY

a		*ū*		*ī*		*ā*		*ē*		*e*		*ō*	
ሀ	*ha*	ሁ	*hū*	ሂ	*hī*	ሃ	*hā*	ሄ	*hē*	ህ	*he*	ሆ	*hō*
ለ	*la*	ሉ	*lū*	ሊ	*lī*	ላ	*lā*	ሌ	*lē*	ል	*le*	ሎ	*lō*
ሐ	*ḥa*	ሑ	*ḥū*	ሒ	*ḥī*	ሓ	*ḥā*	ሔ	*ḥē*	ሕ	*ḥe*	ሖ	*ḥō*
መ	*ma*	ሙ	*mū*	ሚ	*mī*	ማ	*mā*	ሜ	*mē*	ም	*me*	ሞ	*mō*
ሠ	*ša*	ሡ	*šū*	ሢ	*šī*	ሣ	*šā*	ሤ	*šē*	ሥ	*še*	ሦ	*šō*
ረ	*ra*	ሩ	*rū*	ሪ	*rī*	ራ	*rā*	ሬ	*rē*	ር	*re*	ሮ	*rō*
ሰ	*sa*	ሱ	*sū*	ሲ	*sī*	ሳ	*sā*	ሴ	*sē*	ስ	*se*	ሶ	*sō*
ቀ	*qa*	ቁ	*qū*	ቂ	*qī*	ቃ	*qā*	ቄ	*qē*	ቅ	*qe*	ቆ	*qō*
በ	*ba*	ቡ	*bū*	ቢ	*bī*	ባ	*bā*	ቤ	*bē*	ብ	*be*	ቦ	*bō*
ተ	*ta*	ቱ	*tū*	ቲ	*tī*	ታ	*tā*	ቴ	*tē*	ት	*te*	ቶ	*tō*
ኀ	*ḫa*	ኁ	*ḫū*	ኂ	*ḫī*	ኃ	*ḫā*	ኄ	*ḫē*	ኅ	*ḫe*	ኆ	*ḫō*
ነ	*na*	ኑ	*nū*	ኒ	*nī*	ና	*nā’*	ኔ	*nē*	ን	*ne*	ኖ	*nō*
አ	*'a*	ኡ	*'ū*	ኢ	*'ī*	ኣ	*ā*	ኤ	*'ē*	እ	*'e*	ኦ	*'ō*
ከ	*ka*	ኩ	*kū*	ኪ	*kī*	ካ	*kā*	ኬ	*kē*	ክ	*ke*	ኮ	*kō*
ወ	*wa*	ዉ	*wū*	ዊ	*wī*	ዋ	*wā*	ዌ	*wē*	ው	*we*	ዎ	*wō*
ዐ	*ʿa*	ዑ	*ʿū*	ዒ	*ʿī*	ዓ	*ʿā*	ዔ	*ʿē*	ዕ	*ʿe*	ዖ	*ʿō*
ዘ	*za*	ዙ	*zū*	ዚ	*zī*	ዛ	*zā*	ዜ	*zē*	ዝ	*ze*	ዞ	*zō*
የ	*ja*	ዩ	*jū*	ዪ	*jī*	ያ	*jā*	ዬ	*jē*	ይ	*je*	ዮ	*jō*
ደ	*da*	ዱ	*dū*	ዲ	*dī*	ዳ	*dā*	ዴ	*dē*	ድ	*de*	ዶ	*dō*
ገ	*ga*	ጉ	*gū*	ጊ	*gī*	ጋ	*gā*	ጌ	*gē*	ግ	*ge*	ጎ	*gō*
ጠ	*ṭa*	ጡ	*ṭū*	ጢ	*ṭī*	ጣ	*ṭā*	ጤ	*ṭē*	ጥ	*ṭe*	ጦ	*ṭō*
ጰ	*p̣a*	ጱ	*p̣ū*	ጲ	*p̣ī*	ጳ	*p̣ā*	ጴ	*p̣ē*	ጵ	*p̣e*	ጶ	*p̣ō*
ጸ	*ṣa*	ጹ	*ṣū*	ጺ	*ṣī*	ጻ	*ṣā*	ጼ	*ṣē*	ጽ	*ṣe*	ጾ	*ṣō*
ፀ	*ḍa*	ፁ	*ḍū*	ፂ	*ḍī*	ፃ	*ḍā*	ፄ	*ḍē*	ፅ	*ḍe*	ፆ	*ḍō*
ፈ	*fa*	ፉ	*fū*	ፊ	*fī*	ፋ	*fā*	ፌ	*fē*	ፍ	*fe*	ፎ	*fō*
ፐ	*pa*	ፑ	*pū*	ፒ	*pī*	ፓ	*pā*	ፔ	*pē*	ፕ	*pe*	ፖ	*pō*

THE LABIALIZED VELAR SERIES

ኰ	*kua*	ኲ	*kuī*	ኵ	*kue*	ኳ	*kuā*	ኴ	*kuē*
ጐ	*gua*	ጒ	*guī*	ጕ	*gue*	ጓ	*guā*	ጔ	*guē*
ቈ	*qua*	ቊ	*quī*	ቍ	*que*	ቋ	*quā*	ቌ	*quē*
ኈ	*ḫua*	ኊ	*ḫuī*	ኍ	*ḫue*	ኋ	*ḫuā*	ኌ	*ḫuē*

ETRUSCAN

INTRODUCTION

The Etruscan League of City States, bounded by the Apennines, the Tiber, the Arno, and the sea, was Rome's northern neighbour throughout the latter half of the first millennium BC. The Etruscans appear in history about 900 BC. Their period of greatest political, economic, and ideological power lay in the eighth to sixth centuries BC. The following centuries saw a gradual decline in their influence, though the city states were not finally absorbed into the Roman Empire until the first century BC. The language ceased to be used for sacral purposes at about the same time. There is no way of knowing how long it survived as a spoken language.

In spite of repeated efforts to link Etruscan with Indo-European, with agglutinative languages of the Uralic type, and with Caucasian languages, no definite relationship with any other language family has ever been established. Etruscan was written in a Greek-type script which can be read without any great difficulty. The extant material consists of:

1. The Agram mummy-wrapping in the National Museum at Zagreb; the 281 lines contain about 1,300 words.
2. Several medium-length texts, e.g. the Capua tablet (250 words), the Perugia tablet (125 words), and the Lemnos tablet (35 words).
3. Several thousand short stereotyped inscriptions of a votive or funerary nature.

Thanks to the repetitive nature of these short inscriptions, it has been possible to allot meanings – a few with certainty, many tentative – to some hundreds of words, and to identify, again often tentatively, a number of inflectional endings and syntactic linking agents. Certain kinship terms such as *ati* 'mother', *clan* 'son', *seχ/kh* 'daughter', *puia* 'wife', and a few other words like *zilc* 'official', *spura* 'town', *rasna* 'Etruria', may be taken as authenticated beyond reasonable doubt. Failing the discovery of a substantial digloss, an Etruscan Rosetta Stone, the most promising line of attack on the undeciphered remainder would seem to lie in the so-called 'combinatorial method'. This involves the close collation of inscriptions containing both known nuclei and undeciphered material with the artefacts bearing them, in the hope that a recurrent feature in the artefact may prove to be accompanied by a similarly recurrent item in the text. In this way, new lexical items and syntactic formants – affixes, particles, etc. – may be isolated and tentatively interpreted.

SCRIPT

West Greek in origin, written from right to left. Individual forms vary over the 700 years of usage. From the sixth century onwards, words were divided from each other by markers consisting of three or four points. There is some evidence to suggest that Etruscan was originally written in a syllabic script. *See* **Latin Script**.

PHONOLOGY

Pfiffig (1969) gives the following inventory:

Consonants

labials: p, ph, f, v, m
dentals: t, th, n, l, r
velars: k/q, kh, h
silbilants: z, s, ś = /ç/

There are four signs for /s/ in the Etruscan script. It is to be noted that the Greek letters χ, θ, Ø used in transliterated Etruscan, represent the aspirated stops /kh, th, ph/, not the fricatives /χ, ð, f/.

Vowels

i, e, a, u figure in the script; it is assumed that /o/ was also present and notated as *u*.

MORPHOLOGY AND SYNTAX

Noun

There was, apparently, no grammatical gender. The fundamental opposition seems to have been between human and non-human categories. In late Etruscan, female proper names show a gender-related inflection: *-i/-ia*. The singular nominative is not specifically marked. The plural marker is -(V)*r*, with possible change of stem vowel, which also appears in the gentive:

clan 'son' – gen. *clens* – pl. *clenar*
spura town' pl. *spurer*

For *spura* Pfiffig gives the following declension:

	Singular	*Plural*
nom./indefinite acc.	spura	spurer
definite acc.	spureni	spureri
genitive	spureś- spural	—
locative	spurethi	

There seems to have been no dative case in the Indo-European sense. Genitive endings may be compounded.

Adjective

Few adjectives are known. The qualitative adjective was formed from the noun by affixation:

-*ul*-*iu*: cf. *ais* 'god', *aisiu* 'divine';
-*n*V: cf. *suthi* 'grave', *suthina* 'funerary';
-*cva*/*khva*, etc. (allophones depending on stem-final): cf. *math* 'intoxicating drink', *mathcva* 'intoxicating'.

Pronoun

The following forms are known: first person singular *mi*, with definite accusative *mini*; third person singular *an* 'he/she', gen. *enaś*, for example:

mini tur(u)ce larth apunas velethnalas
'larth apunas gave (*tur*(*u*)*ce*) me (*mini*) to the velethna'

POSSESSIVE PRONOUN

Forms in -*sa*/*śa* (3rd p. sing.): e.g. *arnth veluś velusa* = *Arnth Veluś* 'he of Vel'.

DEMONSTRATIVE PRONOUN

Nominative and indefinite accusative forms *ca*/*ta*, plural *cei*/*tei*, may refer to different degrees of distance. The genitive forms are *cla*/*tla*, pl. *clal*, with definite accusative *cn*/*tn*; pl. *cnl*. The locative ending is -*thi*. Examples: *cn turce murila hercnas* 'Murila Hercnas gave this' (*tur*- 'to give'); *clthi śuthiti* 'in this grave'.

INTERROGATIVE PRONOUN

ipa 'who?'; with gen. *ipas*.

RELATIVE PRONOUN

ipa.

Numerals

1–6 inclusive are known with some certainty: *thu*, *zal*, *ci*, *sa*, *makh*, *huth*. 8 is probably *cezp*; *semph* and *nutph* may be 7 and 9. 10 *śar*; 20 *zathrum*; 19 *thunem zathrum*; 18 *eslem zathrum*; 30 *cialkh*; 40 *śealkh*; 50 *muvalkh*; 70 *semphalkh*. The word for 100 is not known. The ordinal for l is *thunśna*.

Verb

The basic opposition seems to be between aspects: imperfective and perfective. From the repetitive and stereotyped nature of the Etruscan votive and funerary inscriptions, it follows naturally that few finite verbal forms occur. The only regularly recurrent forms are the first and third persons singular perfective, and the second person singular imperative.

The verbal base is often a closed monosyllable. The Agram text yields such bases as *ar* 'to make', *rakh* 'to take', *puth* 'to place, put'. This base is also the base for adjectives and nominals: e.g. from *zikh* 'to write', *zikhina* 'appertaining to writing', *zikhu* 'scribe'.

The third person singular perfective (or preterite) is one of the most securely established identities in Etruscan: *-ce*: e.g. *tur.ce* 'he/she gave'; *sval.ce* 'he/she lived'; *zilakh.ce* 'he was praetor'. The first person form is *-cun*: e.g. *thapicun* 'I cursed'. A frequent form in *-a* may be a present/imperfective third person singular: e.g. *hecia* 'he puts'; *ara* 'he makes'; *mena* 'he brings/ gives'.

An optative form in *-e* has been identified: e.g. *satene* 'let him keep'; *ame* 'let him be'.

CAUSATIVE

A formant is *-eth-*: e.g. *ac-* 'to make, do', causative *ekheth-*. For this stem, an archaic preterite has been identified: *ekh.eth.ai.*

THE COPULA

The following forms are known: *am-* 'to be': 3rd p. sing. *ama*; preterite *amce*; optative *ame* 'let him be'. *-in* has been interpreted as a medio-passive formant: e.g. *thezin* 'is sacrificed'; *zikh.un.ce* 'was written'; *utince* 'was carried out'.

SUFFIXES

Examples:

-thur indicates local origin: e.g. *velthur* 'from Vulci' (*vel-* 'Vulci');
-cla makes collectives: e.g. *sacni* 'holy'; *sacnicla* 'holy place' (where holy things are);
-tra identifies the group; e.g. *Vipinal.tra* 'people/followers of the Vipinei'
-za forms diminutives: e.g. *murś* 'urn', *murza* 'a small urn'.

Some Etruscan stems:

tin	'day', 'Jupiter'	*calus*, pl. *calusur*	'dead'
cath	'sun-god'	*cilth*	'people', 'nation'
ais	'god'	*fufluns*	'the Etruscan Dionysos'
suthi	'grave'	*fler*	'sacrificial animal'
zamathi	'gold'	*flere*	'numen'
neri	'water'	*sacni*	'holy'
aita	'Hades'	*mekh rasna*	'res(mekh) publica'
cver	'boy'	*vel.thur*	'son of Vel'
tul	'stone'	*clucthra*	'beverage'
nacna	'great'	*avil*	'year', 'age'

EVEN

INTRODUCTION

Known also as Lamut, this dialect complex belongs to the Northern Tungusic branch of the Altaic group of languages. Even is spoken in the Okhotsk region of the Khabarovsk Kray, in the Magadan Oblast, and Kamchatka, by some 7,000 Evens, i.e. about half of the total Even population.

A few religious texts in Even appeared in the middle of the nineteenth century. The present literary standard is based on the Ola dialect.

SCRIPT

Since the 1930s the Cyrillic script has been used, with the addition in 1958 of ң, and θ/θ̈.

PHONOLOGY

Consonants

stops: p, b, t, d, k, g (q)
affricates: ts, tʃ, dʒ
fricatives: ß/w, s, j, χ, γ, h
nasals: m, n, ɲ, ŋ
laterals: l, ɫ, ʎ
roll: r (→ d/^{d}r/r^{d})

Vowels

The vowel system shows a symmetrical division between five soft ('bright') vowels and five hard ('dark').

hard: ı, e, a, o, u
soft: i, ė, ə, ȯ, u̇

All ten are short, long, or diphthongized, giving 20 + values, inadequately notated in the script: e.g. /i, iː, ı, ıː/ are all notated as и in Cyrillic. The Even vowel-harmony system depends on the contrast between the hard and soft series, the hard vowels being lower in pitch and more tense than their soft counterparts. According to Novikova (1968), the hard vowels tend to be pharyngealized in some Eastern Even dialects.

In non-initial position, short vowels tend to be reduced or shed, a reductionism which also distinguishes many Even words from their Evenki congeners: cf. Evenki *sāre* 'they know', Even *hār.*

Stress

On long syllables; if none, on word-final syllable.

MORPHOLOGY AND SYNTAX

The orthography used here is that of Rishes and Cincius in their *Russko-Evenskij Slovar'* (1952).

Noun

As in Evenki, the plural marker is *-l/-r* (stem-final *-n* drops): e.g. *dyū* 'house', pl. *dyūl*; *oron* 'reindeer', pl. *oror.* The following affixes are also used to mark plurality: *-til*, *-nil*, *-sil* (vowel harmony variable): e.g. aman 'father', pl. *amtıl*; *even* 'Even', pl. *evesel.*

SPECIMEN DECLENSION

dyū 'house' (notated as *ʒū* by Novikova (1968) and Benzing (1955)).

accusative	dyūv	ablative I	dyūduk
dative	dyūdū	ablative II	dyūgīč
adessive	dyūtkī	instrumental	dyūč
locative	dyūlā	comitative	dyūnyun

There are also specific endings to express motion along something: *-līl-klī.* Plural is *dyūl* + case affixes as singular.

POSSESSIVE SUFFIXES

Three-fold series depending on stem-final; e.g. the series following a final vowel is: sing. 1 *-v*, 2 *-s*, 3 *-n*; pl. 1 excl. -(*w*)*un*, incl. *-t*, 2 *-san*, 3 *-tan.* Examples: *dyū.v* 'my house', *dyū.s* 'your house'. These affixes are added to case affixes: e.g. *dyūdūv* 'to my house'.

To express contingent/alienable possession, the relative infix *-ng-* is used. Rishes and Cincius (1952) give the following example: *min dəlu* 'my (own) head'; *min dəla**ng**u* 'my head (of animal killed by me)'. For *min*, *see* **Pronoun**, below.

Adjective

As attribute, adjective precedes noun and is in concord with it for case: e.g. *ōmat dyū* 'new house'; *nyamdū dyūdū* 'in the warm house'; *bi kučukən bisəm* 'I am small'; *bū kučukər bisu* = we are small (i.e. concord for number).

COMPARATIVE

E.g. *muran oronduk əgdedmər* 'the horse is bigger than the reindeer', where

-duk is the ablative case, and *-dmər* is an intensifying affix following *əgde(n)* 'big'.

Pronoun

PERSONAL INDEPENDENT

Sing.: 1 *bī*, 2 *hī*, 3 *nongan*; pl. 1 inc. *mut*, excl. *bū*, 2 *hū*, 3 *nongartan*. These are declined in all cases, with suppletive bases in oblique first singular and exclusive plural: e.g. for first person singular, *bī*: acc. *minu*, gen. *min*, dat. *mindu*, abl. *minduk*, loc. *mindulə̄*, comitative *miññun* with three directional cases, an instrumental and an elative; e.g. *Nongan mindulə̄ dagamrīn* 'He came up to me.'

DEMONSTRATIVE PRONOUN

ərə̄k 'this', pl. *ərəl*; *tarāk* 'that', pl. *taral*. Declined in all cases.

INTERROGATIVE PRONOUN

ngī 'who?'; *yak* 'what?' Declined in all cases.

Numerals

1–10: *umən, dyūr, yelan, dıgən, tunngan, nyungən, nadan, dyapkan, uyūn, mēn*; 11 *mēn-umən*; 12 *mēn-dyūr*; 20 *dyūrmēr*; 30 *yelanmēr*; 100 (*umən*) *nyama*.

Verb

The Even verb is marked for aspect, voice, mood, tense, person, number. Non-finite forms behave partly as verbs, partly as nominals.

ASPECT

Over a dozen markers generate various aspectual meanings in stems. For example, *-l-* is inceptive: cf. *hōng.dāy* 'to weep', *hōng.a.**l**.dāy* 'to burst into tears'; *-dyan-/-dyen-* is reiterative: cf. *ngəndə̄y* 'to go', *ngən.e.dyen.də̄y* 'to keep on going'.

VOICE

The active voice has no special marker. The passive voice has *-v-*, *-u-*, *-m-*: e.g. *baktāy* 'to find', *Oron mindu bak.a.**v**.ran* 'The reindeer was found by me' (*mindu* is dative of *bi* 'I').

CAUSATIVE

-vkan-/-vken-: e.g. *ōdāy* 'to do', *ōvkan* 'cause to be done'; *hādāy* 'to know', *hāvkan* 'let something be known'.

RECIPROCAL

-mač-/-meč-, with variants: e.g. *ukčə̄ndə̄y* 'to talk': *ukčə̄n.məč.t-ə̄y* → *ukčə̄n.məttə̄y* 'to converse'.

MOOD

There are indicative, imperative, subjunctive, potential, and presumptive moods. Tense is distinguished only in the indicative (present, past, future) and in the imperative (present, future).

Imperative: the present-tense markers are *-li*/*-ni* (2nd person sing.), *-lra*/*-lrə* (2nd person pl.), *-(n)g*/*kar*/*-(n)g*/*kər* (1st person pl.), e.g. *gu.li* 'say! speak!' (sing.), *gu.lrə* (pl.); *gu.ngər* 'let us say!'

Future tense: the marker is *d*/*t* + *a*/*ə* + personal endings: e.g. *ha.da.n* 'he is to know'; *nongartan ha.da.tan* 'they are to know'.

Potential: *-k-* + *a*/: *nongan ha.ka.n* 'he may (get to) know'.

Necessitative: *-nna*/: *bi ha.nna.v* 'I have to know'; *nongan ha.nna.n* 'he has to know'.

Presumptive: *-mna*/: *bi ha.mna.v* 'presumably I shall know'.

Conditional: the marker may begin with *r, t, d, s or* Ø, followed by *a*/*ə k*: *bi ha.r(ə).ku.v* 'if I know/knew'.

TENSE

Unless the present tense is specifically marked for an imperfective aspect (e.g. inceptive, reiterative) it can be translated as present or past: e.g. *bi bakram* 'I find/I found'; the reasoning being that the action, if not inceptive etc., is complete.

Novikova (1968) distinguishes three classes of verb based on present indicative: (a) active verbs with affix based on *-r*(*a*) or variant; (b) stative verbs, with affix based on *-s*(*a*) or variant; (c) verbs denoting change of state, transfer, etc. with affix based on *-d*(*a*), etc. Examples: (a) *ma.**ra**.m* 'I kill(ed)'; (b) *en.**sa**.m* 'I am sick'; (c) *nē.**da**.m* 'I put'.

SPECIMEN CONJUGATION

Indicative present, past, and future of *ngəndə̄y* 'to go':

			Present	*Past*	*Future*
sing.	1		ngən.**rəm**	ngən.rī.**v**	ngən.dī.**m**
	2		ngən.**ənri**	ngən.rī.**s**	ngən.dī.**nri**
	3		ngən.**rən**	ngən.rī.**n**	ngən.dī.**n**
plural	1	*incl.*	ngən.**rəp**	ngən.rī.**t**	ngən.dī.**p**
		excl.	ngən.**ru**	ngən.rī.**vun**	ngən.dī.**ru**
	2		ngən.**əs**	ngən.rī.**sən**	ngən.dī.**s**
	3		ngən.**rə**	ngən.rī**tən**	ngən.dī.**r**

NEGATIVE FORMS

The negative verb *ədə̄y*, conjugated for person, tense, and mood, is used with a stable participial form of the sense-verb (based on *-r*/*s*/*d-*, see above): e.g. *bi hāram* 'I know', *bi əsəm hār* 'I don't know'; similarly, *hi əsənri hār, nongan əsni hār; bi əsəm dukra* 'I don't write'; *bi əču dukra* 'I didn't write'; *bi ətə̄m dukra* 'I shan't write'.

As in Evenki, *ač-* is an existential negator: e.g. *nongan ač hutlə̄* 'she has no children'.

PARTICIPIAL FORMS

These are tense-related, e.g. forms in *-ri, di*/*ti, si* with the present, in *-ča*/*čə* with the past, in *dnga/dnge* with the future. In the absence of a relative pronoun, these forms provide the framework for qualifying/modifying information sited on left hand of verb: e.g. *bi knigav tang.ri.v nyārīkām ittın* 'I saw the boy (who was) reading the book' (*tang.ri* is participial form + *-v* acc. marker).

Concomitant action is expressed by *-niqan/-niken*: e.g. *nongan, tetniken, gunin*... 'while dressing, he said...'. *-mi* 'when.../if...': e.g. *Ngən.mi hinu ittan* 'When he came he saw you.'

Postpositions

Most of these are nouns in the locative case + possessive marker *-n*: e.g. *do* 'interior' + loc. *-lā*: *dyū dolān* 'in the house'; *oy* 'upper side': *stol oylān* 'on the table'.

There is also an extensive inventory of emotive and evaluative affixes.

Word order

SOV

EVENKI

INTRODUCTION

Also known as Tungus, Evenki belongs to the Northern Tungusic branch of Altaic. There are are about 22,000 Evenki, and roughly half of them speak the Evenki language. The Evenki National Region is in area not far short of 1 million square kilometres, and in addition the Evenki live in the Buryatia Republic, in northern China, and elsewhere, spread over a vast wilderness extending from the Nenets area on the Yenisei to the Sea of Okhotsk and Sakhalin Island in the east. The many dialects are grouped in Northern, Southern, and Eastern main divisions. A key distinction between them lies in their respective treatment of sibilants: e.g. the verb 'to know' is *xami* in Northern, *sami* in Eastern, and *sami* or *šami* in Southern Evenki. Similarly, 'woman' is *axi* in Eastern and Northern dialects, *asi* or *aši* in Southern.

Written Evenki dates from 1931. Several Russian classics have been translated into a literary standard based on s-type dialects.

SCRIPT

After a period of romanization in the 1930s, Cyrillic was adopted; ң is used to represent the velar nasal (here notated as *ng*).

PHONOLOGY

Consonants

stops: p, b, t, d, k, g
affricate: tʃ, dʒ
fricatives: (f) ß, s, x, j, γ
nasals: m, n ɲ, ŋ
lateral: l
roll: r

Assimilation takes place at junctures; e.g. affix initial after a nasal: *oron.vo* → *oronmo* (accusative of *oron* 'reindeer').

Vowels

short: i, a, ə, o, u
long: i, e, a, ə, o, u

For purposes of vowel harmony, the vowels are classified as (a) hard: /a, aː, eː, o, oː/; soft: /ə, əː/; neutral: /i, iː, u, uː/. Vasiljevich (1958) describes Evenki vowel harmony as 'stepped'; i.e., short vowels are sensitive to an immediately preceding long vowel, and as a result vowel harmony may switch register more than once in the course of a long word.

Stress

Free; varies according to presence or absence of long vowels.

MORPHOLOGY AND SYNTAX

Noun

No grammatical gender, no articles. There are two numbers, with plural in *-l/-r*: e.g. *oron* 'reindeer', pl. *oror*; *bira* 'river', pl. *biral.*

DECLENSION

The endings given here for illustrative purposes have hard vowels, i.e. are in concord with roots having back vowels: case marker follows number marker:

definite accusative: *-va/-pa/-ma*;
indefinite accusative: *-ya/-a*;
dative, locative: *-dū/tū*, eg. *biradū bidem* 'I live on the river';
directional: *-tki*;
allative: *-lā/-dulā*, e.g. *xargilā* 'into the forest';
ablative: *-duk*; *-git/-kit/-ngit*;
instrumental: *-t/-di*, e.g. *adilit* 'with a net'.

There are further locative and directional cases.

POSSESSIVE AFFIXES

	Singular	*Plural*
1	-v/m	*excl.* -wun; *incl.* -t
2	-s	-sun
3	-n	-tin

A specific set of possessive suffixes with the *-ng*(*i*) marker is used to denote contingent and alienable possessions: e.g. *guləngiv* 'my hut' (= the hut I happen to be using).

In the possessive relationship, the possessed noun, with proper affix, follows possessor: e.g. *oron dili**n*** 'reindeer its-head' = 'the reindeer's head'; *čalban awdannali**n*** 'the leaves of the birch-tree'.

Adjective

As attribute, adjective precedes noun and is inflected for number and case: e.g. *ayaldū ōmaktaldū guləldū* 'in nice new houses' (*aya* 'good'; *ōmakta* 'new'; *gulə* 'house').

COMPARATIVE

Made with *-tmar/-mar/-dimar* (with harmonic variants): e.g. *aya* 'good', *ayatmar* 'better'.

Pronoun

PERSONAL INDEPENDENT FORMS

	Singular	*Plural*
1	bi (oblique base, *min-*)	*excl.* bū, *incl.* mit
2	si (oblique base, *sin-*)	su
3	nungan	nungartin

These are declined in all cases.

DEMONSTRATIVE PRONOUN

ər 'this', *tar* 'that'; plural forms: *əril*, *taril*. In subdordinate clauses, *tar* may represent a personal pronoun: e.g. *tar əmərəkiv* 'when I came' (*əmə* 'to come'; *-rək-* is relative marker; *-v* = 1st p. sing. marker).

INTERROGATIVE PRONOUN

ngī 'who?'; *ēkun* 'what?' (plural forms: *ngīl*; *ēkur*).

RELATIVE PRONOUN

None in Evenki. For relative constructions, *see* **Verb**, below.

Numerals

1–10: *umūn*, *dyūr*, *ilan*, *digin*, *tunnga*, *nyungun*, *nadan*, *dyapkun*, *yegin*, *dyān*; 11 *dyān.umūn*; 12 *dyān.dyūr*; 20 *dyūr.dyār*; 30 *ilan.dyār*; 100 *nyama*. Numerals take a plural noun.

Verb

Roots are transitive or intransitive, and have finite and non-finite forms. Aspect, voice, mood, tense have specific markers; in tenses, person and number are shown by affixes.

ASPECT

Perfective is unmarked, imperfective by, for example *-dya/ča*: *um* 'to drink', *um**dya*** 'to be drinking'.

VOICE

passive marker is *-v-/-p-*, e.g. *surūv* 'to take', *surūv**uv*** 'to be taken';
causative: *-vkān/-pkān/-mukān*, e.g. *gūn* 'to say', *gūn**mukān*** 'to cause to say';
inceptive: *-l*, e.g. *dukū*, 'to write', *dukū**l**im* 'I've just started to write';
reciprocal: *-mat*, e.g. *duku* 'to write', *dukū**mat*** 'to correspond'.

TENSE

The indicative mood has an aspectual present (perfective/imperfective), two past tenses, and three futures. For example, perfective present of root *ngənə* 'to go':

	Singular	*Plural*
1	ngənəm	*incl.* ngənərəp; *excl.* ngənərəv
2	ngənənni	ngənərəs
3	ngənərən	ngənərə

Perfective past: the marker is *-čā*, e.g. *bi nungandūn dukūčāv* 'I wrote to him'; *əməčəv* 'I came'.

Imperfective past: *-ngkī*, e.g. *bi teatrildū bingkīv* 'I used to go to the theatres.'

Future (potential): *-dVngV̄*, e.g. *deng*; *əmədengə̄v* 'I'll come'.

NEGATIVE

The negative copula is ə-, inflected, + sense-verb in participial form: e.g. in present: *əsim*, *əsinni*, *əsin* (etc.) *gunə* 'I (etc.) don't speak.' The negative of the existential verb is *āčin*: e.g. *minngi oron.mi āčin* 'I have no reindeer.'

PARTICIPLES

E.g. perfective in *-čā*: *əməčə̄ bəye* 'the man who came'; imperfective in *-rī*: *bəye əməderīwən ičəm* 'I saw that the man was coming.'

There are also imperative, subjunctive, desiderative, and necessitative moods, plus an inferential or presumptive mood with an aorist and a past tense. The presumptive marker is *-rka*: e.g. *əmərkə bičən* 'He has probably come already.'

The examples given here illustrate only a small selection from the very rich inventory of verbal affixes available in Evenki. Vasiljevich (1958) lists about 500, with examples of their usage.

Postpositions

Most of these are nouns in the locative case. In construct, following a noun, they take personal possessive markers, e.g. the third person singular *-n*: e.g.

oyo 'the highest point of anything', e.g. *mō oyo**n*** 'the top of the tree'; *oyo.li* 'on', e.g. *dyū oyoli**n*** 'above the house'; *dyū oyo**n*** 'on the roof'; *daga* 'near(ness)', *dagadu* 'near', e.g. *dyū dagadu**n*** 'near the house', *dagadu**vun*** 'near us'.

Word order

SOV is normal.

EWE

INTRODUCTION

Ewe belongs to the Ewe-Akan sub-group of the Kwa branch of West Sudanic and is spoken by around 4 million people in Ghana and Togo, also in Benin. A literary form of Ewe (based on the Anlo dialect) has been in use since 1853, when the Norddeutsche Missionsgesellschaft started its missionary activity (Togoland was a German colony from 1884 onwards). Ewe was used as the medium of instruction in schools. Under British administration in western Togoland after the First World War, Ewe was one of five African languages selected to take part in the International African Institute competition in 1932. There is now, since independence (1954), a thriving literature in Ewe (Ferdinand Kwasi Fiawoo, Sam Obianim, S.K. Anika, etc.). The Ewe Club publishes a journal, *Togo Gedzedze* ('Light on Togo').

SCRIPT

Roman; the orthography used here is that of Diedrich Westermann (1930). The script does not reflect the many cases of sandhi assimilation at junctures.

PHONOLOGY

Consonants

Labio-dental /f, v/ are paralleled by bilabial /ɸ, ß/. m is syllabic. There is a retroflex /ɖ/, notated here with subscript dot. The dental series includes /ts, dz/. There are two labio-velars /kp/ and /gb/ with simultaneous closure. Other sounds: /p, b, w; t, d, s, z, l, r, n; ɲ, j; k, g, x, h, ŋ/.

Vowels

a, ɛ, e, i, ɔ, o, u; ə, ɪ

These are usually short. Long vowels are indicated by doubling. All vowels can be nasalized. There are many diphthongs.

Tones

There are three level pitches and two glides: high, mid, low, rising, and falling. Tone change is a concomitant of vowel assimilation: e.g. *á* + *à* → *â* (falling): e.g. *ká así* → *kâsí* 'touch with the hand'. Cf.

elision of initial *a-*: *ḍetí* 'cotton' + *agble* 'farm' > *ḍetígblè* 'cotton farm' (note change in tone);
-*e* + -*a* with transfer of tone: *fla ɸé atí* > *fla ɸáti* 'the king's sceptre' (ɸe is a relationship marker);
elision of 3rd p. sing. marker *e-* following the verb: *édè égbɔ* 'he went to him' becomes *édě gbɔ́*.

Tone in Ewe is phonemic: cf. *wò* 'you (sing.)', *wó* 'they'. Tonal transfer or sandhi is a very complicated matter, to which Westermann (1930) gives twelve pages of rules. Some examples: a high tone in the verb becomes a falling tone preceding a high or middle tone: *tsɔ́* 'to take' + *tú* 'gun': *éstsɔ̂ tú* 'he took the gun'. In compound nouns, a middle-tone syllable raises a following low-tone syllable to middle: *tsò* 'to kill' + *lã́* 'animal': *lã́tsósó* 'slaughter of an animal'.

In Westermann's notation, syllables unmarked for tone are understood to have the tone of the nearest preceding marked syllable; thus, *lã́tsósó* can be written as *lã́tsoso*.

MORPHOLOGY AND SYNTAX

Noun

There is no grammatical gender. Natural gender is distinguished lexically: *tɔ́* 'father', *nɔ* 'mother'; *fõ* 'elder brother', *dă* 'elder sister', or by a coded suffix on the common root: *sɔ́-* 'horse': *sɔ́tsu* 'stallion', *sɔ́nɔ̃* 'mare'; *koklô-* 'poultry': *koklôtsú* 'cock', *koklónɔ́* 'hen'. The third person plural pronominal form *wó* is used as a plural marker: e.g. *ame* 'person', pl. *amewó*; *xɔ* 'house', pl. *xɔ**wó***. This marker may be added to such postpositional items as adjectives and other parts of speech: e.g. *amewó yi* = *ame **wó**yì* 'the people went'; *lã vzɔ̃* 'wild animal', pl. *lã vzɔ̃**wo*** (note change of tone).

CASE

Positional. The possessive connective is *ɸé*: e.g. *fia ɸé xɔ* 'the chief's house'. Direct object follows verb and is followed by indirect object: e.g. *Éfia atí adelá* 'He showed the tree (*atí*) to the hunter (*adelá*).' The verb *ná* 'to give' functions in a dative/benefactive sense: *é.ɸlè sɔ́ nám* 'he bought (*é.ɸlè*) a horse (*sɔ́*) for-me (*ná.m*)' (*see* **Pronoun**, below).

Adjective

As attribute, adjective follows noun: e.g. *xɔ nyuí* 'good house'; *tó kɔ́kɔ siawó* 'these high mountains' (mountain – high – demonstrative + plural sign). Many adjectival meanings are rendered by verbs: e.g. *kɔ́* 'to be high'; *atí kɔ́kɔ* 'high tree'; *atí lá kɔ́* 'the tree is high'.

COMPARISON

One way of expressing comparison is by using *wú* 'to surpass': e.g. *Sɔ́ lolo **wú** tédzi* 'The horse is larger than the donkey.'

Pronoun

Absolute (subject or object):

	Singular	*Plural*
1	nye	míawo
2	wò	miawó
3	éyà, yé	wóawo

These are separated from the verb either by the pronoun *é* 'he, she, it', or by the article *lá* + verb + conjoint resumptive pronoun: e.g. *nyeé kpɔ́è* 'I (am the one who has) seen it' = 'I have seen it'; *nye* ***lá mekp***ɔ́è 'I have seen it'.

The conjoint pronoun forms are (basic forms): sing. 1 *me*, 2 *è*, 3 é; pl. 1 *míe*, 2 *mìe*, 3 *wó*.

The possessive forms are close to the absolute. They may precede (in which case they have a rising tone) or follow the noun: cf. *nyě xɔ* = *xɔ́ nye* 'my house'. Preceding verbal nouns they are objective: *é.kpɔ.kpɔ* 'the looking at him', i.e. 'his appearance'.

1st and 2nd p. singular possessive pronouns can be infixed in compound nouns: *nɔvíŋutsù* 'brother': *nɔví****nye****ŋutsù* 'my brother'.

DEMONSTRATIVE PRONOUN

si(*a*) 'this'; pl. *siawó*; *á*, *lá* 'the, this': e.g. *atí lá* = *atía* 'the tree'.

INTERROGATIVE PRONOUN

kâlka 'who, which?'; pl. *kawó*.

RELATIVE PRONOUN

sì, pl. *siwó*: e.g. *lã́kle sì míekpɔ etsɔ lá* 'the leopard which we saw yesterday'; *lã́kle siwó míekpɔ etsɔ lá* 'the leopards which we saw yesterday'.

Numerals

1–10: *ḍeká*, *eve*, *etɔ̃*, *ene*, *atzɔ̃́*, *adé*, *adré*, *enyí*, *enyíḍe*, *ewó*; 11 *wúìḍekɛ́*; 12 *wúìeve*; 20 *bláavè*; 21 *bláavè vɔ́ ḍekɛ́*; 30 *bláàtɔ̃*; 40 *bláanè*; 100 *aláfá ḍeká*.

Verb

Stems are invariable and are used transitively and intransitively. Tense and mood are generated externally. There is no passive. Examples from *yi* 'to go':

- aorist: sing. *meyi*, *èyì*, *éyì*; pl. *míeyì*, *mieyi*, *wóyì*;
- future: formed by prefixation of *á-*: e.g. *m.á.yì* 'I shall go', *m.á.wɔ̀.dɔ́* 'I shall (do) work'; *á.ɸò.m* 'he will strike me'.
- habitual: *-na* suffix, e.g. *meyina* 'I generally go';
- progressive: *le* 'to be' + sense-verb + *-ḿ* suffix, e.g. *mele yiyiḿ* 'I am going'; pret. *nɔ* (aorist of *le*) + sense-verb + *ḿ*, e.g. *menɔ yiyiḿ* 'I was in the habit of going'; *é.nɔ̀ yiyim* 'he was in the habit of going';

intentional: progressive + *gé* replacing *ḿ*, e.g. *mele yiyi gé* 'I'm about to go';
imperative: *yi!* 'go!', pl. *miyi*;
jussive: *náyì* 'you are to go';
prohibitive: *ga* infix between pronoun and verb, e.g. *mé**gà**yi!* 'do not go!';
verbal noun (formed by reduplication): *yiyi* 'act of going'.

VERB + PRONOMINAL OBJECT
E.g. with verb *ɸo* 'to strike':

éɸòm 'he strikes/struck me'	éɸò mí 'he strikes/struck us'
éɸò wo 'he strikes/struck you'	éɸò mi 'he strikes/struck you'
éɸòe 'he strikes/struck him'	éɸò wó 'he strikes/struck them'

NEGATION
The marker is *me/ma*. The *me* form is used with finite verbs: in the 1st p. sing. and the 3rd p. pl. as an infix: *nye.**mé**.yì.**o*** 'I don't/didn't go' (with *-o* final); in 2nd and 3rd sing. *me* precedes the verb: ***mé**.yi* < *me.è.yi*, 'you don't/didn't go'. In 1st and 2nd pl. *me* is often omitted.

The particle *ma* negates the verbal noun/adjective: *wɔwɔ* 'the (act of) doing' neg. ***ma**.wɔ.**ma**.wɔ*; *wɔ nú ame* 'to do something (*nú*) to someone (*ame*): negative verbal noun: *nu.**ma**.wɔ.ma.wɔ.e* 'the not doing/having done something'.

Postpositions

Ewe uses various nouns of place, e.g. *ŋgɔ* 'front', as postpositions in a locative (> temporal) sense: *élè xɔ ŋgɔ* 'he is in front of the house'. Similarly, *me* 'inside, in', *dzi* 'upper part, on', *nu* 'mouth, in, in front, according to', *tá* 'head, over, above'. These may appear as infixes in polysyllabic compounds: *gbé.**mè**.lã*, literally 'bush-in-animal', i.e. 'wild animal'.

Word formation

COMPOUNDS
Noun + article: e.g. *agble* 'farm', *agbleá* 'farmer', *agble.delá.nyényé* 'the being a farmer', where *nyényé* is the reduplicated verbal noun of *nyé* 'to be'; *ade* 'hunt', *adeá* 'hunter'. Other formants may be inserted, e.g. *de* 'to go to': *tɔ́ɸò* 'water', *tɔ́ɸòdeá* 'boatman'.

APPOSITION
E.g. with *tɔ́* 'owner', *agbletɔ́* 'farmer' ('owner of farm'); with *nɔ* 'female, subject to'; *dɔnɔ* 'invalid' (subject to sickness); noun + verb + noun, e.g. *atítsògbe* 'day for felling trees'; *dɔwuame* 'starvation' ('hunger-kill-man').

MULTIPLE COMPOUND
E.g. *ḍuamewòádzekpoe* 'bite-man-he-will-go-mad' = 'scorpion'.

Word order

SVO is normal. O may precede V for emphasis: *lãkle míewù* ‘a leopard (*lãkle*) we killed’.

Ta 1.

Le gọmedžedžea me Nyaa le, eye Nya la kple Mawu ele, eye Nya la eye nye Mawu.
2 Eyea ke kple Mawu le gọmedžedžea me.
3 Wowọ nuwo katã le eyea ńûti, eye wo mekplẽ nẹ di wọ nadeke de ke, ši wowọ na wò.
4 Eyea me agbèa le, eye agbèa eye nye amẹwo ŵe kẹkẹli.
5 Eye kẹkẹli la eye klẹ na le fifiti me, eye fifiti la, eye mekpee do wò.
6 Amade fa dšọ, ši dšo Mawu gbọ eńkọ enye Johane.
7 Eyea fẹ dase di ge, bena nẹ ye adi dase le kẹkẹli la ńũti, bena nẹ amẹwo katã nẹ woaχọ ase le eńûti.
8 Menye eyea enye kẹkẹli la wò, hafi efa dase di ge le kẹkẹli ńûti.

FAEROESE

INTRODUCTION

Originally inhabited by Celts, the Faeroe Islands were invaded in the early Middle Ages by Scandinavian settlers speaking a form of Old Norse. The development of Faeroese as a specifically divergent form of Scandinavian dates from the mid-sixteenth century, when Danish was imposed as the official language of the colony. It might be said that Faeroese is Old or Middle Norwegian as modulated by Danish. In 1947 Faeroese was given official status as the 'chief language' of the islands, which have autonomous status under the Danish crown. Faeroese is spoken by about 50,000 islanders. The language is divided geographically into two dialect clusters: (a) that spoken on the northern and central islands by about $\frac{3}{4}$ of the total population, and (b) the southern dialect of Suderø.

A standardized orthography was first provided by the Faeroese linguist and writer V.U. Hammershaimb in the middle of the nineteenth century. Up to that point, a fairly rich folk literature had been transmitted orally. The first newspaper appeared in 1890, the first novel in 1909. The twentieth century produced some outstanding names, such as Jens Djurhuus and Heðin Brú. On the other hand, two writers of international stature, who are in fact Faeroese, Jørgen-Frantz Jacobsen and William Heinesen, have chosen to write in Danish, which still enjoys widespread usage and considerable prestige in the Faeroes.

SCRIPT

Roman with additional symbols: *œ*, *ø*, *ð*.

PHONOLOGY

Consonants

stops: p, b, t, d, k, g
affricates: tʃ, dʃ
fricatives: f, v, s, ʃ, j, h
nasals: m, n
lateral and flap: l, r

Written *x* = /ks/.

Vowels

The written inventory, with phonetic values in brackets:

Short vowels: *a* (a); *á* (ɔ); *e* (ä); *i*/*y* (ɪ); *o* (ɔ); *ó* (œ); *u* (u); *ú* (ö > ü) (i); *æ* (a); *ø* (œ).

Long vowels (most of these tend to be diphthongized): *a* (äa); *á* (oa); *e* (eə); *i*/*y* (i); *í*/*ý* (ui); *o* (oə); *ó* (ou); *u* (ū); *ú* (iw); *æ* (äa); *ø* (œə).

In Faeroese, there is a considerable discrepancy between the etymologically purist orthography and the actual pronunciation. Some examples are given:

ð = /j/, /w/, or /ø/: e.g. *leiða* 'lead', /laija/; *maður* 'man', /mɛawər/; *suður* 'southerly', /suər/. ð is no longer pronounced as /ð/;
g + soft vowel = /dj/ = /dʃ/: e.g. *borgin* 'town', /bordʃin/; *genta* 'girl', /dʃɛnta/; *djór* 'animal', /dʃour/;
k = /tʃ/: e.g. *kirkja* 'church', /tʃirtʃa/; or /k/: e.g. *koma* 'come', /koəma/.
hv = /k°/: e.g. *hvaar* 'where', /k°ɛar/;
a before /n, nk/ → [ɛ]: e.g. *tangi* 'spit of land', /tɛndʃi/.
long *a* → [ɛa]: e.g. *dagur* 'day', /dɛawər/;
a = /oa/: e.g. *bátur* 'boat', /boatər/;
æ in long syllable → /ɛa/: e.g. *klæða* 'clothe', /klɛa/.

Stress is invariably on the first syllable.

MORPHOLOGY AND SYNTAX

Noun

There are strong and weak declensions; 3 genders, 2 numbers, 4 cases. In the strong declension, the genitive singular always ends in a consonant; in the weak declension, all four cases end in a vowel in the singular. For example, the strong declension of *úlvur* 'wolf': weak declension, *eyga* 'eye':

	Singular	*Plural*	*Singular*	*Plural*
nom.	úlvur	úlvar	eyga	eygu(r)
gen.	úlvs	úlva	eyga	eygna
dat.	úlvi	úlvum	eyga	eygum
acc.	úlv	úlvar	eyga	eygu(r)

There are many variants, depending on stem and phonetic composition. The umlaut classes: *bók* – *bøkur*, *sonur* – *synir*, *gata* – *gøtur* are found.

Article

The independent definite article is masc. *hin*, fem. *hin*, nt. *hitt*, with plural forms *hinir*, *hinar*, *hini*. These are fully declined. As in Icelandic, these are rarely used; mainly if an attributive adjective is present: e.g. *hin gamli maður* 'the old man'.

The definite article is usually added in truncated form to the noun: e.g. *úlvurin* 'the wolf'; *drottning.ar.innar* 'of the queens'.

Adjective

As attribute, adjective precedes noun and takes strong or weak declension: e.g. *sjúkur maður* 'sick man', *hin sjúki maður(in)* 'the sick man'. Cf.

hin stóri maður(in) 'the big man'
hin unga gentan 'the young girl'
hitt góða barni 'the good child'

or with demonstrative pronoun:

tann góði maður(in)
tann unga gentan
tað stóra húsið

Strong adjective: *sjúkur*, fem. *sjúk*, neuter *sjúkt*.

Writing in the 1930s Ernst Krenn could record such examples of strong concord as: e.g. *góðs manns barn* 'a good man's child', *góða manna børn* 'the children of good people'. The modern tendency here (as Krenn notes) is for the genitive to be replaced by the accusative or by a prepositional circumlocution.

COMPARATIVE

-*(a)ri*, often with umlaut: e.g. *stórur* 'big' – *størri*. Some bases are suppletive: e.g. *góður* 'good' – *betri*; *illur* 'bad' – *verri*. The comparative has a strong declension, but is not declined following the indefinite article: *ein vakrari maður, ein vakrari genta, eitt vakrari barn* 'a more handsome man, girl, child'.

Pronoun

The third person personal pronoun distinguishes gender: sing. 1 *eg*, 2 *tú*, 3 *hann*, *hon*, *tað*; pl. 1 *vit*, 2 *tit*, 3 *teir*, *tær*, *tey*. These are declined in four cases; the oblique base of the first person plural is *okk*-: *okkara*, *okkum*. A polite second person is *tygum*, plural *tykkum*.

POSSESSIVE PRONOUN

	Singular	*Plural*
1	mín/mín/mitt	vár/vár/várt
2	tín...	tykkara (indeclinable)
3	sín...	teirra

Cf. *á okkara døgum* 'in our days'.

DEMONSTRATIVE PRONOUN

Masc./fem. *tann*; nt. *tað*. Plural as third personal plural.

INTERROGATIVE PRONOUN

hvør, /k°œɐr/ 'who?' The neuter form is *hvørt*.

RELATIVE PRONOUN

sum (indeclinable): e.g. *tey gomlu kvœðini, sum eru dansivísur* 'the old *kvœði*, which are dance songs'.

Numerals

1–3 inclusive: *ein, tveir, tríggir*, are declined. 4–10: *fýra, fimm, seks, sjey, átta, níggju, tiggju*; 11 *ellivu*; 12 *tólv*; 20 *tjúgu*, 30 *tríati*; 40 *fýrati*; 100 *hundrað*.

Verb

The infinitive is marked by *at*: e.g. *at sova* 'to sleep', *at skriva* 'to write'. There are active, passive, and middle voices, the latter in *-st*; indicative, subjunctive, and imperative moods; eight tenses, including perfect, pluperfect, future perfect, and past conditional. The present and imperfect tenses are simple, all the others are composite.

There are strong and weak conjugations.

STRONG CONJUGATION

Examples of ablaut classes: infinitive – third person singular present – first person singular and plural imperfect – past participle:

renna 'to run' – rennur – rann/runnu – runnin
sita 'to sit' – situr – sat/sótu – sitin
standa 'to stand' – stendur – stóð/stóðu – staðin
njóta 'to enjoy' – nýtur – neyt/nutu – notin

Personal endings: present, e.g. from *renna*: sing. 1 *renni*, 2/3 *rennur*; pl. 1, 2, 3 *renna*.

Past imperfect: sing. 1 *rann*, 2 *ranst*, 3 *rann*; pl. 1, 2, 3 *runnu*.

WEAK CONJUGATION

E.g. *brenna* 'to burn', *telja* 'to count':

brenna – brennir – brendi/brendu – brendur
telja – telur – taldi/taldu – taldur

AUXILIARIES

hava, vilja, skula, munna, etc.: e.g. *eg havi runnið* 'I have run'; i.e. auxiliary + neuter past participle.

PASSIVE

E.g. *eg verði heilsaður = eg eri heilsaður* 'I am greeted'; *vit verði heilsaðir = vit eru heilsaðir* 'we are greeted'.

The middle voice is generally reciprocal: *vit heilsast* 'we greet each other'.

Prepositions

These take accusative, dative, or both; some take accusative + genitive. Note the presence of a periphrastic genitive, made with the preposition *á* + dative: e.g. *hondin á honum* 'his hand'.

There are a few postpositions, e.g. *millum* 'among': *teirra millum* 'among them'.

Word order

SVO; VSO if adverbial material initiates sentence.

Í fyrstuni var orðið, og orðið var hjá Guði, og orðið var Guð.

2 Hetta var í fyrstuni hjá Guði.

3 Allir lutir eru vorðnir til við tí, og uttan tað varð einki til av tí, sum til er vorðið.

4 Í tí var lív, og lívið var ljós menniskjunnar.

5 Og ljósið skínur í myrkrinum, og myrkrið tók ikki við tí.

6 Maður kom, sendur frá Guði, hann æt Jóhannes.

7 Hesin kom til vitnisburðar, til tess at hann skuldi vitna um ljósið, fyri at allir skuldu trúgva við honum.

8 Hann var ikki ljósið, men hann skuldi vitna um ljósið.

FIJIAN

INTRODUCTION

Fijian belongs to the Melanesian sub-group of Malayo-Polynesian. The separation of Fijian and related languages from the mainstream of Malayo-Polynesian seems to have taken place in the second millennium BC. There is an East/West dialect split, the standard literary language being based on the Bauan (Eastern) dialect. The official language of Fiji is English, but about 350,000 people speak Fijian, many as their second language. Local broadcasting is in Fijian, and there is a high degree of literacy in the language. Printing in Fijian (Biblical texts) dates from the 1830s.

SCRIPT

Roman, minus *h*, *x*, *z*. The pre-nasalized consonants are denoted as follows: /mb/ by *b*, /nd/ by *d*, /ng/ by *q*. /ð/ is notated as *c*, /ŋ/ as *g*, /nr/ as *dr*. *F*, *j*, *p* occur only in borrowed words.

PHONOLOGY

Consonants

stops: p, t, k; pre-nasalized voiced: ^{m}b, ^{n}d, ^{n}g; palatalized t′, d′ occur
fricatives: β, ð, s
nasals: m, n, ŋ
roll: r, ^{n}r
lateral: l
semi-vowels: w, j

Vowels

short and long: i, ɛ, a, ɔ, u

Final vowels → Ø (all Fijian words end in vowels). Vowel sequences tend to become diphthongs.

Stress

Long syllables attract stress, which in their absence tends towards penultimate. Stress is phonemic.

MORPHOLOGY

Typical Malayo-Polynesian division into bases and particles. Particles adhere in pre- or postposition to base, which is nominal or verbal depending on the valencies in the complex whose nucleus it forms.

Noun

No gender, but *see* **Class markers**. There are two articles: *o*/*ko* precedes proper nouns: e.g. *o Viti* 'Fiji'; the definite/indefinite article for all other nouns is *na*: e.g. *na waqa* 'a/the canoe'.

NUMBER

Common bases have a plural marker *vei* which also forms collectives: e.g. *na tiri* 'mangrove' – *na veitiri* 'mangrove swamp'; *na siga* 'day' – *na veisiga* 'days'.

Adjective

As qualifier, adjective follows noun: e.g. *vinaka* 'good': *draki vinaka* 'good weather'; *na waqa vinaka* 'the good canoe'.

Pronoun

The subject pronouns used with verbs are:

	Singular		*Dual*	*Trial*	*Plural*
1	(k)au.u	*excl.*	keirau	keitou	keimami
	–	*incl.*	(e)daru	(e)datou	(e)da
2	(k)o		(k)o drau	(k)o dou	(k)o nī
3	–		(e)rau	(e)ratou	(e)ra

The objective forms are very similar. Subjective forms precede the base; objective forms follow it.

POSSESSIVE PRONOUN

The possessive pronouns precede bases, and have singular, dual, trial, and plural forms. The first person excl. row is *noqu* – *neirau* – *neitou* – *neimami*. The second person base (sing.) is *nomu*, the third *nona*: e.g. *na nona vale* 'his house': *na nodratou vale* 'their (three people) house'.

These forms are used in the equivalent of the verb 'to have': e.g. *E dua na nona waqa* 'his canoe is one' = 'He has a canoe.'

CLASS MARKERS

The classes are: 1 neutral, 2 edible, 3 potable, 4 integral. The markers are: class 1 sing. *no*, dual, etc. *nei*; class 2 sing. *ke*/*qau*, dual, etc. *kei*; class 3 sing. *me*, dual, etc. *mei*.

In class 4 the class marker is suffixed to the base, which denotes a natural integration – the family, the body, a plant, etc. There are detailed rules for the proper use of terms referring to parts of these natural wholes: e.g. in kinship terms, relative status, age, degree of kinship must all be taken into account: *tama* 'father'; *tamaqu* 'my father'.

The markers are prefixed to the possessive pronominal base. Thus, *nona* in the third person refers to a neutral object – 'house': *na no**na** vale*; similarly *na **kena** uvi* 'his yam(s)', in edible class; *na **mena** wai* 'his water', in potable class; *na dalo **kei** Pita* 'Peter's taro' (edible class).

DEMONSTRATIVE PRONOUN

Three-term gradation related to person: *oqō* 'this' (near first person); *oqori* 'that' (near second person); *(k)oya* 'that' (near third person): e.g. *e na vale oqō* 'in this house (where I am)'; *e na vale oqori* 'in that house (where you are)'.

INTERROGATIVE PRONOUN

cei 'who?'; *cava* 'what?'

RELATIVE PRONOUN

ka (referring to subject); *kina/kaya* (referring to oblique case): e.g. *na waqa ka* . . . 'the canoe which . . . '; *na waqa eratou ā lako **kina*** 'the canoe in which they sailed . . . '.

Numerals

These are verbal bases: 1 *e dua na*; 2 *e rua na*; similarly, between *e* and *na*, the following are inserted for 3–10: *tolu*, *vā*, *lima*, *ono*, *vitu*, *walu*, *ciwa*, *tini*: e.g. *e dua na waqa* 'one canoe' (lit. 'the canoe is one'); *e na vale e rua oqō* 'in these two houses'. 20 *ruasagavulu*; 21 *ruasagavulu ka dua*; 30 *tolusagavulu*; 100 *dua na drau*.

Verb

Transitive and intransitive. Transitive verbs may be formed by adding -*Ca* to the base or by lengthening the final vowel: e.g. *gunu* 'to drink', *gunu**va*** 'to drink it'; *kila* 'know', *kil**ā*** 'to know it'. The intransitive form plus an object amounts to a stative verb: e.g. *eratou gunu yaqona* 'they are-kava-drinking' but *eratou gunu**va** **na** yaqona* 'they are drinking the kava'. -*a* → -*i* before a proper object: e.g. *eratou ā raici Viti* 'they saw Fiji'.

Tense markers precede base: *ā* for past, *na* for future: e.g. *era ā lako* 'they (pl.) went'; *era na lako* 'they (pl.) will go'.

NEGATIVE

sega is a general negative marker: e.g *e ā sega ni lako* 'he didn't go'; *au sega ni raica* 'I haven't seen it'; *e sega ni vinaka* 'it's not good'.

MODAL PARTICLES

E.g. durative *tiko*; potential *rawa*; reiterative *tale*; *E cakacaka tiko mai Suva* 'He's working in Suva.'

PASSIVE

-*a* → -*i*: e.g. *e vaka-yagatak**a*** 'he uses it', *e vaka-yagatak**i*** 'it is used'. Cf. *au* *nanuma na vanua* 'I remember the land', *sā nanumi na vanua* 'the land is remembered'.

A number of particles, e.g. *dui* 'all', *dē* 'possible', *vei* (reciprocal marker), precede the verbal base; others, e.g. *vata* 'together' (comitative marker), follow.

CAUSATIVE

The formant is *vaka*: e.g. *mate* 'die' – *vaka.mate.a* 'kill'. The circumfix *vaka... taka* forms transitives: e.g. *mārau* 'happiness' – *vaka.mārau.taka* 'amusing'. *Vaka-* also indicates possession of something: e.g. *vaka.vale* 'having a house'; *na vosa vakaviti* 'the Fijian language'.

Word order

VSO; SVO.

**O KOYA na Vosa sa bula
e nai vakatekivu, a rau
sa tiko kei na Kalou ko koya
na Vosa, a Kalou ko koya na
Vosa.
2 Sai koya oqo e rau sa tiko vata kei na Kalou mai nai
vakatekivu.
3 Sa cakava na ka kecega
ko koya: a sa sega e dua na
ka sa cakavi, me sega ni cakava ko koya.
4 Sa tu vua na bula; ia na
rarama ni tamata na bula.
5 Sa cila mai na rarama e
na butobuto; a sa sega ni
kunea na butobuto.
6 ¶ E dua na tamata sa ta-
la mai vua na Kalou, a yaca-
na ko Joni.
7 O koya oqo sa lako mai
me dautukutuku, me tukuni
koya na Rarama, me ra vaka-
bauta na tamata kecega e na
vukuna.
8 Ia ka sa sega na Rarama
dina ko koya, a sa talai mai
me tukuna na Rarama ko ya.**

FINNISH

INTRODUCTION

A member of the Balto-Finnic group of Finno-Ugric. Finnish is the official language of Finland (jointly with Swedish), and joint official language of the Karelia Republic. Finnish is spoken in Finland by around 5 million, with considerable *emigré* bilingual communities abroad, e.g. over half a million in North America.

The main dialectal split is into Western (South-Western, centred on Turku, and the Häme dialect, spoken by the *hämäläiset*) and Eastern (e.g. Savo dialect, spoken by the *savolaiset*). Differences between dialects are largely phonological: e.g. the /k, t, p/ stops can precede /r, l/ in Eastern forms: cf. Western *kaula* 'neck' – Eastern *kakla*; Western *eilen* 'yesterday' – Eastern *eklen*; Western *peura* 'wild reindeer' – Eastern *petra*. Also the labial final in third person singular present: Western *juo* 'he drinks' – Eastern *juop(i)*. The modern literary standard represents a successful compromise between the main dialect forms.

Finnish literature begins in 1544 with the *Rukouskirja Bibliasta* of Michael Agricola, followed in 1548 by his translation of the New Testament. Little of note followed until 1835 when Elias Lönnroth published the first version of his *Kalevala* material. The mythopoeic, ethnological, and linguistic riches revealed in *Kalevala* and its companion volume *Kanteletar* added more than one new dimension to Finnish self-awareness.

From the 1880s onwards, Finnish has been the vehicle for a rich literature in prose and verse, often fervently nationalistic but showing acute awareness of cultural crises on a European scale. Some notable names are Mika Waltari, Toivo Pekkanen, Pentti Haanpää, Paavo Haavikko, Väinö Linna, and Veijo Meri.

SCRIPT

Latin alphabet, minus *b, c, f, q, w, x, z*; plus *ä* (= /æ/), *ö* (= /œ/); *b, c,* and *f* are used in loanwords.

PHONOLOGY

Consonants

stops: p, t, d, k
fricatives: v, j, ş, h
nasals: m, n, ŋ

lateral and flap: l, r

CONSONANT GRADATION

This is a crucially important element in Finnish phonology and morphology, affecting all declension and conjugation patterns. A 'strong' consonant, or consonant cluster initiating an open syllable, is mutated into its 'weak' correlative, when the syllable is closed by the addition of a consonant. The phenomenon (which has many complexities) can be illustrated by comparing nouns in the nominative singular (open syllable) with their genitive forms (closed by addition of the genitive marker *-n*); or by comparing infinitives (strong grade) with the first person singular (weak):

Strong	*Weak*	*Example*
pp	p	loppu – lopun 'end'
tt	t	ottaa – otan 'to take'
kk	k	kukka – kukan 'flower'
mp	mm	enempi – enemmän 'more'
t	d	katu – kadun 'street'
p	v	apu – avun 'help'
k	Ø	lukea – luen 'read'

There are some important exceptions to this general rule: e.g. mutation does not take place before a long vowel (e.g. *katu* – illative *katuun*) or before the personal possessive affix (e.g. *puku* 'clothes' – *pukunsa* 'his clothes').

The process works in reverse also, i.e. strong grade is restored, for example, in the plural form of the adjective with weak grade in the singular: *rakas* 'dear' – pl. *rakkaat*.

Vowels

long and short: i, e, ɛ, a, o, œ, u, y

Length is phonemic. Long consonants and vowels are notated by gemination. There are sixteen diphthongs: three rising – /ie, uo, yœ/, the rest falling, ending in /i, u/ or /y/.

Not more than one consonant can figure as syllable-initial (this goes even for foreign words: e.g. Stockholm becomes Tukholma), except in recent borrowings, e.g. *standartti*, *spontaaninen*, *stratosfään*, and words can end only in a vowel or one of the letters /l, n, r, s, t/. Final vowels tend to be aspirated.

VOWEL HARMONY

Back vowels /a, o, u/ are followed by back; front /ɛ, œ, y/ by front; /i/ and /e/ are neutral. Thus, *kymmenen* 'ten'; ***omena*** 'apple'; ***talossa*** 'in the house'; ***meressä*** 'in the sea'.

Formative affixes vary in orthography and pronunciation according to vowel harmony: e.g. *tuntem**a**t**o**n* 'unknown'; *kärsim**ä**t**ö**n* 'impatient'.

MORPHOLOGY AND SYNTAX

Noun

No articles, no gender. The plural marker is *-t*, with an /-i-/ infix in the oblique cases (other than the accusative).

CASE

There are 15 cases; as illustration, the paradigm for a back-vowel noun, *talo* 'house':

	Singular	*Plural*
nominative	talo	talot
accusative	talo	talot
genitive	talon	talojen
essive	talona	taloina
translative	taloksi	taloiksi
partitive	taloa	taloja
inessive	talossa	taloissa
elative	talosta	taloista
illative	taloon	taloihin
adessive	talolla	taloilla
ablative	talolta	taloilta
allative	talolle	taloille
abessive	talotta	taloitta
comitative	–	(taloinensa)
instrumental	(talon)	taloin

Most of the cases are self-explanatory. Among the uses of the partitive are:

(a) to express indefinite quantity: e.g. *pieniä ja isoja puita* 'small and large trees';
(b) after a negative: e.g. *täällä ei ole ihmisiä* 'there's nobody here'; *en lue kirjaa* 'I don't read a/the book';
(c) after numerals: e.g. *kaksi kirjaa* 'two books';
(d) 'some': e.g. *lasi vettä* 'a glass of water'.

The adessive in *-lla/-lle* is used to express the verb 'to have', which is missing in Finnish: e.g. *minulla/meillä on/ei ole ystäviä* 'I/we have (no) friends'.

Adjective

As attribute, adjective precedes noun, and agrees with it in number and case: e.g. *pieni poika* 'small boy'; *pienet pojat* 'small boys'; *suuren kaupungin/suurten kaupunkien* (*ulkopuolella*) '(outside) the large town/s'.

COMPARATIVE

-mpi added to genitive minus *-n*: e.g. *Minä olen vanhempi kuin sinä* 'I am older than you' (*kuin* 'than').

Pronoun

Personal subject (nominative) forms: sing. 1 *minä*, 2 *sinä*, 3 *hän*; pl. 1 *me*, 2 *te*, 3 *he*. These are declined in eleven cases; e.g. the accusative forms are: *minut*, *sinut*, *hänet*; *meidät*, *teidät*, *heidät*.

POSSESSIVE AFFIXES

Sing. 1 *-ni*, 2 *-si*, 3 *-nsa/nsä*; pl. 1 *-emme*, 2 *-nne*, 3 as singular. These are added after case endings: e.g. *talossani* 'in my house'.

DEMONSTRATIVE PRONOUN/ADJECTIVES

Two-degree distinction: *tämä* 'this'; *tuo* 'that', with plural forms *nämä*, *nuo*. *Se*, pl. *ne* is neutral. All forms are declined in 12 cases.

INTERROGATIVE PRONOUN

kuka 'who?'; *mikä* 'what?' Declined in 12 cases, the plural forms being *kutka*, *mitkä*. For all cases, the base for *kuka* is *ken-*.

RELATIVE PRONOUN

joka, pl. *jotka*, declined in 12 cases. Examples: *Tunnen kaikki, jotka asuvat tässä talossa* 'I know all those who live in this house'; *Han on mies, jonka sanaan voi luottaa* 'He is a man whose word can be relied on.'

Numerals

1–10: *yksi*, *kaksi*, *kolme/li*, *neljä*, *viisi*, *kuusi*, *seitsemän*, *kahdeksan*, *yhdeksän*, *kymmenen*; 11 *yksitoista*; 12 *kaksitoista*; 20 *kaksikymmentä*; 21 *kaksikymmentäyksi*; 30 *kolmekymmentä*; 100 *sata*.

Verb

The Finnish verb has active and passive voices and four moods: indicative, imperative, conditional, and potential. Tenses are simple (present, imperfect) or compound (e.g. perfect). There is no future tense. The language has an extensive apparatus of inflected participial and gerundial forms, including four infinitives. Compound tenses are made with the auxiliary *olla*, whose present tense is sing. *olen*, *olet*, *on*; pl. *olemme*, *olette*, *ovat*; the past tense is sing. *olin*, *olit*, *oli*; pl. *olimme*, *olitte*, *olivat*.

There is only one conjugation for all Finnish verbs; anomalies are phonological. The positive version is parallelled by a negative one. The negative marker is conjugated for person and number: sing. *en*, *et*, *ei*; pl. *emme*, *ette*, *eivät*: thus, *sanon* 'I say'; *en sano* 'I do not say'; *sanoo* 'he says'; *ei sano* 'he does not say', i.e. the sense-verb remains uninflected in the present. For past tense, see below.

Specimen conjugation of *sanoa* 'to say':

present tense: sing. *sanon*, *sanot*, *sanoo*; pl. *sanomme*, *sanotte*, *sanovat*; negative, *en sano*, etc.;
past imperfect: e.g. sing. *sanoin*, *sanoit*, *sanoi*; here, the negative version is made with the past participle which is marked for number: e.g. *en sanonut*, *et sanonut*, *emme sanon**eet***, *ette sanon**eet***;
perfect: e.g. *olen sanonut*, negative *en **ole** sanonut*, *emme **ole** sanon**eet***;

Conditional and potential tenses are constructed on the same principles: the former with an *-is-* infix, e.g. *sano**is**in*, *sano**is**it*; the latter with an *-e* ending, e.g. *sanonen*, *sanonet*, and the auxiliary *lienee* in the past, e.g. *lienen sanonut*.

Imperative: 2nd sing. *sano*; 2nd pl. *sano**kaa***; in the negative, the auxiliary is *älä/älkää*: *älä sano*, *älkää sano**ko***.

All parts of the Finnish verb can be constructed from three base forms – the infinitive, the first person singular present, and the third person singular past: e.g. *sanoa* – *sanon* – *sanoi*. In this example, the *-n* is stable: a mutating example is *tehdä* – *teen* – *teki* 'to do'.

PASSIVE VOICE

The passive stem is made from the active by the addition of *-ta/-tä*, *-tta/-ttä*: e.g. *sanoa* 'to say', *sano**tta*** 'to be said'. The passive voice is impersonal: *sanotaan* 'it is being said' → 'people say...'; cf. *Yöllä nukutaan*, lit. 'at-night it-is-being-slept' = 'People sleep at night'; *ei lauleta* 'there is no singing'; *Täällä eletään hauskasti* lit. 'here it-is-being-lived well' = 'Here one lives well'; *Antakaat, niin teille annetaan* 'Give and it shall be given unto you' (Luke 6.38).

PARTICIPLES

(a) Present active in *-va/vä*; provides one way of making relative clauses: e.g. *Näen hänen tule**van*** 'I see him coming'; *Luulen hänen tulevan* 'I think he is coming'; *suomea puhu**va** ulkomaalainen* 'a foreigner who speaks Finnish'.
(b) Present passive: passive stem + *-va/-vä*: e.g. *Kuulen näin sanottavan*... 'I hear it's being said...'; *lue**ttava** kirja* 'a book that has to be read'; *minun on teh**tävä***... 'I have to do' (where *minun* is the genitive case of *minä*).
(c) Past active: *-nut/-nyt/-neet*; used for example in formation of compound tenses, see above.
(d) Past passive: formed from passive stem by changing *-a-* to *-u-*, *-ä-* to *-y-*. The partitive singular of this participle indicates anterior action in the past: e.g. *Syö**tyä** lähde**ttiin***, lit. 'there-having-been-something-of-an-eating it-was-gone' = 'After eating, I/you/he (etc.) went away.'

The following examples show how inflected impersonal forms are used to express modality, purpose, etc.: *mitä he ovat teke**mässä*** 'What are they doing?'; *Menin Amerikkaan opiskele**maan*** 'I went to America to study'; *Minulla ei ole mitään teke**mistä*** 'I've nothing to do'; *teke**mällä*** 'by working';

*teke**mättä*** 'without working'. Motivation for the endings will be found by reference to the declension table above.

Prepositions and postpositions

Finnish has a few prepositions: e.g.

ilman 'without' with partitive, e.g. *ilman aihetta* 'without cause', *ilman rahaa* 'without money';
paitsi 'besides, except' with partitive, e.g. *Paitsi häntä en nähnyt ketään* 'Apart from him, I saw no one.'

Postpositions usually follow the genitive case:

jälkeen 'after', e.g. *juosta jonkun jälkeen* 'to run behind someone';
kanssa 'with', e.g. *lapsen kanssa* 'with the child';
aikana 'during', e.g. *kahden viikon aikana* 'during two weeks';
edessä 'in front of', e.g. *ikkunan edessä* 'in front of the window'.

Word formation

By formant affix: e.g. nouns from verbs:

-mo/-mö 'place where': *leipomo* 'bakery', *panimo* 'brewery';
-ja/-jä indicates agent: *lukea* 'to read', *lukija* 'reader';
-ri indicates agent: *juoda* 'to drink', *juomari* 'drinker'.

Nouns from nouns: e.g.

-sto/-stö: collective affix: *kirja* 'book', *kirjasto* 'library';
-nen is a diminutive: *kukkanen* 'little flower';
-tar/-tär mythopoeic female formant: *luonnotar* 'goddess of nature'; *onnetar* 'goddess of fortune'.

In a privative sense either the postposition -(*ma*)*ton* or the preposition *epä-*: *ajattelematon* 'thoughtless'; *epäluonnollinen* 'unnatural'.

-(*t*)*taa*/(*t*)*tää* makes verbs from any part of speech: *paimentaa* 'to tend, herd' (*paimen* 'flock, herd'); *ylittää* 'to exceed' (*yli* 'over, above').

Word order

SVO is normal but other sequences are possible; e.g. VS may follow adverbial material beginning sentence.

1 Alussa oli Sana, ja Sana oli Jumalan luona.
Sana oli Jumala, [2]ja hän oli alussa Jumalan
luona. [3]Kaikki on luotu hänen kauttaan, eikä mitään ole luotu ilman häntä. [4]Hänessä oli elämä,
ja elämä oli ihmisten valo. [5]Valo loistaa pimey-
dessä, mutta pimeys ei ole sitä koskaan käsittänyt.
[6]Jumala lähetti Johannes-nimisen miehen [7]todis-
tamaan valosta, että kaikki kuulisivat häntä ja us-
koisivat. [8]Hän ei ollut itse valo, hän vain todisti
valosta.

FRAFRA

See **Gurenne**.

FRENCH

INTRODUCTION

French belongs to the Italic branch of Indo-European. The official language of France is spoken by over 50 million in the Republic itself, by a further 4 million Walloons in Southern Belgium, and by about 6 million in Switzerland, where it is one of the four official languages. Further afield, about 6 million French speakers live in Quebec, where they form something like 80 per cent of the population, while the Francophone element in New England numbers about 1 million. For most of the 5 million inhabitants of Haiti the everyday language is Creole (*see* **Pidgins and Creoles**), but theoretically French is the official language of the island. Finally, there are the sixteen Francophone states running across Central Africa, in all of which French provides an official administrative and commercial medium *vis-à-vis* numerous indigenous colloquials. The total number of French speakers, including those who use it regularly as a second language, is in excess of 200 million.

Dialects

In France itself there is a broad north/south division between *langue d'oïl* (langue d'œil) and *langue d'oc*, or *occitane*; in some ways, the latter is closer to Catalan than it is to the northern dialects. Gascon in the south-west of the country is a markedly divergent Occitan outlier. The sub-dialect of the Isle-de-France, known as *francien*, is the basis for the modern literary standard.

It is not too much to say that since the eleventh century French literature has provided models and set standards for the western world: an all-pervasive influence which spread in the nineteenth and twentieth centuries beyond the confines of Europe to Africa and the Far East. The history of French literature falls readily into the following six periods:

1. Eleventh to thirteenth centuries: the *chansons de geste*, including the *Chanson de Roland*; the *romans* (Arthurian cycle, *Roman de la Rose*).
2. Sixteenth century: Rabelais and Montaigne.
3. Seventeenth century: Malherbe, Descartes, Pascal, Boileau; Corneille, Molière, Racine.
4. Eighteenth century: Montesquieu; the Enlightenment and L'Encyclopédie; Voltaire, Rousseau.
5. Nineteenth century: Chateaubriand; de Vigny, Lamartine; Baudelaire, Mallarmé, George Sand, Victor Hugo, Alexandre Dumas, Gustave Flaubert, Emile Zola.

6. Twentieth century.

SCRIPT

Latin alphabet, with three accents, circumflex, acute, and grave, and cedilla.

In the Old French period, many lexemes were, at least in writing, closer to their Latin originals than they are in Modern French, and the orthography was correspondingly more rational, with a closer correlation between sound and symbol: cf. OF *vedeir* 'see' > MF *voir*.

The period from the fourteenth to the sixteenth century brought accelerated phonetic change in which monosyllabism was a key feature, along with a consciously archaizing and sometimes misguided attempt to restore Latin orthography: e.g.

OF doit	>	MF doi**g**t	(Latin di**g**itum)
OF pie	>	MF pie**d**	(Latin pe**d**em)

The result is that the overall correspondence between pronunciation and notation in Modern French is weak; for example, /ɛ/ is notated in half a dozen different ways, and the proportion of mute letters is high. In this respect, French joins Portuguese in sharp contrast to Italian and Spanish.

In the nineteenth and twentieth centuries several attempts were made at achieving a limited rationalization of the orthography: e.g. the Beslais commissions in 1952 and 1965 which proposed *inter alia* a standardized plural marker in *-s* (i.e. the abolition of the *-x* marker) and the reduction of superfluous geminates. No action has been taken on these points.

PHONOLOGY

Consonants

stops: p, b, t, d, k, g
fricatives: f, v, s, z, ʃ, ʒ, ʁ
nasals: m, n, ɲ
lateral: l/l̥
semi-vowels: j, w

Vowels

(a) Oral: i, y, e, ø, œ, ɛ, a, ə, ɔ, o, u + many diphthongs/triphthongs involving /j/, /w/, and /ɥ/.
(b) Nasal: ɛ̃, ɔ̃, ã, œ̃.

Some important features in the development of French phonology since the Old French period:

1. Loss of affricates and of /h/.
2. Strong tendency towards monosyllabism, involving 3 (below).

3. In Latin forms of $C_1V_1C_2(C_3)V_2C_4$ type, early loss of C_4 followed by loss in spoken French of V_2, thus generating a new final C_2/C_3.

By the rules of French prosody, final syllables which are mute in spoken French are given their full value in verse, e.g. if followed by a consonantal initial.

LIAISON

In word sequences whose components are closely linked by sense, e.g. article + noun, adjective + noun, verb + personal pronoun, etc., there is a follow-through between a final consonant (normally mute) and an initial vowel; in these circumstances, a voiceless fricative is voiced:

nous allons à Paris = /nuzalɔ̃**z**apari/ 'we are going to Paris'
ils ont appris = /i(l)**z**ɔ̃**t**apri/ 'they have learned'

Stress

Stress tends to fall on the final syllable in citation form; in connected speech, on the focused item.

MORPHOLOGY AND SYNTAX

French has two genders – masculine and feminine – and two numbers.

Noun

Certain nominal endings are coded for gender, e.g. the following are always feminine: *-sion/-tion/-xion*; *-aison*, *-ance*; and most nouns in *-ment* are masculine. Essentially, however, gender in French is unpredictable.

A distinction between nominative (direct) and oblique case persisted throughout the Old French period, and most nouns in Modern French are derived from the oblique forms:

Latin	*Old French*	*Modern French*
noctem	> noit	> nuit
hominen	> hom	> homme
gentem	> gent	> gens

The plural marker is *-s*; a few nouns ending in *-eu/eau/ou* take *-x*: e.g. *le feu* 'fire' – *les feux*.

Modern French has lost all trace of declension; all syntactic relationship are expressed by means of prepositions, e.g. *de*, *à*, *pour*, etc.

Article

French has two articles. Both the definite and the indefinite article are marked for gender in the singular, and for number:

	Masculine	*Feminine*	*Plural*
definite	le	la	les (before vowel, *le/la→l'*)
indefinite	un	une	des 'some'

The preposition *de* coalesces with the definite article to produce the partitive articles: *de + le → du*; *de + les → des*; (*de + la* gives *de la*): thus, *du pain* '(some) bread'; *des livres* '(some) books'. But these forms are reduced to *de* if an adjective precedes the noun: e.g. *des mirois* 'mirrors': ***de** grands miroirs* 'big mirrors'; *vers de nouveaux rivages* (Lamartine) 'towards new shores'.

The indefinite and partitive articles have a single negative form, *de*: e.g. ***Il** y a du pain* 'There is bread'; ***Il** n'y a pas **de** pain* 'There is no bread'.

Coalescence of the definite article with the preposition *de* was illustrated above. In the same way, *a + le → au, a + les → aux*. Unlike Italian, French does not permit coalescence of *de/a* with the feminine article (cf. It. *della, alla*).

Adjective

As attribute, the adjective usually follows its noun, but a few very common adjectives always precede: e.g. *bon* 'good', *mauvais* 'bad', *grand* 'big', *petit* 'small', etc. In either position, the adjective agrees with the noun in gender and number. Often, the siting of an adjective is a matter of style: cf.

un emploi déréglé et passionnel du stupéfiant image (Aragon)
'a wild and passionate use of the stupefying image'

Feminine forms normally add *-e*: e.g. *lourd – lourde* 'heavy'. On the phonological plane, this addition very often involves activation of a mute consonant:

Masculine	*Feminine*
grand /grã/ 'big'	grande /grã**d**/
blanc /blã/ 'white'	blanche /blã**š**/
bon /bõ/ 'good'	bonne /b**ɔn**/

COMPARATIVE

Made with *plus* 'more': e.g. *belle* 'beautiful (fem.)' – *plus belle.* Irregular suppletive forms are: *bon* 'good' – *meilleur*; *mauvais* 'bad' – *pire*.

Pronoun

(a) Conjunctive: first and second person have nominative and oblique forms; third person has nominative + two oblique forms, direct and indirect, with gender distinguished in nominative forms.

		Singular	Plural
1		je – me	nous – nous
2		tu – te	vous – vous
3	masc.	il – le – lui	ils – les – leur
	fem.	elle – la – lui	elles – les – leur

The second person plural, *vous* is used as a polite form of address for singular.

The sequential order of the conjunctive pronouns is fixed: *me, te, nous, vous* (also the reflexive *se*) precede *le, la, les*, which, in turn, precede *lui, leur*. Following all of these come the third person oblique forms: *y* (dat.) and *en* (gen.), which are used primarily with non-human referents: e.g. ***J'y*** *vais* 'I'm going there'; *Je n'**en** ai jamais entendu* 'I've never heard of it.'

Pronominal order changes in the imperative mood: cf. *je le/les lui/leur ai donné* 'I gave it/them to him/her/them'; but *donne-le-moi* 'give it to me'. *Moi* in the last example is the first person singular disjunctive oblique.

(b) The forms for the remaining persons are: *toi, lui/elle*; pl. *nous, vous, eux/elles.* These are used mainly with prepositions and for emphasis: e.g. *pour moi* 'for me'; *à toi* 'to you'; *avec eux* 'with them (masc.)'.

POSSESSIVE ADJECTIVES

The singular forms show the gender of the possessed object in all three persons: *mon – ma – mes*, etc.: *mon frère* 'my brother' – *ma sœur* 'my sister'; pl. common: *mes frères.* The plural forms, *notre, votre, leur*, are not marked for gender: e.g. *leur frère/sœur*; but show number of the possessed object: *nos, vos, leurs.*

DEMONSTRATIVE ADJECTIVE

ce/cet (masc.) – *cette* (fem.) – *ces* (pl.) 'this/that'.

DEMONSTRATIVE PRONOUN

celui-ci/celle-ci 'this one', *celui-là/celle-là* 'that one'; pl. *ceux-ci/là*; *celles-ci/là*. That is, the distal member is expressed by replacing *ci* of the proximate by *là*.

INTERROGATIVE PRONOUN

qui 'who?'; *quoi* 'what?'; *qu'est-ce qui/que.*

RELATIVE PRONOUN

qui/que; *ce qui/ce que*; with oblique forms, e.g. *dont* (gen.): *un homme qui sait le français* 'a man who knows French'; *Montrez-moi les livres que vous avez achetés* 'Show me the books you have bought'; *C'est un homme que je ne connais guère* 'He's a man I scarcely know'; *une classe dont l'utilité social a disparu* 'a class whose social usefulness has vanished'.

Numerals

1–10: *un/une, deux, trois, quatre, cinq, six, sept, huit, neuf, dix*; 11 *onze*; 12

douze; 13 *treize*; 14 *quatorze*; 15 *quinze*; 16 *seize*; 17–19, *dix* + unit; 20 *vingt*; 21 *vingt et un*; 22 *vingt-deux*; 30 *trente*; 40 *quarante*; 100 *cent*.

Verb

There are three main conjugations, with infinitive forms ending in *-er*, *-ir*, and *-re*. *-ir* verbs are further sub-divided into (a) verbs like *finir* 'to finish', which take the infix *-iss-* in the plural forms of the indicative and subjunctive present and imperfect, and in the imperative; and (b) those like *ouvrir* 'to open', which do not.

There are indicative, imperative, and subjunctive moods. A passive voice is formed analytically by means of the auxiliary verb *être* 'to be' plus the past participle of the sense-verb: e.g. (*ses comédies*) *n'ont pas été écrites pour la scène* '(his comedies) were not written for the stage'.

Compound tenses are made with the auxiliary *avoir* 'to have', except for verbs of motion and reflexive verbs, which use *être* 'to be': e.g. *j'ai donné* 'I have given'; *je suis allé* 'I have gone/I went'; *Il s'est couché de bonne heure* 'He went to bed early.' Both *avoir* and *être* are highly irregular.

Specimen paradigms: *donner* 'to give' and *finir* 'to finish'; forms in regular use in modern literary and spoken French:

Present indicative:

singular	1	je donne	je finis
	2	tu donnes	tu finis
	3	il/elle donne	il finit
plural	1	nous donnons	nous fin**iss**ons
	2	vous donnez	vous fin**iss**ez
	3	ils/elles donnent	ils fin**iss**ent

Imperfect: *je donn-ais, -ais, -ait; -ions, -iez, -aient; je finiss-ais,* etc.

Future: infinitive + the following endings: sing. *-ai, -as, -a*; pl. *-ons, -ez, -ont*: e.g. *je donnerai, il finira*.

Conditional: infinitive + imperfect endings: e.g. *je donner.ais, nous finir.ions*, etc.

Present subjunctive: sing. and 3rd p. pl. as present indicative (+ *-iss-* if present in indicative plural), 1st and 2nd pl. as imperfect: e.g. *que je donne*; *qu'il finisse*; *que nous donnions*; *qu'ils finissent*.

Imperative: *donne – donnons – donnez*; *finis – finissons – finissez*.

PARTICIPLES

Present: *donnant*, *finissant*; past: *donné*, *fini*. The past participle of verbs in *-re* is made with *-u*: e.g. *vendu* 'sold', *rompu* 'broken'.

These are regular verbs; there are, of course, many irregular verbs, some of which can be grouped, e.g. verbs in *-eler*, in *-yer*, in *-cer/-ger*.

A striking feature of these paradigms (and of French conjugation in general) is the homophonic nature of first, second, and third singular, usually shared by third plural as well. Thus, *donnais*, *donnais*, *donnait*, *donnaient*, are all pronounced as /dɔnɛ/; *donne*, *donnes*, *donne*, *donnent* as /dɔn/. It follows from this that the personal conjunctive pronouns have to be used to identify subject, a role in which they are often supported by use of the disjunctive series as well: e.g. *Moi, je veux vivre à la campagne* '(Me,) I want to live in the country.'

The subject pronoun cannot be omitted, even where, as in first person plural, the verb form itself provides sufficient identification: e.g. ***nous*** *avons mangé* 'we have eaten' (contrast It. *abbiamo mangiato*, and Sp. *hemos comido*).

The past historic tense (or, simple past) is found in formal literary style, though no longer in spoken or informal written style; e.g. of *donner*: sing. *je donnai, tu donnas, il donna*; pl. *nous donâmes, vous donâtes, ils donnèrent*.

The present subjunctive is used in subordinate clauses, following main verbs expressing emotion, doubt, opinion, prohibition, fear, etc.; also after certain subordinating conjunctions: *afin que* 'in order that', *quoique* 'although', *avant que* 'before', etc.: e.g. *Je crains qu'il (ne)* ***soit*** *mort* 'I'm afraid he may be dead'; *quoiqu'il* ***soit*** *pauvre*... 'although he is poor...'; *J'approuve qu'il le* ***fasse*** *immédiatement* 'I agree he should do it at once.' The imperfect subjunctive is virtually obsolete.

NEGATION

The standard negator is *ne...pas*: e.g. *je ne sais pas* 'I do not know'. There is an increasing tendency, especially in spoken French, to drop the pre-verbal *ne*: e.g. *Je suis pas malade* (Sartre) 'I'm not ill'; *C'est pas ça qui manque* (Sartre) 'That's not what we are short of.' In older literary style, *pas* was often omitted: e.g. *je ne sais comment cela se fait* (Maurois) 'I don't know how one does that.'

Prepositions

Apart from their function as spatial and temporal indicators – *dans le jardin* 'in the garden', *sur la table* 'on the table', *après moi* 'after me', *à la campagne* 'in the country', etc. – certain prepositions, notably *à* and *de*, are syntactically bound to specific verbal constructions:

commander ***à*** *défendre* ***à*** *quelqu'un* ***de*** *faire quelque chose* 'order/forbid someone to do something';
enseigner quelqu'un ***à*** *faire quelque chose* 'teach someone to do something'.

Word order

SVO is basic. Simple or complex inversion occurs in certain syntactic situations.

1 Avant que Dieu crée le monde, la Parole existait déjà;
la Parole était avec Dieu, et la Parole était Dieu. 2 La
Parole était donc avec Dieu au commencement. 3 Dieu a fait
toutes choses par elle; rien de ce qui existe n'a été fait sans
elle. 4 En elle était la vie, et cette vie donnait la lumière aux
hommes. 5 La lumière brille dans l'obscurité, et l'obscurité ne
l'a pas reçue.

6 Dieu envoya son messager, un homme appelé Jean. 7 Il
vint comme témoin, pour parler de la lumière. Il vint pour
que tous croient grâce à ce qu'il disait. 8 Il n'était pas lui-
même la lumière, il était le témoin qui vient pour parler
de la lumière.

FULANI (Fulbe)

INTRODUCTION

This language (also known as Fulfulde) belongs to the West Atlantic branch of the Benue-Congo family. The total number of Fulani speakers is estimated at *c.* 15 million, the great majority of whom live in northern and eastern Nigeria. Others are scattered over a dozen West African states, from Chad to the seaboard.

Under the Fulani emirate of Adamawa (1806–1901) literature was mainly in Arabic. From the mid-eighteenth century onwards, a main centre of *ajami* Fulani poetry was in what is now Guinea.

PHONOLOGY

Consonants

stops: p, b, ḅ, t, d, ḍ, k, g, q, ʔ
affricates: tʃ, dʒ, dz
nasals: m, n
fricatives: f, s, h
lateral and flap: l, r
semi-vowels: j, w
unvoiced /j̥/ is also present

Initial and medial /b, d, g, dʒ, j/ are frequently nasalized; notated by prefixed *m*/*n*. Note tendency to transfer nasalization to preceding long vowel: CV̄ + nasalization → CV̄̃. *ḅ* and *ḍ* can also be written as ɓ and ɗ.

PAIRED CONSONANTS

This a very striking feature of Fulani structure. The paired sets are:

b	w	dʒ	j
p	f	tʃ	s
d	r	g	w
		k	h

That is, stops are paired with their relative fricatives. *See* **Noun**, below.

Vowels

short: a, ə, ɛ, ɪ, ɔ, u
long: a, e, i, o, u

There are seven glide diphthongs onto /j, w/.

Stress

Stress tends to long vowels.

MORPHOLOGY AND SYNTAX

Noun

No article or gender, no case system: case by position. The fundamental dichotomy in the language is human/non-human.

PLURAL

Two classes of noun are distinguished, personal and non-personal. The plural of personal nouns is formed by changing the initials as follows: stop (affricate) to fricative:

b	→ w/g	j/dʒ	→ y
ch/tʃ/	→ s	k	→ h
d	→ r	p	→ f
g	→ w/y		

and adding *-ḇe* or *'en*: e.g. ***gorko*** 'male person', pl. ***worḇe***; ***konōwo*** 'warrior'; pl. ***honōḇe***; ***demōwo*** 'farmer', pl. ***remoḇe***. These changes are reversed in the plural formation of non-personal nouns: fricative to stop (affricate):

w	→ b/g	f	→ p
h	→ k	y	→ j/g
s	→ ch/tʃ/	r	→ d

Non-personal endings vary very widely: cf. *jōḓirgal* 'stool', pl. *jōḓirḓe*; ***hōre*** 'head', pl. ***kō'e***; *sūdu* 'house, hut', pl. ***chūḓi***; *ngēlōba* 'camel', pl. *gēlōḓi*. Unvoiced *ḇ, ḓ, y̥*, the nasalized consonants, and the initials of loanwords do not change in either class.

Genitive relationship is indicated by construct: *puchu lāmiḓo* 'the king's horse'; *puchu bāba māko* 'his father's horse'.

Dative precedes accusative noun, follows accusative pronoun.

Adjective

Verbal forms supply predicative adjectival sense: an attributive form is then supplied by the neutral participle, normally in *-ḓum*, often in *-dʒum* (spelled *-jum*): e.g. *wōḓi* 'it is good', ***bōḓḓum*** 'good'; *woji* 'it is red', ***bodējum*** /bodēdʒum/ 'red'.

The *-jum* class of noun has a personal singular form in *-jo*, with plural in *-'en* or *-ḇe*: e.g. *danējo* 'white man'; plural ***ranēḇe***.

The *-jum* affix can be added to any word to form an adjectival derivative: e.g. *hande* 'today'; *handējum* 'today's', 'actual'.

A nasal initial in the noun is resumed in the adjective: cf. *mbōdi mboḍēri* 'a red snake', pl. *boḍḍe boḍēje*; *yēso woḍēwo* 'a red face', pl. *gese boḍēje.*

COMPARATIVE

Made with *ḅura* 'to excel': e.g. *Puchu ḅuri nagge* 'A horse is better than a cow'; *Leggal ḅuri towugo dou sūdu* 'The tree is taller than the house' (*dou* 'over').

Pronoun

PERSONAL INDEPENDENT PRONOUN

Sing. 1 *min*, 2 *an*, 3 *kanko*; pl. incl. *enen*, excl. *minin*, 2 *onon*, 3 *kamḅe.* These are not used with verbs. Instead, the conjunctive forms are used:

	Singular			*Plural*	
	Nominative	*Accusative*		*Nominative*	*Accusative*
1	mi	yam	*inc.*	en	en
			excl.	min	min
2	a	ma		on	on
3	o	mo		ḅe	ḅe

POSSESSIVE FORMS

E.g. sing. 1 *am*, 2 *ma/māḍa*, 3 *māko*. These follow the noun: e.g. *puchu māko* 'his horse'; cf. *oyi' i mo* 'he saw him'; *o dilli bē māko* 'he went with him'.

DEMONSTRATIVE PRONOUN

o/ḍo 'this', pl. *ḅe*; *on/ḍon* 'that', pl. *ḅen*; *to/oya* 'that (further away)', pl. *ḅeya.*

INTERROGATIVE PRONOUN

moi 'who?', pl. *ḅeye*; *ḍuma* 'what?'

RELATIVE PRONOUN

mo, pl. *ḅe*: e.g. *tigōwo* ***mo*** *a yi'i kengya* 'the merchant whom you saw yesterday'.

Numerals

1–5: *gōtel/go'o, ḍiḍi, tati, nai, jow*; 6–9 are based on 5: *jowēgo, jowēḍiḍi, jowētati, jowēnai.* 10 *sappo*; 11 *sappo e go'o*; 20 *nōgas*; 30 *chappanḍe tati*; 40 *chappanḍe nai*; 100 *temerre.*

Verb

The verb has three voices: active with infinitive in *-ugo*; passive with infinitive in *-ēgo*; middle with infinitive in *-āgo.*

Perfect and imperfective aspectual system rather than tense. Thus the perfect endings in the active voice are *-i*, negative *-ai*; imperfective: *-a,-ata*, *-an*. *No* may be added to fix action in past.

Initial of stem changes for number: e.g. *o **w**indi* 'he wrote', *ɓe **mb**indi* 'they wrote'.

SPECIMEN PARADIGM

Present: *mi ɗon **w**inda* 'I am writing', negative *mi **w**indata*; *min ɗon **mb**inda* 'we are writing', negative *min **mb**indata*.

Imperfect: *mi ɗonno **w**inda* 'I was writing', negative *mi **w**indatāno*; *min ɗonno **mb**inda* 'we were writing', negative *min **mb**indatāno*.

Future: *mi **w**índata* 'I shall write', negative *mi **w**indáta*; *min **mb**indata*

.

Preterite I: *mi windi*, negative *mi windai*.

Preterite II: *mi windino*, negative *mi windaino*.

Imperative: *windu – mbinde*, negative *tā windu – tā mbinde*.

PARTICIPLES

(a) Imperfective or present: personal *bindaiɗo*, pl. ***w**indaiɓe* 'about to write', 'writing'; neutral *bindaiɗun*.

(b) Perfective: personal *binduɗo*, pl. ***w**induɓe*; neutral *binduɗum*.

VOICE

Passive: not much used, active forms being preferred. Pronominal forms and initial concord as for active voice.

Middle: pronominal forms and initial concord largely as for active voice.

DERIVATIVE STEMS

There are five of these:

-ina is always transitive: e.g. *o andi* 'he knew', *o andini mo* 'he informed him';

-ra, *-r*V is instrumental; *see* **Word formation**, below;

*-t*V is intensive, or expresses the contrary of stem meaning: e.g. *maɓɓugo* 'to shut', *maɓɓitugo* 'to open';

*-d*V has various meanings: e.g. *o jangi* 'he read', *o jangidi* 'he read through and finished'.

There are several other formants of this kind, e.g. *-tira/-indira* expressing reciprocity: e.g. *hōfna* 'to greet, *ɓe **k**ōfnindiri* 'they greeted each other'.

Prepositions

There are a couple of dozen of these: e.g. *diga* 'from', *tana* 'without', *bāwo* 'behind', *fāgo* 'for'; e.g. *batākewol fāgo hā alkāli* 'a letter for the judge'.

Word formation

Formation of nouns from verbs: e.g. *-ōwo* 'agent': *winda* 'to write', *bindōwo* 'writer', pl. *windōɓe*.

Noun of instrument formed from *-ra-* derived stem, with neutral endings *-ḓum*, pl. *-ḓe*; *-gal*, pl. *ḓe*; *-gol*, pl. *ḓi*: thus from *winda* 'to write': ***b**indirgol* 'pen', pl. *bindirḓi*; ***w**indirde* 'office', pl. *bindirḓe*; ***b**induki* 'writing'.

Word order

Normally SVO.

1 Har fuɗɗam Wolde wonno, Wolde ɗonno wondi be Allah, Wolde nde Allah. 2 Har fuɗɗam o ɗonno wondi be Allah; 3 kala hunde fuh e mako lati; kala ɗum ko lati fuh ɗum lataki bila mako. 4 Nder mako ngēndam wonno; ngēndam ɗām ɗam annora 'yimɓe. 5 Annora kā e yaino nder nyiɓre; nyiɓre jālaki ka.

6 Wodino gorko nulaɗo ibgo e Allah, inde muɗum Yuhanna. 7 Kaŋko o wari ngam sedamku, ha o sedna annora kā, ngam ha moɓgal fuh nuɗɗina ngam mako. 8 Kaŋko o lataki annora kā, amma o wari ngam o sedna annora kā.

GAELIC

See **Scottish Gaelic**.

GAGAUZ

INTRODUCTION

Gagauz is a member of the Oguz-Bulgar sub-group of Western Turkic (Baskakov's (1966) classification). At present, there are about 150,000 speakers of Gagauz in Moldova and in the Odessa area of Ukraine, with a few in Bulgaria and Romania. It was from north-eastern Bulgaria that the Gagauz moved *en masse* in the early nineteenth century, and it is to the Turkic dialects spoken there that the language is most closely related – so much so, indeed, that several authorities have considered Gagauz to be a dialect of Turkish. Structurally, this is the case, but Gagauz has been influenced by Slavonic and Romanian.

Gagauz has adopted a great many Slavonic and Moldavian/Romanian loanwords.

SCRIPT

In 1957 a script was introduced on a Cyrillic base + *ö* (= /œ/), *ӱ* (= /y/), *ä* (= /ɛ/). Very little use has been made of this script.

PHONOLOGY

Consonants

The consonantal inventory is standard Turkish but includes, in addition, the velar fricative /x/ and the dental affricate /ts/.

A notable feature of Gagauz pronunciation is the marked palatalization of consonants before front vowels: e.g. *köpek* 'dog' is [k′œp′ek′].

Vowels

front: i, e, ɛ, œ, y
back: ı, ɛ, a, o, u

All occur both long and short. A long vowel may be primary or secondary, i.e. due to the elision of intervocalic consonant, either historically present or still written but dropped in pronunciation: e.g. *sābi* < *sahibi* (Arabic *ṣāḥib*).

VOWEL HARMONY

Standard; /o, œ/ do not appear in affixation.

MORPHOLOGY AND SYNTAX

In general, standard Turkic, with small variations in spelling and pronunciation. Consonant elision leads to some unfamiliar forms, e.g. in the declension of *inek* 'cow': gen. *inā̄n*, dat. *inā̄*, but loc. *inektä*.

The comparative degree of adjectives is made with *tā*: *tā uzun* 'longer'.

Personal pronoun: the base forms for first and second singular have the broad vowel *ä*: e.g. *bän*, *sän*, reverting to the narrower form in the oblique cases: *benim*, *beni*, etc.

A unique form is provided by the potential modal marker *nižä*: e.g. *var nižä* 'possible, can do'; *yok nižä* 'not possible, can't do'; *var nižä gideyim* 'I can go'; *yok nižä gidäsin* 'you (sing.) can't go'; *yoktu nižä gitsinnär* 'they can't go'.

Word order

Under Slavonic influence; SVO.

1 Келямъ ибтидаде мевджудъ иди, ве келамъ Аллахӂнъ нездинде иди, ве келамъ Аллахъ иди;

2 бу келамъ ибтидаде Аллахӂнъ нездинде иди.

3 Херъ шей анӂнъ васитасийле вуджуде гелди, ве вуджуде гелмишъ оланлардanъ ансӂзъ биръ шей вуджуде гелмеди.

4 Хаятъ анде иди, хаятъ дахи адемлеринъ нурӂ иди.

5 Ве нуръ зулметде зия вериръ, зулметъ дахи анӂ идракъ етмезъ иди.

6 Аллахъ тарафӂнданъ ирсалъ олунмушъ Иоанисъ исминде биръ адемъ варъ иди.

7 Ишбу адемъ шехадетъ ичунъ гелди, таки нурӂнъ хакӂнда шехадетъ етмесийле, джумле адемлеръ анӂнъ васитасӂйле имана гелсилнеръ.

GAN

See **Chinese Dialects**.

GARO

INTRODUCTION

This language belongs to the Baric group of Tibeto-Burman. The ethnonym is Achik. Garo is spoken in the Garo Hills area of Assam, and in adjacent parts of Bangladesh, by about 500,000 people.

SCRIPT

The Bengali script was originally used for the language (Bible translation, etc.); the Roman alphabet is now in use for some literary activity, including a long-running weekly newspaper.

PHONOLOGY

Consonants

The labial, dental, and velar series are represented by unvoiced and voiced stops + associated nasals: e.g. /p, b, m/. /ts, tʃ/ and /dz/dʒ/ are present, also /s, r/l/ and the glottal stop. The nasals /m, n, ŋ/ and /r/ have glottalized allophones.

Burling (1961) points out that in citation or word-final form morphemes ending in the glottal stop take a kind of echo of the root vowel: e.g. *do'* 'bird' pronounced /do'.o/; *wa'* 'bamboo', pronounced /wa'a/. The echo vowel is not pronounced in compounds: *do'.ci* 'bird's egg'.

Vowels

The vowels are /i, e, a, o, u/, with intermediate values.

Stress

Stress is phrasal.

MORPHOLOGY AND SYNTAX

Garo has no form of inflection; the accidence is entirely suffixal apart from one prefix. Formally, nominal and verbal bases differ only in their respective valencies: i.e. nominal bases are compatible with nominal affixes, verbal bases with verbal affixes. Some nominal affixes may, however, be attached to verbs expanded by certain verbal affixes.

Noun

PLURALITY

Suffixes, e.g. *-raŋ*, are available, but their use is optional: e.g. *man.de.raŋ* 'men'. Reduplication may also be used to indicate plurality.

CASE MARKERS

E.g. *ko* for objective, *na* dative, *ni* genitive: X *ni* Y 'X's Y'. *Ni* is attached to personal pronoun to make possessive: e.g. *aŋ.ni* 'my'. The *ni* form acts as base for secondary suffixes, e.g. *gim.in* 'about': *naŋ.ni.gim.in* 'about you', *man.de.raŋ.ko nik.a.ha.ma?* 'did you see the men?' where *ko* is the object marker, *nik* 'to see', *a.ha* is the past-tense marker, and *ma* is the interrogative suffix.

A locative is made with *o* which also renders the verb 'to have': e.g. *aŋ.o kitap doŋ.a* 'I have a book'. Like *ni*, *o* also serves as base for further suffixation: e.g. with dative *na*: *an.ti.**o**.na re'aŋ.gen* 'will go to market' (*an.ti* 'market', *re'aŋ* 'to go', *gen* is future marker).

Other case makers are e.g. *ci* 'to/from', *miŋ* 'with'.

NUMERICAL CLASSIFIERS

In Garo these are sited between noun and numeral: e.g. *sak* for human beings: *man.de sak.git.tam* 'three men' (*-git.tam* 'three'). *Ge* is an all-purpose numerical classifier, equivalent to Chinese *ge*; *te* is used for buildings; *poŋ* for long, cylindrical objects, etc., *maŋ* for animals: *moŋ.ma maŋ.sa* 'one elephant'.

Adjective

Treated as verbal base; as attribute, adjective follows noun.

Pronoun

PERSONAL PRONOUN

	Singular	*Plural*
1	aŋ.a	*excl.* ciŋ.a, *incl.* a'n.ciŋ
2	na'.a	na'sim.aŋ
3	bi.a	u.a.maŋ/u.a.raŋ

Aŋ.a and *na'.a* have oblique forms *aŋ*/*na'ŋ* to which suffixes are attached: e.g. *na'ŋ.ko* 'you (acc.)'.

DEMONSTRATIVE PRONOUN/ADJECTIVE

i.a. 'this'; *a.o.a.* 'that'.

INTERROGATIVE PRONOUN

sa.wa 'who?'; *ma.i.ma* 'what?'

RELATIVE PRONOUN

A relative construction with *je* has been borrowed from Bengali: e.g. ***Je**.ko* *dok.a.ha u.an man.de o'ŋ.a* 'That is the man who was hit' (*dok* 'to hit'; *a.ha* = past-tense marker; *u.a* + *-n* = 3rd p.; *o'ŋ.a* 'to be').

Numerals

1–10: these are bound forms following classifiers: *-sa*, *-gin.i*, *-git.tam*, *-bri*, *-boŋ.a*, *-dok*, *-sin.i*, *-cet*, *-sku*, *-ci.kiŋ*. 11 *-ci.sa*; 12 *-ci.gin.i*; 20 *kor.grik*; 30 *kor.a.ci*; 40 *sot.bri*; 100 *rit.ca.sa*.

Verb

Tense and aspect markers are affixed to base: e.g.

- *-eŋ* marks continuous action: e.g. *ca'.eŋ.a* 'am/is/are eating';
- *-man* marks perfective aspect: e.g. *ca'.man.jok* 'has finished eating';
- *-jok* past tense;
- -(*a*).*ha* past tense;
- *-gen* future marker: *aŋ.a re'.aŋ.gen* 'I shall/will go', where *-aŋ-* is the centrifugal indicator (opposite is *-ba-*).

NEGATION

The marker is (*gi.*)*ja*; e.g. *ca'.ja.ha* 'did not eat'.

IMPERATIVE

bo; negative imperative: *da* + V + *bo*.

Subordinate verbs and adverbs can be further added to base + tense markers; e.g. *on* makes temporal subordinate clauses; *u.a sok.ba.on* 'when he comes' (*sok* 'to arrive'; *ba* is a directional marker, 'hither'). There is a large inventory of adverbial affixes like *ba*; for example, *aŋ* is the 'thither' counterpart of *ba*, indicating motion away from first person; *-pir-* plus *ta.i.ta.i* (*ta.i* = 'again') suggests recapitulation, reiteration of an action (*pir* is presumably borrowed from Bengali or Assamese); *-rim-* is comitative; *-grik-* suggests reciprocity.

Causative verbs are constructed with the affix *-at-*: e.g. *aŋ.a u.ko ca'.**at**.jok* 'I made him eat'; *-cim-*, desiderative marker: e.g. *ca'.gin.ok.cim* 'feel(s) like eating' (where *gin.ok* is an intentional future marker).

FORMANTS

E.g. *-gip.a-*, agent: e.g. *ca'.gip.a man.de* 'the person who eats'. *-ram-* marks locus of action: e.g. *ca'.ram* 'eating place'.

Word order

SOV is normal.

1 Chengon Kata gnangchim, aro ua Kata Isol baksachim, aro ua Kata Isolchim.
2 Uan chengon Isol baksachim. 3 Uachin
pilakan ongaha; aro uni griode onggiminoni
onggipa mingsaba dongja. 4 Unon janggi
gnangchim, aro ua janggi manderangna seng a
ongachim. 5 Seng a andalao tengsua; aro
andala uko rim jachim. 6 Isolni watata mande
saksa rebaaha, uni bimung Johan. 7 Antang-
chi maikai darangan beberana mangen, seng ani
gimin saki on na ine ua saki ongna rebaaha.
8 Uan seng a ongjachim, indiba seng ani gimin
saki on na (rebara).

GE'EZ

See **Ethiopic**.

GEORGIAN

INTRODUCTION

Georgian belongs to the South Caucasian (Kartvelian) group of languages, and is spoken by about 3½ million in Georgia. It has been a literary language since the sixth century AD. The Old Georgian period extends from the beginnings to the twelfth/thirteenth centuries; this period is rich in translation, mainly of religious works, and culminates in the work of the greatest Georgian poet, Shota Rustaveli, the author of the heroic epic *Vepkhis Tqaosani*, 'The Man in the Tiger Skin'.

It was not until the early eighteenth century that Georgia began to recover from the ravages of the Mongol conquest: King Vakhtang VI edited and completed the corpus of chronicles covering the dark period, known as *Kartlis Tskhovreba*, 'The Life of Georgia'. In the 1860s the drive for a unified literary language was led by three distinguished writers – Prince Ilia Chavchavadze, Akaki Tsereteli, and Vazha-Pshavela. Among modern writers, Niko Lortki-Panidze and K. Gamsakhurdia are worthy of special mention.

SCRIPT

See **Script** at end of article.

PHONOLOGY

Consonants

Central to the Georgian phonological system is the contrast between voiced, voiceless aspirate, and voiceless ejective phonemes (the latter notated with subscript dots in the text), found in the stops (three series) and the affricates (two series):

stops: b, p, p̣; d, ṭ, t'; g, k, ḳ; q
affricates: dz, ts, ṭṣ; dʒ, tʃ, ṭ'ʃ̣'
fricatives: v, s, z, ʃ, ʒ, x, γ, h
nasals: m, n
lateral and flap: l, r
semi-vowel: j

In the above inventory, /p, t, k/ are aspirates; /p̣, ṭ, ḳ/ are ejectives (glottalized). Similarly for the affricates. Multiple clusters are frequent in Georgian; an example of a six-term cluster, given by Comrie and Hewitt

(1981), is *mçvrtneli* 'trainer'. Such clusters have single or dual/triple release (involving shwa) depending on whether the components are homogeneous or not.

Vowels

i, ɛ, a, ɔ, u

Stress

On first syllable of disyllabics; in longer words, stress tends to fall on first and antepenultimate syllables.

MORPHOLOGY AND SYNTAX

Noun

There is no grammatical gender; if it is necessary to distinguish between sexes, defining terms may be added, e.g. for *švili* 'child': *važi.švili* 'boy–child' = 'son'; *kali.švili* 'girl–child' = 'daughter'.

There is no definite article. The numeral *ert* 'one' may be used as indefinite article.

NUMBER

The plural marker is *-eb-* following stem, preceding case markers: e.g. *çigni* 'book', pl. *çig**neb**i*; *mta* 'mountain': *mt**eb**ši* 'in the mountains'. There is also an older literary plural in *-ni*: e.g. *dzma* 'brother', pl. *dzmani.*

DECLENSION

The following endings are added to consonant stems:

nominative	-i	instrumental	-it
ergative	-ma	adverbial	-ad
accusative/dative	-s	ablative	-dan
genitive	-is	locative	-ši

Vocalic stems drop *-i*, and take *-m* in the ergative.

Examples: *kalaki* 'town': *kalakši* 'in the town'; *samšoblo.dan* 'from the homeland'; *maṭareblit* 'with the train'; *Petres çigni* 'Peter's book'. The ergative in *-m*(*a*) is the case of the logical subject with a transitive verb in the aorist (*see* **Verb**, below).

Adjective

The attributive adjective precedes the noun, and is, in the main, invariable. Consonant stems, however, drop *-i* in the dative (e.g. *didi* 'big', becomes *did*) and take the ergative *-ma*: cf. *pataraØ bavš**ma*** 'by a small child'; *did**ma** bavšma* 'by a big child'; *ahal çigni* 'new book'; *ahal muzeumši* 'in the new museum'.

Pronoun

PERSONAL PRONOUN

Independent, with subject, direct and indirect pronoun markers, and possessives:

		Independent	*Subject marker*	*Direct object*	*Indirect object*	*Possessive*
sing.	1	me	v-	m	mi	čemi
	2	šen	(h) Ø-	g	gi	šeni
	3	is	-s	Ø	u	misi
pl.	1	čven	v . . . t	gv	gvi	čveni
	2	tkven	Ø . . . t	g . . . t	gi . . . t	tkveni
	3	isini	-en/-n	Ø	u	mati

Examples: *me* ***v****.c̣er* 'I write'; *is c̣er.s* 'he writes'; *čven* ***v****.c̣er.****t*** 'we write'; direct object with *xatav* 'to paint'; *šen* ***m****.xatav me* 'you paint me'; *isini.****gv****.xatav.****en*** *čven* 'they are painting us'.

The subject marker of the first person ***v-*** is always dropped before the second person object marker *-g-*: i.e. ****v.g****.xatav šen* → ***g****.xatav šen* 'I paint you'. That is, the absence of a subject marker, plus the presence of second person object marker, identifies the verb form as first person: ***g****.xedav* 'I see you'.

The independent forms, *me, šen, is,* etc., are declined, with little change in form; e.g. *me* is both nominative and ergative.

DEMONSTRATIVE PRONOUN/ADJECTIVE

As in Armenian, there are three degrees of distance, associated with the three persons: *es* (first person) 'this', *eg* (second person) 'that', *igi* (third person) 'that yonder'. These are declined and used for both numbers. The oblique base of *is* is *ama-*.

INTERROGATIVE PRONOUN

vin 'who?'; *ra* 'what?'; *romeli* 'which?': e.g. *Vin aris es ḳaci?* 'Who is this man?'; *Vis xatav.****s*** *axla es mxatvari?* 'Whom is this painter painting now?'

RELATIVE PRONOUN

-c is added to the interrogative forms: *romelic, vinc, rac*: e.g.

is c̣erili, romelic me gamo.v.gzavne Tbilisidan
'this letter which I sent from Tbilisi'

Ik iqo dγes **imdeni** sṭudenṭebi, **ramdenic** ik iqo gušin
'There were as many students here today as there were yesterday'

Numerals

1–10: *erti, ori, sami, otxi, xuti, ekvsi, švidi, rva, cxra, ati*; 11 *tert.meṭi* (*ati* → *t*

+ *ert* + *meṭi* 'more'); 12 *tormeṭi*. 20–99 are constructed modulo 20: thus, 20 *oci*; 30 *oc.da.ati*; 40 *or.m.oci*; 60 *sam.m.oci*. 100 *asi*.

Verb

1. In sharp contrast to the relatively simple nominal system, the Georgian verbal system is extremely complicated and difficult to describe in brief. There are two basic contrasts: verbs are (a) static or dynamic, and (b) transitive or intransitive: the latter category includes passive and middle verbs. All static verbs are intransitive; dynamic verbs may be either transitive or intransitive. Transitive verbs require the ergative construction to be used with their aorist forms, i.e. with a direct object in the *nominative* case.
2. Georgian verbs are mono- or polypersonal. For personal indices, *see* **Pronoun**, above.
3. *Conjugation*: four types are distinguished:

I This is an active voice, and stems conjugated in it are usually transitive. Aspect is distinguished.
II Stems conjugated in this model are mostly intransitive; the second conjugation also offers one way of making passives. Aspect is distinguished.
III Denominatives are conjugated according to III. Aspect is not distinguished.
IV This is a specific conjugation for indirect verbs, whose grammatical subject is in the dative.

There is a certain amount of interchange between conjugations; e.g. verbs handled according to IV may borrow forms from II.

4. *Series and screeves*: the term 'screeve' (in Georgian *mc̣krivi*) was coined by the Georgian linguist A. Šanidze to denote a finite verbal form which may be temporal (i.e. a tense), modal, or aspectual. The screeves are arranged in three series:

(a) the present–future series, comprising the following screeves: present – future – past imperfective – conditional – first subjunctive present – first sunjunctive future;
(b) the aorist series: aorist – second subjunctive (optative);
(c) the perfect series: perfect – pluperfect – third subjunctive.

5. *Version*: marked by the pre-radical vowels: (Ø), *a*, *i*, *u*: Ø is neutral; *i* denotes 'for oneself'; *u* denotes action for third party; *a* is the so-called super-essive marker: action on something. Cf.

c̣er.s 'he writes' (neutral: no specific referential deixis);
i.*c̣er.s* 'he writes for himself', ***mi***.*c̣er.s* 'he writes something for me';
u.*c̣er.s* 'he writes something for him (third party)';
*v.**a**,c̣er* 'I write something on something'.

6. *Preverbal markers*: e.g. *a-*, *ga-*, *gada-*, *da-*, *mi-/mo-*, *čamo-*. These function as (a) aspect markers, and (b) directional markers: e.g.

me ***v****.çer* 'I write': *me* ***da.v****.çer* 'I shall write' = 'have written' (cf. Russian perfective-present form = future);
me ***mi****.v.divar teatr****ši*** 'I am going to the theatre' (*mi-* 'thither');
me ***mo****.v.divar sadguri****dan*** 'I am coming from the station' (*mo-* 'hither').

Cf. if speaker is at X: *gada.v.atrev* 'I drag something towards Y'; *gadmo.v.atrev* 'I drag something towards X' (point of origin).

NEGATION

The general marker is *ar*: e.g. *arapers ar vaķeteb* 'I do nothing' (double negative).

Some examples:

(a) Series forms of a I conjugation verb: root *çer* 'to write':

		Singular	*Plural*
present screeve:	1	me **v**çer = **I** am writing	čven **v**çer**t**
	2	šen **Ø**çer	tkven **Ø**çer**t**
	3	is çer**s**	isini çer**en**
past imperfective:	1	me **v**çer**di**	čven **v**çer**dit**
	2	šen **Ø**çer**di**	tkven çer**dit**
	3	is çer**da**	isini çer**dnen**

For the conditional, the imperfective forms are preceded by ***da-***: e.g. ***da.v****.çer.****di***.

(b) Series forms: aorist with logical subject in ergative: e.g. ***me da.v****.çer.****e*** 'I wrote' (*me* is the ergative case of *me* 'I'); *sțudenț****.ma da****.çer.****a*** 'the student wrote'. Optative: *sțudenț****.ma*** *unda* ***da****.çer.****os*** 'the student has to write' (*unda* 'must'; *-o-* is the optative characteristic).

(c) Series: perfect: the screeves in this series differ from those in (a) and (b) in that the 'perfect' forms are essentially inferential or presumptive (cf. the Turkic *-miş-* tenses). The following example, from Tschenkeli Bd. 1: 491, exhibits the difference:

imperfect: *sțudenți çer.d.a çerilebs* 'the student wrote/was writing letters';
aorist: *sțudenț****.ma*** (ergative) *da.çer.a çerili* 'the student wrote the letter'.

Both of these sentences are factual and positive. In the perfect screeve, however, we have: *sțudențs da.****u****.çer.i.****a*** *çerili* 'the student has, it would appear, written the letter', where the *-u-* marker refers to the logical subject (the student) which is in the dative/accusative case, while the *-a* marker refers to the logical object (*çerili* 'the letter'). The inferential nature of this form is usually underlined by adding the adverb *turme* 'apparently'.

The 'perfect' form is also used to notate action presumably initiated in the past, the consequences of which are now, in the present, manifest: cf. *sṭudenṭ.**s** da.**u**.ҫer.i.**a** Mariam.**is**.tvis ҫerili* 'the student, it appears, has written a letter to Maria' (where *-tvis* is the postposition 'for', governing the genitive case in *-is*). Here, the speaker has not actually witnessed the writing of the letter, but takes its present existence as acceptable evidence. Such a sentence will often begin with the phrase *rodesa.c me ga.**v**.ige* or *rogor.c me **v**.hedav* 'as I see . . . ', 'evidently'.

When a positive sentence with a (b) class aorist tense is negated, a (c) class form replaces the aorist: cf.

aorist; *da.ҫer.e šen ukve ҫerili* 'have you already (*ukve*) written the letter?;
aorist; *ki, me da.v.ҫer.e is* 'Yes, I've written it';
but perfect: *ara, me ar da.mi.ҫer.i.a is* 'no, I haven't written it'.

POLYPERSONAL VERBS WITH SUBJECT AND OBJECT INDICES

The grid for the present screeve, for example (either transitive or intransitive), shows 28 forms, made up as follows: four each for first and second person singular and plural; plus six each for third person singular and plural. As several of these forms would otherwise be identical, the independent forms are added: cf. *is mas **Ø**ehmareb.a* 'he helps him' *is mat **Ø**ehmareba* 'he helps them'; *me mas **v.Ø.ehmarabi*** 'I help him'; ***me tkven g.ehmarabit*** 'I help you (pl.)' (for ***v*** → **Ø**, *see* **Pronoun**); *tkven čven **gv**.ehmarebit* 'you (pl.) help us' (final *-t* is subject marker; *gv-* is object marker).

PASSIVE

The marker is *-i-*, *-d-*, or *-ebi-*: e.g. from *ҫer* 'to write': ***i**.ҫer.eb.a* 'is being written'. The subject is marked by the postposition *mier* which governs the genitive case. Cf. *ҫerili i.ҫer.eb.a sṭudenṭis mier* 'the letter is written by the student'. Other forms: future: *da.i.ҫer.eb.a* 'it will be written'; imperfect: *i.ҫer.eb.od.a* 'it was being written'; aorist: *da.i.ҫer.a* 'it was written'; optative: *unda da.i.ҫer.os* 'it has to be written'. *-d-* is used with denominatives: e.g. *γame* 'night': *γam.**d**.eba* 'it becomes night' = 'night falls'.

Postpositions

These may be affixed to words in genitive, dative, or ablative case: e.g. *-tvis* 'for', affixed to genitive: *Qvela ertisa**tvis**, erti qvelasa**tvis*** 'All for one, one for all'; *-gan* 'from', affixed to genitive: *Vis**gan** aris es ҫerili?* 'From whom is this letter?'

Affixed to dative: e.g. *-ši* 'in', *-ze* 'on', 'at', *-tan* 'with', 'at' ('*chez*'): *kalak**ši*** 'in the town'; *kreba**ze*** 'at the meeting'; *dedas**tan*** 'at one's mother's'.

Independent postpositions following genitive case:

šemdeg 'after', e.g. *gaḳvetilis šemdeg* 'after the lesson';
šesaxeb 'about', e.g. *Ris šesaxeb laparaḳobs es moҫape?* 'What is this pupil talking about?';
dros 'during': e.g. *omis dros* 'during the war'.

Word order

Relatively free: SVO, SOV, OSV all occur.

1. პირველითგან იყო სიტყჳა, და სიტყჳა იგი იყო ღჳთისა თანა, და ღმერთი იყო სიტყჳა იგი.
2. ესე იყო პირველითგან ღჳთისა თანა.
3. ყოველივე მის მიერ შეიქმნა, და თჳნიერ მისა არცა ერთი რა იქმნა, რაოდენი რა იქმნა.
4. მის თანა ცხოვრება იყო, და ცხოვრება იგი იყო ნათელ კაცთა.
5. და ნათელი იგი ბნელსა შინა ჰსჩანს, და ბნელი იგი მას ვერ ეწია.
6. იყო კაცი მოვლინებული ღჳთისა მიერ, და სახელი მისი იოანე.
7. ესე მოვიდა მოწამედ, რათა ჰსწამოს ნათლისა მისთჳს, რათა ყოველთა ჰრწმენეს მისგან.
8. არათუ იგი იყო ნათელი, არამედ რათა ჰსწამოს ნათლისა მისთჳს.

SCRIPT

Georgia was converted to Christianity in the middle of the fourth century; and a need to make the Gospels accessible to the Georgians in their own language must have fostered the creation of a Georgian alphabet, which followed early in the fifth century. According to tradition, St Mesrop Mashtotz, the creator of the Armenian script, was also, at least in part, responsible for the Georgian alphabet. Like the Armenian, the Georgian alphabet is clearly based on a Greek model, for example in the order of the letters. But the Georgian phonological inventory is very different from the Greek; and this first classification and notation of Caucasian phonemes – a classification which remains valid today – must rank as a linguistic achievement of the first order.

This early Georgian alphabet is known as *xucuri*. In the eleventh century, it was replaced by the *mxedruli* 'civil' script. Seven of the original forty *mxedruli* letters are now obsolete. The thirty-three letters now in use are shown in the table. Punctuation follows the West European model.

THE GEORGIAN SCRIPT

THE ALPHABET

ა	*a*	რ	*r*
ბ	*b*	ს	*s*
გ	*g*	ტ	*ṭ*
დ	*d*	უ	*u*
ე	*e*	ფ	*ph*
ვ	*v*	ქ	*kh*
ზ	*z*	ღ	*γ*
თ	*th*	ყ	*q̣*
ი	*i*	შ	*ʃ*
კ	*ḳ*	ჩ	*čh*
ლ	*l*	ც	*ts*
მ	*m*	ძ	*dz*
ნ	*n*	წ	*ṭs*
ო	*o*	ჭ	*tʃ*
პ	*p̣*	ხ	*χ*
ჟ	*ž*	ჯ	*dž*
		ჰ	*h*

GERMAN

INTRODUCTION

A member of the West Germanic branch of Indo-European and the official language of Germany (over 76 million speakers), German is also spoken in Austria (over 7 million) and is one of the national languages of Switzerland (*c.* 4 million). In addition, there are large numbers of German speakers in the former Soviet Union (about 1 million), in Romania (½ million), and in Alsace-Lorraine (1½ million). The world total of German speakers is around the 120,000,000 mark.

Dialects

The Second (Germanic) Sound Shift is of fundamental importance here. During the first millennium AD, part – but not all – of the continuum of emergent German speech-forms underwent a series of phonetic mutations which can be summarized as follows:

> Proto-Germanic unvoiced stops became homorganic fricatives or affricates: i.e. /p, t, k/ > /f, s, x/ç/ *or* /pf, ts, kx/; voiced stops were mutated to unvoiced: /b, d, g/ > /p, t, k/.

Where these mutations were consistently carried through, the language form known as High or Upper German resulted; its emergence can be dated to, roughly, the fifth to seventh centuries. The same mutations made a partial penetration into the central German area, but left the northern dialect area untouched. Some illustrative examples:

High German	*Low German*	*English*
i**ch**	i**k**	I (Anglo-Saxon: i**c**)
ma**ch**en	ma**k**en	ma**k**e
hei**ss**	hei**t**	ho**t**
A**pf**el	a**pp**el	a**pp**le
Schi**ff**	ski**p**	shi**p**

As the central German area gradually accepted the High German forms, the dialect situation was reduced to a basic opposition between High and Low German. The latter, also known as Plattdeutsch, has been used as a literary language, e.g. by Fritz Reuter (1810–74), and Klaus Groth (1819–99).

The historical development of High German falls into four main periods:

1. Old High German: from the conclusion of the Second Sound Shift onwards; attested from the eighth to tenth centuries, notably in the sole surviving Old Germanic heroic ballad, the *Hildebrandslied*.
2. Middle High German: 1100–1350. The rich period of the courtly epic is dominated by Wolfram von Eschenbach, the author of *Parzival*, with its key concept of *mâze* – 'moderation, fittingness'; Gottfried von Strassburg, whose splendid version of the Tristan and Isolde story dates from *c.* 1210; and Hartmann von Aue, the author of *Der arme Heinrich*. The Middle High German period also produced the great Germanic epic of the *Nibelungenlied*, the source of Richard Wagner's *Ring des Nibelungen* tetralogy; and one of Europe's finest lyric poets, Walther von der Vogelweide.
3. Early New High German: 1350–1600: culminating in the Reformation and Martin Luther's translation of the Bible.
4. New High German: seventeenth century onwards.

It was Luther's translation of the Bible into the East Central German dialect (by then largely homogenized with High German) in the mid-sixteenth century that provided a firm basis for a standardized literary language. As he says in his *Sendbrief vom Dolmetschen* (1530): '*Ich hab mich des geflissen im Dolmetschen, das ich rein und klar Deutsch geben möchte*', which may be freely translated: 'The task to which I have applied myself as interpreter has been to provide pure, clear German.' Luther succeeded; and his 'pure, clear German' became the language of the *Aufklärung*, and of Classical Weimar (Goethe and Schiller; Hölderlin), the language of *Bildung*, 'self-cultivation'. Through the nineteenth and early twentieth century it was the language of scholarship, of great prose (Adalbert Stifter, Theodor Fontane, Thomas Mann) and of some sublime poetry (Rainer Maria Rilke), until the days of the Third Reich, when German lost touch with both *mâze* and *Bildung*. In 1933 Karl Kraus ended his last poem with the line: *Das Wort entschlief, als jene Welt erwachte.*

SCRIPT

Until the twentieth century the Gothic script was used for German, both in print and in handwriting. Roman is now standard. Voiceless /s/ is notated as ß in word-final position, before final *-t*, and following a long vowel or diphthong: e.g. *groß* 'big'; *läßt* 'lets'; *füße* 'feet'. The most recent spelling reform has further restricted the use of ß.

PHONOLOGY

Consonants

stops: p, b, t, d, k, g, ʔ
fricatives: f, v, s, z, ʃ, ʒ, ç, x, h; [ç/x] are positional variants
nasals: m, n, ŋ
lateral and flap: l, r, ʀ

semi-vowel; j

The phonemes /ts, ps, ks, pf/ also occur, and are variously classified as affricates or as clusters.

[ç/x] as positional variants: cf. *ich* 'I' /iç/; *Buch* 'book' /bux/. The diminutive suffix *-chen* is invariably /çɛn/ whatever the preceding phoneme.

Voiced stops in word-final position are devoiced; e.g. *gab* 'gave' /gaːp/; *Tod* 'death' /toːt/.

Vowels

front: i, iː, y, yː, e, eː, œ, œː, ɛ, ɛː
central: ə, a, aː
back: u, uː, o, oː
diphthongs: ai, oi, au

MORPHOLOGY AND SYNTAX

German has three genders and two numbers. The noun has four cases.

Noun

Nominal endings are very largely coded for gender. Thus, all nouns in *-heit*, *-keit*, *-schaft*, *-ung*, and *-ion* are feminine (a very numerous class), and most nouns in *-e* are also feminine. Nouns in *-ling*, *-ich*, *-ig* are masculine; nearly all nouns in *-nis*, *-tum* are neuter (one or two exceptions), as are all nouns with the diminutive suffixes *-chen* and *-lein*. Further, most nouns with the prefix *Ge-* are neuter: e.g. *das Gebäck* 'pastry', *das Gebirge* 'range (of mountains)'.

PLURAL FORMATION

By affix: *-e/-en/-er/-s*; by stem mutation; by stem mutation + ending: e.g. *der Hund* 'dog' – *die Hunde*; *der Strahl*; 'ray' – *die Strahl**en***; *das Kind* 'child' – *die Kind**er***; *das Wort* 'word' – *die Wört**er***; *der Bruder* 'brother' – *die Br**ü**der*; *die Tochter* 'daughter' – *die T**ö**chter*.

Some nouns have two plural forms differing in sense; e.g. *das Wort* 'word': pl. *die Worte* 'words in connected utterance', *die Wörter* 'words' (as a plurality, e.g. in *Wörterbuch* 'dictionary').

Article

DEFINITE ARTICLE

der, die, das (masc., fem., neut.). These are fully declined in four cases; the accusative is distinguished only in the masculine; the following paradigm illustrates the declension of the article and the noun, as well as the weak declension of the adjective ('the good man/woman/book'):

	Masculine	*Feminine*	*Neuter*
sing. nom.	der gute Mann	die gute Frau	das gute Buch

acc.	**den** guten Mann	die gute Frau	das gute Buch
gen.	**des** guten Mann**es**	**der** guten Frau	**des** guten Buch**es**
dat.	**dem** guten Mann	**der** guten Frau	**dem** guten Buch
pl. nom.	die guten Männer	die guten Frauen	die guten Bücher
acc.	die guten Männer	die guten Frauen	die guten Bücher
gen.	**der** guten Männer	**der** guten Frauen	**der** guten Bücher
dat.	**den** guten Männer**n**	**den** guten Frauen	**den** guten Bücher**n**

A few dozen nouns take -*(e)n* in all cases except the nominative (all masculine): e.g. *der Mensch* 'human being': *den, des, dem Menschen*; pl. *die Mensch**en***.

INDEFINITE ARTICLE

masculine: *ein, einen, eines, einem*;
feminine: *eine, eine, einer, einer*;
neuter: *ein, ein, eines, einem.*

Adjective

As attribute, adjective precedes noun and shows concord in gender, number, and case. There are two declensions: weak, when the adjective is preceded by the definite article or other qualifier marking gender, number, and case (which is illustrated above) and strong, which is used in the absence of such a qualifier; the adjective itself then takes on the requisite markers: e.g.

	Masculine	*Feminine*	*Neuter*
nom.	gut**er** Wein	gute Frau	gut**es** Brot
acc.	gut**en** Wein	gute Frau	gut**es** Brot
gen.	gut**en** Wein**es**	gut**er** Frau	gut**en** Brot**es**
dat.	gut**em** Wein	gut**er** Frau	gut**em** Brot

The plural endings for all three genders are: *-er, -e, -er, -en.*

There is also a mixed declension used after the indefinite article, the possessive adjectives *mein, dein*, etc., and the negating adjective/pronoun *kein*: cf. *eine**m** gute**n** Wein* 'to a good wine'; *eine**r** gute**n** Frau* 'of a good woman'.

COMPARATIVE

-er added to positive: several very common monosyllables also mutate the stem vowel: e.g. *langsam* 'slow' – *langsamer*; *lang* 'long' – *l**ä**nger*; *gro**ß*** 'big' – *gr**öß**er*. Suppletive: *gut* 'good' – *besser.*

Pronoun

	1	*2*	*3*
singular	ich	du	er (masc.), sie (fem.), es (neut.)
plural	wir	ihr	sie (all 3 genders)

These are fully declined in three cases: e.g. for first person singular *ich*, acc. *mich*, dat. *mir*.

The genitive forms, e.g. *mein(er)*, *dein(er)*, etc. are very sparingly used in modern German, e.g. *es waren ihrer zehn* 'there were ten of them', though frequent in classical poetry:

Ich denke dein, wenn mir der Sonne Schimmer vom Meere strahlt (Goethe)
'I think of you when shimmering sunlight shines towards me from the sea'

Du and *ihr* are familiar second person singular and plural, restricted in use to certain specific sociolinguistic categories (family, school-friends, etc.). The polite form of address is *Sie* (sing. and pl.) with plural concordance; dat. *Ihnen*.

The neuter pronoun *es* is used as demonstrative and complement with the verb *sein* 'to be':

Sind **es** deine Brüder? – Ja, sie sind **es**
'is it/are these your brothers? – Yes, it is they'

DEMONSTRATIVE PRONOUN/ADJECTIVE

dieser/diese/dieses; pl. *diese* 'this, these'; *jener/jene/jenes*; pl. *jene* 'that; those': e.g. *in dieser Welt* 'in this world'; *in jenen Tagen* 'in those days' (dative endings after preposition *in*: *see* **Prepositions**).

The neutral form *dies* may be used as an all-purpose demonstrative pronoun: e.g. *dies sind meine Schwestern* 'these are my sisters' (cf. Russian, *eto*).

INTERROGATIVE PRONOUN

wer 'who?', *was* 'what?'

Wer has accusative and dative forms: *wen*, *wem*; both *wer* and *was* have a genitive: *wessen*

RELATIVE PRONOUN

Two forms are used: (a) *der*, *die*, *das*; pl. *die*; (b) *welcher*, *welche*, *welches*; pl. *welche*. The (a) form is more usual; the masculine and neuter genitive form is *dessen*; the feminine and plural genitive form fluctuates between *deren* and *derer*: e.g. *es folgten acht Monate, während derer*... 'eight months followed, during which ...'.

The extended form, *derjenige/diejenige/dasjenige*, pl. *diejenigen*, is also available.

Numerals

1–10: *eins, zwei, drei, vier, fünf, sechs, sieben, acht, neun, zehn*; 11 *elf*; 12 *zwölf*; 13 *dreizehn*; 14 *vierzehn*; 20 *zwanzig*; 21 *einundzwanzig*; 22 *zweiundzwanzig*, etc. 30 *dreißig*; 40 *vierzig*; 100 *hundert*.

The numeral *eins*, when used before a noun, takes the form *ein/eine/ein*, and is declined like the indefinite article: e.g. *das kostet nur eine Mark* 'that costs only one mark'; *einer der Beamten* 'one of the officials'; *eines Morgens* ... 'one morning ...'.

Verb

German verbs are transitive or intransitive; formally, weak or strong, There are three moods: indicative, subjunctive, and imperative, in two voices: active or passive. The active voice has two simple tenses, present and past, and several compound tenses, made with such auxiliaries as *haben* 'to have', *sein* 'to be', *werden* 'to become'. The passive voice is entirely analytical.

All transitive and many intransitive verbs are conjugated with *haben*. Reflexive verbs are also conjugated with *haben*, apart from a few cases where reciprocity is expressed, e.g. with *begegnen* 'to meet': *wir sind uns in der Stadt begegnet* 'we met each other in town'. *Haben* is also used with impersonal verbs: *es hat geregnet* 'it's been raining/has rained'.

With the verbs *liegen* 'to lie', *sitzen* 'to sit', *stehen* 'to stand' *haben* is preferred in North German, *sein* in South German usage. Intransitive verbs denoting change of state or place, and involving directed motion, are conjugated with *sein*, as are a few verbs like *geschehen* 'to happen', *bleiben* 'to remain.

Verbs like *spalten* 'to split', *schmelzen* 'to melt', *reissen* 'to tear', which can be (a) transitive or (b) intransitive, take *haben* for (a) and *sein* for (b).

In some instances, change of auxiliary involves a change in meaning: cf. *er ist mir gefolgt* 'he followed me' (directed motion); *er hat mir gefolgt* 'he obeyed me' (extension of base meaning).

WEAK VERBS

The past tense is formed by adding *-te* to the stem; the past participle by prefixing *ge-* to the stem, i.e. the infinitive minus *-en*. For example, infinitive: *mach**en*** 'to make'; stem: *mach-*; past tense: *mach**te***; past participle: ***ge**macht*. Similarly: *holen* 'to fetch' – *holte* – *geholt*; *sagen* 'to say' – *sagte* – *gesagt*.

STRONG VERBS

The past tense is made by ablaut, i.e. mutation of stem vowel. The past participle may resume either the stem vowel or the past-tense vowel, or may exhibit a further mutation: cf.

	Past	*Past participle*
lesen 'read'	l**a**s	gelesen
fließen 'flow'	fl**o**ß	gefl**o**ssen
empf**e**hlen 'recommend'	empf**a**hl	empf**o**hlen

g**e**hen 'go' g**i**ng geg**a**ngen

Specimen paradigms of indicative present and past tenses of weak (*holen*) and strong (*gehen*) verbs.

		Singular	*Plural*	*Singular*	*Plural*
present:	1	ich hole	wir holen	ich gehe	wir gehen
	2	du holst	ihr holet	du gehst	ihr gehet
	3	er holt	sie holen	er geht	sie gehen
	1	ich holte	wir holten	ich ging	wir gingen
	2	du holtest	ihr holtet	du gingst	ihr ginget
	3	er holte	sie holten	er ging	sie gingen

Certain stem vowels also mutate in the second and third persons singular of the present tense of strong verbs: e.g.

/ē > ī/: *lesen* 'read': *ich lese, du* ***lie****st, er* ***lie****st.*
/a > ä/: *fangen* 'catch': *ich fange, du f****ä****ngst, er f****ä****ngt.*
/o > ö/: *stoßen* 'push': *ich stoße, du st****ö****ßt, er st****ö****ßt.*

The present subjunctive is always regular: e.g. of *tragen* 'to carry': *ich trage, du tragest,* **er trage**; *wir tragen, ihr traget, sie tragen.*

The past subjunctive adds *-e* to the past indicative first and third persons singular, and mutates the stem vowel of possible: e.g. *ich tr****ü****ge, du tr****ü****gest, er tr****ü****ge*, etc.

German verbs, transitive and intransitive alike, are simple, as *tragen*, or take a separable or inseparable prefix. The following prefixes are inseparable, *be-*, *emp-*, *ent-*, *er-*, *ge-*, *ver-*, *zer-*, and, therefore, do not take prefixed *ge-* to form the past participle:

empfehlen 'recommend': ich empfehle – ich empfahl – ich habe **emp**fohlen;
geschehen 'happen': es geschieht – es geschah – es ist **ge**schehen.

The following prefixes are variable, i.e. separable or inseparable: *über-*, *durch-*, *hinter-*, *unter-*, *um-*, *voll-*, *wider*, *miß-*, *wieder-*. A verb which is used with one of these nine prefixes in an inseparable capacity has normally a secondary or derived sense. Compare with *legen* 'to lay', *setzen* 'put, place':

separable:

wir setzten (mit der Fähre) **über**
'we crossed (by ferry)'

sie hatte dem Kinde eine Decke über**ge**legt
'she had laid a blanket over the child'

inseparable:

er **über**setzte das Buch/er hat das Buch über**Ø**setzt

'he translated the book'

ich habe es mir noch mal über**Ø**legt
'I had second thoughts about it'

Prepositions

The prepositions in German govern the genitive, the dative, or the accusative. Nine very common prepositions take either the accusative or the dative, depending on sense. For example:

with gen. während **des** Krieges 'during the war'
with dat. seit **dem** Krieg(e) 'since the war'
with acc. er ging durch **den** Wald 'he went through the wood'

variable: e.g. *in*:

er wohnt in **der** Stadt 'he lives in the town' (locus of action does not change)
er ist in **die** Stadt gefahren 'he drove to town' (change of locus)
das Buch liegt auf **dem** Tisch 'the book is lying on the table'
er hat das Buch auf **den** Tisch hingelegt 'he laid the book on the table'

Word order

The rules governing German word order are strict, especially as regards the relative positioning of verbal components:

1. In a principal clause; basic order with a simple tense is SVO: e.g. *Ich gebe ihm das Buch* 'I give him the book.' If the tense is compound, the non-finite component goes to the end: e.g. *Ich habe ihm das Buch* ***gegeben*** 'I have given/gave him the book.' If the sentence is introduced by anything other than the subject, e.g. by adverbial material, inversion is obligatory: e.g. *Gestern* ***habe ich*** *ihm das Buch gegeben* 'Yesterday I gave him the book.'

Use with modal verb; e.g *müssen* 'to have to': e.g. *Er muß in die Stadt fahren* 'He has to go to town.'

If a compound tense is used, both sense-verb and modal auxiliary close the sentence in infinitive form: e.g. *Er* ***hat*** *in die Stadt* ***fahren müssen*** 'He (has) had to go to town.'

2. Relative clause: the auxiliary in a compound verb form now follows the participle: e.g. *Ich weiß, daß er in die Stadt* ***gefahren ist*** 'I know that he has gone to town'. But the auxiliary precedes the sense-verb if a modal verb is used: e.g. *Ich weiß, daß er in die Stadt* ***hat fahren müssen*** 'I know that he (has) had to go to town'; *In unserem Kreise* ***hat*** *er sich nicht mehr* ***sehen lassen können*** 'He was not able to let himself be seen again in our circle.'

In *oratio obliqua* the subjunctive is used: e.g.

Assertion:
Das billigt er nicht, aber er kann es verstehen
'He does not approve of this, but he can understand it.'

Reported speech:
Er billige das nicht, aber er **könne** es verstehen.

1 Im Anfang war das Wort, und das Wort war bei Gott, und Gott war das Wort.
2 Dasselbe war im Anfang bei Gott.
3 Alle Dinge sind durch dasselbe gemacht, und ohne dasselbe ist nichts gemacht, was gemacht ist.
4 In ihm war das Leben, und das Leben war das Licht der Menschen.
5 Und das Licht scheint in der Finsternis, und die Finsternis hat's nicht ergriffen.
6 ¶Es war ein Mensch, von Gott gesandt, der hieß Johannes.
7 Der kam zum Zeugnis, um von dem Licht zu zeugen, damit sie alle durch ihn glaubten.
8 Er war nicht das Licht, sondern er sollte zeugen von dem Licht.

GERMANIC LANGUAGES

INTRODUCTION

Towards the close of the second millennium BC, tribes speaking the Proto-Germanic dialect of Indo-European seem to have been located in the Baltic area centring on southern Sweden. When and whence these tribes reached this habitat remains something of a mystery (*see* **Indo-European Languages**).

It is significant, however, that, *vis-à-vis* the parent stock, Germanic is one of the most divergent of all the twelve branches of Indo-European. The divergence is evident both on the lexical and on the phonological plane. At least 30 per cent of the vocabulary of Common Germanic is non-Indo-European in origin, and, surprisingly, this sub- or adstrate third is largely made up of everyday words connected with hunting, sea-faring, farming, social organization, etc. – all of these being semantic fields amply furnished elsewhere with Indo-European roots. The case here for linguistic miscegenation is strong.

PHONOLOGY

Consonants

Evidence for this is also forthcoming on the phonological plane. The phonological watershed between the Indo-European matrix and the Proto-Germanic language is marked by

(a) the First or Germanic Sound Shift;
(b) a concomitant or closely subsequent shift to initial primary stress;
(c) a consequent erosion in, and ultimately loss of, final unstressed syllables.

The crucially important and far-reaching First Sound Shift seems to have been complete by the middle of the first millennium BC. It can be summarized as follows:

1. Unaspirated and aspirated voiceless stops merge to yield the corresponding fricatives in Proto-Germanic; the palatal/velar distinction is lost:

$$\left.\begin{array}{l} /p, t, \hat{k}/q, q^{w}/ \\ /ph, th, \hat{k}h/qh, q^{w}h/ \end{array}\right\} \quad > \quad /f, \theta, \chi^{h}, \chi^{w}/$$

2. Voiced unaspirated stops are unvoiced; again, the palatal/velar distinction is lost:

/b, d, ĝ;/g, g^{w}/ > /p, t, k, k^{w}/

3. The voiced aspirated stops become voiced fricatives:

/bh, th, ĝh/gh, $g^{w}h$/ > /β, ð, γ, γ^{w}/

For example, using Latin and Gothic:

p > f	Latin	**p**ēs	Gothic	**f**otus	English	**f**oot
t > θ		**t**rēs		**þ**reis		**th**ree
k̂ > χ		**c**anis		**h**unds		**h**ound
b > p	IE	*dheu**b**		diu**p**s		dee**p**
d > t	Latin	**d**ecem		**t**aihun		**t**en
g > k		**g**enus		**k**uni		**k**in
g > k		iugum		ju**k**		yo**k**e
bh > β > b	IE	*bhrāter		broþar		brother

The voiced and unvoiced fricatives in Proto-Germanic appear as positional allophones, depending on the position of the primary stress in the Indo-European matrix form. Thus, where /t/ is neither initial nor immediately preceded by the primary strees, it becomes /ð/ in Proto-Germanic; if preceded by stress, it becomes /θ/. For example:

IE **pətér* (Sanskrit *pitár*, Greek *patér*) – Gothic *fāðar*

but

**bhrā́ter* (Sanskrit *bhrā́tr*, Latin *frā́ter*) – Gothic *broþar*

This reflex relationship is known as Verner's Law, after the Danish linguist who first identified it.

Changes in the vocalic structure of Proto-Germanic, relative to the parent stock, can be briefly summarized: the Indo-European short vowels /ă. ŏ, ə̆/, merged to give Proto-Germanic /ă/; /aː/ and /oː/ merged to give /ō/; syllabic /r, l, m, n/ were expanded to yield /ur, ul, um, un/.

The Second Sound Shift is a local German phenomenon, complete by the end of the Old High German period, by which High German became differentiated from the Low and (up to a point) the Central German dialects (*see* **German**).

Historically, the Germanic languages fall into three groups:

(a) North Germanic: represented today by the Scandinavian languages, Icelandic, and Faeroese. The old literary language is known as Old Norse or Old Icelandic. North Germanic is attested in runic inscriptions from the third century onwards.
(b) West Germanic: the contemporary representatives are English, German, Low German (*das Plattdeutsche*), Dutch/Flemish, Frisian, Afrikaans, Yiddish; historical stages of English and German are represented by Anglo-Saxon, Middle English, Old and Middle High German. English has many regional variations which have proliferated on a global scale,

as dialectal differentiation within the confines of Britain itself has shrunk.

(c) East Germanic: the languages of the Goths, Vandals, Burgundians, etc. who installed themselves throughout Southern Europe following the collapse of the Roman Empire. Their languages are all extinct. The earliest connected text in a Germanic language is provided by the Bible translation into Gothic of Bishop Wulfila in the fourth century AD.

The global diffusion of English gives Germanic the widest territorial distribution of any language family. About 450 million people speak Germanic languages, with English accounting for about 75 per cent of this total.

MORPHOLOGY AND SYNTAX

Noun

The Indo-European inventory of three genders, three numbers, and eight cases was reduced to three genders, two numbers, and four cases (nominative, accusative, genitive, dative). Traces of a dual are found in Old Norse and in Old English pronominal forms. The nominal declension system was reduced, with a corresponding gain in the prepositional inventory. The pronominal system remained relatively unaffected *vis-à-vis* the Indo-European model. A Germanic innovation is the formal distinction between strong and weak adjectives, the latter being used with the definite article.

Verb

The rich verbal apparatus of the Indo-European core languages – Sanskrit, Greek, Latin – is cut down in Proto-Germanic and the daughter languages to a formal contrast between past and non-past; a future tense is formed with the help of auxiliary verbs. The medio-passive was lost, except in Old Norse; Gothic retains a passive. The subjunctive mood merged with the optative. The innovatory importance of the sound shift on the phonological plane is matched in the morphology by the highly distinctive ablaut series of strong verbs (*see* **German**, **Gothic**, **Old Norse**, etc.). Germanic weak verbs make their past tenses with the help of a dental formant, /t/d/.

In the older Germanic languages – Gothic, Old Norse, Old and Middle High German, Anglo-Saxon – finite verbal forms were coded for person and number, though not exclusively: i.e. some endings were duplicated. For example, in Old Norse, present and past tenses of *gefa* 'to give':

	Singular			*Plural*		
present:	1 gef	2 gefr	3 gefr	1 gefum	2 gefið	3 gefa
past:	1 gaf	2 gaft	3 gaf	1 gáfum	2 gafuð	3 gáfu

Coded inflection is largely retained in Icelandic and in modern standard German; cf. the corresponding forms of German *geben* 'to give':

	Singular			*Plural*		
present:	1 gebe	2 gibst	3 gibt	1 geben	2 gebt	3 geben
past:	1 gab	2 gabst	3 gab	1 gaben	2 gabt	3 gaben

In English, the three Scandinavian languages, and in Afrikaans, the inflectional system has been greatly reduced by syncretic processes, often to a single form for each tense. Thus, in English, the past tense has *gave* for all six forms; the present tense has *give*, with *-s* added for the third person singular.

GILYAK

See **Nivkh**.

GOṆḌI

INTRODUCTION

Goṇḍi belongs, in Andronov's (1978) classification, to the Gondwana group of the Dravidian family, a group which includes Kui, Kuvi, Koṇḍa, and Pēngō. Goṇḍi is much the largest of the non-literary Dravidian languages, and is spoken at present by at least 1 ½ million people in Madhya Pradesh, Maharashtra, Andhra Pradesh, and Orissa. There are several dialects.

PHONOLOGY

Consonants

stops: p, b, t, d, ṭ, ḍ, k, g
affricates: tʃ, dʒ
fricatives: v, j, s, h
nasals: m, n, ṇ, ŋ
lateral and flap: l, r, ṛ

All stops and affricates have corresponding aspirates: /ph, bh/, etc. Retroflex consonants are notated here with dots.

Vowels

long and short: i, e, a, o, u

Subrahmanyam (1968) points out a kind of vowel harmony in CVCV̄C forms: e.g. *mosōr* 'nose'; *perēk* 'rice'.

Goṇḍi can be written in Devanāgarī (see specimen at end of this article) or in other Indian scripts such as Bengali or Tamil.

MORPHOLOGY AND SYNTAX

Noun

There are traces of a feminine ending in *-āṛ*/*-ī*: e.g. *pōrāṛ* 'mother-in-law', but the opposition masculine/non-masculine is characteristic, and indeed general in the Gondwana group. A typical masculine ending is *-āl*: e.g. *āndāl* 'blind man'.

NUMBER

A masculine plural ending is *-īr*/*-ūr*: e.g. *kāṇḍīr* 'boys'. Non-masculine plural endings are *-ng*, *-(ī)k*: e.g. *ḍuvvālīk* 'tigers'; *marāk* 'trees'; *kork* 'fowls'.

CASE SYSTEM

The case markers are added either to the base or to the base plus augment, this augment being *-d-/t/ṭ/n/* or Ø: e.g.

with accusative/dative ending *-un*: e.g. *ḍuvvāl.**d**.un* 'the tiger (acc.)', 'to the tiger';
with instrumental/locative ending *-e/-ē*: e.g. *nār.**t**.ē* 'in the village'; *nār.k.**n**.ē* 'in the villages';
with ablative ending *-(n)āl*: e.g. *nā(r).**ṭ**.nāl* 'from the village'.

The genitive ending is coded for the masculine/non-masculine dichotomy.

Pronoun

PERSONAL INDEPENDENT PRONOUN

1 sing. *(n)annā*; pl. excl. *(m)ammāṭ/marāṭ*, incl. *aplō*; 2 sing. *imma/(n)immē*; pl. *immāṭ/mirāṭ*. That is, *-a-* is first person marker + *n* (sing.)/*m* (pl.); *-i-* is second person marker.

The third person forms are supplied from the demonstrative series, in which Subrahmanyam (1968) distinguishes proximate and distal forms:

	Masculine	*Non-masculine*
proximate:	sing. vēr, pl. vīr	sing. id, pl. iv
distal:	sing. vōr, pl. vūr	sing. ad, pl. av

INTERROGATIVE PRONOUN

Masc. sing. *bōr*, pl. *būr*; non-masc. sing. *bad*, pl. *bav*.

Numerals

1–7: *undī, ranḍ, mūnd, nālūŋ, siyyūŋ, sārūŋ, ēṛūŋ*: these are non-masculine forms; the masculine forms add *-ī/-ōr* to modified bases. 1 and 2 are suppletive, *vorōr, ivvīr*; 4 *nālvīr*, etc.

From 8 inclusive onwards, Marathi numerals are used: e.g. 8 *āṭh*; 9 *nav*; 10 *daha*.

Verb

Inflected forms are made with base + tense marker + personal ending. The personal endings are (all with several allophones):

		Singular	*Plural*
1		-ōn/-ā	*excl.* -ōm; *incl.* (future only) -āṭ
2		-ī	-īṭ
3	masc.	-ōr	-ēr
	non-masc.	-ā	-āŋ

That is, third person distinguishes gender.

TENSE

Markers are:

past: *-t-/-ṭṭ-*
present/future: *-ānt-/-nt-*
future: *-(a)k/-(ā)n-/-ār-*

Examples: *aṭṭ.ṭ. ōn* 'I cooked'; *un.ṭṭ.ōn* 'I drank'; *vā.**k**.ā* 'I'll come'; *si.**nt**.ōn* 'I' m giving, will give'.

NEGATIVE

The marker is *-v-/-ō-*, the latter for use with non-second person: e.g. *veh.**v**.ī* 'you (sing.) will not tell', pl. *veh.v.īṭ*; *sūṛ.**ō**.n* 'I don't/will not see'; *sūṛ.**ōr*** 'he does/will not see'.

IMPERATIVE

2nd sing./pl. *-ā/-m/-Ø*: e.g. *sūṛ.**ā***, *sūṛ.āṭ* 'see!'

PARTICIPLES

There are several participles; some of the endings are illustrated here: past, *tin.**jī*** 'having eaten'; present, *tin.**jēr*** 'eating'; conditional, *vā.t.**ēkē*** 'if/when you came'.

A verbal noun form in *-māṛ/-vāḷ* (active or passive) is used to make relative clauses: e.g. *veh.**vāl** māynāl* 'the man who tells'; *veh.**vāl** vēsūṛī* 'the story that is told'.

Postpositions

Usually follow the augumented base: e.g.

aggā 'in, near': e.g. *kay.**d**. aggā* 'in the hand';
karūm 'near': e.g. *marā.**t**.karūm* 'near the tree';
tarsō 'with, by': e.g. *vōr.**n**.tarsō* 'with/by him';
phorō 'on': e.g. *marā.**t**.phorō* 'on the tree';
roppō 'inside': e.g. *kuhī.**t**.roppō* 'in the forest'.

Word order

SOV

(१) मुन्ने ते बचन मत्ता अनि बचन परमेश्वर-तू-संगने मत्ता अनि वचन परमेश्वर मत्ता। (२) इद्दे मुन्ने ते परमेश्वर-तू-संगने मत्ता। (३) सब कुछ ओना कैदाल पैदा आता, अनि जो कुछ पैदा आता आपिनाल ओन मीचुक बड़ांगे भी हल्ले पैदा आयो जो पैदा आता। (४) ओन रोपा जीवन मत्ता अनि अद जीवन आदमीड़ा वेर्ची मत्ता। (५) अनि वेर्ची सीकाटीते चमके माइता अनि सीकाटी तान नाश[1] हल्ले केवो॥

(६) परमेश्वर-तू-इगाताल रॉहतल वोड्डुल आदमी वातुल अनि ओना पड़ोल योहन्ना मत्ता। (७) एल आदमी गवाही सीयाले वातुल – अद वेर्ची ता गवाही सीआले, कि सब आदमीड़ ओना द्वारा बिश्वास केवीड़। (८) ओल तना अद वेर्ची हल्ले आयोल, पर परमेश्वर ओन अद वेर्चीता गवाही सीयाले रॉहतुल।

GORONTALO

INTRODUCTION

This Austronesian language is spoken in the north-eastern peninsula of Sulawesi (Celebes) by about 900,000 Muslims. The ethnonym is Holontalo (the sound /r/ is not in the language).

SCRIPT

If written, the Roman alphabet is used.

PHONOLOGY

Consonants

stops: p, b, t, d, k, g, q, ʔ
affricates: tʃ, dʒ
fricative: h
nasals: m, n, ŋ
lateral: l
semi-vowels: w, j

Pre-nasalized stops: e.g. /mb, nt, ŋg/; *-nt-* seems to tend towards /ṇḍ/. /s, n, r/ occur in loanwords.

Vowels

short: i, ɛ, a·, ɔ, u
long: i, ɛ, a, ɔ

All finals are vocalic with diphthong glides, e.g. oö, iö /wə, jə/. Stress is always on the penultimate.

MORPHOLOGY AND SYNTAX

Noun

No gender; stems are potentially nominal or verbal. The singular can be stressed by addition of the numerical *tuwawu*/*tu.a.u* 'one'. There is no plural formant: *dadata* 'many' may be used, and reduplication occurs., e.g. *tau.tau.alo* '(the) men'; *olo.olobu alo* 'buffaloes'.

U is often used as an article, together with demonstrative: e.g. *U alo bo.tie mo.piohu tutu* 'This food (*alo*) is very (*tutu*) good (*mo.piohu*)', where *bo.tie* is the demonstrative pronoun/adjective.

POSSESSION

Positional, e.g. *bihu auhu* 'the shore of the ocean' (*auhu* = Indonesian *laut*). The connecting particle *li* (Malay, Bahasa Indonesia *di*, Buginese *ri*, Tagalog *ni*) may also be used: e.g. *o/u bele li pani* 'the house (*bele*) of the smith'; *loia li amo.lio* 'the speech of his father' (*-lio* is third person suffix).

o- before a noun indicates possessor of that referent: *ti.gulu* (< Sk. *guru*) *o.medja tuwawu* 'the teacher has a table'

Adjective

As attribute, adjective follows noun: e.g. *bele mo.piohu* 'fine house'; *huidu mo.langgato* 'high mountain'; *hualimo talaa* 'silver ring'.

A comparative is made with *laba*: *iö pangola bo wau* /u.a.u/ *laba pangola* 'you are old but I am older'.

Pronoun

Personal independent with enclitic suffixes:

	Singular		Plural	
1	wau/wātija	-(q)u	*incl.* ito, *excl.* ami/	-lami/-to/-nto
2	(j)iö	-mu	timongoli	-limongoli
3	tiö	-(l)io	timongolio	-limongolia

High register suffixes are: sing. 1 *-laatia*, 2 *-nto*; pl. 1 (excl.) *-lamiaatiae.*

DEMONSTRATIVE PRONOUN/ADJECTIVE

Based on stems *ti/ta*: *bo.tia/-tie* 'this, these'; *bo.ito* 'that, those'. These follow the noun: e.g. (*u*) *tau bo.tia* 'this man'.

INTERROGATIVE PRONOUN

ti.ta 'who?'; *wo.lo* 'what?'

RELATIVE PRONOUN

tā: e.g. *wadala tā pangola* 'a horse which is old'; *Wau/wātija tā mo.hama, jiö tā mo.delo* 'I am the one who takes, you are the one who brings'; *Wātija tā mo.mintaqā bulua boito* 'I am the one who will pick up the box.'

Numerals

1–10: *o-ēnta, o-luo, o-tolu, o-pato, olimo, o-lomo, o-pitu, o-walu, o-tio, o-pulu.* 11 *mo.pulu wa u tuau*; 20 *dulo pulu*; 30 *to*(*w*)*ulo pulu*; 100 *mo-hetuto.*

Another word for 'one' is *tuwawu*, which can, as mentioned above, be used as a marker of singularity.

Verb

Prefixes, often compounded, play a crucial role in Gorontalo verb structure.

TENSE MARKERS

Present *he*; past *lo*(*ti*); future *mo*(*ti*) = imperfective marker. Examples: *Tiö he mo.kaladža to ilēngi* 'He works in the garden'; *Tei Ako he mo.luladu* 'Ako is writing now'; *Ti mama he mo.tubu* 'Mother is cooking'; *Wātija lo.tuluhē to bele.lio ohui* 'I slept at his house last night'; *Wātija mo.tuluhē toqutōnu?* 'Where shall I sleep?' Cf. *Ti mama dīla* ***mo****tubu ila* 'Mother isn't going to cook rice' (*dīla* 'not'); *Ti mama dīla* ***lo****tubu ila* 'Mother didn't cook rice.'

Perfective marker is *ma*-: e.g. *teli* 'buy', *mateli* 'have bought'; *Tete ma.ti.lumeteo* 'The cat has run away'. The imperfective marker *mo*- is also used with adjectival verbs: e.g. *Wadala.mu mo.hata* 'Your horse is thin'.

Imperative/necessitative marker is *po*: e.g. *po*(*ti*).*huloqolo!* 'sit down!': *Po.laö jiö ode hulondtalo* 'You have to go to Gorontalo.' This marker is reduplicated for emphasis: e.g. *Dīla popo.langgata batanga tota ngopohidža* 'Do not place yourself above others'.

Future necessitative: *mapopo*-, e.g. *mapopo.teli.ja.mu* 'to be bought by you'.

Potential: *loö*, e.g. *loö.teli* 'be able to buy'.

Passive infix: -*il*-, e.g. *mo.delo* 'to bring', *mo.d.il.elo.lio* 'it was brought by him'.

Causative prefixes: *mopo*-, *lopo*-, *popo*- for present, past, future: e.g. *Tiö mopo.teteqo* 'He will make it run' (= drive a car); *Tiö lopo.teteqo* 'He made it run.'

Prepositions

Li 'of', 'by', e.g. *ilā li Ali* 'eaten by Ali'; *to* 'at', e.g. *to Hulondtalo* 'at/in Gorontalo', *towātija* 'at my house' (= '*chez moi*'); *londto* 'from', e.g. *londto wātija* 'from me'.

Word order

SVO

GOTHIC

INTRODUCTION

Gothic belongs to the Germanic family, and is the only textually attested form of East Germanic. In the fourth century AD the Visigoths were settled along the lower course of the Danube and in neighbouring areas, having moved there from a homeland in southern Sweden; and it was here that Bishop Wulfila worked as a missionary and translator, first north of the Danube, and after 348 south of the river in Roman territory. Wulfila seems to have translated most of the Bible into Gothic, and our knowledge of the language rests on the extensive fragments which have survived. The manuscripts date from about the sixth century and were found in northern Italy, brought there presumably by the Ostrogoths. There are two main collections – the *Codex Argenteus* in Uppsala University, and the *Codices Ambrosiani* in Milan. A form of spoken Gothic survived in the Crimea until the eighteenth century.

SCRIPT

See **Script** at end of article

PHONOLOGY

Consonants

stops: p, b, t, d, k, g
fricatives: f, v, s, θ, ð, z, h, γ
nasals: m, n, ŋ
lateral and flap: l, r
semi-vowels: w, j

/b, d, g/: pronunciation depends on position in word: cf. *barn* /barn/, 'child'; *sibun* /sivun/, 'seven', where /-v-/ is a bilabial [β] *augō* /auγoː/, 'eye'; *dag* /dax/, 'day'; *drigkan* /driŋkan/, 'to drink'. /m, n, s, l, r, θ/ occur geminated. [k˚] and [h˚] occur. /h/ may represent [ç] or [x].

ƕ probably = /h˚/: *ƕeila* /h˚eila/ 'time', Eng. 'while'.

Vowels

i, eː, a, aː, oː, u, uː

/ɛ/ and /ɔ/ were probably present, notated as digraphs *ai* and *au*. /m, n, l, r/ function as vowels in certain words, i.e. as /m̩, n̩, l̩, r̩/.

Digraphs: aí = /ɛ̆/, ái = /ej/, ai = /ɛ̄/; aú = /ɔ̆/, au = /ɔ̄/, áu = /ou/.

These are not marked by Ulfilas (Wulfila), but can be determined by comparison with his spelling of Greek etyma, especially proper names. Cf. *aírþa* /ɛrθa/ 'earth'; *áins* /ɛjns/ 'one'; *haúrn* /hɔ̆rn/ 'horn'; *trauan* /trɔ̄an/ 'trust'; *dáuþus* /douθus/ 'death'.

MORPHOLOGY AND SYNTAX

Noun

Nouns are masculine, feminine, or neuter, singular or plural, with four cases.

a-, *ō*-, *i*-, and *u*- stems follow the standard Indo-European strong-declension model. There is also a weak declension comprising *n*- stems.

Example of *a*- tem declension: *dags* 'day' (masculine):

	Singular	*Plural*
nominative	dags	dagos
accusative	dag	dagans
genitive	dagis	dagē
dative	daga	dagam

Cf. masculine *n*- stem: *atta* 'father', pl. *attans*; feminine *ō*- stem: *giba* /giva/ 'gift', pl. *gibōs*; neuter *a*- stem: *waúrd* /wɔrd/ 'word', pl. *waúrda*; masculine *-nd* stem: sing./plural *frijōnds* 'friend'.

Examples of case usage:

Accusative: *bigētun þana siukan skalk hailana* 'they found the sick servant whole' (*hailana* is acc. of adjective *hails* 'whole'; *þana* is acc. of demonstrative *sa* 'that'); *izwis ni qiþ a skalkans* 'I call you not servants'.

Genitive: *ahmins weihis fulls* 'full of the Holy Ghost'; *hilp meinàziōs ungaláubeinàis* 'help thou my unbelief'.

Partitive genitive: *jah ni was im barnē* 'and they had no children'.

Dative: *jah qaþ du þamma mann þamma gaþaursana habandin handu* (Mark 3.3) 'and he said to the man which had the withered hand' (*du* is preposition 'to'; *habandin* is participle + dat. ending); *wōpida Iēsus stibnái mikilái* 'Jesus cried out with a loud voice'.

Adjective

The adjective has strong and weak declensions (as nouns). Both are exemplified in the sentence above: *bigētun þana siukan skalk hailana* (*siukan* is weak after *þana*, and *hailana* is the strong-declension accusative).

The singular masculine strong declension is illustrated here by *blinds* 'blind': nom. *blinds*; acc. *blindana*; gen. *blindis*; dat. *blindamma*. The singular weak forms are: nom. *blinda*; acc. *blindan*; gen. *blindins*; dat. *blindin*.

COMPARATIVE

The comparative is made with *-iz-/-oz-*: e.g. *swinþs* 'strong', comp. *swinþoza*.

The usual suppletive bases are found: e.g. *gōþs* 'good' – *batiza*; *mikils* 'big' – *máiza*; *ubils* 'bad' – *waírsiza*; *sa afar mis gagganda swinþōza mis ist* 'he that cometh after me is mightier than I'.

Pronoun

PERSONAL PRONOUN

		1st person	*2nd person*	*3rd person*		
				Masc.	*Nt.*	*Fem.*
singular	nom.	ik	þu	is	ita	si
	acc.	mik	þuk	ina	ita	ija
	gen.	meina	þeina	is	is	izōs
	dat.	mis	þus	imma	imma	izai
dual	nom.	wit	–			
	acc.	ugkis/uŋkis/	igqis			
	gen.	–	igqara			
	dat.	ugkis	igqis			
plural	nom.	weis	jus	eis	ija	–
	acc.	uns(is)	izwis	ins	–	ijōs
	gen.	unsara	izwara	izē	–	izōs
	dat.	uns(is)	izwis	im	im	im

DEMONSTRATIVE PRONOUN/ADJECTIVE

sa 'this' (masc.) with nt. *þata*, fem. *sō*. These are declined normally: e.g. *sa*: *þana*, *þis*, *þamma*.

INTERROGATIVE PRONOUN

Masc. *h°as*; neuter *h°a*; fem. *h°o*: fully declined.

RELATIVE PRONOUN

Masc. is provided by the demonstrative *sa*, *þata*, *sō*, with affixed particle *-ei*: *sa.ei*, *þat.ei*, *sō.ei*; fully declined: e.g.

> þu is sunus meins sa liuba, in þuzei waila galeikāida (Mark 1.11)
> 'thou art my beloved Son, in whom I am well pleased'

Numerals

1–10: *áins*, *twái*, *þrija*, *fidwōr*, *fimf*, *saíhs*, *sibun*, *ahtáu*, *niun*, *taíhun*; 12 *twalif*; 14 *fidwōrtaíhun*; 20 *twái tigjus*; 40 *fidwōr tigjus*; 100 *taíhuntēhund*.

Verb

The Gothic verb has two voices, active and passive; two moods, indicative and subjunctive; two tenses, present and preterite; three numbers.

For the indicative and subjunctive present there is a synthetic passive, unique in Germanic, e.g. *nasja* 'I save': pass. *nasjada* 'I am saved'; subj. pass. *nasjaidau*. Elsewhere, the passive voice is made analytically with past participle (passive) plus auxiliaries *wairþan* or *wisan*.

CONJUGATION

Strong or weak according to the form taken by the preterite: strong (a) ablaut: six classes; (b) reduplication; (c) ablaut + reduplication (unique in Germanic); weak: *-da*/*-ta* (this is a Germanic innovation).

Strong:

(a) The ablaut classes can be illustrated by giving the infinitive, the first person singular and plural preterite, and the past participle: e.g.

niman – nam, nēmum – numans 'take'
hilpan – halp, hulpum – hulpans 'help'
giban – gaf, gēbum – gibans 'give'

(b) Reduplicating class: e.g. *háitan* – *háiháit*, *háiháitum* – *háitans* 'call'.
(c) Ablaut + reduplication: *grētan* – *gaigrot* – *grētans* 'weep'.

ga- prefix with perfective or collective nuance: *ga.nasjan* 'to save'; *ga.baíran* 'to bring forth'; *ga.rinnan* 'to hasten together'.

Present indicative and subjunctive: e.g. of *niman* 'take':

Indicative:

sing.	1 nima	2 nimis	3 nimiþ
dual	1 nimos	2 nimats	
pl.	1 nimam	2 nimiþ	3 nimand

Subjunctive:

sing.	1 nimáu	2 nimáis	3 nimái
dual:	1 nimáiwa	2 nimáits	
pl.	1 nimáima	2 nimáiþ	3 nimáina

The first person indicative preterite forms are: sing. *nam*; dual: *nēmu*; pl. *nēmum*; and in the subjunctive: sing. *nēmjáu*; dual; *nēmeiwa*; pl. *nēmeima*.

Passive:

	Singular			*Plural*
indicative:	1 nimada	2 nimaza	3 nimada	1, 2, 3 nimanda
subjunctive:	nimáidáu	nimáizáu	nimáidáu	nimáindáu

The passive dual is not attested.

Imperative: 2nd sing. *nim*; dual; *nimats*; pl. 1 *niman*, 2 *nimiþ*, 3 *nimandáu.*

Weak:

The first person forms of a weak verb, *nasjan* 'to save', are given as illustration:

indicative present: *nasja*; dual: *nasjōs*; pl.: *nasjam*;
subjunctive present: *nasjáu*; dual: *nasjáiwa*; pl.: *nasjáima*;
indicative preterite: *nasida*; dual: *nasidēdu*; pl. *nasidēdum*;
subjunctive preterite: *nasidēdjáu*; dual: *nasidēdeiwa*; pl.: *nasidēdeima*;
passive: *nasjada*; subjunctive passive: *nasjáidáu*.

Use of auxiliary *wisan* 'to be': *was Iōhannēs dáupjands* 'John was baptizing'; *wēsun sipōnjōs fastandans* 'the disciples were fasting'. Passive with *wisan*: *qam Iésus jah daupiþs was fran Iōhannē* 'Jesus came and was baptized by John'; *sabbatō in mans warþ ga.skapans* 'the Sabbath was made for man'.

Prepositions

Prepositions govern accusative or dative or both; e.g. with acc., *undar* 'under', *wiþra* 'against'; with dative, *af* 'from', 'to', *du* 'to'; with both, *afar* 'after'. Some govern both + genitive, e.g. *in* 'in'.

20 Aþþan ni bi þans bidja áinans, ak bi þans galáubjandans
þaírh waúrda izē du mis,
21 ei alláí áin sijáina, swaswē þu, atta, in mis jah ik in þus, ei
jah þái in uggkis áin sijáina, ei sō manasēþs galáubjái þatei
þu mik insandidēs.
22 Jah ik wulþu þanei gaft mis, gaf im, ei sijáina áin swaswē
wit áin siju.
23 Ik in im jah þu in mis, ei sijáina ustaúhanái du áinamma,
jah kunnei sō manasēþs þatei þu mik insandidēs, jah frijōdēs
ins, swaswē mik frijōdēs.
24 Atta, þatei atgaft mis, wiljáu ei þarei im ik, jah þái sijáina
miþ mis, ei saíƕáina wulþu meinana þanei gaft mis, untē
frijōdēs mik faúr gaskaft faírƕáus.
25 Atta garaíhta, jah sō manasēþs þuk ni ufkunþa; iþ ik þuk
kunþa. Jah þái ufkunþēdun þatei þu mik insandidēs.
26 Jah gakannida im namō þeinata jah kannja, ei friaþwa þōei
frijōdēs mik, in im sijái jah ik in im.

(John 17.20–6)

SCRIPT

Basically, a Greek uncial plus graphs from Roman and Runic (*u* and *o*).

THE GOTHIC SCRIPT

THE ALPHABET

a b g d e
q z h θ i
k l m n j
u p r s t
w f ch hw o

GREEK, CLASSICAL

INTRODUCTION

Greek belongs to the Hellenic branch of Indo-European. With a written record extending over 3,400 years, it has the longest attested history of any Indo-European language, and is rivalled globally only by Chinese.

It was early in the second millennium BC that the first wave of Indo-European-speaking invaders reached the Greek Peninsula, the Peloponnese, and some of the islands, and settled. Homer calls them the *Achaioi*. Their speech seems to have formed the basis for the dialect subsequently known as Ionic. Little is known about the autochthonous 'Pelasgian' people whom they displaced or absorbed, but it is to the presumably non-Indo-European Pelasgian language that Greek owes such consonantal clusters as *-nth-* and *-ss-*, which proliferate in place-names and names of plants: e.g. *Korinthos, Zakinthos*; *akantha* (thorny bush).

This Bronze Age civilization, known as Mycenaean, lasted approximately from 1500 to 1100 BC. During this period, the language was notated in the so-called Linear B script, which was based on a non-Indo-European Cretan model (Linear A). The Linear B character was deciphered by Michael Ventris and John Chadwick in 1952.

In the eleventh century BC the Mycenaean civilization was disrupted by the Dorian invasions into western Greece. There followed a considerable redistribution of population involving dispersal of dialects. Linear B ceased to be used. For three centuries there is no written record.

In the ninth/eighth centuries BC the Homeric poems were written in the Ionic dialect and in a new script based on the North Semitic alphabet, with specific signs for the five vowels. Thus the creation of a literary standard in the shape of two of the world's greatest poems coincided with the introduction of what is arguably the world's most efficient and adaptable writing system.

Ionic blended into the Attic dialect of Athens, and the scene was set for the unparalleled period of creativity which followed – the seminal years of the whole of Western culture: a period which includes Aeschylus, Sophocles, Euripides, Aristophanes, Sappho, Anacreon, Pindar, Menander, Plato, Aristotle, Demosthenes, Herodotus, Thucydides, and Xenophon.

Towards the end of the first millennium BC a modified Attic Greek emerged as *hē koinē dialektos*, or 'common speech', a form which was to survive for a thousand years as the language of the Hellenistic period, based first on Alexandria and then on Byzantium. It is this form which provides the basis for the *katharevousa* (*see* **Greek, Modern Standard**).

Dialects

Many dialects flourished in the Classical and Hellenistic periods, and are attested in thousands of inscriptions found all over the Greek world, which includes, apart from Greece itself, Asia Minor, the Adriatic seaboard, Southern Italy, Sicily, Egypt, and parts of the Middle East. Four dialects are important:

1. Ionic, the dialect used in the Homeric poems and in Hesiod.
2. Attic, the language of the Classical period.
3. Doric/Dorian, the language of Sparta. Doric is marked by certain archaic features, e.g. the retention of long *ā* in words like *mātēr* 'mother' where Ionic and Attic have *mētēr*. In Attic literature, Doric was used for choral lyric poetry, and to superb comic effect in the Lysistrata of Aristophanes.
4. The dialect known as Aeolic, spoken in Thessaly and in some of the islands, e.g. Lesbos, was used by Sappho. A curious trait in this dialect is the presence of /p/ for Attic /t/ in such words as *pisyres* 'four' for Attic *tessares*.

PHONOLOGY

Consonants

stops: p, ph, b, t, th, d, k, kh, g
fricatives: s (in later Greek + f (< ph), θ (< th), χ (< kh))
nasals: m, n, ŋ
lateral and flap: l, r

There are three composite fricatives: /zd/, /ks/, /ps/; notated as ζ, ξ, ψ. Note that voiced aspirates are missing.

Vowels

iː, ɪ, ɛː, ɛ, aː, a, ɔː, o, uː, yː, y

Vocalic onset is accompanied by rough (ʿ) or soft (ʾ) breathing. Rough onset is indicated here by h-.

DIPHTHONGS

ai, au, eu, ɛi, ɛu, oi, yi, ɔi

PITCH MARKS

From 200 BC on, under the influence of the Alexandrine grammarians pitch accents are used: high (acute), low (grave), and high to low (circumflex). The tonic stress falls on one of the last three syllables. In the nominal system, accentuation is usually consistent with citation form; in the verbal system, stress is governed by rules and is therefore theoretically predictable.

MORPHOLOGY AND SYNTAX

Greek has three genders and three numbers: the dual is preserved in the

Attic nominal system throughout the classical period; in the verbal system it is practically limited to the second and third person.

Definite article

Masc. *ho*, fem, *hē*, nt. *to*; declined in three numbers and four cases: nominative, accusative, genitive, dative: e.g. masc. *ho – ton – tou – tōi*; fem. *hē – tēn – tēs – tēi*. Dual: nom./acc. *tō*, gen., dat. *toin* are regularly used for all three genders, though specific feminine forms, *tā*, *tain*, existed. Plural: masc. *hoi – tous – tōn – tois*; fem. *hai – tās – tōn – tais*; nt. *ta – ta – tōn – tois.*

The article – especially the neuter plural *ta* – can be used without an overtly expressed referent: e.g. *ta tōn polemiōn* 'the (things, i.e. assets) of the enemy'; *ta en Spartēi* 'the (events) in Sparta'; *pros tous eukolōs ekpherontas* ***ta autōn*** 'to those who talk lightly about their own affairs' (Epictetus: IV, XIII).

Declension

There are three declensions of nominals including adjectives and participles:

1st decl. *ā* stems: masc. *-as/ēs*, fem. *ā/ē*: e.g. masc. *ho politēs* 'the citizen'; fem, *hē xōrā* 'the land', *hē timē* 'the honour'.
2nd decl. *-o/ō* stem: masc. *-os* (with some feminines); neuter *-on*: e.g. masc. *ho logos* 'the word'; fem. *hē nēsos* 'the island'; nt. *to dōron* 'the gift'.
3rd decl. the consonantal declension comprising all nouns not in 1st or 2nd: e.g. masc. *ho phylaks* 'the watchman', *ho salpingks* 'the trumpet', *ho poimēn* 'the shepherd', *ho sōtēr* 'the saviour'; fem. *hē lampas* 'the lamp', *hē elpis* 'the hope'; nt. *to peras* 'the end', *to sōma* 'the body'.

Specimen declension: *ho politēs* 'the citizen':

	Singular	*Dual*	*Plural*
nom.	ho politēs	tō politā	hoi politai
acc.	ton politēn	tō politā	tous politās
gen.	tou politou	toin politain	tōn politōn
dat.	tō politēi	toin politain	tois politais

Declension is, on the whole, remarkably regular and symmetrical; there are, of course, many irregularities.

Some examples of case usage (apart from primary functions):

Accusative:

cognate accusative, e.g. *hamartīma hamartanein* 'to sin a sin', *graʃēn graphesthai* 'to bring an indictment';
accusative of specification: e.g. *Hellēnes eisi to genos* 'they are Greeks by race'.

Genitive:

partitive genitive with many verbs: e.g. *hoi agathoi tōn anthrōpōn* 'the good (ones) among the men';
with verbs of perception: e.g. *eleutheriēs geusamenoi* 'having tasted of freedom' (Herodotus), *toutōn tōn mathēmatōn epithymō* 'I long for this learning' (Xenophon);
with ablative nuance: e.g. *Hē nēsos ou poly diekhei tēs ēpeirou* 'The island is not far distant from the mainland'; *epistēmē khōrizdomenē dikaiosynēs* 'knowledge separated from justice' (Plato);
genitive of cause, source: e.g. *Zdēlō se tou nou, tēs de deilias stygō* 'I envy you for your mind but detest you for your cowardice' (Sophocles: *Electra*).

Genitive absolute (corresponding to Latin ablative absolute):

pneontos anemou tou autou
'with the same wind blowing' (Plato, *Theaet.* 152 B)

tēs gar emporias ouk ousēs
'there being no mercantile traffic' (Thucydides, *Hist. Pel. War*, I, ii)

katastantos de tou Minō nautikou
'when the navy of Minos had been established' (Thucydides, *Hist. Pel. War*, I, viii)

tōn thurōn kekleismenōn
'the doors being closed/when the doors were closed' (Gospel of St John 20.26)

Dative:

of benefit or disadvantage (*dativus commodi et incommodi*): e.g. *Pas anēr autōi ponei* 'Every man labours for himself' (Sophocles: *Ajax*), *Solon Athēnaiois nomous ethēke* 'Solon made laws for the Athenians';
causal and instrumental use: e.g. *logōi* 'in word', *ergōi* 'in deed', *horōmen tois ophthalmois* 'we see with our eyes';
agent: e.g. *eksetasai ti pepraktai tois allois* 'to ask what has been done by the others' (Demosthenes);
time: e.g. *tēi autēi hēmerai apethanen* 'he died on the same day'.

Adjective

The adjective agrees in gender, number, and case with noun, and as attribute, precedes it: e.g. *ho sophos anēr* 'the wise man', gen. *tou sophou andros*, dat. *tōi sophōi andri*, pl. gen. *tōn sophōn andrōn*. Similarly, all participles in *-os*.

Some adjectives are irregular, e.g. *megas* 'big': acc. *megan*, gen. *megalou*. dat. *megalōi*.

COMPARATIVE

In *-teros*/*-tatos*: e.g. *pikros* 'bitter' – *pikroteros*/*pikrotatos*.

Pronoun

PERSONAL PRONOUN

The personal pronouns are:

	Singular	*Dual*	*Plural*
1	egō	nōin	hēmeis
2	sy	sphōin	hymeis
3	autōs/autē/auto	autō/autā/autō	spheis; autoi/autai/auta

These are declined in all cases; e.g. first person singular: *egō – eme – emou – emoi*. The dual accusative = nominative; the genitive/dative forms are first person *nōin*, second *sphōin*.

DEMONSTRATIVE PRONOUN

houtos/hautē/touto; pl. *houtoi/hautai/tauta* 'this, these'; *hode/hēde/tode*; pl. *hoide/haide/tade* 'that, those'. *Ekeinos/-ē/-o* can also be used for 'that, those'. The demonstratives have dual forms and are declined in all cases.

INTERROGATIVE PRONOUN

tis, ti 'who? what?', declined in three numbers and all cases.

RELATIVE PRONOUN

hos, hē, ho; dual *hō* (all three genders); pl. *hoi, hai, ha*: e.g. *egō hos touto epoiēsa* 'I who did this'; *Edēlōse touto* ***hois*** *epratte* 'He showed this by what he did' (pl. dat.); *Touto ouk epoiēsen, en* ***ōi*** *ton dēmon etimēsen an* 'He did not do this in which he might have honoured the people' (Demosthenes).

Numerals

1–4 inclusive: *eis, dyo, treis, tessares/tettares*; these are declined; the feminine of *eis* is mia, the neuter *hen*.

The numbers 5 upwards are indeclinable: 5–10 *pente, heks, hepta, oktō, ennea, deka*; 11 *endeka*; 12 *dōdeka*; 13 *treis kai deka*; 20 *eikosi(n)*; 21 *eis kai eikosi*; 30 *triakonta*; 40 *tessarakonta*; 100 *hekaton*.

Verb

The Greek verb had three voices: active, middle, and passive; medio-passive forms with active meaning are known as deponent verbs.

There are four moods: indicative, imperative, subjunctive, optative; the indicative mood has seven tenses: present, imperfect, perfect, pluperfect, aorist, future, and future perfect.

TENSE SYSTEM

The basic nine stems, with their associated tenses:

1. present: present, imperfect (active, middle, and passive);
2. future: future (active and middle)
3. first aorist: first aorist (active and middle);

4. second aorist: second aorist (active and middle);
5. first perfect: first perfect, pluperfect (active);
6. second perfect: second perfect, pluperfect (active);
7. perfect middle: perfect and pluperfect (middle), future perfect (passive);
8. first passive: first aorist, future (passive);
9. second passive: second aorist, future (passive).

Few verbs have both the first and second forms of any tense; hence, most verbs have only six stems, while many have fewer.

Verbs are further sub-divided into two categories: in (a) the root stem is stable throughout the tense system; in (b) the root stem is specifically modulated to accommodate the various tense stems.

A further division is into (a) vowel stems, e.g. *phile-* 'to love', and (b) consonant stems, e.g. *trib-* 'to rub', *graph-* 'to write', *peith-* 'to prevail upon'.

PRINCIPAL PARTS

Theoretically, all forms of a Greek verb can be constructed from the following items: first person singular of the present, the future, the first aorist, and the perfect in the indicative active; the first person singular of the perfect middle and the aorist (passive); first person singular of second aorist (active or middle) if present. Examples, from *leipō* 'to leave' and *phainō* 'to show':

leipō, leipsō, leloipa, leleimmai, eleiphthēn, elipon
phainō, phanō, ephēna, pephangka/pephēna, pephasmai, ephanthēn

DEPONENT VERBS

The principal parts are the first person singular of the present, the future, the perfect, and the aorist (all indicative); e.g. of *ergazdomai* 'to work':

ergazdomai, ergasomai, eirgasamēn, eirgasmai, eirgasthēn

CONJUGATION

Involves selection of the correct stem, the relevant personal endings in three numbers, the use of the augment in the imperfect and aorist indicative, and the use of the reduplicating prefix in the perfect system. In this way, over 500 forms are generated in a typical conjugation.

Specimen conjugation: *leipō* 'to leave':

1. Present system:

active: present: *leípō*; imperfect: *éleipon*; subjunctive: *leípō*; optative: *leípoimi*; imperative: *leîpe*; infinitive: *leípein*; participle: *leípōn*;
middle: present: *leípomai*; imperfect: *eleipómēn*; subjunctive: *leípōmai*; optative: *leipoímēn*; imperative: *leípou*; infinitive: *leípesthai*; participle: *leipómenos*;
passive: as middle.

2. Future system:

active: future: *leípsō*; optative: *leípsoimi*; infinitive: *leípsein*: participle: *leípsōn*;
middle: future: *leípsomai*; optative: *leipsoímēn*; infinitive: *leípsesthai*; participle: *leipsómenos.*

3. None.
4. Second aorist system:

active: ***é****lipon*; subjunctive: *lípō*; optative: *lípoimi*; imperative: *lípe*; infinitive: *lipeîn*; participle: *lipṓn*;
middle: ***e****lipómēn*; subjunctive: *lípōmai*; optative: *lipoímēn*; imperative: *lipoû*; infinitive: *lipésthai*; participle: *lipómenos.*

5. None.
6. Second perfect and pluperfect:

active: ***lé****loipa*; subjunctive: ***le****loípō*; optative: ***le****loípoimi*; infinitive: ***le****loipénai*; participle: ***le****loipṓs.*

7. Perfect and pluperfect:

middle: ***lé****leimmai*; subjunctive: ***le****leimménos ō*; optative: ***le****leimmēnos eíēn*; imperative: ***lé****leipso*; infinitive: ***le****leîphthai*; participle: ***le****leimménos*;
future perfect: ***le****leípsomai*; optative: ***le****leipsoímēn*; infinitive: ***le****leípsesthai*; participle: ***le****leipsómenos.*

8. First future passive: *leiphthḗsomai*; optative: *leiphthēsoímēn*; infinitive: *leiphthḗsesthai*; participle: *leiphthēsómenos.*
9. First aorist passive: ***e****leíphthēn*; subjunctive: *leiphthô*; optative: *leiphtheíēn*; imperative: *leíphthēti*; infinitive: *leiphthênai*; participle: *leiphtheís.*

The *-th-* characteristic of the passive system is a Greek innovation in the structure of Indo-European.

Certain irregularities are due to internal sandhi in consonant-stem verbs: e.g. from *trībō* 'rub', perfect *****tetribmai*** → ***tetrimmai***, etc.

The vocalic collocations *aō, eō, oō* are contracted in the present and imperfect: e.g. *timaō* → *timō* 'honour'; *dēloō* → *dēlō* 'manifest'.

Verbs in *-mi* form a special class, with irregularities in the present and second aorist systems.

PERSONAL ENDINGS

Basic inventory:

(a) Active

		Primary tenses	*Secondary tenses*
sing.	1	mi (ō)	n
	2	s	s
	3	si (ti)	–
dual	2	ton	ton

	3	ton	tēn
pl.	1	men (mes)	men (mes)
	2	te	te
	3	nsi (nti) asi	n, san

(b) Middle and passive

sing.	1	mai	mēn
	2	sai	so
	3	tai	to
dual	2	(s)thon	(s)thon
	3	(s)thon	(s)thēn
pl.	1	metha	metha
	2	(s)the	(s)the
	3	ntai	nto

Imperative

		Active	*Middle and passive*
sing.	2	thi	so
	3	tō	(s)thō
dual	2	ton	(s)thon
	3	tōn	(s)thōn
pl.	2	te	(s)the
	3	ntōn/tōsan	(s)thōn/(s)thōsan

The primary tenses referred to in the above table are the present, perfect, future, and future perfect; the secondary tenses are the imperfect, the pluperfect, and the aorist.

Oratio obliqua: infinitive construction (marked for tense/aspect): e.g. *phēsi tous andras apelthein* 'he says that the men went away'; *nomizdō se mōron einai*: 'I think you're stupid'; *Apangelleis moi pollous toi epibouleuein* 'You tell me that many are plotting against you' (Diogenes Laertius I.64).

Or tense sequence after *hoti* 'that': following primary tenses, an indicative form retains mood: e.g. *legei hoti graphei/egraphen/egrapsen* 'he says that he is writing/was writing/wrote'. After secondary tenses the optative may replace the indicative forms: e.g. *Eleksan hoti pempseie sfas ho Indōn basileus* 'They said that the king of the Indians had sent them' (Xenophon).

NEGATION

ou is the general negator in both independent and indirect sentences. *Mē* negates the imperative and the subjunctive.

Prepositions

Four – *anti* 'against', *apo* 'from, for', *ek*(*s*) 'out of', *pro* 'before' – take the genitive: e.g. *apo toutou tou khronou* 'from that time' (Xenophon); *onar ek Dios estin* 'the dream comes from Zeus' (*Iliad*).

Two – *en* 'in', *syn* 'with' – take the dative: e.g. *ton Periklea en orgē eikhon* 'they held Pericles in anger' = 'were angry with Pericles' (Thucydides).

Four take the genitive or accusative: *dia* 'through', *kata* 'below', *hyper* 'over', *meta* 'among': e.g. with gen.: *meta zdōntōn* 'among the living' (Sophocles); with accusative: *meta straton ēlas'; Akhaiōn* 'he drove into the army of the Achaeans' (*Iliad*).

Six take genitive, dative, or accusative: *amphi* 'about', *epi* 'on', 'upon', *para* 'by', 'near', *peri* 'around', *pros* 'at', 'by', *hypo* 'under': e.g. *hypo:*

with genitive: *ta hypo gēs* 'the things that are under the earth' (Plato: *Apology*);
with dative: *hypo tēi Akropoli* 'under the Akropolis' (Herodotus);
with accusative: *ēltheth'; hypo Troiēn* 'you came to Troy' (*Odyssey*).

Indeclinable particles

A key element in Classical Greek syntax is provided by the indeclinable particles, such as *de*, *men*, *gar*, *dē*, *oun*, *ara*, etc. The particles accompany the narrative with a kind of connective counterpoint: for example, Subject A + *men* (+ verb) anticipates Subject B + *de* (+ verb); the formal symmetry is accompanied by semantic balance, often implying contrast, and the syntagm can be translated into English as 'On the one hand (A) . . . on the other hand (B)'. *de* by itself is a ubiquitous connective, functioning as the second word in numberless Greek sentences. It can usually be translated simply as 'and'. Formally, it (like *men* and *oun*) can be placed between the article and the noun: *hoi de Thēbaioi* . . . ', 'the Thebans . . . '. Sometimes it seems to act as a focusing agent, like Japanese *wa*. *gar* and *oun* can be translated as 'therefore', 'because of'. Few particles can be finals; *dēta*, an emphatic negative, is one.

A second set of particles, including *ge*, *dē*, *kai dē*, are non-connective, but add various nuances and/or emphasis to the discourse. (Compare the *xū zi*, the 'empty words' in Classical Chinese.)

Some examples follow:

hoi men oun Athēnaioi kai Lakedaimonioi peri tauta ēsan, hoi de Thēbaioi . . .
'So the Athenians and the Lacedaimonians were occupied with these matters. As for the Thebans . . . ' (Xenophon, *Hellenica* VI)

peri men dē tōn theōn
'So, touching the gods' (Xenophon, *Anabasis* II, v)

emoi men gar metriōs . . .
'for me (that) will suffice' (Plato, *Phaedrus*)

pōs legeis touto, ou gar mathainō
'What do you mean by that? I don't follow' (Plato, *Phaedrus*)

tauta men dē houtos exetō

'that may very well be so' (Plato, *Crito*)

ouk ar′ agathon ho ploutos
'so, after all, wealth is not a blessing'

hoi de Thēbaioi ēkouon men tauta
'so, while the Thebans listened to these words . . . ' (Xenophon, *Hellenica*, VI, v)

ou dēta = ou dei dē pou
'certainly not!'
'Why, no!' (Plato, *Crito*)

hoi de legontes hoti . . .
'there are those who say that . . . '

Word order

Generally SVO, but almost any order is possible.

1 III **1** Ἐν ἀρχῇ ἦν ὁ λόγος, καὶ ὁ λόγος ἦν πρὸς τὸν θεόν,
καὶ θεὸς ἦν ὁ λόγος. **2** οὗτος ἦν ἐν ἀρχῇ πρὸς τὸν θεόν.
3 πάντα δι᾽ αὐτοῦ ἐγένετο, καὶ χωρὶς αὐτοῦ ἐγένετο ⸂οὐδὲ
ἕν⸃:. ὃ γέγονεν:¹ **4** ἐν αὐτῷ ζωὴ ⸀ἦν, καὶ ἡ ζωὴ ἦν τὸ φῶς
⸋τῶν ἀνθρώπων⸌· **5** καὶ τὸ φῶς ἐν τῇ σκοτίᾳ φαίνει, καὶ
ἡ σκοτία αὐτὸ οὐ κατέλαβεν.
2 III **6** Ἐγένετο ἄνθρωπος, ἀπεσταλμένος παρὰ ⸀θεοῦ, ⸆
ὄνομα αὐτῷ Ἰωάννης· **7** οὗτος ἦλθεν εἰς μαρτυρίαν ἵνα
μαρτυρήσῃ περὶ τοῦ φωτός, ἵνα πάντες πιστεύσωσιν δι᾽
αὐτοῦ. **8** οὐκ ἦν ἐκεῖνος τὸ φῶς, ἀλλ᾽ ἵνα μαρτυρήσῃ περὶ
τοῦ φωτός.

SCRIPT

Ancient Greek was first written, from *c.* 1400 to the twelfth century BC, in the Mycenaean script known as Linear B. This is the script which was deciphered by Ventris and Chadwick in 1952. An earlier script, associated with the Minoan culture of Crete, has not been deciphered; the language it notates is probably non-Indo-European.

The Mycenaean script was a syllabary, similar in structure to those used in Japanese. Independent vowels could be notated, especially if initial, but not independent consonants. Thus Ancient Greek words appear in Linear B exactly as Anglo-American loanwords do in Japanese katakana: e.g. *elektryōn* appears as *a.re.ku.tu.ru.wo.* In the same way, katakana writes *sukottorando* for 'Scotland', and *happibaasudee* for 'happy birthday'.

The Mycenaean script did not survive the Dorian invasions of Greece. When written Greek re-appears, in the eighth century, it is in an alphabetic script based on a North Semitic model. To begin with, the Semitic direction of writing – right to left – was copied, with frequent use of boustrophedon. After about 500, the left-to-right mode became standardized. Symbols for non-Semitic phonemes were invented. But the truly momentous step was taken when letters for the five vowels a, e, i, o, u were introduced. This far-reaching innovation ensured that the Greek alphabetic script would become – particularly after it came into Roman hands – the most successful and the most practically useful of the world's scripts. Not phonologically the most precise: here, the Graeco-Roman script must take second place to Devanāgarī. But no other script has been called upon to serve so many widely differing sound systems (though the closely related Cyrillic is a close second). The Greek script which was adopted in Athens in 403, and thereafter generalized, was, in terms of Greek dialectology, an Ionic (Eastern) model. The pitch accents – acute, grave, and circumflex – were introduced in the third century. The table shows the Greek letters, upper and lower case, with their ancient and modern pronunciation.

Aeolic also retained the digamma Ϝ = /w/: cf. Mycenaean *woiko* = Aeolic *Ϝoikos* = Attic *oikos* 'house'.

THE GREEK SCRIPT

THE ALPHABET

Capital letter	*Small Letter*	*Ancient phonetics*	*Usual transliteration*	*Modern pronunciation*	*Usual transliteration*
Α	α	[a]	a	[a]	a
Β	β	[b]	b	[v]	v
Γ	γ	[g]	g	[j] (/—i,e)	y
				[ɣ] (elsewhere)	g(h)
Δ	δ	[d]	d	[ð]	d(h)
Ε	ε	[ɛ]	e	[ɛ]	e
Ζ	ζ	[zd]	z	[z]	z
Η	η	[ɛː]	e:, ē	[i]	i
Θ	θ	[t^{h}]	th	[θ]	th
Ι	ι	[i]	i	[i]	i
Κ	ϰ	[k]	k	[k]	k
Λ	λ	[l]	l	[l]	l
Μ	μ	[m]	m	[m]	m
Ν	ν	[n]	n	[n]	n
Ξ	ξ	[ks]	x	[ks]	ks, x (as in *box*)
Ο	ο	[o]	o	[o]	o
Π	π	[p]	p	[p]	p
Ρ	ϱ	[r]	r	[ɾ]	r
Σ	σ (ς)	[s]	s	[s]	s
Τ	τ	[t]	t	[t]	t
Υ	υ	[y]	y, u	[i]	i
Φ	φ	[p^{h}]	ph	[f]	f
Χ	χ	[k^{h}]	ch, kh	[χ]	h, x (IPA value)
Ψ	ψ	[ps]	ps	[ps]	ps
Ω	ω	[ɔː]	o:, ō	[o]	o

Diphthongs and clusters	*Ancient phonetics*	*Usual transliteration*	*Modern pronunciation*	*Usual transliteration*
αι	[ai̯]	ai	[ɛ]	e
αυ	[au̯]	au	[av] (/__ + voice)	av
			[af] (/__ − voice)	af
ει	[eː]	ei	[i]	i
ευ	[ɛu̯]	eu	[ev] (/__ + voice)	ev
			[ef] (/__ − voice)	ef
οι	[oi̯]	oi	[i]	i
ου	[oː]	ou	[u]	u
υι	[yi̯]	yi, ui	[i]	i
γ before γ χ ξ	[ŋ]	n (g, kh, ks)	[ŋ]	n (g, h, ks)
γκ	[ŋk]	nk	[(ŋ)g] (medially)	(n)g
			[g] (initially)	g
μπ/μβ	[mp/mb]	mp/mb	[(m)b] (medially)	(m)b
			[b] (initially)	b
ντ/νδ	[nt/nd]	nt/nd	[(n)d] (medially)	(n)d
			[d] (initially)	d
τζ	-----	-----	[dz]	dz

Source: Joseph, B.D. (1987) 'Greek', in B. Comrie (ed.) *The World's Major Languages*, London: Routledge.

GREEK, MODERN STANDARD

INTRODUCTION

Modern Greek belongs to the Hellenic branch of Indo-European. It is the official language of Greece, where it is spoken by over 10 million people, and joint official language of Cyprus; in addition, there are large Greek-speaking communities in many countries. A dialect of Greek is still spoken in a few villages in Calabria.

For many centuries Greece presented the classic example of a *diglossia*. Two Greek languages were in use: (a) Demotic, the spoken language deriving from the Hellenistic koine, as modulated and developed in the Byzantine period and during the following centuries of Ottoman domination; and (b) Katharevousa, the consciously archaizing language of administration, religion, education, and literature. Katharevousa itself was written on more than one stylistic level, ranging from a semi-puristic register (advocated, for example, by Adamantios Koraïs in the early nineteenth century; a Demotic base plus classical enhancement) to a high-flown literary style which was almost indistinguishable from Classical Greek. Curiously enough, the creation of an independent Greek state in 1830 proved a setback for the pro-Demotic camp, as the linguistic issue became confused with political interests. Thus, from the mid-nineteenth century to the 1970s Greek continued to exist on two or even three linguistic planes, the selective use of which depended on sociolinguistic factors. Key stages in the gradual ascendancy of Demotic are:

1. The 'militant demoticism' of Psycharis (1854–1929): identification of Demotic as the expression of the modern Greek ethos: **γλώσσα και πατρίδα είναι το ίδιο**, 'language and fatherland are one and the same thing'.
2. 1910: Educational Society founded to promote the use of Demotic in education; countered by recognition in the 1911 Constitution of Katharevousa as the official language of the Greek state.
3. 1917: Venizelos government introduces use of Demotic in elementary schools.
4. After several setbacks – e.g. the 1952 Constitution and the Emergency Law of 1967, both of which endorsed the 1911 ruling – Demotic has now been finally and formally recognized as the spoken and written language of Greece.

SCRIPT

The 24 letters of Classical Greek, plus digraphs for certain sounds; e.g.

mp = /b/: *mpaino* = /bɛnɔ/, 'I go in';
nt = /d/: *ntunomai* = /dinɔmɛ/, 'I dress';
gx = /ŋx/: *sugxronos* = /siŋxrɔnɔs/, 'contemporary';
ts = /ts/.

PHONOLOGY

Consonants

stops: p, b, t, d, k, (g) + palatalized k′
affricates: ts, dz, ks/gz, ps
fricatives: f, v, θ, ð, s, z, x, γ
laterals and flap: l, ʎ, r
nasals: m/m′, n/ŋ
semi-vowel: j

g is rare.

Vowels

i, ɛ, a, ɔ, u

The former distinction between long and short vowels has been lost. All unstressed syllables are short; stressed syllables may be slightly longer or half-long. A reduction to /ə/ before or after stressed syllable is frequent. Vocalic reduction has led to considerable divergence between sound and symbol; the sound /i/, for example, is notated in no less than six different ways: η, ι, υ, ει, οι, υι.

If the digraphs *ai*, *oi* are to be pronounced as diphthongs, the *i* is marked by a diaeresis: e.g. *roloï* 'watch'; *kaïmaki* 'cream'. *u* is realized as /f/ in some environments: e.g. αυτό /aftó/, ευχαριœτο /efχaristó/.

Stress

Until recently, stress in both Demotic and Katharevousa was marked by acute, grave, and circumflex accents, a legacy from the musical pitch of Ancient Greek. In 1982, a monotonic system of accentuation was introduced by the Greek Ministry of Education; this uses the acute alone to mark stress. Use of the circumflex seems to be optional. The grave has been discarded along with the aspiration markers (*spiritus asper* and *spiritus lenis*) traditionally provided for vocalic initials.

Sandhi

Sandhi at word juncture is a fundamental feature of Greek pronunciation: e.g.

/n/ + /k/ → [ŋg]: e.g. *ston kipo* [stɔ**ŋg** ipɔ], 'in the garden';
/n/ + /b/ → [mb]: e.g. *ðen mporei* [ðɛ**mb**ɔri], 'he cannot';
/n/ + /ks/ → [ŋgz]: e.g. *ðen ksero* [ðɛ**ŋg** zɛrɔ], 'I don't know'.

Crasis takes place at vocalic junctures.

MORPHOLOGY AND SYNTAX

Noun

Greek has three genders, masculine, feminine, and neuter. Some guidance as to gender may be given by the ending of a word. Thus, words ending in *-os*, *-as*, *-is* are usually masculine; words in *-i*, *-a* are typically feminine; words in *-o*, *-i*, *-ma* typically neuter.

ARTICLES

There are two articles: the indefinite article is: masc. *enas*, fem. *mia*, neut. *ena*. The definite article is: masc. *o*, pl. *oi* /i/; fem. *i*, pl. *oi* /i/; neut, *to*, pl. *ta*. This article is declined: see declension of noun, below.

DECLENSION

There are three declensions according to ending; the consonantal stems, so plentiful in Katharevousa, have been largely reduced to their accusative forms: *i elpis* 'hope' > *elpida*; *filaks* 'guard' > *filaka*.

Three typical paradigms follow: masc., *o pateras* 'father', fem., *i kardia* 'heart', neut., *to vuno* 'mountain':

singular	nom.	o pateras	i kardia	to vuno
	gen.	tou patera	tis kardias	tou vunou
	acc.	ton patera	tin kardia	to vuno
plural	nom.	oi pateres	oi kardies	ta vuna
	gen.	ton pateron	ton kardion	ton vunon
	acc.	tous pateres	tis kardies	ta vuna

Katharevousa formants may reappear in plural endings: e.g. *psaras* 'fisherman' – *psarades.* Notice also such forms as *to kreas* 'meat', gen. *tou kreatos*; *to gramma* 'letter', gen. *tou grammatos.*

Adjective

As attributive, adjective precedes noun, with concord for gender, number, case: e.g.

nom.	o kalos pateras	i kali mitera	to kalo paidi
gen.	tou kalou patera	tis kalis miteras	tou kalou paidiou
	'the good father('s)'	'the good mother('s)'	'the good child('s)'

Most Greek adjectives end in *-os*, *-i/-a*, *-o*. Other endings are found, e.g. *ziliaris* 'jealous' – fem. *ziliara* – neut. *ziliariko*; pl. masc. *ziliarides.*

COMPARATIVE

In *-teros* (inflected) or with *pio* + positive: thus from *psilos* 'high': *psiloteros* = *pio psilos.*

Pronoun

PERSONAL PRONOUN

The personal pronouns have full, oblique, and two short forms, one of which is used as possessive marker, the other as objective pronoun. These forms are:

	Singular			*Plural*		
	Full	*Oblique*	*Short*	*Full*	*Oblique*	*Short*
1	ego	emena	mou, me	emeis	emas	mas
2	esu	esena	sou, se	eseis	esas	sas

The third person is marked for gender: masc. *autos* /**af**tɔs/, fem. *auti* /**af**ti/, neut. *auto.* These are declined like the definite article, except that the feminine plural has *autes* – *auton* – *autes* /**af**tɛs/, etc.

POSSESSIVES

Example: *o pateras mou* /ɔ patɛra**z**.mu/, 'my father'.

DIRECT OBJECT

ðen **m**.*endiaferei* 'It doesn't interest me'; *mas katalave* = 'he understood us'. Also as indirect object: *Sas aresoun ta taksiðia?* 'Do you like travelling?'; *telefonese mas* 'call us'.

DEMONSTRATIVE PRONOUN

autos, auti, auto 'this' (*see* **Personal pronoun**, above). The non-proximate series is *ekeinos, ekeini, ekeino.*

INTERROGATIVE PRONOUN

pyos – *pya* – *pyo* 'who?', with plural forms, e.g. *Pyos eina autos o anthropos?* 'Who is that man?'; *ti* 'what?'

RELATIVE PRONOUN

Is marked for gender, e.g. *o opyos* – *o opya* – *to opyo*; and is declined like *autos.* The alternative forms *pou* and *o, ti* are indeclinable: e.g. *o neos pou irthe* 'the young man who came'; *o neos pou eidha* 'the young man whom I saw'; *o, ti theleis* 'whatever you want'; *to spiti to opyo koitazeis* = *to spiti pou koitazeis* 'the house you are looking at'.

Numerals

1–10: *enas* '1', is fully declined (fem. *mia*) and provides the indefinite article, *duo* '2' /ðiɔ/ is indeclinable; *treis* '3' and *tessereis* '4' are declined. Thereafter indeclinable; 5–10: *pente, eksi, epta, okto, ennea, deka*; 11 *endeka*; 12 *dodeka*; 20 *eikosi*; 30 *trianta*; 40 *saranta*; 50 *peninta*; 100 *ekato.*

Verb

The basic division is into perfective and imperfective aspects. The perfective base is made from the imperfective base by addition of *-s*, with accompanying assimilation depending on stem final: vowel + *s* → *s*; *z* + *s* → *s*; *f* + *s* → *ps*; *g*/γ + *s* → *ks*. Thus:

Imperfective base	*Perfective base*
γrafo 'I write'	γra**ps**o
ðiavazo 'I read'	ðiava**s**o
ðialeγo 'I choose'	ðiale**ks**o

There are two conjugations: in (a) the stress falls on the root syllable preceding the ending; in (b) stress falls on the ending. For conjugation (a) the formation of the perfective aspect, as set out above, is regular; in conjugation (b) the formative element is *-is*: e.g. *milo* 'I speak' – *miliso.*

From the imperfective base the following tenses are made (verb *khano* 'I lose'):

present: sing., *khano, khaneis, khanei*; pl. *khanoume, khanete, khanoun*;
future: auxiliary + present forms: *tha khano*, etc. (*tha* is invariable);
past imperfect: augment in sing. 1, 2, 3, and in pl. 3: e.g. ***e****khana*, ***e****khanes*, ***e****khane*; pl. *khaname, khanate*, ***e****khanan*;
imperfect subjunctive: particle *na* + present: *na khano* 'that I lose';
conditional: auxiliary *tha* + past imperfect forms;
optative: *na* + past imperfect forms;
participle: *khanontas*;
imperative: sing., *khane*, pl. *khanete*; negative: *mi*(*n*) + subjunctive.

Tenses made from perfective base:

past definite: again the augment is in the singular and the third person plural: e.g. sing. ***e****khasa*, ***e****khases*, ***e****khase*; pl. *khasame, khasate*, ***e****khasan*;
future definite: *tha* + perfective base + imperfective endings: e.g. *tha khasoume* 'we shall lose';
perfect subjunctive: *na khaso*;
perfect: auxiliary *ekho* 'I have' + past participle: e.g. *ekho khasei* 'I have lost'.

MIDDLE VOICE

The -V*mai* ending has three distinct functions:

(a) deponent: *kaθomai* 'I sit';
(b) reflexive: *ntunomai* /dinɔmɛ/, 'I dress (myself), get dressed';
(c) passive: *vlepetai* 'it is seen'.

The present-tense endings, e.g. for *khanomai*, are: sing. *khan-omai, -esai, -etai*; pl. *-omaste, -este, -ontai.*

The perfective stem ends in -θ with assimilation: *khaθika*, *khaθikes*, etc.: e.g. *sinantiθikame ksana meta ti sinaulia* 'we met again after the concert'.

PARTICIPLES

Active present *khanontas*, past *khasei*; passive-present *khamenos*, past *khaθei*.

MODAL VERBS

Examples:

prepei na ton vlepo taktika 'I must see him regularly' (*prepei* 'must, should')
prepei na ton ðo simera 'I must see him today' (*ðo* is the suppletive perfective base of *vlepo* 'I see')
θelo na sou ðoso mia simvouli (*θelo* 'I want')
'I want to give you some advice' (*ðoso* is the perfective base of *ðino* 'I give')

mou aresei na ðiavazo vivlia 'I like reading books'; literally: 'to-me is-pleasing that I read (continuous action, present indicative) books'; but, *θelo n'agoraso ena vivlio* 'I want to buy (= have bought) a book'; *m'aresei na maθaino γlosses* 'I like learning languages', but *prepei na maθo ellenika* 'I must learn (= have learnt) Greek'.

Prepositions

Prepositions are simple or compound: e.g.

simple: *se* 'in(to)', which coalesces with the article: e.g. *ston*, *stin*, *sto*; *me* 'with'; *meta* 'after'; *prin* 'before';
compound: e.g. *istera apo* 'after'; *ðipla se* 'alongside'; *pamo se* 'upon'.

Most govern the accusative, five the genitive; one -*kata*- takes either the accusative or the genitive, with change in meaning; e.g. *sto spiti* 'in the house, at home'; *stin Aθina* 'to/in Athens'; *kata ton polemo* 'during the war'; *meta ton polemo* 'after the war'; *apo tin Anglia* 'from England'; *me ta poðia* 'with the feet', i.e. 'on foot'.

Word order

SVO is basic; OV with S understood is frequent: e.g. *tin eiða* 'I saw her'.

1 Απ' όλα πριν υπήρχε ο Λόγος
κι ήταν ο Λόγος με το Θεό,
κι ήταν Θεός ο Λόγος.
2 Απ' την αρχή ήταν αυτός με το Θεό.
3 Μέσον αυτού δημιουργήθηκαν τα πάντα,
κι απ' όσα έγιναν
δεν έγινε τίποτε χωρίς αυτόν.
4 Αυτός ήταν για τα δημιουργήματα η ζωή, [α]
κι ήταν η ζωή αυτή το φως για τους ανθρώπους.
5 Το φως αυτό έλαμψε μέσα στη σκοτεινιά του κόσμου,
μα η σκοτεινιά δεν το δέχτηκε. [β]
6 Ο Θεός έστειλε έναν άνθρωπο που τον έλεγαν Ιωάννη· 7 αυτός
ήρθε ως μάρτυρας για να κηρύξει ποιος είναι το φως, ώστε με τα λόγια
του να πιστέψουν όλοι. 8 Δεν ήταν ο ίδιος το φως, ήρθε όμως για να
πει ποιος είναι το φως.

GUARANÍ

INTRODUCTION

Guaraní belongs to the Tupí-Guaraní group of the Andean-Equatorial family. It is spoken by about 3 million people in Paraguay, where it has semi-official status along with the official language, Spanish. The Paraguayan Guaranís are the descendants of Tupí tribes who migrated to the Paraguay River area in the fifteenth century. Guaraní has been a written language since its use in the Jesuit communities in Paraguay in the sixteenth and seventeenth centuries.

SCRIPT

The Roman alphabet with diacritics. A standardized orthography was agreed at the Montevideo Congress in 1950.

PHONOLOGY

Consonants

stops: ᵐb, p, ⁿd, t, k, g, ʔ
affricate: dʒ
fricatives: v, ʃ, h
lateral and flap: l, r
nasals: m, n ɲ, ŋ
semi-vowels: j, w

Neither /b/ nor /d/ occurs apart from as the pre-nasalized phonemes. /ʃ/ is notated as *x*, /dʒ/ as *j*.

Vowels

i, e, a, o, u, y

All occur nasalized, usually marked in Guaraní script by diaeresis: *ï*, *ë*, etc. Length is not phonemic.

/y/ is a pharyngeal unrounded vowel resembling /ɯ/ or /ɪ/. Guasch (1956) compares it to the Russian ы. Its nasalized allophone is the characteristic Tupí-Guaraní sound.

Stress

Stress is, in general, unmarked on final vowel or diphthong.

MORPHOLOGY AND SYNTAX

Guaraní has no grammatical gender, nor is there a definite article. Increasing use is being made, however, of the two Spanish articles, *la* for the singular, and *lo* for the plural: e.g. *lo mitä* 'the children'. The numeral *peteï* may serve as an indefinite article for a singular noun, *umi* (a plural demonstrative) for the plural: e.g. *peteï mitäkuña paraguai* 'a Paraguayan girl'. Similarly, a demonstrative may be used as a definite article: e.g. *pe kokue jara jagua* 'the farmer's dog' (*kokue* = *chacra* 'small farm'; *jara* 'master'; *jagua* 'dog').

Noun

Initial *t-* and *h-* are movable or 'oscillating' consonants, changing to *r-* after first or second personal pronouns used as possessives, and in the inverse construct which is the Guaraní (and Tupí) genitive: cf. *tova* 'face' – *xe.**r**ova* 'my face' (*xe* = first person pronoun); *tera* 'name' – *xe.**r**era* 'my name'; *oga* 'house' – *Tupa**r**oga* 'house of God'. Many nouns which originally had a *t-* initial are now fixed in the *r-* form.

NUMBER

The plural marker is *-kuera* (→ *nguera* by assimilation, e.g. after nasal vowel): e.g. *jagua* 'dog', pl. *jaguakuera*; *mitä* 'child', pl. *mitä**ng**uera*.

GENITIVE

By juxtaposition, the inverse of the Spanish order, with *t-*/*h-* shift: e.g. *tuva sombrero* 'father's hat'; *Ko **t**apo mba'e yvyra **r**apo.pa?* 'This root is the root of which tree?' (*yvyra* 'tree').

Pe is used to mark a direct or indirect object, and also as a locative marker: e.g. *jagua ojuca mbarakaja**pe*** 'the dog kills the cat'; *Pe karai ome'ë avati kavaju**pe*** 'The man (*karai*) gives maize (*avati*) to the horse'; *i.koty.**pe*** 'in his (*i.*-) room'; *ipo**pe**kuera* 'in his hands' (*po* 'hand').

-gui is an ablative suffix: *mamo.gui.pa re.ju* 'where are you coming from?' (*-pa* interrogative particle; *re-* 2nd p. sing. pronoun marker; *ju* 'to come'); *a.ju Paraguay.gui* 'I come from Asunción' (*a-* 1st. p. sing. pronoun marker).

Adjective

Adjective follows noun: *peteï kure ka'aguy hü* 'a wild black pig'; *Paraguai ñane **r**etä porä* 'Paraguay, our lovely country' (***t**etä* 'country').

A comparative is made with *-ve... gui*: *i.tuja.**ve** xe.he.**gui*** 'he is older than I'.

Pronoun

Subject, possessive, direct and indirect object sets are distinguished (*see also* **Verb** prefixes, below):

			Subject	*Possessive*	*Direct object*	*Indirect object*
sing.	1		xe	xe	xe	xeve
	2		nde	nde	nde/ro	ndeve
	3		ha'e	i/in/ij/h(i)	ixupe	ixupe
pl.	1	*incl.*	ñande	ñande	ñande	ñandeve
		excl.	ore	ore	ore	oreve
	2		peë (pende)	pende	pende/po	peëme
	3		ha'e kuera	*as sing.*	ixupekuera	ixupekuera

Examples: *xe/nde kavaju* 'my/your horse...'; *ñande **ra**'ykuera **rera*** 'the number of our sons' (***ta**'y* 'son', ***t**era* 'number'). The base forms take postpositions: e.g. *xe.hegui* 'of me'; *xe.**re** he* 'for me'; *xe.ndive* 'with me'.

Examples of pronominal subject/object:

xe ha'e ixu.**pe** peteë mba'e 'I say something to him/her'
La Tupasÿ o.ñanga ñande.**rehe** 'The Virgin cares for (*rehe*) us'
ore **ro**.mondo tupao.**pe** 'We (excl.) send you to the church'

DEMONSTRATIVE ADJECTIVE

Ranges through several degrees from *ko/ko'ä* 'this' (here and now), to *aipo(v)a* 'that' (unseen and unknown). Plural forms: *äva*; *umi.*

INTERROGATIVE PRONOUN

avapa 'who?'; *mba'epa* 'what?'

RELATIVE PRONOUN

See **Relative clause**, below.

Numerals

Guaraní forms are used for the first four numerals: *peteï*, *moköi*, *mbohapy*, *irundy.* Thereafter, Spanish numbers are used, though Guaraní forms exist (set out, for example, in Guasch (1956)).

Verb

There is a broad division into two classes of verb, which the Spanish writers in Guaraní call (a) *verbos areales*, and (b) *verbos xendales.*

(a) *Verbos areales*: these are active/transitive, with invariable stem and personal prefixes as subject markers: these are sing. 1 *a-*, 2 *re-*, 3 *o-*; pl. 1 (incl.) *ja-/ña-* (excl.), *ro-*, 2 *pe-*, 3 *o-*. A sub-group has 1 *ai-*, 2 *rei-*, etc.: e.g. (*xe*) ***a**.guata* 'I walk', (*nde*) ***re**guata* 'you walk'.

Tense markers are added: *va'ekue* (past), *va'erä* (future): e.g. ***re**.japo.va'ekue* 'you did'; ***re**.japo.va'erä* 'you will do'. There is also a continuative form: ***a**.japo**aina*** 'I am doing'; *Mba'epa **re**.japo **reina**?* 'What are you doing?'

Objective pronouns: first and second person forms precede the verb, third person forms follow: e.g. *nde* ***xejuhu*** 'you meet me'; *ha'e* ***nde****.juhu* 'he meets you'; *xe ajuhu* ***ixupekuera*** 'I meet them'.

(b) *Verbos xendales*: these are stative forms, in which the independent pronoun precedes an adjectival or nominal stem. If the stem initial is *t-/h-*, the shift to *r-* takes place for first and second persons: e.g. with *tasy* 'sick': *xe* ***rasy*** 'I am sick'; *nde* ***rasy*** 'you are sick'; but, ***hasy*** 'he is sick'.

Both types of verb are negated by means of *nda-...i*, as in Tupí: *nd.ai.pota.i* 'I don't want' *nde.rei.pota.i* 'you don't want'; *nda.ore.rasy.i* 'we are not ill'. *nda* is reduced to *na* before nasals; e.g. *na.ñande.rasry.i* 'we (incl.) are not ill'. The imperative is negated by *ani... tei*.

There are, of course, numerous secondary tenses, e.g. a perfect with *kuri*: ***a****japo/****re****japo kuri* 'I/you have done'; and a second future in *-ne*: ***a****japone* 'I shall do'.

A continuative is made with *ina*, the participle of the root *i* 'to be': *xe a.karu* ***a.ina*** 'I am eating'; *nde rei.karu* ***re.ina*** 'thou art eating'; *ha'e o.karu.****h. ina*** 'he is eating'.

For phonological reasons, verbs with initial consonant *r-/n-*, such as *a.reko* 'to have', *a.raha* 'to carry', *a.ru* 'to pull', take the increment *-gue-* following pronominal *-o*, in the 3rd p. sing. and pl. and in the 1st, p. pl. excl. Thus, *a.reko* 'I have', *re.reko* 'thou hast' but ***o.gue****.reko* 'he has'. Similarly, (*xe*) *a.raha* 'I carry' but *o.gue.raha* 'he carries'. An example with an infixed object pronominal marker in *-o* is: *ndo.****ro.gue****.rovia.i xe* 'I do not believe (*rovia*) you (*ro*)'. That is, the presence of an object pronominal marker in *-o* attracts the use of *gue* in any person of the paradigm.

Guaraní has two verbs meaning 'to be': (a) *aime* 'I am in/at a place'; (b) *aiko* 'I am (+ adverb)'. There is no copula; 'I am' + adjective or noun = juxtaposition: e.g. *xe tujama* 'I am old'. Nouns may be marked for tense (cf. Tupí): *-kue* (past), ***-ra*** (future): *mburuvixa****kue*** '(he) who was boss/chief'; *mburuvixa****ra*** '(he) who will be boss/chief'; *mburuvixa****rangue*** 'someone who was expected to become chief but did not'. Nominals marked for tense can be made from verbal roots with the particle *tembi*: *tembi.pota.py* 'that which is desired'; *tembi.pota.pyre* 'what was desired', *tembi.pota.pyrä* 'what will be desired'.

RELATIVE CLAUSE

va/gua: the referent is the subject or direct object of the relative clause: e.g. *amo karai oho.****va*** *amongotio* 'that man who is going over there' (*oho* is third person singular of irregular verb *aha* 'go'); *amo karai a hexa.****va*** *amo* 'the man I see there'. *Ha* is used with reference to an indirect object: e.g. *amo karai a me'ë.****ha****...* 'the man to whom I give...'; *amo tava aju.****ha****.gui* 'that village from which I come'. Cf. *Kova.pa re.jogua va'erä?* 'Is this what you intend to buy?'; *Kova pa re.jogua va'ekue?* 'Is this what you bought?'

Further examples:

mba'epa la rei.pota.**va** 'what is it that you (*rei*) wish (*pota*)?'
peteï mitä'i hasë.**va** hina 'a child who was crying' (*hina* is the continuative marker, *see* **Verb**, above)
oime i.katu ha ndo.i.pota.i.**va** 'there are those who can (*katu* 'to be able') and do not want to' (for formation of negative, see verb, above)
oime oi.pota.**va** ha i.katu'ÿ.**va** 'others who want to and who can't'

Imperative, conditional, potential, causal, affective moods and several modalities of motion, etc. are expressed with the help of an extensive inventory of particles.

For example:

-se desiderative marker: *ñande ña ma'ë.se* 'we want to see';
-kuaa 'to be able to, know how to': *xe a.yapo.kuaa* 'I can make/do…';
re.ñe'ë.kuaa.pa guaraní.me 'can you speak Guarani?';
ramo gives a conditional tense in subordinate clauses: *re.jogua.se.ramo kesu* 'if you want (*se*) to buy cheese…'.

Word order

SVO, VOS.

Cuando todo comenzó, ya existía la Palabra estaba con Dios y era Dios. En el principio pues él estaba con Dios.

Por medicio de él, Dios hizo todas las cosas; nada de lo que existe fue hecho sin él. En él estaba la vida, y esta vida era la luz para los hombres. Esta luz brilla en la oscuridad, y la oscuridad no ha podido apagaria.

Hubo un hombre a quien Dios envió, llamado Juan, que vino como testigo para hablar de la luz, para que todoscreyeran por medio de lo que él decía. Juan no era la luz; era solamente un testigo enviado para hablar en favor de la luz.

GUJARATI

INTRODUCTION

Gujarati is a Western New Indo-Ayran language and is the official language of the state of Gujarat, where it is spoken by about 25 million people. It also spreads into Maharashtra, and is spoken by Gujarati communities in every major city in India. The total number of speakers is estimated at around 45 million.

Gujarati took shape from the Gurjara Apabhraṁsa between the tenth and thirteenth centuries AD. The literature dates from the fourteenth century with medieval verse centring on the Rādhā–Kṛṣṇa theme.

Modern writing in Gujarati started in the late nineteenth century along with a new literary standard language, based on the Baroda dialect, as its medium. The influence of Mahatma Gandhi's writings in Gujarati can hardly be overestimated. An outstanding modern poet is Umāśankar Jośī.

Bhili and Khandesi, spoken together by around 3½ million people, are usually regarded as variant forms of Gujarati, but by some authorities as languages in their own right. Apart from this questionable point, Gujarati is remarkably homogeneous over its spoken area.

SCRIPT

See **Script** at end of article.

PHONOLOGY

Consonants

stops: p, b, t, d, ʈ, ɖ, k, g; all with aspirated values: ph, bh, etc.
affricates: tʃ, tʃh, dʒ, dʒh
fricatives: v/w, (f), s, ʂ, ʃ, h
laterals and flaps: l, lh, ɭ, r, rh
nasals: m, mh, n, nh, ɳ, ɳh, (ɲ), (ŋ)
semi-vowels: j, w

dʒ/ and /dʒh/ are represented as *j* and *jh*; retroflex sounds with a subscript dot.

Vowels

i, e, ɛ, ə, a, ɔ, o, u

Most occur nasalized. Each vowel is realized in four allophones, depending on position in word. These variants are not phonemic. Vowels may be accompanied by a kind of breathy 'murmur', which is perhaps associated with elision of intervocalic consonants.

Stress

Stress is barely perceptible.

MORPHOLOGY AND SYNTAX

Noun

Gujarati distinguishes masculine, feminine, and neuter genders. Gender may be identifiable from ending: thus, *-o* is typically masculine, *-ī* and *-ā* are feminine, *-ũ* is neuter. An exception is provided by the many nouns of profession, nationality, etc. which have a masculine form in *-ī*: e.g. *kaṇbī* 'peasant', *maḷī* 'gardener'. There are no articles.

NUMBER

The plural marker *-o* is added to the oblique base; this is normally identical to the nominative base, which is also the citation form. Masculine nouns in *-o*, however, make their oblique base in *-ā*: e.g. *ghoḍo* 'horse', obl. base *ghoḍā-*.

DECLENSION

There are six cases. Specimen declension of *kūtro* 'dog':

Singular:

nom. *kūtro*;
gen. *kūtrāno* (masc.), *-nī* (fem.), *-nũ* (neuter) (i.e. the genitive behaves as an adjective coded for gender of possessed object);
acc./dat. *kūtrāne*;
instr. *kūtrāe*;
abl. *kūtrāe*;
loc. *kūtrāmā̃*.

The plural adds the same affixes to the pluralized stem: e.g. *kūtrāo.-no*, *-nī*, *-nũ*, etc.

GENITIVE

Examples: *chokəra.**no** bāp* 'the boy's father'; *ghar.**nī** orḍī* 'the room of the house'; *mahātmā Gandhījī.no āšram* 'Mahatma Gandhi's ashram'.

The ablative may be used in such passive constructions as *bāp**thī** aje kām nahi thāy* 'from father today work not done' = 'father did no work today'; *kuvāmā̃* 'in the well'.

Adjective

Adjectives in *-o* show concord for gender, number, and case. Other adjectives are indeclinable, e.g. *sundar* 'beautiful'.

Variable adjectives, i.e. those in *-u* (citation form) show concord for gender and number: masc. *-o*, fem. *-ī*. In the singular oblique cases of masc. and neuter nouns, a generalized form is used: *-ā* (masc.), *-ā* (neuter); cf. *dholā jhāḍ nīce* 'under an old tree' (*jhāḍ* 'tree', *nīce* 'under': this postposition takes the genitive case).

Pronoun

Personal base forms:

	Singular	*Plural*
1	hũ	ame (*excl.*), āpṇe (*incl.*)
2	tũ	tāme, āp
3	te/ā (demonstratives)	teo/āo

These are declined in five cases. The oblique base of *hu* is *man-*.

POSSESSIVE PRONOUN
Sing. *māro*, *tāro*; pl. *amāro*, *tamāro*; these show concord.

DEMONSTRATIVE PRONOUN
ā 'this', *te* 'that', with plural forms.

INTERROGATIVE PRONOUN
The base form *koṇ* appears as *kyo* (masc.), *kaī* (fem.), *kyũ* (neut.), with plural forms.

RELATIVE PRONOUN
Sing. *je*, pl. *jeo*, declined in all cases, e.g. gen. sing. *jenũ*, pl. *jenmũ*; with correlatives in *t-* form in principal clause: e.g.

je maŋəsne mẽ pəysa apya **te** pəṭel.no bhaī che
'the man to whom I gave the money is the village officer's brother' (*pəṭel* 'village officer')

Jyāre mumbaī jao **tyāre** māre māṭe ā be pustak lāvajo
'When you go to Bombay (*mumbaī*) (then) bring me those two books' (*māṭe* 'for' (postposition); *pustak* 'book')

Numerals

1–10: *ek*, *be*, *traṇ*, *cār*, *pā̃c*, *cha*, *sāt*, *āṭh*, *nav*, *das*; 11 *agiār*; 12 *bār*; 13 *ter*; 14–19 are unpredictable forms; 20 *vīs*; 30 *trīs*; 40 *cāḷīs*. The individual forms for 21–99 are unpredictable, though decade + 9 is always linked to the following decade: e.g. 48 is *aḍtāḷīs* (i.e. based on *cāḷīs*) but 49 is *ogaṇpacās*, based on *pacās* '50'. 100 *so*.

Verb

The infinitive ending is *-ũ*: e.g. *karvũ* 'to do'; this is the citation form. The imperfective participle ends in *-to, -tī, -tũ*; pl. *-tā, -tī, -tā̃*. The perfective participle has two forms:

(a) *-yo*, marked for person and number;
(b) *-elo*, marked for person and number.

MOODS

Indicative, imperative, subjunctive, conditional, presumptive.

Indicative mood: specimen tense formations:

Present: stem + personal inflections: e.g. for *karvũ* 'to do': sing. 1 *hũ karũ*, 2 *tũ kare*, 3 *te kare*; pl. 1 *ame karīe*, 2 *tame karo*, 3 *teo kare*. A progressive form is made from this by using the auxiliary verb *chũ, che, che; chīe, cho, che*: e.g. *hũ karũ chũ, tũ kare che.*

Perfect:

(a) Intransitive verb, *āvvũ* 'to come': perfective participle (two forms), marked for gender and number, + *chũ*: *hũ āvyo/-ī/-ũ chũ* = *hũ āvelo/-lī/-lũ chũ* (*chũ* is conjugated).
(b) Transitive verb: *karvũ* 'to do': subject in oblique (instrumental) case. The participial form agrees with the object in gender and number: e.g. *mẽ karyũ che, tẽ karyũ che* = *mẽ/tẽ karelũ che* 'by-me, by-you was done'.

Past habitual: pronoun + imperfective participle, marked for gender and number: e.g. *hũ karto/-tī/-tũ* 'I was in the habit of doing'; pl. *ame kartā/-tī/-tā̃*.
Past perfective: intransitive: *hũ āvyo/-ī/-yũ* = *hũ āvelo/-lī/-lũ* 'I came'; transitive: *mẽ, tẽ... karyũ/karelũ.*
Future: sing. 1 *hũ karīš*, 2 *tũ karše*, 3 *te karše*; pl. *karīšũ, daršo, karše.*

The presumptive, subjunctive, and conditional moods are made by combining the perfective/imperfective participles with auxiliaries: e.g. in subjunctive: *hũ āvto/-tī/-tũ hoũ* 'I may (not) come'.

PASSIVE

In *-ā-*, e.g. from *karvũ, karāvũ* 'to be done'. Conjugated as in active.

CAUSATIVE

-āv/-āḍ added to stem: e.g. *karāvvũ* 'cause to do'.

NEGATION

The negative form of the copula – sing. *chũ, che, che*; pl. *chīe, cho, che* – is *nathī* /nəhiː/, which is invariable: e.g. *malik ahī̃ nathī* 'the master is not here'; *teo bīmār nathī* 'he is not ill'; *gayo nathī* 'he hasn't gone'. The particles *na* /nə/, *nahi* /nəhi/ negate personal and impersonal forms of the verb in which the copula is not used: e.g. *kuvāmā̃ kapaḍā̃ dhovā̃ nahi* 'clothes are not to be washed in the well' (*kuvo* 'well'; *kapaḍũ* 'cloth'; *dho* 'to wash'). *Mā* is used to form a negative imperative.

Postpositions

These may follow either the base form of the noun, or one of the oblique cases. For example, with *par* 'on', *beso khursī par* 'sit on the chair', where *khursī* is in the base form.

Several postpositions follow the feminine genitive case in *-nī*: e.g. *ā bāḷak.nī taraph* 'in the direction of that boy'.

Word order

SOV is normal.

SCRIPT

Gujarati (Gujarātī) is a New Indo-Aryan language, which took shape from a western form of Middle Indian around the eleventh/twelfth century AD. Literature in Gujarati begins to appear in the fifteenth century, and about the same time in the closely cognate Rajasthani. But whereas Rajasthani stuck to Devanāgarī, Gujarati, for its part, developed a graceful cursive script which dispenses with the superscript bar, characteristic of Devanāgarī. The only other New Indo-Aryan script which is closely similar to the Gujarati is the Kaithi cursive script, sometimes used for writing Hindi in northern India.

The table shows the Gujarati consonantal inventory, and the vowels: the latter (a) in their independent forms, and (b) in combination with the consonant *b*. Like other Brāhmī derivatives, the Gujarati script is syllabic, with short *a* inherent in each consonant.

Conjunct consonants are formed by juxtaposition, partial amalgamation or subscript.

As in Devanāgarī, the inherent vowel is cancelled by virāma ◌્. The final *ḥ* in Sanskrit words is denoted by : visarga, and ◌ં anusvāra marks nasalization which is homogeneous with the following consonant.

THE GUJARATI SCRIPT

CONSONANTS

ક	ખ	ગ	ઘ	ઙ
ka	*kha*	*ga*	*gha*	*nga*
ચ	છ	જ	ઝ	ઞ
ca	*cha*	*ja*	*jha*	*nya*
ટ	ઠ	ડ	ઢ	ણ
ṭa	*ṭha*	*ḍa*	*ḍha*	*ṇa*
ત	થ	દ	ધ	ન
ta	*tha*	*da*	*dha*	*na*
પ	ફ	બ	ભ	મ
pa	*pha*	*ba*	*bha*	*ma*
ય	ર	લ	વ	
ya	*ra*	*la*	*wa, va*	
શ	ષ	સ	હ	ળ
śa	*ṣa*	*sa*	*ha*	*la*

VOWELS

(a) independent

અ	આ	ઇ	ઈ	ઉ	ઊ	ઋ
a	*ā*	*i*	*ī*	*u*	*ū*	*ri*
એ	ઐ	ઓ	ઔ			
ē	*ai*	*ō*	*au*			

(b) in combination with the consonant *ba*

બા	બિ	બી	બુ	બૂ	બૃ
bā	*bi*	*bī*	*bu*	*bū*	*bri*
બે	બૈ	બો	બૌ		
bē	*bai*	*bō*	*bau*		

NUMERALS

૧	૨	૩	૪	૫	૬	૭	૮	૯	૦
1	2	3	4	5	6	7	8	9	0

GURENNE

INTRODUCTION

Known as Frafra to its neighbouring peoples in West Africa, Gurenne belongs to the Gur (Voltaic) group of the Niger-Congo phylum. It is spoken in north-eastern Ghana, with some spread into Burkina Faso and Togo, by about a half a million people.

The following description is based on: Rapp, E.L. (1966) *Die Gurenne-Sprache in Nord-Ghana*, which contains an extensive Gurenne–German vocabulary, and an interesting collection of 363 proverbs.

SCRIPT

Gurenne may be written in Roman script.

PHONOLOGY

Consonants

stops: p, b, t, d, k, g; with two labio-velars: kp, gb and two palatalized: /k′/ = [tj], /g′/ = [dj]
fricatives: f, v, s, z, γ
nasals: m, n, ɲ, ŋ, ŋm
lateral and flap: l, r
semi-vowels: j, w

/h/ occurs in loanwords. /γ/ occurs as an allophone of /g/.

Vowels

short or long: i, ɪ, e, ɛ, a, æ, o, ɔ, u, ʊ

There are two series of long vowels: /iː, eː, aː, oː, uː/, and /i'i, e'e, a'a/, etc., that is, vowel + glottal stop + echo. Both /m/ and /ŋ/ are syllabic and tone-bearing. All vowels are subject to weak or strong nasalization. /ə/, always short, occurs for example between final root consonant and initial consonant of class marker.

Tone

Gurenne has five tones: mid-even, high, low, rising, and falling. Terraced tone is a feature of Gurenne pronunciation: relative to an initial high tone, subsequent high tones tend to drop in pitch through an utterance. Low tones are not affected and remain constant in relative pitch.

Falling tone appears to be mainly associated with interrogation: cf. *fo ye la ba* 'where are you going?'

MORPHOLOGY AND SYNTAX

Noun

Gurenne has five noun classes; these are semantically heterogeneous, and the class marker is affixed to the stem, in contrast to Bantu practice. The classes are:

	Singular	*Plural*	*Example*
1	-a	-ba	nera 'man', *pl.* nereba (*-a* < original *-ka*)
2	-ka	-se	bua (< buka) 'goat', *pl.* buuse
3	-de	-a	yelle (< yelde), 'word, thing', *pl.* yela
4	-ko	-to	zuo (< zuko) 'head', *pl.* zuto
5	-bo	-i	naafo 'cow', *pl.* nii

The class markers for 3 singular and 4 singular and plural have many variants. Class 3 singulars have C + *e/i*; class 4 singulars and plurals have C + *o/u*. Class 3 plural is stable in *-a*.

Many nouns are hybrid as regards class, with singular in one class, plural in another: e.g. *mabia* 'brother' is singular class 2, the plural *mabito* is class 4. Some plurals are suppletive, e.g. *bia* 'child' (class 2), pl. *komma* (class 1).

The class marker is dropped (a) from the possessor noun in the genitive construct: e.g. *na.ba* 'chief', *bia* 'child': *na.***Ø** *bia* 'chief's son'; *Guren.ga* 'Gurenne man', *yire* 'house': *Guren.***Ø** *yire* 'a Gurenne man's house'; and (b) from the noun when an attributive adjective follows. The class marker is then transferred to the adjective: e.g. with *paale* 'new', *nere paale.***ga** 'new man'.

Kinship terms form a special class of noun in Gurenne, and often have a very extensive range of meaning; e.g. *deema* which has over two dozen meanings, ranging from 'mother-in-law'/'father-in-law' to 'husband of mother's brother's daughter's daughter'.

The definite article *la* follows the noun: *nera la dela Guren.ga* 'the man is a Frafra'.

Adjective

Theoretically, the adjective should take all 5×2 class endings, and some in fact do so, e.g. *paale* 'new', *som* 'good'. For most adjectives, however, one singular and one plural ending suffice in all five classes.

Pronoun

PERSONAL PRONOUN

The third person is marked for class:

		Full form	Short form	Object
singular	1	mam	ma	m
	2	fom	fo	f
plural	1	tomam	to	
	2	yamam	ya	

		Singular		*Plural*	
		Full	*Shortened*	*Full*	*Shortened*
3rd p. class	1	enga	a – e	bamma	ba
	2	ka	ka	se	se
	3	de	de	a	a
	4	ko	ko	to	to
	5	bo	bo	i	i

The shortened forms have high tone as possessives, low tone as verbal subjects. Examples: *m puuse fo* 'I thank you (sing)'; *a bote ka* 'he/she loves her/him', neg. *a* ***ka*** *bote ka* (***ka*** = neg. marker); *mam ka nye yebaa la* 'I have not seen the leopard' (*nye* 'to see; *yebaa* 'leopard'; *la* = article).

DEMONSTRATIVE PRONOUN

Proximate: class marker + vowel lengthening + *-na*: e.g. *nere* ***eena*** *wa* 'this man (here)' (*wa* is the demonstrative adjective); similarly *bi* ***kaana*** *wa* 'this child', pl. *bi* ***seena*** *wa* 'these children'; *zi* ***boona*** *wa* 'this fish', pl. *zi* ***iina*** *wa* 'these fish'.

The distal pronoun is formed by duplicating the class marker, with *n/m* linker: thus in cl. 2 sing. *ka.****n****.ka*, pl. *se.****n****.se*; cl. 4 sing. *ko.****n****.ko*, pl.*to.****n****.to*.

INTERROGATIVE PRONOUN

anne 'who?'; *bem* 'what?'

RELATIVE PRONOUN

mina: e.g. *mina n tare lon yinga* 'he who has a single piece of land' (*tare* 'have'; *lon* 'land'; *yinga* 'single'; *n* is a co-ordinating particle).

Numerals

Here, the normal Gurenne order, stem – class marker, is reversed; the numeral stems are added to the class marker. Thus, *-yemena* '1' appears, depending on class, as *ayemena*, *kayemena*, *deyemena*, etc., e.g. *nera ayemena* 'one man'. Similarly with *-yi* '2': *nere.ba ba.yi* 'two men', *bon.se se.yi* 'two donkeys'. The remaining stems 3–9 are: *-ta*, *-naase*, *-nuu*, *-yoobe*, *-yopoe*, *-nii*, *-wœ*; 10 is *pia*, which is invariable for all classes: e.g. *nereba pia* 'ten men', *bonse pia* 'ten donkeys'. 11–19: e.g. *pia la ayemena*. Class is ignored, and *pia* is invariable, though it changes tone (both syllables low when = '10'; both syllables high through teens and upwards). 20 *piseyi*; 30 *pisetã*; 40 *pisenaase*; 100 *kwabega* /kɔbega/.

Verb

The stem is uninflected; tense is indicated by markers: e.g.

present: the affirmative marker is *la*; *la* is discarded when the negating particle *ka* is used: e.g. *m ye la* 'I go', *m ka ye* 'I don't go'; *fo ye la* 'you (sing.) go';

past imperfective: the tense marker is *daa*: e.g. *ka dela* 'he is', *ka daa dela* 'he was', *ka daa dagge* 'he wasn't'. Where a time-fixing adverb is present, no marker is necessary: e.g. with *zaa* 'yesterday': *m zaa kenge* 'I went yesterday' (*kenge* = ye 'go');

perfect: *ya* or *pon* may be used: e.g. *mam pon di* 'I have already eaten', *ka nye ya* 'he has received';

future tense: made with the ingressive particle *wa*: *m wa n kenge* 'I shall go'.

IMPERATIVE

The stem acts as a singular imperative; the plural is stem + *-ya*. An indirect imperative is made with *vam/vamya*: e.g. *Vamya te to kenge daa* 'Let's go to the market' (*te* 'so that'; *to* 'we'; *daa* 'market'). This imperative is negated by *da*: e.g. *da vam te to kenge daa* 'let's not go to market'.

CAUSATIVE

The marker is *se/sa*.

Postpositions

Examples: *zia/zian* 'with', 'at': *to so zian* 'with our father', 'at our father's'; *poore* 'after', 'behind': *taae mam poore na* 'follow me' (*taae* 'follow'; *na* 'hither').

There is a localizer in *-n*: e.g. *daa* 'market': *daan* 'at market'; *moen* 'in the jungle'; *diadeon* 'in the restaurant'.

Word order

SVO: e.g. *a karenge la gongo* 'he reads (*karenge*) a book (*gongo*)', where *la* is a pleonastic affirmative particle following the verb; *sasenga ka deenne la buuse* 'the hyena (*sasenga*) does not (*ka*) play (*deenne*) with the goat (*buuse*)'; *a.ka.bote n doggere a.bote.bala* 'he-doesn't want it begets he-wants-it-thus' i.e. 'he starts by saying he doesn't want it, and ends up saying he'll have it like this'.

HAIDA

See **North American Indian Isolates**.

HAITIAN CREOLE

See **Pidgins and Creoles**.

HAKKA

See **Chinese Dialects**.

HATTIC

INTRODUCTION

This language is also known as Proto-Hittite, which is confusing as the Hattic people who lived in north-east Anatolia throughout the third millennium BC were not Indo-European, and had, beyond cultural contact, nothing to do with the Indo-European-speaking Hittites who invaded their country. Hattic influence on the Hittite-Luwian peoples was particularly strong in the field of religion, and the substantial Hattic element in Hittite vocabulary bears witness to this. By the first millennium BC, Hattic was a dead language. Its existence is known primarily from a small number of tablets found in the royal archives at Hattušaš (*see* **Hittite**). Some of these are bilingual texts, from which about 150 Hattic words have been tentatively identified.

SCRIPT

Hattic was written in the syllabic Akkadian cuneiform, without ideograms.

PHONOLOGY

Consonants

The script gives Hattic the following inventory:

stops: p, t, k
fricatives: z(tʃ), ʃ, ḫ
nasals: m, n
lateral and flap: l, r
semi-vowels: j, w

But it is most unlikely that the clumsy Akkadian syllabary could record with any degree of accuracy the sounds of a non-Indo-European, non-Semitic language like Hattic.

Vowels

There were four vowels:

i, e, a, u

MORPHOLOGY AND SYNTAX

Hattic was an agglutinative language. About twenty formants, in the shape of prefixes and suffixes have been identified. Some of these appear to be case or number markers, others have a pronominal character. Gender seems to be distinguished, in that *-el/-il* appears as a suffix associated with masculine referents, *-aḫ* with feminine.

Hattic verbal complexes have been typologically reconstructed (e.g. by Kammenhuber), and display some similarity with the **Abkhaz-Adyge** model (**q**.v.). The formula comprises four main slots: (1) affective: desirability or otherwise of action; negation; (2) subject group; (3) object group; (4) preverbs and base.

While certain endings have been tentatively identified as accusative (*-šu*), genitive (-V*n*), dative (*-ja*), and ablative (*-tu*), Hattic seems to have no ergative endings. D'akonov (1979) points out that neither Abkhaz-Adyge nor Hattic has an ergative *case*, although the verbal structure of both languages is characteristically ergative.

Some markers appear to have a dual role: e.g. *-e-/-ja-* is a dative ending in nouns, and an indirect-object marker in the verbal complex.

HAUSA

INTRODUCTION

This, the major language of West Africa, belongs to the Chadic branch of the Afro-Asiatic phylum. It is spoken as mother tongue by 25 million people, and used as second language and lingua franca by at least another 10 million, and is one of the official languages of the Republic of Nigeria.

Writing in Hausa dates from the religious and literary revival associated with the Sokoto Empire established by the Fulani Usman dan Fodio in 1809. Hausa was written in Arabic script, and this *ajami* tradition lasted in general until the British occupation of Nigeria introduced the Roman script in the early twentieth century. Locally, in northern Nigeria, *ajami* writing persists. Traditional Hausa literature consists largely of verse chronicles and homiletic tracts. Prose fiction began to appear in the 1930s, drama slightly later. Poetry retains its popularity and is often broadcast.

The Kano dialect is the basis of the literary language. Very many Arabic loanwords have been integrated into Hausa; borrowing from English is also extensive.

SCRIPT

Roman alphabet with modified letters: *ɓ*, *ɗ*, *ƙ*, to notate the glottalized implosives. Neither vowel length nor tones are marked.

PHONOLOGY

Consonants

stops: p, b, t, d, k, g, ˀ; glottalized: ɓ, ɗ, ƙ; palatalized: k′, g′, ƙ′
labialized: k˚, g˚, ƙ˚
affricates: tʃ, dʒ
fricatives: f, s, z, ʃ, f′, h
nasals: n, m, ŋ
lateral: l
flap/roll: r, ɽ
semi-vowels: j, w

All initial vowels have glottal onset (hamza). Retroflex /ɽ/ is notated here with a subscript dot.

Vowels

short and long: i, e, a, o, u

Short /e/ = [ɛ], short /i/ = [ɪ], short /o/ = [ɔ], short /a/ = [ɐ]. Diphthongs: /ai, au/.

Tone

Two main tones, high and low, with a secondary falling tone. Tone is phonemic. Intonation is also of the greatest importance in Hausa: three cardinal intonational patterns are distinguished: declarative (stepped descending), interrogative, and vocative.

MORPHOLOGY AND SYNTAX

Noun

There are two genders, masculine and feminine, identifiable as such only in the singular. Most nouns not ending in *-a*/*-aa* are masculine. Some very common nouns in *-a*(*a*) are masculine: *gidaa* 'house', 'home', *ruwaa* 'water', *naamaa* 'meat'.

The plural takes many forms, usually involving extension and/or rearrangement (on broken plural lines; *see* **Arabic**) of singular ending, plus tonal change. In the following examples, tone is marked for illustrative purposes: *túnkìyáa* 'sheep', pl. *túmáakíi*; *sírdìi* 'saddle', pl. *síràadáa*; *gàrmáa* 'plough', pl. *gárèemáníi*; *gàríi* 'town', pl. *gárúurúwàa*. A frequent formation is the replacement of the final vowel of the singular by *ō*.C.*ī*, where C is the final consonant of the singular or its reflex: e.g. *taasaa* 'bowl', pl. *taas**ooshii***; *kaasuwaa* 'market', pl. *kaasuw**ooyii***. Many words have more than one plural form.

THE CONSTRUCT STATE

That is, linkage by *na* → *n* (masc.), *ta* → *r* (fem.), pl. *-n*. These linking elements are used in the following ways:

(a) To form the possessive relationship: e.g.

masc. *abooki.**n** ubaa* 'the friend of the father' (*abookii* 'friend');
fem. *goona.**r** ubaa* 'the field of the father';
pl. *mutaane.**n** garii* 'the people of the town'.

(b) To link preceding attributive adjective to noun: e.g.

masc. *babba.**n** gidaa* 'the big house' (*gidaa* is masculine, although ending in *-aa*);
fem. *saabuwa.**r** makarantaa* 'the new school';
pl. *saababbi.**n** littattaafai* 'the new books'.

(c) To link noun with enclitic demonstrative: e.g. *gari.**n** nan* 'this town'; *ƙoofa.**r** nan* 'this door'.

(d) To link noun and possessive marker: e.g. *dooki.**n**.sa* 'his horse'; *goona.**r**.mu* 'our farm'.

(e) In relative clause structure (see below).

Adjective

There is no distinction between adjectives and other nominals. Attributive nominals precede the noun they qualify, and are in gender and number concord with it. (See examples, above.)

Pronoun

PERSONAL PRONOUN

			Base form	*Dative*	*Possessive*
singular	1		ni	mini	-na
	2	masc.	kai	maka	-ka
		fem.	ke	miki	-ki
	3	masc.	shi	masa	-sa
		fem.	ita	mata	-ta
plural	1		mu	mana	-mu
	2		ku	muku	-ku
	3		su	musu	-su

The base forms have direct-object forms which are identical except for second singular, *ka*/*ki*; and third feminine, *ta*. The pronominal forms, plus linking element, underlie the verbal tense markers (see below). The possessive enclitics combine with the construct markers to provide separable possessives: *nawa*, *naka*; *tawa*, *taka*, where -*wa* is a variant of -*na*: e.g. *Gida.n na.mu nee* 'This house is ours.'

DEMONSTRATIVE PRONOUN/ADJECTIVE

wannan (masc. and fem.) 'this', pl. *waɗannan* 'these'; *wancan* (masc.), *waccan* (fem.) 'that'; pl. *waɗancan* 'those'. *Nan* 'this', 'these' and *can* 'that', 'those' follow noun + construct marker: e.g. *wannan dookii* = *dooki.n nan* 'this horse'.

INTERROGATIVE PRONOUN

waa 'who?'; *mee* 'what?' These combine with particles *nee* and *cee* to form sing. *waanee*, *waacee*, pl. *su waanee*: e.g. *Su waanee nee suka tafi goona*? 'Who (pl.) went to the field?'

RELATIVE CONSTRUCTION

Two constructions are used:

(a) With *da* (invariable): headword + *n*/*r* link + *da*: e.g. *gida.**n da** sarkii ya gina* 'the house that the chief built' (for *ya gina*, *see* **Verb**, below).

(b) *da* + *wa* → sing. masc. *wanda*, fem. *wadda*, pl. *waɗanda*; here, no linker is used: e.g. *yaaroo wanda ya zoo* 'the boy who came'.

Numerals

1–10: *ɗaya, biyu, uku, huɗu, biyar, shida, bakwai, takwas, tara, gooma.* 11 (*gooma*) *sha ɗaya*, 12 (*gooma*) *sha biyu*; 20 *ashirin*; 30 *talatin*. Arabic forms are used for decades. 100 *ɗarii*.

Verb

All Hausa verbs end in a vowel, and are invariable as regards tense or aspect, person, and number. The final vowel is, however, coded for transitivity and intransitivity, causativity, and certain modal nuances (see below). Specific realizations for aspect, version, person, etc. are generated via preverbal markers (based on the pronominal series) plus auxiliary verbal elements. One classification of Hausa verbs uses the third person plural form of these pronominal markers as indices of the various aspects and versions.

There are perfective, imperative, subjunctive, future, continuative, and habitual aspects; direct (indicative) and relative versions, affirmative, and negative; three singular and three plural + an impersonal form; the second and third singular forms are marked for gender.

DIRECT (INDICATIVE) VERSION

Perfective aspect: the pronominal series used here is illustrated with the stem *zoo* 'to come': sing. 1 *naa zoo*, 2 *kaa/kin zoo*, 3 *ya/ta zoo*; pl. 1 *mun zoo*, 2 *kun zoo*, 3 *sun zoo*. The impersonal form is *an*: e.g. *an zoo* 'one came'.

Formally, the pattern for other aspects is largely similar. Thus, e.g. for the first future, in which the auxiliary *zaa* precedes a specific set of markers:

	Singular	*Plural*
1	zan zoo	zaa mu zoo
2	zaa ka/ki zoo	zaa ku zoo
3	zai/zaa ta zoo	zaa su zoo

The direct continuative uses the auxiliary *naa* following a specific set of markers, and preceding the verbal noun: eg. *inaa zuwaa* 'I am coming'; *kanaa/kinaa zuwaa*; *yanna/tanaa zuwaa*. The continuative paradigm plus *da* is used to express 'to have': *munaa da aiki* 'we have work'. This form is negated by *baa*... *da* with inserted specific personal pronoun: *baa yaa da aiki* 'he has no work'. Cf. *inaa da shii* 'I have it'; *baa ni da shii* 'I haven't got it'.

RELATIVE VERSION

The perfective and the continuative aspects have relative versions which are used in the formation of relative clauses: e.g. sing. 1 *na zoo*, 2 *ka/kika zoo*, 3 *ya/ta zoo*; pl. 1 *muka zoo*, 2 *kuka zoo*, 3 *suka zoo*. Examples: *mutaane**n** da suka zoo jiya* 'the people who came yesterday' (*jiya* 'yesterday'); *abi**n** da ya cee jiya* 'what he said yesterday' (*cee* 'to say'). As the first of these examples shows, even when a nominal head-word is present, the pronominal copy is necessary.

SUBJUNCTIVE

The subjunctive marker is *su*: e.g. *su zoo* 'let them come'.

NEGATIVE

All affirmative forms, some of which are illustrated above, have negative counterparts: e.g. the negative form of the direct perfective *naa zoo*, etc. is *ban zoo ba*, *ba ka zoo ba*, *ba ki zoo ba*, etc. The subjunctive negative is in *kada* + pronominal marker: e.g. *kada in zoo* 'lest I come'.

Hausa has nothing comparable to the derived stem system of Arabic, but certain terminal vowels plus accompanying tonal patterns are associated with specific meanings. By establishing a relationship between terminal vowel, tone pattern, and transitivity/intransitivity, F.W. Parsons (1960) has organized the great majority of Hausa verbs into seven categories, which he calls 'grades'. Thus ˋ*-aa* verbs are always transitive, e.g. *girbaa* 'to harvest'; ˋ*-a* verbs are usually intransitive, e.g. *shìga* 'to enter'. Some in ˋ*-i* have centrifugal meaning, e.g. *tàfi* 'to go away'. Similarly, *-èe* verbs are transitive or intransitive, often with intensification of root meaning; *-ar* verbs are often causative, e.g. *sayar* 'to sell' (= cause to buy); many verbs in *-oo* have centripetal significance, e.g. *zoo* 'to come'; ˋ*u* verbs are intransitive and passive, e.g. *tàaru* 'to be gathered together'.

Prepositions

Prepositions are simple, derivative, or compound. Simple: e.g. *a* 'at', 'in': *zaa ka daɗee a Kanoo?* 'will you stay-long (*daɗee*) in Kano?'; *sai naa daawoo daga Kanoo* 'until (*sai* '(only) then') I return-here (*daawoo*) from (*daga*) Kanoo'. Derivative prepositions are nouns specifying location. They take the construct markers: *cikii* 'stomach': *ciki.n* 'in(side)', 'into': *yaa shiga cikin gidaa* 'he went into the house'; *gabaa* 'breast': *gaba.n* 'in front of': *ƙarƙashin teebur* 'under(neath) the table'. Compound: e.g. *a kan* 'on (top of)': *naa saa a kan teebur* 'I put it on the table'.

Word formation

By affixation or compounding. Examples of affixation: *mai-* denoting presence of object or quality; *maras-* denoting its absence, e.g. *hankalii* 'mind', *mai.hankalii* 'intelligent', *maras.hankalii* 'unintelligent'; *ba-* denoting ethnic origin, profession, e.g. *ba.haushee* 'a Hausa', *ba.tuuree* 'European', 'English'.

Compounding: e.g. noun + noun with construct *-n*: *jirgii* 'boat' + *samaa* 'sky': *jirgi**n** samaa* 'aircraft'; or + *kasaa* 'land': *jirgi**n** ƙasaa* 'train'.

Compound + prefixed form: e.g. *tauraro.mai.wuciya* 'star with a tail' = 'comet'.

Word order

Normally SVO.

1 1 Tun fil azal akwai Kalma. Kalman
nan kuwa tare da Allah yake.
Kalman nan kuwa Allah ne. 2 Shi ne
tun fil azal yake tare da Allah. 3 Dukan
abubuwa sun kasance ta gare shi ne, ba
kuma abin da ya kasance na abubuwan
da suka kasance, sai ta game da shi.
4 Shi ne tushen rai, wannan rai kuwa shi
ne hasken mutane. 5 Haske na has-
kakawa cikin duhu, duhun kuwa bai
rinjaye shi ba.
6 Akwai wani mutum da Allah ya
aiko, mai suna Yahaya. 7 Shi fa ya zo
shaida ne, domin ya shaidi hasken,
kowa yā ba da gaskiya ta hanyarsa.
8 Ba shi ne hasken ba, ya zo ne domin
ya shaidi hasken.

HAWAI'IAN

INTRODUCTION

Hawai'ian belongs to the Eastern Polynesian branch of the Malay-Polynesian family (*see* **Polynesian Languages**). English is the official language of the State of Hawai'i (the fiftieth state of the USA), and 2,000 retain a command of the Hawai'ian language. Some effort is being made to halt its decline. An uncontaminated form of Hawai'ian is still spoken on the island of Ni'ihau.

There is a considerable body of traditional literature; the *Kumulipo* creation myth is especially notable. Bible translation dates from 1839.

Hawai'ian exhibits an extreme case of phonological reductionism, with only eight consonants surviving from the Proto-Polynesian inventory. Together with five vowels, these eight consonants can form 45 of the monosyllabic particles which play a crucial role in Polynesian syntax.

SCRIPT

Roman alphabet + ' for glottal stop.

PHONOLOGY

Consonants

w, m, p, l, n, k, h, ʔ

Vowels

a, e, i, o, u

MORPHOLOGY AND SYNTAX

Noun

For a general note on Polynesian morphology, *see* **Polynesian Languages**. In Hawai'ian, the nominal complex has the following preposited items:

(a) Prepositions: include possessive markers, neutral and emphatic (the *o/a* dichotomy; *see* **Possession**, below); the subjective marker *'o*, the agentive *e*, the relative *i*; the relational particles *me* 'with', *ma* 'at', 'in', *mai* 'from', *aa* 'as far as'.

(b) Determinatives: comprise the articles: *ka/ke*, the definite-article singular, plural *naa*; *he*, the indefinite article; *a*, the personal article.

(c) Number markers: *mau*, *po'e*, *kau* are plural markers. *Wahi* is one of several paucal markers.

Adjective

The adjective is not separately distinguished. Nominal qualifiers follow the noun: e.g. *mauna loa* 'long mountain'; *aloha nui* 'much *aloha*'. Elbert's (1979) term is 'adjectival stative'; it may correspond to English adjective or adverb: e.g. *he kanaka maika'i* 'a *good* man'; *ua hana maika'i* '... worked *well*'.

Pronoun

PERSONAL PRONOUN

Here a dual number is distinguished:

		Singular	*Dual*	*Plural*
1	*incl.*	—	kaaua	kaakou
	excl.	au/wau	maaua	maakou
2		'oe	'olua	'oukou
3		'oia	laaua	laakou

Examples: *'ike kaaua* 'we (= you and I) know'; *'ike 'ia 'oia e kaaua* 'he was seen by us (= you and me)' (*'ia 'oia* = third person subject form; *e* is agentive marker; *ike* 'to see').

POSSESSION

There are three series of possessive pronouns with initial discriminants: *k*-, Ø-, *n*-. The discriminant is followed by the possessive marker, -*a*- for alienable, -*o*- for inalienable possession, and the personal pronoun (often in truncated form): thus, *k.o.aakou* 'ours (yours and mine)', inalienable; *k.aa.na* 'his/hers', alienable. The singular alienable forms of the *k*- series are: *ka'u* 'my', *kaau* 'yours', *kaana* 'his/hers'. The *k*- forms are also possessive adjectives. Ø- forms and *n*- forms are also used, *inter alia*, like the *k*- forms, to express the verb 'to have' which is missing in Hawai'ian: e.g. *he keiki ka'u* 'I have a child'.

Alienable/inalienable possession: as Elbert (1979) puts it, -*a*- forms indicate that ownership has been brought about by the possessor; the -*o*- forms show that the possessive relationship is not primarily due to the contingent possessor: e.g. *kaana keiki* 'his child' (-*a*- form, as the child is begotten by him), *ko'u kupuna* 'my grandparent'; *ka heana **a** ke ali'i* 'the chief's victim' (lit. 'the dead body caused by the chief'), *ka heana **o** ke ali'i* 'the chief's corpse' (examples from Elbert 1979).

In the socio-religious terminology of the traditional Hawai'ian culture, -*a*- forms were characteristic of subordinate relationships; -*o*- forms of dominant relationships, e.g. of divine action.

DEMONSTRATIVE PRONOUN

Three-degree series by relative distance: (*kee*)*ia* 'this' – (*kee*)*naa* 'that' –

(kee)laa 'that (yonder)': e.g. *i keeia kanaka* 'to this person', *ua hale laa* 'that house' (*ua* recapitulates a noun already mentioned).

INTERROGATIVE PRONOUN

wai 'who?'; *aha* 'what?': e.g. *'o wai ke kumu?* 'who is the teacher?'; *'o wai kou inoa?* 'what's your name?'

Numerals

The basic numerals 1–10 are *kahi, lua, kolu, haa, lima, ono, hiku, walu, iwa, 'umi*. These are usually preceded by a general classifier, *'e*. The classifier *'a* is used in the names of days: e.g. *poo'**a**kahi* 'Monday', *poo'**a**lua* 'Tuesday', etc. 11 *'umi kuumaa-kahi*; 12 *'umi kuumaa-lua*; 20 *iwakaalua*; 30 *kana-kolu*; 40 *kanahaa*; 100 *hanele*. Examples: *'elua i'a* 'two fish'; *'elua a'u mau i'a* 'my two fish'.

Verb

Verbal bases are compatible with certain particles, nominal and verbal, which precede it. There is a basic division into active and stative verbs. For nominal particles, see above. The verbal particles include:

aspect:	inceptive	ke
	perfective	ua
	progressive	e...ana
		ke...nei
		ke...na
tense:	past	i
	non-past	e

plus markers for imperative and subjunctive moods, positive and negative. Examples: ***Ua** hele ke kanaka i Lalato'a* 'The man went to Rarotonga' (*hele* 'to go'; *kanaka* 'man'); ***ke** kali **nei** au* 'I'm waiting'; ***E** hele **ana** 'oe?* 'Are you going?'

The passive voice is marked by the particle *'ia* + *e* or *i*: e.g. *Ua inu ke kanaka i ka lama* 'The man drank the rum' (*inu* 'drink'; *lama* 'rum'); *Ua inu **'ia** ka lama **e** ka kanaka* 'The rum was drunk by the man' (*e* is the agentive case marker).

NEGATIVE

'a'ole + verb: e.g. of perfective *'a'ole i hele ke kanaka* 'the man did not go'.

Word formation

Verbs and nouns take certain prefixes which modify the meaning in various ways: e.g. *ho'o* and its alternants are causative: cf. *hele* 'to go', *ho'ohele* 'to cause to go', 'set in motion'; *'ai* 'to eat', *hoo'ai* 'to feed (trans.)'. *Aka* suggests a slow or careful approach: e.g. *aka'ai* 'to eat deliberately'.

The particle *'ana* and the suffix *-na* act as nominalizers: the suffix may have a regressive effect on the stem vowel(s): e.g. *hau* 'to strike', ***haa**una* 'a blow'; *hiki* 'to arrive', *hiki**na*** 'the east'.

Word order

VSO is normal in verbal sentences. S can be fronted for emphasis: SVO.

I KINOHI ka Logou me ke Akua ka Logou, a o ke Akua no ka Logou.
2 Me ke Akua no hoi la i kinohi.
3 Hanaia iho la na mea a pau eia; aole kekahi mea i hanaia i hana ole ia e ia.
4 Iloko ona ke ola, a o ua ola la ka malamalama no na kanaka.
5 Puka mai la ka malamalama iloko o ka pouli, aole nae i hookipa ka pouli ia ia.
6 Hoounaia mai la e ke Akua kekahi kanaka, o Ioane kona inoa.
7 Hele mai la oia i mea hoike, i hoike ai ia no ua malamalama la, i manaoio ai na kanaka a pau ma ona la.
8 Aole no oia ka malamalama, aka ua hele mai ia e hoike i ka malanalama.

HEBREW

INTRODUCTION

In the North-Western branch of Semitic in the first millennium BC, a distinction is made between Canaanite and Aramaic. By far the most important member of the Canaanite group is Hebrew, known from a rich literature which can be broadly periodized as follows:

1. The Bible: earliest material *c.* 1200 BC, latest *c.* 200 BC. This period includes the Babylonian exile, 587–538, and the Persian rule, 538–333.
2. The Dead Sea Scrolls and related material: these are mainly Essene writings dating from the time of the Maccabees around the turn of the millennium.
3. The rabbinical literature of the early centuries AD. By this time, Hebrew was no longer a spoken language, and much of the rabbinical literature, e.g. the *Talmud* and the *Targum*, is in Aramaic and based on oral tradition (cf. the Hadith in Islam). Central to these writings, however, is the *Mishnah*, a first-century collection of Hebrew treatises on Jewish law.
4. The medieval period: the outstanding figure is Moses Maimonides (1135–1204), whose main works in Hebrew are the *Mishne Torah*, a monumental codification of Jewish law, and the *More Nevukhim*, translated by Maimonides himself from his Arabic original *Dalālat al-ḥā'irīn*, the 'Guide for the Perplexed'.

For the modern revival of Hebrew, *see* **Ivrit**.

SCRIPT

See **Script** at end of article.

PHONOLOGY

Consonants

stops: p, b, t, d, ŧ, k, g, q, ˀ
affricate: ts
fricatives: f, β, θ, ð, s, z, ꞩ, ʃ, χ, γ, ʕ, h, ɦ
lateral and flap: r, l
nasals: m, n
semi-vowels: j, w

The stops /b, g, d, k, p, t/ have spirant allophones: [β, γ, ð, x, f, θ] notated in transcription as *ḇ*, *g̲*, *ḏ*, *ḵ*, *p̲*, *ṯ*. The six stops are primarily syllable-initial, and become spirants following vowels: *bayiṯ* 'house': *ba.ḇayiṯ* /bə.βajiθ/, 'in a house'.

The dotted letters *ṭ*, *ṣ* are the emphatics; *ḥ* represents /ɦ/.

Vowels

long and short: i, e, a, o, u + shwa /ə/ and shwa augments /$ə^a$, $ə^o$, $ə^u$/

Stress

Stress is generally on the final syllable, otherwise on penultimate. Stress can be marked in the script.

MORPHOLOGY AND SYNTAX

Noun

Hebrew has two genders (masculine and feminine) and three numbers; the dual is used mainly for naturally paired items, e.g. parts of the body: *einayim* 'two eyes'; *reglayim* 'two feet'.

Masculine nouns often end in a consonant and have *-im* plural marker: e.g. *ṣuṣ* 'horse', pl. *ṣuṣim*. Irregularly, some masculine nouns have the feminine plural marker *-oṯ*, e.g. *'aḇ* 'father', pl. *'aḇoṯ*; others have a modified stem: *'iš* 'man', pl. *'anašim*.

Typical feminine singular endings are *-ah*, *eṯ/aṯ*, but many nouns with consonantal endings are feminine: e.g. *'eš* 'fire', *'erec* 'earth', *yaḏ* 'hand', *regel* 'foot', *nep̱eš* 'soul', *ḥereḇ* 'sword'. The feminine plural marker is *-oṯ*: e.g. *nep̱eš* 'soul', pl. *nep̱ešoṯ*.

The dual endings are masc. *-ayim*, fem. *-aṯayim*.

DEFINITE ARTICLE

h- + V, where V is a vowel depending on the nature of the following initial and its vocalization: cf. *hā.'iš* 'the man'; *ha.ḥereḇ* 'the sword'; *he.hārim* 'the mountains'; *he.ḥāg* 'the festival'.

Certain consonants are geminated following the definite article: e.g. *meleḵ* – *ha.m.meleḵ* 'the king'.

CASE

The accusative is marked by the particle *'eṯ*: e.g. *bərešiṯ bara' 'elohim 'eṯ ha.šamayim v'eṯ ha.'arec* 'In the beginning (*resiṯ*) God created (*bara'*) heaven and earth.'

The genitive relationship is expressed by means of the construct formula: the noun denoting the possessed object, shortened or compressed as far as possible, precedes the possessor: e.g. *qol ha.'elohim* 'the voice of God'. The feminine construct form restores the *-ṯ* ending: e.g. *torah* 'law', construct, *toraṯ-*: *toraṯ YHVH* 'the law of Jehovah'; *'iššeṯ ha.'iš ha.toḇ* 'the wife of the good man'. As in Arabic, the noun in construct cannot take the article. The masculine plural and dual ending in the construct is *-ei*: e.g. *'elohei ha.šamayim və 'elohei ha.'arec* 'the God of heaven and of earth'. Cf. *dāḇār*

> *dəb̲ar*, construct plural *dəb̲rei*: *dəb̲rei nəb̲'ei ha.elohim* 'the words of the prophets of the Lord'.

Adjective

As attribute, the adjective follows the noun, with concord in number and gender. If the noun is definite, the article is resumed with the adjective: e.g. *ha.'iš ha.ṭob̲* 'the good man'; *ha.'iššah ha.ṭob̲ah* 'the good woman'; *ha.'anašim ha.ṭob̲im* 'the good men'. As predicate, the adjective usually precedes the noun: *ṭob̲ ha.'iš* 'the man is good'. Adjectival qualification may also be expressed by construct noun plus nominal: e.g. *har ha.qodeš* 'mountain of holiness' = 'the holy mountain'.

Pronoun

Independent personal forms with enclitics (possessive):

		Singular		*Plural*	
		Independent	*Enclitic*	*Independent*	*Enclitic*
1		'ani/'anok̲i	-i	'anaḥnu	-enu
2	masc.	'attah	-k̲a	'attem	-k̲em
	fem.	'att	-ek̲	'atten	-k̲en
3	masc.	hu'	-o	hem/hemmah	-am
	fem.	hi'	-ah	hennah	-an

The possessive enclitics are added to the construct form: e.g. *dab̲ar* 'word', *dəb̲ar.i* 'my word', *dəb̲ar.enu* 'our word'; with feminine noun, e.g. *šanah* 'year', *šənat̲.i* 'my year', *šənat̲.enu* 'our year'. For plural of possessed object, yodh appears in the possessive suffix: *dəb̲ar.einu* 'our words'.

DEMONSTRATIVE PRONOUN/ADJECTIVE

Masc. *zeh*, fem. *zot̲*, pl. *'elleh* (common) 'this', 'these'; masc. *hu'*, pl. *hem*; fem. *hi'*, pl. *hen*(*nah*) 'that', 'those'. These follow the noun and take the article: e.g. *ha.'iš ha.zeh* 'this man'; *ha.'iššah ha.zot̲* 'this woman'.

INTERROGATIVE PRONOUN

mi 'who?'; *mah* 'what?' These are indeclinable. *Ha-* in various forms, depending on phonetic follow-up, initiates an interrogative sentence (cf. Arabic *hal*): e.g. ***ha***.*tob̲ah ha.'arec?* 'Is the land good?'

RELATIVE PRONOUN

'ašer, indeclinable: e.g. *vayasem šam 'et̲ ha.ad̲am 'ašer yacar* 'and he put there the man whom he had formed' (Genesis 2.8); *ha. 'ir'ašer yaṣə'u mim.mennah*; literally 'the city which they came from it'. A participial construction may also be used: e.g. *ha.'iš ha.yošeb̲* 'the man who is sitting'.

Numerals

1–19 have masculine and feminine forms; 1–10 have both construct and absolute forms. Thus, for '2':

	Absolute	*Construct*
masculine	šənayim	šənei
feminine	šətaim	šətei

Example: *va.yaʿaš elohim 'et̲.šənei ha.mə'orot̲ ha.gəd̲olim* 'and God made the two great lights' (*ma'or* 'light': masc. noun with fem. pl.).

3–10: masculine forms in singular absolute; these forms modify *feminine* nouns: *šaloš, 'arbaʿ, ḥameš, šeš, šeb̲aʿ, šəmoneh, tešaʿ, ʿešer*. The feminine form adds *-ah* to a slightly modified form of the masculine: e.g. from *šeš*, fem. *šiššah*. The feminine forms qualify *masculine* nouns: compare ***šeš*** *našim* 'six women', ***šiššah*** *'anašim* 'six men'; ***šaloš*** *banot̲* 'three daughters'; ***šəlošet*** *banim* 'three sons'.

Verb

Hebrew verbs are strong or weak: in the former, the (triliteral) root is stable throughout the base conjugation and the derived forms. Weak verbs belong to any one of the following categories: (1) one radical is a guttural; (2) first or third radical is aleph; (3) first radical is nun; (4) first radical is yodh or waw; (5) hollow verb (second radical is yodh or waw); (6) geminated verbs.

The Hebrew verb, like the Arabic, is marked for aspect rather than tense; i.e. perfective contrasts with imperfective. Aspect coalesces with tense in the sense that the perfective aspect is very often equivalent to a past tense, the imperfective to a present or future.

The two aspects combine and complement each other in the narrative tense known as the waw-consecutive, which is a cardinal feature of Old Testament Hebrew. The first verb in such a narrative sequence is in the perfective, while following verbs, continuing the narrative, are in the imperfective – even with switch of subject. In this way, successive actions are effectively linked to initial action: the effectiveness is, of course, lost in translation, e.g. *qam ha.'iš wa.y.yomer.* 'and the man arose and **says**' (= said)... '. Conversely, a future-orientated proposition starts with an imperfective verb, and continues with perfective forms. The consecutive-waw, as the conjunction is called, is followed by gemination of the imperfective personal prefixes (*see* **Conjugation**, below) except in the first person singular, where the vowel of waw is lengthened before *'e-*. The sequence is broken by a negative (the negative particle is *lo*), and must then be re-initiated by a perfective or imperfective take-off point.

Variations arising in the conjugation of weak and irregular verbs are mostly phonological, such as lengthening of vowels and assimilation of consonants (e.g. in *nat̲an* 'to give', where the final *-n* of the stem is assimilated to the initial /t/ of the subject pronominal suffix: *nəṯattem* 'you (masc. pl.) gave'). Biconsonantal stems: e.g. *bā'* 'he came' and *qām* 'he arose': *bā'ṯi* 'I came', *bā'ṯem* 'you (plural) came', *bā'ū* 'they came'.

In verbs with identical second and third radicals, the second-stem radical becomes *-o-*, with gemination of the second radical: *saḇaḇ* 'he went around': *sabboṯi* 'I went around', *sabbonu* 'we...'.

CONJUGATION

The basic *binyan* or 'structure' of the Hebrew verb is known as the *qal* form. Here, as illustration, the perfective and imperfective aspects of the root *KTB* 'write':

			Perfective	*Imperfective*
singular	3	masc.	**kāṯaḇ** 'he wrote'	yi**ḵtōḇ** 'he writes/will write'
		fem.	kāṯəḇah	tiḵtōḇ
	2	masc.	kāṯaḇta	tiḵtōḇ
		fem.	kāṯaḇt	tiḵtəḇi
	1		kāṯaḇti	'eḵtōḇ
plural	3		kāṯəḇu	masc. yiḵtəḇu, fem. tiḵtoḇnah
	2	masc.	kəṯaḇtem	tiḵtəḇu
		fem.	kəṯaḇten	tiḵtōḇnah
	1		kāṯaḇnu	niḵtōḇ

The other *binyanim*, the derived 'structures', are:

1. *niphal*: this is the passive of the *qal*, and is marked by the prefix *n-*: e.g. ***ni**ḵtaḇ ha.daḇar* 'the word was written'.
2. *piel*: this is the factitive of the *qal*, forming transitive verbs: it is marked by gemination of the second radical, thus corresponding to Arabic II: *qadeš* 'holy', ***qiddaš*** 'to sanctify'. It also forms verbs from nouns: e.g. *daḇar* 'word', *di**bb**er* 'to speak'.
3. *pual*: the passive of the *piel*: e.g. *biqqeš* 'to seek', ***bu**qqaš* 'he was sought'.
4. *hiphil*: the marker is a prefixed *h-*: the causative of *qal*: e.g. *šama'* 'to hear', ***hi**šmi'a* 'he caused to hear'.
5. *hophal*: the passive of the *hiphil*: e.g. ***ho**ḵtaḇ* 'it was caused to be written'.
6. *hithpael*: reflexive of *piel*; also reciprocal: e.g. ***hiṯ**ra'u* 'they looked at one another'. Cf. *hiṯqadeš* 'to sanctify oneself', *hiṯgadel* 'to magnify oneself'.

The imperative has forms for second person masculine and feminine, both singular and plural. The jussive coincides largely with the imperfective (slightly truncated), is not used in the first person, and has a specific negative particle: ***al*** *tiqṭol* 'do not kill'. (It is interesting that in Exodus 20 the negative commandments are in the imperfective with the negative particle *lo*: i.e. a general exclusion, rather than contingent prohibition: *lo tircāḥ* 'thou shalt not slay'; *lo tignoḇ* 'thou shalt not steal'. But cf. Exodus 20.16: *dabər-' atāh*

ʿimmānu wa.nišmā ʿāh wa.ʾal.yidaber ʿimmānu ʾelohim 'speak thou with us and we will hear; but let not God speak with us'.

Verb with pronominal-object suffixes: as we have seen above, *'et̲* functions as a direct-object marker. The particle *'et̲* > *'ot̲* also takes personal pronominal endings: *'ot̲i* 'me', *'ot̲o* 'him', *'ot̲anu* 'us', etc. Correlated pronominal endings can also be added directly to the verb: *ra'it̲ihu* 'I saw him' = *ra'it̲i 'ot̲o*. Cf. *šəmarani* 'he watched me', *šəmaro/šəmarahu* 'he watched him', *šəmaranu* '... us'.

PARTICIPLES

The active participle of the *qal* has the form *kot̲eb̲* 'writing'; the passive is *kat̲ub̲* 'written'.

Prepositions

(a) Bound forms: *bə* 'in', *lə* 'to', *kə* 'like'. These replace the *h-* of the article: e.g. *be.harim* 'in the mountains'; *la.melek̲* 'to the king'.
(b) Hyphenated forms: e.g. *'el* 'to(wards)', *ʿal* 'on', 'over,' 'against', *taḥat̲* 'under', *'aḥarei* 'after'. These have a specific set of personal pronominal enclitics, e.g. *'elaw* 'to him'.
(c) Free forms: e.g. *lip̲ne* 'near'.

Composite prepositions are made by combining simple prepositions with nouns:

ʿal-dəb̲ar 'because of'; *bə-qereb̲* 'in the midst of';
ʿal-pəne ha.m.mayyim 'upon the face of the waters' (Genesis 1.2).

Word order

VSO is standard, SVO is frequent.

SCRIPT

For most of the first millennium BC, Hebrew epigraphic material is written in an Old Hebrew character, which was adapted from the Phoenician alphabet around 1000 BC. Circa 200 BC, however, a cognate form of Phoenician-based script was borrowed from Aramaic, and all subsequent Hebrew writing is in this 'square' character. The Samaritans alone retained the Old Hebrew form (*see* **Samaritan**).

The first table shows the Hebrew consonants with the Phoenician equivalents. It will be seen that five characters – kaf, mem, nun, pe, and tsade – have two forms: the second form (in parentheses) is word-final only. Originally vowels were not marked. In the pre-Exilic period, three consonants, yod, waw, and he, came to be used as *matres lectionis* for the notation of long final vowels: yod representing /iː, eː/, waw /oː, uː/, and he /aː/. Later, this usage was extended to medial long vowels.

In the seventh century AD, the Masoretes – Jewish scholars working to preserve the Hebrew text of the Old Testament with maximum fidelity – introduced the system of vocalization known as the Masoretic. Since the consonantal structure of the text was held to be sacred, and could not be modified in any way, vowel points were written above or below the consonants (but *see* **Daghesh**, below). The classical vocalization thus preserved represents, therefore, the pronunciation of Hebrew in the seventh century AD, and there are grounds for believing that the original pronunciation of the language was somewhat different. In addition to the *matres lectionis* for long vowels, the Masoretic system marks short /i, e, a, o, u/, plus simple shwa and three shwa augments /ĕ, ă, ŏ/. See the table of Hebrew vowels.

Daghesh. The single point written within a consonant, known as daghesh, has two functions:

(a) it distinguishes a stop from its correlative spirant, which has no point (daghesh lene):

ŧ ת   *t* תּ   *ꝑ* פ(ף)   *p* פּ   *ꝁ* כ(ךְ)   *k* כּ(ךּ)

đ ד   *d* דּ   *ǥ* ג   *g* גּ   *ƀ* ב   *b* בּ

(b) it marks gemination (daghesh forte): e.g.

...qq קּ   *...mm* מּ   *...ww* וּ   *...bb* בּ

The letter shin is pointed at the upper left to notate /s/, at the upper right to notate /ʃ/:

שׂ s   שׁ ʃ

The sign ְ has a dual function: (a) it denotes the shwa vowel /ə̆/; and (b) it marks a medial consonant with null vocalization. In certain cases, there may be some doubt as to the correct reading. A useful rule is that ְ in a syllable following a long vowel always denotes /ə̆/.

Throughout the post-Biblical period and the Middle Ages, the 'vowel letters', waw for *o/u*, yod for *i*, were increasingly used in prose, though verse was more conservative. In the nineteenth and mid-twentieth century, a conservative orthography known as *xaser*, which used classical spelling without pointing, received scholarly sanction. At the same time, however, the press and the public in general stuck to *male*, a simplified orthography making extensive use of the vowel letters.

In 1970 the Hebrew Language Academy published rules for a standardized orthography without pointing.

א 1 בְּרֵאשִׁית הָיָה הַדָּבָר וְהַדָּבָר הָיָה אֵצֶל הָאֱלֹהִים וֵאלֹהִים 1
הָיָה הַדָּבָר. 2 הוּא הָיָה בְּרֵאשִׁית אֵצֶל הָאֱלֹהִים. 3 הַכֹּל
נִהְיָה עַל-יָדוֹ וּמִבַּלְעָדָיו לֹא נִהְיָה כָּל אֲשֶׁר נִהְיָה. 4 בּוֹ הָיוּ
חַיִּים וְהַחַיִּים הָיוּ הָאוֹר לִבְנֵי הָאָדָם. 5 הָאוֹר מֵאִיר
בַּחֹשֶׁךְ וְהַחֹשֶׁךְ לֹא הִשִּׂיגוֹ.
6 אִישׁ הָיָה שָׁלוּחַ מֵאֵת אֱלֹהִים וּשְׁמוֹ יוֹחָנָן. 7 הוּא בָּא
לְעֵדוּת, לְהָעִיד עַל הָאוֹר כְּדֵי שֶׁעַל-פִּיו יַאֲמִינוּ הַכֹּל.
8 הוּא לֹא הָיָה הָאוֹר; הוּא בָּא לְהָעִיד עַל הָאוֹר. 9 הָאוֹר

(John 1.1–18)

THE HEBREW SCRIPT

CONSONANTS

Phoenician (= Old Hebrew)	*Jewish Square* (modern print)	*Cursive* (modern)	*Name*	*Transcription*
𐤀	א	א	alef	*ʔ*
𐤁	ב	ב	bet	*B; b, ƀ ~ v*
𐤂	ג	ג	g'imel	*G; g, ǥ*
𐤃	ד	ד	d'alet	*D; d, đ*
𐤄	ה	ה	he	*H; h*
𐤅	ו	ו	vav	*W; w ~ v, u, o*
𐤆	ז	ז	z'ayin	*Z; z*
𐤇	ח	ח	xet	*Ḥ; ḥ ~ x*
𐤈	ט	ט	tet	*Ṭ; ṭ ~ t*
𐤉	י	י	yod	*Y; y, i,e*
𐤊	כ (ך)	כ (ך)	kaf	*K; k, ꝁ ~ x*
𐤋	ל	ל	l'amed	*L; l*
𐤌	מ (ם)	מ (ם)	mem	*M; m*
𐤍	נ (ן)	נ (ן)	nun	*N; n*
𐤎	ס	ס	s'amex	*S; s*
𐤏	ע	ע	'ayin	ʿ
𐤐	פ (ף)	פ (ף)	pe	*P; p, ᵽ~f*
𐤑	צ (ץ)	צ (ץ)	tsade	*Ṣ; ṣ~c(=ts)*
𐤒	ק	ק	qof	*Q; q~k*
𐤓	ר	ר	resh	*R; r*
𐤔	ש	ש	shin	*Š; š*
𐤕	ת	ת	tav	*T; t, ŧ~t*

VOWELS

(a) The Masoretic vowels (without *matres lections*). C stands for consonant.

qāmeṣ:	subscript lateral plus vertical:	$\underset{\top}{\mathrm{C}}$
ṣēre:	two subscript dots:	$\underset{..}{\mathrm{C}}$
ḥīreq:	one subscript dot:	$\underset{.}{\mathrm{C}}$
ḥolem:	one superscript dot:	$\dot{\mathrm{C}}$
paṯah:	one subscript lateral:	$\underline{\mathrm{C}}$
səghol:	two plus one subscript dots:	$\underset{\because}{\mathrm{C}}$
qibbuṣ:	three subscript dots in right-slanting line:	$\underset{\ddots}{\mathrm{C}}$

See examples below.

(b) The vowels (combining with various consonants).

Long		*Short*	*Ultrashort*
ṭå טָ		*ṭa* טַ	*'ă* עֲ
lēʸ לֵי	*lē* לֵ	*lɛ* לֶ	*ʔĕ* אֱ
mōʷ מוֹ	*rō* רֹ	*ṣå* צָ	*hă* חֳ
tīʸ תִּי		*si* סִ	*zə, z* זְ
	nūʷ נוּ	*nu* נֻ	

Source: Hetzron, R. (1987) 'Hebrew', in B. Comrie (ed.) *The World's Major Languages*, London: Routledge.

HINDI

INTRODUCTION

A New Indo-Aryan language, Hindi has been the official language of India (along with English) since 1947. In terms of numbers it is by far the most important of the New Indo-Aryan languages. It is estimated that as many as 180 million people speak Hindi as mother tongue in the states of Bihar, Haryana, Himachal Pradesh, Uttar Pradesh, Madhya Pradesh, and Rajasthan, and several millions more speak it as a second language. In addition, there are considerable Hindi-speaking communities in many parts of the world.

In origin, Hindi stems from the same Khaṛī Bolī group of dialects which underlies its alter ego – Urdu. For a note on the historical development of these twin forms, *see* **Urdu**.

The *Rāmcaritmānas* of Tulsi Dās (late sixteenth/seventeenth century) written in the Avadhī dialect, is generally regarded as the first outstanding work in the Hindi literary tradition. In Hindi, the transition from traditional poetry to the treatment of contemporary themes in adequate language, lagged, on the whole, behind parallel developments in Bengali and Urdu. The first genuinely modern writer of any stature in Hindi was Hariścandra Bhārtendu (1850–85). With the advent of Premcand (1880–1936) Hindi prose writing, in the shape of the socio-political novel and short story, came of age. During the twentieth century his work was followed by the *āñcalik upanyās* school of novels of social criticism. Through the mid-twentieth century the *nayī kavitā* and *nayī kahānī* – the 'new poetry' and the 'new story' – movements have flourished, both preoccupied with man's predicament in a modern society.

SCRIPT

Devanāgarī, retaining Sanskrit conjuncts. *See* **Sanskrit**.

PHONOLOGY

Consonants

The consonantal grid is essentially as in Sanskrit. The retroflex /ḷ/ is not in Hindi; /f, z, x, γ, q/ occur in loanwords.

The opposition between the aspirate and the non-aspirate series is carefully observed, as is the opposition between the dentals and the retroflex sounds.

Vowels

short: ɪ, ə, ʊ
long: i, e, ɛ, a, ɔ, o, u

All occur nasalized. The digraph *ai* = /æ/; *au* = /ɔ/.

Stress

Stress is not phonemic.

MORPHOLOGY AND SYNTAX

Noun

Hindi has no articles. There are two genders, masculine and feminine. A typical masculine ending is *-ā*: e.g. *laṛkā* 'boy', *beṭā*, 'son'. Typical feminine endings are *-ī*, *-iyā*: e.g. *laṛkī* 'girl' . Nouns with consonantal endings may be of either gender: e.g. *din* 'day' is masculine, *mez* 'table' is feminine. Sanskrit nouns retain their original gender.

CASE SYSTEM

Basically, there are two cases, direct (nominative) and oblique, plus two numbers, singular and plural. Nouns ending in the characteristic vowels *-ā*/*-ī* are declined as follows:

	Masculine		*Feminine*	
	Singular	*Plural*	*Singular*	*Plural*
direct	laṛkā	laṛke	laṛkī	laṛkiyāṁ
oblique	laṛke	laṛkoṁ	laṛkī	laṛkiyoṁ

(nasalized forms like *laṛkoṁ* can also be transcribed as *laṛkõ*).

Athematic nouns like *din*, *mez* do not change for singular oblique, but take *-eṁ* and *-oṁ* in the plural.

This system is extended by a series of postpositional markers: e.g. *ko* which marks the definite direct or indirect object: e.g. *us ādmī* ***ko*** 'to that man'; *Kisān ghoṛe* ***ko*** *ḍhūṁṛh rahā hai* 'The farmer is looking for the horse.'

The genitive relationship is expressed by means of the link *kā*, *kī*, *ke*, depending on gender and number of nouns possessed; this link follows the oblique case: e.g. *laṛ**ke** **kī** pustak* 'the boy's book', *laṛk**oṁ** **kī** pustakeṁ* 'the boys' books'.

Other case relations are expressed with the help of such postpositions as *se* 'from', *meṁ* 'in', *par* 'on', *tak* 'up to', 'as far as', *ne* 'by' following the oblique case: e.g. in *laṛkoṁ kī bahnoṁ ko* 'to the sisters of these boys'.

Adjective

As attribute, adjective precedes the noun; adjectives ending in *-ā* in the masculine singular behave like *kā*: all other adjectives are invariable, i.e. the feminine form in *-ī*, for example, does not change to *-e* in the oblique: e.g. *us choṭe gāṁv meṁ* 'in that small village' (masc.) but, *un choṭī mezoṁ par* 'on these small tables'.

Pronoun

PERSONAL PRONOUN

The basic forms with their oblique cases are: sing. 1 *maiṁ – mujh*; 2 *tū – tujh*; pl. 1 *ham – ham*; 2 *tum – tum*. The third person forms are supplied from the demonstrative series: *yah* 'this', *vah* 'that'. These have oblique forms in *is*/*us*.

A more formal and polite second person form is *āp*, e.g. *āp.ke beṭe* 'your son' (honorific plural) taking plural concord in verb. Used also with reference to third person.

INTERROGATIVE PRONOUN

kaun 'who?', *kyā* 'what?'

RELATIVE PRONOUN

jo, obl. *jis* (declined), with correlative *vah*: e.g. *Jo kitab us mez par hai,* ***vah***... 'The book that is on the table, (it)...'; *ham.**ne** jin ādmiyoṁ.**ko** kal yahaṁ dekhā thā*, ***ve***...'The men we saw here yesterday, (they)...' (for use of agentive case with perfective verb, *ne*, *see* **Verb**, below; *ko* is the accusative particle; *ve* is plural of *vah* 'that').

Numerals

1–10: *ek, do, tīn, cār, pāṁc, chah, sāt, āṭh, nau, das*; 11 *gyārah*; 12 *bārah*; 20 *bīs*; 30 *tīs*; 40 *cālīs*; 100 *sau*.

The intermediate forms are not predictable. As in other New Indo-Aryan languages, decade + 9 anticipates the following decade; thus, 38 is *aṛtīs*, continuing the *tīs* '30' decade, but 39 is *untālīs* anticipating *cālīs* '40'.

Verb

The division into finite and non-finite forms is basic:

Non-finite forms:

infinitive:	-nā	
gerundive:	-nā	
present/imperfective participle:	-tā	declined for gender and number
past/perfective participle:	-ā	declined for gender and number
conjunctive participle:	-kar(ke)	

Finite forms:

1. Synthetic: the Old Indo-Aryan flectional system is represented in Hindi by the following:

(a) The imperative: 2nd sing. = base; 2nd pl. (associated with *tum*) in *-o*. A more formally polite imperative/request is made with *-ie* (associated with *āp*): e.g. *Yah kām abhī kījīe* 'Could you please do this work now.'

(b) The subjunctive: the endings are sing. 1 *-ūṁ*, 2 *-e*, 3 *-e*; pl. 1 *-eṁ*, 2 *-o*, 3 *-eṁ*: e.g. *caleṁ* 'let's go/shall we go?'; *maiṁ kyā karūṁ?* 'What am I to do?'

(c) The future (not, strictly speaking, synthetic) is made by adding the affix *-gā/-gī/-ge* to the subjunctive endings: e.g. *maiṁ dūṁgā* 'I shall give'; *ham caleṁge* 'we shall go'.

2. Compound tenses with auxiliary *hūṁ*:

(a) With imperfective participle (marked for gender and number) + *hūṁ* (inflected):

general present: *maiṁ caltā hūṁ* 'I go/am going'; *ham calte haiṁ* 'we go/are going';
imperfect past: *maiṁ caltā thā* 'I went/was going'; *ham calte the* 'we (masc.) went/were going'.

(b) With perfective participle (marked for gender and number) + auxillary:

perfective present: *maiṁ calā hūṁ* 'I have gone';
perfective past: *maiṁ calā thā* 'I had gone'.

3. Perfective participle conjugated as preterite tense: e.g. *maiṁ calā* 'I went'; *ham calīṁ* 'we (fem.) went'. The perfective participle forms of five irregular verbs are very important: *karnā* 'to do' – *kiyā*; *lenā* 'to take' – *liyā*; *denā* 'to give' – *diyā*; *jānā* 'to go' – *gayā*; *honā* 'to be' – *huā*.
4. Aspectual forms with secondary auxiliaries: stem + aux.^{2} + aux.^{1}: e.g. a durative aspect with *rahnā* 'to remain': *maiṁ cal rahā hūṁ* 'I was going'; *ham cal rahe haiṁ* 'we (masc.) were going' (stressed as ***cá**l.rahā.hūṁ*).
   Similarly, with modal auxiliaries: e.g. *saknā* 'to be able', *cuknā* 'to complete', *milnā* 'to receive': *maiṁ hindī bol saktā hūṁ* 'I can speak Hindi'; *maiṁ khā cukā hūṁ* 'I've finished eating'.
5. Passive voice: perfective participle of sense-verb + *jānā* 'to go' : e.g. *Hindī bhārat meṁ bolī jātī hai* 'Hindi is spoken in India' (*bhārat*).
6. Causative: a formal progression often produces transitive and causative verbs from an intransitive stem; the causative marker is *-vā-*: cf.

marnā 'to die', *m**ā**rnā* 'to kill', *mar**vā**nā* 'to have someone killed';
bannā 'to be made', *banānā* 'to make', *banvānā* 'to have something made'.

AGENTIVE CASE WITH TRANSITIVE VERBS IN PERFECTIVE FORM

The subject is in the oblique case + *ne*, the verb is in concord with the object: e.g. ***Is** laṛke **ne** kitāb paṛhī **thī*** 'The boy read the book' (*kitāb* is fem.). In this construction, the postposition *ne* follows the oblique form of the third personal pronoun, but the nominative (direct) form of the first and second: cf. *maiṁ.ne/tū.ne/us.ne patr likhā* 'I/you/he/she wrote the/a letter', where *likhā* agrees with *patr* (masculine). However, if a definite object marked by *ko* is present, the verbal form is that of third person singular, construed as an impersonal. An example is given in the section on the relative pronoun, above; cf. *maiṁ.**ne** un logon.**ko** pahle dekhā **thā**.* 'I had seen these people before'.

Postpositions

Some of the most important have been mentioned in the foregoing sections. Further examples: *meṁ* 'in': *dillī meṁ* 'in Delhi'; *se* 'from', 'than': *āp mujh se baṛe haiṁ* 'you are bigger than me'; compound postpositions: e.g. *ke aṅdar* 'inside', *ke bāhar* 'outside', *ke sāth* 'with', *ke pās* 'near': *gaṁv ke pās* 'near the village'. In certain postpositions the order of components is inverted: cf. *binā… ke* 'without': *binā paise ke* 'without money'.

Word order

SOV

१ आदि में शब्द* था;—शब्द परमेश्वर
के साथ था और शब्द परमेश्वर था।
२ वह आदि में परमेश्वर के साथ था।
३ उसके द्वारा सब वस्तुओं की उत्पत्ति हुई,
और जो कुछ भी उत्पन्न हुआ उसमें से एक
भी वस्तु उसके बिना उत्पन्न नहीं हुई।
४ उसमें जीवन था +और यह जीवन मनुष्यों
की ज्योति था।
५ ज्योति अन्धकार में प्रकाश देती रही,
परन्तु अन्धकार उस पर कभी विजयी नहीं
हुआ।
६ परमेश्वर ने एक व्यक्ति को भेजा।
उसका नाम यूहन्ना था। ७ यूहन्ना साक्षी देने
के लिए आए कि वह ज्योति की साक्षी दें जिससे
सब लोग उनके द्वारा ज्योति पर विश्वास
करें। ८ वह स्वयं ज्योति नहीं थे, किन्तु
ज्योति के सम्बन्ध में साक्षी देने आए थे।

HITTITE

INTRODUCTION

Hittite is the oldest attested Indo-European language, and the most important member of the Anatolian branch of Indo-European. The other members are Luwian, Palaic, Lydian, and Lycian.

The Hittite-Luwian peoples seem to have entered Anatolia (present-day Turkey and north Syria) late in the third millennium BC, displacing an indigenous population whose language was not Indo-European (*see* **Anatolian Languages**, **Hurrian**). Whether the Hittite invaders came from the east via the Caucasus, or southwards from the Balkans and Greece, is not clear. A Palaic document refers to the sun 'rising out of the sea'. Through the second millennium BC the Hittite kingdom was one of the most powerful in the Near East. The capital city was Hattušaš, the modern Boğazköy, about a hundred miles east of Ankara. From 1905 onwards, excavation at this site yielded over 25,000 clay tablets, many of them inscribed in two known languages, Sumerian and Akkadian; the great majority, however, in a hitherto unknown language. The fact that the same cuneiform character was used for all three made for relatively rapid decipherment of the new language, and during 1915–19 Hrozný demonstrated that 'Hittite' was an Indo-European language.

The Indo-European identity of Hittite was initially obscured by two factors: first the presence of a large non-Indo-European lexical element; and, second, the absence of that degree of synthetic inflection which might reasonably have been expected in an Indo-European language older than Homeric Greek and Vedic Sanskrit.

The exotic element in the vocabulary would be readily explicable as a substratum dating from the transit period or from prolonged sojourn in a non-Indo-European linguistic environment, or both, were it not so extensive – much larger than, for example, the Dravidian element in New Indo-Aryan. Nor is there any convincing explanation for the surprising simplicity of the morphological system.

The Boğazköy material dates mainly from the New Kingdom period of Hittite history (*c.* 1400–1300 BC) though it includes copies, made during this period, of much older material dating from the Old Kingdom, and going back as far as 1800 BC. The Hittite ethnonym was *nešili/nāšili* 'in the language of Nesa'.

In 1984 the first two volumes of the *Hittite Etymological Dictionary* by Jaan Puhvel were published by Mouton in Berlin. Volume 3 followed in 1991,

Volume 4 (words beginning with K) in 1997. The work is now edited by Werner von Winter and Richard A. Rhodes, and is published by Mouton de Gruyter in Berlin. This major work of reference covers the entire corpus of Hittite texts published to date.

SCRIPT

See **Script** at end of article.

PHONOLOGY

Consonants

stops: p, t, k; with geminated series pp, tt, kk
affricate: ts
fricatives: z, ʃ, h/ɦ (notated as ḫ/ḫḫ)
nasals: m, n
lateral and flap: l, r

Geminated consonants are tense.

F. de Saussure's hypothesis (1879) that loss of certain laryngeal sounds, originally present in Proto-Indo-European, could account for regular phonetic differentiations in the daughter languages, seemed to find support in the Hittite phonological system, where *ḫ*/*ḫḫ* appears in positions predicted by the theory; cf.

Hittite *paḫḫur*	Greek *pur*	English *fire*
Hittite *ḫaštai*	Greek *osteon*	Sanskrit *asthi*, Latin *os*

Vowels

i, e, a, u

The absence of /o/ is striking. There are two signs for *u* in the cuneiform script, and some authorities take the simpler graph ◁ to represent /o/. *e* and *i* appear to be in free variation; thus, *e.eš.ḫar* 'blood' can also be written as *i.iš.ḫar*; *pi.eš.ta* 'he gave' as *pi.iš.ta*. A contributory factor here is that, while the script can distinguish between certain syllables, e.g. *mi* and *me*, *il* and *el*, it has only one sign for certain others like *re*, *le*, *ez*, etc.

MORPHOLOGY AND SYNTAX

Noun

In Late Hittite there are two numbers, two genders (common and neuter), and six cases (Old Hittite had eight, counting a vocative). Forms naturally vary over a time-span of 1,500 years; the following table of endings may be taken as typical:

	Singular		*Plural*	
	Common	*Neuter*	*Common*	*Neuter*
nominative	-š/s	-n, Ø	-eš, aš, uš	-a, i, Ø
accusative	-n	–	-uš	–
genitive	-aš	–	-an, aš	–
dative	-ai, a, i, Ø	–	-aš	–
locative	-a, i, Ø	–	-aš	–
ablative	-az	–	-az	–
instrumental	-it	–	-it	–

Specimen nouns:

a/ā stems: *antuḫša-* 'human being', *atta-* 'father', *anna-* 'mother', *išhā-* 'master';
i-stems: *tuzzi-* 'army', *ḫalki-* 'grain';
u-stems: *ḫeu-* 'rain', *LUGAL.u* 'king', *genu-* 'knee';
n-stems: *henkan* 'death'; *tekan* 'earth';
l-stems: *waštul* 'sin'.

In contrast to other Indo-European languages, *r/n* stems are fairly common in Hittite (cf. Latin, *femur – femoris* 'thigh'):

u̯atar 'water', gen. *u̯itenaš*, pl. *u̯idar* (cf. Greek *hudor – hudatos*);
paḫḫur 'fire', gen. *paḫḫwenaš*;
ešḫar 'blood'; gen. *ešḫanaš*.

Examples of case usage:

Dative: *aruna* 'to the sea'; *napiša* 'to the heavens'. In late Hittite, dative and locative coalesce in an *-i* form: *URUHattuši* 'in Hattusas'.

Genitive: cf. *parnaš išḫaš* 'the master (*išḫā-*) of the house'; *ammēl UKU. aš* 'my man'; *attašaš E.ri* 'in the house of her father'. This word order – possessor before possessed – may be reversed if the possessor is denoted by an ideogram; Friedrich gives the example: *LU takšulaš* 'the man of peace' = 'the peaceful man'. This circumlocution is very common in Hittite; cf. (LU) *u̯astulaš* 'man of sin' = 'the sinner'. In this sense, the genitive comes to function independently: cf. *tai̯azilaš* 'of theft' = (he) of theft = 'the thief'.

Partitive apposition may replace the genitive; see Friedrich's detailed analysis of this point (Friedrich 1960: 123).

Ablative: *napiš.az* 'from heaven', *u̯eten.az* 'from the water'; *UD.KAM.az* 'by day', *MI.KAM.az* 'by night'.

Instrumental: *u̯eten.it* 'with water'; *UTU.un IGIḪ.IA.it uškizzi* 'she sees the sun with her eyes'.

Adjectives

In general, inflected as nominals. Thus:

a-/ā- stems: *dannatta-* 'empty', acc. *dannattan*, dat./loc. *dannatti*;
i- stems: *šalli-* 'big', *mekki-* 'many', *karūili-* 'old';
u- stems: *aššu-* 'good', *idālu-* 'bad'.

In general, a comparative form is achieved by syntactic means, using dat./loc./ablative; *ḫūmant-* 'all' is added to express a superlative: *DINGIR*^{MEŠ}*.naš ḫūmandas* ^{d}*Zašḫapunaš šalliš* 'from-among all the gods Z. (is) great'.

Pronoun

	I Singular	*I Plural*	*II Singular*	*II Plural*
nom.	uk (ugga)	u̯eš	zik (zigga)	šumēš
acc.	ammuk	anzāš ammugga	tuk (tugga)	šumāš
gen.	ammēl	anzēl	tuēl	šumēl
dat./loc.	ammuk	anzāš	tuk	šumāš
abl.	ammēdaz	anzēdaz	tuēdaz	šumēdaz

The third person is more fully attested: *apāš* (common), *apāt* (neuter), with oblique cases: gen. *apēl*, dat./loc. *apēdani*, abl. *apēz*, instr. *apit*. The third person plural forms are *apē*, *apūš*.

Enclitic forms for direct and indirect objects:

	Singular	*Plural*
1	-mu	-naš
2	-ta/-du	-šmaš
3	-ši	-šmaš

The possessive enclitics are characteristic of older Hittite: sing. 1 *-mi/-mu*, 2 *-ti/-ta*, 3 *ši*; pl. 2/3 *-smi*. These take case endings: e.g. with *atta-* 'father': *attaššin* 'his father' (acc.).

DEMONSTRATIVE PRONOUN

kāš (1st p. orientated), pl. *ke*, *kuš*; *ap*āš (2nd and 3rd p. orientated), pl. *ape*, *apuš*.

INTERROGATIVE PRONOUN

kuiš 'who?'; pl. *kueš*; *kuiš* is also used as a relative pronoun.

Numerals

In Hittite texts, numerals are virtually always written as digits, and never written out phonetically. Only for 1, 2, 3, 4, and 7 are doubtful pronunciations known: 1 *āšma*, 2 *dā-* (known from use in compounds), 3 **tri-*

(on evidence of an ordinal form) 4 *meu-* (probable base of certain adjectival forms), 7 **šipta* (found in one compound).

Verb

In comparison with Vedic Sanskrit and Homeric Greek, Hittite has a remarkably simple verbal system: there are two voices, active and middle; two moods, indicative and imperative; and two tenses, present–future and past.

INDICATIVE

There are two sets of present–future endings for the singular: *-mi*, *-ši*, *-zi*, and *-ḫi*, *-ti*, *-i*. The two sets coalesce in the plural to give the single set: *-weni*, *-teni*, *-anzi*.

SPECIMEN CONJUGATION

Present-future *iya-* ‘to do’:

	Singular	*Plural*
1	ijami	ijau̯eni
2	ijaši	ijatteni
3	ijazi	ijanzi

Past of *mi-* stem: of *ḫi-* stem:

	Singular		*Singular*
1	-(n)un	1	-ḫun
2	-š(ta)	2	-š(ta)
3	-t	3	-š(ta)

	Common plural
1	u̯en
2	ten
3	er

THE MIDDLE VOICE

Present-future:

	Singular	*Plural*
1	ḫaḫari	u̯aštati
2	tati	dumari
3	tari	antari

The past endings in the middle voice are closely similar to the present series.

IMPERATIVE

Used in both voices; the active endings are: sing. 1 (*a*)*llu*, 2 -Ø, 3 -*du*; plural 1 -*u̯eni*, 2 -*ten*(*tin*), 3 -*andu*. The endings in the middle-voice imperative are close to those of the middle present.

The infinitive ends in -*anzi* or -*anna*. The verbal noun in -*u̯ar* is declined, with a genitive in -*u̯aš*: *pāu̯ar* 'going', gen. *pāu̯aš*; *arnummar* 'bringing', gen. *arnummaš*. This form often behaves like a gerundive; cf. *memijaš* (< *memijan* 'word', 'thing'), *kuiš ijau̯aš* 'something (requiring) to be done'. The participle in -*ant*- is passive in transitive verbs, active in intransitives: cf. *appant*- 'caught' (< *ep*- 'to seize'); *dant*- 'taken' (< *dā*- 'to take').

NEGATION

The indicative is usually negated by the Akkadian *UL*, read in Hittite as *natta*. A prohibitive is made with *lē* plus the present indicative.

The causative formant is -*nu*: cf.

u̯eḫ- 'to turn' (intrans.);
u̯aḫ.nu- 'to turn' (trans.).

PREVERBS

E.g. *anda* 'into', *appa*(*n*)- 'back'; e.g. with *pāi*- 'to go', *anda pāi*- 'to enter', *appa pāi*- 'to go back'.

Postpositions

Some signify either locus or directed motion into/towards that locus: e.g. *piran*: ^{GIŠ}*BANŠUR-i piran* 'before the table' (locus), or 'towards the front of the table'. Similarly, *anda*(*n*) 'in(to)': *E-ri anda*(*n*) 'in(to) the house'.

With other postpositions a distinction is made: e.g. *ḪUR-SAG-i šēr* 'on the mountain'; *ḪUR-SAG-i šarā* 'up to the top of the mountain'.

SCRIPT

Cuneiform, very close to Old Akkadian. That is to say, Hittite was written in a script originally designed to notate a radically different phonological system. Sumero-Akkadian ideograms and determinants appear in it, and these are semantically useful in that they help to determine meaning. At the same time, they give no clue (unless they are accompanied by phonetic *furigana* – *see* **Japanese**) as to how they were pronounced in Hittite. For example, the Sumero-Akkadian phonogram 𒌉 *DUMU* is known to mean 'son', 'child', but its Hittite pronunciation is unknown. Ideograms are also found accompanied by cuneiform phonetic complements indicating case: e.g. *EN* 'lord', 'master'; *EN-an* (acc.), *EN-i* (dat.). The Hittite reading of *EN* is *išḫā*-: nominative singular *iš.ḫa.a.aš* = *EN.aš*. Similarly, the accusative *EN.an* may appear as *iš.ḫa.a.an*, and the plural nominative, *išḫēš*, can be written as *iš.ḫi.e.eš* = *EN*^{MEŠ}. *eš*, where superscript *MEŠ* is a plural marker (i.e. -*eš* is redundant).

Consonantal clusters have to be written in terms of the three syllables permissible in cuneiform: Cv, vC, CvC. Thus, **tri-* appears as *te.ri-*. In polysyllables, variations and inconsistencies in the use of the three available syllables abound. Friedrich gives the example of *arhun* 'I reached', notated both as *a.ar.aḫ.ḫu.un* and *a.ar.ḫu.un*.

In transliteration, Sumero-Akkadian ideograms and phonograms are notated in capitals.

Ideograms remain identical in all cuneiform scripts; thus 𒀭 'God' is read in Sumerian as *dingir*, in Akkadian as *ilu*, in Hittite as *šiuna-*, and in Hurrian as *eni-*.

𒆳 'land' is Sum. *kur*, Akk. *mātu*, Hit. *utnē*, Hur. *umini-*.

HOPI

INTRODUCTION

Hopi belongs to the Pueblo group of the Uto-Aztecan branch of the Aztec-Tanoan phylum. Linguistically, the Pueblo group is heterogeneous, containing, in addition to Hopi, Tewa and Keresan languages and Zuni, whose genetic status is not clear. Culturally, the Pueblo Indians are the modern representatives of the Anasazi-Pueblo civilization – a major Indian culture extending from the early years of the first millennium AD to modern times, which reached its climax in the 'cliff-dwelling' culture of the eleventh to fourteenth centuries. At present Hopi is spoken by about 2,000 Indians in northern Arizona. The language is unwritten. The form described by Whorf (1946) is the Toreva dialect.

Much has been written about the Hopi perception of time and space. Hopi is, of course, not unique in making a distinction between a Heraclitean flux of point events on the one hand, and the relative stability of durative events on the other; but few languages are so well equipped to map this distinction on to their morphological structure. Point events – momentary flashes, sparks, movements, ripples – occur *in* a spatio-temporal field which is not materially altered by them; and Hopi avoids what Whitehead called the fallacy of 'misplaced concreteness' by refusing to confer the stability of nominalization upon them. Rocks, mountains, and the desert are nominals; point events are mapped in the form of verbals, which do not even need umbral indices (contrast English '*it* poured', '*it* flashed'). The same goes for cyclical events: to a Hopi, 'summer' is not a nominal, nor could it be the subject of a sentence; it can only be a temporal adverbial: 'when-it-was-summer'.

Durative events can be nominalized, however, in so far as they (a) are bounded spatio-temporal entities, and/or (b) affect their spatio-temporal locus by superimposing their own determinateness upon it.

PHONOLOGY

Consonants

The plosives /p, t, c, k, k°, q/ are accompanied by their pre-aspirated counterparts /ʿp, ʿt/, etc. and by the nasal series /m, n, ɲ, ŋ, n°/. Further, Whorf (1946) lists what he calls 'desonants': /w̱, m̱, ṉ, ḻ, y̱/, which are described as 'voiceless continuants'. Glottal stop ˀ.

Vowels

a, ɛ, ɪ, ou, œ, i

A following consonant causes a vowel to be abruptly cut off.

There are three tones, high, middle, and low. Elision, contraction, and assimilation are frequent.

MORPHOLOGY AND SYNTAX

Parts of speech (Whorf's special terminology):

Analytics: this is Whorf's term for a group of words comprising adjectives, numeratives, locators, modalizers, tensors, etc. For translation purposes, most of the words in this group can be treated as adverbs.

Ambivalents: Whorf's term for lexemes which can function in either the nominal or the verbal inflectional system (both extensive). Hopi nouns and many ambivalents denote spatio-temporal entities that are (a) durative configurations, and (b) steady-state. Persons can qualify for nominal status by virtue of, for example, the kinship system. Point-events with no durative dimension can be denoted only by a verb or a locator.

Locators: formally, these are case-inflected pronominal bases, functioning mainly as postpositions.

A '**directional locator**' serves to denote (non-verbally) vector motion in terms of field position: 'away', 'up', 'here', 'from'. This contrasts with motion in terms of outline/contour, with no reference to field position; this form of motion is denoted verbally, plus or minus a directional locator: 'running', 'turning', 'wriggling', etc.

Locus: '**punctual locus**' at a '**point-moment**' contrasts with '**tensive**' **locus**, which always involves a plurality/multiplicity of contours, configurations, extensions in four-dimensional space–time. Plurality coheres in tensive locus: thus, pluralization of a singular subject involves the replacement of points (mathematically, scalars) by tensors. See example, below.

Certain case-suffixes have both punctual and tensive forms, e.g. the **super-essive**: *-cvi('o)* punctual, *-cva(a'a)* tensive.

It is noteworthy that a personal agent (denoted by the ergative in many languages) is marked in Hopi by the super-essive inflection.

Eventive predicator: this notates an event which induces change in its force-field, with either temporary or permanent effect. A transitory event is recorded by a verb; a durative change by an ambivalent. The **dynamic eventive** emphasizes the ensuing change, and can be reinforced by the **extended dynamic**. Whorf points out that most Indo-European transitives denoting physical alteration correspond to causatives of *k*-class eventives in Hopi.

Noun

There are three classes: animate, inanimate, vegetative. The noun is inflected for case (nominative/accusative), state (absolute/construct), and, where this does not conflict with Hopi cosmology, for number. Animate and inanimate nouns may be marked for dual, paucal, and multiple number. The vegetative category has one general plural marker, *-qölö*. The Hopi notion of plurality applies to entities that can be simultaneously grouped and counted; clearly, this rules out temporal concepts.

Specimen conjugation for root *pa.sa* 'field' (inanimate):

		Singular		*Plural* (*multiple*)	
		Nominative	*Accusative*	*Nominative*	*Accusative*
absolute		pa·sa	pá·sat	pá·vàsa	pá·vàsat
construct	1	'ivása 'my field'	'ivásay	'ivá·vàsa	'ivá·vàsay
	2	'éˁpàsa	'éˁpàsay	'éˁpà·vasa	'èˁpà·vasay
	3	pá·sa'àt	pá·sayàt	—	—

Further case relationships are expressed by suffixes, e.g. *-mem* (comitative), *-h* (partitive), *-vníˁqaY* (comparative).

Adjective

Adjectives in Hopi are restricted to such qualitative concepts as 'cold', 'rough', etc. They cannot map shape or configuration: point configuration is a verbal, and durative configuration is expressed by an ambivalent form (usually a *k*- class verb, see below).

Pronoun

The personal forms have a base form, three nominal forms (nominative, objective, and possessive), and about a dozen locative/directional forms. The base forms are:

	Singular	*Plural*
1	'ine-	'itame-
2	'e-	'eme-
3	'a-	'ame-

SPECIMEN DECLENSION

First person: nom. *ne*'; obj. *ney*; poss. *'i-*; loc. *'ineˁpe*; all. *'inemi*; ill. *'inemiq*; abl. *'ineŋaq*.

The pronoun *han* (1st person sing. nominative only) encodes, according to Whorf, 'one's unspoken intention', contrasting with 1st person *ne*, the uttering ego.

DEMONSTRATIVE PRONOUN
Examples: base *pá-*; nom. *pam*; pl. *pema*. The base for the oblique cases is *p*V + nasal, e.g. illative *paŋsok*. The demonstrative agrees with the noun in case: thus, *paŋsok kí·soŋmiq* 'into (the interior of) that house' (*-soŋ-* links the root *ki·* 'house' with the suffix *-miq*).

Verb

The verb is intransitive or transitive; in the latter, if no overt direct object is present, a third person object is implied.

Different collocations of stress, extension by suffix, and contraction of stem produce four conjugations. The most important extension is that provided by the *k-* class verbs – the 'eventive' voice, described by Whorf (1946: 173) as 'a rich vocabulary of CVCV roots which denote... characteristic visual outlines and figural arrangements'. The spectrum here extends from momentary manifestations which do not affect their field, to semi-durative configurations which do, qualifying thereby for status as 'ambivalents': verbals with certain nominal properties. An essive voice reports a measure of concretion plus prolongation of an event; the cessative voice records its cancellation. With the 'extended dynamic voice' Hopi is even equipped to notate the switch from a neutral background field to a force-field, exerting influence on the event denoted by the verb. The possessive voice defines a subject in terms of its valencies: e.g. *siwa yta* 'has a younger sister', or with a modifier, 'is younger-sistered'.

Aspects are marked by stem suffixes in ordered sequence. The simplex aspect with Ø marker refers either to a point event or to a durative, depending on the semantic content of the stem. The inceptive aspect is always with reference to a point event; all other aspects are durative.

The ingressive aspect in *-i.va* makes explicit the point of transition from latency ('causal power', described by Whorf as 'an important Hopi concept') to manifestation. Related to this aspect is the impotential modality, which notates an insufficiency of 'causal power' for positive actualization.

The 'segmentative aspect', found only in the *k-* class verbs, converts a point event into a recurrent or cyclical spatio-temporal configuration. Aspects may be compounded to notate even more subtle facets of Hopi perception and Hopi cosmology. In addition, several modes classify spatio-temporal events in terms of concomitance, sequentiality, agency, etc. The transrelative mode copes specifically with subject-switching.

As mentioned above, pluralization of a singular subject involves the replacement of point events by tensive events. In one of the most illuminating passages in his magisterial account of Hopi, Whorf uses the example:

ma.na 'ayám ki.vɛ qatéʼqa 'aŋk wárikìwta

'the girl who lived in yonder house came running'

ma.na: 'girl', nom. sing.;
'ayám: punctual locative of demonstrative pronoun 'yonder';
ki.vɛ: stem of *ki.he* 'house' plus punctual locative suffix *-vɛ*;
qaté 'qa: singular agentive case of *qate*: 'sits, dwells';
'aŋk: ablative case of pronoun: 'from there';
wári.kìw.ta: essive of *k-* class verb *wari*: sing. subject 'runs'.

The punctual referents become tensive on pluralization, and the sentence now reads:

mamaNt 'ayɛ́' kí.kihèt 'aŋ yɛsqam 'ah yéˁte.kiw.yèŋʷa

mamaNt: multiple plural of *ma.na*, with animate suffix *-t*;
'ayɛ': tensive locative of *'ayám*;
kí.kihèt: objective case in *-t* of *ki.kihe*, multiple inanimate, 'houses'; 'houses', being plural, cannot take case inflection, hence use of postposition *'aŋ* 'in', tensive locative;
yɛsqam: paucal suffix *-m* is used for plural of agentives; here added to agentive of *yɛ.sɛ*: plural subjects 'sit', 'dwell';
'ah: partitive signalling distributive/diffuse removal;
yeˁte.kiw.yèŋʷa: *yèŋʷa* is the plural form of *-ta*; the verb form is the essive of *k-* class verb *yeˁte*: plural subjects 'run'.

Word order

SOV

1 1 **Ayáq yayhniwhqat epeq God Lavayiat pay ep'e; pu Lavayi God ámuma; pu pay Lavayi God.**
2 **Pu pay pam hak piw yayhniwhqat epeq God amum yanta.**
3 **Sohsoy himu put ahpiy yukilti; pu qa himu yukiwtaqa put qa ahpiy yukilti.**
4 **Pam nāp nahpiy qatsit pasiwta; pu pay pam qatsi sinmuy amumi tālat anta.**
5 **Noqw tāla qatālat ep tālawva; noqw qatāla put qa tōka.**
6 **Noqw hak tāqa God aṅqw ayatiwa; nihqe John yan mātsiwa.**
7 **Pam hak hihta tuawi'taniqe ōviy pitu, Tālat tuawi'taniqee, sohsoyam put ahpiy tūtuptsiwaniqat ōviy'o.**
8 **Pay pam qa pas pas pám himu Tāla; pam put Tālat tuawi'taniqe ayatiwa.**

HUNGARIAN

INTRODUCTION

Hungarian belongs to the Finno-Ugric branch of Uralic, and is the official language of the Republic of Hungary. There is also a large Hungarian-speaking minority in Transylvania (Erdély) and the total number of speakers is 15 million. The ethnonym is Magyar: *a magyar nyelv* 'the Hungarian language'.

From an original homeland in the Urals, where their closest congeners still live (*see* **Khanty**, **Mansi**) the Magyar tribes moved westwards to reach the Carpathians and the Danube in the ninth century AD. Under the leadership of Árpád, the *honfoglalás* 'settlement' was completed by 896. The oldest monuments in Hungarian are the *Halotti Beszéd* ('Funeral Oration') of *c.* 1200, and the *Ó-Mária Siralom* ('Lament of Mary') dating from about a hundred years later. The fifteenth century saw a brilliant renaissance period in the reign of Matthias I Corvinus. National disaster at Mohács, where the Hungarians were defeated by the Turks, was followed by a long, slow recovery until the early nineteenth century, when the revolutionary movement produced two great poets, Petőfi Sándor and Arany János. The social and economic transformation of Hungary from the 1860s onwards brought the conditions for a tremendous upsurge in cultural creativity, both qualitative and quantitative, and Hungarian can now lay claim to one of the world's great literatures.

SCRIPT

Roman alphabet, minus *q*, *w*, *x*, *y*, plus diacritics for vowel length and quality: peculiar to Hungarian is the notation of long /œ, y/ as *ő*, *ű*.

PHONOLOGY

Consonants

stops: p, b, t, d, ɟ, k, g
affricates: tʃ, dʒ
fricatives: f, v, s, z, ʃ, ʒ j, h
nasals: m, n, ɲ, ŋ
lateral and flap: l, r

All consonants can be long or short; if long, they are written doubled. At junctures, assimilation takes place: unvoiced → voiced before voiced: e.g. *nép* 'people' + *dal* 'song': *népdal* /neː**b**dal/, 'folksong'. And vice versa: voiced →

unvoiced before unvoiced: e.g. *zseb* /ʒɛp/, 'pocket' + *kendő* 'kerchief': *zsebkendő* /ʒɛ**p**kendœ/, 'handkerchief'.

Vowels

For reasons of vowel harmony, the vowels are divided into:

high: i, e, œ, y
low: a, o, u

All have corresponding long values (indicated by acute accent). As regards vowel harmony, /i, iː/ are neutral and can be used with either high or low vowels; e.g. *virág* 'flower', *piros* 'red'. /e, eː/ may also occur with low vowels. In general, however, the front/back opposition is observed: cf.

a ház 'the house', a házb**a**n 'in the house';
a víz 'the water', a vízb**e**n 'in the water';
adt**a**m 'I gave', kért**e**m 'I asked'.

Hungarian short /a/ is close to the value [ɒ]; long /a/ is [aː]. Theoretically, there is a distinction between open and closed short /e/: [ɛ] and [e]. In Budapest Hungarian the distinction is not observed. /œ/ and /y/ are notated here as *ö* and *ü*.

Liaison of final consonant to initial vowel of following word is a marked feature of Hungarian pronunciation: e.g. *nem akarok ebédelni* /ne-ma-ka-ro-ke-bé-del-ni/, 'I don't want to have lunch'.

Stress

Stress is invariably on first syllable.

MORPHOLOGY AND SYNTAX

Noun

There is no grammatical gender; the pronoun *ő*, for example, means 'he/she'. Where necessary, nouns signifying natural distinction of gender may be added: e.g. *a tanár* 'the teacher', *a tanárnő* 'the female teacher' (*nő* 'woman').

The definite article is *a*/*az*, the latter form before vowels: e.g. *az ember* 'the man'. The definite article is invariable for number: e.g. *a kép* 'the picture', pl. *a képek*. The article is assimilated to postpositions, as for example *a ház**ban*** 'in the house': **az.ban a házban* → ***abb**an a házban* 'in that house'.

The plural marker is *-k* linked to consonantal stems by a harmonic vowel: e.g. *a ház**ak*** 'the houses'; *a könyv**ek*** 'the books'; *az ablak**ok*** 'the windows'.

CASE SYSTEM

Agglutinative affixes on stem, with harmonic vowels where necessary. With certain endings, assimilation at juncture takes place (see, for example, comitative case in the following paradigm). In the plural, the endings are added to the *-k* marker.

singular	nominative	*a bor* 'the wine'	*a víz* 'the water'
	accusative	*a bort*	*a vízet*
	dative	*a bornak*	*a víznek*
	illative	*a borba*	*a vízbe*
	comitative	*a borral*	*a vízzel*

The comitative ending is *-val/-vel* → *-ral/-rel* after *-r*, → *-zal/-zel* after *-z*, etc.
Variants: some stems change for certain oblique cases, e.g. *tó* 'lake', acc. *tavat*.

Adjective

As attribute, adjective precedes noun and is invariable: e.g. *piros virág* 'red flower', *piros virágok* 'red flowers'; *egy mezőgazdasági kérdés* 'an agricultural question'; (*megoldás*) *ezek**re** a mezőgazdasági*Ø *kérdések**re*** '(solution) to these agricultural questions'.

All adjectives can be used as nouns, and are then declined fully: e.g. *a magyar nép* 'the Hungarian people'; *a magyar**ok*** 'the Hungarians'.

COMPARATIVE

(Harmonic vowel) + *-bb*: e.g. *nehéz* 'heavy', *nehez**ebb*** 'heavier'. Some comparatives are suppletive, e.g. *sok* 'many', comparative *több.*

Pronoun

	Singular			*Plural*		
	Nominative	*Accusative*	*Enclitic*	*Nominative*	*Accusative*	*Enclitic*
1	én	engem(et)	-m	mi	minket	-unk/ünk
2	te	téged(et)	-d	ti	titeket	-tok/tek
3	ő	őt	-i/e	ők	őket	-ik

Te and *ti* are familiar. The polite second person is *Ön* or *Maga*, with third person concord. Oblique forms are made by adding the enclitic markers to the case endings; e.g. *nek**em*** 'to me', *nek**ed*** 'to you'; *benn**em*** 'in me', *benn**ünk*** 'in us'. The possessive markers are closely similar, but precede the case endings: e.g. *könyv**em*** 'my book'; *ház**unk*** 'our house'; *egy barát**om*** 'a friend of mine'; *zseb**em**ben* 'in my pocket'; *a város**aink**nak* 'of our cities'. These endings also provide the Hungarian equivalent of the verb 'to have': *könyv**em** van* 'I have a book' (lit. 'my-book is'); *könyv**em** nincs* 'I don't have a book'. Where one possessive follows another, the second has the *-nak/-nek* ending: e.g. *a tanár**om** barát**já.nak** a könyv**e*** 'my teacher's friend's book' (where *-já-* marks possession by *tanár**om*** 'my teacher', and ***-nak*** signals the pending possessive ending *-**e***).

DEMONSTRATIVE PRONOUN/ADJECTIVE
ez 'this', pl. *ezek*; *az* 'that', pl. *azok*: e.g. *ez a könyv* 'this book'; *azok a virágok* 'those flowers'; ***ennek** az iskolá**nak** a tanuló**i*** 'the pupils of this school'.

INTERROGATIVE PRONOUN
ki 'who?'; *mi* 'what?'

RELATIVE PRONOUN
aki/ami/amely/amelyik: e.g. *az ember, aki beszél* 'the man who is speaking'; *az ember, aki**ről** beszéltem* 'the man I spoke about'.

Numerals

1–10: *egy, két/kettő, három, négy, öt, hat, hét, nyolc, kilenc, tíz*; 11 *tizenegy*; 12 *tizenkettő*; 20 *húsz*; 30 *harminc*; thereafter by addition of *-van/-ven*: e.g. 40 *negyven*; 50 *ötven*; 100 *száz*.

Numerals are followed by a noun in the singular: e.g. *hat könyv* 'six books'; *tíz ember* 'ten men'.

Verb

Stems are inherently transitive or intransitive, and can be converted or extended by various modal and aspectual formants: e.g.

-tat/-tet makes causatives: *csinál-* 'to do', 'make', *Péter ruhát csinál**tat*** 'Peter has a suit made';
-kozik/kezik/közik makes reflexives: e.g. *véd* 'to defend', *véde**kezik*** 'to defend oneself';
-gat/-get is frequentative: e.g. *beszél* 'to speak', *beszél**get*** 'to converse'.

The passive voice is no longer used in Hungarian; many stems are paired for transitive/active and intransitive/passive meanings: e.g. *nyít-* 'to open' (trans.) – *nyílik* 'to open (intrans.)/be opened'; *rejt-* 'to hide' (trans.) – *rejlik* 'to be hidden'.

There is a very extensive system of preverbal particles or prefixes, which are separable, as in German. Some of the commonest are: *be-* 'into'; *ki-* 'out of'; *le-* 'down'; *át-* 'through'; *vissza* 'back'; *meg-* is the perfective marker. Thus *megy* 'he goes', ***be**megy* 'he goes into'; *lép* 'he steps', ***ki**lép* 'he comes out'; *írja* 'he writes', ***le**írja* 'he writes down'; *fordul* 'he turns', ***vissza**fordul* 'he turns back'.

SEPARABILITY
Illustrated with verb *tenni* 'to do' + *meg-* (present third singular is *tesz*):

hosszú utat tett **meg** 'he's come a long way'
mindent **meg**tenne értem 'he'd do anything for me'
meg kell tennem 'I have to do it'
nem tesz **meg** 'he won't do it'

MOOD
Indicative, conditional, and a subjunctive/imperative.

Indicative: present and past tenses are made by means of personal endings added to the stem. There are two sets of these endings, one for definite, the other for indefinite complement. A subordinate clause introduced by *hogy* 'that', counts as definite. The endings are illustrated with the stem *ad-* 'give':

		Present		*Past*	
		Indefinite	*Definite*	*Indefinite*	*Definite*
singular	1	adok	ado**m**	adtam	adtam
	2	adsz	ado**d**	adtál	ad**tad**
	3	ad	ad**ja**	adott	ad**ta**
plural	1	adunk	ad**juk**	adtunk	ad**tuk**
	2	adtok	ad**játok**	adtatok	adtá**tok**
	3	adnak	ad**ják**	adtak	adtá**k**

Thus *újśagot olvasok* 'I read *a* newspaper'; *az újságot olvaso**m*** 'I read *the* paper.'

First person singular subject + second singular object are encoded in the ending *-lak/-lek*: e.g. *kérlek* 'I ask you'; *szeretlek* 'I love you'.

A future tense is made with the auxiliary *fog-* ('to catch') + infinitive in *-ni*: e.g. *adni fogok/fogom* (depending on whether complement is definite or indefinite) 'I'll give'. The present with *meg-* prefix may also have future sense: e.g. *megkérdezem a tanártól* 'I'll ask the teacher' (lit. 'from the teacher').

Conditional: the marker is *-n-* + harmonic vowel: e.g. *ad**nám*** 'I'd give' (definite object); *kér**nék*** 'they would ask'.

Imperative/subjunctive: the marker is *-j-*: note the sandhi of *j* with certain sibilants: *s* + *j* → *ss*; *sz* + *j* → *ssz*; *z* + *j* → *zz*: e.g. *olvas-* ('read') + *j* → *olvassa* 'read' (definite object). A polite request is made with *legyen szíves* 'please': e.g. *legyen szíves, olvasson* 'please read' (indefinite). *Fontos, hogy megír**jam** a levelet* 'It's important (*fontos*) that I write the letter.'

PARTICIPLES

Imperative in *-ó/-ő*: e.g. *a dolgoz**ó** ember* 'the working man'. The form is much used as a nominal: e.g. a *dolgozók* 'the workers'. The perfective participle is identical with third person singular past indefinite: e.g. *adott* 'he gave' → 'given'; *egy ismert író* 'a well-known writer'.

The participial form in *-va/-ve* denotes a state of affairs; it is often used with the auxiliary: e.g. *Az üzletek **be vannak** csuk**va*** 'The shops are closed'; *A televiziót néz**ve** elaludtam* 'While watching television I fell asleep.'

NEGATIVE

The general marker is *nem*; *ne* is used with the imperative/subjunctive: e.g. *nem megy* 'he doesn't go'; *ne menjen* 'don't go'. Negation is reduplicated: e.g.

Nem dolgoznak sehol sem, lit. 'They're not working nowhere neither' = 'There's nobody working anywhere.'

Postpositions

For example, *mellett* 'beside', *fölött* 'above', *alatt* 'below'. They are reduplicated with demonstratives: e.g. *ez alatt a szék alatt* 'under this chair'. The postpositions take the personal markers, and show a three-way opposition for motion relative to speaker or other referent: e.g. *mellett**em*** 'beside me'; *mell**ém*** 'in my direction'; *mell**ől**em* 'from beside me'; *föl**ött**em* 'above me'; *föl**ém*** '(moving) over me'; *föl**ül**em* 'from above me'.

Word order

SOV is basic, but order is free.

1 1 **Kezdetben volt az Ige, és az Ige az Istennél volt, és Isten volt az Ige.** 2 **Ő**
kezdetben az Istennél volt. 3 **Minden általa lett, és nélküle semmi sem lett,**
ami létrejött. 4 **Benne élet volt, és az élet volt az emberek világossága.** 5 **A**
világosság a sötétségben világít, de a sötétség nem fogadta be. 6 **Megjelent egy**
ember, akit Isten küldött, akinek a neve János. 7 **Ő tanúként jött, hogy bizonyságot**
tegyen a világosságról, és hogy mindenki higgyen általa. 8 **Nem ő volt a világosság,**
de a világosságról kellett bizonyságot tennie.

HURRIAN

INTRODUCTION

This ancient Anatolian language is of unknown affinity. Clearly non-Indo-European, it is very close to Urartian (*see* **Urartian**). The Hurrian people seem to have entered Anatolia and the north Mesopotamian area during the third millennium BC. It is possible that at least one wave of Hurrians came in via Armenia. The apogee of their power was reached in the second millennium BC, when they ruled the kingdom of Mitanni. They disappear from the historical scene in the sixth/fifth century BC. Their language is known from second-millennium texts excavated at a number of places in the Near East – Mari on the Euphrates, Amarna in Egypt, Boğazköy in Turkey, and Ugarit on the Syrian coast.

While attempts to establish a genetic relationship between Urartian-Hurrian and the Karthvelian languages have not met with general agreement, the case for some connection with the Nakh languages of Dagestan seems to be more promising.

SCRIPT

Mainly Akkadian cuneiform. Some Hurrian texts have been found in the Ugaritic proto-alphabet (*see* **Ugaritic**).

PHONOLOGY

Consonants

Paired stops – a surd and its geminate – are characteristic of Hurrian: e.g. /p – pp, t – tt, k – kk/. Sonant and semi-vowel pairs are also found: /w – ww, l – ll, ḫ – ḫḫ, Z – ZZ/.

The sibilant series is indeterminate; notated here by capitals *S*, *Z*.

Other phonemes: /m, n, r, d, g, γ/.

Vowels

i, e, a, o, u, ə

MORPHOLOGY AND SYNTAX

Noun

There is no grammatical gender. The noun has two numbers, with a plural form in *-a-* or *-aZ*. Eight or nine cases are distinguished. Some case endings:

	Singular	Plural
absolute	Ø	-aZ
ergative	-(u)S	-aZuS
genitive	-we	-aZ(w)e
dative	-wa	-aZ(w)a
ablative	-dan	—

ARTICLE

Sing. *-ne*, pl. *-na*. This article usually precedes the case marker, but may follow it. The following example shows an ergative construction with article: *SawuSka.we.na.aZuS Sije.na.aZuS* 'by (the agency of) the waters of (the goddess) Sawuska', where the plural ergative marker follows the article (pl. *-na-*), which, in the first word, follows the genitive marker *we-*: *ardi.ne.we.na Ḫatti.ne.we.na* '(the gods) of the town of Hatti'.

Adjective

There are certain adjectival formants: *-ul-oḫḫe*, e.g. *hijar.oḫḫe* 'golden'; *-ul -ozzi*, e.g. *aStuzzi* 'female'; *-γe*, e.g. *ḫurwo.γe* 'Hurrian'.

Pronoun

First person: the base form is *iSte*, with ergative *iZaS*, genitive *Zowe*. The second person is known only in its ergative form, *weS*, and its genitive, *we.we* and dative: *we.wa*. No third person pronouns are attested.

POSSESSIVE ENCLITICS

	Singular	Plural
1	-iww	iww.aZ
2	-w	—
3	-ija	-ijaZ

DEMONSTRATIVE PRONOUN

andi 'this'; *anni* 'that'.

RELATIVE PRONOUN

(i)ja/je

Numerals

The following are known: 2 *Sin*; 4 *tumni*; 7 *Sinda*; 10 *eman*.

Verb

A Hurrian verbal form is a complex of strictly ordered markers following a (possibly augmented) base. The slot sequence is (D'akonov 1979):

1. extension of base: *-ar/-al/-ug*, etc. (cf. **Urartian**);

2. aspect marker: *-u/oZ-* (perfective), *-ed-* imperfective;
3. this slot has a *-t-* marker when no direct object is present;
4. the *-st-* marker: in Urartian this is perfective; its meaning in Hurrian is doubtful;
5. plural marker;
6. transitive/intransitive markers: *-i-* (trans.), *-u/o-* (intrans.);
7. negation: *-wa-*, *-kk-*;
8. unreal conditional marker;
9. mood marker;
10. subject marker: singular 1 *-(a)f*, 2 *-u/o*, 3 *-(i)a*;
11. subject plural marker: plural 1 *-(a)f.Za*, 3 *-(i)a.Za*.

If the formants *-a* and *-o/u* (stative/intransitive) and *-i* (active/transitive) are added to the base, the resultant form is a participle, whose root may not always be verbal; the form can be made from such nouns as *ewr.i*, 'lord', 'ruler', for example. Similarly, the names of Hurrian gods are sentences in participial form: *un.a.b.TeSSob* 'he who has come' – (the god) Tessob, where *un-* is the root 'to come', *-a-* is the stative marker, and *-b-* is an archaic 3rd person marker. Cf. *un.o.kk.a.lla* 'they do not come' (*-kk-* is the negating marker in slot 7, *-lla* is the 3rd person plural marker).

Source: D'akonov, I.M. in *Jazyki Azii i Afriki*, Vol. 111, 1979. Moscow.

ICELANDIC

INTRODUCTION

Icelandic belongs to the Germanic branch (Scandinavian sub-division) of the Indo-European family. It is the official language of Iceland, where it is spoken by about a quarter of a million people. While its Scandinavian congeners have carried reductionism to extremes, Icelandic remains close to Old Norse. This is partly due to its geographical position as an outlier. More important, however, and the major factor in its linguistic conservatism, was the presence in Iceland of the saga literature of the thirteenth and fourteenth centuries. What was kept alive was not merely a grammatical system, but one of the world's great literatures. The narrative sweep, the moral power, and the sheer human interest of the sagas clearly inform the genre in which modern Icelandic writers have excelled – the epic novel, as practised by Halldor Laxness, Þ. Þórðarson, G. Hagalín, and O.J. Sigurðsson. Modern Icelandic literature has also produced many outstanding poets.

Dialectal differences are not great. The main division is between *harðmæli* in Northern Iceland, and *linmæli* in Southern Iceland (including Reykjavik). This division centres on the pronunciation of the plosives /p, t, k/ between vowels: in *harðmæli* as aspirates [p^h, t^h, k^h] and in *linmæli* as almost voiceless [b̥, d̥, g̊].

SCRIPT

Gothic until the nineteenth century. Now Roman alphabet + *æ*, *ö*, *þ*, *ð*.

PHONOLOGY

Consonants

The core of the Icelandic consonantal system is provided by the five-term series of labial, dental, and velar stops: weak non-aspirate – hard non-aspirate – weak aspirate – strong pre-aspirate – strong post-aspirate: e.g. the labial series /b̥ – p – b̥^{h} – ^{h}p – p^h/. In addition, there is a palatalized velar series, in which, however, the weak aspirated member */g̊^{h}/ is missing. The remaining phonemes in the consonantal inventory are:

fricatives: f, v, þ, ð, s, ç, γ, χ, h
nasals: voiced m, n, ŋ, ŋ′; unvoiced m̥, n̥, ŋ̊, ŋ̊′
lateral and flap: l, l̥, r, r̥
semi-vowel: j

The Icelandic phonological system is of extreme complexity, and the sound–symbol correspondence is correspondingly weak. The graph *k* for example represents the following nine values, depending on phonetic environment: /k, k′, k^{h}, ^{h}k, k′^{h}, g̊, g̊′, χ, Ø/: e.g. *kalla* /k^{h}ad̥la/, *aska* /aska/, *ekla* /ɛ^{h}kla/, *kær* /k′^{h}aiːr̥/, *veski* /vɛsk′i/, >*skammur* /sg̊amːyr/, *skyr* /sg̊′iːr/; *slikt* /sliχt^{h}/, *velkt* /vɛl̥t^{h}/.

Long consonants are pronounced doubled.

Vowels

front: i, ɪ, ɛ
central: ʏ/y, œ, a
back: u, ɔ, o

Vowels tend to be diphthongized (vowel + /i/) before *-gi*/*-gj*: e.g. *boginn* /bɔiγɪn/, 'crooked', 'bent'.

Stress

Always on first syllable, even in loanwords: *prófessor*. Both ablaut and umlaut are very frequent in Icelandic words, the former in the strong-verb system, the latter in declension.

MORPHOLOGY AND SYNTAX

Noun

There are three genders: masculine, feminine, and neuter. The definite article is free or bound. The free article is used with a noun which is also defined by an adjective; the bound article is affixed, e.g. when a possessive pronoun follows the noun: e.g. *hinn góði maður* 'the good man'; *bókin þín* 'your book'. The free article is:

	Masculine	*Feminine*	*Neuter*
singular	hinn	hin	hið
plural	hinir	hinar	hin

These are declined in four cases: the genitive forms are: *hins*, *hinnar*, *hins*, with a common plural for all three – *hinna*.

The bound form is made by dropping the *h*(*i*)- of the free article: *hestur.inn* 'the horse', plural *hestar.nir*.

GENDER

Many endings are specific, e.g. all nouns in *-ir*, *-inn*, *-ingur* are masculine and all nouns in *-ning*, *-ung*, *-ja* are feminine. But no generally applicable rule can be given.

DECLENSION

Weak or strong; the weak declension comprises nouns ending in a vowel.

Typical weak declensions: *tunga* (fem.) 'tongue'; strong: *vetur* (masc.) 'winter'; *hestur* (masc.) 'horse'.

	Singular	*Plural*	*Singular*	*Plural*	*Singular*	*Plural*
nom.	tunga	tungur	vetur	vetur	hestur	hestar
acc.	tungu	tungur	vetur	vetur	hest	hesta
dat.	tungu	tungum	vetri	vetrum	hesti	hestum
gen.	tungu	tungna	vetrar	vetra	hests	hesta

Adjective

The adjective agrees with noun in gender, number, and case. The adjective has strong and weak declensions: weak if the article or a pronoun is present. For example, the strong declension of *glaður* 'glad' is:

singular	glaður	glaðan	glöðum	glaðs
plural	glaðir	glaða	glöðum	glaðra

COMPARATIVE

The comparative is made with -(*a*)*ri*, and is always weak: e.g. *rikari* 'richer'. The usual suppletive forms are found: e.g. *góður* 'good' – *betri*; *gamall* 'old' – *eldri*; *lítill* 'small' – *minni*.

Pronoun

The base forms are:

	Singular	*Plural*	*Honorific plural*
1	ég	við	vér
2	þú	pið	þér

The third person is marked for gender:

singular	hann	hún	það
plural	þeir	þær	þau

These are declined in four cases: e.g. *ég*, *mig*, *mér*, *mín*.

The genitive forms of these personal pronouns – *mín*, *þín*, etc. – are used mainly after prepositions, and as the objective forms after certain transitive verbs: e.g. *ég vænti þín* 'I await you', *ég vænti hennar* 'I await her', *til þín* 'to you', *meðal þeirra* 'among them'. The possessive pronominal adjectives are: masc. *minn*, fem. *mín*, neuter *mitt*; plural *mínir*, *mínar*, *mín*, declined in four cases. They are in concord with the noun they qualify in gender, number, and case: *bróðir minn*, *bókin mín*, *húsið mitt*; *braeður mínir* 'my brothers'. Cf. *í húsi föður míns*... 'in my father's house...' (St John's Gospel 14.2).

DEMONSTRATIVE PRONOUN/ADJECTIVE

Masc/fem. *þessi*, neut. *þetta* 'this'; masc. *sá*, fem. *sú*, neut. *það* 'that'. All these forms are declined in four cases, singular and plural.

INTERROGATIVE PRONOUN

hver /χɛːr/ 'who?'; *hvad* /χaːð/ 'what?'

RELATIVE PRONOUN

sem (indeclinable): e.g. *maðurinn, sem ég sá* 'the man whom I saw'; *maðurinn, sem sá mig* 'the man who saw me'.

Numerals

1–10: 1 to 4 inclusive are marked for gender: 1 *einn/ein/eitt*, 2 *tveir/tvær/tvö*, 3 *þrír/þrjar/þrja*, 4 *fjorir/fjorar/fjögur*. 5–10: *fimm, sex, sjö, átta, níu, tíu*; 11 *ellefu*; 12 *tólf*; 20 *tuttugu*; 21 *tuttugu og einn*; 30 *þrjátíu* (*þrír tugir*); 40 *fjörutíu* (*fjórir tugir*); 100 *hundrað*.

Verb

Verbs in Icelandic are weak or strong. There are active, passive (analytical), and middle (in *-st*) voices; indicative, imperative, and subjunctive moods.

TENSE

The present and preterite are simple; other tenses are formed by means of the auxiliary verbs: *hafa* 'have', *vera* 'be', *verða* 'become', etc. The non-finite forms are: the infinitive, and present and past participles.

WEAK VERB

Four groups are distinguished by phonological criteria; the key forms are the infinitive, the first person singular preterite, and the past participle. Examples of each class are given here; the forms shown are the infinitive, the first person singular present tense, the first person singular and plural preterite, and the past participle in its masculine form:

1. *telja* 'to count' – *tel* – *taldi/töldum* – *talinn*;
2. *heyra* 'to hear' – *heyri* – *heyrði/heyrðum* – *heyrður*;
3. *segja* 'to say' – *segi* – *sagði/sögðum* – *sagður*;
4. *elska* 'to love' – *elska* – *elskaði/elskuðum* – *elskaður*.

Most weak verbs belong to class 4. The present and preterite of *elska* are:

	Singular			*Plural*		
present	1 elska	2 elskar	3 elskar	1 elskum	2 elskið	3 elska
preterite	elskaði	elskaðir	elskaði	elskuðum	elskuðuð	elskuðu

In the subjunctive present, *i* replaces *a* of the indicative present: e.g. *elski, elskir*, etc. The past subjunctive is the same as the indicative past. The present participle is *elskandi*; past participle, *elskaður*.

STRONG VERB

Here there are seven classes, according to seven types of ablaut. The classes are set out here, showing infinitive, first person singular/plural of present, first person singular/plural of preterite, past participle: the ablaut sequence is marked by bold typeface:

1. *líta* 'look' – *lít/lítum* – ***leit-/litum*** – *litið*;
2. *brjóta* 'break' – *brýt/brjótum* – ***braut/briutum*** – *brotið*;
3. *verða* 'become' – *verð/verðum* – ***varð/urðum*** – ***orðið***;
4. *bera* 'bear' – *ber/berum* – ***bar/bárum*** – ***borið***;
5. *gefa* 'give' – *gef/gefum* – ***gaf/gáfum*** – gefið;
6. *fara* 'travel' – *fer/förum* – ***fór/fórum*** – ***farið***;
7. *falla* 'fall' – *fell/föllum* – ***féll/féllum*** – *fallið*.

Conjugation of a strong verb: *gefa* = 'to give' (ablaut class 5):

	Singular			*Plural*		
present	1 gef	2 gefur	3 gefur	1 gefum	2 gefið	3 gefa
preterite	gaf	gafst	gaf	gáfum	gáfuð	gáfu

Subjunctive: present, e.g. *gefi*, *gefir*; past, e.g. *gæfi*, *gæfir*.

hver sem hefir eyru að heyra, hann **heyri**! (Mark 1.6)
'he who has ears to hear, let him hear'

The subjunctive is used in indirect speech with subject switch: cf.

hann hefir lesið bókina
'he has read the book'

hún segir, að hann **hafi** lesið bókina
'she says that he has read the book'

Participles: present, *gefandi*; past, *gefinn*. The past participle of most strong verbs is declined as an adjective: *gefinn* (masc.), *gefin* (fem.), *gefið* (neuter) 'given', and can precede the nominal in this capacity: *mikið lesin bók* 'a much read book'. When conjugated with *vera* 'to be' and *verða* 'to become', the past participle agrees with the subject: *hann er farinn* 'he has gone', *hún er farin* 'she has gone'. With *hafa* 'to have' the neuter participle is used:

þer hafið ekki útvalið mig, heldur hefi ég útvalið yður
'you have not chosen me, but I have chosen you' (John 15.16)

MIDDLE VOICE

The characteristic is *-st*: e.g. *kallast* 'to be called'. The middle voice has reflexive, reciprocal, and passive sense: cf. *klæðast* 'to get dressed': *þeir heilsast* 'they greet each other'; *finnast dæmi til, að*... 'an example can be found for...'; *brjótast fyrir einhverju* 'to fight for something'.

PASSIVE

Auxiliary *vera* 'to be' + past participle of sense-verb, coded for gender: e.g. *bókin var gefin mér* 'the book was given to me'.

MODAL AUXILIARIES

kunna, munu, skulu, mega, eiga/átt, vilja, etc.: e.g.

ég kann ekki að gera það 'I can't do that'
hann sagð**ist** mundu koma 'he said he would probably come'

ég má ekki hugsa til þess 'I can't think about this'

The present tense of *eiga* is: sing. 1 *á*, 2 *átt*, 3 *á*; pl. 1 *eigum*, 2 *eigkð*, 3 *eiga*. Past: sing. 1 *átti*; past participle *átt*. Cf. *hann aetti að gera það* 'he should do that'.

þu átt að læra íslenzku 'you ought to learn Icelandic'

NEGATION

The general negating particle is *ekki* /ɛ^{h}k'iː/ following the verb, e.g. *eg veit ekki* 'I don't know'.

Prepositions

With accusative: *um, á, í, undir, eftir, fyrir*, etc.
With genitive: *til, án*; directionals, *sunnan* 'southwards', *norðan* 'northwards', etc.
With dative: *að, hjá, gegn, handa*, etc.

Examples with accusative: *á borðið* 'on the table'; *ganga á fjöll* 'to go into the mountains'; *hann fer í garðinn* 'he goes into the garden'; *það er gott fyrir sjúklinga* 'that is good for invalids'.

Examples with dative: *hann er hjá mér* 'he's with me'; *kaupa eitthvað handa einhverjum* 'to buy something for someone'.

Word order

SVO.

Í UPPHAFI var Orðið og Orðið var hjá Guði, og Orðið var Guð.
2. Það var í upphafi hjá Guði.
3. Allir hlutir eru fyrir það gjörðir, og án þess er ekkert til orðið, sem til er.
4. Í því var líf, og lífið var ljós mannanna;
5. Og ljósið skín í myrkrinu, og myrkrið meðtók það ekki.
6. ¶ Maður nokkur var sendur af Guði, hann hèt Jóhannes.
7. Þessi kom til vitnisburðar, til þess að vitna um ljósið, svo allir tryðu fyrir hans vitnisburð.
8. Ekki var hann ljósið, heldur átti hann að vitna um ljósið.

IGBO

INTRODUCTION

Igbo is usually assigned to the Kwa group of Niger-Congo languages, though certain affinities with the Bantu language Efik have been pointed out. It is spoken by around 12 million people, in a variety of dialects spread over southern Nigeria, from Onitsha and Owerri to Calabar. 'Central Igbo' is a compromise standard based on the Onitsha-Owerri dialect. Writing in Igbo, as distinct from Bible translation, dates from 1932 when Pita Nwana's story *Omenuko* won a prize in a competition run by the International African Institute. From the 1970s on there has been a steady growth in the output of Igbo novels, plays, and verse. Igbo writers have also been prolific in English.

SCRIPT

Romanization dates from the inception of missionary activities in the mid-1850s. A standardized orthography was introduced in 1961. The sound–symbol correspondence is weak: e.g. the letter *s* represents /s/, s'/, /s̃/, and /s̃'/.

PHONOLOGY

Consonants

stops: /p, ph, b, bh/; these occur palatalized: /p', ph'/, etc.
/t, th, d, dh/; the palatalized dentals: /c, ch, ɟ, ɟh/
/k, kh, g, gh/; the velars occur labialized: /k°, kh°/, etc.
fricatives: /f, v, s, z, γ, h/; these occur (except /γ/) nasalized: /f̃, ṽ/, etc. /s, z, h/ occur both palatalized and nasalized: /s̃', z̃', h̃'/; /h̃/ also labialized, /h̃°/
lateral: l
roll: r
nasals: m, n, n', ŋ, ŋ°
semi-vowels: j, w
implosives: kp, gb

Vowels

i, ɪ, ɛ, a, ɔ, o, ɵ, u

Notated as: *i, ị, e, a, ọ, o, ụ, u*.

VOWEL HARMONY

i, e, o, u are compatible with each other; similarly, *ị, a, ọ, ụ*.

Tone

Three level tones are distinguished: high, mid-, and low. The mid-level tone is constrained in that it can only follow a high, i.e. no monosyllable can be mid-level. Two or more non-level tones, i.e. rising/falling, are also present. Tonal contours are not fixed, and relative pitch varies considerably in the course of an utterance. Furthermore, lexical tone or citation form changes in certain environments.

Tone in Igbo is of cardinal phonemic importance.

In this description, high tone is unmarked, low tone is marked with a grave accent, mid-level with a dash (').

MORPHOLOGY AND SYNTAX

Noun

Nouns fall lexically into tonal classes: e.g. for disyllables, high–high, low–high; high–low, low–low. Similarly for tri- and quadrisyllables. In various syntactic relationships, e.g. in genitive construction and in conjugational patterns, lexical tone is subject to change in specific ways: cf.

m chị̀ anụ 'I bring meat'
m̀ chị̀ anụ 'Do I bring meat?'
m̀ chị̀ anụ́ 'I don't bring meat'

Meaning is thus a function of tonal pattern and word position.

There is no plural form.

Adjective

Adjectives may be formed by tonal modulation from verbs and other parts of speech: e.g. from *ịjọ̀* 'to be bad' is formed *ọjọlọjọọ̀* 'bad'; cf. *ọma* 'good'. There are few words of this type in Igbo. Any nominal can, of course, act as a modifier and follow another nominal; this collocation is equivalent to the genitive relationship: e.g. *ụlọ̀ ezè* 'house-chief' = 'chief's house'; *ụlọ̀ eghù* 'goat-shed'; *àla ụ́dho* 'land of peace'; *àlà ezè* 'chief's domain'.

Pronoun

PERSONAL PRONOUN

		Separable	*Inseparable*
singular	1	mụ, m	m
	2	gị	i/ị
	3	ya	o/ọ

impersonal *e/a*

plural	1	anyị
	2	unù
	3	h̃a

The inseparable forms occur only as bound forms for verbal subject. There is also an emphatic form: ***à**mị̂*, ***à**gị̂*, ***à**yâ*; *anyî*, *unû*, *h̃â*.

The separable forms act also as possessives: tone depends on noun modified: cf. *nn**à** m* 'my father'; *nne **ḿ***; 'my mother'; *nn**à** gị* 'your father'; *nne gị* 'your mother'; *isi **ḿ***; 'my head'; *isi gị* 'your head'.

Examples of object pronoun: *nyètu **ḿ***; *yá* 'give it to me'; ***jù**o y**á*** 'ask him'; *dèe y**á*** 'write it'; *ži y**á** ùwe m* 'show him my clothes'.

DEMONSTRATIVE ADJECTIVES

à 'this', *ahụ̀* 'that'. Emphatic forms: e.g. *àmị̂*, *àgị̂*.

INTERROGATIVE PRONOUN

These have specific tonal patterns: *ònye*/*òchu* 'who?'; *gịnị́* 'what?': e.g. *ònyê bịà-rà*? 'Who came?'

Numerals

1–10: *otù*, *àbụọ́*, *àtọ*, *ànọ*, *ìse*, *ìsii*, *àsaà*, *àsatọ́*, *tolụ́*, *ìri*. 11 *ìri nà otù*; 12 *ìri nà àbụọ*; 20 *ohu*; 30 *ohu nà ìri*; 40 *ohu àbụọ́*; 50 *ohu àbụọ́ nà ìri*; 100 *ohu íse*.

Verb

Formally simple, the Igbo verb structure is of great tonal complexity. The infinitive is marked by the high-tone prefix *i-* or *ị-*, harmonizing, that is, with the stem vowel, which is either middle or low tone: e.g. *i.sí* 'to cook', *ị.nụ́* 'to hear', *i.zù* 'to meet'.

The infinitive is negated by replacing *i-*/*-ị* with *e-*/*a-* (depending on vowel harmony) and adding the suffix *-ghị*/*-ghì*: e.g. *i.kè* 'to distribute', negative ***e.kè.ghì***.

A participial form is made with harmonic prefix *e-*/*a-*; this form is conjugated by one of several auxiliaries, e.g. *ị.nà* 'to do', 'make': *ọ nà.è.sí anụ́* 'she is cooking meat' (tone of prefix changes from *e* to *è*). Simple forms take this participial form to express protracted or habitual action: e.g. *mụ nà.a.chị anụ* 'I (usually) brought meat'.

The exact meaning – aspectual, modal, temporal – of an Igbo verb depends on tone and on the presence or absence of certain prefixes and suffixes; the stem itself is not inflected in any way. Tonal sequence also varies depending on whether a statement is or is not initiatory.

IMPERATIVE

No prefix, certain suffixes may be used: e.g. *gwa ḿ* 'tell me!'; *gà.wa ahịa* 'set off for market!' (where *-wa* is an inceptive suffix).

ASPECT

VSO/SVO imperfective aspectual assertion: a pronominal vowel prefix is used in VSO, absent in SVO: cf. ***a***.*chị m̀ anụ* 'I am/was carrying some meat', *m chị anụ* 'I am/was carrying some meat'.

SVO perfective: with -*r*V suffix, where V copies the stem vowel: cf. *m sì.**rì** anụ* 'I cooked some meat', *m hù.**rù** enyi* 'I saw an elephant'.

The directional suffix *te*/*ta* may be added: e.g. *ọ bù.tè.rè abọ* 'he brought the basket' (to a specific place), where the form *te* is demanded by vowel harmony (within the *i*, *e*, *o*, *u* group) and -*r*V copies it: *te.**re***.

SVO perfective with *e*-/*a*- prefix, plus open vowel suffix and *la*/*le* suffix: e.g. *anyị **è**.sì.**e.le** anụ́* 'we have cooked meat'. The pronominal prefix *e*-/*a*- is dropped if the pronominal subject preceding the verb is monosyllabic: *m sị.e.le anụ́* but *e.sị.e.le ḿ anụ* 'I have cooked meat'.

All affirmative forms have correlative negative forms. The prohibitive usually has the -*le*/-*le* suffix. In negative assertion, *e*-/*a*- is prefixed to the verb, and -*ghi* is added. This *e*-/*a*- is a verbal prefix, not to be confused with the pronominal prefix *e*-/*a*- discussed above: e.g. *Ewu **atá.ghi** ji ányị* 'The goat (*ewu*) didn't eat our yams (*ji*).'

Narrative form: this form takes up the thread of discourse from a preceding primary form, with no recapitulation of subject: absence of overt subject induces tonal change in both verbs and nouns.

Subordinate verb forms, differing from primary forms in tone, are used to make affirmative and negative conditional and relative clauses: e.g. a relative affirmative clause with change of subject:

unù tìsị ùwe 'you wear clothes'
ùwe unu tìsị dị mmà 'the clothes you are wearing are good'

ewû tàrà ji 'the goat ate yams'
ji ewu tàrà rìrì nne 'the yams the goat ate were many'

Prepositions

na/*la* 'on', 'in' is an all-purpose preposition: e.g. *ọ nọ nà London* 'he is in London', where *na* changes to *nà* (low tone) because of following consonant (non-nasal). Preceding a vowel, *na* is assimilated to the vowel in both tone and quality, and is written as *n'*: e.g. *na ụlọ̀ → n'ụlọ̀* 'in the house'.

Word order

See **Verb**, above.

1 NA mbu ka Okwu ahu[3] diri, Okwu
ahu nạ[4] Cineke[5] di-kwa-ra, Okwu ahu
buru[6] kwa Cineke. 2 Onye ahu na
Cineke diri na mbu. 3 Ekere ihe nile[7]
site n'aka-Ya ; ekegh kwa otù[8] ihe ọbula[9]
nke ekeworo[10] ma Ọnọgh ya. 4 Nịme
Ya ka ndu diri ; ndụ ahu buru kwa Ìhè
nke madu(pl). 5 Ìhè ahu we[11] nāmu
n'ọciciri[12] ; ọciciri ahu ejidegh kwa ya.
6 Otù nwoke putara, onye ezitere[13]
site n'ebe[14] Cineke nọ, ahà-ya bu Jọn.
7 Onye ahu biara igba amà,[15] ka ọwe gbara
Ìhè ahu amà, ka madu nile we sịte n'aka-
ya kwere.[16] 8 Ya onweya abugh Ịhè ahu,
kama[17] *ọbiara* ka ọwe gbara Ìhè ahu
ama.

ILOKANO

INTRODUCTION

This Austronesian language (Malayo-Polynesian branch) is spoken in the Philippines (northern Luzon and elsewhere) by 5 million people, i.e. exceeded only by Cebuano and Tagalog. Ilokano is used for press and radio.

SCRIPT

Adapted from Spanish. *c* before *e* and *i* is pronounced as /s/.

PHONOLOGY

Consonants

There is a very simple consonantal inventory of the labial, dental, and velar voiced and unvoiced stops with their associated nasals, plus the semi-vowels /w, j/, and /r, s, l/.

Vowels

i, e, a, o, u

Stress

Stress may be phonemic; *see* **Adjective**, below.

MORPHOLOGY AND SYNTAX

As typically in the languages of the Philippines, noun, pronoun, and verb are correlated in a syntactic nexus determined by the category of focus (*see* **Tagalog**). The Ilokano account of an action will focus the agent, the patient, the beneficiary, or the means or locus of such action; and for each option a specific verb form is available with correlated pronouns.

Noun

Nouns are proper or common, with singular and plural markers: *ni* and *da* for proper nouns, *ti* and *dagiti* for common. The same markers can be used as possessive–relational links: *ni Pedro* 'Peter's'; *ti ubing* 'of the child'; *dagiti ubbing* 'of the children'; *dagiti estudiante* '(some) students'; *dagiti aramaten ti balay* 'household goods' (*balay* 'house').

Nouns with circumfix *pag...an* indicate locus of verbal action: *pag.digos.an* 'bath-house' (*digos* 'to bath(e)').

PLURAL

Mainly by reduplication: e.g. *sabong* 'flower', pl. *sabsabong*. This extends even to loanwords: e.g. *maestra* 'teacher', pl. *mamaestra*. The plural form is not necessary if a plural demonstrative is present: e.g. *balásang* 'lady', pl. *babbalasang*; *balasang dagitoy* 'these ladies'.

Adjective

There are two forms, simplex, e.g. *dakkel* 'big', and *na-* prefix form, e.g. *nalukmeg* 'stout', *napintas* 'beautiful'. Again, the plural form is by reduplication: *dadakkel, lulukmeg*. The adjective and noun are connected by *a* (before consonants) or *nga* (before vowels): e.g. *nalukmeg nga ubing* 'a fat child'. The formula for attributive adjective plus noun is either adjective + ligature + noun, or noun + ligature + adjective: *napintas a balay* = *balay a napintas* 'beautiful house' (*balay* 'house', *napintas* 'beautiful').

COMPARISON

A comparative is made, also by reduplication: cf. *napí**n**pintás* 'more beautiful' (distinguished from *napipintás*, the plural form). Further, the comparative form has two stress points, the plural only one.

Pronoun

There are four series:

(a) Sing. 1 *siak*, 2 *sika*, 3 *isu*; dual. *data*; pl. 1 incl. *datayo*, excl. *dakami*, 2 *dakayo*, 3 *isuda*. These are used for example with 'agent-focus' verbs as subject/nominative pronouns.
(b) The *ak* series: identical to *siak* series minus the *si-/da-*prefix: sing. 3 is Ø.
(c) The *ko* series: sing. *ko, mo, na*; dual *ta*; pl. *mi, tayo, yo, da*. Used for example with *-en* verbs (target-focus). The *ko* pronouns are also possessives: *trabaho.**k*** 'my work', *trabaho.**m*** 'your work'.
(d) The *kaniak* series: e.g. *kaniak, kenka, kenkuana*, the oblique series.

Indirect personal pronouns can be formed with *kada-*: *kada.kayo* 'to/for you (pl.)'; *kada.tayo* 'to/for us (incl.)'. Cf. *kada.giti estudiante* 'to the students'.

DEMONSTRATIVE PRONOUN

Three degrees of distancing, singular and plural forms: *daytoy* 'this', *dayta* 'that', *daydiay* 'that yonder': pl. *dagitoy, dagita, dagidiay.*

INTERROGATIVE PRONOUN

sino 'who?'; *ania* 'what?'

RELATIVE PRONOUN

Example with *ti*: *Siak ti agsurat* 'I am the one who will write.'

Numerals

The native series 1–10: *maysa, dua, tallo, uppat, lima, innem, pito, walo, siam, sangapulo.* 11 *sangapulo ket maysa*; 20 *duapulo*; 30 *tallopuo*; 100 *sangagasut*.
The Spanish numerals are also in use.

Verb

As in Tagalog, Ilokano verbs are classified by their determinant affixes: *ag-/-um-* verbs, *-en* verbs, *i . . . -an* verbs, etc.

ag-/-um- verbs: verbs with these affixes are agent-focused, and use the *(si)ak* pronominal series: e.g. *ag.basa ak* 'I read'; *ag.takder* Ø 'he/she stands'. A progressive form is made by reduplication: e.g. *ag.tak.tak.der* 'he/she goes on standing'. The past form is made with *nag-*: e.g. *nag.saludsod* 'he asked'.

-um- verbs are also agent-focused, and take the *siak* series: e.g. *gatang* 'buy', *g.um.atang ka* 'you buy'; *inom* 'drink', *um.inom tayo* 'we (incl.) drink'. The progressive is again by reduplication: e.g. *tumulong* 'to help', prog. *tumultulong*. Past of *-um-* verb, e.g. from *tumakder* 'to stand': *timmakder*; from *tumulong* 'to help': *timmulong*.

-en verbs are target-focused; they are used with the *ko* series of pronouns: e.g. *lutuen* 'to cook (something specific)', *lutuen ta ti karne* 'we two cook the meat'; *kitaen ti ubing ni Pedro* 'the child looks at Pedro'. Past tense of *-en* verb, e.g. *sapolen* 'to look for': *sinapol.*

i-/iya- verbs are also target-focused. Past tense of *i-* verb, e.g. *irikep* 'to close something': *inrikep.*

pag- verbs are means/instrument-focused: e.g. *pag.surat mo daytoy* 'use this to write with'. The *pag-* verbs use the *ko* series. The past tense is in *pinag-*.

The *i- . . . -an* verbs are used when the beneficiary of an action is in mind: e.g. *i.gatang.an na kami iti singsing* 'he/she buys us (excl.) a ring'. Here, since the beneficiary is focused, the *siak* series is used for 'us' while the agent 'he' is in the *ko* series.

maka- verbs denote (a) ability to perform the action expressed by the stem, and (b) bodily affections and needs: e.g. *maka.pagna* 'to be able to walk'; *maka.turog* 'to feel sleepy'.

VERBAL NOUN

panag- + stem, or *i-* + partial reduplication + base. These forms are used to make future and past-tense formations with the help of marked adverbials, e.g. adverbial + *-nto* (future); + *idi* (past): e.g.

kaan**onto** ti **i**sasangpet **da** = kaan**onto** ti **panag**sangpet **da**?

'When will they arrive?'

kaano **idi** ti **i**sasangpet **da**?
'When did they arrive?'

Word order

VSO/VOS are typical.

1 Idi punganay addan ti Sao ket ti Sao adda iti
Dios, ket ti Sao, Dios. 2 Isu idi punganay adda
iti Dios. 3 Babaen kencuana napaadda dagiti amin
a banag, ket amin a napaaddan saanda a napaadda
no di babaen kencuana. 4 Adda idin kencuana ti
biag, ket ti biag isu ti silaw cadagiti tao. 5 Ket ag-
lawag ti silaw iti sipnget, ket saan nga inabac ti
sipnget.
6 Adda idi maysa a tao a ti naganna Juan a
naibaon nanipud iti Dios. 7 Ket daytoy immay ma-
ipuon iti panangsacsi, tapno mangpanecnec maipapan
iti silaw, tapno babaen kencuana mamati coma dagiti
isuamin. 8 Saan nga isu ti silaw no di ket isu immay tapno mangpanecnec maipapan iti silaw.

INDO-ARYAN LANGUAGES (New)

See **New Indo-Aryan Languages**.

INDO-EUROPEAN LANGUAGES

INTRODUCTION

The Indo-European family of languages comprises the following twelve branches:

1. Indic: including Vedic, Sanskrit, the Prakrits, and the New Indo-Aryan languages (NIA); the Dardic languages form a peripheral and controversial grouping within this branch.
2. Iranian: including Avestan, Old Persian, Middle Iranian (Pehlevi, etc.), the modern Iranian languages (Persian, Kurdish, Pashto, Ossetian, etc.), and the Pamir languages.
3. Anatolian: Hittite, Luvian, Palaic, Lydian, etc.; all extinct.
4. Armenian.
5. Hellenic: including Linear B Greek, Homeric and Classical Greek, New Testament Greek, and Modern Greek.
6. Albanian: formerly regarded as the sole survivor of an Illyrian branch.
7. Italic: including Latin-Faliscan, Oscan-Umbrian, Venetic, the modern Romance languages.
8. Celtic:
   (a) Continental Celtic (in Gaul, the Iberian Peninsula, and Central Europe; Galatian in Anatolia; all extinct);
   (b) Insular Celtic: (i) Goidelic: Irish, Gaelic, Manx; (ii) Brythonic: Welsh, Cornish, Breton.
9. Tocharaic (extinct).
10. Germanic:
    (a) East Germanic: Gothic;
    (b) North Germanic: Old Norse, Icelandic, the modern Scandinavian languages;
    (c) West Germanic: Old and Middle High German, Low German, Anglo-Saxon, English, modern German, Dutch, Frisian, Afrikaans; Yiddish.
11. Baltic: Lithuanian, Latvian; Old Prussian (extinct).
12. Slavonic:
    (a) South Slavonic: Old Church Slavonic, Macedonian, Bulgarian, Serbo-Croat;
    (b) East Slavonic: Russian, Ukrainian, Belorussian;
    (c) West Slavonic: Polish, Czech, Slovak, Lusatian, Slovene.

In terms of their primary expansion, that is, as located about 2,000 years ago, the Indo-European languages covered a territory stretching from Ireland to Assam, and from Norway and central Russia to the Mediterranean, the Persian Gulf, and Central India. Secondary expansion in the last 400 years, by conquest and colonization, has placed Indo-European languages, especially English, Spanish, Portuguese, Russian, and French in every corner of the globe. The sole major language area still largely untouched by Indo-European is that occupied by its sole quantitative rival – Chinese.

As regards textual attestation, the Indo-European languages can be divided into four groups:

1. Primary stratum: centring round the second millennium BC: Hittite, Vedic, Linear B Greek.
2. Secondary stratum: first millennium BC: Greek, Sanskrit, Avestan, Old Persian, Latin, Oscan, Umbrian.
3. Tertiary stratum: first millennium AD: Gothic, Old Irish, Tocharaic, Old Church Slavonic, Armenian, early North and West Germanic.
4. Modern period: from 1000 to present: the medieval and modern New Indo-Aryan languages, Iranian, Romance, Germanic, Slavonic, Celtic, and Baltic languages; Modern Greek, Armenian; Albanian.

The position of Lithuanian in this tabulation is anomalous; though it is attested from no earlier than the fifteenth century AD, it belongs by virtue of its exceptionally archaic structures to the primary or, at least, the secondary stratum.

It is customary to use the IE word for 'hundred' – **kṃtom* – as a base for dividing the languages belonging to strata 1 to 3 inclusive into two groups: the centum group and the satem group. In the centum group, proto-IE *k* was preserved as /k/, giving Latin *centum*, Greek *e.katon*, Old Irish *cet* (*k'ēt*), Tocharian A *känt*; in Germanic, the *k* > *h*, hence Gothic *hund-* (English *hundred*).

In the satem group, common IE *k* was softened to a sibilant: thus we get Sanskrit *śatam*, Iranian *satəm*, Lithuanian *šim̃tas*, Old Slavonic *sʌto*. Albanian has *qind* (*k'ind*), while Armenian has the anomalous form *harjur*. In general, the satem languages, forming the Eastern branch of the family, are more conservative than their western (centum) congeners.

A genetic relationship between the classical languages, Greek, Latin, and Sanskrit, was identified in the late eighteenth century by Sir William Jones, who correctly postulated a 'common source' for these three languages, and suggested that Celtic, Iranian, and Germanic might well be connected. The genetic relationship was first scientifically codified and set out on a comparative basis by Franz Bopp, whose major work – *Vergleichende Grammatik des Sanskrit, Zend, Armenischen, Griechischen, Lateinischen, Lithauischen, Altslawischen, Gothischen und Deutschen* – was published in 1833. ('Zend' in Bopp's title refers to **Avestan**, **q.v.**) In the following half-century, comparative Indo-European linguistics made rapid strides in several fields: phonology (Pott, Saussure), reconstruction of Proto-Indo-European

(Schleicher); lexicography (Fick), and comparative morphology (Brugmann, Delbrück, Rask). This period of comparative Indo-European studies culminates in the great *Grundrisz der vergleichenden Grammatik der indogermanischen Sprachen* (5 vols, 1886–1916) by Karl Brugmann and Berthold Delbrück. The comprehensive, enormously detailed, and theoretically well-ordered picture presented here of Proto-Indo-European and its reflexes, was shaken in some respects by the discovery of Hittite, in the early years of the twentieth century. In particular, a brilliant piece of theoretical insight, put forward by Saussure some fifty years earlier, seemed to find confirmation in the new language. Saussure had argued that certain ablaut sequences in the Classical Indo-European languages could be explained by assuming the presence in the parent language of what he called '*coefficients sonantiques*' – probably laryngeals – which were subsequently lost; and now here was Hittite with two laryngeals, written as *ḫ* and *ḫḫ* in the Akkadian cuneiform script, precisely where the theory predicted they should be found: cf. Hittite *ḫarkiš* 'white' – Greek *argēs.*

Lehmann (1952) notated four laryngeals as /x, γ, h, ˀ/.

Hittite differs, of course, so markedly from its coevals in this oldest stratum of Indo-European (it might be compared to Samoyedic *vis-à-vis* Uralic), and is so evidently under non-Indo-European influence, that not all authorities accept the laryngeal theory as it stands (cf. Krahe 1966: 101). Nevertheless, one to three laryngeals figure in the more recent, authoritative reconstruction of the Indo-European phonological system by O. Szemerényi (1980) which contains:

Consonants

stops: labial, dental, and velar four-term series with four-way distinction of voiced/unvoiced and aspirate/non-aspirate: e.g. /$p – p^h – b – b^h$/. The velar series has palatalized and labialized correlatives: /k', k'^h, g', g'^h; k^w, k^{wh}, g^w, g^{wh}/

fricatives: /s, h/ (a reduction from Brugmann's system)

resonants: /j, w, m, n, l, r/

syllabic liquids: /n̥, m̥, l̥, r̥/, long and short

One to three laryngeals.

Vowels

/i, e, a, ə, o, u/; long and short, except /ə/ which is short only

diphthongs: ei, ai, oi; eu, au, ou

Diachronic reflexes to this basic phonological inventory can be displayed in a series of equations. For example, the reflexes of proto-IE *p, t,* q°:

p: In general, IE *p* is preserved as /p/ in the daughter languages, but in Germanic *p* > *f/b*, though remaining /p/ after /s/; e.g. in the word for 'seven': IE **septm̥*: Sanskrit *saptá*, Greek *eptá*, Latin *septem*, Lithuanian *septyni*; Gothic *sibun*, Anglo-Saxon *sibun* (English 'seven'); 'father': IE *pətēr*:

Sanskrit *pitā*, Greek *patīr*, Latin *pater*; Gothic *fadar* (English 'father'). Here, Armenian has *p* > /h/: *hair*; in Celtic the initial *p* was lost: Old Irish *athir* /āṯhir/.

t: IE *t* was retained as /t/ generally, but in Germanic the reflex is *t* > *þ*, except after a sibilant. Cf. the equation for 'three': IE **trejes*: Sanskrit *trayaḥ*, Greek *treĩs*, Latin *trēs*, Lithuanian *trỹs*, Old Slavonic *trʌje*; Gothic *þreis* (English 'three').

Example of an IE labio-velar: **q°o-/q°e-/q°i-* 'who?':

> k in Sanskrit *kaḥ*, Lithuanian *kas*, Old Slavonic *kʌto*;
> p/t in Greek: *tis*;
> q° in Latin: *quis* (cf. Hittite *kuiš*);
> x°/hw-/h-/g° in Germanic: Old High German *hwer*;

Cf. IE **leiq°o* '(I) leave': Greek *leipō*, Latin *linquō*.

IE *d* is retained everywhere except in Germanic where the reflex is /t/: IE **dekm̥* 'ten': Sanskrit *daśa*, Greek *deka*, Latin *decem*, Lithuanian *dēšimtis*, Old Slavonic *desętʌ*; Gothic *taihun* (English, 'ten').

IE *bh* and *dh* are retained only in Sanskrit; elsewhere > *b*/*d*/(*f*).

IE *m*, *n*, *r*, *l* are stable throughout the family, though in Sanskrit *l* tends to /r/: cf. **leuq-* 'shine', 'be bright', Sanskrit *rōcatē*.

The IE vowel system of short and long vowels is generally stable in transfer to the daughter languages, /e/ *ē* is less so than the others.

These and the many other equations which can be set up for individual sounds present IE inventories as they seem to have been through the first millennium BC. In the following millennium each inherited set of reflexes was to be subjected to further far-reaching changes. *See* **Germanic Languages**, **New Indo-Aryan Languages**, **Romance Languages**, **Slavonic Languages**, etc.

If we take the highly inflected and mythopoetically rich Indo-Iranian reflex as close to, and typical of, the parent language, it is clear that we then have to postulate an anterior period of development lasting some 5,000 years. In its final stage before the break-up, Proto-Indo-European seems to have had three genders, three numbers, and probably eight cases (as in Sanskrit). Adjectives were treated as nouns. First and second personal pronouns were present, with the third personal forms supplied from the demonstrative series; all were declined in all cases. The verb had two voices and four moods, with both finite and non-finite forms, and very elaborate marking for person and number.

Over the two centuries since its identification, the comparative study of the Indo-European family has tended to centre round the great classical languages of India, Greece, and Rome, with Germanic, Celtic, and Slavonic as important auxiliary fields. The discovery of Hittite, a primary stratum language with a phonological and morphological apparatus about as far removed from its coeval Vedic as could well be imagined, has awakened interest in the Anatolian area as an alternative cradle of Proto-Indo-European, which, it was increasingly felt, had been reconstructed perhaps all too exclusively in the Aryan (Indo-Iranian) mould. (For example, of all the Indo-European languages, Sanskrit alone displays a phonological system of almost artificial perfection, with five positional series, each of which has five modes of articulation.)

Typological reconstructions have now been put forward which include four typically Caucasian ejectives (glottalized obstruents) as bases for voiced and unvoiced plain and aspirated stops: e.g. /ṭ – d/d^h – t/t^h/.

A typological equation between a theoretical reconstruction of Proto-Indo-European and languages of the **Abkhaz-Adyge (q.v.)** type does not, of course, imply any sort of genetic relationship. The premise that the proto-language had ejectives, however, does offer promising solutions for certain highly technical problems in the daughter languages; and the ejective model is, in fact, fundamental to the phonological apparatus of the main Indo-European language in the Caucasus area – Armenian.

Pari passu with the reconstruction of the Proto-Indo-European language went the quest for an 'Aryan' homeland, speculation on its nature, and the creation of scenarios for the primary diffusion process. One of the most influential was that advanced by Professor V. Gordon Childe (1926), *The Aryans.* Childe used the archaeological evidence provided by the so-called Corded Ware culture, together with the linguistic evidence of isoglosses – common Indo-European roots delineating the flora, fauna, and climate of the putative homeland – to fix an Aryan radiant in what is now the Ukraine, at a time close to the onset of the Bronze Age. Thus, artefacts were identified with a tribe, the tribe with a language. Today, amplified by much new evidence, the Kurgan thesis (so called after the burial mounds in the Ukraine: the Turkic word *kurgan* means 'tumulus', 'mound') has been given a fresh lease of life in the impressive work of Marija Gimbutas. From a Pontic source, so runs the scenario, mounted warrior-sages fanned out in the late Neolithic period to dispense conjugation and declension, the horse, the wheel, and Indo-European kinship systems, including the husband's in-laws, to agglutinating and isolating humanity. In some ways, this thesis ties up with the image of Aryan superiority built into the Indo-Iranian sector of historical Indo-European. In the *Rig-Veda*, Indra smites dusky Aboriginals: e.g. in Hymn 12 of Book II:

> yo dāsaṃ varṇam adharaṃ guhākaḥ
> '(Indra) who has subjected and made to vanish the non-Aryan colour'
> (where *akar*, the root aorist of *kṛ* to do, has to be understood)

If this point is worth making, it is because the subjugation of more primitive societies by a dominant elite is a feasible mode of language diffusion; and certainly, Indo-European languages spread into India from the north. The account given in the *Rig-Veda* is, naturally, partisan, however. Thus, Indra is also described as: *yo apo vavṛvāṃsaṃ Vṛtraṃ jaghāna* 'who slew Vṛtra who had enclosed the waters', ostensibly a victory for the dominant elite. The fact is, however, that this seems to refer to the destruction of the dams which supplied the great cities of Mohenjo-Daro and Harappa with water: the ruin, that is, of the technologically advanced pre-Aryan Indus civilization by invading pastoral nomads.

Alternative scenarios featuring Anatolia as an Urheimat have been put forward. Thus, T.V. Gamkrelidze and V.V. Ivanov (1986), while accepting a Pontic radiant for Balto-Slavonic, Celtic, Germanic, and Italic contingents, as postulated by Gimbutas, regard this as a *secondary* staging-post for an advance into Europe; the original homeland is placed in Anatolia and the Lake Van area, and antedates the Pontic stage by some 3,000 years. From this viewpoint, Indo-European diffusion falls into three categories: (a) the proto-Europeans move out to sojourn in the Pontic area before starting to colonize Europe *c.* 3000 BC; (b) the proto-Indo-Iranians move eastwards through Iran towards India; (c) the Hittites, the Greeks, and the Armenians stay put: that is, Hellas was colonized by Greeks from Anatolia, not vice versa.

In the total absence of concrete evidence for these speculations, Gamkrelidze and Ivanov rely on comparative reconstruction, pointing to the undoubted presence of Semitic roots in Indo-European, and adducing alleged parallels from various Caucasian languages. Not all linguists find either these parallels or, indeed, the thesis itself convincing.

Colin Renfrew (1988) also places the Urheimat in Anatolia, whence, *c.* 6500 BC, peasant farmers with agrarian and stock-breeding skills, spread slowly (a few kilometres per annum) north and westwards to the Ukraine and to central and northern Europe. In other words, Indo-European languages are *in situ* for thousands of years, instead of being swiftly spread by mounted warriors. Concurrently, farmers (in the exact sense of the word – i.e. not pastoral nomads) speaking Proto-Afro-Asiatic, and, possibly, Proto-Dravidian, make their economically elite way by comparable pathways to North Africa and the East. In both of these scenarios the time-scale changes dramatically; starting about 3000 BC the mounted warrior-sages had taken something over a thousand years to colonize the Indo-European speech area as it appears in the second and first millennia BC; by wheelbarrow it took much longer.

Not that the early Indo-European farmer travelled necessarily on his own. If the Georges Dumézil school is to be believed, both the warrior and the priest, if not actually alongside him, were not far behind. Dumézil saw early Indo-European society as informed throughout by what he called *les trois fonctions.* These are:

(a) the sacerdotal power, or spiritual authority; the indispensable basis of
(b) the temporal and military power;
(c) the sustaining power: the providers and distributors of food.

In the Indian tradition, where they are designated as 'colours' (*varṇa*: see quote from *Rig-Veda*, Book II, Hymn 12, above) the three functions are embodied as follows: (a) *brahman*; (b) *kṣattriya*; (c) *vaiśya*. And a congruent tripartite system is found in the Avesta: (a) *āθravan*; (b) *raθaēštā*; (c) *vāstryō fšuyant*. The terms in (c) form a syzygy, which Emile Benveniste (1969) translates as *celui des pâturages*, and *celui qui s'occupe du bétail*. In the Hellenic sources, Plato (*Critias*) lists the following functions: (a) *hiereis*; (b) *makhimoi*; (c) *geōrgoi* and *dēmiourgoi*. Comparable triads can be found in Umbrian (in the Iguvine Tables), in Ferdousi's Shāh Nāmeh, in Celtic, and elsewhere.

INDONESIAN

INTRODUCTION

Indonesian is a member of the Austronesian family. Two main forms of the Malayan stock are spoken and written in South-East Asia and the islands of the archipelago: (a) Bahasa Indonesia, the official language of Indonesia, spoken by around 170 million; (b) Bahasa Malaysia, the official language of Malaysia, Singapore, and the Sultanate of Brunei, spoken by around 20 million. Phonologically and morphologically, the two forms are virtually identical. Nor is there much variation in vocabulary, though local differences are frequent. The description that follows is specifically of Bahasa Indonesia.

As far back as in the ninth to twelfth centuries AD Malay was in use as the administrative language of Hindu rule in Sriwijaya (south-east Sumatra). It continued to be so used through the following centuries under the Sultans of Malacca: on the one hand, as Classical Malay, the highly organized vehicle of a rich and extensive literature, and on the other as the lingua franca for the many peoples who lived in the area. In this second form it was known as *Melayu Pasar* – 'Bazaar Malay'.

In the early years of the twentieth century it seemed likely that Dutch would emerge as the language of administration, higher education, and the cultural media in the archipelago, and, in line with this, the claims of Dutch were promoted even by Indonesian intellectuals (e.g. the Budi Utomo Association). Resistance to this policy grew *pari passu* with the rise of nationalism, and in 1928, at a conference in Batavia, the ideal of a national language was first promulgated. For such a national language there could be only one base – Malay, by far the most widely used and understood of all the languages of Indonesia. Curiously, by banning the use of Dutch, the Japanese occupation fuelled this movement. On 17 August 1945, Bahasa Indonesia was officially adopted as the national language of the Republic of Indonesia.

SCRIPT

Roman alphabet. A 'perfected spelling' was recommended by the Indonesian Ministry of Education in 1972. The main change here is that *y* everywhere replaces the *j* previously used under Dutch influence: e.g. *jang* > *yang*. *j* and *c* now represent the voiced and unvoiced affricates.

Modern Bahasa Malaysia is also written in *rumi*, the *jawi* (Arabic) script being reserved for religious texts.

PHONOLOGY

Consonants

stops: p, b, t, d, k, g, ʔ
affricates: tʃ, dʒ
fricatives: f, s, ʃ, x, h
nasals: m, n, ɲ, ŋ
lateral and flap: l, r
semi-vowels: j (notated as *y*), w

Vowels

i, ɪ, e, ə, a, ɔ, o, u

The letter *i* represents /i/ and /ɪ/; the letter *e* represents /ɛ/, /ɪ/, or /ə/; *o* represents /o/ or /ɔ/.

Stress

On the penultimate syllable, unless this contains an *e*-pepet (short *e*), no longer specifically marked in Bahasa Indonesian.

MORPHOLOGY AND SYNTAX

Roots are largely disyllabic. In the absence of prefixation, which encodes nominal and verbal properties, it is not possible to tell by inspection whether a disyllable is a noun, an adjective, a verb, or a numeral: cf. *gambar* 'picture' (noun); *hitam* 'black' (adjective/stative verb); *goreng* 'to fry' (verb); *tujuh* 'seven'.

Noun

Nouns are not marked for gender or number. Lexical means may be used to specify gender where necessary; and again, if necessary, number can be shown by reduplication (never if a numeral is present): e.g. *barang-barang itu* 'these things'; *penyakit-penyakit tropis* 'tropical diseases'; *sumber-sumber militer* 'military sources'.

DEFINITE/INDEFINITENESS

There are no articles, but the demonstratives *itu* and *ini* may be used as recapitulatory topicalizers, whose referents are known to the audience: e.g. *Undangan itu akan dipenuhi tahun ini juga* 'The invitation will be taken up this year' (the *undangan* 'invitation', having already been mentioned in the discourse; *akan* is future formant; *tahun* 'year').

All case relations are expressed by means of prepositional constructions or by apposition: e.g. *rumah makan* 'house-eat' = 'restaurant'; *pusat kebudayaan* 'cultural centre'; *buku petunjuk kota* 'guide book to the town'.

NOMINAL FORMATION BY AFFIXATION

Examples:

-an: forms resultatives, e.g. *tulis* 'to write' – *tulisan* 'something written'; *ajar* 'to teach' – *ajaran* 'doctrine'.

ke . . . -an: frequently used to form abstract nouns from adjectives and root nouns, e.g. *bangsa* 'people' – *ke.bangsa.an* 'nationalism'; *berani* 'brave' – *ke.berani.an* 'courage'.

pe-: indicates agent or instrument. The prefix modulates before certain initials as follows:

pe- + *b, f* > *pe.m-*: *baca* 'to read', *pe.m.baca* 'reader'; initial *p-* is elided: *pimpin* 'to lead', *pe.m.impin* 'leader';

pe- + *d, j, c* > *pe.n-*: *dengar* 'to hear', *pe.n.dengar* 'listener'; initial *t* is elided: *tulis* 'to write', *pe.n.ulis* 'writer';

pe- + vowel, *g, h* > *pe.ng-*: *ajar* 'to study', *pe.ng.ajar* 'instructor', 'teacher'. Initial *k* is elided (with some exceptions): *karang* 'to compose', *pe.ng.arang* 'composer'; but cf. *kerja* 'to work', *pe(r)kerja* 'worker';

pe- + *s* > *pe.ny-* with elision of *s*: *sakit* 'sick', *pe.ny.akit* 'disease' (i.e. a departure from the normal connotation of agent or instrument).

per/pen . . . an: abstract nouns formed by these two circumfixes may differ in respect of voice: e.g. from *kembang* 'develop': *per.kembang.an* 'development' (the passive result of a process), *pen.gembang.an* 'development' (the active process of developing something).

Adjective

As attribute, adjective follows noun, though quantifying modifiers precede: e.g. *orang baik* 'good man'; *banyak orang* 'many people'.

COMPARISON

The comparative is made with *lebih . . . dari(pada)*: e.g. *Malam ini lebih dingin daripada kemarin* 'Tonight is colder than yesterday.'

Pronoun

1st person: sing. *saya/aku*; pl. excl. *kami*, incl. *kita*.
2nd person: sing. *kamu/engkau/saudara/anda*; these are also plural forms.
3rd person: sing. *dia/ia*; pl. *mereka*. *Beliau* is a polite third person form.

Saudara is a generally acceptable form of polite address; *anda* is increasingly used when addressing an impersonal audience, e.g. on radio or television. *Aku*, *kamu*, and *dia* have enclitic forms: *-ku*, *-mu*, *-nya*.

Either the full form of the pronoun or its enclitic can be used as possessive: e.g. *rumah saya* = *rumah.ku* 'my house'; also as object, direct or indirect: e.g. *dia sudah menyurati saya* = *dia sudah menyurat kepada saya* = *dia sudah menyurati.ku* 'he has written (to) me'; *saya akan tinggal dengan dia/dengan.nya* 'I shall live with him'.

DEMONSTRATIVE PRONOUN/ADJECTIVE

itu 'this', 'these'; *ini* 'that', 'those'.

INTERROGATIVE PRONOUN

siapa 'who?'; *apa* 'what?' *Apa* is used as an introductory interrogative particle: e.g. *Apa mereka belum makan?* 'Haven't they eaten yet?'

RELATIVE PRONOUN

yang: e.g. *pemilihan yang akan datang* 'the forthcoming election' ('which will come').

Numerals

1–10: *satu, dua, tiga, empat, lima, enam, tujuh, delapan, sembilan, sepuluh*; 11 *sebelas*; 12 *dua belas*; 13 *tiga belas*; 20 *dua puluh*; 30 *tiga puluh*; 100 *seratus.*

Classifiers

The lengthy inventory of numerical classifiers formerly used in Malay has been reduced in both languages, in Indonesian to three: *seorang* for humans; *seekor* for animals; and *sebuah* for things. Even of these, use is optional: e.g. *dia* (*seorang*) *wartawan* 'he is a journalist'.

Verb

The verb in Indonesian is not marked for person, number, or tense. Aspect and tense can be indicated by adverbial markers (see below). There is no copula. Roots are modulated by affixation. Verbs are stative, intransitive, or transitive. A transitive verb takes both a *me*(N)- prefix and a *di-* prefix; i.e. a transitive verb can be both active and passive.

VERBAL FORMANTS

Examples:

1. *ber-*: this is a formant for very many intransitives and statives, e.g. *bermain* 'to play'; *berhenti* 'to pause'; *bersumber* 'to originate in'.
2. *me*(N)-, usually with *-kan* affix: dynamic/transitive formant of wide semantic range. N here stands for a nasal, homogeneous with initial of root word: for sandhi with word initial, see *pe-* in **Nominal formation by affixation**, above. Cf. *jalan* 'walk' – *men.jalan.kan* 'to drive (a car)', 'to carry out'; *hidup* 'to live' – *meng.hidup.kan* 'to enliven', 'to switch on (the radio)'; *luas* 'wide' – *me.luas.kan* 'to spread'; *meng.amuk* 'to run amuck'. Initial *p, t, k, s* are dropped when *men-* is prefixed: e.g. *tangis* → *men.angis* 'to weep, cry'.
3. *mem-* acts as a subject focus marker prefixed to *per-*: cf. *kenal* 'to become friendly with' – *memper.kenal.kan* 'to introduce'; *lihat* 'to see' – *memper.lihat.kan* = *me.lihat.kan* 'to show'.
4. *di-* can be described as an object focus marker, or, in Indo-European terms, as a passive marker: e.g. *di.tunggu ke.datang.an.nya* 'his arrival is expected'; *dutabesar di.terima oleh Menteri Luar Negeri* 'the ambassador was received by the foreign minister' (*oleh* 'by'); cf. *memper.timbang.kan*

'to take into consideration', *di.timbang.kan* 'to be taken into consideration'.

Transitive verbs with direct and indirect object. Cf. *S mem.belikan.**nya** O*: here, *S* is active subject, O is direct object, and the beneficiary B is notated by *-nya*, the 3rd person pronominal enclitic: 'S buys B O'. The same meaning can be expressed in a different construction by dropping *-kan* from the verb, and affixing *-nya* = B to the preposition *untuk* 'for': *S mem.beli.Ø O untuk.nya/B* 'S buys O for B'.

In both of these sentences S is focused. O can be focused as follows: *O **di**.beli S untuk B* 'O is bought by S for B'. The beneficiary may also be construed as the primary object, and is then fronted: *B di.beli.kan S O*; or, *B **di**.beli.kan O oleh* ('by') *S*: 'For B, O is bought by S'.

The prefix *ter-* denotes involuntary, accidental happening or action: *bakar* 'fire', *ter.bakar* 'to catch fire'; *tidur* 'sleep', *ter.tidur* 'to fall asleep', 'drop off'. Here too, the object can be focused: *kopi.mu ter.minum oleh saya* 'I've drunk your coffee by mistake'.

NEGATIVE

The general negating particle is *tidak* preceding the word negated. A negative imperative is made with *jangan(lah)*: e.g. *janganlah baca buku itu* 'don't read that book'.

TENSE MARKERS

Imperfective *masih*, *sedang*; perfective *sudah*. The future-tense marker is *akan*.

Prepositions

Indonesian uses prepositions: e.g. *di* 'in', 'on', 'at'; *untuk* 'for'; *kepada* 'to' (a person).

Word formation

In recent years, many compounds have been formed from the initial syllables of component roots in a name, title, or designation consisting of several words: e.g. *Jatim* = *Jawa Timur* 'East Java': *Dubes* = *duta besar* 'ambassador'; *Hankam* = *Pertahanan dan Keamanan* 'Defence and Security'.

Word order

SVO for subject focus; object focus (restricted to transitive verbs) produces OVS or OSV.

1 Maka pada awal pertama adalah Kalam, dan Kalam itoe bersama-sama dengan Allah, dan Kalam itoelah djoega Allah.
2 Adalah Ia pada moelanja beserta dengan Allah.
3 Segala sesoeatoe didjadikan Oléhnja, maka djikalau tidak ada Ia, tiadalah djoega barang sesoeatoe jang telah djadi.
4 Didalamnja itoe ada hidoep, dan hidoep itoelah terang manoesia.
5 Maka terang itoe bertjahaja didalam gelap, maka gelap itoe tiada sadar akan Dia.
6 Maka adalah seorang jang disoeroeh oléh Allah, namanja Jahja.
7 Ialah datang memberi kesaksian, hendak menjaksikan hal terang itoe, soepaja sekalian orang pertjaja oléh sebab Dia.
8 Maka ia sendiri boekan terang itoe, melainkan hendak menjaksikan hal terang itoe.

INGRIAN

See **Balto-Finnic Minor Languages.**

INUIT

INTRODUCTION

Inuit belongs to the Eskimo-Aleut family. There are two main divisions of Eskimo: Eastern, known as Inuit or Inupiaq, and Western, known as Yupik. Each of these divisions is a dialectal continuum, with a rather sharp dividing line between them. Inuit and Yupik are mutually unintelligible. The dividing line lies roughly along the 64° parallel in Alaska. To the south and west of this line Yupik extends towards the Aleutians, and into Siberia. The main Yupik dialect – Central Alaskan – is spoken by about 15,000 people, and literary and pedagogical material in it is produced under the aegis of the University of Alaska. Obsolescent in most of its territory, Yupik seems to be just holding its own in Central Alaska. The situation as regards Inuit is very different. It is spoken by over 60,000 people, 45,000 of whom are in Greenland, where Inuit is now the official language: *kalaallit oqasii*, 'the language of the Greenlanders'. In Canada the language is spoken by *c.* 16,000, with another 5,000 in Alaska.

West Greenlandic Inuit is the primary language of instruction in schools in Greenland, which means that the number of Inuit speakers is on the increase. Most Greenlanders, especially urbanized adults, are, of course, bilingual in Danish and Inuit.

Literature in West Greenlandic dates back to the religious texts produced in the eighteenth century. Today there is a fairly prolific output in most genres – newspapers, magazines, novels, school books, etc.

SCRIPT

Roman. In the mid-nineteenth century Samuel Kleinschmidt standardized the spelling of Greenlandic words on an etymological rather than a phonetic basis. In 1973 a new, phonetically more accurate, orthography was introduced.

PHONOLOGY

Consonants

stops: p, t, k, q
fricatives: v, s, (ʃ), j, γ, h, ɹ/ʁ
nasals: m, n, ŋ, N
lateral: l

/N/ is a voiced uvular, notated as *rng*.

Vowels

a, i, u (with hamza onset)

These have several allophones induced by phonetic environment. Thus, /a/ → [ɛ], /i/ → [ɪ], /u/ → [ɔ].

MORPHOLOGY AND SYNTAX

Inuit words are divided into nominals, verbals, and particles. Inflection in nominals and verbals is always by affix; there are about 400 affixes in the language (listed in Fortescue 1983).

Noun

The Inuit noun is marked for number, case, and possessive relationship. A noun is in the absolute case when it is the subject of an intransitive verb, in the relative (ergative) case when it is the subject of a transitive verb.

Specimen of inflectional paradigm:

	Singular	*Plural*
absolute	-q/-t/-k/Ø	-(i)t
relative	-(u)p	-(i)t
instrumental	-mik	-nik
allative	-mut	-nut
locative	-mi	-ni
ablative	-mit	-nit
circumstantial	-kkut	-tigut
equative	-tut	-tut

Affix initials are subject to sandhi (assimilation, accommodation) at junctures.

Examples:

allative: *umiarsuar.mut* 'by ship';
ablative: *qiia.nir.nit* 'from the cold' (*-nir* is a nominalizing particle on verbal stem);
instrumental: *savim.mi.nik* 'with his knife';
circumstantial: *ullaa.kkut* 'in the mornings', *unnua.kkut* 'at night'.

POSSESSION

There are two sets of endings, depending on absolute or relative status of head-noun. Possessor precedes possessed. *X.-**p** Y.-**a***: 'the Y possessed-by (*-a*)' (*-p* is a relative marker); *X.-**p** Y.-**ata** Z.-**a***: 'the Z possessed by Y possessed by X' = X's Y's Z; where *-ata* notates the relationship whereby Y is possessed by X, and is the possessor of Z. E.g. *niviarsia.**p** ikinn.uta.**ata** qimmi.**a*** 'the girl's friend's dog' (*niviarsia* 'girl', *ikinng-* 'friend', *qimmi* 'dog'); *ut*(*i*) in this example is the marker of alienable possession. Cf. *piniartu.**p** irnir.**a** pani.**a** lu* 'the hunter's son and daughter' (*lu* 'and'); *piniartu.**p** irnir.**ata** pani.**a**.lu* 'the hunter's son and his (the son's) daughter'. Further, there is a specific set of endings for oblique object possessed.

Adjective

There is no adjective as a separate category in Inuit. The predicative function is discharged by stative verb, the attributive function by the intransitive participle form (nominal): e.g. *illu.at kusanar.puq* 'their house is pretty' (*-at* = 3rd p. poss. abs.; *kusanar* (verb) 'to be pretty'; *puq* = 3rd p. sing. indicative).

Attributive follows noun: e.g. *inuit pikkuris.**su**.t* 'clever people' (*pikkuris* (verb) 'to be clever'; *su* = intrans. participle affix; *t* = pl. marker).

Pronoun

The free personal forms are:

	Singular	*Plural*
1	uanga	uagut
2	illit	ilissi
3	una	uku

The third person forms are demonstratives. These pronouns are declined in all cases. Thus for first person singular: *uanga – uanga – uannik – uannut – uanni – uannit – uakkut – uattut*. For subject/object fused forms in transitive verb, *see* **Verb**, below).

DEMONSTRATIVE PRONOUN

The complex orientational/directional deictic system of Eskimo in general has been reduced in West Greenlandic to a simpler grid based on relative proximity: *manna* 'this' – *una* 'that' – *innga* 'that yonder'; with further series indicative of relative height, compass point, or visibility.

The demonstratives form plurals and are declined in all eight cases in both numbers. *Ta-* may be prefixed to any demonstrative form whose coreferent has already been focused: e.g. ***ta**manna* 'this (here) (item) we've been talking about'.

INTERROGATIVE PRONOUN

kina 'who?'; *suna* 'what?' Declined in eight cases, singular and plural.

RELATIVE PRONOUN

None. *See* **Relative clauses**, below.

Numerals

Native Eskimo words exist for 1–20. For numbers over 12, Danish equivalents are used, pronounced as in Danish or as converted to Inuit phonology. The indigenous series is: 1 *ataasiq*; 2 *marluk*; 3 *pingasut*; 4 *sisamat*; 5 *tallimat*; 6 *arvinillit*; 7 *arvini(q)-marluk*; 8 *arvini(q)-pingasut*; 9

qulingiluat; 10 *qulit*; 11 *aqqanillit*; 12 *aqqani(q)-marluk*. Continued on *aqqani-* base to 15; then *arvirsani-* base + units to 20, which is *arvirsani(q)-tallimat*.

The numerals are declined: e.g. *ukiuni* ***sisamani*** 'in four years'; *qimmit qaqurtut* ***marluk*** *taakku* 'these two white dogs' (*qimmi* 'dog'; *qaqurtu* 'white'). The old Eskimo dual is not used in West Greenlandic.

Verb

Inuit verbs are intransitive, transitive, or semi-transitive. A definite direct object following a transitive verb is in the base case: *tuttu taku.aa* 'he saw the caribou' (*tuttu* 'caribou'; *taku-* 'see'; -(*v*)*aa* inflection encoding transitive action by third person subject on third person object, both singular); an indefinite or non-focused object is in the instrumental case and follows a transitive stem now furnished with intransitive endings: e.g. *tuttu.mik taku.vuq* 'he saw a caribou', where *-vuq* is the intransitive third person ending. The stem *taku-*, with a specific infix, may also behave as a semi-transitive, again with intransitive inflection, and object in the instrumental: *tuttu.mik taku.****nnip****.puq* (with juncture assimilation, *-vuq* → *-puq*). Finally, the word denoting the object can itself take a verbalizing affix, e.g. *-si-*, plus the intransitive endings: e.g. *tuttu.si.vuq* which amounts to 'he caribou-ed', 'he became caribou-seeing'. (See Fortescue 1984: 86.)

PASSIVE VOICE

The marker is *-niqar-*; the object of the active verb becomes the subject of the converted verb, while the subject of the active verb may appear in the ablative case: Fortescue gives the following examples: *Inuit nanuq taku.aat* 'The people saw the polar bear'; *Nanuq* (*inun.****nit***) *taku.****niqar****.puq* 'The polar bear was seen by the people'; cf. *taa.****niqar****.tar.puq* 'it is called' (where *-tar-* is habitual action marker); *apiri.****niqar****.tar.punga* 'I'd be asked'.

MOOD AND TENSE

Inuit has primary (indicative, imperative/optative, interrogative) and several subordinate moods, the latter including a causative and a conditional. With each mood are associated (a) a set of intransitive endings; (b) a set of inflections coded for transitivity, person, and number; and (c) a specific mood marker; e.g. *va/var* (indicative), *gu/ku* (conditional), *li/la* (optative). The intransitive indicative paradigm shows the following endings:

	Singular	*Plural*
1	-vunga	-vugut
2	-vutit	-vusi
3	-vuq	-pput

For example *isu.aqar.punga* 'I think/thought' (the unmarked indicative can be construed as present or past tense, depending on context), while the correlative transitive paradigm has 28 forms notating person and number deixis: e.g. *-vara* (1st p. sing. subject acting on 3rd p. sing. patient; *-varma* (2nd p. sing. subject acting on 1st p. sing. patient). Cf. *nalunggil.ara* 'I know it' (*-vara* > *-ara* after consonant); *paasi.ssa.vaat* 'they will understand him' (*-ssa-* is future marker). Specimen forms from the optative paradigm are: *-lara* (1st p. sing. acting on 3rd p. sing.), *-lakkit* (1st p. sing. acting on 2nd p. sing.). *Sima*, *nikuu* are used as past-tense markers: e.g. *Nuum.miis.sima.vunga* 'I've been to Nuuk.' The future is marked by *-ssa-* (with others): e.g. *aalla.ssa.agut* 'we shall leave'.

Several affixes, e.g. *-qqu-*, *-tit-*, *-sar-*, convert intransitive into transitive verbs.

Conditional: the intransitive singular forms are: 1 *-guma*, 2 *-guit*, 3 *-ppat*: e.g. *ilaa.ssa.guit* 'if you come' (*ssa* is future marker).

There are specific infixed markers for various modal senses, e.g. potential, inceptive, and desiderative: e.g. potential *-sinnaa-*: e.g. *kalaallit qallunaatut uqalus.**sinnaa**.su.t* (where *-su-* is the intransitive participle characteristic, and *-t* is the plural marker) 'Greenlanders (*kalaallit*) who can speak (*uqalus*) Danish (*qallunaatut*)'.

ASPECT

Fortescue (1984) lists about 50 'affixes concerned with aspect'. Some of the markers are:

perfective: *riir*, *tikit*;
imperfective: *riar*;
habitual: *tar*/*sar*;
progressive: *giartur*;
iterative: *qattaar*.

NEGATIVE

nngit negates sentences (sandhi at junctures): e.g. *tuku.**nngil**.aa* 'he didn't see him' (*-aa* is trans. ending for 3rd sbj. acting upon 3rd obj., both sing.); *paasi.**nngil**.aa* 'he didn't understand it'. The infix may be doubled: e.g. *tiki.**nngi**.ssa.**nngil**.anga* 'I'll not not-come' = 'I'll definitely come'.

RELATIVE CLAUSES

Participial forms replace adjective and relative pronoun, both absent in Inuit: e.g. *niviarsiaq kalaallisut ilinnia.lir.**suq*** 'the girl who has begun learning Greenlandic' (*lir* is inceptive marker; *suq* = intrans. participle); *Nuum.miir.**suq**niviarsiaq* 'the girl from Nuuk'; *illu purtusu.nngit.**suq*** 'a house that is not tall'.

Postpositions

Various nominals are used as postpositions: e.g.

ilu 'interior': *illu**p** ilu.a.ni* 'in the house' (*-a-* is poss. marker);
silat 'outside of': *uqaluvvi.**up** silata.a.ni* 'outside the church';
quli- 'above': *quli.tsin.nit* 'above us' (*-tsin*(*ni*) is the 1st plural possessive marker).

Word order

Fairly free.

1 pilerĸârneráne oĸauseĸ ípoĸ, oĸauserdlo Gûtimīpoĸ, oĸau-
-serdlo Gûtiuvoĸ. 2 táuna pilerĸârneráne Gûtimīpoĸ. 3 sùt ta-
-marmik táussumùna píngorput; táussumûna píngitsumik atautsi-
-migdlûnît píngortoĸángitdlat píngortut. 4 inũssut táussumanī-
-poĸ, inùssutdlo inuit ĸáumarĸutigât. 5 ĸáumarĸutdlo târtumut
ĸaumavoĸ, târmiutdle ilasiaríngilât. 6 inuk Gûtip autdlartitarâ
Juánasimik atilik. 7 táuna tikiúpoĸ nalunaiáisavdlune, ĸáumarĸut
nalunaiáissutigísavdlugo, tamaisa táussumûna ugperĸuvdlugit.
8 táuna ĸáumarĸutauvdlune píngilaĸ, kisiáne ĸáumarĸut nalunaiái-
-ssutigísagamiuk.

IRANIAN LANGUAGES

In its origins, this satem branch of Indo-European is very closely associated with the Indic branch. Apart from the evident parallels in religion and mythology, the language of the oldest stratum of the Gathas (*see* **Avestan**) is close enough to Vedic Sanskrit to suggest a fairly recent common ancestor. It seems likely that a stage of Indo-Iranian unity, centred in or near an Indo-European homeland in what is now the Ukraine, lasted into the third millennium BC. Exactly how and when the two groups reached their present locations is not clear; a Caucasian passage is one possibility. By the time the *Rig-Veda* was composed, however, in the middle of the second millennium, the Aryan kindred were already settled in northern India, and a comparable dating for Iranian colonization of Iran seems plausible.

The ethnonym of the Iranian-speaking tribes was *ar*(*i*)*ya* (Sanskrit: *ārya* 'of one's own tribe'; 'honourable', 'noble') from which are derived Modern Persian *Irān*, Tajik *eron*, Ossete *Iron*.

As now distributed, the core languages – Persian, Dari, Baluchi, Pashto, Kurdish – lie in a broad band stretching from Pakistan to Turkey. The outliers are few – Ossete in the Caucasus, Tat in Azerbaijan, and the Pamir language Sarikoli in the CPR. The group can be classified dialectally and diachronically as follows:

(a) South-West Iranian

1. Ancient and middle Iranian: Old Persian; Pehlevi.
2. Modern: Persian, Dari, Tajik, Tat, with several smaller dialects including Luri and Bakhtyari.

(b) North-West Iranian

1. Ancient and middle Iranian: Median, Parthian.
2. Modern: Kurdish, Baluchi, Talysh, with many dialects.

(c) Eastern Iranian

Northern:

1. Ancient and middle Iranian: Avestan, Sogdian, Khwarezmian.
2. Modern: Ossete, Yagnob.

Southern:

1. Ancient and middle Iranian: Khotanese Saka, Bactrian.
2. Modern: Pashto, Pamir languages.

Typological grouping by dialect does not always correspond to present-day geographical location. For example, Ossete is a North-East Iranian language but is, in fact, the most north-westerly member of the family. As a North-West Iranian language, Baluchi is similarly uncharacteristically placed on the south-eastern flank.

PERIODIZATION

Ancient Iranian: end of second millennium BC to fourth/third century BC; Middle Iranian: third century BC to eighth/ninth century AD; Modern Iranian: to the present day.

The close similarity between the oldest strata of Indic and Iranian was pointed out above. With the passage of time, however, the two families diverged very considerably, and no modern Iranian language is intelligible to a New Indo-Aryan speaker, or vice versa (though a special case might be made out for Classical literary Urdu, for example, which had a considerable number of Persian loanwords). Within the Iranian family itself, while Persian, Dari, and Tajik form a closely homogeneous group, the mutual intelligibility factor is, in general, rather low.

Vis-à-vis the Indo-European parent language, Iranian shows the following sound shifts:

1. IE /*p, t, k/ > Iranian /f, θ, x/ (Indic /p, t, k/).
2. IE /*ph, th, kh/ > Iranian /f, θ, x/ (Indic /p, t, k/).

That is, the Indo-European voiceless stops and their aspirated counterparts were collapsed in Iranian to form the series of homorganic fricatives.

3. The voiced aspirated stops */bh, dh, gh/ were unvoiced in Iranian to give /b, d, g/ (in Indic the aspiration was retained).
4. IE *s > Iranian h; s/s after */i, u, r, k/: e.g.

Avestan	***frā***	Sanskrit	***pra-***, Greek ***pro***, Latin ***prō-*** (prefix meaning 'in front of', 'on behalf of', etc.)
Avestan	*yaθa*	Sanskrit	*yathā*, 'as'
Avestan	***brātar***	Sanskrit	***bhrātar*** 'brother'
Avestan	*ahmi*	Sanskrit	*asmi* 'I am'

5. IE /*a, e, o, n̥, m̥/ (all short) > Iranian /a/; the corresponding long values > Iranian /aː/: e.g. IE * *dekm̥* > 'ten' Avestan ***dasa***, Sanskrit ***daśa***; Latin *decem*, OCh. Slav. *deset'*.

   IE /*ə/ > Iranian /i/; e.g. **pəter* > Iranian *pitā*; Latin *pater* 'father'.

In the modern languages, the West Iranian voiced stops /b, d, g/ are represented in East Iranian by the corresponding fricatives /β, ð, γ/; and Western /p/ is represented by /f/: cf. Persian *pedär* – Ossete *fidalfəd*.

Between 90 and 100 million people speak Iranian languages, over half of this total being provided by Persian. As might be expected, all the present-day representatives of the family share a considerable number of Arabic words.

See **Avestan; Persian; Pehlevi; Baluchi; Kurdish; Ossete; Pashto; Pamir Languages; Persian; Shughn-Roshan; Tajik; Talysh; Tat**.

EASTERN MEDIEVAL IRANIAN LANGUAGES

INTRODUCTION

The Iranian imprint in Central Asia dates from the satrapies established beyond the Amu Darya by the Achaeminids: Suguda (in Greek, *Sogdianē*) and Uvarazmish (in Greek, *Chorasmia*). By the time that the Silk Road came to be used for commercial and cultural communication between India, China, and the West (Rome and Byzantium) several of the main staging-posts thereon, such as Kashgar, Yarkand, Khiva, and Khotan, were inhabited by Iranian-speaking populations. Four of their languages, all fairly close to each other, are known to us from archaeological excavations carried out in the twentieth century. They are:

1. Sogdian: after forming part of the Kushan (Tocharian) realm, and sharing in its Mahāyāna Buddhist culture, Sogdiana fell, first to the Sasanids, then to the western Turks (sixth century AD) and finally to the Sāmānid dynasty. The so-called Ancient Letters, which were found on the Great Wall of China date from the fourth century AD, but most of the extant Sogdian material is of much later date (eighth to tenth centuries). The main find was in the Zerafshan valley in 1933. Here, as elsewhere, Buddhist, Christian, and Manichaean religious texts and documents in Sogdian were found. With each of these denominations is associated a specific variety of the Aramaic alphabetic script, and what appears to be a specific sociolinguistic identity. For example, in marked contrast to the Manichaean material aimed at the upper classes, the Christian documents suggest an appeal to the wider masses of Sogdian society (Oranskij 1963, after Henning 1958).

2. Khwarezmian: Chorasmia was conquered by the Arabs in the sixth century, and our main source of textual material in the Khwarezmian language is provided by Arabic works of the twelfth/thirteenth century – e.g. Zamakhšari's *Muqaddimatu'l adab*, which contains Khwarezmian glosses in Arabic script. Khwarezmian glosses, mainly of a legal nature, are also found in the Arabic texts of al-Biruni (tenth/eleventh century). Earlier specimens of the language were found in Khiva, the site of the ancient capital, Khwarazm; these date from the third to the eighth centuries. An earlier Khwarezmian archive, dating from the third century BC, was found in excavations at Toprak-Kala.

3. Khotanese Saka: Khotan, the ancient Hvatana, lies in Chinese Turkestan (Xīnjiāng) between the Kunlun and the Takla Makan desert. Here, and in Tumshuk, a considerable corpus of Buddhist literature, dating from the seventh to the tenth centuries was found, most of it consisting of translations from Sanskrit. Khotanese was written in the Indian Brahmi character.

4. For about 500 years (second century BC to third century AD) Parthian was the official language of the Aršacid Dynasty in the Parthian Empire (south-east of the Caspian Sea). The language is known from many inscriptions on pottery, and from Manichaean texts, some of which – notably the hymns of Mar Ammo – are of high literary value. The language also appears in the bilingual (with a Middle Persian dialect) inscriptions of the successor Sāsānian kings.

   Genetically, Parthian is a North-Western Iranian language; Parthian loanwords in Old Armenian, however, show certain Eastern Armenian traits.

   Phonologically, Middle Persian and Parthian are close to each other. For Middle Persian /h/ Parthian has /f/ or /s/; cf. Middle Persian *dah* 'ten', Parthian *das*; Middle Persian *čahār* 'four', Parthian *čafar*. Middle Persian *yazdah* 'eleven', Parthian *ēvandas.*

MORPHOLOGY

Originally, the Parthian nominal declension had two cases – nominative, with null marker, and oblique with *-u*. By the time of the Manichaean texts, however, the two had fused.

Pronoun

Singular 1 nom. *'z*, **az*, with oblique *mn *man*; 2 *tw*. Plural 1 **ama(h)*. Third person forms were supplied by the demonstratives *hw*, plural *hwyn*.

Manichaean Parthian has the enclitic series:

	Singular	*Plural*
1	-əm	-mān
2	-əð	-tān
3	-əš	-šān

(cf. Modern Persian)

Present-tense endings in Parthian:

indicative singular	1	-am	*subjunctive singular*	1	-ān
	2	-ēh		2	-āh
	3	-ēð		3	-āh
plural	1	-ām	*plural*	1	-ām
	2	-ēð		2	-āð
	3	-ēnd		3	-ānd

Mention should also be made of Bactrian, about which very little is known. In the second century BC, Bactria (on the upper and middle reaches of the Amu-Darya) was occupied by Tocharian and Saka tribes. About the second century AD, the Kushan dynasty, which then ruled Bactria, introduced a variant of the Greek script. A 25-line inscription, found in Northern Afghanistan, contains the name of the Kushan ruler Kanishka.

PHONOLOGY

The Khotanese Saka consonantal inventory has three symmetrical series consisting of surd – voiced stop – voiceless fricative – voiced fricative: /p, b, f, β; t, d, θ, ð; k, g, x, γ/. Also present are the affricates: /ts, dz, tʃ, dʒ/; the fricatives /s, z, ʃ, ʒ/ with the pharyngeal /ħ/; the semi-vowels /j/ and /w/; and /m, n, r, l/.

The Sogdian inventory is closely similar, but here the voiced stops appear to be used only after nasals; /l/ is absent. A Sogdian characteristic is the retention of surd stops in intervocalic position.

MORPHOLOGY AND SYNTAX

Noun

Sogdian had definite and indefinite articles which vary according to gender (masculine or feminine), case, number, and denominational affiliation: e.g. nominative masculine singular: Buddhist *'γw*, Manichaean/Christian *xw*.

SPECIMEN DECLENSION

Khotanese Saka, *dastä* 'hand' (cf. Persian *dast*).

	Singular	*Plural*
nominative	dastä	dasta
accusative	dastu	dasta
genitive	dasti	dastānu
instrumental/ablative	dastäna	dastyau
locative	dīśta	dastuvo
vocative	dasta	dastyau

Feminine nouns: e.g. *kantha* 'town' (nom., acc.), pl. *kanthe*. Oblique endings as in masculine paradigm. The Khwarezmian plural ending was *-ina*.

Adjective

Adjectives are marked for gender and case in both Sogdian and Saka, and partially for number: e.g. Saka *dirä*, fem. *dira* 'bad', declined like *dastä*. The adjectival inflections are unstable, and tend, in later stages of the language, to be omitted. The comparative marker is Saka *-tarä*, Sogdian *-t(a)r*, with many variants: e.g. Manichaean Sogdian *čn škr' n'mr.tr* 'sweeter than honey'.

Pronoun

The personal pronoun has independent forms with two cases, and enclitic forms. The Sogdian paradigm is:

	Independent (singular = plural)		*Enclitic*	
	Direct	*Oblique*	*Singular*	*Plural*
1	'zw	mn'	-my	-mn
2	tγw	tw'	-f(y)	-fn
3	xw	w(y)nyy	-šy(y)/-šw	-šn

These are Manichaean forms. The oblique form of the independent pronouns may be used as a possessive: e.g. *mn' w'xš* 'my words'.

DEMONSTRATIVE PRONOUN

Several variants. In Sogdian, the forms *x-/w-*, each with oblique base, are used as indefinite articles. In Saka, masc. *ṣä*, fem. *ṣa*, pl. *ttä*, *tte*: declined in six cases on base *tt-*.

Numerals

Khotanese Saka 1–10: *śśau* (fem. *śśa*), *duva* (fem. *dvī*), *drai*, *tcahora*, *paṁjsa*, *kṣä(tä)*, *hauda*, *haṣṭa*, *nau*, *dasau*; 20 *bistä*; 30 *därsä*; 100 *satä*. The Sogdian numerals vary according to religious affiliation; e.g. for 3, Manichaean *'ðry(y)*; Buddhist *ðry*; Christian *šy* **θrē*.

Verb

The characteristic Iranian division into present and past bases is found, the former generating the present indicative, the subjunctive, the optative, the imperative, and the present participle. The past tense, the past participle, and the infinitive are formed from the past base.

Sogdian and Khwarezmian retain an imperfect constructed on the present base. Also noteworthy in these two languages is a transitive perfect, formed with the auxiliary verb *ðār* 'to have', from transitive verbs: e.g. *θfart ðāram* 'I gave', *θfart ðārt* 'he gave'.

In all three languages the verb is marked for person, number, tense, and mood; Khotanese Saka adds gender (marked in the past tense) and voice.

Sogdian indicative present: root *var-* 'to carry', 'take':

	Singular	*Plural*
1	varam	varim
2	vari	varta
3	vart	varand

Sogdian imperfect:

	Singular	*Plural*
1	varu	varim
2	var	varθ
3	vara	varand

The negative marker is *nē*; prohibitive, *mā*.

Prepositions and postpositions

All three languages use both pre- and postpositions. Sogdian is perhaps the only known language in which a writer's religion can be identified from the prepositions he uses: cf. Buddhist *čnn*, Manichaean/Christian *čn*, Manichaean *čwn* 'from', 'than' (as used in example in **Adjective** above).

IRISH

INTRODUCTION

A member of the Goidelic branch of Celtic, Irish is the first official language of the Republic of Ireland, with English. The Gaeltacht – the area where Irish is spoken – is not continuous; there is a broad division into a southern belt (Waterford, Cork, Kerry) and a northern (Connemara, Galway, Mayo, Donegal). About 80,000 people speak Irish in one form or another, none of them monoglot. There is a very considerable degree of divergence between the dialects. A standard orthography was adopted in 1948.

The centuries covering the transition from Old Irish to Modern Irish – 1200 to 1600 – produced a lot of fine bardic verse. Thereafter there was a period of decline, relieved by the work of three outstanding poets: Ó Bruadair in the seventeenth century, Aogán Ó Rathaille and Brian Merriman in the eighteenth. There has been a small but significant revival in the twentieth century – e.g. the short stories of Liam O'Flaherty.

SCRIPT

The Old Irish minuscule, formerly used for Irish, has been replaced by the Roman alphabet, minus the letters *j, k, q, v, w, x, y, z*. In the Irish script the spirants were marked by superscript dot; the Latin script uses the letter *h*: thus Irish *ċ* = Latin *ch* /χ/. Long vowels are marked by acute.

PHONOLOGY

Consonants

Eighteen letters represent some sixty phonemes. The basic consonantal inventory is:

stops: b, p, d, t, g, k; palatalized: b′, p′, d′, t′, g′, k′
fricatives: f, v, s, ʃ, x, γ, h; palatalized: f′, x′ (ç), γ′ (→ [j])
nasals: m, n, ɲ; palatalized: m′, n′ ɲ′
lateral and flap: l, r; palatalized: l′, r′
semi-vowel: w

The non-palatalized consonants are associated with the 'broad' vowels, /a, o, u/, long and short; the palatalized with the 'slender' /i, e/. In other words, the vowels determine and indicate the palatal or non-palatal nature of consonants.

Vowel

The vowel series is:

slender: iː, ɪ, eː, ɛ, æ
broad: aː, a, oː, ɔ, uː, u
neutral: /ə/

The notation is highly redundant and inefficient: /oː/, for example, is variously represented as *ó, ói, eo, eoi, omh, omha*(*i*). There are several diphthongs.

Stress

Stress is usually on the first syllable.

Mutation

(a) Lenition: (*see also* **Scottish Gaelic**). In Modern Irish, the stop to spirant mutation is observed in the initial of singular feminine nouns, following the definite article, the singular genitive of masculine nouns, after the singular series of possessive adjectives (except third feminine), after certain prepositions, numerals, and particles in the construct relationship, etc.: e.g.

bean 'woman': *an* ***bh****ean* /ən **v**′æn/, 'the woman';
crann 'tree'; *barr* 'top′: *barr an* ***ch****rainn* /bar.ən **x**rin'/ 'the top of the tree';
mac 'son': *mo* ***mh****ac* /mo **w**ak/ 'my son'; *hata an fhir bhig* /hata ənir′ vig′/ 'the small man's hat'.

(b) Eclipsis (nasalization): this mutation takes place in noun initials after the plural possessive adjectives, after certain numerals, in the dative singular and the genitive plural, after the preposition *i* 'in'; in verbs after certain particles, after the negative relative *nach*, etc.: e.g.

ár 'our'; *cairde* 'friends' (sing. *cara*): *ár* ***gc****airde* /ār gar′d′ə/, 'our friends';
seacht 'seven'; *capall* 'horse': *seacht* ***gc****apall* /śæxt gapəl/, 'seven horses';
i 'in'; *teach* 'house': *i* ***dt****each* /i d′æx/, 'in a house'.

As will be seen from these examples, the sound resulting from eclipsis is marked in the script by a digraph: *p* → *bp, t* → *dt, c* → *gc, b* → *mb, d* → *nd*, etc.

(c) The *h*- prefix: used with vocalic initials, after the article *na*, after *a* 'her', after certain prepositions and particles, and after *de* 'day': e.g.

aos 'age': *a* ***h****aois* /ə hiʃ/, 'her age';
Aoine 'Friday': *De* ***h****Aoine* /d′ē hin′ə/, 'Friday' (lit: 'day of Friday');
ean 'bird': *na* ***h****ein* /nə hēn′/ 'the birds'.

(d) *t*- prefix: in masculine singular nouns with vowel initial, after definite article: e.g.

aran 'bread': *an* ***t****-aran* 'the bread'

and *s*- → *ts*- /t/ in feminine singular nominative and masculine genitive singular: e.g.

seachtan (fem.) 'week': *an* ***ts****eachtain* /ən t′æxtən′/, 'the week'.

MORPHOLOGY AND SYNTAX

Two genders: masculine and feminine. Apart from a few linked endings, gender is not predictable. The definite article is *an* (sing.), *na* (pl.). The phonetic changes outlined above have to be borne in mind when the article is added.

Noun

There are five declensions in the literary standard, with three cases: nominative/accusative – genitive – vocative. A few nouns have specific forms for the dative. Plural forms are divided into (a) strong (one form for all three cases) and (b) weak (nominative/genitive). The following examples show typical plural formations for each declension:

1st declension: *an capall bán* 'the white horse': pl. *na capaill* ***bh****ána*; pl. gen. *na* ***g****capall* ***b****án* 'of the white horses'.
2nd declension: *cloch* 'stone' (fem.): pl. *na* ***cloch****a* *troma* 'the heavy stones'.
3rd declension: *ríocht* 'kingdom': pl. *na ríocht****aí***; *gamhain* 'calf': pl. *na gamh****na***.
4th declension: *iascaire* /iəsgir′i/, 'fisherman': pl. *iascair****i***.
5th declension: *cathair* /kahir′/, 'city': pl. *na cathr****acha***.

CASES

Example: second declension noun, *an chloch* (fem.) 'the stone' (west Munster dialect):

	Singular	*Plural*
nominative/accusative	an chloch	na **c**locha
genitive	na clo**i**che	na **gc**loch
dative	don **ch**loich	dosna **c**loch**aibh**

The vocative has to be learnt: with masculine nouns of the first declension it is the same as the genitive singular; with feminine nouns of the first declension it is the same as the nominative. The preposed vocative particle *a* causes lenition: e.g. *Cáit* > *a Cháit!* 'Hi, Kathy!'

POSSESSIVE CONSTRUCT

As in Semitic, the possessed noun comes first, minus its article: e.g. *fuinneog an t-seomra* 'the window of the room'. In masculine nouns, the initial of the possessor noun is mutated, and a final broad consonant is mutated into the corresponding slender. Thus, from *sagart* 'priest': *teach an tsagai**rt*** /ən tagər′t/, 'the house of the priest'.

Adjective

As attribute follows noun, with concord for gender, number, and case. Thus, *fear mór* 'big man': gen. *fir **mhóir*** 'of a big man'; pl. *fir **mhóra*** 'big men': *fear**aibh** mór**a*** 'to big men'.

Adjectival qualification may also be expressed by prefix: *dea-*, *so-* 'good', *droch-*, *do* 'bad': e.g. *dea.scéal* 'good news'; *droch.bheas* 'bad habit' (cf. Sanskrit *su-*, *dus-*).

In the first three declensions the adjective is modified to form a comparative, e.g. *deacair* 'difficult' – *deacr**a***; *fada* 'long' – *faide. Níos* precedes the comparative in a verbal sentence with *tá* 'is': e.g. *tá* X *níos faide ná* Y 'X is longer than Y'.

Some comparatives are suppletive: *olc* 'bad' – *measa*; *beag* 'small' – *lú*; *maith* 'good' – *fearr*.

Pronoun

PERSONAL PRONOUN

The independent subject forms are:

		Singular	*Plural*
1		mé	muid
2		tú	sibh
3	masc.	sé	siad
	fem.	sí	

These are also the object forms, except in the third person where *e/i* and *iad* replace *sé/sí* and *siad*: cf. *chonaic mé thú* 'I saw you'; *chonaic tú é* 'you saw him'.

POSSESSIVE ADJECTIVES

Sing. 1 *mo/m′*, 2 *do/d′*, 3 *a* (these induce lenition).
Pl. 1 *ár*, 2 *bhur*, 3 *a* (these induce eclipsis, i.e. voicing or nasalizing of initial consonant).

A series of important prepositions combine with the personal pronouns, e.g. *ag* 'at': *agam, agat, aige/aici*… to express 'to have': e.g. *ta leabhar **agam*** /ta l'aur agəm/ 'I have a book' ('a book is at me').

DEMONSTRATIVE PRONOUN/ADJECTIVE

Three degrees of relative distance: *seo* 'this', *sin* 'that', *siúd* 'that yonder': e.g. *an fear seo* 'this man'.

INTERROGATIVE PRONOUN

cé 'who?'; *céard* 'what?': e.g. *Cé/céard a chonaic sé*? 'Whom/what did he see?'

RELATIVE PRONOUN

(a) Direct: *a* + lenition: e.g. *an obair* ***a*** *bhí sibh a dhéanamh* 'the work you were doing' where *dhéanamh* /jeːnə/ is the verbal noun of *deinim* /d′in′im/ 'I do'.

(b) Indirect: *a* + eclipsis, or, *ar* + lenition: e.g. *am buachaill* ***a bh****fuil a athair tinn* 'the boy whose father is ill'.

Numerals

1–10: *a haon, a dó, a trí, a ceathair, a cúig, a sé, a seacht, a hocht, a naoi, a deich* /ə d′e/; 11 *a haon déag*; 12 *a dó dhéag*; 13 *a trí déag*; 20 *fiche*; 30 *tríocha*; 40 *daichead*; 50 *caoga*; 100 *céad*. There is a specific series of numbers, 1–10, for persons. These end in -*(e)ar* < *fear* 'man': e.g. *seis.ear* 'six persons'.

Verb

In striking contrast with Old Irish, most verbs are regular in the modern language. There are two conjugations: I comprising monosyllabic stems with a future tense in -*fidh*/-*faidh* /ə/; and II polysyllabic stems with future tense in -*(e)oidh* /ɔ/. As regards inflection, there is considerable divergence among the various dialects; on the whole, the southern dialects (Munster) are more conservative, and here synthetic forms tend to be retained which are replaced by analytic forms in the north and west.

The tense/mood structure consists of indicative present (progressive or habitual), past habitual, preterite, future; conditional, subjunctive, imperative. Where analytic reductionism has produced an identical form for more than one person, the personal pronouns have to be added.

A key role is played by the verbal noun, whose form is not predictable; over a dozen different formulations are possible. Among the commonest are: -*(e)adh*, -*áil*, -*e*, -*t*. For example, from *bris* 'break', VN *bris****eadh***; from *tóg* 'take', VN *tóg****áil***, from *ith* 'eat', VN *ithe*; from *labhair* 'speak', VN *labhair****t***. Uses of the verbal noun will be illustrated in the following description of the tenses.

Present progressive: auxiliary + subject + *ag* + VN: e.g. *tá mé ag léamh* 'I am reading'; *tá thú ag obair* 'you are working'. The same formula can be used in the past (*tá* → *bhí*) or future (*ta* → *beidh*).

Present habitual: in Galway and the north, only the first person singular and plural have synthetic forms: e.g. from *dún* 'to shut', *dúnaim* and *dúnaimid*. Second and third persons have VN *dúnann* followed by personal pronouns – *tú, sé/sí, sibh, siad*. In Munster, synthetic forms may be retained for second singular and third plural.

Preterite: here again there is dialectal variation: in Galway, the initial is lenited: *dún* – ***dhún***, *mol* – ***mhol***, and this single form is followed by the personal pronouns, *except* in the first person plural, which has the synthetic form *dhún.amar* 'we closed', *mhol.amar* 'we praised'. In Munster, the form is *do dhúnas, do dhúnais*, etc.

Future: the future form, as given above, + personal pronouns, again with an exception for the first person plural: *molfaidh mé/tú/sé/sí*, etc. but *molfaimid* in first person plural. The conditional endings are close to those of the future; the subjunctive is in *-a*/*-e* (depending on whether stem vowel is broad or slender).

Dependent forms: these occur with only a few verbs, but these few have a very high frequency rating, e.g. the auxiliary *tá*, whose dependent forms are:

(a) with negative *ní*: present: *níl*; past: *ni raibh* /n′i ro/;
(b) after interrogative particle *an*: present: *an bhfuil* /ə wil′/, past: *an raibh*;
(c) after negative interrogative particle *nach* (as after interrogative);
(d) after relative link *go* (as b, c).

Thus, *bhí thú ann* 'you were there'; *An* ***raibh*** *tú ann*? 'Were you there?'

The autonomous form: the regular endings for all persons and both numbers are: present: *-t(e)ar*; past: *-adh*; future: *-far* /hər/. The past form does not take lenition. The autonomous form takes an object: *briseadh an fhuinneog* /ən iŋ′oːg/ can be rendered in English as 'they broke the window' or 'the window got broken'. A more exact translation would be 'breaking-occurred with relation to the window': cf. *dúntar an dorus* 'closing-occurs with relation to the door'; *óltar deoch* 'drinking-occurs with relation to a dram'. (Cf. Finnish and Estonian forms like *annetaan*, *räägitakse*, etc.)

Irish has several very common and very irregular verbs, with dependent forms, e.g. *téigh* 'to go', with independent pret. *chuaigh mé*; dependent pret. *ní dheachaigh mé*: future: *rachaidh mé*: VN: *dul*. There are similar thematic complications with *feic* 'to see', pret. *chonaic*; *déan* 'to do', pret. *rinne*; *tar* 'to come', pret. *tháinig*.

Prepositions

We have already seen the preposition coalescing with the personal pronouns to produce forms like *agam* 'I have', *againn* 'we have', etc. Similarly, with *de* 'from': *díom* 'from me', *díbh* 'from you (pl.)', etc.; *i* 'in': *ionam* 'in me', *ionat*, etc. This preposition combines with the article to form *san*: *san ardeaglais* /sən ardæglәʃ/, 'in the cathedral'. Other examples: *ar* 'on': *orm*, *ort*, *air*; *as* 'out of': *asam*, *asat*, *as*.

Word order

VSO is basic.

1 Bhí an Briathar(I) ann i dtús báire
agus bhí an Briathar in éineacht le Dia,
agus ba Dhia an Briathar.
2 Bhí sé ann i dtús báire in éineacht le Dia.
3 Rinneadh an uile ní tríd
agus gan é ní dearnadh aon ní dá ndearnadh.
4 Bhí beatha ann
agus ba é solas na ndaoine an bheatha.
5 Agus tá an solas ag taitneamh sa dorchadas,
ach níor ghabh an dorchadas é.
6 Bhí fear a tháinig ina theachtaire ó Dhia, agus Eoin a ba
ainm dó. 7 Tháinig sé ag déanamh fianaise chun fianaise a
thabhairt i dtaobh an tsolais chun go gcreidfeadh cách tríd.
8 Níorbh é féin an solas ach tháinig ag tabhairt fianaise i dtaobh
an tsolais.

IRISH, OLD

INTRODUCTION

Old Irish is a Q-Celtic language, and the oldest attested form of Goidelic. It is known to us from (a) about 300 inscriptions in the Ogam runic script, dating from the fourth to the eighth centuries, and (b) an extensive corpus of very fine poetry and prose (eighth to twelfth centuries), a central place being taken by the splendid heroic romance, the *Tain bo Cúailnge* (seventh century). The main sources for these early works are the twelfth-century *Leabhar na h-Uidhe* ('The Book of the Dun Cow'), the twelfth-century *Book of Leinster*, and the fourteenth-century *Yellow Book of Lecan*. The ninth-century *Book of Armagh*, containing the most ancient translation of the New Testament into Irish, should also be mentioned.

SCRIPT

The Roman alphabet was introduced in the fifth century. As a notation for Old Irish it is highly inadequate: mutation is only partially marked. The acute accent is used to mark long vowels, e.g. *sin* 'that', *sín* 'weather', and to identify true diphthongs: *céo* 'mist', 'fog'.

The letter *c* serves to notate initial /k/; medial and final post-vocalic plosives /b, d, g/ are notated by *p, t, k*: e.g. *fotae* /fode/, 'long'. Medial and final *b, d, g* notate the homorganic voiced fricatives: /v/β, ð, γ/: e.g. *dub* /duv/, 'black'. /χ, f, θ/ are represented by *ch, ph, th*. Geminated *ll, nn, rr* are energetically pronounced held sounds, represented in transcription by *L, N, R*. Dotted consonants: *ṡ* = /h/, the lenited form of /s/: e.g. *son* 'sound' – *a ṡon* /əhon/; *ḟ* = Ø the lenited resultative of /f/: e.g. *fuil* 'blood' – *a ḟuil* /ə-ul′/.

PHONOLOGY

Consonants

The neutral or basic inventory of consonants is:

stops: p, t, k, b, d, g
fricatives: f, s, θ, ð, χ, γ
nasals: m, n, ɴ
lateral and flap: L, R, l, r

Parallel to the basic series is the palatalized series: /p′, t′, k′/, etc. Certain consonants may also have had a labialized value.

Vowels

long and short: i, e, a, o, u

Plus eight long and three short diphthongs.

Mutation

Lenition: marked for the occlusives *p, t, k* → *ph, th, ch*. The spirant resultatives of lenited *b, d, g,* /v, ð, ɣ/ (between vowels, and as post-vocalic final; cf. *mod* /moð/ 'work'; *cride* /kriðə/ 'hearts'; *ní hed* /Ni:heð/ 'it is not') are not marked in the script, nor are those of other consonants. Similarly, the nasalized (eclipsed) values of the stop series are only partially notated: *b, d, g* → *mb, nd, ng*.

MORPHOLOGY AND SYNTAX

Three genders: masculine, feminine, neuter. Traces of a dual number are preserved, always accompanied by the numeral *da* 'two', with plural concord in the verb, e.g. *a dib crannaib* 'from two trees'; *in da ḟer moir* 'the two big men' (dotted *f* is silent).

DEFINITE ARTICLE

Masc. *in*, fem. *ind*, nt. *a*; pl. *ind – inna – inna*. The article is declined in four cases: nominative, accusative, genitive, dative, with little variation from the nominative form: thus, masc.: *in – (s)in – ind – (s)ind*. The three plural oblique cases have the same forms for all three genders: *inna/isna – inna – (s)naib*.

Noun

The noun is declined in the same cases as the definite article, plus a vocative. About a dozen types of declension are distinguished, according to stem; in several of these, only the genitive singular is significantly inflected. Example: a feminine *ā*-stem: *aram* 'number':

	Singular	*Plural*	*Dual*
nominative/vocative	áram	áirmea	ár(a)im
accusative	áraim	airmea	–
genitive	áirme	áram	áram
dative	ár(a)im	áirmib	áirmib

In general, Old Irish declension shows a gradual levelling out of the nominative/accusative opposition, and a reduction of final vowels to /ə/.

Some nouns are highly irregular, e.g. *ben* 'woman': gen. sing. *mná*; pl. nom. *mná*, gen. *ban*, dat. *mnáib*.

POSSESSIVE CONSTRUCT

Possessed (minus article) precedes possessor: e.g. *claideb iṅd ḟir* /klaðev ind.ir/ 'the man's sword', *claideb inna fer* 'the men's swords'; cf. *son cíuil* 'the sound of music'.

Adjective

As attribute, adjective follows noun, agreeing with it in gender and number. With regard to initial mutation, adjectives behave as nouns do after the article. Like nouns, adjectives are classified according to stem. Examples: *in mathair oac* 'the young mother'; *a crann n-ard* 'the high tree'; *isnaib cathaib móraib* 'in the great battles'.

COMPARISON

A comparative is made by adding -(*i*)*u* to the positive, usually with palatalization: e.g. *sen* 'old' – *siniu*. The dative case follows the comparative: e.g. *ard.u slébib* 'higher than mountains'. Several comparatives are suppletive: e.g. *maith* 'good' – *ferr*; *már* 'big' – *máo*; *olc* 'bad' – *messa.*

Pronoun

The pronominal system can be set out as (a) independent forms, and (b) three sets of infixed/suffixed forms. The independent forms are:

sing. 1 *mé*, 2 *tú*, 3 masc. (*h*)*é*, fem. *sí*, nt. (*h*)*ed*;
pl. 1 *sní*, 2 *sí*, 3 (*h*)*é*.

These have emphatic forms (the spelling varies):

		Singular	*Plural*
1		meisse	snisni
2		tussu	sissi
3	masc.	(h)é.som	(h)ésidi
	fem.	si.ssi	(h)ésidi
	nt.	(h)ed.ón	(h)ésidi

The first set of infixed forms appears as sing. 1 *m*, 2 *t*, 3 *a* – *s* – *a*; pl. 1 *n*, 2 *b*, 3 *s*. These follow most of the preverbal particles: e.g. *ro-cluinethar* 'he hears'; ***romchluinethar*** 'he hears me'.

The second series has a dental prefix *t*/*d*: sing. 1 *tom*/*dom*/*tum*, 2 *tot*/*tat* . . . . It follows certain preverbals such as *ad*, *aith*, *com*: e.g. *ad-cí* 'he sees'; ***atot-chí*** 'he sees you (sing.)'.

The third series has a *d*- prefix + the same endings as the second series; it is used in relative clauses: e.g. *in fer no-**dom-chara*** 'the man who loves me'; *in fer no-**da-cara*** 'the man who loves her'.

All singular forms are followed by lenition, except third person masculine, which is followed by nasalization, as is third person feminine in the first series (*s*); the feminine forms in the other two series do not affect the following consonant.

Third person singular simple verbs may also take suffixed pronominal forms: e.g. ***beirthium*** 'he carries me'; ***beirthiut*** 'he carries you'.

Pronominal markers are attached to certain prepositions: e.g. ***lem*** 'with me', ***dim*** 'from me', *duit* 'to you': e.g. *Scél* ***lem dúib*** 'tidings – with me – to you (pl.)' = 'I have news for you'. Compare the eleventh-century *Invocation of the Holy Spirit* (Murphy 1970: 52):

In Spirut nóeb immun, innunn ocus ocunn
'May the Holy Spirit be about us, in us and with us.

DEMONSTRATIVE PRONOUN/ADJECTIVE

(a) Indeclinable postpositional: *salsa* 'this', *sin* 'that': e.g. *in fer.sin* 'that man'; *ind fir.so* 'these men'.
(b) Deictic particle *-í* added to definite article: e.g. *indí.sin* 'these' (masc.); *donaib-í* 'to those'.

INTERROGATIVE PRONOUN

cía 'who?'; *cid* 'what?' The particle *in* introduces a positive question; the negative form is *in(n)ád*: e.g. *In cruthaigedar Día domun do duiniu*? 'Does God create the world for a man?'

Numerals

1 *oén*: indeclinable, compounds with following noun which is lenited: *oénfer* 'one man'. 2 *da*; 3 *tri*; 4 *cethir*: these are declined. 5–10: *cóic, sé, secht, ocht, noí, deich*: these are indeclinable. 11–19: *déac* (genitive plural of *deich*) is added: e.g. *di huair déac* '12 hours'; *tri fir deac* '13 men'. 20 *fiche*; 30 *tricho*; 40 *cethorcho*: these are nouns followed by genitive plural, e.g. *tri ferdruíd, trí bandruíd* 'three druids and three druidesses'. 100 *cét*.

Verb

The Old Irish verb is immensely complex, and no more than a few pointers to its structure can be attempted here.

1. Verbs are weak or strong; a distinguished feature is the presence or absence of a vocalic ending in the conjunct third person: cf.

   strong: *as.beir***Ø** 'says' (< Indo-European stock);
   weak: *marb****a*** 'kills' (Goidelic innovation).

2. Both strong and weak verbs have absolute and conjunct forms, and stress-dictated prototonic and deuterotonic forms. Absolute forms are not preceded by particles: e.g. *Móraid Conn slógu* 'Conn praises a host.' Conjunct forms are preceded by such particles as *ni* (negating): e.g. *ní móra***Ø** *Conn slóg***Ø** 'Conn does not praise a host.' (Examples from Quin 1975.)
3. Compound verbs are formed by means of prepositional prefix: this acts in the same way as the particles referred to in (2), and the verb is therefore in conjunct form: root *biru* 'bear', 'bring': compound: ***do.biur*** 'I bring'. The form *-biur* is said to be 'bound', as it cannot stand alone.
4. Stems: there are present, subjunctive, *f*- future, *s*- future, *s*- and *t*- preterite stems. The *f*- future and the *s*- preterite are common in weak verbs, the *t*-

preterite in strong verbs, and there is a reduplicated preterite, e.g. *cingid* 'he strides', pret. ***cechaign***: ***Cechain in duine in salm*** 'The man sang the psalm.'

Principal parts of strong verbs: some examples (in third person singular):

	Present	*Present subjunctive*	*Future*	*Preterite*	*Verbal noun (variable gender)*
'sing'	canid, -cain	-cana	-cechna	cechuin	cétal (nt.)
'break'	bongid, -boing	-bó	-biba	bob(a)ig	búain (fem.)
'take'	gaibid, -gaib	-gaba	-géba	ga(i)b	gabá(i)l (fem.)
'run'	rethid, -reith	-ré	-ré	ráith	riuth (masc.)

5. Personal endings: indicative present and preterite of *berid* 'carries':

   present singular: 1 *biru*, 2 *biri*, 3 *berid*; plural: 1 *bermai*, 2 *beirthe*, 3 *berait*; preterite singular (bound form): 1 *biurt*, 2 *birt*, 3 *bert*; plural: 1 *bertammar*, 2 *bertaid*, 3 *bertar*.

6. Verbal particles: e.g. *no/nu* with non-bound forms: e.g. *No marbad firu* 'He was killing men'; *No crenainn ech* 'I bought a horse'; *No scríbmais libru* 'We wrote books'. The particle *ro* has perfective force: e.g. *Ro marb in fer* 'He has killed the man'.
7. Deponent verbs in *-r* (*cf.* **Latin**): e.g. *labraithair* 'speaks'. The passive form is third person only, used as an impersonal verb, which can take an object: e.g. *no.**m**.marbthar* 'there is a killing with reference to me' = 'I am killed'.
8. Relative clause: leniting (after nominative or accusative referent), nasalizing (after accusative referent); the referent must be third singular/plural or first plural. Examples from Quin (1975: 54):

   in fer **ch**eles in claideb 'the man who hides the sword'
   in claideb **ch**eles in fer 'the sword the man hides'
   in fer **nád ch**eil in claideb 'the man who does not hide the sword'

The nasalizing relative is also used to indicate modality, the 'how' of an action: e.g.

in gabál **ng**aibes in catt in lochaid
'the seizing, by-way-of which the cat seizes the mouse'

9. Verb 'to be' (substantive/existential verb):

   sing. 1 *at-to*, 2 *at-tai*, 3 *at-tá*; pl. 1 *at.-táam*, 2 *at.táaid*, 3 *at-táat*.

Negative: *fil* is used + infixed accusative pronoun (original meaning of *fil* is 'sees'):

sing. 1 ***ním**-fil*, 2 ***nít**-ḟil*, 3 ***ní-fil***; pl. 1 ***nín**-fil*, 2 ***níb**-fil*, 3 ***nís**.fil*.

Copula: proclitic:

sing. 1 *am*, 2 *at*, 3 *is*; pl. 1 *ammi*, 2 *adib*, 3 *it*, cf. *is mé do-gní insin* 'it is I who do that'. This formula is constant for sing. 1, 2, 3 and pl. 1, 2, with change of pronoun (*mé, tú, é, sí*; *sní, sí*); in pl. 3, however, the verb takes pl. concord: *it é do-gní**at** insin* 'it is they who do that'.

Bound form: sing. *-ta, -ta*, -Ø; pl. *-tam, -tad, -tat*: e.g. in negative: *ni.ta* etc.: e.g. *Adib céili, nítad ríg* 'You are companions, not kings.'

Prepositions

Prepositions take various cases: e.g. (*h*)*i* takes the accusative for motion into something, the dative for rest in a place. *Co* 'with' takes the dative: e.g. *co claidbib* 'with swords'. Examples: *is.ind fid* 'in the wood'; *a dib crannaib* 'out of two trees'; *a sidib* 'from the fairy mounds'; *cen brón, cen dube, cen bás* 'without sorrow, without grief, without death' (description of *Tír nan Óg* 'Land of Youth').

Word order

VSO is basic.

ITALIAN

INTRODUCTION

Belonging to the Italic branch of Indo-European, Italian is the official language of the Republic of Italy and is spoken today by over 50 million people, if the dialect form spoken in Sardinia is included. In addition, Italian is one of the three official languages of Switzerland, and is spoken in large communities in North and South America, in North Africa, and elsewhere, which probably add 5 or 6 million to give an overall total of about 60 million.

A dialectal division of Italy running roughly along the line of the Northern Appennines has long been recognized (see, for example, Dante, *De Vulgari Eloquentia*, X). To the north of this line are Piedmontese, Lombardian, Venetian, etc.; to the south lie Tuscan, Umbrian, Neapolitan, Calabrese, and Sicilian. In spite of the homogenizing influence of the standard language used by the media, most of the dialects are still very much alive, and many Italians use the language on two socio-linguistic levels – the local dialect in the family circle and among friends, Standard Italian on all more formal occasions. A celebrated modern example of a successful symbiosis between literary standard and dialect is provided by Carlo Gadda's novel *Quer pasticciaccio brutto de via Merulana* (1967). Certain dialectal features differ markedly from the standard norm, e.g. in the north, the palatal fricative reflex of Low Latin *pl-* as /tʃ/: e.g. /tʃatsa/ for standard *piazza*; and, in the south, the interdental fricatives of Tuscan, e.g. /θ/.

The earliest textual example of written Italian dates from the tenth century. In the ensuing 300 years, poetry was written in several dialects, until Tuscan was suddenly transmuted into one of the world's great literary languages by the genius of Dante Alighieri (1265–1321); the *Divina Commedia* was written between 1310 and 1314. Petrarca and Boccaccio complete the trio of great fourteenth-century writers. The prestige thus conferred upon Tuscan – specifically Florentine – usage ensured its adoption in the nineteenth century, when political union brought the question of a unified national language to a head. Alessandro Manzoni, who presided over the committee (1868) which took this decision, was himself impelled to rewrite his masterpiece *I Promessi Sposi* in Florentine Tuscan (the original version was in Manzoni's native Lombardian dialect; Tuscan version 1840). *See also* **Romance Languages**.

SCRIPT

Latin alphabet; *j, k, w, x, y* appear in foreign words only. The grave accent is used to mark stress on a final syllable: *città* 'town', *unità* 'unity'. The grave also serves to differentiate between homonyms: cf. *di* 'of', *dì* 'day'; *la* (article), *là* 'there', *si* 'oneself', *sì* 'yes'.

PHONOLOGY

The Florentine standard inventory is given.

Consonants

stops: p, b, t, d, k, g; labialized /k/: [k°]
affricates: ts, dz, tʃ, dʒ
fricatives: f, v, s/z, ʃ
nasals: m, n, ɲ, (ŋ)
lateral and flap: l, ʎ, r
semi-vowel: j, w

/ɲ/ is notated as *gn*: e.g. *ogni* 'each' = /ɔɲi/; /k/ is notated as *c*/*ch*; /w/ is notated as *uo*: *uomo* 'man' = /wɔmo/, or *ua*: *acqua* 'water' = /akwa/. The letter *z* is unvoiced /c/ or voiced /dz/: e.g. *zucchero* /tsukɛrɔ/ 'sugar'; *zelo* /dzɛlo/ 'zeal'. The distinction may be phonemic. *c* + *e*/*i* is /tʃ/; with hard vowels, *c* is /k/; similarly, *g* + *e*/*i* is /dʒ/: thus *cena* 'supper' is /tʃe:na/; *giro* 'circle' is /dʒi:ro/.

To preserve the /k/ value of *c*, and the /g/ value of *g* before soft vowels, *h* is inserted: *chi* /ki:/ 'who?'; *ghiaccio* /gijatʃo/ 'ice'.

/ʎ/ is notated as *gl*: *gli* /ʎi:/ 'to him'.

Vowels

i, e, ɛ, a, ɔ, o, u

/e, ɛ/ and /o, ɔ/ contrast in stressed syllables. Typically, Italian words end in vowels.

Stress

Stress is frequently on the penultimate syllable, but there are many exceptions: e.g. the third person singular past definite is always stressed on the final, as are many words marked with final grave: e.g. *virtù*, *caffè*, etc. Antepenultimate stress appears in infinitives like *vèndere* 'to sell', in the third person plural present indicative form (*màndano* 'they send'), and in many words like *mèdico* 'doctor', *àngelo* 'angel', *piròscafo* 'steamer'.

MORPHOLOGY AND SYNTAX

Italian has two genders and two numbers.

Noun

Nominal endings are, up to a point, coded for gender: e.g. most nouns in *-o* are masculine with plural in *-i*: e.g. *il bambino* 'the child' – *i bambini*; and most nouns in *-a* are feminine with plural in *-e*: e.g. *la stella* 'the star' – *le stelle.* These categories are not exclusive, however: cf. *la mano* 'the hand', pl. *le mani*; *il poeta* 'the poet', pl. *i poeti.*

Most nouns in *-e* are masculine: e.g. *il fiume* 'the river' – *i fiumi*, and all in *-zione*, *-gione*, *-udine* are feminine.

There is no declensional system; syntactic relationships are expressed by prepositions which typically coalesce with the articles: e.g.

a 'to' + *il* → *al*: similarly, *ai*, *agli*, *alla*, *alle*;
in 'in' + *il* → *nel*: similarly, *nei*, *negli*, *nella*, *nelle*;
con 'with' + *il* → *col*: similarly, *coi*, *cogli*, *colla*, *colle.*

ARTICLES

The definite article is marked for gender and number: masc. *il* – *i*; fem. *la* – *le.* Before vocalic initial, both *il* and *la* become *l'*; *lo* is the form taken by the masculine article before such frequent initials as /ɲ/ and *s* + consonant: conditions which also change the plural *i* to *gli*: e.g. *lo squillo* 'ringing', *gli scopi* 'the aims'.

The indefinite article is masc. *un*(*o*), fem. *un*(*a*), with pl. forms: masc. *dei*/*degli*, fem. *delle.*

Adjective

The adjective agrees in gender and number with the noun, which it may precede or follow; some adjectives, e.g. of nationality, colour, always follow. A few very common adjectives have shortened forms used before masculine nouns beginning with a consonant (subject to the same constraints as those affecting the use of the definite article): e.g. *un bel dì* 'a fine day'; *un bello specchio* 'a beautiful mirror'.

COMPARATIVE

più + *di*: e.g. *Questa ragazza e più bella di quella* 'This girl is prettier than that one.'

The customary suppletive forms are found with very common adjectives: *buono* 'good' – *migliore*; *cattivo* 'bad' – *peggiore*; *poco* 'little' – *meno*; *grande* 'big' – *maggiore.*

Pronoun

The Italian pronominal system has (a) independent forms, showing a formal/informal distinction in the second and third persons. Thus, second person singular *tu* is informal, contrasting with *voi* 'you' (sing. or. pl. informal). In the third person formal *egli*/*ella* are distinguished from informal *lui*/*lei*; the plural of both is *loro.* The form chosen as the most acceptable for polite address, however, is *Lei* (sing.), pl. *Loro* with accusative *La*: *La vedremo domani* 'We shall see you tomorrow', though *voi* is acceptable, especially in the south.

Secondly (b) sets of disjunctive and conjunctive pronouns, the latter sub-divided into accusative and dative forms. Thus:

		Singular			*Plural*		
independent:		1 io	2 tu	3 lui, lei	1 noi	2 voi	3 loro
disjunctive:		me	te	lui, lei	noi	voi	loro
conjunctive:	acc.	mi	ti	lo, la	ci	vi	li, le
	dat.	mi/me	ti/te	gli/glie/le	ci/ce	vi/ve	loro

The *-e* forms are used before *lo, la, li, le,* and *ne* 'of it' (= Fr. *en*): e.g. *gli* + *lo* → *glielo*: *glielo diedi* 'I gave it to him'.

Conjunctive forms follow an infinitive, whose object they form: e.g. *volevo dar.glie.lo* 'I wanted to give it to him'.

Pronominal complexes, consisting of *si* → *se* or *ci* → *ce* + *la* or *ne,* follow certain verbs: e.g. *dar.se.la a gambe* 'to take to one's heels'; *metter.ce.la* 'to do one's utmost'.

POSSESSIVE ADJECTIVES

These are accompanied by the article, precede the noun, and show number and gender, except *loro* 'your/s', 'their/s', which is invariable: e.g. *il mio, la mia, i miei, le mie,* etc. but *il Loro, la Loro, i Loro,* etc.

DEMONSTRATIVE PRONOUN/ADJECTIVE

questo 'this', *quel(lo)* 'that'. These are marked for gender and number: e.g. *questo/quel ragazzo* 'this/that boy'; *quella ragazza* 'that girl'.

INTERROGATIVE PRONOUN

chi 'who?'; *che* 'what?'

RELATIVE PRONOUN

il quale, la quale, i quali, le quali; *che* (indeclinable): e.g. *la ragazza che vedi* 'the girl (whom) you see'; *il libro che sto leggendo* 'the book which I am reading'.

Numerals

1–10: *uno/una, due, tre, quattro, cinque, sei, sette, otto, nove, dieci*; 11 *undici*; 12 *dodici*; 13 *tredici*; 20 *venti*; 30 *trenta*; 40 *quaranta*; 100 *cento.*

Verb

Italian verbs may be conveniently divided into three conjugations: (a) verbs in *-are*; (b) verbs *-ere*; and (c) verbs in *-ire*. Verbs in *-e* are further sub-divided into two classes, depending on whether the stem or the ending is stressed: e.g. *chièdere* 'to close'; *sedère* 'to sit'. Verbs in *-i* may be regular or may take a stem augment, *-isc-*, e.g. *finisco* 'I finish': 3rd person *finisce*, plural *finiscono.* The *-sc-* augment does not appear in the 1st and 2nd persons plural: *finiamo,* *finite*. An important group of *-e* verbs has irregular forms in the past definite: e.g. *prendere* 'take' – *presi*.

Verbs are transitive or intransitive, and there are indicative, imperative, and subjunctive moods. Both the indicative and the subjunctive have present and imperfect tenses; the indicative has in addition a past definite, a future, and a conditional. The non-finite forms include the infinite, a gerund, and present and past participles. The gerund and the past participle combine with auxiliaries such as *stare* 'be', *avere* 'have', *essere* 'be' to form composite tenses: e.g. a progressive: *sto scrivendo* 'I am writing'; *stavo dicendo* 'I was saying'; and a perfect: *abbiamo mangiato* 'we have eaten'; *sono andato* 'I went'.

The basic verbs of motion – *andare* 'go', *venire* 'come', *partire* 'depart', *entrare* 'enter', etc. – are always conjugated with *essere*. Some verbs expressing motion, e.g. *correre* 'run', may be conjugated with either *avere* or *essere*, depending on sense.

SPECIMEN PARADIGM

1st conjugation verb, *mandare* 'to send':

Indicative mood:

present: *mand-o, -i, -a*; *-iamo, -ate, -ano* (stress on penultimate syllable, except in third person plural where it moves to the antepenultimate);
imperfect: *mandav-o, -i, -a*; *-amo, -ate, -ano*;
past definite: *mandai, mandaste, mando*; *mand-ammo, -aste, -arono*;
future: *mander-o, -i, -a*; *-emo, -ete, -anno*;
conditional: *mandere-i, -sti, -bbe*; *-mmo, -ste, -bbero*.

Subjunctive mood:

present: *mand-i, -i, -i; -iamo, -iate, -ino*;
imperfect: *mandass-i, -i, -e*; *-imo, mandaste, mandassero*;
imperative mood: *manda, mandi*; *mandiamo, mandate, mandino*;
gerund: *mandando*; past participle: *mandato*.

PASSIVE

Can be made analytically by means of such auxiliaries as *essere, venire, andare* followed by the past participle: e.g. *Il manoscritto è andato perduto* 'The manuscript has been lost'; *Le città vengono bombardate* 'The cities are being bombed.'

Wherever possible, Italian prefers the impersonal construction with *si*: e.g. *Si parla inglese qui* 'English is spoken here.'

NEGATION

The general negating particle is *non* preceding the verb; negation may be duplicated or triplicated: e.g. *Non voglio niente* 'I don't want anything' (lit. 'nothing'); *Non lo vuole nessuno* 'No one wants it' (lit. 'doesn't want').

Prepositions

Simple, e.g. *di*, *a*, *con*, *per*, etc.; or compound: *davanti a* 'in the presence of', 'in front of'; *di lato a* 'beside'; *al di sopra di* 'above'. As in French, certain verbs take specific prepositions before a following infinitive: e.g. *dimenticare* ***di*** 'to forget', *cominciare* ***a*** 'to begin to': e.g. *mi sono dimenticato* ***di*** *avvertirti* 'I forgot to let you know'; *cominciare* ***ad*** *andare* 'to start walking'.

Word order

Depending on emphasis, SOV, VOS, VSO are all possible.

1 1 Al principio,
prima che Dio creasse il mondo,
c'era colui che è « la Parola ».
Egli era con Dio;
Egli era Dio.
2 Egli era al principio con Dio.
3 Per mezzo di lui Dio ha creato ogni cosa.
Senza di lui non ha creato nulla.
4 Egli era vita
e la vita era luce per gli uomini.
5 Quella luce risplende nelle tenebre
e le tenebre non l'hanno vinta.
6 Dio mandò un uomo:
si chiamava Giovanni.
7 Egli venne come testimone della luce
perché tutti gli uomini,
ascoltandolo,
credessero nella luce.
8 Non era lui, la luce:

ITELMEN

INTRODUCTION

Itelmen was formerly known as Kamchadal. The Itelmen live or lived – they are now virtually extinct – in the Koryak National Okrug in Kamchatka: the ethnonym is *itənmə'n* 'the existent ones', 'the living'. The agglutinative language belongs to the Chukotko-Kamchatkan group, and was unwritten, apart from a brief experimental period in the 1930s.

PHONOLOGY

Consonants

The consonantal inventory is rather more elaborate than those of Chukchi and Koryak. The voiced plosives are missing but /p, t, k, q/ + their palatalized counterparts occur, as does the glottal stop.

fricatives: s, z, x, γ, χ
affricates: tʃ, tʃ′
laterals:
  unvoiced: l′
  voiced: l, l′
nasals: m, n, ɲ, ŋ

Vowels

The vowel system is simple:

i, e, a, ə, o, u

MORPHOLOGY AND SYNTAX

Noun

Nouns are classified as human or non-human. Seven or eight cases are formed; the plural marker is *'n*: *č′ozaq* 'ant', plural *č′oza**kə'n***; final -*č* drops: e.g. *sleč* 'eagle', pl. *sle'n*.

Specimen declension: *wač* 'stone'; singular:

nominative	wač
locative	wač.ank
instrumental	wa.l

dative	wač.anke
ablative	wačan.x'al
comitative	k'wa.čom
causative	wačan.ket

The plural nominative is *wa'n*; locative *wa'nk*, etc.

An adjectival formant is *-laχ*: *atx.laχ* 'white'; *as.laχ* 'high'.

Pronoun

PERSONAL PRONOUN

Sing. 1 *kəmma*, 2 *kəzza*, 3 *'ənna*; pl. 1 *muza'n*, 2 *tuza'n*, 3 *itχ*. These are declined in 14 cases, including an ergative.

INTERROGATIVE PRONOUN

k'e' 'who?', *əŋqa'* 'what?'

Numerals

Only 1–4 have been retained: *kŋiŋ*, *kasχ*, *č'oq*, *č'aaq*.

Verb

Transitive verbs are animate or inanimate.

Monopersonal verbs may be intransitive or transitive non-animate, with six personal forms; polypersonal verbs are transitive animate, with 28 personal forms in each of three moods: indicative, subjunctive, and imperative/optative.

TENSE AND ASPECT

The past-tense marker is Ø; present *-s/z-*; future, *-al'-*. The aspect marker precedes the tense marker: e.g. *-kzo-* is the durative aspect marker, so present tense in durative aspect is marked by *-kzo.s-*. The past imperfective is marked by *-kzo.Ø*; in the past perfective both aspect and tense have the null marker; thus: *t.skə.**kzo.Ø**.čen* 'I was doing something'; *t.skə.**Ø.Ø**čen* 'I did something'; *t.skə.**kzo.s**.čen* 'I do something continually'.

Examples of polypersonal paradigm of *ančpəs* 'to teach someone':

1st person – 2nd	*t.ančp.γen* 'I teach you'
2nd person – 1st	*Ø.ančp.məŋk* 'you teach me'
3rd person – 1st	*Ø.ančp.γomnen* 'he teaches me'
1st plural – 2nd	*n.ančp.γen* 'we teach you'
3rd plural –1st	*n.ančp.γomnen* 'they teach me' *n.ančp.γomne'n* 'they teach us'

NEGATION

Formed analytically, e.g. by means of the negating particle *qam* preceding the sense-verb in the invariable form in *-kaq*: *qam vetatkaq* 'I don't work/did not work'; 'you don't/did not work', etc. Person and tense are inferred from the context.

INFINITIVE

Transitive: *-s*: *ančpə.*s 'to teach someone'; intransitive: *-kə.s*: *vetat.kə.s* 'to work'.

Prepositions

There are no native prepositions, but Itelmen has borrowed a few from Russian.

Word order

SVO, SOV both occur. If S is a personal pronoun, it is in the ergative case: cf. *kmәlvәn tančpčen p'eč* 'I taught the boy', where *kmәlvәn* is the ergative case of *kәmma*, the first person pronoun.

IVRIT

INTRODUCTION

Modern Hebrew, or Ivrit, belongs to the Semito-Hamitic branch of the Afro-Asiatic phylum. The rebirth of Hebrew, as a spoken language, from the literary Hebrew which was used in the Mediterranean area for a thousand years, began in Eastern and Central Europe in the mid-nineteenth century, as the hopes nourished by the Haskalah, the Jewish Enlightenment movement, of assimilation on the basis of shared German–Hebrew/Russian–Hebrew Bildung faded. The decline of Haskalah coincides with the renewed persecution of the Jews in Russia in the 1880s, and with the emergence of Chaim Nachman Bialik (1873–1934), the national Hebrew poet, whose career covers the intermediary period between the end of Haskalah and the onset of the Palestinian period (1924–1947). The Palestinian period saw a vigorous campaign for the renewal of Hebrew as the spoken and written language of a new Jewish society centred on Palestine. Notable writers include Abraham Shlonsky and Uri Zvi Greenberg. With the creation of the State of Israel in 1948, this ideal was realized, as Hebrew became once again a national language, spoken and written within its own national frontiers. (*See* **Hebrew**, **Yiddish**.)

Essentially, Ivrit is the Hebrew of the *Torah*, plus enormous lexical expansion and many phonological and morphological modifications. These modifications are more or less radical, depending on the register of speech or writing. Thus, formal literary style may use forms approximating to Classical Hebrew, which are quite inappropriate in colloquial parlance. For example, the rules governing the alternation of consonants are observed in literary style, ignored in the colloquial. In step with this division, two varieties of orthography are in use: *xaser*, conservative, i.e. classical, spelling without the pointing; and *male*, used in the press, with the vowels /o/ and /u/ written with *vav*, /i/ with *yod*. The pronunciation represents a compromise between Ashkenazi (Northern and Eastern) and Sephardic (Southern, specifically of Spain) models.

The thousands of new items with which the Hebrew lexicon has been enriched are in part derived from Semitic roots, in part loanwords.

SCRIPT

Classical Hebrew basis.

PHONOLOGY

Consonants

stops: p, b, t, d, k, g, ʔ
affricates: ts
fricatives: f, v, s, ʃ, z, x, h
nasals: m, n
lateral and flap: l, r, ʀ
semi-vowel: j

Ivrit has a very extensive range of initial and medial clusters: e.g. /gz, cd, pc, pg, cx/. Certain clusters are realized with the help of a schwa vowel: thus, *nd-* /n^{c}d/. /tʃ, dʒ/ occur in loanwords.

Vowels

i, ɪ, e, a, o/ɔ, u, ə
diphthongs: /oa/ = [oə], /ua, ea, ia/

MORPHOLOGY AND SYNTAX

Noun

Ivrit has two genders, masculine and feminine; and three numbers, singular, dual, and plural. The dual is used mainly for naturally paired objects: the ending is *-aim*: *eynaim* 'two eyes'; and units of time: *šnataim* 'two years'. The dual takes the plural form of the verb. The masculine plural ending is *-im*, fem. *-ot*: e.g. *xaver* 'comrade', pl. *xaverim*. There are a few exceptions, e.g. *'avot* 'fathers'.

The definite article is *ha-*.

CONSTRUCT FORMS

Many nouns governed by a following noun, or by a personal pronominal suffix, undergo a kind of stretto modification: thus, *šalom* 'peace', 'welfare', ***šlom*** *ha.mišpaxa* 'the welfare of the family'; *bayit* 'house', ***bet*** *ha.sefer* 'house of the book' ('school'); *braxa* 'blessing', ***birkat****.i* 'my blessing'; *'erec* 'country', *'****arc****.i* 'my country' (in *birkati*, the *-t-* is the Semitic feminine ending which reappears in the construct).

The construct, which is the natural Semitic way of expressing the genitive relationship, is giving way (as in Maltese) to an analytical construction with the particle *šel*: e.g. *ha.bayit* ***šelo*** 'his house', *ha.bayit šel Dov* 'Dov's house'.

ACCUSATIVE

A definite object after a transitive verb is signalled by the particle *et*: e.g. *ten.li et.ha.sefer* 'give me the book'; *tisgor et.ha.delet* 'close the door' (*sefer* 'book'; *delet* 'door').

Adjective

The attributive adjective follows the noun, and agrees with it in gender and number, i.e. the adjective will normally add *-a* for the feminine, *-im* for the masculine plural, *-ot* for the feminine plural. The article is resumed: e.g. *ha.binyan* ***ha****.gadol* 'the big building'; pl. *ha.binyanim ha.gədolim*. Adjectives have construct forms.

COMPARISON

A comparative is made with *yoter* + *mi* 'from': e.g. *Dov yoter xazak mi.Moše* 'Dov is stronger than Mose.'

Pronoun

The basic personal forms are followed here by their objective and possessive suffix forms:

	Singular				*Plural*		
1		ani	oti	-i	anu	otanu	-enu
2	masc.	ata	otxa	-xa	atem	etxem	-xem
	fem.	at	otax	-ex	aten	etxen	-xen
3	masc.	hu	oto	-o	hem	otam	-am
	fem.	hi	ota	-a	hen	otan	-an

An alternative set of objective forms is affixed to the verb. These are almost identical to the possessive forms; the first person singular is *-ni* instead of *-i*.

The possessive forms are added to nouns in the construct: e.g. *Ma šlom.xa?* 'How is your health?' (to a man); *ma šlom.ex?* (to a woman).

Objective forms: cf. *yekabel otxa* = *yekablexa* 'he will receive you (masc.)'.

DEMONSTRATIVE PRONOUN/ADJECTIVE

ze (masc.), *zot* (fem.), pl. *'ele* (common), following the noun, and taking definite article: e.g. *ha.sefer ha.ze* 'this book'; *ha.anišim ha.'ele* 'these people'.

INTERROGATIVE PRONOUN

mi 'who?'; *ma* 'what?'

RELATIVE PRONOUN

Classical Hebrew *ašer* is represented in Ivrit by *še-* prefixed to the following verbal: *ha.yeled še.diber ivrit* 'the boy who spoke Hebrew'.

Numerals

Ivrit has two sets of cardinal numbers:

1. A set with formally feminine endings: this set functions, however, as the masculine set, used in the enumeration of masculine referents: cf. *šloša batim* 'three houses', where the noun *bait* is masculine, while the adjectival ending *-a* is feminine. This set is also used for non-referential counting. It runs, 1–10, as follows: *exad, šnaim, šloša, arbaa, xamiša, šiša, šiv'a, šmona, tiš'a, asara*.
2. The formally masculine set functions as the feminine set, used to enumerate feminine referents: cf. *šaloš oniot* '3 ships' (*onia* 'ship' is

feminine). This set runs: *axat, štaim, šaloš, arba, xameš, šeš, ševa, šmone, teša, eser.*

Certain numerals have alternative feminine forms, e.g. *šlošet ha.-* 'three of...', *arba'at ha.-* 'four of...', *xamešet ha.-* 'five of...': *šlošet ha.oniot* 'the three ships'.

The teens are expressed by construct forms preceding *esre*: *axat esre* 11, *šteym esre* 12, *šloš esre*, 13, etc.

Apart from *exad/axat*, which follows the noun, the cardinals precede it. The two sets tend to be used interchangeably.

20–100: the decades take the *-im* plural ending: *esrim* 20, *šlošim* 30, *arbaim* 40, etc. Following the decade markers the numerals 1–9 are marked for gender: e.g. *esrim ve-xamiša sfarim* '25 books', where the feminine form *xamiša* is used with the masculine noun *sefer* 'book', pl. *sfarim*.

100 is *mea* (invariable).

Verb

As in other Semitic languages, the radical is usually a triliteral, though two- and four-literal radicals abound.

Formally, the aspectual system of the Classical Hebrew verb is retained, but this is construed in Ivrit as a tense system with past- and future-tense forms. There is also a present tense formed on different lines. The derived versions of the stem (the binyanim, *see* **Hebrew**) are also retained.

THE TENSE SYSTEM

Past tense: stem + affix, marked for person and number, additionally, in second and third persons singular and plural, for gender.

Future tense: prefix + stem + affix (in second and third masculine/feminine plural and second feminine singular).

Present: *me-* is prefixed to the masculine singular imperative; marked for gender and number.

As illustration, the tense system of *DBR* 'to speak':

Imperative: masc. sing. *daber*; fem. sing. *dabri*, masc. pl. *dabru*, fem. pl. *daberna*.

			Singular	*Plural*
future:	1		**a**. daber	**ne**.daber
	2	masc.	**te**.daber	**te**.dabr.**u**
		fem.	**te**.dabr.**i**	**te**.daber.**na**
	3	masc.	**ye**.daber	**ye**.dabr.**u**
		fem.	**te**.daber	**te**.daber.**na**

past:	1		dibar.**ti**		dibar.**nu**
	2	masc.	dibar.**ta**		dibar.**tem**
		fem.	dibar.**t**		dibar.**ten**
	3	masc.	diber		dibr.**u**
		fem.	dibr.**a**		dibr.**u**
present:		masc. sing.	**me**daber	masc. pl.	**me**dabr.**im**
		fem. sing.	**me**dabe**ret**	fem. pl.	**me**.dabr.**ot**

THE BINYANIM

For more detail, *see* **Hebrew**. Here are some examples of Ivrit usage.

(a) *nif'al*: the prefix is *ni-*: the form expresses the passive or intransitive of the *pa'al* (active) form: *patax* 'he opened' – *niftax* '...was opened'; *moxer* 'he sells' – *nimkar* '...is sold'; *šalxu oti la.malon* 'they sent me to the hotel'; *nišlaxti la.malon* 'I was sent to the hotel'.
(b) *hif'il*: the prefix is *h-*; *hif'il* is itself the causative binyan of *pa'al*; it is used to form causatives: e.g. *šama'ti* 'I heard' – *hišma'ati* 'I proclaimed'; *gadal* 'he grew' – *higdil* 'he enlarged (something)'.
(c) *hitpa'el*: the prefix is *hit-*, with extensive assimilation at junctures. The form makes intransitive verbs from transitives, with extension to passive sense: e.g. *šina* 'he changed something' – *hištana* 'he changed' (intrans.); *šiamem* 'he bored someone' – *hištaamamti* 'I was bored'.

There are several examples in the above of consonant alternation, involving *b/v*, *p/f*, *k/x*. In this context, the alternation affects first and second radicals. The general rule is that initial *b*, *p*, *k* become *v*, *f*, *x* in non-initial position and in specific phonological environments:

***p**tax* 'open!' (imperative) – *ti**f**tax* 'you will open';
***b**ikašti* 'I asked' – *le.vakeš* 'to ask';
***p**ne* 'turn!' (imperative) – *ti**f**ne* 'you will turn'.

NEGATION

The general marker is *lo*: e.g. *hu yaqia maxar* 'he'll arrive tomorrow'; *hu lo yaqia maxar* 'he'll not arrive tomorrow'. *'eyn* negates the existential verb *yeš* 'there is/are', and the present: e.g. *ani medaber* 'I speak' – *'eyneni medaber* 'I do not speak'; *eyn lak adam še.eyn lo šaa*, lit. 'there is not to you (*lak*) a man (*adam*) that (*še*) has not his hour (*šaa*)', i.e. 'no man but has his hour'.

Prepositions

These take the personal possessive affixes: e.g. with *avur* 'for': *avuri* 'for me', *avurenu* 'for us'. Some fuse with the article, e.g. *le* 'to': *le* + *ha* → *la*, e.g. *la.doar ha.merkazi* 'to the main post-office'.

Word order

SVO is basic; a pronominal S is, of course, not always necessary.

1,2לפני שנברא העולם היה המשיח עם אלוהים. הוא היה עם
אלוהים מבראשית, והוא עצמו אלוהים.• 3הוא ברא את כל הקיים — אין
דבר שלא נברא על-ידו. 4יש בו חיי נצח, וחיים אלה העניקו אור לבני-
האדם. 5חייו הם האור הזורח והמאיר בחשכה, והחשכה אינה יכולה
להתגבר על אור זה.
6,7אלוהים שלח אדם בשם יוחנן להעיד שישוע המשיח הוא האור
האמיתי, כדי שכולם יאמינו בו. 8,9יוחנן עצמו לא היה האור; הוא רק
נשלח לזהות את האור האמיתי שבא לעולם כדי להאיר לכל בני-האדם.

JAPANESE, LITERARY

INTRODUCTION

The Neolithic culture known as the Joomon lasted about 6,000 years in Japan, to be followed in the third century BC by the Yayoi neolithic culture, which lasted about 500 years. According to one school of thought, the Joomon people were the Aboriginal inhabitants of Japan, and the ancestors of the Ainu people. The archaeological evidence is not conclusive, however, and little or nothing is known about either the Joomon or the Yayoi language. What is clear is that Old Japanese, as it first appears in the eighth-century documents, is characterized by a sparse phonological system, a polysyllabic lexical structure, and an agglutinative morphology, features which qualify the language equally well for inclusion in either the Altaic or the Malayo-Polynesian areal type. Japanese philologists are much concerned with identifying 'Yamato' words – i.e. pristine Japanese words – as the core of their language. As attested, however, even the oldest Japanese stratum does not seem to be entirely free of Chinese loanwords.

PERIODIZATION OF CLASSICAL JAPANESE

1. *c.* AD 400–794: this is the Nara period, including the 180 years when the Yamato court had its seat in the then new city of Nara. To this period belong the oldest known works in Japanese – the *Man'yooshuu* (an anthology of about 4½ thousand short poems) and the *Kojiki* ('Record of Ancient Things'), a collection of myths and pseudo-history. Both of these works were compiled in the eighth century.

2. In 794 the court moved to Heian. The Heian period, which lasted until 1191, saw the great efflorescence of Classical Japanese literature. A major formal innovation was the introduction of narrative prose for fiction and the essay/diary. At its best, this literature is often of extraordinary charm and refinement: it is enough to mention the *Genji Monogatari* and the *Murasaki Shikibu Nikki*, both by the Lady Murasaki Shikibu (*c.* 1000) and the delightful 'Pillow Book' (*Makura no Sooshi*) by the Lady Sei Shoonagon, who was at the Heian court between 990 and 1000.

It was in the Heian period that the gradual bifurcation into written and spoken registers of Japanese made itself felt; though it can still be said that the language of the Genji Monogatari, for example, is often quite close to contemporary educated speech.

The written register, however, crystallized into *bungo*, the literary Japanese language, which was to endure as a kind of katherevousa from the eleventh to the twentieth century: used not only by writers and scholars, but also for governmental, legislative, legal, and scientific purposes. As regards literature in the Japanese Middle Ages, mention should be made of the various *monogatari* ('about this and that') collections: e.g. *Senki Monogatari*, the war tales of the thirteenth to fifteenth centuries, culminating in the *Heike Monogatari*, the saga of the doom-laden Taira dynasty; and the historical tales of the *Rekishi Monogatari*, all of these in a more or less formal *bungo*. Three outstanding figures are: the Noo dramatist Zeami (1363–1443), the Kabuki playwright Chikamatsu Monzaemon (seventeenth/eighteenth century), and the seventeenth-century poet and diarist Matsuo Basho.

Two key figures in the Meiji period (nineteenth century), who played an important part in the incipient swing away from the use of *bungo* must be mentioned. Fukuzawa Yukichi (1835–1901) was instrumental in introducing the emergent middle classes to rationalized – i.e. non-traditional – ways of thought. His *Gakumon no susume* 'The Encouragement of Learning' (1872–76), defining a rationalized and liberalized society, was written in a greatly simplified style, expressly designed to be accessible to the middle classes. Three million copies were sold.

Fukuzawa prepared the ground for Futabatei Shimei (1864–1905) whose novel *Ukigumo*, 'Floating Cloud' (1887–89), marked a decisive break with tradition. For the first time in Japanese literature, everyday themes drawn from everyday middle-class existence were treated in colloquial language. Futabatei was strongly influenced by the Russian novelists, particularly Turgenev and Gogol.

SCRIPT

See **Script** at end of article.

PHONOLOGY

Consonants

Heian Japanese had the following consonantal inventory:

stops: p, b, t, d, k, g
fricatives: (f) – h, s, z
nasals: m, n
flap: r
semi-vowels: j (usually notated as *y*), w

Vowels

In its earliest stages, the language had an eight-vowel system consisting of /i, e, a, o, u/, plus allophones of [i, e, o], which are notated in the literature on Old Japanese as *ï*, *ë*, *ö*. These seem to have been lower, less tense than *i*, *e*, *o*. Many words now written with *o*, for example, had *ö* in Old Japanese: cf.

tökörö 'place', Modern Standard Japanese *tokoro*; *kökörö* 'heart', Modern Standard Japanese *kokoro*.

By the late Heian period, this eight-vowel system had been reduced to five, with the reduction of /i/ï/ to /i/, /e/ë/ to /e/, /o/ö/ to /o/.

Combining the consonantal and vocalic rows, we get a grid of open syllables which provide the phonemes of Japanese. In early Old Japanese there were about a hundred such syllables, reduced in Heian Japanese to about 70: e.g. for the series based on *k*, *ka – ki – ku – ke – ko*.

MORPHOLOGY AND SYNTAX

Japanese words were traditionally divided into two categories: indeclinable words (including nouns, pronouns, particles, adverbs, conjunctions, interjections) and declinable words (comprising verbs and adjectives). There are no articles; gender is absent.

Noun

NUMBER

The noun is neutral as to number: *kaze* 'wind(s)', *michi* 'road(s)', *yama* 'mountain(s)'. Certain pluralizers are available, e.g. *-tachi*, *-domo*, *-ra*; *kami.tachi*, 'gods'.

Since the noun is uninflected, syntactic relationships have to be expressed by means of particles. The main case particles are: *nö/no*, *ga*, *wo*, *ni*, *to*, *tsu*, *he*, *yori*, *made*.

nö > *no* is the most frequently used case marker, occurring over 5,000 times in the *Man'yooshuu*, for example. In Classical Japanese it functions as an attributive/genitive particle:

tsuki no to no hito ga 'the people of the capital (*to*) of the moon'
tsuki no yo 'a moonlit night'
mukashi no tera 'ancient temples'
umi.be nö jadö ni 'in a cottage on the sea-shore'
ashibiki no yama no anata ni 'on the other side of the feet-tiring mountain' (more on *anata* and *ashibiki* in **Pronoun** and **Adjective**, below)
Hito no kuru wo shiru 'I know a person's coming', i.e. 'I know that someone is coming.'

ga: originally a genitive particle, and consistently used as such, *ga* came to be used as a conjunctive particle 'coordinating but not necessarily contrasting two propositions' (Sansom 1928). Thus, as genitive after pronoun:

a.ga ko tobasitsu 'my child flew away' (i.e. died)
kimi ga kokoro 'your heart'

Comparison of *no* and *ga*: Sansom gives the excellent example:

Masamune no katama 'a Masamune sword'
Masamune ga katama 'Masamune's sword'

wo: generally used throughout the history of Japanese in both registers as a particle marking the object of a verbal proposition, i.e. the accusative. Originally, it seems to have been an emphatic marker or exclamatory particle, and as such is frequent in the *Man'yooshuu*:

terishi tsuku.yo wo! 'lo, the shining moonlight!', VII, 112 (*teru* 'to shine')
Tomo no urami wo! 'Oh for the shore of Tomo!', VII, 116
imo matsu are wo! 'behold me waiting for my mistress!'

In this sense *wo* is notated in the *Man'yooshuu* as 乎 the Chinese exclamatory particle *hŭ*.

wo as accusative marker: *hito no kuru wo matsu* 'to await the coming of someone'.

ni: this particle is used in a dative, locative, and instrumental sense; prefixed to the predicative verb *aru*/*ari*, it functions as a copula: *imo mo ware mo hitotsu nareba ka mo* 'perhaps it is because my sister and I are really one person' (see Waley 1946: 21), where *nareba* is the concessive form from *nari*: 'because... is/are'. Cf. *hito no ko yuye ni* 'because of a child of man' (Waley 1946: 20).

ni with locative:

aki no no-hara ni 'on the autumn moor'
yume ni mitsu 'saw in a dream'

ni marking agent in instrumental:

haha ko ni nakaru 'the mother was wept-for by the child'
hana ni mai 'dancing because of the flowers'

Other particles such as the terminative *made* and the ablative *yori* are used much as in Modern Standard Japanese.

Compounds are readily formed: e.g. *yama.bito* 'mountain people' (*hito* → *bito*); *matsu.kaze* 'wind in the pines'.

Adjective

There are two categories of adjective – inflected and uninflected. Inflected adjectives are conjugated on the following model: stem *yo-* 'good':

predicative: *yo.shi*;
conjunctive: *yo.ku*;
imperfect: *yo.ku* (i.e. not as yet realized);
attributive: *yo.ki*;
perfect: *yo.kere* < (*yo.kare*).

Examples:

predicative: *kokoro yoshi* '(his) heart is-good';
attributive: *yoki kokoro* 'a good heart';
conjunctive: *yo.ku neru* 'to sleep well';

imperfect: *samu.ku mo* 'even if it turns out to be cold';
perfect: *ashi.kari.shi hito* 'someone who was bad'.

The uninflected adjective, consisting of stem plus suffix (e.g. *-ka*, *-ge*) requires the presence of a verbal form, e.g. *naru*:

shizu.ka naru tokoro 'a quiet place'
kono tokoro wa shizu.ka nari 'this place is quiet'
shizu.ka nari.shi tokoro 'a place that was quiet'
shizu.ka narazu 'it is not quiet'

Uninflected adjectives are also provided by a small group of honorific (closed) prefixes such as *oo-* and *mi-*:

oo.kimi 'great king'
mi.yako 'capital city'
mi.kado 'august gateway' > 'Majesty'
mi.nema.shiki 'performing august slumber' (i.e. 'asleep')

goto- denotes similarity:

nagaruru gotoshi 'seem(s) to flow'
mukashi no hito wo ai-miru gotoshi 'like meeting face to face with the men of yesteryear'
oni no gotoki nari 'they are like devils'

A favourite stylistic device in early Japanese poetry is the *makura-kotoba*, 'pillow-word', the fixed epithet. For example, in the *Man'yooshuu*, Prince Ootsu describes the mountain where he has an assignment as *ashi.biki no yama* 'foot-dragging mountain', i.e. 'tiring to the feet' (*biki* is from *hiku* 'to drag'). A city appears as *momo.shiki* 'having a hundred towers'. A wood is *momo.ki.nasu* 'where a hundred trees grow'. A wanderer who has to sleep rough says he is *kusa.makura tabi ni* 'on a "grass-as-pillow" journey' (*tabi* = 'journey'). Elsewhere in the *Man'yooshuu* obeisance is done to *taka.hikaru waga hi no mi.ko* 'our august Son of the high-shining Sun'.

The *makura-kotoba* is usually of four, five, or six syllables. All the above examples are from the *Man'yooshuu*.

Pronoun

True personal pronouns appear in the language of the Nara period, and two or three of these continue to be used in the Heian classics. By the Edo period all had been ousted by the periphrastic forms which are now characteristic of standard Japanese, e.g. *wata(ku)shi* and *anata*: the former seems to refer to an interior locus of identity self > 1st person; *anata* means 'on that (other) side' > 2nd person.

The Nara forms are *a(re)*, *wa(re)* for 1st person sing./pl. and *na(re)* for 2nd. No 3rd person pronoun is definitely attested, though a form *shi* has been tentatively identified.

The particle *ga*, now used as a subject marker, functions in the early language as a possessive particle: *(w)a.ga* 'my', 'our': *waga yado wa* 'as for my house'; *waga* persists in Modern Standard Japanese. Cf.

> a.ga ko tobasitsu 'my child flew away' (i.e. 'died')
> wa.ga imo(ko) 'my little sister', i.e. 'my mistress'
> ware wa sabishi 'I am lonely'

The Japanese tendency to avoid the use of 2nd person pronouns is already present in the Nara language, and may reflect an original *tabu*; *nare* is, however, used. Thus the Lady of Sakanoye (eighth century) complains that *na wo to wa wo Hito zo saku-naru* 'it is other people who have separated you and me'. Cf. *na wo mireba* 'when I look at you'; *na.bito* 'thou-person' also occurs. The respectful *kimi* 'Sir', 'Lord' can be used for 2nd and 3rd person.

The personal pronoun was relatively unimportant in Literary Japanese as verbs were themselves so coded for varying degrees of respect and deference that deixis was usually manifest: deferential expressions were naturally first-person orientated, while respectful or honorific language could only imply a second person addressed, or a third person referred to. *See* **Honorific language**, below.

DEMONSTRATIVE PRONOUN

Proximate *ko*(*re*), distal *so*(*re*). The demonstrative adjective is *ko.no*, *so.no*; proximate *ko*(*re*), distal *so*(*re*).

INTERROGATIVE PRONOUN

tare 'who?', *nani* 'what?'

> ko wo tare ka shiru? 'who knows this?' (*Man'yooshuu*)
> nani no saga zo mo? 'of what can this be an omen?'

RELATIVE PRONOUN

None; for formation of relative clause, *see* **Verb**, below.

Numerals

The earliest numerals show an ablaut relationship with their doubles: 1 *pitö*, 2 *puta*; 3 *mi*, 6 *mu*; 4 *yö*, 8 *ya*; this does not apply to *itsu* 5, and *nana* 7. The number 9 is represented by the rarely attested form *kokonotsu*; 10 is *töwo*. The teens are formed by adding the word *mari* (= plus) to *töwo*, followed by the relevant digit: e.g. *töwo.mari.yö* 14.

Verb

The verb has neither person nor number. Stems are not 'conjugated' in the sense in which this word is used with regard to, for example, Indo-European languages. They are modulated in two stages:

Stage 1: stems are differentiated into six aspectual/modal bases: e.g. from the stem *yuk-* 'to go', the six bases are (1) *yuk**u***, (2) *yuk**u***, (3) *yuk**i***, (4) *yuk**a**-*, (5) *yuke*, (6) *yuke*. Not all verbs make their bases in the same way; thus, for *tabe-*

'to eat' the series is *tab**u***, *tab**uru***, *tabe*, *tabe-*, *tab**ure***, *tabe*. These bases have specific functions:

1. Base 1 is predicative/affirmative: *yuku* 'go/goes', *kaku* 'write/s', e.g. *waga uma nadum**u*** 'my horse stumbles'; *kari ga kaer**u*** 'wild geese are returning'; *hototogisu nak**u*** 'the cuckoo(s) is/are singing'.
2. Base 2 provides the attributive form which precedes nouns and is used in the formation of relative clauses: e.g. *ware no yuk**u** tokoro* 'the place I go to'; *waga omo**u** hito wa* 'the person I care for'.
3. This base provides the conjunctive or suspended form, used to hold verbs in a serial utterance until the last verb, which alone can be inconclusive, i.e. predicative, form (base 1). (Cf. the role of the participle in Altaic languages, especially **Turkic languages**.) A simple example: *Hana saki tori nak**u*** 'While flowers bloom the birds sing.'
4. Imperfective base: action has not taken place or will not. Hence it is also the base used for the negative. This is the only base that can never be used independently; it is always followed by a temporal or modal particle: e.g. *tabe.mu* 'will eat'; *tabezu* 'does not eat'; *tabe.ba* 'if... eat(s)'; *waga koromo iro ni simete.mu* 'my garment will be dyed'.
5. The perfective form: usually followed by *ba* or *do*(*mo*): e.g. *kake*/*kakeba* 'has/have written'.
6. Imperative (rare).

Stage 2: the first four primary bases take auxiliary verbal suffixes expressing tense, voice, plus certain nuances. Some of these suffixes have already been seen in the illustrations to base 4, above: *mu*, *zu*, *ba*. There is a distinction here, however: some suffixes, e.g. *mu* and *zu*, are themselves declinable, and are therefore subject to the primary modulation; *ba* is not declinable.

Suffixes following the verbal stem as modulated for base are coded for aspect, tense, or modality. They can be divided (e.g. by Sansom) into (a) suffixes denoting affirmed realization, i.e. related to the perfective aspect: e.g. *-tsu*, *-tari*, *-nu*; (b) past-tense suffixes, e.g. *-keri*, *-ni*; (c) future-tense suffixes, e.g. *-mu*, *-meri*; (d) suffixes expressing conjecture, likelihood: e.g. *-beshi*, negated by *-maji*; *-ramu*, *-rashi*.

Examples:

-tsu has attributive *-tsuru*, conjunctive *-te*:

hototogisu naki.tsuru kata wo naga.mureba
'when I gaze towards the place (*kata*) where the cuckoo sang' (O'Neill 1968: 125)

hani saki.te tori naku
'flowers having blossomed, the birds sing'

-tari (< *-te ari*) marks action initiated in the past, and now continuing:

pisakata (= *hisakata*) nö tsuki.pa teri.tari

'the moon of heaven goes on shining' (*Man'yooshuu*)

-nu is used predicatively and attributively in an affirmative sense; the attributive form is *-nuru*. Sansom gives an example from the *Man'yooshuu*:

hisakata no ame shira.shi.nuru kimi
'my Lord who ruleth in Heaven'

töki.nö yu.kereba mi.yako.tö nari.nu
'when the time came you became a city' (*Man'yooshuu*)

... aki ki.nu to
'... that autumn has indeed come' (*Kokin shuu*)

-keri (< *-ki* + *ari*), *-keru*, *-kera*, *-kere*: as simple past: *ima wa mukashi T. to ieru mono ari.keri* 'once upon a time there was a man called T'.

-keri often suggests present perception and evaluation of action initiated in the past: *wakaki no ume wa/hana saki.ni.keri* 'the young plum tree (once transplanted) has now at last blossomed' (Waley 1946: 83).

-ki: attributive *-shi*, perfect *-shika*, negative base *-se*; no conjunctive.

kikite.shi hi yori 'since the day when (I) heard (it)'
yama.ni yuki.shika.ba 'when we went into the hills'

-mu, *-meri*: these express both probability and uncertainty:

mukame ka yuka.mumachi.ni ka mata.mu
'shall (I) go to meet (him) or shall (I) go on waiting?' (Sansom)

iye ni shite/ware wa koi.mu na
'shall we make love indoors?' (negative response expected)

-be: predicative form *-beshi*, attributive *-beki*:

yuku.beshi 'he'll go'
wa.ga seko ga ku.beki yoi nari 'it is the night for my lover to come'

-be is negated by *-maji*:

aru.maji.ki koto 'something unlikely or undesirable'
yuku beki hito 'someone who will very probably go'
yuku.majiki hito 'someone very unlikely to go'
ku.beki haru ka wa *lit.* 'is there a sure-to-come spring?'
wasurete aru.beki mono wa 'an ought-to-have-been-forgotten thing' (*wasuru* 'to forget')

-ramu and *-rashi* imply plausible conjecture or inference; 'looks as though':

tsuki wo miru.ramu 'I suppose... is/are moon-gazing'
yama.ni shigure furu.rashi 'it looks as though there's a shower falling on the mountain'

Negative suffixes are *zu* (predicative: attributive *nu*, conjunctive *zu*, perfect *ne*(*ba*)) and *ji*, which is not declined:

yoku mo ara.zu 'though it is not good'
shira.nu michi 'an unknown road'
shira.zu '(I) don't know'
michi-yuki shira.ji 'will not know the way to go' (*Man'yooshuu*)

PASSIVE VOICE

in -(*ra*)*ru*(*ru*) (< *uru* 'to get')

The earliest formant is *-ay-*, with animate agent in *-ni*:

ka yukeba pitö.ni itöpaye/kaku yukeba pitö-ni nikumaye
'he goes there – he is unliked by the people; he comes here – he is hated by the people' (*pitö* = *hito*) (*Man'yooshuu*)

-rayu- is also found:

miru.ni shirayenu uma.hito
'a groom not known by sight'

yuki.ni furayete sakeru ume no hana
'plum blossoms that had opened after having been snowed-on'

POTENTIAL MOOD

Formally identical to the passive voice:

yukaruru 'can go'

ukiyo no mono to omowarezu
'cannot think of them as part of this floating (i.e. evanescent) world' (O'Neill 1968), i.e. 'cannot be thought of as…'

CAUSATIVE VOICE

The endings are: (*sa*)*seru*/(*sa*)*suru*/(*sa*)*su*:

yukasu 'cause to go'
misasu 'enable to see'

AUXILIARY VERBS (*ARU* AND *SURU*)

aru is the equivalent of the Chinese *yŏu* 'there is/are'; its forms (with predicative *ari*) have not changed in the fifteen hundred years that have elapsed since the Nara period. It can function as a principal verb: *sake ari mata sakana ari* 'there is drink and so is there food', and as auxiliary: *kono hana wa shiroku ari* > *shirokari*, which can be glossed as 'as regards these flowers, whiteness exists'.

The negative of *aru* is *naku* + *aru* > *nakaru*: *shiru hito no naki* 'there is none that knows'.

suru 'to do', 'make' is much used in the formation of compound verbs consisting of Chinese *kanji* plus *suru* as auxiliary (cf. use of Arabic nominals plus *etmek*, etc. in Turkish, or *kardan* in Persian). *suru* is used in this sense in the *Man'yooshuu*: cf. Hitomaro: *to-gari-suru kimi* '(you) my Lord, who are bird-hunting' (*gari* = *kari* 'hunt').

Honorific language

Both literary and spoken Japanese have a large repertory of inflected and uninflected forms coded to cover sociolinguistic situations involving social status. The repertory is much more extensive in the literary than in the spoken language, and is particularly characteristic of the Heian classics, though honorific language is found in earlier Japanese.

Various registers of honorific language may be distinguished, ranging from the merely polite to the deeply respectful and the humble. Thus, use of *tatematsuru* to express the notion of 'giving' identifies the donor as socially much inferior to the recipient. Relative status in the social scale is similarly coded in verbs such as *makaru* 'to come/go', *haberi* 'to serve', 'exist as', *moosu* 'to say', 'do', *uketamawaru* 'hear', 'receive'; *saburoo*, for example, denotes 'to serve a person of high rank'. See Ikeda (1975: 146–90) for many good examples of coded verbs.

A striking feature of literary Japanese is the use of passive and causative forms as honorifics (see Sansom: 165). Thus Akahito (mid-eighth century) has: *Masurao wa/Mi-kari ni tatashi* 'The men of valour have betaken themselves to the lordly (honourable) hunt', where *tatashi* is from *tatasu* 'to cause to start' and *mi-* is an honorific prefix (*see* **Adjective**, above); *masurao* = 'warriors', *kari* = 'hunt'.

In the Heian language, a verb often used to denote 'to humbly accept' is *tamawaru*, the passive form of *tamau*, itself a verb denoting 'to receive from a superior'.

Certain auxiliary verbs have honorific status, e.g. *-mesu*: *kiko.shi.mesu* 'deign to hear' or 'partake of food, drink'; *shirashi.mesu* 'deign to know'.

Similarly, *-masu* is used in the *Man'yooshuu*, where Hitomaro has *Kimi ga ki.masa.mu* 'My Lord will deign to come'; *-masa.mu* is the future of the honorific auxiliary *-masu*, following the root *ki-* 'come'.

Word Order

Basically SOV. OSV is possible.

SCRIPT

The Chinese morphemic script reached Japan via Korea in the third/fourth century AD. For Japanese, a polysyllabic and highly inflected language, a logographic script such as the Chinese character, perfectly adapted to a monosyllabic isolating language devoid of inflections, could be utilized in either or both of two ways:

(a) Chinese characters could be used to designate their Japanese semantic equivalents. This is known as the *kun* method. For example, the Chinese character 山 /shan/ in Chinese, meaning 'mountain', could be read as *yama*, the Japanese semantic equivalent. Early *kun* 訓 texts often stick awkwardly close to the syntactically alien Chinese text: e.g. negation markers are found preceding verbs, a word order which is characteristic of Chinese, not of Japanese. The artificial language thus produced is known as *kanbun* 漢文. A modified form of *kanbun* known as *hentai kanbun*, while retaining the principle of semantic transfer, tended to replace Chinese syntax with Japanese.

(b) *man'yoogana*: the *kun* method worked up to a point with bare stems. For the representation of Japanese inflections and particles, the *man'yoogana* 万葉仮名 method was developed: this involved selecting Chinese characters, regardless of meaning, as phonetic approximations: for example, the Japanese genitive/relative particle の /no/ is often represented in *kanbun* by 之 (zhi), its Chinese semantic equivalent. In *man'yoogana* writing, /no/ is represented by a Tang Chinese character, selected on grounds of phonetic similarity. In the same way, a Japanese polysyllabic word could be represented by a concatenation of Chinese phonetic approximations. It was an unwieldy method of writing, and there was no consistency in the selection of Chinese characters: at least a dozen Chinese graphs are used to denote the Japanese particle *ka*.

(c) The ninth century saw the introduction of the *okototen* 乎己止点 system, whereby Chinese characters used as *kun* (see above) were supplied with peripheral dots indicating which Japanese inflections or particles were to be added to complete the sense. Thus, if we use a square □ to represent a Chinese character, a dot at the upper right-hand corner □˙ indicates that the Japanese object marker (*w*)*o* is to be added. Similarly, a dot at the lower right-hand corner signals addition of the nominalizer *wa*, while a dot at the bottom left-hand corner marks the Japanese participial form in *-te*, and so on. At least eight key markers in Japanese morphology and syntax could be specified in this way.

(d) At the same time, the two Japanese syllabaries, *katakana* and *hiragana*, were beginning to take shape. *Katakana* originated in abbreviated forms of Chinese characters, used as a kind of shorthand for mnemonic purposes. The elegant and aesthetically pleasing *hiragana* syllabary derives from the cursive writing of Chinese characters. Through the late Heian and the Kamakura periods – i.e. well into the Japanese Middle Ages – literature continued to be produced in a variety of scripts: in *kanbun* (mainly by Buddhist priests), in pure Chinese and in *katakana* (by male scholars and courtiers), and in *hiragana* (by ladies of the imperial court, among whom the Lady Murasaki Shikibu and the Lady Sei Shoonagon cannot fail to be mentioned). By the close of the Heian period, however, the so-called *wabun* 和文 style, based on *hiragana* plus a limited use of Chinese characters, had established itself as the most satisfactory medium for the notation of Japanese. Printing was imported from Korea in 1593. Early books are set in *wabun* style, the kanji being accompanied by furigana (phonetic glosses in *hiragana*), where required.

Modern Japanese (*hyoojungo* 'standard language') is written in a combination of Chinese characters and the two syllabaries. Hiragana is used for verbal inflection, nominal particles, and many native Japanese words. *Katakana* is used for foreign words, particularly the Anglo-American words which proliferate in modern Japanese. It is also the script for telegraphese. Chinese characters function as root words, both verbal and nominal. For example, in the complex verb form *asobanakereba narimasen* 'has/have to play', the root *aso-* 'play' is notated as the Chinese character 遊 (Chinese *you* 'to play') while the remaining ten syllables (final *-n* is syllabic), conveying the negative conditional and the negative present indicative, are in *hiragana*. Most Chinese characters used in Japanese have more than one pronunciation; as at the outset, over a thousand years ago, the basic distinction is still between the Sino-Japanese reading (the *on-yomi*) and the native Japanese reading (the *kun-yomi*). For example, the *on-yomi* reading of the character meaning 'to play', given above, is *yū*. Reference to this character in the dictionary (Nr 4726 in Nelson's *Japanese–English Dictionary*) will show that out of about eighty compounds listed, only 25 per cent or so give 遊 its *kun-yomi* pronunciation (*aso-*); everywhere else, the *on-yomi* reading *yū-* is used.

In 1946, an official list of 1,850 Chinese characters was adopted as the desirable inventory for everyday purposes. In 1981, this list was extended to almost 2,000. Chinese characters not included in this list are accompanied, when used in print, by their *hiragana* readings.

The *hiragana* and *katakana* syllabaries are set out in the tables. For the structure of Chinese characters, *see* **Chinese**.

Extensive adoption of American-English loanwords has led in recent years to the introduction of several innovative *katakana* forms, denoting, for example, /ʃe/, /tʃɛ/, /wi/.

THE JAPANESE SCRIPT

THE SYLLABARIES

HIRAGANA

あ	か	が	さ	ざ	た	だ	な	は	ば	ぱ	ま	ら
a	*ka*	*ga*	*sa*	*za*	*ta*	*da*	*na*	*ha*	*ba*	*pa*	*ma*	*ra*
い	き	ぎ	し	じ	ち	ぢ	に	ひ	び	ぴ	み	り
i	*ki*	*gi*	*shi*	*ji*	*chi*	*ji*	*ni*	*hi*	*bi*	*pi*	*mi*	*ri*
う	く	ぐ	す	ず	つ	づ	ぬ	ふ	ぶ	ぷ	む	る
u	*ku*	*gu*	*su*	*zu*	*tsu*	*zu*	*nu*	*fu*	*bu*	*pu*	*mu*	*ru*
え	け	げ	せ	ぜ	て	で	ね	へ	べ	ぺ	め	れ
e	*ke*	*ge*	*se*	*ze*	*te*	*de*	*ne*	*he*	*be*	*pe*	*me*	*re*
お	こ	ご	そ	ぞ	と	ど	の	ほ	ぼ	ぽ	も	ろ
o	*ko*	*go*	*so*	*zo*	*to*	*do*	*no*	*ho*	*bo*	*po*	*mo*	*ro*
や	きゃ	ぎゃ	しゃ	じゃ	ちゃ	ぢゃ	にゃ	ひゃ	びゃ	ぴゃ	みゃ	りゃ
ya	*kya*	*gya*	*sha*	*ja*	*cha*	*ja*	*nya*	*hya*	*bya*	*pya*	*mya*	*rya*
ゆ	きゅ	ぎゅ	しゅ	じゅ	ちゅ	ぢゅ	にゅ	ひゅ	びゅ	ぴゅ	みゅ	りゅ
yu	*kyu*	*gyu*	*shu*	*ju*	*chu*	*ju*	*nyu*	*hyu*	*byu*	*pyu*	*myu*	*ryu*
よ	きょ	ぎょ	しょ	じょ	ちょ	ぢょ	にょ	ひょ	びょ	ぴょ	みょ	りょ
yo	*kyo*	*gyo*	*sho*	*jo*	*cho*	*jo*	*nyo*	*hyo*	*byo*	*pyo*	*myo*	*ryo*

KATAKANA

ア	カ	ガ	サ	ザ	タ	ダ	ナ	ハ	バ	パ	マ	ラ	ワ	ファ	ン
a	*ka*	*ga*	*sa*	*za*	*ta*	*da*	*na*	*ha*	*ba*	*pa*	*ma*	*ra*	*wa*	*fa*	*n*
イ	キ	ギ	シ	ジ	チ	ヂ	ニ	ヒ	ビ	ピ	ミ	リ		フィ	
i	*ki*	*gi*	*shi*	*ji*	*chi*	*ji*	*ni*	*hi*	*bi*	*pi*	*mi*	*ri*		*fi*	
ウ	ク	グ	ス	ズ	ツ	ヅ	ヌ	フ	ブ	プ	ム	ル			
u	*ku*	*gu*	*su*	*zu*	*tsu*	*zu*	*nu*	*fu*	*bu*	*pu*	*mu*	*ru*			
エ	ケ	ゲ	セ	ゼ	テ	デ	ネ	ヘ	ベ	ペ	メ	レ		フェ	
e	*ke*	*ge*	*se*	*ze*	*te*	*de*	*ne*	*he*	*be*	*pe*	*me*	*re*		*fe*	
オ	コ	ゴ	ソ	ゾ	ト	ド	ノ	ホ	ボ	ポ	モ	ロ		フォ	ヲ
o	*ko*	*go*	*so*	*zo*	*to*	*do*	*no*	*ho*	*bo*	*po*	*mo*	*ro*		*fo*	*o*
ヤ	キャ	ギャ	シャ	ジャ	チャ	ヂャ	ニャ	ヒャ	ビャ	ピャ	ミャ	リャ			
ya	*kya*	*gya*	*sha*	*ja*	*cha*	*ja*	*nya*	*hya*	*bya*	*pya*	*mya*	*rya*			
ユ	キュ	ギュ	シュ	ジュ	チュ	ヂュ	ニュ	ヒュ	ビュ	ピュ	ミュ	リュ			
yu	*kyu*	*gyu*	*shu*	*ju*	*chu*	*ju*	*nyu*	*hyu*	*byu*	*pyu*	*myu*	*ryu*			
ヨ	キョ	ギョ	ショ	ジョ	チョ	ヂョ	ニョ	ヒョ	ビョ	ピョ	ミョ	リョ			
yo	*kyo*	*gyo*	*sho*	*jo*	*cho*	*jo*	*nyo*	*hyo*	*byo*	*pyo*	*myo*	*ryo*			

Long vowels are notated in Hiragana by adding あ, い, う, え, or お, e.g.

おかあさん *okā-san;*

and in Katakana by adding ー, e.g.

テーブル *tēburu.*

Syllabic final consonants other than /n/ are notated

by つ in Hiragana

and by ツ in Katakana, e.g.

いった *itta*, and マッチ *matchi.*

JAPANESE, MODERN STANDARD

INTRODUCTION

(For a note on genetic affinity, *see* **Japanese, Literary**). Today, Japanese is spoken by about 120 million, in Japan and by large Japanese communities in several parts of the world. The Ryu-Kyu language spoken in the Okinawa Prefecture is a dialect of Japanese. In Japan itself, several local dialects persist, some of which are unintelligible to outsiders, but all Japanese in Japan are taught *hyoojun.go*, the 'standard language'.

For a note on the early literature, *see* **Japanese, Literary**.

The political, economic, and social upheaval brought about by the Meiji Restoration in 1868 could not fail to be reflected in new attitudes to literature in Japan, and the ensuing century saw a remarkable efflorescence of the novel as the relevant medium both for the naturalistic narrative and for social and psychological analysis. Themes were drawn from Sino-Japanese sources and from a great variety of Western models, ranging from Zola and the Russian novelists to Kafka and Rilke, and Japanese treatment of this material is equally eclectic, covering the familiar fields of naturalism, surrealism, alienation, and existentialism, and adding a peculiarly Japanese vein of morbid lyricism. Distinguished names abound; the following cannot fail to be mentioned: Natsume Sooseki, Shimazaki Tooson, Mori Oogai, Abe Kooboo, Kawabata Yasunari, Akutagawa Ryuunosuke, Mishima Yukio.

SCRIPT

See **Japanese, Literary**.

PHONOLOGY

Consonants

stops: p, b, t, d, k, g
fricatives: s, z, h
nasals: m, n, ŋ
flap: r
semi-vowels: j, w

Vowels

i, e, a, o, u

These provide the basic inventory in terms of the vowel X consonant grid (*see* **Japanese, Literary**). However, allophones arise in the grid: in the *s* series the fricative /ʃ/, in the *t* series the affricates /ts/ and /tʃ/, and in the *z* series the affricate /dʒ/. These are notated in the usual transcription, and here, as *sh*, *ts*, *ch*, *j*. Thus, *hajimemashite* 'how do you do' is /hadʒimemaʃte/. For the complete grid, see the Japanese script chart.

Again, for all consonants apart from /d/ and /w/ there is a three-term palatalized series: e.g. *kya*, *kyu*, *kyo*. In the *s* row the palatalized values are realized as /ʃa – ʃu – ʃo/; in the *t* row as /tʃa – tʃu – tʃo/, and in the *z* row as /dʒa – dʒu – dʒo/.

Final *-n* is realized as nasal [ŋ], without nasalization of the preceding vowel. That is to say, final *n* is syllabic: *Nihon* 'Japan' is pronounced /ni.ho.ŋ/.

In the transcription used here, long vowels are written doubled: e.g. *oo*. They are twice the length of single vowels; the difference is phonemic.

There are several diphthongs. When final or in contact with an unvoiced consonant: /u/ is reduced to Ø: e.g. *suki* 'likes', 'is fond of' → /ski/; *arimasu* 'is' → /arimas/.

Stress

Japanese has a pitch-accentuation pattern in place of tonic stress. Syllables flow evenly: a long syllable is two moras, a short syllable is one mora. Pitch is not marked; if it were, the marker would be on the last syllable of a high-pitch sequence, preceding a drop: e.g. *wakarimasen deshita* 'didn't understand': /wa^{karimase}n.^{deshita}/. Other patterns are possible.

MORPHOLOGY AND SYNTAX

There is no grammatical gender; no articles. A plural marker exists but this is used mainly with pronouns. Reduplication is possible. The word *takusan* 'many' is often used: e.g. *Kuruma ga takusan arimasu ne?* 'There are lots of cars, aren't there?'; *shashin o takusan torimashita* 'took lots of photographs'.

Noun

Nouns are invariable. Syntactic relationships are expressed by means of particles. The most important of these are:

wa: this is a focusing agent, which identifies or recapitulates the topic, e.g. *watashi no kaisha* ***wa*** *Oosaka ni arimasu* '(as for) my business (it) is in O'.

ga: subject marker, e.g. *soto* ***wa*** *ame* ***ga*** *futte imasu* '(as for) outside, the rain is falling'; *ano hito* ***wa*** *se* ***ga*** *takai desu* '(as for) that man, stature is tall' = 'that man is tall'.

ni: locative, aditive, dative, e.g. *kooen ni* 'in the park'; *imooto ni* 'to sister'; *sakura o mi* ***ni*** *ikimasu* 'go to see the cherry blossom'.

o: object marker, e.g. *asa-gohan* ***o*** *tabemashita* 'ate breakfast'; *e-hagaki* ***o*** *takusan kaimashita* 'bought many postcards'.

no: genitival relationship, e.g. *watashi* ***no*** *heya wa* 'my room'; *Tookyoo wa Nippon* ***no*** *shuto desu* 'Tokyo is the capital of Japan'.
de: instrumental, e.g. *hikooki* ***de*** 'by plane'; *denwa* ***de*** 'by phone'; *daigaku de* 'at university'; *resutoran de* 'in a restaurant'.

Adjective

See **Stative verbs**, below. An attributive adjective precedes the noun: e.g. *yuumei-na haiku wa* 'a famous haiku'; *takai yama wa* 'a high mountain'.

Pronoun

In general, pronouns are avoided in Japanese, especially as regards the second person. Here, the addressee's name followed by *san* should be used: e.g. *Oota.san wa nani o tabemasu ka?* 'What are you having (to eat)?' (addressing Mr Oota).

Watashi, pl. *watashitachi* are acceptable first person forms; *anata* has restricted use as a second person form.

Third person: *anohito* or *anokata* 'he/she'; *kare* 'he', *kanojo* 'she'.

DEMONSTRATIVE PRONOUN

kore 'this', *sore* 'that', *are* 'that' (further away). The demonstrative adjectives are *kono* 'this', *sono* 'that', *ano* 'that' (further away).

INTERROGATIVE PRONOUN

dare 'who?'; *nani* 'what?' The final particle *ka* makes a sentence interrogative: e.g. *Sono hito wa Nippon-jin desu* ***ka*** 'Is that man (is he) a Japanese?'

RELATIVE PRONOUN

See **Verb**, below.

Numerals

There are two parallel sets of numbers, native Japanese and Chinese: 1–10: Jap. *hito-*, *futa-*, *mi-*, *yon-*, *itsu-*, *mu-*, *nana-*, ya-, *kokono-*, *too*; Ch. *ichi*, *ni*, *san*, *shi*, *go*, *roku*, *shichi*, *hachi*, *ku/kyu*, *juu*. In enumeration, the Chinese numerals have to be combined with appropriate classifiers, e.g. *-hon* for long objects, *-satsu* for books, *-nin* for people. There are a couple of dozen of these, usually with assimilation at junctures: e.g. with *-hon*: ***ippon*** 'one' (e.g. pencil); *ni**hon*** 'two' (pencils); *san**bon*** /sa**mb**on/, 'three' (pencils). Numeral + classifier usually follow the referent: e.g. *Ki* ***ga roppon*** *arimasu* 'There are six trees' (*roku* + *hon* → *roppon*).

11 *juu-ichi*; 12 *juu-ni*; 20 *ni-juu*; 30 *san-juu*; 100 *hyaku*; 1,000 *sen*.

Verb

There are three classes of verb: vowel stems, consonantal stems, and a small class of irregular verbs (six members). For inflectional purposes, the six bases of Classical Japanese are retained in slightly modified form:

Base	*1*	*2*	*3*	*4*	*5*	*6*
vowel class	mi	mi	miru	mire	miro	miyoo
consonant class	kaka	kaki	kaku	kake	kake	kakoo
irregular	shi/sa	shi	suru	sure	seyo/siro	shiyoo

Base 1: this is used in the formation of the negative, e.g. *mi**nai*** 'not to see', and the causative, e.g. *kaka**seru*** 'to cause to write'.

Base 2: provides the base for the present and past polite forms, and the desiderative: e.g. *mi**masu*** 'sees' and 'will see'; *mi**mashita*** 'saw', *mi**tai*** 'wants to see'.

Base 3: citation form, used as infinitive. Plain present tense.

Base 4: provides the conditional form in *-ba*, e.g. *mire**ba*** 'would see'; *kake**ba*** 'would write'.

Base 5: imperative plain form, e.g. *kake!* 'write!'; this is permissible only in reported speech.

Base 6: prospective or hortative, e.g. *motto benkyoo **shiyoo** to omotte imasu* 'I'm thinking of doing some more studying' (*benkyoo*). This form is associated with first person only (but citation form + *deshoo* – base 6 of *da* 'to be' – is general: e.g. *Taroo wa kyoo kuru deshoo* 'Taroo will probably come today').

THE -TE/-DE (GERUND) FORM

In verbs ending in *-ru*, *-te* replaces *-ru*: *deru* – *de**te*** 'having gone out'. In *-u* verbs, root *k/g* are elided, *-de* appears after a sonant: *kaku* 'write' – *ka**ite***; *shinu* 'die' – *shi**nde***; *narabu* 'line up' – *nara**nde***. There are some irregular forms: *suru* 'do' – ***shite***; *kuru* 'come' – ***kite***.

This form is much used with the auxiliary *iru/aru* to express a continuing state of affairs: e.g. *Nani o shite imasu ka* 'What is/are . . . doing?'; *kekkon.shite.imasu* 'I'm married'. It is also used as a holding suffix in a serial utterance involving several verbs; each of these then ends in *-te/-de*, the final verb alone taking the finite ending:

Hiru-gohan o tabe**te**, oka ni nobot**te**, machi o mimashita
'Having eaten lunch, we climbed up the hill and looked at the town.'

Tamago o too kat**te**, niwa e de**te**, hiru-gohan o tabemashita
'(I, we, etc.) bought ten eggs, went into the garden and had lunch.'

The parallel with the Turkic languages is striking.

PRESENT AND PAST POLITE FORMS, POSITIVE AND NEGATIVE

Present: *-masu* /mas'/, e.g. *kaki**masu*** 'writes'; neg. *kaki**masen*** 'doesn't write'.

Past: *-mashita* /mash'ta/, e.g. *kaki**mashita*** 'wrote'; neg. *kaki**masen deshita*** 'didn't write'.

There is a great wealth of agglutinative affixes; some of the most important are:

-ba: conditional, e.g. *ame ga fure**ba*** 'if it rains';
-tara: temporal, e.g. *hiru-gohan o tabe**tara*** 'when (I, we, etc.) eat, have eaten lunch';
negative base + *-ba* + *ikemasen/narimasen*: obligation, e.g. *Watashiwa Tookyoo e ikanakereba narimasen* 'I have to go to Tokyo';
-tai: desire, e.g. *Watashi moo tabetai desu* 'I want to eat too.'

PASSIVE

Infixes *-are-*, *-rare-*, e.g. *tabe**rare**ru* 'be eaten'; *kak**are**ru* 'be written'. An agent, if overtly expressed, takes the postposition *ni*: e.g. *Watashi wa kinoo ame **ni** fur**are**ta* 'By the rain (*ame*) I-was-rained-on yesterday.'

CAUSATIVE

The infixes are *-ase-*, *-sase-*, e.g. *tabe**sase**te imasu* 'is feeding (trans.)'. Passive and causative may be combined: e.g. *Watashi wa ka-choo-san **ni** Oosaka e ik.**ase.rare**.mashita* 'I was made to go to Osaka by my department boss.'

STATIVE VERBS

Examples: *takai* 'it is high'; *omoshiroi* 'it is interesting'. As attributes, these precede the noun. As predicates they are conjugated: past *omoshiro.katta* 'it was interesting'; negative past *omoshiro**ku**.nakatta* 'it wasn't interesting'.

RELATIVE CLAUSES

Relative clauses are placed in attributive position to the left of the head-word: e.g. using *o-tenki* 'weather', *warui* 'bad', *tokoro* 'place', *o-tenki ga warui tokoro* 'a place where the weather is bad'. Ambiguity may arise, as the deixis is not specific in Japanese: e.g. *tegami o okutta hito wa* 'the man who sent us the letter', *or* 'the man to whom the letter was sent'.

Nominalizing agents such as *toki* 'time', *koto* 'thing' are used to form other types of relative clause (verb in plain form): e.g. *asa hito ni atta toki ni wa*... 'when you meet someone in the morning...' (*asa* 'morning'; *au* 'to meet'); *Kare wa sensoo ga owatta **to iu koto** o shiranakatta* 'He didn't know (the thing) that the war had ended.' In such relative adjectival clauses, the verb is in the plain form: *Nihon e **itta** koto ga arimasen* literally 'to-Japan – gone-affair – is not', i.e. '(I, etc.) have never been to Japan'.

HONORIFIC PREFIXES

O-, *go-* are attached to nominals and to adjectives: e.g. *Anata no **o-too-san** no **go**-iken wa doo desu ka?* 'What is your (hon.) father's (hon.) opinion?' A verbal form is made honorific by substituting *o-/go-* + base 2 + *narimasu*: *Yamada-san wa kore o **o-kaki ni** narimashita* 'Mr Yamada wrote this'; cf. for first person (never hon.): *watashi wa kore o kakimashita* 'I wrote this'.

Giving and receiving: among social equals *yaru* is a status-neutral verb meaning 'to give'. Several other verbs which express a donor–recipient relationship are coded for social status. For example, *ageru* (or *sashiageru*) can be used if the recipient (a) is 2nd or 3rd p., and (b) occupies a 'superior' rank in the social hierarchy; it cannot be used with a 1st p. recipient. Thus *watashi wa Yamada sensei ni kono hon o agemashita* 'I gave Professor Yamada the book'. Where a 1st p. recipient is concerned, *kureru* or *kudasaru* may be used; either encodes the superior status of the donor: *Yamada sensei ga watashi ni kono hon o kudasaimashita* 'Professor Yamada gave me the book.' *itadaku* is similarly coded, and appears in polite, set expressions, e.g. *itadakimasu*, said before a meal: 'I am grateful for the food you have provided'. These and other verbs encoding social status are used with verbs denoting benefactive action such as teaching: *watashi wa Taroo san ni Eigo o oshiete agemasu* 'I am teaching Mr Taroo English' but, *Taroo san ga watashi ni Nippon.go o oshiete kuremasu* 'Mr Taroo is teaching me Japanese'.

Postpositions

Examples: *kara* 'from', *made* 'as far as', *de* 'in', 'with'.

Compound words of many types proliferate in Japanese: cf. *hana.mi* 'flower-viewing'; *matsu.yama* 'the summer mountains'. Verbal stems can be compounded: e.g. *toru* 'take' plus *kaeru* 'change' > *tori.kaeru* 'exchange'; *toru* plus *kesu* 'extinguish' > *tori.kesu* 'cancel'.

The verbal formant -*gar*(*u*) is added to adjectival stems to express affective reaction:

inu wo kowa.gar.imasu 'is afraid of dogs'

danboo ga nai no de, minna samu.gatte.imasu
'as there is no heating, everyone is cold'

Word order

Typically SOV. OSV is also possible.

1 初めに言(ことば)があった。 言は神と共に
あった。言は神であった。

2 この言は初めに神と共にあった。

3 すべてのものは，これによってできた。できたものの
うち，一つとしてこれによらないものはなかった。

4 この言に 命があった。 そして この命は 人の光で
あった。
5 光はやみの中に輝いている。 そして，やみはこれ
に勝たなかった。
6 ¶ ここにひとりの人があって，神からつかわされて
いた。その名をヨハネと言った。
7 この人はあかしのためにきた。 光についてあかしを
し，彼によってすべての人が信じるためである。

8 彼は光ではなく，ただ，光についてあかしをする
ためにきたのである。

JAVANESE

INTRODUCTION

Javanese belongs to the Malayo-Polynesian branch of Austronesian, and is spoken by 75 million people in central and eastern Java. The language has been influenced, first by Sanskrit, then, from the fifteenth century onwards by Arabic, and finally, since about 1600, by Dutch. The influence of Malay, in the shape of Bahasa Indonesian, has increased since the latter became the official language of Indonesia.

For the older language and literature, *see* **Javanese, Old**. By the thirteenth/fourteenth century Old Javanese was no longer a spoken language, though it continued to be used for literature. Of particular interest in the Middle Javanese period is the *babad* literature dealing with the traditional history of Java. This period culminates in the impressive figure of Jasadipura, the eighteenth-century court poet whose work was a major factor in the emergence of the Surakarta, or Solo, dialect as the basis of modern literary Javanese.

The *wayang* – the traditional Javanese puppet theatre – draws on both Hindu and Islamic sources for its themes: e.g. on Jasadipura's reworking of the Old Javanese version of the *Mahābhārata*, Book III (*Vanapurvan*).

The twentieth century has seen the growth of the social novel and other Western genres; certain influential writers in this field, e.g. Senggono and Subagijo, use *ngoko* (*see* **Speech levels**, below). In general, however, Javanese has been more conservative than Bahasa Indonesian.

SCRIPT

The *čarakan* script was used exclusively until replaced by romanization in the twentieth century. In 1926 a standardized orthography was adopted, and revised in 1972. *See* **Javanese, Old**.

Speech levels

Javanese is a two-tier language. The sociolinguistic constraints which operate in many languages with regard to pronominal usage, for example, are applied in Javanese to all parts of speech, nouns, verbs, adjectives, prepositions. The two main levels are: *ngoko* or colloquial; *krâmâ* /krɔmɔ/, 'elevated'.

Ngoko is basic Javanese in the sense that it is picked up by the child at home. From school age on, however, the Javanese child has to acquire the additional and rather extensive *krâmâ* lexicon for use in certain prescribed sociolinguistic situations – by young people to their elders, on formal occasions, when addressing strangers or social superiors, and so on. A compromise solution is increasingly being developed in the shape of *krâmâ madya* – more formal than *ngoko*, less stilted than *krâmâ*.

All three forms have virtually identical grammar and syntax; the differences are purely lexical. For any given referent, krâmâ may have the same word as *ngoko*, an enhanced form, or a completely different word: e.g.

Ngoko	*Krâmâ*	*English*
wit	wit	tree
prakara	prakawis	occasion
asu	segawon	dog
omah	griya	house
wong	tiyang	man

Use of *ngoko* is steadily encroaching on the *krâmâ* preserve. The Javanese press uses *ngoko* in general. *Krâmâ* itself has more than one register.

PHONOLOGY

Consonants

stops: p/b, t/d, ṭ/ḍ, k/g, ʔ
affricates: tʃ/dʒ/, t′/d′
fricatives: w, s, j, h
nasals: m, n, ɲ, ŋ
lateral and trill: l, r

Since the voiced/unvoiced values are almost indistinguishable, the stops and affricates are set out in pairs. According to Uhlenbeck (1949), the voiced member is slightly aspirated. Initial /k/ = [q]; final /k/ = /ʔ/. No final is voiced.

Vowels

i, ɪ, e, ɛ, a, ə, ɔ, o, u

/ə/ is known as *e*-pepet; it appears in unstressed syllables, /a/ in penultimate and final syllables → [ɔ]: e.g. *nagara* /nəgɔrɔ/, 'country'.

There are no diphthongs; contingent vowels are pronounced separately.

Stress

Stress is on the penultimate syllable unless this is *e*-pepet: e.g. *berás* 'polished rice'.

MORPHOLOGY AND SYNTAX

(N = *ngoko*, K = *krâmâ*.)

Noun

No gender; there are no articles or plural markers; to suggest plurality N *akeh*, K *kathah* 'many' may be used. A collective can be made by reduplication: e.g. *sedulur-sedulur* (sometimes written '*sedulur 2*') 'a group of friends'.

POSSESSIVE RELATIONSHIP

See **Pronoun**, below.

Adjective

The attributive adjective follows the noun and is invariable: e.g. N *omah gedhé* = K *griya ageng* '(a/the) big house'.

COMPARATIVE

N. *luwih*, K *langkung*: e.g. N *luwih dhuwur* = K *langkung inggil* 'higher'.

Pronoun

Independent personal forms and possessive enclitics:

	Personal	*Possessive*
1	N aku, K kula	N -ku, K kula
2	N kowé, K sampéyan	N -mu, K sampéyan
3	N dhèwèké, K piyambakipun	N -e, K -ipun

There are no specifically plural forms: e.g. N *omah**ku*** = K *griya kula* 'my house(s)', 'our house(s)'; N *omahé* = K *griya**nipun*** 'his house(s)', 'their house(s)'; cf. N *sapi**né** wong iki* = K *lembun**ipun** tiyang punika* 'that man's cow'.

DEMONSTRATIVE PRONOUN

N *iki*, K *punika* (pronounced /menikɔ/): 'this', 'that'.

INTERROGATIVE PRONOUN

N *sapa*, K *sinten* 'who?'; N *apa*, N *punapa* /menɔpɔ/ 'what?' The introductory interrogative particle is N *apa*, K *punapa*.

RELATIVE PRONOUN

N *kang/sing*, K *ingkang*: e.g. N *Iki wong kang arep adol omahe* = K *Punika tiyang ingkang badhé sade griyanipun* 'That is the man who wants to sell his house' (*arep* = *badhé* 'will'; *adol* = *sade* 'sell').

Numerals

For the cardinals 1–5 there are distinct N/K sets: N *siji*, *loro*, *telu*, *papat*, *lima* = K *setunggal*, *kalih*, *tiga*, *sekawan*, *gangsal*; 6–9 show common N/K forms: *enem*, *pitu*, *wolu*, *sanga*. 10 = N *sepuluh*, K *sedasa*; 11 = N/K *sewelas*; 12–15 separate N and K forms; 16–19 common forms; 20 is N *rongpuluh*, K *kalihdasa*; 30 N *telungpuluh*, K *tigangdasa*; 100 N/K *saratus*.

Verb

A few Javanese verbal stems are used in primary form, e.g. N *takon* = K *taken* 'ask'; N *ana* = K *wonten* 'be located', but the great majority of stems undergo initial nasalization before they can function as verbs. Vocalic initials take prefix *ng-*, e.g. *iris* – ***ngiris*** 'to cut'; consonantal initials take homorganic nasal, e.g. *buru* – ***mburu*** 'to hunt'; *sapu* – ***nyapu*** 'to sweep'; *rembat* – ***ngrembat*** 'to yoke'. These stems are neutral as to tense or aspect, and, since there is nothing resembling a conjugational system, adverbial markers preceding the verb may be used to indicate tense, e.g. N *tau* = K *nate* for remote past; N *wis* = K *sampun* for past; N *bakal, arep* = K *badhé, adyeng* for future. Example: K *Ratu sampun.nitih mengsah.hipun* 'The prince has overcome his enemy' (*mengsah* 'enemy').

THE -I SUFFIX

This establishes a directional relationship between a verb and its locus of action or its direct object: e.g. *lungguh* 'to sit' – *nglunggihi* 'to sit on (something)'; *-tulis* 'to write' – *nulisi kertas* 'to write on paper'. An objective complement must be overtly expressed.

PASSIVE

In general, the passive construction is preferred in Javanese, and there are several passive forms:

(a) The personal passive: the prefixes are N 1 *tak-*, 2 *ko(k)-*, 3 *di-*; K 1 *kula*, 2 *sampeyan*, 3 *dipun*. Thus, *tak/dak.tulis* 'written by me' or 'written by us'; *ko(k).tulis* 'written by you' (singular or plural); *di.tulis* 'written by him/her, them', i.e. 'I/we write', 'you write', etc. For person to be expressed thus by a prefix is unique in the Javanese verbal system, cf. N *Layang iki **tak**tulis* 'This letter is being written by me'; N *Woh iki **di**pangan wong iki* = K *Woh punika **dipun** tedha tiyang punika* 'This fruit is being eaten by this man.'

(b) Neutral passive: this is characteristic of the literary style – *-in-* infix, e.g. ***tin**ulis* 'to be written'.

(c) Chance or accidental passive: formed with *ke*... *an* circumfix, e.g. N *maling* 'thief' – ***kemalingan*** 'to be robbed', K *pandung* 'thief' – ***kepandungan*** 'to be robbed'; N *udan* 'rain' – ***kodanan*** 'to be caught in the rain', K *jawah* 'rain' – ***kejawahan*** 'to be caught in the rain'.

(d) Two passives are coded for aspect: *ka-* perfective; *-um-* imperfective.

IMPERATIVE

In N only, as imperative forms would be incompatible with K usage. The N suffixes are *-a*, *-(n)en* for passive verbs, *-ana* for *-i* verbs.

CAUSATIVE

The suffixes are N *-aké-*, K *-aken*: e.g. N *sopir itu nglakok**aké** montore* = K *sopir punika nglampah**aken** montor**ipun*** 'the driver starts his engine'.

NEGATIVE

N *ora*/K *mboten* negate verbs: N *dudu*/K *sanès, dede* negate nouns: e.g. N *aku dudu wong Inggeris* = K *kula sanès tiyang Inggeris* 'I'm not English'; N *aku ora bisa basa Jawi* = K *kula mboten saged basa Jawi* 'I don't speak Javanese'.

AFFIXES

Examples:

-an, an all-purpose affix, usually with loss of initial nasalization; often indicates result of verbal action, or the instrument used: e.g. *nimbang* 'to weigh' – *timbangan* 'scales'.

ka... an makes abstract nouns, e.g. *sugih* 'rich' – *kasugihan* 'wealth'.

pa- indicates agent, e.g. N *nulis* 'to write' – *panulis* 'writer'; K *nyerat* 'to write' – *panyerat* 'writer'.

pa... an: locus of action, e.g. N *turu* 'to sleep' – *paturon* 'bedroom'.

sa + *pa-*: extent, range, e.g. *mbedhil* 'to shoot' – *sapambedhil* 'range limit for a shot' → 'as far as...'.

Suffix *-en* forms adjectives, e.g. *uwan* 'grey hair' – *uwanen* 'grey-haired'.

Prepositions

Examples: *ing* 'in', *saking* 'from'. Composite prepositions like *ing duwur* 'up', *ing isor* 'down' are also adverbials.

Word order

Varies according to whether construction is active or passive. S normally precedes V.

1 Ing kala purwa Sang Sabda iku ana, déné Sang Sabda iku nunggil karo Gusti Allah, sarta Sang Sabda iku Gusti Allah. 2 Wiwitané Pandjenenganė iku nunggil karo Gusti Allah. 3 Samubarang kabèh dumadiné déning Sang Sabda, lan samubarang kang dumadi ora ana sawidji-widjia kang ora didadèkaké déning Sang Sabda. 4 Sang Sabda kang kedunungan urip, sarta urip iku kang dadi pepaḍanging manungsa. 5 Anadéné Sang Paḍang nelahi sadjroning pepeteng, lan ora kalinḍih déning pepeteng iku. 6 Ana prija rawuh kautus déning Allah asmané Jokanan. 7 Rawuhé dadi saksi, kapatah neksèni bab Sang Paḍang, supaja dadia lantarané wong kabèh paḍa pratjaja. 8 Pandjenenganė iku dudu Sang Paḍang pijambak, mung kapatah neksèni bab Sang Paḍang.

JAVANESE, OLD (Kawi)

INTRODUCTION

This is the only Austronesian language whose earlier forms are attested in written record in the shape of an extensive corpus of texts. Herein lies the great importance of Old Javanese. The language makes its first appearance in a legal document dated AD 804, and it reaches its apogee in the rich output of creative literature and re-creation of Sanskrit originals, which continued from the tenth to the fifteenth century. These are the centuries of Indic cultural domination in Sumatra and Java, and it is hardly surprising to find that about a third of Kawi vocabulary consists of Sanskrit roots (always in base form). This imported element does not, however, prevent the language from being, structurally, pure Malayo-Polynesian, close, in many respects, to Modern Javanese. Even the Sanskrit roots are acclimatized, so to say, in a Javanese setting; one might compare the harmonious symbiosis of Arabic words and Persian syntax.

The great period of Old Javanese writing is bound up with the Śailendra and Majapahit Dynasties in eastern Java. On the collapse of the latter, in the face of advancing Islam, the centre of gravity of Old Javanese culture moved to Bali, where it is still preserved as a living entity.

THE LITERATURE

Three main divisions may be recognized:

(a) Recensions of parts of the *Mahābhārata*. These are never exact translations – rather, one might call them restatements of the epic material in Javanese terms.
(b) Didactic fables or cautionary tales, loosely based on such sources as the *Pañcatantra* and the *Jātakas*.
(c) Narrative texts: these combine the myth and history of the Javanese people: e.g. the *Pararaton*, an account of the Majapahit Dynasty which contains the *ken angrok* saga, important for an understanding of the Old and Middle Javanese world-view, and the *Tantu Panggĕlaran*, which is a creation myth.

SCRIPT

See **Script** at end of article.

PHONOLOGY

Consonants

stops: p, b, ʈ/ʈh, ɖ/ɖh, t/th, d/dh, k, g
affricates: tʃ, dʒ
fricatives: s, ʂ, ʃ, j, w, h
nasals: m, n, ɲ, ŋ
lateral and flap: l, r

Retroflex consonants are notated here as *ṭ*, *ḍ*, *ṣ*. The distinction between *s*, *ṣ*, and *ʃ* is relevant for Sanskrit loanwords only. In Old Javanese they were probably all realized as /s/.

Vowels

a, aː, i, uː, ə, e, o, œ, ɽ, ɭ

/ɽ/ and /ɭ/ were probably realized as [rə], [lə], that is, as consonant (r/l) plus /ə/; *ĕ* as /ɐ/.

Little is known about the actual pronunciation of Old Javanese. Long vowels are indicated by a macron in the following text, e.g. *ū*.

Sandhi in compounds and elsewhere is partly Sanskrit and partly Javanese.

MORPHOLOGY AND SYNTAX

No gender, number, or case: e.g. *wwang* 'man/people'. If greater precision is necessary, an indefinite article can be made with the numeral 'one': e.g. *sa.tunggal wwang* 'a man'; pl. with *akweh* 'many': *akweh wwang* 'people'.

The particle *ng/ang* is used as a topicalizing device, suggesting that the noun to which it is affixed is definite, and known to listener or reader, e.g. *ang kathā* 'this story (which is well-known to all of you)'. *kathā* is a Sanskrit loanword. The all-purpose preposition *i*, with variants *ning*, *ing*, *ring*, *ri*, *ni*, serves as a linking particle in possessive relationships: e.g. *wwe ning samudra* 'the waters of the ocean'; *warna ning kuda* 'the horse's colour'.

DERIVATIVE NOUNS

Examples:

pa-: *naḍah* 'to eat' – *pa.naḍah* 'eating' (noun);
-an: *dum* 'to divide' – *duman* 'a part';
ka-: *pĕjah* 'to die' – *kapĕjah* 'death', *doh* 'remote' – *kadohan* 'a far-off place';
ka...*an* makes abstract nouns: *panas* 'hot' – *ka.panas.an* 'heat', *ling* 'word' – *ka.ling.an* 'intention', *pa.kadang.an* 'friendship'.

Adjective

Invariable, follows noun: e.g. *sila item* 'black rock' (cf. Indonesian *hitam* 'black').

Pronoun

Not marked for number or gender:

	Singular and plural	*Enclitics*
1	aku, dak, tak, kami, sun	-ku/-ngku
2	ko, kamu, sira, kita	-mu
3	ya, sira	-nya/-(n)ira

Plus an inventory of honorific and periphrastic forms. The enclitics are sometimes used to replace a verb: e.g. *nātha ling.nya* 'the king his-word' = 'the king said'.

DEMONSTRATIVE PRONOUN

iki 'this' – *iku* 'that' – *ika* 'that yonder'.

INTERROGATIVE PRONOUN

syapa 'who?'; *apa* 'what?'

RELATIVE PRONOUN

Simple apposition may be used: *tan hana wwang* **Ø** *tumahenaken prabhawa.-nya* 'not exist man able-to-resist his-might', i.e. 'there was noone who could . . . '. Demonstratives with *-ng* also function as relatives, e.g. *ikang*:

> Mangaliwati sire**ng** Ksīrārṇawa ikang punuter de ning dewāsura
> 'They sailed across the (sea of) K, which the gods and the asuras had made stormy.'

Numerals

1–10: *tunggal*, *rwa*, *telu*/*tiga*, *pat*/*papat*, *lima*, *nem*, *pitu*, *wwalu*, *sanga*, *sapuluh*; 11 *sawĕlas*; 12 *rwa wĕlas*; 20 *likur*; 21 *salikur*; 30 *telu**ng** puluh*; 100 *atus*.

Verb

The Kawi verb has no tenses, nor is it marked for person; the context is the only guide.

Active and passive voices are, however, formally distinguished by affixation or infixation. For example, (*m*)*a*N-, where N represents the homorganic nasal – *m*, *n*, *ɲ*, *ŋ* – of following initial, is a prefix, e.g. *rengö* 'to hear', *mang.rengö*; *-um-* is an infix, forming active transitive verbs from nouns. Both (*m*)*a*N- and *-um-* also function as intransitive formants: e.g. *laku* 'way' – ***lum**aku* 'to go'. Certain initials, especially labials, are discarded when the prefix is added: cf. *panas* 'warm' – *am**Ø**anas.i* 'to heat'; *santwa* 'respect' – ***sum**antwa* 'to show respect to'. The passive is made either by *-in-* infix, or by *ka-* prefix: e.g. *ton* 'to see' – ***tin**on* = ***ka**ton* 'to be visible'; *-in-* is agent-focused, *ka-* is object-focused. *Paha* → *maha* makes transitives/causatives: e.g. *lĕbā* 'pleasant' – *mahalĕbā* 'to make desirable'.

-akĕn, *-i*: these important suffixes signal the presence of direct object(s), locus of verbal action, and accompanying dynamic movement or change: e.g. *hana* 'there is/are': *mang.han.ākĕn* 'to create'; *ya tanuwuh.akĕn krodha sang gurupatni* 'this arouses the anger (*krodha*, Sanskrit loanword) of the teacher's wife (*gurupatni*, Sanskrit loanword)'; *wwang mangaliwat.i Yamuna* 'people swimming across the Jumna'.

NEGATIVE

The particle is *tan* (with variants): e.g. *Sugyan tan wruha kita ri kami* 'Perhaps you do not know me' (*sugyan* 'perhaps', 'if'; *wruh-* 'to know').

The last sentence illustrates one usage of the linking particle *i/ri/ning*, etc., i.e. to mark the direct or indirect object: e.g. *ri kami* '(to) us'. This particle has many prepositional usages, e.g. *ing hawan* 'on the road'; *i sedeng* 'at that time'; *i sor* 'down below'; *in gruhur* 'above'. Its role as a genitival linking particle has already been mentioned.

Word order

SVO/VSO; when the latter is used, the exact meaning has usually to be elucidated from associated particles and from the context: cf. the sentence given above in illustration of the relative pronoun, where both components – the principal and the relative clause – are verb-initial.

Illustrative passage from the *Tantu Panggĕlaran* (Zurbuchen 1976: 70):

> . . . ndah pahenak tang.denta mang.rengo ring kacaritanikā nusa Jawa ring asitkāla. Iki manusā tanana, nguniweh sang hyang Mahāmeru tan hana ring nusa Jawa; kunang kahananira sang hyang Maṇḍalagiri, sira ta gunung magöng aluhur pina.ka.linggan.ing bhuwana, mungguh ring bhūmi Jambudipa. Ya ta matang.nyān henggang henggung hikang nusa Jawa, sadakāla molah marayegan, hapan tanana sang hyang Mandaraparwata, nguniweh janma manusa. Ya ta matang.nyān mangadeg bhaṭāra Jagadpramanā, rep mayugha ta sira ring nusa Jawadipa lawan bhatārī Parameswari; ya ta matang.nyān hana ri Dihyang ngaranya mangke, tantu bhatāra mayugha nguni kacaritanya.

SCRIPT

The Old Javanese literary language is attested from the tenth century AD. It is known as Kawi (< Sanskrit *kavi* 'sage', 'seer', 'poet'), and it was written in a script which is clearly based on Brāhmī. The same script was used for Old Balinese and Sundanese. Typically Indic features in the script are: (a) its syllabic character: as in Devanāgarī the vowel /a/ inheres in all base-form consonants; (b) the consonantal inventory is ordered in positional (velar, palatal, dental, labial) rows, each of five terms (*see* **Devanāgarī**); in Kawi, however, the retroflex series is represented by *ṭa* and *ḍa* only.

Also characteristically Indic is the presence of signs for /ṛ/ and /ḷ/ and for the three sibilants /s/, /ʃ/, and /ṣ/; also for anusvāra, visarga, and virāma (*see* **Devanāgarī**).

An innovation in Kawi is the presence of signs for short and long /ə/, absent in the Brāhmī model.

With 31 consonantal and 20 vocalic symbols, the Kawi script was well equipped to notate a literary language, about 90 per cent of whose vocabulary consisted of Sanskrit loanwords.

In Kawi, C_2, the second component of a consonantal conjunct C_1C_2, could be written, in somewhat modified form, under C_1. Thus developed through the medieval period the secondary forms, known as *pasangan* in modern Javanese. Other modifications took place: many letters changed in shape, and several, e.g. those denoting the aspirates, were discarded as irrelevant to the needs of modern Javanese. Punctuation signs were also introduced.

Column 1 in the table of consonants shows the primary *aksårå*, column 2 their *pasangan* forms. As noted above, *a* > /ɔ/ is inherent in the *aksårå*. The table of vowels shows the *sandangan* ('clothed') signs used to notate the vowels *e, i, o, u* in post-consonantal position, and certain other phonemes.

In addition, the Classical Javanese script had a series of 'large' or capital letters, for use in the names and titles of distinguished personages.

THE JAVANESE SCRIPT

CONSONANTS

1	*2*	*Name*	*Value*
ꦲ ꦲ	꧀ꦲ ꧀ꦲ	hå	h (mute)
ꦤ ꦤ	꧀ꦤ ꧀ꦤ	nå	n
ꦕ ꦕ	꧀ꦕ ꧀ꦕ	cå	tʃ
ꦫ ꦫ	꧀ꦫ ꧀ꦫ	rå	r
ꦏ ꦏ	꧀ꦏ ꧀ꦏ	kå	k (as final > ʔ)
ꦢ ꦢ	꧀ꦢ ꧀ꦢ	då	d
ꦠ ꦠ	꧀ꦠ ꧀ꦠ	tå	t
ꦱ ꦱ	꧀ꦱ ꧀ꦱ	så	s
ꦮ ꦮ	꧀ꦮ ꧀ꦮ	wå	w
ꦭ ꦭ	꧀ꦭ ꧀ꦭ	lå	l
ꦥ ꦥ	꧀ꦥ ꧀ꦥ	på	p
ꦝ ꦝ	꧀ꦝ ꧀ꦝ	ḍå	ɖ
ꦗ ꦗ	꧀ꦗ ꧀ꦗ	jå	dʒ
ꦪ ꦪ	꧀ꦪ ꧀ꦪ	yå	j
ꦚ ꦚ	꧀ꦚ ꧀ꦚ	ñå	ɲ
ꦩ ꦩ	꧀ꦩ ꧀ꦩ	må	m
ꦒ ꦒ	꧀ꦒ ꧀ꦒ	gå	g
ꦧ ꦧ	꧀ꦧ ꧀ꦧ	bå	b
ꦛ ꦛ	꧀ꦛ ꧀ꦛ	ṭå	ʈ
ꦔ ꦔ	꧀ꦔ ꧀ꦔ	ngå	ŋ

Source: Bohatta, H. (n.d.) *Praktische Grammatik der Javanischen Sprache*, Vienna.

VOWELS AND OTHER SYMBOLS

Sign	*Name*	*Value*
◌ꦼ ◌ꦼ	pěpět	ě
◌ꦶ ◌ꦶ	wulu	i
◌ꦸ ◌ꦸ	suku	u
ꦺ◌ ꦺ◌	taling	é/è
ꦺ◌ꦴ ꦺ◌ꦴ	taling-tarung	o (circumfix)
◌꧀ ◌꧀	pangkon Kr., patěn Ng.	cancels inherent vowel; corresponds to Devanagari virāma
◌ꦾ ◌ꦾ	pingkal	marks palatalized consonant
◌ꦿ, ◌ꦿ ◌ꦿ ◌ꦿ	cåkrå	post-consonantal r
◌ꦽ ◌ꦽ	kěrět	rě following a consonant
◌ꦂ ◌ꦂ	layar	syllabic final r
◌ꦃ ◌ꦃ	wigñan	syllabic final h
◌ꦁ ◌ꦁ	cěcak	syllabic final ŋ
ꦉ ꦉ ꦉ ꦉ	pa-cěrěk	rě
ꦋ ꦋ ꦋ ꦋ	ngå-lělět	lě

Vowels in isolation: these occur mainly in foreign words:

ꦄ ꦄ a ꦌ ꦌ e ꦆ ꦆ i

ꦎ ꦎ o ꦈ ꦈ u

In the vowel table above, Kr. refers to *kråmå* /krɔmɔ/ 'polite, formal speech'; Ng. refers to *ngoko* 'colloquial speech'.

Source: Bohatta, H. (n.d.) *Praktische Grammatik der Javanischen Sprache*, Vienna.

JUANG (Cuəŋ)

INTRODUCTION

A member of the Juang-Dai branch of the Tai family, Juang 僮 enjoys official status as a major minority language of the People's Republic of China (along with Tibetan, Mongolian, Uighur, and Korean), and is spoken by about 13 million people in the Juang Autonomous Region of Guangxi (established in 1958). Other groups of Juang live in Yunnan, Guizhou, and Guangdong. All Juang are bilingual. The literary standard is based on Wuming usage (Northern dialect).

SCRIPT

Until the 1950s Juang was occasionally written in a script based on Chinese, in which Chinese characters were freely and arbitrarily adapted, truncated, and compounded. The closest parallel is perhaps with the *chữnom* script used formerly in Vietnam (*see* **Vietnamese**). In the 1950s a roman-based script with additional signs was adopted. Among the additional letters are five indicating tones 2–6. In this article, the Arabic numerals are used.

PHONOLOGY

As in Chinese, the phonemes of Juang are divided into two classes – initials and finals. A Juang syllable may be (a) a vowel or diphthong; (b) an initial consonant + vowel or diphthong; (c) as (b) + a permissible final; (d) vowel or diphthong + permissible final. Permissible finals are the nasals and the stops /p, t, k/ which are not released; that is, they become implosives. Chinese students of Juang have established a Thai-type connection between tone and initial consonant. Thus, for words with initial *b, d, j, w, h*, tones 1, 3, 5 are normal; for all other initials, 2 and 4 are normal.

Consonants

stops: p, b, t, d, k, ʔ; k′, k°
fricatives: f, ç, s > θ, h
nasals: m, n, ɲ, ŋ, ŋ°
laterals: l, r/γ
semi-vowels: j, w

The Serdyučenko (1961) table of consonants includes /ʔ/, but it is not clear whether this is indeed a glottal stop or a hamza-type onset /ʕ/, e.g. preceding *j, w, b, d*: /ʕj, ʕw, ʕb, ʕd/. *g* is also absent from the Serdyučenko table, but figures in his text, e.g. *gou* 'I', denoting the half-voiced non-aspirate /g̥/.

There is no dental /s/; *ç* is used to notate a palatalized /c/.

In some Juang dialects, initial clustering of the Thai type is tolerated: e.g. *ml, pl*; in the standard language, these tend to be reduced and palatalized; e.g. /pl/ > [p′].

The labialized /ŋ°/ is a characteristic Juang sound.

Vowels

The basic vowels are:

i, e, ə, a, ɯ, o, u

All may be long or short, except /e/ and /a/ which are short only. Short /o/ is notated as *θ*.

Tone

Some authorities specify six tones, others eight including two 'checked tones' used with /p, t, k/ finals. The tone markers are placed immediately after words, e.g. *wun*2 'man'; *ma*4 'horse'. Tone 2 is low falling, 3 high even, 4 falling, 5 mid-rising, 6 low rising.

MORPHOLOGY AND SYNTAX

Noun

As in Chinese, the parts of speech in Juang may be classified in terms of nominals, verbals, and particles. A further division is into free and bound forms. Apart from many lexical items, Juang has borrowed from Chinese certain structural features, e.g. the relational particle *-de* (the Juang form is *ti*6), e.g. to form a genitive case which coexists with the standard Juang appositional genitive: cf. *səɯ kou* ('book – I') = *kou də səɯ* 'my book'. Other case relations are positionally determined. A plural form may be made for nouns denoting persons by means of a specific classifier.

Juang has a great many classifiers. These precede the noun, e.g. *bon*3 for books, *diu*2 for rivers, *lau*4 for old people, generalized, as in Chinese, to provide a familiar mode of addressing people of any age. The classifier *ən* has become an all-purpose classifier, equivalent to the Chinese *ge*. A specific classifier may replace its referent nominal: e.g. *bon*3 *kou* 'my book' (the classifier *bon*3 fixes the referent as a book), *bon*3 *hən*4 'that book'.

Adjective

Adjective follows noun as in Thai: e.g. *va diŋ* 'red flower'; *ko saŋ* 'high tree'. It may be intensified by reduplication: e.g. *diŋdiŋ* 'brilliant red'.

Pronoun

The personal pronouns are:

	Singular	*Plural*
1	kou/gou	tou, rəu2
2	muɯŋ2	sou
3	te	k′əŋte

As possessive forms these follow the noun: e.g. *na*2 *kou* 'my field'; *bi*6 *sou* 'your clothes'.

DEMONSTRATIVE PRONOUN

*nei*4 'this'; *hən*4 'that'. Again as in Thai, these follow the noun.

INTERROGATIVE PRONOUN

*bou*4 *ləɪ*2 'who?'; *ki*6 *ma*2 'what?'

Numerals

1–10: *te*, *soŋ*, *sam*, *sei*5, *ha*3, *rŏk*, *cət*, *bet*, *kou*3, *cip*; 11 *cip it*; 12 *cip soŋ*; 20 *ŋei*6 *cip*; 30 *sam cip*; 40 *sei*5 *cip*; 100 *bak* (Chinese *băi*).

Verb

Stems may be simple or compound: e.g. *gu*6 'do', *sieŋ*3 'think'; *ro*4*nau* 'know' (*ro*4 'know' + *nau* 'speak'). Stems may be reduplicated – type xxyy is common: e.g. *bəibəimama* 'come'.

There are no tenses or personal endings; hence, personal pronouns are always necessary. Tense is inferred from the context (e.g. the presence of adverbial indicators) and from certain aspectual markers, e.g. *lo* denoting completed action (cf. Chinese *le*); other perfective markers are *kwa*5 and *liu*4/*leu*: e.g. *kɯn* 'eat' – *kɯn.liu*4 'ate up'.

*to*4/*ta*3 may be prefixed to a stem to denote customary action: e.g. *ta*3*təm* 'to plough'.

Juang has an elaborate system of modal co-verbs (resultative, directional, potential, etc.): e.g. *tei*3 = *kam*3 'be able to'; *ɪŋdaŋ* 'have to' (Chinese); *n′ien*6 'want to'.

COPULA

/tɪk/, notated as *duɯg*, is used between nominals: e.g. *soutu rəu*2 *duɯg Bəkgiŋ* 'our capital is Beijing'; *ən ran*2 *nei*4 *duɯg hakdaŋ* 'this building is a school'.

NEGATION

The negating particle *bou*3 precedes verb: e.g. *bou*3 *gu*6 'not work'.

Prepositions

Examples: *da*3 'from', 'out of'; *vi*6 'for'; *vi*6*liu*4 'on account of'. *Doi*5 is used to indicate an indirect object: e.g. *doi*5 *te gaŋ*3 'to tell him'.

Vocabulary

The basic Tai stock is supplemented with many borrowings, both ancient and modern, from Chinese.

Basic Tai words are: *bo*6 'father', *me*6 'mother', *wun*2 'man', *ma* 'dog'. Ancient Chinese loanwords include *mu* 'eye', *lu* 'way', *ma*4 'horse'. Modern Chinese loanwords: e.g. *ciŋciu* = Ch. *zhèngzhì* 'politics'; *ban6fap* = Ch. *bànfă* 'method', 'procedure'.

An interesting group of compounds takes the form AB, where A is a general generic term particularized by B: e.g. for birds the generic term is *rŏg*: e.g. *rŏggum*3 'female quail'; *rŏgbieghag* 'white crane'; *rŏgbit* 'duck'.

Word order

SVO

KABARD-CHERKES

INTRODUCTION

Kabard-Cherkes belongs to the Abkhaz-Adyge group of North-West Caucasian, and is spoken by between 300,000 and 350,000 people in the Kabardino-Balkaria Republic and in the Karachaevo-Cherkessia Republic. A literary norm, based on the dialect of Bol′šaya Kabarda dates from 1924.

SCRIPT

Since the late 1930s, Cyrillic + *I*, which is used to mark the ejective consonants.

PHONOLOGY

Consonants

plosives: b, p, p', d, t, t', g°, k°, k°', q, q', q°, q°', ʔ
affricates: dz, ts, t's, dʒ, tʃ, t'ʃ
fricatives: v, f, f', z, s, ź, ś, ś', ʒ, ʃ, γ, x, x°, ʁ, χ, ʁ°, χ°, h/ħ
nasals: m, n
lateral and flap: l, ɬ, l', r

In the following description, the ejective consonants are marked with subscript dot: i.e. /t'/ is notated as *ṭ*. The alveo-palatal series of fricatives /ź, ś, ś'/ is notated here as *z̄*, *s̄*, *s̄'*.

In the Cyrillic script, the ejective palatal affricate /t'ʃ/ is notated as K*I*; in this article as *č̣*. Cyrillic *KIy*, however, is /k'°/, *ḳ°*.

Vowels

Kabardian has been variously described as vowel-less (Kuipers 1960), as having a basic opposition between /ə/ and /a/aː/ (Jakovlev 1923), and as having one single vowel /a/. Šagirov (1967) gives the following list:

high: i, u
middle: e, ı, o
low: ɛ, a

This is also the inventory given by Kardanov in the 1955 Russian-Kabard dictionary.

The basic Kabardian vowels seem to be /a, ı, ɛ/; the other vowels as listed by Šagirov are secondary formations involving the semi-vowels /j, w/. In this entry, *a* is used as a generalized sign for the basic Kabardian vowel sound, whose values range over /a, ı, ɛ/.

MORPHOLOGY AND SYNTAX

Noun

Nouns are definite or indefinite. All nominals are declined in three cases, according to one paradigm: nom. in *-r*, erg. in *-m*, instr. in *-ç̌a*.

CASE

The ergative figures as logical subject with a transitive verb; the logical object is in the nominative case: e.g. *š̄aḳ°**em** š̄ıhır **yu**č̣aš̄* 'by the hunter – the deer – killed'. The *-m* form may also be the direct or indirect object with both transitive and intransitive verbs, depending on the opposition between dynamic and stative versions: e.g. *ş̄aler radio**m** yoda'we* 'the boy listens to the radio'; *sa thılım sodže* 'I read the book'.

Postpositional or instrumental case: in *-ç̌a*, e.g. *qarandaš̄.ç̌a* 'with a pencil' (Russian loanword).

NUMBER

The plural marker is *-xa*: e.g. *žıg* 'tree', pl. *žıg.xa.r*; *wuner* 'house', pl. *wunaxar/wunexer*.

Adjective

As attribute, adjective follows noun: e.g. *psı š̄ı'a* 'cold water'; *zawe š̄ı'a* 'cold war'.

COMPARISON

A comparative is made with *neχra*: e.g. *neχ jən* 'bigger'; *Mo wınem neχra mı wıner neχ jənš̄* 'This house is bigger than that one.'

Pronoun

	Singular	*Plural*
1	sa/se	da/de
2	wa/we	fa/fe

These have no specific ergative forms. The possessive adjective forms are sing. *si – wi*, pl. *di – fi*: e.g. *si q°eš* 'my brother'.

The third person pronouns are: sing. *ar*, pl. *axer*. These have ergative forms: *abı*, *abıxem*. The third person possessive pronouns, sing. *i*, pl. *ya*, are always preceded by these ergative forms: *abı i wune* 'his house'; *mı wune.r abı ey.š̄* 'this house is his'; *abıxem ya wune* 'their house'.

DEMONSTRATIVE PRONOUN/ADJECTIVE

ar 'this'; *mır* 'that'; *mor* 'that' (further away); *a/mı thılır* 'this/that book'.

INTERROGATIVE PRONOUN

xet 'who?'; *sıt* 'what?'

RELATIVE PRONOUN

The same as the interrogative; or participial construction may be used: e.g. *sto**łm** teł thıłır* 'the book which is lying on the table' (Russian loanword).

Numerals

1–10: *zı, ṭu, ṣ̄ı, pḷı, txu, xı, blı, yi, bγu, pṣ̄ı. Zı* precedes the noun; 2–10 inclusive follow noun in affixed form: e.g. *wune.ṣ̄* 'three houses'; *çıx°ıpṣ̄* 'ten men'. 11 *pṣ̄ı.ḳ°.z*; 12 *pṣ̄ı.ḳ°.ṭ*; 20 *ṭoṣ̄*; 30 *ṣ̄aṣ̄*; 100 *ṣ̄a*.

Verb

The Kabardian verbal system is very complicated and rather confusing; only a brief outline can be attempted here. There are two basic oppositions: (a) transitive/intransitive, and (b) dynamic/stative. However, many roots are labile, and function equally as transitive or intransitive. Both transitive and intransitive verbs may be dynamic or stative, though the latter are mainly intransitive. Thus, for example, *sa s.o.ẑe(r)* 'I await him' is construed as intransitive, polypersonal, dynamic; while *sa sı.ṣ̄ısṣ̄* 'I sit' is intransitive, monopersonal, stative. All transitive verbs are polypersonal; intransitives may be either mono- or polypersonal.

Since the verb is not marked for person, personal pronominal markers are used; normally, the independent personal pronoun is also used: e.g. ***sa*** *s.o.tx.e* 'I write', ***fe*** *f.o.tx.e* 'you (pl.) write'. The full personal pronominal prefix inventory is:

1st person: sing. *s(ı)/z(ı)*; pl. *d(ı)/t(ı)*;
2nd person: sing. *w(ı)/b/p/p̣*; pl. *f(ı), f̣/v(ı)*.

The 3rd person prefix is Ø in stative verbs, *ma/me* in monopersonal intransitives, and *i-* (sing.)/*ya-* (pl.) with transitive verbs. Cf. ***Ø****ṣ̄ısṣ̄* 'he sits'; ***me.****laẑe* 'he works'; *abıxem* ***ya.****tx* 'they write'.

Transitive verbs: the subject is in the ergative case; the direct object in the nominative:

ṣ̄aḳ°e**m** ṣ̄ıhı**r** yuçaṣ̄ 'the hunter (*ṣ̄aḳ°e*) killed the deer (*ṣ̄ıh*)'

In the present tense of both transitive and intransitive verbs, 1st and 2nd persons have an *-o-* characteristic: examples with the intransitive verb *edžen* 'to read' (polypersonal):

sa thıłım **s.o.**dž.e 'I read the book'
we thıłım **w.o.**dž.e 'you (sing.) read the book'
fe thıłım **f.o.**dž.e 'you (pl.) read the book'

With polypersonal verbs, the 3rd person takes the *-o-* characteristic, with which it is incompatible in the case of monopersonal verbs:

ar thıłım **y.o.**dž.e 'he reads the book'

The present tense is negated by suffixed *-r.qım*; the *-o-* characteristic becomes *-e-*:

sa thıłım **s.e.**dž.e.rqım 'I don't read the book'

PAST TENSE

There are several past tenses, each of which represents a specific segmentation of past time in terms of aspect/tense: typical characteristics are *-a-* (perfective), *-γa-* (perfective in distant past). The participial base marker *-š̄* is affixed: cf.

sa thıłım **s.**e.dž̄.**a.š̄** 'I read the book'
sa **s.**ı.tx.**a.**γ**a.š̄** 'I had written'

These are negated by *-qım*; *-š̄* drops:

sa thıłım **s.**e.dž.**a.qım** 'I did not read the book'
sa **s.**ı.tx.**a.**γ**a.qım** 'I had not written'

A past anterior is also made with *-at*: *de dı.lež̄.**at*** 'we had already worked'.

FUTURE TENSE

The characteristic is *-nu-* plus *š̄*:

sa **s**ı.lež̄.e.**nu.š̄** 'I shall work/have worked', negative: sa **s**ı.lež̄.**qım**
axer **Ø**.lež̄.e.**nu.š̄** 'they will work/have worked'

The same apparatus of personal pronominal markers and formal characteristics is used to conjugate nominals. Cf. *sa sı.X.š̄* 'I am X', where X is a nominal, e.g. *selet* 'soldier', *lež̄ak̦°e* 'worker'. Similarly, *sa sı.X.**aš̄*** 'I was an X'; *sa sı.X.**nu**.š̄* 'I shall be an X'.

IMPERATIVE

For the 1st person, a basic formula is: personal marker plus prefix *-re-* plus stem (minus *-n* of the infinitive): *sı.re.k̦°e* 'let me go!' For the 2nd person, the stem suffices: *k̦°e* 'go!' The 3rd person singular/plural imperative is made with *ire-*: *ire.laže* 'let him/them work!'

PREVERBS

Prefixed to verbs these generate many nuances of mode, manner, place: e.g. with *de-/dı-/xe-/xı-*:

mašına.r weramı**m d**etš 'the car is standing in the street'
psı**m xa**.sın 'stand in the water'
thılır stolım **te**.ł.š̄ 'the book is lying on the table'
ş̄ı**m xe**łın 'to lie on the earth'
š̄heγubže**m de**.płın 'to look out of the window'

PARTICIPLES

An active participle is provided by the stem, minus *-n* of the infinitive: e.g.

from *txen* 'to write', *txe.r* 'writing', '(he) who writes'; *tx.**a**.r* '(he) who wrote', *txe.**nu**.r* '(he) who will write'.

The transitive active formant is *zı-*: *zı.hır* 'he who bears'; *zı. šar* 'he who leads'.

Passive participle: typical markers are *zı-/za-/zar-*: e.g. in

present: *sa sı.ze.džer* 'being read by me';
past: *sa sı.ze.dž**a**r* 'read by me';
future: *sa sı.ze.dže.**nu**.r* 'to be read by me'.

GERUND

Examples: ***sa**.dž.aw* 'I (while) reading . . . '; ***da**.dž.aw* 'we (while) reading . . . '.

Postpositions

In Kabardian these are not clearly differentiated from nominals and verbals; they may be declined. Examples: *dež* 'at', 'of', e.g. *nıbžeγ°m dež* 'at/of (my) friend', *Muhamad i ḳ°ašım dež šı' aš* 'Muhamad was at his brother's place'; *nes* 'as far as', 'up to', e.g. *qalam nes ḳ°e* 'go to the town'. In these examples, *nıbžeγ°.m* and *ḳ°aši.m* are both in the *-m* case.

Word order

SOV is basic.

KACHIN

INTRODUCTION

Burmic group of Sino-Tibetan. The Kachin area forms the northern-most administrative unit in Myanmar (Burma) (capital Myityina). There are about 160,000 speakers in Myanmar, and possibly 80,000 in China. The ethnonym is Tsingpho. The many dialects can be grouped in three main divisions: (a) Tsingpho, (b) Maru, (c) Nung.

SCRIPT

A Roman alphabet with diacritics was provided for Kachin by O. Hanson in 1896. The diacritics mark the reduced vowels; the tones are not marked. A revised and simplified script for Kachin as spoken in China was worked out in the 1950s. Hanson's script, used here, marks the aspirates as *hp*, *ht*, *hk*.

PHONOLOGY

Consonants

stops: non-aspirate: p, b, t, d, k, g, ʔ; aspirate: p', t', k'; retroflex p̣, ḅ, ḳ, g̣; aspirate p̣', ḳ'
affricates: ts, tʃ, dʒ
fricatives: f, v, s, z, ʃ, ʒ, h
nasals: m, n, ŋ, m′, n′
lateral: l
semi-vowels: w, j
palatalized: p′, b′, k′, g′
aspirated: p', t', k', p̣', ḳ'
aspirated and palatalized: p'′, k'′

Vowels

i, e, ə, ă, a, ɑ, o, u

Tone

The dialect described by Puzitski (1968) has three tones (not marked): mid-level, high-level, mid-falling. Tone is phonemic.

MORPHOLOGY AND SYNTAX

Noun

Nouns are indeclinable, and there is no grammatical gender. If necessary, lexical means are used to specify male/female, e.g. *-la-* for male, *-num-* for female: pre- or post-positive: e.g. *kăsha* 'child': *lakăsha* 'boy', *numkăsha* 'girl'; *myenla* 'Burmese man', *myennum* 'Burmese woman'. A similar pair for animals is *la/yi*: e.g. *gumrala* 'stallion', *gumrayi* 'mare'.

The particle *ni* acts as a pluralizer: e.g. *măsha ni* 'people'; *gumra ni* 'horses'. A plural may also be made by reduplication.

Adjective

Invariable; adjective may precede or follow noun; if preceding, it takes relative marker *ai*: e.g. *sănat gălu* 'long rifle'; *gălu ai sănat* 'long – which-is – rifle'.

COMPARATIVE

Made with *hta grau* 'more than': e.g. *Ngai a kumra gaw wora hta grau kăba ai* 'My horse is bigger than that one' (*ngai a*, *see* **Pronoun**, below; *gaw*, subject marker; *wora*, demonstrative pronoun; *kăba* (verb) 'to be big').

Pronoun

PERSONAL INDEPENDENT

	Singular	*Dual*	*Plural*
1	ngai	an	anhte(ng)
2	nang	nan	nanhte(ng)
3	shi, hkri	shan, hkan	shanhte(ng), hkanhte

The *hk-* forms are colloquial.

POSSESSION

First and second person singular have specific possessive forms, *nye*, *na*: e.g. *nye nta* 'my house'; *na sha* 'your child'. All three persons also make a possessive by means of the particle *a*/*ai*: e.g. *nang a nta* 'your house'; *shi a gumra* 'his horse'.

DEMONSTRATIVE PRONOUN

Three-degree graduation: *ndai* 'this' – *dai* 'that' – *waw* 'that yonder'; with a plural, *ndaini* 'these'. Another series of demonstratives takes into account position in vertical plane relative to speaker: e.g. *wora* (on the same level as speaker), *htawra* (higher than speaker), *lera* (lower). Example: *ndai laika* = *laika ndai* 'this book'.

INTERROGATIVE PRONOUN

Kădai 'who?'; *kăra* 'what?'; with plural in *-ni*, or reduplication.

RELATIVE PRONOUN

ai is used: e.g. *ngai hpe karum ai masha* 'the man (*masha*) who (*ai*) helps (*hpe karum*) me'.

Numerals

1–10: *lăngai, lăhkawng, măsum, măli, mănga, kru, sătnit, măsat, chăhku, shi*; 20 *nkum/hkum*; 30 *sum shi*; 40 *măli shi*; 100 *lă sa*.

Numerical classifiers are used: collectives (e.g. *hpun* 'a herd') and measure words (e.g. *lin* 'a vessel'). The numeral follows the classifier: e.g. *saupa lin lahkawng* 'two measures of water'.

Verb

The invariable base is followed by grammatical markers which generate distinctions of aspect, mood, tense, and – exceptionally for a Sino-Tibetan language – person. For example, in imperfective aspect, *galaw* 'to do', present tense:

	Singular	*Plural*
1	ngai gălaw nngai	anhte gălaw gă ai
2	nang gălaw ndai	nanhte gălaw mă ndai
3	shi gălaw ai	shihte gălaw mă ai

In perfective aspect, past tense: e.g. sing. 1 *ngai gălaw sa ngai* 'I did'; pl. 1 *anhte gălaw sa ga ngai* 'we did'.

These grammatical markers are also coded for subject/object relationship; e.g. *de ai* encodes action by 1st p. sing. on or for 2nd p. sing.: *ngai nang hpe jaw de ai* 'I give you this' (*hpe* (postposition) 'to', 'for'); *mi ai* encodes action by 2nd or 3rd p. sing. on 1st p. sing.: *shanhte ngai hpe tsun mi ai* 'they speak to me'. Similarly in hortative mood and interrogative version: *shi sa u ga!* 'let him go!'; *Shi hpa ra ai ta* 'What does he want?' Cf. *Nang namsi sha n ni* 'Do you eat fruit?' (imperfective aspect; *n ni* = 2nd on 3rd); *Nang namsi sha sa ni* 'Did you eat the fruit?' (perfective aspect: *sa ni* encodes action by 2nd on 3rd; *sha* 'eat', cf. Tibetan /za.ba/).

TENSE MARKERS

Future *na*, e.g. *shi sa na ai* 'he will come'; past *yu*.

MODAL AFFIXES

Continuative *nga*; inchoative *wa*; terminative *tawn*; potential *lu/dang*: e.g. *ngai gălaw lu nngai* 'I can do this'; *ngai gălaw lu na* 'I shall have to do this'.

NEGATIVE

The marker *n* precedes the verb, e.g. *n gălaw* 'not to work'. The prohibitive marker is *hkum*: e.g. *hkum sa!* 'don't go!'

Word order

Fixed SOV; indirect object precedes direct.

1 Shawng npawt ē, Mungga nga ai, dai
Mungga mung, Kărai Kăsang hte rau nga
ai rai nna, dai Mungga gaw, Kărai Kăsang
2 rē ai rai. Dai gaw shawng npawt ē, Kărai
3 Kăsang hte rau nga ai. Shi kaw nna arai
yawng măyawng tai wa ai rē; shi hta nna,
ntai ai arai lăngai mi muk, n tai ai rai.
4 Shi hta nsoi nsa rawng ai; dai nsoi nsa
5 chyawm gaw, măsha ni a nhtoi rē. Dai
nhtoi gaw, nsin hta a htoi nga ai; nsin
chyawm gaw, dai hpe n hkap la wu ai.
6 Kărai Kăsang shăngun dat ai, Yawhan
7 mying ai măsha lăngai mi, sa ra ai. Dai
wa gaw sakse tai na sa ai; mahkra shi kaw
nna kam mu ga, dai nhtoi a lam shi sakse
8 hkam na rai. Shi gaw dai nhtoi n rai, dai
nhtoi a lam sakse hkam na shi sa ai.

KALMYK

INTRODUCTION

Kalmyk belongs to the Oyrat branch of Mongolian. In the seventeenth century the Kalmyk left their Central Asian homelands and moved westwards, finally to settle along the lower Volga; it is here that most of them now live, in the Kalmykia Republic. The number of speakers is put at *c.* 140,000. During the Second World War, the Kalmyk were one of the minority peoples deported to Central Asia on a charge of collaboration with the enemy. The Kalmyk Autonomous Soviet Socialist Republic was re-established in the late 1950s.

There is a sizeable Kalmyk population, probably around 5,000, in the Xinjiang-Uigur Autonomous Region of the CPR.

SCRIPT

Till the mid-seventeenth century a variety of the vertical Mongolian script was used. Cyrillic was adopted in 1924, and again in 1939, after the experimental romanization in the 1930s. Non-initial short vowels are not notated in the script: thus *uls* = /uləs/. Additional letters: *h, җ, ц, ә, ɵ, ү, ң*.

PHONOLOGY

Consonants

stops: (p), b, t, d, k, g
affricates: ts, tʃ, dʒ
fricatives: (f), s, (z), ʃ, ʒ, j, x, h
nasals: m, n, ŋ
lateral and flap: l, r

Vowels

long and short: i, ɛ, ə, a, y, œ, o, u

There are no diphthongs. /y/ is notated here as *ü*; /œ/ as *ö*.

VOWEL HARMONY

Front vowels followed by front, back by back, with /i/ neutral. /ɛ, o, œ/ long and short, are found only in first syllables; in following syllables they tend to be neutralized, /ɛ/ and /œ/ to /y/ or /ə/, /o/ to /a/ or /u/.

MORPHOLOGY AND SYNTAX

Noun

The noun is marked for number and case. Vocalic stems take a plural marker *-s*: e.g. *xarada* 'swallow', pl. *xaradas.* Other pluralizing affixes are *-ud/-üd*, *-mud/-müd*, *-čud/-čüd*: e.g. *nökəd* 'comrade', pl. *nökədmüd*; *-nr*: e.g. *bagš* 'teacher', pl. *bagšnr* /bagʃənər/.

There are nine cases, including the nominative base with null marker; the other cases may be illustrated with noun *mal* 'cattle': gen. *malin*; dat./loc. *mald*; acc. *malig*; instr. *malar*; abl. *malas*; conj. *malla*; com. *malta*; adit. *malur.* The same endings are added to the plural: e.g. *nökədmüdin* 'of the comrades'.

As in Khalkha (*see* **Mongolian**, **Modern**), the reflexive possessive (*-n* added to inflected stem, e.g. *malasən* 'from one's own cattle') and the double declension (especially genitive + comitative) are frequent.

Adjective

Adjective precedes the noun as attribute and is invariable.

Pronoun

Independent forms with oblique bases and possessive markers:

	Singular			*Plural*		
	Nominative	*Oblique base*	*Possessive*	*Nominative*	*Oblique base*	*Possessive*
1	bi	nan-	-m	bidn	man-	-mdn
2	či	čam-	-čn	tadn	tan-	-tn

The first person plural has an alternative nominative form, *madn.* Third person forms are supplied from the demonstrative series: *ẹn* 'this', *ter* 'that'.

INTERROGATIVE PRONOUN

ken, 'who?'; *yun* 'what?'

Numerals

1–10: *negn*, *xoyr*, *hurvn*, *dörvn*, *tavn*, *zurhan*, *dolan*, *nəəmn*, *yisn*, *arvn*; 20 *xörn*; 30 *hučn*; 40 *döčn*; 100 *zun*. Decimal system.

Verb

In general, close to Khalkha (*see* **Mongolian**, **Modern**). The Kalmyk verb is marked for aspect (durative, intensive, etc.), five voices (active, passive, hortative, reciprocal, co-operative), two moods (indicative, imperative), tense, person, and number. Overt tense marking is restricted to the indicative mood and the participial forms.

INDICATIVE MOOD

Present and past-tense forms are distinguished. The markers are: general present *-na/-nə*; past *-v*; past anterior *-la/-lə*. To the stem and tense marker is added the personal affix for first or second person:

	Singular	*Plural*
1	-v	-vdn
2	-č	-t

Thus, *naad.na.v* 'I play'.

A progressive present is made with the participial form in *-č/-dž* + shortened auxiliary: e.g. *bič.dž.ənəv* 'I am writing'.

The participles and gerunds, or converbs, express various modes and stages of conjoint, contemporary, anterior, successive action; for detail of the closely similar Khalkha system, *see* **Mongolian, Modern**.

A general negating particle is *ẹs.*

Postpositions

Follow nominative, genitive, or comitative cases.

Word order

SOV is basic.

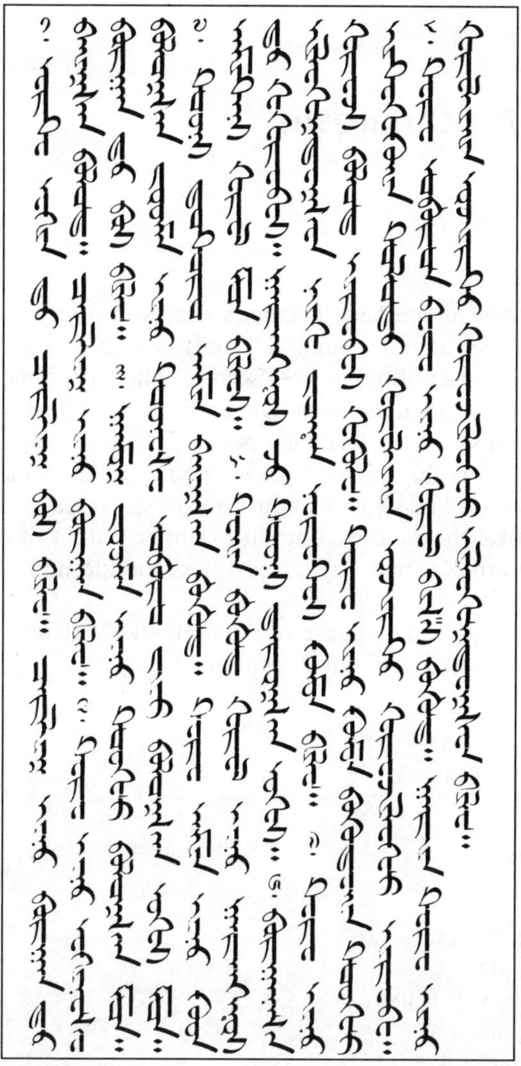

KANNADA (Kanarese)

INTRODUCTION

As regards number of speakers, Kannada comes in third place among the Dravidian languages after Telugu and Tamil; as regards age and quality of literary tradition, it runs Tamil a close second. The most important work in the early period is the *Kavirājamārga*, a rhetorical Sanskritized treatise, enlivened by glimpses of the Kannada people and their customs. Worthy of particular mention is the splendid *vacana* poetry of the Vīraśaiva saints – free verse of mystical and gnomic import in colloquial Kannada – produced in the tenth to twelfth centuries. With its extensive output of novels, drama, and verse, Modern Kannada literature is one of the most flourishing in southern India.

Kannada is the official language of the State of Karnataka. The number of speakers is estimated at about 27 million.

SCRIPT

See **Script** at end of article.

PHONOLOGY

Consonants

stops: p, b, ʈ, ɖ, t, d, k, g
affricates: tʃ, dʒ
fricatives: v, s, ʂ, l̲, ʃ, j, h
nasals: m, n, ɲ, ŋ, ɳ
lateral and flap: l, ɭ, r, r̲

/l̲/ is the retroflex fricative which tends to be pronounced as [l] in Modern Kannada. Similarly, /r̲/ tends to [r]. The stops have aspirated values, not usually found in pure Kannada words. The affricates also have aspirated values. Retroflex phonemes are notated here with a dot: e.g. /ɖ/ = *ḍ*.

Vowels

long and short: i, e, a, o, u
diphthongs: ai, au

Stress

Light stress on first syllable. All Kannada words end in vowels.

Sandhi

/j/ and /v/ are widely used in vocalic juncture: e.g. *guru* + *-u* → *guruvu* 'guru', 'teacher'; *ā* + *ūṭa* → *āvūṭa* 'that food'; *huli* 'tiger' + *-inda* (instr. affix) → *huliyinda* 'by the tiger'.

MORPHOLOGY AND SYNTAX

Noun

Kannada has three genders: masculine, feminine, and neuter. A typical masculine ending is *-anu*, typical feminine *-aḷu*. Plural markers are *-aru*, *-kaḷu/gaḷu*. Thus, *sēvaka.nu* 'male servant', and *sēvaka.ḷu* 'female servant', share the plural form *sēvaka.ru*: cf. *maravu* 'tree', pl. *mara.gaḷu*; *ūru* 'village', 'town', pl. *ūru.gaḷu*. A reduplicated plural of respect is found: e.g. *dēv.aru.gaḷu* 'gods'.

DECLENSION

There are seven cases: given here is the specimen declension of *sēvaka* 'servant':

	Singular
nominative	sēvakanu
accusative	sēvakanannu
instrumental	sēvakaninda
dative	sēvakanige
genitive	sēvakana
locative	sēvakanalli
vocative	sēvakanē

Plural forms are as singular, with *-r-* replacing *-n-*: e.g. nom. *sēvakaru*, acc. *sēvakarannu*.

Adjective

As attribute, adjective is invariable, preceding noun: e.g. *doḍḍa ūru* 'a big town'.

Pronoun

The first person singular is *nān(u)/nā*, with pl. *nāvu*; similarly, the second person forms are sing. *nīnu/nī*, with pl. *nīvu*. The third person forms are marked for gender: masc. *avanu/ivanu*; fem. *avaḷu/ivaḷu*, in the singular; they share a common plural form: *avaru/ivaru*. The neuter third person form is sing. *adu/idu*, pl. *avu(gaḷu)/ivu(gaḷu)*.

In the declension of the first person singular form, *nān(u)* the base for the oblique cases remains *nann-*: e.g. gen. *nanna*, acc. *nannannu*.

DEMONSTRATIVE PRONOUN

ī/intha 'this'; *ā/antha* 'that'

INTERROGATIVE PRONOUN

Masc. *yāvanu*, fem. *yāvaḷu*; they coalesce as *yāru* 'who?'; *yāvudu* 'what?'

RELATIVE PRONOUN

None in Kannada; *see* **Verb**, below, for formation of relative clause.

Numerals

The numerals 1–5 inclusive have each two forms reflecting gender. The neuter series is *ondu, eraḍu, mūru, nālku, aidu*; the corresponding masculine/feminine forms are *obba, ibbaru, mūvaru, nālvaru, aivaru*. From 6 onwards, there is only one form for each numeral. Numbers 6–10: *āru, ēḷu, eṇṭu, ombhattu, hattu*. 11 *hannondu*; 12 *hanneraḍu*; 13 *hadimūru*; 20 *ippattu*; 21 *ippattondu*; 30 *muvattu*; 40 *nālvattu*; 100 *nūru*.

Verb

Fundamental to the structure of the Kannada verb is the verbal noun series comprising the infinitive, the gerunds, and the participles. For the stem *māḍu* 'to do', 'make', the forms are:

infinitive: *māḍa*;
gerunds: present *māḍuttā*, past *māḍi*, negative *māḍade*;
participles: present *māḍuva*, past *māḍida*, negative *māḍada*.

For many Kannada verbs, the form of the verbal noun is not predictable: cf. *koḍu* 'to give' – *koṭṭu*; *koḷḷu* 'to take' – *koṇḍu*; *nagu* 'to laugh' – *nakku*.

There are three moods: indicative, imperative, suppositional.

INDICATIVE MOOD

Present tense (marker -(*u*)*tt*); past tense (marker -(*i*)*d*); future tense (marker -(*u*)*v*). Thus, from stem *māḍu* 'to do':

		Present			*Past*			*Future*	
		Sing.	*Pl.*		*Sing.*	*Pl.*		*Sing.*	*Pl.*
1	māḍu**tt**.	-ēne	-ēve	māḍ**id**	-ēnu	-evu	māḍu**v**	-enu	-evu
2		-īye	-īri		-e	-iri		-e	-iri
3	masc.	-āne	-āre		-anu	-aru		-anu	-aru
	fem.	-āḷe			-aḷu			-aḷu	
	nt.	-ade	-ave		māḍitu	-uvu		-udu	-uvu

NEGATIVE CONJUGATION

The personal affixes are added directly to the root, without infixed marker. The negative form thus produced does duty for all three tenses: thus, the present, past, and future negative indicative of *māḍu* is:

		Singular	Plural
1		māḍenu	māḍevu
2		māḍe	māḍiri
3	masc.	māḍanu	māḍaru
	fem.	māḍaḷu	
	nt.	māḍadu	māḍavu

IMPERATIVE MOOD

Here the verb is marked for three persons, singular and plural, without distinction of gender in the third person: e.g. sing. 1 *māḍuve*, 2 *māḍu*, 3 *māḍali*; pl. *māḍōṇa* (with variants), *māḍiri*, *māḍali*.

SUPPOSITIONAL MOOD

Made by adding the personal affixes to the stem extended by the past-tense characteristic vowel *-i*: e.g. *māḍ.**i**.y.ēnu* 'I may/might do'.

NON-FINITE FORMS

Present-future participle: *māḍuva* 'doing', 'is doing', 'will be doing'. Past participle: *māḍida* 'was doing'. Pronominal endings may be attached to these forms to produce verbal nouns marked in third person for gender: e.g. *māḍuva.v.anu* 'he who does'; *māḍuva.v.aḷu* 'she who does'. The Kannada participle is negated by affixing *-ada* to the root: *māḍ(u)-* – *māḍada*. This form can be coded for gender and number by adding the relevant markers: -(*v*)*anu* (masculine), -(*v*)*aḷu* (feminine), *-du* (neuter), -(*v*)*aru* (plural): *māḍada.v.anu* 'he who does/did not', *māḍada.v.aru* 'they who . . .'.

The participial forms are used in the formation of relative clauses; the forms themselves are neutral as to voice: cf. *pāṭhavannu ōdida huḍuganu* 'the boy who read the lesson'; *huḍuganu ōdida pāṭhavu* 'the lesson read by the boy'.

Postpositions

Nouns, participles, pronouns, etc. governed by postpositions are usually in the genitive case: e.g. *oḍane* 'along with', *nanna* + *oḍane* → *nannoḍane* 'along with me'; *horatu* 'apart from', *nanna horatu* 'apart from me'.

Word order

SOV

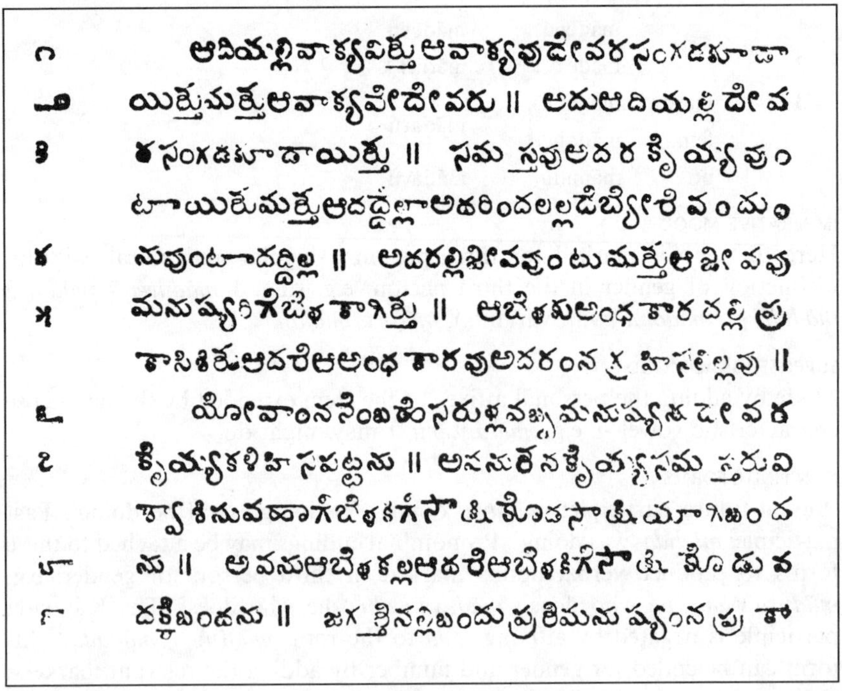

SCRIPT

The Kannada (also known as Kanarese) script is a derivative of Brāhmī. Between the Brāhmī source and the Kannada script, as it appears from the fourteenth century onwards, a transitional script was in use which also underlies Telugu (**q.v.**). The table shows the modern Kannada inventory of consonants and vowels: the latter (a) independent (initial only), and (b) as applied to the consonant /k/. As in most Indian scripts, the short vowel /a/ is inherent in each base consonant: thus ಕ is /ka/.

Conjunct consonants are in general formed by subscription of the second component, which is often abbreviated.

THE KANNADA SCRIPT

CONSONANTS

ಕ *ka*	ಖ *kha*	ಗ *ga*	ಘ *gha*	ಙ *nga*
ಚ *ca*	ಛ *cha*	ಜ *ja*	ಝ *jha*	ಞ *nya*
ಟ *ṭa*	ಠ *ṭha*	ಡ *ḍa*	ಢ *ḍha*	ಣ *ṇa*
ತ *ta*	ಥ *tha*	ದ *da*	ಧ *dha*	ನ *na*
ಪ *pa*	ಫ *pha*	ಬ *ba*	ಭ *bha*	ಮ *ma*
ಯ *ya*	ರ *ra*	ಲ *la*	ವ *va*	
ಶ *śa*	ಷ *ṣa*	ಸ *sa*	ಹ *ha*	ಳ *la*

VOWELS

ಅ *a*	ಆ *ā*	ಇ *i*	ಈ *ī*	ಉ *u*	ಊ *ū*	ಋ *ru*
ಎ *e*	ಏ *ē*	ಐ *ai*	ಒ *o*	ಓ *ō*	ಔ *au*	

Vowel signs: here illustrated as applied to *ka*

ಕಾ *kā*, ಕಿ *ki*, ಕೀ *kī*, ಕು *ku*, ಕೂ *kū*, ಕೃ *kru*, ಕೆ *ke*,
ಕೇ *kē*, ಕೈ *kai*, ಕೊ *ko*, ಕೋ *kō*, ಕೌ *kau*

NUMERALS

೧	೨	೩	೪	೫	೬	೭	೮	೯	೦
1	2	3	4	5	6	7	8	9	0

KARACHAY-BALKAR

INTRODUCTION

Baskakov's (1966) classification puts this language in the Kipchak-Oguz subdivision of the Kipchak group of Turkic languages. Both the Karachays and the Balkars use the ethnonym *alan*, which would link them to the Scythian tribes who inhabited the area between the Black Sea and the Danube in the Middle Ages. The language of the fourteenth-century *Codex Cumanicus* is close to Karachay-Balkar.

Today, about 160,000 people speak Karachay-Balkar in the Karachaevo-Cherkessia Republic and in the Kabardino-Balkaria Republic; the language is used in local media, radio, and newspapers, and some books have been published. Loanwords from Ossete, Kabardian, Arabic, and Persian are fairly numerous.

SCRIPT

Cyrillic + *ý* which denotes the bilabial sonant /β/.

PHONOLOGY

Consonants

The consonantal inventory is standard Turkic (*see* **Turkic Languages**).

Vowels

front	rounded: y, œ
	unrounded: i, e
back	rounded: u, o
	unrounded: ı, a

This division underlies the vowel harmony system of Karachay-Balkar: front is followed by front vowel, back by back, and rounded by rounded: e.g. *kyok.yubyuz* 'our sky'.

Stress

Stress is on the final syllable, displaced by affixation: e.g. by negative marker to preceding syllable: *kelmék* 'to come', *kél.me.gen.di* 'he didn't come'.

MORPHOLOGY AND SYNTAX

Noun

In general, standard Turkic. The plural marker is *-la/-le*, i.e. with loss of final *-r*, which reappears, however, in medial position: e.g. *atla* 'horses', *atlarım* 'my horses'.

The genitive and accusative ending is *-n*V^4, i.e. *-n* + one of four possible vowels; the dative affix has nine variants by assimilation and vowel harmony.

The predicative personal endings and the possessive markers are all standard, the latter varying from two possible forms in the third person plural – *-ları/-leri* – to eight in the second and first persons plural and third person singular: cf. *ana.gız* 'your (pl.) mother'; *džurt.uγuz* 'your (pl.) homeland'.

Adjective

Standard; a comparative is made in *-raq/-rek*: e.g. *Umar Xalit**den** uzun.raq.dı* 'Umar is taller than Xalit' (ablative case). As in Turkish, intensification is expressed by partial reduplication, with harmonic consonant: e.g. *sap.sarı* 'very yellow'; *qap-qara* 'pitch-black'.

Pronoun

Standard, but note third person plural *ala*, with loss of final *r*.

Numerals

Standard, but there is some wavering between the decimal and the vigesimal systems: thus, *on* is 10; 20 may be *eki on* = 2 × 10, or *bir džıyırma* (cf. Turkish *yirmi*); 40 is *tyört on* = 4 × 10, or *eki džıyırma* = 2 × 20.

Verb

Standard Turkic pattern, with passive in -V^{10}*l/n*; causative in *-d/t*V^4*r*; reciprocal in -V^5*s*; reflexive in -V^5*n*, with variants: e.g. *ayı**nl*** 'be separated'; *kel**tir*** 'to bring' ('cause to come').

TENSE STRUCTURE

The present-future tense has a link vowel between stem and ending:

Singular	*Plural*
bar.a.ma 'I go'	bar.a.bız
bar.a.sa	bar.a.sız
bar.a.dı	bar.a.dıla

The past definite marker is *-dı-*: e.g. *ayt.dı.m* 'I said'; *ayt.dın*... 1st pl. *ayt.dı.**q***. The auxiliary *tur-*, plus the gerund in *-a/-e/-i/-y* is used to make the present progressive: e.g. *išley **tur**.a.ma* 'I am working at present'.

There are two futures: the first, or presumptive, future tense has the infix

-ır/ir: e.g. *al.ır.bız* 'we shall (probably) take'. The second, or definite, future has *-lıq/-nıq/-rıq*: e.g. *al.lıq.bız* 'we shall take'.

Postpositions

These govern all cases except the accusative. E.g. with dative: *deri* 'up to', 'as far as', e.g. *yüj.ge deri bar.dı.m* 'I reached home'; with ablative: *arı* 'beyond', e.g. *kyöpyür.den arı* 'beyond the bridge'; with genitive: *amaltın* 'because of', e.g. *seni amaltın* 'because of you'.

Word order

As normal in Turkic.

1. Исса келиб синагогагъа киреди; анда уа къолу къурушхан биреу бар эди.

2. Алайдагъыла, Исса шабаткюн аны сау этгени болса, аны сылтау этиб Иссаны терслер акъыл бла, Аны ызындан къарайдыла.

3. Исса ол къолу къурушханнга: ортагъа чыкъ—дейди.

4. Алайдагъылагъа да: шабаткюн игилик этгенми игиди, огъесе джаманлыкъ этгенми? Джанны къутхаргъанмы, огъесе аны джойгъанмы? Алай болгъанлыкъгъа ала, джукъ айтмай, тынглайдыла.

5. Тёгерекдегилени джюреклерини къатылыгъына ачый, алагъа хыны къарай, Исса ол сакъатха: къолунгу узат—дейди. Ол да къолун узатады, олсагъат огъуна сакъат къолу ол башха къолу кибик, сау болады.

6. Фарисейле, тышына чыгъыб дженгил огъуна иродчула бла бирге, Иссаны джояр ючюн кенгеш этедиле.

7. Алая Исса Кесини сохталары бла бирге алайдан тенгиз таба кетеди; Аны ызындан Галилеядан, Иудеядан,

8. Иерусалимден, Идумеядан эм да Иорданны арыджанындан кёб халкъ джыйын болуб тебредиле. Аны кибик, Тир бла Сидонну тёгереклеринде джашагъанла да, Аны неле этгенлерин эштиб, уллу джыйын болуб Аннга келе эдиле.

(Mark 3.1–8)

KARAKALPAK

INTRODUCTION

In Baskakov's (1966) classification, Karakalpak is placed in the Kipchak-Nogay sub-division of the Kipchak group of Western Turkic languages. It is spoken by about 300,000 people in the Karakalpak Republic (created in the 1930s), which lies to the south and west of the Aral Sea. There are two main dialects, which are not widely divergent. The literary standard is based on the North-Eastern dialect. The language is used in the local media – radio, television, newspapers, and periodicals – and some books are published.

SCRIPT

Karakalpak was first written (from 1924 onwards) in an adapted Arabic script. The experimental romanization period in the 1930s was followed by an expanded Cyrillic script, which, as amended in 1957, is in use today. The additional non-Cyrillic letters are: ә, ғ, қ, ң, ө, ү, ў, ҳ.

PHONOLOGY

Consonants

stops: p, b, t, d, k, g, q
affricates: ts, tʃ
fricatives: w, v, f, s, z, ʃ, ʒ, j, ɣ, x, h
nasals: m, n, ŋ
lateral and flap: l, r

Vowels

front: i, ɛ, ə, œ, y; back: ɨ, a, ɔ, u

VOWEL HARMONY

Back–back and front–front sequence is rigorously observed. Theoretically, rounded should always be followed by rounded, and unrounded by unrounded, but according to Baskakov this is only partially observed.

MORPHOLOGY AND SYNTAX

In general, Karakalpak is close to standard Turkic model (*see* **Turkic Languages**; **Turkish**).

The plural marker is *-lar/-ler*: e.g. *Qaraqalpaqlar* 'the Karakalpaks'.

Assimilation in the declension system yields several initials for most case affixes, plus harmonic change in vowel; thus, the genitive takes the following forms: *-nıŋ*, *-niŋ*, *-dıŋ*, *diŋ*, *-tıŋ*, *-tiŋ*. Hereafter, the index convention is followed.

The possessive affixes are standard. The adjective makes a comparative in *-ıraq/-irek*.

The first person singular pronoun is *men*, with oblique cases formed on this same base.

The numerals are standard, with some variant spellings, e.g. *žeti* 7 = Turkish *yedi*; *žigirma* 20 = Turkish *yirmi*.

Verb

Four voices with standard markers, e.g. -V*n/l* for passive: ***alın*** 'to be taken', *-t/d.i/ı.r* for causative: *kel**tir**-* 'bring' (*kelmek* 'to come').

Frequentative or irregular action can be marked by *-qıla*^{4}: e.g. *at-* 'to shoot', *at**qıla**-* 'to fire at intervals'. An intensifying infix is *-ıŋqıra-*^{2}.

There is a large inventory of participial and gerundial forms, marking tense, aspect, and mood: e.g. *al**ıp*** 'having taken'; *al**a*** 'taking'.

There are two sets of personal endings, full and truncated. The full endings are used, for example, in the simple present, e.g. *al.a.man* 'I take'; and in the present progressive with the auxiliary *žatır*, e.g. *men alıp.žatır.man* 'I am taking'; and again the future tense with the future participial marker *-žaq*, e.g. *men al.a.žaq.man* 'I shall take'.

The short endings appear, for example, in the past definite: e.g. *men al.dı.m* 'I took'. Other forms: *men al.ar edim* 'I'd have taken'; *al.sam* 'if I take'; *al.γay.man* 'let me take'.

As in Turkic generally, the participial forms are used in the construction of relative clauses: e.g. *Men seniŋ bar.ma.i.žaγın.dı bilemen* 'I know that you won't go', where *seniŋ* is the genitive of the second person singular pronoun *sen*; *-ma-* is the negative infix; *-žaq/žaγ-* is the future marker; *-n* is the genitive inflection; *-dı* marks the accusative; *bil.e.men* 'I know'.

Postpositions

Standard Turkic inventory.

KARELIAN

INTRODUCTION

Karelian belongs to the Balto-Finnic group of Finno-Ugric. Makarov in *JaNSSSR*, Vol. III, 1966, traces the *karja-* root to Baltic *garja-*, meaning 'wooded and/or hilly country': /g > k/ + *-la*; the language is known to its speakers as *karjalan kieli*. There are about 120,000 speakers in the Karelian Republic. It is not known even approximately when Finno-Ugric speaking tribes reached and settled in the Karelian Isthmus, but they were certainly there in the early Middle Ages, when *karjalaiset* are first mentioned in Russian chronicles of the twelfth century. The following centuries saw Karelian expansion towards the White Sea, and southwards towards Lakes Ladoga and Onega and the Valdai Hills. In 1323 a new frontier line between Novgorod Russia and Sweden divided the Karelians into two groups: those to the east of it are the ancestors of the present-day Karelians, while those to the west of it merged with other groups to form the nucleus of the modern Finnish nation.

The earliest record of Karelian is a spell against lightning, scratched on a piece of birch-bark dating from the thirteenth century. Apart from some translation of religious texts, Karelian has never been used for written literature. It should be pointed out, however, that it was in Karelia, particularly in the Uhtua area, that Elias Lönnroth was able to draw on the vast riches of Karelian folklore for the material which he subsequently reworked to form the *Kalevala*. Post-Lönnroth collections often preserve more clearly the Karelian nature of the texts.

There are three main dialects: Karelian proper, Olonets (*aunuksen kieli*), and Lud, the latter being close to Veps (*see* **Balto-Finnic Minor Languages**). The three dialects vary in their treatment of consonant gradation; it is close to the Finnish standard in Karelian proper, and virtually absent in Lud (cf. Veps). The dialects also vary in lexicon: e.g. Karelian *kirpu* 'flea' (Finnish *kirppu*) is *čonžoi* in Olonets and *sonzar'* in Lud.

The official languages for administration, education, and the media in the Karelian Republic are Finnish and Russian.

SCRIPT

If written, Karelian uses a Roman base plus diacritics.

PHONOLOGY

As compared with literary Finnish, Karelian shows the following characteristics: (a) the presence of the voiced stops *b*, *g*, *d* (in initial position), and the voiced fricative *z*: e.g. Finnish *tupakka*, Karelian *dabakka*; Finnish *karpalo*, Karelian *garbalo* 'cranberry'; (b) the affricate *tʃ* and the fricatives *ʃ* and *ʒ*: Finnish *uskon*, Karelian *užon* 'I believe'; Finnish *metsä*, Karelian *meccä* 'forest'; (c) palatalization: Finnish *lehti*, Karelian *leht'i* 'leaf'.

CONSONANT GRADATION

In Karelian proper, consonant gradation is largely as in Finnish standard (for detail, *see* **Finnish**), i.e. strong grade in open syllables, weak grade in closed. As examples of divergence from Finnish standard:

	Genitive	*Finnish*	
meččä 'forest'	mečän	metsä	metsän
jogi 'river'	joven	joki	joen
šada 'hundred'	šuan	sata	sadan
hammaš 'tooth'	hambahan	hammas	hampaan

Vowels

i, e, ε, a, œ, o, y, u

All combine to form diphthongs. /ε/ is notated here as *ä*, /œ/ as *ö*, /y/ as *ü*.

VOWEL HARMONY

/a, o, u/ followed by like; similarly /ε, œ, y/. /e/ and /i/ are neutral.

MORPHOLOGY AND SYNTAX

Noun

The plural marker is *-t* in nominative and accusative; in oblique cases *-i-* is infixed, extended to *-loi-*/*-l'öi-* in certain phonetic environments: e.g. from *mua* 'earth' (Finnish *maa*), ablative *mualoida*.

DECLENSION

Thirteen cases are made by agglutinative suffixation. There is one general paradigm for all nouns, anomalies occurring in the partitive only. There are, of course, phonetic variants. As an example, *hammaš* 'tooth': the consonant gradation is *-mm-*/*-mb-*, with *-mm-* appearing in nominative, accusative, and partitive singular only. Thus, for example gen. *hambahan*, partitive singular *hammasta*, iness. *hambahašša*, abl. *hambahalda*; plural: *hambahat*, gen. *hambahin*, part. *hambahie.*

Adjective

As attribute, adjective precedes noun, and has concord in case and number. A comparative is made in *-mbi-*: e.g. *l'evie* 'wide' – *l'eviembi.*

Pronoun

PERSONAL INDEPENDENT

	Singular	*Genitive*	*Plural*	*Genitive*
1.	mie	miwn	müö	miän
2	šie	šiwn	t′üö	t′iän
3	hiän/že	hän′en/žen	hüö	hiän

These are declined with five oblique cases e.g. of *mie*, *miwn*: acc. *miwn*, ill. *miwh*, adess. *miwla*, part. *milma*.

DEMONSTRATIVE PRONOUN

t′ämä 'this', *tua* 'that', *že* 'that' (already mentioned). Plurals in *n′ämä*, *nua*, *n′e*. Declined with three oblique cases.

INTERROGATIVE PRONOUN

ken 'who?'; *mi* 'what?' Three oblique cases. The interrogative pronouns are also used as relative pronouns.

POSSESSIVE PRONOMINAL MARKERS

2nd sing. *-š*, 3rd sing. *-h* are added only to nouns denoting close kin: *tuatto.**š*** 'your father'. The 1st person singular marker *-(z′e)n′i* lends a nuance of familiarity and affection: *muamo**z′en′i*** 'mama', 'mum'.

oma is affixed to the genitive of relevant pronoun: e.g. *miwn-oma* 'my', *šiwn-oma* 'your'.

Numerals

1–10: *üks′i*, *kakši*, *kolme*, *n′el′l′ä*, *viiz′i*, *kuwži*, *šeiččimen*, *kahekšan*, *ühekšän*, *kümmenen*; 20 *kakšikümmen′d′ä*; 100 šada.

Verb

Finite and non-finite forms; active and passive voices; positive and negative versions. There are four moods; the indicative mood has four tenses, two simple and two compound. The subjunctive and the potential moods have two tenses each. The fourth mood is the imperative, present only.

SPECIMEN CONJUGATION

šanuo 'to say'; indicative mood, present tense:

	Positive		*Negative*	
	Singular	*Plural*	*Singular*	*Plural*
1	šanon	šanomma	en šano	emmä šano
2	šanot	šanotta	et šano	et′t′ä šano
3	šanow	šanotah	ei šano	ei **šanota**

IMPERFECT

Sing. *šanoin*, *šanoit*, *šano*; pl. *šanoimma*, *šanoja*, *šanottih*. The negative is *en*, *et*, etc., *šanon*, with distinctive form in third plural *ei* ***šanottu***. The perfect and pluperfect are made with the auxiliary *olen*, *olet*, etc. Again, the third person plural has a specific form: *ei olla šanottu* (perfect).

SUBJUNCTIVE

šanoz'in, *sanoz'it*; neg. *en*, *et šanois'*

POTENTIAL

šanonnen, *šannonet*; neg. *en*, *et šanonne*; both with distinctive forms in third person plural: *ei sanottais'*, *šanottanne.*

IMPERATIVE

šanokko(*is*), pl. *šanokkua*(*kkois*); neg. *el'a šano*, *el'giä šanokkua.*

Participial and gerundial forms and usage correspond closely to those in Standard Finnish: e.g. the inessive of the declined infinitive, in *-eššal-eššä*, expresses concomitant action; the illative in *-mahl-mäh* inceptive action, the elative in *-maštal-mäštä* motion from or out of something: e.g. *Hiän tulow l'eikkuamašta* 'He comes back from the reaping.'

Prepositions and postpositions

Karelian uses both prepositions and postpositions: e.g. postposition: *miwda vaššen* 'in relation to me'; preposition: *ennen üöd'ä* 'before nightfall'. The case system is, of course, rich enough to express many meanings requiring prepositions or postpositions in other languages: e.g. *talvekši* 'in winter'.

Compounding

As in Finnish, compounding is a highly productive source of lexical enrichment: noun (in nom. or gen.) + noun, adjective/adverb + noun: cf. *keviä.vihma* 'spring rain'; *vihma-keviä* 'a rainy spring'. The first component is usually a noun in the nominative, but combinations with the genitive are also found: *jumalan.l'ehmän'e* 'ladybird', where *jumalan* is the genitive of *jumala* 'God'.

Word order

As in Finnish.

A translation of St Matthew's Gospel was published in St Petersburg in 1820 (translated into Karelian by Zolotinski and Vedenski). It seems possible that other translations appeared after 1870.

KAREN

INTRODUCTION

Spoken by about 2 million people in south-east Burma and western Thailand, this language complex is certainly of Tibeto-Burman stock, but typologically diverges up to a point – e.g. in word order – from its Bodic, Baric, and Burmic congeners. The main forms are Sgaw and Pho Karen. There is a sizeable body of religious and pedagogic literature in Sgaw, which also has periodicals and some creative writing, along with a local radio service. The description of Sgaw Karen, given here, is based on Jones (1961).

SCRIPT

A Latin-based notation for Sgaw Karen dates from the mid-nineteenth century. The Mon script has also been used.

PHONOLOGY

Consonants

The dental series is represented by /t, th, d, θ, n, l, r, s, sh, z/, where /th/ and /sh/ are aspirates. The labial, palatal, and velar series have unvoiced unaspirate and aspirate stops + associated nasals; the labial series has in addition the voiced stop /b/. The glottal stop and *h* are present, also the semi-vowels *j* and *w*, and the fricative /γ/.

Vowels

i, e, ɛ, ʉ, ə, a, ɔ, o, u

Tones

High, mid, and low. Tone is affected by a final glottal stop. Tone is phonemic: e.g. *pγa* 'person', *pγà* 'old'.

MORPHOLOGY AND SYNTAX

There are five main classes of word. Nominal and verbal bases are not formally distinguished, and differ only in terms of their valencies. The class of attributes (adjectives) is included in the verb. The other three main classes are: pronouns, numerical classifiers, and particles.

Noun

Nouns are simple or compound: *γí'* 'house', *tàsháγí'* 'hospital' (*tà* 'item'; *shá* 'sick').

Attributes follow the noun in genitive or adjectival relationship: e.g. *kə'sə̀phó* 'hill people' (*kə'sə̀* 'mountain'); *lì'* *γɔ tə' bé' 'i* 'this red book' (*lì'* 'book'; *γɔ* 'red'; *tə'* 'one'; *bé'* = numerical classifier for books).

There is a very large inventory of classifiers, which follow the numeral.

Pronoun

The pronoun has topical (independent) forms, which are, for the first and second persons singular, *jɛ́, nɛ́*, plural *wɛ́, θúwɛ́*. The subject/possessive and objective forms are:

		Subject/possessive	*Objective*
singular	1	jə'	ja
	2	nə'	na
plural	1	pə'	pγa ('person')
	2	θú	θʉ

The third singular subject form is *'ə'wɛ́* to which the plural adds the pluralizing suffix *θé'*.

Cf. topical form plus subjective: *jɛ́ jə'.kə' phɔ'ɔ'* 'as for me, I shall cook'.

Example of possessive: *jə' dɔ'thɔ' jə'.kə'θé'* 'I was riding my horse'. This sentence also exemplifies the continuous action marker *dɔ'*.

DEMONSTRATIVE PRONOUN/ADJECTIVE

'i 'this'; *ne'* 'that'. These follow noun + attribute phrase.

INTERROGATIVE PRONOUN

mə'ta(γa) 'who?'; *mə'* 'what?'; *dí'* 'what?'

RELATIVE PRONOUN

The all-purpose particle *lə́* is used: e.g. *'ə'má lə́'ə'dó'tà γe tə'γa* 'a wife who is pretty' (lit. 'whose figure is good').

Numerals

1–10: *tə́, khí, θə́, lwì, jɛ̀, xý, nwí, xɔ', khwí, tə'shi.* These precede the classifiers.

Verb

In a typical verbal complex the main verb occupies the nucleus, with modal verbs and auxiliaries to the left, and attributes, auxiliary verbs, and aspectual markers to the right.

The modal verbs include *θá* expressing intention; *plɛ́* expressing permission. Auxiliary verbs: e.g. *θé/kɛ́*, both expressing potentiality: 'can', 'be able'. Modal and aspectual auxiliaries: *wi* perfective; *di'* imperfective; *dɔ'* continuous action; *kə'* future.

Other examples: *pə'kə'lɛ shúzé* 'we'll go to market'; *jɛ́ jə'kə'lɛ kha'tà* 'as for me, I'll go hunting'; *di'* imperfective: *jə' kɛ́ di' x* 'I was still acting as/doing X'; *wi* perfective: *'ə'wɛ́né' wi nə'ma mə'nulɛ́'* 'that finished, what did you do?'; *plɛ́* as main verb: *lə́ kə'plɛ́ ja lə́ jə'kə'kə́ matà lə́ kɔpə'jɔ pu* '... which/that will permit me to (I) will return to work in Burma' (for infinitive 'to return' Karen uses the finite form '(that) I will return').

NEGATION

Expressed by *tə'* (... *bá'*): e.g. *kə' lɛ bá'* 'will definitely go' (*bá'* is the aspectual auxiliary emphasizing action); *lɛ tə' θé* 'cannot go'; *tə' lɛ bá'* 'definitely did not go'; *lɛ tə' γe!* 'don't go!' (lit. 'go not good').

Prepositions

Lə́ is a general preposition with several meanings (used also as relative pronoun): e.g. *lə́wètə'kú'* 'in Rangoon'. Exceptionally for a Tibeto-Burman language, Karen has no postpositions.

Word order

Again, exceptionally for a Tibeto-Burman language, SVO.

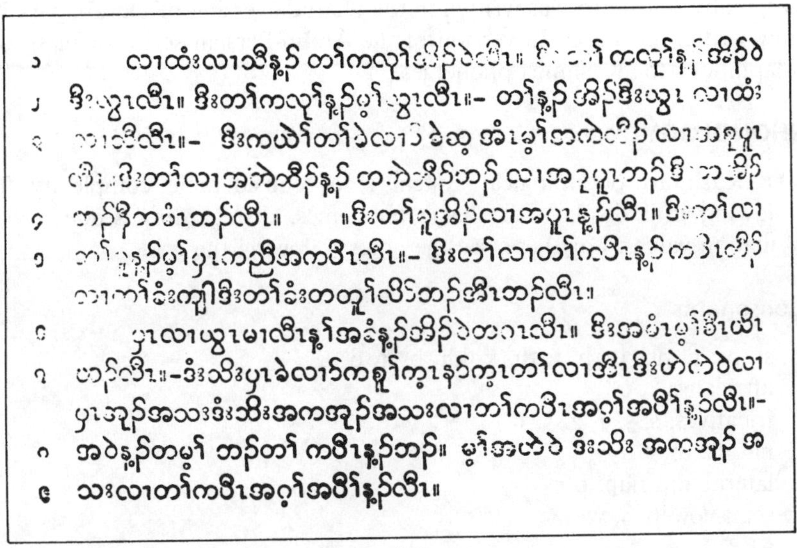

(Sigaw dialect)

KASHMIRI

INTRODUCTION

By far the most important of the Dardic languages, Kashmiri is the official language of the Indian states of Jammu and Kashmir. The number of speakers is estimated at 3 million. The ethnonym is /k′aʃiːr^y/. For controversy surrounding the exact genetic status of Kashmir and the other Dardic languages, *see* **Dardic Languages**.

Alone among the Dardic languages, Kashmiri has a literary tradition dating from the thirteenth/fourteenth century. The earliest Kashmiri poetry was written by the female poet Lal Ded in the fourteenth century; later, two of the best writers in a specifically Kashmiri genre, the *lol* ('love') lyric, were also women – Haba Khotun in the sixteenth century and Arnimal in the eighteenth century.

SCRIPT

Originally, Kashmiri was written in the Sharada version of Devanāgarī. It is now written in the Urdu version of the Arabo-Persian script, with specific adaptations for Kashmiri phonemes.

PHONOLOGY

The Kashmiri phonological system is of considerable complexity. The following grid displays the basic phonemes, disregarding secondary articulation values. For these, see the notes following the grid.

Consonants

stops: p, ph, ṭ, ṭh, t, th, k, kh, b, ḍ, d
affricates: c, č
fricatives: s, ṣ, ʃ, z, ʒ, h
nasals: m, n
lateral and flap: l, r
semi-vowels: j, w

Notes

1. Stops: this is the familiar NIA series, minus the voiced aspirate member. All stops (including the aspirates) occur palatalized: /p′, ph′, b′/, etc., and all, except the labials, occur labialized: /t°, th°/, etc.

2. Affricates: Kashmiri has a dual series of affricates: (a) a dental series (single focus) based on /c/ pure and aspirated, each of these with palatalized and labialized correlatives: /c, c′, c°, c', c'′, c'°/ (six terms); (b) a palatal series based on /č/, pure and aspirate, with labialized correlatives (four terms). The base phoneme (dual focus) for this series is represented by Zakhar′in and Edel′man (1971) as *čǰ*.

   The Kashmiri affricates appear to have a homorganic sibilant fricative onset. Examples given in Zakhar′in and Edel′man include (here simplified): *bučh* 'it stung', 'bit', transcribed as /b°u-ʊ-ś-čh/. Similarly, for a voiced affricate: *baji* 'more', 'bigger', /b°əʒdʒi/.

3. Initial clusters are articulated with the help of epenthetic vowels, which harmonize with the stem vowel: *drog* 'dear' /d**o**roʊg°/.

4. /s, z, h, l, r, w/ occur palatalized; /s, z, ʃ, h, l, r/ occur labialized.

5. /m′, n′, n°/ are present.

The complete grid comprises 69 phonemes. In this entry, the retroflex phonemes are denoted by subscript dot: e.g. /ɖ/ = *ḍ*.

Vowels

short: ɪ, ə, a, o, u, œ, y
long: iː, eː, aː, oː, uː

These are basic values; all occur nasalized, and all, especially the short vowels, have many variants. Close transcription of Kashmiri is exceedingly complicated; here, a simplified approximation is used. (Long vowels are notated here as *ī*, *ē*, etc.)

The Kashmiri vocalic system has two distinctive features:

(a) Regressive assimilation, whereby the root vowel is modified by the affix (cf. *Uygur*): e.g. *pūth′* 'book'; oblique base, *poṭh′ɪ*.
(b) The so-called matra vowels – ultra-short medial and final vowels – historically present; now mute, they nevertheless induce the regressive assimilation described in (a). The matra vowels are written in index position: e.g. *host^{u}* 'bull elephant'.

MORPHOLOGY AND SYNTAX

Noun

Kashmiri has two genders, masculine and feminine. Gender is very unstable. A typical masculine ending is -^{u}; fem. -$^{i/ü}$: both of these matra vowels mark palatalization of the preceding consonant.

Virtually all nouns ending in the singular in a palatalized consonant are feminine.

PLURAL FORMATION

Some examples illustrating affixation and stem change: *māl* 'garland', plural *māl.ɪ*; *wat* 'way' – *wat.ɪ*; *mōl* 'father' – *məl'*; *rāt* 'night' – *rəc*; *bud* 'old woman' – *budžɪ*.

Where singular and plural do not differ, plurality is indicated by verbal concord: e.g. singular *cūr čhuh ā.mut* 'the thief came'; plural *cūr čhɪh ā.mɪt'* 'the thieves came'.

DECLENSION

Four models: two masculine (-^{u} and non -^{u}) and two feminine: e.g. masculine in -^{u}:

	Singular	*Plural*
nominative	gur^u 'horse'	guri^i
oblique I	guris	guren
oblique II	guri }	guryau
agentive	gur^i }	

Oblique I provides the direct object; oblique II and the agentive are used as subject of transitive verb.

	Singular		*Plural*
	Masculine	*Feminine*	*Masculine and feminine*
oblique I dat./acc.	-ɪs/ -as	-e/-ɪ	-en/-an
oblique II instr./abl.	-ɪ/-a	-ɪ	-au
agentive	-ɪ/-an	-ɪ	-au

GENITIVE

The inflected postpositions -*h*/*sund*, -*un*, -*uk* are used. Some examples: *məl' sund gur* 'father's horse'; *məl'sɪnd' gur^i* 'father's horses'; *məl'sɪnd'ɪs gur'ɪs p'aṭh* 'on father's horse'; *māl'an.hɪnd'aw gur'aw p'aṭh* 'on the horses of the fathers'.

Adjective

As attribute, the adjective precedes the noun with which it is in concord for gender, number, and case: e.g. nom. *boḍ^u mahanyuv^u* 'big man'; obl. I *bɪḍis mahanvis*; pl. *baḍ^i mahaniv^i*. Cf. *bɪḍɪs gāmas manz* 'in the big village'; *baḍ'aw gāmaw manz* 'from big villages'. Cf.

yɪh čhuh boḍ garɪ 'this is a big house'
boḍāh čhuh wanān šur'ɪs 'the grown-up said to the boy'
bəḍ'an 'to the big ones' (plural oblique I)
baḍ'aw 'from the big (ones)' (plural oblique II)
baḍ'aw šahɪraw manzɪ 'from big towns' (plural oblique II)

COMPARATIVE

Example: *yɪh gur hum'ɪ gur'ɪ čhuh boḍ* 'this horse is bigger than that one', where *hum'ɪ gur'ɪ* is in obl. II.

Pronoun

	Singular		*Plural*	
	Nominative	*Oblique*	*Nominative*	*Oblique*
1	boh	me	as^{i}	ase
2	cə	ce	toh^{i}	tohe

The third person forms are supplied from the demonstrative series.

The personal pronouns have enclitic forms used with verbs: e.g. *di.m* 'give me' (where *.m* marks the first person indirect object); *wuč*h^{u}*.h.as* 'they saw me'.

Enclitic pronominal forms:

	Singular			*Plural*		
Person	*1*	*2*	*3*	*(1)*	*2*	*3*
series I	-Vs	-Vkh				
series II	-Vm	-Vth	-Vn		-Vw	-Vkh
series III		-Vy	-Vs			
		-Vyı				

-Vkh and *-Vth* may > *h* before an enclitic: *n'u-h-as* 'they took from him'; *sūz-n-as* 'he sent me'; *dop-n-as* 'he said to him'; *dop-ukh* 'they said'; *anō-n* 'we'll bring this'.

DEMONSTRATIVE PRONOUN

The series has five degrees of relative distance, ranging from *yıh* 'this' (close at hand) to *suh* (remote, invisible). All are fully declined.

INTERROGATIVE PRONOUN

k'āh 'who', 'what?'

RELATIVE PRONOUN

Masc. *yus*, fem. *yossa*, inanimate *yıh*; pl. *yım* (masc.), *yıma* (fem.).

Numerals

1–10: *akh*, *z*^{a}*h*, *trih*, *cor*, *panc*, *ṣah*, *sath*, *aiṭh*, *nav*, *dah*; 11 *kāh*; 12 *bāh*; 13 *truwāh*; 20 *wuh*; 21 *akawuh*; 22 *z*^{a}*tōwuh*; 29 *kunatr*^{a}*h*; 30 *tr*^{a}*h*; 100 *hath*.

From 2 onwards, the numerals are declined, with plural oblique I and II and agentive. In the oblique forms of *zı*(*h*) = 2, the old Sanskrit initial *dv*/*dw*- surfaces: oblique I *dvan*, oblique II/agentive *dvaw*.

Verb

Non-finite forms:

infinitive in *-un*: e.g. *wučhun* 'to see';
present participle in *-ān*: e.g. *wuchān* 'seeing'; this form is invariable;
past participle: four forms covering recent to remote past: e.g. *wučh*ᵘ; to these forms, the perfective aspect marker *-mut*ᵘ*-* (inflected for gender and number) can be added;
gerund in *-ıth*: *wučhıth* 'having seen', 'seeing'.

Synthetic forms inherited from Indo-Aryan are represented in Kashmiri by the present-future tense with the following personal endings: singular 1 *-a*, 2 *-akh*, 3 *-i*; plural 1 *-aw*, 2 *-iw*, 3 *-an*, and by the imperative mood.

All other tenses are constructed by conjugating the relevant participle with an auxiliary, *čhus/ās*, marked for person, gender, and number. The present tense of *čhus* has, for example, the following first person forms: singular, masculine *čhus*, feminine *čhes*; plural, masculine *čhıh*, feminine *čheh*: e.g. *čhus wuchān* 'I see'; *čhıh wučhān* 'we see'. The negative form is *wučhan.ay.*

Future *ās-* + participle: *āsı wučhān* 'I shall see'.

The past tense of the auxiliary is based on *os-/əs-*: e.g. *ōsus wučhān* 'I was seeing'. In the past tenses, the non-finite form (apart from the present participle) agrees with the subject of an intransitive verb, with the object of a transitive. The subject of the transitive verb is then in the agentive case (*see* **Pronoun**, above) and may be recapitulated by a personal enclitic marker affixed to the participle: e.g. *me wučhu.**m*** 'I saw him' (i.e. *me* 'by me'; *wučh*ᵘ past participle of verb 'to see'; Ø third person implied; *-m* first person oblique enclitic).

Irregularities due to phonetic accommodation, vowel harmony, and other requirements abound in the system.

čhus wučhān 'I see'
čhəh wuchan 'she sees'
ōs wučhān 'he was seeing', 'he saw'
ə̄s'wı wučhān 'we were seeing'
āsı wučhān 'I shall see'
ās′ı wučhān 'he will see'
prat dᵘahı ōs yı gačhān ək′ıs jangal′ıs manz 'every day he was going into a forest'
so ōs pātšāh akh 'there was an emperor'
su pātšāh ōs sōnuyı mōl 'that emperor was our father'
yi ōs on 'he was blind'

Participle in *-ıth*:

wıchıth 'having seen'
kānh čhu nı kə̄m kər′ıth h′akan 'no one can do this work'
mə̄l′ıs h′okun nı akh lafaz wən′ıth 'father could not say a word'

Declined past participle: *wučh-* 'to see':

	Singular	*Plural*
masculine	wučhmut	wičhmɪth
feminine	wɪčhmɪc	wɪčhɪmɪcɪ

panɪn′ rə̄ wmɪc g°ɪr wučhɪt/wɪčhɪth 'having seen his lost mare'
at′ l′ūkhmut r°opyes pə̄nc hat′ 'on it was written "500 rupees" '

SUBJUNCTIVE

First person forms:

	Present/future	*Past*	*Past durative*
singular 1	wučhɪ	wučhahə̄	āsahə̄ wučhān
plural 1	wučhau	wučhahə̄w	āsahə̄w wučhān

hargā ki su pātšāh so tr′eš čayɪh′ə, su mar′ih′ə
'if the emperor had drunk this potion, he would have died'

PASSIVE

The oblique case of the infinitive combines with the verb *yun* 'to come': e.g. *wučhana yun*^{u} 'to be seen'.

NEGATIVE

nɪ: this negative particle precedes or follows the finite verb:

ōs-nɪ 'was not'
čhu-nɪ karān 'he is not doing'
nɪ bōz′an yɪhunzɪ kathɪ 'he did not hear their words'
kānh ōs nɪ tas k′anh d′ɪwān 'no one was giving him anything'

mā/ma-ti: this appears in prohibition, with subjunctive or imperative forms of verb; also in context of doubt, uncertainty, unease:

mā ās-ɪm 'can't be for me!'
mā-tɪ nɪ-tan curɪ 'they couldn't have stolen (it)'

pɪ follows the finite verb or the finite element of a composite tense form:

d′ututh-pɪ 'you didn't give'
ə̄s′-pɪ gačhān 'they weren't going'
chu-pɪ karān 'he doesn't do'
mar′ɪh′ə-pɪ 'he wouldn't have died'

Postpositions

There are very few simple postpositions in Kashmiri: e.g. *k′at* 'in', 'on', *sɪt′* 'with', *p′ath* 'on', *puch′* 'for', *k′ut* 'for'. The possessive markers *-uk*, *-un*, *-h/sund* are included here. Many compound postpositions are made by combining nouns in either of the oblique cases with simple postpositions (denominals).

Use of *-h/sund*: cf. *m′ōn′ɪs mə̄l′sɪnd′ɪ garɪ manzɪ* 'from my father's house'; *mə̄l′sɪnd′ɪ garuk brōr* 'father's house-cat'; *brə̄r′sund* 'feline': cf.

paranas-k′ut garı 'house for reading', i.e. 'reading-room'
parun-k′ut akhbār 'newspaper for reading'
m′a čhah pūth′ parın′ 'to-me the book is requiring-to-be-read', i.e. 'I have to...'

Additional examples:

tas čhuh gur 'to him is a horse', i.e. 'he has a horse'
əm′ısıyı əs′ zı g°ır′ tı akh g°ır 'he had two horses and a mare'
yım pātšāzādı zı ə̄s′ 'there were two of these princes'
nə̄yan dop pādšāhas 'the barber said to the emperor'
ci h′ndustānas gachakh 'you (sing.) are going to India'
zanānas dop 'say to the woman'
tam′ wıčh kor′ı 'he saw the girl'
ōs ak′is vanas manz 'in a certain forest lived (was)...'
ək′ıs mohn′ıw′ıs ə̄s′ zı n′acıw′ 'a man had two sons'
yal′ı šahrı wāpas āw 'when he returned from the town'
suh ōs garı dur 'he was far from home'
k′ısanah šahar drāw 'a peasant went to town'
məl′ısk′ut gur 'a stallion for the father'
mə̄l′ısk′ic gur 'a mare for the father'
kōr′ı-puch′ı garı manzı 'from the girls' house'
n′acıw′-sınd′ı khə̄tırı 'for the sons'
kōr′an-sınd′ı bāpat 'for the sake of the daughters'
mə̄l′ıs tı mā̌jı-hund kār 'a matter for father and mother'
gur′ıs-k′ut kharıč 'food for the horse'
gur′an-hınd′ı puch′ pōn 'water for the horses'
gamas manz ōs akh gāṭul mohan′uw 'in the village there lived/was a wise man'
gāṭıl′ dop gar′ības 'the wise (man) said to the poor (man)'

Word order

Rather free; SVO is frequent.

ا ب ۱ ۞ در اِبتِدا اۆس کلام تہٕ کَلام اۆس خُدائِس سٟتِ تہٕ کَلام
۲ ۳ اۆس خُدا ۞ یِہی اۆس در اِبتِدا خُدائِس سٟتِ ۞ سآری چیز بَنیٖن
تِہٕندی وسیلہٕ سٟتِ پَیدٕہ تہٕ تِہٕندِ بغیر بَنیٖن نہٕ کِہنہ تہٕ پَیدٕہ یہٕ پَیدٕہ
۴ سَپُن ۞ زِندگی آس تَس اَندَر تہٕ سُہ زِندگی آس اِنسانَن ہُند نوٗر
۵ ۶ ۞ تہٕ نوٗر چھُ تارِیکیِ اندر پرٕزلان تہٕ تاریکیِ کرٕ نہٕ سُہ دریافت ۞ اَکھ
شخصہٕ اۆس خُدایہٕ سَندِہ طَرفہٕ سوٗزنہٕ آمُت یَس یُوحنّا ناو
۷ اۆس یِیہ آو گواہیِ ہَندِہ خاطرِ زِہ نوٗرَس پیٹھ دِیہ گواہی
۸ یُتھ سآرِی تَمِسَندِہ وسیلہٕ اِعتِقاد اَنَن ۞ سُہ اۆسنہٕ سُہ نوٗر
۹ بَلکہ نوٗرَس پیٹھ اۆس گواہی دِنہٕ آمُت

KASHUBIAN

This member of the Lekhitic or Pomeranian branch of West Slavonic is spoken by about 150,000 people in the region of the Gulf of Danzig. The Lekhitic group, whose most important member is, of course, Polish, included Polabian (extinct since the eighteenth century) and Slovincian (still spoken by a few people in the 1900s). Of the smaller members of the group, Kashubian alone has, to some extent at least, resisted assimilation to German- and Polish-speaking populations. The Poles regard Kashubian as a dialect of Polish.

Three dialects of Kashubian are recognized. Phonologically the most interesting is the northern dialect which has movable stress and phonemic quantity. In the central dialect, stress is on the penultimate as in Polish; in the southern, on the initial as in Czech and Slovak.

A striking feature of the verbal system is the analytical perfect with the verb 'to have' as auxiliary, as in German: e.g. *ja mom widzel* = Gm. *ich habe gesehen* 'I have seen'.

In the late nineteenth and early twentieth centuries some attempt was made to establish a literary standard in Kashubian. Since 1956 the Organyzacia Zrzeszenia Kaszubskiego has been publishing the periodical *Kaszube*.

KAWI

See **Javanese, Old**.

KAZAKH

INTRODUCTION

In Baskakov's (1966) classification, Kazakh is placed in the Kipchak-Nogay group of Western Hunnic Turkic. There are over 5 million speakers in Kazakhstan, and about 1 million in the Xinjiang-Uygur Autonomous Region of the CPR. The Kazakh literary language dates from the early nineteenth century (Abay Kunanbayev, 1845–1904, is regarded as its founding father), though traditional folk-poetry is older.

SCRIPT

Until the 1930s Kazakh was written in the Arabic script (*see* **Arabic**). A period of experimental romanization followed. Since 1940, Cyrillic with nine additional letters: ә, ғ, қ, ң, ө, ұ, ү, һ, і.

PHONOLOGY

Consonants

stops: p, b, t, d, k, g, q
affricates: ts, tʃ/dz′
fricatives: f, v, s, z, ʃ, ʒ, x, γ, h
nasals: m, n, ŋ
lateral and flap: l, r
semi-vowels: w, j

Vowels

front unrounded: i, e
rounded: œ, y
back unrounded: ı, a
rounded: o, ŭ

/œ/ and /y/ are here notated as *ö* and *ü* respectively. Assimilation, both progressive and regressive, takes place, internally and at junctures.

VOWEL HARMONY

(a) Palatal vowel harmony is strictly observed: front with front, back with back: cf. front, *mektep.ler.imiz.niŋ* 'of our schools'; back, *qalam.dar.-ımız.nıŋ* 'of your pens'.

(b) Labial: the rounded/unrounded opposition is less strictly observed, certainly less so than in Kirgiz or Altay, and is usually disregarded beyond the third syllable of a word: e.g. *önerpaz.darımız* 'our skilled workmen'.

Stress

Stress tends to be on the final syllable, but never on copula affixes.

MORPHOLOGY AND SYNTAX

In declension, formation of plural, treatment of adjective, the pronominal system, and the numerals, Kazakh conforms to the general Turkic pattern. The plural marker is *lar*^{6} (i.e. six variants), with *l/d/t* initial and *a/e* according to vowel harmony.

Noun

Examples of declension, showing phonetically variant affixes: *oquši* 'pupil', *köse* 'street', *kitap* 'book'; singular:

nominative	oquši	köse	kitap
genitive	oquši.nıŋ	köse.niŋ	kitap.tıŋ
dative	oquši.γa	köse.ge	kitap.qa
accusative	oquši.nı	köse.ni	kitap.tı
locative	oquši.da	köse.de	kitap.ta
ablative	oquši.dan	köse.den	kitap.tan
comitative	oquši.men	köse.men	kitap.**p**en

Some examples of case usage:

Genitive: e.g. *el.imiz.diŋ astana.sı* 'the capital of our country'.
Accusative: distinguishes definite object from indefinite, e.g. *Men kitap oqıdım* 'I read (past) a book'; *Men kitap**tı** oqıdım* 'I read the (specific) book'.
Dative of purpose: e.g. *Bala.lar balıq alauγa ketti* 'The boys went to catch fish.'
Locative: may express possession, coupled with verb 'to be', e.g. *Sašada qızıq kitap var* 'Sasha has an interesting book.'
Ablative: e.g. *Üy kirpišten salındı* 'The house is built of brick.'
Instrumental/comitative in *-men*^{3}: e.g. *qarındašpen* 'with a pencil'; *men poez.**b**en keldim* 'I came by train'.

Pronoun

The base forms are:

	Singular	*Plural*
1	men	biz(der)
2	sen	sen/siz(der)
3	ol	olar

The possessive pronominal markers are:

	Singular	*Plural*
1	-m^2	-ımız^4
2	-ŋ^2	-ınız^4
3	-s^3	-(lar^6)ı^2

Verb

COPULA

The endings are: sing. 1 *mın*^{6}, 2 *sıŋ*^{2}, 3 Ø; pl. 1 *mız*^{6}, 2 *sızdar*^{2}, 3 Ø. These are negated by *emes*: e.g. *men qazaqpın* 'I am a Kazakh'; *ol qızmetši emes* 'he isn't a worker'.

A simple present is made for only four verbs: *tur-* 'to stand'; *otır* 'to sit'; *žür-* 'to go'; *žatır-* 'to lie'. A compound present and several other tenses are made by means of the *-p*/*-ıp*^{2} gerund of the sense-verb plus inflected form of one of these four auxiliaries: e.g. *žazıp otır* 'he is writing', *oqıp otırsızdar* 'you (sing./pl.) are reading'; negative *oqıp otır.γan žoqsız*.

The first person singular affixes are *-mın*^{4}; pl. *-mız*^{6}; second person *-sıŋ*^{2}; pl. *-sıŋdar*^{4}. The third person form has a null affix, except in the past tense, where it has *-dı*^{4}.

Past definite: synthetic form with *-dı-* marker: e.g. *kör.di.m* 'I saw'; analytical form: *γan*^{4} + copula: e.g. *žaz.γan.sıŋ* 'you were writing', where *γan*^{4} is the past participial marker (with allophones *gen*, *qan*, *ken*): cf. *ber.il.gen* 'given', where *-il-* is the passive marker (*see* **Turkic Languages**); *kel.gen* '(who) came'.

A presumptive future is made with the marker *-ar*^{3}- + the copula: e.g. *bar.ar.sıŋ* 'you will (presumably) go'; a definite or intentional future with *-maq*^{6} + copula: usually with *-šı*^{2}- infix: e.g. *kel.mek.ši.siŋ* 'it is up to you to come/your intention is to come'.

As elswhere in Turkic, the participles are used to make forms corresponding to relative clauses in other languages: e.g. the present participle in *-tın*^{2}: *kel.e.tin kisi* 'the man who is coming'.

Gerund: important endings are: *-e*^{3} for concomitant action: *kör.e* 'seeing', *al.a* 'taking', and *-ıp*^{3} for completed action: *al.ıp* 'having taken', *kör.ip* 'having seen'.

The citation form of the verb is in *-u*: *bar.u* 'to go', *kel-u* 'to come', *al.u* 'to take'. A linking vowel is discarded: *oqı* + *-u* > *oq.u* 'to read'. The form is also the verbal noun, and can be declined.

Composite verbs: *al.ıp baru* 'having taken – go', i.e. 'to take away'; *al.ıp kelu* 'to bring'.

NEGATIVE

The negative marker is *ma*[6]: e.g. *al.ma.dı* 'he didn't take'; *emes* and *žoq* are used with compound tenses: *ol kel.gen žoq* 'he didn't come'.

Postpositions

Many are standard Turkic: e.g. *sabaqtan soŋ* 'after the lesson'; *qanndaš stol üstinde žatır* 'the pencil is lying on the table' (note vowel harmony neutralization in *üstinde*); *bala.m turalı əngime* 'a story about my son'.

Word order

SOV

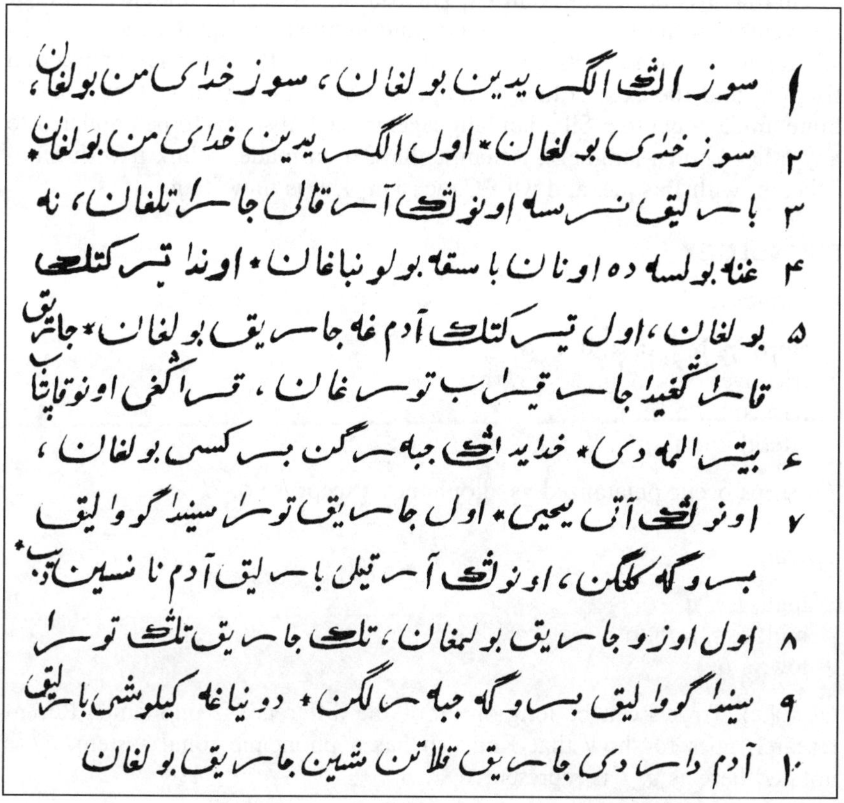

١ سوز اتك الگس يدين بولغان ، سوز خدای من بولغان ،
٢ سوز خدای بولغان • اول الگس يدين خدای من بولغان
٣ باسليق نرسه اونونك آرقالى جاسالتلغان ، نه
٤ غنه بولسه ده اونان باسقه بولونباغان • اوندا تيرشلك
٥ بولغان ، اول تيرشلك آدمغه جاريق بولغان • جاريق
قاراڭغيدا جارقيراپ تورغان ، قاراڭغى اونو قاپتا
٦ بيتسالماه دی • خدايدانك جبرلگن بر كسى بولغان ،
٧ اونونك آتى يحيى • اول جاريق توراسيندا گواليق
بروگه كلگن ، اونونك آرتيل باسليق آدم نانسين دب *
٨ اول اوزو جاريق بولمغان ، تك جاريق تلك تورا
٩ سيندا گواليق بروگه جبرلگن • دونياغه كيلوشى باسليق
١٠ آدم داسى جاريق تلاتن شين جاريق بولغان

KET

INTRODUCTION

This is the sole remaining representative of the Yeniseyan group of languages, the other members of which – Arin, Assan, and Kott – died out in the early nineteenth century. The Kets live along the middle reaches of the Yenisei in the Krasnoyarsk Kray, and number less than a thousand. In several ways – e.g. in its class system of nouns, the presence of internal flection, and the extraordinary complication of the verbal system – Ket is quite unlike any other Siberian language; indeed, it seems to be unrelated to any other known language. Attempts have been made to link it with Sino-Tibetan, with Basque, and with Caucasian. Ket is unwritten.

PHONOLOGY

Consonants

stops: p, b, t, d, k, g, q, ɢ, ʔ
fricatives: v, s, s′, j, x, γ, ʁ, (h)
nasals: m, n, ɲ, ŋ
lateral and flap: l, l′, r, r′

All stops occur palatalized as allophones, except /q, ɢ, ʔ/.

Vowels

high: i, ɪ, u
mid: e, ɛ, ʌ, ɔ, o
low: a (æ)

/a/ = [æ]. Vowels can be long or short; the difference is phonemic. Recent research goes to show that Ket also has a phonemic tonal system. /ɛ/ is notated here as ę; ъ is represented by ə.

Stress

Stress is movable, and again may be phonemic, in that it distinguishes, for example, number and person.

MORPHOLOGY AND SYNTAX

Noun

Three noun classes are distinguished: masculine, feminine, and neuter. The class of masculine nouns includes, apart from male humans, most male animals, some birds, nearly all fishes, some insects, all trees, large wooden objects, and the moon; the feminine class includes some animals (fox, hare, squirrel, etc.), three kinds of fish, and the sun. Everything else is in the neuter class. Nouns themselves are not overtly marked for class; concord is established via verbal forms, predicative adjectives, etc.

NUMBER

The plural is formed in several ways: masculine and feminine classes coalesce in the plural:

(a) by suffixation: (vowel) + *n*/*n′*, e.g. *ut′* 'mouse', pl. *ut′n′*; *am* 'mother', pl. *amaŋ*;
(b) internal flection: e.g. *tip′* 'dog', pl. ***ta**p′*;
(c) by vowel lengthening;
(d) by stress transfer;
(e) by suppletion: e.g. *k′ẹt* 'person', *d′ẹŋ* 'people'; *dɪl′* 'child', *kʌt* 'children'.

CASE SYSTEM

Seven cases are distinguished by suffixation: e.g.

the dative/aditive case has dental + (harmonic?) vowel + *ŋa*: e.g. *am* 'mother' – *amdiŋa*; *op* 'father' – *o**b**daŋa*;
ablative: dental + vowel + *-l′*: e.g. *amdil′* 'from the mother';
benefactive: dental + vowel + *-nt′* (often + *-œn*), e.g. *amdiŋt′* = *amdiŋtœn* 'on behalf of', 'for the mother'. Cf. in plural: *amiŋ.naŋt′* 'for the mothers'.

Adjective

A petrified formant, *-l′*, is found in some adjectives: e.g. *s′ẹl′* 'bad'; *xol′* 'short'; *qil′* 'wide'. The attributive adjective precedes the noun, and may take a plural marker. The predicative adjective is marked for person, and, in the third person, for class: e.g. *at′ qœ.r′i* 'I am big'; *u qœ.γu* 'you are big'; *bu qœ.r′u* 'he is big'; *bu qœ.r′œ* 'she is big'.

Pronoun

PERSONAL INDEPENDENT

		Singular	*Plural*
1		at′	ət′n′
2		u/uk	əkŋ
3	common:	bu	buŋ

These are declined in five cases: e.g. for 1st sing., aditive *aviŋa*, ablative *avil′*, locative *aviŋt′*, comitative *ar′as′*.

Personalizing prefixes marking possession, relatedness to, etc.:

		Singular	Plural
1		(a)b-	na/næ, ət′næ
2		(u)k-	na/næ, əknæ
3	masc.	da-/dæ, buræ-	na/næ, buŋnæ
	fem.	d-, bur-	–

Examples: *(a)**b**am* 'my mother'; *(u)**k**am* 'your mother'.

DEMONSTRATIVE PRONOUN

Three degrees of relative distance ('this' – 'that' – 'that yonder') are distinguished, fully declined: masculine series: *kir′ – tur′ – qar′*; fem. *kir′œ – tur′œ – qar′œ*; pl. *kin′œ – tun′œ – qan′œ*.

INTERROGATIVE PRONOUN

anœ(t) 'who?', pl. *anœtœŋ*; *akus′* 'what?' The interrogative series is fully declined.

Numerals

The forms for 1–5 inclusive have class markers:

neuter: *qus′am, ɪn′œm, doŋœm, siγœm, qaγœm*;
masculine: *qogd′, ɪn′aŋ, do:ŋ, si:ŋ, qa:ŋ*;
feminine: *qogd′œ*.

6–10 have one form for all three classes: 6 *as′*, 7 *on′s*, 8 is *ɪn′œm bəns′aŋ qus′* '10 minus 2', 9 is *qus′œm bəns′aŋ qus′* '10 minus 1', 10 *qūs′*.

Verb

The main features of the very complicated system described by Kreinovič (1968) are here set out.

Roots are integral or split; the following four models are found:

(a) integral root in final position; all deixis by prefixation;
(b) split root consisting of two root morphemes;
(c) split root with derivatory element preceding root; deixis by prefix/infix;
(d) split root with derivative element following root; deixis by prefix/infix.

The complete table of personal prefixes and infixes shows 64 forms. Formally, they can be divided into two groups of first and third person forms: the D-group and the B-group:

D-group				*B-group*			
Prefixes		*Infixes*		*Prefixes*		*Infixes*	
1	2	3	4	1	2	3	4
d-/d-	di-/du-	-r-/-a-	-r-/Ø-	ba-/bu-	bo-/bu-	-ba-/a-	-bo/o-

That is, the first person singular markers are D *d-*, *di-*, *-r-*, *-r-* and B *ba-*, *bo-*,

-ba-, *-bo-*; the third person markers are: D *d-*, *du-*, *-a-*, *-∅-* and B *bu-*, *bu-*, *-a-*, *-o-*. These third person forms are masculine; there are feminine and neuter correlatives.

The first person plural infixes under both D 3 and 4 are *-dæŋ-*, which is also both the prefix and infix form for the whole of the B row. The second person plural forms are again based on *k*. In the plural, the third person forms are not marked for class.

D-group:

1: subject exponents in verbs of all types;
2: subject exponents in base-final verbs;
3: subject and object exponents;
4: subject exponent in intransitive verb; object exponent in intransitive/reflexive verb.

B-group:

1 and 2: subject exponent;
3 and 4: subject and object exponent.

In base-final verbs, both series precede the base; in split-root verbs (bases X and Y) first series precedes base X, second series follows; base Y is final.

Examples:

(a) D-group exponent as subject: base *-it* 'to sneeze' (base-final): ***di****.j.it*, ***ku****.j.it*, ***du****.j.it* 'I sneeze', 'you sneeze', 'he sneezes'.
(b) Base + derivative: *di-* 'hide oneself': *di.****ri****.tn*, *di****u****.tn* 'I'll hide', 'you'll hide'.
(c) D-group exponents as subject and object; split base: *usqit* 'to warm', ***d****.us.qi.****r****.it* 'he warms me': ***d****.us.qi.****u****.t* 'he warms you'.
(d) B-group as subject exponent; *sa:l* 'to spend the night': ***ba****.γ.i.s.sœl* 'I spend the night'; ***ku****.γ.i.s.sœl* 'you spend the night'.
(e) B-group exponent as direct object; base *-uŋ* 'to see': ***ba****.t.uŋ* 'sees me'; ***ku****.t.uŋ* 'sees you'; ***dœŋ****.t.uŋ* 'sees us'.

Plurality of subject can be marked at the end of the verbal complex by (γ) + vowel + *-n/ŋ*: e.g. from base *totœt* = 'to praise': *to.****ba****.γœ.t.iγ****in*** 'they praise me'.

Since Ket has no accusative case, the subject/object relationship has to be elucidated by the personal exponents within the verbal complex. Kreinovič gives an example involving the word *bis'œp* 'sibling' (male or female):

bis'æp bis'æp d.i.t.uŋ 'the brother sees the sister'
bis'æp bis'æp dæ.a.t.uŋ 'the sister sees the brother'

In the first sentence, *d.i.* indicates action by third masculine on third feminine: 'he – her'; in the second sentence, *dœ.a.* indicates action by third feminine on third masculine.

MOOD AND TENSE

In origin, *l*, *l′*, *n*, *n′* were perfective markers. They now appear as indicative past-tense markers, and are also used in the imperative mood. The indicative mood has a present/future tense marked by Ø, -*s*-, or -*a*-.

don′.s.i.vit 'I (shall) make-a-knife'
don′l′.i.vit 'I made/was-making-a-knife'

Imperative: the initial is *i-/a-*: *i.ndoq* 'fly!' (cf. *di.r.oq* 'I fly'; *di.n.doq* 'I flew'). The imperative forms are marked for subject and object of action (in transitive verbs) showing person, class, and number, and for modality (single or repeated action, etc.). Other modalities of action – inceptive, terminative, semelfactive, etc. – may also be expressed.

NEGATIVE

bən′ precedes the verb: e.g. *bu bən′ daʁij* 'he doesn't laugh'; *bu bən′ daʁol′ij* 'he didn't laugh'.

The elaborate participial and gerundial apparatus characteristic of so many Siberian languages is completely absent in Ket, but the infinitive has a great many forms, both primary and derivative.

Postpositions

Nominal derivatives with possessive affix are used.

Word order

SOV occurs, as in the example given above: *bis′œp bis′œp d.i.t.uŋ* 'the brother sees the sister', though this could also be construed as OSV. OVS also occurs; Kreinovič gives the following example: *abam dūtœt b′ep* 'brother/son-in-law (*b′ep*) beats (*dūtœt*) my mother (*abam*)'.

KHAKAS

INTRODUCTION

Classified by Baskakov (1966) as a member of the Uygur-Oguz group of Turkic languages. There are between 50 and 60 thousand speakers in the Khakasia Republic, which lies just north of the Tuva Republic in Krasnoyarsk Kray. The name 'Khakas' dates from the 1920s; previously, the Khakas were known as Abakan or Minusinsk Tatars. Use of a literary standard also dates from the early years of Soviet rule. The language is now used in local radio and television and the press, and there is a small literature.

SCRIPT

Cyrillic was adopted in 1939, after an experimental period of romanization. There are seven additional letters: і, ö, ÿ, ғ, ҷ, ң, ҷ.

PHONOLOGY

Consonants

stops: p, b, t, d, k, g
affricates: ts, tʃ, dʒ
fricatives: f, v, s, z, ʃ, ʒ, j, x, γ
nasals: m, n, ŋ
lateral and flap: l, r

Vowels

front: i, e, œ, y
back: ı, a, o, u

Consonants are either hard – associated with back vowels – or soft – associated with front vowels. Two /i/ sounds are distinguished by relative degree of closure, the more narrow being denoted in the script by the Cyrillic letter и, the half-narrow by the Roman *i*. /i/ is short only; all other vowels can be either long or short. Here, the difference between the two soft /i/ sounds is ignored. /œ/ is notated as *ö*, /y/ as *ü*.

VOWEL HARMONY

Normal Turkic pattern, /i/ is neutral. Labialization of endings is not notated in the script: cf. *tülgü* + *-ni* = /tylgyny/ 'the fox' (acc.).

MORPHOLOGY AND SYNTAX

See also **Turkic Languages**.

Noun

The plural marker is *lar*^{6} (*l-/n-/t-* + *a/e*): e.g. *tura.lar* 'houses'.

DECLENSION

Standard Turkic endings, with allophones varying from eight in the dative to two in the instrumental. To the usual six cases, Khakas adds an aditive in -*sar*^{4}, and an instrumental in -*naŋ*^{2}.

The possessive affixes and the predicative affixes are standard: e.g. *min toγısčı***bın** 'I am a worker'; *ol toγısčı***Ø** 'he is a worker'.

Pronouns

The pronominal system is standard Turkic for the most part; a relative pronoun exists (*kem* 'who', *nime* 'what'), though relative clauses are made, as is usual in Turkic, by means of participial forms: *see* **Verb**, below.

Numerals

Standard: 1 *pir*; 2 *iki*; 3 *üs*. 20 is *čibirgi*; 40 *xırıx*; 100 *čüs*.

Verb

Five moods, four voices; the present-tense system has three forms, the past-tense system has six, and there is a future.

The voice markers are standard Turkic: e.g. passive -*il/-ıl*: e.g. *pas-* 'to write', *pazıl* 'to be written'. Causative: -*tir*^{4}, e.g. *al-* 'to take', *aldır* 'to cause to be taken'.

PARTICIPIAL FORMS

Examples: *uzup.čatxan ōlax* 'the sleeping boy/the boy who is asleep'; *čōxtaγ an* → *čōxtān kizi* 'the man who was speaking/had spoken'; *kiligen mašina* 'the car that is coming'.

Postpositions

Standard Turkic, as is word order.

KHALKHA

See **Mongolian, Modern**.

KHANTY

INTRODUCTION

Khanty belongs to the Ob′-Ugric branch of Finno-Ugric (along with Mansi and Hungarian). In the nineteenth century the people and the language alike were known as Ostyak. There are at present about 15,000 speakers of the language in the Khanty-Mansii Autonomous Area and the Yamalo-Nenets Automonous Area. Khanty shows marked dialectal variation. In particular, one dialect – Vakh – is highly idiosyncratic, in that it has vowel harmony based on a rigid opposition between back and front vowels, with no neutral middle ground, and, in addition, a semi-ergative construction, unique in Uralic. The agent of a Vakh transitive verb is marked by the locative ending *-nə* – but the direct pronominal object is in the accusative, and the verb is in concord with the agent-subject.

Here the Central Ob′ dialect is described.

SCRIPT

Early missionary attempts to provide a script for Khanty covered several dialects, and were in general on a Roman basis. Since 1937 Khanty has been written in Cyrillic + a hooked *n* (ң) for /ŋ/ (notated here as *ng*). The reduced vowel /ə/ is notated as ы or и.

PHONOLOGY

Consonants

stops: p, t, k + palatalized t′
fricatives: s, ʃ, s′, x
nasals: m, n, ɲ, ŋ
lateral and flap: l, r
semi-vowels: j, w

Vowels

The vocalic system is based on two oppositions. (a) Between the long vowels: /eː, aː, oː, uː/; and the short vowels: /i, a, o, u/. All of these occur with pre-palatalization: /ji, je, ja/, etc. (b) Between all the above vowels and the reduced vowel /ə, jə/ which is never initial. In this article, /ə/ is notated as *ẹ*.

MORPHOLOGY AND SYNTAX

Noun

Khanty has three numbers: singular, dual, and plural. The dual marker is *-ngẹn*; the plural *-t/-ẹt*.

DECLENSION

Three cases: nominative (unmarked), dative/aditive, locative/instrumental: e.g. *xot* 'house':

	Singular	*Dual*	*Plural*
nominative	xot	xotngẹn	xotẹt
dative/aditive	xota	xotngẹna	xotẹta
locative/instrumental	xotnẹ	xotngẹnnẹ	xotẹtnẹ

POSSESSIVE ENDINGS

The grid shows singular/dual/plural possessor with singular/dual/plural possessed object, for all persons, i.e. 27 possible forms. Example for first person with singular, dual, and plural referents: *misem* 'my cow'; *misemẹn* 'my two cows'; *misew* 'my cows'; cf. *misngẹtuw* 'our (pl.) two cows'; *mistatẹn* 'our (dual) cows'. The possessive forms are declinable.

Adjective

As attribute, adjective is invariable. There is no comparative form. A denominal formant is *-ẹng*: *yur* 'strength', *yur.ẹng* 'powerful'. The affix *-tẹ* denotes lack of the quality expressed by the noun: *yur.tẹ* 'powerless'.

Pronoun

There are singular, dual, and plural personal forms:

	Singular nominative	*Dual nominative*	*Plural nominative*
1	ma	min	mung
2	nang	nẹn	nang
3	tuw	tẹn	tẹw

These have accusative and dative cases: e.g. for *ma*: acc. *manẹt*, dat. *manẹm*.

DEMONSTRATIVE PRONOUN/ADJECTIVE

tamẹ 'this', *tomẹ* 'that', *sit* 'that' (yonder). A shortened form is used attributively before nouns: e.g. *tam xot* 'this house'.

INTERROGATIVE PRONOUN

xoy 'who?'; *muy* 'what?'; fully declined.

Numerals

1–10: *yit/yiy*, *katn/kat*, *xutẹm*, *nyatẹ*, *wet*, *xut*, *tapẹt*, *nẹvẹt*, *yaryang*, *yang*. 11

yixosyang; 12 *katxosyang* (where -*xos′*- is a postposition meaning 'around'); 20 *xus*; 30 *xutẹmyang*; 100 *sot*.

Verb

Like Mansi and Hungarian, Khanty has definite and indefinite conjugations. The inflections of the definite conjugation are coded for person and number for both subject and object, and are very similar to the inflections of the possessive declensions. Cf. *tusem* 'I brought him'; *tustam* 'I brought them'; *tusemẹn* 'we two brought him'; *pontẹttẹn* 'you two will place them'. Both intransitive and transitive verbs may be conjugated in the indefinite conjugation.

The Central Ob′ dialect has indicative and imperative moods, and the indicative mood has two tenses: present-future and past. As illustration, the present-future endings, indicative mood, of *tuta* 'to bring' (indefinite conjugation):

	Singular	*Dual*	*Plural*
1	tutẹm	tutmẹn	tutuw
2	tutẹn	tuttẹn	tuttẹ
3	tut	tutngẹn	tutẹt

The definite present tense of *tuta* is as follows:

	Singular	*Dual*	*Plural*
1	tutem	tutemẹn	tutew
2	tuten	tuttẹn	tuttẹn
3	tutte	tuttẹn	tutet

The characteristic of the past tense is -*s*-: e.g. from *tuta*: *tusẹm* 'I brought' – *tusẹn* – *tus*; dual: e.g. *tusmẹn*; pl. e.g. *tusuw*.

PASSIVE VOICE

The characteristic is -*ai*/*ẹi* infix + indefinite conjugation endings: e.g. present-future *kitt.**ai**.m* 'I am/shall be sent'; past *kit.s.**ai.m*** 'I was sent'; *kit.s.**ai**.tẹn* 'you two were sent'.

IMPERATIVE

Second person only, in all three numbers and both conjugations. The dual and plural forms are not differentiated for definiteness/indefiniteness.

NON-FINITE FORMS

The infinitive is in -*ta*. Participles: present in -*tẹ*, past in -*ẹm*: e.g. *wertẹ* 'doing/being done'; *manẹm* 'having gone'. Gerund is in -*man*: e.g. *werman* 'doing'. These participial forms can be conjugated with personal affixes and case endings: e.g. *wertẹmnẹ* 'when I do'; *wertewnẹ* 'when we do'; *wertemẹnnẹ* 'when we two do'; *wermemnẹ* 'when I did'. They are used attributively: e.g. *rupittẹ xo* 'working man', 'man who works'; *rupitẹm xo* 'a/the man who worked'.

ASPECT

The inchoative characteristic is *-mẹ-*: e.g. *xuxẹtta* 'to run' – *xuxẹt.**mẹ**.ta* 'to start running', 'run off'. The semelfactive characteristic is *-ẹmt/-emẹ*; the reiterative has *-jit-*.

The general negating particle is *ant-* preceding the verb: *ant mantẹm* 'I shan't go'. The imperative is negated by *at*: e.g. *at mana!* 'don't go!'

Postpositions

Examples:

> *xosi* 'at', 'around', e.g. *xop xosi* 'at the boat';
> *xuwat* 'along', e.g. *yoxan xuwat* 'along the river';
> *pata* 'for', e.g. *tow pata* 'for the horse'.

Word order

SOV is normal.

9 Nen sidy sagat poikśat: muṅ azieu, turmet ochtyna ultot! nyṅ jemyṅ nemen muṅ choźa jemyṅ at ull;
10 At jogodl nyṅ turum nubten; nyṅ kažen at ull i mu ochtyna chody turum ochtyna;
11 N'aṅ muṅ mosta levypaseu mija muṅeu tam chadl ochtyja;
12 I esla muṅeu muṅ kreklau, chody i muṅ eslylu kuteuna kreklau;
13 Pa al esla muṅeu chuzipsaja pidta, no muṅeu šavyja kul' el'ta; nyṅ choźa ull turum nubyt i vey i symyltypsa nubyt chuvat, jena.
14 Chun channe-chojeta ly kreklal eslta pidleta, i nen turum azen esll nyṅylana;
15 A chun channe-chojeta ly kreklal eslta an pidleta, i nen turum azen an esll nen kreklan.

(Matthew 6.9–15)

KHASI

INTRODUCTION

Khasi is usually classified as a branch of the Mon-Khmer family of Austro-Asiatic languages. It is spoken in northern Assam by anything up to half a million people. There are four dialects, the main one being the Pnar dialect.

SCRIPT

A Roman script was provided by missionaries in the nineteenth century, and this has been utilized in the twentieth century to provide a small literature. Devanāgarī is also used.

PHONOLOGY

Consonants

The main framework is provided by the series /p, ph, b; t, th, d; k, kh, Ø/; with their associated nasals /m, n, ŋ/, though the voiced velar is missing. /dʒ/ is present with its nasal /ɲ/. Further, the sonants /r, l/, the sibilants /s, ʃ/, the semi-vowels /w, y/, the glottal stop /ʔ/, and the fricative /h/.

Rabel (1961) analyses Khasi lexemes in terms of 'major' and 'minor' syllables. Major syllables may be independent lexemes, such as *'uu* 'he', *rii* 'country', or they may require additional syllable(s) to achieve lexeme status. They take such forms as: consonant/cluster – vowel – (consonant): e.g. *luom* 'mountain', *dieng* 'tree', *thliem* 'leech', *dkhiw* 'ant'. The syllable CV is usually a bound morpheme: *ka* – feminine gender marker, *la* – past-tense marker.

A minor syllable consists of any Khasi consonant plus one of the sonants *r, l, m, n, ŋ* (i.e. excluding *ɲ*). Here, the sonant functions as a vowel. Such a syllable is a pre-formant. Many Khasi bi-/trisyllabic lexemes consist of a minor syllable (pre-formant) followed by a major syllable/lexeme: cf. *kn.maaw* 'to remember': *pn.kn.maaw* 'to remind' (*pn-* is the causative marker).

Vowels

Basically:

i, ɪ, e, ɛ, a, o, ɔ, u

These can be short, long, half-long, raised, lowered. In her grammar of Khasi, Rabel (1961) lists 32 phonemic values of the basic vowels.

Stress

Stress tends towards final syllable of both word and phrase. Syllabic stress in citation form is overruled by sentence rhythm.

MORPHOLOGY AND SYNTAX

Roots in Khasi are largely ambivalent and can be treated as nominals or verbals. However, initial *pn-* identifies the following syllable(s) as verbal. *jiŋ-* and *noŋ-* are nominal markers: *jiŋ.buon.kam* 'activity'; *jiŋ.buon.kam joŋ ŋa* 'my activity'.

Noun

There are two numbers, singular and plural; and two genders, masculine and feminine/neuter. The gender markers, *'uu* for masculine and *ka* for feminine/neuter are also the third person pronouns: the common plural is *kii*. Examples: *'uu kpaa* 'father', 'the/a father'; *ka kmi* 'mother', 'the/a mother'; *'uu khlaa* 'tiger'; *ka miaw* 'cat'; *'uu bseɲ* 'snake'. *'ii* can be used as a marker expressing endearment: e.g. *'ii miaw* 'pussy'.

POSSESSION

The possessive relating particle is *ǰoŋ* /dʒon/: e.g. *'uu khuon ǰoŋ ka knthey* 'the woman's son'; *ka kmi joŋ phii* 'your mother'. All attributes follow headword.

Pronoun

		Singular	*Plural*
1		ŋa	ŋii
2	polite	phii	phii
	familiar	pha	
3	masc.	'uu	kii
	fem.	ka	

DEMONSTRATIVE PRONOUN

These are compound forms, the personal pronouns being prefixed to six bases which give four degrees of relative distance plus two of relative locus above or below that of the speaker. Thus, for example *'uutu 'uu briw* 'that man (near you)', *katu* 'that woman/thing'.

INTERROGATIVE PRONOUN

These are compounds made from the personal pronouns plus the interrogative base *'ey*: *'uu'ey* 'who?' (male), *ka'ey* 'who?' (female)/'what?'.

RELATIVE PRONOUN

ba can be used with recapitulation of the personal marker: e.g. *kii khuon kii ba*... 'the children who...'.

Numerals

1–10: *wey/šii, 'aar, laay, saaw, san, hnriw, hnɲew, phra, khndaaw, khat*. 11–19: *khat-* + units. 20 *'aarphew* (where *-phew* is another word for 10); 30 *laayphew*; 100 *šiispa'*.

Verb

There is no inflection. The following tense markers are used:

customary action in past:	*la*
perfective	*la'*: *phii la' dep* 'you have finished'
future	*'n/sa* (*'n* is affixed to the pronominal subject: *na.n 'aay* 'I shall give')
continuous	*na*

ya is an object marker, optional where one object is concerned, obligatory in the case of two: e.g. *'uu hiikay* ***ya*** *ŋa ka ktien pharen* 'he teaches me English'. (Rabel 1961: 124).

The verb is negated by *'m*, which is affixed to the pronoun if there is a pronominal subject, to the verb if not. In the past tense, *šm* replaces *la*: e.g. *ŋi.****m šm*** *yatip* 'we didn't know'.

MODAL MARKERS

ya reciprocal; *pn* causative: e.g. *tip* 'to know' – ***pn****tip* 'to make known'. Bound forms may be pre- or post-verbs: e.g. with the verb stem *baam* 'to eat': *naŋ.baam* 'to keep on eating'; *šaj baam* 'to be accustomed to eating'. Examples of post-verbs: *kaay* 'to do (something) for pleasure'; *lem* 'to share'; *baam kaay* 'to eat for eating's sake'; *lej lem* 'to go together'.

Prepositions

Examples of directional prepositions: *na, ha, ša*. These are used with or without gender marker/article: e.g. *'uu lej ša ka skul* 'he goes to the school'.

Word formation

Compounds are freely made: noun–noun, noun–verb, verb–verb, verb–noun: e.g. *ka šnon* 'village' + *ka kndon* 'corner': *ka šnon.kndon* 'an out-of-the way village'. Imitative compounds are based on such patterns as Ab-Ac, Abc.Abd: e.g. *khuon.kur khuon.kmi* 'respectable people' (*kur* 'mother's relatives'); *kren thu'.khana kren thu'.khade'* 'to gossip' (*kren* 'to speak'; *thu'.khana* 'to tell a story').

Reduplication is much used in Khasi, e.g. in an open class of adverbs, often with ablaut; Rabel (1961) gives several examples, e.g. *khliŋkhliŋ khlaŋkhlaŋ* 'to look around'.

Word order

SVO; inversion is possible in the principal clause, if preceded by the subordinate clause.

১ কাবানুংকং কাক্তিন লাডন্ কাক্তিন বংওব্লেই রঙ্কাট
২ লাডন্ পাতেং কাক্তিন ওব্লেই হি। কাতা মিন্নুংকং
৩ রঙ্কাট বংওব্লেই লাডন। বস্তু কাজিংবু ডাকাডা
লালাথাও পাতেং কাটং লালাথাও হাপ্ডেং জুংকা
কাৰেই কাজিংবুরু গ্লেম্কাতা কাবালাথাও কাম্চুম্লং।
৪ হাপ্ডেং জুংকা কাবাইম কাতা কাবাইম কাজুংকিব্রুও
৫ কাবাসায়। কাতা কাবাসায় হাকাবাইয়ংডেঞ্জ
লালাসায় পাতেং কাবাইয়ংডেঞ্জ কাতা কাম্চুম্রি।
৬ ওয়োহন হাকাকর্তেং ওৰেই নাওব্লেই ওবালাফা
৭ ওলাডন্ বস্তু ডাওতা ওডেইং নাপুনকানে ওতা কাজুং
কাবাসায় কাপ্রুযান বান্আয় ওৰেই ওসাক্ষী বাল্লং
৮ ওলাওআন। ওতা কাতা কাবাসায় এম্ পাতেং কাজুং
কাতা কাবাসায় কাপ্রুযান বান্আয় ওলালাডন।

KHMER

See **Cambodian.**

KIRGIZ

INTRODUCTION

In Baskakov's (1966) classification, Kirgiz appears as the Kirgiz-Kipchak sub-group of Eastern Hunnic. The language is spoken by 1½ or 2 million people in Kirghizia, and in adjacent areas of Uzbekistan, Tajikistan, and Kazakhstan. The Kirgiz also live in the Xinjiang-Uigur Autonomous Region of the CPR, and in western regions of Mongolia. Smaller communities are found in Afghanistan and Pakistan.

In the eighth/ninth century AD the Kirgiz were located in the Upper Yenisei region, and it is presumably to their culture that we owe the Orkhon-Yenisei inscriptional material discovered there in the seventeenth century. (*See* **Orkhon-Yenisei**.)

Kirgiz folk literature possesses one of the world's longest poems – the *Manas* epic – which runs in one version to half a million lines. The epic mixes heroic myth with a colourful account of actual happenings in the history of the Kirgiz people. Sections of the *Manas* are sung on festive occasions by *manasčiler*.

The modern literature dates from the 1920s. Primary and secondary education are provided in Kirgiz, which is also used in local media, radio, television, and journalism.

SCRIPT

Originally Arabic; Cyrillic since 1940.

PHONOLOGY

Consonants

stops: p, b, t, d, k, g (q)
affricates: ts, tʃ, dʒ
fricatives: (f, v), s, z, ʃ, (ʒ) j, x, (γ)
nasals: m, n, ŋ
lateral and flap: l, r

Vowels

Kirgiz has one of the most symmetrical vowel systems in Turkic:

	Unrounded	*Rounded*
front	(ə, əː), ɛ, ɛː, i, iː	œ, œː, y, yː
back	a, aː, ɪ, ɪː	o, oː, u, uː

/œ/ is notated here as *ö*, /y/ as *ü*. Long vowels are indicated in the text by macrons: e.g. *ī*.

VOWEL HARMONY

Is systematically observed: front with front, back with back, rounded with rounded: cf. declensions of *konok* 'guest' and *töö* 'camel':

nominative	konok	töö
accusative	konoktu	töönü
genitive	konoktun	töönün
dative	konokko	töögö
locative	konokto	töödö
ablative	konokton	töödön

The accusative marker *-nı* appears in twelve variants: four with *n-* initial, four with *d-*, and four with *t-*; the locative and ablative in eight.

MORPHOLOGY AND SYNTAX

Declension, the personal affixes, the possessive markers, the treatment of adjectives, the pronominal system, and the numerals are all standard Turkic in pattern and individual forms (*see* **Turkic Languages**). The verb has simple and composite (participial) forms. Unusually, the third person plural of the first preterite takes an *-iš-* infix: e.g. *kaldı* 'he remained': *kal.ıš.tı* 'they remained'; *kal.ıš.pa.dı* 'they did not remain'.

Adjective

As attribute, adjective precedes noun and is invariable. Comparative in *-irek*^{2}, with compared form in ablative: e.g. *kara at***tan** *tez***irek** 'faster than the black horse'.

Pronoun

Standard Turkic forms. The third person shows optional forms, *al/ol* (sing.), with oblique cases, e.g. gen. *anın/onun*, and pl. *alar/olor*, gen. *alardın/olordun*.

The possessive markers are standard: e.g. *at***ım** 'my horse'; *kiteb***im** 'my book'; *emgekči.ler.***din** *el aralık kün***ü** 'the international day of the workers' (*el* 'nation'; *ara.lık* 'between').

DEMONSTRATIVE PRONOUN/ADJECTIVE

bul/bu 'this'; *usul* 'that'; declension is standard.

INTERROGATIVE PRONOUN

kim 'who?'; (*n*)*emne* 'what?'; declension is standard.

Numerals

Standard; 20 is *ǰıyırma* = Turkish *yirmi.*

Verb

Standard Turkic pattern throughout (*see* **Turkic Languages**).

The personal endings can be sub-divided into (a) full forms, and (b) short forms:

	Singular		*Plural*	
	Full	*Short*	*Full*	*Short*
1	-min	-m	-biz	**-k**
2	-siŋ/-siz	-ŋ/ŋiz	-siz(der)	-ŋer/ŋizder
3	(-t)	—	—	—

NEGATION

The copula, which is expressed in positive sentences by a specific set of pronominal endings: sing. 1 *min*, 2 *siŋ/siz*, 3 Ø; pl. 1 *biz*, 2 *siŋer/sizer*, 3 Ø, is negated by *emes*, sited between the nominal and the ending: e.g. *men emgekči.min* 'I am a worker', *al emgekči.Ø* 'he is a worker'; *men emgekči emes.min* 'I am not a worker', *al emgekči emes* 'he is not a worker'. The existential verb 'there is/are' is expressed by *bar*, and negated by *jok*: *jurnal bar bı* 'is there a magazine?', *jurnal jok* 'there is no magazine'.

The standard Turkic negative marker (Turkish *-ma-/-me-*) appears in Kirgiz as *-b/p/m*V-. Some examples are given below.

Examples of verb formation:

- present/future definite: *-e/a-*, e.g. *jaz.a.m* 'I write', 'I'll write';
- future presumptive: *-er/ar*, e.g. *kal.ar.bız* 'we'll (presumably) stay', *Kal.ba.s.sıŋar* 'You won't stay?';
- present progressive: gerund of sense-verb + auxiliary *tur-/jat-*, e.g. *okup turam* 'I'm reading now';
- past definite: *-dı/di-*, e.g. *kaldım* 'I stayed', *kal.ba.dı.ŋızdar* 'you didn't stay';
- conditional: *-se/sa-*, e.g. *kelsem* 'if I come';
- desiderative/optative: *-gey/gay-* + auxiliary *ele-*.

Passive, causative, and reciprocal markers are standard.

The negative particle *emes* is conjugated to negate certain tenses: e.g. *okuču emesmin* 'I was not in the habit of reading' (*okuču-* is past habitual). Note the form *-gende*, etc. which makes temporal clauses of concomitant action: e.g. *karıganda* 'when he grows old . . . '.

Postpositions

Standard, governing base case, ablative, dative, or accusative.

بدايت‌ده كلمت بار ايردي و كلمت خداي‌ده
ايردي و كلمت خدا ايردي ✿ ٢ و همان بدايت‌ده ايردي
الله‌ده ✿ ٣ وسيله‌سي برله هر نرسه بولدي و آنيسيز هيچ بر
نرسه بولمادي كه بولدي ✿ ۴ آنده حيات بار ايردي و
اول حيات آدم‌لارننك روشنيسي ايردي ✿ ٥ و اول روشني
قرانكلق‌ده يالدورايب دورا و قرانكلق آني (ايچنده)
توتمادي ✿ ٦ بر آدم خدادان مرسول بولدي كه اسمي
يحيا ايردي ✿ ٧ همان شهادت اوچون كيلدي (يعني)
نورغه شهادت بيرمک اوچون كه سببندان همه ايمان
كيلدورالار ✿ ٨ شول نور داكول ايردي لكن شول نورغه
شهادت بيرمک اوچون كيلدي ✿

KOMI

INTRODUCTION

The Permic branch of Finno-Ugrian includes, apart from Udmurt, the two forms of Komi: Komi-Zyryan and Komi-Permyak. They are mutually intelligible. Most Komi-Zyryan live in the Komi Republic in the northern Urals; the Komi-Permyak live further to the south, in the Komi-Permyak Autonomous Area. The total number of speakers of both forms is put at about 360,000.

Komi is one of the two Uralic languages whose past history is actually documented. In the second half of the fourteenth century St Stephen of Perm, Bishop of the Russian Orthodox Church and missionary to the Permic peoples, translated parts of the Bible and the liturgy into Komi, using a script which he himself had prepared from Greek and Cyrillic elements. Both script and literary language were known to no more than a few clerics, and both, accordingly, were soon forgotten. The extant material is, however, of great philological importance, as it represents by far the oldest written record of a Uralic language (if the markedly divergent and therefore unrepresentative Hungarian is discounted). This material falls into two divisions: (a) late seventeeth/eighteenth-century copies in Cyrillic script containing passages from the Acts of the Apostles and from St John's gospel, along with some liturgical material; (b) texts in St Stephen's script inscribed on two ikons – the Holy Trinity Ikon in the church of Vožem and the Pentecost Ikon (now lost).

The language of the Old Permic texts is quite close to Modern Komi.

From the middle of the nineteenth century onwards, Komi has produced a small but flourishing literature with one or two outstanding figures, e.g. the poet I.A. Kuratov, who translated several English, French, and German authors into Komi.

The forms described in this article are those of Komi-Zyryan.

SCRIPT

Cyrillic with additional letters *i* and *ö*.

PHONOLOGY

Consonants

stops: p, b, t, d, k, g; t′, d′
affricates: (dz), tʃ, tʃ′, dʒ, dʒ′

fricatives: v, s, z, ʃ, ʒ, s′, z′, j
nasals: m, n, ɲ
laterals and flap: l, l′, r

Consonants marked with the palatalization sign ′ differ materially in articulation from their non-palatalized counterparts.

Vowels

i, e, ı, œ, a, o, u

/œ/ → [ə].

A dental consonant may be followed by a palatalized or a non-palatalized /i/. In the former case, /i/ is denoted by the Cyrillic letter и; in the latter case, by the letter *i*. In this article, hard /i/ is denoted by a dot under the preceding consonant. Semi vowel: *j* (= /y/).

Stress

Theoretically, stress is on the first syllable, but is mobile and non-phonemic.

MORPHOLOGY AND SYNTAX

Noun

The noun has two numbers, the plural marker being *-yas*: e.g. *kerka* 'house', pl. *kerkayas*; *vöv* 'horse', pl. *vövyas.*

Sixteen cases are distinguished in the literary language; for *yort* 'comrade', e.g. gen. *yortlön*, dat. *yortlı*, acc. *yortös*, instr. *yortön*. The possessive affixes are sing. 1 *-öy*, 2 *-ıd*, 3 *-ıs*; pl. 1 *-nım*, 2 *-nıd*, 3 *-nıs*. These affixes may precede or follow the case ending; cf. *yort**öy**lön* 'of my comrade'; *yorttög**ıd*** 'without your comrade'. The plural marker *-yas* precedes them: *vöv.yas.ıd* 'your horses'.

Adjective

As attribute, adjective precedes noun and is invariable: e.g. *bur mortlön* 'of the good man'. The predicative adjective tends to be in the instrumental, and may have a specific plural form in *-ös′*: e.g. *vövyas yonös′* 'the horses are strong'.

Pronoun

Personal: sing. 1 *me*; 2 *te*; 3 *ṣiyö*; pl. 1 *mi*; 2 *ṭi*; 3 *nayö*. These are declined in all cases, e.g. for *me*: gen. *menam*, dat. *menım*, acc. *menö.*

DEMONSTRATIVE PRONOUN

tayö 'this'; *ṣiyo* 'that'

INTERROGATIVE/RELATIVE PRONOUN

koḍi 'who?'; *mıy* 'what?'

Numerals

1–10: *ötik, kık, kuim, nyol′, vit, kwayt, sizim, kökyamıs, ökmıs, das*; 11 *das öti*; 12 *das kık*; 20 *kız′*; 30 *komın*; 40 *nelyamın*; 100 *syo*.

The numerals are followed by the singular case: *kık mort* 'two men'. Cf. *nyol′nan.ım* 'the four of us'.

Verb

The verb has aspect, mood, voice, tense, number, and person; positive and negative versions. As specimen, the present indicative, affirmative and positive, of *gižnı* 'to write':

	Positive		*Negative*	
	Singular	*Plural*	*Singular*	*Plural*
1	giža	gižam	og giž	og gižöy
2	gižan	gižannıd	on giž	on gižöy
3	gižö	gižönı	oz giž	oz gižnı

The future tense is closely similar in the affirmative, identical in the negative. There are two past tenses, one of which is an inferential: e.g. *gižis* 'he wrote'; *gižöma* '(it seems that) he wrote'. This inferential tense has no first person form.

NEGATION

As will be seen from the above example, the verb is negated by means of a conjugated negative auxiliary, plus a stem form marked for number.

ASPECT

Semelfactive, reiterative aspects are marked, but the distinction between perfective and imperfective is not observed.

VOICE

Causative with a dental marker, e.g. *-öd*; reflexive with a sibilant. The infinitive can take personal endings: e.g. *munnım og vermı* 'I can't go'; *munnıd on vermı* 'you can't go'.

Postpositions

Komi uses postpositions: e.g. *berd-* 'near', *vör berdın* 'near the forest'; *dıryi* 'during', *voina* (Russian loanword) *dıryi* 'during the war'; *gögör* 'about', *vit lun gögör* 'about five days'; *moz* 'like', *udžalö oš moz* 'he works like a bear'.

Word order

SVO seems usual.

Въ началѣ было Слово, и Слово было у Бога, и Слово было Богъ.

2. Оно было въ началѣ у Бога.

3. Все чрезъ Него начало быть, и безъ Него ни что не начало быть, чтò начало быть.

4. Въ Немъ была жизнь, и жизнь была свѣтъ человѣковъ.

5. И свѣтъ во тьмѣ свѣтитъ, и тьма не объяла его.

6. Былъ человѣкъ, посланный отъ Бога; имя ему Іоаннъ.

7. Онъ пришелъ для свидѣтельства, чтобы свидѣтельствовать о свѣтѣ, дабы всѣ увѣровали чрезъ него.

8. Онъ не былъ свѣтъ, но былъ *посланъ*, чтобы свидѣтельствовать о свѣтѣ.

KOREAN

INTRODUCTION

Korean has been variously connected with Dravidian, Austronesian, Palaeo-Asiatic, Chinese, and, most convincingly, with the Altaic languages, with which it certainly shares many grammatical features. How many of these resemblances are areal or typological, however, is a moot point, and the exact genetic affinity of Korean remains questionable. The Chinese element is very large but essentially alien. Comparison with Japanese yields a surprising wealth of morphological and syntactical similarities, but the two languages seem to have developed in parallel, rather than to be derived from a common genetic source.

Modern Korean derives from the ancient Korean Han dialect, which ousted its rival congeners thanks to the rise to political dominance of the Silla state, where it was spoken. It is spoken today by 63 million people in North and South Korea, and in Korean colonies in China, Japan, and elsewhere. The literary norm is based on the Seoul dialect.

Until the nineteenth century Chinese was the main language of literature in Korea, and little seems to have been written in Korean. A favourite genre was the *sijo* – a kind of rubaʿi, with seven- (three + four) or eight-syllable lines. Among the most famous exponents of the *sijo* were Yun Səndo (seventeenth century), Chəng Ch'əl (sixteenth century), and Kim Sijang (eighteenth century). In the twentieth century the novel has become the main forum for the literary handling of social issues. The best-known practitioners include Yi Kwangsu and Yi Injik.

SCRIPT

See **Script** at end of article.

PHONOLOGY

Consonants

stops: /p, t, k/, with aspirates /ph, th, kh/, and glottalized /p', t', k'/. The glottalized values are written as *pp, tt, kk*, and are sometimes described as 'implosives'. The same triad is found in the affricates: /tʃ, tʃh, tʃ'/.
fricatives: s, s', h
nasals: m, n, ŋ
lateral and flap: l, r
semi-vowels: j, w

In final position, members of the dental triad, the affricates and the sibilants are all realized as /t/; final /k, kh, k'/ → /k/; final /p, ph, p'/ → /p/. Intervocalic /p, t, k/ → [b, d, g].

Korean has an elaborate system of consonantal assimilation: e.g. stops preceding a nasal are assimilated to that nasal: e.g. *pakmulkwan* 'museum' → /panmulgwan/. In this article, /tʃ/ and its allophone /dʒ/ are notated as *c*, /tʃh/ as *ch*, /tʃ'/ as *ch'*.

Vowels

The basic inventory is:

i, e, ɛ, ɪ, ə, a, u, o

plus allophones /œ, y/. The script provides for notation of the vowels preceded by /j/ and by /w/, i.e. palatalized and labialized series. [ɔ] and [ʌ] are allophones of /ə/. Korean shows some traces of vowel harmony.

MORPHOLOGY AND SYNTAX

Noun

The nominative/subject particle, corresponding to the Japanese *ga*, is *-i* (following a consonant) or *ka* (following a vowel): e.g. *saram.**i*** 'the man'. Six oblique cases are formed by agglutinative affix (not inflection):

genitive	saramıi
accusative	saramıl
dative	sarameke
locative	(saramesə)
instrumental	saramıro
comitative	saramkwa

In itself the noun is neutral as to number. A plurality marker is *-tıl/-dıl*. A focusing agent or topicalizer, corresponding to Japanese *wa*, is -(*n*)*ın*: e.g. *Kı saram.ın Hankuk mal.ıl kalıchi.lə kassımnita* 'As for that man, he went to teach Korean.' (*Hankuk.mal* 'Korean language'; *kalıchi-* 'to teach'; *-lə* 'in order to': *see* **Modal constructions**, below.)

Compound nouns are readily formed by apposition: e.g. *chaek.pang* 'book-store'; *chaek-sdang* 'reading table'; *chaek.kaps* 'price of books'; *Hankuk.salam* 'Korean person'.

Adjective

A participial form in *-n* provides attributive adjectives which precede the noun: e.g. *khı.ta* 'to be big': *khı**n*** 'big', *khın kənmul* 'big building'; *pissa.ta* 'to be expensive': *pissa**n*** 'dear', *pissan chaek* 'expensive book'.

Pronoun

Until comparatively recently personal pronouns were avoided in Korean in favour of various circumlocutions, e.g. with *mom* 'body': *i mom.i* 'this body' = 'I'. In the modern language, pronouns are respect-graded: first and second person singular forms in respectful/formal language are: *cə*, *tangsin*; *na* is an acceptable form for first person singular in more informal language. For the third person the demonstrative *kɪ* is used, often plus *saram*, *puin*: e.g. *kɪ saram.ɪn* 'he', *ki puin.i* 'she' (cf. *ano hito wa* in Japanese). A polite form of address is *sənsaeng* = Chinese *xiānsheng*.

The pluralizing marker *-tɪl* can be added.

DEMONSTRATIVE PRONOUN/ADJECTIVE

Three degrees: *i* 'this', *chə* 'that', *kɪ* 'that yonder'.

INTERROGATIVE PRONOUN

nugu 'who?', *myəch* /myət/, 'what?'

RELATIVE PRONOUN

None; *see* **Relative constructions** in **Verb**, below.

Numerals

The indigenous Korean numerals 1–10 are: *han(a)*, *tu(l)*, *se*, *ne*, *tasəs*, *yəsəs*, *ilkop*, *yətəl*, *ahop*, *yəl*. For the teens, these are added to *yəl*: e.g. 11 *yəl-hana*. 20 *sɪmu(l)*; 30 *səlhɪn*; 40 *mahɪn*; 100 *paek*.

paek is used as *bǎi* in Chinese to mean an indefinitely large number, 'many'; cf. *paek.hwa.cəm* 'hundred-goods-store', 'supermarket'.

A Chinese series 1–10 is also used: *il*, *i*, *sam*, *sa*, *o*, *yuk*, *chil*, *phal*, *ku*, *sip*.

Verb

With half a dozen basic agglutinative components which can be added to the stem, plus a large number of possible affixes, a Korean verb can appear in literally hundreds of forms. The basic structure can be set out as: stem – grade marker – tense/mood/aspect marker – finite indicative or interrogative marker: e.g. *kalɪchi – si – kess.imni – ta* 'will teach' (honorific register).

Neither person nor number is marked; i.e. failing a nominal subject, the personal pronoun must be used.

STEM

This can be one-, two- or three-syllable: e.g. *mək-* 'eat'; *pissa-* 'be expensive'; *kalɪchi-* 'teach'. Compounds are made with *ha-/hae-* 'to do', *po-* 'to see', and other verbs, following either a noun or a verbal form: e.g. with noun: *kongpu ha-* 'to study' (Japanese *benkyō suru*); with verbal: *mul po-* 'to inquire' (*mu.ta* 'inquire', *pota* 'to see').

GRADE

There are several sociolinguistic levels; a broad division is into plain, informal polite, formal polite, and honorific. For example, in the present tense, the informal polite style has a form close to the stem, + *yo*; the formal polite style has the infixed characteristic *-mn-*: cf.

Stem	*Informal polite*	*Formal polite*	*Respectful*
ha 'to do'	hae yo	ha**mn**ita	has**ɯ**mnita
iss 'to be'	issə yo	iss**ɯmn**ita	issɯsɯmnita
o- 'to come'	wa yo	o**mn**ita	os**ɯ**mnita/wassimnita

Some verbs have suppletive stems for respectful/honorific usage: e.g. *mək* 'to eat': hon. *capsusita* – *capsusɯmnita* 'eat(s)'. The plain style has its own specific set of endings, used in the family and at school: senior to junior, elder to younger, and so on.

TENSE MARKERS

The informal and formal style present has been illustrated above. The past-tense characteristic is *-ss-*; past anterior *-ssəss-*; future *-kess-*: e.g. in formal polite style: *ilkəssɯmnita* 'read' (past tense); *patə**ssə**ssɯmnita* 'had taken'; *kalɯchi.si.**kess**.ɯmnita* 'will teach' (hon.).

IMPERATIVE/HORTATIVE MOOD

Typical endings are *-iyo* and *-ita*: e.g. *cusipsiyo* 'please give'; *kapsita* 'let's go'. The verb stem + *ki* is a verbal noun: *Hankukmal*(*ɯl*) *paeu**ki*** '(the) learning (of) Korean'.

NEGATION

There are several interesting constructions:

1. *an* preceding finite form: e.g. *hakkyo.e kamnita* 'goes to school', *hakkyo.e an kamnita* 'doesn't go to school';
2. stem + *ci-* + *anh-*: e.g. *ka.ci anh.simnita* 'doesn't/don't go';
3. stem + *ci-* + *mot hamnita*: e.g. *kaci mot hamnita* 'doesn't/don't go';
4. stem in *-l* form + *su* + *əps*: e.g. ***kal*** *su əpsɯmnita* 'can't go', *əps.ta* 'not exist'; literally, 'ability to go is not'.

INTERROGATIVE

The general characteristic is *-kka*, *kka yo*: e.g. *əti.e kasɯmnikka* 'Where is/are... going?'; *Tapang.e kal kka yo* 'How about going to a tearoom?'

MODAL CONSTRUCTIONS

There are many of these: e.g.

-(*i*)*lə* 'in order to', e.g. *Hankuk mal.ɯl paeu.**lə*** 'in order to learn Korean'; *chinku.lɯl mannalə wassɯmnita* 'came to meet a friend' (*chinku*).
-(*i*)*ly ko* + *ha-*: 'intend to', e.g. *Hankuk.e kalyəko haessɯmnita* 'intended to go to Korea'.
-ko + *siph-*: 'want to', e.g. *yənghwa.lɯl poko siphsɯmnita* 'wanted to see a film'.
-myən: 'if', e.g. *Hankuk.e ka.myən* 'if... go(es)/went to Korea'; *maekcu.lɯl wənhasi**myən*** 'if you'd like a beer'.
stem in *-l* + *su iss-*: 'be able to', e.g. *kal su issɯmnita* 'can go'.

-(*i*)*ni kaa*: 'because', e.g. *ton.i əpsɪmikka* 'because... has/have no money'.

-(*i*)*l kka ha-*: prospective/contemplative: *i.pən.e.nɪn pæ.lo ka.l.kka.hamnita* 'this time (*pən* 'time', 'occasion') by-boat (*pæ* 'boat') thinking-of-going', i.e. 'this time (I/you, etc.) thinking of going by boat'.

-*ko iss-*: continuative: *kɪ.ttae.e Səul.esə sal.ko issəssə yo* 'at that time (*ttae* 'period of time') (I/you, etc.) living in Seoul'.

-*ssimyən coh-*: desiderative: *Hankuk.ɪl kukyəng.haessəmyən coh.kess.ɪmnita* '(I, etc.) would like to see Korea' (*kukyəng hada* 'go sight-seeing');

-*n/ɪn/nɪn* + *kəs*: nominalization of verb (cf. Japanese *koto*: e.g. *Nihongo.o hanasu koto wa* 'the speaking of Japanese'): *Səul.esə san.ɪn kəs.ɪl coha.hamnikka* 'do you like living in Seoul?'

-(*ɪ*)*lyə.myən*: conditional desiderative: *wekyokwan.i twə.lyəmyən wekuk mal.ɪl cal.hae.ya.hamnita* 'if want to be a diplomat, must be good at foreign languages' (*wekyokwan* < Chinese *wài.jiāo.guān* 'diplomat'; *twə.da* 'to become'; *wekuk* < Chinese *wài.guó* 'foreign country'; *cal.hata* 'be good at'; *ya* is the necessitative marker: 'must').

RELATIVE CONSTRUCTIONS

Participial forms in -*n* (for present and past) and -*l* (future) are used attributively: e.g. *nae.ka paeu.nɪn mal* 'the language which I am learning'; *nae.ka ilk.ɪl chaek* 'the book which I'm going to read'; *hal il.i manhsɪmnita* 'the work which has to be done is much' = 'there's a lot of work to be done'. These forms can be passive: e.g. *mannal salam* 'people who are going to be met'.

Postpositions

Examples: *hakkyo aph e* 'in front of the school'; *i nyən cən.e* 'before two years' = 'two years ago'; *Səul esə Pusan kkaci* 'from Seoul to Pusan'.

Word order

SOV is normal.

처음에도가이스되도가 하ᄂᆞ님과함긔하니도난곳 하
나님이라이도가처음에 하나님과함긔하미만믈이말미
여다지ᄆᆡ스니지은바는하나투말미지안코지으미업나니
라ᄂᆞᆫ에싱명이이스니이싱명이사람의빗치되여빗치어두
온데빗치우되어두오디나아지못하다라한사람이기스니
하나님이보낸바일홈은요인니라와서간증이되문빗출위
하여간증하여뭇사람이텨로말미여믿기하ᄂᆞ텨가빗치간
이요오직빗출위하여간증하엿나니라

SCRIPT

Buddhist missionaries from China, and Buddhist texts in Chinese reached Korea around the turn of the millennium, and by the fifth century Korea was a Buddhist state using Chinese as the language of administration and culture. The subsequent spread of Confucianism in the Korean Middle Ages reinforced the status and the use of Chinese. It is not surprising that after nearly two thousand years of unremitting exposure to Chinese influence, well over 50 per cent of Korean vocabulary consists of Chinese borrowings.

By the seventh century, however, scholars were looking for ways of using Chinese characters to notate native Korean words. Among the earliest examples extant are the *hyangga* folksongs. The problem of adapting the morphemic Chinese script to the requirements of a highly inflected, agglutinative language was being faced at very much the same time in Japan; and, as in the analogous case of Japanese, three possible paths were explored: (a) semantic transfer: a Chinese character was used to denote its Korean semantic equivalent; in a language as heavily sinicized as Korean this must have seemed an attractive solution; (b) phonetic representation: Chinese characters were used to 'spell' Korean words; (c) Chinese characters, functioning as semantic nuclei, were supplied with phonetic diacritics to indicate the additional material (inflections, particles) required by Korean grammar and syntax (cf. the *okototen* system in Japanese).

A practical solution, such as was developed in Japan in the shape of the elegant and tractable *wabun* script, eluded the Korean scholars. In the middle of the fifteenth century, however, a group of scholars under the aegis and direction of the fourth monarch of the Yi Dynasty, King Sejong (reigned 1418/19–1450) produced the phonetic syllabary of 28 letters known as *Hangŭl*. Within a year or two of its promulgation, the new script had been used in the poetical work *Yong.pi ŏch'ŏn ka* (Dragon(s) Flying to the Heavens).

The Korean syllabary has been described as 'one of the most scientific alphabets in use in any country' (*Encyclopaedia Britannica*). In fact, however, for the next 400 years, little use was made of it. Chinese remained as before the status language of the educated and influential classes. Of all the written material produced in Korea between the invention of the *Hangŭl* syllabary and the late nineteenth century, less than 1 per cent is in Korean: the rest is in Chinese.

Towards the end of the nineteenth century, the so-called 'mixed script' began to gain ground. In this system, much as in modern Japanese, Chinese characters function as root morphemes, while the syllabary is used for inflections and particles. Since the late 1940s, use of Chinese characters has been discontinued in North Korea, while in South Korea mixed script continues to be used.

The syllabary is set out in the accompanying tables. The most interesting feature of *Hangŭl* is the way in which consonants and vowels combine in their base forms to form syllables. That is to say, vowels following consonants do not assume secondary forms as in Devanāgarī, nor are the consonants themselves modified as in Ethiopic. The consonantal inventory takes into account the three-fold division of Korean stops into lax, aspirated, and tense. The tense consonants are geminates of the lax: cf. ㄱ /k/, ㄲ /kk/; ㅂ /p/, ㅃ /pp/. To distinguish aspiration the consonant is marked: ㄱ /k/, ㅋ /k^{h}/, while palatalization is notated in the vocalic series: 가 /ka/, 갸 /kya/. Vowels cannot stand alone, but must be supported by the bearer ㅇ (not to be confused with the consonantal sign for /n/): thus 아 /a/, 오 /o/.

THE KOREAN SCRIPT

THE SYLLABARY

Letter	*Transcription*	*Letter*	*Transcription*
Pure vowels:			
ㅣ	/i/	ㅡ	/ŭ/
ㅔ	/e/	ㅓ	/ə/
ㅐ	/æ/	ㅏ	/a/
ㅟ	/ü/	ㅜ	/u/
ㅚ	/ö/	ㅗ	/o/
Compound vowels:			
ㅑ	/ya/	ㅘ	/wa
ㅒ	/yæ/	ㅙ	/wæ/
ㅕ	/yə/	ㅝ	/wə/
ㅖ	/ye/	ㅞ	/we/
ㅛ	/yo/	ㅢ	/ŭi/
ㅠ	/yu/		
Consonants:			
ㄱ	/k/	ㅇ	/ŋ/
ㄴ	/n/	ㅈ	/c/
ㄷ	/t/	ㅊ	/c^{h}/
ㄹ	/l/	ㅋ	/k^{h}/
ㅁ	/m/	ㅌ	/t^{h}/
ㅂ	/p/	ㅍ	/p^{h}/
ㅅ	/s/	ㅎ	/h/
Double consonants:			
ㄲ	/k'/	ㅆ	/s'/
ㄸ	/t'/	ㅉ	/c'/
ㅃ	/p'/		

Source: Kim, N.K. (1987) 'Korean', in B. Comrie (ed.) *The World's Major Languages*, London: Routledge.

Two sample rows follow:

(a) C +V

가	갸	거	겨	고	교	구	규	그
ka	***kya***	***kə***	***kyə***	***ko***	***kyo***	***ku***	***kyu***	***kŭ***
기	개	걔	게	계	괴	귀	긔	과
ki	***kæ***	***kyæ***	***ke***	***kye***	***ko***	***ki***	***kwi***	***kwa***
궈	괘	궤						
kwə	***kwæ***	***kwe***						

C + V + C (phonetic realizations)

각	간	갇	갈	감	갑	갓	강
kak	***kan***	***kat***	***kal***	***kam***	***kap***	***kat***	***kang***
갖	갗	같	갚	갛	갉	값	갔
kat	***kat***	***kat***	***kap***	***ka'***	***kak***	***kap***	***kat***

KORYAK

INTRODUCTION

In terms of numbers this is, after Chukchi, the largest member of the Chukotko-Kamchatkan group of Palaeo-Siberian languages. It is spoken by about six thousand people in the Koryak Autonomous Area in north Kamchatka, and along the Bering Sea coast as far as Cape Navarin. Since 1936, a written form, based on the Chavchuven dialect, has been notated in Cyrillic script with additional letters for /q/ and /ŋ/.

Two closely related languages, Alyutor and Kerek, both now virtually extinct, were until recently regarded as dialects of Koryak.

It is noteworthy that not all neologisms in the language are straight loans from Russian; many are calques on Russian words, using native Koryak resources.

PHONOLOGY

Consonants

stops: p, t, k, q, ʔ
affricate: tʃ
fricatives: w, v, j, γ, ʕ
nasals: m, n, ŋ
lateral: l

/t, n, l/ also occur palatalized: /t′, n′, l′/.

Vowels

i, ɪ, e/ɛ, a, o, u

In this article, /ɛ/ is represented as *ẹ*.

VOWEL HARMONY

Very close to that of Chukchi (*see* **Chukchi**).

MORPHOLOGY AND SYNTAX

Noun

The minimum sense-bearing unit in Koryak is the disyllable; hence, root monosyllables are reduplicated to form lexemes: **ya* 'house', citation form *ya.ya*; **gil* 'ice' – *gil.gil*. Similarly, monosyllabic loanwords are homogenized for Koryak usage by reduplication: Russian *čaj* 'tea' – Koryak *čaj.čaj*. The root monosyllable may appear, however, as the nucleus of a denominative verb: *ta.**ya**.ŋ.k.ı* 'to build a house'.

A dual number is distinguished throughout the grammatical system, though, in the noun, it is formally marked only in the absolute/nominative case. Elsewhere in the nominal declension it seems to be identical to the plural. Human and non-human categories are distinguished, giving two declensions: the first comprises all nouns in the non-human category, plus nouns denoting humans in so far as they are general, i.e. do not refer to specific persons. These are covered by the second declension.

The dual marker is *-t* or *-u*/*-ẹ*: e.g. *qoya.t* 'two reindeer'; *kayŋı.t* 'two bears'.

For nouns ending in a vowel, the plural marker is *-v*' (with variants); *-u* is added to nouns ending in a consonant. Both plural endings tend to be realized as /w/: e.g. *ŋavıqqalyu.v*' 'girls'; *tınup.u* 'hills'.

DECLENSION

The first declension has eleven cases which are neutral as to number, apart, of course, from the nominative or absolute case which is marked for dual or plural. Thus, for *qoyaŋa* 'reindeer', dual *qoyat*, plural *qoya.v*' /qoyaw/, the paradigm shows, for example, an ergative *qoya.ta*; a locative *qoya.k*; an ablative *qoya.ŋqo*; a comitative *ga.qoya.ma.*

In the second declension, the plural forms are distinguished from the singular by the presence of *-yık*(*a*)-; and the ergative and locative cases, separate in the first declension, share a single form: e.g. for *appa* 'father':

	Singular	*Plural*
ergative/locative	appa.nak	appa.yık
ablative	appa.na.ŋqo	appa.yıka.ŋqo
dative	appa.na.ŋ	appa.yık.ıŋ
aditive	appa.na.ytıŋ	appa.yıka.ytıŋ

The second declension has eight cases.

Adjective

Qualitative adjectives are constructed on the model *nı* + stem + *qin*: e.g. *nı.mẹyıŋ.qin* 'big'; *nı.ŋlı.qẹn* 'smoky'. These forms are then conjugated for person and number: e.g. *nı.X.y.gım* 'I am X', *nı.X.y.gi* 'you (sing.) are X', where X is a quality. Similarly with nouns: e.g. *ẹn'piči.y.gım* 'I am a father', *ẹn'piči.y.gi* 'you (sing.) are a father'. There are corresponding negative versions.

Pronoun

	Singular	*Dual*	*Plural*
1	gımmo	muyi	muyu
2	gıčči	tuyi	tuyu
3	ınno	ıčči	ıčču

These are fully declined: e.g. the ergative of first person singular is *gımnan*, of first person plural *močgınan*.

DEMONSTRATIVE PRONOUN

Three degrees: *v'uččin* 'this' (proximate) – *ınnin* 'that' – *ŋaen* 'that yonder'.

INTERROGATIVE PRONOUN

męki 'who?' (declined in second declension); *yınnı* 'what?'

Numerals

1–10: *ınnęn, ŋıččeq, ŋıyoq, ŋıyaq, mıllıŋęn, ınnan.mıllıŋęn, ŋiyaq.mıllıŋęn, ŋiyoq.mıllıŋęn, qon'ʕayčıŋkęn, mıngıtkęn.*

Verb

The infinitive ending is *-k(kı)*; there are indicative, subjunctive, and imperative moods. The indicative has a present, two past tenses, two futures. The dual is everywhere formally distinguished. The conjugational system is essentially one of prefix – stem – personal ending, e.g. from *tılęk* 'to go':

present:

	Singular	*Dual*	*Plural*
1	tıku.lę.ŋ	mıt.ku.lę.ŋ	mıt.ko.la.laŋ
2	Øku.lę.ŋ	Øku.lę.ŋtık	Øko.la.laŋtık
3	Øku.lę.ŋ	Øku.lę.ŋi	Øko.la.laŋ

Here *lę* is the stem of the verb and *la* is an allophone.

Similarly for other tenses and moods: e.g. the perfective past has a *t-* prefix in the singular, *mıt-* in dual and plural; the suffixes end in *-k/-i*. The imperative has *mı.lę.k* 'that I may go', 'let me go'; *qı.lę.gi* 'go!'

TRANSITIVE VERB + OBJECT

The endings encode subject/object deixis: e.g. with verb *lıʕuk* 'to see':

tıku.lʕu.gi 'I see you (sing.)'
tıku.lʕu.ŋtık 'I see you two'
kinę.lʕu.ŋ 'you (sing.) see me'
nęku.lʕu.gi 'he sees you'
nęku.lʕu.gım 'they see me'

The complete grid has over 80 forms.

ERGATIVE CONSTRUCTION

Agent in instrumental case: e.g. *igę tımnęn qoyaŋa* 'the wolf killed the reindeer' (*-ę* is instr. ending for bases ending in a consonant; *qoyaŋa* is abs./nom. case; *tımnęn* 'he/it killed him/it').

NEGATION

The Koryak verb is negated by combining a negative marker (*uiŋẹ*), the *ẹ/a . . . ke/ka* form of the sense-verb, and a conjugated auxiliary (transitive or intransitive): e.g. *ınno uiŋẹ ẹ.yemk.ẹ itti* 'he didn't come'; *gımmo uiŋẹ avẹtat.ka titık* 'I didn't work'; *ınno uiŋẹ avẹtat.ka itti* 'he didn't work'.

Word order

Free; SVO is normal.

KPELLE

INTRODUCTION

Kpelle belongs to the Mande group of Niger-Congo. It is spoken by around 600,000 people in Liberia, with some spill-over into Guinea.

PHONOLOGY

Consonants

In addition to /p, b, f, v, w, m/, there are labio-velars /kp/ and /gb/. In the dental series, /s/ and /z/ tend to palatal fricatives /ʃ, ʒ/. There are two *d* sounds, one of which alternates with *l* and *r*. The fricative /γ/ and the nasals /ɲ/ and /ŋ/ are present. Nasals + stops are subject to sandhi at junctures, e.g. /-n/ + /t-/ → [nd]. Clustering occurs, e.g. *kplikpli* 'cat-fish'.

Vowels

The phonemes are:

long or short: i, ɪ, ɛ, a, ɔ, o, u

Vocalic length is phonemic, though homonyms are also usually distinguished by tone. Nasalized vowels in contact with a non-nasal consonant are marked: *ã*, *ɛ̃*, etc.

Tone

High, low, rising, falling; not usually marked in script.

MORPHOLOGY AND SYNTAX

Noun

There is no grammatical gender. A noun is made definite by mutation of initial and addition of *-i*: e.g. a voiceless initial mutates to its voiced counterpart: e.g. *folo* 'sun' – ***voloi*** 'the sun'. Nasal consonants do not mutate but add *-i*: e.g. *nyɛ* 'fish' – ***nyɛi*** 'the fish'. Further examples: *ba* 'rice' – ***mbai*** 'the rice'; *lɔwɔ* 'bush' – ***ndɔwɔi*** 'the bush'; *wulu* 'tree' – ***ŋgului*** 'the tree'.

PLURAL

-ŋa is added: e.g. *ta* 'town'; *taŋa* 'towns'; ***daŋai*** 'the towns'. Plural marking is largely optional. A generic plural is made with *-bela*: e.g. *kpɛlɛnu* 'a Kpelle man'; pl. *kpɛlɛ**bela*** 'Kpelle people'.

GENITIVE

Appositional; possessor precedes possessed: e.g. *kaloŋ ta* 'chief's town'. The personal pronoun may be interpolated: *kaloŋ* ***a*** *ta*.

Adjective

As attribute, adjective follows noun, e.g. *wulu koya* 'high tree', and takes the same mutations: *ŋgului* ***goyai*** 'the high tree'.

Pronoun

The independent forms used with the copula/existential verb are:

	Singular	*Plural*
1	nyá	kwiá
2	yɛ́	ká
3	nyà	diá

Example: *kpɛlɛnu ba nyà* 'I am a Kpelle'.

SUBJECT, OBJECT, AND DATIVE FORMS

The past-tense set (*see also* aorist tense in **Verb**, below):

	Singular			*Plural*		
	Subject	*Object*	*Dative*	*Subject*	*Object*	*Dative*
1	ŋá	ŋá	mê	kú	kú	kúà
2	í	í	ya	ká	ká	kâ
3	è	**Ø** (see below)	mè	dí	dí	díà

The third person singular object pronoun is indicated by mutation (as in nominals) of the initial of the verb: e.g. *kâ* 'to see' – *dí* ***gà*** 'they saw him'; *paa* 'to kill' – *dí* ***baa*** 'they killed him'.

DEMONSTRATIVE PRONOUN/ADJECTIVE

Examples: *ŋɛi* 'this'; *tí* 'that'.

INTERROGATIVE PRONOUN

gbɛ 'who?'; pl. *gbɛni* 'what?'

There is no relative pronoun; a relative clause is indicated by raised tone + *-i* final: e.g. *bɛlɛi nyin a lɔmui* 'the house which he enters' (*nyin* 'that', demonstrative; *lɔ* 'enter'; *mu* 'lower part', 'under', cf. *bɛlɛi mu* 'in the house').

Numerals

1–5: *taaŋ*, *felɛ*, *saba*, *naaŋ*, *lɔlu*; 6 *lɔl mai da*; 7 *lɔl mai felɛ*; 10 *pu*; 11 *pu kao tɔnɔ*; 20 *pu felɛ*; 100 *pu pu*.

Verb

There is no inflection. Tenses are generated by tonal change in root + specific sets of pronominal markers + auxiliaries:

aorist: pronominal series sing. *ŋà*, *yà*, *à*; pl. *kwà*, *kà*, *dà* + root, e.g. *pa – à pá* 'he has come';
past: subject series (as above, *see* **Pronoun**) + root, e.g. *è pà* 'he came' (note change of tone in root);
progressive: aorist series + root + *-i*, e.g. *à pái* 'he's coming';
future: *pai* is placed before root; aorist pronominal series, + *-i*: e.g. *ŋà pái kái* 'I shall see'.

NEGATION

The general negative marker is the circumfix *fé... -ni*: e.g. *ŋa fé pani* ' I did not come'; ***vè*** *pani* 'he did not come' (*vè* < *a.fe*).

There are various ways of emphasizing a tense form, e.g. the aorist by means of *gba*: this produces a perfective aspect. Similarly, the verb *kɛ* 'to do' can reinforce another verb: e.g. *na* (*fe*) *kɛ mɛni* 'I heard/did not hear'.

Postpositions

Examples: *su* 'in' – *zu* 'in him'; *pol* 'behind' – ***bol*** 'behind him'; *pɔ* 'with' – *bɔ* 'with him'; – *bɛlɛi pol* 'behind the house'.

Word order

SVO: e.g. *sulɔno e kwɛni pili* 'The boy threw a stone' (*sulɔno* 'boy'; *pili* 'stone'; *kwɛni* 'throw'; *e* is the third person pronoun copying the nominal subject). A pronominal indirect object may be final: e.g. *e* X *fe me* 'he gave X to me'.

**1 Gɔ́ɔ pelanii Ŋóoi e kɛ̀ naa. Ŋóoi nyaŋ e kɛ̀
Ɣâla kɔlɛ. Nyaŋ Ŋóoi e kɛ̀ a Ɣâla. 2 E kɛ̀ Ɣâla
kɔlɛ a gɔ́ɔ pelanii. 3 Sɛŋ kélee e kpɛ̀tɛ zârai. Sɛŋ
da kelee fe kɛ ni a gbɛtɛɛ ŋ̀ɛ́i pôlu ma nyii kɛ̀ a
gbɛtɛɛi. 4 Fúlu-laa e kɛ̀ gbonôi. Nyaŋ vúlu-laai e
kɛ̀ a núu-kpune ŋɔkwaa-ponɔɔ. 5 Gwaa-ponɔɔi a
fòlo gbínii su. Nyaŋ gbínii fe tá niiŋ ni.**

**6 Núu tɔ̀nɔ e kɛ̀ naa. Ɣâla e dɛ̀ɛ. Ǹáa ɓe kɛ̀ a
Zɔ̃̀ɔ. 7 E pà sêre-faa kɛ mɛni ma, e gwaa-ponɔɔi
maa sêre-faa kɛ, a gɛɛ núu kelee é láa la zârai.
8 Ve kɛ ni a gwaa-ponɔɔi. Kɛ́lɛ, e pà a gɛɛ é gwaa-
ponɔɔi maa sêre-faa kɛ́.**

KUMYK

INTRODUCTION

Kumyk belongs to the Kypchak-Polovets group of Turkic languages (Baskakov's (1966) classification). With 200,000 speakers in the Dagestan Republic, Kumyk is one of the six literary languages of Dagestan.

SCRIPT

Following initial experiments with Arabic and romanization, Cyrillic has been used since the late 1930s. The Cyrillic hard and soft signs are used to modify base letters; thus, *o* + soft sign = /œ/, *u* + soft sign = /y/, notated here as *ö* and *ü* respectively.

PHONOLOGY

/c/ figures in an otherwise standard Turkic inventory (*see* **Turkic Languages**), plus the glottal stop which is, for example, a realization of script *t*: e.g. *atlı* /aˀlı/, 'rider'.

VOWEL HARMONY

Both palatal and labial, e.g. *qızardaš.ım* 'my sister', *güčlüsüz* 'you are strong (pl.)'.

MORPHOLOGY AND SYNTAX

Standard Turkic models throughout; *see* **Turkic Languages**.

Noun

In the nominal declension, the genitive case ending is -*n*V^4, i.e. the normally present final -*n* has been dropped, making the genitive and accusative forms identical: *atnı* 'of the horse/the horse (acc.)'.

Verb

Some examples of tense structure:

present: *gel.e.men* 'I come';
past (a): *gel.gen.men* 'I have come';
past (b): *geldim* 'I came';
imperf.: *gel.e.edim* 'I was coming';
future: *gel.er.men* 'I shall come';

conditional: *gel.sem* 'if I come'.

PARTICIPLES

gel.e.gen 'coming', 'who is coming'; *gel.gen* 'who came'; *gel.e.žek* 'who will come'.

INFINITIVE

gel.mek 'to come'; negative: *gel.me.mek* 'not to come'.

٣١ صونك, آننك آناسی وقارداشلاری کلدیلر, و
(اوی ننك) قیر یاننده توروب, آنی چاقرمغه آدم
٣٢ یباردیلر. وآننك آیلانه سنده اولتورغان خلق, اوغار
آیتدیلار: «مونه حاله, آنانك وقارداشلارنك کلوب,
٣٣ قیرده سغه قارایلار». اول ده اولارغه جواب
بروب: «آنام وقارداشلارم کیملر در؟» دیدی.
٣٤ وآیلانه سنده اوتورغان لارغه قراب, «مونه حاله,
٣٥ آنام وقارداشلارم. زیرا هر کیم الله ننك مُرادین تمام
ایتسه; اُولدر قارداشم وقزقارداشم وآنام» دیدی.

(Mark 3.31–5)

!KUNG (!Xu)

INTRODUCTION

!Kung belongs to the Northern Khoisan group of languages. It is spoken by upwards of 10,000 Bushmen in the Botswana, Angola, Namibia frontier regions, on the north-western fringes of the Kalahari Desert.

The language has been reduced to writing in various forms of notation. An official orthography was approved by the Language and Publications Board of South West Africa in 1969. The orthography adopted in this article follows that of Snyman (1970).

PHONOLOGY

Consonants

About a hundred consonantal phonemes are distinguished, evenly divided between egressive (non-click) and ingressive (click) inventories. This large number of phonemes (the world record, as far as is known) is achieved in both inventories by means of extensive secondary articulation.

The egressive inventory has bilabial, alveolar, palatal, and velar series. The aveolar series, for example, is based on the simple plosives /t/ and /d/. Velar aspiration is added to give /tx/, laryngeal aspiration to give /th/, and ejective velar aspiration to give /tx'/; the voiced correlatives are /dγ/ and /d'h/; this latter phoneme is preceded by unreleased glottalization.

Analogous surd and voiced sets, each with from four to seven members, are provided by the bilabial plosives (based on /p/, /b/), the velar plosives (based on /k/, /g/), the alveolar affricates (based on /ts/, /dz/) and the palatal affricates (based on /tʃ/, /dʒ/). Together, these sets provided 31 phonemes.

The fricatives are relatively simple: /β, s, z, ʃ, ʒ, x, ɦ/. There are six phonemes based on /m/, including a laryngeal aspirate /mɦ/, glottalized onset /ˀm/, and two phonemes involving 'interruption': *m.m* = /m'm/, where ' represents a kind of glottal *Bebung*, and *m̭.m̭* = /m'm/ in which pharyngeal friction is added to interruption (*see* **Vowels**, below).

The ingressive or click inventory has dental, alveolar, and palatal rows. The dental row has ten fricatives and three nasals based on the dental click, which is notated as |. The alveolar row has eleven plosives and three nasals based on the alveolar click ǂ. The palatal row has eleven plosives based on the palatal plosive click !, and eleven africatives and six nasals based on the palatal fricative and nasal click ||.

The palatal plosive series is given here in illustration:

!	!x	!h
!?	!x?	!?h
g!	g!γ	g!h
	g!γ?	g!?h

Vowels

Here the basic division is into nasal and non-nasal (oral) series.

short vowels: i, e, a, o, u

/a/ and /o/ also occur accompanied by pharyngeal friction to produce a kind of croaking sound. Snyman (1970) calls these 'pressed vowels', and notates them as a̭ and o̭. The long vowels include all the short vowels except /e/ – iː, aː/, etc.

A third series of vowels involves interruption; notated as *a.a* or *a'a*.

The above sets are oral. The nasal sets include: (a) short vowels: as oral without /e/; (b) long vowels: /ãː, ã̭ː, õ̭ː, õː, ũː/; (c) rising and falling diphthongs: e.g. /eĩ, oĩ, wã/; (d) interrupted homorganic or disparate pairs: e.g. /ã.ã/.

MORPHOLOGY AND SYNTAX

A detailed and very finely differentiated taxonomy of the Bushman habitat is reflected in the vocabulary of !Kung.

Noun

Singular and plural numbers are not normally distinguished, but plural markers are available if required, e.g. *-mhi*, *-si/-sĩ*: *ǂ'aama* 'snake', pl. *ǂ'aamhi*; *!a'o* 'leopard', pl. *!a'osi*.

There is no inflection for case. Syntactic relationships are expressed by means of postpositions: e.g. *n!om !'o* 'on the rock'; *n!om dĩ* 'under the rock'; *tš'u n!eng* 'inside the house'; *tš'u ts'i* 'in front of the house'.

Adjective

Modifier follows modified, attached to it by a *-wa/-ya* glide, which behaves very like the Iranian *ezafe*; e.g. *|ao* 'buffalo' + *|xwa* 'alive': *|ao**wa*** *|xwa* 'the live buffalo'; *|hwe* 'horse' + *|'lom* 'beautiful': *|hwe**ya*** *|'hom* 'the beautiful horse'. The plural connective is *-sa*; e.g. *|ao**sa*** *|xwa* 'the live buffaloes'; *|hwe**sa*** *|'hom* 'the beautiful horses'.

Any verb in !Kung can function thus, as what Snyman calls 'adnouns' in modifier position connected by glide link, and it is in this way that relative clauses are made: e.g. *|hwe* + *'m* → *|hwe**ya*** *'m* 'the horse which is grazing'; *žu.**wa*** *kwa̭ n!'hei* 'the person (*žu*) who fears (*kwa̭*) a lion (*n!'hei*)'.

Pronoun

PERSONAL PRONOUN

	Singular	*Plural*
1	mi	e!a, m!a (with variants)
2	a	i!a, i
3	ha	(dependent on class: see next section)

Singular and plural forms of the third person are related to specific Bushman taxonomies which are not always identifiable in Indo-European terms. The *ha-* (sing.) – *si* (plural) class comprises human beings; the *ha–hi* class covers birds, reptiles, insects; the *ha–ha* class covers articles of everyday use. There are many sub-groupings, which are presumably explicable in terms of specific features of the environment. Some examples from Snyman:

		Class
žu|'hwã	'Bushman'	ha–si
da'ama	'child'	ha–si
||a'e	'monkey'	ha–hi
!wã!wã	'arrow shaft'	ha–ha
šamanga	'maize'	hi–hi
‡'aama	'snake'	ka–ka

These class distinctions are reflected in the possessive contructions: e.g. *mi hisi* 'my...' (plural objects belonging to the *ha–si* class); *a masi* 'your...' (plural objects belonging to the *ha–ha* class).

DEMONSTRATIVE PRONOUN AND ADJECTIVE

he, ke 'this'; *to'a* 'that'; *uuto'a* 'that yonder'. The *-wa/-ya* glide is used as a connective: e.g. *n|ei* 'head' – *n|ei**ya** ke* 'this head'.

INTERROGATIVE PRONOUN

hažwe/hažwĩ 'who?'; *hatše/hatšiĩ* 'what?' These require the general interrogative marker *re, ba, xae* (with variants): e.g. *Hatše* ***ba*** *‡'aama n!ei?* 'What does the snake bite?'

Numerals

1 *n|e'e* or *n|wi*; 2 *tsã*; 3 *n!eni*. Examples: *žu n|e'e* 'one person'; *e tsã* 'we two'; *gumi n!eni* 'the three animals'.

Verb

Verbs are transitive or intransitive. There is no inflection, nor are there any auxiliary verbs. Regular transitive verbs do not show concord with the object: cf. *zo n!ei !'hwã* 'the bee stings the man'; *zo n!ei n||a̭e* 'the bee stings the men'. But, irregularly, concord may be shown with the number of the object: e.g. *mi g!xa g!we* 'I take off the shoe'; *mi* ***šwe*** *g!we****si*** 'I take off the shoes'.

A causative is made with *n≠ei*: e.g. *N!aro-kx'ao n≠ei-ge'eya de'ebi* 'The teacher (*n!aro-kx'ao*) makes the children (*de'ebi*) sing (*ge'eya*).'

TENSE

In the absence of inflection of any kind, temporal adverbs are necessary. Some of these may precede or follow the subject. Some examples from Snyman: *ka |ao !haa-tsi* 'the buffalo is charging now (*ka*)'; *|ao n||aãha !haa-tsi* 'the buffalo charged long ago'.

IMPERATIVE

The imperative is usually followed by a benefactive pronoun, e.g. *na* 'to/for me', *ko* 'for other': cf. *eiya na 'msi* 'mother gives me food'; *na 'msi* 'give me food'.

NEGATIVE

The verb is generally negated by negative adverbs, e.g. *|wa*, *|wi*, *|ao:mi ho !'hwã* 'I see the man'; *mi |wa ho !'hwã* 'I do not see the man'.

COPULA

o; e.g. *g!heĩ o mi ga* 'the tree is mine'; *g!heĩsi o mi gasi* 'the trees are mine'; *mi o žu|'hwã* 'I am a Bushman'.

Postverbal particles generate modal senses – reciprocal, comitative, instrumental, benefactive.

Word order

SVO

31. Te Yesu ||' ã ha ta̱e kota ha tsīsī tsia ha, xabe siḷa |wa g̱la'ma tš'u te ||xwaa žú te hi ḷ'eu ha.
32. Te žúsa ǂhhi ḷhoo n||homi ha, te siḷa ḷwa te ko: Ye'ao, a ta̱e kota a tsīsī gea ts'i te ḷ'eu a.
33. Xabe ha meni siḷa te ko: Hažwe re o mi ta̱e te hažwe si ne o mi tsīsī?
34. Te ha se n||homi ha l'e ko žú te ko: Sḷlasa he o mi ta̱esī kota mi tsīsī.
35. Khhama žwa du tšisa ḷXu ku kare o mi ḷo kota mi ḷwui kota mi tsī kota mi ta̱e.

(Mark 3.31–5)

KURDISH

INTRODUCTION

Kurdistan, where this North-West Iranian language is mainly spoken, covers large contiguous areas of Turkey, Syria, Iraq, and Iran. Kurds are also resident in north-eastern Iran (Khorasan), Baluchistan, and in Armenia, Azerbaijan, and Turkmenistan. Estimates as to the total number of speakers vary widely; possibly around 14 million people speak one or another form of Kurdish. The main dialects are Sorani (Iraq and Iran) and Kurmandji (Armenia, Azerbaijan, Turkey, Turkmenistan, and Syria).

Political and social fragmentation is reflected in the language, which has no recognized standard form, and which is or has been written in a variety of scripts – Arabic, Cyrillic, Roman, Armenian. Sorani has semi-official status in Iraqi Kurdistan, where it is the language of primary education and of the local media. Poetry has been written in Kurdish since the thirteenth century.

SCRIPT

Sorani Kurdish is written in Arabic script plus the Iranian innovations and two letters for the specifically Kurdish sounds r̲ and l̲: inverted circumflex on Arabic *r*, *l*. The inverted circumflex is also used on a *y* or *w* bearer to denote the vowel phonemes /o/, /ə/, /ɛ/. Arabic *hā* is used to denote /ĕ/; thus, for example, the word *ferheng* 'dictionary' is written as فەرهەنگ.

In Cyrillic, /ɪ/ is represented by the Cyrillic soft sign ь; /ə/ by ə. In Sorani, the orthography is that codified by Taufiq Wahby in the 1920s, as subsequently modified by Iraqi Kurdish scholars. Treatment of certain phonemes, for example of medial and final /iː/ and /uː/, is not always consistent.

PHONOLOGY (OF SORANI)

Consonants

stops: p, b, t, d, k, g, q, ʔ; k, p, t are aspirated
affricates: tʃ, dʒ
fricatives: f, v, s, ʃ, z, ʒ, x, γ, ħ, h, ʕ = Arabic ʿain.
nasals: m, n, ŋ
laterals and flaps: l, l̲ /ɫ/, r, r̲ /r/
semi-vowels: j, w

/k/ and /g/ have palatalized allophones. *r* is single-flap /ɾ/; *r̲* is rolled /r/.

Kurmandji makes a distinction between the non-aspirates /p, t, k, ʃ/ and their aspirated counterparts /ph, th/, etc.

Vowels

short: ɪ, ɛ, ʊ
long: i, e /ɛ:/, a, o, u

ö is a diphthong, /əɛ/. The short vowels are unstable. Long vowels are indicated here by a macron, e.g. *ō*.

MORPHOLOGY AND SYNTAX

Noun

The definite article is -*(y)eke*: e.g. *bazar̲.eke* 'the market'; *dē.yeke* 'the village'. The indefinite article is *ēk/ē*: e.g. *pē.yēk* 'a foot'.

Gender is not distinguished grammatically; if necessary, natural gender can be marked lexically: e.g. *shēr.ī.nēr* 'lion', *shēr.ī.mē* 'lioness'. In Kurmandji, gender (masculine, feminine, common) is distinguished and marked by correlative changes in the ezafe (*see* **Persian**).

NUMBER

The usual plural marker is *-an*: e.g. *wul̲at.an* 'countries'. The definite article precedes *-an*: e.g. *žin.ek.an* 'the women'.

POSSESSION

The ezafe *-ī/-y* links two nouns in genitive relationship: e.g. *xel̲k.i.r̲ožhel̲at* 'the peoples of the Middle East'; *mela.y.mizgewt* 'the mullah of the mosque'. The ezafe is to be distinguished from the linking vowels, *e, ö, a, o, ē*, used for example in composite nouns: *būm.e.lerze* 'earthquake' (here, the linker *e* coalesces with the Arabic article: *al.arḍ* 'the earth'); *kič.e.čaw.r̲eš.eke* 'the black-eyed girl' (*čaw* 'eye'; *r̲eš* 'black').

(In the Kurdish spoken in the former Soviet Union nouns form oblique cases: e.g. *gavan* 'shepherd', oblique, *geven*.)

Adjective

As attribute, adjective follows noun and is invariable. It is linked to its noun by the ezafe: e.g. *utel.i.bāš* 'good hotel'; *šar.ek.i gewre.y taze* 'a big modern town'; *žin.ek.i kurd.i ǰiwan* 'a beautiful Kurdish woman'.

COMPARISON

A comparative is made with *-ter*: e.g. *sūr* 'red' – *sūr.ter*.

Pronoun

The personal pronouns with their enclitics are:

	Singular		*Plural*	
1	min	-(i)m	ēme	-man
2	to	-(i)t	ēwe	-tan
3	ew	-ī	ewan	-yan

The verb 'to be' is expressed by the following enclitic endings: sing. 1 *-m*, 2 *-y*, 3 *-ye*; pl. 1 *-yn*, 2 *-n*, 3 *-n*. The negative form is *nim* 'I am not', *nit*, etc.

The enclitic forms are used as possessive affixes, e.g. *čaw.an.it* 'your eyes', and as direct-object forms between prefix and root in the present tense and the subjunctive mood: e.g. *de.**m**.bīn.ē* 'he sees me' (*de* is the present-tense marker).

DEMONSTRATIVE PRONOUN

em.e (proximate), *ew.e* (non-proximate); pl. *ewane.*

DEMONSTRATIVE ADJECTIVE

em – ew; in Kurmandji a circumfix, e.g. *'əm.pyaw.ə* 'this man'.

INTERROGATIVE PRONOUN

či 'who?'; *čī* 'what?'

RELATIVE PRONOUN

Normally, definite marker plus *ke*: e.g. *ew kitēb-**e.y ke** to de.**y**.bīn.ī* 'the book which you see (it)'. *ke* may be omitted: *shar.e.y dīt.man* 'the town (which) we saw it (*y*)'.

Numerals

1–10: *yek, dū, sē, čuwar, pēnč, šeš, ħewt, hešt, no, de.* 11 *yazde*; 12 *duwazde*; 20 *bīst*; 30 *sī*; 40 *čil*; 100 *sed.*

Verb

As in Persian, the Kurdish verbal system is built up on the two-base pattern, the present base underlying the present-future tense, the present subjunctive, and the imperative; the past base supplies the three past tenses. The past base is obtained by dropping the *-in* ending of the infinitive; the present base is not predictable: e.g.

girtin	'to catch'	– girt	– gir
kuštin	'to kill'	– kušt	– kuž
dītin	'to see'	– dīt	– bīn

The personal endings for intransitive verbs are: sing. 1 -(*i*)*m*, 2 *-ī*/*y*(*t*), 3 *ē*(*t*); pl. 1 *īn*, 2 *-in*, 3 *-in*. Some examples of verb forms:

Present tense: *de* + present stem + personal ending, e.g. *de.kew.im* 'I fall'; in negative version *na* replaces *de*: *na.kew.im*.

Present subjunctive: *bi* + present stem + personal ending, e.g. *bi.kew.im* 'I may fall'.

Preterite: past stem + personal ending – third person marker here is **Ø**, e.g. *kewt.im* 'I fell', *kewt* 'he fell'; negative: *ne.kewt(im)*.

Perfect: past stem + *-uw-* + personal ending, e.g. *kewt.uw.im* 'I have fallen'; negative: *ne.m.kewt(im)*.

Imperfect: *de* + past stem + personal ending, e.g. *de.kewt.im* 'I was falling'; negative: *ne.de.kewt.im.*

A pluperfect is made with the past stem of *hebun* 'to be', e.g. *kewt.i.bū.m* 'I had fallen'.

An unreal conditional with the particle *-aye*, e.g. *bi.kewt.im.aye* 'if I had fallen'.

TRANSITIVE VERB

In the past tense the transitive verb is in concord with the object, and the agent is denoted by personal affix attached to that object; if no object is present, the agent marker is attached to the verb: cf. with object: *name.yek.**im** nūs.ī* 'I wrote a letter'. The agent markers are the enclitic forms of the personal pronouns (see above): cf. *nard.it.im* 'you (sing.) sent me'; *nard.im.it* 'I sent you (sing.)'; *nard.man.in* 'we sent you/them'. Examples with no object present: *xward.im* 'I ate', *xward.man* 'we ate'; neg. *ne.m.xward* 'I didn't eat', *ne.man.xward* 'we didn't eat'.

PASSIVE

The characteristic is *-r-*, with *-ē* for the present, *-a* for the past; thus, from *nūsīn* 'to write': ***nūsran*** 'to be written'; past stem: ***nūsra***; present stem: ***nūsrē.***

The causative characteristic is *-din*: e.g. *šikan* 'to break' (intrans.) *-šikandin* 'to break' (trans.).

The past participle is made by adding *-ū*/*-w* to the past base. Enclitic personal markers are added to this participle to form the perfect tense: e.g. *hat.uw.im* 'I have come'.

Prepositions

Prepositions may be simple, e.g. *be* 'to', *bo* 'for'; or complex, e.g. the circumfix *le... da* 'in': ***le** kurdistan.i.emro **da*** 'in modern Kurdistan', where the circumfix encloses the ezafe phrase, which is felt as a unit. Similarly, *legel... da* 'with': e.g. *legel dostim da* 'with my friend'.

Word order

SOV is normal.

له ابتدا کلمه بو و آو کلمه له لای خدا بو

هر آو کلمه خدا بو ۲ هر آوه له ابتدا له

لای خدا بو ۳ و بجز خواهش آوه چشتی

له موجودات وجود نات ۴ له آوه حیات

بو و حیات نور انسان بو ۵ و نور له تاریکی

تابان بو و تاریکی آوه ادراک نکرد ۶ شخصی

له لای خدا هات و رسالت ناوی یحیی بو

۷ آوه ازای شهادت هات تا و نور شهادت

بیت تا گشت له واسطه آوه ایمان بارن ۸

آوه آو نور نبو بلکه هات تا و نور شهادت

بیت